THE OXFORD HANDBOOK OF

COGNITIVE
LINGUISTICS

THE OXFORD HANDBOOK OF

COGNITIVE LINGUISTICS

Edited by

DIRK GEERAERTS
AND HUBERT CUYCKENS

OXFORD
UNIVERSITY PRESS

OXFORD
UNIVERSITY PRESS

Oxford University Press, Inc., publishes works that further
Oxford University's objective of excellence
in research, scholarship, and education.

Oxford   New York
Auckland   Cape Town   Dar es Salaam   Hong Kong   Karachi
Kuala Lumpur   Madrid   Melbourne   Mexico City   Nairobi
New Delhi   Shanghai   Taipei   Toronto

With offices in
Argentina   Austria   Brazil   Chile   Czech Republic   France   Greece
Guatemala   Hungary   Italy   Japan   Poland   Portugal   Singapore
South Korea   Switzerland   Thailand   Turkey   Ukraine   Vietnam

Published by Oxford University Press, Inc.
198 Madison Avenue, New York, New York 10016

www.oup.com

First issued as an Oxford University Press paperback, 2010

Oxford is a registered trademark of Oxford University Press

Library of Congress Cataloging-in-Publication Data
The Oxford handbook of cognitive linguistics / edited by Dirk Geeraerts
and Hubert Cuyckens.
p. cm.
Includes bibliographical references and index.
ISBN 978-0-19-973863-2 (pbk.)
1. Cognitive grammar.   I. Geeraerts, Dirk, 1955–   II. Cuyckens, H.
P165.O974 2007
415—dc22   2006051728

1   3   5   7   9   8   6   4   2
Printed in the United States of America
on acid-free paper

PREFACE

....

In the past decade, Cognitive Linguistics has developed into one of the most dynamic and attractive frameworks within theoretical and descriptive linguistics. With about fifty chapters written by experts in the field, the *Oxford Handbook of Cognitive Linguistics* intends to provide a comprehensive overview of the entire domain of Cognitive Linguistics, from basic concepts to practical applications.

We thank the publisher, Oxford University Press, and its responsible editor, Peter Ohlin, for the initiative they took to commission this reference work and for the subsequent freedom they gave us in shaping it. The overall design and organization of the book, the selection of the topics to be treated, and the identification of the experts to treat them, were predominantly the work of the first editor of this volume, Dirk Geeraerts. The second editor, Hubert Cuyckens, was responsible for the inevitably long and painstaking task of guiding the authors from the initial versions of their texts, over numerous revisions on the content-side as well as on the formal side, to the published versions.

At various moments in the course of this huge editorial task, Hubert received help from Koen Plevoets, Hendrik De Smet, Gert De Sutter, José Tummers, An Van Linden, and Sofie Van Gijsel. We thank all of them for their generous support. A special word of thanks also goes to Daniela Kolbe (University of Hannover) for her meticulous help in formatting the references.

In addition, we particularly thank the authors for their chapters: if the Handbook achieves its goal of providing a uniquely wide-ranging and authoritative coverage of the most significant topics and viewpoints in Cognitive Linguistics, it will be through the professional and expert nature of the authors' contributions.

Contents

PART V LINGUISTIC VARIATION AND CHANGE

CONTRIBUTORS

MICHEL ACHARD (PhD 1993) is associate professor of French studies and linguistics at Rice University. His interest in Cognitive Linguistics dates from his days as a graduate student at the University of California, San Diego, where he was a student of Ronald Langacker. He was part of the 2001 International Cognitive Linguistics Conference organizing committee and organized the 2002 Conference on Conceptual Structure, Discourse, and Language with Suzanne Kemmer. His main research interests include the semantics and syntax of complement systems, the argument structure of predicates, and first and second language acquisition. He has published several articles as well as a monograph (1998) on different aspects of French complementation from a Cognitive Grammar perspective. He also published edited volumes on language acquisition (with Susanne Neimeier, 2000), second language acquisition and pedagogy from a cognitive perspective (with Susanne Niemeier, 2003), and language, culture, and mind (with Suzanne Kemmer, 2004). His current research is concerned with split intransitivity and impersonal constructions. Michel Achard can be reached at achard@rice.edu.

RONNY BOOGAART (PhD 1999) is professor of Dutch linguistics at the Free University Amsterdam and at the University of Leiden. His dissertation was titled *Aspect and Temporal Ordering: A Contrastive Analysis of Dutch and English* (1999). His publications include "Aspect and Aktionsart" in *Morphologie / Morphology* (2004). His current research focuses on the semantics and pragmatics of modal constructions, in particular modal auxiliaries in Dutch. Ronny Boogaart can be reached at rju.boogaart@let.vu.nl.

JOAN BYBEE (PhD 1973) is distinguished professor of linguistics at the University of New Mexico. She has been involved in usage-based analysis and cognitive-based explanations throughout her career. In 1976 she first wrote about frequency effects in language change; in 1979 at a conference on the cognitive representation of speech, she first proposed lexically specific exemplar representations for words in memory. Her 1985 book *Morphology* documents semantically based iconic relations in the morphological structures of the languages of the world. Her 1994 book on grammaticization (*The Evolution of Grammar*, with Revere Perkins and William Pagliuca) studies the universal paths of semantic development in grammaticization in a worldwide sample of languages. Her 2001 edited book *Frequency and the Emergence of Linguistic Structure* (with Paul Hopper) studies usage-based effects at all levels of grammar. Her *Phonology and Language Use* (2001) applies usage-based and cognitive principles to phonology, as well as the interaction of phonology with morphology and syntax. Bybee directed the 1995 Linguistic Institute. She was the chair of the Department of Linguistics at the University of New Mexico from 1999 to 2002 and was president of the Linguistic Society of America in 2005. Joan Bybee can be reached at jbybee@unm.edu.

ALAN CIENKI (PhD 1988), formerly of Emory University in Atlanta, Georgia, now teaches in the Department of Language and Communication, Faculteit der Letteren, Vrije Universiteit, Amsterdam. His research has encompassed such topics as the nature of image schemas, the semantics of spatial language, metaphorical extensions of spatial language to abstract domains (such as possession and honesty), and the expression of conceptual metaphors in gesture with speech. He is author of *Spatial Cognition and the Semantics of Prepositions in English, Polish, and Russian* (1989) and coeditor of *Conceptual and Discourse Factors in Linguistic Structure* (with Barbara Luka and Michael Smith, 2001) and *Metaphor and Gesture* (with Cornelia Müller, forthcoming). His current research concerns the multimodal nature of spoken interaction, metaphor and framing in political discourse, and methodology in metaphor research. Alan Cienki can be reached at a.cienki@let.vu.nl.

DAVID CLARKE (PhD 1975, 1987) is professor of psychology, and former head of the School of Psychology, at the University of Nottingham, England. He is director of the Action Analysis Group, and codirector of the Accident Research Unit within the School. He read medical sciences and psychology at Cambridge, before doing a DPhil in psychology at Oxford, and later a PhD in social and political sciences at Cambridge. He is a Chartered Psychologist, a Fellow of the British Psychological Society, and the author of about 90 papers, chapters, and books. His research interests include temporal patterns in language, and methods for detecting languagelike structures in episodes of other behavior. David D. Clarke can be reached at david.clarke@nottingham.ac.uk.

WILLIAM CROFT (PhD 1986) is professor of linguistics at the University of New Mexico. His main research interests are in typology, Construction Grammar, and Cognitive Semantics, especially verb semantics. His publications include *Typology and Universals* (1990; 2nd ed., 2003); *Syntactic Categories and Grammatical Relations: The Cognitive Organization of Information* (1991); *Explaining Language Change: An Evolutionary Approach* (2000); *Radical Construction Grammar: Syntactic Theory in Typological Perspective* (2001); and *Cognitive Linguistics* (with D. Alan Cruse, 2004). His involvement with Cognitive Linguistics dates from the 1980s, when his PhD presented an early cognitive linguistic account of what is now known as argument structure and an analysis of parts of speech that anticipated certain aspects of Construction Grammar. Since that time, he has endeavored to bring cognitive linguistic and typological theory together, particularly in the area of grammatical representation, and also to develop a thoroughly usage-based approach to language using an evolutionary model. William Croft can be reached at wcroft@unm.edu.

HUBERT CUYCKENS (PhD 1991) is professor of English language and linguistics at the University of Leuven, where he is a senior member of the "Functional Linguistics

Leuven" research unit (see http://wwwling.arts.kuleuven.be/fll for more information). His interest in Cognitive Linguistics dates from the 1980s, when he started investigating the importance of prototype theory for the analysis of such highly polysemous items as prepositions. He has published a substantial number of articles on the cognitive semantics of prepositions in English and Dutch. He has also published several edited volumes on cognitive lexical semantics and on the study of adpositions, including *Polysemy in Cognitive Linguistics* (with Britta Zawada, 2001); *Cognitive Approaches to Lexical Semantics* (with John Taylor and René Dirven, 2003); *Perspectives on Prepositions* (with Günter Radden, 2003); and *Adpositions of Movement* (with Walter de Mulder and Tanja Mortelmans, 2005). His recent research is concerned with issues in the diachrony of English from a cognitive-functional perspective; these include grammaticalization phenomena and the development of complementation patterns in the history of English. He is a former board member of the International Cognitive Linguistics Association. Hubert Cuyckens can be reached at hubert.cuyckens@arts.kuleuven.be.

WALTER DE MULDER (PhD 1992) is professor of French and general linguistics at the University of Antwerp. His main research interests involve the semantics and pragmatics of demonstratives, tenses, and prepositions. He has published several articles on these topics, among others, in *Travaux de Linguistique* and *Verbum* and has edited several volumes, including the special issue "Coherence and Anaphora," *Belgian Journal of Linguistics* (with Liliane Tasmowski-De Ryck and Carl Vetters, 1996). His interest in Cognitive Linguistics dates from the end of the 1980s, when he started working on the semantics of prepositions. His current research topics include grammaticalization phenomena, such as the development of the (French) definite article or the evolution of (French) prepositions—see the issue "Linguistique diachronique, grammaticalisation et sémantique du prototype," *Langue française* (edited with Anne Vanderheyden, 2001) and the issue "Grammaticalisation: Le cas des prépositions locatives," *Linguisticae Investigationes* (edited with Michèle Goyens, 2002). He is also currently working on a cognitive theory of (French) past verb tenses—see, e.g., the article "The French *imparfait*, Determiners and Grounding," in *Grounding* (with Carl Vetters, 2002). Walter De Mulder can be reached at walter.demulder@ua.ac.be.

RENÉ DIRVEN (PhD 1971) is emeritus professor of English linguistics at the University of Duisburg, Germany. He set up the Linguistic Agency—first at the University of Trier and from 1985 at the University of Duisburg (LAUD)—organizing annual linguistic symposia and publishing linguistic preprints. As professor emeritus, he continues his research and work in international projects and organizations such as LAUD (Preprint series and symposia at the Universities of Duisburg-Essen and Koblenz-Landau), Languages in Contact and Conflict in Africa, and the International Association of Cognitive Linguists (president from 1995 to 1997). He initiated and edited the collective volume *Cognitive Exploration of Language and Linguistics* (1998, 2004), which offers cognitive introductions to language and linguistics and has appeared in eight European languages and Korean. He coauthored *Cognitive English Grammar* (with Günter Radden, 2006). He initiated and is working on the annual expansions of two electronic bibliographies: METBIB, on metaphor, metonymy, and other figurative conceptualization (2005), and COG-BIB, on Cognitive Linguistics (2006). His research focuses on grammatical conceptualizations in the areas of attribution, complementation, and conditionality; on figurative conceptualizations via metaphor and metonymy; and on sociocultural dimensions of conceptualization as manifested in language attitudes, language policies, and ideology—an area of study becoming known as cognitive sociolinguistics. René Dirven can be reached at rene.dirven@pandora.be.

GILLES FAUCONNIER (PhD 1971) is distinguished professor in the Department of Cognitive Science at the University of California, San Diego. He was one of the founders of Cognitive Linguistics in the 1970s through his work on pragmatic scales and mental spaces. Fauconnier is author of a number of books on linguistics and cognitive science, including *Mental Spaces* (1985), *Mappings in Thought and Language* (1997), and *The Way We Think* (with Mark Turner, 2002). A former Guggenheim Fellow, Fellow of the American Philosophical Society, and Fellow of the Center for Advanced Study at Stanford, Fauconnier was a professor at the Ecole des Hautes Etudes en Sciences Sociales in Paris, the University of Paris VIII, and a visiting professor at many universities in Europe, Japan, North and South America, and Africa. His recent research explores conceptual integration, compression of conceptual mappings, and emergent structure in language and beyond. Gilles Fauconnier can be reached at faucon@cogsci.ucsd.edu.

MARGARET H. FREEMAN (PhD 1972) is emeritus professor of English at Los Angeles Valley College. She and her husband are currently engaged in creating the Myrifield Institute for Cognition and the Arts in Heath, Massachusetts, where they now live. She has been reading in the field of Cognitive Linguistics since its inception and moderates COGLIT, an Internet discussion list for people interested in cognitive linguistic approaches to literature. She has published articles on cognitive approaches to poetry in several journals and is working on a book-length cognitive guide to reading the poetry of Emily Dickinson. Margeret H. Freeman can be reached at freemamh@lavc.edu.

JOSÉ M. GARCÍA-MIGUEL (PhD 1992) teaches general linguistics at the University of Vigo. Since the beginning of his career, his research interests have centered around clause structure, seeking semantic (functional and cognitive) explanations for syntactic constructions. His publications include the monographs *Transitividad y complementación preposicional en español* (1995) and *Las relaciones gramaticales entre predicado y participantes* (1995). He has also published several articles on the structure and meaning of clausal constructions, grammatical relations and case, middle voice, diathesis alternations, preferred argument structure, and more. His recent research is concerned with diathesis alternations in Spanish and the integration of verb meaning into alternate constructional schemas using an empirical, corpus-oriented basis, and he is leading a project (ADESSE) aiming at developing a database of diathesis alternations of Spanish verbs. José M. García-Miguel can be reached at gallego@uvigo.es.

DIRK GEERAERTS (PhD 1981) is professor of linguistics at the University of Leuven, where he is the head of the research unit Quantitative Lexicology and Variational Linguistics (see http://wwwling.arts.kuleuven.be/qlvl for more information). His main research interests involve the overlapping fields of lexical semantics, lexicology, and lexicography. His publications include the following monographs: *Wegwijs in woordenboeken* (with Guy Janssens, 1982); *Paradigm and Paradox* (1985); *Woordbetekenis* (1986); *Wat er in een woord zit* (1989); *The Structure of Lexical Variation* (with Stefan Grondelaers and Peter Bakema, 1994); *Diachronic Prototype Semantics* (1997); *Convergentie en divergentie in de Nederlandse woordenschat* (with Stefan Grondelaers and Dirk Speelman, 1999), and *Words and Other Wonders* (2006). He is also editor-in-chief of the 14th edition of the *Van Dale Groot Woordenboek der Nederlandse Taal*, which is the major contemporary dictionary of Dutch. His involvement with Cognitive Linguistics dates from the 1980s, when his PhD was one of the first in Europe to explore the possibilities of a prototype-theoretical model of categorization. As the founding editor of the journal *Cognitive Linguistics*, he played an important role in the international expansion of Cognitive Linguistics. He organized the 1993 International Cognitive Linguistics Conference and was president of the International Cognitive Linguistics Association from 1999 to 2001. Dirk Geeraerts can be reached at dirk.geeraerts@arts.kuleuven.ac.be.

RAYMOND W. GIBBS, JR. (PhD 1980) is professor of psychology at the University of California, Santa Cruz. He received his PhD from the University of California, San Diego, and did postdoctoral research in cognitive science at Yale and Stanford Universities before joining the faculty at UC Santa Cruz. Gibbs's research focuses on language, thought, and embodied experience, especially in relation to pragmatics and figurative language. He is author of *The Poetics of Mind: Figurative Thought, Language, and Understanding* (1994), *Intentions in the Experience of Meaning* (1999), and *Embodiment and Cognitive Science* (2006), all published by Cambridge University Press. He is also coeditor of *Metaphor in Cognitive Linguistics* (with Gerard Steen, 1999) and is currently editor of the journal *Metaphor and Symbol*. Gibbs became interested in Cognitive Linguistics because of his studies on idiom and metaphor processing, and more general concern with the relations between thought, language, and the body. Raymond W. Gibbs, Jr., can be reached at gibbs@ucsc.edu.

JOSEPH E. GRADY (PhD 1996) is a principal and cofounder of Cultural Logic LLC, a research firm that applies principles of the cognitive and social sciences to the question of how citizens learn about and engage with public interest issues. His main academic research interests include metaphor, lexical semantics, and conceptual structure. Grady's publications have looked closely at the fundamental conceptual units and relations that participate in metaphorical mappings (particularly, primary metaphors), as well examining the nature and typology of these concepts and relations and their implications for broader questions about cognition and experience. Grady received his doctoral degree at the University of California, Berkeley, where he worked closely with George Lakoff, Eve Sweetser, and other prominent scholars in the field of Cognitive Linguistics. Joseph E. Grady can be reached at joegrady@cox.net.

STEFAN GRONDELAERS (PhD 2000) is associate professor at the Université Libre de Bruxelles. In his PhD thesis, he examined the sociolexicology, pragmatics, and psycholinguistics of Modern Dutch presentative *er* 'there'. Grondelaers is coauthor of *The Structure of Lexical Variation* (with Dirk Geeraerts and Peter Bakema, 1994) and *Convergentie en divergentie in de Nederlandse woordenschat* (with Dirk Geeraerts and Dirk Speelman, 1999). He is on the editorial board of the journal *Corpus Linguistics and Linguistic Theory*. Grondelaers mainly investigates language-structural and contextual variation in the lexicon and in syntax, building on corpus-linguistic and psycholinguistic research methods. He is a strong advocate of a full integration of Cognitive Linguistics and psycholinguistics. Stefan Grondelaers can be reached at sgrondel@ulb.ac.be.

PETER HARDER (PhD 1996) is professor of English language at the University of Copenhagen. He is based in a European tradition of functional and structural linguistics, and living through the rise of generative and formal linguistics and the subsequent pragmatic and cognitive developments kindled his interest in foundational issues (see his 2003 article "The Status of Linguistic Facts," *Mind and Language*). His research interests focus on relations between functional and cognitive dimensions of language, and his main work is *Functional Semantics* (1996). He was a visiting scholar at the University of California, San Diego, in 1994 and at the University of California, Berkeley, in 2003. His current research includes developmental patterns in the encoding of perspective and the nature of clausal embedding (see his forthcoming "Complement-Taking Predicates: Usage and Linguistic Structure," with Kasper Boye, in *Studies in Language*). Peter Harder can be reached at harder@hum.ku.dk.

RICHARD HUDSON (PhD 1961) is emeritus professor of linguistics at University College London. His main research interests involve the overlapping fields of lexical semantics, syntax, morphology, speech processing, and sociolinguistics. His publications include the textbook *Sociolinguistics* (1981, 1996) and the following monographs: *English Complex Sentences: An Introduction to Systemic Grammar* (1971); *Arguments for a Non-transformational Grammar* (1976); *Word Grammar* (1984); and *English Word Grammar* (1990). He also has a strong interest in applying linguistics in education. He was elected a Fellow of the British Academy in 1993. For more biographical information, see http://www.phon.ucl.ac.uk/home/dick/home .htm. His involvement with Cognitive Linguistics dates from the 1970s, when he first heard about prototypes in a lecture by George Lakoff at a time when he was also learning about knowledge representation in Artificial Intelligence and was developing a rather cognitive view of sociolinguistics; since then, his research and ideas have converged increasingly on those of the leading cognitive linguists, and they now fit comfortably in this tradition. He has been a consulting editor of the journal *Cognitive Linguistics* since its foundation. Richard Hudson can be reached at dick@ling.ucl.ac.uk.

LAURA JANDA (PhD 1984) is professor of Slavic linguistics at the University of North Carolina at Chapel Hill (http://www.unc.edu/~lajanda) and director of the Slavic and East European Language Resource Center (http://www.seelrc.org). Her main research interests involve the semantics of Slavic morphological categories, particularly case and aspect. Her publications include the following monographs: *A Semantic Analysis of the Russian Verbal Prefixes ZA-, PERE-, DO- and OT-* (1986); *A Geography of Case Semantics: The Czech Dative and the Russian Instrumental* (1993); *Back from the Brink: A Study of How Relic Forms in Languages Serve as Source Material for Analogical Extension* (1996); *Common and Comparative Slavic* (with Charles E. Townsend, 1996); *Czech* (with Charles E. Townsend, 2000); and *The Case Book for Russian* (with Steven J. Clancy, 2002). Her 1984 dissertation was among the first in the United States in the framework of Cognitive Linguistics, and she is cofounder of the Slavic Cognitive Linguistics Association. Laura Janda can be reached at janda@unc.edu.

THEO JANSSEN (PhD 1976) is professor of Dutch language and linguistics at the Vrije Universiteit Amsterdam, where he is the head of the Linguistic Research master's program (http://www.let.vu.nl/master/linguistics/). His research interests concentrate on the field of semantics, particularly deixis (demonstratives and tense). His publications include *The Function of Tense in Texts* (edited with Jadranka Gvozdanović, 1991); *Reported Speech: Forms and Functions of the Verb* (edited with Wim van der Wurff, 1996); *Cognitive Linguistics: Foundations, Scope, and Methodology* (edited with Gisela Redeker, 1999); and "Deixis and Reference" in *Morphologie / Morphology* (2004). He has been involved with Cognitive Linguistics since the founding of the International Cognitive Linguistics Association in 1989. Since 1990, he has been a consulting editor of the journal *Cognitive Linguistics*. Together with Gisela Redeker, he organized the 1997 International Cognitive Linguistics Conference at the Vrije Universiteit Amsterdam. More information on Janssen can be found at http://www.let.vu.nl/staf/thajm.janssen. Theo Janssen can be reached at thajm.janssen@let.vu.nl.

RONALD W. LANGACKER (PhD 1966) is professor emeritus and research professor at the University of California, San Diego. Early in his career, major areas of research included generative syntax and the comparative-historical grammar of the Uto-Aztecan family of Native American languages. Over the last quarter century, his main concern has been to develop and progressively articulate a radical alternative to generative theory. A basic statement of the framework appeared as a two-volume work, *Foundations of Cognitive Grammar*, in 1987 and 1991. Other monographs presenting the model are *Concept, Image, and Symbol* (1990) and *Grammar and Conceptualization* (1999). He has further published a substantial number of articles dealing with a broad array of issues in Cognitive Linguistics. He was a founding member of the International Cognitive Linguistics Association and served as its president from 1997 to 1999. He was chair of the 2001 International Cognitive Linguistics Conference organizing committee. He was an original coeditor of the monograph series Cognitive Linguistics Research and is a member of numerous editorial and advisory boards. Ronald W. Langacker can be reached at rlangacker@ucsd.edu.

BARBARA LEWANDOWSKA-TOMASZCZYK (PhD 1972, Dr habil. 1987) is professor of English language and linguistics at the University of Łódź, where she holds the position of professor ordinarius and chair of the Department of English Language. Her research interests are primarily in semantics and pragmatics of natural language, corpus linguistics, and their applications in translation studies and lexicography. She has published books and papers in the area of Cognitive Linguistics, including *Depth of Negation: A Cognitive Linguistic Study* (1996) and *Cognitive Linguistics Today* (edited with Kamila Turewicz, 2002), and has organized numerous international conferences and seminars. Over the years, she has been invited to read papers at international conferences and to lecture and conduct seminars at European and American universities. She served in the Board of Consulting Editors for *Cognitive Linguistics* until 1998 and has been president of the Polish Cognitive Linguistics Association since 2002. Barbara Lewandowska-Tomaszczyk can be reached at blt@uni.lodz.pl.

RICARDO MALDONADO (PhD 1992) is professor of syntax, semantics, and Cognitive Linguistics at the Universidad Nacional Autónoma de México and a guest professor at the Universidad Autónoma de Querétaro, Mexico. Maldonado did his PhD work on middle voice in Spanish, under the supervision of Ronald Langacker. He has published a book on Spanish middle voice (1999) as well as a variety of papers on reflexive, middle, impersonal, and causative constructions in Spanish. He has also done research on the objectivity-subjectivity continuum in datives and possessives in Huastec and Spanish, as well as on the development of pragmatic and discourse markers from adverbs (with María Jesus Fernández) and on quantifiers (with Alejandra Vigueras). Maldonado has also studied category formation in the acquisition of agentive nouns (with Alejandra Auza) and of tense-aspect verbal morphology (with Donna Jackson). His current field of interest is the study of cross-linguistic syntactic voice patterns in Romance and Mexican indigenous languages. Ricardo Maldonado can be reached at msoto@servidor .unam.mx.

TANJA MORTELMANS (PhD 1999) teaches German linguistics at the University of Antwerp. Her main research interests include modality, grammaticalization, grounding, and subjectification. Her involvement with Cognitive Linguistics (more specifically, with Cognitive Grammar) goes back to her PhD, in which she investigated whether and to what extent the German modals qualify as "grounding predications." She has published a number of articles on this subject. More recently, her field of interest has also come to include tense and mood markers in German, on which she has published as well. Tanja Mortelmans can be reached at tanja.mortelmans@ua.ac.be.

GEOFF NATHAN (PhD 1978) is associate professor of English in the Linguistics Program at Wayne State University in Detroit, Michigan. He began working on phonology in Cognitive Grammar after reading early drafts of Lakoff's *Women, Fire, and Dangerous Things*. He has published several articles on various aspects of how phonology would work within Cognitive Grammar (see Nathan 1986, 1989, 1996, and 1999 in the Reference section of chapter 23) and is completing a textbook on the subject for the Cognitive Linguistics in Practice series. Current research includes an experimental and theoretical examination of the usage-based model, Optimality Theory, and further explorations of how phonology relates to other skilled motor behavior. He is also interested in the history of linguistics and comparative phonological theories. Geoff Nathan can be reached at geoffnathan@wayne.edu.

BRIGITTE NERLICH (PhD 1985) is a principal research officer at the Institute for the Study of Genetics, Biorisks, and Society (IGBiS) at the University of Nottingham, United Kingdom. She has published numerous books and articles on the history of semantics and pragmatics, cognitive semantics, figurative language, polysemy, and semantic change. She now studies the uses of metaphorical models in the discourses about cloning, designer babies, GM food, stem cells, and genomics. She has recently concluded a project on the social and cultural impact of foot and mouth disease in the United Kingdom, and she will shortly start work on a new project "Talking Cleanliness in Health and Agriculture," which deals with MRSA and avian flu from a sociological and applied linguistics perspective. Like the foot and mouth project, this project is funded by the Economic and Social Research Council. Brigitte Nerlich can be reached at brigitte.nerlich@nottingham.ac.uk.

JAN NUYTS (PhD 1988) is professor in the Linguistics Department of the University of Antwerp, Belgium. His main research interests are in cognitive-functional semantics and syntax. His focus of attention is on the analysis of modal notions (evidentiality, epistemic, and deontic modality) and their linguistic expression and its implications for our understanding of the relations between language and thought. His publications include the books *Aspects of a Cognitive-Pragmatic Theory of Language* (1992) and *Epistemic Modality, Language and Conceptualization: A Cognitive-Pragmatic Perspective* (2001). "Raised" as a functional linguist, he has, from his early publications on, shown a strong interest in the cognitive structure of language and the relations between language and conceptualization, which explains his (long-standing) concern with Cognitive Linguistics and its relations to Functional Linguistics. Jan Nuyts can be reached at jan.nuyts@ua.ac.be.

TODD OAKLEY (PhD 1995) is associate professor of English and cognitive science at Case Western Reserve University in Cleveland, Ohio. His principle areas of scholarship are in rhetoric, linguistics, and cognitive science. He has published several scholarly articles and book chapters on these topics. He has also coauthored several articles and coedited a special issue of *Cognitive Linguistics* on conceptual blending with Seana Coulson. Currently, Oakley and Coulson are coediting another special issue on blending for the *Journal of Pragmatics*. His interest in Cognitive Linguistics dates from the early 1990s, when he began investigating the conceptual basis of rhetorical effect, a project that drew heavily on Langacker's Cognitive Grammar and Fauconnier's Mental Spaces Theory. This project has since expanded to focus on the relationship between attention and meaning construction in general, hence its title, *Elements of Attention: Explorations in Mind, Language, and Culture*. Todd Oakley can be reached at todd.oakley@case.edu.

GARY B. PALMER (PhD 1971) is emeritus professor of anthropology at the University of Nevada, Las Vegas. His main research interests involve the overlap of cultural categories and polysemy in lexical constructions as an approach to ethnosemantics. He has published research on polysemy in Tagalog (Austronesian) verbal prefixes, cultural determinants of Shona (Bantu) noun classifiers, and polysemy in Snchitsu'umshtsn (Salish) spatial prefixes. His publications include *Toward a Theory of Cultural Linguistics* (1996); *Languages of Sentiment: Cultural Constructions of Emotional Substrates* (edited with Debra J. Occhi, 1999); *Cognitive Linguistics and Non-Indo-European Languages* (edited with Gene Casad, 2003); and the special issue "Talking about Thinking across Language" (edited with Cliff Goddard and Penny Lee; *Cognitive Linguistics*, 2003). His involvement with Cognitive Linguistics dates from his first encounter with Langacker's *Foundations of Cognitive Grammar*, which he first read in the late 1980s. Gary B. Palmer can be reached at gary.palmer@unlv.edu.

KLAUS-UWE PANTHER (PhD 1976) is professor of English linguistics at the University of Hamburg. He has had a long-standing interest in pragmatics and its influence on grammatical structure culminated in two monographs. With Linda Thornburg, he was one of the first scholars in Cognitive Linguistics to recognize the importance of conceptual metonymy as a natural inference schema that underlies much of pragmatic reasoning (see, e.g., *Metonymy and Pragmatic Inferencing*, with Linda Thornburg, 2003). He is a member of the editorial board of *Cognitive Linguistics* and is on the advisory/referee board of several other journals. He is also a member of the editorial board of Benjamins's Cognitive Linguistics in Practice series. Currently, he is the president of the International Cognitive Linguistics Association. Klaus-Uwe Panther can be reached at panther@uni-hamburg.de.

ERIC PEDERSON (PhD 1991) is associate professor of linguistics at the University of Oregon. The overarching theme of his research is the relationship between language and conceptual processes. He was a student at the University of California, Berkeley, working within Cognitive Linguistics with George Lakoff, Dan Slobin, Eve Sweetser, and Leonard Talmy since 1980. He joined the Max Planck Institute for Psycholinguistics in 1991 until 1997, where he began working on issues more specific to linguistic relativity. Relevant publications include "Geographic and Manipulable Space in Two Tamil Linguistic Systems" (1993); "Language as Context, Language as Means: Spatial Cognition and Habitual Language use" (1995); "Semantic Typology and Spatial Conceptualization" (with Eve Danziger, Stephen Levinson, Sotaro Kita, Gunter Senft, and David Wilkins, 1998); "Through the Looking Glass: Literacy, Writing Systems and Mirror Image Discrimination" (with Eve Danziger, 1998); and "Mirror-Image Discrimination among Nonliterate, Monoliterate, and Biliterate Tamil Speakers" (2003). In addition to linguistic relativity, his general interests include semantic typology, field/descriptive linguistics (South India), and the representation of events. Eric Pederson can be reached at epederso@uoregon.edu.

FRANK POLZENHAGEN (PhD 2005) is a member of a research and dictionary project on West African English in progress at Humboldt University Berlin, where he earned his doctorate. His PhD thesis explores cultural conceptualizations in West African English. In his work, he seeks to combine the cognitive linguistic approach with concepts from anthropological linguistics and with corpus-linguistic methods and to apply this framework to the study of what has been termed "New Englishes" in sociolinguistics. His further research interests include Critical Discourse Analysis, metaphor theory, intercultural communication, and verb morphology. Frank Polzenhagen can be reached at frank.polzenhagen@rz.hu-berlin.de.

MARTIN PÜTZ (PhD 1987, Dr habil. 1993) is professor of linguistics and English language at the University of Koblenz-Landau (Campus Landau, Germany). He taught for several years at the Universities of Duisburg, Düsseldorf, Greifswald, and Groningen. His main research interests involve the fields of applied Cognitive Linguistics, multilingualism, and foreign language teaching/learning. Among his publications are several edited volumes, including *The Construal of Space in Language and Thought* (with René Dirven, 1996); *Applied Cognitive Linguistics*, 2 vols. (with Susanne Niemeier and René Dirven, 2001); *Cognitive Models in Language and Thought: Ideology, Metaphors and Meanings* (with René Dirven and Roslyn Frank, 2003); *Language, Discourse and Ideology* (with JoAnne Neff-van Aertselaer and Teun van Dijk, 2004); and *'Along the Routes to Power': Explorations of Empowerment through Language* (with Joshua A. Fishman and JoAnne Neff-van Aertselaer, 2006). He is the review editor and an editorial board member of the journal *Cognitive Linguistics*. In 1989, he organized, with René Dirven, the First International Cognitive Linguistics Conference at the University of Duisburg, Germany. Since the year 2000, he has been the main organizer of the biannual International LAUD Symposium, held at Landau University, Germany. Martin Pütz can be reached at puetz@uni-landau.de.

TIM ROHRER (PhD 1998) took his PhD in the philosophy of Cognitive Science at the University of Oregon under the guidance of Mark Johnson. Since 1987, when he first saw the potential of using cognitive semantics as a tool to analyze the political rhetoric of international peacemaking negotiations, he has been an active researcher and frequent contributor to the field. In 1994, he founded the online Center for the Cognitive Science of Metaphor at the University of Oregon to disseminate cognitive semantics research on the World Wide Web. He has recently held a Fulbright Fellowship at the Center for Semiotic Research in Aarhus, Denmark (where he collaborated with Per Aage Brandt and Chris Sinha on Embodiment Theory), and a NIH Fellowship to the Institute for Neural Computation and the Department of Cognitive Science at the University of California, San Diego, where he conducted ERP and fMRI studies on conceptual metaphor. Currently, he is at work on a book tentatively titled *Sensual Language: Embodiment, Cognition and the Brain* and directs the Colorado Advanced Research Institute. Tim Rohrer can be reached at rohrer@cogsci.ucsd.edu.

TED SANDERS (PhD 1992) is professor of Dutch language use and discourse studies at Utrecht University, Netherlands. His research concentrates on discourse structure and coherence. Striving for an interdisciplinary approach, he combines Cognitive Linguistics and text linguistics with the psycholinguistics of discourse processing, as well as with his interest in text and document design. He is currently the head of a research project on "Causality and Subjectivity in Discourse and Cognition," funded by the Dutch organization for scientific research (NWO). He is the (co-)author of several articles published in edited volumes and international journals, such as *Cognitive Linguistics, Discourse Processes, Journal of Pragmatics, Reading and Writing, Text,* and *Written Communication.* He recently coedited special issues of *Cognitive Linguistics* and *Discourse Processes,* and with Joost Schilperoord and Wilbert Spooren, he edited *Text Representation: Linguistic and Psycholinguistic Approaches* (2001). Ted Sanders can be reached at ted.sanders@let.uu.nl.

HANS-JÖRG SCHMID (PhD 1992) holds the chair of Modern English Linguistics at Munich University, Germany. His interest in Cognitive Linguistics dates back to the late 1980s, when he started working on his PhD thesis on categorization as a basic principle of semantic analysis, published in 1993. Together with Friedrich Ungerer he wrote the first book-sized introductory text to the whole field of Cognitive Linguistics, *An Introduction to Cognitive Linguistics* (1996; rev. 2nd ed., 2006). He has published articles on categorization, metaphor, compounding from a cognitive linguistic perspective, and the methodology of prototype theory, as well as on the reifying and encapsulating functions of abstract nouns, which are investigated in detail in his monograph *English Abstract Nouns as Conceptual Shells: From Corpus to Cognition* (2000). His most recent book, *Englische Morphologie und Wortbildung: Eine Einführung* (2005), includes a new cognitive linguistic perspective on English word-formation. Schmid initiated the foundation of the Interdisciplinary Centre for Cognitive Language Research at Munich University. Hans-Jörg Schmid can be reached at hans-joerg.schmid@anglistik.uni-muenchen.de.

GUNTER SENFT (PhD 1982) is senior research fellow at the Max Planck Institute for Psycholinguistics in Nijmegen and extraordinary professor of general linguistics at the University of Cologne (see http://www.mpi.nl/world/persons/profession/gunter.html for more information). His interest in Cognitive Linguistics dates from the 1980s, when he started investigating the system of nominal classification in Kilivila, the Austronesian language of the Trobriand Islanders of Papua New Guinea. He has been studying the language and the culture of the Trobriand Islanders since 1982 (including 37 months of fieldwork so far). His main research interests include Austronesian (especially Oceanic) and Papuan languages, anthropological linguistics, pragmatics, lexical semantics, the interface between language, culture, and cognition, the conceptualization of space, and the documentation of endangered languages. His publications include the following books: *Sprachliche Varietät und Variation im Sprachverhalten Kaiserslauterer Metallarbeiter* (1982); *Kilivila: The Language of the Trobriand Islanders* (1986); *Classificatory particles in Kilivila* (1996); *Referring to Space: Studies in Austronesian and Papuan Languages* (1997); and *Systems of Nominal Classification* (2000). He is senior editor of *Pragmatic,* the journal of the International Pragmatics Association, and was one of the founding members of the European Society for Oceanists and of the Gesellschaft für bedrohte Sprachen. Gunter Senft can be reached at gunter.senft@mpi.nl.

CHRIS SINHA (PhD 1988) is professor of psychology of language in the Department of Psychology, University of Portsmouth, United Kingdom. His first degree was in developmental psychology, and he remains (if critically) a devotee of the grand narratives of Baldwin, Piaget, Vygotsky, and Wallon, as well as finding lasting inspiration in the work of Jerry Bruner and Colwyn Trevarthen. His involvement with Cognitive Linguistics was triggered by reading Langacker and Lakoff, and by the first International Cognitive Linguistics Conference in Duisburg in 1989, organized by René Dirven. These enlightening experiences convinced him that Cognitive Linguistics was indispensable for interdisciplinary work in the cognitive and language sciences. His central research interest is in the developmental relations between language, cognition, and culture, and he co-organized the International Conference on Language, Culture, and Mind at Portsmouth in 2004. A main aim of his research is to integrate Cognitive Linguistic with sociocultural approaches to language acquisition and development. He was the initiator of Project SCALA, which pioneered a cognitive semantic-based approach to language acquisition and development, focusing on the cross-linguistic and cross-cultural study of the development of spatial language and cognition. He is author of *Language and Representation: A Socio-naturalistic Approach to Human Development* (1988) and of numerous articles in cultural and developmental psychology, linguistics, education, evolutionary and comparative biology, and anthropology. Chris Sinha can be reached at chris.sinha@port.ac.uk.

DIRK SPEELMAN (PhD 1997) is associate professor at the Department of Linguistics, University of Leuven, where he teaches corpus linguistics and ICT for language students. In his PhD, he explored possibilities for cross-fertilization between theoretical concepts from Cognitive Linguistics (notably prototype theory) and empirical methods from quantitative corpus linguistics. Speelman is coauthor of *Convergentie en divergentie in de Nederlandse woordenschat* (with Dirk Geeraerts and Stefan Grondelaers, 1999). He also is author of several software tools in support of quantitative corpus-based or corpus-driven analysis of language (e.g., the tool *Abundantia Verborum*). His main research interest lies in the fields of corpus linguistics, computational lexicology, and variationist linguistics in general. Much of his work focuses on methodology and on the application of statistical and other quantitative methods to the study of language. Dirk Speelman can be reached at dirk.speelman@arts.kuleuven.be.

WILBERT SPOOREN (PhD 1989) is professor of language and communication at the Vrije Universiteit Amsterdam, Netherlands. His research focuses on issues of text structure and coherence. He is interested in combining insights from the fields of Cognitive Linguistics, text linguistics, and psycholinguistics, and in doing so, applies various research methodologies (both qualitative and quantitative—the latter comprising corpus studies, experiments, and survey studies). In order to stimulate the interdisciplinary discussion of issues of text structure, he has, since 1995, been involved in the organization of a series of international biannual workshops called Multidisciplinary Approaches to Discourse (MAD). He has published on discourse structure, genre, interestingness, and persuasiveness, in edited volumes and in journals such as *Cognitive Linguistics, Discourse Processes*, and *Journal of Research in Reading*. Together with Ted Sanders and Joost Schilperoord, he edited a book volume on *Text Representation* (2001). Wilbert Spooren can be reached at w.spooren@ let.vu.nl.

SOTERIA SVOROU (PhD 1988) is professor of linguistics at San José State University, California. Her main research interests lie with the intersection of lexical semantics, semantic typology and universals, and grammaticalization. Her involvement with Cognitive Linguistics dates from the 1980s, when she started to investigate the expression of spatial relations across languages. Her monograph, *The Grammar of Space* (1994), represents an example of how the theoretical tools of Cognitive Linguistics can be used to analyze synchronic, cross-linguistic, and diachronic aspects of spatial grammatical forms. It was followed by other published work on issues of semantic typology and grammaticalization of spatial grammatical forms. Her current research interests include the syntax and semantics of multiverb constructions across languages. Soteria Svorou can be reached at ssvorou@email .sjsu.edu.

LEONARD TALMY (PhD 1972) is professor of linguistics and adjunct professor of philosophy and was director of the Center for Cognitive Science for thirteen years through summer 2004 at the University at Buffalo, State University of New York. His broader research interests cover Cognitive Linguistics, the properties of conceptual organization, and cognitive theory. His more specific interests within linguistics center on natural language semantics, including: typologies and universals of semantic structure; the relationship between semantic structure and formal linguistic structures—lexical, morphological, and syntactic; and the relation of this material to diachrony, discourse, development, impairment, and culture. Additional specializations are in American Indian and Yiddish linguistics. Over the years, he has published several articles on these topics, which have been collected in the two-volume set, *Toward a Cognitive Semantics*: volume 1, *Concept Structuring Systems*; volume 2, *Typology and Process in Concept Structuring* (2000). He is currently working on a book for MIT Press titled *The Attention System of Language*. He was elected a Fellow of the Cognitive Science Society in its 2002 inaugural selection of Fellows (and had been a founding member of the society). He is on a number of journal and governing boards. He is included in *Outstanding People of the 20th Century* and in *International Who's Who of Intellectuals* (13th ed.). Leonard Talmy can be reached at talmy@buffalo.edu.

JOHN R. TAYLOR (PhD 1979) is senior lecturer in linguistics at the University of Otago, New Zealand; previously he was at the University of the Witwatersrand, Johannesburg, and the University of Trier, Germany. His interest in Cognitive Linguistics dates from the 1980s, when, after having completed his doctoral thesis on acoustic phonetics, he chanced upon a preprint of some chapters of Langacker's *Foundations of Cognitive Grammar*. He is author of *Linguistic Categorization* (1989; 2nd ed., 1995; 3rd rev. ed., 2003; and translated into Japanese, Korean, Italian, and Polish), *Possessives in English* (1996), and *Cognitive Grammar* (which appeared in 2003 in the Oxford Textbooks in Linguistics series). He has also coedited two volumes: *Language and the Cognitive Construal of the World* (with Robert MacLaury, 1996) and *Current Approaches to Lexical Semantics* (with Hubert Cuyckens and René Dirven, 2003). Since 1996, he has been one of the editors (alongside Ronald Langacker and René Dirven) of the series Cognitive Linguistics Research, published by Mouton de Gruyter. His main research interests are lexical semantics, the syntax-semantics interface, and phonetics/phonology in a Cognitive Linguistics perspective. John R Taylor can be reached at john.taylor@stonebow.otago.ac.nz.

LINDA L. THORNBURG (PhD 1984) taught linguistics at California State University, Fresno, and Cognitive and Functional Linguistics at Eötvös Loránd University, Budapest. She has been an occasional lecturer in the Department of English and American Studies at Hamburg University. Her interest in semantic and pragmatic explanations in historical linguistics, a topic pursued in her dissertation on syntactic reanalysis in early English, led her quite naturally to Cognitive Linguistics. Since 1994 she has been collaborating with Klaus-Uwe Panther on various projects on the role of metonymy in conceptual and grammatical structure and language use. Thornburg and Panther's key ideas on the role of metonymy in pragmatic inferencing were laid out in an article in the *Journal of Pragmatics* (1998) and applied and refined in many subsequent publications culminating in their edited volume *Metonymy and Pragmatic Inferencing* (2003). They are currently working on an edited volume *Metonymy and Metaphor in Grammar*. Thornburg serves on the advisory boards of several (cognitive linguistic) journals, and she is a board member of the Linguistic Association of Canada and the United States. She is coeditor (with Janet M. Fuller) of the forthcoming *Studies in Contact Linguistics: Essays in Honor of Glenn G. Gilbert*. Linda L. Thornburg can be reached at lthornburg@alumni.usc.edu.

MICHAEL TOMASELLO (PhD 1980) is codirector of the Max Planck Institute for Evolutionary Anthropology in Leipzig. His major research interests include processes of social cognition, social learning, and communication from a developmental, comparative, and cultural perspective, with special emphasis on aspects related to language and its acquisition. His current theoretical focus involves processes of shared intentionality. Major publications include *First Verbs: A Case Study of Early Grammatical Development* (1992); *The Cultural Origins of Human Cognition* (1999); and *Constructing a Language: A Usage-Based Theory of Language Acquisition* (2003). Michael Tomasello can be reached at tomas@eva.mpg.de.

DAVID TUGGY (PhD 1981) has been a member of the Summer Institute of Linguistics (SIL) since 1970. He studied at the University of California, San Diego, and wrote one of the first dissertations within the Space Grammar (later Cognitive Grammar) framework. It was the first to be based on a non-Indo-European language. He has published a number of articles from a Cognitive Linguistics perspective and has taught Cognitive Grammar at a number of universities and workshops in Latin America, the United States, and elsewhere. He has published (in Spanish) a grammar of Orizaba Nawatl (available at http://www.sil.org/~dtuggy) and is coordinator of the Mexico Web site of SIL (http://www.sil.org/mexico). Among his research interests are Nahuatl, inadvertent blends and other bloopers (a forthcoming book is titled *My Brain Has a Mind of Its Own*), and lexicography. David Tuggy can be reached at david_tuggy@sil.org.

MARK TURNER (PhD 1983) is institute professor at Case Western Reserve University. He took his PhD in English language and literature and his MA in mathematics from the University of California, Berkeley. His books include *Death Is the Mother of Beauty: Mind, Metaphor, Criticism* (1987); *Reading Minds: The Study of English in the Age of Cognitive Science* (1991); *The Literary Mind: The Origins of Thought and Language* (1996); and *Cognitive Dimensions of Social Science: The Way We think about Politics, Economics, Law, and Society* (2001). He has been a visiting professor at the Collège de France and a fellow of the Institute for Advanced Study, the John Simon Guggenheim Memorial Foundation, the Center for Advanced Study in the Behavioral Sciences, the National Humanities Center, and the National Endowment for the Humanities. In 1996, the Académie française awarded him the *Prix du Rayonnement de la langue et de la littérature françaises*. His Web page address is http://turner.stanford.edu. Mark Turner can be reached at mark .turner@case.edu.

FRIEDRICH UNGERER (PhD 1964) is emeritus professor of English linguistics at the University of Rostock, Germany. He was attracted to Cognitive Linguistics in the early 1990s and has worked mainly in the fields of lexical categorization, metaphor, and iconicity. Apart from his coauthorship of *An Introduction to Cognitive Linguistics* (with Hans-Jörg Schmid, 1996), he has edited *Kognitive Lexikologie* (1998), a collection of essays, and has published a number of articles in the above areas, the most recent one on the cognitive function of derivational morphology (2002). Other current research areas are applied grammatical description and media linguistics. Friedrich Ungerer can be reached at friedrich.ungerer@philfak.uni-rostock.de.

JOHAN VAN DER AUWERA (PhD 1980) is professor of English and general linguistics at the University of Antwerp. His research interests have always concerned language universals, but whereas he initially approached them from a logical and philosophical point of view, he has progressively become more involved in typology and, more particularly, grammatical semantics. A major focus is the study of mood and modality. Book-length results of his work include *Language and Logic* (1985) and the edited volumes *The Germanic Languages* (with Ekkehard König, 1994) and *Adverbial Constructions in the Languages of Europe* (1998). His present activities are embedded in a center that brings together cognitive and typological linguistics, the Antwerp Center for Grammar, Cognition and Typology (http://webhost.ua.ac.be/cgct/). His Web pages address is http://webhost.ua.ac.be/vdauwera. Johan van der Auwera can be reached at johan.vanderauwera@ua.ac.be.

KAREN VAN HOEK (PhD 1992) studied Cognitive Linguistics and the acquisition of American Sign Language at the University of California, San Diego. Her dissertation, "Paths Through Conceptual Structure: Constraints on Pronominal Anaphora," was published by Chicago University Press as *Anaphora and Conceptual Structure* (1995). The work was a groundbreaking demonstration that Cognitive

Grammar could explain constraints on pronominal anaphora more insightfully than generative grammar accounts based on c-command. She currently works in the field of accent reduction for the company Your American Voice and does research on the application of cognitive semantics and frame theory to political arguments and speechwriting. Karen can Hoek can be reached at kvh@umich.edu.

WILLY VAN LANGENDONCK (PhD 1970) is professor of linguistics at the University of Leuven. He started as a structuralist, became a generativist, turned to Generative Semantics, and got interested in cognitive linguistic theories, such as Word Grammar, Cognitive Grammar, and Radical Construction Grammar. His main research interests include markedness and iconicity, reference and semantics (especially proper names), and grammatical categories such as definiteness, genericness, number, grammatical relations, prepositions, dependency syntax, and word order. In these fields he has published a substantial number of articles in journals, readers, and handbooks. Recent titles include *Word Grammar* (with Richard Hudson, 1991); *Ikonizität in natürlicher Sprache* (with W.A. de Pater, 1992); "Determiners as Heads?" (1994); "The Dative in Latin and the Indirect Object in Dutch" (1998); and "Neurolinguistic and Syntactic Evidence for Basic Level Meaning in Proper Names" (1999). He has also published two edited volumes on the dative (with William Van Belle, 1996, 1998). His recent research is concerned with the role of iconically formed relator constructions in cross-linguistic word order. Willy Van Langendonck can be reached at willy.vanlangendonck@arts .kuleuven.be.

ARIE VERHAGEN (PhD 1986) has been the chair of Dutch Linguistics at the University of Leiden since 1998. He received his PhD at the Free University of Amsterdam on a study of word order, presenting an account in terms of perceptual independence based on linear precedence. Soon afterwards, he started to participate in the emerging community of cognitive linguists. From his dissertation work onwards, he has been especially interested in linking up the study of grammar with the use of language in discourse. He has taught at the Free University of Amsterdam, Utrecht University, and the University of Leiden. His publications include the following books: *Linguistic Theory and the Function of Word Order in Dutch* (1986), *Usage-Based Approaches to Dutch* (edited with Jeroen van de Weijer, 2003), *Constructions of Intersubjectivity. Discourse, Syntax, and Cognition* (2005). He was editor of the major Dutch linguistics journal *Nederlandse taalkunde* (and one of its predecessors) from 1981 until 1999 and editor-in-chief of the journal *Cognitive Linguistics* from 1996 until 2004. His research focuses on relations between language use and language structure, synchronically and diachronically, in a usage-based, evolutionary approach to construction grammar; special topics include (inter)subjectivity, causation, and stylistics. His Web site address is http://www .arieverhagen.nl. Arie Verhagen can be reached at arie.verhagen@let.leidenuniv.nl.

SHERMAN WILCOX (PhD 1988) is professor of linguistics at the University of New Mexico. His main research interests are the theoretical and applied study of signed languages. His theoretical work focuses on iconicity, gesture, and typological studies of signed languages. He is widely recognized as an advocate for academic acceptance of American Sign Language in universities in the United States. He also has taught signed language interpreting for many years and most recently has begun to demonstrate the application of Cognitive Linguistics to interpreting theory. He is author of several books and articles, including *The Phonetics of Fingerspelling* (1992); *Gesture and the Nature of Language* (with David F. Armstrong and William C. Stokoe, 1994); *Learning to See: Teaching American Sign Language as a Second Language* (with Phyllis Perrin Wilcox, 1997); and several edited collections. Sherman Wilcox can be reached at wilcox@unm.edu.

HANS-GEORG WOLF (PhD 1994, Dr habil. 2001) is associate professor in the English Department and coordinator of the Program in Language and Communication at the University of Hong Kong. He has published a book on *English in Cameroon* (2001) and one on *The Folk Model of the 'Internal Self' in Light of the Contemporary View of Metaphor: The Self as Subject and Object* (1994). His research interests include sociolinguistics, Cognitive Linguistics, corpus linguistics, and pragmatics, and he tries to weave them into a coherent whole in his studies of cultural variation in second language varieties of English. Hans-Georg Wolf can be reached at hanswolf@hkucc.hku.hk.

JORDAN ZLATEV (PhD 1997) is assistant professor at the Center for Languages and Literature, Lund University, Sweden (see http://asip.lucs.lu.se/People/Jordan .Zlatev for more information). In his PhD dissertation "Situated Embodiment: Studies in the Emergence of Spatial Meaning," he presented a synthetic biocultural conceptual framework for the study of language and cognition and its application to spatial meaning. He has continued this line of work with respect to language acquisition, "epigenetic robotics," and most recently the evolution of language and its relation to gesture. He has published chapters related to spatial semantics in several volumes dealing with Cognitive Semantics, as well as articles in interdisciplinary journals (e.g., his 2001 "The Epigenesis of Meaning in Human Beings, and Possibly in Robots," *Minds and Machines*). His engagement with Cognitive Linguistics began in 1992, while visiting the University of California, Berkeley, and collaborating with Terry Regier on the connectionist modeling of spatial language. Jordan Zlatev can be reached at jordan.zlatev@ling.lu.se.

Abbreviations

1	First person	IMPERF	Imperfective
2	Second person	IMPERS	Impersonal
3	Third person	IND	Indicative
ABL	Ablative	INF	Infinitive
ABS	Absolutive	INST	Instrumental
ACC	Accusative	INTR	Intransitive
ADVZ	Adverbializer	INV	Inverse
AF	Agent focus	IRR	Irrealis mood
ALL	Allative	LF	Location in focus
AP	Antipassive	LG	Ligature
ART	Article	LOC	Locative
BEN	Benefactive	LRM	Light reflexive marker
BF	Beneficiary in focus	M	Masculine
CL	Classifier	MID	Middle
COMP	Complementizer	N	Noun
COMPL	Completive	NC	Non-control
COND	Conditional	NCL	Noun classifier
COP	Copula	NEG	Negative
DAT	Dative	NOM	Nominative
DEF	Definite	NOMZ	Nominalizer
DEM	Demonstrative	OBJ	Object
DET	Determiner	OBL	Oblique
DIR	Direct	OBSRV	Observer
DS	Directional suffix	OBV	Obviative
EMPH	Emphatic	PART	Partitive
EPISTNEC	Epistemic necessity	PASS	Passive
ERG	Ergative	PERF	Perfective
EUPH	Euphonic	PL	Plural
F	Feminine	PM	Predicate marker
FIN	Finite	POSS	Possessive
FOC	Focus	POT	Potential
FUT	Future	PP	Past participle
FUTPST	Future past	PRED	Predicative
GEN	Genitive	PRÊT	Preterite
HON	Honorific	PRO	Anaphoric pronoun
HRM	Heavy reflexive marker	PROL	Prolative case

PROX	Proximal	SG	Singular
PRS	Present	SITNEC	Situational necessity
PST	Past	SPC	Specific
PSTSUBJ	Past subjunctive	SPON	Spontaneous
R	Imperfective reduplication	STAT	Stative
REFL	Reflexive	SUBJ	Subjunctive
REM	Remote deictic	TF	Theme in focus
REP	Repetitive	TOP	Topic
RLS	Realis mood	TR	Trajector
SFP	Sentence final particle	TRNS	Transitive

THE OXFORD HANDBOOK OF

COGNITIVE
LINGUISTICS

CHAPTER 1

INTRODUCING COGNITIVE LINGUISTICS

DIRK GEERAERTS
AND HUBERT CUYCKENS

1. INTRODUCTION

Cognitive Linguistics as represented in this *Handbook* is an approach to the analysis of natural language that originated in the late seventies and early eighties in the work of George Lakoff, Ron Langacker, and Len Talmy, and that focuses on language as an instrument for organizing, processing, and conveying information. Given this perspective, the analysis of the conceptual and experiential basis of linguistic categories is of primary importance within Cognitive Linguistics: the formal structures of language are studied not as if they were autonomous, but as reflections of general conceptual organization, categorization principles, processing mechanisms, and experiential and environmental influences.

In this introductory chapter, we will sketch the theoretical position of Cognitive Linguistics together with a number of practical features of the way in which research in Cognitive Linguistics is organized: Who are the people involved in Cognitive Linguistics? What are the important conferences and the relevant publication channels? Are there any introductory textbooks? Throughout this theoretical and "sociological" introduction to Cognitive Linguistics, we will emphasize that Cognitive Linguistics is not a single theory of language, but rather a cluster of broadly compatible approaches. This recognition also determines the practical organization of the present *Handbook*, which will be presented in the fourth section of the chapter. The penultimate and the final sections deal with two specific questions: can we explain the apparent appeal of Cognitive Linguistics, and what would be important questions for the further development of the framework?

2. THE THEORETICAL POSITION OF COGNITIVE LINGUISTICS

Because Cognitive Linguistics sees language as embedded in the overall cognitive capacities of man, topics of special interest for Cognitive Linguistics include: the structural characteristics of natural language categorization (such as prototypicality, systematic polysemy, cognitive models, mental imagery, and metaphor); the functional principles of linguistic organization (such as iconicity and naturalness); the conceptual interface between syntax and semantics (as explored by Cognitive Grammar and Construction Grammar); the experiential and pragmatic background of language-in-use; and the relationship between language and thought, including questions about relativism and conceptual universals.

Crucially, there is no single, uniform doctrine according to which these research topics (all of which receive specific attention in the chapters of this *Handbook*) are pursued by Cognitive Linguistics. In this sense, Cognitive Linguistics is a flexible framework rather than a single theory of language. In terms of category structure (one of the standard topics for analysis in Cognitive Linguistics), we might say that Cognitive Linguistics itself, when viewed as a category, has a family resemblance structure (Lewandowska-Tomaszczyk, this volume, chapter 6): it constitutes a cluster of many partially overlapping approaches rather than a single well-defined theory.

Even so, the recognition that Cognitive Linguistics has not yet stabilized into a single uniform theory should not prevent us from looking for fundamental common features and shared perspectives among the many forms of research that come together under the label of Cognitive Linguistics. An obvious question to start from relates to the "cognitive" aspect of Cognitive Linguistics: in what sense exactly is Cognitive Linguistics a cognitive approach to the study of language?

Terminologically, a distinction imposes itself between Cognitive Linguistics (the approach represented in this *Handbook*), and (uncapitalized) cognitive linguistics (all approaches in which natural language is studied as a mental phenomenon). Cognitive Linguistics is but one form of cognitive linguistics, to be distinguished from, for instance, Generative Grammar and many forms of linguistic research within the field of Artificial Intelligence. What, then, determines the specificity of Cognitive Linguistics within cognitive science? The question may be broken down in two more specific ones: what is the precise meaning of *cognitive* in *Cognitive Linguistics*, and how does this meaning differ from the way in which other forms of linguistics conceive of themselves as being a cognitive discipline? (The latter question will be answered specifically with regard to Generative Grammar.)

Against the background of the basic characteristics of the cognitive paradigm in cognitive psychology, the philosophy of science, and related disciplines (see De Mey 1992), the viewpoint adopted by Cognitive Linguistics can be defined more precisely. Cognitive Linguistics is the study of language in its cognitive function, where *cognitive* refers to the crucial role of intermediate informational structures in our encounters with the world. Cognitive Linguistics is cognitive in the same way that cognitive psychology is: by assuming that our interaction with the world is mediated through informational structures in the mind. It is more specific than cognitive psychology, however, by focusing on natural language as a means for organizing, processing, and conveying that information. Language, then, is seen as a repository of world knowledge, a structured collection of meaningful categories that help us deal with new experiences and store information about old ones.

From this overall characterization, three fundamental characteristics of Cognitive Linguistics can be derived: the primacy of semantics in linguistic analysis, the encyclopedic nature of linguistic meaning, and the perspectival nature of linguistic meaning. The first characteristic merely states that the basic function of language involves meaning; the other two characteristics specify the nature of the semantic phenomena in question. The *primacy of semantics* in linguistic analysis follows in a straightforward fashion from the cognitive perspective itself: if the primary function of language is categorization, then meaning must be the primary linguistic phenomenon. The *encyclopedic nature of linguistic meaning* follows from the categorial function of language: if language is a system for the categorization of the world, there is no need to postulate a systemic or structural level of linguistic meaning that is different from the level where world knowledge is associated with linguistic forms. The *perspectival nature of linguistic meaning* implies that the world is not objectively reflected in the language: the categorization function of the language imposes a structure on the world rather than just mirroring objective reality. Specifically, language is a way of organizing knowledge that reflects the needs, interests, and experiences of individuals and cultures. The idea that linguistic meaning has a perspectivizing function is theoretically elaborated in the philosophical, epistemological position taken by Cognitive Linguistics (see Johnson 1987; Lakoff 1987; Geeraerts 1993). The *experientialist* position of Cognitive Linguistics vis-à-vis human knowledge emphasizes the view that human reason is determined by our organic embodiment and by our individual and collective experiences.

Given this initial characterization of the cognitive nature of Cognitive Linguistics, we can now turn to the second question: how can it be that Cognitive Linguistics and Generative Grammar both proclaim themselves to be cognitive enterprises?

Essentially, the two approaches differ with regard to the epistemological role of natural language. They both agree (and this is their common cognitive parentage) that there can be no knowledge without the existence of a mental representation that has a constitutive, mediating role in the epistemological relationship between subject and object. But while, according to Cognitive Linguistics, natural languages precisely embody such categorial perspectives onto the outside world, the generative linguist takes natural language as the object of the epistemological relationship, rather than as the intermediate link between subject and object. Cognitive Linguistics is interested in our knowledge of the world and studies the question how natural language contributes to it. The generative linguist, conversely, is interested in our knowledge of the language and asks the question how such knowledge can be acquired given a cognitive theory of learning. As cognitive enterprises, Cognitive Linguistics and Generative Grammar are similarly interested in those mental structures that are constitutive of knowledge. For the Cognitive approach, natural language itself consists of such structures, and the relevant kind of knowledge is knowledge of the world. For the generative grammarian, however, the knowledge under consideration is knowledge of the language, and the relevant mental structures are constituted by the genetic endowment of human beings that enables them to learn the language. Whereas Generative Grammar is interested in knowledge *of* the language, Cognitive Linguistics is so to speak interested in knowledge *through* the language.

The characterization that we just gave of the "cognitive" nature of Cognitive Linguistics in comparison with the cognitive nature of Generative Grammar suggests that there are two ways in which a direct confrontation of Cognitive Linguistics and Generative Grammar can be achieved.

In the first place, taking into account the formalist stance of Generative Grammar, Cognitive Linguistics should try to show that an adequate description of the allegedly formal phenomena at the core of generative theory formation involve semantic and functional factors that are beyond the self-imposed limits of the generative framework. In this sense, Cognitive Linguistics is characterized by a specific working hypothesis about natural language, namely, that much more in natural language can be explained on semantic and functional grounds than has hitherto been assumed (a working hypothesis that it shares, to be sure, with many other pragmatically and functionally oriented linguistic theories). Any time a particular phenomenon turns out to involve cognitive functioning rather than just formal syntax, the need to posit genetically given formal constraints on possible syntactic constructions diminishes. A prime example of this type of argumentation can be found in van Hoek's chapter 34 of this *Handbook*.

In the second place, Cognitive Linguistics should develop a nonautonomist theory of language acquisition embodying the predictions, first, that language acquisition often involves mechanisms and constraints that are not specific to natural language, and second, to the extent that there do exist constraints on learning that are restricted to natural language acquisition, that these will at least to some extent draw on "informational substance" supplied by cognitive systems other than the linguistic. In chapter 41 of the present *Handbook*, Tomasello illustrates how this program is actually carried out.

To summarize, what holds together the diverse forms of Cognitive Linguistics is the belief that linguistic knowledge involves not just knowledge of the language, but knowledge of the world as mediated by the language. Because of this shift in the type of knowledge that the approaches focus on in contrast with Generative Grammar, and specifically because of the experientialist nature of Cognitive Linguistics, it is sometimes said that Cognitive Linguistics belongs to the "second cognitive revolution," whereas Generative Grammar belongs to the "first cognitive revolution" of the 1950s; see Sinha, this volume, chapter 49, for an elaboration.

3. THE PRACTICAL ASPECTS OF COGNITIVE LINGUISTICS

Scientific frameworks are not just sets of concepts, models, and techniques: they also consist of people, activities, and channels of communication. Thinking in terms of people, the key figures of Cognitive Linguistics are George Lakoff, Ronald W. Langacker, and Leonard Talmy. Around this core of founding fathers, who originated Cognitive Linguistics in the late 1970s and the early 1980s, two chronologically widening circles of cognitive linguists may be discerned. A first wave, coming to the fore in the second half of the 1980s, consists of the early collaborators and colleagues of the key figures, together with a first generation of students. Names that come to mind include those of Gilles Fauconnier, Eve Sweetser, Mark Johnson, Mark Turner, Ray Gibbs, Bill Croft, Adele Goldberg, Dave Tuggy, Laura Janda, Suzanne Kemmer, Sally Rice, Ricardo Maldonado, and Karen van Hoek. Simultaneously, a number of people in mostly Western and Central Europe took up the ideas of Cognitive Linguistics and contributed to their international dissemination. Names include those of René Dirven, Brygida Rudzka-Ostyn, John Taylor, Chris Sinha, Arie Verhagen, Barbara Lewandowska-Tomaszczyk, Peter Harder, Günter Radden, and the editors of this *Handbook*. The 1990s witnessed a second wave of expansion, directed largely toward Asia and the south of Europe.

Organizationally, the contacts between the people working in the Cognitive Linguistics framework are facilitated by the ICLA or International Cognitive Linguistics Association. The Association (see http://www.cognitivelinguistics.org/), which has a number of local and regional affiliates, organizes the biannual conferences in Cognitive Linguistics that constitute the rallying point for people working in the field. The first ICLC conference was organized in 1989 in Duisburg by René Dirven (whose role in giving Cognitive Linguistics an organizational structure can hardly be underestimated). Later venues include Santa Cruz (1991), Leuven (1993), Albuquerque (1995), Amsterdam (1997), Stockholm (1999), Santa Barbara (2001), Logroño (2003), Seoul (2005), Krakow (2007), and Berkeley (2009).

Given the theoretical aspects of Cognitive Linguistics as described in the previous paragraph, it is easy to appreciate that the demarcation of Cognitive Linguistics in terms of people is somewhat arbitrary. Sociologically speaking, cognitive linguists would be those people who belong to the Cognitive Linguistics community—who interact with like-minded researchers and who attend the ICLC conferences. But if we think in terms of common perspectives and purposes, even if only partially shared, many more names could be mentioned. For instance, in terms of seminal ideas and actual influence, Charles Fillmore should be considered on a par with the three founding fathers, even though he would probably not describe himself as a cognitive linguist.

The journal *Cognitive Linguistics*, which was founded by Dirk Geeraerts in 1990, is the official journal of the ICLA. In 2003, a second journal specifically devoted to research in Cognitive Linguistics, the *Annual Review of Cognitive Linguistics*, was launched under the auspices of the Spanish branch of the ICLA. Book series dedicated to Cognitive Linguistics are published by two major publishing houses in linguistics: Mouton de Gruyter of Berlin publishes the Cognitive Linguistics Research series, and John Benjamins Publishing Company of Amsterdam publishes the Cognitive Linguistics in Practice series.

Primers in Cognitive Linguistics, in the form of introductory textbooks, include (in chronological order of first appearance), Taylor (1989), Ungerer and Schmid (1996), Dirven and Verspoor (1998), Lee (2001), Croft and Cruse (2004), and Evans and Green (2006). The Dirven and Verspoor volume has been translated in several languages. A collection of basic texts by leading representatives of Cognitive Linguistics may be found in Geeraerts (2006a).

An extended bibliography of work in Cognitive Linguistics, edited by Hans-Georg Wolf, René Dirven, Rong Chen, Ning Yu, and Birgit Smieja, has appeared online and on CD-ROM at Mouton de Gruyter, Berlin in 2006. The *Cognitive Linguistics Bibliography* (*CogBib*) consists of a database covering monographs, journal articles, book series, dissertations, MA theses, proceedings, working papers, and unpublished work relevant to the study of Cognitive Linguistics and adjacent disciplines. It consists of 7,000 entries and aims at an annual growth of 1,000 items. The first release of the database is fully indexed and will be available for subscribers to *Cognitive Linguistics*.

4. THE ORGANIZATION
OF THE *HANDBOOK*

The organization of the present *Handbook* reflects the prototypical structure of Cognitive Linguistics that was described above. In terms of people, the contributions come predominantly from first-generation cognitive linguists, together with some members of the second generation, and a number of fellow travelers who would perhaps not consider themselves cognitive linguists *pur sang*, but who are close enough to Cognitive Linguistics to shed an illuminating light on some of its subdomains. And, of course, the key figures are represented. We regret that George Lakoff was not able to contribute to this *Handbook* (with a projected chapter on the relationship between Cognitive Linguistics and neuroscience).

In terms of content, the absence of a single unified theoretical doctrine means that a handbook of this type cannot simply start off with an exposé on the architecture of Cognitive Linguistics as a theory. Rather, we start, under the heading "Basic Concepts of Cognitive Linguistics," with a set of chapters that discuss different conceptual phenomena that are recognized by Cognitive Linguistics as key concepts: prototypicality, metaphor, metonymy, embodiment, perspectivization, mental spaces, and the like each constitute a specific principle of conceptual organization as reflected in the language. Many of these notions are far from exclusive for Cognitive Linguistics, but even then, Cognitive Linguistics subjects them to specific forms of analysis.

The second part of the *Handbook*, "Cognitive Linguistic Models of Grammar," deals with different frameworks that bring together a bigger or smaller number of the basic concepts into a particular theory of grammar and a specific model for the description of grammatical phenomena. The models discussed include Ron Langacker's Cognitive Grammar, Construction Grammar, and Word Grammar. The fact that theory formation in Cognitive Linguistics is not yet completely stabilized (or, to put it more constructively, the fact that Cognitive Linguistics is a flexible framework that allows for a number of competing frameworks to be developed in parallel) shows up in the relationship between Cognitive Grammar and Construction Grammar. On the one hand, the chapter on Construction Grammar describes a family of approaches and suggests that Cognitive Grammar as founded by Langacker is a member of that family. On the other hand, Cognitive Grammar was a well-established model of grammar well before Construction Grammar emerged. Moreover, it is without any doubt the most developed, both empirically and conceptually, of all approaches that could be grouped under the heading of Construction Grammar. The example shows how related theoretical models are developed in parallel within the broad framework of Cognitive Linguistics.

As we have seen, demarcation problems may exist at the edges of Cognitive Linguistics as a whole, just as they exist with regard to the boundary between different approaches within Cognitive Linguistics. To get a better grip on the position of Cognitive Linguistics within the landscape of linguistics at large, the section "Situating Cognitive Linguistics" compares Cognitive Linguistics with other forms of linguistic research: functional linguistics (its closest ally), autonomous linguistics (its declared enemy), and the history of linguistics (its often forgotten ancestry). Here again, the reader will notice that things are not always as simplistic as they might seem at first sight. The chapter on autonomous linguistics, for instance, suggests that the distance between Cognitive Linguistics and the contemporary developments in Chomskyan linguistics need not be in all respects unbridgeable.

The first three sections of the book constitute an initial introduction to Cognitive Linguistics. Readers who have gone through the twenty-one chapters of the first three sections will have acquired a fairly thorough knowledge of the fundamental analytic concepts and descriptive models of Cognitive Linguistics and their background. The following three sections of the *Handbook* apply these basics to various more specific domains. The section "Linguistic Structure and Language Use" illustrates how Cognitive Linguistics deals with the traditional subdomains of grammar, ranging from phonetics and morphology over lexicon and syntax to text and discourse. Separate chapters are devoted to topics that have received special attention in Cognitive Linguistics.

The chapters in the section "Linguistic Variation and Change" focus on different types of variation within and between languages. Next to diachronic change and sociolinguistic variation, these include typological variation (with related chapters on anthropological linguistics and linguistic relativity) and language acquisition (seen as variation in the individual's knowledge of the language). A chapter on sign language may also be placed within this section, given that sign language involves a change in the medium of communication.

The final section groups chapters that deal with "Applied and Interdisciplinary Perspectives." The interdisciplinary links with fields of research like philosophy and psychology are very important for Cognitive Linguistics. As it is one of the tenets of Cognitive Linguistics that linguistic knowledge is not separated from other forms of cognition, the disciplines studying those other aspects of human knowledge will be natural conversation partners for Cognitive Linguistics.

5. The Appeal of Cognitive Linguistics

Cognitive Linguistics is definitely a success in terms of academic appeal. The ICLC conferences, to give just one example, have grown into major events with more than 500 attendees. The openness and flexibility of theorizing in Cognitive Linguistics probably contributes to its attractiveness: as we have stressed, Cognitive Linguistics is a building with many rooms, and it may thus draw the attention of researchers with diverse interests. We think, however, that more is at stake. We would like to argue that Cognitive Linguistics combines a number of tendencies that may also be found in other contemporary developments in theoretical linguistics and, by combining them, taps into the undercurrent of contemporary developments more than any other theoretical framework.

More specifically, while *decontextualization* appears to be a fundamental underlying characteristic of the development of grammatical theory in twentieth-century linguistics, a number of current developments involve a *recontextualization* of grammar. And Cognitive Linguistics, we contend, embodies this recontextualizing tendency more than any other approach.

The logic behind the decontextualization of twentieth-century grammar may be grasped if we take our starting point in Saussure. The Saussurean dichotomy between *langue* and *parole* creates an internally divided grammar, a conception of language with, so to speak, a hole in the middle. On the one hand, *langue* is defined as a social system, a set of collective conventions, a common code shared by a community (Saussure [1916] 1967: 25). On the other hand, *parole* is an individual, psychological activity that consists of producing specific combinations from the elements that are present in the code (30). When *langue* and *parole* are defined in this way, there is a gap between both: what is the mediating factor that bridges the distance between the social and the psychological, between the community and the individual, between the system and the application of the system, between the code and the actual use of the code?

The Chomskyan distinction between competence and performance formulates the fundamental answer to this question: the missing link between social code and individual usage is the individual's knowledge of the code. Performance is basically equivalent with *parole*, but competence interiorizes the notion of the linguistic system: competence is the internal grammar of the language user, the knowledge that the language user has of the linguistic system and that he or she puts to use in actual performance.

Remarkably, however, Chomsky introduces a new gap into the system. Rather than the trichotomy that one might expect, he restricts his conception of language to a new dichotomy: the social aspects of language are largely ignored. In comparison with a ternary distinction distinguishing between *langue*, competence, and *parole*/performance (between social system, individual knowledge of the system, and individual use of the system), the binary distinction between competence and performance creates a new empty slot, leaving the social aspects of language largely out of sight.

Relegating the social nature of language to the background correlates with a switch toward the phylogenetic universality of language. The Chomskyan emphasis on the genetic nature of natural language links up logically with his apparent lack of interest for language as a social semiotic. Where, in particular, does the individual knowledge of the language come from? If the source of linguistic knowledge is not social, what else can it be than an innate and universal endowment? If the language is not learned through acculturation in a linguistic community (given that a language is not primarily a social code), what other source could there be for linguistic knowledge except genetics?

The link between the Chomskyan genetic perspective and the absence of any fundamental interest in language as a social phenomenon engenders a stepping-stone development, leading by an internal logic to an isolation of grammar. Let us go through the argument in the form of the following chain of (deliberately succinct and somewhat simplistic) propositions.

First, *if natural language is not primarily social, it has to be genetic*. This is the basic proposition that was described in the previous paragraph. The relationship could, of course, be construed in the other direction as well. As presented above, the Chomskyan predilection for a genetic perspective in linguistics follows from his lack of interest for the social side of language. But in actual historical fact, Chomsky's preference for a genetic conception of language seems to have grown more from his discussion with behaviorist learning theory (Skinner in particular) than from a confrontation with Saussure. Because the amazing ability of young children to acquire language cannot be explained on the basis of a stimulus-response theory—so the argument goes—an innate knowledge of language has to be assumed. But if one of the major features of language is its genetic nature, then of course the social aspects of language are epiphenomenal. Regardless of the direction in which the link is construed, however, the effects are clear.

Second, *if natural language is primarily a genetic entity, semantics or the lexicon cannot be part of the core of linguistics*. Meanings constitute the variable, contextual, cultural aspects of language par excellence. Because social interaction, the exchange of ideas, and changing conceptions of the world are primarily mediated through the meaning of linguistic expressions, it is unlikely that the universal aspects of language will be found in the realm of meaning. Further, if the lexicon is the main repository of linguistically encoded meaning, studying the lexicon is of secondary importance. Here as before, though, it should be pointed out that the actual historical development is less straightforward than the reconstruction might suggest. The desemanticization of the grammar did not happen at once (nor was it absolute, for that matter). Triggered by the introduction of meaning in the standard model of Generative Grammar (Chomsky 1965), the "Linguistic Wars" (see Harris 1993) of the late 1960s that opposed Generative Semantics and Interpretive Semantics basically involved the demarcation of grammar with regard to semantics. The answer that Chomsky ultimately favored implied a restrictive stance with regard to the introduction of meaning into the grammar, but this position was certainly not reached in one step; it was prepared by severe debates in the generativist community.

Third, *if semantics or the lexicon cannot be part of the core of linguistics, linguistics will focus on formal rule systems*. The preference for formal syntax that characterizes Generative Grammar follows by elimination from its genetic orientation: formality is required to keep out meaning, and studying syntax (or more generally, the rule-based aspects of language) correlates with the diminished interest in the lexicon. It should be added that the focus on rules is not only determined by a negative attitude with regard to meanings, but also by a focus on the infinity of language: language as an infinite set of sentences requires a rule system that can generate an infinity of sentences.

Finally, if linguistics focuses on formal rule systems, the application of the rule systems in actual usage is relatively uninteresting. If the rules define the grammar, it is hard to see what added value could be derived from studying the way in which the rules are actually put to use. The study of performance, in other words, is just as secondary as research into the lexicon.

This chain of consequences leads to a decontextualization of the grammar. It embodies a restrictive strategy that separates the autonomous grammatical module from different forms of context. Without further consideration of the interrelationship between the various aspects of the decontextualizing drift, the main effects can be summarized as follows:

a. through the basic Chomskyan shift from langue to competence, linguistics is separated from the social context of language as a social code;

b. through the focus on the genetic aspects of the language, linguistics is separated from the cognitive context that shows up in the semantic side of the language;

c. through the focus on formal rule systems, linguistics is separated from the situational context of actual language use.

In terms of the subdisciplines covered by linguistics, this means that the core of linguistics in Chomskyan terms respectively excludes sociolinguistics, semantics and the lexicon, and pragmatics. This does not mean, however, that these disciplines, which would be considered peripheral from the generativist point of view, disappeared altogether. In fact, the generativist era witnessed the birth, in the 1960s and 1970s, of approaches that autonomously developed the aspects that were rejected or downplayed by Generative Grammar: sociolinguistics (including the sociology of language, the ethnography of speaking, and sociohistorical linguistics, next to sociolinguistics in the narrow, Labovian sense), pragmatics (including discourse linguistics and conversational analysis), and formal semantics.

None of the approaches mentioned here, however, overcomes the autonomist restrictions in any fundamental sense. Sociolinguistics and pragmatics exist alongside grammatical theory rather than interacting with it intensively, and the conception of meaning that lies at the basis of formal semantics is too restricted to consider it a truly recontextualized grammar. In other words, the recuperation of the contextual aspects rejected by Generative Grammar could go further, and this is exactly what is happening in a number of contemporary trends in linguistics.

From roughly 1985 onwards, in fact, a number of trends in linguistics appear to link the grammar more closely to the contextual aspects that were severed from it by generative theorizing. The peripheral aspects that were being developed largely separately and autonomously are now being linked up more narrowly with the grammar itself (which can then no longer be autonomous). When we have a look at the relevant developments, we will see that Cognitive Linguistics plays a role in each of them.

First, the *reintroduction of the lexicon into the grammar* is probably the most widespread of the tendencies to be mentioned here; it is, in fact, relatively clear within Generative Grammar itself. This lexicalist tendency in grammatical theory is triggered by the recognition that describing grammatical rules appears to imply describing the lexical sets that the rules apply to. Reversing the descriptive perspective then leads to a description of the valence of the lexical items (i.e., the structures that an item can appear in). The lexicalist tendency appears in various forms in the more formal approaches to grammar: one may think of the projections and theta-roles of Generative Grammar, of the central role of the lexicon in Lexical-Functional Grammar, and of the lexically driven grammar developed in the framework of Head-Driven Phrase Structure Grammar. In the context of Cognitive Linguistics, the relexification of the grammar is most outspoken in Construction Grammar (Goldberg 1995; Croft 2001), which starts from the recognition that there is a continuum between syntax and lexicon: constructions are syntactic structures that may contain lexical material.

Second, Cognitive Linguistics at large is the most outspoken current attempt to *give meaning a central position in the architecture of the grammar*. In contrast with formal semantics, however, the conception of meaning that lies at the basis of this approach is not restricted to a referential, truth-functional type of meaning. Linguistic structures are thought to express conceptualizations, that is, conceptualization is central for linguistic structure—and conceptualization goes further than mere reference. It involves imagery in the broadest sense of the word: ways of making sense, of imposing meaning. Also, the conceptualizations that are expressed in the language have an experiential basis, that is, they link up with the way in which human beings experience reality, both culturally and physiologically. In this sense, Cognitive Linguistics embodies a fully contextualized conception of meaning. Again, there are other approaches that develop a meaning-based approach to grammar, like Hallidayan Systemic-Functional Grammar, but Cognitive Linguistics is undoubtedly the most outspoken example of this tendency.

And third, the *link between linguistic performance and grammar* is reestablished by those functionalist approaches that try to find (potentially universal) discourse motivations for grammatical constructs. Discourse is then no longer the mere application of grammatical rules, but the grammatical rules themselves are motivated by the discourse functions that the grammar has to fulfill. The existence of passives in a given language, for instance, is then explained as a topicalization mechanism: grammars contain passives because topicalizing direct objects is a useful function in discourse. Seminal publications within this approach include Givón (1979), Hopper and Thompson (1980), and Hopper (1987). In the realm of Cognitive Linguistics, this tendency takes the form of an insistence on the idea that Cognitive Linguistics is a usage-based model of language (as it is aptly called by Barlow and Kemmer 2000). Importantly, the model is also applied to language acquisition. Specifically in the work done by Tomasello and his group (see this volume, chapter 41), an alternative is presented for the Chomskyan genetic argument. These researchers develop a model of language acquisition in which each successive stage is (co)determined by the actual knowledge and use of the child at a given stage, that is, language acquisition is described as a series of step-by-step usage-based extensions of the child's grammar. The grammar so to speak emerges from the child's interactive performance. Finally, language use is becoming an increasingly important factor in grammatical change, witness Traugott's (1988) studies on the role of speaker-hearer interaction in grammaticalization; Croft's (2000) usage-based theory of language change (and grammatical change, in particular); and Bybee's (2001) and Krug's

(2000) work on such usage-based factors as entrenchment and frequency in grammatical change.

To conclude, if we can agree that contemporary linguistics embodies a tendency (a cluster of tendencies, to be more precise) toward the recontextualization of linguistic enquiry, we may also agree that Cognitive Linguistics embodies this trend to an extent that probably no other theoretical movement does. It embodies the resemanticization of grammar by focusing on the interplay between language and conceptualization. It embodies the recovery of the lexicon as a relevant structural level by developing network models of grammatical structure, like Construction Grammar. And it embodies the discursive turn of contemporary linguistics by insisting explicitly on the usage-based nature of linguistics. Other approaches may develop each of these tendencies separately in more detail than Cognitive Linguistics does, but it is the latter movement that combines them most explicitly and so epitomizes the characteristic underlying drift and drive of present-day linguistics. We would like to suggest, in short, that it is this feature that constitutes one of the fundamental reasons behind the success of Cognitive Linguistics.

6. The Future of Cognitive Linguistics

The recognition that Cognitive Linguistics is not a closed or finished doctrine implies, obviously, that there is room for further developments. The contributions brought together in this *Handbook* not only give an idea of the achievements of Cognitive Linguistics, but they also point to a number of underlying issues that are likely to shape the further elaboration of Cognitive Linguistics. Three issues that we would like to highlight are the following.

1. Readers will have noticed that a fourth type of context mentioned in our description of the decontextualizing tendencies of twentieth-century linguistics was absent from our overview of recontextualizing tendencies that apply to Cognitive Linguistics. In fact, Cognitive Linguistics, by its very "cognitive" nature, has a tendency to look at language from a psychological point of view, that is, language as (part of) the organization of knowledge in the individual mind. However, a number of researchers (Palmer 1996; Sinha and Jensen de López 2000; Harder 2003; Itkonen 2003; Tomasello 2003, and others) emphasize that the experientialist nature of Cognitive Linguistics does not only refer to material factors (taking a notion like "embodiment" in a physical and physiological sense) but that the cultural environment and the socially interactive nature of language should be recognized as primary elements of a cognitive approach.

This emphasis on the *social aspects of language*, however, will have to be turned into a an actual research program exploring social cognition and sociovariational phenomena. If Cognitive Linguistics develops an interest in language as a social phenomenon, it should pay more attention to language-internal variation. Sociolinguistic research, however, is probably the least developed of all linguistic domains within Cognitive Linguistics. Recently, though, we witness some developments toward cognitive sociolinguistics.

For one thing, variational phenomena are being studied empirically in work such as Kristiansen (2003) on phonetic variation, Berthele (2004) on differences in syntactic construal between dialects, and Grondelaers (2000) on grammatical phenomena whose distribution is determined by a combination of internal (structural or semantic) and external (contextual or sociolinguistic) factors. More examples may be found in Kristiansen and Dirven (2007). Usage-based and meaning-based models of grammar in fact introduce more variation into the grammar than a rule-based approach tends to do: the language-internal or discourse-related factors that influence the use of a particular construction may be manifold, and the presence or absence of a construction is not an all-or-none matter. In the analysis of this type of variation, it often appears that the variation is codetermined by "external" sociolinguistic factors: the variation that appears in actual usage (as attested in corpora) may be determined simultaneously by grammatical, discursive, and sociolinguistic factors. Disentangling those different factors, then, becomes one methodological endeavor: in the actual practice of a usage-based enquiry, grammatical analysis and variationist analysis will go hand in hand.

For another, there is an interest in cultural models and the way in which they may compete within a community: see, for instance, many of the papers collected in Dirven, Frank, and Pütz (2003). In work such as Lakoff (1996), this approach takes on a critical aspect that brings it close to the tradition of ideological analysis known as Critical Discourse Analysis. Some researchers are applying the theory of conceptual metaphors and cultural models to questions of social identity and the role language plays in them: see the collective volumes edited by Dirven, Frank, and Ilie (2001), Dirven, Frank, and Pütz (2003), and Dirven, Hawkins, and Sandikcioglu (2001). It has recently been pointed out (Berthele 2001; Geeraerts 2003) that such metaphorical models may also characterize the beliefs that language users entertain regarding language and language varieties. In this way, Cognitive Linguistics may link up with existing sociolinguistic research about language attitudes.

These developments show that the interest in sociovariational analysis in Cognitive Linguistics is on the rise, but at the same time, it has to be recognized that the final contextual gap that we discussed in the previous section still has to be filled properly.

2. If we understand *empirical methods* to refer to forms of research (like corpus linguistics, experimentation, and neurological modeling) that do not rely on introspection and intuition but that try to ground linguistic analysis on the firm basis of objective observation, then we can certainly witness a growing appeal of such empirical methods within Cognitive Linguistics: see the argumentation of Gibbs (2006) and Geeraerts (2006b) in favor of empirical methods, and compare the practical introduction provided by Gonzalez-Marquez, Mittelberg, Coulson,

and Spivey (2007). The theoretical background of this development is provided by the growing tendency of Cognitive Linguistics to stress its essential nature as a usage-based linguistics—a form of linguistic analysis, that is, that takes into account not just grammatical structure, but that sees this structure as arising from and interacting with actual language use. The central notions of usage-based linguistics have been programmatically outlined in different publications (Langacker 1990; Kemmer and Barlow 2000; Tomasello 2000, 2003; Bybee and Hopper 2001b; Croft and Cruse 2004), and a number of recent volumes show how the program can be put into practice (Barlow and Kemmer 2000; Bybee and Hopper 2001a; Verhagen and van de Weijer 2003). The link between the self-awareness of Cognitive Linguistics as a usage-based form of linguistic investigation and the deployment of empirical methods is straightforward: you cannot have a usage-based linguistics unless you study actual usage—as it appears in corpora in the form of spontaneous, nonelicited language data or as it appears in an online and elicited form in experimental settings.

Also, if Cognitive Linguistics belongs to cognitive science, it would be natural to expect the use of techniques that have proved their value in the cognitive sciences at large. Experimental psychology, for instance, has a long tradition of empirical studies of cognition. So, one might count on the use of the same methods in Cognitive Linguistics. And obviously, the growing interest in the link between Cognitive Linguistics and neuroscience (headed by the Neural Theory of Language Group of George Lakoff and Jerome Feldman) goes in the same direction.

The recent rise of interest in empirical methods does not imply, to be sure, that empirical approaches were absent in the earlier stages of Cognitive Linguistics. The methodology of European studies in Cognitive Linguistics in particular has tended to be more corpus-based than the early American studies, which were predominantly introspective. The use of corpus materials (which seems to have come to the attention of the broader community of Cognitive Linguistics only since Kemmer and Barlow 2000) was already part of early European studies like Dirven and Taylor (1988), Rudzka-Ostyn (1988), Schulze (1988), Goossens (1990), and Geeraerts, Grondelaers, and Bakema (1994). Early experimental studies, on the other hand, are represented by the work of Gibbs (1994, and many more) and Sandra and Rice (1995). In this respect, what is changing is not so much the presence of empirical research as such, but rather the extent to which the belief in such a methodology is shared by cognitive linguists at large.

However, the empirical aspects of usage-based linguistics still often remain programmatic: in many cases, a lot more methodological sophistication will have to be brought in than is currently available. In the realm of corpus research, for instance, the type of quantitatively well-founded investigations that may be found in the work of Gries (2003), Stefanowitsch (2003), Gries and Stefanowitsch (2006), and Stefanowitsch and Gries (2003) and in that of Grondelaers, Speelman, and Geeraerts (2002), and Speelman, Grondelaers, and Geeraerts (2003) is still rather exceptional. (For an overview of the methodological state of affairs in usage-based linguistics, see Tummers, Heylen, and Geeraerts 2005.)

More generally, the rising interest in empirical methods is far from being a dominant tendency, and overall, there is a certain reluctance with regard to the adoption of an empirical methodology. While the reasons for this relative lack of enthusiasm may to some extent be practical (training in experimental techniques or corpus research is not a standard part of curricula in linguistics), one cannot exclude the possibility of a more principled rejection. Cognitive Linguistics considers itself to be a nonobjectivist theory of language, whereas the use of corpus materials involves an attempt to maximize the objective basis of linguistic descriptions. Is an objectivist methodology compatible with a nonobjectivist theory? Isn't any attempt to reduce the role of introspection and intuition in linguistic research contrary to the spirit of Cognitive Linguistics, which stresses the semantic aspects of the language—and the meaning of linguistic expressions is the least tangible of linguistic phenomena. Because meanings do not present themselves directly in the corpus data, will introspection not always be used in any cognitive analysis of language? (For an explicit defense of such a position, albeit in terms of "intuition" rather than "introspection," see Itkonen 2003.)

There seems to exist a tension, in other words, between a broad methodological tendency in Cognitive Linguistics that considers introspection the most or perhaps the only appropriate method for studying meaning and a marginal but increasing tendency to apply empirical methods that are customary in the other cognitive sciences. Resolving that tension is likely to be on the agenda of Cognitive Linguistics in the near future.

3. As we mentioned and illustrated several times in the course of this introductory chapter, Cognitive Linguistics is far from being a unified and stabilized body of knowledge. We have tried, in the course of compiling and editing this *Handbook*, not to make the enterprise of Cognitive Linguistics look more unified than it actually is. Nevertheless, *theoretical unification* may be expected high on the future research agenda of Cognitive Linguistics. In this respect, we hope that the survey of Cognitive Linguistics that is offered in the present volume will not only introduce novices to the full richness and dynamism of research in Cognitive Linguistics, but that it may also help the cognitive linguistic community at large to define the directions for the future more clearly.

REFERENCES

Barlow, Michael, and Suzanne Kemmer, eds. 2000. *Usage-based models of language.* Stanford, CA: CSLI Publications.

Berthele, Raphael. 2001. A tool, a bond or a territory: Language ideologies in the US and in Switzerland. LAUD Paper, no. 533. Essen, Germany: Linguistic Agency, Universität Duisburg-Essen.

Berthele, Raphael. 2004. The typology of motion and posture verbs: A variationist account. In Bernd Kortmann, ed., *Dialectology meets typology: Dialect grammar from a cross-linguistic perspective* 93–126. Berlin: Mouton de Gruyter.

Bybee, Joan L. 2001. *Phonology and language use.* Cambridge: Cambridge University Press.

Bybee, Joan L., and Paul Hopper, eds. 2001a. *Frequency and the emergence of linguistic structure.* Amsterdam: John Benjamins.

Bybee, Joan L., and Paul Hopper. 2001b. Introduction. In Joan L. Bybee and Paul Hopper, eds., *Frequency and the emergence of linguistic structure* 1–24. Amsterdam: John Benjamins.

Chomsky, Noam. 1965. *Aspects of the theory of syntax.* Cambridge, MA: MIT Press.

Croft, William. 2000. *Explaining language change: An evolutionary approach.* London: Longman.

Croft, William. 2001. *Radical construction grammar: Syntactic theory in typological perspective.* Oxford: Oxford University Press.

Croft, William, and D. Alan Cruse. 2004. *Cognitive linguistics.* Cambridge: Cambridge University Press.

De Mey, Marc. 1992. *The cognitive paradigm: An integrated understanding of scientific development.* Chicago: University of Chicago Press.

Dirven, René, Roslyn Frank, and Cornelia Ilie, eds. 2001. *Language and ideology.* Vol. 2, *Descriptive cognitive approaches.* Amsterdam: John Benjamins.

Dirven, René, Roslyn Frank, and Martin Pütz, eds. 2003. *Cognitive models in language and thought: Ideology, metaphors and meanings.* Berlin: Mouton de Gruyter.

Dirven, René, Bruce Hawkins, and Esra Sandikcioglu, eds. 2001. *Language and ideology.* Vol. 1, *Theoretical cognitive linguistic approaches.* Amsterdam: John Benjamins.

Dirven, René, and John R. Taylor. 1988. The conceptualisation of vertical space in English: The case of *tall.* In Brygida Rudzka-Ostyn, ed., *Topics in cognitive linguistics* 379–402. Amsterdam: John Benjamins.

Dirven, René, and Marjolijn Verspoor. 1998. *Cognitive exploration of language and linguistics.* Amsterdam: John Benjamins. (2nd ed., 2004)

Evans, Vyvyan, and Melanie Green. 2006. *Cognitive linguistics: An introduction.* Edinburgh, UK: Edinburgh University Press.

Geeraerts, Dirk. 1993. Cognitive linguistics and the history of philosophical epistemology. In Richard Geiger and Brygida Rudzka-Ostyn, eds., *Conceptualizations and mental processing in language* 53–79. Berlin: Mouton de Gruyter.

Geeraerts, Dirk. 2003. Cultural models of linguistic standardization. In René Dirven, Roslyn Frank, and Martin Pütz, eds., *Cognitive models in language and thought: Ideology, metaphors and meanings* 25–68. Berlin: Mouton de Gruyter.

Geeraerts, Dirk, ed. 2006a. *Cognitive linguistics: Basic readings.* Berlin: Mouton de Gruyter.

Geeraerts, Dirk. 2006b. Methodology in cognitive linguistics. In Gitte Kristiansen, Michel Achard, René Dirven, and Francisco J. Ruiz de Mendoza Ibáñez, eds., *Cognitive linguistics: Current applications and future perspectives* 21-49. Berlin: Mouton de Gruyter.

Geeraerts, Dirk, Stefan Grondelaers, and Peter Bakema. 1994. *The structure of lexical variation: Meaning, naming, and context.* Berlin: Mouton de Gruyter.

Gibbs, Raymond W., Jr. 1994. *The poetics of mind: Figurative thought, language, and understanding.* Cambridge: Cambridge University Press.

Gibbs, Raymond W., Jr. 2006. Introspection and cognitive linguistics: Should we trust our own intuitions? *Annual Review of Cognitive Linguistics* 4: 135–151.

Givón, Talmy. 1979. *On understanding grammar.* New York: Academic Press.

Goldberg, Adele E. 1995. *Constructions: A construction grammar approach to argument structure*. Chicago: University of Chicago Press.

Gonzalez-Marquez, Monica, Irene Mittelberg, Seana Coulson, and Michael J. Spivey, eds. 2007. *Methods in cognitive linguistics*. Amsterdam: Benjamins.

Goossens, Louis. 1990. Metaphtonymy: The interaction of metaphor and metonymy in expressions for linguistic actions. *Cognitive Linguistics* 1: 323–40.

Gries, Stefan Th. 2003. *Multifactorial analysis in corpus linguistics: A study of particle placement*. London: Continuum Press.

Gries, Stefan Th., and Anatol Stefanowitsch, eds. 2006. *Corpora in cognitive linguistics: Corpus-based approaches to syntax and lexis*. Berlin: Mouton de Gruyter.

Grondelaers, Stefan, Dirk Speelman, and Dirk Geeraerts. 2002. Regressing on *er*: Statistical analysis of texts and language variation. In Annie Morin and Pascale Sébillot, eds., *Sixth International conference on the statistical analysis of textual data* 335–46. Rennes, France: Institut National de Recherche en Informatique et en Automatique.

Harder, Peter. 2003. The status of linguistic facts: Rethinking the relation between cognition, social institution and utterance from a functional point of view. *Mind and Language* 18: 52–76.

Harris, Randy A. 1993. *The linguistics wars*. Oxford: Oxford University Press.

Hopper, Paul. 1987. Emergent grammar. *Berkeley Linguistics Society* 13: 139–57.

Hopper, Paul J., and Sandra A. Thompson. 1980. Transitivity in grammar and discourse. *Language* 56: 251–99.

Itkonen, Esa. 2003. *What is language? A study in the philosophy of linguistics*. Turku, Finland: Åbo Akademis tryckeri.

Johnson, Mark. 1987. *The body in the mind: The bodily basis of meaning, imagination, and reason*. Chicago: University of Chicago Press.

Kemmer, Suzanne, and Michael Barlow. 2000. Introduction. In Michael Barlow and Suzanne Kemmer, eds., *Usage-based models of language* vii–xxviii. Stanford, CA: CSLI Publications.

Kristiansen, Gitte. 2003. Referencia exofórica y estereotipos lingüísticos: Una aproximación sociocognitiva a la variación alofónica libre en el lenguaje natural. PhD dissertation, Universidad Complutense de Madrid.

Kristiansen, Gitte, and René Dirven, eds. 2007. *Cognitive sociolinguistics*. Berlin: Mouton de Gruyter.

Krug, Manfred. 2000. *Emerging English modals: A corpus-based study of grammaticalization*. Berlin: Mouton de Gruyter.

Lakoff, George. 1987. *Women, fire, and dangerous things: What categories reveal about the mind*. Chicago: University of Chicago Press.

Lakoff, George. 1996. *Moral politics: What conservatives know that liberals don't*. Chicago: University of Chicago Press.

Langacker, Ronald W. 1990. *Concept, image, and symbol: The cognitive basis of grammar*. Berlin: Mouton de Gruyter.

Lee, David. 2001. *Cognitive linguistics: An introduction*. Oxford: Oxford University Press.

Palmer, Gary B. 1996. *Toward a theory of cultural linguistics*. Austin: University of Texas Press.

Rudzka-Ostyn, Brygida. 1988. Semantic extensions into the domain of verbal communication. In Brygida Rudzka-Ostyn, ed., *Topics in cognitive linguistics* 507–54. Amsterdam: John Benjamins.

Sandra, Dominiek, and Sally Rice. 1995. Network analyses of prepositional meaning: Mirroring whose mind—the linguist's or the language user's? *Cognitive Linguistics* 6: 89–130.

Saussure, Ferdinand de. [1916] 1967. *Cours de linguistique générale*. Paris: Payot.

Schulze, Rainer. 1988. A short story of *down*. In Werner Hüllen and Rainer Schulze, eds., *Understanding the lexicon: Meaning, sense and world knowledge in lexical semantics* 394–410. Tübingen, Germany: Max Niemeyer Verlag.

Sinha, Chris, and Kristine Jensen de López. 2000. Language, culture and the embodiment of spatial cognition. *Cognitive Linguistics* 11: 17–41.

Speelman, Dirk, Stefan Grondelaers, and Dirk Geeraerts. 2003. Profile-based linguistic uniformity as a generic method for comparing language varieties. *Computers and the Humanities* 37: 317–37.

Stefanowitsch, Anatol. 2003. Constructional semantics as a limit to grammatical alternation: The two genitives of English. In Günter Rohdenburg and Britta Mondorf, eds., *Determinants of grammatical variation* 413–44. Berlin: Mouton de Gruyter.

Stefanowitsch, Anatol, and Stefan Th. Gries. 2003. Collostructions: Investigating the interaction between words and constructions. *International Journal of Corpus Linguistics* 8: 209–43.

Taylor, John R. 1989. *Linguistic categorization: Prototypes in linguistic theory*. Oxford: Clarendon Press. (3rd ed., 2003)

Tomasello, Michael. 2000. First steps toward a usage-based theory of language acquisition. *Cognitive Linguistics* 11: 61–82.

Tomasello, Michael. 2003. *Constructing a language: A usage-based theory of language acquisition*. Cambridge, MA: Harvard University Press.

Traugott, Elizabeth Closs. 1988. Pragmatic strengthening and grammaticalization. *Berkeley Linguistics Society* 14: 406–16.

Tummers, José, Kris Heylen, and Dirk Geeraerts. 2005. Usage-based approaches in Cognitive Linguistics: A technical state of the art. *Corpus Linguistics and Linguistic Theory* 1: 225-261.

Ungerer, Friedrich, and Hans-Jörg Schmid. 1996. *An introduction to cognitive linguistics*. London: Longman. (2nd ed., 2006)

Verhagen, Arie, and Jeroen van de Weijer, eds. 2003. *Usage-based approaches to Dutch*. Utrecht, Netherlands: LOT.

PART I

BASIC CONCEPTS

CHAPTER 2

EMBODIMENT AND EXPERIENTIALISM

TIM ROHRER

1. INTRODUCTION

The *basic* problem of language is childlike in its simplicity: How can we understand one another? How is it that I can make some noises, you can hear them, and we can arrive at some shared meaning? How can we ever be sure we are really thinking the same thought as a result of our communication?

Two broad approaches to answering this question divide those who study language and semantics. One might, as many traditions of philosophy and linguistics do, choose to answer such questions by positing meaning as something abstract, propositional, and symbolic. For example, *Está lloviendo* and *It is raining* are taken to be propositional claims which are abstractly equivalent when considered from a symbolic standpoint. Thus, these two expressions, drawn from different languages, have an identical meaning that can be true or false in reference to the current state of affairs actually existing in the world. The more nuanced and complex language of actual speech is thought to result from the logical combination of such atomic propositions. In this model, adopted by most analytic philosophers of language and Chomskyan linguists, semantics is believed to be purely referential and syntactic structures ultimately resolve to logical relations, while pragmatics is seen as the primary source of ambiguity, subjectivity, and error. In its more extreme forms, such as that found in proposals by Frege and Plato, an independent and prior realm of universal ideas is postulated to ensure that reference proceeds entirely objectively and completely devoid of ambiguity. Broadly speaking, such approaches can be lumped together as forming the Objectivist tradition.

On the other hand, we might choose to answer such questions with an empirical examination of what *constitutes* shared meaning. Rather than seeking some idealized set of atomic propositions supposedly well suited to solving problems like ambiguous reference or translation between different languages, we might look at language as it is actually used. For instance, we might observe how language is learned and used within the child-parent dyad and so realize that the single-word utterances naming objects or events (e.g., *Bird!*, *Kitty!*, *Rain!*) are pragmatic requests to establish joint attention between parent and child. These are not simple or pure cases of ostensive reference—the sort of word-world reference relationship Objectivist Semantics would like to take as fundamental—but instead are utterances embedded within a cognitive and social situation wherein one subject wants to direct the intentionality of another. From this standpoint, the primary purpose of language is not the objective description of the world, but instead to communicate and share experiences.

A focus on what people find meaningful necessitates investigating the cognitive, physical, and social embodiment that shapes and constrains meaningful expression. Such a focus requires evaluating findings from the various cognitive sciences and doing linguistic theory in a way that it is consonant with them. For example, we know from cognitive psychology that people find most categories meaningful in terms of prototypes, not in terms of necessary and sufficient conditions. In Cognitive Linguistics, we have developed a theory of radial categorization consonant with both the psychological evidence and wide ranges of linguistic examples. From cognitive neuroscience we know that the physical brain does not process visual information in a disembodied, nonimagistic way, but instead maintains the perceptual topology of images presented to it, and then re-represents increasingly abstract spatial and imagistic details of that topology. In Cognitive Linguistics, such findings have motivated a theory of image schemas whose topologies provide links between different clusters of prototypes in radial categories and whose topologies motivate the cross-domain mappings of systematic conceptual metaphors. Just as in the case of using language to establish joint attention, such factors can and have been shown to shape and constrain what shared meaning emerges when people speak and listen.

One of the most central questions Cognitive Linguistics asks thus has a somewhat Kantian ring to it: how does the bodily apparatus itself shape our linguistic categorization and conceptualization? The spirit of this transition from the Objectivist traditions to a more inclusive Cognitive Semantics is perhaps best captured in a thought experiment proposed by Langacker to characterize the process of linguistic change known as subjectification. He writes:

> Consider the glasses I normally wear. If I take them off, hold them in front of me, and examine them, their construal is maximally objective . . . they function solely and completely as the *object of perception*, and not at all as part of the perceptual apparatus itself. By contrast, my construal of the glasses is maximally subjective when I am wearing them and examining another object, so that they fade from my conscious awareness despite their role in determining the nature of my perceptual experience. The glasses then function exclusively as part of the

subject of perception—they are one component of the perceiving apparatus, but are not themselves perceived. . . . Of course, such extreme polarization represents an ideal that may seldom be achieved in practice. To some extent, for example, I can perceive my glasses even while wearing them while looking at something else, and to that extent their perceptual construal is slightly objective and less than fully subjective. Subjectivity/objectivity is often variable or a matter of degree, and it is precisely such cases that hold the greatest interest linguistically. (Langacker 1990: 316)

Langacker's point in this passage is double-edged. At one level of analysis, he endeavors to change the scope of which utterances are to count as both legitimate and paradigmatic for a theory of meaning—expanding the scope from the atomic propositions of the maximally objective descriptions privileged by Objectivist Semantics to include expressions in which degrees of both subjectivity and objectivity are expressed in how a situation is construed by a speaker (e.g., *I insist that she is innocent*). Yet at a metalevel of analysis, Langacker's example of the glasses illustrates another central concern of Cognitive Linguistics. When we take off our glasses and examine them as an object, and then put them back on and attend to how our glasses, now functioning as a part of our perceptual apparatus, change other objects of our perception, we are performing an act profoundly analogous to what we do as cognitive linguists. In Cognitive Linguistics, we examine how our "glasses"—that is, our physical, cognitive, and social embodiment—ground our linguistic conceptualizations.

At this point, several of the most difficult and hotly contested theoretical concepts in Cognitive Linguistics are already on the table. In the remainder of this chapter, I survey the many ways in which the term "embodiment" has been cashed out by various researchers in Cognitive Linguistics. I then retrace some of the history of the embodiment hypothesis and show how its scope expanded to encompass topics as diverse as the grounding of meaning, the motivating factors of semantic change, experientialism, experimental cognitive psychology, and cognitive neuroscience. I close by offering a theoretical framework inspired by related work in the philosophy of cognitive science and intended to serve as a useful organizational tool for situating and making connections between these varying research projects.

2. THE SENSES OF EMBODIMENT

In its broadest definition, the *embodiment* hypothesis is the claim that *human physical, cognitive, and social embodiment ground our conceptual and linguistic systems*. The hypothesis is intended as an empirical one, albeit lodged at such a level of theoretical abstraction that it is difficult to prove or disprove with a single study or experiment. As such, it is a very live question as to whether the embodiment hypothesis is an empirical scientific hypothesis, a general theoretical orientation, a metaphysics, or some combination of all of these. However, the evidence which led to the hypothesis was empirical evidence, and new bodies of empirical evidence are continually being added to the list of research supporting the hypothesis.

By my latest count, the term "embodiment" can be used in at least twelve different important senses with respect to our cognition. Because theorists often (and sometimes appropriately, given their purposes) conflate two or more of these senses, it is important to get a clear picture of as many of the different dimensions of variability as possible. This list is not intended to be entirely exhaustive of the term's current usage, nor are the dimensions necessarily entirely independent of each other or even entirely distinct from one another. Thus, it is important to note that this survey is not intended to be a prescriptive definition of the term, but instead is intended only to catalog the contemporary usages of the term in a way that reveals the most relevant dimensions to which one must be responsive in order to develop a general theoretical framework for the embodiment hypothesis of Cognitive Linguistics.

   a. Confusion about the use of the term "embodiment" in Cognitive Linguistics begins with two often conflated senses that stem from Lakoff and Johnson's (1980: 112) initial formulation of the embodiment hypothesis as a constraint on the directionality of metaphorical structuring. More accurately, this sense of "embodiment" could be termed the *directionality of metaphorical mappings*. In this strong directionality constraint, they claim that we normally project image-schematic patterns of knowledge unidirectionally from a more embodied source domain to understand a less well understood target domain. In other words, they claim that each and every mapping between the elements of the source and the elements of the target is unidirectional; the logic of the image schema is projected from the source to the target, and not from target to source.

   b. Yet in its original formulation, the embodiment hypothesis also contains a generalization about the kinds of basic conceptual domains which ordinarily serve as the source domains for conceptual metaphors. We might call this second sense of embodiment *the directionality of explanation* in order to distinguish it from the previous sense. This sense is stated more explicitly in Lakoff and Turner's "grounding hypothesis," in which it is argued that meaning is grounded in terms of choosing from a finite number of semantically autonomous source domains (Lakoff and Turner 1989: 113–20).

   c. "Embodiment" is also used as a shorthand term for a counter-Cartesian *philosophical* account of mind and language. Descartes took problems within geometric and mathematical reasoning (such as the meaning of the term *triangle*) as model problems for the study of mind and language and concluded that knowledge is disembodied—that is, fundamentally independent of any particular bodily sensation, experience, or perspective. His thought experiments strongly influenced the traditions of analytic philosophy and Objectivist Semantics. From this perspective, the philosophy of language typically involves (i) mapping the reference relations between idealized mental objects of knowledge and the objects or "states of affairs" in the real world (as in Truth-conditional Semantics), and (ii) discussing the logical internal structure of the relations which hold between these mental objects ("syntax"). Of course, Descartes was by no means unique or alone within Western philosophy in claiming this position (held in varying forms by Pascal, Russell, the young Wittgenstein, Quine, Chomsky, and many others), but Descartes' extraordinary clarity has garnered him the laurel of becoming metonymic for that package of assumptions (Lakoff and Johnson 1980, 1999; Geeraerts 1985; Johnson 1987; Damasio 1995; Rohrer 1998; Johnson and Rohrer 2007).

d. "Embodiment" is also used to refer to the *social* and *cultural* context in which the body, cognition, and language are perpetually situated. For example, such context can include factors such as governmental language policy, cross-cultural contact/aversion, or the influence of historical scientific models and theories on individual language learners (Geeraerts and Grondelaers 1995). Similarly, the context can include the *cultural artifacts* that aid and manifest cognition—many of which are not only constrained by but are also extensions of the body (Hutchins 1995, 2005; Fauconnier and Turner 2002).

e. "Embodiment" has a *phenomenological* sense in which it can refer to the things we consciously notice about the role of our bodies in shaping our self-identities and our culture through acts of conscious and deliberate reflection on the lived structures of our experience (Brandt 1999, 2000). The conscious phenomenology of cognitive semiotics can be profitably contrasted with the cognitive unconscious of cognitive psychology (see sense 9 below).

f. "Embodiment" can also refer to the particular subjective vantage point from which a *perspective* is taken, as opposed to the tradition of the all-seeing, all-knowing, objective and panoptic vantage point. While this sense of the term can be seen as partly philosophical (as in Nagel 1979: 196–213; Geeraerts 1985; Johnson 1987; Rohrer 1998), the idea of considering the embodied viewpoint of the speaker has linguistic implications which may impact the role of perspective in subjective construal (Langacker 1990; MacWhinney 2003).

g. In yet another important sense, "embodiment" can refer to the *developmental* changes that the organism goes through as it transforms from zygote to fetus or from child to adult. One prominent area of such work would be research on "normal" language acquisition, while another would be research on developmental disorders of language (Tomasello 1992; MacWhinney 1999). As an example of a cognitive cross-cultural language acquisition study, Sinha and Jensen de López (2000) research embodiment by investigating the acquisition course of spatial relation terms in body-part locative languages in order to determine whether such terms were first acquired as names for body parts or as spatial relations terms or whether these two senses were acquired independently of each other.

h. An equally important temporal sense of the term "embodiment" refers to the *evolutionary* changes a species of organism has undergone throughout the course of its genetic history. For example, an account of the gradual differentiation of perceptual information into separate multiple maps, each representing a different frame of reference in the visual system of mammals, could provide an evolutionarily embodied explanation of the multiple frames for spatial reference found in human languages. Or on an even grander scale: human beings have presumably not always had a language capability, and so evidence from studies on the evolutionary dimension of embodiment may often prove crucial to understanding why, for example, language processing in the brain does not appear to be exclusively concentrated as an autonomous module but instead draws on numerous subsystems from the perceptual modalities (see for treatments Donald 1991; Edelman 1992; Deacon 1997; MacWhinney 1999).

i. Additionally, "embodiment" can mean what Lakoff and Johnson (1999) have recently called the *cognitive unconscious*. Here, "embodiment" refers to the ways in which our conceptual thought is shaped by many processes below the threshold of our active consciousness, as revealed through experimental psychology. Gibbs (1980, 1986, 1992, 1994) provides important reviews of the interface between experimental cognitive psychology and Cognitive Linguistics.

j. In a *neurophysiological* sense, the term "embodiment" can refer to measuring the particular neural structures and regions which accomplish feats like metaphorical projection, the integration of image schemas, object-centered versus viewer-centered frames of reference in the visual system, and so on (Rohrer 2001, 2005; Coulson and Van Petten 2002).

k. "Embodiment" can also refer to *neurocomputational* models of language, particularly with respect to conceptual metaphor or spatial language. Such neural networks may be said to be embodied in several different ways. First, they may more or less closely model the actual neurobiology of the neural circuitry whose function they seek to emulate. Second, they may use as their input structures the output from maps of better understood embodied neural structures, typically from within the perceptual modalities (Regier 1992, 1996; Bailey 1997; Narayanan 1997; Lakoff and Johnson 1999;

Feldman and Narayanan 2004). Third, they can be taken to be models of experiential activity at a conceptual or psychological level of processing (Zlatev 1997, 2003; this volume, chapter 13).

l. Finally, the terms "embodiment" and "embodied cognition" are now also widely used in cognitive robotics. While "embodiment" is often associated there with humanoid robot projects, it can also refer to cases where the work done by the robot depends on the particular *morphological* characteristics of the robot body (morphology is used here in its biological and not its linguistic sense). For example, Cornell University's Passive Dynamic Walker uses no motors and no centralized computation but instead relies on gravity, mechanical springs, and cleverly designed limb morphology to "walk." By exploiting the capacities of the morphology, cognition is off-loaded onto the body—a design principle that is consonant with both evolutionary theory and embodiment theory within Cognitive Linguistics (Brooks 1997; Pfeifer and Scheier 1999; Bertram and Ruina 2001; Collins, Wisse, and Ruina 2001).

This descriptive list illustrates that the scope of the embodiment hypothesis requires thinking through evidence drawn from a multiplicity of perspectives on embodiment and, therefore, drawn from multiple methodologies. Of course, almost no researcher or research project can attend to all these different senses of the term and produce sound scientific findings; but research projects that build bridges or perform parallel experiments across these differing dimensions are of particular interest.

Once the descriptive work has been done, however, it can be seen that many of these senses cluster about at least two poles of attraction. As I show in subsequent sections, critiques of the embodiment hypothesis have given rise to two broad usages of the term "embodiment." These two could be well described as "embodiment as broadly experiential" and "embodiment as the bodily substrate." Thus, in one cluster the term refers to dimensions that focus on the specific subjective, cultural, and historical contextual experiences of language speakers. Senses (c)–(f) of my enumeration of the term's usages would typically cluster in this realm, while senses (h)–(l) would often cluster about the pole which emphasizes the physiological and neurophysiological bodily substrate. But not all the senses can be so clearly clustered, given that the attention to temporal character which characterizes the developmental (sense g) and evolutionary (sense h) dimensions can place them about either pole. For example, Sinha and Jensen de López (2000) show how both culturally specific experiential child-rearing practices and physiologically universal bodily interactions with space affect the course of language acquisition for terms which can indicate both spatial relations and body parts (e.g., *head* and *foot*). At a minimum, an adequate theoretical framework for Cognitive Linguistics will have to acknowledge both the experiential and bodily substrate senses of "embodiment" and provide a nonreductionistic manner of reconciling research which measures in all these different dimensions.

3. Origins of the Embodiment Hypothesis

To understand how the differing readings of embodiment have emerged, it is helpful to examine the genealogy of the term within a single strand of Cognitive Linguistics. Here, I will trace it in terms of metaphor theory; elsewhere, I have discussed its genealogy and application in terms of spatial and linguistic frames of reference (Rohrer 2001). For some time, the conceptual metaphor and embodiment hypotheses were nearly inextricable. Beginning in the late 1970s with a mass of empirical linguistic examples of metaphor, Lakoff and Johnson (1980) discovered that much of the ordinary language we use to characterize a wide variety of experiences is systematically shaped by a relatively small number of metaphors (see also Grady, this volume, chapter 8). Their work called into question the traditional distinction between the deeply conventionalized, "dead" metaphors on one hand and the more creative, literary "live" metaphors on the other hand. In a series of electrifying examples, they showed that linguistic expressions which were supposed to be "dead" metaphors are in fact part of larger systematic metaphors which also have very noticeable "live" metaphorical extensions. They argued that the "live" metaphorical expressions are the inferential and creative extensions of an underlying metaphor, while the "dead" metaphorical expressions comprise the core of the metaphor—so well understood that they are hardly noticeable to us as we listen to everyday speech. They dubbed this more systematic notion of metaphor "conceptual metaphor," both in order to distinguish it from the prior tradition of "linguistic metaphor" (or "literary metaphor") and in order to emphasize that metaphors are a matter of cognition and conceptual structure rather than a matter of mere language.

Yet the systematicity of conceptual metaphors was neither the most important nor the most controversial discovery stemming from Lakoff and Johnson's groundbreaking research. What was even more intriguing was the fact that the relatively small number of conceptual metaphors draw primarily on domains stemming from bodily experience and that these bodily source domains do the vast majority of the work of structuring more abstract human concepts. In its earliest formulation, the embodiment hypothesis came from a generalization about the directionality of metaphorical projection. Metaphors tended to characterize the abstract in terms of the concrete:

> First, we have suggested that there is *directionality* in metaphor, that is, we understand one concept in terms of another. Specifically, we tend to structure the less concrete and inherently vaguer concepts (like those for emotions) in terms of more concrete concepts, which are more clearly delineated in our experience. (Lakoff and Johnson 1980: 112)

In the immediately subsequent section, Lakoff and Johnson (1980: 117–19) identified three sources for these more concrete concepts. They argued these more concrete concepts constitute the "natural kinds of experience" and are composed of "experiential gestalts" more basic than other concepts because they are the natural products of our bodies, our interactions with the physical environment, and our interactions with other people in our culture. Reserving judgment for future research, they also indicated that while some of these natural kinds of experience might be universal, others might very well vary from culture to culture. They explicitly pointed out that they were using the terms "nature" and "natural" in a sense which encompasses at least the possibility of cultural variation, and not in the sense of the standard "nature-culture" distinction. Lakoff and Johnson concluded this section by arguing that these more concrete concepts can be used in the "metaphorical definition" of more complex concepts. In short, they argued that these three natural kinds of experience—experience of the body, of the physical environment, *and* of the culture—are what constitute the basic source domains upon which metaphors draw. All of these factors are cognitively represented, though they may also be physiological or sociocultural in origin, and this fact led to the appellation "*cognitive* linguistics" (Fesmire 1994). From the outset, then, the term "embodiment" was intended to cover research on both the experiential and bodily substrates of language.

4. ELABORATIONS AND EXTENSIONS OF THE EMBODIMENT HYPOTHESIS

Over the ensuing twenty years, the notions of experientialism, embodiment, and a directionality to conceptual metaphor received much scrutiny, generated much controversy, and consequently received much elaboration. More systematic surveys undertaken during the mid-1980s at Berkeley and elsewhere showed that bodily source domains were prevalent not only for the semantics of English, but also for languages as distant from it as Japanese and Mixtec. However, it is equally important to note that the languages *did* vary cross-culturally as to which *particular* bodily source domains were used to understand a given target domain and with respect to how these patterns were represented linguistically.

With respect to historical semantic change, Sweetser has argued that the direction of such change is motivated by the embodiment hypothesis. For instance, she documented a directionality within Indo-European languages for metaphors such as KNOWING IS SEEING, arguing that the terms which came to be the ordinary ones for abstractions such as knowing were at an earlier time restricted to embodied perceptual capabilities, such as seeing, grasping, hearing, smelling, tasting, and feeling. In a now standard example, she traces the transition of the Indo-European root **weid* 'see' through the Greek *eidon* 'to see' and, in its perfective form *oida* 'sight, know', to the English terms *idea*, *wit*, and *witness*, which retain none of their visual sensibility to most native English speakers (1990: 23–48). By observing how a wide range of embodied perceptual terms systematically lose their perceptual connotations as they acquire their intellectual meaning, she proposed that there exists a large-scale temporal constraint on the directionality of semantic change. In the following quote, she compares this new constraint with the well-established constraint in linguistics on the directionality of phonological shifts from /b/ to /p/ and /g/ to /k/.

> If we are willing to look at such large-scale, systematic historical connections between domains of meaning, it becomes evident that not all of semantic change is as whimsical and perverse as has often been assumed. True, prediction of any individual change remains impossible and seems unlikely to become possible in the future. Phonological and morphological change cannot be predicted on an individual basis either, so surely no one expects specific-case predictions for semantic or syntactic change. However, in many semantic domains it seems possible to determine what would be natural as opposed to unnatural directions of change, just as in phonology we know that voiced stops would be likely to devoice in final position or to become fricatives in intervocalic position, rather than the other way around. (Sweetser 1990: 46–47)

The direction of semantic change is for languages to utilize terms for perception as terms for knowing, rather than from terms for knowing to terms for perception. We understand knowing as seeing, but not seeing as knowing. Historical semantic change may thus be said to be strongly motivated by the embodiment hypothesis, though it may not be exactly predicted by it—much in the same way as the historical phonological shifts exhibit motivated regularities.

In the preface to *The Body in the Mind*, Johnson (1987: xii–xiii) presented six converging bodies of evidence for the embodiment hypothesis understood as a directional constraint on meaning. This list included not only cross-cultural research on metaphor and historical semantic change but also work on prototypes in categorization, the framing of concepts, polysemy, and inferential patterns in metaphor. Near the same time, other research in Cognitive Linguistics (such as Langacker's 1987, 1991 cognitive theory of grammar—a theory motivated by spatial relations) contributed to an increasing focus on the role of the body in shaping linguistic and conceptual structure generally, and not just within a thread of semantic theory. In work that also appeared that same year, Lakoff (1987) characterized the experientialism (or experiential realism) at the core of the embodiment hypothesis as including

> everything that goes to make up the actual or potential experiences of either individual organisms or communities of organisms—not merely perception, motor movement, etc., but especially the internal genetically acquired makeup of the organism and the nature of its interactions in both its physical and social environments. (Lakoff 1987: xv)

Experiential realism, as Lakoff defined it, was to be in direct contrast with the traditional philosophical conception of meaningful thought and reason as the manipulation of symbols that correspond to an objective reality that is independent of the particular kind of embodiment of the organism. By 1987, the embodiment hypothesis had explicitly grown much more ambitious in scope than in its more humble origins as a generalization about the directionality of metaphors. Physiology, temporal development, and organism-environment interactions as well as linguistic evidence were explicitly expected to play a role in an increasingly broad theoretical hypothesis which purported to explain an ever larger amount of linguistic phenomena.

The enlarging scope of the embodiment hypothesis led to criticisms that its central tenets were underspecified. For example, the idea of embodied "experiential gestalts" as natural kinds of experience needed further explanation. Building on work done at Berkeley by Talmy (1985, 2000) on the role of force-dynamic patterns in shaping syntactic constructions, Johnson developed a theory of *image schemas*. He defined an image schema as a recurrent pattern, shape, or regularity in, or of, our actions, perceptions, and conceptions. He argued that "these patterns emerge primarily as meaningful structures for us chiefly at the level of our bodily movements through space, our manipulation of objects, and our perceptual interactions" (1987: 29). For example, the CONTAINMENT schema structures our regular recurring experiences of putting objects into and taking them out of a bounded area. We can experience this pattern in the tactile modality with physical containers, or we can experience this pattern visually as we track the movement of some object into or out of some bounded area or container. It is particularly important to see that an image schema can also be experienced cross-modally; for example, we can use the visual modality to guide our tactile and kinesthetic experience when we reach into a container and grasp an object.

Johnson argued that these patterns can then be metaphorically extended to structure nonphysical, nontactile, and nonvisual experiences. In a particularly striking set of examples, he traced many habitual notions of containment we might experience during the course of a typical morning routine: we wake up *out of* a deep sleep, drag ourselves *up out of* bed and *into* the bathroom, where we look *into* the mirror and pull a comb *out from inside* the cabinet. Later that same morning we might wander *into* the kitchen, sit *in* a chair at the breakfast table, and *open up* the newspaper and become lost *in* an article. Some of these experiences are spatial and physical but do not involve the prototypical CONTAINMENT image schema (as in the example of sitting *in* a chair), while some of these experiences draw on purely metaphorical extensions of CONTAINMENT (as in the example of getting lost *in* the newspaper article).

Such image schemas are *preconceptual* embodied structures of meaning in at least two important ways. First, image schemas are developmentally prior to conceptual thinking, at least insofar as conceptual structure is accessible to us by means of language. Johnson drew on work by the developmental psychiatrist Daniel Stern (1985) and the developmental psychologist Andrew Meltzoff (summarized in Meltzoff 1993). Stern argued that the activation, buildup, and release of emotional tension is among the earliest and most foundational of our prelinguistic experiences:

For instance, in trying to soothe the infant the parent could say, "There, there, there . . . ," giving more stress and amplitude on the first part of the word and trailing off towards the end of the word. Alternatively, the parent could silently stroke the baby's back or head with a stroke analogous to the "There, there" sequence, applying more pressure at the onset of the stroke and lightening or trailing it off toward the end . . . the infant would experience similar activation contours no matter which soothing technique was performed. (Stern 1985: 58)

As infants we experience these patterns of feeling (image schemas) before we develop a linguistic self, and these image schemas are not unique to any one perceptual modality but have a structure which is shared across them.

Second, Johnson argued that image schemas are preconceptual in that they can underlay multiple different conceptual metaphors. We can extend—by means of metaphor—these directly emergent experiences to characterize nonspatial experiences, such as falling *into* a depression or getting lost *in* the newspaper. Further, we can project the inference patterns of the CONTAINMENT schema into the metaphorically structured domain. For example, just as we reason that the deeper an object is in a container the harder it will be to get it out, we reason that the deeper someone is in a depression the harder it will be to get them out of their depression. It is important to note that image schemas serve as the preconceptual basis for metaphors in both a developmental and a structural sense. The embodiment hypothesis is thus not only a hypothesis about how image schemas and conceptual metaphors structure adult cognition, but about the ontogenetic acquisition of metaphorical structure as humans develop from infants to adults.

Though calling patterns which are supposed to be cross-modal "images" may seem to be a little misleading, Johnson fortuitously chose the term "image schemas" in accordance with burgeoning research in the cognitive sciences on the role of images in our embodied mental conceptualization. In the early 1970s, the psychologists Shepard and Metzler (1971) asked experimental subjects to determine whether a pair of two-dimensional pictures of three-dimensional objects were identical. They discovered that subjects rotated these objects mentally at a fixed speed of approximately 60 degrees each second, suggesting that humans manipulated the images as a whole. Their discovery touched off a powder keg of controversy, as the then prevalent view of the mind as a symbol manipulation system favored a theory in which perceptual images were decomposed into image-independent propositional representations, much as they would have been represented in the computers of that time (Kosslyn 1980, 1994).

Shepard and Metzler's (1971) original work on visual imagery was one of the key factors which led to a revolution in the cognitive sciences in which the mind and brain are now increasingly understood to be organized in terms of image-like wholes. This revolution has been most dramatically borne out by convergent evidence from cognitive neuroscience (Kosslyn 1994; Kosslyn et al. 1995). In particular, researchers using neuroimaging and neuroanatomic techniques have been able to isolate regions of the cortex which maintain topologically consistent images of, for example, the visual field as perceived, top-down visual imagery, and spatial (i.e., nonvisual, tactile, or kinesthetic) imagery. As the Shepard and Metzler results suggest, humans have topologically mapped neural circuitry for both the visualization and the visual perception of spatial form. Similarly, starting in the 1930s, the neurosurgeon Wilder Penfield and colleagues had shown that the somatosensory and motor regions of the human cerebral cortex topologically map the body's tactile and kinesthetic experience. Such image-like maps are considered to be topological because they preserve the contours of perceptual experience.

Similar topological maps of perceptual experience have been found for the other sensory modalities, such as pitch maps for auditory experience. We now know that these topological maps are refined into more selective maps which respond to higher-order and more selective kinds of contour patterns. Though recent work on grasping schemas in humans and monkeys is promising (Gallese and Lakoff 2005), the current state of cognitive neuroscience stops short of specifying neural maps embodying the exact sets of perceptual contour patterns Johnson identifies as image schemas. This is especially true when image schemas are considered as perceptuolinguistic structures, though several recent experiments comparing linguistic and perceptual stimuli have shown promise (Hauk, Johnsrude, and Pulvermüller 2004; Rohrer 2005). At present, the possible neurophysiological instantiation of image schemas remains an intriguing area for future research. Yet the embodiment hypothesis's proposal of image schemas is still highly consistent both with the known facts about neurophysiology, particularly the ways in which the visual system and other perceptual modalities map perceptual experience, and with the kinds of structures we observe in linguistic conceptualizations.

5. CONTEMPORARY FORMULATIONS OF THE EMBODIMENT HYPOTHESIS

In their recent work, Lakoff and Johnson have turned much of their attention away from embodiment defined broadly as experientialism and toward investigating how the bodily substrate shapes language, although they would certainly argue for the importance of continued research on the cultural and social dimensions. It is crucial to see that their current neural conception of the embodiment hypothesis is much more than the simpleminded argument that our conceptual structure must have *some* neural instantiation. Introducing their most recent formulation of the embodiment hypothesis, Lakoff and Johnson observe that while even the traditional view of the disembodied mind maintains the minimal position that concepts must have some neural representation, the embodiment hypothesis must go much farther: "Advocates of the disembodied mind will, of course, say that conceptual structure must have a neural *realization* in the brain, which just *happens* to reside in a body. But they deny that anything about the body is essential for characterizing what concepts are" (Lakoff and Johnson 1999: 37). To work in cognitive science, this version of the embodiment hypothesis makes an analogy which argues that conceptual and perceptual processes share many of the same physiological and neurophysiological subprocesses.

To see the analogy clearly, consider some more examples drawn from the literature on mental imagery. In an experiment done by Stephen Kosslyn and colleagues (Kosslyn et. al. 1995; see also Kosslyn 1994), the subjects were either asked to form a mental image within a grid on a computer screen or presented with an equivalent visual image on a computer screen. By comparing the two experimental conditions in a brain-imaging PET study, these researchers were able to show that many of the same areas of the brain were active both under the imagery and the perceptual task conditions. The results of Kosslyn and his colleagues show that a "top-down" volitional task such as mental imagery (visualization) utilizes the same subprocesses as a "bottom-up" task like visual perception. Similarly, language may well share common subprocesses with the portions of perceptual systems.

This idea of shared bodily subprocesses which underlie both cognition and perception is at the core of the present formulation of the embodiment hypothesis. The analogy between the form of the argument for the embodiment hypothesis and the form of the foregoing argument about visual imagery and visual perception can be made explicit: just as visual imagery shares and builds upon the processes the brain and body use to perceive visual images, so conceptual structure generally shares and builds upon perceptual processes. Of course, the argument that *per*ceptual and *con*ceptual structure share the same subprocesses is much more ambitious in scope than the foregoing argument about two kinds of tasks which take place in one modality (i.e., vision). However, Lakoff and Johnson currently formulate the embodiment hypothesis in precisely this fashion:

> The embodied-mind hypothesis therefore radically undercuts the *perception/ conception* distinction. In an embodied mind, it is conceivable that the same neural system engaged in *perception* (or in bodily movement) plays a central role in *conception*. That is, it is possible that the very mechanisms responsible for perception, movements, and object manipulation could be responsible for conceptualization and reasoning. (Lakoff and Johnson 1999: 37–38)

What is crucial to the argument of the embodiment hypothesis is that the *same* neural mechanisms which are responsible for "lower-level" activities like perception and movement are taken to be *essential* to "higher-level" cognitive abilities, namely to our reasoning and conceptualization. Thus, on their view Lakoff and Johnson argue "that the very properties of concepts *are created* as a result of the way the brain and body are structured and the way they function in interpersonal relations and in the physical world" (1999: 37). The way these properties are created is by means of conceptual metaphors which project cross-domain image-schematic patterns, which in turn are drawn from the more specific structures within visual perception, locomotion, object manipulation, and so on. At some of the "top levels" of investigation—studies on language and categorization in linguistics and philosophy—the research which has already been done on metaphorical structuring provides the largest bodies of evidence in favor of the embodiment hypothesis. There is considerable evidence that we do categorize and organize our linguistic structure in ways which are shaped by these kinds of phenomena. What remains to be done, however, is the project of establishing how *specific* neural and physiological mechanisms are recruited to provide that conceptual organization and how they develop and vary in differing physical environments and cultures.

Though they admit that much of their current research paradigm is far less a neurophysiological model and more a computational model of what such mechanisms might be, Lakoff and Johnson summarize recent efforts in the neurocomputational modeling of metaphor and semantic structure that show how low-level image-schematic structure can be preserved by structured connectionist models that draw on known neural structures for the types of information taken as inputs. For example, Regier (1992, 1996) has investigated how spatial relations terms such as *up*, *down*, and *above* can be learned by structured connectionist networks that utilize low-level schematizations which have plausible neural analogues in the neuroanatomy of visual perception. Although the other research (Bailey 1997; Narayanan 1997) in this approach to the neurocomputational modeling of language, resting on mathematically reducible analogues to "pure" neural network models, is even more distant from identifying its plausible neural analogues, Lakoff and Johnson also cite that work as support for the embodiment hypothesis. Although thus far they have largely omitted the discussion of actual neurophysiology in favor of discussing such computational models, that deficiency speaks more about the paucity of the current research on the neurophysiology of meaning. They are quite explicit in acknowledging both its importance and their inability to do full justice to the neurophysiological issues at this early stage of the research.

Over the course of this brief history of the embodiment hypothesis, I have traced the evolution of several senses of the term. I have traced its gradual evolution and expansion from simply a hypothesis about the grounding of conceptual metaphors to one which has grown increasingly large in scope throughout its dialogue with other branches of cognitive science. This increase in scope has led to the present confusion as to what exactly the term "embodiment" is to mean within Cognitive Linguistics. For example, some theorists have argued for a return to a more culturally situated theory of embodiment (Zlatev 1997; Sinha 1999), while others press onward with attempts to ask what embodiment means in its physiological and neural senses (Lakoff and Johnson 1999). What we have lacked is a coherent framework which can tie these differing senses of the term together. While Lakoff and Johnson (1999: 112–13) offered a three-tiered proposal with cognitive, neurocomputational, and neurobiological levels of investigation, the usefulness of their proposal is limited by its tight focus on their particular research program, the Neural Theory of Language. In the following section, I argue for adopting a more sophisticated and widely used theoretical framework from the cognitive sciences as an aid in clarifying the full range of current research of Cognitive Linguistics.

6. THE 'LEVELS OF INVESTIGATION' THEORETICAL FRAMEWORK

In developing a broader theoretical framework for use in Cognitive Linguistics (see table 2.1), I have made use of Posner and Raichle's (1994) schematization of the levels of investigation in cognitive science. The most basic organizing criterion of this theoretical framework is the scale of the relative physical sizes of the phenomena which produce the different kinds of social, cognitive, or neural events to be studied. Physical size (expressed in meters) is mapped vertically in the rows of the table, providing a relative distribution of the "higher to lower" levels of cognitive processes. The first column presents examples of what the relevant physiological structures are at a given physical scale, while I give a general name to each level of investigation in the next column. For instance, at the communicative, cultural, and social level, we primarily study language as it is used between people, and hence at a physical size scale of roughly 1 m and up when we make observations as to the emergence or frequency of a particular metaphor in a videotaped or written corpus, and so on. Alternatively, it is possible to focus on a single individual's performance on linguistic tasks via measures which focus on the individual's body, such as the reaction time elapsed or the galvanic skin response conducted when the individual reads an emotionally salient metaphor. Similarly, we could also conduct experiments designed to measure either neuroanatomic regions or single-cell activity in response to analogous linguistic tasks. Thus, I describe the level of investigation in accordance with the kinds of cognitive processes measurable given the methodologies used at that order of physical size.

In order to preserve Posner and Raichle's insight that it is profitable to consider how the inquiries into similar questions change at various levels of investigation due to the constraints of the observational apparatus and method, the "Tasks" column of this theoretical framework specifies for Cognitive Linguistics in particular some typical relevant experimental or explanatory tasks. The next column lists some of the relevant theoretical constructs operative at each level of investigation, while the final column presents some of the various methods used to study phenomena at each level.

This framework can be used to situate the wide methodological array of studies on various topics of interest to cognitive linguists, such as metaphor, mental imagery, categorization, frames of reference, emotions, and so on. This type of theoretical framework is now fairly common within much of cognitive science, but Cognitive Linguistics has been slow to give explicit attention to the problem of how we are to theoretically situate and reconcile these different levels of investigation.

I have explicitly included a level of cultural and communicative analysis. By choosing to include a level situated at the "1 m and up" physical size scale, I mean to highlight that human language should be considered not just in terms of the physiological size of the central nervous system, but also in terms of the standard scale of the interactional distance we use in speaking with one another. Language is

Table 2.1. **Theoretical framework for the embodiment hypothesis in cognitive science as applied to Cognitive Linguistics**

Size (in m)	Physiological Structures	Level of Investigation	Typical Cognitive Linguistics Theory Explanatory Tasks	Sample Operative Theoretical Constructs	Sample Methods of Study
1 and up	Multiple central nervous systems	**Communicative and cultural systems** in anthropology, language, science, and philosophy	Uses of widespread cultural metaphors in interpersonal communication; syntactic and semantic change	Complex conceptual metaphor, conceptual blends, disanalogy, subjectification	Linguistic analysis, cross-linguistic typology, discourse analysis, cognitive anthropology
.5 to 2	Central nervous systems	**Performance domain:** Cognitive, conceptual, gestural, and linguistic systems as performed by individual subjects	Understanding metaphors, extending metaphorical inferences to novel cases, facilitation of related information; use of slang; testing choice of syntactic form given extralinguistic semantic task	Complex conceptual metaphor, conceptual blends, disanalogy, primary metaphor, metaphor mappings, inference generalizations	Verbal report, observational neurology, and psychiatry, cognitive, and developmental studies examining reaction time (RT)

(continued)

Table 2.1. (continued)

10^{-1} to 10^{-2}	Gross to medium size neural regions (anterior cingulate, parietal lobe, etc.)	**Neural systems**	Activation course in somatosensory, auditory, and visual processing areas when processing conceptual metaphor or multimodal perceptual experiences	Conceptual metaphor mappings, primary metaphor, conceptual blends, disanalogy, image schemas, topological maps	Lesion analysis, neurological dissociations, neuroimaging with fMRI and PET, ERP methods, neurocomputational simulations
10^{-2} to 10^{-4}	Neural networks, maps and pathways	**Neuroanatomy:** Neural circuitry in maps, pathways, sheets	Neuroanatomical connections from visual, auditory, somatosensory regions to language areas	Image schemas, primary metaphor, topographic maps, convergence zones	Electrocellular recording, anatomical dyes, neurocomputational simulations
10^{-3} to 10^{-6}	Neurons, cortical columns	**Neurocellular systems:** Cellular and very small intercellular structures	Fine neuroanatomical organisation of particular structures recruited in lang. processing	Orientation-tuning cells; ocular dominance columns	Electrocellular recording, anatomical dyes, neurocomputational simulations
Less than 10^{-6}	Neuro-transmitters, ion channels, synapses	**Subcellular systems:** Subcellular, molecular, and electrophysical	None—beyond theoretical scope	Neurotransmitter, synapse, ion channels	Neuro-pharmacology, neurochemistry, neurophysics

not learned in isolation nor are words uttered in a vacuum, and research in Cognitive Linguistics should include this level of investigation. Investigations at the cultural level are occasionally given short shrift by some strains of cognitive science, but this has been and should remain a strong point of Cognitive Linguistics.

While this table representing the framework gives a good overview of the relationship between body, brain, and culture, it is not as illustrative for issues pertaining to evolutionary, historical, and developmental time scales, which may be considered at any of these levels. For example, both diachronic semantic change and the evolution of the larynx are important to Cognitive Linguistics. However, this failing is more a limitation of the imagery of a two-dimensional table than of the theoretical framework itself. If we were to add another axis for time perpendicular to the surface plane of the table, we could then imagine this framework as a rectangular solid. I have omitted representing this dimension because such an illustration would make it difficult to label the levels, but I make it explicit here because both the developmental and evolutionary time courses of these phenomena are crucial components of understanding how studies at these levels interact. An obvious example in language research is the fact that a study on second-language acquisition at one of these levels of investigation done at one point in stage of development would likely differ from a very similar study at the same level, but at another developmental stage. Such temporal concerns are an important, if sometimes neglected, dimension of variability.

Elsewhere, I have discussed the details of the pragmatic application of this framework to issues such as spatial frames of reference (Rohrer 2001), but for a briefer example of its application, consider some of the research done on the embodiment and conceptualization of anger. Kövecses (1986, 1995) has argued that the conceptual metaphor ANGER IS THE HEAT OF A FLUID IN A CONTAINER has a physiological basis in universal bodily experiences such as the elevated skin temperatures of the anger response, as measured by Ekman (1982, 1999). However, in a more experientialist vein, Geeraerts and Grondelaers (1995) critiqued Kövecses's research as ahistorical and acultural, arguing that historical lexicography shows that these metaphors have been inherited from the humoral theory of medieval Western science. Yet their critique seems at least partially rebutted by several cross-cultural analyses of the metaphors for anger in non-Indo-European languages, such as Matsuki's (1995) study of Japanese, where somewhat similar HEATED FLUID metaphors have been found.

Note that this controversy, centering on the question of change across time and culture, evokes the "universalist-relativist" philosophical debate on objectivity; however, and as the American pragmatist philosopher John Dewey (1917) noted, such debates are notoriously unhelpful to the continued inquiry that characterizes a *genuine* objectivity. A more pragmatic response might be to see these studies as the result of using differing methodologies at different levels of investigation to study the embodiment of anger. Applying this theoretical framework, we could seek to identify questions which investigate multiple dimensions. We might then expand the scope of the inquiry from the bodily and performative level of the framework to the communicative and cultural level: Was the humoral theory also physiologically motivated? Does this metaphor exist in any Indo-European linguistic evidence which predates the appearance of humoral theory? Did the Japanese metaphor arrive via Western contact, or did it emerge independently? And, to what extent does the Japanese conceptualization rely on shared underlying conceptual metaphors such as THE BODY IS A CONTAINER? Alternatively, a cognitive psychologist might frame a further inquiry at the performative level by measuring, via reaction times, heart rates, and/or skin temperature, whether Japanese and Indo-European language speakers exhibit similar physiological responses to differing variants of this metaphor. Or one might also measure whether subjects who were recently taught humoral theory would be quicker to use (or comprehend) passages containing this anger metaphor than other anger metaphors.

Thus, this controversy, along with many others in Cognitive Linguistics, is not simply a matter of "either-or," with one position being correct to the exclusion of the other. Instead, and from the perspective of this theoretical framework, the controversy results from measuring different but equally important dimensions of human embodiment. Once we recognize this fact, we can take concrete steps to investigate how these dimensions interact on a particular question. We are as unlikely as ever to resolve the "relativism-universalism" debate, so it is better to situate our questions, specify the scale and scope of our investigations, and look at how the conscious, experiential embodiment and the physiological embodiment interact in language.

7. Conclusions

If the answer to the basic problem of language—How do we share meaning?—could only be as simple and childlike as the question, then there might be no controversy about defining, in precise and narrow terms, what exactly the term "embodiment" means. The actual details of science are rarely neat and tidy, however, and even the most widely accepted scientific maxims are only incontrovertible so long as serious attention is placed elsewhere. We have barely begun to investigate the mechanics of how embodiment shapes and constrains meaning, of testing and validating the claims made by Cognitive Linguistics at the psychological and neurophysiological levels, of examining how embodiment shapes cultural artifacts such as watches, dials, and gauges, and of how the social and cultural context alters what embodied source is being used by a particular speaker. This project has necessarily enlisted anthropologists, sociologists, psychologists, and neuroscientists to work alongside linguists. The complexity of the survey that I have given will only be deepened by the details in the chapters which follow.

REFERENCES

Bailey, David. 1997. When push comes to shove: A computational model of the role of motor control in the acquisition of action verbs. PhD dissertation, University of California at Berkeley.

Bertram, John E. A., and Andy Ruina. 2001. Multiple walking speed-frequency relations are predicted by constrained optimization. *Journal of Theoretical Biology* 209: 445–53.

Brandt, Per Aage. 1999. Domains and the grounding of meaning. In José Luis Cifuentes Honrubia, ed., *Estudios de Lingüística Cognitiva* 467–78. Alicante, Spain: Dept. de Filología Española, Lingüística General y Teoría de la Literatura, Universidad de Alicante.

Brandt, Per Aage. 2000. Metaphor, catachresis, simile: A cognitive and semiotic approach and an ontological perspective. MS, Center for Semiotic Research, University of Aarhus, Denmark.

Brooks, Rodney A. 1997. From earwigs to humans. *Robotics and Autonomous Systems* 20: 291–304.

Collins, Steven H., Martijn Wisse, and Andy Ruina. 2001. A 3-D passive-dynamic walking robot with two legs and knees. *International Journal of Robotics Research* 20: 607–15.

Coulson, Seana, and Cyma Van Petten. 2002. Conceptual integration and metaphor: An event-related potential study. *Memory and Cognition* 30: 958–68.

Damasio, Antonio. 1995. *Descartes' error: Emotion, reason, and the human brain.* New York: Basic Books.

Deacon, Terrence. 1997. *The symbolic species: The co-evolution of language and the brain.* New York: W. W. Norton.

Dewey, John. 1917. The need for a recovery of philosophy. In Jo A. Boydson, ed., *John Dewey: The middle works, 1899–1924.* Vol. 10, *1916–1917*, 3–48. Carbondale: Southern Illinois University Press.

Donald, Merlin. 1991. *Origin of the modern mind: Three stages in the evolution of culture and cognition.* Cambridge, MA: Harvard University Press.

Edelman, Gerald M. 1992. *Bright air, brilliant fire: On the matter of the mind.* New York: Basic Books.

Ekman, Paul. 1982. *Emotion in the human face.* 2nd ed. Cambridge: Cambridge University Press.

Ekman, Paul. 1999. Basic emotions. In Tim Dalgleish and Mick Power, eds., *The handbook of cognition and emotion* 45–60. Chichester, UK: John Wiley & Sons.

Fauconnier, Gilles, and Mark Turner. 2002. *The way we think: Conceptual blending and the mind's hidden complexities.* New York: Basic Books.

Feldman, Jerome, and Srini Narayanan. 2004. Embodied meaning in a neural theory of language. *Brain and Language* 89: 385–92.

Fesmire, Steven A. 1994. What is "cognitive" about cognitive linguistics? *Metaphor and Symbolic Activity* 9: 149–54.

Gallese, Vittorio, and George Lakoff. 2005. The brain's concepts: The role of the sensory-motor system in conceptual knowledge. *Cognitive Neuropsyhcology* 22: 455–79.

Geeraerts, Dirk. 1985. *Paradigm and paradox: Explorations into a paradigmatic theory of meaning and its epistemological background.* Leuven, Belgium: Leuven University Press.

Geeraerts, Dirk, and Stefan Grondelaers. 1995. Looking back at anger: Cultural traditions and metaphorical patterns. In John R. Taylor and Robert E. MacLaury, eds., *Language and the cognitive construal of the world* 153–79. Berlin: Mouton de Gruyter.

Gibbs, Raymond W., Jr. 1980. Spilling the beans on understanding and memory for idioms in conversation. *Memory and Cognition* 8: 449–56.

Gibbs, Raymond W., Jr. 1986. Skating on thin ice: Literal meaning and understanding idioms in conversation. *Discourse Processes* 9: 17–30.

Gibbs, Raymond W., Jr. 1992. Categorization and metaphor understanding. *Psychological Review* 99: 572–77.

Gibbs, Raymond W., Jr. 1994. *The poetics of mind: Figurative thought, language, and understanding.* Cambridge: Cambridge University Press.

Hauk, Olaf, Ingrid Johnsrude, and Friedemann Pulvermüller. 2004. Somatotopic representation of action words in human motor and premotor cortex. *Neuron* 41: 301–7.

Hutchins, Edwin. 1995. *Cognition in the wild.* Cambridge, MA: MIT Press.

Hutchins, E. 2005. Material anchors for conceptual blends. *Journal of Pragmatics* 37: 1555–77.

Johnson, Mark. 1987. *The body in the mind: The bodily basis of meaning, imagination, and reason.* Chicago: University of Chicago Press.

Johnson, Mark, and Tim Rohrer. 2007. We are live creatures: Embodiment, American pragmatism and the cognitive organism. In Tom Ziemke, Jordan Zlatev, and Roz Frank, eds., *Body, Language and Mind,* vol. 1, *Embodiment* 17–54. Berlin: Mouton de Gruyter.

Kosslyn, Steven. 1980. *Image and mind.* Cambridge, MA: Harvard University Press.

Kosslyn, Steven. 1994. *Image and brain: The resolution of the imagery debate.* Cambridge, MA: MIT Press.

Kosslyn, Stephen, William L. Thompson, Irene J. Kim, and Nathaniel M. Alpert. 1995. Topographic representations of mental images in primary visual cortex. *Nature* 378: 496–98.

Kövecses, Zoltán. 1986. *Metaphors of anger, pride, and love: A lexical approach to the study of concepts.* Amsterdam: John Benjamins.

Kövecses, Zoltán. 1995. Anger: Its language, conceptualization, and physiology in the light of cross-cultural evidence. In John R. Taylor and Robert E. MacLaury, eds., *Language and the cognitive construal of the world* 181–96. Berlin: Mouton de Gruyter.

Lakoff, George. 1987. *Women, fire, and dangerous things: What categories reveal about the mind.* Chicago: University of Chicago Press.

Lakoff, George, and Mark Johnson. 1980. *Metaphors we live by.* Chicago: University of Chicago Press.

Lakoff, George, and Mark Johnson. 1999. *Philosophy in the flesh: The embodied mind and its challenge to Western thought.* New York: Basic Books.

Lakoff, George, and Mark Turner. 1989. *More than cool reason: A field guide to poetic metaphor.* Chicago: University of Chicago Press.

Langacker, Ronald W. 1987. *Foundations of cognitive grammar.* Vol. 1, *Theoretical prerequisites.* Stanford, CA: Stanford University Press.

Langacker, Ronald W. 1990. *Concept, image, and symbol: The cognitive basis of grammar.* Berlin: Mouton de Gruyter.

Langacker, Ronald W. 1991. *Foundations of cognitive grammar.* Vol. 2, *Descriptive application.* Stanford, CA: Stanford University Press.

MacWhinney, Brian. 1999. The emergence of language from embodiment. In Brian MacWhinney, ed., *The emergence of language* 213–56. Mahwah, NJ: Lawrence Erlbaum.

MacWhinney, Brian. 2003. The emergence of grammar from perspective-taking. Manuscript, Carnegie Mellon-University, Pittsburgh, PA.

Matsuki, Keiko. 1995. Metaphors of anger in Japanese. In John R. Taylor and Robert E. MacLaury, eds., *Language and the cognitive construal of the world* 137–51. Berlin: Mouton de Gruyter.

Meltzoff, Andrew. 1993. Molyneux's Babies: Cross-modal perception, imitation and the mind of the preverbal infant. In Naomi Eilan, Rosaleen McCarthy, and Bill Brewer, eds., *Spatial representation: Problems in philosophy and psychology* 219–35. Oxford: Basil Blackwell.

Nagel, Thomas. 1979. *Mortal questions.* Cambridge: Cambridge University Press.

Narayanan, Srini. 1997. KARMA: Knowledge-based active representations for Metaphor and aspect. MS thesis, University of California at Berkeley.

Ortony, Andrew, ed. 1993. *Metaphor and thought.* 2nd ed. Cambridge: Cambridge University Press.

Pfeifer, Rolf, and Christian Scheier. 1999. *Understanding intelligence.* Cambridge, MA: MIT Press.

Posner, Michael, and Marcus Raichle. 1994. *Images of mind.* New York: Scientific American.

Regier, Terry. 1992. The acquisition of lexical semantics for spatial terms: A connectionist model of perceptual categorization. PhD dissertation, University of California at Berkeley.

Regier, Terry. 1996. *The human semantic potential: Spatial language and constrained connectionism.* Cambridge, MA: MIT Press.

Rohrer, Tim. 1998. When metaphors bewitch, analogies illustrate, and logic fails: Controversies over the use of metaphoric reasoning in philosophy and science. PhD dissertation, University of Oregon.

Rohrer, Tim. 2001. Pragmatism, ideology and embodiment: William James and the philosophical foundations of cognitive linguistics. In Esra Sandikcioglu and René Dirven, eds., *Language and ideology,* Vol. 1, *Theoretical cognitive approaches* 49–81. Amsterdam: John Benjamins.

Rohrer, Tim. 2005. Image schemas in the brain: fMRI and ERP investigations into embodiment and conceptual metaphor. In Beate Hampe, ed., *From perception to meaning: Image schemas in cognitive linguistics* 165–96. Berlin: Mouton de Gruyter.

Shepard, Roger N., and Jacqueline Metzler. 1971. Mental rotation of three-dimensional objects. *Science* 171: 701–3.

Sinha, Chris. 1999. Grounding, mapping, and acts of meaning. In Theo Janssen and Gisela Redeker, eds., *Cognitive linguistics: Foundations, scope, and methodology* 223–55. Berlin: Mouton de Gruyter.

Sinha, Chris, and Kristine Jensen de López. 2000. Language, culture, and the embodiment of spatial cognition. *Cognitive Linguistics* 11: 17–41.

Stern, Daniel. 1985. *The interpersonal world of the infant.* New York: Basic Books.

Sweetser, Eve. 1990. *From etymology to pragmatics: Metaphorical and cultural aspects of semantic structure.* Cambridge: Cambridge University Press.

Talmy, Leonard. 1985. Force dynamics in language and thought. *Chicago Linguistic Society* 21, vol. 2 (parasession): 293–337.

Talmy, Leonard. 2000. *Toward a cognitive semantics.* Vol. 1, *Concept structuring systems.* Cambridge, MA: MIT Press.

Tomasello, Michael. 1992. *First verbs: A case study of early grammatical development.* Cambridge: Cambridge University Press.

Zlatev, Jordan. 1997. *Situated embodiment: Studies in the emergence of spatial meaning.* Stockholm: Gotab Press.

Zlatev, Jordan. 2003. Polysemy or Generality? Mu. In Hubert Cuyckens, René Dirven, and John R. Taylor, eds., *Cognitive approaches to lexical semantics* 447–94. Berlin: Mouton de Gruyter.

CHAPTER 3

CONSTRUAL AND PERSPECTIVIZATION

ARIE VERHAGEN

1. INTRODUCTION

A fundamental principle in Cognitive Linguistics is that semantics is, indeed, primarily cognitive and not a matter of relationships between language and the world (or truth conditions with respect to a model). This principle becomes especially manifest in the research into facets of meaning and grammatical organization which crucially makes use of notions such as "perspective," "subjectivity," or "point of view." What these notions have in common is that they capture aspects of conceptualization that cannot be sufficiently analyzed in terms of properties of the *object* of conceptualization, but, in one way or another, necessarily involve a *subject* of conceptualization. A strong incentive for this type of research stems from the awareness that the more linguistic problems can be solved by making use of these notions, the more (heuristically) successful the fundamental principle is; in addition, this research is motivated by the awareness that the best way to make these notions relevant for linguistic analysis is not given a priori and thus requires empirical investigation. It is therefore not surprising that there is in fact quite a large body of research into such nonobjective facets of linguistic meaning.

The cover term that has come to be used for different ways of viewing a particular situation is "construal." At a very elementary level, construal is a feature of the meaning of all linguistic expressions, if only as a consequence of the fact that languages provide various ways for categorizing situations, their participants and features, and the relations between them. Speaking thus always implies a choice:

> A speaker who accurately observes the spatial distribution of certain stars can describe them in many distinct fashions: as a *constellation*, as a *cluster of stars*, as *specks of light in the sky*, etc. Such expressions are semantically distinct; they reflect the speaker's alternate construals of the scene, each compatible with its objectively given properties. (Langacker 1990a: 61)

The fact *that* a particular situation can be construed in alternate ways should, from a cognitive linguistic perspective, not come as a big surprise or require extensive justification. What is more important linguistically is that languages systematically provide means for different *kinds* of construal. For instance, the distinct descriptions of a single phenomenon given in the quotation from Langacker above differ in (among other things) the *frames* of knowledge with respect to which the conceived situation is characterized: a particular distribution of stars is only considered a constellation in a culturally shared traditional frame of knowledge about the structure of the sky, while this framework is not required for conceptualizing it as a cluster. So one type of construal involved in these examples crucially involves frames of knowledge (or "Idealized Cognitive Models"). Another type, also involved here, focuses on the *compositionality* of the conceptualization: both *a cluster of stars* and *specks of light in the sky* evoke their objects of conceptualization by combining several elements into a whole in some particular way, while the lexical item *constellation* does not. Then again, *specks of light in the sky* (with the plural noun *specks* as its head) focuses on the multiplicity of the phenomenon observed, whereas *constellation* and *a cluster of stars* impose the construal of a coherent unit (with *the cluster* constituting a "multiplex" one in the sense of Talmy 2000a: 59).

This simple example already shows that there are several dimensions along which construals may vary. Cognitive linguists, most notably Langacker and Talmy, have proposed a number of classification schemes for construal phenomena, in attempts to organize them into a relatively small number of basic types. However, these classificatory systems seem to exhibit a substantial amount of arbitrariness. This is partly due to the fact that research into construal phenomena, while ubiquitous in ordinary language and therefore highly important, has at the same time led to a large increase in the number of known distinct construal operations. Therefore, it is useful to consider a few more types of construal before considering the classification proposals. It should be evident, though, that this cannot be a comprehensive list of construal phenomena.

2. The Diversity of Construal Phenomena

One of the first construal operations to have been recognized as linguistically highly relevant is the "Figure/Ground" distinction, well known from studies in Gestalt psychology. It was introduced into Cognitive Linguistics (even before it was known under that name) through the work of Talmy (1978). In visual perception, one element may be the focus of attention—the "Figure"; it is perceived as a prominent coherent element and set off against the rest of what is in the field of vision—the "Ground." This psychological distinction is reflected in many linguistic distinctions, lexical as well as grammatical. Consider, for instance, the expressions *X is above Y* and *Y is below X*; while these expressions denote the same spatial configuration, they are semantically distinct in that they reflect different selections of the participant that is to provide the Ground, with respect to which the other participant, as Figure can be located. A well-known example of a grammatical alternation in which the construal of a participant as either Figure or Ground constitutes part of the semantic difference is the active/passive contrast.

The meanings of lexical items quite generally include a subtype of this Figure/Ground construal. Consider the meaning of the word *uncle*, which presupposes a background network of kinship relations, and foregrounds one particular node in it. More generally, a lexical item usually designates, or "profiles" (in Langacker's terminology), a substructure within a larger structure (the "base"), and knowing what larger structure is involved is part of knowing the meaning of that item. The words *finger* and *thumb*, while profiling different substructures, share the conception of a hand as their base; the same holds for *ceiling* and *floor* with respect to a room, and so on. A general linguistic reflex of this phenomenon is found in constraints on expressions denoting part-whole relationships; these may not "bypass" base-profile relations. While *The hand of this animal has three fingers* is felicitous, ?*The arm of this animal has three fingers* is definitely awkward, and *This animal has three fingers* has an entirely different meaning.

Profile-base distinctions also exist in the domain of time. The flow of time constitutes (part of) the base of the meaning of verbs. Different lexical verbs may profile different "slices" of time, backgrounding and foregrounding different features (thus producing different "aspectual" profiles). For example, *think* and *read* present processes that are construed as ongoing, not involving a change in the period of time being focused on, while *arrive* and *promise* present processes that crucially involve a change at the time being focused on. Grammatical constructions may impose a particular kind of profile on the temporal interpretation of a situation. For example, the English progressive construction (*be* + *V-ing*) can be said to impose a particular profile on the interpretation of the clause, backgrounding any boundaries (beginning and end point) of the designated process, irrespective of the meaning of the verb (see also Michaelis 2004; Boogaart and Janssen, this volume, chapter 31).

Another important construal operation is based on the fact that objects and situations can be perceived at different levels of "resolution," or "granularity." One linguistic correlate of this cognitive feature is the fact that lexical categories may form taxonomic hierarchies consisting of various levels of specificity (e.g., *Palomino, horse, mammal, animal, living thing, thing*). Each of these levels corresponds to our perception of things at different degrees of granularity. This in itself already allows language users to describe events at different levels of specificity (or, conversely, schematicity). Some of the most common verbs in a language are highly schematic (e.g., English *be, have, do,* and *make*), allowing a speaker to characterize a situation without paying attention to all the details of the specific state or process involved. Thus, the same objective situation can be described as *The young physicist wrote an original book, The physicist wrote a book, The scientist produced a publication, The woman made something,* or *She made something.* Often, the role of verbs in a construction is to provide specifics to the schematic conceptualization evoked by the construction. For example, *They made their way through the forest*, although itself a specific case of a transitive template, still evokes a rather schematic image of overcoming resistance and movement, while *They cut their way through the forest* provides more details about the means of "way-making." The function of modifiers is to allow for representations with a high degree of specificity on the basis of (clausal and nominal) templates that are in themselves only rather schematic for types of events— that is, modifiers also make specificity possible without the need for more templates.

An example of grammatical construal involving different levels of granularity is provided by those causative constructions which code the causal and the result components of an event separately (e.g., English *to make something happen*). Such a construction construes an event with a higher degree of resolution than a causal lexical verb would; compare, for instance, *to make someone believe something* with *to tell someone something.* This, in turn, allows variation in explicit, highly granular construals of causal relationships, with distinctions such as those between *to make someone believe something* and *to let someone believe something.*

The construal phenomena discussed so far variously impose *structure* on conceptualizations in ways that do not immediately follow from their content, which is why they are considered cases of construal in the first place. Another form of construal consists in understanding one conceptualization *in relation to* another one. For example, tense marking in a finite clause in English relates the situation mentioned in the clause to the conceptualization of the communicative situation (roughly, as overlapping or not), which is why the category of tense is considered "deictic"—along with such elements as personal pronouns (with *I* and *you* identifying participants in the conceived situation as communicative participants and third-person pronouns identifying situation participants as *not* participating in the communicative process) and adverbs like *here, now, there,* and *then.* Other ways of understanding one conceptualization in relation to another are by establishing similarity or any sufficiently salient contingent connection—these two constitute the basis (albeit not exhaustively) for metaphor and metonymy, respectively—or by establishing contrast (e.g., negation) or scalarity (e.g., comparison).

Not only can construals of events be different within languages, but also across languages; that is, there exist typological distinctions in terms of construal—an issue related to the issue of linguistic relativity. For example, languages may not only have different means available to organize spatial relations, they may also differ radically in the way space is conceptually structured. In such cases, individual speakers have little or no freedom of choice to pick one construal over another, as their language simply lacks some of the "options." Nevertheless, what is involved is still different construals of similar experiences or phenomena.

One type that has traditionally received much attention is the different ways motion events are expressed linguistically in languages such as English, on the one hand, and languages such as Spanish, on the other (see Talmy 2000b: 21–67, for a recent comprehensive overview). In English, the verb in a sentence expressing a motion event usually also encodes (features of) a "co-event," such as manner (*to slide, to roll, to bounce*, etc.) or cause or instrument (*to push, to blow, to chop, to pound*, etc.), while the direction of movement may be indicated by optional adjuncts (*into the water*, etc.). In Spanish, on the other hand, the verb is mostly required to mark some aspect of directionality, and factors such as manner or instrument may be expressed by means of adjuncts (. . . *entró a la casa bailando* ' . . . entered the house dancing'). Spanish, encoding the path component of motion in the verb, is called a "verb-framed language," while English is called a "satellite-framed language." Since verbs are obligatory elements in clauses expressing events, the two types of languages conventionally impose different construals on the conceptualization of motion events. It is findings of this type that have given rise to a research program, especially executed by Talmy, into the questions of what the typological variation in construal among languages is and what kind of factors are involved in it.

Another highly intriguing question triggered by this kind of typological results concerns the influence of conventional construal patterns in a language on the thought processes of its speakers (see Bowerman 1996; Levinson 2001). With respect to the distinction between satellite-framed and verb-framed languages in the domain of motion events, Slobin has developed his concept of "thinking for speaking"; the idea is that the grammatical patterns of a native language force its learners to habitually pay attention to those features of events that are necessary for expression in linguistic communication (Slobin 1996)—this issue is developed further by Pederson in chapter 38 of the present *Handbook*.

In view of the multitude of possible construal operations and their diverse uses across languages—which has become apparent even from this brief overview—a number of interrelated questions can be raised. How are construal operations related to each other? Are there basic types of construal? Which construal relations share which properties? Can linguistic expressions be exhaustively characterized as belonging to certain types and not others? One additional consideration that gives rise to these questions is the fact that certain phenomena systematically seem to allow for more than one classification. For example, the fact that a phenomenon allows for construal at different levels of specificity is at least to some extent related to the fact that it can be seen as similar to other phenomena: the higher the schematicity, the more general the category to which it is assigned, and thus the larger the set of phenomena that are considered similar. Or consider the English progressive above, which was characterized in terms of profiling (backgrounding of the boundaries of a process unfolding in time); an alternative way of characterizing the progressive might be in terms of viewpoint: the position from which the situation is viewed is contained in the ongoing process itself (so that any boundaries are not "in view"). Considerations like these also make the question which types of construal operations there are, and how they are connected, an urgent one. So let us now turn to the issue of classifying construal phenomena.

3. Classifications of Construal Operations

Langacker (1987: 116–37) proposed the following threefold classification of construal operations (then called "focal adjustments"):

a. Selection
b. Perspective
c. Abstraction

The first category concerns language users' capacity to selectively attend to some facets of a conceptualization and ignoring others. The second comprises linguistic manifestations of the position from which a situation is viewed, and is divided into four subtypes: (i) Figure/Ground alignment, (ii) Viewpoint, (iii) Deixis, and (iv) Subjectivity/Objectivity. The third major category relates to our ability to establish commonalities between distinct phenomena and abstracting away from differences, and thus to organize concepts into categories. Langacker has since revised his classification, which now[1] looks as follows (see Langacker, this volume, chapter 17):

a. Specificity
b. Prominence
c. Perspective
d. Dynamicity

The first class (Specificity) roughly corresponds to the previous class Abstraction. The new category of Prominence comprises especially Figure/Ground phenomena and the phenomena formerly categorized under Selection. Perspective has remained the same, except that of the subtype Figure/Ground has now been placed in the Prominence category. Dynamicity is an additional category and concerns the development of a conceptualization through processing time (rather than through conceived time). It is first of all connected to the inherent temporal nature of linguistic utterances: presenting elements of a conceptualization in a different order results in differences of meaning. But a dynamic, sequential conceptualization may also result from the application of a dynamic concept to an object of conceptualization that is not inherently dynamic itself (as in *The road winds through the valley*).

Talmy (1988) originally proposed the following "imaging systems" as the major classes of construal phenomena:

a. Schematization
b. Perspective
c. Attention
d. Force Dynamics

There is a considerable overlap between this proposal and the one by Langacker, which in itself is indicative of the relevance of these classes. Thus, Talmy's Schematization largely corresponds to Langacker's Specificity; both have a category Perspective comprising similar phenomena, and Talmy's category Attention overlaps with Langacker's Prominence. Force Dynamics, though, is absent from Langacker's classification.

Talmy (2000a: 40–84) has now also revised his classification, yielding the following major categories:

a. Configurational Structure
b. Perspective
c. Distribution of Attention
d. Force Dynamics[2]

Perpendicular to these four "schematic systems," as they are now called, there is a "schematic category" called Domain, which includes only a very limited number of major dimensions of construal, namely, "space" and "time."[3] As such, a single specific construal operation from the schematic system "configurational structure" (e.g., ± boundedness) may apply to several domains. For example, in the domain of space as well as that of time, concepts may be construed as discrete (i.e., as objects in space and acts in time) or as continuous (as masses in space and activities in time). This way of cross-combining construal operations is linguistically justified by the fact that in nominalization (which converts concepts from the domain of time to the domain of space) acts are construed as objects and activities as mass, witness such pairs as in (1) and (2):

(1)   John called me – John gave me a call.
(2)   John helped me – John gave me some help.

In Langacker's approach, Talmy's domains of "space" and "time" correspond to the conceptual distinction between nouns and verbs. In particular, Langacker (1987, 2005) views nouns as "things," understood as a construal resulting from conceptual grouping and reification, and verbs as "processes," understood as a construal resulting from sequential scanning of a temporally manifested relationship. However,

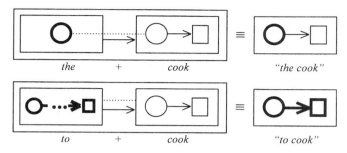

Figure 3.1. "Nominal" and "verbal" construal of the same content in different constructions

Langacker does not treat the noun-verb distinction as reflecting a fundamental schematic category in itself, but rather as a special instance of Figure/Ground organization (in particular, the profile-base organization) and of categorization. The English noun and verb *cook*, for example, have a shared conceptual content, but in one class of constructions (*the cook*, etc.), a different part of this content is "profiled" than in constructions (*to cook*, etc.) that encode a processual construal (schematically presented in figure 3.1).

Because of these (and other) patterns, the English word *cook* can be regarded as having a schematic sense that does not impose a particular profile and thus serves as a superordinate category for the specific nominal and verbal uses of the word (Langacker 2005). Figure 3.2 provides a schematic representation.

It is clear from the foregoing that, while the concepts employed in Langacker's and Talmy's analyses play a rather different role in their respective frameworks, their approaches basically capture the same insights. Furthermore, they both embrace the idea that several dimensions of construal can be involved in the meaning of a single linguistic expression. What these two points suggest is that any classification of construal phenomena in a particular language is likely to be at least to some extent arbitrary, if only because linguistic units often participate in more than a single kind of construal.

Croft and Cruse (2004: 43–46) also indicate that a classification of construal phenomena is to some extent arbitrary or cannot be entirely motivated. For one thing, they observe that the classifications proposed by Langacker and Talmy share a number of features, but also that it is not obvious how the differences can be reconciled. Furthermore, they point out that from both classifications, some dimensions of construal (e.g., image schemas) are still missing and their integration into the proposed classifications is not immediately evident. Building on an earlier comparison of construal classifications (Croft and Wood 2000), Croft and Cruse (2004: 45) then state that the main categories in such a classification should correspond to psychological processes and capacities that have been established independently, by psychologists and phenomenologists. But this requirement had, of course, already motivated Langacker's and Talmy's classifications. Thus, it is no surprise that the classification proposed by Croft and Cruse overlaps with those by Langacker and

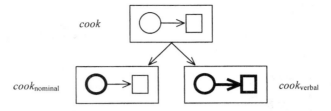

Figure 3.2. The word stem *cook* categorizing nominal and verbal construal

Talmy. Aside from some (smaller) reassignments of specific kinds of construal to other major categories, the main difference between Croft and Cruse's classification and those of Langacker and Talmy is that the former is more comprehensive than the latter ones. The main categories, according to Croft and Cruse, are:

a. Attention/Salience
b. Judgment/Comparison
c. Perspective/Situatedness
d. Constitution/Gestalt

Category (a), Attention/Salience, in general comprises the same types of construals as the ones subsumed under Talmy's Attention category (and Langacker's Prominence), but it also contains as subcategories certain construal phenomena that had the status of major categories in (some version of) Langacker's and Talmy's work; specifically, it includes Langacker's Abstraction and Talmy's Schematization ("scalar adjustments") and Langacker's Dynamicity. In addition, it contains the subcategory Scope (including referent accessibility; see Ariel 1990), a category which was not explicitly discussed by Langacker or Talmy.

The second category, Judgment/Comparison, contains the subcategories Categorization, Metaphor, and Figure/Ground. As such, we can observe that Figure/Ground has been reassigned from the category Attention/Prominence in Talmy's and Langacker's work. Furthermore, Categorization is not viewed as a Schematization phenomenon, as Talmy had it—despite the intimate connection between the two. Then again, the inclusion of Metaphor in the classification of construal phenomena makes this classification more comprehensive than previous ones.

The Perspective category is the one that is obviously most similar to that in the other proposals. The category Constitution/Gestalt, finally, overlaps with Talmy's (2000a) category Configurational Structure, but also includes Force Dynamics.

What conclusions can be drawn from this survey of classifications? First of all, although all classifications share the requirement that they should reflect general and well-established psychological abilities, they still turn out to be considerably different.

The proposal by Croft and Cruse, who formulate this requirement most emphatically, actually raises the same kind of questions as those that were raised by the other proposals; the assignment of particular construal operations under one rubric rather than another cannot always be clearly motivated (e.g., why, for instance,

Fictive Motion should be subsumed under Attention/Salience and not under Constitution/Gestalt?). The increase in coverage of construal operations in Croft and Cruse's classification in fact goes hand in hand with a further decrease of its transparency. It looks as if any new construal operation being discovered requires its own new category. Obviously, this does not mean that certain construal operations must therefore be excluded from the theory, but rather that construal operations may vary in so many different respects that attempts at an exhaustive classification necessarily have a considerable degree of arbitrariness. In fact, in his contribution to the present *Handbook*, Langacker states that his "classification of construal phenomena is... mostly for expository convenience" (chapter 17, note 22).

An additional reason for taking up this position is the fact that these taxonomies not only serve to classify the construal operations, but also the linguistic elements that express them. Now, what has not been taken into account in any of the classification schemes considered is the fact that the type of construal linguistic expressions reflect may gradually change. But precisely this observation casts considerable doubt on the feasibility of a psychologically realistic classification scheme. We can illustrate this with the phenomenon, well known from grammaticalization studies, that markers of perfectivity may change into markers of past tense. Such a change involves a transfer from the category of configurational construal operations (imposing boundedness on the conceived event) to the category of perspectival, deictic ones (marking the conceived event as preceding the communicative event). However, the meaning of a linguistic unit does not shift from one class of construal operations to another one overnight; semantic change is gradual. The diachronic development implies that for many speakers of a language for a long time (normally spanning several generations), these perfective expressions reflect both types of construal, in the sense that both types remain distinguishable for analysts. For the speakers themselves, however, it makes more sense to assume that they operate with a complex but unitary ("Gestalt-like") construal operation in which the effect on the structure of the event ('completed') is immediately associated with an effect on the relation of the event to the communicative situation ('past'). In other words, it is part of these speakers' knowledge of the conventions of their language that the unit involved conveys this complex construal. It is thus psychologically unrealistic to want to assign this particular construal operation to one category rather than another. For the speakers, it simply is a category in its own right, possibly sharing more or less prototypical characteristics of several other types of construal, some "configurational," some "perspectival." In fact, such conclusions soon appear inevitable on the basis of research into the details of the working of any particular kind of construal operation in actual usage (see Cornelis 1997 on construals effected by passive constructions).

Thus, it is precisely from a cognitive point of view that one should not expect that classifications of construal operations can be set up that are exhaustive and complete. From this perspective, it is therefore quite appropriate that the chapters to follow simply present the most important and well-studied types of construal operations successively.

The insight that a general classification scheme for construal operations is not feasible should not obscure the fact that the set of these operations definitely exhibits structure—it is not a list of totally unrelated notions. Some subsets of construal operations share more features with each other than with other ones, and as such the entire set of construal phenomena is amenable to a structure comprising some general rubrics under which they can be subsumed on the basis of their recurrent or shared features.

There is one such rubric that stands out as a more general dimension of construal than other ones, namely, perspective. In view of the differences between the different classification systems discussed above, it is striking that they show agreement about the relevance of a class of perspectival construal operations. Actually, this is hardly surprising since the concept of "construal" was introduced to capture aspects of conceptualization that cannot be adequately analyzed in terms of the object of conceptualization but require reference to a *subject's* perception, choice, or point of view. Accordingly, I will assume that perspective is a central part of the entire range of possible construal relations, in fact a definitional aspect of prototypical instances of construal.

We may think of the general rubrics under which construal operations can be subsumed as establishing a kind of "conceptual space" for construal. A linguistic element conventionally conveying a specific kind of construal may in principle occupy any position in this space; elements sharing features can be thought of as close together, forming "clusters" in this space without necessarily belonging in preestablished, bounded regions. Starting from fundamental features of the notion "construal" itself, the remainder of this chapter will develop a general conceptual framework in terms of which construal operations may be characterized, as an alternative to different classification schemes discussed before. On the one hand, this framework will not provide a new exhaustive classification (nor is it intended as one); on the other hand, it will allow us to see that still more (especially grammatical) phenomena may crucially involve construal (especially perspectivization) than have already been considered so far.

4. A General Framework for Characterizing Construal Operations

Langacker (1987: 487–88) defines the *construal relationship* as follows: "The relationship between a speaker (or hearer) and a situation that he conceptualizes and portrays, involving focal adjustments and imagery." In this definition, the construal

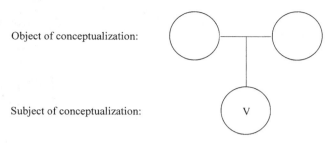

Object of conceptualization:

Subject of conceptualization:

Figure 3.3. A viewing arrangement

relation basically involves an individual (speaker *or* hearer), on the one hand, and a conceived situation, on the other. Thus, it corresponds closely to Langacker's "viewing arrangement" (see Langacker 1987: 129; 1993: 454). Diagrammatically, this relationship can be represented as in figure 3.3.

This configuration, being two-dimensional, already embodies one very basic distinction between construal types. As was pointed out in section 2, some construals involve the imposition of *structure* on the object of conceptualization, while others consist in one conceptualization being understood *in relation to* another one, in particular the communicative situation. Different sorts of structure (attentional, force-dynamic, etc.) involve the higher, horizontal level of figure 3.3, while different sorts of relations to the communicative situation (deixis, viewpoint, etc.) concern the vertical relation.[4]

Langacker subsequently identifies the lower, horizontal level of figure 3.3 as the "ground" (Langacker 1987: 126; 1990b: 9), which he defines as the ensemble of the communicative event, its participants, and its immediate circumstances.[5] Although in this definition, the ground includes participants—in plural—rather than a singular "viewer," no distinction is made between *different* speech act participants, and the graphic representations given still represent only a single "viewer" (or "subject" of conceptualization).[6] Moreover, while the configuration, as depicted in figure 3.3, is amenable to providing a wide array of cognitive abilities with respect to various objects of conceptualization, it does not accommodate one highly human capacity, namely, to take into account *other minds* in relation to an object of conceptualization. Indeed, it is a characteristically human trait to be able to identify deeply with conspecifics. In characterizing biologically determined cognitive differences and similarities between young humans and other primates, Tomasello (1999: 14–15) writes:

> There is just one major difference, and that is the fact that human beings 'identify' with conspecifics more deeply than do other primates. This identification is not something mysterious, but simply the process by which the human child understands that other persons are beings like herself . . . and so she sometimes tries to understand things from their point of view. . . . For purposes of exposition

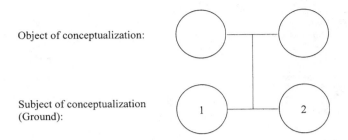

Object of conceptualization:

Subject of conceptualization
(Ground):

Figure 3.4. The construal configuration and its basic elements

> I refer to this process generally as 'understanding others as intentional (or mental)
> agents (like the self).'[7]

Language use, which is dependent on mutually shared knowledge of conventions, is crucially dependent on recognizing others like oneself. So, certainly with respect to linguistically coded conceptualizations, Langacker's initial way of construing the construal relationship may be treated as a special case of a somewhat more complex configuration that incorporates the insight that language use comprises more than one subject of conceptualization.[8] Consider figure 3.4.

The "ground" of any linguistic usage event consists of two conceptualizers—the "communicator" (conceptualizer 1 in figure 3.4), who takes responsibility for the utterance, and the "addressee" (conceptualizer 2 in figure 3.4), with whom the communicator enters into a coordination relation—and the knowledge that they mutually share, including models of each other and of the discourse situation. On this view, the ground is essentially "common ground" (see Clark 1996; also Sinha 1999 for further psychological and philosophical considerations motivating this view of "ground" and Verhagen 2005 for linguistic considerations). The point of a linguistic utterance is, generally speaking, that the first conceptualizer invites the second to jointly attend to an object of conceptualization in some specific way and to update the common ground by doing so; that is, both conceptualizers are involved in coordinating cognition by means of language, with one conceptualizer taking the initiative in each specific instance. This coordination relationship between the two conceptualizers is indicated by the lower horizontal line in figure 3.4, and the relation of joint attention between the conceptualizers and the object of conceptualization by the vertical line.

Figure 3.4 represents a conceptual space which can be organized in different ways and which is reflected in different linguistic expressions. Extreme cases at one end are those in which the meaning of the expression does not in any respect involve an element of the ground and which may thus be labeled maximally "objective." Schematically, the first type of situation may be represented as in figure 3.5.

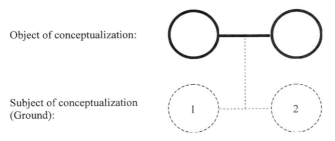

Object of conceptualization:

Subject of conceptualization
(Ground):

Figure 3.5. Construal configuration in maximally "objective" expressions

The use of dotted lines in figure 3.5 indicates that, although the ground may be said to figure in the interpretation of any utterance (in some "tenuous sense"; Langacker 1990b: 9), it is not signaled by the conventional meaning of "maximally objective" linguistic units. That is to say, these linguistic units wholly pertain to the level of the object of conceptualization, which is indicated by the use of bold lines: they "profile" aspects of the object of conceptualization, but none at the level of the subjects of conceptualization or of the relation between the two levels. Such "pure" cases are relatively rare, and artificial. One might think of "common nouns and verbs considered in isolation (for example *lamp, tree*, . . .)" (Langacker 1990b: 9) or a label like "bathroom" on a door (Theo Janssen, p.c.). Even a noun phrase such as *the horse* or a simple tensed sentence (*John owns a horse*) are not purely objective in this sense, as the identity of the referent or the time of the described event are accessed via the communicative situation (which is why the article and the tense marking are called "grounding predications"). Note also that, even though in specific utterances, a single common or proper noun may be used to attract an interlocutor's attention (*Wolves!*) or to invite him/her to respond in a particular way (*John?*), this occurrence of cognitive coordination is not due to the meaning of the nouns, so the ground is not said to be profiled by these elements.

The construal configuration, as represented in figure 3.4, may be used to indicate differences between linguistic units in the same language, but also between seemingly similar elements in different languages or at different historical stages of a language (with one element conventionally marking only certain elements of the construal configuration, and the other some other, or more, elements). This is the way this representation will be used in the remainder of this chapter. The extreme case at the other end involves the mirror image of the situations depicted in figure 3.5, that is, expressions in which only elements of the ground and/or the relationship between them are profiled, and no aspect of an object of conceptualization is marked linguistically. This is represented in figure 3.6.

Examples of such purely subjective utterances are interjections, as in greetings (*Hi*), apologies (*Sorry*), or calls for attention (*Hey*). Even more simple configurations

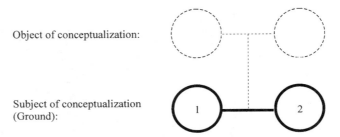

Object of conceptualization:

Subject of conceptualization
(Ground):

1   2

Figure 3.6. Construal configuration in highly "subjective" expressions

may be possible in which only one element is really profiled, as in noninteractional
signs of disgust or frustration (*Yuck, Damn*). In actual usage, however, these subjective utterances also involve aspects of language users' experience that function as
objects of conceptualization (such as what triggered the apology or the bad taste of
some piece of food), but these objective elements are not indicated by the conventional meanings of these elements, which only express a subjective reaction or
organize the relationship between speaker and addressee.

The fact that maximally objective and maximally subjective expressions constitute only restricted kinds of language use demonstrates, in fact, that the normal
situation is for linguistic expressions to construe some specified features of an
object of conceptualization in relation to one or more facets of the ground. Labeling
objects and producing interjections constitute the opposite extremes on a continuum from maximally objective to maximally subjective expressions, and thus the
exceptions; expressions in the "middle part" of this continuum are the rule.

It will be recalled that many of the construal operations presented in sections 2
and 3 reflect cognitive abilities relating only to the *object* level of conceptualization.
Still, the fact that the classifications of construal operations were in agreement on
the importance of a class of perspectival construal phenomena suggests that the
structure of the basic construal configuration cannot be complete without a *subject*
level of conceptualization. Indeed, expressions evoking perspectival phenomena
make explicit reference to the subject level of this configuration, and/or its relation
to the object level, while other expressions of construal do not refer to the ground
(although, of course, the decision to *use*, or to refrain from using, any expression,
normally involves the ground as it is made by speakers on the basis of an assessment of their interlocutors and the rest of the communicative situation). I have
furthermore suggested that the basic construal configuration should be seen as
involving a relation of intersubjective coordination, reflecting the typically human
cognitive ability to identify with conspecifics and thus to conceive of things from
other points of view. I will now develop the latter point further, showing that it not
only covers traditionally recognized perspectival construals, but may also extend to
other construals in a natural way.

5. Perspectivization

5.1. General Grounding

We have seen that a particular spatial configuration of two entities X and Y can be encoded as X *is below* Y and as Y *is above* X, and therefore that the semantics of these expressions necessarily involves an element of construal, in this case Figure/Ground organization. Another dimension of construal is involved in similar uses of these expressions, as exemplified in (3) and (4):

(3)   The ballroom is below.
(4)   Write to the address above for full details.

In each of these cases, the landmark with respect to which the trajector is located is part of the ground of the utterance. The position of the ballroom in (3) is calculated from the common position of the speech participants or the position of the addressee (for example, when (3) is uttered as an instruction over the telephone). Likewise, if (4) is a sentence in a particular document currently relevant for the speech participants (i.e., part of the common ground), then the location of the address is calculated from the position of sentence (4) in this document. So, in each of these cases, we have a situation, unlike the ones discussed so far, in which a relation between the ground and the object of conceptualization actually *is* profiled in the interpretation of the expressions. This is indicated in figure 3.7 by the bold vertical line representing the construal relation.

Profiling a relationship with the ground is obviously not a necessary condition for the use of such lexical items as *below* and *above*, but it is a necessary condition in constructions where the landmark is not represented linguistically. In particular, spatial expressions indicating the position of specific text portions relative to the currently relevant one, as illustrated by (4) and similar sentences such as *Further instructions are below*, may be considered a conventional pattern. Thus, it has become a convention of English that the items *below* and *above* allow for such a perspectivized construal, and it is this construal which distinguishes them from other items such as *beside*, which does not participate in a construction of the type X *be beside* to indicate a position to the side of some element of the ground. Note also that there do not seem to be specific restrictions on the interpretation of an entity's location relative to the ground, as long as it is computable from the context in which the utterance is interpreted.

Another example in English of an expression whose landmark *may* be construed as an element of the ground is *across*, as is illustrated in (5) and (6).

(5)   Vanessa is sitting across the table.
(6)   Vanessa is sitting across the table from Veronica.

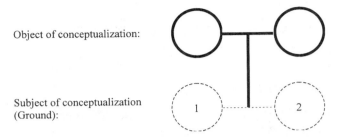

Object of conceptualization:

Subject of conceptualization (Ground):

Figure 3.7. Construal configuration in (minimally) "perspectivized" expressions

In (5), the position with respect to which Vanessa is being located is an element of the ground (the speaker), while it is an element of the object of conceptualization in (6). Possibly, there is a difference in degree of conventionality between examples (3) and (4) and examples (5) and (6): the usage of *below* and *above* in (3) and (4) represents a special subtype of their "normal" use, whereas, in (5) and (6), it is the subjective construal of *across* in (5) that can be considered prototypical, and the "objectified" use in (6) a special subtype. For relative spatial indications such as *to the left/right*, construal with respect to the ground is always possible, even when an explicit reference point is mentioned. In (7), Vanessa may obviously be sitting at Veronica's right-hand side, but the relative order of Veronica and Vanessa may also be "left-to-right" from a conceptualizer's point of view (even though Vanessa might be at Veronica's left-hand side from Veronica's point of view, e.g., when they are facing the conceptualizer).

(7)   Vanessa is sitting to the right of Veronica.

From the foregoing examples, it appears, then, that there are differences in the degree of conventionality with which a construal configuration such as in figure 3.7 may be associated with a specific linguistic form. There are also linguistic items that *always* comprise a construal with respect to the ground as part of their semantic characterization. The referent of *yesterday*, for example, can never be determined without using knowledge about the time of the ground. With linguistic items of this kind, we enter the realm of what is traditionally called "deictic" elements (see Brisard 2002, for explorations of deixis from a cognitive point of view). When viewing deixis as a type of construal, however, one no longer restricts it to something limited to and determined by a specific class of linguistic items (so-called "deictic" morphemes). As we have seen, construal with respect to an element of the ground is something that can be associated with different elements to different degrees of conventionality. Of course, one may want to identify the class of elements in a language whose meanings *necessarily* invoke elements of the ground as deictic, but that should not imply that deixis does not occur elsewhere.

Other examples of elements whose meaning requires calculation with respect to *some* element of the ground, that is, as deictic in a broad sense, are the verbs *come* and *go* and the simple past tense (in English and several other languages). A particular situation can be described both as *Santa Claus came in* and as *Santa Claus went in*;

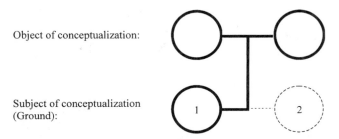

Object of conceptualization:

Subject of conceptualization
(Ground):

Figure 3.8. "First-person deixis" construal configuration

the different lexicalizations reflect different construals with respect to a "point of view" identifiable for the conceptualizers (*come* involves a point of view inside the space entered by Santa Claus; *went* a point of view outside that space). The choice of this point of view is not further constrained; it may be the speaker's or the hearer's, but also that of some participant whose point of view has been introduced explicitly into the discourse (see below, at the end of section 6.2). Slightly differently, the past tense locates an event outside the ground, thus outside the scope of the immediate experiences of the conceptualizers in the ground, without differentiating between them (see Boogaart and Janssen, this volume, chapter 31, for further discussion).

5.2. Specific Grounding

In addition to the deictic elements indicating a general type of grounding, there are other deictic elements that indicate a different, more specific kind of construal. Consider figure 3.8.

This configuration characterizes instances of what may be called first-person deixis and is present in expressions such as *here*, *now*, and *this/these*. For example, while the expression *yesterday* does invoke the ground, it does not *profile* a temporal point of the ground, and it does not invoke a specific conceptualizer as distinct from another. The expression *now*, on the other hand, does profile a time overlapping with that of the ground (i.e., the time envisaged by conceptualizer 1 as the time of communication—not necessarily the moment at which the utterance is physically produced).

Counterparts of first-person deixis expressions are *there*, *then*, and *that/those*. The latter are usually characterized as "distal," while the former are called "proximate." The terms "proximate" and "distal" suggest that these sets of expressions express different distances between the conceptualizer and the object of conceptualization. However, as Janssen (2002, 2004) has argued, the terms actually have more to do with the construal relationship between conceptualizer and object of conceptualization than with the distance between them. For instance, when a physician investigating a sore spot on a patient utters *Is this where it hurts?* and the patient responds with *Yes, that is where it hurts*, the difference between *this* and *that*, and especially the patient's

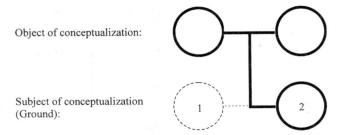

Object of conceptualization:

Subject of conceptualization
(Ground):

Figure 3.9. "Second-person deixis" construal configuration

use of *that*, cannot be adequately characterized in terms of (non)proximity, since the spot referred to is on the patient's body. Rather, what the patient does is to indicate that the spot referred to is *not* as much in his/her focus of attention as it is in somebody else's, in this case, the physician's (Janssen 2002: 172–73). In this respect, Janssen quotes a suggestion from C. Lyons to the effect that the difference between *this* and *that* can be related to the category of person; indeed, in the situation described, a proper paraphrase of the meaning of *that* would be 'the spot *you* are focusing on', so that it would involve a construal configuration as indicated in figure 3.9.

However, although figure 3.9 represents the natural construal configuration for expressions such as *that, there,* and *then* in many contexts, it is not applicable to *all* of their uses. In other contexts these expressions can also profile entities, moments, and locations which have neither the speaker's *nor* the addressee's immediate attention. Thus, the general rule here is that linguistic items expressing this construal are defined *negatively* with respect to the ground, specifically conceptualizer 1.

Similarly, so-called third-person personal pronouns (*he, she, they,* and their oblique and possessive counterparts) are defined negatively with respect to the ground and specifically with respect to both conceptualizers 1 and 2. Still, the identification of their referents has to take place via the ground; they are still objects of shared attention (as first and second persons are by participating in the communicative situation), either established ostensively or as prominent discourse referents (see van Hoek 2003).[9]

6. COORDINATION OF PERSPECTIVES

6.1. Implicit Multiple Perspectives

I have characterized the horizontal line between the conceptualizers in the basic construal configuration of figure 3.4 as representing a process of coordinating cognition. This coordination relation does not play a role in the perspectivized construals discussed so far, but it is crucial in an important class of linguistic expressions, namely, sentential negation and related expressions. Consider, for instance, (8) and (9), each of which is a possible description of a person feeling sad.

(8)   Mary is not happy.
(9)   Mary is unhappy.

Both expressions may be said to invoke the notion of happiness serving as the Ground for the characterization of Mary's actual state of mind (the Figure). In this dimension of construal, (8) and (9) do not differ, so the difference must involve yet another type of construal. The relevant dimension here is defined by the specific human ability to entertain other points of view in the same way as one's own, which we explicitly incorporated into the construal configuration by distinguishing two subjects of conceptualization (the bottom part of figure 3.4). In particular, it is the coordination relation between the conceptualizers that appears to be crucially involved in distinguishing (8) from (9). It is only sentence (8) that profiles *two* distinct views with respect to the proposition *Mary is happy* (or two "mental spaces" in the sense of Fauconnier 1985; see also Fauconnier, this volume, chapter 14), that is, only (8) involves two conceptualizers with an opposite epistemic stance toward this proposition (conceptualizer 1 rejects the positive epistemic stance of conceptualizer 2).[10] This can be observed from the behavior of the phrase *on the contrary* (Verhagen 2005: 31–32):

(10)   Mary is not happy. On the contrary, she is feeling really depressed.
(11)   #Mary is unhappy. On the contrary, she is feeling really depressed.

The use of the negation *not* in (10) evokes a second mental space: it profiles the contrast between the stance toward 'Mary being happy' in some other mental space and the speaker's (the so-called "base" space of conceptualizer 1). It is this evoked second mental space to which the discourse marker *on the contrary* can relate: Mary's being depressed is contrary to the idea of her being happy, not to her not being happy (which is what conceptualizer 1 has just asserted). Morphological negation with *un-* lacks this power to evoke a second mental space contrasting with the base space, and this is what makes (11) incoherent. Sentential negation thus yields a typical and quite general case of the construal configuration depicted in figure 3.10.

What the negative morpheme *not* itself profiles is just the relation between the perspectives of the two conceptualizers, namely, a relationship of opposition, such that the view of the conceptualizer 2 should be replaced by that of conceptualizer 1. However, it is part of the conventional use of *not* that an object of conceptualization has to be specified (so that it may actually more adequately be regarded as a construction, unlike the negative element *No*, which precisely *cannot* be applied to linguistic material profiling an object of conceptualization). This is why the construal configuration for sentential negation is represented as in figure 3.10 rather than as in figure 3.6. Furthermore, other construal phenomena may be operative with respect to the object of conceptualization as represented in the utterance, determining, for example, Figure/Ground-alignments, temporal deixis, and so on.

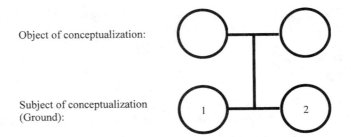

Object of conceptualization:

Subject of conceptualization
(Ground):

Figure 3.10. Construal configuration for coordination of perspectives

So while any linguistic usage event involves two conceptualizers as part of its ground, sentential negation (as well as a phrase such as *on the contrary* in English) actually *profiles* two viewpoints being brought into coordination *in* the linguistic material. In the language of adult speakers, and in particular in fairly complex discourse, the point of view being rejected does not have to be the *actual* addressee's, and not even a specific person's, but even when it is not precisely "anchored" in the actual communicative situation, it remains a profiled mental space in which a different epistemic stance toward the proposition is entertained than in the space of conceptualizer 1. Another type of construction to which the same general characterization applies is that of concessive connectives (see Verhagen 2000; 2005: chapter 4).

Viewing sentential negation as a case of construal—profiling the coordination relation between two epistemically distinct conceptualizers with respect to the same object of conceptualization—has the advantage of allowing for a natural extension to other elements that behave conceptually and linguistically like negation, even though they may differ from negation in terms of truth conditions. For example, the expressions *few linguists* and *a few linguists* may refer to sets of exactly the same size (whether absolute or relative), but only the former construes the relationship between the two conceptualizers with respect to the object of conceptualization as one of opposition. It exhibits the grammatical behavior of negation (witness contrasts in the context of polarity items, e.g., *any*: *Few linguists have any idea about evolutionary theory* vs. **A few linguists have any idea about evolutionary theory*). The same holds for its discourse behavior, witness the naturalness of the exchange in A–B in (12) in contrast with the exchange in (13), in which A–B is not natural, but A–B' is.

(12)   A: Few linguists still believe in transformations.
        B: So you think they won't be around much longer?
        B': #So you think they'll still be around for some time?

(13)   A: A few linguists still believe in transformations.
        B: #So you think they won't be around much longer?
        B': So you think they'll still be around for some time?

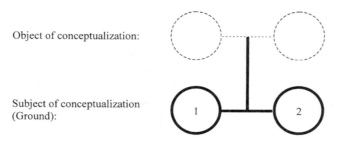

Object of conceptualization:

Subject of conceptualization
(Ground):

Figure 3.11. Construal configuration for epistemic interpretation

This parallelism between grammatical and discourse properties clearly demonstrates that what is profiled by sentential negation, as well as other "negative" elements, is a relation of epistemic opposition between two conceptualizers, conceptualizer 1 rejecting the cognitive state of conceptualizer 2 in the process of representing it (for further elaboration and discussion, see Verhagen 2005: chapter 2). It should be noted, though, that this brief discussion can hardly scratch the surface of the complexities involved in negation and polarity, especially in relation to the scalar inferences invited by many expressions in natural languages (see Israel 1998, and especially various studies by Horn, of which Horn 1996 is illustrative).

Yet another subtype of expressions that instantiate this type of construal are modal verbs and adverbs, as exemplified in (14) and (15).

(14)   Some theoreticians may deny the relevance of these results.

(15)   Frankly, some theoreticians deny the relevance of these results.

In a sentence like *Someone with such a track record may say things like this*, the modal auxiliary *may* designates a relationship of permission in the *object* of conceptualization ('being allowed', the so-called deontic reading).[11] But the natural interpretation of *may* in (14) is that it designates a relationship in the ground; it evokes the views that some theoreticians deny the relevance of the results and that some do not, and profiles conceptualizer 1 as the ground element endorsing that the former possibility is the one to be reckoned with. It appears, then, that epistemic construal shares properties with sentential negation in profiling parts of the ground but differs from sentential negation in that, besides evoking two conceptualizers with distinct epistemic stances, it also makes a *definite* claim about the object of conceptualization. Although epistemic *may*, as in (14), operates on an object of conceptualization, it does not, in this sense, designate an element of the object of conceptualization, but *only* of the ground; its construal is of the type depicted in figure 3.11.[12]

Similarly, the adverb *frankly* in (15) does not designate the presence of frankness in one of the participants in the conceptualized event. Rather, it profiles both the present speaker's frankness in saying this, as well as an attempt to acknowledge the fact that the addressee may not like the implications.[13] The reading in which *frankly* profiles an aspect of the object of conceptualization rather than the ground is more natural with another word order and intonation contour (*Some theoreti-cians frankly deny the relevance of these results*). The fact that in front position *frankly* takes elements of the ground (the utterance itself and how it may be taken by the addressee) as its base and not the object of conceptualization implies that the construal relation itself is in this case even less profiled than in the case of epistemic *may*, so that this *frankly*-sentence exemplifies the highly subjective construal configuration of figure 3.6 rather than that of figure 3.11. Yet, the highly subjective nature of a construal is certainly a matter of degree, as the use of *frankly* still imposes a constraint on the nature of the object of conceptualization: it must be some piece of discourse.

Some elements in a language may allow objective as well as epistemic, and "speech act" construals. This has been proposed, for example, for some causal connectives (e.g., *because* in English) by Sweetser (1990). Consider the following examples.

(16)   John typed her thesis because he really loves her.
(17)   John really loves her, because he typed her thesis.
(18)   What are you doing tonight? Because there's a good movie on.

In (16), *because* profiles a causal relationship as part of the object of conceptualization; in (17), it construes an element of the object of conceptualization (the fact that John typed her thesis) as an argument for the addressee to accept the conclusion that John's love for her must also be part of the object of conceptualization (an epistemic construal of the type depicted in figure 3.11); and in (18), it justifies an element of the ground itself, namely, the speech act of asking.

What we have seen, then, is that these are all linguistic expressions—just like the spatial markers *below* and *across*—that as such allow both relatively objective and relatively subjective construals. The actual type of construal varies depending on several contextual features (for an illuminating discussion of such factors in the case of modals, see Heine 1995). Whether there are *constraints* on the types of construal allowed for specific linguistic items is a matter of (historically developed) convention. As Sweetser noted, there are languages in which an objective or an epistemic construal of a causal relationship requires distinct causal connectives; the fact that *because* can be used in these different, historically developed ways, is thus a convention of modern English. We will briefly return to this issue in section 7, on subjectification.

6.2. Explicit Multiple Perspectives

The use of modal auxiliaries and adverbs as in (14) and (15) is sometimes called "speaker-oriented" and paraphrased by means of complement constructions with a first-person subject in the matrix clause (e.g., *I consider it possible that . . . , I frankly say to you that . . .*). This raises the issue what aspects of the construal configuration are profiled by such complement constructions themselves. Until fairly recently, it was usually (explicitly or implicitly) assumed that complement clauses are subor-

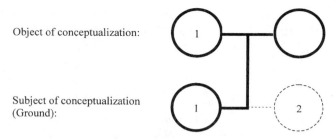

Object of conceptualization:

Subject of conceptualization
(Ground):

Figure 3.8'. Construal configuration with "first person" as object of conceptualization

dinate structures, occupying an argument position of the predicate in the "main" clause and are thus subordinate (e.g., Jespersen 1933; Noonan 1985, among many others). In cognitive linguistic work, this view has also been the starting point of a number of analyses; for example, Langacker (1991: 436) states: "Complement clauses are prototypical instances of subordination; . . . *I know she left* designates the process of knowing, not of leaving." As the example demonstrates, such a view suggests that the main clause of a complement construction (also when it involves an element of the ground) describes an event in the same way as a simple clause does, that is, as an object of conceptualization. Recent research, however, suggests that in many important cases this is actually a misconception. Studying child language acquisition, Diessel and Tomasello (2001) have shown that, apparently, children's first complement constructions contain "complement-taking predicates" of the type *I think* and *you know*, which function "as an epistemic marker, attention getter, or marker of illocutionary force," and that the whole complex utterance "contains only a single proposition expressed by the apparent complement clause" (97). Thus, the complement-taking predicates do *not* contribute to profiling an object of conceptualization; rather, they instantiate the construal configuration of figure 3.11, only profiling (parts of) the ground. It is only at later stages that children start saying things like *I thought* and *She knows*, in which someone's thinking or knowing may be construed as an object of conceptualization (see figures 3.5 and 3.7) and the complement-taking predications as "main clauses" to which the "complement" is "subordinated."[14] Once this ability has developed, it also becomes possible for a conceptualizer, in uttering *I think*, to construe his own thinking as an object of conceptualization for specific purposes, as in *I think he will arrive on time, but I am not sure/but John is skeptical* (especially with *I* or *think* stressed in the first conjunct). While the use of *I think* as an epistemic marker constitutes an instance of figure 3.11, its construal as an object of conceptualization is a special case of figure 3.8. It is a case of first-person deixis (belonging to the same family as *now, here,* and *this*), but with conceptualizer 1 as an element of the object of conceptualization in the construal configuration. It may thus be called an instance of "objectification,"[15] whereby the primary subject of conceptualization is construed as part of its own object of conceptualization; see figure 3.8'.

However, such a "detached" view of one's own cognitive state cannot be considered a very normal use for these constructions. In fact, the analysis by Diessel and Tomasello entails that even after the development of the ability to construe the content of a complement-taking predicate as a possible object of conceptualization, phrases such as *I think, I/You see* simply continue to be used as markers of epistemic stance, attention-getting, or illocutionary force. This is strongly corroborated, at least for conversational interaction, in a study by Thompson (2002), showing that participants in conversation organize important aspects of their interaction, and of their (common) personal relationships with the things being talked about, by means of such complement-taking predicates, and that this organizational role in fact exhausts the function of these fragments of discourse. The analysis by Thompson actually provides the basis for an explanation of the correlation noted by Diessel and Tomasello (2001: 136) between the first complement-taking predicates in children's utterances and their frequency in the ambient language produced by their parents and caretakers.

Such results, then, show that not only lexical items but also grammatical constructions—including complementation constructions, which are generally considered a core part of syntax—may exhibit variation that can be captured in terms of the general construal configuration, with a crucial role for its subjective part, the ground. This conclusion need not really be surprising for a framework recognizing a continuum between lexicon and grammar and adopting an essentially cognitive view of linguistic semantics, but it still had to be demonstrated.

One specific use of these grammatical constructions is that they may assign an object of conceptualization to a conceptualizer in a particular way. While sentential negation and modal verbs and adverbs implicitly evoke another mental space besides that of conceptualizer 1, complement constructions may to some extent put another mental space "on stage" (but cf. note 13).[16] When they do, they provide the conceptualization of the ground entering into a construal relationship with the content of the subordinated clause; in that case, these complement constructions are not directly interpreted as construed by the *actual* producer of the discourse, but by the *represented* subject of conceptualization. Consider a simple case such as (19).

(19)   The president is afraid that he might not be re-elected.

The actual speaker of (19) may have a certain knowledge about the president's re-election (for example, when the speaker is in charge of the election process and has just completed the count of the votes). The use of *might* relates to the epistemic stance of the president. The alternative mental space evoked by *might*—and the same would go for the negation *not*—are construed with respect to the latter stance and not the epistemic stance of the actual producer of the utterance.

Note that different elements behave differently in such constructions. For example, the first-person pronoun in a complement clause always designates the person responsible for the whole utterance (*The president was afraid that I might fail*), while the "proximate" demonstrative *this* is ambiguous. (In *The president was afraid that he might fail at this point*, *this* either refers to the point that is in 'his' focal attention or that is in 'mine'—the former reading in effect boils down to construing a "free indirect speech" representation.) Shifting of the deictic center occurs not only in the context of complement constructions, although this constitutes the prime grammaticalized instrument for a deictic shift. In principle, any explicit introduction of another person's state of mind in a discourse may produce such a shift, as illustrated by (20).

(20)   I looked through the window and saw that the children were very nervous. In few minutes, Santa Claus would come in.

The question what constitutes the ground with respect to the elements *few* and *come* should be directly construed, and how this relates to the ground of the producer of the entire discourse may involve considerable complexities (see Sanders 1994). But whatever the details, the very fact that such differential construals are generally possible is a major motivation for characterizing the construal configuration in terms of the slightly abstract roles of "conceptualizers" (e.g., conceptualizers 1 and 2, with the first being interpreted as taking the initiative), rather than in terms of the concrete roles of actual speaker and hearer (see Talmy 2000b: 337). The actual speaker of (20) does not have to be taken as expressing any personal uncertainty or anxiety concerning Santa Claus's arrival (imagine that *I* refers to the person playing the role of Santa Claus), but *few* still evokes the subjective stance and *come* the deictic origin of the conceptualizer responsible for the thought of Santa's entering, that is, the children.

7. Subjectification

So far we have used the different profiling patterns in the basic construal configuration of figure 3.4 as ways of capturing recurring features in the meaning and use of several kinds of expressions. It has already been hinted at (in the beginning of section 4 and in section 6.2) that relationships between different profiling patterns can also be conceived of as the outcome of dynamic processes. In the course of children's language development, for example, complement-taking predicates start out as purely epistemic markers and later acquire the potential of designating an object of conceptualization. Such a process may appropriately be characterized as one of objectification: initially, an expression does not profile any element of an object of conceptualization, but in the end it does.

The reverse process is that of subjectification. In its pure form, subjectification may involve an expression initially profiling no part of the ground or not profiling the construal relationship and then acquiring the potential of profiling, in one or more respects, the construal relationship and/or parts of the ground (a possible example is the shift from marking perfectivity to marking past tense as discussed at the end of section 3). But it may also consist in an *increase* of the role of the construal relation or the ground in the profile of an expression, or (what ultimately may be part of the same process) a *decrease* of the role of the object of conceptualization.

The phenomenon of subjectification is a highly regular and characteristic feature of many processes of language change, as demonstrated in a considerable body of work by Traugott (e.g., Traugott 1989, 1995, and especially the comprehensive Traugott and Dasher 2002). Traugott defines subjectification as a pragmatic-semantic process whereby "meanings become increasingly based in the speaker's subjective belief state/attitude toward the proposition" (Traugott 1989: 35; 1995: 31). Notice two features of this definition: subjectification refers to a *historical process* producing a change, and it is semasiological, that is, it is concerned with linguistic symbols (or assemblies of symbols) and with what they mean. Thus, the development of English *will*, from expressing a desire or intention on the part of the referent of its grammatical subject to expressing a prediction by the speaker of the utterance, is a clear case of subjectification under this definition.

It should be noted, in order to avoid confusion, that the term "subjectification" is used here in a way that is different from, albeit related to, the one proposed by Langacker (1990b: 17). For Langacker "subjectivity" and "subjectification" refer not to expressions, but primarily to the way an element of a conceptualization is perspectively construed, namely, objectively or subjectively (cf. Langacker 1999: 150). For example, the difference between *Vanessa is sitting across the table from me* and *Vanessa is sitting across the table* according to Langacker is that the same content (the speaker as the landmark of the *across*-relation) is "objectively construed" in the former because it is put on stage by the expression *me* (similarly to another nominal expression (see 5 above), whereas it is "subjectively construed" in the latter because it remains offstage as the implicit locus of conception (see 6 above). Accordingly, Langacker uses the term "subjectification" to refer to an increase in subjectivity in this sense, namely, the increased construal of some notion as functioning implicitly in the ground rather than on stage, in the conceived situation; subjectification is "the realignment of some relationship from the objective axis to the subjective axis" (Langacker 1990b: 17), where "subjective axis" refers to the construal relationship.

Although Langacker's and Traugott's notions of subjectification are related, each is clearly useful in its own domain, the former primarily in the area of semantic analysis, the latter in that of semantic change. There has been some discussion of the precise relation between Langacker's and Traugott's notions (see several contributions in Stein and Wright 1995; Langacker 1999: 149–50; Traugott and Dasher 2002: 97–98). Still, it seems that when restricted to phenomena of semasiological change—which Langacker evidently wants to include under his rubric of subjectification—at least the extensions of the two notions coincide: whenever a new meaning is more based in the speaker's belief state/attitude than the old one, some realignment from the objective to the subjective axis has apparently taken place. In this section, I am concerned with a certain kind of shift in the meanings of linguistic items, which is why my use of the term here is basically the same as its use in studies of semantic change.

Diachronic subjectification exhibits "unidirectionality": the meaning of a linguistic expression (in a semasiological perspective) is much more likely to develop from relatively objective to more subjective than the other way around. Thus, one repeatedly finds a verb of desire and/or intention developing into a marker of future (e.g., English *will*), but seldom a future marker developing into a verb denoting intention. Temporal connectives regularly develop adversative meanings (e.g., English *while*, as in *Mary likes oysters while Bill hates them*), but adversative connectives seldom, if ever, develop into temporal ones (see Bybee, this volume, chapter 36). What is it that makes subjectification largely unidirectional? The answer to that question must lie in the actual processes that produce the changes. For several cases, Traugott has shown that the relevant cognitive and communicative mechanisms involve inferences that are first "only" pragmatic, that is, related to specific instances of use in a particular context, and then become associated with the linguistic expression as such, in other words, "conventionalized." For example, when the actual relevance of mentioning the co-temporality of two events by means of *while* lies in its unexpectedness and hearers/readers assume that it is this unexpectedness that the speaker/writer intended, the association between *while* and unexpectedness may be reinforced to the extent that it becomes conventionalized (i.e., the marker of co-temporality can be used to mark unexpectedness without the hearer having to compute the answer to the question 'Why is the speaker marking co-temporality here?'), even to the extent that co-temporality may become unnecessary. The process of the conventionalization of pragmatic inferences explains unidirectionality in that even if the original conventional meaning of an expression at some point in time does not profile a feature of the ground, the communicative acts in which it is used will always comprise participants making inferences— hearers constructing interpretations of what the speakers intended and speakers anticipating those interpretations—so that there are always (more) subjective elements in actual interpretations that may end up getting conventionalized.

The general unidirectionality of subjectification points to a fundamental asymmetry in the construal configuration. The actual *use* of any linguistic utterance always entails that one conceptualizer is trying to influence another one's cognition in a particular way by means of that specific utterance so that some (further) inferences from the object of conceptualization to the ground are always relevant.[17] But knowing what kind of coordination relationship is at stake in a specific communicative event does not as such license inferences concerning the object of conceptualization. Any expression, even if it does not profile the construal relationship or the ground, *evokes* the basic construal relation of figure 3.4 in a particular way when it is actually used, and the recurrence of such features may gain prominence and become conventional. In this essentially usage-based perspective, all linguistic utterances display subjectivity of some sort, and subjectification may consist in the gradual diminishing of the "weight" of objective features of conventional meaning in favor of subjective ones. For example, consider the difference between (21) and

(22), containing instances of the objective and of the subjectified (epistemic) use of the speech act verb *promise*, respectively.

(21)   John promised to be back in time.
(22)   The debate promised to be interesting.

It is not the case that only (22) conveys a positive anticipation by the speaker. This is just as much true for (21); witness the kind of inferences (21) licenses with respect to the ground: it counts as a positive answer to the question 'Do you think that John will be back in time?', and it would not be felicitous in a context in which the person asking that question obviously does *not* desire John's timely return. Furthermore, there are also in-between cases such as (23) and (24).

(23)   The newspaper promised to publish the results.
(24)   The new strategy promised to produce interesting results.

These examples differ from each other and from (21) and (22), not so much in the dimension "subjective, positive anticipation" (which they all share), but in the degree to which a promise is considered to be (also) a part of the object of conceptualization. It is easier for the newspaper in (23) than for the strategy in (24) to be construed as metonymically or metaphorically related to human beings who are conceptualized as committing themselves to something, and this is totally impossible for the debate in (22). Thus, it actually seems better to characterize the cline from (21), via (23) and (24), to (22) in terms of decreasing objectivity than in terms of increasing subjectivity (see Langacker 1999 and Verhagen 1995 for further discussion, including syntactic correlates of the semantic differences).[18] In any case, the differences and changes can all be construed as "shifts" in the degree of profiling of elements and relations in the basic construal configuration.

At the same time, this analysis once more demonstrates that it is crucial to distinguish between the conventional forms of construal made available by the resources of a language, and the construal conveyed in a particular instance of use. In the domain of perspectivization discussed in this section, the phenomenon of semantic change precisely consists in usage becoming conventionalized, which therefore presupposes the distinction.

8. CONCLUSION

Construal operations are central to language and cognition. They involve cognitive abilities of humans with clear linguistic reflexes, but there seems to be no way to organize them all in terms of an exhaustive classification system. Although the basic construal configuration presented in this chapter is not a comprehensive classification system, it incorporates the typically human ability to identify deeply with conspecifics and provides a unifying conceptual framework in terms of which many semantic phenomena involving different kinds of "perspective" and "subjectivity" can be captured. The dimensions and elements of the configuration may be considered general and universal, but the actual distinctions drawn in this conceptual space differ from one language to another and are variable over time, in individual development as well as historically (in communities). The general unidirectionality of historical processes of subjectification can be taken as indicative of the basic asymmetry between subject and object of conceptualization.

NOTES

I wish to thank the Netherlands Institute for Advanced Study (NIAS) for providing me with the opportunity, as a Fellow-in-residence, to write this chapter. I would also like to thank Peter Harder, Theo Janssen, Ronald Langacker, and Mirna Pit, as well as the editors of this volume, for useful comments on the first draft of this chapter. Any remaining errors and misconceptions are entirely my own responsibility.

1. In his 1993 paper, Langacker arranged ("[if] only for expository purposes," 448) construal into the following five general dimensions: specificity, scope, prominence, background, and perspective.

2. It has been suggested (Croft and Cruse 2004: chapter 3) that in his recent work, Talmy dropped Force Dynamics as a separate construal category. Still, although Force Dynamics is not treated separately in chapter 1 of Talmy (2000a), it is clear from the structure of the book that Talmy intended to maintain it (see also Talmy 2000a: 41).

3. While Talmy proposes Domain as a schematic category perpendicular to his four types of "schematic systems," Croft and Cruse (2004: chapter 3) rather suggest that Domain is an additional system. Talmy (2000a: 47) mentions one additional member of the category Domain, namely, "identificational space," to accommodate such differences as those between *you* and *they* in their indefinite uses (the former indicating identification with the speaker, the second nonidentification).

4. The object of conceptualization is represented as having at least some complexity (there are two elements, connected in one way or another) precisely because of the structural construal normally imposed on it.

5. Langacker's term "ground" is not to be confused with the term "Ground" in "Figure/Ground alignment."

6. In later work in Cognitive Grammar (e.g., Langacker 1999, van Hoek 2003), one does sometimes find representations in which the roles of S(peaker) and H(earer) are distinguished.

7. For a more recent, and more subtle view, see Tomasello, Call, and Hare (2003a, 2003b).

8. In practice, many instances of construal configurations in the literature exhibit this structure, as in Langacker (1990b) and van Hoek (2003).

9. Van Hoek (1997) provides a cognitive account of the way third-person pronouns find their antecedents in sentences and in discourse, partly drawing on the inherent link between first-person and third-person pronouns as markers of "other first persons."

10. A possible semantic difference is also that (8) need not entail (9), while the reverse entailment holds, so that (9) is, strictly speaking, more informative than (8). However, in actual usage, one seldom, if ever, uses (8) to convey that Mary's position on the scale of happiness is right in the middle. This actually leads to an interesting observational question: Why do language users so often choose an apparently less informative question when a more informative one is readily available? The answer is given in the analysis in the text (a detailed discussion can be found in Verhagen 2005: 32–35, 70–75).

11. With some interpretive effort, it is also possible to impose a deontic interpretation on (14), e.g., when *some theoreticians* is understood as referring to a group that has a special status for one reason or another, which justifies their being allowed certain kinds of behavior.

12. Langacker (1990b: 14) characterizes modals, also in their epistemic senses, as profiling the object of conceptualization (schematically). He mentions in this connection that modals may function as clausal pro-forms (*She may, You must*). However, this possibility is specific for English and may possibly be ascribed to the existence in the grammar of English of the general pattern Subject + Auxiliary (with the function of indicating a clausal pro-form), so that the function of the epistemic modal itself may still be said to involve only the construal relationship and the ground itself.

13. As such, it represents a case of what Traugott calls "intersubjectification," i.e., the development of a meaning which not (only) profiles a speaker's subjective attitude toward a proposition, but also his/her assessment of his/her relationship with the addressee in the production of the utterance. Other instances of intersubjectification are *tu/vous*-type distinctions in second-person address forms and honorifics (cf. Traugott and Dasher 2002).

14. In fact, I argue in Verhagen (2001, 2005) that it is *normal* for all complements, also in written texts, to contain the information which an utterance actually contributes to a discourse, even if the main clause may be read as independently designating an event (of communication, cognition, or the like) distinct from the ground. For instance, these main clauses rarely participate in the coherence relations of the discourse (unlike the complements); rather, they serve to specify in what way the information of the complement relates to the perspective of conceptualizers 1 and/or 2 (as someone else's, as something hoped for, as a possibility, etc.). Further consequences, especially for the grammatical properties of the constructions, are discussed in Verhagen (2005: chapter 3).

15. The content of this concept as I use it here is similar, if not identical, to that of Langacker's (1987). As I see it, the difference is that Langacker indiscriminatingly considers all uses of the pronoun *I* as instantiating the configuration of figure 3.8'—in which conceptualizer 1 "is also the primary object of conceptualization" (131), while I consider many normal uses of the pronoun in such patterns as *I think* as well as in performative utterances as indicating only conceptualizer 1, without turning him/her into an object of conceptualization.

16. Another type of construction with a similar function is conditionals; see Dancygier and Sweetser (1997) and especially Dancygier and Sweetser (2005).

17. For a discussion of the theory of communication underlying this view, see Verhagen (2005: chapter 1).

18. It remains true, of course, that to the degree that objective conceptualization fades as part of the meaning of an expression, the *relative* weight of subjectivity automatically increases.

REFERENCES

Ariel, Mira. 1990. *Accessing noun-phrase antecedents*. London: Routledge.

Bowerman, Melissa. 1996. The origin of children's spatial semantic categories: Cognitive versus linguistic determinants. In John J. Gumperz and Stephen C. Levinson, eds., *Rethinking linguistic relativity* 145–76. Cambridge: Cambridge University Press.

Brisard, Frank, ed. 2002. *Grounding: The epistemic footing of deixis and reference*. Berlin: Mouton de Gruyter.

Clark, Herbert H. 1996. *Using language*. Cambridge: Cambridge University Press.

Cornelis, Louise H. 1997. *Passive and perspective*. Amsterdam: Rodopi.

Croft, William, and D. Alan Cruse. 2004. *Cognitive linguistics*. Cambridge: Cambridge University Press.

Croft, William, and Esther J. Wood. 2000. Construal operations in linguistics and artificial intelligence. In Liliana Albertazzi, ed., *Meaning and cognition: A multidisciplinary approach* 51–78. Amsterdam: John Benjamins.

Dancygier, Barbara, and Eve Sweetser. 1997. *Then* in conditional constructions. *Cognitive Linguistics* 8: 109–36.

Dancygier, Barbara, and Eve Sweetser. 2005. *Mental spaces in grammar. Conditional constructions*. Cambridge: Cambridge University Press.

Diessel, Holger, and Michael Tomasello. 2001. The acquisition of finite complement clauses in English: A corpus-based analysis. *Cognitive Linguistics* 12: 97–141.

Fauconnier, Gilles. 1985. *Mental spaces: Aspects of meaning construction in natural language*. Cambridge, MA: MIT Press. (2nd ed., Cambridge: Cambridge University Press, 1994)

Heine, Bernd. 1995. Agent-oriented vs. epistemic modality: Some observations on German modals. In Joan L. Bybee and Suzanne Fleischman, eds., *Modality in grammar and discourse* 17–53. Amsterdam: John Benjamins.

Horn, Laurence R. 1996. Exclusive company: *Only* and the dynamics of vertical inference. *Journal of Semantics* 13: 1–40.

Israel, Michael. 1998. The rhetoric of grammar: Scalar reasoning and polarity sensitivity. PhD dissertation, University of California at San Diego.

Janssen, Theo A. J. M. 2002. Deictic principles of pronominals, demonstratives and tenses. In Frank Brisard, ed., *Grounding: The epistemic footing of deixis and reference* 151–93. Berlin: Mouton de Gruyter.

Janssen, Theo A. J. M. 2004. Deixis and reference. In Geert Booij, Christian Lehmann, Joachim Mugdan, and Stavros Skopeteas, eds., *Morphologie / Morphology: Ein internationales Handbuch zur Flexion und Wortbildung / An international handbook on inflection and word- formation* 2: 983–98. Berlin: Mouton de Gruyter.

Jespersen, Otto. 1933. *Essentials of English grammar*. London: Allen and Unwin.

Langacker, Ronald W. 1987. *Foundations of cognitive grammar*. Vol. 1, *Theoretical prerequisites*. Stanford, CA: Stanford University Press.

Langacker, Ronald W. 1990a. *Concept, image, and symbol: The cognitive basis of grammar*. Berlin: Mouton de Gruyter.

Langacker, Ronald W. 1990b. Subjectification. *Cognitive Linguistics* 1: 5–38.

Langacker, Ronald W. 1991. *Foundations of cognitive grammar*. Vol. 2, *Descriptive application*. Stanford, CA: Stanford University Press.

Langacker, Ronald W. 1993. Universals of construal. *Berkeley Linguistics Society* 19: 447–63.

Langacker, Ronald W. 1999. Losing control: Grammaticization, subjectification, and transparency. In Andreas Blank and Peter Koch, eds., *Historical semantics and cognition* 147–75. Berlin: Mouton de Gruyter.

Langacker, Ronald W. 2005. Construction grammars: Cognitive, radical and less so. In Francisco J. Ruiz de Mendoza Ibáñez, and M. Sandra Peña Cervel, eds., *Cognitive Linguistics: Internal dynamics and interdisciplinary interaction* 101–59. Berlin: Mouton de Gruyter.

Levinson, Stephen C. 2001. Covariation between spatial language and cognition, and its implications for language learning. In Melissa Bowerman and Stephen C. Levinson, eds., *Language acquisition and conceptual development* 566–88. Cambridge: Cambridge University Press.

Michaelis, Laura A. 2004. Type shifting in Construction Grammar: An integrated approach to aspectual coercion. *Cognitive Linguistics* 15: 1–67.

Noonan, Michael. 1985. Complementation. In Timothy Shopen, ed., *Language typology and syntactic description* 2: 42–140. Cambridge: Cambridge University Press.

Sanders, José. 1994. Perspective in narrative discourse. PhD dissertation, Tilburg University.

Sinha, Chris. 1999. Grounding, mapping and acts of meaning. In Theo Janssen and Gisela Redeker, eds., *Cognitive linguistics: Foundations, scope, and methodology* 223–55. Berlin: Mouton de Gruyter.

Slobin, Dan I. 1996. From "thought and language" to "thinking for speaking." In John J. Gumperz and Stephen C. Levinson, eds., *Rethinking linguistic relativity* 70–96. Cambridge: Cambridge University Press.

Stein, Dieter, and Susan Wright, eds., 1995. *Subjectivity and subjectivisation: Linguistic perspectives*. Cambridge: Cambridge University Press.

Sweetser, Eve. 1990. *From etymology to pragmatics: Metaphorical and cultural aspects of semantic structure*. Cambridge: Cambridge University Press.

Talmy, Leonard. 1978. Figure and ground in complex sentences. In Joseph Greenberg, ed., *Universals of human language*, vol. 4, *Syntax* 625–49. Stanford, CA: Stanford University Press.

Talmy, Leonard. 1988. The relation of grammar to cognition. In Brygida Rudzka-Ostyn, ed., *Topics in cognitive linguistics* 165–205. Amsterdam: John Benjamins.

Talmy, Leonard. 2000a. *Toward a cognitive semantics*. Vol. 1, *Concept structuring systems*. Cambridge, MA: MIT Press.

Talmy, Leonard. 2000b. *Toward a cognitive semantics*. Vol. 2, *Typology and process in concept structuring*. Cambridge, MA: MIT Press.

Thompson, Sandra A. 2002. 'Object complements' and conversation: Towards a realistic account. *Studies in Language* 26: 125–64.

Tomasello, Michael. 1999. *The cultural origins of human cognition*. Cambridge, MA: Harvard University Press.

Tomasello, Michael, Josep Call, and Brian Hare. 2003a. Chimpanzees understand psychological states—the question is which ones and to what extent. *Trends in Cognitive Sciences* 7: 153–56.

Tomasello, Michael, Josep Call, and Brian Hare. 2003b. Chimpanzees versus humans: It's not that simple. *Trends in Cognitive Sciences* 7: 239–40.

Traugott, Elizabeth Closs. 1989. On the rise of epistemic meanings in English: An example of subjectification in semantic change. *Language* 65: 31–55.

Traugott, Elizabeth Closs. 1995. Subjectification in grammaticalisation. In Dieter Stein and Susan Wright, eds., *Subjectivity and subjectivisation: Linguistic perspectives* 31–54. Cambridge: Cambridge University Press.

Traugott, Elizabeth Closs, and Richard B. Dasher. 2002. *Regularity in semantic change.* Cambridge: Cambridge University Press.

van Hoek, Karen. 1997. *Anaphora and conceptual structure.* Chicago: University of Chicago Press.

van Hoek, Karen. 2003. Pronouns and point of view: Cognitive principles of coreference. In Michael Tomasello, ed., *The new psychology of language: Cognitive and functional approaches to language structure,* 2: 169–94. Mahwah, NJ: Lawrence Erlbaum.

Verhagen, Arie. 1995. Subjectification, syntax, and communication. In Dieter Stein and Susan Wright, eds., *Subjectivity and subjectivisation in language* 103–28. Cambridge: Cambridge University Press.

Verhagen, Arie. 2000. Concession implies causality, though in some other space. In Elizabeth Couper-Kuhlen and Bernd Kortmann, eds., *Cause—condition—concession—contrast: Cognitive and discourse perspectives* 361–80. Berlin: Mouton de Gruyter.

Verhagen, Arie. 2001. Subordination and discourse segmentation revisited; or, Why matrix clauses may be more dependent than complements. In Ted Sanders, Joost Schilperoord, and Wilbert Spooren, eds., *Text representation: Linguistic and psycholinguistic aspects* 337–57. Amsterdam: John Benjamins.

Verhagen, Arie. 2005. *Constructions of intersubjectivity: Discourse, syntax, and cognition.* Oxford: Oxford University Press.

CHAPTER 4

....

SCHEMATICITY

....

DAVID TUGGY

1. INTRODUCTION

....

One of the most intellectually fertile concepts of Cognitive Grammar has been that of *schemas*.[1] The aim of this chapter will be to characterize this concept, relate it to some of the other concepts discussed in the surrounding chapters of this book, and illustrate some of the many ways it is used under Cognitive Grammar. Particular attention is given to how it allows Cognitive Grammar to explicate such traditional concepts as polysemy, syntactic categories, rules, analogy, figurative language, headship and valence, and composition, in useful and intuitively satisfying ways. These phenomena under other models must be handled by separate mechanisms, but recognizing them as manifestations of schematicity allows Cognitive Grammar to handle them in an integrated manner.

The concept in itself is not a novelty attributable to Cognitive Grammar, but some of its applications are, and especially novel is the theoretical unification it affords. In particular, Cognitive Grammar handles, by this single cognitive mechanism, both phenomena which are linguistic in the strict sense (the categories and generalizations in speakers' minds which constitute part of languages) and meta-linguistic phenomena (such as the categories linguists use to talk about language and languages).

2. The Nature of Schematicity

2.1. The Basic Idea

The use of the term in Cognitive Grammar has numerous historical roots,[2] but the basic idea is an ancient, commonsensical one. Briefly, a *schema* is a superordinate concept, one which specifies the basic outline common to several, or many, more specific concepts. The specific concepts, which are called *elaborations* or *instantiations* or *subcases* of the schema, fill in that outline in varying, often contrastive ways. Both Langacker's and Lakoff's usages of the term have been quite influential in Cognitive Linguistics circles; they will be examined briefly in the next two sections.

2.2. Langacker's Characterization

Langacker considers the ability to generalize, which he equates with the extraction of schemas, to be one of the most central human cognitive capabilities. It involves the recognition of core commonalities, abstracting away from less important (for the cognitive task at hand) details which may differ from one concept or cognitive experience to another. This ability may be operative in any domain or combination of domains of cognition (Langacker 1987a: 132), and it in fact pervades our thought relative to them all. The relationships of schematicity thus established are one of the main kinds of relationships that structure the "inventory of conventional linguistic units" which constitutes a language (73–75).[3]

> The notion of schematicity pertains to level of specificity, i.e. the fineness of detail with which something is characterized; the notion always pertains, primarily if not solely, to precision of specification along one or more parameters, hence to the degree of restriction imposed on possible values along these parameters. A schema is thus abstract relative to its . . . elaborations in the sense of providing less information and being compatible with a wider range of options. . . . The difference is akin to that between representing a structure by plotting it on a fine grid (where even minor features show up) and on a coarse grid (where only gross features are preserved). . . . Our cognitive ability to conceptualize situations at varying levels of schematicity is undeniable. It is manifested, for instance, . . . linguistically in the existence of terms for superordinate as well as subordinate terms. . . . The linguistic significance of this ability is hard to overstate. (Langacker 1987a: 132–35)

Schemas are constituted as such by virtue of their relationship to their elaborations, the specific subcases that give the same information at a higher level of detail. It does not make sense to call a concept a "schema" or say it is "schematic" except in the context of specific cases relative to which it is abstract or whose information it represents at a coarser level of detail. Similarly, it makes no sense to speak of an "elaboration" except in the context of a concept which is schematic for it.

All human concepts are schematic in some degree, abstracting away from the differences in the particular experiences or thoughts on which they are based.[4] They "allow a range of variation rather than pinning things down to an exact value. Without this inherent imprecision and the flexibility it affords, language could hardly have become a viable instrument of thought and communication" (Langacker 1987a: 132–33). The "terminal nodes" or most specific concepts we can express are not different in kind, but only in degree, from the relatively abstract and even very highly abstract concepts with which we think and which we communicate on a day-to-day basis.

Since schematicity is a relative matter and all concepts communicated linguistically are schematic in some degree, it should not surprise us to find hierarchies of schematicity, with one concept schematic relative to others, but itself serving as an elaboration of yet more highly schematic concepts. Thus, Langacker gives TALL → OVER SIX FEET TALL → ABOUT SIX FEET FIVE INCHES TALL → EXACTLY SIX FEET FIVE AND ONE-HALF INCHES TALL, or THING → ANIMAL → MAMMAL → RODENT → SQUIRREL → GROUND SQUIRREL, or MOVE → LOCOMOTE → RUN → SPRINT (1987a: 132–35).[5]

An arrow is used to graphically represent the schematicity relationship, with the schema at the tail and its elaboration at the head of the arrow; thus → can be read as 'is schematic for', and ← as 'is an elaboration of'. At each step, alternative elaborations are possible; for instance, instead of LOCOMOTE above we might have had CONTRACT or WAVE or FALL; instead of RUN we might have had WALK or CRAWL or (purposely) ROLL; instead of SPRINT we might have had JOG or TROT. Note also that schematicity is a "transitive" concept, in the logical sense: A → B and B → C logically necessitates that A → C; thus MOVE → SPRINT and GROUND SQUIRREL ← THING.[6]

In sum, for Langacker any concept that abstracts away from differences among similar subcases may be properly called a schema.

2.3. Lakoffian "Image Schemas"

Lakoff rarely speaks of schemas in this general sense, but often uses the related term "image schema" (which he credits Langacker with helping to elucidate; Lakoff 1987: 68) in a more restricted sense.

> Image schemas are relatively simple structures that constantly recur in our everyday bodily experience: CONTAINERS, PATHS, LINKS, FORCES, BALANCE, and in various orientations and relations: UP-DOWN, FRONT-BACK, PART-WHOLE, CENTER-PERIPHERY, etc. These structures [image-schematic together with "basic-

level"] are directly meaningful, first, because they are directly and repeatedly experienced because of the nature of the body and its mode of functioning in our environment. (Lakoff 1987: 267–68)

These are certainly schemas in the Langackerian sense, but perhaps the only characteristic necessary for making them so is that they are "relatively simple." The characteristics that draw Lakoff's attention are things like their constant recurrence, their basis in bodily experience and thus their direct meaningfulness, their gestaltish nature (1987: 272), their "preconceptual structuring" (292–93), their universality in human experience (302, 312), and their ubiquity in language use (272), particularly as structuring concepts for the metaphors so central to human understanding (283). Thus, for Lakoff, image schemas are "central truths" (296). Many, doubtless most, Langackerian schemas will not exhibit these qualities to any high degree: there are multitudinous concepts in the minds of speakers of every language under the sun which are simple relative to other concepts but recur relatively rarely, are not based in bodily experience, are not directly meaningful, are limited to one or a few cultures, and so on. They also are well worth investigating and considering—Lakoff agrees, saying of such "noncentral truths" that "to me, this is the most interesting kind of truth" (297).

In the rest of this chapter, we will follow the Langackerian definition. This is not to discount in any way the importance of the concepts that Lakoff is examining, the subset of schemas which are in fact experientially basic, directly meaningful, and so on. They are in fact the theme of Oakley (this volume, chapter 9). But the commonality of these with all other direct abstractions is significant and worth discussing.

2.4. The Ubiquity of Schematicity

As noted above, many particular schemas, under the Langackerian definition, are far from universal. For instance, the concept of an OPENING, in chess-nuts' usage, is a schema including KING-PAWN and QUEEN-PAWN OPENINGS (along with such less common ones as KING'S KNIGHT or QUEEN'S ROOK–PAWN OPENINGS) and such cross-classifying concepts as GAMBIT; and each of these is schematic over many different families of openings (e.g., QUEEN-PAWN OPENING → QUEEN'S GAMBIT → QUEEN'S GAMBIT DECLINED → CAMBRIDGE SPRINGS DEFENSE, etc.), and each of these in turn has many subpatterns over which it schematizes. None of these schemas can be expected to exist in all the world's languages, much less among all the speakers of all those languages (though, of course, as the culture of chess spreads, they may be expected to spread with it).

What is ubiquitous in the world's languages is this kind of relationship: that is, schematicity itself. Every language will have some concepts which are relatively specific and others which designate the same sort of entity but are less specific as to details. The following discussion will serve to illustrate this contention.

3. SCHEMATICITY AND SIMILARITY; FULL AND PARTIAL SCHEMATICITY

Schematicity relations arise when cognizers compare mental structures and perceive similarities between them. The act of comparison is asymmetrical, comparing a *target* structure to a *standard*. The resulting judgment of similarity or nonsimilarity can be thought of as a sort of vector relationship, in which the degree to which the standard can be recognized in the target is a major parameter of magnitude along which different comparisons may differ. The human cognitive apparatus is apparently of such a nature that as this degree approaches complete recognition, the system experiences a state of heightened excitation; we notice (whether consciously or not) when the standard's specifications are entirely preserved in the target concept.

It follows for the same reasons that schematicity at a smaller *elaborative distance*, where the schema has many specifications which are recognized and the target structure adds few details, is likely to be more salient (produce higher excitation) than an elaboratively distant schematicity. Thus, for example, RODENT → SQUIRREL will naturally be a more salient schematicity relation than THING → SQUIRREL.

Full schematicity (represented by the previously mentioned solid arrow from standard to target, S → T) occurs in just the case when all the standard's features are preserved in the target, that is, when there is 100 percent coincidence. When there is not such full coincidence, where there is omission, contravention, or distortion of the standard's specifications, some degree of *partial schematicity* or *extension* obtains (represented by a dashed-line arrow, S --→ T). Most comparisons, obviously, yield judgments of partial rather than full schematicity; very many involve so much distortion that there is little reason to talk of even partial schematicity. But as they approach the limiting case of full schematicity, their cognitive (and linguistic) importance increases.[7]

Nothing prohibits a simultaneous or subsequent converse comparison, taking the erstwhile target as standard and the erstwhile standard as target. When there is partial schematicity in one direction, there may well be the same in the other (A --→ B and B --→ A may both obtain). Where there is full schematicity (A → B), the converse comparison predictably yields partial schematicity (B --→ A) except in the limiting case of identity or *correspondence*, where each concept's specifications are fully exhibited in the other. Thus, since RUN → SPRINT and the two concepts are not identical, it is predictable that a converse comparison will yield the judgment SPRINT --→ RUN: some of SPRINT's specifications are omitted from RUN.

As mental comparisons and schematicity judgments of these sorts are repeated, especially repeated saliently (forcefully), in a person's thinking, they become *entrenched* in his or her mind, and their ease of reactivation is thereby enhanced. As usage events that presuppose or even assert them occur, their *conventionality* is established, and they become part of that subset of the person's cognitive repertoire which constitutes the language he or she shares with other speakers; see the discussion of entrenchment and salience in Schmid (this volume, chapter 5).

Consequently, nonlinguistic cognitive structures start to become linguistic as soon as they are used as part of a phonological or semantic structure, that is, the minute language users start to talk about or with them. They are unlike more central structures only in their lesser degree of entrenchment and/or conventionalization. (They cannot be conventionalized without being entrenched, though they can be entrenched without being conventionalized.)

Langacker points out (1987a: 372–75) that any act of comparison which yields a judgment of partial schematicity necessarily involves activation of the specifications that the compared entities have in common. To the extent that those specifications form a coherent concept, it will tend to be schematic for both the compared entities, and to the extent that it recurs, and especially as it proves useful in other contexts, it will become cognitively entrenched and conventionalized. In this way, the relationship A --→ B tends strongly to facilitate the establishment of C, the schema subsuming A and B, in the cognitive network which constitutes the language.[8] And, of course, the establishment of C facilitates its use for communicative purposes, which in turn establishes its conventionality and further entrenches it. By repeated occurrences of this sort of process, quite extensive and complex subnetworks can be built up (see section 4.1, figure 4.3a).

Schemas have the important and paradoxical property of being *immanent* to their elaborations. Since all the specifications of C are, by definition, fulfilled in A and in B, whenever A or B is activated, C is being activated as well. (Any time language users think or speak of a SQUIRREL, they are thinking of or mentioning a RODENT, a MAMMAL, an ANIMAL, etc.) Thus, the representation in figure 4.1b, where the curved and dashed *lines of correspondence* indicate identity, is entailed by 4.1a. This renders obvious an awkwardness or inaccuracy of diagrams using the arrow conventions. For analytic purposes, we are representing in separate boxes (using the CONTAINER metaphor, in fact), on a piece of paper, structures which are not as discrete as the representation might suggest, whose link to each other is much more like identity. It is important not to let this analytic convenience unduly influence the way we understand the relationship. Langacker's comments in chapter 17, page 433, though prompted by the specific issue of polysemy, are apropos for all schematic networks.

It is also important to remember that the arrows used in diagrams of this sort are a notational summary over correspondences between the structures involved. A more complete (and potentially more confusing) version of figures 4.1a and 4.1b would be like figure 4.1c,[9] where specifications x, y, z, and q correspond in all three boxes, but A and B have other specifications which are not matched in each other or in C. For many purposes, notably for teasing out the specifics of blending mechanisms (see section 4.12), it may be necessary to attend carefully to those individual correspondences or noncorrespondences.

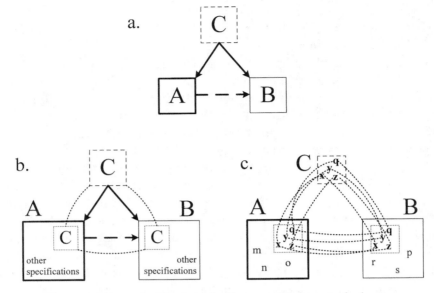

Figure 4.1. Extension tends to facilitate establishment of schemas

4. FUNCTIONS OF SCHEMAS IN THE COGNITIVE GRAMMAR MODEL

A number of phenomena which other theories treat in quite disparate ways are claimed, within Cognitive Grammar, to be manifestations of schematicity. This fundamental insight of Cognitive Grammar, that all these phenomena are, at bottom, the same thing, affords a conceptual unification that is an attractive feature of the model.

4.1. Categorization: "Classical" and Prototype-Based Categories

The relationship of schematicity is central to the characterization of categories of any sort in the Cognitive Grammar model.

"Classical" categorization (to use Taylor's 1995: 21–37 term for it) has, since Aristotle's day, assumed categories with fairly rigid and predictable boundaries, including all and only those structures which meet their definitions. They are defined either by a single abstract characterization or, in some versions, by a combination of abstract features. Thus, the category MAN (i.e., HUMAN) can be defined as consisting of all and only featherless bipeds, or, nearly equivalently, all and only those entities which exhibit the combination of features [−FEATHERED] and [+BIPED].

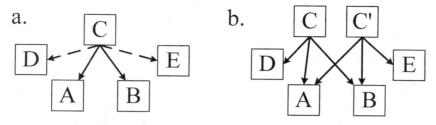

Figure 4.2. Classical categories modeled by schemas

Such categories can be easily modeled using schemas. All that is necessary is to restrict one's attention to relations of full schematicity and ignore relations of extension. Thus, in figure 4.2a, the relations of full schematicity from C to A and B mean they are members of the classical category defined by C, while the relations of partial schematicity from C to D and E mean they are not. In figure 4.2b, the two schemas C and C' are the functional equivalents of features: each defines a classical category, and A and B would be in the classical category defined by the overlap of the two categories they define.[10]

Classical categories have no gradations of membership: all members have equal claim to their status as such (Taylor 1995: 24). This again can be modeled in, or read off, structures such as those in figure 4.2. However, as Schmid indicates in chapter 5 (this volume), structures are expected under Cognitive Grammar to vary in their degree of *salience* or cognitive prominence (i.e., the energy with which they occur in the mind, generally closely paralleling the degree of their entrenchment). This parameter of differentiation means that when a category is activated, some members of it are likely to be more strongly or inevitably activated than others.

In our diagrams, we will represent differences of salience by increasing the thickness of the box lines for cases of relatively high salience and by the use of dashed lines for cases of relatively low salience. Thus, in figure 4.1, A is more salient than B, which is more salient than C. Ignoring such differences, as the representation in figure 4.2 does, gives a "flat" structure like that assumed by classical categorizations; including them means that some members are more highly entrenched, and thus more salient, than others.

It is natural for comparisons to be made from what is familiar to what is less so; it is therefore quite common for a strongly entrenched and highly salient concept to anchor many relations of full or partial schematicity. In such cases, this strongly entrenched concept serves as the center of a category constructed on the *prototype* model (see Lewandowska-Tomaszczyk, this volume, chapter 6). By repeated applications of the process represented in figure 4.1, there may come to be a single schema uniting the whole or a small number of schemas covering large overlapping parts of the category, but they will tend not to be as salient as the prototype and will thus be less important cognitively and linguistically. This will be despite the natural salience that they gain from the fact that the relationships they anchor are

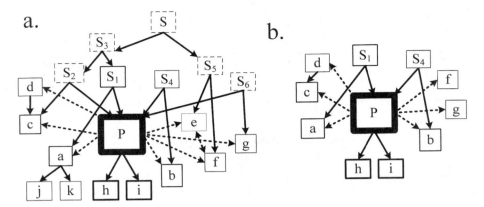

Figure 4.3. A prototype in a schematic network

relationships of full (as opposed to partial) schematicity. Figure 4.3a exemplifies this sort of structure, with P as prototype and S as highest-level schema.[11]

By raising the threshold of salience in figure 4.3a to such a degree that the schemas in dashed-line and thin-line boxes are ignored, the structure in 4.3b will result. This structure is essentially equivalent (except for retaining the relatively salient schemas S_1 and S_4 and the elaborate structures h and i) to the prototype-based "radial" category structures proposed by Lakoff and others (Lakoff 1987: 84; Lewandowska-Tomaszczyk, this volume, chapter 6; note the common use of diagrams such as the one in Aitchison 1990: 54). Categorization by schema and categorization by prototype are, accordingly, not incompatible, but rather can be seen as different views of or readings off the same complex cognitive structures.

Part of the nature of such structures as figure 4.3a is the possibility of layers of categories, the idea that higher-order categories and subcategories are natural in human cognition and thus in language. Positing a category which consists of S (with its subcases) does not preclude the existence or minimize the possible importance of such subcategories as S_3, which in turn does not preclude or downgrade S_1 or S_2, which in their turn do not by their existence eliminate or denigrate a and P, and so forth.

Linguistic categories of all sorts, whether those in speakers' minds or in linguists', will be represented, under Cognitive Grammar, in these ways. An obvious kind of example are the semantic poles of lexical items (see note 11), where the complexity of the structure will be the record of the lexical item's polysemy. Other linguistic categories will also fit the model, including syntactic categories with their subcategories and sub-subcategories, functional categories of all sorts, other semantically based categories besides the semantic poles of lexical items, phonological categories, and so on.

This way of viewing categories gives ease to certain theoretical or analytic problems of long standing. As one example, the traditional, commonsensical definition of a *noun* as a word designating a 'person, place, or thing' has been rejected by many linguists because it would exclude many, even—if *thing* is understood in its prototypical sense of '(inanimate) physical object'—most, nouns. None of the four (or six) nouns in the first sentence of this paragraph fits the definition at all well, for instance. Many have therefore concluded that the category 'noun' can have no semantic basis, but must be characterized only in terms of the syntactic environments words are allowed to occur in (e.g., possible co-occurrence with *the*, ability to head a noun phrase which can be subject or object of a verb, etc.).[12] Assuming for the moment that this is true of the category as a whole (though another possibility is presented in section 4.2), it is quite possible under Cognitive Grammar to represent this in a schema. Syntactic behavior is, to be sure, an extrinsic rather than intrinsic quality of lexical items, much as the combinatory behavior of chemicals is a quality extrinsic rather than intrinsic to them, but such extrinsic qualities can be a part of or practically make up the whole of the content of a schema. The syntactic nature of the extrinsic relations in this case does not make them different in kind from other extrinsic specifications. Given such a highest-level schema, it remains clear that under Cognitive Grammar it can perfectly well coexist with a prototype or set of prototypical subcases, such as HUMAN BEING, SPATIAL LOCATION (= PLACE), and INANIMATE PHYSICAL OBJECT, which presumably all would agree are defined on semantic grounds. The traditional definition 'a person, place, or thing' can therefore be seen as a good rough-and-ready approximation to or useful handle on the prototypical center of the category. One can see both why it worked as well as it did and why it was incomplete. One is forced neither to the intuitively dubious conclusion that the category has no semantic basis, nor to the clearly wrong claim that all nouns do, or should in principle, share all the semantic characteristics of the most prototypical ones. Figure 4.4 is an (obviously incomplete) representation of some of the concepts in the THING category and their relationships.

4.2. Superordinate Concepts and the Substantive Nature of Schemas

Classical categories have sometimes been portrayed as by nature void of intrinsic content or substance, as constituted only by essentially arbitrary inclusions and exclusions.[13] Thus, in Figure 4.2a, the claim would be that from the point of view of linguistic theory there is, or at least need be, no commonality between A and B for them to be includable in a category C. The Cognitive Grammar claim is rather that, if there is a schema C which subsumes A and B, that schema must by definition include what is common to them, and will, to that extent, be substantive, having that nonarbitrary content. It is, of course, cognitively possible for an extremely heterogeneous category to be set up in which the only common quality is the highly

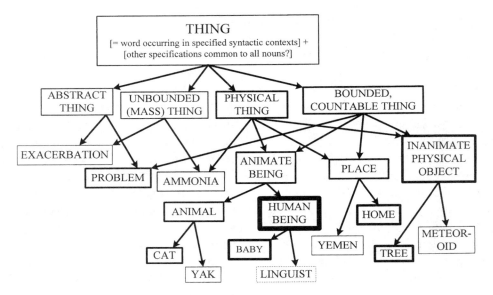

Figure 4.4. The THING category

extrinsic and ad hoc quality of having been selected to be in the category: that selectedness would then be construed as the content of the schema C characterizing the class (see Langacker 1987a: 199–200). Doubtless, there are categories in which a comparably extrinsic specification is a part of the nature of C. The schema THING in figure 4.4 would, if characterized solely in terms of syntactic behavior, be such a category, and there are other kinds of categories defined by common syntactic behavior or morphological marking for which more intrinsic semantic characterizations are highly elusive. However, in the nature of things, such schemas will be less likely to be communicatively useful or easy to maintain as conventional over time. The vast majority of useful categories will have more specifications, and particularly more intrinsic specifications, which characterize the commonality of the subcases and therefore will be part of the schema subsuming them. In short, although it is possible under Cognitive Grammar for completely arbitrary categories to be set up, they are very much the exceptional case, and substantive characterization of the schemas defining important categories is a very important theoretical endeavor.

Categories, then, are typically defined by schemas which express the commonality of their subcases. Such schemas are precisely what are traditionally labeled superordinate, or hyperonymous, concepts. As such concepts are named (linked symbolically to a phonological structure) to form lexical items; they will enter into lexical hierarchies such as those in sections 2.2 or 2.4.

But other kinds of superordinate concepts that linguists use are also schematic in nature. For instance, consider the hierarchy CONSONANT → STOP → VOICELESS STOP → /p/ → [pʰ]. This, as it occurs in a linguist's mind, fits the definition for a relationship of schematicity at each step. (Each step also corresponds to a category including other structures beyond just the one subcase represented, of course, but that is not the point here.)

A major difference between such superordinate concepts as CONSONANT or VOICELESS STOP and those in a lexical hierarchy is that these, for many speakers, do not function as the semantic pole of any commonly used word or other lexical structure. However, they may function in other ways in the language, for instance as part of the structure of entrenched generalizations (rules). In any case, for the group that knows and uses the terms, the naming of them (as *consonant, voiceless stop*, etc.) makes them indeed the semantic pole of a lexical item. Metalanguage is language, and the meanings of its words are not different in kind from those of other words.[14]

Schematic hierarchies can be posited for other concepts with a long history of linguistic utility. For instance, in a sequence such as *Hilary Rodham Clinton* ← **Woman's Name** ← **Name** ← **Noun**,[15] or *be running* ← **Continuous Action Verb** ← **Imperfective Verb** ← **Verb**, the notions **Woman's Name**, **Name**, and **Noun**, are superordinate concepts which might be posited by a linguist. If so, they are schemas occurring in the linguist's mind, and, again, as soon as they are named they begin to be entrenched as semantic structures of the corresponding phonological (or graphical) forms, and as they become entrenched in other speakers' minds, they become part of the language.

They may also, however, correspond to structures already entrenched in speakers' minds, and the more pervasive and useful ones are likely to be so. Linguists' categories which do not correspond to speakers' categories are a naturally occurring phenomenon that can be modeled in Cognitive Grammar, but only those which in fact do correspond to speakers' categories are likely to be valuable for building the theory, enhancing our understanding of what is actually happening in speakers' minds.

Langacker has argued extensively (1987b, 1991: 13–50) that the meanings of the basic terms *noun* and *verb* can be characterized by schemas which are almost certainly linguistically universal, grounded in the nature of our cognitive apparatus (thus image schemas of the Lakoffian type; see section 2.3). The cognitive schema for the semantic pole of *noun* (i.e., NOUN), which he calls THING,[16] is characterized as "a region in some cognitive domain," where "region" is "a set of interconnected entities" (1987a: 189, 198; 1991: 15). That of *verb* he characterizes as PROCESS, which involves tracking a RELATION or cognitive interconnection through conceived time.[17] Similarly, other "basic syntactic categories" would be characterized by high-level schemas, as in figure 4.5 (see Langacker 1987a: 249). Reference to these categories in more complex generalizations (e.g., syntactic rules; see section 4.3) will be a matter of reference to these schemas. Insofar as this view is correct, the ubiquity, if not universality, of these categories is accounted for, the different behavior of nouns and verbs reflects the differences in those cognitive constructs, and cases of referential overlap (e.g., where the same situation can be described by a noun and a verb) are allowed for. Langacker's superschema ENTITY, which perhaps may

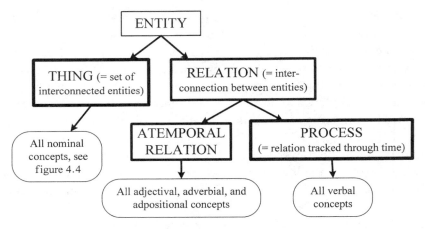

Figure 4.5. Schematic hierarchy of major syntactic classes

be thought of as the semantic pole of the word *concept*, neutralizes the distinction between these and is schematic for them and every other cognitive structure one might wish to talk about.

Whether one agrees with all the details of these proposals or not, it is clear that if these are to be viable theoretical constructs within Cognitive Grammar, they will have to be of this nature, that is, they will have to be schemas.

What all this means is that under Cognitive Grammar, when we speak of nouns, verbs, modifiers, and so forth, or consonants, syllables, phonemes, and so on, we are not dealing with empty, arbitrary, node, or category labels. We are employing cognitive structures which, although highly schematic, consist of positive, substantial content which characterizes the essential commonality of the structures which elaborate them.[18]

4.3. Generalizations: Rules, Patterns, and Constructions

Superordinate concepts (the semantic poles of superordinate terms) are one kind of generalization, but there are many others. All of them will, under Cognitive Grammar, exist in the mind as schemas. Just about anything that is called a "rule," a "pattern," or a "template" in other linguistic theories will be handled within Cognitive Grammar by positing a schema (or schemas). This will include syntactic rules, phonological rules, diachronic rules, semantic rules, syllabic or word-level or phrasal rules, lexical rules, morphological rules and templates, phonological templates or patterns, case frames, and other such constructs.[19] For each of these, it will be in principle an empirical matter whether it actually forms part of speakers' linguistic systems or not; if it does it will be a schema in speakers' minds, otherwise only in the linguist's.

For instance, the classic "phrase-structure rule" $S \rightarrow NP\ VP$ (Chomsky 1957: 26, 111) can be viewed as an expression of a schematic relationship, where S would be the schema generalizing over sentences, $NP\ VP$ would be the schema generalizing over sentences consisting of a subject and verb-phrasal predicate, and the arrow would be reinterpreted as representing the schematicity relationship itself.[20] $NP\ VP$ is itself, of course, a high-level schema, which could be further elaborated by relatively specific patterns, such as those represented in figures 4.6a.ii and 4.6a.iii (of which only the latter is a pronounceable sentence, of course).[21] Similarly, for the classic "transformational rule" of Passive $[NP_i\ Aux\ V\ NP_j] \dashrightarrow [NP_j\ Aux\ be\ V\text{-}en\ by\ NP_i]$ (Chomsky 1957: 43, 112), one could posit schemas for the active and passive structures, but in this case certain specifications of the active structure are contravened by specifications of the passive structure. Therefore, the arrow connecting them would not be a solid arrow representing full schematicity, but rather a dashed arrow of partial schematicity or extension; that is, the rule would be something like 4.6b.i. As in the other case, this schema can be elaborated by more specific structures such as 4.6b.ii and 4.6b.iii, of which only the latter is a pronounceable sentence.

Although these and other "rules" can be expressed as schemas, some important differences between these schemas and other theories' rules need to be emphasized.

a. There is no presumption that schemas must, should, or will be in any way absolute or exceptionless. A schema generalizes over the cases it generalizes over, and the fact that there may be similar structures that contravene its specifications is neither surprising nor problematic. There is only a difference in degree, not a difference in kind, between "major" and "minor rules"; there is neither reason nor expectation that a class of exceptionless generalizations should exist, much less that it should form a coherent subpart of a language, amenable to description apart from the more normal schematic structures. Exceptionless generalizations are not *ipso facto* more important in the language than those that do have exceptions.

b. Many have thought that once a rule (generalization) was made, the particulars were thereby rendered redundant and theoretically objectionable and should be excised from the grammar. In the 1960s and 1970s, when simplicity was almost universally held up as the indispensable criterion for deciding between competing models, the phrase "listing the particulars means losing the generalization" became almost a mantra. Cognitive Grammar emphatically states that if the particulars are learned (entrenched and conventional), they are part of the language and cannot be omitted from a complete description, regardless of whether they could be predicted or built starting from other structures. In fact, all things being equal, lower-level generalizations (at least down as far as a relevant *basic level*; see Schmid, this volume, chapter 5) are more likely than high-level schemas to

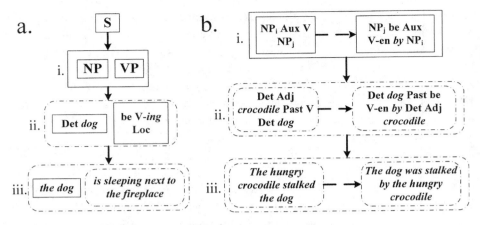

Figure 4.6. Syntactic rules as schemas

be cognitively useful and therefore entrenched. This, together with the natural salience of elaboratively close schematic relationships (see section 3) has the result that high-level schemas (and categories) can be expected, *a priori*, not to be as salient in speakers' minds as low-level schemas (and their categories). In this way, the configuration of figure 4.2a is typical. Schemas do not, in general, explain away their elaborations. It is not the case that the schema is the linguistically "real" or "basic" element and the elaboration (necessarily) only contingent, computed, or derived but not itself part of the linguistic system.

c. One aspect of this refusal to give unquestioned pre-eminence to schemas is that rules couched in the "process metaphor" fit at best uncomfortably within Cognitive Grammar. To say that A "becomes" B, "is rewritten as" B, and so on, while not impossible within Cognitive Grammar, makes it hard to see B as other than contingent, completely dependent for its existence on the more "basic" A. Such a relationship should not be assumed unless good reason can be found for it.

d. As previously observed, generalizations which exist in linguists' minds but are not entrenched in other people's cognitive systems are at best marginally part of the language. The fact that a rule may elegantly cover and in some degree account for a large amount of data does not of itself guarantee it a place in the grammar.

e. Schemas which are part of the language are (it has been claimed) subject to the *content requirement* (Langacker 1987a: 53–54): they either must be themselves directly used in linguistic expressions or they must be fully schematic for structures that are. Thus, linguists' generalizations that violate this constraint are, if Cognitive Grammar is right on this point, not linguistic in the sense of being part of the language. This is related to the contention urged in section 4.2 that schemas are substantive.

Among the types of rules and templates posited by linguists, the constructions of the construction-grammar approaches (Croft 2001; this volume, chapter 18) show an especially close affinity to the Cognitive Grammar conception of syntactic (and other) rules. Constructions are clearly schemas, and Cognitive Grammar can be classed as a kind of construction grammar (Langacker, this volume, chapter 17, section 1; Croft, this volume, chapter 18, section 5.3).

4.4. Interpretation of Classes: Coherence and the Gradation between One and Two

As emphasized above, schemas do not explain away their elaborations. One aspect of this is that a structure may perfectly well elaborate more than one schema at the same time. In other words, it may be a member of more than one category or an example of more than one rule or pattern, and to have found a rule that accounts for it or a category that includes it does not mean that it is thereby fully characterized or accounted for. And, diachronically, new schemas, implying new similarities, can be extracted from particular elaborate structures that are already established as subcases of older schemas.

This is a point on which schematic hierarchies such as the one represented in figure 4.4 differ from taxonomic hierarchies, which they resemble and with which they have sometimes been confused. In a well-behaved taxonomic hierarchy, the lines from superordinate to subordinate categories do not cross, and each daughter category has only one mother category. Once bats, butterflies, and bullfinches have been classified into the three different categories of mammal, insect, and bird, it is superfluous and even objectionable to introduce a crosscutting category of fliers into the classification scheme. In Cognitive Grammar, it is entirely natural.

If speakers of a language do indeed make (and conventionalize) a cross-cutting generalization, that generalization is a schema, and a complete description of the language must include it. Investigation indicates that overlapping, cross-cutting categorial structures like that of figure 4.4 are extremely common. The hierarchy in figure 4.5, for instance, leaves out an important schema ATEMPORAL ENTITY, which would cross-classify THING and ATEMPORAL RELATION together, in contrast to PROCESS. And, of course, the lower reaches of that schematic network can be expected to have many cross-classifying schemas, such as those in the THING subcategory as already represented in figure 4.4. Further, Langacker argues (1987a: 258–61) that important schemas unite the COUNTABLE THING schema with the PERFECTIVE PROCESS subcategory of verbs, and MASS THING with IMPERFECTIVE PROCESS. These cross-cutting classificatory schemas are represented in figure 4.7.

One kind of classification which traditionally was expected to manifest such cross-categorization was classification by features (see the discussion of figure 4.2b). In theory, all values of all features might be expected to coincide in particular subcategories, and at times substantial weight was given to the theoretical beauty

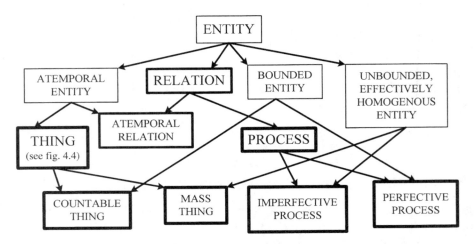

Figure 4.7. Fuller hierarchy of major syntactic classes

or economy of an analysis which utilized all the possibilities. Thus, two binary features could be expected to define four subclasses, and three would define eight (2^3) subclasses. Such cases can easily be modeled by schematic hierarchies, but the concept of the schematic hierarchy does not lead one to expect *a priori* that all combinations must occur. If a particular subcase can be shown to be established, and it elaborates more than one schema, that is fine, but the fact that two schemas might coincide in some subcase does not mean that they necessarily do so. So in figure 4.7, one might logically expect there to be subcases of the ATEMPORAL RELATION schema which would manifest the BOUNDED-UNBOUNDED distinction so prominent in the THING and PROCESS categories, but there is under Cognitive Grammar no strong pressure for this to be the case.

All of this leads to the observation that schema-based classifications typically rather than exceptionally involve interpenetrating classes, and a classification that is rendered salient in one context may be backgrounded and another emphasized in a different context. The term "network" is a natural one for describing a collection of schematic-elaborative relationships because it suggests this interpenetration and multiplicity of relationships. A category achieves coherence "to the extent that its members are densely linked by . . . categorizing relationships [i.e., full or partial schematic-elaborative relationships] of minimal distance" (Langacker 1987a: 388). But coherence is a matter of degree. A lexical item, for instance, is a kind of coherent category, existing "to the extent that a semantic network with common symbolization approximates a coherent category . . . the definition allows a single network to be divided into lexical items in multiple and mutually inconsistent ways. I regard this as a realistic characterization of the phenomena in question" (388).

This grading of categories into each other, combined with differences of salience among the cohering structures, allows for a gradual rather than an abrupt

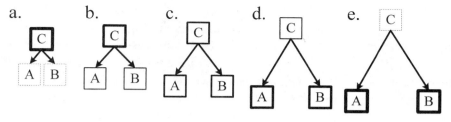

Figure 4.8. The gradation between one and two (by way of three)

distinction between a single category and two or more separate categories. The gradation represented in figure 4.8 has been used to represent the gradation between ambiguity (two separate, noncohering meanings; figure 4.8e) via polysemy (separable but coherent meanings; figure 4.8c) to vagueness (one coherent meaning; figure 4.8a) (see also Tuggy 1993; Lewandowska-Tomaszczyk, this volume, chapter 6), but it finds application in many other areas of linguistic categorization as well.[22] In particular, diachronic changes involving a single category (figure 4.8a) splitting into two (figure 4.8e)—or two categories converging into one—are easily represented as gradual under such a model.

4.5. Sanction: the Mechanism of Generativity

An important insight of Cognitive Grammar is that the schematicity relationship confers legitimacy, that to the extent that a schema is a legitimate (entrenched and conventionalized) part of the grammar of a language, its subcases are *sanctioned* by it and share in its legitimacy. More technically, (i) sanction varies directly with the degree of conventional entrenchment of the schema; (ii) a relationship of full schematicity provides full, or direct sanction, but relationships of partial schematicity provide only weaker, partial sanction (whose strength increases as the relationship approaches full schematicity); and (iii) the strength of sanction also varies inversely with the *elaborative distance* (see section 3) between the schema and the subcase (Langacker 1987a: 66–71).

Any structure sanctions itself to the degree that it is established in the language—i.e., that it is entrenched and conventionalized (point (i) above). It legitimizes itself fully (point (ii) above), and it does so at the minimum possible elaborative distance, namely zero (point (iii) above). If another well-established structure is schematic to it, the self-sanctioning structure receives additional sanction from that relationship, making it even more firmly a part of the language. Often, however, speakers will construct novel structures, which, since they are not conventionally entrenched, are not self-sanctioning. Such nonestablished structures will be judged as well formed to the degree that they are sanctioned by structures that are well established.

Thus, for instance, the word *can-opener* or the phrase *Here's Johnnie!* are conventionally entrenched for millions of American English speakers. The sanction they receive from well-entrenched [**Object-Process**-*er*] or [*Here's* **Name**!] schemas reinforces their legitimacy as parts of the English language. Those same schemas will also sanction such nonestablished (perhaps more accurately, not-yet-established) structures as *beetle-smasher* or *Here's Hortense!* These structures do not sanction themselves, but the sanction they receive from the schemas qualifies them as acceptable English. For the (presumably novel) word *beetle-collector*, there is also direct sanction from the elaboratively closer schemas **Small.Item**-*collector* and (perhaps) **Insect**-*collector*,[23] and partial (indirect) sanction from *butterfly-collector* and (perhaps) *bug-collector* and others, making it more strongly sanctioned than *beetle-smasher* would be. Similarly, *Here's Jennie!* will receive significantly more sanction from the established *Here's Johnnie!* than will *Here's Hortense!*, because the sanction is more nearly (though not fully) direct.

This is the mechanism by which Cognitive Grammar accounts for the occurrence of novel formations. Schematic patterns sanction both established and novel structures, and a novel structure is automatically acceptable to the degree that it directly elaborates a well-established, elaboratively close schema or set of schemas. The sanction it receives "is [the] measure of [its] well-formedness, i.e. how closely it conforms to linguistic convention" (Langacker 1987a: 66). Although a schema in such a case is a kind of rule, it is not the schema but the speaker who, taking advantage of the sanction afforded by that rule, creates the new structure.

"Creative" as opposed to "rule-governed" production of new forms will be evidenced by novel structures which depend more on partial than on full sanction, or whose sanction comes only from elaboratively distant sources. In extreme cases, there may even be no clear sanction, and a structure will simply be invented out of the blue and through constant repetition become established. Much more commonly there is some degree of sanction. If someone were to say *Over there's Herman!* it would be rather odd, because there is not clear sanction for usage of *over there* as opposed to *there* or (better) *here* in a presentational structure. But it would still have some sort of indirect sanction from such structures with *here* and *there*. If it were *Over there's Johnnie!*, especially if said with the proper intonation and timing, the sanction would be significantly stronger and the usage, though creative and norm-bending, more nearly in line with the norms for English. Of course, if such a structure is used enough, it will become established in its own right and can become a source of sanction for other, even more divergent, structures.

4.6. Analogy under a Schema-Based Model

Under many other models, rule-based and analogy-based accounts of linguistic creativity are seen as strict alternatives, theoretically distinct, and relegated to different modules of the grammar. Under Cognitive Grammar, the difference between them is one of degree, and the two types may often be simultaneously active.

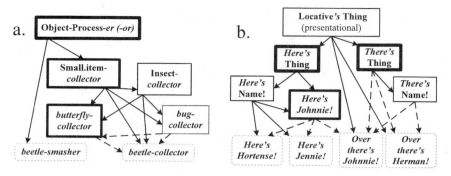

Figure 4.9. Sanction of established and novel structures

For example, the word *ink-jet* was originally coined to designate a device that squirted droplets of ink onto paper.[24] This was the central and distinctive mechanism for a particular type of printing device, which was then called an *ink-jet printer*, often shortened to *ink-jet* and dehyphenated to *inkjet*. It contrasted with such other types as dot-matrix, daisy-wheel, and thermal-paper printers and was superior to most of them in its ability to quickly and quietly print graphics-intensive copy on standard paper. Later, the terms *deskjet* and *laserjet* were coined on the analogy of *inkjet* as names for particular brands of printers;[25] a DESKJET is actually a kind of INKJET, but a LASERJET is not. Assuming that *deskjet* was the first of the two new formations,[26] we can represent what happened as an extension from the established *inkjet* to the nonestablished *deskjet*, with the relationship of partial schematicity mediating sufficient sanction to warrant the new formation. This is represented below in figure 4.10a. It was a "creative," norm-bending formation, but it caught on and became established. In accordance with what was said in section 3 and diagrammed in figure 4.1, this partial sanction entailed the activation of the specifications common to the two structures, thus facilitating the establishment of the schematic structure (figure 4.10a.i) consisting of those specifications. Also in Figure 4.10a is represented the subsequent extension from this group of structures to the novel *laserjet*, with the concomitant activation of a new schema for the whole category. This schema (4.10a.ii), which designates a high-tech, graphics-friendly printer with a name **Noun**-*jet*, can, to the extent that it becomes established, be used to directly sanction such new formations as *DesignJet*, *PaintJet*, and *OfficeJet*. Further extensions and schematizations allow **Verb**-*jet* formations like *ThinkJet* and (taking *design* and *paint* as verbs) *DesignJet* and *PaintJet*, **Adjective**-*jet* formations like *QuietJet*, and names for not-only-printer and nonprinter computer peripherals like *CopyJet* and *ScanJet*. These extensions are represented in figure 4.10b.

"Analogy" is most clearly to be invoked where there is no preestablished schema to directly sanction the newly coined structure. But the very notion of analogy implies that the ways in which the new structure is analogous, or similar, to the old

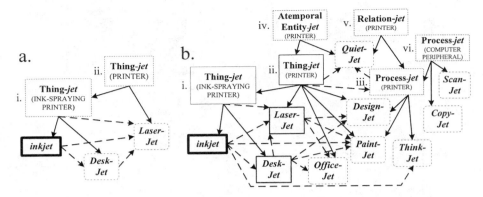

Figure 4.10. Examples of analogy

are crucial to the new formation. That is, there must be some basis for the analogy; and that basis will constitute an incipiently established schema. Such are the schemas represented in figures 4.10b.iii–vi. To the extent that such schemas become entrenched and begin to participate directly in sanctioning the formation of new structures, the mechanism of rule-based creativity is active. Such is the case of 4.10b.ii (a more entrenched 4.10a.ii) vis-à-vis *OfficeJet*, *PaintJet*, and *DesignJet*. But as long as such partially schematic relationships as those from *deskjet* or *laserjet* to *PaintJet* and *OfficeJet* are also important for establishing the latter, the mechanism of analogy is also at work, reinforcing the entrenchment of 4.10b.ii in the process.

The distinction between a schema-based and an analogy-based account of novel formations "comes down to whether the schema [rule] has previously been extracted, and whether this has occurred sufficiently often to make it a[n established] unit." "If the notion of analogy is made explicit, and if rules are conceived as schemas, there is no substantial difference between analogical and rule-based descriptions. The model therefore achieves a significant conceptual unification" (Langacker 1987a: 447).

4.7. Figurative Language

Under Cognitive Grammar, figurative usages of language involve the same sorts of structures we have been seeing repeatedly. Thus, metaphors (this volume, chapter 8) and metonymies (this volume, chapter 10) involve extension from a standard (the "literal" sense) to a target (the "figurative" sense). Their whole configuration, including both senses, will constitute the semantic pole of the expression in its figurative usage. Thus, in *the cat (is) out of the bag* the literal meaning CAT OUT.OF BAG is extended to mean INFORMATION OUT.OF CONCEALMENT, as represented in figure 4.11a (see Langacker 1987a: 93).

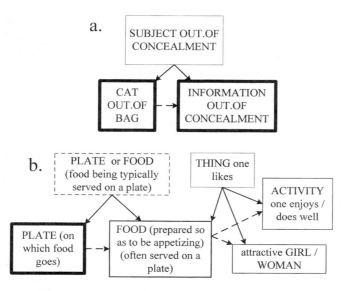

Figure 4.11. Examples of metaphor and metonymy

The categories of metaphor and metonymy overlap and grade into each other and often coincide, but the major difference between them in the clear cases is that for metaphors the designated cognitive configuration (the *profile* in Langacker's terms) can be seen as holding steady while the cognitive background (*base*) shifts dramatically, and in metonymy the base holds steady while the profile shifts. This has the result that for metaphors the extraction of a coherent schema with both literal and figurative senses (standard and target) as subcases, as in figure 4.1, is generally possible, whereas for metonymies it is more problematic (see the discussion in the next section). For instance, for most speakers of modern American English, the primary sense of *dish* is closely synonymous with the primary sense of *plate*, designating the physical, usually round and slightly concave, object on which food is typically placed for eating, and the sense FOOD PREPARED IN A CERTAIN MANNER is an extension from it. The profiling shifts from the object on which food is placed to the food (bounded in domains of quality and manner of preparation instead of, or typically besides, in space). Figure 4.11b diagrams this: it also provides a couple of additional examples of metaphor, where an activity one excels at or a good-looking girl or woman is called a *dish*.

4.8. Domains

Some concepts expressed in alternative terms are easily reducible to a schema: thus GIRL/WOMAN in figure 4.11b is intended as a shorthand for (PHYSICALLY MATURE) FEMALE HUMAN. It is not similarly easy to conceive of a schema containing the common essence of PLATE and FOOD. A common base for the two concepts can be characterized, however, and the dashed-line schema in 4.11b may be taken as identifying such a concept. (Perhaps we might paraphrase it as 'Thing prominent in the typical scenario of well-prepared food being offered to humans for consumption'.) This is problematic, however: at least prototypically, the profiling of subcase and schema must match for there to be full schematicity, and we do not have that in this case. Rather, either the base is devoid of profiling, or it has some sort of alternative profiling.[27]

It may, in the end, be a matter of definition, but it seems reasonable to posit that people can, as one of the "focal adjustments" they make to a conceived scene (Langacker 1987a: 116–37), disengage the profiling from any particular entity within the scene. Such a construct in the case of PLATE and FOOD certainly abstracts from the differences and retains the commonality of the two concepts, which makes it rather difficult to deny that it is a schema with respect to them. Accepting it as such would make it natural for us to view metaphor and metonymy as similar cognitive phenomena, yet the difference in the kind of focal adjustment (despecification of significant parts of the base for metaphor; despecification of the identity of the profile for metonymy) will allow us to appropriately distinguish the two phenomena as well. Such conceptual unification of closely related phenomena is surely a desirable result.

This sort of schema (if that is the proper name for it) is probably rightly to be equated with the idea of a *cognitive domain*, which in turn is very close if not identical to what people mean by such terms as "script," "scene," "frame," "ICM," "scenario," "semantic field of potential," or "mental space"; for some, this is a, if not the primary, meaning for the term "schema" (see Schank and Abelson 1977; Adams and Collins 1979: 3; Chafe 1987: 29; Cienki, this volume, chapter 7; Fauconnier, this volume, chapter 14). For Langacker at least, domains are ubiquitous: "Semantic units are characterized relative to cognitive domains, and any concept or knowledge system can function as a domain for this purpose" (1987a: 63, 147–82). This echoes Fillmore's (1975: 124) statement that a scene can be "any kind of coherent segment of human beliefs, actions, experiences or imaginings." For other authors, only a subset of concepts, generally highly schematic and ubiquitous in cognition, or otherwise especially prominent, cognitively independent, and so on, may be deemed worthy of being called a domain (or frame, etc.) (see Croft 1993: 337–45).[28] By whatever name, what we are talking about is a coherent set of interrelated concepts within which or in relation to which entities may be singled out for profiling. It is a specialized kind of schema with no profiling prespecified.[29]

It does not follow that schemas of this type are of high salience. It is difficult in most cases to think of them as meanings of the structures involved. Although I can entertain the schematic concept of the food-served-on-a-plate scenario, devoid of any profiling, it is significantly more difficult to think of it as a meaning of *dish*. It would seem that such profile-less concepts are difficult to maintain as objects of conception and, as a result, unlikely to be entrenched in specific cases of metonymy. The partial schematicity relation involved in the same configuration (i.e., in the example, PLATE --→ FOOD) suffers under no such disadvantages and is more likely to be well entrenched.

The requisite domain or scenario for establishing a metonymy commonly characterizes not the prototypical meaning of a lexical item, but a more elaborate but less prominent subcase. It is only a subcase of BAG, and not a very salient one for most people nowadays, that features the notion of 'bringing game home from the field in a bag'. But that base scenario is the one that underlies the metonymic change to the verb *bag* meaning 'to successfully hunt or capture', or to the noun *bag* meaning 'the game' in such a case.

When we speak of domains we use nominal structures (e.g., nouns such as *domain, scenario*, etc.) which profile the domain as a whole. That is a rather different thing from the kind of profile-less concept we have been discussing. It is much like profiling a place: a (profiled) location is not schematic for the things in it. There is a similar difficulty in conceiving of a domain or situation which one has just named and thereby profiled as schematic for the elements which can be located in it. Whether or not profile-less domains are to be considered schemas for the elements in them, profiled domains are not.

This is particularly relevant to cases of part-to-whole or whole-to-part metonymy (synecdoche or meronymical metonymy), where one of the two concepts involved is largely coextensive with the common base for the two concepts. Thus, in the case of WHEELS --→ VEHICLE, the common base would be a vehicle with its wheels, but it would be a vehicle which is neither profiled itself nor has any subpart profiled. Such a concept could still be claimed to be activated as a schema for the two metonymically related meanings, but the meaning VEHICLE, which profiles the whole, is a different concept precisely because it is profiled.

4.9. "Elaboration Sites" and Syntactic Coherence

Relationships of schematicity are, in the Cognitive Grammar model, important for syntagmatic valences. Always some (sub)structure in one entity is identified with the neighboring entity or a substructure of it. Usually when the whole of the one entity is identified with a substructure of the other, there is a clear relationship of schematicity between the two. The schematically characterized substructure is in such cases called an *elaboration site* or *e-site*. Most typically, a central participant in a Relation functions as an e-site for a Thing. Thus, the process ATE has as central participants a schematically characterized eater and some schematically characterized food. In figure 4.12a, those substructures are identified with, and elaborated by, the Things JOHN WAYNE and THE TOAST, respectively.

To the extent that an e-site is salient within the meaning of a structure and its elaborative distance from its target (its syntagmatic partner) is great, the structure

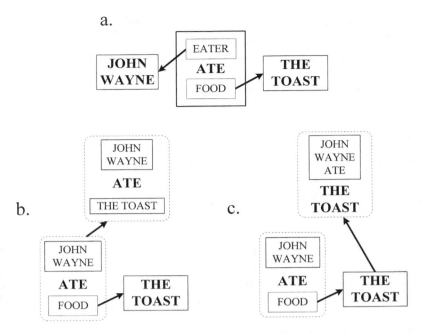

Figure 4.12. The elaboration of e-sites, profile determinance

containing that e-site is said to *depend* on its syntagmatic partner. Thus, in figure 4.12a ATE depends quite strongly on JOHN WAYNE and on THE TOAST.[30] Dependence is a central element for characterizing the range of kinds of valences (Langacker 1987a: 298–310).

4.10. Profile Determinance and the Complement-Modifier Distinction

Figures 4.12b and 4.12c represent two possible results of combining THE TOAST with JOHN WAYNE ATE,[31] preserving the same dependence relationship (of JOHN WAYNE ATE on THE TOAST). In one case, the composite structure designates the same entity as JOHN WAYNE ATE, and in the other the same entity as THE TOAST. In Cognitive Grammar terms, JOHN WAYNE ATE is *profile determinant* in the one case and THE TOAST is profile determinant in the other.

Profile determinance is the major factor in what has traditionally been called *headship*.[32] Thus, JOHN WAYNE ATE is the head of the construction in figure 4.12b (the semantic pole of *John Wayne ate the toast*) and THE TOAST in figure 4.12c (the semantic pole of *the toast John Wayne ate*). Profile determinance amounts to a schematicity relationship in which the composite structure elaborates the profile determinant component.

When the profile determinant within a construction depends on its syntagmatic partner(s), as in figure 4.12b, a *head-complement* construction obtains. Conversely, when the nonhead depends on the profile determinant, as in figure 4.12c, it is a *head-modifier* construction (Langacker 1987a: 309–10). Schematicity is thus central to the definitions, within Cognitive Grammar, of these important syntactic notions.

4.11. Schemas and the Component-Composite Relationship

The profile determinant, in clear cases, is fully (or very nearly fully) schematic for the structure of which it is a component. It thus sanctions the formation of the composite structure. But nonprofile determinant components also sanction particular substructures or aspects of the composite structure. Thus, in figure 4.13a, which represents in slightly greater detail the same structure as figure 4.12b, the nonhead is represented as sanctioning a subpart of the composite structure.

In figure 4.13a, THE TOAST is virtually, if not totally, the same within the composite structure as in its solitary state as a component. It is thus quite easy to construe it as simply embedded within the structure or as added to its syntagmatic companion to form that structure. This is a very common and a prototypical kind of component-composite relationship, and its predominance is what makes plausible the commonly assumed BUILDING-BLOCK *metaphor*, which construes complex structures as composed completely and exclusively of the components, much as a brick wall consists entirely and exclusively of bricks. One of the implications of this mental model is that the bricks (e.g., lexical items) and their patterns of integration (syntax) are very difficult to construe as anything but completely different sorts of entities.

Typically there are small discrepancies, however. In figure 4.13b (= 4.12c), there is such a discrepancy: the structure JOHN WAYNE ATE comes with a strong expectation that a phonologically subsequent noun phrase will elaborate the concept of the eaten substance; that is, the phrase is strongly transitive, but its counterpart in the composite structure is not. It is for that reason that the relationship between the component structure and its counterpart in the composite structure is represented by a dashed rather than a solid-line arrow.

This difference, though in a sense minor and quite understandable, even fully expectable,[33] is a very mild case of something that can be seen more clearly in other cases where the independent meaning of a structure differs significantly from its meaning as a component in a composite structure. For instance, the noun *toast* alone designates (at least for most American English speakers) sliced (and otherwise initially untreated) bread the surface of which has been toasted, that is, browned by being held close to a source of radiant heat. In *French toast*, the composite structure designates sliced bread which has been browned, but only after it has been dipped in a milk-and-egg batter, and the manner of the browning is by

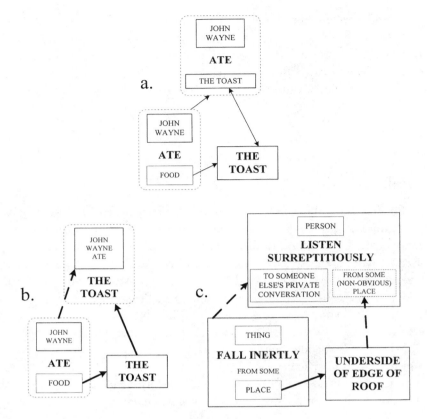

Figure 4.13. Sanction by components

being placed on a hot surface (i.e., the bread is fried rather than toasted). *Toast* is still usefully identified as the head (profile determinant) of the composite structure, but its relation to the composite meaning is one of partial rather than full schematicity. The other component, *French*, does not correspond clearly to anything at all salient in the composite structure. Most speakers will suppose that this method of preparing bread for eating originated in France, but that is a quite peripheral and even a somewhat doubtful specification. The building-block metaphor does not work very well in such a case, and of course there are even more egregious examples: *English horn*, for instance, which is a kind of large oboe (one of the least horn-like of wind instruments) and which is not particularly English in origin or distribution, or *eavesdrop* (see figure 4.13c), which is an action of listening to what is not addressed to one and has nothing obvious to do with *eaves* or with *drop*ping (though since *drop* designates a process it is more nearly schematic for the composite and thus identifiable as head).[34]

Such discrepancies between the components and the composite are entirely unproblematic under the Cognitive Grammar model. Instead of the building-block model, it is helpful to adopt a *scaffolding* metaphor: "component structures are seen as scaffolding erected for the construction of a complex expression" (Langacker 1987a: 461). Their structural specifications and modes of integration will generally parallel and suggest the shape of the composite structure, but (even from the beginning and vastly more so as it becomes entrenched in its own right) it exists independently of them and may vary from them in significant ways (Langacker 1987a: 460–64).

By accounting for composition in terms of schematicity relations, the Cognitive Grammar model handles such variations of compositionality with no further machinery. The prototype for composite structures has a clear and fully schematic relationship from the head to the composite structure and identical or fully schematic relationships from nonhead components to clearly identifiable subparts of the composite structure. The prototypicality of this configuration accounts for the plausibility and pervasiveness of the building-block model. But the existence of such structures does not preclude others where the headship is less easy to determine and where the contributions of the components to the composite structure are difficult to recognize—to the point where it might be posited that they are not components at all. The differences between these kinds of constructions are all matters of degree rather than differences of kind: no new syntactic or lexical machinery is needed to account for the full range of attested types.

4.12. Blends

A powerful theoretical tool wielded by many practitioners of Cognitive Linguistics has been the idea of blending mental spaces to achieve a new kind of combined space with emergent properties (see Fauconnier, this volume, chapter 14; Turner, this volume, chapter 15). At least in clear cases, blending structures are easily seen as a particular kind of schematic network.

Coulson and Oakley (2000: 178) describe the conceptual integration network as central to conceptual blending theory:

> These networks consist of two or more *input* spaces structured by information from discrete cognitive domains, a *generic* space that contains structure common to all spaces in the network, and a *blended* space that contains selected aspects of structure from each input space, and frequently, emergent structure of its own. Blending involves the establishment of partial mappings between cognitive models in different spaces in the network, and the projection of conceptual structure from space to space.

This can be expressed in a schematic network as in figure 4.14a. Figures 4.14b–d represent three kinds of blends. Figure 4.14b represents a high-level blend referenced in several publications by Fauconnier (e.g., 1997), in which the concepts of

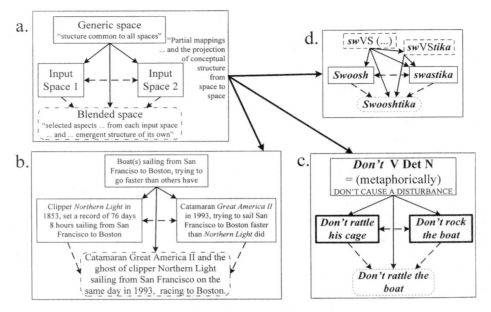

Figure 4.14. Blends

two ships sailing from San Francisco to Boston a century and a half apart are blended into a race between one ship and the ghost of the other.[35] Figure 4.14c gives an example of an inadvertent phrasal blend, and figure 4.14d (adapted from Kemmer 2003, which gives an excellent discussion of schemas as tools for analyzing lexical blends) represents the graphicophonological pole of a purposeful lexical blend. In each case, the blend clearly fits the pattern (schema) of 4.14a, which is itself composed of schemas.

Sweetser (1999) and others (e.g., Fauconnier 1999) have stressed that the mechanisms of blending must often be invoked for the analysis even of such everyday grammatical structures as Adjective-Noun constructions. Having these structures already analyzed in terms of schematicity relationships among components and composite structure makes this sort of proposal much more natural and obviously right than it would be under other theoretical models.

It is probably feasible to claim that all cases of blends consist of appropriately configured arrays of schematic and partially schematic relationships among cognitive structures, elaborating or differing in various ways from the prototype characterized in figure 4.14a. Such a claim does not, of course, obviate the necessity of specifying more fully what kinds of correspondences (figure 4.1c) are involved in the partially schematic mappings which are so important to the blending or of explicating what kinds of emergent structures show up in the blended spaces and how they do so. But at the very least, it seems clear that schematicity relationships are crucially involved in the mechanism of blending.

5. SUMMARY

The foregoing discussion is far from exhaustive: there are other ways schematicity relations function in language and many other subtleties in the functions I have discussed. It should be clear, however, that:

a. relationships of schematicity are pervasive in language;
b. recognition of them is crucial, at least under the Cognitive Grammar model, to understanding many of the most central kinds of structures which constitute the grammars of languages;
c. in particular, a number of other seminal and widely utilized concepts within Cognitive Linguistics, such as image schemas (this volume, chapter 9), constructions (this volume, chapter 18), blends (this volume, chapter 15), metaphor (this volume, chapter 8), and (perhaps) frames, ICMs, domains, and mental spaces (this volume, chapters 7, 14), are usefully seen as particular kinds (subcases) or arrangements of schemas;
d. by recognizing schematicity in these different areas, the Cognitive Grammar model achieves significant conceptual unification and appropriate simplification of the theoretical machinery;
e. our understanding of certain long-standing problems for linguistic analysis is considerably aided by adopting this perspective.

NOTES

1. The etymologically correct plural *schemata* is also used. I here follow the usage of Langacker (1987a, 1991) and Lakoff (1987) in preferring *schemas*.

2. Dictionary definitions of the term are close to the Langackerian meaning we will use in this chapter; e.g., "a summarized or diagrammatic representation of something, an outline" (*The American Heritage Dictionary of the English Language*, 1978). The term's use in Cognitive Linguistics traces back, at least in part, to Rumelhart's (1975) work with computational schemas; see also this volume, chapter 9, section 2 for a fuller discussion and references.

3. The other relationships mentioned in this regard are component-composite relationships, symbolization relationships between phonological and semantic structures, and syntagmatic relationships between co-occurring forms. Of these, the component-composite and syntagmatic relationships in their turn depend heavily on schematicity for their characterization (sections 4.9, 4.10, and 4.11; Langacker 1987a: 73–75).

4. Although this point is relevant to the question of whether there exist linguistic "primitives" or "atoms" (e.g., Wierzbicka 1996), it is not exactly the same issue. For instance, Wierzbickan-style primitives, while they are to be understood as being both cognitively and linguistically universal, make no pretense of being cognitively, but only linguistically, atomic. (They have a lot in common with Lakoffian "basic-level" and "image-schematic" concepts; see section 2.3.) A true conceptual (cognitive) atom would

probably be something like a single neuron firing or (if we admit a slightly higher neurological level) a message to contract a single muscle or the perception that a particular single point of the skin has been touched. But it is improbable that such cognitive structures are ever the meanings of any linguistic structures. Rather, it is much higher-level patterns of such cognitive events that we are conscious of and use in our communications. Such patterns are, by definition, schemas.

5. Although Langacker used italics instead of small caps, he clearly is talking about the relationships between the concepts, the meanings which constitute the semantic poles of the lexical items in question. I am following the tradition of representing such purely semantic constructs in small caps.

6. It does not follow that there can be no difference between a mediated schematic relationship A → B → C and a direct one A → C. For instance, in figure 4.9a, an arrow is represented directly from **Small.Item**-*collector* to *butterfly-collector* besides a relationship mediated through INSECT-*collector*. This reflects my judgment that whether or not a speaker activates the **Insect**-*collector* schema on a given occasion (or even has such a schema), *butterfly-collector* is likely to be coactivated and compared directly with **Small.Item**-*collector* and to be strongly sanctioned by it.

7. In particular, unless there is some special factor at work, casual comparisons which yield few or no similarities are highly unlikely to ever become cognitively entrenched in the first place, much less conventionalized among a group of speakers.

8. In Figure 4.1, A might be DOG and B HYENA; C would be a schema which we might call DOG-LIKE CARNIVORE, which would tend to become established by the mental activity of construing hyenas as a (deviant) kind of dogs.

9. Figure 4.1c does not indicate, as 4.1a and 4.1b do, the direction of comparison; i.e., it represents a comparison A ◄-- B as much as A --► B.

10. In figure 4.2a, A and B might be MAN and WOMAN, C FEATHERLESS BIPED, D CHICKEN, and E DOG. Similarly in 4.2b, C might be BIPED and C' FEATHERLESS THING, while the other identifications remain constant.

11. Figure 4.3 might represent meanings of the English word *baby* as follows: P = HUMAN INFANT, a = NEWBORN/VERY YOUNG ANIMAL, b = YOUNGEST OF A SET OF SIBLINGS, c = GIRLFRIEND, d = GIRL OR YOUNG WOMAN ADDRESSED WITH FAMILIARITY, e = PET PROJECT, f = CHERISHED OBJECT (e.g., CAR), g = OF SMALLER THAN NORMAL SIZE, h = MALE INFANT, i = FEMALE INFANT, j = PUPPY, k = CHICK, S = OBJECT OF INTEREST/AFFECTION, S_1 = NEWBORN/VERY YOUNG ANIMATE BEING, S_2 = HUMAN OBJECT OF TENDERNESS/AFFECTION, S_3 = ANIMATE OBJECT OF TENDERNESS/AFFECTION, S_4 = (NEAR) YOUNGEST MEMBER OF FAMILY, S_5 = INANIMATE OBJECT OF INTEREST/CARE, S_6 = (THING) OF SMALLER THAN NORMAL SIZE. Note that even S is not schematic for all the concepts, as it does not include S_4 and b, nor S_6 and g, nor d.

12. Pinker (1994: 106), for one, holds that "a noun, for instance, is simply a word that does nouny things; it is the kind of word that comes after an article, can have an 's stuck onto it, and so on." The major problem with this statement for a cognitive grammarian is the word "simply." Pinker's summary statement is that "a part of speech, then, is not a kind of meaning; it is a kind of token that obeys certain formal rules." My argument here is that obeying such rules should be counted as a kind of meaning, but I also follow Langacker in contending, below, that there is other semantic material in the overall schema for the category, and certainly in its prototypical subschemas.

13. Many cite Saussure's ([1916] 1996) seminal notion of "oppositions" in this regard: a category is defined not by what it includes but by what it contrasts with, and thus excludes. Some substantive characterizations are also selective to the point of near vacuity. For

instance, the often-cited choice of bipedality and featherlessness as the criterial features for
defining humanity involves ignoring many substantive qualities of humans which are
intuitively more central, such as cognitive and particularly linguistic abilities, manual
dexterity and technological skill, facial appearance and general bodily shape, complex
social behaviors (again including language), and so on.

14. A type of phonological class which deserves special mention is that of phonemes.
They are usefully modeled as near-classical categories in which less salient elaborate
structures (allophones) are largely subsumed under highly prototypical schemas with little
overlap. Traditionally problematic issues, such as aberrant allophones, contextual neu-
tralizations, and "archiphonemes," can be naturally and insightfully modeled in schematic
hierarchies including such structures. Similarly, phonological features can be modeled as
schemas, and their behavior, including those aspects that have been problematic for other
theories, fits the model well (Langacker 1987a: 388–94; this volume, chapter 17, section 5;
Nathan, this volume, chapter 23).

15. Note that to be true schemas for the lexical item *Hilary Rodham Clinton*, these
structures must be bipolar *symbolic structures*, with a SIGNIFIÉ/*signifiant* structure; that
is, a complete representation would have something like [HILARY RODHAM CLINTON /
'hɪləri rɑ :dəm klɪntn̩] ← [WOMAN'S NAME / X] ← [NAME / X] ← [THING / X]. We will use
bolded lettering with initial capitals (e.g., **Woman's Name**) to indicate structures of
this sort: too schematic to be lexical, but neither solely semantic nor solely phonological.

16. THING may be thought of as the meaning of *thing* in contexts such as *anything
at all*.

17. The differences between the schemas THING, RELATION, and PROCESS, in Langacker's view, are thus matters of construal (see this volume, chapter 3) rather than
necessarily of identity of the entities referred to. The verb or adjective *parallel* (both
relations, one processual and the other not) and the noun *parallel(s)* (a thing) can thus be
used of the same pair of lines; the differences are not differences of truth values or of what
situation is referred to, but are, nonetheless, semantic distinctions. Nominal/verbal pairs
denoting events or other processes (e.g., the noun *love* and the verb *love*, or the noun
distribution and the verb *distribute*) are handled similarly; the differences in meaning
consist of different construals imposed on a set of interconnected entities, designating
either the set as a whole or the interconnections (evolving over time) which help constitute
it as a set.

18. As usual, it is difficult to discuss these matters without recourse to the "content
metaphor." We could perhaps reword this statement to say "the structures involved are
linked to definite cognitive routines which constitute their semantic poles."

19. "Spell-out rules" would be an exception: Cognitive Grammar holds that the relationship between a meaning and the phonological structure associated with it is not one
of schematicity but of a different, associative rather than comparative, linkage. Not coincidentally, spell-out rules are one case where what is called a "rule" is not a generalization, but rather an idiosyncratic fact about a single lexical item.

20. NP, VP, and the like are of course shorthand for more substantive characterizations of the sort required under Cognitive Grammar, with the definition of an NP centered
on that of an N (i.e., it will have the schema THING as its semantic pole) and that of
VP centered on that of a V (i.e., the schema PROCESS as its semantic pole). Similar
substantive characterizations would be necessary for **Aux**, the uninflected verb represented
as **be**, the past-participial inflection represented as **-en**, the **Det**erminer, the **Loc**ative
element schema, and so forth.

21. In figure 4.6 and later diagrams, we follow the convention of using boxes with dotted-dashed lines and rounded corners to indicate structures which are novel or near-novel, that is, not yet established in their own right even though, as in this case, they may be grammatical in the sense of being *sanctioned*—see section 4.5—by established schemas.

22. In figure 4.8, and not elsewhere in this chapter, an attempt has been made to render the parameter of cognitive distance by physical distance between represented entities: thus, in 4.8a the schema is much closer to its elaborations and they to each other than in 4.8e.

23. The parenthesized *perhaps* is meant to indicate that there may well be a good many speakers for whom the structures in question are not well established in their own right. To the extent that any of them is established, it contributes its bit of legitimacy to *beetle-collector*; if it is not, the lack of its sanction does not mean the novel structure is therefore ill formed. The sanction from *bug-collector* is very nearly direct, since BEETLES are a prototypical kind of BUGS; it is only the phonological specifications of *bug* and *beetle* that conflict.

24. Presumably, this involved analogy with words like *water-jet* or *air-jet*. An analysis similar to the one given in the text below would apply to the case of *inkjet* as well. The sanction received from such high-techy words as *ram jet*, *turbojet*, *Lear Jet*, etc., or from schemas derived from them, will not be further mentioned but is certainly a real factor in the discussion that follows.

25. *DeskJet*, *LaserJet*, *CopyJet*, *OfficeJet*, *PaintJet*, *QuietJet*, *ScanJet*, and *ThinkJet* are all trademarks of the Hewlett-Packard Company. *Deskjet*, and to a lesser extent *laserjet*, seem to have achieved the marketing nirvana of being common nouns for the type of product as well as specific names for the brand.

26. The historical order of these coinages is an interesting but nondeterminative question. If the (historical) order was different from the one presented here, this order can be taken as representing the experience of a hearer like me who first learned the terms in the order given.

27. I will not pursue further the issue of whether a schema can consist of a disjunctive "either-or" structure or the closely related question of whether a list of alternatives may function in certain ways as a schema would. I have argued elsewhere (Tuggy 1992: 254–55) that the answer to the second question, in certain instances at least, is yes.

28. "In practice, we are more likely to call a semantic structure a domain if there are a substantial number of concepts profiled relative to that structure. . . . The term 'domain' implies a degree of cognitive independence not found in a dimension" (Croft 1993: 340).

29. Lakoff and Turner (1989: 103) appear to use the words "domain" and "schema" interchangeably in discussing metaphor and metonymy: "In *metaphor* there are two conceptual domains, and one is understood in terms of the other. . . . Metonymy involves only one conceptual domain. A metonymic mapping occurs within a single domain, not across domains . . . via metonymy one can refer to one entity in a schema by referring to another entity in the same schema . . . one entity is taken as standing for one other entity in the same schema, or for the schema as a whole."

30. Since John Wayne is a human being, there is in the encyclopedic semantic structure attached to his name a strong, though not particularly salient, expectation that he eats food (and engages in other typical human activities). THE TOAST, in contrast, contains a clear and salient expectation that the designatum was produced in order to be eaten. These specifications function as e-sites to which ATE corresponds. However, (i) neither is as salient within or central to JOHN WAYNE and THE TOAST as ATE's e-sites are to it, and (ii) there is little elaborative distance between them and ATE. Thus, the dependence of the

noun phrases on the verb is much less than the verb's dependence on them. These relatively subtle points are not represented in figure 4.12.

31. Although it is typical for standard transitive clauses in English to combine the verb with its object, forming a verbal phrase constituent, before combining that phrase with the subject, it is not necessary under Cognitive Grammar (and certainly not definitional for subjecthood vs. objecthood, as in some other theories). Combination of the verb with its subject first, as implied in figures 4.12b and 4.12c, will produce the same composite structure and will in fact be favored in some syntactic environments. This particular constituency is chosen here in the interest of expository clarity.

32. Where there is a great disparity between a highly schematic profile determinant (typically an affix) and a highly elaborate nonprofile determinant (stem), linguists tend to dispute whether headship should be accorded to the lightweight affix or to the semantically heavier stem. Thus, it may be mooted whether ASSIGN or MENT is the "head" of AS-SIGNMENT. Under the Cognitive Grammar conception, profile determinance is a central kind of semantic weight, and the prototypical head is both profile determinant and semantically heavier than its syntagmatic partners. It becomes a matter of definition which is "head" when the profile determinance and overall semantic weight do not line up.

33. If transitivity is a need for further specification of the nature of the object (*landmark*) of a process, the elaborative link from the FOOD specification to THE TOAST fulfills that need, and further elaboration is likely to be unneeded, perhaps even problematic. Yet another language, or even certain dialects of English, might well allow or require an object nonetheless, giving something like *the toast John Wayne ate it*.

34. Most speakers will agree that *English* and *horn* are components of *English horn*, and that *eaves* and *drop* are components of *eavesdrop*; that is, the participation of these words in the construction is clear even though the nature of their participation is not. In other cases, the participation itself is not clear: for instance, few speakers think of *halter* as saliently composed of *halt* and *-er*, and fewer still would recognize the morphemes *rue* and *-th* in the *ruth* of *ruthless*. Space precludes full discussion of such cases here, but analyzing compositionality in terms of schematicity relationships automatically provides for such variations in analyzability, allowing them to fit with perfect ease within the gamut of constructional types (Langacker 1987a: 457–66).

35. The solidness of the boxes around the two input spaces and the generic space in figure 4.14b is accurate only in the particular context in which the blend arose, where those concepts were established in the minds of the author and most readers. They are not widely established structures of English.

REFERENCES

Adams, Marilyn Jager, and Allan Collins. 1979. A schema-theoretic view of reading. In Roy O. Freedle, ed., *New directions in discourse processing* 1–22. Norwood, NJ: Ablex.

Aitchison, Jean. 1990. *Words in the mind: An introduction to the mental lexicon.* Oxford: Basil Blackwell. (2nd ed., 1994; 3rd ed., 2003)

Chafe, Wallace L. 1987. Cognitive constraints on information flow. In Russell S. Tomlin, ed., *Coherence and grounding in discourse* 21–51. Amsterdam: John Benjamins.

Chomsky, Noam. 1957. *Syntactic structures.* The Hague: Mouton.

Coulson, Seana, and Todd Oakley. 2000. Blending basics. *Cognitive Linguistics* 11: 175–96.

Croft, William. 1993. The role of domains in the interpretation of metaphors and metonymies. *Cognitive Linguistics* 4: 335–70.

Croft, William. 2001. *Radical construction grammar: Syntactic theory in typological perspective*. Oxford: Oxford University Press.

Fauconnier, Gilles. 1997. *Mappings in thought and language*. Cambridge: Cambridge University Press.

Fauconnier, Gilles. 1999. Methods and generalizations. In Theo Janssen and Gisela Redeker, eds., *Cognitive linguistics: Foundations, scope, and methodology* 95–127. Berlin: Mouton de Gruyter.

Fillmore, Charles J. 1975. An alternative to checklist theories of meaning. *Berkeley Linguistics Society* 1: 123–31.

Kemmer, Suzanne. 2003. Schemas and lexical blends. In Hubert Cuyckens, Thomas Berg, René Dirven, and Klaus-Uwe Panther, eds., *Motivation in language: Studies in honor of Günter Radden* 69–97. Amsterdam: John Benjamins.

Lakoff, George. 1987. *Women, fire, and dangerous things: What categories reveal about the mind*. Chicago: University of Chicago Press.

Lakoff, George, and Mark Turner. 1989. *More than cool reason: A field guide to poetic metaphor*. Chicago: University of Chicago Press.

Langacker, Ronald W. 1987a. *Foundations of cognitive grammar*. Vol. 1, *Theoretical prerequisites*. Stanford, CA: Stanford University Press.

Langacker, Ronald W. 1987b. Nouns and verbs. *Language* 63: 53–94.

Langacker, Ronald W. 1991. *Foundations of cognitive grammar*. Vol. 2, *Descriptive application*. Stanford, CA: Stanford University Press.

Pinker, Steven. 1994. *The language instinct: How the mind creates language*. New York: William Morrow.

Rumelhart, David. 1975. Notes on a schema for stories. In Daniel G. Bobrow and Allan M. Collins, eds., *Representation and understanding: Studies in cognitive science* 211–36. New York: Academic Press.

Saussure, Ferdinand de. [1916] 1996. *Cours de linguistique générale*. Ed. Eisuke Komatsu. Trans. George Wolf. Oxford: Pergamon.

Schank, Roger C., and Robert P. Abelson. 1977. *Scripts, plans, goals and understanding*. Hillsdale, NJ: Laurence Erlbaum.

Sweetser, Eve. 1999. Compositionality and blending: Semantic composition in a cognitively realistic framework. In Theo Janssen and Gisela Redeker, eds., *Cognitive linguistics: Foundations, scope, and methodology* 129–62. Berlin: Mouton de Gruyter.

Taylor, John R. 1995. *Linguistic categorization: Prototypes in linguistic theory*. 2nd ed. Oxford: Clarendon Press. (3rd ed., 2003)

Tuggy, David. 1992. The affix-stem distinction: A cognitive grammar analysis of data from Orizaba Nahuatl. *Cognitive Linguistics* 3: 237–300.

Tuggy, David. 1993. Ambiguity, polysemy, and vagueness. *Cognitive Linguistics* 4: 273–90.

Wierzbicka, Anna. 1996. *Semantics: Primes and universals*. Oxford: Oxford University Press.

CHAPTER 5

ENTRENCHMENT, SALIENCE, AND BASIC LEVELS

HANS-JÖRG SCHMID

1. INTRODUCTION

One of the basic tenets of Cognitive Linguistics is that the human capacity to process language is closely linked with, perhaps even determined by, other fundamental cognitive abilities. This chapter is concerned with possible manifestations of such abilities—most notably among them perception, memory, and attention allocation—in linguistic competence and use. It deals with mechanisms that influence the storage of concepts and constructions in long-term memory and with factors involved in the retrieval and activation of concepts and constructions from memory during ongoing language processing.

This chapter falls into seven sections. Following this introduction, section 2 illustrates the use of the notions of *entrenchment* and *salience* in Cognitive Linguistics and provides initial definitions. Section 3 deals with the role of entrenchment in the emergence, sanctioning, and blocking of linguistic units. More specific linguistic effects of entrenchment and salience in the lexicon are discussed in section 4. Section 5 reviews an attempt to measure the relative entrenchment of categories in lexical taxonomies. Section 6 deals with effects of entrenchment and salience in the area of syntax, and section 7 offers an outlook on future research in this area.

2. The Notions of *Entrenchment* and *Salience* in Cognitive Linguistics

2.1. Entrenchment

When speakers encode their conceptualizations in words and sentences, they utilize their *competence*, that is, the linguistic knowledge of phonological, semantic, grammatical, and collocational properties of words and syntactic structures. This knowledge is stored in their long-term memory. It is fairly unlikely, however, that speech processing is always carried out in a creative, generative fashion in the sense that language users always have to actively, or even consciously, search their memory for means of encoding what they have in mind or decoding what they hear or read. Presumably, a lot of what speakers say is available in memory in some kind of prepackaged, ready-made format. Convincing evidence for this claim are the words of a language, since these represent nothing else than conceptualizations that have been fossilized by convention in a speech community. We hardly ever stop to think what language would be like without prepackaged concepts readily encodable by words. To refer to a dog that we see running across a meadow, there is no need to consciously construe an appropriate conceptual unit from scratch, because words like *dog* or *poodle* are readily available. The question of how to name this entity will not reach a level of conscious awareness, and the activation of concepts matching our experience of the dog will hardly require cognitive effort. The reason is that familiar concepts like 'dog' or 'poodle' are deeply *entrenched* in our memory so that their activation has become a highly automated routine.

When we are faced with a more exotic animal, say a tapir in a zoo, the situation will be different, because the cognitive processes relating the perceptual input that determines the target conceptualization to the corresponding phonological unit are less well entrenched. We are likely to need more time to identify and categorize the animal by considering some of its most prominent attributes before we can even begin to search our mental lexicon for a word matching this cognitive category. Clearly, then, the conceptual unit 'tapir', which is represented by this cluster of attributes, is less well entrenched than the cognitive unit 'dog'.

Cognitive units come to be entrenched and their activation automated to the extent that they have been used before. According to Langacker (1987: 59), there is a

> continuous scale of entrenchment in cognitive organization. Every use of a structure has a positive impact on its degree of entrenchment, whereas extended periods of disuse have a negative impact. With repeated use, a novel structure becomes progressively entrenched, to the point of becoming a unit; moreover, units are variably entrenched depending on the frequency of their occurrence.

Langacker conceives of entrenchment as being fostered by repetitions of cognitive events, that is, by "cognitive occurrences of any degree of complexity, be it the firing of a single neuron or a massive happening of intricate structure and large-scale architecture" (1987: 100). As a result, the degree of entrenchment of a cognitive or linguistic unit correlates with its frequency of use. Geeraerts, Grondelaers, and Bakema (1994) argue for a more refined version of this idea (see section 5). On their account, it is not frequency of use as such that determines entrenchment, but frequency of use with regard to a specific meaning or function in comparison with alternative expressions of that meaning or function.

Entrenchment of concepts or constructions not only depends on the frequency of activation by individual speakers (and in that sense is not a completely private matter), but it also applies to languages as such and whole speech communities, because the frequency of occurrence of concepts or constructions in a speech community has an effect on the frequency with which its members are exposed to them. The (tacit rather than explicit) implication is that this results in some kind of collective automatization effect, which makes it possible to talk of the degree of entrenchment of a concept or construction in a given language.

In short, the notion of entrenchment is thus used in Cognitive Linguistics—and especially in Langacker's influential framework of Cognitive Grammar (1987, 1991; this volume, chapter 17)—to refer to the degree to which the formation and activation of a cognitive unit is routinized and automated.

2.2. Salience

The notion of *salience* is employed in Cognitive Linguistics in two closely related ways, yet distinct enough to call for differentiation.

The first usage, called "cognitive salience," concerns the activation of concepts in actual speech events. Cognitive units must be activated when they are required for speech processing, and this may result from either one of two mental processes: the activation of a concept may be controlled by a conscious selection mechanism, whereby the concept enters a person's focus of attention and is being processed in current working memory (Anderson 1983: 118–20; Deane 1992: 35); alternatively, a concept may be activated through *spreading activation*, which occurs when the activation of one concept (e.g., 'dog') facilitates the activation of others (e.g., 'bark', 'tail wagging', 'fur', 'poodle', 'alsatian', 'collie', etc.) (see Collins and Quillian 1969; Collins and Loftus 1975; Anderson 1983: 86–125; and Deane 1992: 34). Irrespective of how a cognitive unit has been activated, it is said to be *salient* if it has been loaded, as it were, into current working memory and has thus become part of a person's center of attention. Since the use of concepts that are already activated requires minimal cognitive effort, a high degree of cognitive salience correlates with ease of activation and little or no processing cost. Currently inactive concepts, on the other hand, are nonsalient.

The second usage of the notion of *salience*, "ontological salience," is not related to temporary activation states of concepts but to more or less stable properties of entities in the world. The idea is that by virtue of their very nature, some entities are better qualified to attract our attention than others and are thus more *salient* in this sense. The obvious link between *ontological salience* and *cognitive salience* is that mental concepts of salient entities have a better chance of entering our focus of attention. As a consequence, ontologically salient entities are more likely to evoke corresponding cognitively salient concepts than ontologically nonsalient ones. For example, a dog has a better attention-attracting potential than the field over which it is running. Therefore, it is likely that observers of the scene will be more aware of the dog and its actions than of the field.

The notion of *salience* may thus denote both a temporary activation state of mental concepts (*cognitive salience*) and an inherent and consequently more or less permanent property of entities in the real world (*ontological salience*).

It follows from these definitions that there is a two-way relationship between salience and entrenchment. On the one hand, ontologically salient entities attract our attention more frequently than nonsalient ones. As a result, cognitive events related to the processing of ontologically salient entities will occur more frequently and lead to an earlier entrenchment of corresponding cognitive units, or concepts. This is perhaps most noticeable in the early stages of language acquisition when active, movable, or otherwise interesting—and therefore salient—entities such as people, animals, or colorful and noisy toys, which have a relatively high potential of attracting children's attention, stand a better chance of early entrenchment as cognitive units than less salient entities, such as walls or carpets. It must be emphasized, however, that there is no one-to-one causal link between ontological salience and entrenchment, because from a certain point onwards, children acquire the ability of adults to conceptualize one entity, say a given dog, via a whole range of differently entrenched concepts such as 'dog', 'poodle', 'mongrel', 'animal', or 'creature'. This shows that it is, of course, not real-world entities themselves that get entrenched but possible concepts of entities.

On the other hand, deeply entrenched cognitive units are more likely to become cognitively salient than less well entrenched ones. The reason is that a smaller amount of spreading activation will suffice to activate them. The question of which factors determine the choice from a range of concepts that are entrenched to an intuitively similar degree ('dog', 'poodle', 'animal') will be discussed in more detail in sections 4 and 5. What sections 1 and 2 have shown so far is that there is no general agreement on how to define the concepts underlying the terms *entrenchment* and *salience*. However, unlike in other areas, the terminological unclarity is not the result of a long-standing debate but rather a symptom of the novelty of the concepts involved (see also Geeraerts 2000).

3. The Role of Entrenchment in the Emergence, Sanctioning, and Blocking of Linguistic Units

As shown in the previous section, the term *entrenchment* designates the storage of concepts and constructions as (variably) routinized items in long-term memory. By the same token, it accounts for the emergence of linguistic items with a high degree of unit-hood, that is, symbolic associations between semantic and phonological structures (Langacker 1987: 57–59) with little perceived internal complexity. Indeed, although the size of linguistic units can vary from single morphemes to quite elaborate syntactic constructions, it is the hallmark of fully entrenched units that they are conceived of as single gestalts. As Langacker (1987: 59) points out, "When a complex structure coalesces into a unit, its subparts do not thereby cease to exist or be identifiable as substructures.... Its components do become less salient, however, precisely because the speaker no longer has to attend to them individually."

It is by virtue of their Gestalt-like nature that, despite their possible internal complexity, units are relatively easy to process and manipulate and that they require little effort to combine with, or integrate into, other structures. This is the main cognitive advantage of entrenchment. Note, however, that as there are degrees of entrenchment, a linguistic item's unit status may also be variable, that is, there are no discrete boundaries between units and nonunits.

As already hinted at, it is not only lexical concepts that get entrenched with repeated use, but also collocational patterns, or *constructions* in the Construction Grammar sense of the term (see Croft, this volume, chapter 18), and syntactic structures. For example, given their high frequency of usage, lexical bundles like *I don't know*, *I don't think*, *do you want*, or *and I said* (Biber et al. 1999: 994) are likely to be highly entrenched, and so are frequently recurring clause patterns such as 'abstract NP as subject + copula + *that*-clause' (e.g., *the thing/fact/point/problem is that*...) or 'abstract NP as subject + copula + *to*-infinitive' (e.g., *the aim/job/task/ idea is to*...; see Schmid 2000).

Firmly entrenched units play a crucial role in the emergence of novel linguistic structures, a process which is known as *sanctioning* in Cognitive Grammar (see Langacker, this volume, chapter 17). If the way to the establishment of novel structures in the repertoire of individual speakers and in the lexicon and grammar of a language is paved by similar structures that are already well entrenched, their entrenchment (i.e., of these novel structures) will be facilitated in turn. On the other hand, well-entrenched structures can inhibit or even block the adoption of novel structures (Langacker 1991: 162). This occurs, for example, in the field of word-formation, where the entrenchment of potential novel structures like English *stealer* or German *Bauer* (as a derivation of the verb *bauen* 'build') is blocked by the established words *thief* and *Bauer* 'farmer' respectively.[1]

4. SALIENCE AND ENTRENCHMENT EFFECTS IN THE LEXICON: BASIC LEVELS OF CATEGORIZATION

According to the theory of spreading activation, many more words than those that are uttered in a given speech act are activated during the process of lexical retrieval. This claim is supported by association and priming experiments, which suggest that whole networks of concepts that can be related to a target word in various ways (e.g., synonyms, antonyms, superordinates, subordinates, collocates, elements of one frame) achieve some level of activation during lexical retrieval (Aitchison 2003: 84–101). It is from these networks that the most suitable means of encoding the conceptualization to be conveyed, the *active node* (Langacker 1987: 384; 1991: 159–60), is selected during speech production.

This suggests that the stage of conceptual categorization, which is part of lexical retrieval (see Levelt 1989: 222–34), may involve two levels of activation: the activation of a conceptual network and the activation of the active node from the options provided by the network. The two steps result in the allocation of different degrees of salience across possible concepts, and this, in turn, raises the question as to the factors determining this allocation process. Arguably, the degree to which concepts are entrenched in long-term memory will play a crucial role in both stages. All other things being equal—for example, the match between the target conceptualization and the concepts—well-entrenched concepts have a better chance of being selected as active nodes than less well entrenched ones.

What is known about the differences between categories with regard to their degree of entrenchment? While it is of course difficult to make justified assessments about the entrenchment of individual concepts (but see section 5), there is a long-standing tradition in anthropology, cognitive psychology, and linguistics in trying to attribute degrees of entrenchment to certain types of cognitive categories. According to research to be reviewed in the following, it is on the so-called *basic level of categorization* that the most deeply entrenched categories are found.

Before the term *basic level* itself was introduced into cognitive psychology by Rosch et al. (1976), there was evidence that categories were not on a par with regard to their entrenchment levels. In a seminal study, Berlin and Kay (1969) collected data from twenty languages suggesting that there is a set of *basic color terms* whose extension on the color spectrum is similar across languages of different developmental states. They hypothesized the existence of *focal colors*, areas in the spectrum that are particularly likely to be named by basic color terms in different languages. Their research proved to be an important inspiration for cognitive linguists, because it indicated that there was a much closer and more direct tie between perception and naming than had previously been assumed. Later, Kay and McDaniel (1978) supported the universalist notion of basic color terms by showing that there is a correspondence between at least some focal colors and human color receptors, but other attempts to account for the existence of focal colors of variable universality have also been made (see, e.g., Wierzbicka 1990).

Looking at plant taxonomies in Tzeltal, a language spoken in southern Mexico, Berlin and his collaborators (Berlin, Breedlove, and Raven 1973, 1974; Berlin 1978) found that there was one level of abstraction at which the largest number of category names were available. This was the so-called *generic level*, situated in the center of the taxonomies between *unique beginners* (e.g., PLANT) and *life forms* (TREE) at the more general end, and *specific* (WHITE BEAN) and *varietal* (RED COMMON BEAN) categories at the more specific end. The generic level, which included categories like PINE or WILLOW, not only provided speakers of Tzeltal with the widest range of terms (471 terms as opposed to 4 for life forms, 273 for specific categories, and 8 for varietal categories), but it was also the level chosen most frequently for naming plants. In addition, the generic level stood out from the other taxonomic levels on two further scores: (i) the terms used to name these generic categories were short and morphologically simple, and (ii) many generic-level categories, such as CORN and BEAN, were culturally highly significant and biologically important—some were not even seen as subordinate to more general life-form categories. All these findings point in the same direction: category divisions at the generic level seem to carve up reality in such a way that it is convenient to name things at this level. This, in turn, suggests that the generic level of categorization may play a special role in cognitive processing.

The term *basic level of categorization* was first used for the central level in taxonomies by Rosch et al. (1976) to reflect this cognitive importance. Their study also provided the first and most important pieces of systematic psychological evidence concerning this level. Rosch et al. (1976) carried out a set of experiments with the aim of confirming the idea "that there is one level of abstraction at which the most basic category cuts are made" (382). The taxonomies used as experimental stimuli had three levels, superordinate, basic, and subordinate, and comprised such categories as illustrated in (1):

(1)   superordinate level   FRUIT, FURNITURE
      basic level   APPLE, PEACH, GRAPES, etc.   TABLE, LAMP, CHAIR, etc.
      subordinate level   DELICIOUS APPLE, MACINTOSH APPLE, etc.
      KITCHEN TABLE, DINING ROOM TABLE, etc.

The experiments yielded the following results (see, e.g., the surveys in Rosch 1977; Lakoff 1987: 46–54; Taylor 1995: 46–51; Ungerer and Schmid 1996: 69–71):

a. Basic-level categories strike an ideal balance between specificity of conceptual information and variety and range of members. In contrast, categories at the superordinate level give little specific information but collect a wide range of different members. And subordinate categories give highly specific information but pick out only small sets of members.

b. Similarly, basic-level categories carve up reality at a level of abstraction keeping an ideal balance between intracategorial similarity and intercategorial difference. On the superordinate level, the difference between category members (e.g., chairs, tables, sofas, and cupboards as members of the category FURNITURE) is so great that only very few category-wide attributes, which may be useful for measuring intracategorical similarity, can be found. Then, again, at the subordinate level, the similarities between neighboring categories outweigh the differences between them. For example, the attributes 'has a seat', 'is used to sit on', and 'has a back' are shared by both 'kitchen chair' and 'living room chair'.

c. In experiments, subjects could name the largest number of motor movements typically carried out in interaction with objects, when they were confronted with basic-level terms. While FURNITURE did not elicit more than 'scan with the eyes', basic-level categories such as CHAIR evoked specific descriptions of movements like 'sitting down', which involve subactions like 'turning one's head', 'bending one's knees and waist', and 'moving one's body backwards'.

d. Basic-level categories are the most inclusive categories that allow for the construal of a visual Gestalt image of a category schema which is compatible with most category members. For example, the outer shapes of most members of the category DOG are so similar that it is possible to imagine a picture of a dog "as such." This is clearly impossible for superordinate categories, because their members' outer shapes are too divergent.

What these and other findings indicate is that the basic level of categorization is basic in a number of respects:

a. it is perceptually basic because it allows for Gestalt perception;
b. it is mnemonically basic because it organizes knowledge about things in an ideal balance between specificity of information and cognitive effort;
c. it is functionally basic because it captures shared kinds of interactions with objects; and
d. it is linguistically basic because basic-level terms tend to be morphologically simpler, to be acquired earlier by children (Brown 1958, 1965), to be used as the unmarked choice for introducing referents into discourse (Cruse 1977), and to provide the raw material for extensions of the lexicon by means of metaphor, metonymy, and word formation (Schmid 1996a).

In sum, it seems to be cognitively advantageous to divide reality into categories at the basic level, and this is why basic-level categories of persons, animals, living organisms, and concrete objects are considered the most deeply entrenched categories at our disposal. Not only are they more deeply entrenched than either superordinate or subordinate concrete categories, but they are also more deeply entrenched than categories subsuming actions, events, properties, and abstract ideas, for they seem to provide the earliest and most fundamental way of comprehending the world around us. Arguably, basic-level categories are acquired as early as in

Piaget's sensorimotor stage, when children begin to interact with the objects around them and find out about their similarities and differences by touching and bodily interacting with them (Deane 1992: 195).[2] There have been attempts to ascribe a similar kind of basicness to certain event categories (Rifkin 1985), speech act categories (Verschueren 1985), locomotive categories (Ungerer and Schmid 1996: 103), and property categories on a central level of abstraction (Ungerer and Schmid 1996: 106), but the extent to which these categories really derive their basicness from an ontologically early and deep cognitive entrenchment is debatable.

5. MEASURING THE RELATIVE ENTRENCHMENT AND SALIENCE OF CATEGORIES IN LEXICAL TAXONOMIES

In the previous section, the entrenchment of basic-level categories was mainly accounted for in terms of cognitive factors like perception, conceptual structure, and early acquisition. It will be recalled, however, that the degree of entrenchment of concepts is also thought to correlate with the frequency with which they are activated: the more frequently a concept is activated, the more entrenched it will become, and, vice versa, the more entrenched a concept is, the easier and therefore more frequently it will be activated. While the correlation between entrenchment and frequency of usage had essentially already been noted by Brown (1965: 321) and Rosch et al. (1976: 435), it was first investigated with a closed controlled corpus of running texts in a study of oral narratives by Downing (1977). Confirming Brown's and Rosch's expectations, Downing found that "it is basic level names which are most frequently used to refer to concrete objects in actual discourse" (476).

Much later, Geeraerts, Grondelaers, and Bakema (1994) took up the variable of frequency in order to measure the degree of entrenchment of the concepts underlying the Dutch lexical field of clothing terms. Their method was not based on the analysis of running text but on a comparison between pictures of clothing items in magazines and the lexical items used to describe these items in the captions or texts accompanying the pictures. A large parallel database was set up, consisting of, on the one hand, referential information about such parameters as type of garment, material, cut, length, and so on, and, on the other hand, of lexical information about the word naming the particular item of clothing. Among other things, this parallel setup allowed the researchers to measure the degree of entrenchment, or *onomasiological salience* in their terminology, by counting how often a certain type of garment, for example tight cotton pants reaching down to the calves, was conceptualized as a particular concept and named by corresponding words, for example *kledingstuk* 'garment', *broek* 'pants', or *legging* 'leggings'. Loosely speaking, entrenchment was thus measured in terms of relative frequency of naming.[3] This is a very early example of how entrenchment and salience can be operationalized, making use of a corpus of authentic language use, and can then be employed to explain the actual choices of lexical construal that language users make. Geeraerts, Grondelaers, and Bakema's hypothesis was that if "a referent (or set of referents) is expressed more readily ... by an item with a higher entrenchment value" (1994: 11) and if basic-level concepts were indeed more fully entrenched than concepts at other levels of specificity, then words encoding basic-level concepts should occur more frequently as names for a particular type of garment than words encoding other types of concepts.

This hypothesis was not fully confirmed by their findings. While on the whole basic-level categories did turn out to have a higher entrenchment value than superordinate and subordinate categories, Geeraerts, Grondelaers, and Bakema (1994: 144–46) drew particular attention to one area that casts doubt on the basic-level hypothesis, namely the field of terms denoting different kinds of pants. Here, it turned out that the subordinate terms *short/shorts* 'shorts', *bermuda* 'bermuda shorts', and *legging/leggings* 'leggings' scored roughly the same entrenchment values as the basic-level term *broek* 'pants'. More strikingly, the category JEANS, encodable in Dutch by the terms *jeans*, *jeansbroek*, and *spijkerbroek*, had a considerably higher entrenchment value than *broek*. The subordinate category JEANS thus seems to be more firmly entrenched than the basic-level category BROEK, and this clearly runs counter to the expectation that basic-level categories are more deeply entrenched than other types of categories. Geeraerts, Grondelaers, and Bakema (1994: 146) conclude that the basic-level model may not be universally valid.

There is, however, a second possibility of interpreting their findings (Schmid 1996b: 82–83): if the category JEANS is indeed more firmly entrenched than the category BROEK, then why cannot 'jeans' belong to the basic level as well? For this interpretation to be acceptable, one has to sacrifice the idea that cognitive taxonomies are based on the logical principle of class inclusion, because from that point of view there can be no doubt that JEANS is subordinate to BROEK; after all, all jeans are pants, but not all pants are jeans. But it must not be taken for granted that natural everyday taxonomies, as opposed to artificial and logical scientific ones, are indeed based on class inclusion. There is in fact some evidence that natural conceptual hierarchies are fairly messy and not organized in a particularly consistent manner. As was briefly indicated above, the Tzeltal plant taxonomy, for example, contains a number of particularly important generic terms which are not affiliated to superordinate terms, a phenomenon that is known in lexical field theory as a *generalization gap* (Lipka 1980: 108). Furthermore, conceptual hierarchies do not even seem to be stable: there is evidence from attribute-listing experiments that categories may move from the subordinate to the basic level when they gain in cultural importance (see Ungerer and Schmid 1998: 84–91; also Ungerer and Schmid 1996: 92–95). Words like *(motor)car* or *(air)plane*, for instance, which started out as subordinates in the field of vehicles, have since clearly acquired basic-level status. A similar process is plausibly at work with the category JEANS in Dutch (and possibly other languages), because of the enormous cultural importance of these types of pants.

If the logical principle of class inclusion is declared invalid—at least for natural conceptual hierarchies—as a determinant of category status at the vertical level, this has consequences on the horizontal level as well: categories at the same level of categorization need not always be mutually exclusive. Even if PANTS and JEANS can operate at the same cognitive level in the conceptual hierarchy (though not the same taxonomic level from a logical point of view), this does not preclude conceptualizing a pair of pants as a member of either of these categories. In view of the cross-classifications, gaps, inconsistencies, and other signs of cognitive flexibility, which are eschewed in scientific taxonomies but part and parcel of many everyday conceptual hierarchies (see Geeraerts, Grondelaers, and Bakema 1994: 137; Ungerer and Schmid 1996: 80–83), this claim does not seem implausible.

As already mentioned, Geeraerts, Grondelaers, and Bakema's study ushered in what can be called a quantitative turn in the investigation of entrenchment and salience effects. More recently, the quantitative approach has been extended to other grammatical fields, for example, to phonology (and to some extent morphology) by Bybee (2001) and to syntax by Grondelaers (2000) and Grondelaers et al. (2002). Further illustrations of this trend include my work (Schmid 2000) on abstract nouns based on the COBUILD corpus, Gries's (2003) corpus study on particle placement, and the theme session on the use of corpora in Cognitive Linguistics at the Eighth International Cognitive Linguistic Conference in La Rioja, Spain, convened by Stefan Gries and Anatol Stefanowitsch. What is particularly exciting about the quantitative studies is that they contribute to making the cognitive linguistic approach a testable theory of language.

6. Entrenchment and Salience Effects in Syntax

6.1. Figure/Ground Alignment

The examples of quantitative studies referred to in the previous section illustrate that different degrees of salience of concepts are not only seen to be reflected in the lexical choices provided by languages, but also in their grammars. It is one of the most fundamental ideas in Cognitive Linguistics that grammatical structures encode and control the distribution of attention across the entities involved in a given scene (see Talmy, this volume, chapter 11; De Mulder, this volume, chapter 12). Quite plausibly, for example, in (2) the book is highlighted for attention, while the table serves as a point of reference for the location of the book.

(2)   Look at that book on the table.

Such patterns of attention distribution have been explained by cognitive linguists in terms of different degrees of salience or prominence. The most common terms for the two entities involved in such relations, which are borrowed from the terminology of Gestalt psychology, are *Figure* and *Ground* (see, e.g., Ungerer and Schmid 1996: 156–60; Talmy 2000: 311–44). The Figure is regarded as the most salient entity in a given configuration, while the Ground has secondary prominence. If a grammatical structure includes more than two elements, it is either decomposed into several layers of Figure/Ground pairings or both Figure (with primary prominence) and Ground (secondary prominence) are seen as standing out from the background, which is the least prominent part of the scene.

Figure/Ground organization provides a cognitive basis for a range of linguistic structures, most notably among them relational predications expressed by prepositions (as in (2)) and basic clause patterns consisting of subjects and complements. What all these structures share is the idea that language allows speakers to highlight certain aspects of conceptualized scenes while backgrounding others.

6.2. Relational Configurations Encoded by Prepositions

In Cognitive Grammar (see Langacker, this volume, chapter 17) and in Lindner's (1981), Lakoff's (1987: 416–61), and Brugman's (1981) work, the terms *trajector* and *landmark* are used as specific manifestations of the Figure/Ground principle in relations encoded by prepositions (see Zlatev, this volume, chapter 13; Svorou, this volume, chapter 28). Thus, the first nominals in sentences (3) to (5) are trajectors in the relational configuration and the second landmarks.

(3)   The car crashed into the wall.
(4)   Milton Keynes is close to London.
(5)   The sugar is in the red jar.

Here we will follow the practice of linguists such as Talmy (2000: 311–44) and continue using the terms *Figure* and *Ground* to emphasize the similarity between the processes in relations encoded by prepositions and those expressed by other syntactic relations.

Especially in examples (4) and (5), which, unlike (3), do not describe dynamic motion events but stative relations, the question may arise why it is that Figure has more salience than Ground. The answer lies in the arrangement of the two entities involved in the relation. As a general rule, at least in English and related languages, it is the entity that is mentioned first by the speaker that will be accorded the higher degree of salience. This can easily be shown by reverting example (5), as shown in (6):

(6)   The red jar contains sugar.

In (6), the hearer's attention is first drawn to the red jar and then to its content; in (5), which describes the same container-content relation, the sugar is more salient. In short, the salience of nominals is determined by their positions in clause structures, and these, in turn, are allocated by speakers according to their perspective on a scene. It depends on the speaker's subjective perception of a real-world scene, or the conception of the scene before the speaker's mental eye, how Figure and Ground will be distributed.

While speakers have thus, in principle, a good deal of freedom in organizing Figure/Ground alignment, it turns out that their choice is in fact severely restricted by the linguistic means available to them. As such, Figure/Ground reversals of the type illustrated for (5) are more difficult, in fact even problematic, for (3) and (4). Attempts to swap the positions of Figure and Ground in (3) and (4) are given in (7) and (8):

(7)   ?London is close to Milton Keynes.
(8)   a. The wall was hit by the car.
       b. ?The wall absorbed the motion energy of the car.
       c. *The wall received the car.

The questionable status of (7) derives from fact that London is both larger and more familiar than Milton Keynes, and therefore more suitable as a reference point.[4] Examples (3) and (8) show that it is impossible to preserve propositional content while reversing Figure and Ground: (8a) omits the description of the actual process of the car hitting the wall and the vehemence of the process encoded in the verb *crash*; both (8b) and (8c) are odd, to say the least, and focus on the state resulting from the crash rather than on the process itself. With regard to (5) and (6), then, (5) is felt to be much more "natural" in depicting the scene than (6), which is stylistically formal. So even here there seem to be tendencies for marked and unmarked ways of describing scenes.

These examples indicate that the range of options provided by English for Figure/Ground alignment is fairly limited. The basis for this limitation is arguably cognitive and resides in the way people perceive and conceive events. Apparently, most real-world situations are inherently predisposed toward one specific kind of perception and, as a consequence, are strongly suggestive of one kind of Figure/Ground alignment. This is partly due to the fact that some entities, namely, ontologically salient ones (see section 2 above), qualify as better Figure entities than others. It must be added, however, that the properties of prototypical Figure entities in relational configurations are not necessarily the same as those that qualify for early entrenchment as concepts. The cognitive basis for lexical entrenchment is not identical with the one for salience in grammatical structures. The concept 'London', for example, is clearly more deeply entrenched in most people's minds than the concept 'Milton Keynes', and yet it is the latter that is the more natural Figure at least when the two are connected by the preposition *near* as in example (4).

Table 5.1. Typical characteristics of Figure and Ground (based on Talmy 2000: 315)

Figure	*Ground*
Properties inherent in the entities	
(a) more movable	more permanently located
(b) smaller	larger
(c) geometrically simpler	geometrically more complex
Properties related to the perception to the entities vis-à-vis each other	
(d) less immediately perceivable	more immediately perceivable
(e) more salient, once perceived	more backgrounded, once Figure is perceived
(f) more dependent	more independent
Properties related to the activation status of the concepts	
(g) more recently on the scene/in current awareness	more familiar
(h) of greater concern/relevance	of lesser concern/relevance

What, then, are the typical characteristics of prototypical Figure and Ground entities? A list of such characteristics has been put forward by Talmy (2000: 315–16; see also Talmy 1978). Table 5.1 is based on his list.

These properties explain the questionable status of the Figure/Ground reversals in (7) and (8). The fact that properties (b), (c), (d), and (g) are flouted accounts for the oddness of example (7), while property (a) accounts for the difficulties in reversing Figure and Ground in (3). Table 5.1 shows, furthermore, that the characteristics of Figure and Ground are not absolute but relative in nature, and that not all of them pertain to the entities themselves or to how people tend to perceive them.

Another caveat is in order here: the principles of Figure/Ground alignment apply to cases of *unmarked coding* (Langacker 1991: 298). The ontological properties (a)–(c) and the perceptual properties (d)–(f) can easily be overruled by other cognitive factors related to information processing and previous discourse or world knowledge. For instance, the question whether example (6) is indeed the marked construction and (5) the unmarked one largely hinges upon the previous context. If it is the red jar that is already in the focus of attention, then (6) is clearly the unmarked choice. A further illustration is given in (9):

(9)   A: Where is the station?
        B: The station is near my car.

While B's answer clearly clashes with properties (a)–(f), it could still be used appropriately in a situation where A and B were together when they parked the car and, possibly after some time spent wandering through the city, speaker A has to catch a train and needs to know where the station is. In this case, it would not be entirely unnatural of B to choose the car as a reference point, which means that property (g) can thus take precedence over properties (a)–(f).

6.3. Figure/Ground Alignment in Simple Clause Patterns

In the examples discussed in the previous section, it was always the case that the Figure in the relational configuration coincided with the subject constituent in the clause. As Figure entities function as anchor points of relations and subjects are known to function as starting points for clauses, this syntactic arrangement seems natural enough. It is thus hardly surprising that the idea of Figure/Ground alignment and the underlying principle of the deployment of salience are also applied to simple clause patterns.

In cases of unmarked coding, subjects are regarded as Figure entities in the relational configurations encoded by simple clauses. To refer to the subject function in clauses, various terms have been used, such as *primary figure* (Langacker 1991: 323), *relational trajector* or *figure* (Langacker 1990), and *syntactic figure* (Ungerer and Schmid 1996: 173). An additional complement to the basic clause pattern, such as direct object or subject complement, makes up the ground in the relation expressed by the verb and is referred to by terms such as *secondary figure* (Langacker 1991: 323) or *syntactic ground* (Ungerer and Schmid 1996: 173). Subject and objects are seen as *focal participants* (Langacker 1991: 301), which are accorded the highest level of prominence in the clause. When there are two obligatory complements in addition to the subject, two analyses are possible, that is, to postulate several layers of Figure/Ground pairings or a tripartite Figure-Ground-background arrangement (see section 6.1).

Since salience is at issue in this chapter, the main question in this context concerns once more the principles that guide speakers in mapping the participants of an event onto clause constituents representing different degrees of salience. "To characterize subjects in terms of cognitive salience is largely vacuous unless we can say more precisely what *kind* of salience is supposedly involved" (Langacker 1991: 306). Taking recourse to work by Givón (1984), Langacker claims that this mapping is determined by a factor called *topicality* (1991: 306). This concept can be broken down into several parameters, one of which is of course Figure/Ground alignment. This means that the mapping of participants is partly determined by the properties listed in table 5.1. Participants with good Figure-properties are more likely to occupy the subject position, while participants with good Ground-properties more likely to be allocated the object function. Quite obviously, it is the very fact that Figure/Ground alignment codetermines subject and object mapping that motivates terms such as *primary* or *syntactic figure* for the traditional notion of subject.

A second topicality factor is an entity's semantic role in a given event. This idea can be traced back to Fillmore's (1968) Case Grammar and his suggestion that there is a case hierarchy determining the mapping of deep cases to surface constituents. According to Fillmore, the case hierarchy is *Agent > Instrument > Patient*. This means that if the setup of an event includes an Agent as a participant, it will be the unmarked choice for the subject constituent. If an Instrument (rather than an

Agent) is included, this will turn out to be the subject, and so on. The relation between case hierarchy and salience is quite apparent. In fact, in later work, Fillmore accounts for the case hierarchy by introducing what he calls a "saliency hierarchy" (1977: 78): Agents, who are the willful instigators of changes in the environment and constitute the starting points of energy with regard to the action chains encoded by clauses (see Langacker 1991: 301), clearly play the most salient parts in dynamic events. That they are encoded as the most prominent clause constituent in unmarked cases is a natural consequence from a cognitive point of view. Patients, on the other hand, tend to be less salient and be mapped onto less prominent clause constituents as a consequence.[5]

Semantic roles play an important part in cognitive linguistic approaches to syntax, because they seem to capture highly fundamental aspects of how humans perceive and understand the external world. Indeed, Fillmore had already ventured the claim that deep cases could be sets "of universal, presumably innate, concepts, which identify certain types of judgements human beings are capable of making about the events that are going on around them" (1968: 24). Langacker introduces the term *role archetypes* for notions like Agent, Patient, Instrument, Experiencer, and Mover "in order to call attention to their primal status and nonlinguistic origin" (1991: 285). He considers these roles "so basic and experientially ubiquitous that their manifestation in language is for all intents and purposes inevitable." The fundamental nature of role archetypes also lends itself to an explanation in terms of entrenchment: obviously, they are firmly entrenched in individual and collective memory. However, role archetypes are not individual concepts comparable to those encodable by means of single words, but are deeply entrenched conceptual distinctions that assist us in making sense of our environment and encoding our experience (see Deane 1992: 194–95).

This brings us to the third topicality factor affecting the mapping of entities on clause constituents, namely, the position of the entities on the scale of ontological salience or *empathy* (Langacker 1991: 306). While role archetypes are roles of entities vis-à-vis other entities in events, ontological salience captures properties that are inherent in the entities themselves (though they must, of course, be perceived or construed by the speaker). Scales of ontological salience or empathy have their ultimate source in feature hierarchies suggested by Silverstein (1976, 1981) to explain some universal aspects of case-marking and ergativity. The common idea is that entities can be ranked according to their potential for attracting a person's interest and empathy. The hierarchy suggested by Langacker (1991: 307) is given in (10):

(10)   *speaker > hearer > human > animal > physical object > abstract entity*

Since speakers are of most immediate concern to themselves, they make up the starting point of this hierarchy, followed by hearers, persons outside the immediate speech event, and so on. Many grammatical phenomena seem to point to a ranking of entities of this type that is deeply entrenched in our cognitive system; this has led authors such as Deane (1992: 194–205) to use the term *entrenchment hierarchies* for rankings derived from Silverstein's hierarchy.

Finally, the salience of participants is presumably influenced by the *definiteness* of the experience to be encoded and the corresponding linguistic expressions (Langacker 1991: 307–8). A likely hierarchy based on the brief suggestions by Langacker is given in (11), but systematic research into the contribution of definiteness to salience is yet to be carried out. In particular, the role of such contrasts as concrete vs. abstract, singular vs. plural, individual vs. collective, count vs. mass, bounded vs. unbounded, and a few others has to be clarified.[6]

(11)   *definite (proper name) > definite (definite description) > specific indefinite > non-specific indefinite*

The parameterization of the relative salience of clause constituents in terms of Figure/Ground alignment, semantic role, entrenchment/empathy hierarchy, and definiteness allows for a description of prototypical manifestations of the focal clause constituents. Thus, prototypical subjects are Figure entities in the profiled relation, Agents, human, and definite; prototypical direct objects are Grounds in the profiled relation, Patients, physical objects, and specific indefinite (Langacker 1991: 308, 323). It must be added, however, that the status of these factors may differ considerably. While the correspondences Figure-subject and Ground-object are highly stable across clause and discourse types, it remains open which conception of prototypicality is involved in the three other factors. For example, it does not seem reasonable to regard Agents as prototypical subjects in expository texts on abstract topics, where persons do not tend to feature prominently at all. It appears, then, that the prototypes outlined above can only be applied to an idealized type of discourse that is of maximum conceptual simplicity. They are part of some kind of basic, uncorrupted child-like language that is limited to the description of concrete events and is tacitly seen as providing the cognitive foundation for more elaborate discourse genres and text types.

6.4. Salience in Reference-Point Constructions

One further area of syntax where salience effects have been described can only be mentioned in passing: the encoding of possessive relations. Here, salience is seen as affecting the choice of *reference points* (in the Cognitive Grammar sense of the term; see note 4). According to Langacker, the basic cognitive principles at work here include that "a whole is more salient than its parts; a physical object is more salient than an abstract entity; and a person has maximal cognitive salience" (1991: 171). Other principles derived from the entrenchment and empathy hierarchy described in the previous section can easily be added; for example, a person is more salient than an animal or an object, an animal is more salient than an object, and so on. Principles of this kind account for the unacceptability or markedness of the (b)-versions in examples (12)–(15):

(12)   a. the girl's neck
        b. *the neck's girl

(13)   a. the cat's mat
     b. *the mat's cat
(14)   a. the boy's bicycle
     b. *the bicycle's boy
(15)   a. the man's problem
     b. *the problem's man

A more comprehensive view of reference-point constructions is given in Langacker (1993) and in Taylor (2000).

7. CONCLUSION

This chapter has introduced the cognitive phenomena *entrenchment* and *salience* and illustrated a number of their linguistic manifestations. While it may be unlikely that entrenchment and salience are the only cognitive processes governing the linguistic observations discussed here, they would still appear to provide a starting point for a plausible and psychologically realistic explanation of many of these observations. In the future, it will be important to pursue the investigation of entrenchment and salience phenomena from both the linguistic and the psychological end. Starting out from language, further linguistic rules and regularities should be made amenable to explanations in terms of entrenchment and salience; in particular, effects of the exigencies of discourse processing on syntactic and lexical choices should be investigated. A step forward in this direction has been made by Deane (1992), but more research is clearly needed. In particular, the relation between cognitive linguistic accounts of salience phenomena and theories of information processing, such as Accessibility Theory (Ariel 1990, 2001) or the Givenness Hierarchy (Gundel, Hedberg, and Zacharski 1993), needs further clarification. Some pioneering work in this area has been done by van Hoek (1997). And starting out from the mind, more research should go into what determines the wiring-in of conceptual and linguistic information into the cognitive system and the activation of concepts from it.

NOTES

1. Two complementary types of blocking are involved here, synonymic and homonymic blocking: *stealer* is blocked by an entrenched linguistic form encoding the concept 'person who steals', while *Bauer* is blocked because this form is already entrenched as a means of encoding a different concept (see Schmid 2005: 116–17). It should also be mentioned that both forms can, of course, occur as ad-hoc formations, which, by definition, are nonentrenched uses of words.

2. The notion of *generative entrenchment* should be mentioned in this context, which has been used in evolutionary biology and ethnology as a refinement of the controversial notion of innateness (Wimsatt 1986), which allows for the possibility of treating environmental information as part of innate concepts. Interestingly, like *entrenchment* in Cognitive Linguistics, *generative entrenchment* is considered to be a matter of degree (189). A further parallel is that *generatively entrenched* conceptual features are considered to be basic for the acquisition of later features (198). See Pienemann (1998) and Schwartz (1998) for later work on *generative entrenchment* from the field of language acquisition.

3. For a more detailed description of the problems involved in using frequency as a criterion, see Geeraerts, Grondelaers, and Bakema (1994: 138–43).

4. The term *reference point* is used here in its everyday meaning; it must be noted that the term is part of the special terminological system introduced by Langacker in his Cognitive Grammar framework. It will be used in the latter sense in section 6.4. below (see also, e.g., Langacker 1991: 170–72; 1993; this volume, chapter 17).

5. Fillmore (1977: 76–79) introduces four saliency conditions defining the saliency hierarchy, which have an obvious affinity to the topicality factors proposed by Givón and Langacker: humanness, change of location, definiteness, and totality.

6. It should be added that there is, of course, a difference between the notions of *subject* and *topic*, which is not discussed here for reasons of space. What should be mentioned, however, is Deane's assumption that the prominence of subjects is due to spreading activation rather than selective attention-focusing (see section 2 above). This claim is interesting and useful because it resolves an irritating discrepancy between Langacker's syntax-oriented view, which contributes maximum salience to the subject, and discourse-oriented views of attention-distribution in sentences, which have traditionally seen the focus of attention in the rhematic, that is, the later, parts of sentences (see, e.g., Halliday 1994: 37–38). The two views can be reconciled by claiming that subjects/topics/themes are salient in that they tend to be already activated, while complements/comments/rhemes are salient because they introduce new information that requires a selective focus of attention.

REFERENCES

Aitchison, Jean. 2003. *Words in the mind: An introduction to the mental lexicon.* 3rd ed. Oxford : Basil Blackwell.

Anderson, John R. 1983. *The architecture of cognition.* Cambridge, MA: Harvard University Press.

Ariel, Mira. 1990. *Accessing noun-phrase antecedents.* London: Routledge.

Ariel, Mira. 2001. Accessibility theory: An overview. In Ted Sanders, Joost Schilperoord, and Wilbert Spooren, eds., *Text representation: Linguistic and psycholinguistic aspects* 29–87. Amsterdam: John Benjamins.

Berlin, Brent. 1978. Ethnobiological classification. In Eleanor Rosch and Barbara B. Lloyd, eds., *Cognition and categorization* 9–26. Hillsdale, NJ: Lawrence Erlbaum.

Berlin, Brent, Dennis E. Breedlove, and Peter H. Raven. 1973. General principles of classification and nomenclature in folk biology. *American Anthropologist* 75: 214–42.

Berlin, Brent, Dennis E. Breedlove, and Peter H. Raven. 1974. *Principles of Tzeltal plant classification.* New York: Academic Press.

Berlin, Brent, and Paul Kay. 1969. *Basic color terms: Their universality and evolution.* Berkeley: University of California Press.

Biber, Douglas, Stig Johannson, Geoffrey Leech, Susan Conrad, and Edward Finegan. 1999. *Longman grammar of spoken and written English.* Harlow, UK: Pearson Educated.

Brown, Roger. 1958. How shall a thing be called? *Psychological Review* 65: 14–21.

Brown, Roger. 1965. *Social psychology.* New York: Free Press.

Brugman, Claudia. 1981. Story of *Over.* MA thesis, University of California at Berkeley. (Published as *The story of Over: Polysemy, semantics, and the structure of the lexicon.* New York: Garland, 1988)

Bybee, Joan L. 2001. *Phonology and language use.* Cambridge: Cambridge University Press.

Collins, Allan M., and Elizabeth Loftus. 1975. A spreading-activation theory of semantic processing. *Psychological Review* 82: 407–28.

Collins, Allan M., and M. Ross Quillian. 1969. Retrieval time from semantic memory. *Journal of Verbal Learning and Verbal Behavior* 8: 240–47.

Cruse, D. Alan. 1977. The pragmatics of lexical specificity. *Journal of Linguistics* 13: 153–64.

Deane, Paul D. 1992. *Grammar in mind and brain: Explorations in cognitive syntax.* Berlin: Mouton de Gruyter.

Downing, Pamela. 1977. On 'basic levels' and the categorization of objects in English discourse. *Berkeley Linguistics Society* 3: 475–87.

Fillmore, Charles J. 1968. The case for case. In Emon Bach and Robert T. Harms, eds., *Universals in linguistic theory* 1–88. London: Holt, Rinehart & Winston.

Fillmore, Charles J. 1977. The case for case reopened. In Peter Cole and Jerrold M. Sadock, eds., *Syntax and semantics.* Vol. 8, *Grammatical relations* 59–81. New York: Academic Press.

Geeraerts, Dirk. 2000. Salience phenomena in the lexicon: A typology. In Liliane Albertazzi, ed., *Meaning and cognition* 125–36. Amsterdam: John Benjamins.

Geeraerts, Dirk, Stefan Grondelaers, and Peter Bakema. 1994. *The structure of lexical variation: Meaning, naming, and context.* Berlin: Mouton de Gruyter.

Givón, Talmy. 1984. *Syntax: A functional-typological introduction.* Vol. 1. Amsterdam: John Benjamins.

Gries, Stefan Th. 2003. *Multifactorial analysis in corpus linguistics: A study of particle placement.* London: Continuum Press.

Grondelaers, Stefan. 2000. De distributie van niet-anaforisch *er* buiten de eerste zinsplaats: Sociolexicologische, functionele en psycholinguïstische aspecten van *er*'s status als presentatief signal [The distribution of non-anaphoric *er* in non-sentence-initial position: Sociolexcicological, functional, and psychological aspects of the status of *er* as a presentative marker]. PhD dissertation, University of Leuven, Belgium.

Grondelaers, Stefan, Marc Brysbaert, Dirk Speelman, and Dirk Geeraerts. 2002. *Er als* accessibility marker: On- en offline evidentie voor een procedurele interpretatie van presentatieve zinnen [*Er* as an accessibility marker: On- and offline evidence for a procedural interpretation of presentative sentences]. *Gramma/TTT* 9: 1–22.

Gundel, Jeannette K., Nancy Hedberg, and Ron Zacharski. 1993. Cognitive status and the form of referring expressions in discourse. *Language* 69: 274–307.

Halliday, Michael A. K. 1994. *An introduction to functional grammar.* 2nd ed. London: Edward Arnold. (3rd ed., 2004)

Kay, Paul, and Chad K. McDaniel. 1978. The linguistic significance of the meanings of basic color terms. *Language* 54: 610–46.

Lakoff, George. 1987. *Women, fire, and dangerous things: What categories reveal about the mind*. Chicago: University of Chicago Press.

Langacker, Ronald W. 1987. *Foundations of cognitive grammar*. Vol. 1, *Theoretical prerequisites*. Stanford, CA: Stanford University Press.

Langacker, Ronald W. 1990. Settings, participants, and grammatical relations. In Savas L. Tsohatzidis, ed., *Meanings and prototypes: Studies on linguistic categorization* 213–38. Oxford: Routledge.

Langacker, Ronald W. 1991. *Foundations of cognitive grammar*. Vol. 2, *Descriptive application*. Stanford, CA: Stanford University Press.

Langacker, Ronald W. 1993. Reference-point constructions. *Cognitive Linguistics* 4: 1–38.

Levelt, Willem J.M. 1989. *Speaking: From intention to articulation*. Cambridge, MA: MIT Press.

Lindner, Susan. 1981. A lexico-semantic analysis of English verb-particle constructions with OUT and UP. PhD dissertation, University of California at San Diego. (Published as A lexico-semantic analysis of English verb-particle constructions, LAUT Paper, no. 101. Trier, Germany: Linguistic Agency of the University of Trier, 1983)

Lipka, Leonhard. 1980. Methodology and representation in the study of lexical fields. In Dieter Kastovsky, ed., *Perspektiven der lexikalischen Semantik: Beiträge zum Wuppertaler Semantikkolloquium vom 2.–3.12.1977* 93–114, Bonn: Bouvier.

Pienemann, Manfred. 1998. Developmental dynamics in L1 and L2 acquisition: Processability theory and generative entrenchment. *Bilingualism: Language and Cognition* 1: 1–20.

Rifkin, Anthony. 1985. Evidence for a basic level in event taxonomies. *Memory & Cognition* 13: 538–56.

Rosch, Eleanor. 1977. Human categorization. In Neil Warren, ed., *Studies in cross-cultural psychology* 1: 1–49. London: Academic Press.

Rosch, Eleanor, Caroline B. Mervis, Wayne D. Gray, David M. Johnson, and Penny Boyes-Braem. 1976. Basic objects in natural categories. *Cognitive Psychology* 8: 382–439.

Schmid, Hans-Jörg. 1996a. Basic level categories as basic cognitive and linguistic building blocks. In Edda Weigand and Franz Hundsnurscher, eds., *Lexical structures and language use* 1: 285–95. Tübingen: Max Niemeyer.

Schmid, Hans-Jörg. 1996b. Review of Geeraerts, Grondelaers, and Bakema 1994. *Lexicology* 2: 78–84.

Schmid, Hans-Jörg. 2000. *English abstract nouns as conceptual shell. From corpus to cognition*. Berlin: Mouton de Gruyter.

Schmid, Hans-Jörg. 2005. *Englische Morphologie und Wortbildung: Eine Einführung*. Berlin: Erich Schmidt.

Schwartz, Bonnie. 1998. On the 'wrong-headedness' of generative entrenchment. *Bilingualism: Language and Cognition* 1: 34–35.

Silverstein, Michael. 1976. Hierarchy of features and ergativity. In Robert M. W. Dixon, ed., *Grammatical categories in Australian languages* 112–71. Canberra: Australian Institute of Aboriginal Studies.

Silverstein, Michael. 1981. Case marking and the nature of language. *Australian Journal of Linguistics* 1: 227–44.

Talmy, Leonard. 1978. Figure and ground in complex sentences. In Joseph Greenberg, ed., *Universals of human language*, vol. 4, *Syntax* 625–49. Stanford, CA: Stanford University Press.

Talmy, Leonard. 2000. *Toward a cognitive semantics*. Vol. 1, *Concept structuring systems*. Cambridge, MA: MIT Press.

Taylor, John R. 1995. *Linguistic categorization: Prototypes in linguistic theory*. 2nd ed. Oxford: Clarendon Press. (3rd ed., 2003)

Taylor, John R. 2000. *Possessives in English: An exploration in cognitive grammar*. Oxford: Oxford University Press.

Ungerer, Friedrich, and Hans-Jörg Schmid. 1996. *An introduction to cognitive linguistics*. London: Longman.

Ungerer, Friedrich, and Hans-Jörg Schmid. 1998. Englische Komposita und Kategorisierung. *Rostocker Beiträge zur Sprachwissenschaft* 5: 77–98.

van Hoek, Karen. 1997. *Anaphora and conceptual structure*. Chicago: University of Chicago Press.

Verschueren, Jef. 1985. *What people say they do with words: Prolegomena to an empirical-conceptual approach to linguistic action*. Norwood, NJ: Ablex.

Wierzbicka, Anna. 1990. The meaning of color terms: Semantics, culture, and cognition. *Cognitive Linguistics* 1: 99–150.

Wimsatt, William C. 1986. Constraints, generative entrenchment, and the innate-acquired distinction. In William Bechtel, ed., *Integrating scientific disciplines* 185–208. Dordrecht, Netherlands: Martinus Nijhoff.

CHAPTER 6

POLYSEMY, PROTOTYPES, AND RADIAL CATEGORIES

BARBARA LEWANDOWSKA-TOMASZCZYK

1. INTRODUCTION

One of the most fundamental phenomena observed in language is the existence of a diversity of related meanings expressed by the same word form. Relatedness of meanings is not a new discovery in linguistics. That some words have more than one meaning and that these meanings are related was first observed in ancient Greece (see Nerlich and Clarke 1997). The term "polysemy" was first introduced in nineteenth-century semantics by Bréal (1897) as part of his study on meaning change—a field of study which provided a major impetus for the study of semantics (see Nerlich and Clarke, this volume, chapter 22). In the twentieth century, the interest in polysemy was uneven. In the first half of the century, structuralism introduced a shift from diachronic semantics to a synchronic semantic framework with psychological and sociological groundings but did not study polysemy intensively. In the second half of the century, Transformational Generative Grammar practically denied the existence of polysemy on theoretical grounds (Postal 1969),[1] providing instead lists of identical (homonymic) word forms with their partly overlapping feature matrices. By contrast, one of the major distinguishing features of Cognitive Linguistics as it emerged in the 1980s is precisely the renewed interest it carries in the analysis of meaning. As stated by Wierzbicka (1985: 11), "It goes without saying that polysemy must never be postulated lightly, and that it has always to be justified on language-internal grounds; but to reject polysemy in a dogmatic and a priori fashion is just as foolish as to postulate it without justification." In this respect, Cognitive Linguistics tries to do justice to earlier opinions like that of Stephen Ullmann (whose 1951 book is an excellent overview of the development of linguistic semantics from its nineteenth-century beginnings to the middle of the twentieth century), who stated that polysemy is "the pivot of semantic analysis" (1951: 117).

The specific perspective taken by Cognitive Linguistics in the study of polysemy is to analyze polysemy as a form of categorization. In the course of this chapter, I will present four features that are crucial for the cognitive linguistic approach and its relation to polysemy: the flexibility of meaning, the prototype-theoretical model of semantic structure, the radial set model, and the schematic network model.[2] I will conclude by presenting major open questions for Cognitive Linguistics as well as prospects and areas of possible future research on these matters.

Given the wide range of the material to be considered, it would be impossible to exhaust the topic at hand (polysemy, radial sets, and schematic networks), but an attempt will be made to present some main features of cognitive linguistic theorizing with reference to these semantic issues. Cognitive Linguistics, in fact, has been prolific in studying semantic questions. Even though classical polysemy refers first of all to lexis, Cognitive linguistic tools make it possible to observe polysemic effects in phonology, morphology, and syntax (e.g., Taylor 1989). Polysemic words abound in the language used in early childhood in language development (see Tomasello 1992) and in language games.[3] The phenomenon of polysemy also accounts for a great number of cases of historical change in language by explaining synchronic variation as resulting from diachronic change. Numerous scholars have employed the Cognitive Linguistics paradigm (and its approach to polysemy) to show the direction of lexical change in language (see, e.g., Sweetser 1990; Lewandowska-Tomaszczyk 1992; Cuyckens 1995, 1999; Geeraerts 1997; Blank and Koch 1999; Bybee 2000; Nerlich and Clarke 2003).[4] Newman (1996: 270), in his study of *give* verbs across languages, uses the examples of the semantics of *give* in English to postulate the existence of connections between, or interrelatedness of, the numerous polysemic chains evident in individual languages. Such studies encompass both the diachronic and synchronic dimensions. Research on polysemy and prototypes in Cognitive Linguistics is extensive.[5] Cognitive Linguistics opens a whole new vista on these issues, whereby it is assumed that there exist no clear boundaries between linguistic and encyclopedic meanings and that boundaries between categories are blurred. How exactly, then, does Cognitive Linguistics proceed?

2. POLYSEMY TESTS AND THE FLEXIBILITY OF MEANING

The descriptive models of polysemy that Cognitive Linguistics focuses on (prototypicality, radial sets, schematic networks) share a concern for the flexibility of meaning. As a first step, we may have a look at existing polysemy tests and the way they reveal the flexibility of meaning. A number of tests, thoroughly discussed in Geeraerts (1993), Tuggy (1993), and Dunbar (2001) and conveniently summarized in Ravin and Leacock (2000), have been proposed in the logical, philosophical, and linguistic literature to distinguish polysemy from vagueness. An examination of these tests shows that they do not necessarily detect the same meaning phenomena: what has to be considered a different meaning is not a self-evident matter.

2.1. The Logical Test

The diagnostic polysemy test proposed by Quine (1960) states that *a word is polysemic if an assertion involving that word can be both true and false of the same referent.* Quine's test shows that vague meanings (i.e., meanings that are unmarked for a certain category distinction) do not pass the logical test. If the word *student* were polysemic between a reading 'male student' and 'female student', then it would be possible, according to the test, to truthfully utter sentence (1); that is, for any given student, only one of the readings would be applicable. The awkwardness of (1) shows, however, that *student* is vague or unmarked rather than polysemic with regard to the distinction between 'male student' and 'female student'.

(1)   I gave the book to a student but not to a student.

Analyzing the status of the form *port*, on the other hand, Geeraerts (1993: 229) shows that it passes the test, so it is polysemic between the two readings 'harbor' and 'certain type of fortified wine':

(2)   Sandeman is a port (in a bottle) but not a port (with ships).

As (2) shows, Quine's test does not seem to discriminate between polysemy and homonymy, given that the two readings of *port* are homonymous. A similar example with the word *light* provided by Quine (1960: 129) also passes the polysemy test:

(3)   The feather is light (not heavy) but not light (dark).

Quine (1960: 129) concludes that "an ambiguous term such as *light* may be at once clearly true of various objects (such as dark feathers) and clearly false of them." In this case, the ambiguity involves readings that are etymologically unrelated; the two readings are homonyms rather than polysemes. In fact, the distinction between *polysemy* and *homonymy* is traditionally made by invoking historical criteria. Identical forms with historically related meanings are polysemic items and are distinguished from those words, usually referred to as *homonyms*, whose forms happen to be identical for historical reasons but whose meanings are etymologically unrelated.

In some cases, originally homonymic forms may be reanalyzed as being conceptually related: a conceptual connection may be synchronically established between word meanings that are not historically related. Langacker (1987: 387) gives the following example:

> Sometimes, as with the central senses of *tree*, the similarities are cognitively salient and would likely be noticed even in the absence of common symbolization. In other instances the resemblance is quite tenuous. Many speakers treat the meaning of *ear* implied by *ear of corn* as an extension from the prototypical value of *ear* as a body-part term; it is doubtful that the concepts would ever be compared were it not for their identical symbolization. The cognitive distance and entrenchment of such categorizing relationships are obviously variable. Homonymy represents a limiting case, where the comparison of two identically symbolized concepts reveals no similarity that is salient or plausible enough to establish a categorization achieving unit status. For a speaker who fails to notice any special resemblance among the meanings of *bill* (proper name; request for payment; protrusion on a bird, cap, or platypus), the semantic units do not unite to form a network and are connected only via their common symbolic correspondent.

An analysis of the semantic reanalysis processes that take place in such cases may be found in Geeraerts (1997: 130–50). Taylor (1989) and Blank (2003) present examples of the converse case, when words that are historically related come to be perceived as unrelated by contemporary users of the language. Taylor (1989) mentions English *a pupil at school* and *the pupil of the eye*; Blank (2003: 276) mentions French *voler* 'to fly' and *voler* 'to steal' and German *Schloss* 'lock' and 'castle'. What can be observed here then is the diachronic flexibility of meaning, specifically regarding the borderline between polysemy and homonymy: meanings that are historically unrelated may come to be perceived as related, and, conversely, existing perceptions of semantic relatedness may wither.

2.2. The Linguistic Ambiguity Test

A second diagnostic test for polysemy was originally formulated by Zwicky and Sadock (1975) and later rephrased by Cruse (1986). This test is of a linguistic nature. One version of the test says that *when polysemic words are used in one sentence, they result in a zeugmatic combination*, as in the example of the word *expire*:

(4)   ?Arthur and his driving license expired last Thursday.

Discussing the word *dissertation*, Cruse showed that the incompatibility of readings (which would establish polysemy) is heavily context-bound and is thus a question of degree rather than an all-or-nothing matter:

(5)   ?Judy's dissertation is thought provoking and yellowed with age.
(6)   Judy's dissertation is still thought provoking although yellowed with age.

According to (5), the material and the abstract reading of *dissertation* (referring either to a book as a concrete volume or to a body of knowledge as an intellectual achievement) appear to be polysemicly incompatible. The context presented in (6), however, suggests that the two interpretations do not constitute different senses.

Another version of the linguistic test involves the use of the anaphoric *so do* construction as in:

(7)   I was busy dressing, and so were they.

The use of a polysemic item in the two clauses (e.g., *dressing* in the sense of putting on a dress, etc., in the first clause, and *dressing* in the sense of, say, military troops coming to the proper alignment, in the *so do* part) renders a zeugmatic combination. However, when the sense of *dressing* in both of the clauses is simply *vague* between putting on different kinds of clothes, the sentence is acceptable.

2.3. The Definitional Test

Finally, there is the most classical, *definitional* test, whose origin can be traced back to Aristotle's *Metaphysics*. A word is considered polysemic *if more than a single definition is needed to account for its meaning*. In semantic field theories and their extensions involving feature matrices (Katz and Fodor 1963), this principle was interpreted in terms of sets of necessary and sufficient conditions for category membership. In other words, if no single set of necessary and sufficient conditions suffices to account for the meaning of a word, the word is considered polysemic. Basic criticism, referred to as *Plato's Problem* by Laurence and Margolis (1999: 14), which has been leveled against the Classical Theory of concepts, states that for most concepts definitions are difficult to give.

We see, to conclude, that none of the three basic tests as such is without problems. On top of the problems that issue from the contextual flexibility of meaning, we may note that the three tests do not necessarily yield the same results. One of the examples mentioned by Geeraerts (1993) involves autohyponymous words.[6] In such words, a general sense includes a more specific one, such as *egg* 'reproductive body from various animals', 'egg from a bird, with a yellow yolk, surrounded by a hard shell', and so on (see Lehrer 2003: 229) or *dog* 'member of the species Canis familiaris' (general reading) and 'male member of the species Canis familiaris' (restricted reading). The distinction between the two readings of *dog* can be established by means of the logical test, given that a sentence like *Mirza is a dog but not a dog* is fully acceptable when Mirza is female. The definitional test, however, cannot establish a distinction between both readings, because the more restricted reference is always included in the more encompassing definition. The fact that there is no complete correspondence between polysemy tests, then, suggests that meaning is a flexible phenomenon and that the boundaries between homonymy, polysemy, and vagueness are not rigid.

3. PROTOTYPE THEORY

The suggestion that categorial meaning is flexible receives an initial expression in prototype theory. (The term "initial expression" is used here because we will see later on that a further extension toward a schematic network model of semantic structure is necessary.) The starting point of the prototypical conception of categorial structure is summarized in the following statement:

> When describing categories analytically, most traditions of thought have treated category membership as a digital, all-or-none phenomenon. That is, much work in philosophy, psychology, linguistics, and anthropology assumes that categories are logical bounded entities, membership in which is defined by an item's possession of a simple set of criterial features, in which all instances possessing the criterial attributes have a full and equal degree of membership. In contrast, it has recently been argued . . . that some natural categories are analog and must be represented logically in a manner which reflects their analog structure. (Rosch and Mervis 1975: 573–74)

The traditional conception rejected in this statement is sometimes referred to as the Classical Theory of concepts, which has had a long history in philosophy dating back to antiquity (e.g., Aristotle 1984; Plato 1981; Locke [1697] 1960; Carnap 1978). Its main tenet is that concepts have definitional structure in the sense that they encode necessary and sufficient conditions for their application.[7] For example, the concept 'bachelor' can be interpreted in terms of the Classical Theory as a complex mental representation that is composed of a set of features (semantic markers) such as MALE, ADULT, and NOT MARRIED (see Katz and Fodor 1963). In this section, I will discuss the way in which Cognitive Linguistics developed a prototype-based conception of semantic structure that goes against the Classical Theory. Two basic steps need to be taken: the identification of various prototype effects and the development of a radial set model of semantic structure as a generic model underlying the prototype effects—and which at the same time applies to polysemic sets of meanings. The third part of this section presents a number of additional issues concerning prototypicality and radial sets.

3.1. Prototype Effects

In contrast with the so-called Classical Theory, features that are frequently mentioned as typical of a prototype-theoretical conception include the following (first proposed by Geeraerts 1989):

a. Prototypical categories exhibit degrees of typicality; not every member is equally representative for a category.
b. Prototypical categories are blurred at the edges.
c. Prototypical categories cannot be defined by means of a single set of criterial (necessary and sufficient) attributes.
d. Prototypical categories exhibit a family resemblance structure, or more generally, their semantic structure takes the form of a radial set of clustered and overlapping readings.

Let us have a closer look at these four characteristics. Feature (a) involves the recognition that category membership may be graded: some members of a category are better, more typical members of the category than others. One of the first contributions pointing to this was Berlin and Kay's (1969) discovery of *focal colors*, that is, the best examples of basic colors, which showed that these categories are not uniform and contain central and peripheral members. Berlin and Kay's studies were found to match Eleanor Rosch's experiments (Heider 1971, 1972), where she showed that such central colors were psychologically real even for the speakers of the languages which do not name such colors at all. They function as special *cognitive reference points* and "best examples" or *prototypes*, more representative of the category than other members. These asymmetries between the prototypical and peripheral category members were experimentally confirmed to be present in direct goodness-of-examples rating, true-false reaction times, production of examples, asymmetries in similarity ratings, and generalization. The discoveries concerning graded category membership were first modeled by Zadeh (1965) in a form of set theory known as *fuzzy set theory*, in which additional values between 0 and 1 are allowed to capture category membership gradation.

When the attention is shifted from the center of a conceptual category to the periphery, it appears that membership gradience may involve two different situations. Some categories like BIRD have rigid boundaries, in the sense that both sparrows and penguins are clearly within the category boundaries, even though the former are better exemplars of the category than the latter. Some other categories, on the other hand, such as colors or OLD PERSON, do not have rigid boundaries and the graded category membership correlates with uncertainty concerning the borderline of the concept: where exactly does old age begin? This leads to characteristic (b): in some cases, the boundaries of a concept may be vague.

Characteristics (a) and (b) both involve the members (exemplars or subclasses) of a concept: some members are more typical than others, and sometimes membership status may be unclear. Characteristic (c) looks at the definitional structure of the category rather than the membership structure. It involves the absence of classical definitions for a category: if no definition in terms of necessary and sufficient attributes is available for a category, then that category is defined less rigidly than the classical model of definitions predicts. Instead of a single description consisting of individually necessary and jointly sufficient features, the definition takes the form of a cluster of partial descriptions. Suggestions in this direction were first formulated within philosophy by Wittgenstein (1953) and Quine (1953, 1960), then in psychology by Rosch (1973), and others. Wittgenstein showed that a concept such as 'game' could not be adequately defined according to the classical model. Instead, the members of such categories are related by what he called *family resemblance*. Family resemblance involves a *polythetic*, or *similarity classification*, where members of a class share some of the characteristics, none of which, however, is sufficient for class membership. Such cases contrast with what is called in science *monothetic classes*, characterized by sets of discrete, singly necessary and jointly sufficient criteria. Polythetic classification may be schematically represented as a pattern, where, for instance, three categories *A*, *B*, and *C* display different but overlapping sets of properties: *A*: *p*, *q*, *r*; *B*: *r*, *s*, *t*; *C*: *t*, *u*, *v* (see Needham 1972). Members of class *A* share one property with class *B*, which shares one property with class C, even though class *A* and *C* have no common characteristics. No common core can thus be identified for all category members (see, e.g., Fodor 1981 for the analysis of *paint* and Fillmore 1982 for the discussion of *climb*). Another line of criticism concerning the Classical Theory (after Laurence and Margolis 1999) is associated with the problem of analyticity and analytic inferences it was to account for. In his critique of analyticity in "Two Dogmas of Empiricism," Quine (1953) successfully argued that there is no tenable analytic-synthetic distinction that would underlie the Classical Theory.

It will be clear that characteristics (c) and (d) are mutually related: it is precisely the absence of a classical definition as signaled by (c) that leads to a definition in terms of family resemblances, as indicated by (d). If we cannot find a set of features shared by all birds that is sufficient to distinguish birds from non-birds, then our definition of 'bird' will have to take the form of a cluster of overlapping sets of features that each describe classes of birds. In contrast with the example just given, however, there might well be a set of common features (like the fact that all birds are born from eggs), but the set of common features is not sufficient to distinguish birds from other specifies (like reptiles, as far as the reproductive system is involved). Such common features, even though they are jointly not distinctive enough for the category as a whole, will carry more structural weight in the definition of 'bird' than the features that are shared by only a subset of birds. And even among the features that are not common to all birds, some will be more frequent than others: not all birds have wings (think of the kiwi) and not all birds can fly (think of the ostrich and the chicken), but still, having wings or being able to fly are salient features of the category BIRD. We see, in other words, that the elements of a family resemblance definition need not carry equal weight: some features or clusters of features may be more important for the description of the category than others.

3.2. Radial Sets and Polysemy: The Extended Version of Prototype Theory

Characteristic (d) is applied even more broadly in the context of Cognitive Linguistics. Note, as argued in Geeraerts (1987), that the so-called absence of classical definitions as such does not suffice to establish the nonorthodox, prototype-based nature of lexical categories. Even in the classical model, the absence of a single definition in terms of necessary and sufficient attributes is a regular feature of lexical categories; in fact, in those cases where they are polysemic, if a polysemic category is conceived of as one that cannot be adequately described by means of a single definition, then it necessarily fits the description of (c) mentioned above. This means that characteristic (c) is only a nontraditional feature of lexical meaning when it applies to *each* of the polysemic readings of a lexical item. For the polysemic lexical item *as a whole*, characteristic (c) simply coincides with the definitional test of polysemy that was introduced earlier.

But then what about characteristic (d) when we look at a polysemic lexical item as a whole, and not at each of the polysemic readings separately? One of the most fruitful insights of Cognitive Linguistics is the recognition that the definitional structure of a polysemic lexical item is similar to the definitional structure of a single meaning. When we look at the relationship between different meanings of a lexical item, we are likely to encounter the same phenomena that are typical of single meanings. For one thing, there may be demarcation problems: it may not be easy to draw a sharp line between one meaning and the other. (This is in line, of course, with what we said earlier about the relationship between the different polysemy tests.) For another, one meaning may carry more structural weight than others, in the sense that it directly or indirectly lies at the basis of other meanings. Observe, for instance, that *bird* might be used metaphorically to indicate an airplane (as in *A gigantic silver bird approached from the west*). That metaphorical extension from the 'biological species' reading would certainly be less salient than the latter as such. This is true from a logical point of view (to the extent that the metaphorical reading is a semantic extension of the former), from a psychological point of view (to the extent that the metaphorical reading is less likely to be permanently stored in the mental lexicon of the language user), and from a statistical point of view (to the extent that the metaphorical reading is less common than the literal one).

The recognition that the same structural characteristics that apply to single meanings also apply to polysemic sets of meanings is the basis for the *radial set* model of conceptual structure. According to Kleiber (1990), the shift from single meanings to polysemic clusters of meanings introduces the second stage of the development of prototype theory. The first stage, dubbed the *standard version* of prototype theory by Kleiber, involves members of one category and thus represents an *intracategorial* perspective. The second stage (*an extended version*, in Kleiber's parlance) represents cases of *intercategorial polysemy* and involves members of more than one category.

Brugman and Lakoff (1988; see also Lakoff 1987) describe the radial set model in the following terms. Polysemic words consist of a number of radially related categories even though each of the polysemic senses can itself display a complex prototype structure. The central radial category member provides a cognitive model that motivates the noncentral senses. The extended senses clustered around the central category are related by a variety of possible links such as image schema transformations, metaphor, metonymy, or by partial vis-à-vis holistic profiling of distinct segments of the whole sense.

Some subtypes of, for instance, the category MOTHER are (predictable) extensions of the central member of the category (e.g., biological mother or stepmother). Some others, however, develop when the central category does not productively generate a new subcategory, but rather when convention and culture condition the development of an unpredictable category. Such new submembers are considered members of *radial models of categorization*. Lakoff (1987: 83) gives an example of the Trobriands radial extension of the concept 'mother' to cover cases where a biological mother gives her child to an older woman in the community to bring it up or, as in traditional Japanese culture, to the mother's sister. What Lakoff proposes is that "the center, or prototype, of the category is predictable. And while the noncentral members are not predictable from the central member, they are 'motivated' by it, in the sense that they bear family resemblances to it" (65).

The main properties of radial structures have been characterized by Lakoff (1987: 379) as follows:

a. A radially structured category possesses no single representation. Both central and noncentral subcategories have their own representations, and no properties of subcategories can be predicated from the central subcategory. The noncentral categories can be treated as variants of a prototypical (central) model with no one core in common. All subcategories can be seen as bearing family resemblance to one another.

b. The noncentral subcategories are *motivated* by the central member; they are neither predictable nor arbitrary.

c. An experientialist theory of thought and reason employing all kinds of cognitive models (i.e., propositional, metaphorical, metonymic, and image-schematic) is needed to account for the types of links between the central and noncentral category members.

The concept of radial categorization may have interesting theoretical implications for the relationship between language and culture. The Triobrands' *mother*, extended to include non-mothers in the European sense, can be considered a polysemic extension from the perspective of European culture. However, in the Trobriand culture, it could be treated as a full-fledged central category member. Radial structures, as observed by Lakoff (1987), provide one of the strongest arguments against the objectivist treatment of cognition and semantics. Radial categories do not *objectively* exist in the outside reality. Instead, together with the existence of polysemic chains, they provide evidence for a theory of cognitive models that are shaped in accordance with the speakers' perspective and their *construal of the scene* (see Langacker 1987, 1991). The cognitive models at work in radial categories, in other words, may be culturally specific; they do not so much reflect how reality is carved up objectively, but rather how the mind creates different realities. Such cases as the English *adoptive mother* and *surrogate mother* and the Japanese classifier *hon* constitute culture-bound category variants according to Lakoff. The variants, however, are not arbitrary even though they are not predictable. They are motivated and constrained by the central subcategory: a plausible explanation for the peripheral extensions can be provided a posteriori.

In addition to lexical concepts such as 'anger' (Lakoff and Kovecses 1987), 'truth', and 'knowledge', linguistic categories like 'nouns' and 'verbs' and linguistic constructions like *there is* have been shown to possess a polysemic radial structure. For instance, Janda (1990) discusses the radial structure of the category of grammatical case in Czech and shows the dynamic nature of the category with the category members, which enter both stable and new dynamic alliances. In fact, as Lakoff (1987: 463) notes, in a cognitively based grammar, all grammar "will be a radial category of *grammatical constructions*, where each construction pairs a cognitive model (which characterizes meaning) with corresponding aspects of linguistic form." He further proposes to account for the theory of grammatical constructions in terms of a general theory of symbolic models, which are understood as "pairings of models of form with other cognitive models" (467). "Grammatical constructions," in Lakoff's wording, "are organized via prototype theory, using radially structured constructional categories" (584).

3.3. Additional Features of Prototypicality

There are three more things to mention regarding prototypicality: we have to look into the sources of prototypicality, we have to examine the relationship between the Geeraerts's (1989) characteristics (a)–(d), and we have to say something about the application of prototype theory outside the lexical realm in which it was originally developed.

To begin with, it is generally taken for granted that the different prototype effects enumerated in characteristics (a)–(d) may have different sources. Two major explanations stand out.

First, prototype effects (and gradience in particular) may result from the fact that concepts function as mental reference points. When we come across new phenomena, we tend to interpret them in terms of existing categories (see Geeraerts 1997 for an extended discussion in terms of efficiency and cognitive economy). These categories then function as Idealized Cognitive Models, as Lakoff (1987) calls them; they are, so to speak, the yardstick by which we measure new objects and events. In the case of *gradience*, then, different degrees of matching can be observed between an Idealized Cognitive Model referring to a given object or event and the particular object and event. In the concept 'bachelor', discussed first by Katz and Fodor (1963) in terms of feature matrices, then by Fillmore (1982) and Lakoff (1987) in the cognitive framework, a partial fit is observed between an Idealized Cognitive Model of 'bachelor' and the concept of 'bachelor' as applied, for instance, to the pope.

Second, prototypicality may involve cognitive economy in yet another sense. Categories exist at different levels, and some of the levels were discovered to be more basic than others. Berlin, Breedlove, and Raven (1974) and Hunn (1977) showed, for instance, that the level of the biological genus in Tzeltal plant and animal taxonomies is psychologically basic—that is, more salient than other category levels, more readily acquired, recalled, etc. (see Rosch and Mervis 1975; Schmid, this volume, chapter 5). It is precisely at these basic levels that categories exhibit a maximization of perceived similarities among category members and a minimization of perceived similarities among different categories. As such, the features of such basic-level categories have high cue validities: they are good predictors of whether something belongs to the category or not. More generally, the prototype categories may find their source in an overall attempt to maximize cue validity, in other words, to group things together in such a way that the members of a category are maximally similar within the category and maximally dissimilar with regard to other categories.

Let us now turn toward a closer examination of the relationship between features (a)–(d). Following Geeraerts (1989), we may observe that the features (a)–(d) are not necessarily coextensive; they do not always co-occur. There is now a consensus in the linguistic literature on prototypicality that the characteristics enumerated above are prototypicality effects that may be exhibited in various combinations by individual lexical items and may have very different sources. Also, the four features are systematically related along two dimensions. On the one hand, characteristics (a) and (c) take into account the referential, extensional structure of a category. In particular, they have a look at the members of a category; they observe, respectively, that not all members of a category are equal in representativeness for that category and that the referential boundaries of a category are not always determinate. On the other hand, these two aspects (nonequality and nondiscreteness) recur on the intensional level, where the definitional rather than the referential structure of a category is envisaged. For one thing, nondiscreteness shows up in the fact that there is no single definition in terms of necessary and sufficient attributes for a prototypical concept. For another, the clustering of meanings that is typical of family resemblances and radial sets implies that not every reading is structurally equally important (and a similar observation can be made with regard to the components into which those meanings may be analyzed). If, for instance, one has a family resemblance relationship of the form AB, BC, CD, DE, then the cases BC and CD have greater structural weight than AB and DE.

The concept of prototypicality, in short, is itself a prototypically clustered one in which the concepts of nondiscreteness and nonequality (either on the intensional or on the extensional level) play a major distinctive role. Nondiscreteness

Table 6.1. The main prototype effects and their mutual relationships

	EXTENSIONALLY *(on the referential level)*	*INTENSIONALLY* *(on the level of senses)*
NON-EQUALITY (salient effects, internal structure with core and periphery)	[a] differences of salience among members of a category	[b] clustering of readings into family resemblances and radial sets
NON-DISCRETENESS (demarcation problems, flexible applicability)	[c] fluctuations at the edges of a category	[d] absence of definitions in terms of necessary and sufficient attributes

involves the existence of demarcation problems and the flexible applicability of categories. Nonequality involves the fact that categories have internal structure: not all members or readings that fall within the boundaries of the category need have equal status, but some may be more central than others; categories often consist of a dominant core area surrounded by a less salient periphery.

The distinction between nondiscreteness (the existence of demarcation problems) and nonequality (the existence of an internal structure involving a categorial core versus a periphery) cross-classifies with the distinction between an intensional perspective (which looks at the senses of a lexical item and their definition) and an extensional perspective (which looks at the referential range of application of a lexical item or that of an individual sense of that item). The cross-classification between both relevant distinctions (the distinction between nondiscreteness and nonequality and the distinction between an intensional and an extensional perspective) yields a two-dimensional conceptual map of prototypicality effects, in which the four characteristics mentioned before are charted in their mutual relationships. Table 6.1 schematically represents these relationships.

Characteristic (a) illustrates the extensional nonequality of semantic structures: some members of a category are more typical or more salient representatives of the category than others. Characteristic (b) instantiates intensional nonequality: the readings of a lexical item may form a set with one or more core cases surrounded by peripheral readings emanating from the central, most salient readings. Characteristic (c) manifests the notion of extensional nondiscreteness: there may be fluctuations at the boundary of a category. And characteristic (d) represents intensional nondiscreteness: the definitional demarcation of lexical categories may be problematic when measured against the classical requirement that definitions take the form of a set of necessary attributes that are jointly sufficient to delimit the category in contrast with others.

4. SCHEMATIC NETWORKS

Prototypicality and the radial set model do not exhaust the insights into the structure of polysemy developed within Cognitive Linguistics. A further step to be taken involves the notion of schematic networks (see also Tuggy, this volume, chapter 4).

4.1. Parsimony or Polysemy?

To see how a prototype-theoretical, radial set model of semantic structure ties in with the notion of schematic network, we may start from the granularity question: Which level of detail is most appropriate for semantic description? The challenge of polysemy for language theorists is to find out whether it is possible to predict the polysemic chains a given word can build up, to identify the mechanisms that underlie such extensions, and to account for the motivation which makes it possible for a language user to interpret the meanings in context. But it also involves the question of *the granularity of definition*, of the level at which the relatedness of the senses can be best observed and captured.

The question of the granularity of definition touches upon one of the most important properties of semantic analysis. It involves a discussion of whether it is the monosemy, the polysemy, or the homonymy approach which most adequately accounts for lexical meanings. The *monosemy* approach strives for more schematicity in semantic analysis and more parsimonious schematic definitions. The polysemy approach prefers fine-grained, maximally specific analyses, while the homonymy approach does not assume any relatedness of meanings between items having the same form.[8]

One can detect a radical *homonymy* position in generative analyses of lexical senses (Katz and Fodor 1963), where a practical disregard for the polysemy-homonymy distinction can be observed. Lexical meanings are represented there as sets of matrices of linguistic (semantic-syntactic) properties, strict subcategorization features (semantic markers), and their combinatorics (accounted for by selectional restriction rules). Cognitive linguists (e.g., Langacker 1991; Geeraerts 1993; Tuggy 1993; Sandra and Rice 1995) have put forward arguments in favor of basically the *polysemy* position in semantic analysis. The *monosemy* position is represented by work such as that by Ruhl (1989), who takes issue with Lakoff and Johnson (1980) about the polysemy stand. The monosemy position, as presented by Ruhl, argues in favor of the distinction between a lexical item's semantic part—an abstract, minimum representation of its meaning—and an identifying part of the meaning that is contextual (i.e., pragmatic). This approach is grounded in the structuralist tradition (see Bierwisch 1983 for similar views)[9] and makes a clear division between (abstract) semantics and (elaborated) pragmatics in the form of contextual implication and world knowledge (see also Dunbar 2001: 9 and, more recently, Tyler and Evans 2003 for their concept of a *protoscene*).[10]

There are several diachronic arguments against such a concept of monosemy. First of all, the diachronic study of the world's languages rather unambiguously suggests that the direction of semantic development is from the concrete to the abstract (Traugott 1982; Sweetser 1990) and not vice versa. Secondly, polysemy usually develops from the more salient to the less salient sense.[11] In his seminal article, in which he takes issue with Sandra (1998) and to a certain extent with Croft (1998), Tuggy (1999) presents further evidence for polysemy and identifies what he calls "an open-minded preference or pre-expectation of polysemic analyses" over either monosemic or homonymic accounts (356–57). His justification involves three points, two of which are methodological. First, as Tuggy has it, it is harder to prove a negative ("there is no mental connection between meanings") than a positive ("there are some connections"). Second, it is reasonable to assume that the majority of cases fall in the middle of a continuum (the continuum, that is, between absolute monosemy and radical homonymy) rather than at the extremes. And finally, linguistic evidence *for* polysemy is abundant.[12]

This does not mean, however, that attempts to account for polysemy in terms of a single common structure are absent in the cognitive linguistic framework. Lakoff (1987), Brugman (1981), Brugman and Lakoff (1988), and, more recently, Janssen (2003) posit similar configurational image schemas to underlie the relationships between polysemic senses (see Brugman 1990, Lakoff 1990, and Turner 1990 for the discussion of the Invariance Hypothesis). The schemas supposedly preserve their Gestalt configuration across diverse polysemic senses of the same lexical form. Underlying the meaning of such forms is a core set of image schemas, such as: CONTAINER, SOURCE, GOAL, LINK, UP, and DOWN, and image schema transformations. Furthermore, Lakoff (1987: 440) proposes that there exist natural relationships among image schemas and that these motivate polysemy. Examples here include the schema transformations between MULTIPLE and MASS schemas or the relationship between the image schemas PATH and END OF PATH (see Bennett 1975, quoted in Lakoff 1987):

(9)   Sam walked *over* the hill. (PATH)
(10) Sam lives *over* the hill. (END OF PATH)

However, whereas the radical monosemy position defends an abstract, minimal semantic representation for a decontextualized general sense from which polysemic instances are derived by contextual (pragmatic) constraints, Cognitive Linguistics tends to defend the view that polysemic senses of one lexical item form interrelated sets. Whereas monosemy assumes a minimal, narrow semantic representation, Cognitive Linguistics tends to favor a rich form of representation in which each lexical meaning is an access point to a *network* of related categories. Radial sets constitute one type of network, but the *schematic network model* as developed by Langacker (1987) and presented in detail in Tuggy (this volume, chapter 4) goes one step further: it introduces different levels of abstraction into the model. Within a semantic network, readings that are separate at one level of granularity may be subsumed under an overarching reading at a less specific level. The discussion between a monosemy stand and a polysemy stand then receives an answer not in terms of an either-or opposition, but in terms of an and-and complementarity. If there is an abstract schema that overarches the more concrete readings, it may coexist with the latter at a different hierarchical level of the network. In such a framework, the definitional test of polysemy can be regarded as a search for a schema subsuming related senses (see Tuggy 1993).[13] It is not exactly clear, though, whether a more schematic reading need always consist of a definition in terms of necessary and sufficient conditions; in the actual practice of applying the schematic network model, this is certainly not always the case. Also, the knowledge base captured by the schematic network is dynamic, whereas a monosemy approach is static. Cases of reanalysis (e.g., *light* or *ear*) can naturally be accounted for in such an approach. In other words, the categorization underlying linguistic meanings, as any other kind of categorization, is not given once and for all; rather, the categorization process is a dynamic creative activity, both for an individual and for a linguistic.[14]

Polysemy, as understood in cognitive terms, is an exponent of the absence of clear boundaries between semantics and pragmatics (as it is an exponent of the absence of clear boundaries between lexicon and syntax; see note 14). Indeed, the thesis of the encyclopedic nature of linguistic meaning and semantic description and, concomitantly, the rejection of a strict dichotomy between encyclopedic and linguistic meaning clearly lead to the rejection of a parsimonious monosemic approach to the advantage of the polysemy position (see Geeraerts 1993). According to this approach, homonymy, polysemy and vagueness form a continuum.[15] The place on the continuum depends on two factors as formulated by Tuggy (1993): (i) the presence of a subsuming schema and (ii) the relative conceptual distance of such a schema from the structures. A token example of English homonymy such as in the *Bank of England* and *river bank* can be said to be subsumed by the well-entrenched THING schema but the instantiations are, as Tuggy proposes, fairly distant from each other, both conceptually and from the point of view of elaboration. Vagueness, also called "systematic polysemy," "(partial) segment profiling," or "allosemy" (Deane 1988), on the other hand, involves meanings which are not well entrenched, such as the gender distinction (female/male) in the English word *student*, but whose schematic meaning is relatively well entrenched and elaboratively close.

4.2. Comparing the Representational Formats

In the course of the previous pages, we have come across three different models of lexical semantic structure that are current in Cognitive Linguistics: the overlapping sets (or family resemblance) model, the radial set model, and the schematic net-

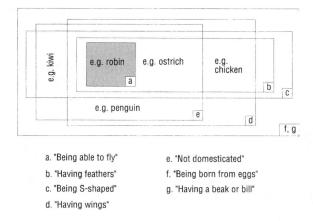

a. "Being able to fly"   e. "Not domesticated"

b. "Having feathers"   f. "Being born from eggs"

c. "Being S-shaped"   g. "Having a beak or bill"

d. "Having wings"

Figure 6.1. The overlapping set structure of the category BIRD

work model. Following Geeraerts (1995), we will now present a comparison of the three models. By way of example, let us start from the following meanings of *bird*:

   i. Any member of the class *Aves*
   ii. A clay disk thrown as a flying target
  iii. Shuttlecock as used in badminton
  iv. A rocket, guided missile, satellite, or airplane
   v. A young woman

The *overlapping sets model* is illustrated by figure 6.1, reprinted from Geeraerts (1995: 25). Early applications may be found in studies such as Geeraerts (1990), Cuyckens (1991), and Schmid (1993). The basic elements in this representational format are the members of a category (such as the types of birds in figure 6.1), or, in some cases, instances of use of the category as found in a text corpus. These basic elements are grouped together on the basis of the features that they share or the senses that they exemplify. Each grouping is typographically represented by means of a Venn-diagram. The different groupings may overlap; the area in the figure where the sets overlap maximally constitutes the prototypical center of the category. The *radial set model* was introduced in Lakoff (1987), as described in the previous pages. Early examples may be found in the work of Brugman (1981), Janda (1990), Nikiforidou (1991), Goldberg (1992), and others. The basic elements in a radial set representation are the meanings or senses of a category; these are connected by means of relational links that indicate how one reading is an extension of an other. In the *bird* example, as represented by figure 6.2, all links from the central biological reading to the peripheral readings are motivated by metaphorical similarity. (The motivational link is not the same, though. In senses [ii], [iii], and [iv], the 'flying thing' aspect is dominant, while the metaphor behind sense [v] would

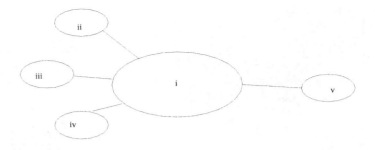

Senses of *bird* in a radial set model

i.   Any member of the class *Aves*

ii.   A clay disk thrown as a flying target

iii.   A shuttlecock as used in badminton

iv.   A rocket, guided missile, satellite, or airplane.

v.   A young woman

Figure 6.2. An abstract representation of a radial set

rather be something like 'pretty, lively thing', perhaps with the overtone of serving as prey.) The typographical distribution of the various readings on the page illustrates the prototypical structure of the category: the prototypical sense is situated roughly in the middle of the figure, while the extensions that emanate from this central sense are grouped radially around it.

The *schematic network model* is described in detail by Langacker (1987, 1991). Early illustrations may be found in the work of Rudzka-Ostyn (1985, 1989), Tuggy (1987, 1993), Taylor (1992), Casad (1992), Schulze (1993), and others. The basic elements in the schematic network model may be meanings or members of a category. As in the radial set model, these elements are connected by means of relational links, but a systematic distinction is maintained between two kinds of links: links of schematization and links of extension. Schematicity involves the relationship between a subordinate node and a superordinate node in a taxonomical hierarchy. The category BIRD, for instance, is schematic with regard to ROBIN, SPARROW, OSTRICH, and other types of birds. Extension, on the other hand, involves partial schematicity: assuming that the subset comprising robins, sparrows, and blackbirds (among others) constitutes the prototypical center of the category 'BIRD', the subset comprising chickens is an extension from that prototype. Chickens do not fall within the prototypical subset, but the concept 'chicken' can be seen as an extension (based on a relationship of similarity) of the prototypical sense. (And the same holds, obviously, for 'kiwi', 'ostrich', and 'penguin'.) Precisely because the example involves similarity, the relation is one of partial schematicity.

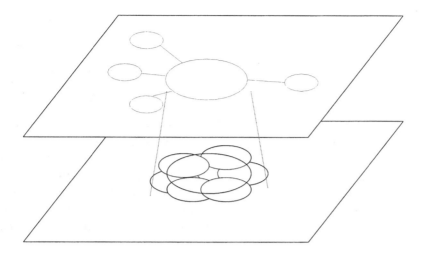

Figure 6.3. A schematic network as combining the radial set model and
the overlapping sets model

We will not present an example of a schematic network as it is usually drawn; ample illustrations will be found in Tuggy (this volume, chapter 4). Given our example, though, it will be easy to appreciate that the schematic network representation is able to combine the overlapping sets representation and the radial network representation. In the radial network presentation of figure 6.2, reading (i) is schematic with regard to the analysis presented in figure 6.1: the prototype-based, family resemblance representation in figure 6.1 is an analysis of reading (i) in figure 6.2, at a higher level of granularity than what is presented in the radial network presentation of figure 6.2. A schematic network representation intends to capture both levels at the same time. An informal representation (informal in the sense that it does not use the typographical conventions specifically developed for schematic networks; again, see Tuggy, this volume, chapter 4) of the levels in the schematic network and the relationship between them might look like figure 6.3, where the lowest level presents the family resemblance analysis of figure 6.1 and where the higher level corresponds with figure 6.2.

It will be clear, then, that the representational formats are not incompatible, but rather focus on different aspects of semantic structure as discussed in the previous pages: the overlapping sets representation deals primarily with the "standard version" of prototypicality, in Kleiber's terms. The radial set representation is well suited for the extended version of prototypicality, while the schematic network representation adds the recognition that the level of abstractedness at which categories are conceptualized is contextually flexible.

5. FURTHER RESEARCH

Let us summarize. Cognitive models of polysemy reveal that vagueness, polysemy, and homonymy represent a cline of diminishing schematicity and increasing instance salience. Polysemy is an instance of categorization, and category members form a user-dependent chain of related senses. They are built around centers which share relevant information, where contrasting information is taken as irrelevant. Categorization is not static, given once and for all, but it is dynamic and creative. These facts direct present and future research toward refining the cognitively based concept of lexical meaning. There is, however, still much to be learned about the exact identification and characterization of linguistic meaning. In this concluding paragraph, we will identify three topics that are likely to be high on the agenda for future research.

First, Prototype Theory, as well as the concept of prototype itself, has given rise to numerous controversies since the time it was first proposed (see, e.g., Osherson and Smith 1981). The inherent dynamism of the concept prototype is, for example, captured in a different manner by MacLaury's Vantage Theory (MacLaury 1992; Taylor and MacLaury 1995), which is one of the possible reformulations of the theory of prototypes. Other contemporary theories of concepts extend and refine other aspects of the prototype theory or resort to and modify classical theories of concepts (see Laurence and Margolis 1999; Margolis and Laurence 1999 for the presentation and analyses of Neoclassical Theories, the Theory-Theory, and Conceptual Atomism). The systematic comparison of theoretical models, then, should be an essential concern for the further development of semantics in Cognitive Linguistics.

Second, another pertinent issue in Cognitive Linguistics is related to the mechanisms of *"online" meaning construction* involving dynamic categorization and re-categorization (see, e.g., Coulson 2001). Current accounts of polysemy require further elaboration along these lines. In all those questions, more *experimentation* and *neurobiological evidence* of neural activity is welcome (see Coulson 2004), based on such measures as, for instance, the event-related brain potential (ERP) derived from the encephalogram. Some issues relevant to polysemy are discussed in the papers on ERP elicited by lexical ambiguities (Van Petten and Kutas 1987, 1991). Measures of brain activity that implement the cognitive processes, together with a description of language based on authentic language data (namely, *Corpus Linguistics methodology*; see Lewandowska-Tomaszczyk 1997), are likely to present more convincing arguments for the theoretical constructs proposed by cognitive linguists.

Third, the major task for Cognitive Linguistics remains the search for *establishing cognitive reality* of different kinds of schemas governing the presence of meaning relatedness among identical linguistic forms, as well as the examination of possible conceptual constraints on the number and type of polysemic senses. Apart from individual introspection and intuition, then, linguists look for various kinds of evidence. First of all, there is a substantial body of linguistic evidence to examine (see Langacker 1987: 157). Furthermore, one has to resort to *experimental findings* and *acquisitional data* (as in Dowker 2003 or Nerlich, Todd, and Clarke 2003). There exist numerous *empirical techniques* worth mentioning here. Sandra and Rice (1995), for instance, used sorting tasks, which show the relatedness between words and sentences at different levels of granularity by means of hierarchical clustering analysis, similarity judgments involving a scale between "completely different" and "absolutely identical," and acceptability judgments. There are also attempts to use eye-tracking techniques to determine what representation people initially access at the word processing level, as well as important psychological findings on salience in literal and nonliteral uses (see Giora 1997; Giora and Gur 2003).[16] Geeraerts, Grondelaers, and Bakema (1994) use *referential analysis* rather than an experimental empirical technique. Ambiguity and polysemy have also been at the center of attention of *computational linguists*, who study word senses and propose models of semantic tagging (e.g., Rayson 1995) and word sense disambiguation (e.g., Pustejovsky 1991). In her doctoral dissertation on systematic polysemy, Lapata (2000) uses *statistical methodology* to disambiguate polysemic word combinations and proposes a probabilistic model for selecting the dominant meaning. The presence of elements of synchrony in diachrony and diachrony in synchrony justifies the use of *historical linguistic methodology* in cognitive linguistic analyses (see Tyler and Evans 2003: 108 for the concept of a primary sense in their analysis of propositional polysemy), enriched by *cross-language comparisons* and *variationist* studies.

However, no convincing evidence has yet been forthcoming on the adequacy of different methods in determining the complex nature of a predominant, primary, or sanctioning sense, and we still have to find out which particular instance of a lexical form more exactly counts as a distinct sense and which of the two—that is, a partial or full-specification approach to polysemy—has a higher cognitive reality. Even though, as we have recently been reminded by Tyler and Evans, "all linguistic analysis is to some extent subjective"; more rigorous methods and tools are needed in Cognitive Linguistics to secure "replicability of findings, a prerequisite for any theoretically rigorous study" (2003: 104).

NOTES

1. The purpose of the semantic description included in early Transformational Grammar (see Katz and Fodor 1963) was to account for ambiguity—in the sense of homonymy—(see, e.g., *I observed the ball*, Postal 1969: 32). Some researchers within the generative framework investigated the nature of the lexicon and lexical categories (see, e.g., Fillmore 1970, "The grammar of *hitting* and *breaking*") or made attempts to answer the question concerning the status of word meanings (Perlmutter 1970). It may be noted that an interest in semantics existed outside linguistics: researchers outside linguistics pointed to a significant role the study of polysemy can bring to illuminate the mechanisms of human cognition (cf. Brown and Witkowski 1983).

2. A topic that we will not be able to pursue in detail is the demarcation between different types of meaning. Different types of meaning relatedness of the same form have, in fact, been identified and labeled. One such case of lexical ambiguity is "classical polysemy" or "polycentric categorization" (see Taylor 1989, 2003), in which, for example, the English word *chest* can mean the 'upper front part of the human body', 'a case or a box with a lid', or a 'treasury of a public institution'. In such cases, as noted by Dunbar (2001: 2), "the extensions do not overlap, but there is a conceptual relationship." Classical polysemy, understood in this way, should be distinguished from what is usually known as "vagueness," where a word is unmarked for a certain category, as in the English word *doctor*, which is vague with reference to gender. The distinction between vagueness and polysemy is blurred as the same lexical forms can also *profile* parts of different domains in their respective semantic base. For instance, the adjective *fast* in *a fast car* as opposed to *fast* in *a fast drink* or the noun *window* understood either as a glass pane or a wooden frame evoke different domains and profile different attributes of the things they refer to. Such examples as *fast* or *window* involve profiling of parts associated with an object within one conceptual domain and are called "natural" (Lewandowska-Tomaszczyk 2002), "systematic," or "complementary polysemy" (see Pustejovsky 1991; Pustejovsky and Boguraev 1999; Pustejovsky and Bouillon 1999). Another class representing related senses involves conceptual categories such as BIRD, which embraces all varieties of birds, from prototypical category members such as sparrows or robins, through eagles and owls, to peripheral category exemplars such as penguins or ostriches.

3. Nerlich, Todd, and Clarke (1998) report cases of young children who tell one another jokes such as these: Why does the teacher wear sunglasses? Because her class is so bright; or, What's the hardest thing when learning to ride a bike? The road.

4. For instance, in his important book on diachronic prototype semantics, Geeraerts (1997) proposes two major causes of semantic change, "expressivity" and "efficiency." Efficiency is shaped by two counteracting principles: the principle of isomorphism (avoidance of polysemy and homonymy) and the principle of prototypicality, which, as Geeraerts showed in a number of case studies, secures the structural stability of concepts with the simultaneous maintenance of informational density and their flexible adaptability.

5. The following topics are examples of those researched in Cognitive Linguistics: category chaining of classifiers in Japanese (Lakoff 1987; Matsumoto 1993) and Shona (Palmer and Woodman 1999); nominal categories in Dutch (Geeraerts, Grondelaers, and Bakema 1994), Dyirbal (Dixon 1968; Lakoff 1987), and English (Sweetser 1987); verbal categories in Australian and Austronesian (Wilkins and Hill 1995), French (Hewson 1997), Dutch (Verhagen 1992), Portuguese (Soares da Silva 2003), Cora (Casad 2001), and Polish (Lewandowska-Tomaszczyk 1995, 1996); cross-language perspectives (Raukko 1995; Newman 1996); Finnish conjunctions (Herlin 1998); adverbs and prepositions in English (Lindner 1981; Herskovits 1986; Lakoff 1987; Brugman 1981; Langacker 1987, 1991; Schulze 1988; Dirven 1993; Sandra and Rice 1995), French (Vandeloise 1991), Dutch (Cuyckens 1991, 1995), Polish (Kalisz 1990; Krzeszowski 1990), and Czech, Russian, and other Slavic languages (Janda 1990); adjectives and possessives in English (Taylor 1992, 1996), semantics of Mesoamerican color terms (MacLaury 1992); evidential categories in Wanka Quechua (Floyd 1999); verbs in Orizaba Nahuatl (Tuggy 2003); and various grammatical categories, such as case (Janda 1990), modality (Sweetser 1990), and passives (Verhagen 1992). Mangasser-Wahl (2000) contains a history of the concept of prototypicality and its linguistic use.

6. His conclusion is weakened somewhat by Dunbar (2001), who claims that linguistic and logical criteria adequately capture the distinction between polysemy (ambiguity) and

vagueness provided their use is restricted to denotational rather than referential phenomena.

7. See Laurence and Margolis (1999: 9): "A concept encodes the conditions that are single necessary and jointly sufficient for something to be in its extension."

8. Monosemy as opposed to polysemy can be perceived in terms of the "minimalist/maximalist" difference and the "abstractivist/cognitivist" difference (for a discussion, see Nerlich and Clarke 2003).

9. About two decades ago, the productivity of polysemy mechanisms was discussed in terms of general linguistic functions and cognitive principles (Nunberg 1978; Norrick 1981; Ross 1981). Lehrer (1990) shows the inadequacy of such a radical generative stand and proposes that even though a number of regularities can be identified, some meanings, even though motivated in Lakoff's (1987) sense, are unpredictable by general rules alone. They should instead be accounted for by more specific cognitive principles interacting with a variety of other functions and principles.

10. See also Tyler and Evans (2003: 95) for the concept of a "protoscene": an abstract, primary meaning component. Tyler and Evans argue for a basically monosemic analysis of polysemy in Cognitive Linguistics and propose a dividing line between "what counts as a distinct sense conventionalized in semantic memory, and a contextual inference produced on-line for the purpose of local understanding" (106).

11. Cecil Brown (1983), an anthropologist, quotes examples of languages where 'eye' (the more salient element) was extended to cover 'face', but not vice versa. This process is frequently accompanied by assigning overt marking to this extended form and the polysemy is then dropped.

12. However, Zlatev (2003) rejects a distinction between polysemy and monosemic *generality*: he dispenses with the polysemy analysis in the case of spatial prepositions in Indo-European languages and argues against positing a constant "basic meaning." Criticism of a polysemy position which—in some cases—does allow for an analysis in terms of "the same psychologically primitive concept," comes from such researchers as Rakova (2003), who argues for a "no polysemy" view of conceptual structure.

13. See Lewandowska-Tomaszczyk (2004: 408): The consequence of Bierwisch's *two-level model* to the analysis of polysemic items is "a postulate of the existence of the identical semantic, i.e. monosemous, level with alternative conceptual interpretations, limiting thus, in fact, the range of polysemy in language. Bierwisch's model is consonant with the modularity thesis concerning the division of work between linguistic and other cognitive faculties of the mind. The semantic representations Bierwisch postulates have a predicate-argument structure and are based on semantic primitives that underlie them. Even though Langacker's and Bierwisch's models are cognitive models, they refer in fact to different realities. In both models polysemic items involve relatedness of senses. While, however in Langacker's network model, the subsuming schema, to use Tuggy's term (1993), if of a similar cognitive character as its instantiations, in the two-level model, the two are qualitatively different—the 'superschema' represents a unitary linguistic meaning, while the instantiations, which carry meanings differences, are conceptual in nature."

14. It may be interesting to note that such processes can be modeled in the connectionist architecture systems of neural activation as constraint-satisfaction rather than rule systems (MacWhinney 2000: 142–43). Such systems, as MacWhinney (1989) explains, can deal with violations in word combinatorics. He gives the combination *another sand* as an example. "Typically," MacWhinney says, "the word *another* requires a count noun and *sand* is a mass noun. However, when the listener is confronted with this particular combination, it is still possible to retrieve an interpretation by treating *sand* as a count noun.

This can be done by thinking of bags of sand, types of sand, alternative meanings of the word *sand*, or even the act of applying sandpaper to something" (2000: 143). MacWhinney (1989) discusses these semantic extension effects in terms of the process of "pushy polysemy." These and similar cases of polysemy are accounted for by some cognitive linguists in terms of *Construction Grammar* (Fillmore 1985; Goldberg 1995; Croft, this volume, chapter 18). Brugman (2001), for instance, analyzes polysemy of English light verbs in terms of force-dynamic relations, in which the semantic-syntactic function of grammatical constructions, expressed by aspect/Aktionsart and semantic roles, contributes to the polysemic interpretation of individual verbal senses.

15. It is worth noting that some linguists with a structuralist rather than a cognitive background, for instance Cowie (1982) or Lipka (1986, 1988), also argued that the distinction between polysemy and homonymy is a matter of degree.

16. Giora (1997) put forward the "graded salience hypothesis," which says that "salient meanings should always be activated initially, even when they are incompatible with contextual information.... Factors contributing to degrees of salience are, e.g., conventionality, frequency, familiarity and prototypicality" (Giora and Gur 2003: 307).

REFERENCES

Aristotle. 1984. *The complete works of Aristotle*. Ed. Jonathan Barnes. Rev. Oxford trans. 2 vols. Princeton, NJ: Princeton University Press.

Bennett, David C. 1975. *Spatial and temporal uses of English prepositions: An essay in stratificational semantics*. London: Longman.

Berlin, Brent, Dennis E. Breedlove, and Peter H. Raven. 1974. *Principles of Tzeltal plant classification*. New York: Academic Press.

Berlin, Brent, and Paul Kay. 1969. *Basic color terms: Their universality and evolution*. Berkeley: University of California Press.

Bierwisch, Manfred. 1983. Semantische und konzeptuelle Repräsentation lexikalischer Einheiten. In Rudolf Ruzicka and Wolfgang Motsch, eds., *Untersuchungen zur Semantik* 61–99. Berlin: Akademie-Verlag.

Blank, Andreas. 2003. Polysemy in the lexicon and in discourse. In Brigitte Nerlich, Zazie Todd, Vimala Herman, and David D. Clarke, eds., *Polysemy: Flexible patterns of meaning in mind and language* 267–93. Berlin: Mouton de Gruyter.

Blank, Andreas, and Peter Koch, eds. 1999. *Historical semantics and cognition*. Berlin: Mouton de Gruyter.

Bréal, Michel. 1897. *Essai de sémantique: Science des significations*. Paris: Hachette.

Brown, Cecil H. 1983. Polysemy, overt marking, and function words. Manuscript, Department of Anthropology, Northern Illinois University.

Brown, Cecil H., and Stanley R. Witkowski. 1983. Polysemy, lexical change, and cultural importance. *Man* 18: 17–89.

Brugman, Claudia. 1981. Story of *Over*. MA thesis, University of California at Berkeley. (Published as *The story of Over: Polysemy, semantics, and the structure of the lexicon*. New York: Garland, 1988)

Brugman, Claudia. 1990. What is the invariance hypothesis? *Cognitive Linguistics* 1: 257–66.

Brugman, Claudia. 2001. Light verbs and polysemy. *Language Sciences* 23: 551–78.

Brugman, Claudia, and George Lakoff. 1988. Cognitive topology and lexical networks. In Steven L. Small, Garrison W. Cottrell, and Michael K. Tanenhaus, eds., *Lexical ambiguity resolution: Perspectives from psycholinguistics, neuropsychology, and artificial intelligence* 477–508. San Mateo, CA: Morgan Kaufmann.

Bybee, Joan L. 2000. The phonology of the lexicon: Evidence from lexical diffusion. In Michael Barlow and Suzanne Kemmer, eds., *Usage-based models of language* 65–85. Stanford, CA: CSLI Publications.

Carnap, Rudolf. 1978. The elimination of metaphysics through logical analysis of language. In Alfred J. Ayer, ed., *Logical positivism* 60–81. Westport, CT: Greenwood Press. (First published as "Uberwindung der Metaphysik durch logische Analyse der Sprache," *Erkenntnis* 2 (1932): 219–41)

Casad, Eugene H. 1992. Cognition, history, and Cora *yee*. *Cognitive Linguistics* 3: 151–86

Casad, Eugene H. 2001. Where do the senses of Cora *va'a-* come from? In Hubert Cuyckens and Britta Zawada, eds., *Polysemy in cognitive linguistics* 83–114. Amsterdam: John Benjamins.

Coulson, Seana. 2001. *Semantic leaps: Frame-shifting and conceptual blending in meaning construction.* Cambridge: Cambridge University Press.

Coulson, Seana. 2004. Electrophysiology and pragmatic language comprehension. In Ira Noveck and Dan Sperber, eds., *Experimental Pragmatics* 187–206. Basingstoke, UK: Palgrave Macmillan.

Cowie, Anthony P. 1982. Polysemy and the structure of lexical fields. *Nottingham Linguistic Circular* 11: 51–65.

Croft, William. 1998. Linguistic evidence and mental representations. *Cognitive Linguistics* 9: 151–73.

Cruse, D. Alan. 1986. *Lexical semantics.* Cambridge: Cambridge University Press.

Cuyckens, Hubert. 1991. The semantics of spatial prepositions in Dutch: A cognitive-linguistic exercise. PhD dissertation, University of Antwerp.

Cuyckens, Hubert. 1995. Family resemblance in the Dutch spatial prepositions *door* and *langs*. *Cognitive Linguistics* 6: 183–207.

Cuyckens, Hubert. 1999. Grammaticalization in the English prepositions 'to' and 'for'. In Barbara Lewandowska-Tomaszczyk, ed., *Cognitive perspectives on language* 151–61. Frankfurt am Main: Peter Lang Verlag.

Deane, Paul, D. 1988. Polysemy and cognition. *Lingua* 75: 325–61.

Dirven, René. 1993. Dividing up physical and mental space into conceptual categories by means of English prepositions. In Cornelia Zelinsky-Wibbelt, ed., *The semantics of prepositions: From mental processing to natural language processing* 73–97. Berlin: Mouton de Gruyter.

Dixon, Robert M. W. 1968. Noun classes. *Lingua* 21: 104–25.

Dowker, Ann. 2003. Young children's and adults' use of figurative language: How important are cultural and linguistic influences? In Brigitte Nerlich, Zazie Todd, Vimala Herman, and David D. Clarke, eds., *Polysemy: Flexible patterns of meaning in mind and language* 317–32. Berlin: Mouton de Gruyter.

Dunbar, George. 2001. Towards a cognitive analysis of polysemy, ambiguity, and vagueness. *Cognitive Linguistics* 12: 1–14.

Fillmore, Charles J. 1970. The grammar of *hitting* and *breaking*. In Roderick A. Jacobs and Peter S. Rosenbaum, eds., *Readings in English transformational grammar* 120–33. Waltham, MA: Ginn and Company.

Fillmore, Charles J. 1982. Frame semantics. In Linguistic Society of Korea, ed., *Linguistics in the morning calm* 111–37. Seoul: Hanshin.

Fillmore, Charles J. 1985. Frames and the semantics of understanding. *Quaderni di Semantica* 6: 222–54.

Floyd, Rick. 1999. The structure of evidential categories in Wanka Quechua. Dallas, Texas: Summer Institute of Linguistics.

Fodor, Jerry A. 1981. *Representations: Philosophical essays on the foundations of cognitive science.* Brighton, UK: Harvester Press.

Geeraerts, Dirk. 1987. On necessary and sufficient conditions. *Journal of Semantics* 5: 275–91.

Geeraerts, Dirk. 1989. Prospects and problems of prototype theory. *Linguistics* 27: 587–612.

Geeraerts, Dirk. 1990. The lexicographical treatment of prototypical polysemy. In Savas L. Tsohatzidis, ed., *Meanings and prototypes. Studies in linguistic categorization* 195–210. London: Routledge.

Geeraerts, Dirk. 1993. Vagueness's puzzles, polysemy's vagaries. *Cognitive Linguistics* 4: 223–72.

Geeraerts, Dirk. 1995. Representational formats in cognitive semantics. *Folia Linguistica* 29: 21–41.

Geeraerts, Dirk. 1997. *Diachronic prototype semantics: A contribution to historical lexicology.* Oxford: Clarendon Press.

Geeraerts, Dirk, Stefan Grondelaers, and Peter Bakema. 1994. *The structure of lexical variation: Meaning, naming, and context.* Berlin: Mouton de Gruyter.

Giora, Rachel. 1997. Understanding figurative and literal language: The graded salience hypothesis. *Cognitive Linguistics* 7: 183–206.

Giora, Rachel, and Inbal Gur. 2003. Irony in conversation: Salience, role, and context effects. In Brigitte Nerlich, Zazie Todd, Vimala Herman, and David D. Clarke, eds., *Polysemy: Flexible patterns of meaning in mind and language* 297–315. Berlin: Mouton de Gruyter.

Goldberg, Adele. 1992. The inherent semantics of argument structure: The case of the English ditransitive construction. *Cognitive Linguistics* 3: 37–74.

Goldberg, Adele E. 1995. *Constructions: A construction grammar approach to argument structure.* Chicago: University of Chicago Press.

Heider, Eleanor (Eleanor Rosch). 1971. "Focal" color areas and the development of color names. *Developmental Psychology* 4: 447–55.

Heider, Eleanor (Eleanor Rosch). 1972. Universals in color naming and memory. *Journal of Experimental Psychology* 93: 10–20.

Herlin, Ilona. 1998. *Suomen kun* [The Finnish conjunction kun]. Suomalaisen Kirjallisuuden Seuran Toimituksia 712. Helsinki: Suomalaisen Kirjallisuuden Seura [Finnish Literature Society].

Herskovits, Annette. 1986. *Language and spatial cognition: An interdisciplinary study of the prepositions in English.* Cambridge: Cambridge University Press.

Hewson, John. 1997. *The cognitive system of the French verb.* Amsterdam: John Benjamins.

Hunn, Eugene S. 1977. *Tzeltal folk zoology: The classification of discontinuities in nature.* New York: Academic Press.

Janda, Laura A. 1990. The radial network of a grammatical category—its genesis and dynamic structure. *Cognitive Linguistics* 1: 269–88.

Janssen, Theo A. J. M. 2003. Monosemy versus polysemy. In Hubert Cuyckens, René Dirven, and John R. Taylor, eds., *Cognitive approaches to lexical semantics* 93–122. Berlin: Mouton de Gruyter.

Kalisz, Roman. 1990. *The pragmatics, semantics and syntax of the English sentences with 'that' complements and the Polish sentences with 'że' complements: A contrastive study.* Gdańsk: Wydawnictwo Uniwersytetu Gdańskiego.

Katz, Jerrold J., and Jerry A. Fodor. 1963. The structure of a semantic theory. *Language* 39: 170–210.

Kleiber, Georges. 1990. *La sémantique du prototype: Catégories et sens lexical.* Paris: Presses Universitaires de France.

Krzeszowski, Tomasz P. 1990. Prototypes and equivalence. *Papers and Studies in Contrastive Linguistics* 21: 5–20.

Lakoff, George. 1987. *Women, fire, and dangerous things: What categories reveal about the mind.* Chicago: University of Chicago Press.

Lakoff, George. 1990. The invariance hypothesis: Is abstract reason based on image-schemas? *Cognitive Linguistics* 1: 39–74.

Lakoff, George, and Mark Johnson. 1980. *Metaphors we live by.* Chicago: University of Chicago Press.

Lakoff, George, and Zoltán Kövecses. 1987. The cognitive model of anger inherent in American English. In Dorothy Holland and Naomi Quinn, eds., *Cultural models in language and thought* 195–221. Chicago: University of Chicago Press.

Langacker, Ronald W. 1987. *Foundations of cognitive grammar.* Vol. 1, *Theoretical prerequisites.* Stanford, CA: Stanford University Press.

Langacker, Ronald W. 1991. *Foundations of cognitive grammar.* Vol. 2, *Descriptive application.* Stanford, CA: Stanford University Press.

Lapata, Maria. 2000. The acquisition and modeling of lexical knowledge: A corpus-based investigation of systematic polysemy. PhD dissertation, University of Edinburgh.

Laurence, Stephen, and Eric Margolis. 1999. Concepts and cognitive science. In Eric Margolis and Stephen Laurence, eds., *Concepts: Core readings* 3–81. Cambridge, MA: MIT Press.

Lehrer, Adrienne. 1990. Polysemy, conventionality, and the structure of the lexicon. *Cognitive Linguistics* 1: 207–46.

Lehrer, Adrienne. 2003. Polysemy in derivational affixes. In Brigitte Nerlich, Zazie Todd, Vimala Herman, and David D. Clarke, eds., *Polysemy: Flexible patterns of meaning in mind and language* 217–32. Berlin: Mouton de Gruyter.

Lewandowska-Tomaszczyk, Barbara. 1992. Cognitive and interactional conditioning of semantic change. In Gunter Kellermann and Michael D. Morrissey, eds., *Diachrony within synchrony: Language history and cognition* 228–50. Frankfurt am Main: Peter Lang Verlag.

Lewandowska-Tomaszczyk, Barbara. 1995. Worldview and verbal senses. In Braj B. Kachru and Henry Kahane, eds., *Cultures, ideologies, and the dictionary: Studies in honor of Ladislav Zgusta* 223–35. Tübingen: Max Niemeyer Verlag.

Lewandowska-Tomaszczyk, Barbara. 1996. *Depth of negation: A cognitive semantic study.* Łódź: Łódź University Press.

Lewandowska-Tomaszczyk, Barbara. 1997. Lexical meanings in language corpora. In Barbara Lewandowska-Tomaszczyk and Patrick James Melia, eds., *PALC '97: Practical applications in language corpora* 236–56. Łódź: Łódź University Press.

Lewandowska-Tomaszczyk, Barbara. 2002. Polysemy: Research methodology and mechanisms. In Barbara Lewandowska-Tomaszczyk and Kamila Turewicz, eds., *Cognitive linguistics today* 81–96. Frankfurt am Main: Peter Lang Verlag.

Lewandowska-Tomaszczyk, Barbara. 2004. Review of *The Lexicon-encyclopedia interface*, edited by Bert Peeters. *Cognitive Linguistics* 15: 406–19.

Lindner, Susan. 1981. A lexico-semantic analysis of English verb-particle constructions with OUT and UP. PhD dissertation, University of California at San Diego. (Published as *A lexico-semantic analysis of English verb-particle constructions.* LAUT Paper, no. 101. Trier, Germany: Linguistic Agency of the University of Trier, 1983)

Lipka, Leonard. 1986. Homonymie, Polysemie, oder Ableitung im heutigen Englisch. *Zeitschrift für Anglistik und Amerikanistik* 34: 28–38.

Lipka, Leonard. 1988. A rose is a rose is a rose: On simple and dual categorization in natural languages. In Werner Hüllen and Rainer Schulze, eds., *Understanding the lexicon: Meaning, sense and world knowledge in lexical semantics* 355–66. Tübingen: Max Niemeyer Verlag.

Locke, John. [1697] 1960. *An essay concerning human understanding*. Abr. and ed. A. S. Pringle-Pattison. Oxford: Clarendon Press.

MacLaury, Robert E. 1992. From brightness to hue: An explanatory model of color category evolution. *Current Anthropology* 33: 137–86.

MacWhinney, Brian. 1989. Competition and lexical categorization. In Roberta Corrigan, Fred Eckman, and Michael Noonan, eds., *Linguistic categorization* 195–241. Amsterdam: John Benjamins.

MacWhinney, Brian. 2000. Connectionism and language learning. In Michael Barlow and Suzanne Kemmer, eds., *Usage-based models of language* 121–49. Stanford, CA: CSLI Publications.

Mangasser-Wahl, Martina. 2000. *Von der Prototypentheorie zur empirischen Semantik*. Frankfurt am Main: Peter Lang Verlag.

Margolis, Eric, and Stephen Laurence, eds. 1999. *Concepts: Core readings*. Cambridge, MA: MIT Press.

Matsumoto, Yo. 1993. Japanese numeral classifiers: A study of semantic categories and lexical organization. *Linguistics* 31: 667–713.

Mervis, Carolyn B., and Eleanor Rosch. 1981. Categorization of natural objects. *Annual Review of Psychology* 32: 89–115.

Needham, Rodney. 1972. *Belief, language, and experience*. Oxford: Basil Blackwell.

Nerlich, Brigitte, and David D. Clarke. 1997. Polysemy: Patterns in meaning and patterns in history. *Historiographia Linguistica* 24: 359–85.

Nerlich, Brigitte, and David D. Clarke. 2003. Polysemy and flexibility: Introduction and overview. In Brigitte Nerlich, Zazie Todd, Vimala Herman, and David D. Clarke, eds., *Polysemy: Flexible patterns of meaning in mind and language* 3–30. Berlin: Mouton de Gruyter.

Nerlich, Brigitte, Zazie Todd, and David D. Clarke. 1998. The function of polysemous jokes and riddles in lexical development. *Cahiers de psychologie: Current psychology of cognition* 17: 343–66.

Nerlich, Brigitte, Zazie Todd, and David D.Clarke. 2003. Emerging patterns and evolving polysemies: the acquisition of *get* between four and ten years. In Brigitte Nerlich, Zazie Todd, Vimala Herman, and David D. Clarke, eds., *Polysemy: Flexible patterns of meaning in mind and language* 333–57. Berlin: Mouton de Gruyter.

Nerlich, Brigitte, Zazie Todd, Vimala Herman, and David D. Clarke. eds. 2003. *Polysemy: Flexible patterns of meaning in mind and language*. Berlin: Mouton de Gruyter.

Newman, John. 1996. *Give: A cognitive linguistic study*. Berlin: Mouton de Gruyter.

Nikiforidou, Kiki 1991. The meanings of the genitive: A case study in semantic structure and semantic change. *Cognitive Linguistics* 2: 149–205

Norrick, Neal R. 1981. *Semiotic principles in semantic theory*. Amsterdam: John Benjamins.

Nunberg, Geoffrey. 1987. *The pragmatics of reference*. Bloomington: Indiana University Linguistics Club.

Osherson, Daniel N., and Edward E. Smith. 1981. On the adequacy of prototype theory as a theory of concepts. *Cognition* 9: 35–58.

Palmer, Gary, and Claudia Woodman. 1999. Ontological classifiers as polycentric categories, as seen in Shona class 3 nouns. In Martin Puetz and Marjolijn Verspoor, eds.,
Explorations in linguistic relativity 225–49. Amsterdam: John Benjamins.

Perlmutter, David M. 1970. The two verbs *begin*. In Roderick A. Jacobs and Peter S.
Rosenbaum, eds., *Readings in English transformational grammar* 107–19. Waltham,
MA: Ginn.

Plato. 1981. Euthryphro. In *Five Dialogues* 5–22. Trans. G. M. A. Grube. Indianapolis, IN:
Hackett.

Postal, Paul M. 1969. Underlying and superficial linguistic structure. In David A. Reibel
and Sanford A. Schane, eds., *Modern studies in English: Readings in transformational
grammar* 19–37. Englewood Cliffs, NJ: Prentice-Hall.

Pustejovsky, James. 1991. The generative lexicon. *Computational Linguistics* 17: 409–41.

Pustejovsky, James, and Branimir Boguraev. 1999. Introduction: Lexical semantics in
context. In James Pustejovsky and Branimir Boguraev, eds., *Lexical semantics: The
problem of polysemy* 1–14. Oxford: Clarendon Press.

Pustejovsky, James, and Pierrette Bouillon. 1999. Aspectual coercion and logical polysemy.
In James Pustejovsky and Branimir Boguraev, eds., *Lexical semantics: The problem of
polysemy* 133–62. Oxford: Clarendon Press.

Quine, Willard Van Orman. 1953. Two dogmas of empiricism. In Willard Van Orman
Quine, *From a logical point of view* 20–46. Cambridge, MA: Harvard University Press.

Quine, Willard Van Orman. 1960. *Word and object*. Cambridge, MA: MIT Press.

Rakova, Marina. 2003. *The extent of the literal: Metaphor, polysemy and theories of concepts*.
Houndmills, UK: Macmillan.

Raukko, Jarno. 1995. What do we get for get in Finnish? *The New Courant* 3: 179–80.

Ravid, Dorit, and David Hanauer. 1998. A prototype theory of rhyme: Evidence from
Hebrew. *Cognitive Linguistics* 9: 79–106.

Ravin, Yael, and Claudia Leacock. 2000. Polysemy: An overview. In Yael Ravin and Claudia
Leacock, eds., *Polysemy: Theoretical and computational approaches* 1–29. Oxford:
Oxford University Press.

Rayson, Paul. 1995. The ACAMRIT semantic tagging system. http://www.comp.lancs.ac
.uk/ucrel/acamrit/acamrit.html.

Rosch, Eleanor. 1973. Natural categories. *Cognitive Psychology* 4: 328–50.

Rosch, Eleanor, and Carolyn B. Mervis. 1975. Family resemblances. *Cognitive Psychology* 7:
573–605.

Ross, John D. 1981. *Portraying analogy*. Cambridge: Cambridge University Press.

Rudzka-Ostyn, Brygida. 1985. Metaphoric processes in word-formation: The case of prefixed words. In Wolf Paprotté and René Dirven, eds., *The ubiquity of metaphor* 209–41.
Amsterdam: John Benjamins.

Rudzka-Ostyn, Brygida. 1989. Prototypes, schemas, and cross-category correspondences:
The case of *ask*. *Linguistics* 27: 613–62.

Ruhl, Charles. 1989. *On monosemy: A study in linguistic semantics*. Albany: State University
of New York Press.

Sandra, Dominiek. 1998. What linguists can and can't tell you about the human mind:
A reply to Croft. *Cognitive Linguistics* 9: 361–78.

Sandra, Dominiek, and Sally Rice. 1995. Network analyses of prepositional meaning: Mirroring whose mind—the linguist's or the language user's? *Cognitive Linguistics* 6: 89–130.

Schmid, Hans-Jörg. 1993. *Cottage und Co., idea, start vs. begin: Die Kategorisierung als
Grundprinzip einer differenzierten Bedeutungsbeschreibung*. Tübingen: Max Niemeyer
Verlag.

Schulze, Rainer. 1988. A short story of *down*. In Werner Hüllen and Rainer Schulze, eds., *Understanding the lexicon: Meaning, sense and world knowledge in lexical semantics* 394–410. Tübingen: Max Niemeyer Verlag.

Schulze, Rainer. 1993. The meaning of *(a)round*: A study of an English preposition. In Richard A. Geiger and Brygida Rudzka-Ostyn, eds., *Conceptualizations and mental processing in language* 399–431. Berlin: Mouton de Gruyter.

Soares da Silva, Augusto. 2003. Image schemas and coherence of the verb category: The case of the Portuguese verb *deixar*. In Hubert Cuyckens, René Dirven, and John R. Taylor, eds., *Cognitive approaches to lexical semantics* 281–322. Berlin: Mouton de Gruyter.

Sweetser, Eve. 1987. The definition of lie: An examination of the folk models underlying a semantic prototype. In Dorothy Holland and Naomi Quinn, eds., *Cultural models in language and thought* 43–66. Cambridge: Cambridge University Press.

Sweetser, Eve. 1990. *From etymology to pragmatics: Metaphorical and cultural aspects of semantic structure.* Cambridge: Cambridge University Press.

Taylor, John R. 1989. *Linguistic categorization: Prototypes in linguistic theory.* Oxford: Clarendon Press. (2nd ed., 1995; 3rd ed., 2003)

Taylor, John R. 1992. Old problems: Adjectives in cognitive grammar. *Cognitive Linguistics* 3: 1–36.

Taylor, John R. 1996. *Possessives in English: An exploration in cognitive grammar.* Oxford: Oxford University Press.

Taylor, John R. 2003. Cognitive models of polysemy. In Brigitte Nerlich, Zazie Todd, Vimala Herman, and David D. Clarke, eds., *Polysemy: Flexible patterns of meaning in mind and language* 31–48. Berlin: Mouton de Gruyter.

Taylor, John R., and Robert E. MacLaury, eds. 1995. *Language and the cognitive construal of the world.* Berlin: Mouton de Gruyter.

Tomasello, Michael. 1992. *First verbs: A case study of early grammatical development.* Cambridge: Cambridge University Press.

Traugott, Elizabeth Closs. 1982. From propositional to textual and expressive meanings: Some semantic-pragmatic aspects of grammaticalization. In Winfred P. Lehmann and Yakov Malkiel, eds., *Perspectives on historical linguistics* 245–71. Amsterdam: John Benjamins.

Tuggy, David. 1987. *Scarecrow* nouns, generalizations, and Cognitive Grammar. In Scott DeLancey and Russell S. Tomlin, eds., *Proceedings of the Annual Meeting of the Pacific Linguistics Conference* 307–20. Eugene: Department of Linguistics, University of Oregon.

Tuggy, David. 1993. Ambiguity, polysemy, and vagueness. *Cognitive Linguistics* 4: 273–90.

Tuggy, David. 1999. Linguistic evidence for polysemy in the mind: A response to William Croft and Dominiek Sandra. *Cognitive Linguistics* 10: 343–68.

Tuggy, David. 2003. The Nawatl verb *kîsa*: A case study in polysemy. In Hubert Cuyckens, René Dirven, and John R. Taylor, eds., *Cognitive approaches to lexical semantics* 323–62. Berlin: Mouton de Gruyter.

Turner, Mark. 1990. Aspects of the invariance hypothesis. *Cognitive Linguistics* 1: 247–55.

Tyler, Andrea, and Vyvyan Evans. 2003. Reconsidering prepositional polysemy networks: The case of *over*. In Brigitte Nerlich, Zazie Todd, Vimala Herman, and David D. Clarke, eds., *Polysemy: Flexible patterns of meaning in mind and language* 95–159. Berlin: Mouton de Gruyter.

Ullmann, Stephen. 1951. *The principles of semantics.* Oxford: Basil Blackwell.

Vandeloise, Claude. 1991. *Spatial prepositions: A case study from French.* Chicago: University of Chicago Press.

Van Petten, Cyma, and Marta Kutas. 1987. Ambiguous words in context: An event-related potential analysis of the time course of meaning activation. *Journal of Memory and Language* 26: 188–208.

Van Petten, Cyma, and Marta Kutas. 1991. Electrophysiological evidence for the flexibility of lexical processing. In Greg B. Simpson, ed., *Understanding word and sentence* 129–74. Oxford: North-Holland.

Verhagen, Arie. 1992. Praxis of linguistics: Passives in Dutch. *Cognitive Linguistics* 3: 301–42.

Wierzbicka, Anna. 1985. *Conceptual analysis and lexicography*. Ann Arbor, MI: Karoma.

Wilkins, David P., and Deborah Hill. 1995. When "go" means "come": Questioning the basicness of basic motion verbs. *Cognitive Linguistics* 6: 119–57.

Wittgenstein, Ludwig. 1953. *Philosophical investigations*. Trans. G. E. m. Anscombe. Oxford: Basil Blackwell.

Zadeh, Lofti. 1965. Fuzzy sets. *Information and Control* 8: 338–53.

Zlatev, Jordan. 2003. Polysemy or generality? Mu. In Hubert Cuyckens, René Dirven, and John R. Taylor, eds., *Cognitive approaches to lexical semantics* 447–94. Berlin: Mouton de Gruyter.

Zwicky, Arnold, and Jerry Sadock. 1975. Ambiguity tests and how to fail them. In John Kimball, ed., *Syntax and Semantics* 4: 1–36. New York: Academic Press.

CHAPTER 7

FRAMES, IDEALIZED COGNITIVE MODELS, AND DOMAINS

ALAN CIENKI

1. INTRODUCTION

Constructs such as frames, Idealized Cognitive Models (ICMs), and domains have been central to various methods of analysis in Cognitive Linguistics. Each of them provides a way of characterizing the structured encyclopedic knowledge which is inextricably connected with linguistic knowledge—that assertion being an important tenet in much of the cognitive linguistic research. Frames, ICMs, and domains all derive from an approach to language as a system of communication that reflects the world as it is construed by humans, rather than as it might be represented from some god's-eye point of view. This chapter presents an overview of these three topics, including their origins and development, their interrelation, and their role as foundational ideas in Cognitive Linguistics.

2. FRAMES

The notion of "frame" has been used over the years in various fields, not only in linguistics, but also in areas such as psychology and Artificial Intelligence. Here, the focus will be on the specific role(s) it has played in Cognitive Linguistics, where Charles J. Fillmore's work has been particularly influential. As explained in the following overview, Fillmore began using the term solely on the level of linguistic description, and later, he and others extended its use to include characterization of knowledge structures, thus linking the analysis of language to the study of cognitive phenomena.

In his papers "Frame semantics" (1982a) and "A private history of the concept 'Frame'" (1987), Fillmore reveals the influences which led to his formulation and development of the notion. In the 1950s, he was exploring the principles behind the co-occurrence of strings of words, influenced by Fries (1952), and later by Pike's (1967) work on "tagmemic formulas." Fillmore's early work on transformational syntax led him into researching the distributional properties of individual verbs (e.g., Fillmore 1961). This research involved looking at the substitutability of words, within what could be called syntactic frames, while preserving the meaning of the utterance. But soon the use of "frame" extended from syntax to semantics. Fillmore (1982a: 114) reflects that by the late 1960s, "I began to believe that certain kinds of groupings of verbs and classifications of clause types could be stated more meaningfully if the structures with which verbs were initially associated were described in terms of the semantic roles of their associated arguments." Trying to adapt Transformational Generative Grammar to this way of thinking, he proposed deep-structure valence descriptions for verbs. These "case frames" (Fillmore 1968) specified the semantic roles of the nominals which could occur with a given verb.

However, even "this theory of semantic roles fell short of providing the detail needed for semantic description; it came more and more to seem that another independent level of role structure was needed for the semantic description of verbs in particular limited domains" (Fillmore 1982a: 115). He adds that rather than developing an account in terms of truth conditions, which was customary at the time, "it seemed to me more profitable to believe that there are larger cognitive structures capable of providing a new layer of semantic rule notions."

His first attempt at describing such a cognitive structure appeared in his 1971 paper on "verbs of judging." Here he makes the claim that verbs such as *blame, accuse*, and *criticize* highlight a person who forms a judgment on the worth or behavior of some situation or individual (which he calls "the Judge"), a person whose behavior is being judged ("the Defendant"), and some situation in which judgment seemed relevant ("the Situation"). So use of the verb *accuse* asserts that the Judge, presupposing the badness of the Situation, claimed that the Defendant was responsible. However, with the verb *criticize*, one asserts that the Judge, presupposing the Defendant's responsibility for the Situation, presented arguments for believing that the Situation was in some way blameworthy, and so forth. Note how this differs from the earlier idea of a case frame in that "we have here not just a group of individual words, but a 'domain' of vocabulary whose elements somehow presuppose a schematization of human judgment and behavior involving notions of worth, responsibility, judgment, etc." (Fillmore 1982a: 116). This draws on the speaker's/addressee's background knowledge about what would likely be relevant in such a Situation, or as he came to call it in a more generic sense, the relevant "scene."

In response to the dominant semantic theories in American linguistics in the 1970s, in which linguists tried to capture word meanings in terms of sets of necessary and sufficient conditions, Fillmore proposed "an alternative to checklist theories of meaning" (Fillmore 1975). Here he presented a "scenes-and-frames paradigm." Fillmore notes, "I use the word *scene* in a maximally general sense, including not only visual scenes but also familiar kinds of interpersonal transactions, standard scenarios defined by the culture, institutional structures, enactive experiences, body image" (1975: 124)—in short, what in some ways will be captured in later years by the term *domain*. He continues, "I use the word *frame* for any system of linguistic choices—the easiest cases being collections of words, but also including choices of grammatical rules or linguistic categories—that can get associated with prototypical instances of scenes." Though frames are talked about from a linguistic viewpoint, it is noteworthy that they are not presented as an independent approach to linguistic analysis, but rather as one part of a paradigm, integrally linked to the idea of scenes.

The connection made between frames and scenes is made even clearer with his examples in that paper, such as the following. The English word *write* and the Japanese word *kaku* are commonly considered translation equivalents, but since the overall scenes associated with the words in their respective cultures differ, the linguistic frames within which each word is used also differ coordinately. The scene associated with the English word entails that it is some form of language that is written, while the scene linked to the Japanese word is less specific and could include various kinds of drawing. Thus, the frame for answering the question "What did you write?" would be limited to expressions for "a linguistic communication scene," while in Japanese the frame for answering the coordinate question about *kaku* affords a broader range of possibilities.

In the analysis of the "commercial event," Fillmore (1977) shows that a large set of English verbs are related to each other by how they evoke the same general scene in different ways. Verbs such as *buy, sell, spend,* and *cost* entail an understanding of the relevant roles (buyer, seller) and elements (goods, money) in terms of which the actions of buying, selling, spending, and costing are construed. The argument made is that with verbs of judging, verbs of commercial transaction, and many others, "nobody can really understand the meanings of the words in that domain who does not understand the social institutions or the structures of experience which they presuppose" (Fillmore 1987: 31).[1]

In his 1985 paper, Fillmore makes a distinction between theories concerned with the semantics of truth (T-semantics) and those based on language understanding (U-semantics) and concludes that "both the notion of truth and the uses of negation needed for a formal T-semantics are secondary to the understanding of those notions that arise from a study of U-semantics" (223). In contrast to the dictionary-like notion of meaning inherent in (particularly American) formalist approaches to semantics in the 1970s, the theory of linguistic frames embraces an encyclopedic view of meaning (223), which continues in Cognitive Linguistics to this day. The work on frames also developed in opposition to purely compositional approaches to semantics, according to which the meaning of a text is simply deter-mined by the integration of the meanings of its component words and sentences. Fillmore (1986: 52) points out, "While the *task* of linguistic semantics must be to explain how text meanings are developed, the *knowledge* which is called on for achieving this task is not limited to linguistic knowledge."

Fillmore's work was thus integrally connected with other advances in Cog-nitive Linguistics as the field developed. He was influenced by the ongoing research on prototypes (e.g., citing Rosch 1973), and in his 1975 paper, Fillmore makes a bid for linking research on frames and prototypes, since "in some cases the area of ex-perience on which a linguistic frame imposes order is a prototype" (123). He notes in his 1982a paper that often the frame against which a word is understood involves a schematized prototype of what some part of the world is like. He uses the word *orphan* as an example. We can say the word refers to a child whose parents are no longer living, but "the category ORPHAN does not have 'built into it' any speci-fication of the age after which it is no longer relevant to speak of somebody as an orphan, because that understanding is a part of the background prototype" (118). This idea of frames as drawing on background prototypes sounds like what Lakoff will later call Idealized Cognitive Models, and in 1985, Fillmore makes an explicit comparison between his notion of *scene* and constructs (223), such as Lakoff's (1982) *cognitive model*, Lakoff and Johnson's (1980) *experiential gestalt*, and Langacker's (1984) *base* (in contrast to *profile*).

Influenced by work in the 1970s on pragmatics and speech acts, Fillmore also claimed that we not only employ cognitive frames to produce and understand lan-guage, but also to conceptualize what is going on between the speaker and addressee, or writer and reader. This introduced the idea of framing on another level, in terms of "interactional frames." Such interactional frames provide a tool for talking about the background knowledge and expectations one brings to bear for the production, and interpretation, of oral or written discourse, particularly in relation to accepted genre types. Knowing that a text is a business contract, a folktale, or marriage pro-posal, one employs specific structures of expectations which help lead to a full inter-pretation of the meaning, and also help one know when the text is ending, and how to respond, if that is appropriate (Fillmore 1982a: 117).

Though the notion of frames developed in cognitive psychology independently in the 1970s (Fillmore 1987), Fillmore (1975: 124 and elsewhere) acknowledges con-nections between his use of the term and earlier uses by others. Andor (1985) pro-vides an overview of the use of *frame* and related terms in linguistics, psychology, and computer science. Tannen (1985: 327) comments on use of the notion of frames in anthropology and sociology, à la Bateson (1972) and Goffman (1974), and notes that there it may be better understood as "frames of interpretation" (see also Tannen 1993). However, the common thrust behind these different framings of the term "frame," namely that knowledge schemas guide and structure our use of lan-guage, is of greater significance than the distinctions between the various uses of the term in different disciplines. In later work, Fillmore (1986: 49) admits having given up on maintaining a differentiation between the terms *frame, schema, scene, script* (a standard event sequence found in a specific context, as described by Schank and Abelson 1977), and so on. Rather, all of these reflect different levels of frame knowledge. The idea that language has a frame-like structure as a natural reflection of the ways in which we frame knowledge led to the "frame-semantic treatment of various classes of grammatical constructions" (Fillmore 1986: 55)—which became known as Construction Grammar (Goldberg 1995). Hudson (1985, 1986) concurs that, unless proven to the contrary, a viable working assumption is that linguistic structure works the same way as nonlinguistic conceptual structure, and he proposes his Word Grammar (Hudson 1984) as an integrative theory which embraces this position. For similar reasons, Langacker (1987, 1991), drew on frame semantics in the development of Cognitive Grammar. (See chapters 17, 18, and 19 of the present *Handbook* on each of these theories of grammar.)

As frame semantics developed in the 1970s and early 1980s, it perhaps had more influence as a theoretical construct, and as a stimulus to think about semantics in a different way, than it had as an analytic tool in empirical research (Õim and Saluveer 1985: 295). However, if the *MLA International Bibliography* is an accurate indication, more studies have been published since the late 1980s to the present which use a frame approach in research in specific areas of lexical semantics, particularly in cross-linguistic research (see, for example, Petruck 1995; Rojo López and Valenzuela 1998; and Croft, Taoka, and Wood 2001). Frame semantics portends later research on first-language acquisition, such as approaches to grammar as templates, and Tomasello's (1992) "Verb Island hypothesis." It also has implications for research in historical linguistics. Often a change in linguistic label for something is a consequence of a change in the linguistic frame in which it plays a part. A case in point is "*World War I*, which was not called *World War I* until there was a World War II to get the counting frame started" (Fillmore 1985: 239).

Finally, framing has found important application in recent years with increasing awareness of the persuasive effects that can be achieved by reframing, or using alternative framings, of an issue. "From a frame semantics point of view, it is frequently possible to show that the same 'facts' can be presented within different framings, framings which make them out as different 'facts'" (Fillmore 1982a: 125). We also see use of the word *frame* in Reddy ([1979] 1993) and Schön ([1979] 1993) to refer to ways of thinking about an issue which are reflected in the use of metaphorical language. The manner in which one frames an issue can have practical implications for social policy and for politics. Witness Schön's point that different solutions may seem more logical when one calls a low-income neighborhood a diseased area versus when one considers it to be a natural community; in the former case the neighborhood should be removed, whereas in the latter it should be nurtured and developed. (See also the papers in Dirven, Frank, and Ilie 2001 for analyses of ideologies in discourse in terms of frames and models.) Framing is now being used explicitly as an analytic tool by organizations such as the FrameWorks Institute (Washington, DC), which strives to advance the nonprofit sector's communications capacity through research on framing public discourse about social problems, and the Rockridge Institute (Berkeley, CA), which endorses reframing public debate in the United States in support of progressive politics.

3. IDEALIZED COGNITIVE MODELS

The notion of Idealized Cognitive Models was preceded by a theoretical exploration of the application of Gestalts in linguistics, namely in a new approach dubbed "experiential linguistics." The basic claim of experiential linguistics, as Lakoff (1977: 237) proposes, is that "a wide variety of experiential factors—perception, reasoning, the nature of the body, the emotions, memory, social structure, sensorimotor and cognitive development, etc.—determine in large measure, if not totally, universal structural characteristics of language." This way of thinking sets the stage for many later developments, which come to be known collectively as Cognitive Linguistics. Lakoff continues: "What I would ultimately like to show (or see other people show) is that thought, perception, the emotions, cognitive processing, motor activity, and language are all organized in terms of the same kinds of structures, which I am calling *gestalts*" (246).

He notes that while his use of the term bears some relation to the concept developed by the Gestalt psychologists, it is not intended to refer to exactly the same thing. The following are some of the many properties which Lakoff (1977: 246–47) ascribes to Gestalts:

- Gestalts are structures that are used in cognitive processing;
- Gestalts are wholes whose component parts take on additional significance by virtue of being within those wholes;
- Gestalts have internal relations among parts, which may be of different types;
- Gestalts may have external relations to other Gestalts;
- there may be partial mappings of one Gestalt onto another, or embedding of one within another;
- a Gestalt analysis need not necessarily make claims about the ultimate parts into which something can be decomposed, since such analysis would be guided by cognitive purposes and viewpoints, and thus different analyses may be possible; but
- Gestalts must distinguish prototypical from nonprototypical properties; and
- Gestalts are often cross-modal.

Instantiations of Gestalts in language may involve a number of types of properties, such as grammatical, pragmatic, semantic, and/or phonological ones.

All of this comprises an alternative to the formal syntactic rules of Transformational Generative Grammar, which essentially try to handle grammar in a mathematical framework. Instead, the characterization of linguistic Gestalts stems from what is (or was in the 1970s) being discovered about general processes of cognition, and of categorization in particular. The Gestalt approach supports the view that grammar does not rely on absolute rules, but rather involves flexible patterns and notions like partial similarity, or partial mapping to a pattern.

The phenomenon of "Patient subjects" provides a case in point. Lakoff (1977: 248–54) and van Oosten (1977) discuss how in certain sentences, the usual object of a transitive verb (the Patient) can be used as a subject with an active verb, as in *This car drives easily* or *Bean curd digests easily*. But this is not possible with all verbs, and thus sentences like *Bean curd eats easily* are semantically strange (as indicated by the asterisk). They claim that the grammatical property of subjecthood prototypically pairs with the semantic properties of 'primary responsibility', 'control', and 'volition', as one typically finds in Agent-subject sentences. In Patient-subject sentences, one finds that the properties of the Patient are more responsible for what happens than those of the Agent. So 'primary responsibility' is the most important property paired with subjecthood, to the extent that it can have priority even if 'control' and 'volition' are not involved (i.e., cars and beans do not have independent control or volition). Another factor that is relevant in the formulation of such sentences is which properties of the Agent or the Patient the speaker is putting into focus. Regarding the verbs *digest* and *eat*, properties of the Patient can be primarily responsible for whether digestion takes place, but not for whether eating takes place. So the sentence *Bean curd eats easily* is infelicitous because of the conflict inherent between Patient focus (with the subject *bean curd*) and Agent focus (with the verb *eats*). In this way, linguistic Gestalts involve perspective (in terms of Agent- or Patient-focus)—another way in which the theory is based on factors of human (cognitive and embodied) experience. The linguistic Gestalts of the special-purpose Patient-subject sentences, described above, and the more common type of sentences (in which the Patient is the object of the verb), also bear partial similarity to further types of sentence constructions, such as those with reflexive-Patient-subjects (e.g., *Those dresses practically sell themselves*). In sum, the syntax of a language is structured by numerous overlapping Gestalts, the knowledge of which guides speakers (or writers, or signers) in their production of language and guides addressees in their comprehension.

This notion of Gestalts provided the underpinnings for the development of Idealized Cognitive Models (ICMs) in Cognitive Linguistics. The first detailed explication of ICMs appeared in Lakoff (1987), as part of a synthesis of existing research on categorization within the various branches of cognitive science. ICMs are proposed as a way in which we organize knowledge, not as a direct reflection of an objective state of affairs in the world, but according to certain cognitive structuring principles. The models are *idealized*, in that they involve an abstraction, through perceptual and conceptual processes, from the complexities of the physical world. At the same time, these processes impart organizing structure—for example, in the form of conceptual categories. The use of models in cognitive processing that are idealized in the ways described below also makes sense from an evolutionary perspective. They provide an advantageous means of processing information because they are adapted to human neurobiology, human embodied experience, human actions and goals, and human social interaction.

An example which Lakoff uses helps illustrate the concept of ICMs. The English word *bachelor* has provided semantic fodder for linguists for decades. At least in American English, it has largely been replaced by the gender-neutral *single*, but many aspects of the analysis below carry over to the word *single* as well. Katz and Postal's (1964) analysis of the semantics of *bachelor* led to its frequent citation as an example of the successful transferal of markedness theory from phonology to semantics (using [HUMAN], [MALE], [ADULT], and [NEVER MARRIED] as semantic features). However, Fillmore (1982b) points out that the word and the analysis of it in terms of necessary and sufficient conditions assumes a certain frame of background knowledge, including expectations about marriage and requirements of eligibility for it. Fillmore (1982b: 34) observes, "male participants in modern long-term unmarried couplings would not ordinarily be described as bachelors" and "[Pope] John Paul II is not properly thought of as a bachelor." Lakoff (1987) highlights the point that this word is defined with respect to a model of the world in which certain expectations hold (such as opposite-sex partnership, typical marriageable age, etc.), and this model is *idealized* in that it ignores many possible aspects of the real world (same-sex partnerships, a role in a religious institution which requires a vow of chastity, etc.). Thus, *bachelor* (and in many of the same ways, the word *single* as used in parallel contexts) is defined with respect to an ICM. It is worth noting that currently the word is used far less frequently on its own and usually occurs in a few conventionalized collocations, such as *eligible bachelor* or *bachelor party* (for the groom-to-be on the eve of his wedding). Yet, these set collocations in which the word remains in use today also highlight specific elements of that ICM. So *eligible bachelor* makes the eligibility requirement salient, and a *bachelor party* accentuates the licentious behavior that is part of a stereotype of a man's life before marital responsibilities.

The example above shows only some aspects of what can constitute an ICM. Lakoff (1987: 284) enumerates the following as five basic types of ICMs: propositional, image-schematic, metaphorical, metonymic, and symbolic. Let us consider each in turn in more detail.

3.1. Propositional ICMs

Lakoff (1987: 284–87) describes propositional models as having to do with entities, their properties, and the relations between the entities. What differs here from the objectivist assumptions of semantic theory based in symbolic logic is that propositional models are not claimed to correspond directly to slices of reality. Rather, as cognitive models, the entities and the relations between them are mental constructs. Lakoff, furthermore, points out that the propositional structure of ICMs may be of various types, among them: the simple proposition, the scenario (or script), the feature bundle, the taxonomy, or the radial category. He describes each of these in the following way.

A *simple proposition* consists of arguments and a predicate, and more complex examples involve operations known from logical theory, such as quantification, conjunction, negation, and so on. A propositional ICM structured according to a *scenario* will be about an initial state, a sequence of events, and a final state. Typically, scenarios concern the states and activities of people; thus, the events are structured by the motivation of their purposes. We can think of Schank and Abelson's (1977) "restaurant script" as a scenario-based ICM. This *script* specified the specific knowledge of the events which typically take place when one visits a restaurant and the objects and events playing a role in these restaurant events, all of which were characterized in a form appropriate for a computer program. In this way, we can see connections between Artificial Intelligence research and theories of cognitive models, as well as the continuing influential role of Fillmore's frame semantics.

If a *feature bundle* is a collection of properties, then a propositional ICM structured in this way can be seen as what has been called a "classical category," that is, a category with clear boundaries defined by the properties common to all of its members. This is the folk model of how categories work, which is often employed in everyday reasoning without our realizing it. "Categorical statements," which make uniform claims about all members of a category, represent this type of reasoning.

Taxonomic propositional ICMs consist of hierarchically structured classical categories. A higher-order category is a whole, and the immediately lower categories are the parts of which it is composed, with no overlap of the categories at each level. Since a classical category is structured by a feature bundle ICM, higher-level categories must include all the features of their lower-level parts. Taxonomies of natural things—such as plants, animals, or minerals—represent this kind of categorization (see also Schmid, this volume, chapter 5).

A *radially* structured propositional ICM describes a category with its subcategories structured as containers within it. But this type of model is distinctive in that one subcategory is the center, and the other subcategories are connected to it by various kinds of links. The result is a center-periphery structure. Noncentral subcategories can be subcenters in that they may have other subcategories linked to them, in a smaller center-periphery structure. This approach has been applied in semantic analyses of many lexical items, morphemes, and grammatical constructions (see Lewandowska-Tomaszczyk, this volume, chapter 6). With the radially structured ICM, we already begin to go beyond the scope of the propositional ICMs in that the links between subcategories often involve metaphor or metonymy, whereas the other types of propositional ICMs use these devices less if at all.

3.2. Image schemas and ICMs

Johnson (1987: xiv) characterizes an image schema as "a recurring, dynamic pattern of our perceptual interactions and motor programs that ·gives coherence and structure to our experience"; he elaborates on approximately thirty image schemas which he considers to be the most important ones (see Oakley, this volume, chapter 9, for details). Drawing on this work, Lakoff (1987) demonstrates the structuring role which image schemas play in various types of ICMs.[2] One set of examples is the propositional ICMs, discussed above: a simple proposition is structured according to a PART-WHOLE schema in terms of the relation of the predicate to the proposition, of which it is a part; a scenario-based propositional ICM is structured by a PATH schema in the domain of time, normally with a "source" (an initial state) and a "goal" (a final state); and a radially structured propositional ICM is characterized by a CENTER-PERIPHERY schema.

Lakoff implies that image schemas themselves can be the major structuring elements of certain ICMs by virtue of the fact that each represents a simplified (idealized) abstraction of some pattern in our bodily experience which we use as a model for conceptualizing other (more abstract) aspects of our lives. But even such models necessarily employ metaphorical mappings to link the image schemas to relevant target domains. So the CONTAINER image schema, with its structural elements of 'interior', 'boundary', and 'exterior', provides a model for conceptualizing basic logic, such as the Boolean logic of classes. We understand not only classical categories, but also states of being and many other abstract entities as "containers" via metaphorical extensions from the image schema. Other image schemas serve as the basis for other cognitive models via metaphorical and metonymic extensions, as Johnson (1987) discusses in detail.

3.3. Metaphor and ICMs

Conceptual metaphors (see Grady, this volume, chapter 8) are usually cited for the structuring role they can play in ICMs, rather than being claimed to constitute ICMs in and of themselves. Thus, in one case study, Lakoff (1987) shows the important structuring role that metaphor plays in our ICM of 'anger'. But other structuring principles are also at work, such as prototypical scenarios in which anger can arise. As Emanatian (1999) points out, the degree to which metaphor can play a role in a model can differ vastly depending on the domain in question, from little or none (as in the American schema of what one does when going to a laundromat) to essentially exhausting a model (as in our ways of understanding and describing an abstract domain like 'thought' itself, which is difficult to do without metaphors).

3.4. Metonymy and ICMs

Lakoff (1987: 78) uses the term *metonymic model* to refer to an ICM which contains relation(s) in which one thing stands for another. As an example, Lakoff and Johnson (1980, chapter 8) discuss how we make sense out of sentences like *The White House isn't saying anything* by invoking the common metonymy whereby a place may stand for an institution or people located at that place. The ICM provides the framework for allowing one to make metonymic reference, in that it provides a limited search domain which the addressee can use to identify the metonymic referent. Social stereotypes are one example of how certain salient members of a category can be used to represent the entire category (part stands for whole), with the inherent danger that inferences can be made about the entire category of people based on the characteristics associated with the one subgroup.

3.5. Symbolic ICMs

The association of symbolic units, such as linguistic forms, with the conceptual elements in ICMs is the criterion for identifying an ICM as symbolic (Lakoff 1987: 289–92). In terms of linguistic form, our understanding of what constitutes a lexical item, a grammatical category, and a grammatical construction is claimed to be structured by ICMs. So the concept of 'noun' is a radial category based on the central (prototypical) subcategory of names for physical entities. But ICMs are also relevant in terms of the connection between symbol (linguistic form) and meaning. Lakoff also draws on the Figure/Ground distinction and recasts the findings of Fillmore's work on frame semantics to say that the meaning of each lexical item is represented as an element in an ICM, or conversely, an ICM provides the background against which a word is defined.

3.6. ICMs: Closing Points

ICMs have been used as analytic tools in research on lexical and morphological semantics, polysemy (particularly of prepositions, verb particles, and verbal prefixes), and the syntax and semantics of grammatical constructions. The three case studies in Lakoff (1987) give a sense of this work. One is a semantic analysis of *over* as a preposition and verb particle (developing on Brugman 1981); one provides a coherent account of English constructions with *there*, which sometimes refer to relative location and sometimes to existence (and this analysis invokes the work on frame semantics); and one explicates the ICM of 'anger' (drawing on work with Kövecses). The cross-linguistic studies on cognitive models of emotions that use ICMs as a basis (such as Lakoff and Kövecses 1987; Kövecses 1995) take us into research on cultural models (e.g., Holland and Quinn 1987; Quinn 1991; D'Andrade and Strauss 1992).

Implied, but not mentioned in the explications above, is a relation between ICMs and "mental spaces" (Fauconnier 1985). Mental spaces have been described as "small conceptual packets constructed as we think and talk, for purposes of local understanding and action" (Fauconnier and Turner 2002: 40; see also Fauconnier, this volume, chapter 14). Thus, "any fixed or ongoing state of affairs as we conceptualize it is represented by a mental space" (Lakoff 1987: 281). ICMs provide ready-made ways of structuring mental spaces. If one encounters a situation in which several salient elements evoke a known ICM, that model can provide a framework for filling in potentially relevant details. For example, hearing verbal formulas which introduce a story can invoke the "storytelling ICM," which can help one construct relevant mental spaces more easily to understand the story (Lakoff 1987: 281–82).

One of the critiques of research promoting ICMs as an analytic tool has been that it does not take account of the central role of culture in cognition (e.g., Quinn 1991). While the research on cognitive models and cultural models does not present them as two names for the same thing, the relation between the two sides cannot be ignored (Gibbs 1999). In this regard, Shore (1996) provides a detailed analysis of the many types of models which go into making up what we call "a culture." Shore points out that while some ICMs are really mental models, others are models constructed in the world in terms of social institutions and/or practices (334). Also note that the focus in this chapter, as in the extant literature on the subject, has been on linguistic instantiations of ICMs. But since such models are meant to be part of our general cognitive abilities, we can also find nonlinguistic versions of the various types of ICMs (e.g., various kinds of symbolic models, models employing metonymic reference via iconic images, etc.).

4. DOMAINS

Two main contexts in which the notion of "domains" has been used as a theoretical construct in cognitive linguistic research include conceptual metaphor theory and Cognitive Grammar. Though the term appears to have developed independently in these two lines of inquiry, an exploration into use of the term reveals that it can most profitably be understood by consideration of both contexts.

Lakoff (1993) makes it clear that the mappings in conceptual metaphors are between two "domains of experience," such that a target domain (of experience) is understood in terms of a source domain (of experience). What exactly constitutes a domain remained implicitly understood for some time by many who used the theoretical framework beginning with Lakoff and Johnson (1980), since the term was not yet used in that work. But even initially it was apparent that *domains*, as employed in conceptual metaphor theory, are something broader than *mental spaces*, as mentioned earlier. Whereas mental spaces involve conceptualizations enlisted by the individual in a specific context for a specific purpose, domains encompass many aspects of an experience that are conceptualized as associated.

A more explicit treatment of domains appears with the application of the notion in Cognitive Grammar. Langacker (1987: 488) defines "domain" within this framework as "a coherent area of conceptualization relative to which semantic units may be characterized." This use of "domain" covers a range of types of cognitive entities, from mental experiences, to representational spaces, concepts, or conceptual complexes (147). The notion is at the heart of the encyclopedic view of linguistic semantics in Cognitive Grammar; if knowledge is encyclopedic, rather than dictionary-like, domains provide a way of carving out the scope of concepts relevant for characterizing the meanings of linguistic units. The following is a brief summary of properties of different kinds of domains (based on Langacker 1987: chapter 4).

Domains, as understood in Cognitive Grammar, may be basic or abstract. "Basic domains" cannot be fully reduced to any other domains, and in this way they can be thought of as primitive dimensions of cognitive representation. Our sensory capacities are examples of several different basic domains. A domain which is not basic, "any concept or conceptual complex that functions as a domain for the definition of a higher-order concept" (Langacker 1987: 150), is called an *abstract domain*. For example, an understanding of what an *elbow* is requires knowledge about the domain of 'arm', but 'arm' is itself clearly not a basic domain, and so in this framework it qualifies as an abstract domain. In a footnote, Langacker (1987: 150) says that an abstract domain is essentially equivalent to an ICM, a frame, scene, schema, or possibly a script. However, given the various ways in which the terms listed have been understood, as described in the previous sections of this chapter, it might be best to understand "abstract domain" based on Langacker's own description of it.

In Cognitive Grammar, basic domains are recognized as having one or more dimensions. Thus, while time, pitch, and temperature are understood as one-dimensional, since each entails a single, consistent ordering, domains like kinship relations and color involve multiple dimensions (for kinship relations: intra- versus intergenerational relations; and for color: brightness, saturation, and hue). In addition, a domain can be described as locational or configurational. Examples of locational domains include temperature and color, since each is defined by a location on one or more scales. A configurational domain is one which can "accommodate a number of distinct values as part of a single gestalt" (Langacker 1987: 153). For example, we can have a two-dimensional or a three-dimensional conceptualization of the domain of space, and so it is a configurational domain.

Domain should also be distinguished from what is called a *dominion* in Cognitive Grammar. This is something specific to discussions about "reference points," which can be any entities that are used to establish mental contact with another (see Langacker 1993). In this context, the dominion is the conceptual region or set of entities to which a particular reference point affords direct access (Langacker 1991: 170). A dominion is therefore a concept localized to a specific type of context, and rather different from the broader notion of domains.

Croft (1993) reflects on the understanding of domains in the analysis of conceptual metaphors and metonymies in light of Langacker's work. He begins with Langacker's distinction between a profile and a base. If a profile is the entity designated by a semantic structure, then a base is the ground with respect to which that entity is profiled. He recalls Langacker's (1987: 183–84) example of an arc of a circle: not every curved line is an arc, as an arc presupposes the concept of a circle for its definition. Thus, a circle serves as the base, the background, against which we understand what an arc is (and in this case an arc is the relevant profile). Given this, "we can now define a domain as a semantic structure that functions as the base for at least one concept profile" (Croft 1993: 339).

Croft (1993) moves on to relate domain, as defined in this way, to the study of metaphor and metonymy. First, many concepts presuppose several different domains. So a human being is defined relative to domains such as physical objects, living things, volitional agents, and others. "The combination of domains simultaneously presupposed by a concept such as [HUMAN BEING] is called a domain matrix" (340). Metaphor, then, is a mapping between two domains that are not part of the same matrix (348). Croft notes, "If you say *She's feeling down*, there is no spatial orientation domain in the matrix of the metaphorical concept of emotion being expressed; HAPPY IS UP involves two different concepts with their own domain structures underlying them" (348). However, metonymy normally involves mapping within a domain matrix (see also Panther and Thornburg, this volume, chapter 10). This construal of metonymy helps make sense of previous analyses which claim that metonymy involves a relation of 'contiguity', and explains how metonymy is often used for purposes of reference to something which is related in a contextually salient way. Thus, the notion of domain, though applied in different ways in different avenues of Cognitive Linguistics, is important in several respects to linguistic analysis because it is such a basic cognitive construct.

5. CONCLUDING ISSUES

One criticism that might be leveled against these notions is that in any specific analysis, it is not necessarily clear how to demarcate what is or is not part of a given frame, ICM, or domain. Because they are cognitive constructs, their scope is going to be determined in any instance by contextual factors as well as the subjective nature of construal. So, while they provide useful ways of thinking about the cognitive bases of linguistic structures and the relations of form to meaning, their inherent nature can make them tricky to use as analytic tools in a reliable, replicable fashion. Whether, and if so, how, these notions can be better operationalized for applied research remains to be seen.

In addition, because each of the terms "frame," "ICM," or "domain" can refer to a kind of knowledge structure which can serve as a background for interpreting the meaning of linguistic forms, there is sometimes overlap in how they are used by different researchers. However, each term seems to find its best functional home within one or two specific theoretical frameworks. In this regard, we saw above that frame theory paved the way for particular theories of grammar (such as Construction Grammar). ICMs have been a useful way of capturing the role of background knowledge for certain kinds of semantic analyses, particularly as they relate to questions of categorization (as espoused by Lakoff 1987). Domains play an especially prominent role in conceptual metaphor theory and in Cognitive Grammar. The different theoretical contexts in which frames, ICMs, and domains are used accentuate the nuances of the differences between them.

The development of all of the basic notions outlined in this chapter helped lay the groundwork for what has come to be known as Cognitive Linguistics. They reflect a common view of the study of language which Lakoff (1990: 40) characterizes in terms of "a commitment to make one's account of human language accord with what is generally known about the mind and the brain, from other disciplines as well as our own." The research on frames, ICMs, and domains reflects this commitment in how it has both drawn on and influenced work in various branches of cognitive science, such as psychology, anthropology, and philosophy. Because of the fundamental roles these basic concepts have in cognitive linguistic theory, the original research on them will continue to remain influential in future work in the field.

NOTES

1. It is interesting to note this early connection made between the cognitive and the sociocultural—a concern which was alien to work in American linguistics at the time within the generative paradigm and was ahead of its time in relation to Cognitive Linguistics, which initially did not give much attention to the social aspects of language use.

2. Lakoff (1987: 68) claims to be discussing image-schematic structure as described in Langacker's (1987) Cognitive Grammar, but Langacker does not present a theory of image schemas, and Langacker's notion of "schemas" is not the same as that of Johnson's "image schemas." Lakoff is really referring to the image schemas explicated in Johnson (1987).

REFERENCES

Andor, József. 1985. On the psychological relevance of frames. *Quaderni di Semantica* 6: 212–21.

Bateson, Gregory. 1972. *Steps to an ecology of mind.* New York: Ballantine.

Brugman, Claudia. 1981. Story of *Over.* MA thesis, University of California at Berkeley. (Published as *The story of Over: Polysemy, semantics, and the structure of the lexicon.* New York: Garland, 1988)

Croft, William. 1993. The role of domains in the interpretation of metaphors and metonymies. *Cognitive Linguistics* 4: 335–70.

Croft, William, Chiaki Taoka, and Esther J. Wood. 2001. Argument linking and the commercial transaction frame in English, Russian, and Japanese. *Language Sciences* 23: 579–602.

D'Andrade, Roy G., and Claudia Strauss, eds. 1992. *Human motives and cultural models.* Cambridge: Cambridge University Press.

Dirven, René, Roslyn Frank, and Cornelia Ilie, eds. 2001. *Language and ideology.* Vol. 2, *Descriptive cognitive approaches.* Amsterdam: John Benjamins.

Emanatian, Michele. 1999. Congruence by degree: On the relation between metaphor and cultural models. In Raymond W. Gibbs, Jr., and Gerard J. Steen, eds., *Metaphor in cognitive linguistics* 205–18. Amsterdam: John Benjamins.

Fauconnier, Gilles. 1985. *Mental spaces: Aspects of meaning construction in natural language.* Cambridge, MA: MIT Press. (2nd ed., Cambridge: Cambridge University Press, 1994)

Fauconnier, Gilles, and Mark Turner. 2002. *The way we think: Conceptual blending and the mind's hidden complexities.* New York: Basic Books.

Fillmore, Charles J. 1961. *Indirect object constructions in English and the ordering of transformations.* The Hague: Mouton.

Fillmore, Charles J. 1968. The case for case. In Emmon Bach and Robert T. Harms, eds., *Universals in linguistic theory* 1–88. New York: Holt, Rinehart and Winston.

Fillmore, Charles J. 1971. Verbs of judging: An exercise in semantic description. In Charles J. Fillmore and D. Terence Langendoen, eds., *Studies in linguistic semantics* 273–89. New York: Holt, Rinehart and Winston.

Fillmore, Charles J. 1975. An alternative to checklist theories of meaning. *Berkeley Linguistics Society* 1: 123–31.

Fillmore, Charles J. 1977. Topics in lexical semantics. In Roger Cole, ed., *Current issues in linguistic theory* 76–138. Bloomington: Indiana University Press.

Fillmore, Charles J. 1982a. Frame semantics. In Linguistic Society of Korea, ed., *Linguistics in the morning calm* 111–37. Seoul: Hanshin.

Fillmore, Charles J. 1982b. Towards a descriptive framework for spatial deixis. In Robert J. Jarvella and Wolfgang Klein, eds., *Speech, place, and action: Studies in deixis and related topics* 31–59. New York: John Wiley.

Fillmore, Charles J. 1985. Frames and the semantics of understanding. *Quaderni di Semantica* 6: 222–54.

Fillmore, Charles J. 1986. "U"-semantics, second round. *Quaderni di Semantica* 7: 49–58.

Fillmore, Charles J. 1987. A private history of the concept 'frame.' In René Dirven and Günter Radden, eds., *Concepts of case* 28–36. Tübingen, Germany: Gunter Narr Verlag.

Fries, Charles C. 1952. *The structure of English.* New York: Harcourt, Brace and World.

Gibbs, Raymond W., Jr. 1999. Taking metaphor out of our heads and putting it into the cultural world. In Raymond W. Gibbs, Jr., and Gerard J. Steen, eds., *Metaphor in cognitive linguistics* 145–66. Amsterdam: John Benjamins.

Goffman, Erving. 1974. *Frame analysis: An essay on the organization of experience.* New York: Harper and Row.

Goldberg, Adele E. 1995. *Constructions: A construction grammar approach to argument structure.* Chicago: University of Chicago Press.

Holland, Dorothy, and Naomi Quinn, eds. 1987. *Cultural models in language and thought.* Cambridge: Cambridge University Press.

Hudson, Richard. 1984. *Word grammar.* Oxford: Basil Blackwell.

Hudson, Richard. 1985. Some basic assumptions about linguistic and non-linguistic knowledge. *Quaderni di Semantica* 6: 284–87.

Hudson, Richard. 1986. Frame semantics, frame linguistics, frame...? *Quaderni di Semantica* 7: 85–101.

Johnson, Mark. 1987. *The body in the mind: The bodily basis of meaning, imagination, and reason.* Chicago: University of Chicago Press.

Katz, Jerrold J., and Paul M. Postal. 1964. *An integrated theory of linguistic descriptions.* Cambridge, MA: MIT Press.

Kövecses, Zoltán. 1995. Metaphor and the folk understanding of anger. In James A. Russell, José-Miguel Fernández-Dols, Antony S. R. Mantead, and Jane C. Wellenkamp, eds., *Everyday conceptions of emotions* 49–71. Dordrecht, Netherlands: Kluwer.

Lakoff, George. 1977. Linguistic gestalts. *Chicago Linguistic Society* 13: 236–87.

Lakoff, George. 1982. Categories: An essay in cognitive linguistics. In Linguistic Society of Korea, ed., *Linguistics in the morning calm* 139–93. Seoul: Hanshin.

Lakoff, George. 1987. *Women, fire, and dangerous things: What categories reveal about the mind.* Chicago: University of Chicago Press.

Lakoff, George. 1990. The invariance hypothesis: Is abstract reason based on image-schemas? *Cognitive Linguistics* 1: 39–74.

Lakoff, George. 1993. The contemporary theory of metaphor. In Andrew Ortony, ed., *Metaphor and thought* 202–51. 2nd ed. Cambridge: Cambridge University Press.

Lakoff, George, and Mark Johnson. 1980. *Metaphors we live by.* Chicago: University of Chicago Press.

Lakoff, George, and Zoltán Kövecses. 1987. The cognitive model of anger inherent in American English. In Dorothy Holland and Naomi Quinn, eds., *Cultural models in language and thought* 195–221. Cambridge: Cambridge University Press.

Langacker, Ronald W. 1984. Active zones. *Berkeley Linguistics Society* 10: 172–88.

Langacker, Ronald W. 1987. *Foundations of cognitive grammar.* Vol. 1, *Theoretical prerequisites.* Stanford, CA: Stanford University Press.

Langacker, Ronald W. 1991. *Foundations of cognitive grammar.* Vol. 2, *Descriptive application.* Stanford, CA: Stanford University Press.

Langacker, Ronald W. 1993. Reference-point constructions. *Cognitive Linguistics* 4: 1–38.

Õim, Haldur, and Madis Saluveer. 1985. Frames in linguistic descriptions. *Quaderni di Semantica* 6: 295–302.

Petruck, Miriam R. L. 1995. Frame semantics and the lexicon: Nouns and verbs in the body frame. In Masayoshi Shibatani and Sandra Thompson, eds., *Essays in Semantics and Pragmatics* 279–97. Amsterdam: John Benjamins.

Pike, Kenneth L. 1967. *Language in relation to a unified theory of the structure of human behavior.* The Hague: Mouton.

Quinn, Naomi. 1991. The cultural basis of metaphor. In James W. Fernandez, ed., *Beyond metaphor: The theory of tropes in anthropology* 56–93. Stanford, CA: Stanford University Press.

Reddy, Michael J. [1979] 1993. The conduit metaphor: A case of frame conflict in our language about language. In Andrew Ortony, ed., *Metaphor and thought* 164–201. Cambridge: Cambridge University Press.

Rojo López, Ana, and Javier Valenzuela. 1998. Frame semantics and lexical translation: The risk frame and its translation. *Babel: Revue Internationale de la Traduction / International Journal of Translation* 44: 128–38.

Rosch, Eleanor. 1973. Natural categories. *Cognitive Psychology* 4: 328–50.

Schank, Roger C., and Robert P. Abelson. 1977. *Scripts, plans, goals, and understanding.* Hillsdale, NJ: Erlbaum.

Schön, Donald A. [1979] 1993. Generative metaphor: A perspective on problem-setting in social policy. In Andrew Ortony, ed., *Metaphor and thought* 137–63. Cambridge: Cambridge University Press.

Shore, Bradd. 1996. *Culture in mind: Cognition, culture, and the problem of meaning.* Oxford: Oxford University Press.

Tannen, Deborah. 1985. Frames and schemas in interaction. *Quaderni di Semantica* 6: 326–35.

Tannen, Deborah, ed. 1993. *Framing in discourse.* New York: Oxford University Press.

Tomasello, Michael. 1992. *First verbs: A case study of early grammatical development.* Cambridge: Cambridge University Press.

van Oosten, Jeanne. 1977. Subjects and agenthood in English. *Chicago Linguistic Society* 13: 459–71.

CHAPTER 8

....

METAPHOR

....

JOSEPH E. GRADY

1. INTRODUCTION

....

Metaphor has been a central topic within Cognitive Linguistics since the field was
born and the term coined in the 1970s. This is partly a historical consequence of
George Lakoff's dominant role and major contributions—metaphor was his focus
at the time he and a number of colleagues were defining the field of Cognitive
Linguistics, and continues to be today. But the importance of metaphor studies
within the discipline is also a reflection of the nature of Cognitive Linguistics as it is
understood by its practitioners. If Cognitive Linguistics is the study of ways in
which features of language reflect other aspects of human cognition, then metaphors provide one of the clearest illustrations of this relationship. Since the 1950s,
Chomskyan linguists have been devising theories of syntax which largely exclude
references to the meanings of linguistic structures; it is nearly impossible, though,
to conceive of metaphor without taking into account the connections between
lexical semantics, usage, and our understanding and perceptions of the world.
Metaphors provide rich evidence about the ways in which some aspects of our lived
experience are associated with others, for reasons that reflect basic aspects of perception, thought, and possibly neurological organization.

Within Cognitive Linguistics the term *metaphor* is understood to refer to a pattern of conceptual association, rather than to an individual metaphorical usage or a
linguistic convention. Lakoff and Johnson (1980: 5) describe metaphor as follows:
"The essence of metaphor is understanding and experiencing one kind of thing
in terms of another." When Robert Frost refers to the "road less traveled," he uses
the words *road* and *traveled* in metaphorical ways; in conventional usage, this

phrase is "the metaphor," but for cognitive linguists the more important object of study (and, according to typical usage within the discipline, "the metaphor") is the underlying pattern of thought which allows the phrase to have the meaning it does. Since this pattern involves associations at the conceptual level, it can be expressed by many different lexical means—metaphorical uses of *path, fork in the road, direction*, and numerous other terms reflect the same basic set of associations, between traveling and making life choices.

The emphasis within Cognitive Linguistics on this conceptual dimension suggests a view in which metaphor is not inherently a linguistic phenomenon. In fact, cognitive linguists do conceive of metaphors as patterns of thought which can be expressed on nonverbal ways, such as pictures and gestures. Diagrams, for example, generally follow the convention that "higher" numbers and quantities should be represented higher on a physical surface (e.g., linguistic usages such as *Crime has risen dramatically*). In the artistic realm, M. Johnson (1987: 83) considers the notion of pictorial "balance" and observes that "in Kandinsky's *Accompanied Contrast . . .*, there is an exquisite balance in the work that can be made sense of only by interpreting 'weight,' 'force,' 'location,' and 'value' metaphorically, based on a schema whose structure specifies forces or weights distributed relative to some point or axis." Johnson is suggesting that visual images may stand metaphorically for physical masses and forces.

Cognitive Linguistics is hardly the first area of scholarship to treat metaphor as a serious object of study. Aristotle (1996) and St. Thomas Aquinas (1947) wrote on the subject, as did Vico ([1744] 1961) (see M. Johnson 1981, for a summary of philosophical scholarship on metaphor). More immediate and direct predecessors included Anderson (1971), who explored ways in which understandings of spatial relationships are extended to other kinds of relations expressed in grammar, and Reddy (1993), whose discussion of metaphors for communication Lakoff and Johnson cite as a catalyst for their own interest in the subject. Reddy's paper, in fact, appeared in an important volume of papers treating metaphor from a variety of scholarly perspectives (Ortony 1979). Cognitive Linguistics' unique contribution has been to treat metaphorical language as data to be examined systematically and to be considered in connection with other basic aspects of mental activity. Even more importantly, scholars in the field have recognized the thorough pervasiveness of metaphor even in "ordinary" language and thought.

The starting point for a discussion of metaphor within the field of Cognitive Linguistics must be the approach initiated in Lakoff and Johnson's (1980) seminal *Metaphors We Live By* and elaborated by cognitive linguists since that time (Paprotté and Dirven 1985;[1] M. Johnson 1987, 1993; Lakoff 1987; Lakoff and Turner 1989; Sweetser 1990; Turner 1991; Lakoff and Johnson 1999; Kövecses 2002; etc.).

2. BASICS OF CONCEPTUAL METAPHOR THEORY

The most fundamental notion of conceptual metaphor theory (CMT) is the *mapping*.[2] This term borrowed from mathematics refers to systematic metaphorical correspondences between closely related ideas. For example, the common conceptualization of a nation (or other political body) as a ship includes correspondences between the ship and the state conceived as wholes, but also between the course of the ship and the historical progression of the state; the seas traversed by the ship and the political and other circumstances with which the state is faced; and so forth. Rather than existing as isolated specimens, the metaphorical usages within a passage like the following depend on this conventional pattern of conceptual associations.

> The blueprints drafted last week will ensure that the *ship* of the Commonwealth truly remains one for the ages.... The House Budget ... will allow the state to withstand even the *stormiest weather*.... Continued commitment to our most needy and the Commonwealth's most essential obligations is critical *ballast* for every successful *ship* of state. (from Massachusetts State Representative Paul Casey's Web page: http://www.winchestermass.org/pcasey051999.html; emphasis mine)

In the CMT system, the course of the ship is said to "map" or "be mapped" (or "projected") onto the historical progression of the state, and other elements of the conceptual domain of ships and navigation (the 'source' domain) are likewise "mapped" onto elements of the conceptual domain of nations and politics. The source domain of a metaphor (here, SHIPS AND NAVIGATION) supplies the language and imagery which are used to refer to the domain which is actually at issue in the discourse (the "target" domain—in this case, POLITICS AND STATES). As it is used in popular discourse, the metaphor includes at least the following conventional cross-domain correspondences (see Grady, Oakley, and Coulson 1999):

STATE	SHIP
State's policies/action	Ship's course
Determining policies/actions	Steering the ship
Success/improvement of the state	Forward motion of the ship
Failures/problems	Sailing mishaps (e.g., foundering)
Circumstances affecting the state	Sea conditions
(e.g., on the political or economic levels)	

Other conventional metaphorical patterns involving multiple correspondences between source and target domains include DEATH IS A REAPER (where people are plants to be harvested, etc.) and LIFE IS A JOURNEY (where difficulties are obstacles, objectives are destinations, etc.; see Lakoff and Turner 1989).[3] Note that some patterns are quite a bit more specific than others; for example, LIFE IS A JOURNEY is a very broad pattern, of which LOVE IS A JOURNEY (*We have reached a **crossroads** in our relationship*) might be considered a special case. That is, metaphors exist in hierarchies of specificity, in which a more specific pattern can be said to *inherit* a more general one. In each metaphorical pattern, the mapping between source and target is constrained by what cognitive linguists have called the *invariance principle* (Lakoff and Turner 1989; Brugman 1990; Lakoff 1990; Turner 1991; etc.): the requirement that the mapping not violate the basic topological structure of the target domain (see Oakley's discussion of "Image Schemas"; this volume, chapter 9).

The systematic projection of elements from one conceptual domain onto elements of another involves not merely the objects and properties characteristic of the domain (e.g., buildings, sturdiness vs. flimsiness, etc.) but also the relations, events, and scenarios that characterize the domain. In short, CMT is concerned with the mapping of inferences from source to target. If a person "blows off steam," then the person should feel a reduced intensity of anger afterwards. If one "gets past obstacles" in one's work, then he or she should achieve greater success in his or her objectives. On one level, inference mapping is another illustration of the richness of the conceptual structures upon which metaphorical usages are based. On another, it is a strong demonstration that metaphor is more than an innovative use of language or of the figurative application of a single term to a new referent.

Besides systematicity, the asymmetrical directionality of conceptual metaphors is one of the features most strongly emphasized by Lakoff and Johnson and cognitive linguists since. While a term like *weather* may be used metaphorically to refer to a set of economic and political circumstances, the reverse metaphor is not possible, linguistically or conceptually (e.g., the nonsensical idea of referring to an actual storm as a recession). Likewise, it is meaningful to refer to a person as *warm* but meaningless to refer to a cup of tea as *affectionate*, meaningful to refer to the *foundations* of a theory but meaningless to refer to the *postulates* of a building. Note that this usage is not only unconventional but uninterpretable. We can guess what *white-hot anger* might be like even if we have never heard the phrase, thanks to the underlying conceptual pattern that projects heat onto intense emotions; there is no corresponding pattern which allows us to understand parts of a building in terms of postulates or other elements of logic.

This directionality is more than an interesting and characteristic feature of metaphorical conceptualizations; it is evidence against a traditional and still common view of metaphor, in which a metaphorical usage is most fundamentally a reflection of "similarity" between the source and target ideas. If the ultimate basis for the Theories-as-Buildings pattern (see discussions in Lakoff and Johnson 1980; Clausner and Croft 1997; and Grady 1997b) is an underlying similarity (called a *ground*, in some philosophical studies), metaphorical substitutions might be just as valid in either direction; clearly they are not. More importantly, there are cases where it is hard to identify what the similarity might be between the source and target concepts in a metaphor, even in a simple and familiar pattern such as the understanding of happiness as brightness. We refer to a *sunny disposition* and a *bright future*, but what could the similarity be between a mood and a degree of luminance? Or between physical coldness and lack of emotion? Philosopher John Searle acknowledged this puzzle when he wrote:

> I think the only answer to the question, "what is the relation between cold things and unemotional people that would justify the use of 'cold' as a metaphor for lack of emotion?" is simply that as a matter of perceptions, sensibilities, and linguistic practices, people find the notion of coldness associated in their minds with lack of emotion. The notion of being cold just is associated with being unemotional. (1981: 267)

Coldness and lack of emotion are not "similar" in any straightforward way, yet cognitive linguists have been able to point to a more particular reason than Searle recognizes in this passage: the conceptual domains of temperature and emotion are associated in our experience, for instance, because intimate interactions can entail physical proximity which leads to body heat being shared.

The emphasis on "experiential motivation" is another of the central principles of CMT, and one which most sharply distinguishes the approach from alternative theories. Lakoff and Johnson (1980), for example, discuss motivations for the metaphorical pattern they call MORE IS UP. In their account, elevation and quantity are conceptual domains closely related in experience, since whenever we see a pile of objects or liquid in a contained space, we are aware of the connection between the height which the pile (or whatever) reaches and the number of objects or amount of the liquid. In this way, the mapping between quantity and height is well motivated, rather than arbitrary, but does not depend on similarity per se. This experiential analysis is typical of Cognitive Linguistics' concern with metaphors not only as interesting linguistic phenomena requiring explanation, but as important elements of conceptual structure and reflections of ways in which humans experience the world.

3. PRIMARY METAPHORS AND "NEURAL CMT"

There is a set of pervasive conceptual metaphors which seem to reveal with special directness the deep relationships between word usage, conceptual structure, and the way we experience the world. *Primary metaphors* (Grady, Taub, and Morgan 1996; Grady 1997a; Lakoff and Johnson 1999; etc.) are simple patterns, like Lakoff and Johnson's MORE IS UP, which map fundamental perceptual concepts onto equally fundamental but not directly perceptual ones. Source concepts for primary metaphors include UP, DOWN, HEAVY, BRIGHT, FORWARD, BACKWARD, SWEET, various simple "force-dynamic" concepts (in the sense of Talmy 1988), and so on. Corresponding target concepts are such basic building blocks of mental experience as DOMINANT, SAD, DIFFICULT, HAPPY, SUCCESS, THE PAST, APPEALING, and COMPULSION. (Many of the metaphors for emotion discussed by Kövecses 1990 are primary metaphors.) These metaphors appear to arise directly from experience in ways that more complex metaphors such as THEORIES ARE BUILDINGS do not. There are experiential correlations between quantity and height, as we have seen, and likewise between other concepts paired in primary metaphors: happiness and brightness (we feel safer and more content in sunshine than in the dark); difficulty and heaviness (we experience strain when we try to support or manipulate heavy objects); and so forth. There are no such experiential correlations between theories and buildings, ships and nations, or between various other complex concepts which are linked in conventional metaphorical pairings.

The unidirectionality of primary metaphorical patterns is consistent and absolute. In each case, the perceptual concept is the source and is mapped onto the nonperceptual target concept. Success is easily spoken of and conceived as motion forward (e.g., *We've made great strides forward this year*), but simple forward motion is not thought of as success (consider a car rolling slowly downhill because its brake has not been set). An important matter is *heavy* or *weighty*, but we cannot communicate that one laptop computer is heavier than another by saying it is more *important*.[4] This strong unidirectionality is especially significant given that there are many metaphors which are not asymmetrical in exactly the ways emphasized within most CMT accounts. For instance, Lakoff and Turner (1989: 89–96) discuss a category of "image metaphors," which depict one thing in terms of another based on shared perceptual features (visual or otherwise): "My wife... whose waist is an hourglass," "My horse with a mane made of short rainbows," and so on. In each of these cases, the target-source relationship can be reversed and still yield a perfectly understandable metaphor, if not as poetic an image: the "waist" of an hourglass, a rainbow as a horse's mane, and so on.[5] There are also metaphors which appear to be based on shared qualities which are not perceptual: when we refer to a person as some type of animal based on a personality trait, for example (e.g., as a "pig," "snake," or the more classical, not to mention complimentary, "lion"), we are apparently invoking a commonality which we believe unites the person and the animal (or some stereotype of the animal).[6] Like image metaphors, these are based on conceptual relationships which can be reversed and still be meaningful: we refer to lions as the "king of beasts" and might even equate a particular lion with a particular human exemplar of stout-heartedness.

Strict unidirectionality, then, appears to be a special feature of correlation-based primary metaphors. Complex metaphors which are also thoroughly asymmetrical, like THEORIES ARE BUILDINGS, appear to be analyzable as elaborations of conceptualizations which are, at bottom, primary metaphors—for example, one in which logical organization is understood as physical part-whole structure and another in which continued functionality or existence is understood as persisting in a standing position (Grady 1997b). Each of these metaphorical patterns is entirely unidirectional and can plausibly be accounted for in terms of recurring correlations

in experience. (An account on these lines also has the important advantage of explaining why many of the most salient aspects of buildings from the point of view of the human interacting with them—floors, walls, occupants, rent, and so on—are not parts of the conventional understanding of theories; the metaphors are about understanding complex abstract entities as erect physical structures, rather than as buildings per se.)

Given that humans everywhere share the basic patterns of perception and experience that are reflected in primary metaphors, these patterns ought to show up in languages around the world.[7] In fact, it does appear that primary metaphors are widespread across languages that are not related genetically, areally, or culturally. An example of a pattern with broad (if not universal) cross-linguistic distribution is the semantic extension from 'large' to 'important', observed in senses of Hawaiian *nui* , Malay *besar*, Russian *krupnij*, Turkish *büyük*, and Zulu *-khulu*, for example (cf. uses of English *big*, such as *Today is a big day for the company*). In each case, a basic word referring to size is conventionally used to refer to importance in utterly nonphysical situations (presumably based on the frequent correlation in our experience between the size of an object and its salience or importance to us). Additional patterns found broadly across languages include '(spatially) close' for 'intimate', '(spatially) close' for 'similar', and 'warm/hot' for 'agitated' (Grady 1999b). Primary metaphors, then, are natural or even inevitable consequences of recurring associations in daily life.

Analysis in terms of primary metaphors was one of several concurrent developments that led to the "Neural Theory of Language," and more specifically, a "neural" version of CMT (Lakoff and Johnson 1999). Within this framework (which represents cognitive structures in computational "neural nets"; see the discussion of computational models of metaphor below), the mappings that constitute primary metaphors are treated as neural circuits linking representations of source and target concepts—circuits which are automatically established when a perceptual and a nonperceptual concept are repeatedly co-activated. This automaticity effect within Neural CMT is an implementation of hypotheses about the origins of metaphor in children's thought and language. The concepts linked in primary metaphors are so closely associated with each other in experience that conflated representations may arise as integrated wholes in conceptual structure even before they are understood as associations between distinct ideas. C. Johnson (1999) has shown that children may have no basis for distinguishing between literal and metaphorical senses of a term like *see* based on the ways in which they hear the term used. If parents and others regularly use *see* in contexts where it can mean either 'perceive visually' or 'learn; find out'—as in *Let's see what's in the box* versus *Let's see what this bell sounds like*—children may hypothesize a sense of the term which conflates literal and metaphorical meanings from the adult point of view, and later need to perform a process of *deconflation* before they understand that there are two distinct senses of the word, linked by a conventional pattern of metaphor. Such a developmental trajectory may be natural for many or most terms with conventional senses that are licensed by primary metaphors.

4. THE COGNITIVE REALITY
OF CONCEPTUAL METAPHORS

Are the mappings identified within CMT cognitively "real," rather than mere clever inventions of the analyst trying to account for data (like competing phonological analyses which share nothing except that they can generate the same set of forms)? This is a more crucial question within Cognitive Linguistics than it is within other areas of linguistics, since practitioners of Cognitive Linguistics take seriously the idea that they are describing relationships between language and other cognitive functions. There are several types of evidence that conceptual metaphor mappings are psychologically real. First, there is the fact of systematicity itself; if sets of terms and ideas from particular conceptual domains are systematically and predictably associated with such sets from other domains, it is easier to conclude that the domains are connected on some level of understanding than that mere accidents of usage have led to the data patterns or that the patterns have arisen through analogy, one lexical item at a time. The fact that we can often immediately grasp novel metaphorical usages like *white-hot anger* also suggests that the underlying conceptual patterns are real.

Another compelling confirmation of the reality of metaphors on a conceptual (rather than merely a lexical) level is the way in which gestures often appear to be motivated by metaphorical understandings for which we have evidence in spoken language. McNeill (1992) has used the term "metaphorics" to refer to gestures which are metaphorically motivated. His recorded examples include a gesture used by a mathematician during a conversation with a colleague about the technical concept of limits: while committing a speech error by mentioning "inverse limits" rather than the direct limits he has in mind, the speaker nonetheless makes the hand gesture associated with direct limits (an abrupt motion and stopping of the hand, at the "end point"), showing that his gesture is in fact motivated by his conceptualization of the topic—that is, an understanding in which a quantitative limit is treated as a physical obstacle or stopping point—and specifically *not* by the word he is uttering at the time. It would be difficult to argue that examples like this are motivated by mere analogy with language; instead, they appear to reflect the same underlying patterns of conceptualization which motivate metaphorical uses of words.

Evidence from experimental psychology also helps confirm the cognitive reality of conceptual metaphors. Gentner (2001) has reported on a series of experiments designed to test whether people actually invoke metaphorical conceptualizations when they think and speak about time. Her results indicate that when people switch from one metaphorical system for understanding time to another, there is a cost in reaction time. Subjects were first asked a question framed in terms of either the so-called "ego-moving" model of time or the "time-moving" model. In the ego-moving model, time is conceptualized as the path or landscape through which we move, with the future lying in front of us (e.g., *Is Boston ahead or behind us time-wise?*). The time-moving model frames time independently of the observer (e.g., *Is it later or earlier in Boston than it is here?*), as a series of objects following each other through space; in this model, a later time follows and is therefore "behind" an earlier time. When the first and second questions were framed in terms of conflicting models, response times were slower than when they were framed in terms of the same model. Furthermore, in the "conflicting" condition, subjects often reformulated the second question for themselves, apparently in order to make it easier to understand and reply to; this reformulation did have the effect of significantly speeding up response times. Gentner draws the conclusion that the metaphorical systems are playing a real role in subjects' conceptualization of time and their understanding of temporal language. In a subsequent series of ingenious experiments involving rigorous testing of alternative hypotheses, Boroditsky (2000) demonstrates even more clearly that spatial schemas play a role in structuring temporal thought.

Another kind of evidence comes from Gibbs (1994: 163–64), who has reported that there are consistencies in the mental images described by experimental subjects interpreting metaphorical idioms which go beyond the information supplied in the idioms themselves. Conversely, metaphorical idioms suggest the same set of inferences to people, even when those inferences go far beyond what is expressed in the words themselves; subjects agree that when you *blow your stack*, "the expression of anger is unintentional and is done in an abrupt, violent manner."

Despite the range of evidence in favor of the view of metaphors as entrenched conceptual patterns, there are challenges to this position from a number of directions. One common view which runs contrary to CMT perspectives is that metaphorical thought and language are essentially unconstrained. Philosopher Donald Davidson (1981), for instance, has suggested that any two things can be understood, when juxtaposed, as bearing a metaphorical connection.[8] If one person states that "Life is a kiwi fruit," another will be clever enough to point out the shared features which make these two entities comparable and which provide the ground for the metaphorical mapping of one onto the other. In some sense, the range of possible metaphorical correspondences would appear to be limitless, or to be limited only by our imagination and our ability to interpret expressions based on pragmatic context. In fact, Davidson goes so far as to claim that metaphors have no meaning and that they merely invite us to infer whatever appropriate message we can. Obviously, such a view has no room for conventional metaphors—lasting structures which may narrow in advance the possible interpretations of a given expression and which in practice also limit the metaphors we produce. Other philosophers, such as Black (1955), offer a variety of accounts of metaphor which often have little in common except for the assumption that metaphors are essentially unconstrained. Psychologists, too, have typically assumed that there are no metaphorical relationships with a special status, instead looking for parameters which make individual metaphorical sentences more "apt" or more comprehensible, for instance (see Katz 1989 and MacCormac 1985, among many others).

These philosophical and psychological accounts generally neglect the fact that certain conceptual pairings tend to recur and to motivate a great percentage of the actual metaphorical language we encounter. While there may be no such thing as an "impossible metaphor," metaphor scholars have had no difficulty in identifying sets of particularly common patterns or in offering compelling accounts of the motivations for these frequently encountered mappings. For example, understanding is regularly associated with vision and with grasping in English and other languages of the world, but there are no such widespread mappings between understanding and fighting, for instance. If metaphor is not constrained in an absolute sense by underlying cognitive mechanisms, then at least there are patterns to be explained in the metaphors which tend to arise as opposed to those which do not. Proponents of CMT would argue that these more-likely metaphors are, crucially, better motivated. In short, traditions which focus on metaphor as an expression of similarity have downplayed the conventionalized, structured aspects of metaphor, while CMT scholars have focused particular attention on patterns which become entrenched in language and conceptualization, often as a result of recurring associations in experience (see Grady 1999a).

Another type of experimental finding which is sometimes interpreted as casting doubt on the role of stored conceptual metaphors relates to processing time of metaphorical versus literal language. One intuitively appealing view of how people might process metaphorical language involves several stages: when we encounter a metaphorical statement, we first try to interpret the statement as a literal one, then seek alternate interpretations once we realize that the statement either does not make sense or clearly does not relate to the current topic of discourse (see Searle's 1981 discussion of this "pragmatic" model of processing). To arrive at these alternate interpretations, we might use stored knowledge of metaphorical patterns of usage, among other tools. Some reaction-time data, however, shows that metaphorical utterances can be understood as quickly as literal ones, or even quicker (e.g., Pollio et al. 1984). Such results have led researchers to question whether stored metaphors are accessed during speech processing. What such data suggest to other researchers, however, is that under the right contextual conditions we are "primed" to identify a metaphorical meaning for a sentence. We may even be slower to recognize literal meanings in such cases.[9]

Another apparent challenge to the CMT view of metaphor is what Lakoff and Johnson (1980: 106–10) characterize as the "abstraction" position, namely, that usages which might be identified as metaphorical are actually literal; an abstractionist view of a word's sense holds that it is much more general and inclusive than metaphor theorists allow. Jackendoff and Aaron (1991) provide a good illustration of such a position in their review of Lakoff and Turner's (1989) *More Than Cool Reason*. Jackendoff and Aaron propose a test for metaphors based on the premise that they necessarily involve semantic incongruity on their literal readings. Statements which fit naturally into the following formula involve incongruity and may therefore be considered true cases of metaphor: "Of course A isn't B, but if it were, you might say that _____" (Jackendoff and Aaron 1991: 326). The following sentence, for example, shows that the idea of a romantic relationship which has reached a *dead end* is truly metaphorical: "Of course, relationships are not journeys, but if they were, you might say ours is at a dead end." On the other hand, Jackendoff and Aaron find the following sentence odd: "Of course, states aren't locations, but if they were, you might say I've gotten through my depression." The article argues that this sentence is problematic because there is no need for a hedge in a statement like "I've gotten through my depression." The statement is literally true, since *gotten through* may literally refer to events other than spatial motion. For Jackendoff and Aaron, this and many other expressions that CMT scholars would identify as metaphors are instead reflections of "thematic relations"—abstract categories whose language refers primarily to concrete and spatial experience but whose content is much more general and abstract. "Being Circumstantially in a state is the thematic parallel of being spatially in a location" (328). Jackendoff and Aaron argue that such usages should properly be seen as ordinary and literal. Langacker (1987) raises similar questions about whether particular usages of *go* are really metaphorical (e.g., *This milk is about to go sour*). He proposes

> a generalized notion of extensionality that is not specifically tied to our conception of physical space. It is a property of many domains, both basic and abstract, though the spatial domain stands out among them for its prototypicality and cognitive salience. By making this distinction between extensionality in general and physical space in particular, we can characterize "motion" in abstract terms applicable to any extensional domain, without prejudging the extent to which spatial metaphor is constitutive of these domains. (169–70)

Neither of these compelling proposals about the relationship between spatial location and other conceptual domains, however, refutes the idea that there is a conventional and metaphorical association between the domains of space and states (for instance). Both discussions refer to usages of semantically weak terms like *go* and *get*; a sentence like *I've managed to crawl up out of my depression* passes Jackendoff and Aaron's test and clearly evokes a vivid metaphorical image.

5. CONCEPTUAL INTEGRATION/ BLENDING

In 1994, Fauconnier and Turner introduced a new analytic framework which treats metaphors as products of a more general process of human cognition. This operation, which Fauconnier and Turner call "conceptual integration" (or "blending") involves the combination, often but not always figurative, of selected conceptual material from two or more distinct sources. Like metaphor in CMT terms, blending is understood as a pervasive phenomenon in human thought, one which shows its effects regularly in everyday language. A fuller treatment of the blending framework is provided by Turner (this volume, chapter 15), but it is useful here to briefly consider how the blending account of metaphor adds to, and is different from, the CMT approach. In order to do so, we need to have in mind a few basics of the theory.

Fauconnier and Turner's model involves four "spaces," rather than the two conceptual domains (source and target) which participate in a CMT mapping. Each of these spaces is understood as a mental space in the sense of Fauconnier (1985, 1997; this volume, chapter 14); that is, a coherent bundle of information activated in the mind at a particular time, representing an understanding of a scenario, real or imagined. For example, when an artist creates a variant of Leonardo da Vinci's *Mona Lisa* (or *la Gioconda*) in which the original subject's face has been replaced by Monica Lewinsky's, he is cleverly blending elements from our knowledge of the famous painting with ones from our knowledge about Monica Lewinsky.[10] As we take in this picture, our mental representations of each of these phenomena constitutes an "input space"—one real and one based on an artistic image—projecting material into a third space, the "blend space" represented in the magazine cover. The fourth space in Fauconnier and Turner's scheme is the "generic space," containing material shared by the two inputs; in this case, for example, the image of a dark-haired young woman wearing a subtle and knowing smile. (Like CMT, blending theory is concerned with nonlinguistic as well as linguistic examples.)

Monica Lewinsky and the Mona Lisa are counterparts in the respective input spaces; without such counterparts to establish relations between the inputs, a blend cannot "get off the ground."

Like the Leonardo da Vinci/Lewinsky cover, many of the examples discussed by blending scholars are not exactly metaphorical, though they may be figurative in some sense. Some blends simply involve a juxtaposition of elements that do not co-occur in reality; Fauconnier and Turner (1994) have discussed a blend, for example, in which a modern philosopher is engaged in a figurative "debate" with Immanuel Kant. The philosophers are real and literal, as are the philosophical issues and arguments. The only figurative aspect of the imagined scene is that the discourse takes the form of an in-person debate rather than two sets of writings from different places and historical periods.

In this framework, metaphors are treated as a subset of conceptual blends, characterized by particular kinds of relations holding among the various spaces. Fauconnier and Turner (1998) present a typology of blends in which metaphors are defined by an asymmetry in the degree to which two inputs provide the conceptual frames that structure the blend. In Ship-of-State blends, the input space of ships would be said to provide a structuring frame (including elements such as weather, heading, and so forth) within which such topics as elections and policy are depicted. Grady, Oakley, and Coulson (1999) characterize metaphorical blends as ones involving "fusion" of corresponding elements from the two inputs, where a target concept is excluded from explicit representation in the blend in favor of its counterpart from the source.[11] In a Ship-of-State blend, for example, the nation

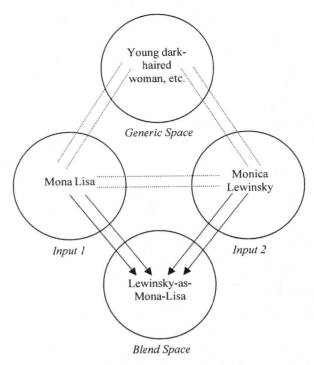

Figure 8.1. Diagram of the Leonardo da Vinci's *Mona Lisa*/Lewinski blend

itself is not represented in the blend; the ship image takes its place (but maintains its conceptual linkage with the state in the target input space). It is this fusion with "accommodation" that leads to the mental experience which Lakoff and Johnson (1980: 5) describe as "understanding and experiencing one kind of thing in terms of another."

A noteworthy advance of blending theory is that it allows analysts a way of describing examples in which the metaphorical image cannot be a straightforward projection of source onto target. Following Coulson (2001), Fauconnier and Turner (1998) discuss examples of the common English idiom *digging [one's] own grave*, which map imagery from the domain of death and burial onto scenarios involving (nonlethal) failure of various sorts.[12] The key point from the blending analyst's point of view is that digging a grave (one's own or anyone else's) does not cause death; yet instances of the idiom always refer to scenarios in which people *cause themselves harm* through their own actions. The causal structure of the source space is not projected into the blend; instead, the blended space contains the causal structure of the target domain, and the imagined scenario is one that would make no sense within the logic of the source input. The blending framework is obviously more powerful than CMT for describing such cases.[13] Within a blending account, we can say that particular elements from each domain are counterparts (e.g., failure and death), and we can identify source and target, but we can also describe the overall structure of the resulting conceptualization, which draws in complex ways from both.

The blending framework also makes it straightforward to record ways in which multiple metaphorical patterns are combined within a single complex conceptualization. For example, while the conventional understanding of nations as ships has nothing to say about right-left (or starboard-port) directionality, it is possible to find examples such as the following, in which the sides of the ship correspond to political orientations: "With Trent Lott as Senate Majority Leader, and Gingrich at the helm in the House, the list to the Right could destabilize the entire Ship of State" (see Grady, Oakley, and Couson 1999: 108).[14] This blend enlists a conventional association which we would ordinarily not think of as "part of" the Ship-of-State metaphor, and the framework allows us to treat this mapping as just another of the counterpart relations exploited by the blend.

Another contribution of blending theory is that it affords an explicit means of reflecting ways in which metaphors may lead to reconceptualization of source domains (see Black's 1955 discussion of "interaction" and Ricoeur's 1978 discussion of "reverberation"). Since blending analyses take the form of linked networks of representations, they are not directional in the same sense as CMT mappings and allow for "feedback" from a blended space to any of its inputs. A hypothetical reference to a current military conflict as a "new Vietnam," intended to frame the contemporary situation in a particular way, can also lead to new insights about the Vietnam war: see also Coulson's (2001) blending analysis of the "Menendez Brothers virus" joke.

A final distinction between blending theory and CMT is that the former is conceived as a description of online processing. That is, where CMT is concerned primarily with conventional patterns of association—patterns which we can think of as objects stored in long-term memory—blending is, in principle, a dynamic process. Blending scholars refer to "elaborations" of a blend—spontaneous developments of the basic scenario constituting a blend. For instance, the Leonardo da Vinci/Lewinsky cover may suggest subsequent events such as the figure's appearance at a congressional hearing, and so on. Since any conceptual blend depends upon identification of counterpart elements in the two input spaces, it is possible to think of conceptual metaphors (as identified within CMT) as preconditions for certain blends; entrenched conceptual metaphors provide one type of counterpart relationship on which blends can be based (see Grady, Oakley, and Coulson 1999). For instance, in the *digging one's own grave* examples, it is clear that one original inspiration for the conceit must have been the conventional metaphorical association between failure and death. Following the establishment of this basic connection between the two spaces, a process of selective projection leads to the more complex metaphorical structure with which we are familiar.

6. COMPUTATIONAL MODELS
OF METAPHOR

Researchers interested in either the ongoing enterprise to model cognitive functions in computational terms (Artificial Intelligence) or the more specific effort to devise computational systems which accurately reproduce aspects of linguistic structure and performance (computational linguistics) have created a number of models of metaphor interpretation and production. Srini Narayanan, one of the analysts working within the Neural Theory of Language project at the University of California at Berkeley, has developed a model, for instance, which is able to generate inferences about the target domains of politics and economics from linguistic input taken from newspapers and using the language of source domains such as physical motion (e.g., "the Government is currently stumbling in its efforts to implement the liberalization plan"). In Narayanan's (1999) model, source domain knowledge is represented as networks of "x-schemas," representing cognitive models of bodily activities, such as walking. These hypothesized schemas are understood as guiding bodily action, but also triggering mental simulations when the relevant concepts are evoked. The model assumes that physical domains involving such activities as walking are much more richly represented in the mind than more abstract domains such as economics. Target domains are represented as "belief nets," that is, networks representing understandings about the current state of the world (or some hypothetical world). One of the central purposes of metaphor, in this view, is to take advantage of rich knowledge structures relating to physical activity in order to make it easier to think about more abstract target domains. "Since knowledge of moving around or manipulating objects is essential for survival, it has to be highly compiled and readily accessible knowledge" (Narayanan 1999: 121). Crucially, Narayanan's model includes "metaphor maps," stored functions which connect source domain representations (x-schemas) to elements of target domains (belief nets). For example, one metaphor map associates a source domain event of 'stumbling' with a target domain representation of 'failure'. (This is a piece of a larger map encompassing a wide range of concepts related to physical motion, representing what Lakoff 1993 has called the "Event Structure Metaphor.") As elaborated in the Neural Theory of Language, this framework has been extended to capture not just metaphorical associations between concepts, but also the types of relations inherent in more basic grammatical constructions, as well as the more elaborate networks of association treated by blending theory (see above).

Another computational model which assumes representations of particular metaphorical mappings as part of its architecture is ATT-Meta, developed by Barnden (Barnden 2001; Lee and Barnden 2001). Like Narayanan, Barnden assumes that an important function of metaphor is to allow reasoning about such richly known conceptual domains as possession or physical motion to be applied to more abstract target domains. If the system is given a metaphorical sentence, such as *I've inherited his thoughts and ideas*, it first generates a set of inferences using only source domain logic (i.e., reasoning goes on within a *pretence cocoon*, as though the sentence were about literal inheritance): for instance, person A possessed something which B now possesses, A and B had a close relationship, and so on. All inferences which can apply to the target situation (in this case, one sports coach replacing another) are then transferred, becoming knowledge about the target domain. The projection from source to target is guided by *metaphorical views* implemented in the system, describing relationships between a variety of source and target domains which are conventionally linked in the minds of English speakers—in this case the idea that the logic of possession may be projected onto ideas.

Other computational approaches assume no prior associations between particular domains and instead seek to infer these relations based on shared properties between stored representations of large sets of concepts. Several models developed by Gentner and colleagues—notably SME (for "Structure Mapping Engine") and its successor MAC/FAC (for "Many Are Called, Few Are Chosen")—operate by seeking similarities between structural properties, either when presented with two inputs (in SME, an interpretation model) or when presented with one input and given the task of finding an appropriate analogue (in MAC/FAC, a production system) (see Falkenhainer, Forbus, and Gentner 1989; Gentner and Forbus 1991; Forbus, Gentner, and Law 1995). Veale's Sapper system (Veale, O'Donoghue, and Keane 1995) also finds its own analogues, but looks at attributes of individual elements, as well as relational properties; the Sapper system also memorizes correspondences which are rich in parallels and stores them as likely candidates for future mappings (i.e., it can gradually learn a set of "conventional" metaphors). In effect, the models of Narayanan and Barnden are informed by theories which posit an inventory of stored conceptual mappings, while Gentner's models focus on the capacity for interpreting and generating novel metaphorical mappings based on the perception of shared features. Veale's model is an attempt to simulate both.

While none of these early models claims to fully replicate the human capacity for creating or interpreting metaphors, such models will inevitably grow richer as the data from psychological and linguistic analyses becomes more refined, as computational power continues to multiply, and as findings about neurological structure continue to inform the architecture of cognitive simulations.

7. METAPHOR AND CULTURE

An emphasis on cognitive perspectives has led to a relative lack of attention to cultural issues within cognitive linguistic metaphor research. With certain major exceptions, researchers have been more interested in the ways that human biology and (species-wide) cognitive predispositions shape conceptualization than in the ways that cultural factors shape those conceptualizations. Of course, this trend is partly in response to decades (or centuries) of special interest in metaphors as distinct literary or cultural objects—characteristic products of unique societies and individual styles. Still, Cognitive Linguistics' cognitive emphasis is complemented and enriched when scholars attend to the ways in which metaphor and culture interact. (See Dirven, Wolf, and Polzenhagen, this volume, chapter 46, for a broader discussion of the relationship between Cognitive Linguistics and culture.)

One general question which presents itself to linguists interested in the relationship between culture and patterns of metaphorical conceptualization is: which metaphors (if any) are culture-specific, or narrowly distributed across cultures, and which ones (if any) are universal or broadly distributed?[15] As we have seen, primary metaphors are patterns that have a high likelihood of being found in any language, regardless of location, cultural affiliation, or historical period. On the other hand, there are long lists of metaphors which appear in some languages and societies but not others, and Lakoff and Johnson did not ignore this fact even in their earliest work. Here is part of their discussion of the metaphorical pattern TIME IS MONEY:

> Time *in our culture* is a valuable commodity. . . . Because of the way that the concept of work has developed *in modern Western culture*, where work is typically associated with the time it takes and time is precisely quantified, it has become customary to pay people by the hour, week, or year. . . . This isn't a necessary way for human beings to conceptualize time; *it is tied to our culture. There are cultures where time is none of these things.* (Lakoff and Johnson 1980: 8–9; emphasis mine)

Linguists may also disagree about the degree to which cultural and universal factors contribute to the genesis of a particular metaphorical pattern. There are reasons to see ANGER IS HEAT, for example, as the product of the universal physiological correlation between the emotion and elevated skin temperature; but the humoral theory of emotions probably also played a role in the development, conventionalization, and elaboration of the pattern in Western languages.[16]

There has now been a substantial amount of metaphor research in languages other than English (including work on signed languages, particularly American Sign Language; e.g., Wilcox 1993; Taub 2001). For instance, a recent special issue of *Cognitive Linguistics*, devoted to cross-linguistic study of terminology within the semantic domain of thought and ideas, includes a number of discussions of metaphors in other languages (particularly, Yu's 2003 study of Chinese). And the field is increasingly characterized by studies which treat the metaphor-culture relationship more centrally. Much of Michele Emanatian's work, for example, has focused on culture-specific metaphorical patterns. She has described American models of "flexibility" as a highly valued trait (Emanatian 1998) and associations between food and sex that underlie linguistic usages in Chagga (a Bantu language of Tanzania) and motivate cultural practices and taboos (Emanatian 1996). In an adjacent academic discipline, anthropologist Bradd Shore (1996) has incorporated some cognitive linguistic perspectives into his work on the schemas that characterize particular cultures—schemas which make up cultural knowledge and are distributed in both the public world of material culture and in individual minds. A characteristically American schema like "modularity," for example, shapes such disparate institutions as the hamburger and skyscraper (each with literal part-whole structure) and the college curriculum, made up of abstract "parts."[17]

Cross-linguistic and cross-cultural variation, of course, can occur at any level of generality. Hiraga (1991) has observed that English and Japanese have similar lexical expressions, based on similar conceptual mappings, linking the domains of time and money; but they frame life metaphorically in terms of different sports (baseball in the case of American English, Sumo in Japanese) and have very distinct metaphors for other conceptual domains—for example, the head and mind are the seat of intentionality for English speakers, while for Japanese speakers it is the *hara* 'belly'. As more comparative metaphor studies of this sort are carried out, we can expect that they will yield a clearer picture of similarities and differences between conceptual systems of people living in different cultural environments.

The CMT framework has also been applied fruitfully to studies of the models operative within a single culture. Lakoff's (1996) *Moral Politics*, for example, is an in-depth study of American moral and political worldviews in terms of metaphorical models which underlie them; and Kövacses's (1986 and elsewhere) studies of emotion concepts discuss the role of metaphor in defining cultural models of emotion. Scholars in fields as diverse as anthropology, literary criticism, archeology, and legal studies have found the theory to be a very useful tool for analyzing the metaphorical patterns that define and permeate shared cultural understandings.

8. Additional Directions and Questions for Metaphor Research

This brief essay can only provide an overview of some of the most central issues in metaphor research from the Cognitive Linguistics perspective. The following is a suggestion of several additional research areas where progress is being made, including implications of metaphor research for the understanding of other fields.

8.1. Metaphor and Attested Data

Since the beginnings of the field, metaphor research within Cognitive Linguistics has often relied on "introspective" data, examples generated by the analysts themselves. While there is nothing suspect in principle about such data, which is produced by native speakers and subject to confirmation by both editors and readers, the potential for refinements and additional insights to be arrived at through analysis of metaphorical language (and images, etc.) produced by "real" speakers and writers is self-evident. A number of research projects have worked exclusively with attested data. Cienki's (1998) analyses of metaphorical gestures, for example, are based on examples elicited during interviews. A larger-scale project involving the participation of a number of analysts and aimed at creating a consistent method for the identification and analysis of metaphors encountered in literature and corpus data is directed by Steen (1999); see also Freeman's discussion of Literary studies (this volume, chapter 45). Such research can shed light on the types of metaphors which real speakers and writers are most (or least) likely to produce, the effect of context on the production of metaphors, and the discourse functions served by metaphors.

8.2. Metaphor and Neuroscience

One of the most inviting frontiers for any twenty-first-century researcher investigating aspects of behavior is the possibility of finding neurobiological correlates for observed patterns of mental operation. The field of cognitive neuroscience is opening new doors through which increasing numbers of metaphor analysts are bound to pass. Cognitive linguists have regularly referred to the work of neuroscientists Antonio Damasio (e.g., 1999) and Gerald Edelman (e.g., 1991) in connection with hypotheses about how schemas and concepts might be represented and associated in the brain. There has also been significant research demonstrating correlations between particular types of brain activity and exposure to particular types of semantic, including metaphorical, content; see, for example, Coulson's work on N400 effects in subjects exposed to novel metaphors (Coulson 2001; Coulson and Van Petten 2002).[18] Such work confirms that bridges, or at least the beginnings of bridges, can be built between the study of metaphorical language and the study of the brain.

8.3. Boundaries of Metaphor

A number of scholars have concluded that it is difficult or impossible to make neat distinctions between metaphorical and nonmetaphorical language. For example, there is no sharp line between metaphor and cases where a category is "stretched" to accommodate a new item, and the difference between metaphor and literal language can be seen as a matter of degree rather than a qualitative distinction. At bottom, these difficulties arise because it is often (perhaps usually) not possible to give precise definitions for individual concepts or conceptual domains. As examples of these problems, Broström (1994) cites uses of color terms to indicate race (e.g., *white* skin); the use of *navigate* in an aeronautical context; the use of *disease* in reference to various externally caused conditions in plants, and so on. In all these cases, she argues, there is no clear answer as to whether metaphor is involved. She also cites the following set of sentences, observing that for at least some speakers, there is no way to draw a definite line between the literal and the metaphorical among the examples: *Life is a mystery / Life is a riddle / Life is a question.* Instead, our judgments about the literal truth of the statements depend on how far we are willing to stretch the categories 'Mystery', 'Riddle', and 'Question'; and such categorization gradually shades into metaphor, rather than being distinct from it. Nevertheless, there is a massive body of indisputably metaphorical examples to serve as materials for study; the "central" cases are clear. Continuing research will help to clarify the status of peripheral ones and the exact nature of the parameters which most accurately define the phenomenon.

8.4. Metaphor Genesis

Current accounts of the origins of conceptual metaphor patterns require further confirmation and elaboration. C. Johnson's (1999) data on developmental patterns for particular lexical items is compelling, as is Gentner's (1988) research on children's developing ability to understand figurative comparisons (and their preferences for particular types). No evidence has yet been forthcoming, however, from these studies or others, on the exact nature of the emergence of metaphorical patterns in children's speech or on their developing awareness of the metaphoricity of usages with which they are already familiar. It is possible, in principle, to trace the spread of a given metaphorical idiom (e.g., phrases coined by Shakespeare which have entered the general lexicon), but there is still much to be learned about the ways in which metaphorical patterns of conceptualization evolve within individual minds and spread from person to person.

Readers interested in pursuing the topic of metaphor further will discover interesting work in many areas not touched on here, including the implications of metaphor research for Western philosophy (e.g., Lakoff and Johnson 1999), for the analysis of particular conceptual domains such as mathematical thought (Lakoff and Nuñez 2000), and for readings of literature (e.g., Turner 1991; M. Freeman 1995; D. Freeman 1998); the ways in which metaphors feed into the development of grammatical systems (e.g., Brugman 1983; Svorou 1989); issues translators must face in dealing with metaphors (e.g., Mandelblit 1995); the diachronic trajectory of metaphorical patterns (e.g., Sweetser 1990); the relationship between metaphor and sound symbolism (e.g., Rhodes and Lawler 1981); and between metaphor and synesthesia (e.g., Takada, 2000).[19] The variety of questions and issues yet to be fully addressed is commensurate with metaphor's pervasive role in thought and language.

NOTES

I would like to thank the editors of this volume, as well as George Lakoff and Zoltan Kövecses, for their helpful comments on an earlier draft of this article.

1. Paprotté and Dirven's (1985) collection of papers reflects the rapid adoption of Lakoff and Johnson's approach by European linguists.

2. A number of terms have been applied to this approach—including 'the contemporary theory' (Lakoff 1993), etc. For a recent and very readable book-length discussion of metaphor from a cognitive linguistic perspective, see Kövecses (2002). For a wide-ranging set of detailed metaphor analyses in the CMT framework, see Lakoff and Johnson (1999).

3. The CMT tradition is to capitalize names of metaphorical patterns.

4. The motivation for such mappings cannot be that they frame the "unfamiliar" in terms of the "familiar," as various accounts of metaphor have suggested, since target concepts like HAPPINESS, DIFFICULTY, and SIMILARITY are every bit as real and familiar to us as the corresponding source concepts. The advantages offered by the metaphors must be of other kinds—e.g., they allow faculties of thought and attention normally devoted to perceptual information to be applied to nonperceptual domains; see Grady (1997a) and the discussion of Narayanan's work in section 6 below.

5. The product of such a reversal is a distinct metaphor; that is, it would be improper to say that the metaphor itself is symmetrical. Rather, in such cases, metaphorical relationships between two concepts may hold in both directions, *based on the same shared feature*.

6. Psychologist Dedre Gentner (1988) distinguishes between metaphors based on "attributes" and "relations" (but does not consider metaphors which might be based on experiential correlation rather than any sort of shared property).

7. Grady and Johnson (2002) refer to these recurring correlations in experience as *primary scenes*.

8. For example, "There are no unsuccessful metaphors, just as there are no unfunny jokes" (Davidson 1981: 200).

9. See Gibbs (1994) for a helpful summary of a number of arguments and sources of evidence on this point, and Gentner (2001) for a more recent discussion of experimental data.

10. See Dean Rohrer's cover for the *New Yorker*, February 8, 1999.

11. See Turner (this volume, chapter 15) for more discussion of the basic principles and operations of blending.

12. Fauconnier and Turner refer to Coulson's unpublished dissertation, which later became the Cambridge volume cited here.

13. CMT offers tools for analyzing some of the particular correspondences within the "digging ones own grave" scenario—such as the connection between death and failure, and possibly a connection between digging a hole (as though digging *for* a desired object) and trying to achieve a purpose. Blending theory offers a framework for combining a number of distinct associations into a whole and representing inferences that do not emerge from any single metaphorical correspondence.

14. From Carol R. Campbell, "Cave Man Bill and the Doleful State of American Politics," published by *The Written Word*, an online journal of economic, political, and social commentary.

15. On an even more fundamental level, of course, there are questions about the extent to which the concepts and conceptual domains linked in metaphorical patterns are themselves created and determined by culture.

16. See Kövecses (1986) and Lakoff and Johnson (1980) for presentations of the "physiological" view, and Geeraerts and Grondelaers (1995) and Kövecses (1995) for an exchange on the issue.

17. For several papers on the relationship between culture and conceptual metaphor, see Gibbs and Steen (1999).

18. A negative component in the brain's electrical waveform, located mainly in the posterior region of the right hemisphere, peaking at about 400 milliseconds following stimulus, occurs in subjects exposed to words which require a special degree of interpretation—as in isolated words, sentence-initial words, or the punch-lines of jokes.

19. See other chapters of this *Handbook* for discussion of a number of these topics.

REFERENCES

Anderson, John M. 1971. *The grammar of case: Towards a localistic theory*. Cambridge: Cambridge University Press.

Aquinas, St. Thomas. 1947. *The Summa Theologica of Thomas Aquinas*. Trans. the English Dominican Fathers. New York: Benziger Bros.

Aristotle. 1996. *Poetics*. Trans. with introduction and notes by Malcolm Heath. Harmondsworth, UK: Penguin Books.

Barnden, John. 2001. Application of the ATT-Meta metaphor-understanding approach to various examples in the ATT-Meta project databank. Technical report CSRP-01-02, School of Computer Science, University of Birmingham, UK.

Black, Max. 1955. Metaphor. In *Proceedings of the Aristotelian Society*, N.S. 55: 273–94. (Repr. in Mark Johnson, ed., *Philosophical Perspectives on Metaphor* 63–82. Minneapolis: University of Minnesota Press, 1981)

Boroditsky, Lera. 2000. Metaphoric structuring: Understanding time through spatial metaphors. *Cognition* 75: 1–28.

Broström, Sofia. 1994. *The role of metaphor in cognitive semantics*. Lund University Cognitive Studies, no. 31. Lund, Sweden: Lund University Cognitive Science.

Brugman, Claudia. 1983. The use of body-part terms as locatives in Chalcatongo Mixtec. In Alice Schlichter, Wallace Chafe, and Leanne Hinton, eds., *Survey of California and other Indian languages* 235–90. Studies in Mesoamerican Linguistics. Report no. 4. Berkeley: University of California at Berkeley.

Brugman, Claudia. 1990. What is the invariance hypothesis? *Cognitive Linguistics* 1: 257–66.

Cienki Alan. 1998. Metaphoric gestures and some of their relations to verbal metaphoric expressions. In Jean-Pierre Koenig, ed., *Discourse and cognition: Bridging the gap* 189–204. Stanford, CA: CSLI Publications.

Clausner, Timothy, and William Croft. 1997. Productivity and schematicity in metaphors. *Cognitive Science* 21: 247–82.

Coulson, Seana. 2001. *Semantic leaps: Frame-shifting and conceptual blending in meaning construction*. Cambridge: Cambridge University Press.

Coulson, Seana, and Cyma Van Petten. 2002. Conceptual integration and metaphor: an event-related potential study. *Memory and Cognition* 30: 958–68.

Damasio, Antonio. 1999. *The feeling of what happens: Body and emotion in the making of consciousness.* New York: Harcourt Brace.

Davidson, Donald. 1981. What metaphors mean. In Mark Johnson, ed., *Philosophical perspectives on metaphor* 200–19. Minneapolis: University of Minnesota Press. (Also published in *Critical Inquiry* 5 (1978): 31–47)

Edelman, Gerald M. 1991. *Bright air, brilliant fire: On the matter of the mind.* New York: Basic Books.

Emanatian, Michele. 1996. Everyday metaphors of lust and sex in Chagga. *Ethos* 24: 195–236.

Emanatian, Michele. 1998. Metaphor clustering in discourse. Poster presented at The Fourth Conference on Conceptual Structure, Discourse, and Language (CSDL-4), Emory University, Atlanta, GA, October 10–12.

Falkenhainer, Brian, Kenneth D. Forbus, and Dedre Gentner. 1989. The structure-mapping engine: Algorithm and examples. *Artificial Intelligence* 41: 1–63.

Fauconnier, Gilles. 1985. *Mental spaces: Aspects of meaning construction in natural language.* Cambridge, MA: MIT Press. (2nd ed., Cambridge: Cambridge University Press, 1994)

Fauconnier, Gilles. 1997. *Mappings in thought and language.* Cambridge: Cambridge University Press.

Fauconnier, Gilles, and Mark Turner. 1994. Conceptual projection and middle spaces. UCSD Cognitive Science Technical Report, no. 9401. University of California, San Diego.

Fauconnier, Gilles, and Mark Turner. 1998. Conceptual integration networks. *Cognitive Science* 22: 133–87.

Forbus, Kenneth, Dedre Gentner, and K. Law. 1995. MAC/FAC: A model of similarity-based retrieval. *Cognitive Science* 19: 141–205.

Freeman, Donald. 1998. Catch(ing) the nearest way: *Macbeth* and cognitive metaphor. In Jonathan Culpeper, Mick Short, and Peter Verdonk, eds., *Exploring the language of drama* 96–111. London: Routledge.

Freeman, Margaret. 1995. Metaphor making meaning: Dickinson's conceptual universe. *Journal of Pragmatics* 24: 643–66.

Geeraerts, Dirk, and Stefan Grondelaers. 1995. Looking back at anger: Cultural traditions and metaphorical patterns. In John R. Taylor and Robert E. MacLaury, eds., *Language and the cognitive construal of the world* 153–79. Berlin: Mouton de Gruyter.

Gentner, Dedre. 1988. Metaphor as structure mapping: The relational shift. *Child Development* 59: 47–59.

Gentner, Dedre. 2001. Spatial metaphors in temporal reasoning. In M. Gattis, ed., *Spatial schemas in abstract thought* 203–22. Cambridge, MA: MIT Press.

Gentner, Dedre, and Kenneth Forbus. 1991. MAC/FAC: A model of similarity-based retrieval. *Proceedings of the Thirteenth Annual Conference of the Cognitive Science Society.* Hillsdale, NJ: Lawrence Erlbaum, 504–9.

Gibbs, Raymond W., Jr. 1994. *The poetics of mind: Figurative thought, language, and understanding.* Cambridge: Cambridge University Press.

Gibbs, Raymond W., Jr., and Gerard J. Steen, eds. 1999. *Metaphor in cognitive linguistics.* Amsterdam: John Benjamins.

Grady, Joseph. 1997a. Foundations of meaning: Primary metaphors and primary scenes. PhD dissertation, University of California at Berkeley.

Grady, Joseph. 1997b. THEORIES ARE BUILDINGS revisited. *Cognitive Linguistics* 8: 267–90.

Grady, Joseph. 1999a. A typology of motivation for conceptual metaphor: Correlation vs. resemblance. In Raymond W. Gibbs, Jr., and Gerard J. Steen, eds., *Metaphor in cognitive linguistics* 79–100. Amsterdam: John Benjamins.

Grady, Joseph. 1999b. Crosslinguistic regularities in metaphorical extension. Paper presented at the Annual Meeting of the Linguistics Society of America, Los Angeles, CA, January 6–9.

Grady, Joseph, and Christopher Johnson. 2002. Converging evidence for the notions of *subscene* and *primary Scene*. In René Dirven and Ralf Pörings, eds., *Metaphor and metonymy in comparison and contrast* 533–54. Berlin: Mouton de Gruyter.

Grady, Joseph, Todd Oakley, and Seana Coulson. 1999. Metaphor and blending. In Raymond W. Gibbs, Jr., and Gerard J. Steen, eds., *Metaphor in cognitive linguistics* 101–24. Amsterdam: John Benjamins.

Grady, Joseph, Sarah Taub, and Pamela Morgan. 1996. Primitive and compound metaphors. In Adele E. Goldberg, ed., *Conceptual structure, discourse and language*. Stanford, CA: CSLI Publications.

Hiraga, Masako. 1991. Metaphor and comparative cultures. In Paul George Fendos, Jr., ed., *Cross-cultural communication: East and west*, vol. 3: 140–66. Tainan, Taiwan: National Cheng-Kung University.

Jackendoff, Ray, and David Aaron. 1991. Review of *More than cool reason*, by George Lakoff and Mark Turner. *Language* 67: 320–38.

Johnson, Christopher. 1999. Metaphor vs. conflation in the acquisition of polysemy: The case of *see*. In Masako Hiraga, Chris Sinha, and Sherman Wilcox, eds., *Cultural, typological, and psychological perspectives in cognitive linguistics* 155–69. Amsterdam: John Benjamins.

Johnson, Mark, ed. 1981. *Philosphical perspectives on metaphor*. Minneapolis: University of Minnesota Press.

Johnson, Mark. 1987. *The body in the mind: The bodily basis of meaning, imagination, and reason*. Chicago: University of Chicago Press.

Johnson, Mark. 1993. *Moral imagination: Implications of cognitive science for ethics*. Chicago: University of Chicago Press.

Katz, Albert. 1989. On choosing the vehicles of metaphors: Referential concreteness, semantic distances, and individual differences. In *Journal of Memory and Language* 28: 486–99.

Kövecses, Zoltán. 1986. *Metaphors of anger, pride, and love: A lexical approach to the study of concepts*. Amsterdam: John Benjamins.

Kövecses, Zoltán. 1990. *Emotion concepts*. New York: Springer Verlag.

Kövecses, Zoltán. 1995. Anger: Its language, conceptualization, and physiology in the light of cross-cultural evidence. In John R. Taylor and Robert E. MacLaury, eds., *Language and the cognitive construal of the world* 181–96. Berlin: Mouton de Gruyter.

Kövecses, Zoltán. 2002. *Metaphor: A practical introduction*. Oxford: Oxford University Press.

Lakoff, George. 1987. *Women, fire, and dangerous things: What categories reveal about the mind*. Chicago: University of Chicago Press.

Lakoff, George. 1990. The invariance hypothesis: Is abstract reason based on image-schemas? *Cognitive Linguistics* 1: 39–74.

Lakoff, George. 1993. The contemporary theory of metaphor. In Andrew Ortony, ed., *Metaphor and thought* 202–51. 2nd ed. Cambridge: Cambridge University Press.

Lakoff, George. 1996. *Moral politics: What conservatives know that liberals don't*. Chicago: University of Chicago Press.

Lakoff, George, and Mark Johnson. 1980. *Metaphors we live by*. Chicago: University of Chicago Press.

Lakoff, George, and Mark Johnson. 1999. *Philosophy in the flesh: The embodied mind and its challenge to Western thought*. New York: Basic Books.

Lakoff, George, and Rafael Nuñez. 2000. *Where mathematics comes from: How the embodied mind brings mathematics into being.* New York: Basic Books.

Lakoff, George, and Mark Turner. 1989. *More than cool reason: A field guide to poetic metaphor.* Chicago: University of Chicago Press.

Langacker, Ronald W. 1987. *Foundations of cognitive grammar.* Vol. 1, *Theoretical prerequisites.* Stanford, CA: Stanford University Press.

Lee, Mark G., and John A. Barnden. 2001. Reasoning about mixed metaphors with an implemented AI system. *Metaphor and symbol* 16: 29–42.

MacCormac, Earl. 1985. *A cognitive theory of metaphor.* Cambridge, MA: MIT Press.

Mandelblit, Nili. 1995. The cognitive view of metaphor and its implications for translation theory. In Marcel Thelen and Barbara Lewandowska-Tomaszczyk, eds., *Translation and meaning, part 3* 483–95. Maastricht, Netherlands: Universitaire Pers Maastricht.

McNeill, David. 1992. *Hand and mind: What gestures reveal about thought.* Chicago: University of Chicago Press.

Narayanan, Srini. 1999. Moving right along: A computational model of metaphoric reasoning about events. *Proceedings of the National Conference on Artificial Intelligence (AAAI-99)* 121–28. Menlo Park, CA: AAAI Press.

Ortony, Andrew, ed. 1979. *Metaphor and thought.* Cambridge: Cambridge University Press. (2nd ed., 1993)

Paprotté, Wolf, and René Dirven, eds. 1985. *The ubiquity of metaphor: Metaphor in language and thought.* Amsterdam: John Benjamins.

Pollio, Howard, Michael Fabrizi, Abigail Sills, and Michael Smith. 1984. Need metaphoric comprehension take longer than literal comprehension? *Journal of Psycholinguistic Research* 13: 195–214.

Reddy, Michael. 1993. The conduit metaphor: A case of frame conflict in our language about language. In Andrew Ortony, ed., *Metaphor and Thought* 164–201. 2nd ed. Cambridge: Cambridge University Press.

Rhodes, Richard, and John Lawler. 1981. Athematic metaphor. *Chicago Linguistic Society*: 318–42.

Ricoeur, Paul. 1978 The metaphorical process as cognition, imagination, and feeling. In Sheldon Sacks, ed., *On metaphor.* Chicago: University of Chicago Press.

Searle, John R. 1981. Metaphor. In Mark Johnson, ed., *Philosophical perspectives on metaphor* 248–85. Minneapolis: University of Minnesota Press. (Also published in John R. Searle, *Expression and meaning* 76–116. Cambridge: Cambridge University Press, 1979)

Shore, Bradd. 1996. *Culture in mind: Cognition, culture, and the problem of meaning.* Oxford: Oxford University Press.

Steen, Gerard J. 1999. From linguistic to conceptual metaphor in five steps. In Raymond W. Gibbs, Jr., and Gerard J. Steen, eds., *Metaphor in cognitive linguistics* 57–77. Amsterdam: John Benjamins.

Svorou, Soteria. 1989. The Evolution of spatial grams. PhD dissertation, State University of New York, Buffalo.

Sweetser, Eve. 1990. *From etymology to pragmatics: Metaphorical and cultural aspects of semantic structure.* Cambridge: Cambridge University Press.

Takada, Mari. 2000. Conceptualization of sound: An analysis of synesthetic sound metaphor. Paper presented at the Japanese Cognitive Science Society Annual Meeting, Hamamatsu, Japan, June 30–July 2.

Talmy, Leonard. 1988. Force dynamics in language and cognition. *Cognitive Science* 12: 49–100.

Taub, Sarah. 2001. *Language from the body: Iconicity and metaphor in American Sign Language.* Cambridge: Cambridge University Press.

Turner, Mark. 1991. *Reading minds: The study of English in the age of cognitive science.* Princeton, NJ: Princeton University Press.

Veale, Tony, Diarmuid O'Donoghue, and Mark T. Keane. 1995. Epistemological issues in metaphor comprehension: A comparison of three models. Paper presented at the 4th International Cognitive Linguistics Conference, University of New Mexico, Albuquerque, July 17–21.

Vico, Giambattista. [1744] 1961. *The new science.* Trans. of *Scienza Nuova* by T. G. Bergin and M. H. Fisch. Ithaca, NY: Cornell University Press.

Wilcox, Phyllis P. 1993. Metaphor in American Sign Language. PhD dissertation, University of New Mexico, Albuquerque.

Yu, Ning. 2003. Chinese metaphors of thinking. *Cognitive Linguistics* 14: 141–65.

CHAPTER 9

IMAGE SCHEMAS

TODD OAKLEY

1. INTRODUCTION

Performing a mundane activity, such as walking to a library, selecting a book from the collection, bringing it to the circulation desk, checking it out, and taking it home, is of complexity far outstripping any known formal description of it. Such routines involve the coordination of multiple acts of sensing, perceiving, moving, and conceptualizing in a three-dimensional world. It is these mundane activities that are most likely to reveal the basic features of human thought and language. Walking to the library already depends on a long history of simpler experiential patterns filtered through culture and the individuals it claims as its own. The exact nature and number of these simpler patterns is still not well understood, but one entity proposed as a supporting structure for human thought and language has become a touchstone notion for all cognitive linguists. This entity is known as an *image schema*.

The locus classicus of image schema theory is Lakoff and Johnson's (1980) conceptual theory of metaphor. Since then, image schema theory has helped Johnson (1987, 1993) establish an epistemology and moral philosophy and has helped Lakoff (1987) articulate a theory of categorization. Subsequently, image schema theory has played a major role in several areas of study: in psycholinguistic investigations by Gibbs (1994) and Gibbs and Colston (1995), in cognitive development by Mandler (1992), in poetics by Lakoff and Turner (1989) and literary criticism by Turner (1987, 1991), in linguistic theories of grammar by Langacker (1987) and Talmy (1983), in mathematics (Lakoff and Núñez 2000), and in computational modeling by the Neural Theory of Language Group.

Briefly, an image schema is a condensed redescription of perceptual experience for the purpose of mapping spatial structure onto conceptual structure. According to Johnson (1987: 29), these patterns "emerge as meaningful structures for us chiefly at the level of our bodily movements through space, our manipulations of objects, and our perceptual interactions."

Image schemas behave as "distillers" of spatial and temporal experiences. These distilled experiences, in turn, are what Cognitive Linguistics regards as the basis for organizing knowledge and reasoning about the world. Accordingly, going to the library and getting a book can be conceptually grouped with a number of instances with little in common save for exhibiting the same image-schematic structure.

This chapter constitutes a primer to the notion of image schemas in Cognitive Linguistics by presenting a preliminary sketch of its terminological history, reviewing a range of studies illustrating the application of image schemas, as well as reviewing studies that establish the psychological and neuropsychological reality of image schemas. I conclude this chapter with a brief discussion of some general theoretical issues concerning the nature of image schemas.

2. PRELIMINARY DISTINCTIONS

2.1. Schemas, Images, and Image Schemas

Image schemas are neither images nor schemas in the familiar senses of each term as used in philosophy, cognitive psychology, or anthropology. Therefore, I will "reverse engineer" this composite structure, examining each component part before reconsidering it in its composite form. I will begin with the second term.

Johnson (1987) credits Immanuel Kant with devising the notion of *schema* as a way of relating percepts to concepts. For Kant, schemas are structures of the imagination, and imagination is the mental faculty that mediates all judgment; hence, imagination is the faculty for synthesizing different modes of representation (sensory percepts, images, concepts, and so on) into concepts. A Kantian schema is a structure of the imagination shared by individuals, but irreducible to conceptual and propositional content. The notion of schema is something like "rationality without rules" (161). For example, Kant argues that "the empirical conception of a *plate* is homogenous with the pure geometrical conception of a *circle*, inasmuch as the roundness which is cogitated in the former is intuited in the latter." Kant then uses this example to posit schemas as "mediating representations" with no empirical content "yet [which] must on the one side be *intellectual*, on the other *sensuous*" ([1781] 1990: 100–101). Schemas, then, are fixed templates superimposed onto perceptions and conceptions to render meaningful representations.

Schemas as "fixed templates" for generating meaningful representations did not originate with Kant, however. The Greek origin of the term *schema* and its plural *schemata* should tip readers off that the very notion has a long intellectual history in the West. Meaning 'form' or 'figure', *schema* provided Greek and Roman rhetoricians with a name for a class of linguistic devices for generating or embellishing arguments. Rhetorical schemas were often contrasted with tropes and figures of thought—for example, metaphor and metonymy—primarily because schemas exploit formal syntactic patterns, while tropes do not. Richard Lewontin's now-famous quip "Just as there is no organism without an environment, there is no environment without an organism" is a prime example of *antimetabole*, a template for replicating the nouns from the first colon in inverse grammatical slots in the second colon. Once available, such schemas can generate new and memorable expressions. Ancient rhetoricians regarded these forms as more-or-less static templates superimposed onto language.

In addition to philosophy and rhetoric, the notion of schema is now a permanent addition to the anthropology and cognitive science lexicons. Even though researchers look slightly differently at the notion of schema and related concepts like "script," "scene," and "scenario," a definition of schema as "a cognitive representation comprising a generalization over perceived similarities among instances of usage" (Kemmer and Barlow 2000: xviii) would likely elicit widespread agreement among them. By repeatedly "activating" a set of properties in a particular way, individuals develop "top-down" frames for construing different facets of experiences, with each repeated instance becoming "an organized framework of objects and relations which have yet to be filled in with concrete detail" (D'Andrade 1995: 122). For example, walking into my campus library activates my schema for UNIVERSITY LIBRARY that includes slots for such roles as 'librarian', 'patron', 'student', 'faculty', any of which can be filled with specific values.

Human beings generate mental images all the time. In Cognitive Linguistics, the term image implicates perception in all acts of conceptualization. Concepts (even abstract concepts) develop from representations of a perceptual conglomeration of visual, auditory, haptic, motoric, olfactory, and gustatory experiences. Images are always analogue representations of specific things or activities.

While immediate perceptions form the basis of mental imagery, the images themselves are abstractions in which the individual can fill in details as he or she frames new experiences. A detailed mental model of my own campus library is specific only to that institution and no other; which is why I know I am in this library and not some other library. Experiences with a particular institution, however, can serve as an imaginative base for creating a "schematized" mental image of a library.

To summarize thus far, a schema has been historically defined as a fixed template for ordering specific information, whereas an image has been defined as a representation of specific patterns capable of being rendered schematically.

As a composite notion, image schemas are neither fixed nor specific, even as they manifest characteristics of each. Many image schemas have "topological" characteristics, insofar as they constitute "spaces" sectioned into areas without specifying actual magnitude, shape, or material. Lack of specificity and content makes image schemas highly flexible preconceptual and primitive patterns used for reasoning in an array of contexts (Johnson 1987: 30).

Johnson (1987: 126) lists the most important image schemas as follows (rendered according to convention in small capitals): CONTAINER; BALANCE; COMPULSION; BLOCKAGE; COUNTERFORCE; RESTRAINT REMOVAL; ENABLEMENT; ATTRACTION; MASS-COUNT; PATH; LINK; CENTER-PERIPHERY; CYCLE; NEAR-FAR; SCALE; PART-WHOLE; MERGING; SPLITTING; FULL-EMPTY; MATCHING; SUPERIMPOSITION; ITERATION; CONTACT; PROCESS; SURFACE; OBJECT; COLLECTION.

On analysis, complex conceptualizations like the library routine fit an image-schematic profile, a combination of image schemas that comprises the topological structure and which allows it to be grouped with other instances of 'going and getting'. For instance, going to the library fits the following image-schematic profile: SOURCE-PATH-GOAL—CONTAINER—COLLECTION—PART-WHOLE—TRANSFER—ITERATION. The library exists as the end point to a path. It also has an inside and an outside, and thus is capable of containing people and objects. Since the objects it contains are of the same kind, the library exploits the notion of collection, which piggybacks on the opposition between part and whole. Physically possessing one of these contained objects in the collection exploits the TRANSFER schema, and its repeatability exploits the ITERATION schema. The above profile represents some of the most conceptually assessable schemas used to structure a working notion of library.

2.2. Image-Schema Transformations

Abstract reasoning depends on the ability to map perceptual categories onto higher-order conceptual categories. Our conceptualizations involve transformations of image schemas (see Johnson 1987: 25–27; Lakoff 1987: 440–44; Turner 1991: 177; Gibbs and Colston 1995; Palmer 1996: 68–74;). Most simple events and actions involve transformations of image schemas. Lakoff (1987: 443) identifies four primary transformations (see also Johnson 1987: 26):

a. *Path focus to end-point focus.* Imagine the path of a moving object and then focus attention on the point where it comes to rest or where it will come to rest.

b. *Mutiplex to mass.* Imagine a cluster of objects. Now imagine moving away from the cluster until the individual objects start to appear as a homogenous mass. Then move back to the point where the mass turns into a cluster again.

c. *Trajectory.* Mentally traverse the path of a continuously moving object.

d. *Superimposition.* Imagine a large sphere and a small cube. Now, increase the size of the cube until the sphere can fit inside it. Now reduce the size of the cube until it fits back inside the sphere.

Consider these transformations from the perspective of the library routine discussed above. Walking to the library involves a *path focus to end-point focus* transformation, whereby one can imagine moving along a path and then shift focus to the point where one is to stop, or where one meets resistance, such as a set of locked doors (Johnson 1987: 26). Selecting a book from a large shelf of books can proceed by a *mass to multiplex* transformation. In this case, the shelf appears first from a distance as a single homogenous mass that turns into a cluster of individual items as one moves closer. Remembering the familiar path to the library involves a *trajectory* transformation, whereby one mentally scans the environment along the way. Finally, imagine removing two books, one larger than the other, from the shelf. Shuffle the two books so that at one moment the folio text supports the quarto text, at another moment the quarto text supports the folio text, producing alternating experiences of superimposition. At one moment, the quarto text is fully actualized visually while the folio text is partially occluded visually; at another moment the quarto text is fully occluded visually and the folio is fully actualized visually. The *superimposition* transformation is one way the mind registers Figure/Ground organization, asymmetry, and dependence. In these instances, image-schema transformations capture dynamic properties of ongoing activities; they are properties of action, and their experience is made real only with respect to a dynamic routine.

3. Image Schemas in Cognitive Linguistics

Cognitive linguists assume that grammar is inherently meaningful, that the lexical and grammatical items reside on a continuum of meaning from specific to schematic, and that all linguistic structures are instantiated as parts of Idealized Cognitive Models (Lakoff 1987: 113–14). An Idealized Cognitive Model for library consists of a prototype and several less-than-prototypical instances (e.g., noncirculating libraries) constituting a radial semantic network of interrelated meanings. Image schemas and their transformations operate as structuring principles of the Idealized Cognitive Model: they "glue" these complex networks together.

If Idealized Cognitive Models and the image schemas that make them possible constitute a fundamental means by which human beings structure knowledge, then they must also make language possible. This is the position of Cognitive Grammar, the predominant theoretical framework used in the studies reviewed below. According to Langacker (1987, 1991), all grammatical structures are meaningful, however schematic. For something to count as a grammatical item in Cognitive Grammar, it must meet the *content requirement* of a symbolic structure, which includes a phonological and a semantic component (or "poles"), specific categorizing relationships for integrating these components with other structures, and schemas for organizing and extending these structures into different (and usually increasingly abstract) domains. The English preposition *from* is a symbolic structure whose semantic component has been schematized so as to be extendable across a wide range of conceptual domains. Specifically, the meaning of this preposition issues from the image-schematic component SOURCE in a SOURCE-PATH-GOAL schema, thereby allowing it to function as an "elaboration site" for orienting attention to an entity. The prepositional phrase *from the library* construes the library as a point of departure for a destination as a salient dimension of its meaning.

Image schema theory plays an important role in studies of the polysemy of individual words or constructions, of related words or constructions, and of semantic change and grammaticalization. It has also been used in literary and textual analysis.

3.1. Studies of the Polysemy of Individual Words or Constructions

This section presents a review of specific studies of words and constructions relying on image schema theory. Every study seeks to show how the symbolic structure in question forms a complex network of related senses, each of which profiles a slightly different feature of an Idealized Cognitive Model. The following review of lexical to grammatical items will necessarily be brief and incomplete but sufficient to provide a general map of the critical terrain.

Casad (1998) conducted an extensive study of the verb 'give' (variations of the verb stem *P^wéihve'e*) in Cora, a Southern Uto-Aztecan language. He found four different types of giving, each with its own specific image-schematic characteristics. The four types of giving include personal interest giving, transport giving, enabling giving, and terminative giving, each a variation of a prototype of giving that entails "one person, using his hands, who physically transfers a discrete entity into the hands of a second person, and, by doing so, also transfers to that second person control over the entity in question" (Casad 1998: 138). The Idealized Cognitive Model for personal interest giving matches the prototype and includes three entities, a giver, a thing, and a recipient, with salient attention focused first on the giver and thing and subsequently on the recipient and thing, and with attention also paid to the motion of the thing from giver to recipient. In sum, personal interest giving regularizes as a canonical instance of the SOURCE-PATH-GOAL schema. A related model focuses attention not on the thing itself but on the CONTAINER of the thing given, as in a vessel of drinking water. This is an instance of transport giving. The third type is of the enabling variety. With this type, an "instigative agent" does something that will enable the recipient to do some other action. Thus, a giver may transfer a vessel of water to a recipient, but focusing attention is on the subsequent enabled actions of the recipient. A fourth type of giving, terminative giving, involves the use of a motion verb and the applicative suffix *-ira* with the agent giver and patient recipient encoded morphologically into the verb. The focus is most salient on some aspect of the recipient with only secondary focus on the transported object, as in *I am going to give it back to him.*

Pauwels's (1995) study of the verb *put* suggests that the CONTAINMENT schema and its entailments are crucial for understanding this verb's various metaphorical usages: from those profiling an inferred destination, as in *put in a good word for me*, to those profiling a loss of control, as in *put out a statement.*

In Cienki's (1998) study of *straight*, he presents evidence that STRAIGHT is an image schema as it represents a recurrent pattern of action, perception, and conception. Cienki offers evidence, mostly from English and Russian (variants of *prjamo*), that sensory-perceptual meanings of *straight* are metaphorically extended into abstract domains of speech, thought, time, and behavior. Both Russian and English evidence *straight* as either an object or location metaphor. For instance, speech, thought, time, and behavior can be expressed as straight objects (e.g., *a straight answer*) or alternately as self-propelled motions along a rectilinear path (e.g., *Say it straight to my face!*). Cienki argues that *straight* has much in common with VERTICALITY schemas, and *straight* correlates strongly in these languages with UP, while antonyms like *bent* correlate with DOWN. *Straight* marks a recurring regularity with our everyday perceptual interaction with the world, which, in turn, provides reason to believe that it patterns our everyday social interactions as well. Even non-Indo-European languages like Hungarian and Japanese evidence regular extensions of *straight* into abstract domains of speech and morality, such that maximally INFORMATIVE SPEECH IS STRAIGHT and MORALITY IS STRAIGHT, while its opposites are *bent, curved, convoluted,* or *crooked.*

Ekberg (1995) analyzes various linguistic manipulations of the VERTICALITY schema in English and Swedish and argues that there are five principles of transformation of the canonical VERTICALITY image schemas. The first principle is the cognitive operation of transforming a vertical axis into a horizontal one by "tipping" it over. Such transformations allow for the extended use of Swedish *upp* 'up' and *ner* 'down' along a horizontal plane; thus, one can say *Han gick upp och ner i korridoren* 'He walked up and down the corridor', even though the objective axis is horizontal. A second principle is end-point focusing where *upp* indexes a location at the end of a mentally traceable vertical trajectory, as exemplified in *Hon bodde en trappa upp* 'She lived one floor up'. A third principle is the metaphorical mapping from the physical to the temporal; thus, expressions like *tankar som når upp i vår egen tid* 'thoughts that reach up into our own time' understand time as a mover along a vertical path. The other two principles include the transformation of a zero-dimensional entity tracing a path to a one-dimensional extended entity and deictic orientation according to the "me-first" principle, with the former principle exemplified in *Klänningen nådde ner till anklarna* 'The dress reached down to the ankles' and the latter exemplified in usages where inanimate objects acquire characteristics of human bodies, such as *Han satt längst upp vid bordet* 'He sat at the head of the table'. Ekberg offers an array of linguistic evidence to support the notion that image-schematic characteristics pervade the meaning structures of even the most commonplace grammatical items.

Serra-Borneto (1995a) argues that image schemas can be used to explain certain exceptions to the general rule governing the use of dative and accusative case markers for two-way prepositions in German, such as *an, auf, hinter,* and *in*. In general, the dative case applies to static relationships between participants while the accusative applies to dynamic relations. This rule works fine for examples like *Hans geht in den Garten* 'Hans goes into the garden', with accusative *den* signaling a dynamic relationship, and *Hans sitzt im Garten* 'Hans sits in the garden', with dative *im* signaling a static relationship. The rule does not seem to apply for examples like *Das Flugzeug über der Stadt* 'The airplane over the city' because the dative *der* marks an ostensive dynamic relationship. Serra-Borneto shows how the entailments of CONTAINMENT— protection from, limits, fixity of location, opaqueness—motivate the different uses of dative markings in two-way prepositions. It makes sense to use the dative in the above example when speakers mean that the plane stays within the city's airspace.

In a similar fashion, Smith (2002) analyzes the many meanings of the third-person neuter pronominal *es* in German, whose range of use extends well beyond the prototype as a grammatical anaphor, referring to nonneuter antecedents and whole settings, both concrete and abstract. Smith argues that *es* reflects an abstraction of the CONTAINMENT schema in which it profiles not only entities within a region but the whole region in which an event or state of affairs occurs.

Watters's (1995) study of Tepehua, a Totonacan language spoken in eastern Mexico, analyzes the various uses of applicative forms for stative and nonstative verbs based on image schema theory. His study focuses specifically on the suffix -*ni* and prefixes *pu*- and *łi*-. When applied to a stative verb, *ni*- means something like *at*, which functions image-schematically like a Ground in a Figure/Ground relationship. When applied to a nonstative verb, *ni*- means something like the GOAL component of an SOURCE-PATH-GOAL schema. As with other grammatical instances, the spatial meaning of these forms is basic, as is especially the case with -*pu*, where the basic directional meaning is extended to include duration.

3.2. Studies of the Polysemy of Related Words or Constructions

In addition to studies of individual items, several studies of closely related words— such as Delbecque's (1995) on the Spanish prepositions *por* and *para*—show how differences in image-schematic structures account for their different meanings. Here is a brief description of two such studies.

Serra-Borneto (1995b) explored the image-schematic constraints governing the use of the German locative verbs *liegen* 'to lie' and *stehen* 'to stand' in perceptual and nonperceptual contexts. The data suggest that *stehen* encodes verticality and *liegen* encodes horizontality, but also that *stehen* can apply to objects with a 'base', while *liegen* applies to cases where either horizontality is the one salient dimension or where referents lack dimensional saliency altogether, such as in cases referring to nonperceptual and "geotopographical" locations. For instance, one can say *Der Punkt liegt auf der Gerade* but not **Der Punkt steht auf der Gerade* 'The point is on the line', and one can say *Frankfurt liegt am Main* but not **Frankfurt steht am Main* 'Frankfurt is on the Main', since a point in space or on a map possesses no salient vertical dimension. As with the other studies discussed above, Serra-Borneto shows how image schema theory provides a cognitive explanation for subtle meaning differences leading to different grammatical realizations.

Williams (1992) also shows this in his treatment of *over*, *under*, and *out* in English comparatives like *overdone*, *underinsured*, and *outmaneuvered*. Williams argues that the particles *over* and *under* prompt us to project two entities (one of which is often implicit) or events against some pragmatic scale for assessing and comparing the target value. The meaning of adjectives *overdone* and *underdone*, for instance, involves relative scales of doneness in cooking. In contrast, *outmaneuver* exploits the notion of CONTAINMENT, with *out* locating and relating entities with respect to a domain of influence. Thus, if a forward in ice hockey *outmaneuvers* the goalie, we understand that the forward (at that moment) occupies an area of speed and skill not within the control of the goalie.

3.3. Studies of Semantic Change and Grammaticalization

The studies reviewed in this section focus on issues of semantic change.

Rhee (2002) proposes four processes involved in semantic change—metaphor, generalization, subjectification, and frame-to-focus variation—as demonstrated by his analysis of the English preposition *against*. Evidence suggests that the original meaning of physical directionality expanded to cover relationships of temporal proximity and approximation; thus, semantic change occurs through metaphorical mapping from the spatial to the temporal domains. Semantic change also occurs through generalization, with *against* initially applying only to tangible entities in opposition and subsequently applying to less tangible and associated entities. Rhee's principal argument is that semantic change involves image schemas and their transformations. When meaning changes, details of source images are generally ignored but schematic structures are preserved. This is one reason *against* can acquire seemly contrasting meanings: each meaning profiles a different image-schematic component of a scene. 'Toward'-*against* focuses on an entity moving along a path, 'opposed'-*against* focuses on a countering force moving in the opposite direction from a moving entity, while 'near'-*against* is a consequence of our ability to construe a scene 'from afar', whereby the entire scene reduces to a small dimension with no visible path.

Both Smith's (1999) study of the Russian instrument marker (*om*) and Verspoor's (1995) study of predicate adjunct constructions make essentially the same argument, that semantic change preserves image-schematic structure. For instance, Smith claims that the prototype of an action chain where the instrument is a conduit for energy flow accounts for some puzzling uses of the instrument marker in Russian, such as to indicate impermanence and irrealis. Similarly, Verspoor offers a detailed explanation for why *Michael wiped the table clean* and *Michael considers the table clean* instantiate the same grammatical construction. The same schema is preserved in both sentences, in that the act of "considering XY" is metaphorically understood in terms of moving an entity from one place to another, thereby altering its state.

The hypothesis that semantic change involves image schema preservation is not without controversy among cognitive linguists, however. Matsumoto (1995) shows that the hypothesis is challenged by the development of two causal markers in Japanese, *ni-yotte* and *tame*, and therefore argues that, at best, only a weak form of this hypothesis is partially viable. Indeed, the development of *ni-yotte* from cause to purpose does not preserve the CAUSAL CHAIN schema; rather, the meaning change seems motivated by the opposite attributive schema of tracing back to a source. Certainly, image schemas are important theoretical notions for studying semantic change and grammaticalization; however, the notion that semantic change involves image schema preservation is a matter of considerable debate.

3.4. Literary and Textual Analysis

Image schema theory has also been instrumental in the development of cognitive approaches to literary and textual criticism, most notably with Turner's work on the nature of linguistic creativity in both everyday and highly artistic contexts. In one noted article, Turner (1992) argues that the *invariance principle* accounts for much of what is systematic about metaphor, using bare equations like *Kingdoms are clay* and *Language is a virus* as they occur in artistic and inartistic contexts. The invariance principle states that the mapping from the source cannot violate the image-schematic structure of the target. For instance, speakers of English are likely to interpret *Kingdoms are clay* as pertaining to the impermanence and temporary nature of the target subject; hence the interpretation 'Kingdoms crumble like clay', insofar as we can understand kingdoms as coming into and going out of existence; or 'Kingdoms can be molded out of clay', insofar as we can understand them as being shaped. What would not be a likely interpretation is 'Kingdoms have a reddish-brown hue', since colorful objects are not a salient part of the underlying schematic structure of the target domain.

Turner's larger point is to counter a prevailing assumption among contemporary critical and literary theorists that no stable or reliable forms of communication actually exist. Freeman (1995, 2002) assumes the same critical perspective, but instead of seeking to reveal the nature of the human imagination generally, she seeks to show how image schema theory can in fact produce better, more reliable literary interpretations. In a recent article, Freeman (2002) counters the common assumption that the poet Robert Frost had a clear poetics that runs throughout his oeuvre but that Emily Dickinson did not. Freeman suggests that image schema theory helps show that Dickinson's oeuvre can be interpreted as the careful working out of a poetics quite distinct from Frost's. In essence, Frost uses the schemas of PATH and BALANCE, while Dickinson uses the schemas of CONTAINER, CHANGE, CYCLE, and CIRCLE to structure her poetic imagery.

Other work in textual analysis focuses on the metaphorical structure of non-literary domains or disciplines and their textual instantiations. Romaine (1996) and Boers and Demecheleer (1997) have each studied conventional metaphors structuring discourse about economics and conflict. To take just one example, Boers and Demecheleer conducted extensive corpus analysis of economic discourse in English, French, and Dutch and found three general conventional metaphorical models accounted for the data, the most prevalent in English being the PATH metaphor, as exemplified in such common metaphors as PROGRESS IS MOVING FORWARD, DECISION MAKING IS CHOOSING A DIRECTION, and so on.

4. PSYCHOLOGICAL CONSIDERATIONS

This section reviews a selection of studies in psycholinguistics, cognitive development and language acquisition, and neurocomputational modeling for the psychological reality of image schemas.

4.1. Psycholinguistics

Gibbs et al. (1994) explored the polysemy of *stand* in a series of four interlocking experiments with the explicit aim of empirically supporting the notion that image schemas organize experience and as such organize semantic structure.

First, after a brief period of standing up, moving around, bending over, crunching, and stretching, subjects were read descriptions of 12 different image schemas related to acts of standing and were then asked to rate the relevance of each image schema to their own experience. The experimenters found five primary image schemas associated with subjects' sense of standing: BALANCE, VERTICALITY, CENTER-PERIPHERY, RESISTANCE, and LINKAGE. Second, subjects were asked to judge the similarity for 35 different senses of *stand*, sorting them into five groups. The experimenters found that subjects did not separate physical senses of *stand* from nonphysical or figurative senses, grouping *stand at attention* with *to stand the test of time*, for example. Third, after another activity period associated with their bodily experiences of standing, subjects were presented with verbal descriptions of the five image schemas, shown a list of 32 senses of *stand* and asked to rate the relevance of each image schema to each sense. From their responses, the experimenters constructed an "image-schematic profile" for each of the 32 uses of stand, with *it stands to reason* and *as the matter now stands* having the same profile of LINKAGE—BALANCE—CENTER-PERIPHERY—RESISTANCE—VERTICALITY (in order of importance). In contrast, *don't stand for such treatment* and *to stand against great odds* exhibit the profile of RESISTANCE—CENTER-PERIPHERY—LINKAGE—BALANCE—VERTICALITY. In both profiles, the least relevant schema for each use was VERTICALITY, which linguists conducting post hoc analysis would likely mark as a primary image schema of *stand*. On the other hand, data showing VERTICALITY as the primary image correlated with expressions not typically associated with this schema, like *the barometer stands at 30 centimeters* or *got stood up for a date*. The data also showed a strong correlation between VERTICALITY and BALANCE as the two most salient profiled schemas in expressions where the subject is a single intentional agent (e.g., *He stands at attention*) and a strong correlation between VERTICALITY and some other image schema, such as CENTER-PERIPHERY, in cases of collective subjects (e.g., *standing ovation*) or artifacts with no moving parts (e.g., *house*). Importantly, subjects did not sort by context, suggesting to the experimenters that similarity of situation did not factor as a primary means of categorizing instances.

4.2. Cognitive Development and Language Acquisition

Infants use image schemas to generalize across perception and find commonalities of experiences. This is the principal claim staked out by Mandler (1992) and supported by Gibbs and Colston (1995).

Gibbs and Colston argue that the transformation of LANDMARK—BLOCKAGE—REMOVAL OF BLOCKAGE back to LANDMARK subtend a 4.5-month-old's demonstration of object permanence, whereas 3.5-month-old children do not demonstrate such a capacity. "One could argue," write Gibbs and Colston (1995: 367), "that development of the notion of object permanence can be thought of as the development of several different image schemas, and the workings of transformations between them."

Infants as young as four months can distinguish between caused motion and self-motion with experiments of subjects observing one ball hitting another ball, causing the second ball to move, and experiments of subjects observing two balls moving independently of one another (Gibbs and Colston 1995: 365). The authors conclude that these infants employ a well-developed TRAJECTOR—PATH image schema within a trajectory schema transformation, such that the end point of the first trajector becomes the starting point of the second trajector. When this pattern does not appear, the ensuing motion of the second trajector is understood in terms of self-motion rather than caused motion.

Another set of findings that has implications for image schema theory is synaesthesia experiments conducted by Wagner et al. (1981). For this study, they paired perceptual events that share no physical features or history of co-occurrence, such as visual markings and musical tones. For example, one-year-olds looked longer at dotted lines than at solid lines when presented with a pulsing tone. Likewise, they looked longer at a downward arrow when presented with a descending tone than with an ascending tone, and vice versa. They also found that children as young as four already conceive similarities between pitch and brightness and between loudness and brightness.

For human beings to have meaningful experiences, conclude Gibbs and Colston (1995: 370), regular patterns of action and perception must develop early in development. The empirical evidence so far suggests that young children possess the ability to discover abstract relations among a diverse range of sensory perceptual events consistent with the general description of image schemas.

While Gibbs and Colston focus attention on the bodily origin of image schemas, more recent work in language acquisition focuses more attention on the manipulation of objects in a material culture. Certainly Johnson and Lakoff, both collectively and individually, acknowledge the importance of varying social environments to cognitive and linguistic development. Indeed, Gibbs and Colston (1995) acknowledge that infants are born into a world which allows them to readily observe simple acts of containment, as would be afforded through cups, bottles, and dishes, which they readily see objects and substances disappear into and reappear out of. Thus, in their words, "it might be easier to analyze the sight of milk going in and out of a cup than milk going in and out of one's mouth" (366). Their suggestion that artifacts in material culture may, in fact, constitute the material substrate for the development of notions of CONTAINMENT means that comparative studies of differing social environments should enjoy greater attention of cognitive linguists.

Cross-linguistic research in first-language acquisition epitomized by Sinha and Jensen de López (2000) calls on cognitive linguists to rethink just where image schemas come from. The authors argue against a strong version of the embodiment hypothesis, which states that bodily experience structures most if not all psychological and interpersonal domains through metaphorical projection. Their studies of English-acquiring, Danish-acquiring, and Zapotec-acquiring children as they acquire and use locatives, and tests using language comprehension and action imitation tasks, suggest an equally strong role for sociocultural context in cognitive development. The Zapotec language, for instance, exhibits no morphological distinction between the nominal English equivalent to *stomach* and its locatives meaning 'in' or 'under'. English and Danish, on the other hand, distinguish *in* from *under*, and acquisition patterns and experiments suggest that there exists a definite bias among English- and Danish-acquiring children in favor of using *in* for good examples of CONTAINMENT and toward regarding *under* as a special case—implying occlusion and immobility but without implying complete enclosure. Zapotec-acquiring children, on the other hand, evince no '*in*-bias' in their use of locatives.

As the history of the Zapotec language attests, the role of the human body is a salient source for linguistic concepts, as is evidenced by the fact that body-part terms acquire locative functions. However, this may be an historical effect of indirect cognitive consequence, for Sinha and Jensen de López's study suggests that it is not only bodily experience which is the driving force for linguistic constructions of space and for the acquisition of spatial terms but also sociocultural context and the artifactual composition of cultural settings. Unlike Danish- and English-acquiring children, who, for the most part, are born into a world of richly diverse sets of artifacts, each of which perform highly specific functions, Zopatec-acquiring children grow up in material cultures with few artifacts, and, therefore, make use of them in more flexible ways. One salient artifact of containment in Zapotec cultures of southern Mexico is baskets. The child enters a world in which baskets are used as often to *cover something up* (e.g., tortillas, for storage, for catching chickens) as they are used to *place an object in*. The inverted orientation of the basket is a defining part of their material culture. In Zapotec culture, containment via baskets counts equally in its "inverted" orientation (*under*) as it does in its canonical orientation (*in*) orientation. The same is not true for English or Danish speaking cultures.

Sinha and Jensen de López (2000: 20) tentatively attribute Zapotec-acquiring children not evincing the same *in*-bias in their responses as English-acquiring and Danish-acquiring children to the fact that baskets (the artifact used in all the experiments) are not used in the same canonical way. As such, there is evidence that containment may be universal but the diversity of nonlinguistic practices from one culture to the next brings about different conceptualizations of language reflected in the language acquisition process itself.

4.3. Image-Schematic Dimensions of Computational Modeling

If conceptual structure arises from spatial perceptual analysis of the immediate environment, as suggested above, then it may be possible to model such a learning process. Such is the aim of the Neural Theory of Language Project initiated by George Lakoff and Jerome Feldman. In this section, I will describe briefly some image-schematic features of this project and how they apply to specific models of language comprehension.

According to Bailey et al. (1997), current Neural Theory of Language projects begin with the representation of human-like actions. The computational feature representing action is the "execution schema" (or x-schema), a representation of actions in an environment used to simulate specific execution patterns. For instance, one model enacts a DROP-schema in order to simulate the act of dropping an object; its components (or "control transitions") include 'start', 'ongoing', 'finish', and 'done', where in the simulation 'start' binds with an agent supporting an object who then withdraws support. The removal of support triggers a FALL-schema, simulating the decreasing height of the object along a vertical trajectory until it hits the ground. These programs include static representations of the possible outcomes or consequences, known as a "feature structures," of an x-schema. A feature structure (or "f-struct"), which in turn binds with, for instance, the DROP-schema, produces the inference that the object will either bounce or break upon reaching the ground.

Although Bailey and his associates make no mention of the image-schematic characteristics of the DROP-schema/FALL-schema simulation, they would doubtless agree that these interlocking schemas exploit basic notions of RESTRAINT REMOVAL, SOURCE-PATH-GOAL, MOMENTUM, and VERTICALITY schemas.

Narayanan (1999) extends the same x-schema protocol to model metaphorical reasoning about political economy. For Narayanan, x-schemas connect source domain structures together in order to be mapped onto a target domain. For the mapping of the source domain of walking maps onto the target domain of liberal economy, this means, then, that x-schemas used to simulate walking combine to form the source domain for conceptualizing political economy (see Narayanan 1999), as exemplified in the sentence, *While great strides were made in the first few years, the Government [of India] is currently stumbling in its efforts to implement the liberalization plan.* Implementation begins with a WALKING-schema and its components 'ready', 'start', 'ongoing', 'finish', and 'done'. At the point the program settles on the 'ongoing' component, it introduces the concept of 'bump', whereby the WALKING-schema is interrupted by a FALL-schema, integrating a different sort of 'start', 'ongoing', 'finish', and 'done' sequence, with 'done' binding to the VERTICALITY component 'down'. At this point, a GET UP-schema and its associated sequence of events runs concurrently with the STABILIZE-schema, complete with its own 'ready', 'start', 'ongoing', 'finish', and 'done' sequence. The source domain that will eventually structure information in the target domain implements x-schemas for WALK and FALL which run sequentially—the first interrupting the second—at the same time that it implements x-schemas for GET UP and STABILIZE, which run concurrently with each other and with the WALK-schema.

As with the previous example, the image-schematic character of these x-schemas can be made readily apparent. The most salient image schemas influencing the walking-stumbling domain would be SOURCE-PATH-GOAL, BALANCE, VERTICALITY, SURFACE, CONTACT, COUNTERFORCE, and ITERATION. To the extent that all x-schemas represent actions in the world, the SOURCE-PATH-GOAL schema is likely to be of fundamental importance when representing mobile agents. The BALANCE schema comes into play negatively with the notion of *stumble*, which implies CONTACT with an entity of COUNTERFORCE impeding forward progress. Since the intention is to keep going, the GET UP and STABILIZE schemas depend on our experiences of VERTICALITY relative to a landmark, and regaining of one's BALANCE allows the WALKING-schema to be resumed, thus experienced as an ITERATION of the same action.

Finally, consider in brief Regier's (1996) computational model for categorizing spatial relations in English, Russian, and Mixtec. The program parses a movie of schematic trajector and landmark relations and judges each one as a poor or excellent example of English *through*, Russian *iz-pod*, or Mixtec *sini*. Principal computational features of this model include a specification for a beginning point, an end point, and an inferred trajectory between them. Computationally, the program matches a "current buffer" with discrete snapshots of information in a "motion buffer," an element of the program structured by a tripartite trajectory representation with three subrepresentations, each of which matches the image-schematic components of SOURCE-PATH-GOAL: a beginning representation, or the initial configuration of trajector relative to a landmark, an end-point representation of the final static relation between trajector and landmark, and an integrated representation of a path running between the initial and final trajectors. The inspiration for Regier's SOURCE-PATH-GOAL-based program comes from studies of apparent motion. When presented with an object displayed at one point in a visual field, then with a copy of the object at another point in a visual field, human subjects will perceive one object as moving from one point to the next.

5. CONCLUSION: A FEW ISSUES OF GENERAL THEORETICAL IMPORTANCE

Consider once again the mundane activity of going and getting a library book, an activity with the image-schematic profile that includes our concepts of SOURCE-PATH-GOAL, CONTAINMENT, COLLECTION, PART-WHOLE, TRANSFER, and ITERATION. But why not stipulate the image schemas for BALANCE, COUNTERFORCE CONTACT, COMPULSION, and NEAR-FAR as equally a part of the profile? Surely one can imagine facets of this complex activity involving each of these schemas: walking entails BALANCE, opening the library doors entails COUNTERFORCE, transfer entails CONTACT, estimating one's progress along a path to a destination entails certain NEAR-FAR orientations, and so on. Therefore, should we conclude that my image-schematic profile is insufficient? Perhaps, but that only begs other questions, such as: What counts as an exhaustive image-schematic account of a familiar activity? Is there consensus on the exact number of image schemas? What are the constraints on postulating image schemas? At present, I see no widespread agreement on these matters, especially regarding the exact number of image schemas or even regarding the question whether some of the items appearing on Johnson's authoritative list, such as ENABLEMENT, are bona fide image schemas.

Adequate answers to the fundamental questions mentioned above have yet to appear. However, a suite of questions of a less fundamental nature do seem to have some promising answers that may help cognitive linguists answer these more fundamental questions. Some of these questions are: What properties are shared by the "most important" image schemas, and how can they be grouped? Are there levels of schematization? How do noncognitive linguistic theories use image schemas? How might the graphic representation of image schemas influence linguistic analysis? This concluding section addresses briefly each of these issues. Perhaps we can regard some image schemas as more general and others as more specific. Cienki (1997), for instance, argues that PROCESS, PATH, OBJECT, and CONTAINER comprise known general schemas, each of which has a set of more specific schemas, such as STRAIGHT, SCALE, ITERATION, and CYCLE for PATH and FULL-EMPTY, SURFACE, and CENTER-PERIPHERY for CONTAINER.

Or perhaps we can group some according to criterion of "super-imposability," whereby they can only be understood relative to other image schemas. The CYCLE schema, for example, can be understood as the superimposition of a PATH whose GOAL and SOURCE are identical points in space due to ITERATION. This "Gestalt" grouping of image schemas with other image schemas leads to the tentative conclusion that some image schemas are perceptually more primary (e.g., PATH), while others suggest a more complex structure; thus, distinguishing between recurring perceptual experience and gestalt complexes of perceptual experiences is crucial, despite their treatment as synonyms in much of the literature.

Distinguishing the developmental trajectory of image schemas may be another way of grouping them. Some image schemas may be developmentally more basic than others. According to Mandler (1992), conceptual development arises from perceptual analysis; by this mechanism, perceptual information is conceptualized, with the resulting notions of ANIMACY, INANIMACY, AGENCY, and CONTAINMENT guiding the initial phases of conceptual development. Image schemas for PATH, COMPULSION, LINK, COUNTERFORCE, CONTACT, SURFACE, and OBJECT may be ontogenetically basic, because each requires one or more of these forms of perceptual analysis.

Now consider what known image schemas have in common.

All image schemas can be construed as dynamic or static scenes, as processes or states (see Cienki 1997, for a review). For example, we can construe the experience of BALANCE as a state of equilibrium or as an act of maintaining balance. The static versus dynamic characteristics of image schemas references Langacker's (1987: 145) distinction between summary and sequential scanning. When we construe a complex scene as one in which all facets are "conceived coexistent and simultaneously available," we are relying on static realizations of image schemas; then again, when we construe a complex scene as a series of states in which one successively transforms into another, we are relying on dynamic realizations of image schemas.

Krzeszowski (1993: 310) discusses in some detail an important characteristic shared by all image schemas: the plus-minus parameter. That is, all image schemas exhibit a bipolar property of conferring positive or negative associations. In other words, image schemas all have euphoric or dysphoric characteristics, and it is this "axiological parameter" that is "responsible for the dynamism of the metaphorization processes inherent in the formation of concepts based on the relevant schemata" (310). Thus, balance is positive/plus, while imbalance is negative/minus; whole is positive while part is negative. These euphoric and dysphoric properties are imperative for forming axiological concepts like 'good', 'beautiful', 'true', 'bad', 'ugly', and 'false' (325).

Even with these distinguishing and common features, image schemas seem to exhibit such a wide variety of instantiations that systematic investigation may seem impossible. This is where Kreitzer's (1997) study of schematization may come in handy.

Taking the case of *over* as his point of departure, Kreitzer distinguishes between three levels of schematization: the component level, the relational level, and the integrative level. The component level refers to particular schematized elements of a spatial scene, such as surfaces, lines, and points. They are geometrically schematic, allowing for an image schema to apply to a wide variety of objects and relations. For example, the SUPPORT and CONTACT schemas, realized linguistically by the preposition *on*, are schematized as points of a mass in contact with a surface. The relational level organizes components into specific spatial relations. The prototype for *over* requires motion and a trajectory traversing the boundaries of a landmark. This means that contact with the landmark is not relevant at the component or relational level of schematization. At the integrative level, multiple image schemas unite. Kreitzer gives the following example, taken from Lakoff (1987): *The city clouded over*. In this case, the PATH schema integrates with a static COVERING schema, but the crucial point is that the COVERING schema is not a part of the PATH schema at the relational level, for the construed relation is static not dynamic, hence no end-point focus transformation occurs (Kreitzer 1997: 307). The main advantage of Kreitzer's levels is that it offers principled criteria for specifying different components of image schemas, with different lexical meanings arising from different integrations of relational schemas. For instance, *over* exhibits three different relational schemas: the first specifying a static relation along the vertical axis; a second specifying a dynamic relation along the vertical and horizontal axes; and a third specifying a static relation defined egocentrically. Kreitzer argues that the component level determines the basic primitives of spatial conceptualization.

The term "spatial conceptualization" brings up an interesting issue regarding how image schemas are understood outside the cognitive linguistic community. Jackendoff's (1996) treatment of the "linguistic-spatial interface" makes mention of image schemas as "abstract representations from which a variety of images can be generated" (9). In his scheme of representational modularity, Jackendoff places image schemas within the module of spatial representation, which is largely "invisible" to conceptual structure. Strictly speaking, image schemas are useful descriptions of spatial representation, providing three-dimensional models of spatial properties, but their influence on conceptual structure and linguistic structure are minimal. Jackendoff's theory of representation modularity is at once an acknowledgment of the power of image schemas as a theoretical notion and a denial that image schemas play a significant role in conceptualization and grammar.

In addition, Jackendoff (1996: 26) is quick to argue that "it is not obvious that places and paths are encoded in imagistic representation because we do not literally *see* them except when dotted lines are drawn in cartoons." This seemingly off-handed remark, however, brings up an important issue regarding the graphic representation of image schemas, namely that these conventions may subtly channel cognitive linguistic investigations in ways that can bias theory and analysis in certain directions. This argument is made explicitly in Mandler (1992) and implicitly in Dewell (1994).

Diagrams for motion in notation systems for Cognitive Grammar usually include straight lines. But such a representation does not help us distinguish between animate motion, self-propelled motion, and inanimate and caused motion, distinctions that are essential for perceptual analysis, as outlined in Mandler (1992). The manner in which something traverses a path is an important, if unstated, element of image schema theory; that is, there are probably distinct schemas for animate and inanimate motion.

Dewell (1994) argues that typical accounts of *over* in Cognitive Linguistics posit several features, such as the shape of and contact with a landmark, as well as positing ACROSS and ABOVE as subschemas, which Dewell regards as separate schemas altogether. Although Dewell does not make this connection explicit, one can see that Lakoff's and Brugman's decision to make 'flat trajectory' examples of *over* the prototype stem, in part, from the tendency to represent trajectories as straight lines. But, as Dewell points out, the best linguistic evidence (e.g., *The dog jumped over the fence*) suggests that the most typical examples of *over* involve an ARCHED PATH schema, and from it he accounts for all the uses of *over* without specifying extraneous features, such as 'contact'. ACROSS and ABOVE are not subschemas of *over* but distinct schemas with their own inference generating capacities and grammatical realizations. Close examination of Lakoff's (1987: 419) case study reveals that he builds his analysis around an initial 'above and across' representation, with an oval marked trajector placed along a straight dotted arrow which runs from left to right and is placed over a square marked landmark, and that all subsequent graphic representations and analyses issue from that basic representation. Dewell, on the other hand, builds his analysis around a semicircular path with an arched arrow partially enclosing a rectangle (1994: 355). To summarize, graphic conventions of many image schema–based studies represent motion in a straight line as the default prototype, but as Mandler and Dewell argue, motion and paths are not prototypically straight. It is open for debate as to how the conventions of image-schematic representations actually bias theory and analysis. These two studies at least hint that this is an issue, as are the others mentioned above, that is worth our attention.

REFERENCES

Bailey, David, Jerome Feldman, Srini Narayanan, and George Lakoff. 1997. Modeling embodied lexical development: Neural theory of language publications. http://www.icsi.berkeley.edu/NTL/papers/cogsci97.pdf. Accessed February 8, 2001.

Boers, Frank, and Murielle Demecheleer. 1997. A few metaphorical models in (Western) economic discourse. In Wolf-Andreas Liebert, Gisela Redeker, and Linda Waugh, eds., *Discourse and perspective in cognitive linguistics* 115–29. Amsterdam: John Benjamins.

Casad, Eugene H. 1998. Lots of ways to GIVE in Cora. In John Newman, ed., *The linguistics of giving* 135–74. Amsterdam: John Benjamins.

Cienki, Alan. 1997. Some properties and groupings of image schemas. In Marjolijn Verspoor, Kee Dong Lee, and Eve Sweetser, eds., *Lexical and syntactical constructions and the construction of meaning* 3–15. Amsterdam: John Benjamins.

Cienki, Alan. 1998. STRAIGHT: An image schema and its metaphorical extensions. *Cognitive Linguistics* 9: 107–49.

D'Andrade, Roy. 1995. *The development of cognitive anthropology*. Cambridge: Cambridge University Press.

Delbecque, Nicole. 1995. Towards a cognitive account of the use of the prepositions *por* and *para* in Spanish. In Eugene H. Casad, ed., *Cognitive linguistics in the Redwoods: The expansion of a new paradigm in linguistics* 249–318. Berlin: Mouton de Gruyter.

Dewell, Robert B. 1994. *Over* again: Image schema transformations in semantic analysis. *Cognitive Linguistics* 5: 351–80.

Ekberg, Lena. 1995. The mental manipulation of the vertical axis: How to go from "up" to "out" or from "above" to "behind." In Marjolijn Verspoor, Kee Dong Lee, and Eve Sweetser, eds., *Lexical and syntactical constructions and the construction of meaning* 69–88. Amsterdam: John Benjamins.

Freeman, Margaret H. 1995. Metaphor making meaning: Dickinson's conceptual universe. *Journal of Pragmatics* 24: 643–66.

Freeman, Margaret H. 2002. Momentary stays, exploding forces: A cognitive linguistic approach to the poetics of Emily Dickinson and Robert Frost. *Journal of English Linguistics* 30: 73–90.

Gibbs, Raymond W., Jr. 1994. *The poetics of mind: Figurative thought, language, and understanding.* Cambridge: Cambridge University Press.

Gibbs, Raymond W., Jr, Dinara Beitel, Michael Harrington, and Paul Sanders. 1994. Taking a stand on the meaning of *stand*: Bodily experience as motivation for polysemy. *Journal of Semantics* 11: 231–51.

Gibbs, Raymond W., Jr., and Herbert L. Colston. 1995. The cognitive psychological reality of image schemas and their transformations. *Cognitive Linguistics* 6: 347–78.

Jackendoff, Ray. 1996. The architecture of the linguistic-spatial interface. In Paul Bloom, Mary A. Peterson, Lynn Nadel, and Merrill F. Garrett, eds., *Language and space* 1–30. Cambridge, MA: MIT Press.

Johnson, Mark. 1987. *The body in the mind: The bodily basis of meaning, imagination, and reason.* Chicago: University of Chicago Press.

Johnson, Mark. 1993. *Moral imagination: Implications of cognitive science for ethics.* Chicago: University of Chicago Press.

Kant, Immanuel. [1781] 1990. *Critique of pure reason.* Translated by J. M. D. Meiklejohn. Buffalo, NY: Prometheus Books.

Kemmer, Suzanne, and Michael Barlow. 2000. Introduction. In Suzanne Kemmer and Michael Barlow, eds., *Usage-based models of language* vii–xxviii. Stanford, CA: CSLI Publications.

Kreitzer, Anatol. 1997. Multiple levels of schematization: A study in the conceptualization of space. *Cognitive Linguistics* 8: 291–325.

Krzeszowski, Tomasz P. 1993. The axiological parameter in preconceptual image schemata. In Richard Geiger and Brygida Rudzka-Ostyn, eds., *Conceptualization and mental processing in language* 307–29. Berlin: Mouton de Gruyter.

Lakoff, George. 1987. *Women, fire, and dangerous things: What categories reveal about the mind.* Chicago: University of Chicago Press.

Lakoff, George, and Mark Johnson. 1980. *Metaphors we live by.* Chicago: University of Chicago Press.

Lakoff, George, and Rafael Núñez. 2000. *Where mathematics comes from: How the embodied mind brings mathematics into being.* New York: Basic Books.

Lakoff, George, and Mark Turner. 1989. *More than cool reason: A field guide to poetic metaphor.* Chicago: University of Chicago Press.

Langacker, Ronald W. 1987. *Foundations of cognitive grammar.* Vol. 1, *Theoretical prerequisites.* Stanford, CA: Stanford University Press.

Langacker, Ronald W. 1991. *Foundations of cognitive grammar.* Vol. 2, *Descriptive application.* Stanford, CA: Stanford University Press.

Mandler, Jean. 1992. How to build a baby: II. Conceptual primitives. *Psychological Review* 99: 597–604.

Matsumoto, Yo. 1995. From attribution/purpose to cause: Image schema and grammaticalization of some cause markers in Japanese. In Marjolijn Verspoor, Kee Dong Lee, and Eve Sweetser, eds., *Lexical and syntactical constructions and the construction of meaning* 287–307. Amsterdam: John Benjamins.

Narayanan, Srini. 1999. Moving right along: A computational model of metaphoric reasoning about events. *Proceedings of the National Conference on Artificial Intelligence (AAAI-99)* 121–28. Menlo Park, CA: AAAI Press.

Palmer, Gary B. 1996. *Toward a theory of cultural linguistics.* Austin: University of Texas Press.

Pauwels, Paul. 1995. Levels of metaphorization: The case of *put.* In Louis Goossens, ed., *By word of mouth: Metaphor, metonymy and linguistic action in a cognitive perspective* 125–58. Amsterdam: John Benjamins.

Regier, Terry. 1996. A model of the human capacity for categorizing spatial relations. *Cognitive Linguistics* 6: 63–88.

Rhee, Seongha. 2002. Semantic changes of English prepositions against a grammaticalization perspective. *Language Research* 38: 563–83.

Romaine, Suzanne. 1996. War and peace in the global greenhouse: Metaphors we live and die by. *Metaphor and Symbolic Activity* 1996: 175–94.

Serra-Borneto, Carlo. 1995a. Two-way prepositions in German: Image and constraints. In Marjolijn Verspoor, Kee Dong Lee, and Eve Sweetser, eds., *Lexical and syntactical constructions and the construction of meaning* 187–204. Amsterdam: John Benjamins.

Serra-Borneto, Carlo. 1995b. *Liegen* and *stehen* in German: A study of horizontality and verticality. In Eugene H. Casad, ed., *Cognitive linguistics in the Redwoods: The expansion of a new paradigm in linguistics* 459–505. Berlin: Mouton de Gruyter.

Sinha, Chris, and Kristine Jensen de López. 2000. Language, culture, and the embodiment of spatial cognition. *Cognitive Linguistics* 11: 17–41.

Smith, Michael B. 1999. From instrument irrealis: Motivating some grammaticalized senses of the Russian instrumental. In Katarzyna Dziwirek, Herbert Coats, and Cynthia M. Vakareliyska, eds., *Annual workshop on formal approaches to Slavic linguistics.* Vol. 7, *The Seattle meeting 1998* 413–33. Ann Arbor: Michigan Slavic Publications.

Smith, Michael B. 2002. The polysemy of German *es*: Iconicity and the notion of conceptual distance. *Cognitive Linguistics* 13: 67–112.

Talmy, Leonard. 1983. How language structures space. In Herbert L. Pick, Jr., and Linda P. Acredolo, eds., *Spatial orientation: Theory, research, and application* 225–82. New York: Plenum Press.

Turner, Mark. 1987. *Death is the mother of beauty: Mind, metaphor, criticism.* Chicago: University of Chicago Press.

Turner, Mark. 1991. *Reading minds: The study of English in the age of cognitive science.* Princeton, NJ: Princeton University Press.

Turner, Mark. 1992. Language is a virus. *Poetics Today* 13: 725–36.

Verspoor, Marjolijn. 1995. Predicate adjuncts and subjectification. In Marjolijn Verspoor, Kee Dong, and Eve Sweetser, eds., *Lexical and syntactical constructions and the construction of meaning: Proceedings of the bi-annual ICLA meeting in Albuquerque, July 1995* 433–49. Amsterdam: John Benjamins.

Wagner, Susan, Ellen Winner, Diane Cicchetti, and Howard Gardner. 1981. Metaphorical mappings in human infants. *Child Development* 52: 728–31.

Watters, James K. 1995. Frames and the semantics of applicatives in Tepehua. In Eugene H. Casad, ed., *Cognitive linguistics in the Redwoods: The expansion of a new paradigm in linguistics* 971–96. Berlin: Mouton de Gruyter.

Williams, Darrell. 1992. English comparative compounds with OVER, UNDER and OUT. *Proceedings of the Eastern States Conference on Linguistics* 9: 272–81.

CHAPTER 10

··

METONYMY

··

KLAUS-UWE PANTHER AND
LINDA L. THORNBURG

1. INTRODUCTION

··

Metonymy is a cognitive phenomenon—not just a figure of speech—whose role in the organization of meaning (semantics), utterance production and interpretation (pragmatics), and even grammatical structure is considerable. The same metonymic principles that relate different senses of a word serve to create and retrieve novel meanings in actual language use. The ubiquity of metonymy can be interpreted as an indication that there is a continuum between linguistic meaning and communicative use rather than a strict division of labor between two autonomous components, semantics and pragmatics. Furthermore, the interpretation of grammatical structure (construction meaning) seems to be sensitive to metonymic principles. Finally, metonymic processes play a crucial role in semantic change and in grammaticalization.

This chapter is organized as follows: after a brief—and necessarily nonexhaustive—summary of the rhetorical tradition in section 2, various cognitive linguistic approaches to metonymy are discussed in section 3. A working definition of metonymy is developed in section 4, which is applied in the subsequent sections. Section 5 reports some work that demonstrates the interaction of metonymy with metaphor and the experiential grounding of metonymy. Section 6 is concerned with the role of metonymy in referential, predicational, propositional, and illocutionary acts. Section 7 considers metonymy in relation to pragmatic inferencing, that is, implicature and explicature, and discusses some of its discourse-pragmatic functions. In section 8, the interaction of metonymy with grammatical structure is explored. Section 9 reports on work that compares the exploitation of metonymies cross-linguistically. Section 10 describes the role of metonymy in dia-chronic change, in particular, semantic change and grammaticalization. Section 11 briefly considers the role of metonymy in language production, comprehension, and acquisition. Section 12 concludes the chapter with a discussion of unresolved problems, an analysis of the taxonomic structure of one high-level metonymy, and suggestions for future research.

2. THE RHETORICAL TRADITION

Metonymy (Greek μετονυμια, Latin *denominatio*) is one of the major figures of speech recognized in classical rhetoric. One of the earliest definitions of meton-ymy is attributed to the treatise *Rhetorica ad Herennium* (see Koch 1999: 140). The anonymous author characterizes metonymy as "a trope that takes its expression from near and close things ['ab rebus propinquis et finitimis'] by which we can comprehend a word that is not denominated by its proper word" (translation by Koch 1999: 141). This ancient characterization already points to the notions of *con-tiguity* and *association* that have ever since been criterial in distinguishing meton-ymy from metaphor.

There is a rich tradition of research on metonymy in the historical-philological tradition of linguistics. As pointed out by Geeraerts (1988), the psychological ori-entation of much of nineteenth-century philology, such as the works of Michel Bréal and Hermann Paul, is theoretically very close to present-day Cognitive Semantics. Furthermore, the study of etymology almost inevitably leads to an interest in the general principles of semantic change including the role of metonymy (and met-aphor) in the development of new meanings.

The concept of metonymy has remained remarkably constant since antiquity: a typical twentieth-century definition of metonymy that is not essentially different from the one given by the author of *Rhetorica ad Herennium* is found in Geeraerts (1994: 2477): "[Metonymy is] a semantic link between two senses of a lexical item that is based on a relationship of contiguity between the referents of the expression in each of those senses."

Traditionally, then, metonymy has been regarded as a *stand for* relation in which the name of one thing (henceforth, the *source* or *vehicle*) is used to refer to another thing (henceforth, the *target*) with which it is associated or to which it is contiguous. This view can be called the *substitution theory* of metonymy. A corol-lary of the substitution theory is that the source and the target are, at some level of analysis, considered to be equivalent ways of picking out the same referent. For example, in the sentence *Buckingham Palace issued a statement this morning*, the place name *Buckingham Palace* (source) may be said to stand for the British queen or one of her spokespersons (target). Under this view, the source expression indirectly achieves the same referential purpose as the more direct referring expression *the Queen*. The substitution theory is, however, too simplistic in at least two respects. First, it typically focuses only on cases of *referential* metonymy, neglecting evidence that metonymy is also found on the predicational and illocutionary levels (see section 6). Second, as Radden and Kövecses (1999: 18) point out, metonymy involves more than just an operation of substitution. For example, in *She is just a pretty face*, the noun phrase *a pretty face* is not used referentially but predicatively; as well, it is not just a substitute expression for *a pretty person* but also highlights the prettiness of the person's face, from which the prettiness of the person can be inferred. Thus, the above sentence expresses more content than 'She is just a pretty person'.

The attempt to develop a sufficiently narrow definition of metonymy leads to the question of how it is to be delimited from other figures of speech and thought. The two tropes in relation to which metonymy is normally seen are metaphor and synecdoche. In traditional rhetoric, synecdoche is regarded as "quite distinct from metonymy" (Bredin 1984: 46). More recently, however (see, e.g., Jakobson [1956] 1971), synecdoche has come to be considered a subtype of metonymy. Jakobson's by now famous distinction between metaphor and metonymy links the former to paradigmatic selection in terms of similarity and contrast and the latter to the syntagmatic combination of semantically contiguous elements. A rather idiosyncratic theory has been put forward by the *Groupe de Liège* or *Groupe μ* (Dubois et al. 1970), where synecdoche is considered as the fundamental trope with both metaphor and metonymy as derivative categories (Schofer and Rice 1977; Bredin 1984: 45).

3. METONYMY IN COGNITIVE LINGUISTICS

In Cognitive Linguistics, metonymy and synecdoche are often believed to instantiate the same conceptual phenomenon (Lakoff 1987).[1] Lakoff and Johnson (1980) see metonymy (including synecdoche) as a predominantly referential shift phenomenon within one cognitive domain—much in line with the traditional conception of metonymy (see section 2 above). In contrast, they regard metaphor as a mapping from one conceptual domain onto another distinct conceptual domain, where the structure of the target is isomorphic to that of the source (Invariance Hypothesis).

Most contemporary accounts in Cognitive Linguistics have built on Lakoff and Johnson's (1980) original distinction between metaphor as a cross-domain mapping and of metonymy as a mapping within one cognitive domain. One influential attempt to elaborate Lakoff and Johnson's characterization is Croft's (1993: 348) proposal that metaphor is "a mapping between two domains that are not part of the same matrix," whereas metonymy is a mapping within one "domain matrix." The notion of domain matrix goes back to Langacker's (1987) insight that the meaning of an expression can often only be determined against the background of a set of overlapping domains that jointly serve as a base against which the meaning of an expression is profiled. Croft (1993: 348) defines metonymy as a process of *domain highlighting* "since the metonymy makes primary a domain that is secondary in the literal meaning." Thus, in the utterance *The Times hasn't arrived yet*, the noun phrase *The Times* metonymically highlights a subdomain of the semantic frame it evokes—such as, a journalist writing for the newspaper—which is usually only secondary. This case is contrasted with the interpretation of the definite description *this book* in *This book is heavy*, where both subdomains of book as a physical object and as a bearer of content are argued to be of equal importance and therefore nonmetonymic.

Ruiz de Mendoza (2000) proposes that metonymic mappings, which are usually considered to be whole-part, part-whole, or part-part mappings, can be reduced to two kinds: either the source of the metonymic operation is in the target ("source-in-target" metonymy) or the target is in the source ("target-in-source" metonymy). For example, for *The ham sandwich is waiting for his check*, Ruiz de Mendoza argues (2000: 114–15) that the contiguity link between HAM SANDWICH and RESTAURANT CUSTOMER is not a part-part relation in the domain RESTAURANT but rather a source-in-target metonymy where THE HAM SANDWICH is conceptualized as being within the target domain THE CUSTOMER. As an example of target-in-source metonymy, Ruiz de Mendoza (2000: 127) cites *I broke the window*, which in most situations conveys that it is not the window as a whole but typically only the windowpane that was broken.

Various scholars have claimed that metonymy is as pervasive a phenomenon in language and thought as metaphor. Lakoff (1987) stresses the cognitive importance of metonymic models alongside propositional, image-schematic, and metaphorical cognitive models (called "Idealized Cognitive Models," or ICMs), and in recent volumes (e.g., Panther and Radden 1999b; Barcelona 2000a; Dirven and Pörings 2002), it has been argued that the conceptual and linguistic significance of metonymy is comparable to that of metaphor. Furthermore, some scholars (e.g., Barcelona 2000b; Radden 2000; Ruiz de Mendoza 2000; Ruiz de Mendoza and Campo 2002) have claimed that the borderline between metaphor and metonymy is blurred. Nevertheless, there are clear and agreed-upon cases of metonymy (and metaphor) and it is on these prototypical cases that the present chapter focuses.

A widely accepted definition of metonymy inspired by Langacker (1993) is the one proposed by Radden and Kövecses (1999: 21): "Metonymy is a cognitive process in which one conceptual entity, the vehicle, provides mental access to another conceptual entity, the target, within the same cognitive model." The notion of cognitive model is taken in its broadest sense, encompassing three "ontological realms" (23): concepts, forms (especially linguistic), and things and events in the "real world." Over these realms, five potential metonymic relations are defined: (i) the sign relation between form and concept (e.g., the relation between the form *house* and the concept HOUSE); (ii) three "referential" relations (Form-Thing/Event, Concept-Thing/Event, and the relation between Concept-Form and Thing/Event) (e.g., the relation between the form *house* or the concept HOUSE and the actual referent, i.e., a concrete house or the set of houses), and (iii) the relation between one sign (Concept-Form) and another sign (Concept-Form), which they call "concept metonymy" (e.g., BUS–*bus* standing for BUS DRIVER–*bus driver*). To these types, the authors add other relations such as the substitution of one form for another (e.g., euphemisms like *shoot* for *shit*, or *gosh* for *God*). In what follows, the focus will be on type (iii) of Radden and Kövecses's typology ("concept metonymies"), that is, those cases that most cognitive linguists would recognize as genuine instances of metonymy.

4. METONYMY AS A CONTINGENT AND DEFEASIBLE RELATION

A common denominator of the work reported on in section 3 is that metonymy is a cognitive process that operates within *one* cognitive domain or domain matrix and links a given *source content* to a less accessible *target content*. What constitutes *one* domain has to date not been satisfactorily elucidated in the literature and certainly remains a topic for further research (see section 12). An interesting proposition has been put forth by Barcelona (2003: 231), who proposes that speakers rely on *conscious* folk models of what constitutes a single domain versus two separate domains for the purposes of metonymy and metaphor, respectively. In this perspective, the decision of what constitutes a single domain cannot be made *a priori* on logicosemantic grounds alone but has to be based on empirical research on how speakers and, more generally, speech communities conceptually structure their universe.

The source content and the target content of a metonymy are linked by *conceptual contiguity* (see Dirven 1993). Metonymies that satisfy this criterion are henceforth called *conceptual metonymies*. "Content" should be understood in its broadest sense, including lexical concepts (words) but also thoughts (propositional contents). When the source content is expressed by a linguistic sign (a lexeme or a syntagmatic combination of lexemes), one can speak of a *linguistic metonymy*. The focus of this chapter is on linguistic metonymies.

The characterization of metonymy as a contiguity relation or as a process whereby a source concept provides mental access to a target concept is perhaps too general. In an attempt to constrain the scope of metonymy, we proposed that the relation between the metonymic source and the metonymic target should be regarded as *contingent*; in other words, under this view, metonymic links do not exist by conceptual necessity (Panther and Thornburg 2002, 2003a). This assumption entails that a metonymic relation is, in principle at least, *defeasible* or *cancelable*. For example, in a hospital context where one nurse says to another, *The ulcer in room 506 needs a special diet*, the link between *the ulcer in room 506* and *the patient with an ulcer in room 506* is a contingent link; it is not conceptually necessary that the ulcer belongs to the patient in room 506. The standard examples of metonymy such as RESULT FOR ACTION, PROCUCER FOR PRODUCT, PART FOR WHOLE, or CAUSE FOR EFFECT all appear to fall under the generalization that the relation between source and target is based on contingent conceptual contiguity.

From the assumption that metonymy is based on conceptual contiguity, it follows that the sign relation between form and meaning cannot be considered metonymic since this relation is usually arbitrary. However, Lakoff and Turner (1989: 108) and Radden and Kövecses (1999: 24) take the view that words/forms metonymically stand for the concepts they express.

The contingency criterion also implies that the notion of mental *access* from a source to a target concept has to be constrained. For example, in the sentence *The loss of her diamond ring chagrined Mary*, the subject noun phrase provides mental access to the concept NONPOSSESSION; this concept, however, follows by necessity from the concept LOSS. Given the contingency criterion, the link between LOSS and NONPOSSESSION does not qualify as a metonymic connection; the converse relation may, however, be used for metonymic purposes since it is contingent: *Oh, I don't have my wallet* may metonymically stand for *Oh, I lost my wallet*, but the latter is not entailed by the former.

Another demarcation problem is how meaning *specialization* and *generalization* relate to metonymy. In the philological-historic tradition (see, e.g., Paul [1880] 1975: 81–82, 97–98) and in modern semantics, specialization (called "autohyponymy" by Cruse 2000: 110–11) and generalization ("autosuperordination" in Cruse's 2000: 111 terminology) are usually regarded as distinct from metonymy. It should be noted, however, that some cognitive linguists, such as Radden and Kövecses (1999: 34), consider specialization (e.g., *the pill* for 'birth-control pill') and generalization (e.g. *aspirin* for 'any pain-relieving tablet') as genuine instances of metonymy. Lakoff (1987) postulates a metonymic relation between the concept MOTHER and the more specialized concept HOUSEWIFE MOTHER (see section 7.1).[2] In view of the constraint on metonymy proposed above, it is problematic to regard generalization as a metonymic process since *aspirin* is a hyponym of *pain-relieving tablet* and therefore *x is aspirin* entails *x is a pain-relieving tablet* (at least under one interpretation of *aspirin*). Specialization, however, does not immediately qualify as nonmetonymic since a superordinate concept does not semantically imply any of its hyponyms: for example, *x is a flower* does not entail *x is a rose*; that is, the relation between hyperonym and hyponym is contingent.

The contingency criterion is obviously not a sufficient criterion for distinguishing metonymy from metaphor and from pragmatic relations such as implicature (see section 7.1), because the latter two also involve contingent (i.e., in principle defeasible) relations between source and target and *implicans* and *implicatum*, respectively. However, it is a *necessary* criterion because it sets metonymy apart from relations that are based on conceptual necessity such as hyponymy (on the concept level) and entailment (on the propositional level).

From a semiotic perspective, metonymy is related to *indexicality*. If, for example, Mary has rented a parking space and finds out that her parking space has been taken by another car, she might become red in the face. An outside observer might interpret this as an index (more specifically, a symptom) that Mary is angry. The same observer might also verbalize his thinking by saying *Mary is red in the face*, thereby metonymically evoking the target content 'Mary is angry'. This metonymic reading is induced by the BODILY REACTION FOR EMOTION metonymy, which is a special case of the more general EFFECT FOR CAUSE metonymy (see section 12.2).

A further important property of a prototypical metonymy is that it *highlights* or *foregrounds* its target content and, accordingly, backgrounds its source content. For example, in the already given utterance *The ulcer in room 506 needs a special diet*, the patient suffering from an ulcer is highlighted, that is, the patient forms the topic of the utterance and can be subsequently referred to by the pronouns *she* or *he* (see section 7.4). By this criterion, in the utterance *Mary built a new garage last year*, the subject *Mary* is not a good example of a metonymy even if the usual inference is that she did not build the garage herself but had the work done by some workmen she hired. Intuitively, the utterance is about Mary, that is, *Mary* is foregrounded, not her workmen. This analysis is corroborated by the fact that . . . *and this year she* (= Mary) *went on a long vacation* is a completely natural continuation of the first utterance (see Panther and Thornburg 2003a), whereas . . . *and then they* (= the workmen) *did some work on the house* sounds somewhat disruptive.

The accessibility of the target from the source appears to correlate with the *strength of the metonymic link* between source and target. In turn, the strength of the metonymic link seems, at least partially, to depend on what one may call the *conceptual distance* between source and target and the *salience* of the source (Panther and Thornburg 1998). For example, the compound *redhead* seems *a priori* more likely to designate a person than the term *toenail* for the simple reason that the former is more salient and conceptually closer (in a meronymic organization of body parts) to the concept PERSON than the latter.

Summarizing the above remarks, an adequate definition of conceptual metonymy should contain at least the following components:

a. Conceptual metonymy is a cognitive process where a source content provides access to a target content within one cognitive domain.
b. The relation between source content and target content is contingent (conceptually nonnecessary), i.e., in principle defeasible.
c. The target content is foregrounded, and the source content is backgrounded.
d. The strength of the metonymic link between source and target content may vary depending, among other things, on the conceptual distance between source and target and the salience of the metonymic source.

5. METONYMY AND METAPHOR

5.1. The Interaction of Metonymy and Metaphor

Like metaphor, metonymy is a means by which concepts with relatively little content may be conceptually elaborated and enriched, as amply demonstrated by, for example, Kövecses (1995), Lakoff (1987), and Niemeier (2000) on emotion concepts such as LOVE or ANGER, and by Feyaerts (1999, 2000) on STUPIDITY in colloquial German. An important result of this research is that, for many concepts, metonymy and metaphor interact in complex ways. For example, Lakoff (1987: 382), who heavily relies on work by Kövecses (1986), postulates metonymies such as BODY HEAT FOR ANGER and INTERNAL PRESSURE FOR ANGER that motivate utterances like *Don't get hot under the collar* and *When I found out, I almost burst a blood vessel*, respectively. These expressions exemplify the more general metonymy SYMPTOM FOR CAUSE, which itself is a subcase of the high-level metonymy EFFECT FOR CAUSE (see section 12.2). Lakoff (1987: 383) argues that the folk theory of physiological effects (especially HEAT) forms the basis for the general metaphor ANGER IS HEAT, which in combination with the metaphor THE BODY IS A CONTAINER FOR THE EMOTIONS gives rise to expressions such as *I had reached the boiling point* and *Simmer down!*

Goossens (1990, 2002) has coined the term *metaphtonymy* to cover the interplay between metonymy and metaphor. He discusses four types of such interaction: metaphor from metonymy, metonymy within metaphor, demetonymization within a metaphor, and metaphor within metonymy. As example of the first category, Goossens (1990: 328; 2002: 356) cites *"Oh dear," she giggled, "I'd quite forgotten,"* where *giggled* stands for 'say something lightheartedly while giggling'. Goossens argues that this metonymic reading is the basis for a metaphorical interpretation involving a mapping from a nonlinguistic domain into the domain of linguistic action.

Goossens's influential work has inspired a rich body of research on the interaction of metonymy and metaphor. Ruiz de Mendoza and his collaborators have investigated various figurative expressions that typically involve the metonymic elaboration of the source and/or the target domains of metaphorical mappings. For example, Ruiz de Mendoza and Díez Velasco (2002: 526–27) analyze the idiomatic expression *Don't bite the hand that feeds you* as involving a source domain that contains the concepts ANIMAL, BITE, and HAND (that feeds you), the last metonymically evoking the agentive concept of a person that feeds you, or FEEDER. This metonymically elaborated source domain is then metaphorically mapped onto the target domain with the figurative meaning 'Don't turn against a person that supports you', with straightforward metaphorical mappings from ANIMAL to PERSON, BITE to TURN AGAINST, HAND (that feeds you) via FEEDER to SUPPORTER.

In a similar vein, Geeraerts (2002) analyzes various types of metaphorical and metonymic interaction. His "prismatic model" enables him to distinguish between the paradigmatic and the syntagmatic dimensions in the interpretation of figurative and idiomatic expressions. On the syntagmatic axis, the (compositional) relation between the meanings of constituent parts and what they contribute to the meaning of the whole expression is defined—both on the literal and on the figurative levels. On the paradigmatic axis, the relation between literal and figuratively derived meaning is described. These relations can be more or less transparent: Geeraerts refers to (the degree of) transparency on the paradigmatic level as "motivation," and to (the degree of) transparency on the syntagmatic level as "isomorphism." For example, the exocentric Dutch compound *schapenkop* 'dumb person' (literally 'sheep's head'; cf. German *Schafskopf*) is both highly *motivated* (on the paradigmatic level) and *isomorphic* (on the syntagmatic level). Paradigmatically, the overall meaning of *schapenkop* comes about through a metaphorical mapping from '(stupid-looking) sheep's head' to '(stupid-looking) human head' followed by a PART FOR WHOLE metonymy that induces the reading 'stupid person' (Geeraerts 2002: 456). Syntagmatically, there is a modifier-head relation on both the literal and figurative levels of interpretations.

In Panther and Thornburg (2002: 289), we demonstrate the interplay of metaphor and metonymy in numerous *-er* nominals. For example, the meaning of *hoofer* is motivated through a metaphor (that itself contains a number of metonymic elaborations) from 'hoof' to '(human) foot'—with the latter metonymically evoking the activity of 'dancing'. This target sense combines with the agent meaning of *-er* to yield the specialized meaning 'professional (vaudeville/chorus) dancer'.

The research of the authors cited above suggests that metaphorical and metonymic mappings are, to a certain extent, intrinsically ordered to achieve an intended interpretation. However, as Geeraerts (2002: 460) points out with the example of the Dutch compound *badmuts* 'bald person' (literally 'swimming cap'), the relative ordering of metaphorical and metonymic operations need not always be fixed to arrive at an identical interpretation. Either the reading 'swimming cap' is metonymically elaborated into 'person with a swimming cap', which itself is metaphorically mapped onto the interpretation 'bald person', that is, 'a person that looks as if he was wearing a swimming cap'; or there is first a metaphorical interpretation of 'swimming cap' as 'bald head', which, in turn, metonymically maps onto 'bald person.'

5.2. The Experiential Grounding of Metonymy and Metaphor

In addition to the interaction of metonymy and metaphor, some thought has been given to the question of the experiential grounding of metonymy and metaphor. Lakoff and Johnson (1980) attribute an experiential basis to many metaphors; Grady (1997), Lakoff and Johnson (1999), and Grady and Johnson (2002) claim that humans from very early on form experiential correlations, which they call "primary metaphors." As instances of such basic metaphors AFFECTION IS WARMTH, DIFFICULTIES ARE BURDENS, and KNOWING IS SEEING, among others, have been proposed. A feeling of warmth is often concomitant with an affectionate embrace, lifting a burden correlates with a feeling of discomfort, and a fundamental source of information (acquisition of knowledge) is visual perception. The above authors see primary metaphors as the atomic building blocks of more complex metaphors. Other authors (e.g., Barcelona 2000b; Radden 2000, 2002) claim that such experiential correlations are metonymic.

For example, Radden (2002) argues that the experiential correspondences between UP and DOWN and HAPPY and SAD, respectively, are metonymic rather than metaphorical. The controversy between the "metaphorists" and the "metonymists" is not purely terminological but empirical in nature. The outcome of this discussion hinges, among other things, on an empirically validated answer to the further question of what the *semiotic* status of such experiential correlations is. If it turns out that, for instance, warmth is interpreted as an indexical *sign* for affection, then it makes sense to regard the experiential correlation between warmth and affection as metonymic rather than metaphorical.

Riemer (2002) argues that many expressions that look metaphorical, because their respective source domains and target domains are clearly separate, originate as metonymies. For example, the idiom *beat one's breast* 'make a noisy open show of sorrow that may be partly pretence', which Goossens (2002: 362) analyzes as a metaphtonymy (i.e., metaphor from metonymy), is better regarded as a metonymy whose source names a social practice that no longer exists. Riemer (2002: 395–97) calls such "truncated" metonymies *post-metonymies*.

The problem of whether metonymic or metaphorical processes lead to changes in meaning is especially acute in diachronic semantics. A case in point is the origin of the systematic polysemy of modal auxiliaries in present-day English and other languages. Sweetser (1991: 49–51) argues that the "root" (deontic) sense and the epistemic sense of modals are linked through a metaphorical mapping from the sociophysical domain into the domain of knowledge and reasoning. Thus, the epistemic *must* in *You must have been home last night* 'The available (direct) evidence compels me to the conclusion that you were home last night' is regarded as a metaphorical extension of the deontic *must* as in *You must come home by ten* 'The direct force (of Mom's authority) compels you to come home by ten' (Sweetser 1991: 61). Yet Goossens (1999, 2000) provides historical evidence for a contextually driven step-by-step dissociation of epistemic meanings from deontic meanings, which would rather point to a metonymic relation between the deontic and epistemic senses of modals.[3]

6. METONYMY AND SPEECH ACT FUNCTIONS

In section 2, it was proposed that metonymy is not merely a referential phenomenon but serves other pragmatic purposes as well. In analogy to the three pragmatic functions that are familiar from speech act theory (see Searle 1969), one may classify metonymies into the following types: (i) referential metonymies, (ii) predicational metonymies, and (iii) illocutionary metonymies. These pragmatic types, which can occur in combination, are illustrated in the following sections (see Thornburg and Panther 1997; Panther and Thornburg 1998; and Brdar and Brdar-Szabó 2003, 2004).

6.1. Referential Metonymy

As discussed in sections 2 and 3 above, traditionally metonymy has been regarded as a means of indirect reference. Well-known examples are referential noun phrases such as *the subway* in *The subway is on strike* referring to the subway personnel or *The saxophone isn't performing tonight* with *the saxophone* referring to the saxophone player.

6.2. Predicational Metonymy

Predicational metonymy is exemplified by utterances such as *The saxophone player had to leave early*, which, in many contexts, metonymically induces the interpretation 'The saxophone player left early'. In this case, a past obligation to leave early, predicated of the referring expression *the saxophone player*, is interpreted as an actually occurring past action predicated of the saxophone player. This case instantiates a large class of phenomena that involve a high-level metonymy where a potential event stands for an actual event.

6.3. Propositional Metonymy

When a referential metonymy is combined with a predicational metonymy, the result can be called a propositional metonymy. An example is *The saxophone had to leave early*, whose target meaning 'The saxophone player left early' comes about through the metonymies MUSICAL INSTRUMENT FOR MUSICIAN (referential) and OBLIGATORY ACTION FOR ACTUAL ACTION (predicational).

6.4. Illocutionary Metonymy

Gibbs (1994, 1999), Thornburg and Panther (1997), Panther and Thornburg (1998), and Pérez Hernández and Ruiz de Mendoza (2002) argue that illocutionary acts, especially indirect illocutionary acts (see Searle 1975), can be analyzed in terms of conceptual frames, scenes, Idealized Cognitive Models, scenarios, and the like. A component of a speech act scenario that is sufficiently "central" can metonymically evoke other components of the scenario and thereby the scenario as a whole. The basic idea is that an attribute of a speech act can stand for the speech act itself, in the same way that an attribute of a person can stand for the person. Thus, a metonymic analysis of an indirect request such as *Can you lend me your sweater?* links a BEFORE component of the request scenario (i.e., the hearer's ability to perform the requested action) to the CORE of the speech act (i.e., the attempt to impose a more or less strong obligation on the hearer).

Gibbs (1994: 354–57) provides experimental evidence that conventional indirect requests such as *Can/will you lend me your sweater?* or *Would you mind lending me your sweater?* are not just random substitute forms for the direct request *Lend me your sweater.* The source expression (and consequently, the source content) is not arbitrarily chosen, but its selection is motivated by the speaker's intention to address potential "obstacles" to the satisfaction of the request (see section 11). Gibbs's work shows that the meaning of the source expression is relevant to the interpretation process as a whole, thus providing strong evidence against the view that a source expression merely stands for a target.

6.5. Cross-Functional Metonymies

Conceptual metonymies often cut across the pragmatic types discussed in sections 6.1–6.4. A given conceptual metonymy may function referentially, predicationally, and illocutionarily. For example, a referential use of the metonymy ABILITY FOR ACTUALITY is illustrated in ***Her ability to convince the board of trustees*** *impressed everyone*, but the same metonymy may also be operative on the predicational level, as in *She was* ***able to convince the board of trustees***. In both cases, there is a metonymically induced target meaning that the act of convincing the board of trustees *actually* occurred. A version of the above metonymy also exists on the illocutionary level. For example, in uttering ***I can assure*** *you that your application will be taken into consideration,* in most contexts the speaker *actually* does assure the addressee of the content of the complement clause despite the use of the modal hedge *can*.

7. Metonymy, Pragmatic Inferencing, and Discourse Functions

7.1. Metonymy and Implicature

The property of defeasibility likens metonymy as a cognitive process to pragmatic inferencing, in particular, conversational implicature in Gricean and Neo-Gricean pragmatics (Grice 1975; Levinson 2000; Panther and Thornburg 2003c). Metonymic links can be used for *reasoning* or *inferencing* purposes.[4] Like implicatures, metonymies can become completely *conventionalized*, that is, end up as senses in a polysemous word. Metonymy therefore cuts across the traditional semantics-pragmatics distinction. A metonymy may, on the one hand, statically relate different senses of a word, but it may also be productively used in actual communication situations to produce novel meanings. For example, *potbelly* has two entrenched lexical meanings 'large round stomach' and 'person with large round stomach', which are related by the metonymy SALIENT BODY PART FOR PERSON; this same metonymy can also be used productively to yield pragmatically derived meanings as, for instance, *balloonnose, fatface, skinnylegs*, and so on. The productive use that speakers make of this metonymy can be considered evidence that it is not a "dead" metonymy but a cognitively real process.[5]

Given that metonymic reasoning is pervasive in language use, some authors have argued that the concept of metonymy should be integrated into a general theory of pragmatic reasoning. Ruwet (1975) even claims that "real" metonymy is a rare phenomenon and many cases of "metonymy" (or "synecdoche," which he treats alike in this respect) are probabilistic inferences drawn on the basis of world knowledge. According to Ruwet, in an utterance like *Voilà une voile à l'horizon* 'There's a sail on the horizon', the speaker means quite literally what is said, namely, that there is a *sail* on the horizon (375). The "metonymic" or "synecdochic" interpretation that there is a *boat* or *ship* on the horizon is a plausible though defeasible pragmatic inference. Ruwet's conclusion that the notion of metonymy is of limited theoretical interest is, however, not warranted since a theory of pragmatic inferencing must surely establish the kinds of *inference schemas* that participants use in actual communication to arrive at utterance meanings and these inference schemas are, to a considerable extent, based on metonymic contiguities.

There are some interesting parallels between what Lakoff (1987) calls "metonymic models" and what Levinson (2000: 37) refers to as the *I*-Heuristic (where *I* stands for "Informativeness") in his theory of generalized conversational implicature. Lakoff points out that, for example, the concept MOTHER metonymically evokes the subconcept HOUSEWIFE MOTHER. Levinson (2000: 37) argues that lexical items routinely implicate stereotypical pragmatic default readings: "What is expressed simply is stereotypically exemplified." Levinson relates this heuristic to Grice's (1975) second Maxim of Quantity, "Do not make your contribution more informative than is required." For example, a defeasible I-Implicature of *secretary* is the attribute 'female'. Defeasibility also holds for the metonymically evoked stereo-typical meanings discussed by Lakoff (1987: 77–84). Although the concept HOUSEWIFE MOTHER is almost automatically activated when the word *mother* is used in linguistic communication, the metonymic link between the two concepts can be explicitly canceled without contradiction: *She is a mother of two daughters, but she is not a housewife* is semantically well formed. A meaning that, in cognitive linguistic terms, is stereotypically evoked via metonymy (see Radden and Kövecses 1999: 27)—or, in Neo-Gricean parlance, via a generalized conversational implicature—is generally not expressed through a separate lexical item; for example, there are no simple lexemes for the concepts HOUSEWIFE MOTHER or FEMALE SECRETARY.

Metonymic links can be regarded as natural inference schemas available to the participants in a communication situation (see Thornburg and Panther 1997; Panther and Thornburg 1998, 2003c). Conversational implicatures, according to Grice, must be capable of being "worked out." As natural inference schemas, metonymies easily meet this requirement.

7.2. Metonymy and Explicature

Relevance theorists have generally been very critical of cognitive linguistic approaches to metonymy (and metaphor). Papafragou (1996) and Song (1997), following Ruwet (1975) in this respect, argue that metonymy, and other figures of speech, can be subsumed under general principles of pragmatic inferencing (in their framework, deductive inferences) and that there is no need to postulate the existence of a separate domain of metonymic reasoning. Papafragou (1996: 181) criticizes the cognitive "associationist" approach to metonymy as suffering "from serious drawbacks on both descriptive and explanatory levels" because this approach supposedly cannot handle creative ad hoc uses of "metonymy." However, as with conceptual metaphor (see Lakoff and Johnson 1999), there might be less creativity in metonymic language use than Papafragou and Song assume. There is at least some initial plausibility that interactants resort to a relatively restricted set of metonymic inference schemas that are exploited again and again (see, e.g., Norrick's 1981 typology of metonymies). Papafragou does not grant any special status to metonymic elaborations but regards them as *explicatures* whose purpose is to allow the reconstruction of the explicit content of an utterance. From a cognitive linguistic perspective, Ruiz de Mendoza and Pérez Hernández (2003), while insisting on the cognitive reality of conceptual metonymy, agree with the view that metonymic elaborations of the sense of an utterance serve to identify its *explicit* content.

7.3. Some Discourse-Pragmatic Functions of Metonymy

So far, little attention has been paid to the pragmatic function of metonymic shifts. Why would speakers use metonymies at all when they could just as well employ nonmetonymic means of referring, predicating, and performing illocutionary acts? For the use of indirect speech acts, sociopragmatic reasons, such as politeness, have been adduced (e.g., Brown and Levinson 1987). In general, a careful analysis of naturally occurring discourse data suggests that metonymic source and metonymic target are not pragmatically equivalent in all respects, nor are metonymies with the same target but different sources mere stylistic variants of each other (see section 6.4).

Papafragou (1996) sees two communicative reasons for using metonymies: (i) the extra processing effort caused by a metonymy is set off by a gain in contextual effects (additional implicatures); or (ii) the processing effort may be smaller than that for a literal expression of the metonymic sense. The latter case occurs quite frequently in the setting of routinized communicative interaction, such as at work: in a restaurant where the waitresses do not know the names of customers, it is common to refer to individuals or groups as, for example, *table five*. In the given context, this is the most economical way to refer to otherwise unknown individuals. As an example of contextual gains consider the sentence *Now it **can** happen* uttered by Richard Williams, father of the tennis-playing sisters Venus and Serena Williams when they reached the final of the US Open tennis tournament in 2001. Why would the speaker choose the modal *can* in a situation where he *knows* that his daughters *will be* the finalists in the tennis tournament? The reason may be that the source concept (POTENTIALITY) has—in the given situation—more contextual effects than the target concept (FUTURE ACTUALITY). The greater cognitive effort resulting from the metonymic coding of the utterance is largely compensated by the richness of conceptual information that it evokes. The potentiality modal *can* and the time adverbial *now* convey pragmatic implications of 'obstacles' that have been 're-moved' by strenuous efforts; such connotations are not conveyed by the predictive modal *will*.

In a similar vein, Song (1997: 101) shows that metonymies with the same target but different source domains yield different contextual effects and can therefore not be regarded as discourse-pragmatically equivalent. For example, in Japanese the two utterances *konogoro kuruma-ni notte-inai* 'I have not ridden wheels recently' and *konogoro handoru-wo nigitte-inai* 'I have not held a steering wheel recently' conventionally stand for 'I have not driven a car recently'. According to Song (1997: 102), "the hold-a-steering-wheel metonymy highlights the controlling aspect while the ride-on-wheels metonymy highlights mobility." The two metonymies are thus appropriate in different contexts.

7.4. Metonymy and Coreference

A particularly intriguing property of metonymy is its interaction with anaphoric coreference in discourse (see Nunberg 1978, 1995; Fauconnier 1985; Kleiber 1995; Stirling 1996). A plausible hypothesis is that an anaphoric pronoun should be coreferential with the metonymically targeted referent of a noun phrase, rather than with the source referent. This hypothesis is confirmed by sentences like (i) **The harpsichord** *is on maternity leave;* **she/#it** *will be back next year*, where the MUSICAL INSTRUMENT FOR MUSICIAN metonymy leads to the interpretation of the subject noun phrase as 'the musician playing the harpsichord'. The anaphoric pronoun is coreferential with this targeted referent. However, in sentence (ii) **Laura** *is sun-burned;* **she** *probably took a vacation in Greece/#it* (= *her skin*) *needs dermato-logical treatment* where usually *Laura* is regarded as a WHOLE FOR PART metonymy for 'Laura's skin,' it is puzzling that the antecedent for the anaphoric pronoun must be the source—hence the selection of *she* instead of *it*. To account for the difference between sentences like (i) and (ii), Nunberg (1995) proposes that in (ii) there is no referential shift of the subject noun phrase *Laura* but rather a *predicate transfer*, that is, a property that is usually attributed to skin is transferred to persons. Thus the obligatory occurrence of the anaphoric pronoun *she* (vs. #*it*) is accounted for.

Nunberg's (1995) explanation has been criticized by various linguists (e.g., Kleiber 1995; Panther and Radden 1999a) on the grounds of its counterintuitive assumption that a sentence like *Linda is parked on the lower deck* involves no reference shift. Ruiz de Mendoza and Pérez Hernández (2001: 351) and Ruiz de Mendoza and Díez Velasco (2004) have suggested a *domain availability principle* that requires the anaphoric pronoun to be coreferential with the matrix domain—be it the source or the target of the metonymic operation. In sentence (i), a source-in-target metonymy is operative, that is, the target domain is the matrix domain ('the harpsichord player'), which selects the anaphoric pronoun. In contrast, in sentence (ii) the metonymic target ('Laura's skin') is part of the source domain ('Laura') (target-in-source me-tonymy), which thus constitutes the matrix domain that is the antecedent of the anaphoric pronoun *she*. The theory of Ruiz de Mendoza and his coauthors has the advantage of accounting for the difference between sentences (i) and (ii) without abandoning the intuitively plausible assumption that both cases involve meto-nymic shifts of reference of the subject noun phrase.

8. METONYMY AND GRAMMAR

Conceptual metonymy, especially predicational metonymy (see section 6.2), inter-acts with grammatical structure. In what follows, some instances where grammatical constructions are sensitive to metonymically induced interpretations are presented.

In Cognitive Linguistics, it is generally assumed that grammatical constructions are carriers of meaning independent of the lexical items they contain (Goldberg 1995; Croft 2001). The lexical items used in a construction, especially the meanings of the verb and its argument structure, have to be fitted into the construction frame, but there are cases where a conflict between constructional meaning and lexical meaning arises. Two interpretive strategies emerge in such cases: either the utterance is rejected as uninterpretable (semantically anomalous) or the semantic and/or syntactic conflict is resolved by a meaning *shift* (Talmy 2000: 324–29) or *coercion* (Pustejovsky 1991). In general, the construction imposes its meaning on the verb meaning. For example, according to Goldberg (1995: 38), the ditransitive construction in English exemplified in *Mary gave Bill the ball* has the central sense 'Agent successfully causes Recipient to receive Patient'. Given this construction meaning, the transitive verb *kick* 'hit with the foot' in *Mary kicked Bill the ball* is in syntactic and semantic conflict with the syntax and the meaning of the ditransitive construction. The resolution of this conflict consists in a semantic shift: the basically transitive verb *kick* is construed ditransitively and coerced into the interpretation 'cause to receive *by means of* hitting with the foot'. This meaning shift is possible because there is an independently motivated conceptual metonymy MEANS OF ACTION FOR ACTION that makes the intended interpretation available to the hearer even if her or she has never before encountered the use of *kick* in the ditransitive construction.

In a similar vein, we considered *stative* predicates in 'action' constructions, such as imperatives or certain infinitival complement clauses (Panther and Thornburg 2000). We showed that, despite the semantic conflict between stativity and action, such sentences are possible if the state expressed by the predicate can be interpreted as the *result* of an action (see figure 10.1 below). In such cases, the imperative construction forces an action interpretation on the stative predicate. Thus, the slogan of the American news network CNN *Be the first to know* is acceptable because the verb phrase *be NP* is interpretable as the effect of an intentional act of the hearer ('Do something [namely, watch CNN] so that, as a result, you are the first to know'). The conceptual shift at work here is based on the RESULT FOR ACTION metonymy. In contrast, the imperative *Be tall!* is pragmatically odd: an action interpretation induced by the RESULT FOR ACTION metonymy is hardly conceivable because 'tallness' is not seen as the outcome of an intentional act.

Ruiz de Mendoza and Pérez Hernández (2001: 340), following Pustejovsky (1991, 1993) in this respect, suggest a metonymic interpretation for complement noun phrases as in *John enjoyed the beer*, which has the default reading 'John enjoyed drinking the beer', but may, in varying contexts, also mean something like 'John enjoyed bottling the beer', 'John enjoyed pouring the beer', and so on. The common denominator of all these readings is that the object denoted by the noun phrase (a salient participant) is involved in some event, which itself has to be metonymically inferred. Possibly, however, as Copestake and Briscoe (1995: 32) argue, the above sentence might be an example of sense modulation (constructional polysemy) that involves "an appropriate aspect of the meaning, rather than a change in the meaning of the NP itself." In other words, the variety of possible contextual meanings of *the beer* could be due to vagueness, rather than to metonymic shifts that would result in clear-cut polysemy.

Langacker (2000: 200, 329–32) argues that a metonymy such as (SALIENT) PARTICIPANT FOR EVENT IN WHICH PARTICIPANT IS INVOLVED is also found in "raising" constructions like *Don is likely to leave*. Strictly speaking, likelihood cannot be predicated of the individual Don, but only of the activity the individual is involved in, which in Langacker's terminology constitutes the "active zone" of the nominal referent *Don* in the above utterance.[6] Brdar and Brdar-Szabó (2004) show that the use of the (SALIENT) PARTICIPANT FOR EVENT IN WHICH PARTICIPANT IS INVOLVED metonymy is fairly restricted in languages like German, Croatian, and Hungarian that do not allow "raising" as freely as in English. Compare, for example, *Don is sure to come* with German **Don ist sicher zu kommen*.

Metonymic coercion also seems to play a role in the interpretation of other nonfinite clauses, which, in Generative Grammar, involve the problem of "control" (see Panther 2001). For example, in *Paula asked John to leave*, the usual (unmarked) interpretation is that John, the referent of the main clause object, is supposed to leave—that is, the object of the main clause "controls" the reference of the understood subject in the infinitive clause; whereas in *Johnny asked the teacher to go to the bathroom*, the referent of the main clause subject is most likely coreferential with the understood subject of the nonfinite clause, that is, Johnny will go to the bathroom. The latter interpretation may be explained on the basis of a metonymic elaboration where the propositional form expressed by the verb phrase in the infinitive clause ('going to the bathroom') is interpreted as 'being allowed to go to the bathroom'. The infinitive highlights the intended pragmatic effect of such an act of permission, which itself is not expressed in the sentence but is easily accessed metonymically in the given context. In other words, the interpretation of this sentence heavily relies on a subtype of the RESULT FOR ACTION metonymy, namely, PRAGMATIC EFFECT OF SPEECH ACT FOR SPEECH ACT.

A clear case of an impact of metonymy on grammatical structure is provided by the use of names (paragons) as common nouns that denote a whole class of individuals (see Barcelona 2004). In *A real Shakespeare would never use those trite images*, the selection of the indefinite article in the subject noun phrase is clearly motivated by a metonymic shift from an individual (Shakespeare) to a whole class of individuals that have essentially the same relevant properties. The target concept determines the grammatical behavior; in this example, the target property of countability determines the possibility of using *Shakespeare* with an indefinite article or even pluralizing it (e.g., *the Shakespeares of the twentieth century*).

As a last example, consider Nikiforidou's (1999: 143) work on nominalizations. Nikiforidou shows that there is a cross-lexemic regularity concerning the interpretation of nominalizations in English. For example, the nominalized form *performance* in its basic sense profiles an action (*The performance lasted for two hours*), but it may also highlight certain subdomains of the profile such as MANNER (*The performance was impressive*) or PRODUCT (*The performance is available on CD*). As Nikiforidou points out, the latter two interpretations can be regarded as active zone phenomena in the sense of Langacker (see above).

9. METONYMIES ACROSS LANGUAGES

So far, relatively little work has been done on how metonymies are exploited across languages. Some of the questions that await answers include: Are there conceptual metonymies that have the status of universals? Can languages be typologically classified according to the metonymies they do or do not exploit? How do these typologies compare with the more traditional morphosyntactic typologies? In what follows, some studies that have begun to explore these issues are presented.

Brdar and Brdar-Szabó (2003) show that the MANNER FOR (LINGUISTIC) ACTION metonymy is much more systematically exploited in English than in Croatian and Hungarian, where usually the linguistic action has to be coded explicitly in the verb. Thus, English allows a sentence such as *I must be open with her*, where only the manner in which the speech act is performed is indicated, leaving it up to the hearer to metonymically infer the linguistic action itself. In contrast, in Hungarian the same content is rendered as *Nyíltan kell vele **beszélnem*** 'I must *speak openly* with her'; a literal translation of the English sentence **Nyíltnak kell vele lennem* is unacceptable in Hungarian.

We have conducted a comparative study of English and Hungarian in which we demonstrate that the POTENTIALITY FOR ACTUALITY metonymy is exploited more extensively in English than in Hungarian (Panther and Thornburg 1999); in the domain of perception, the metonymy is systematically exploited in English but blocked in Hungarian. Thus, English *Can you see him?* for 'Do you see him?' contrasts with Hungarian *Látod?* 'Do you see him?'. In another comparative study (2003b), based on parallel text corpora, we showed that English makes a more extended use than French of two related metonymic principles: THE ONSET FOR THE WHOLE EVENT metonymy and THE INCIPIENT PHASE FOR THE WHOLE EVENT metonymy, where "onset" refers to the starting point and "incipient phase" to the initial time span of an event. An example of the contrasting use of the latter metonymy is seen in a sentence from André Gide's novel *L'immoraliste* and its English translation: *Puis il **plut*** (coding of the whole event) versus *Then it **began to rain*** (coding of the incipient phase metonymically evoking the whole event).

10. Metonymy and Language Change

10.1. Metonymy and Semantic Change

The significance of metonymic processes in the change of meaning of lexical items has been long noted by historical linguists and amply demonstrated since the nineteenth century (see references in Ullmann 1962). More recently, Koch (1999) has shown how meaning changes can be accounted for by relating components in a conceptual frame. For example, there is a quite systematic cross-linguistically observable metonymic shift within the MARRIAGE frame from, for instance, getting engaged or setting up house to marriage. Examples (from Koch 1999: 148) include: Latin *sponsus, -a* 'fiancé(e), hence: bride(groom)' > Popular Latin 'husband/wife' as in Spanish *esposo, -a*, French *époux, -se*; Latin *vota* 'vows' > Spanish *boda(s)* 'wedding'; Old English *weddian* 'to engage' > Modern English *wed* 'marry'; Polish *s'lub* 'vow', hence: 'marriage.' Such examples provide support for the view that metonymies are intradomain mappings.

10.2. Metonymy and Grammaticalization

It has been argued by various authors (e.g., Heine, Claudi, and Hünnemeyer 1991; Traugott and König 1991; Hopper and Traugott 1993) that metonymy plays a crucial role in grammaticalization processes. According to Hopper and Traugott (1993: 80–86), metonymy is instrumental in the development of grammatical meanings from lexical meanings. For example, the historical change of *be going to* into a future marker, which in colloquial English is often contracted to *be gonna*, is based on a conceptual contiguity between the concept PURPOSE and the notion of FUTURE. A sentence such as *I am going to visit my sister* with the reading 'I am going for the purpose of visiting my sister' conversationally implicates 'I will visit my sister'. As Hopper and Traugott (1993: 82) point out, this implicature is defeasible, but still the conceptual link between PURPOSE and FUTURE is so strong that the implicature has become conventionalized in the case of *be going to/be gonna*.

As a further example of metonymically induced grammaticalization, one may cite the development of an abstract causal meaning out of a more concrete temporal meaning, as in the causal use of the conjunctions *since* < Old English *siþþan* 'from the time that'. The metonymic motivation of this shift is that events that are temporally contiguous or overlapping are often seen as causally related. The cognitive reality of the underlying metonymy TEMPORAL CONTIGUITY FOR CAUSAL LINK becomes manifest in such utterances as *I couldn't work when the television was on* that convey the implicature 'I couldn't work *because* the television was on' (see Traugott and König 1991: 197).

11. Metonymy in Language Production, Comprehension, and Acquisition

That metonymic processes play an important part in utterance interpretation is amply demonstrated in Gibbs (1994, 1999). As pointed out in section 6.4, the interpretation of indirect speech acts can be accounted for on the basis of metonymic principles. Gibbs (1994: 345–51; 1999: 73) adduces experimental evidence that people interpret colloquial tautologies (e.g., *Boys will be boys*) on the basis of shared metonymic models (stereotypes). Especially, tautologies containing human nouns are more easily interpretable than *tautologies* with concrete nouns (*Telephones are telephones*) because stereotypes about humans are conceptually richer and more entrenched than stereotypes about things.

To date, hardly any work has been done on how children produce and understand metonymies, with the notable exception of Nerlich, Clarke, and Todd (1999: 368). The phenomena that they call "synecdochical" or "metonymical" over-extensions such as *Papa* for 'father, grandfather, mother' (recorded at age: 1;0) or *choo-choo* for 'train' (age: 1;7) are perhaps best not regarded as genuine examples of synecdoche and metonymy, respectively, because it is not clear that the child in question really exploits a contiguity link between two concepts. At a later age (from about 5 years), however, the data of Nerlich, Clarke, and Todd show a remarkable increase of what they call "creative metonymical shrinking," cognitive shortcuts to express novel ideas as in *I really like being a sandwich*, pronounced by a five-year-old child with the intended meaning 'I like being part of the children who, instead of having school dinner, are allowed to bring their own lunch box with sandwiches'.

12. Areas of Future Research

12.1. Constraints on Metonymy

Little systematic research has been done on what kind of conceptual, pragmatic, and grammatical constraints limit the linguistic exploitation of metonymy. Are there potential conceptual links that are never exploited or unlikely to be exploited by language users? One constraint on the exploitability may be the conceptual distance between source and target content: the more conceptually distant the source from the target, the less likely a metonymic operation will come about (see section 4 for discussion and examples). Alternatively, one might surmise that

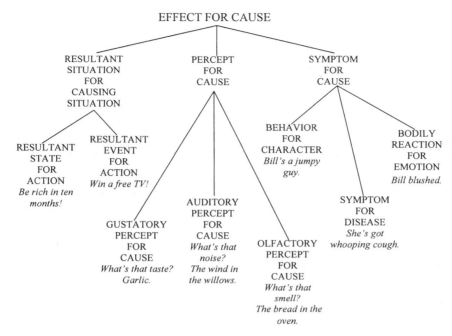

Figure 10.1. A tentative taxonomy of the EFFECT FOR CAUSE metonymy

properties of metonymic targets that are felt to be intrinsic or essential are likely to be exploited more systematically than properties than are seen as accidental.

Often the use of metonymies is restricted in more idiosyncratic ways. For example, *We need some young brains on our faculty* is completely natural, but *A young brain entered the library looking for Grimm's Dictionary* seems less felicitous. Some metonymic uses are highly formulaic such as *a sail* (for 'boat') *on the horizon*, but a nonformulaic usage such as *All the sails sank in the storm* is odd.

12.2. Metonymic Systems

Lakoff and Johnson (1980, 1999) and others have shown that metaphors are organized in rich conceptual systems. Metaphorical systems are presumably based on a relatively small number of basic (primary) metaphors (Grady 1997). For metonymy, various lists of high-level metonymies have been proposed in the twentieth century (e.g., Ullmann 1951; Norrick 1981; Radden and Kövecses 1999; see Nerlich, Clarke, and Todd 1999 for a brief discussion), but these hardly qualify as articulated taxonomies or classifications in the strict sense.

An exhaustive classification of metonymies remains a project for the future, but it is plausible to assume that metonymies are, at least, hierarchically structured from fairly abstract "high-level" metonymies to more and more specific subtypes.

This can be demonstrated for the fairly pervasive high-level metonymy EFFECT FOR CAUSE, which exhibits at least a three-layered taxonomic structure (see figure 10.1).

The most specific instances of the metonymy are situated in the third level of figure 10.1. There is a relation of hyponymy from bottom to top, with the more specific metonymies semantically implying the more generic ones. In what follows, some of the illustrative examples are briefly commented upon. The first two sentences on the far left of figure 10.1 exemplify the RESULTANT SITUATION FOR CAUSING SITUATION metonymy; for example, *Be rich in ten months!* is an exhortation to act in such a way (ACTION) in order to be rich (RESULT). Note that the imperative construction *coerces* a metonymic action interpretation of *be rich* in this case (see section 8). Another pervasive metonymic principle is illustrated by the PERCEPT FOR CAUSE metonymy: the question *What's that **noise*** is about the *cause* of the noise and the subsequent noun phrase identifies the source of the noise, that is, the CAUSE, here a natural force. Related to this metonymy is the metonymy that connects a SYMPTOM to its CAUSE, where the cause ranges from diseases and emotions to more permanent character traits. When a person blushes, this is routinely interpreted as indicating some emotional state (such as shame or embarrassment). Bodily symptoms play an important role in identifying diseases; it is therefore not surprising that many ailments such as *whooping cough* are conventionally named by their symptoms. Finally, character traits are also quite naturally metonymically inferred from overt behavior. Thus, *jumpy* is nowadays conventionally used to convey the meaning 'nervous' and even seems to have acquired the status of a post-metonymy in the sense of Riemer (2002) (see section 5.2).

In conclusion, metonymy is an extraordinarily rich source for the construction of new meanings whose impact on language use and conceptual structure and whose interaction with grammatical form is comparable to that of metaphor. Among the desiderata for future research, the following are especially significant: (i) to establish criteria that permit distinguishing between metonymic intradomain mappings and metaphorical interdomain mappings; (ii) to remove, or at least reduce, some of the terminological heterogeneity in the naming of metonymies; (iii) to search for high-level metonymies from which the rich array of lower-level metonymies can be derived; (iv) to do more comparative work on the exploitation of specific high-level metonymies across languages; (v) to explore the role metonymy plays in the acquisition of the lexicon; and (vi) to carry out experimental work testing the cognitive reality of metonymic processes in language production and comprehension.

NOTES

1. An exception is Seto (1999), who argues that taxonomic relations (hyponymy and hyperonymy) cannot constitute the basis for metonymic mappings. In this respect, Seto's approach appears to be in accord with *Rhetorica ad Herennium*, where synecdoche is restricted to MEMBER-SET or SUBSET-SET relations (see Burkhardt 1996: 177–78). According

to Seto, synecdoche is based on hyponymically organized conceptual relations, whereas
metonymy is grounded in spatiotemporal "real-world" contiguities and, by extension,
contiguity relations among abstract concepts. Thus, cases such as *ticket* for 'traffic ticket'
(HYPERONYM FOR HYPONYM) or *(daily) bread* with the target meaning 'food' (HYPONYM
FOR HYPERONYM) do not qualify as metonymies in Seto's (1999: 114) sense but are regarded
as instances of synecdoche. Seto's terminology is, however, somewhat at odds with the
normal understanding of the terms "synecdoche" as a part-whole and whole-part and
"metonymy" as contiguity relation like cause-effect, producer-product, essential property–
thing, etc.

2. Dirk Geeraerts (p.c.) argues against this view as being based on the metalinguistic
(metaphorical) conceptualization of concepts as sets.

3. It should be noted that Goossens himself is reluctant to call these meaning shifts
metonymic.

4. In argumentation theory (see Feyaerts 1999: 318, who cites van Eemeren et al. 1996 in
this regard), the ubiquity of reasoning by association or by contiguity relations such as
'cause' and 'effect' or 'a person X' and 'X's actions' is well known.

5. An analogous argument is developed in Lakoff and Johnson (1999: 66–67) with
regard to "dead" metaphors.

6. The difference between *John enjoyed the beer* and *Don is likely to leave* is, however,
that in the former case the metonymic target, John's enjoying the *drinking* of the beer,
is not at all coded in the sentence, whereas in the latter case the target, *Don's leaving*, can
be directly read off the sentence itself.

REFERENCES

Barcelona, Antonio, ed. 2000a. *Metaphor and metonymy at the crossroads*. Berlin: Mouton
    de Gruyter.
Barcelona, Antonio. 2000b. On the plausibility of claiming metonymic motivation for
    conceptual metaphor. In Antonio Barcelona, ed., *Metaphor and metonymy at the
    crossroads: A cognitive perspective* 22–58. Berlin: Mouton de Gruyter.
Barcelona, Antonio. 2003. Metonymy in cognitive linguistics: An analysis and a few modest
    proposals. In Hubert Cuyckens, Thomas Berg, René Dirven, and Klaus-Uwe Panther,
    eds., *Motivation in language: Studies in honor of Günter Radden* 223–55. Amsterdam:
    John Benjamins.
Barcelona, Antonio. 2004. Metonymy behind grammar: The motivation of the seemingly
    "irregular" grammatical behavior of English paragon names. In Günter Radden and
    Klaus-Uwe Panther, eds., *Studies in linguistic motivation* 357–74. Amsterdam: John
    Benjamins.
Brdar, Mario, and Rita Brdar-Szabó. 2003. Metonymic coding of linguistic action in En-
    glish, Croatian and Hungarian. In Klaus-Uwe Panther and Linda Thornburg, eds.,
    Metonymy and pragmatic inferencing 241–66. Amsterdam: John Benjamins.
Brdar, Mario, and Rita Brdar-Szabó. 2004. Predicate adjectives and grammatical-relational
    polysemy: The role of metonymic processes in motivating cross-linguistic differences.
    In Günter Radden and Klaus-Uwe Panther, eds., *Motivation in grammar* 321–55.
    Amsterdam: John Benjamins.
Bredin, Hugh. 1984. Metonymy. *Poetics Today* 5: 45–58.
Brown, Penelope, and Stephen C. Levinson. 1987. *Politeness: Some universals in language
    use*. Cambridge: Cambridge University Press.

Burkhardt, Armin. 1996. Zwischen Poesie und Ökonomie: Die Metonymie als se-
mantisches Prinzip. *Zeitschrift für Germanistische Linguistik* 24: 175–94.

Copestake, Ann, and Ted Briscoe. 1995. Semi-productive polysemy and sense extension.
Journal of Semantics 12: 15–67.

Croft, William. 1993. The role of domains in the interpretation of metaphors and metonymies. *Cognitive Linguistics* 4: 335–70.

Croft, William. 2001. *Radical construction grammar: Syntactic theory in typological perspective.* Oxford: Oxford University Press.

Cruse, D. Alan. 2000. *Meaning in language: An introduction to semantics and pragmatics.*
Oxford: Oxford University Press.

Dirven, René. 1993. Metonymy and metaphor: Different mental strategies of conceptualisation. *Leuvense Bijdragen* 82: 1–28.

Dirven, René, and Ralf Pörings, eds. 2002. *Metaphor and metonymy in comparison and
contrast.* Berlin: Mouton de Gruyter.

Dubois, Jacques, Francis Edeline, Jean-Marie Klinkenberg, Philippe Minguet, François
Pire, and Madelin Trinon. 1970. *Rhétorique générale.* Paris: Larousse.

Fauconnier, Gilles. 1985. *Mental spaces: Aspects of meaning construction in natural language.* Cambridge, MA: MIT Press. (2nd ed., Cambridge: Cambridge University Press,
1994)

Feyaerts, Kurt. 1999. Metonymic hierarchies: The conceptualization of stupidity in German
idiomatic expressions. In Klaus-Uwe Panther and Günter Radden, eds., *Metonymy
in language and thought* 309–32. Amsterdam: John Benjamins.

Feyaerts, Kurt. 2000. Refining the inheritance hypothesis: Interaction between metaphoric
and metonymic hierarchies. In Antonio Barcelona, ed., *Metaphor and metonymy at
the crossroads: A cognitive perspective* 59–78. Berlin: Mouton de Gruyter.

Geeraerts, Dirk. 1988. Cognitive grammar and the history of lexical semantics. In Brygida
Rudzka-Ostyn, ed., *Topics in cognitive linguistics* 647–77. Amsterdam: John Benjamins.

Geeraerts, Dirk. 1994. Metonymy. In R. E. Asher, ed., *The encyclopedia of language
and linguistics* 5: 2477–78. Oxford: Pergamon.

Geeraerts, Dirk. 2002. The interaction of metaphor and metonymy in composite expressions. In René Dirven and Ralf Pörings, eds., *Metaphor and metonymy in comparison
and contrast* 435–65. Berlin: Mouton de Gruyter.

Gibbs, Raymond W., Jr. 1994. *The poetics of mind: Figurative thought, language, and understanding.* Cambridge: Cambridge University Press.

Gibbs, Raymond W., Jr. 1999. Speaking and thinking with metonymy. In Klaus-Uwe
Panther and Günter Radden, eds., *Metonymy in language and thought* 61–76.
Amsterdam: John Benjamins.

Goldberg, Adele E. 1995. *Constructions: A construction grammar approach to argument
structure.* Chicago: University of Chicago Press.

Goossens, Louis. 1990. Metaphtonymy: The interaction of metaphor and metonymy in
expressions for linguistic actions. *Cognitive Linguistics* 1: 323–40.

Goossens, Louis. 1999. Metonymic bridges in modal shifts. In Klaus-Uwe Panther and
Günter Radden, eds., *Metonymy in language and thought* 193–210. Amsterdam: John
Benjamins.

Goossens, Louis. 2000. Patterns of meaning extension, "parallel chaining," subjectification,
and modal shifts. In Antonio Barcelona, ed., *Metaphor and metonymy at the crossroads:
A cognitive perspective* 149–69. Berlin: Mouton de Gruyter.

Goossens, Louis. 2002. Metaphtonymy: The interaction of metaphor and metonymy in
expressions for linguistic action. In René Dirven and Ralf Pörings, eds., *Metaphor and
metonymy in comparison and contrast* 349–77. Berlin: Mouton de Gruyter.

Grady, Joseph. 1997. Foundations of meaning: Primary metaphors and primary scenes. PhD dissertation, University of California at Berkeley.

Grady, Joseph, and Christopher Johnson. 2002. Converging evidence for the notions of *subscene* and *primary scene*. In René Dirven and Ralf Pörings, eds., *Metaphor and metonymy in comparison and contrast* 533–54. Berlin: Mouton de Gruyter.

Grice, H. Paul. 1975. Logic and conversation. In Peter Cole and Jerry Morgan, eds., *Syntax and semantics*, vol. 3, *Speech acts* 41–58. New York: Academic Press.

Heine, Bernd, Ulrike Claudi, and Friederike Hünnemeyer. 1991. *Grammaticalization: A conceptual framework*. Chicago: University of Chicago Press.

Hopper, Paul J., and Elizabeth Closs Traugott. 1993. *Grammaticalization*. Cambridge: Cambridge University Press. (2nd ed., 2003)

Jakobson, Roman. [1956] 1971. Two aspects of language and two types of aphasic disturbances. In Roman Jakobson and Morris Halle, eds., *Fundamentals of language* 67–96. The Hague: Mouton.

Kleiber, Georges. 1995. Polysémie, transferts de sens et métonymie intégrée. *Folia Linguistica* 29: 105–32.

Koch, Peter. 1999. Frame and contiguity: On the cognitive bases of metonymy and certain types of word formation. In Klaus-Uwe Panther and Günter Radden, eds., *Metonymy in language and thought* 139–67. Amsterdam: John Benjamins.

Kövecses, Zoltán. 1986. *Metaphors of anger, pride and love: A lexical approach to the study of concepts*. Amsterdam: John Benjamins.

Kövecses, Zoltán. 1995. Anger: Its language, conceptualisation, and physiology in the light of cross-cultural evidence. In John R. Taylor and Robert E. MacLaury, eds., *Language and the cognitive construal of the world* 181–96. Berlin: Mouton de Gruyter.

Lakoff, George. 1987. *Women, fire, and dangerous things: What categories reveal about the mind*. Chicago: University of Chicago Press.

Lakoff, George, and Mark Johnson. 1980. *Metaphors we live by*. Chicago: University of Chicago Press.

Lakoff, George, and Mark Johnson. 1999. *Philosophy in the flesh: The embodied mind and its challenge to Western thought*. New York: Basic Books.

Lakoff, George, and Mark Turner. 1989. *More than cool reason: A field guide to poetic metaphor*. Chicago: University of Chicago Press.

Langacker, Ronald W. 1987. *Foundations of cognitive grammar*. Vol. 1, *Theoretical prerequisites*. Stanford, CA: Stanford University Press.

Langacker, Ronald W. 1993. Reference-point constructions. *Cognitive Linguistics* 4: 1–38.

Langacker, Ronald W. 2000. *Grammar and conceptualization*. Berlin: Mouton de Gruyter.

Levinson, Stephen C. 2000. *Presumptive meanings: The theory of generalized conversational implicature*. Cambridge, MA: MIT Press.

Nerlich, Brigitte, David D. Clarke, and Zazie Todd. 1999. "Mummy, I like being a sandwich": Metonymy in language acquisition. In Klaus-Uwe Panther and Günter Radden, eds., *Metonymy in language and thought* 362–83. Amsterdam: John Benjamins.

Niemeier, Susanne. 2000. Straight from the heart—metonymic and metaphorical explorations. In Antonio Barcelona, ed., *Metaphor and metonymy at the crossroads: A cognitive perspective* 195–213. Berlin: Mouton de Gruyter.

Nikiforidou, Kiki. 1999. Nominalizations, metonymy, and lexicographic practice. In Leon G. Stadler and Christoph Eyrich, eds., *Issues in cognitive linguistics* 141–63. Berlin: Mouton de Gruyter.

Norrick, Neal R. 1981. *Semiotic principles in semantic theory*. Amsterdam: John Benjamins.

Nunberg, Geoffrey. 1978. *The pragmatics of reference*. Bloomington: Indiana University Linguistics Club.

Nunberg, Geoffrey. 1995. Transfers of meaning. *Journal of Semantics* 17: 109–32.

Panther, Klaus-Uwe. 2001. Syntactic control. In Neil J. Smelser and Paul B. Baltes, eds., *International encyclopedia of the social and behavioral sciences* 15397–401. New York: Elsevier.

Panther, Klaus-Uwe, and Günter Radden. 1999a. Introduction. In Klaus-Uwe Panther and Günter Radden, eds., *Metonymy in language and thought* 1–14. Amsterdam: John Benjamins.

Panther, Klaus-Uwe, and Günter Radden, eds. 1999b. *Metonymy in language and thought.* Amsterdam: John Benjamins.

Panther, Klaus-Uwe, and Linda Thornburg. 1998. A cognitive approach to inferencing in conversation. *Journal of Pragmatics* 30: 755–69.

Panther, Klaus-Uwe, and Linda Thornburg. 1999. The POTENTIALITY FOR ACTUALITY metonymy in English and Hungarian. In Klaus-Uwe Panther and Günter Radden, eds., *Metonymy in language and thought* 333–57. Amsterdam: John Benjamins.

Panther, Klaus-Uwe, and Linda Thornburg. 2000. The EFFECT FOR CAUSE metonymy in English grammar. In Antonio Barcelona, ed., *Metaphor and metonymy at the crossroads: A cognitive perspective* 215–31. Berlin: Mouton de Gruyter.

Panther, Klaus-Uwe, and Linda Thornburg. 2002. The roles of metaphor and metonymy in English -er nominals. In René Dirven and Ralf Pörings, eds., *Metaphor and metonymy in comparison and contrast* 279–319. Berlin: Mouton de Gruyter.

Panther, Klaus-Uwe, and Linda Thornburg. 2003a. Introduction: On the nature of conceptual metonymy. In Klaus-Uwe Panther and Linda Thornburg, eds., *Metonymy and pragmatic inferencing* 1–20. Amsterdam: John Benjamins.

Panther, Klaus-Uwe, and Linda Thornburg. 2003b. Metonymy and lexical aspect in English and French. *Jezikoslovlje* 4: 71–101.

Panther, Klaus-Uwe, and Linda Thornburg, eds. 2003c. *Metonymy and pragmatic inferencing.* Amsterdam: John Benjamins.

Papafragou, Anna. 1996. Figurative language and the semantics-pragmatics distinction. *Language and Literature* 5: 179–93.

Paul, Hermann. [1880] 1975. *Prinzipien der Sprachgeschichte.* Tübingen: Max Niemeyer Verlag.

Pérez Hernández, Lorena, and Francisco José Ruiz de Mendoza. 2002. Grounding, semantic motivation, and conceptual interaction in indirect directive speech acts. *Journal of Pragmatics* 34: 259–84.

Pustejovsky, James. 1991. The generative lexicon. *Computational Linguistics* 17: 409–41.

Pustejovsky, James. 1993. Type coercion and lexical selection. In James Pustejovsky, ed., *Semantics and the lexicon* 73–96. Dordrecht, Netherlands: Kluwer.

Radden, Günter. 2000. How metonymic are metaphors? In Antonio Barcelona, ed., *Metaphor and metonymy at the crossroads: A cognitive perspective* 93–108. Berlin: Mouton de Gruyter.

Radden, Günter. 2002. How metonymic are metaphors? In René Dirven and Ralf Pörings, eds., *Metaphor and metonymy in comparison and contrast* 407–34. Berlin: Mouton de Gruyter.

Radden, Günter, and Zoltán Kövecses. 1999. Towards a theory of metonymy. In Klaus-Uwe Panther and Günter Radden, eds., *Metonymy in language and thought* 17–59. Amsterdam: John Benjamins.

Riemer, Nick. 2002. When is a metonymy no longer a metonymy? In René Dirven and Ralf Pörings, eds., *Metaphor and metonymy in comparison and contrast* 379–406. Berlin: Mouton de Gruyter.

Ruiz de Mendoza Ibáñez, Francisco José. 2000. The role of mappings and domains in understanding metonymy. In Antonio Barcelona, ed., *Metaphor and metonymy at the crossroads: A cognitive perspective* 109–32. Berlin: Mouton de Gruyter.

Ruiz de Mendoza Ibáñez, Francisco José, and José Luis Otal Campo. 2002. *Metonymy, grammar, and communication.* Albolote, Granada: Editorial Comares.

Ruiz de Mendoza Ibáñez, Francisco José, and Olga Isabel Díez Velasco. 2002. Patterns of conceptual interaction. In René Dirven and Ralf Pörings, eds., *Metaphor and metonymy in comparison and contrast* 489–532. Berlin: Mouton de Gruyter.

Ruiz de Mendoza Ibáñez, Francisco José, and Olga Isabel Díez Velasco. 2004. Metonymic motivation in anaphoric reference. In Günter Radden and Klaus-Uwe Panther, eds., *Studies in linguistic motivation* 293–320. Amsterdam: John Benjamins.

Ruiz de Mendoza Ibáñez, Francisco José, and Lorena Pérez Hernández. 2001. Metonymy and grammar: Motivation, constraints and interactions. *Language & Communication* 21: 321–57.

Ruiz de Mendoza Ibáñez, Francisco José, and Lorena Pérez Hernández. 2003. Cognitive operations and pragmatic implication. In Klaus-Uwe Panther and Linda Thornburg, eds., *Metonymy and pragmatic inferencing* 23–49. Amsterdam: John Benjamins.

Ruwet, Nicolas. 1975. Synecdoques et métonymies. *Poétique* 6: 371–88.

Schofer, Peter, and Donald Rice. 1977. Metaphor, metonymy, and synecdoche revis(it)ed. *Semiotica* 21: 121–47.

Searle, John. 1969. *Speech acts: An essay in the philosophy of language.* Cambridge: Cambridge University Press.

Searle, John. 1975. Indirect speech acts. In Peter Cole and Jerry Morgan, eds., *Speech acts* 59–82. New York: Academic Press.

Seto, Ken-ichi. 1999. Distinguishing metonymy from synecdoche. In Klaus-Uwe Panther and Günter Radden, eds., *Metonymy in language and thought* 91–120. Amsterdam: John Benjamins.

Song, Nam Sun. 1997. Metaphor and metonymy. In Robyn Carston and Seiji Uchida, eds., *Relevance Theory: Applications and implications* 87–104. Amsterdam: John Benjamins.

Stirling, Lesley. 1996. Metonymy and anaphora. In *Belgian Journal of Linguistics* 10: 69–88.

Sweetser, Eve. 1991. *From etymology to pragmatics: Metaphorical and cultural aspects of semantic structure.* Cambridge: Cambridge University Press.

Talmy, Leonard. 2000. *Toward a cognitive semantics.* Vol. 2, *Typology and process in concept structuring.* Cambridge, MA: MIT Press.

Thornburg, Linda, and Klaus Panther. 1997. Speech act metonymies. In Wolf-Andreas Liebert, Gisela Redeker, and Linda Waugh, eds., *Discourse and perspectives in cognitive linguistics* 201–19. Amsterdam: John Benjamins.

Traugott, Elizabeth Closs, and Ekkehard König. 1991. The semantics-pragmatics of grammaticalization revisited. In Elizabeth Closs Traugott and Bernd Heine, eds., *Approaches to grammaticalization* 1: 189–218. Amsterdam: John Benjamins.

Ullmann, Stephen. 1951. *The principles of semantics.* Oxford: Basil Blackwell.

Ullmann, Stephen. 1962. *Semantics: An introduction to the science of meaning.* Oxford: Basil Blackwell.

van Eemeren, Frans H., Rob Grootendorst, Ralph H. Johnson, Christian Plantin, Charles A. Willard, David Zarefsky, J. Anthony Blair, A. Francisca Snoeck Henkemans, Erik Krabbe, John H. Woods, and Douglas Walton. 1996. *Fundamental argumentation theory: A handbook of historical backgrounds and contemporary developments.* Mahwah, NJ: Lawrence Erlbaum.

CHAPTER 11

....

ATTENTION PHENOMENA

....

LEONARD TALMY

1. INTRODUCTION

....

1.1. Content of the Study

This chapter introduces new work on the fundamental attentional system of language (Talmy, forthcoming), while in part providing a framework in which prior linguistic work on attention can be placed. In a speech situation, a hearer may attend to the linguistic expression produced by a speaker, to the conceptual content represented by that expression, and to the context at hand. But not all of this material appears uniformly in the foreground of the hearer's attention. Rather, various portions or aspects of the expression, content, and context have differing degrees of salience (see also Schmid, this volume, chapter 5). Such differences are only partially due to any intrinsically greater interest of certain elements over others. More fundamentally, language has an extensive system that assigns different degrees of salience to the parts of an expression or of its reference or of the context. In terms of the speech participants, the speaker employs this system in formulating an expression; the hearer, largely on the basis of such formulations, allocates his or her attention in a particular way over the material of these domains.

This attentional system in language includes a large number of basic factors, the "building blocks" of the system, with over fifty identified to date. Each factor involves a particular linguistic mechanism that increases or decreases attention on a certain type of linguistic entity. The mechanisms employed fall into some ten categories, most with subcategories. The type of linguistic entity whose degree of salience is determined by the factors is usually the semantic referent of a constituent, but other types occur, including the phonological shape of a constituent or the vocal delivery of the utterance. Each factor contrasts a linguistic circumstance in which attention is increased with a complementary circumstance in which it is decreased. A speaker can use a factor for either purpose—or in some cases for both at the same time. For some factors, increased attention on a linguistic entity is regularly accompanied by additional cognitive effects, such as distinctness, clarity, and significance, while decreased attention correlates with such converse effects as meldedness, vagueness, and ordinariness. The bulk of this chapter, section 2, presents in highly excerpted form some of the attentional factors in their taxonomy.

Although able to act alone, the basic factors also regularly combine and interact—whether in a single constituent, over a sentence, or through a discourse—to produce further attentional effects. Several such factor patterns are presented in abbreviated form in section 3.

Many further aspects of language's attentional system cannot be examined in this short chapter, but a few can be touched on here to give a fuller sense of the system. First, language-specific and typological differences occur in the use of attentional devices. For a language-specific example, some individual languages (like Tamil) manifest factor Ca1 (see section 2.3) by using special morphemes to mark an adjacent constituent for foregrounding as topic or focus. Other languages (like English) do not use this mechanism at all. For a typological example, sign languages (see Talmy 2003b) appear to differ systematically from spoken languages in the use of a special mechanism for attentional disregard. To illustrate with American Sign Language (ASL), consider that I want to sign that a particular wall was architecturally moved farther out to enlarge a room. To represent the wall in its initial position, I begin the sign by holding my hands horizontally before me joined at the fingertips, with the flattened hands oriented vertically, palms toward myself. If the wall was physically moved along the floor while still standing, I would then move my hands horizontally away from myself with a steady deliberative movement. But the wall may instead have been removed and set up again at the more distant position. In that case, I now move my hands through a quick up-and-down arc, in effect showing them "jump" into the new more distant position. This quick arc-gesture signals that one is to disregard the spatial path that the hands are seen to follow and to take into consideration only the initial and final hand positions. Thus, this gesture can be regarded as a linguistic form with the function of calling for reduced attention to—in fact, for the disregard of—the path of the hands, which would otherwise be understood as a semantically relevant constituent. In addition to individual mechanisms of this last type, signed languages also have unique factor combinations. In ASL, for example, the nondominant hand can sign a specific topic and then be held fixed in position throughout the remainder of the clause as the dominant hand signs the comment (see Liddell 2003). That is, the nondominant hand maintains some of the viewer's background attention on the identity of the topic, even as the dominant hand attracts the viewer's attentional foreground to certain particulars of content. No obvious counterparts of these attentional devices occur in spoken languages.

Next, in the developing theoretical account of the attention system in language, some broad properties are already evident. For example, in terms of the qualities of attention per se, linguistic attention functions as a gradient, not as a dichotomous all-or-none phenomenon. The particular level of attention on a linguistic entity is set in terms of foregrounding or backgrounding relative to a baseline for the entity, rather than absolutely on a zero-based scale. And the linguistic aspects realized in the course of a discourse range along a gradient of "access to attention," from ones with "interruptive" capacity, able to supplant whatever else is currently highest in attention, to ones that basically remain unconscious. Further, in terms of attentional organization, a number of the factors and their combinations accord with—perhaps fall out of—certain more general principles. By one such principle, attention tends to be more on the reference of some linguistic material—that is, on its semantic content—than on the form or structure of the material. And by a related principle, attention tends to be more on higher-level units of such content than on lower-level units. For example, attention is characteristically more on the overall literal meaning of a sentence than on the meanings of its individual words, and still more on the contextual import of that sentence's meaning than on the literal meaning of the sentence.

Finally, the attentional properties found in language appear to have both commonalities and differences with attentional properties in other cognitive systems. An example of commonality is that greater magnitude along a cognitive parameter tends to attract greater attention to the entity manifesting it. This is seen both in language, say, for stronger stress on a linguistic constituent, and in visual perception, say, for large size or bright color of a viewed object. On the other hand, one mechanism in the attentional system of language is the use of special morphemes—for example, topic and focus markers—dedicated to the task of directing attention to the referent of an adjacent constituent. But the perceptual modalities appear to have little that is comparable. Contrariwise, abrupt change along any sensory parameter is one of the main mechanisms in the perceptual modalities for attracting attention to the stimulus exhibiting it. But it has a minimal role in the attentional system of language.

Thus, the larger study, which this chapter only introduces, covers the linguistic system of attentional factors and their patterns of interaction, a theoretical framework that includes the universal and typological aspects of this system, the general principles that the system is based on, and a comparison between this linguistic attentional system and that of other cognitive modalities.

1.2. Context of the Study

Much previous linguistic work has involved the issue of attention or salience. Areas within such work are familiar under terms like topic and focus (e.g., Lambrecht 1994), focal attention (e.g., Tomlin 1995), activation (e.g., Givón 1990; Chafe 1994), prototype theory (e.g., Lakoff 1987), frame semantics (e.g., Fillmore 1976, 1982), profiling (e.g., Langacker 1987), and deictic center (e.g., Zubin and Hewitt 1995). My research on attention has included: the relative salience of the "Figure" and the "Ground" in a represented situation (Talmy 1972, 1978a, 2000a: chapter 5); the "windowing" of attention on one or more selected portions of a represented scene, with attentional backgrounding of the "gapped" portions (Talmy 1976, 1983, 1995b, 1996b, 2000a: chapter 4); the attentional backgrounding versus foregrounding of concepts when expressed by closed-class (grammatical) forms versus by open-class (lexical) forms (Talmy 1978c, 1988b, 2000a: chapter 1); the "level" of attention set either on the whole of a scene or on its componential makeup (Talmy 1988b, 2000a: chapter 1); the differential attention on the "Agonist" and the "Antagonist," the two entities in a force-dynamic opposition (Talmy 1988a, 2000a: chapter 7); "fictive motion," in which a hearer is linguistically directed to sweep his or her focus of attention over the contours of a static scene (Talmy 1996a, 2000a: chapter 2); the backgrounding versus foregrounding of a concept when it is expressed in the verb complex versus by a nominal complement (Talmy 1985, 2000b: chapter 1); the backgrounding versus foregrounding of a proposition when it is expressed by a subordinate clause versus by a main clause (Talmy 1978b, 1991, 2000a: chapter 6); the conscious as opposed to unconscious processes in the acquisition, manifestation, and imparting of cultural patterns (Talmy 1995a, 2000b: chapter 7); and attentional differences between spoken and signed language (Talmy 2003a, 2003b). However, the present study may be the first with the aim of developing a systematic framework within which to place all such prior findings—together with a number of new findings—about linguistic attention. In fact, this study is perhaps the first to recognize that the linguistic phenomena across this whole range do all pertain to the same single cognitive system of attention.

The theoretical orientation of this study is, of course, that of Cognitive Linguistics. This linguistic approach is centered on the patterns in which and the processes by which conceptual content is organized in language. Cognitive Linguistics addresses this linguistic structuring of conception not only with respect to basic physical categories like space and time, force and causation, but also with respect to cognitive categories—the ideational and affective categories ascribed to sentient agents. These forms of conceptual structuring fall into several extensive classes, what I termed "schematic systems" (Talmy 2000a: chapter 1). One such system is that of "configurational structure," which comprises the schematic structuring or geometric delineations in space or time (or other qualitative domains) that linguistic forms can specify (Talmy 2000a: chapters 1–3; 2000b: chapters 1–4). Another schematic system is "force dynamics," which covers the structural representation of two entities interacting energetically with respect to opposition to a force, resistance to opposition, and overcoming of resistance, as well as to blockage, hindrance, support, and causation (Talmy 2000a: chapters 7–8). And a third schematic system is that of "cognitive states and processes," which includes the structural representation of volition and intention, expectation and affect, and perspective and attention (Talmy 2000a: chapters 1, 4, 5, 8). Thus, the present study of attention is an elaboration of one subportion within the extensive conceptual structuring system of language. In turn, the properties that attention is found to have in language can be compared with those of attention as it operates in other cognitive systems, such as in the various perceptual modalities, in the affect system, in the reasoning/inferencing system, and in motor control. This kind of comparative procedure was introduced in Talmy (2000a), designated as the "overlapping systems model of cognitive organization." Accordingly, it is assumed that the findings on attention in language will enable corroborative investigation by the methods of other fields of cognitive science, including the experimental techniques of psycholinguistics, the brain-imaging techniques of cognitive neuroscience, and the simulation techniques of artificial intelligence. The present study can thus help to develop a framework within which attentional findings from a range of research disciplines can be coordinated and ultimately integrated.

2. Some Linguistic Factors That Set Strength of Attention

2.1. Factors Involving Properties of the Morpheme (A)

A morpheme is here quite generally understood to be any minimal linguistic form with an associated meaning. This thus includes not only simplex morphemes, but also idioms and constructions (e.g., the English auxiliary-subject inversion meaning 'if').

Formal Properties of the Morpheme (Aa)

Factor Aa1: Expression in One or Another Lexical Category

A concept tends to be more or less salient in accordance with the lexical category of the form representing the concept. First, open-class categories in general lend more salience than closed-class categories. Further, within open-class categories, nouns may tend to outrank verbs while, within closed-class categories, forms with phonological substance may tend to outrank forms lacking it. Accordingly, lexical categories may exhibit something of the following salience hierarchy:

open-class (N > V) > closed-class (phonological > aphonological)

Only the open-class/closed-class contrast is illustrated here. Consider a case where essentially the same concept can be represented both by a closed-class form and by an open-class form. Thus, English tense is typically represented for a verb in a finite clause by a closed-class form, either an inflection or a modal, as in (1a) with an *-ed* for the past and (1b) with an *-s* or *will* for the future. But a nominal in a prepositional phrase cannot indicate tense in that way. If relative time is to be indicated here, one must resort to open-class forms, as in (2a), with the adjectives *previous* to mark the past and (2b) with *upcoming* to mark the future. The concepts of relative time seem much more salient when expressed by adjectives than by closed-class forms (see Talmy 2000a: chapter 1).

(1)   a. When he arriv*ed*, ...
      b. When he arriv*es/will* arrive, ...
(2)   a. On his *previous* arrival, ...
      b. On his *upcoming* arrival, ...

Factor Aa2: Degree of Morphological Autonomy

The term "degree of morphological autonomy" here refers to the grammatical status of a morpheme as free or bound. A concept tends to receive greater attention—and abetted by that attention, greater distinctness and clarity—when it is represented by a free morpheme than by a bound morpheme. Thus, the English free verb root *ship* and the bound verb root *-port* have approximately the same sense in their concrete usages, 'convey bulky objects by vehicle over geographic distances', and they appear in constructions with comparable meanings, such as *ship in*, *ship out*, *ship away*, *ship across*, and *import, export, deport, transport*. However, because, at least in part, of the difference in morphological autonomy of these two verb roots, *ship* foregrounds its concept with clarity and distinctness to a greater degree than *-port* does with its otherwise similar concept.

Componential Properties of the Morpheme (Ab)

Factor Ab1: Solo versus Joint Expression of a Component in a Morpheme

When a concept constitutes the sole and entire referent of a morpheme, it tends to have greater salience and individuated attention, but when it is conflated together with other concepts in a morpheme's reference, it tends to be more backgrounded and to meld with the other concepts. For example, the concepts 'parent' and 'sister' each receive greater individual attention when expressed alone in the separate morphemes *parent* and *sister*, as in *one of my parents' sisters*. But they receive less individual attention when expressed together in the single morpheme *aunt*, as in *one of my aunts*.

Factor Ab2: The Ensemble versus the Individual Components of a Morpheme's Meaning

In general, a language user directs more attention to the combination or ensemble of the semantic components that make up the reference of a morpheme than to the individual components themselves. That is, more attention is on the Gestalt whole of a morpheme's meaning than on its parts. Even where the components are all essential to the morpheme's use, a speaker or hearer is typically little aware of them, attending instead to their synthesis.

Consider the English verb *pry* as in (3a). Analysis shows that certain semantic components are part of the meaning of *pry* and must all be matched in the referent situation for this verb to apply to it. If any component does not fit the situation, a speaker must switch to some lexical neighbor of *pry*. A series of alterations to the situation reveals the essential components. Thus, if there is a one-foot board stuck vertically to a wall with a handle near the top and I tug on the handle, I cannot say (3a) but rather something like (3b). Sentence (3a) becomes acceptable here if instead of using the handle I levered the board away from the wall. Accordingly, one semantic component essential to the use of *pry* is that the force for removal of a Figure object from a Ground object comes from a third object inserted and pivoted between them. But now say that I do insert and pivot a lever between them so that the board comes away from the wall, but the board is hinged at the bottom and had been loosely upright against the wall. I now must say something like (3c). Sentence (3a) again becomes appropriate only if the Figure is fixed to the Ground and resists removal: the second essential component. But these two components are still not enough. Let us now say that the board is fixed to the wall and that I use a lever between them, but the board comes away from the wall all at once. A more apt sentence is now that in (3d). Sentence (3a) now becomes apt again only if the Figure moves gradually and progressively away from the Ground because it has some flexibility: a third essential component. But now say that instead of a board, a wide foot-long strip of masking tape is stuck to the wall and that I am progressively removing it with a lever inserted between the tape and the wall. Now I must say something like (3e). A fourth essential component is thus that the Figure must be rigid (though with enough give to be somewhat flexible). What should here be noticed in this whole analysis is that most of the components just identified do not come readily to mind on hearing the verb *pry*.

(3)　　a. I pried the board off the wall.
　　　　b. I pulled the board off the wall.
　　　　c. I flipped the board off the wall.
　　　　d. I popped the board off the wall.
　　　　e. I peeled the masking tape off the wall.

The point here is not to work out a specific semantic decomposition but to observe that, on hearing a morpheme, one may have a vivid sense of its meaning as a whole but have little conscious access to the particular components essential to that meaning. Such components typically do not spontaneously appear in our consciousness— so attentionally backgrounded are they—but instead require specialized linguistic techniques of analysis for us to become aware of them.

Factor Ab3: Weighting among the Components of a Morpheme's Meaning

Under factor Ab3, one semantic component within the meaning of a morpheme can be more salient than another. That is, the semantic components expressed by a morpheme can have different attentional weightings. This attentional allocation must be understood as part of the morpheme's lexicalization pattern. For example, while the verb *eat* includes both the components of 'chewing' and of 'swallowing', the 'chewing' component appears to be more salient in one's regard of the eating process than the 'swallowing' component, even though the latter can be shown to be criterial. This observation is perhaps corroborated by the fact that manner adverbs with *eat* tend to pick out the 'chewing' component rather than the 'swallowing' component as the target of their qualifications. Thus, the sentences *You should eat carefully/faster* would not generally be taken to mean that you should swallow carefully or faster, but more likely that you should apply those manners to your chewing.

A consequence of factor Ab3 is that two different morphemes—or two distinct senses of a polysemous morpheme—can have roughly the same semantic components, but can be weighted differently. Hence, a particular semantic component can be more salient in one member of such a pair than in the other member. An example is the semantic component 'multiple intentional causal agency' in the two polysemously related verbs, transitive *pass* and intransitive *pass*. The reference of both these verbs includes the same three semantic components: 'a Figure object' (in 4 below, a goblet), 'multiple intentional causal agency' (below, diners around a table), and 'the motion of the Figure in transit from the grasp of one Agent to that of another'. But transitive *pass* is lexicalized to foreground the 'agency' component, in correlation with its representation as subject, as in (4a). By contrast, intransitive *pass*, as in (4b), is lexicalized to foreground the Figure as subject, while the agency is now comparatively backgrounded. In fact, this verb has no ready complement structure in which to represent the agency.

(4) a. They slowly passed the goblet of wine around the banquet table.
     b. The goblet of wine slowly passed around the banquet table.

Frame and Prototype Properties of the Morpheme (Ac)

Factor Ac1: A Morpheme's Direct Reference versus Associated Concepts

Factor Ac1 involves the distinction between a morpheme's scope of direct reference and outside concepts only associated with that reference. Under it, more attention is on the direct than on the associated concepts. At the same time, the associated concepts are activated into the "midground" of attention. In one type of frame, the associated concepts augment the direct reference because, on the one hand, they add some related conceptual material to it but, on the other hand, they are incidental to it in that they could be dropped or replaced by alternative concepts. To illustrate, the morphemes *north* and *east* in their 'path' sense, as in *I kept flying north* and *I kept flying east*, on initial hearing seem semantically identical except for the compass orientation. But then one may realize that I can fly eastward indefinitely, circling the globe repeatedly, but that I can fly northward only until reaching the

North Pole, after which I am flying south. With respect to differences in salience, it seems clear that the concept of compass orientation is foregrounded in attention, while greatly backgrounded are the concepts of boundedness for *north* and unboundedness for *east*. Further, in addition to being backgrounded, these latter concepts seem not to be an intrinsic part of the direct lexicalized references of the morphemes, but only incidentally associated with them. First, for most local terrestrial usage today—and certainly for the usage of past centuries before knowledge of the global earth—*north* and *east* in fact differ only as to compass orientation and do not depend on any concept of polar terminuses, which could then be dropped from their associative ambit. Second, such polar terminuses are themselves a convention that could be otherwise. For example, geographers might have instead agreed to designate travel that starts northward along longitudes in the Western Hemisphere as remaining continuously northward around those great circles, while travel in the reverse direction would be southward. Our present understanding about longitudes and polar terminuses, therefore, appears to be a conception only incidentally associated with 'north', not necessary to it.

A second type of frame involves a set of concepts, ones within a particular structured interrelation, that co-entail each other. A morpheme can be so lexicalized as to refer directly to just one portion of such a set of co-entailed concepts, while treating the remainder as concepts merely associated with the direct portion. Two different morphemes can involve the same structured set of co-entailed concepts, while selecting different portions of it for their direct references. The portion in the morpheme's direct reference is foregrounded relative to the associated concepts, while the associated concepts come into the midground of attention. Both Fillmore's (1976, 1982) term "frame" and Langacker's (1987) term "base" apply to such a structured set of co-entailed concepts in the midground of attention. Further, Fillmore's term "highlighting" and Langacker's term "profiling" both refer to the foregrounding of one portion of the set in a morpheme's direct reference.

Morphemes of this co-entailment type differ as to whether the associated concepts must be co-present with the direct reference in both space and time, in only one of these domains, or in neither. Thus, Langacker's (1987) example of *hypotenuse* does not merely entail the existence of a right triangle in the midground of attention while referring directly to a particular side of such a triangle in the foreground of attention, it also requires that the co-entailed triangle be co-present with the hypotenuse in space and time, with its parts in the proper arrangement. An isolated length of line is not a hypotenuse but a *line segment*. Adapting Husserl's (1970: 455–57) example, it can next be noted that, in a monogamous context, the English nouns *husband* and *wife* both evoke a married couple in the midground of attention, while each directly refers in the foreground to one or the other member of such a pair. Here, the use of, say, *wife* does not require that the co-entailed husband be co-present in space, but does require that he be co-present in time, or else the referent would not be a wife but a *widow, divorcee*, or *fiancée*. Finally, Fillmore's (1976) 'commercial scene' is a structured set of co-entailed concepts, including a seller, a buyer, goods, money, and their transfers, that any of a number of verbs—such as *sell, buy, spend, pay, charge, cost,* and so on—refer to in the midground of attention, while referring directly in the foreground to a particular subset of the scene's components. Here, though, many of these components can be separated in both space and time, as seen in (5).

(5)   I bought her old banjo from her over the phone—she'll mail it to me next week, and I'll send her a check for it after it arrives.

Factor Ac2: Degree of Category Membership

In general, when an addressee hears a morpheme, more of his or her attention is on the prototype member of that morpheme's referent, or on an entity with a greater degree of membership, than on a peripheral or lower-degree member (see, e.g., Fillmore 1975, Lakoff 1987 for linguistic prototypes and some of their attentional correlates). Thus, on hearing the word *bird,* an American is likelier to have a robin in consciousness than an ostrich. Comparably, a prototype or higher-degree member gets more attention than the referential scope of a morpheme as a whole. Thus, if one hears *bird,* a robin is likelier to be in consciousness than the whole range of birds.

Polysemy Properties of the Morpheme (Ad)

Factor Ad1: Size of the Polysemous Range of a Morpheme

A concept tends to be more salient when it is expressed by a morpheme that has a smaller polysemous range and that accordingly can express fewer other concepts, than when it is expressed by a morpheme with a larger polysemous range covering more concepts. To illustrate with closed-class forms, the concept 'higher than and vertically aligned with' is expressed by both the prepositions *above* and *over* as in (6a). But *above* can refer to relatively few other concepts, whereas *over* can express a rather larger set of other concepts, including, for example, that of 'covering a surface' as in *There is a tapestry over the wall* (see Brugman and Lakoff 1988). It accordingly appears that the verticality sense is more prominently, clearly, and unambiguously evoked by *above* than by *over.* This difference is especially observable in a case where the context does not readily eliminate the other senses of the morpheme with the larger polysemous range, as in (6b).

(6)   a. There is a light above/over the chair.
       b. There is a poster above/over the hole in the wall.

Factor Ad2: Weighting among the Senses
of a Polysemous Morpheme

The various senses of a polysemous morpheme can be differently weighted with respect to how readily they are evoked by the morpheme. That is, when a listener hears the morpheme, some of its senses may come to mind more strongly, while other senses are more obscure. Accordingly, if the target concept that a speaker wishes to convey is one of the less salient senses, it might get overwhelmed by more salient senses unless the context strongly selects for the target concept. Note the difference between the present factor, Ad2, and factor Ab3. Factor Ad2 pertains to the salience of a whole concept when it is one sense of a morpheme, relative to the other senses; factor Ab3 pertains to the salience of one component of a single concept relative to the remaining components of that concept.

To illustrate with open-class forms, the concept 'the particulate material that plants grow in' is perhaps the most salient of the senses of the noun *soil*—certainly more salient than its sense of 'land, country' as in *my native soil* or of 'farmland (as contrasted, e.g., with an urban setting)', as in *I live on the soil*. By contrast, the target concept is less readily evoked by the noun *dirt*, which on the contrary allocates greatest salience to another of its senses, that of 'grime'. Similarly, the target concept is relatively weak in the polysemous range of the noun *earth*, which rather accords greater salience to the sense 'this planet' or the sense 'the surface land mass', as in *It settled to earth*. Where a context clearly selects for the target concept, as in (7a), a speaker can easily use any of the three nouns. But in an underdetermined context, as in (7b)—where a morpheme's most salient sense tends to be the one that first pops into attention—a speaker might best use the noun *soil* to evoke the target concept with minimal confusion.

(7)   a. I need to put more soil/dirt/earth in the planter.
       b. The soil/?dirt/?earth is slowly changing color.

2.2. Factors Involving Morphology and Syntax (B)

Grammatical and Constructional Properties (Ba)

Factor Ba1: Positioning at Certain Sentence Locations versus Other Locations

Each language may have certain locations within a sentence—for example, initial position or preverbal position—that tend to foreground the referent of a constituent placed there. Such added salience usually accompanies or facilitates a further cognitive effect, such as making that referent the target of a conceptual contrast. Many properties of topic and focus, as these have been regarded in the literature, are often engaged by such special positioning. To illustrate, a sentence like (8a) has its constituents in their basic locations. But the initial position of the temporal referent in (8b) foregrounds that referent and suggests a contrast: some other time would be all right. And the initial position of the Patient referent in (8c) foregrounds *that* referent and suggests a new contrast: another kind of music would be all right.

(8)　a.　I can't stand this kind of music right now.
　　b.　Right now I can't stand this kind of music.
　　c.　This kind of music I can't stand right now.

Factor Ba2: Expression in One or Another Grammatical Relation

A cline from greater to lesser prominence tends to be associated with nominals in accordance with their grammatical relation in a sentence as follows: subject > direct object > oblique. Consider for example, the two sentences in (9) that can refer to the same situation involving a landlord and a tenant, but that represent these two entities oppositely with subject or oblique nominals. In the referent situation, the landlord and the tenant are equally agentive. The landlord has perhaps prepared the apartment for new occupancy, advertised it, and interviewed interested parties. The tenant has perhaps checked newspaper listings, made phone calls, and visited other vacancies. But greater attention tends to be focused on the entity mentioned as subject. Associated with this attention is a greater sense that the subject entity is the main Agent, the one that is the more active and determinative in the situation, whose volition and intentions initiate and carry forward the reported action, and whose assumed supplementary activities are taken to be the relevant ones.

(9)　a.　The landlord rented the apartment to the tenant.
　　b.　The tenant rented the apartment from the landlord.

Factor Ba2 underlies much of the Figure/Ground phenomena described in Talmy (2000a: chapter 5). It was noted there—to take just one sector of the phenomena—that a predicate like *be near* is not symmetrical, since a sentence like that in (10a) is semantically distinct from the sentence in (10b). The reason is that, in such sentences, the subject nominal and the oblique nominal have different roles, those of Figure and of Ground, respectively. The Figure is a moving or conceptually movable entity whose path, site, or orientation is conceived as a variable the particular value of which is the relevant issue. And this variable is characterized with respect to the Ground, a reference entity that has a stationary setting relative to a reference frame. These are the definitional characteristics. In addition, there are a number of typically associated characteristics, some of which pertain to attention. Thus, the Ground is more familiar and expected, while the Figure is more recently in awareness. The Figure is of greater relevance or concern than the Ground. The Figure is less immediately perceivable than the Ground, but, once perceived, it is more salient, while the Ground is less salient once the Figure is perceived. Because of the associated characteristics, a bike is a more natural Figure than a house, given everyday circumstances, hence the oddity of (10b).

(10)　a.　The bike is near the house.
　　b.　?The house is near the bike.

Compositional Properties (Bb)

Factor Bb1: The Composition versus Its Components

It was proposed under factor Ab2 that the overall meaning of a morpheme is more in attention than the semantic components analyzable as making it up. In a parallel way, there seems to be a general tendency for more attention to go to the meaning of the whole of a composition than to the meanings of the linguistic constituents that make it up. This tendency manifests itself at two levels of linguistic organization: the morphemes that make up a word and the words that make up a phrase or clause. The tendency perhaps applies more strongly to the former of these. Thus, a speaker or hearer typically might well be more aware of the overall meaning of the form *uneventfulness* as a unified word than of the separate meanings of the four morphemes that make it up, which tend not to stand out individually. This direct observation may be corroborated by the possibility that there would be only a small difference in the contents of our consciousness if this complex word were replaced by a monomorphemic word with roughly the same meaning, like *calm* (full synonymy of course being virtually impossible), as in a sentence like (11).

(11)   The uneventfulness/calm in our household that morning was in stark contrast with the commotion of the night before.

Although less clearly so than for the word-internal case, more speaker or hearer attention seems to be on the overall meaning of a portion of discourse than on the meanings of the words and constructions that make it up. For example, the overall meaning of the sentence *Everyone there gathers in the yard to start the school day* may evoke a Gestalt conception more salient than any of the constituent word meanings—say, 'day', 'yard', or 'school'. And this Gestalt conception may even be more salient than the sum of all the word meanings and of all the constructions that the words are in.

Factor Bb2: An Idiomatic versus a Compositional Meaning

An idiom is a linguistic form consisting of two or more morphemes in a construction whose overall meaning is not derivable by compositional means from the meanings of the component morphemes in that construction. Factor Bb2 holds that, once such a form has been selected by a speaker or identified by a hearer as in fact being an idiom, its overall meaning is stronger in consciousness than any compositional meaning that might otherwise be attempted for it. For example, once the *turn down* in (12a) is determined—in this case by the context provided by its direct object—to be an idiom basically with the meaning 'reject', that meaning is stronger in attention than the compositional meaning 'rotate (something) in a downward direction'. For comparison, just such a compositional meaning does emerge in the context of sentence (12b).

(12)   a. I turned the offer down.
        b. I turned the propeller blade down.

2.3. Factors Involving Forms That Set Attention Outside Themselves (C)

The attentional factors outside category C generally involve properties of a linguistic unit that set the level of attention for that unit itself. For example, by factor Aa1, a morpheme's lexical category affects the attentional strength of its own referent. By contrast, in the factors of category C, a certain linguistic unit sets attention for some linguistic unit or nonlinguistic phenomenon fully outside itself.

Specific Linguistic Forms with an Attentional Effect outside Themselves (Ca)

Factor Ca1: A Form Designating an Outside Referent as the Object of Attention

A morpheme or construction can set the level of attention on the referent of a constituent outside itself. Considering here only the case of foregrounding, an example of a simplex morpheme with this effect is the Tamil particle *-ee*, which is cliticized to the constituent whose referent it foregrounds. One of several attention-directing particles, *-ee* is mostly associated with the marking of a semantic contrast, as exemplified by the sentence in (13), taken from Asher (1985).

(13) *avan   kaaley-iley-ee   va-nt-aan*
      he   morning-LOC-EMPH   come-PST-M
      'He came in the *morning* (and not at some other time of day)'

Factor Ca2: A Form Designating a Concomitant of an Outside Referent as the Object of Attention

Whereas forms under factor Ca1 set attention for the referent of an outside constituent, those of factor Ca2 direct attention to attributes of an outside constituent apart from its referent. Examples of such attributes are the phonological shape of the constituent, its vocal delivery, its exact composition, and its shape-referent linkage. In directing some attention away from the direct referring function of the constituent—its default function—such forms establish a certain degree and kind of metalinguistic awareness of the constituent.

For example, the linguistic form *be called* (compare the monomorphemic German form *heiss[en]*) as in (14a) directs the hearer to attend not just to the referent of the following constituent, but especially to the phonological shape of that constituent and to the linkage of that shape with that referent. By contrast, when the same constituent appears in a sentence like (14b) without a form like *be called*, its presence has the hearer attend simply to its referent.

(14) a. This gadget is called a pie segmenter.
      b. Please hand me that pie segmenter.

As a further example, the current youngsters' expression *be like*, as in (15), though often frowned on, is actually unique in English. It presents the expression that follows as an enactment of an utterance—either an actual utterance or what likely would be the utterance if the subject's state of mind were verbalized. The particular intonation pattern and vocal tones of the expression's delivery are necessarily divergent from a neutral delivery. The form thus directs a hearer's attention not only to the overall referent of the utterance, but also to its style of delivery and, hence, to the affective state of the subject inferable from that style.

(15)   So then I'm like: Wow, I don't believe this!

Factor Ca3: A Form Designating an Outside Entity or Phenomenon as the Object of Attention

A form covered by factor Ca1 or Ca2 sets attention only for a linguistic constituent outside itself, and it indicates which constituent this is to be by its sentential positioning relative to it. A form covered by factor Ca3 also indicates the setting of attention for something outside itself. But that something can be any entity or phenomenon within local space or time, not just another linguistic constituent. Further, the form does not directly indicate which outside entity or phenomenon is to be the object of attention through its sentential positioning. Rather, it denotes that some other mechanism is to indicate the object of attention. There is a taxonomy of such mechanisms. These include temporal proximity (combined with the relative salience of the intended object of attention), bodily movements by the speaker, and the speaker's physical manifestation. All these types are illustrated below. The category of deictics traditionally termed "demonstratives" is generally the type of forms covered by factor Ca3. In English the simplex forms of this sort are basically *this (these)*, *that (those)*, *here*, *there*, *yonder*, *now*, *thus*, *yea*, and stressed *he*, *she*, and *they*.

For the function of singling out one entity from among others, one mechanism is the temporal proximity of its occurrence to the moment of speaking, combined with that object's own intrinsic salience relative to the remainder of the field. This mechanism works for virtually any sense modality. For example, one person can say to another: *That's a cruise ship* as they both stand on a pier watching vessels sail by; *That's a fog horn* on hearing such a sound; *That's diesel fuel* on catching a whiff of its smell; or *That's the east wind* on feeling the air blowing on his or her skin.

Another mechanism for singling out the speaker's intended object of attention is a bodily movement by the speaker. Though the hearer typically views such a movement, it could be felt (or in some cases even heard). With such a movement, say, a pointing finger, the object of attention can be a thing or an activity (*That's my horse/a gallop*), a region of space (*My horse was over there*), or a direction (*My horse went that way*).

Third, the speaker's sheer bodily presence or verbal activity can function to single out a sufficiently coarse-grained component of the surroundings from alternatives. Thus, where the region of space around the speaker's body does not need the finer differentiation that the demonstratives described above can provide, uttering the word *here*, as in (16), is enough to identify that region without additional bodily motion.

(16)   a. Pull your wagon over here.
     b. There are plenty of restaurants around here.

Comparably, where the temporal interval around the speaker's current act of talking needs no finer differentiation than, say, the length of a sentence, uttering the word *now*, as in (17), is enough to identify that interval.

(17)   a. The telephone is available now.
     b. I was sick, but I'm fine now.

On the other hand, if the interval to be singled out is shorter than the length of a sentence, a speaker can use a finer-grained temporal demonstrative mechanism. This mechanism is the counterpart of body movements for finer-grained spatial singling out. Each word in a sentence occupies a specific temporal location in the stream of time. Designating the word that is coincident with it can single out some point of that stream. The means for designating the relevant word include stressing it as well as introducing pauses and stretches in the lead-up to it, as seen in (18).

(18)   a. You can save my life if you push the green button . . . riiiiight . . . NOW!
       (adapted from Fillmore 1997)
     b. The time is exactly . . . 3 . . . o'CLOCK!

Context with an Attentional Effect outside Itself (Cb)

Factor Cb1: Context Designating One Sector of a Morpheme's Extended Reference as the Object of Attention

To explain factor Cb1, I begin by observing that there is no known principled way to distinguish what might be inside a morpheme's reference "proper" and what might be outside and only associated with it. I will use the term "extended reference" to cover this whole range (since Fillmore's 1976 term "frame" tends to suggest only external associations). In accordance with one's conceptualization of it, a morpheme's extended reference can have indefinitely many different aspects, parts, or sectors. By the process at issue here, some one or a few of these can selectively be given more attention than the remainder. The current process is driven by the morpheme's context, whether linguistic or nonlinguistic. When a morpheme occurs as a particular token in an utterance, its context may indicate the current relevance of only certain elements of the morpheme's extended reference. Such context thus largely determines where greater attention is to be located within this extended reference. This process fits under group Cb factors because the context directs attention outside itself, namely, with respect to the morpheme for which it is the context.

This idea is advanced in Fillmore's (1976, 1982) "frame semantics." This proposes that every morpheme is associated with a network of concepts, any of which can be invoked by a question or additional comment outside the morpheme. Thus, the English verb *write* has an associated conceptual frame. Reference to a writing implement, as in (19a), directs greater attention to a particular aspect of that frame, namely, to the physical realization of the writing process. Reference to a language, as in (19b), foregrounds another aspect of writing, namely, the fact that it is always a linguistic phenomenon. And reference to a topic, as in (19c), foregrounds attention on a third aspect of writing, namely, that it communicates conceptual content.

(19)   I wrote . . .
     a. . . . with a quill
     b. . . . in Russian
     c. . . . about daffodils.

Comparably, Bierwisch (1983) observed that different contexts can single out at least two different aspects of the referent of a word like *university* in a systematic way—hence, not as different senses of a particular polysemous morpheme. Thus, attention is directed to the character of a university as a physical entity in *The university collapsed in the earthquake*, and as an institution in *He got his PhD from that university*.

In a similar way, Langacker's (1984) notion of an "active zone"—though it is not characterized in terms of differential attention—designates the particular portion of a morpheme's extended reference that "participates most directly" in a relationship. This relationship is expressed by a morpheme or morphemes outside the affected one. For example, in *My dog bit your cat*, the outside morpheme *bit* determines that, of the extended reference of the morpheme *dog*, it is the teeth and jaws that are most directly involved, and also that only some (unspecified) portion, not the whole, of the cat is involved.

Factor Cb2: Context Designating One of a Morpheme's Multiple Senses as the Object of Attention

A particular morphemic shape in a language can have—and typically does have—a number of distinct referents, whether these are judged to be the related senses of a single morpheme's polysemous range or the separate senses of distinct homophonous morphemes. Yet in any given portion of discourse, a hearer is usually aware of only one sense for each morphemic shape. This apparently results from two complementary operations of our linguistic cognition. One operation is to pick out the one sense of a morphemic shape that seems the most relevant in the current context and foreground this sense in attention. The selection phase of this operation is remarkable for its speed and efficacy. The second operation is to background all the remaining senses. This second operation is here termed "masking": all but the one apparently relevant sense are masked out from attention.

The pertinent context of a morphemic shape often largely consists of other morphemic shapes around it. Hence, in processing an expression, linguistic cognition must determine the single sense within each of the assembled morphemic shapes that are contextually relevant to each other and mask out all the remaining senses within each morpheme. Thus, factor Cb2 can be regarded either as operating on a single morpheme at a time, a morpheme for which all the surrounding morphemes are context, or interactively on the group of morphemes as a whole, which thus forms its own "co-context." This process accordingly can be seen as yielding either a succession of sense selections or a mutual disambiguation.

To illustrate, each of the five open-class forms in (20) has at least the several senses listed for it.

(20)   *check*, V:
    a. 'ascertain'
    b. 'write a checkmark beside'
    c. 'inscribe with a checkerboard pattern'
    d. 'deposit for safekeeping'
    e. 'stop'
    market, N:
    a. 'outdoor area of vendors selling food'
    b. 'store for selling food'
    c. 'institution for financial exchange'
    figure, N:
    a. 'shape'
    b. 'diagram'
    c. 'personage'
    d. 'number'
    stock, N:
    a. 'soup base'
    b. 'stored supply'
    c. 'rifle part'
    d. 'line of descendants'
    e. 'farm animals'
    f. 'fragrant flowered plant species'
    g. 'financial instrument'
    down, A:
    a. 'closer to earth's center'
    b. 'reduced'
    c. 'recorded'
    d. 'glum'

But when these five forms are combined, as in (21), by the operation of factor Cb2, the hearer typically settles swiftly on one sense for each form. In this example, the likeliest selection—especially in an otherwise financial context—is of the 'ascertain' sense of *check* (a); the 'financial exchange' sense of *market* (c); the 'number' sense of *figure* (d); the 'financial instrument' sense of *stock* (g); and the 'reduced' sense of *down* (b).

(21)   I checked the market figures—my stock is down.

2.4. Phonological Factors (D)

This category of factors covers all phonological properties within an utterance, including those of individual morphemes (not covered in the first category). For reasons of space, only one subcategory is presented.

Phonological Properties of Intrinsic Morphemic Shape (Da)
Factor Da1: Morpheme Length

The phonological length of a morpheme or word tends to correlate with the degree of salience that attaches to its referent. One venue in which this correlation is evident is where basically the same concept is expressed by morphemes or words of different lengths. Here, a longer form attracts more attention to the concept, while a shorter form attracts less attention. Thus, roughly the same adversative meaning is expressed by the English conjunctions *nevertheless* and *but*. Despite this, apparently the greater phonological length of *nevertheless* correlates with its fully imposing and prominent effect on narrative structure, while the brevity of *but* correlates with its light backgrounded touch, as in (22).

(22)   They promised they would contact me. Nevertheless/But they never called back.

Factor Da2: Phonological Similarity to Other Morphemes in the Lexicon

The phonological shape of an uttered morpheme may activate other morphemes in the language's lexicon that sound similar. Here, "activate" means (to make possible) to raise attention. This effect can be desirable where the activated morphemes enhance the communicative intention, or undesirable if they detract from it. To illustrate the desirable case, a new product name like *Nyquil* for a medication to aid sleep was presumably coined because it phonologically suggests the words *night* and *tranquil*, whose meanings suit the product's intended image. Also, undesirable associations may have motivated people who used to stress the second syllable of *Uranus* and *harass* to switch to stressing the first syllable.

2.5. Factors Involving Properties of the Referent (E)

All the factors in this chapter outside those in group E raise or lower attention on an object regardless of its identity or content. The E factors raise or lower attention on an object because of the identity or content of that object.

Factor E1: Referential Divergence from Norms

A referent's divergence from certain norms tends to foreground it. Such norms, and deviations from them, include ordinariness versus unusualness, neutral affect versus affective intensity, and genericness versus specificity.

To illustrate this, relative to cultural and other experiential norms, a more unusual referent tends to attract greater attention than a more ordinary referent, as the referent of *hop* does relative to that of *walk*, as in (23a). Similarly, a referent with greater affective intensity tends to evoke greater attention than one with lesser intensity, as the referent of *scream* does relative to that of *shout*, as in (23b). Finally, a more specific referent tends to attract greater attention than a more general referent, as the referent of *drown* does relative to that of *die*, as seen in (23c).

(23) a. He hopped/walked to the store.
      b. She screamed/shouted to him.
      c. He drowned/died.

Factor E2: Direct Reference to Attention in the Addressee

All the other factors presented in this chapter exert their effect on the hearer's attention by acting directly on the cognitive mechanisms of the hearer that automatically direct and set attention with respect to some element within his or her experiential field. For example, heavy stress on a form automatically engages the hearer's attention on the referent of the form. Only factor E2 explicitly refers to the dimension of attention itself and to some value along it and prescribes how the hearer is to direct and set his or her attention. The effectiveness of this factor relies not on the triggering of automatic cognitive mechanisms, but on a further cognitive mechanism of the hearer, one that is under his or her conscious control and that can affect the directing and setting of attention deliberately.

Simply as part of their basic meaning, many predicative morphemes refer to higher or lower attention in the sentient referent of their subject NP, as in *I paid attention to/ignored what he said*, as well as in the sentient referent of their object or other complement, as in *I alerted her to the risk*. When such morphemes are used as directives to the addressee—for example, in (active or passive) imperative, hortative, or modal forms—they directly call on the hearer to allocate either more or less attention to an indicated entity, as seen in (24a) and (24b), respectively.

(24) a. Pay attention to the movie!
         Be alerted that this is only a copy of the original painting.
         You should note their sincerity.
      b. Nevermind what I said!
         Disregard their appearance.

2.6. Factors Involving the Relation between Reference and Its Representation (F)

There appears to be a general attentional bias in language users toward content over form. The hearer typically attends to what the speaker means or can be inferred to mean, more than to what the speaker has actually said in order to represent this meaning. The hearer even strains against distractions to stay attuned to the speaker's meaning—though as they increase, such distractions can garner progressively more of the hearer's attention.

Factor F1: The Reference versus Its Representation

Factor F1 captures what appears to be a general and default attentional tendency for both speaker and hearer: more attention goes to the concept expressed by a linguistic form than to the shape of that form. That is, a form's reference is more salient than how the form is constituted as a representation. This holds for forms ranging from a single morpheme to an expression (or to an extended discourse, for that matter). For example, at the single morpheme level, if a wife says (25a) to her husband, the occurrence of the morpheme *sick* is likely to direct the husband's attention more to its referent 'sickness' than to its phonological representation consisting of the sound sequence [s]-[ɪ]-[k]. This same phonological point can be made at the level of the whole expression in (25a). In addition, though, if the "representation" of an expression as covered by factor F1 can be taken also to include the particular words and constructions selected to constitute the expression, a further observation follows. The husband in this example is later more likely to remember the general reference of the sentence than its specific wording. Thus, he might well be able to recall that his wife telephonically learned from her sister of her illness earlier that day, but he might not be able to recall whether this conception was represented, say, by (25a), (25b), or (25c) (here, knowing that *Judy* is her sister's name). If the pattern of memory of an event correlates at least in part with the pattern of attention on an event during its occurrence, then findings like the present type would be evidence for greater attention on a reference than on its representation.

(25)   a. My sister called and said she was very sick this morning.
       b. My sister called this morning to tell me that she was feeling really sick.
       c. Judy said she was very ill when she called today.

Factor F2: Intended versus Actual Reference and Representation

A speaker's actual linguistic expression often poorly represents the conceptual complex that he or she had intended to express. It can even literally represent a somewhat different complex. Using background and contextual knowledge, a hearer in this circumstance can often infer the conceptual complex that the speaker had intended to express. He or she can also infer the well-formed linguistic expression that might have best represented that complex. By factor F2, the hearer's attention tends to go more to the speaker's inferably intended reference and its presumed well-formed representation. It tends to go less to the speaker's actual representation and its literal reference.

As noted, a speaker's actual expression can literally represent a conception somewhat different from the inferably intended one. In one type of this phenomenon, the speaker uses a form whose referent does not correspond to the surrounding physical context, as in (26a) and (26b) (both constructed examples). Here, in processing the discrepancy, the hearer generally infers that the speaker must have meant to refer to the actual elements of the situation and so attends more to that probably intended reference than to the expressed one. Here, as in all the following examples, the hearer might not even notice the flawed reference and be aware only of the likely intended reference.

(26)   a. How can you stand there and tell me you have no time?!
           <said to someone sitting>
       b. Here, hand this to the baby.
           <passing spoon of applesauce to spouse to feed to baby>

In another type of misrepresentation, words with the appropriate referents are present but in the wrong locations in the expression, as in the case of the lexical spoonerism in (27) (an overheard example). Here, the hearer notices a conflict between the literal reference and his or her background knowledge of conceptual complexes that are more frequent or make more sense. He or she infers that the latter was the speaker's intended reference and attends more to that than to the literal reference.

(27)   Students believe that every solution has a problem.

Other cases involve poor, rather than literally incorrect, representation. In one such type, the speaker talks around a forgotten term. Thus, the speaker of (28) (heard on radio) presumably would have wanted to say *Haven't those negotiations been overtaken by events* but was momentarily unable to retrieve the predicate expression and so, through several false starts, found another way to convey roughly the same idea. Perhaps most hearers did not notice the false starts and circumlocution but attentionally honed to the concept the speaker aimed to express.

(28)   Haven't those negotiations [pause] sort of passed by events, [pause]—aren't they outdated?

Factor F3: Degree of Deviation by the Actual Representation from the Intended One

For each way that a speaker's expression can deviate from a presumed intended one, there may be a certain approximate "grace" degree of divergence that would typically attract virtually no attention from the hearer. Beyond that grace amount, though, it would seem that the greater the degree of deviation, the greater the hearer's attention is on the presence of the deviation, as well as on its shape and perhaps also on its referent. For example, a generous grace deviation seems to be accorded to such discourse phenomena as self-correction, overlap, incompleteness, and low specificity—the kinds of characteristics that stand out in a linguistic transcription of a conversation but that are barely noticed by the interlocutors. On the other hand, some deviations can attract strong attention. Examples might be a speaker's addressing his or her interlocutor by the wrong name or using an inappropriate marker along the familiarity-formality scale in a language that has such forms.

2.7. Factors Involving the Occurrence of Representation (G)

The Inclusion of Representation (Ga)

Factor Ga1: Presence versus Absence of Explicit Representation

By factor Ga1, the presence within discourse of overt linguistic forms explicitly referring to a concept foregrounds the concept. And the absence of forms referring to a concept that might otherwise be represented backgrounds that concept. This is the factor underlying the whole of the "windowing of attention" analysis in Talmy (2000a: chapter 4).

As background for factor Ga1, a speaker in communicating can have a certain conceptual complex that he or she wants to cause to become replicated in the addressee's cognition. The conceptual complex is typically too rich to capture in full scope and detail in a brief enough interval for any cognitively feasible system of representation. For this problem, one of the solutions that seems to have emerged in the evolution of language is a cognitive process of "abstractive representation." By this process, the speaker selects only a subset out of the multiplicity of aspects in his or her more extensive conceptual complex for explicit representation by the linguistic elements of his or her utterance. By a complementary cognitive process of "reconstitution," the hearer then uses this partial explicit representation to reconstitute or "flesh out" a replete conceptual complex sufficiently close to the original one in the speaker. In this reconstitution process, the hearer must assume or infer the inexplicit material, mostly through contextual or background knowledge.

To illustrate this, consider the case in which I am a guest in the house of a host. We are both sitting near an open window, and I am feeling cold. Here, my extended conceptual complex includes general background knowledge, for example, physical knowledge, such as that air is typically colder outside a house than inside and can enter through an aperture; psychological knowledge, such as that a person can feel uncomfortable from contact with colder air; and sociocultural knowledge, such as that a guest typically does not act directly on the property of a host other than that assigned for his or her use.

As noted, even just this most immediately relevant conceptual complex cannot be explicitly represented briefly by language. Instead, by the principle of abstractive representation, I must select a subset of concepts in the complex for overt expression, for example, by saying (29). My host will then reconstitute much of the remainder of my conceptual complex.

(29)   Could you please close the window?

Where factor Ga1 comes in is that the selection of concepts for explicit expression is not an attentionally neutral act, but rather one that foregrounds the selected concepts relative to those in the conceptual complex remaining unexpressed. Moreover, the explicitly represented concepts tend to determine the center of a gradient of attention: greatest at the explicitly represented concepts, less over the remaining concepts within the conceptual complex, and radially decreasing over the rest of one's skein of knowledge. Thus, my utterance will tend to direct my host's attention most on the window and its closing; somewhat less on the likelihood of my feeling cold or on his need to get up from where he is sitting to walk over to the window; and quite little on how his window compares with other window designs.

Factor Ga2: The Occurrent Reference Instead of Alternatives

The process of abstractive representation under factor Ga1 has a corollary. A speaker can generally choose a number of different subsets of aspects from the original conceptual complex, and each of these alternative subsets could be used equally well by the hearer to flesh out something like the original complex. This is a foundational property of language that I termed "conceptual alternativity" (Talmy 2000a: chapter 3). Nevertheless, such alternatives of expression are not attentionally equivalent. Where one expression explicitly represents one set of concepts, leaving the hearer to infer the remaining concepts, another expression would directly express some of the previously inferred concepts, while leaving to inference some concepts previously expressed overtly. Since overtly expressed concepts tend to attract more attention than concepts only inferred, the speaker's choice of one expression among alternatives ends up as a linguistic device for attention setting.

Thus, in the guest-host situation cited above, instead of saying (29), I as guest could alternatively have said (30) to my host. These two sentences select different subsets of aspects out of my extended conceptual complex. In fact, they do not share a single morpheme. But, given his largely comparable contextual and background knowledge, the addressee is likely to reconstruct roughly the same conceptual complex from one sentence as from the other and, indeed, roughly the same one as my own original conceptual complex. Nevertheless, the two reconstructions are not identical since, among other things, the choice in the first sentence to refer to window-closing foregrounds that aspect of the situation, leaving the addressee to infer the backgrounded elements, such as that I am feeling cold, while the second sentence's choice of referring to temperature now foregrounds that aspect, while leaving it to the host to infer the backgrounded notions, such as that he will need to close the window. In addition, the associated radial gradient of attention shifts its center, and hence its penumbra. The speaker choice of referring to window-closing might secondarily raise in salience, say, the path that the host must take to the window, while the choice of referring to the chilliness might secondarily foreground concern over catching cold.

(30)   It's a bit chilly in here.

The Availability of Representation (Gb)

Factor Gb1: Presence versus Absence in the Lexicon of a Morpheme for a Particular Concept

It may turn out that the occurrence of a morpheme, one that represents a particular concept, in the lexicon of a speaker's language makes it possible for the speaker to attend to that concept. There is, of course, no need to have monomorphemic representation of some concept for a speaker to be able to do so. Most concepts, after all, are represented compositionally. Nevertheless, the presence in the speaker's lexicon of a morpheme that represents a certain concept may facilitate that concept's appearance in the speaker's consciousness. For example, the concept 'a warm glow of pleasure from innocent pride in a close kin's (or one's own) accomplishment' can occur in the thought of an English speaker, but it is likelier to do so in the thought of a speaker of Yiddish, whose lexicon includes a morpheme for this concept, *nakhes*.

2.8. Factors Involving Properties of Temporal Progression (H)

The Recency of Representation (Ha)

Factor Ha1: Current versus Prior Forms

One aspect of a hearer's attention, it seems, tends to be more on the linguistic forms currently being uttered by the speaker than on previously uttered forms. One function of this aspect of attention, perhaps in conjunction with working memory, might be to abet the hearer's processing of the forms, including double-checks on the identity of the forms, a first-level sorting of their content, and relating them to what had just preceded.

Optimally, it seems, a hearer's attentional capacity can concurrently cover or can switch fast enough among various aspects of the speaker's discourse. Such aspects can include the currently uttered forms, the significance of previously uttered forms, and the overall conceptual model that the discourse is progressively building up. But these various calls on the hearer's attentional capacity can at times conflict. Thus, if a hearer allocates too much attention, say, to the import of a previously uttered portion of discourse, he or she may miss aspects of the currently uttered portion.

Factor Ha2: Recency of Last Reference or Occurrence

Under factor Ha2, the more recently a phenomenon has been referred to or has occurred, the more hearer attention that remains on that phenomenon or the more readily that his or her attention can be directed back to it. This factor corresponds to the "referential distance" component within the "referential accessibility" described by Givón (1990). He observes that, as the recency of a referent lessens, a speaker refers back to it by selecting a type of linguistic form located progressively further along a certain hierarchy, from a zero form through an unstressed pro-form through a stressed pro-form to a full lexical form. Although treatment of this behavior in the functionalist discourse tradition has seemingly dealt only with the case of prior linguistic reference to a phenomenon, we note that the nonlinguistic occurrence of a phenomenon evokes the same reflex. For example, let us say you are visiting me in my office and a man enters, says a few words to me, and leaves. I can refer to that man using a pronoun if I speak to you within a few minutes after his departure, saying for example, *He's the director of our lab*. But after a while, I would need to use a full lexical phrase, as in *That man who came in and spoke to me was the director of our lab*.

3. ATTENTIONAL EFFECTS RESULTING FROM COMBINING FACTORS

When the basic attentional factors combine and interact, the further attentional effects that result include incremental gradation, convergence, and conflict.

3.1. Gradation in Strength of Attention through Factor Combination

Factors can be incrementally added to produce a gradation in the degree of attention directed to some particular linguistic entity. To illustrate this, let a linguistic entity be the concept of 'agency'. Attention on agency incrementally increases by the successive addition of factors in the following series of otherwise comparable sentences. These sentences are all taken to refer to the same scene in which a group of diners—the agents—hand a goblet of wine from one to another as they sit around a banquet table. In (31a), a minimal background sense of agency is pragmatically inferable from the context (factor Ga1), though not specifically represented by the linguistic forms themselves. Agency is slightly more salient in (31b), where the intransitive verb *pass* includes indirect reference to an agent within its lexicalization (factor Ab3). Still more attention is on agency in (31c), whose passive syntax (in construction with a now transitive verb *pass*) directly represents the presence of an agent (factor Ba4—not included above). A sharp rise in attention on the agent occurs when it is explicitly referred to by an overt pronoun (factor Ga1), the oblique *them* in (31d). The agency is further foregrounded by the occurrence of this pronoun as subject in initial position (factors Ba1 and Ba2) in (31e). And finally, replacement of the pronoun by a full lexical noun (factor Aa1), as in (31f), foregrounds the Agent to the greatest degree.

(31)   a. The goblet slowly went around the banquet table.
　　　　b. The goblet slowly passed around the banquet table.
　　　　c. The goblet was slowly passed around the banquet table.
　　　　d. The goblet was slowly passed around the banquet table by them.
　　　　e. They slowly passed the goblet around the banquet table.
　　　　f. The diners slowly passed the goblet around the banquet table.

3.2. Reinforcement of an Attentional Pattern through Factor Convergence

Several factors can converge on the same linguistic entity to reinforce a particular level of salience, making it especially high or especially low. The grammar of a language is often organized so as to facilitate certain convergences. Thus, as seen in the final example sentence of the preceding series, (31f), English regularly foregrounds the concept of agency strongly through the convergence of all the following factor values: explicit representation (Ga1) by an open-class nominal (Aa1) in initial sentence position (Ba1) as grammatical subject (Ba2) of a verb lexicalized to apply to an Agent subject (Ab3).

3.3. Attentional Resultants of Factor Conflict

Two factors can conflict in their attentional effects, with the resolution usually either that one factor overrides the other or that they are in competition in which case the hearer's attention is divided or wavering between the two claims on it. For an example of override, consider the sentence in (32a). Here, the concept of 'aircraft' is relatively foregrounded in the constituent *plane* through the convergence of four factors. It is expressed in the lexical category highest on the attentional hierarchy, a noun (Aa1); it is the sole concept expressed in its morpheme (Ab1); it is in the prominent sentence-final position (Ba1); and it receives the heavy stress standard for such a final constituent (Dc4). By contrast, the same concept of 'aircraft' is relatively backgrounded within the constituent *flew* in (32b). It is backgrounded there through the same four factors: it appears in a lexical category lower on the attentional hierarchy, a verb; it is joined there by other concepts, namely, 'go' and 'by means of'; it is in a sentence position nonprominent in English, and it receives the relatively low stress of that position. Accordingly, an English speaker may hear this latter sentence as mainly conveying the fact of the journey per se to Key West and as including the idea of aeronautic means only as incidental background information. However, the further application of extra heavy stress (factor Db1) to the verb, as in (32c), now undoes the backgrounding effects of the four convergent factors. It overrides them and forces the foregrounding of the 'aircraft' concept.

(32)   a. I went to Key West last month by plane.
         b. I flew to Key West last month.
         c. I FLEW to Key West last month.

In the competition type of conflict, each of two or more factors calls on the hearer's limited attentional capacity for its own target, with the consequence that one or more of the targets receives less attention than it needs for adequate processing. For example, factor Ha1 calls on the hearer to allocate enough attention to the speaker's currently uttered forms for them to be processed in working memory. But if the speaker had just previously uttered an ill-formed sentence, factor F3 calls on the hearer to allocate enough attention to the discrepancy to puzzle out what the speaker might have intended to say. The hearer may not have enough attentional capacity to act on both factors adequately at the same time. The hearer might attend to the current words and leave the earlier undecipherable discourse unresolved, or he or she may work on the prior discourse while missing what is now being said, or even may allocate some attention to each task, performing neither of them well.

REFERENCES

Asher, Ron E. 1985. *Tamil*. Beckenham, UK: Croom Helm.

Bierwisch, Manfred. 1983. Psychologische Aspekte der Semantik natürlicher Sprachen. In Wolfgang Motsch and Dieter Viehweger, eds., *Richtungen der modernen Semantikforschung* 15–64. Berlin: Akademie Verlag.

Brugman, Claudia, and George Lakoff. 1988. Cognitive topology and lexical networks. In Steven L. Small, Garrison W. Cottrell, and Michael K. Tanenhaus, eds., *Lexical ambiguity resolution: Perspectives from psycholinguistics, neuropsychology, and artificial intelligence* 477–508. San Mateo, CA: Morgan Kaufmann.

Chafe, Wallace. 1994. *Discourse, consciousness, and time: The flow and displacement of conscious experience in speaking and writing*. Chicago: University of Chicago Press.

Fillmore, Charles J. 1975. An alternative to checklist theories of meaning. *Berkeley Linguistics Society* 1: 123–31.

Fillmore, Charles J. 1976. Frame semantics and the nature of language. *Annals of the New York Academy of Sciences: Conference on the Origin and Development of Language and Speech* 280: 20–32.

Fillmore, Charles J. 1982. Frame semantics. In Linguistic Society of Korea, ed., *Linguistics in the morning calm* 111–37. Seoul: Hanshin Publishing.

Fillmore, Charles J. 1997. *Lectures on deixis*. Stanford, CA: CSLI Publications. (First published as *Santa Cruz Lectures on Deixis*. Bloomington: Indiana University Linguistics Club, 1975)

Givón, Talmy. 1990. *Syntax: A functional-typological introduction.* Vol. 2. Amsterdam: John Benjamins.

Husserl, Edmund. 1970. *Logical investigations.* Trans. J. N. Findlay. 2 vols. London: Routledge and Kegan Paul.

Lakoff, George. 1987. *Women, fire and dangerous things: What categories reveal about the mind.* Chicago: University of Chicago Press.

Lambrecht, Knud. 1994. *Information structure and sentence form: A theory of topic, focus, and the mental representations of discourse referents.* Cambridge: Cambridge University Press.

Langacker, Ronald W. 1984. Active zones. *Berkeley Linguistics Society* 10: 172–88.

Langacker, Ronald W. 1987. *Foundations of cognitive grammar.* Vol. 1, *Theoretical prerequisites.* Stanford, CA: Stanford University Press.

Liddell, Scott K. 2003. *Grammar, gesture, and meaning in American Sign Language.* Cambridge: Cambridge University Press.

Talmy, Leonard. 1972. Semantic structures in English and Atsugewi. PhD dissertation, University of California at Berkeley.

Talmy, Leonard. 1976. Semantic causative types. In Masayoshi Shibatani, ed., *Syntax and semantics*, vol. 6, *The grammar of causative constructions* 43–116. New York: Academic Press.

Talmy, Leonard. 1978a. Figure and ground in complex sentences. In Joseph Greenberg, ed., *Universals of human language,* vol. 4, *Syntax* 625–49. Stanford, CA: Stanford University Press.

Talmy, Leonard. 1978b. Relations between subordination and coordination. In Joseph H. Greenberg, ed., *Universals of human language,* vol. 4, *Syntax* 487–513. Stanford, CA: Stanford University Press.

Talmy, Leonard. 1978c. The relation of grammar to cognition—a synopsis. In David Waltz ed., *Proceedings of TINLAP-2* 14–24. New York: Association for Computing Machinery.

Talmy, Leonard. 1983. How language structures space. In Herbert L. Pick, Jr., and Linda P. Acredolo, eds., *Spatial orientation: Theory, research, and application* 225–82. New York: Plenum Press.

Talmy, Leonard. 1985. Lexicalization patterns: Semantic structure in lexical forms. In Timothy Shopen, ed., *Language typology and syntactic description*, vol. 3, *Grammatical categories and the lexicon* 57–149. Cambridge: Cambridge University Press.

Talmy, Leonard. 1988a. Force dynamics in language and cognition. *Cognitive Science* 12: 49–100.

Talmy, Leonard. 1988b. The relation of grammar to cognition. In Brygida Rudzka-Ostyn, ed., *Topics in cognitive linguistics* 165–205. Amsterdam: John Benjamins.

Talmy, Leonard. 1991. Path to realization: A typology of event conflation. *Berkeley Linguistics Society* 17: 480–519.

Talmy, Leonard. 1995a. The cognitive culture system. *The Monist* 78: 80–116.

Talmy, Leonard. 1995b. Narrative structure in a cognitive framework. In Gail Bruder, Judy Duchan, and Lynne Hewitt, eds., *Deixis in narrative: A cognitive science perspective* 421–60. Hillsdale, NJ: Lawrence Erlbaum.

Talmy, Leonard. 1996a. Fictive motion in language and "ception." In Paul Bloom, Mary Peterson, Lynn Nadel, and Merrill Garrett, eds., *Language and space* 211–76. Cambridge, MA: MIT Press.

Talmy, Leonard. 1996b. The windowing of attention in language. In Masayoshi Shibatani and Sandra Thompson, eds., *Grammatical constructions: Their form and meaning* 235–87. Oxford: Oxford University Press.

Talmy, Leonard. 2000a. *Toward a cognitive semantics.* Vol. 1, *Concept structuring systems.* Cambridge: MIT Press.

Talmy, Leonard. 2000b. *Toward a cognitive semantics.* Vol. 2, *Typology and process in concept structuring.* Cambridge: MIT Press.

Talmy, Leonard. 2003a. Recombinance in the evolution of language. *Chicago Linguistic Society 39* (The Panels).

Talmy, Leonard. 2003b. The representation of spatial structure in spoken and signed language. In Karen Emmorey, ed., *Perspectives on classifier constructions in sign language* 169–95. Mahwah, NJ: Lawrence Erlbaum.

Talmy, Leonard. Forthcoming. How language directs attention. Cambridge: MIT Press.

Tomlin, Russell S. 1995. Focal attention, voice, and word order: An experimental, cross-linguistics study. In Pamela Downing and Michael Noonan, eds., *Word order in discourse* 517–54. Amsterdam: John Benjamins.

Zubin, David A., and Lynne E. Hewitt 1995. The deictic center: A theory of deixis in narrative. In Judith F. Duchan, Gail A. Bruder, and Lynne E. Hewitt, eds., *Deixis in narrative: A cognitive science perspective* 129–55. Mahwah, NJ: Lawrence Erlbaum.

CHAPTER 12

....

FORCE DYNAMICS

....

WALTER DE MULDER

1. INTRODUCTION

....

According to Leonard Talmy (2000: 4), Cognitive Semantics is the study of the way conceptual content is organized in language. In Talmy's view, a sentence (or other portion of discourse) does not objectively represent its referent scene, but it evokes in the listener a cognitive representation, defined as "an emergent, compounded by various cognitive processes out of the referential meanings of the sentence elements, understanding of the present situation, general knowledge, and so on" (2000: 93, note 2). Talmy furthermore proposes that the grammatical, closed-class elements in a sentence convey the *structure* of the cognitive representation, while the lexical, open-class elements mainly contribute to sentence content. Across languages, the set of grammatically specified notions "collectively constitutes the conceptual structuring system of language" (2000: 21), which patterns in five schematic systems (formerly called "imaging systems," see Talmy 2000: 40):

- a. "Configurational structure" imposes a particular spatial and temporal structure on referent scenes viewed as composed of entities of a particular nature in particular relationships (Talmy 2000: 47; 467).
- b. "Location of perspective point" adds the point of view from which the scene is conceived, or "ceived" (for the notion of "ceiving," see Talmy 1996a; 2000: 99–175).
- c. "Distribution of attention" concerns the way attention is distributed over aspects of the referent scene and assigns it a Figure/Ground distinction.
- d. "Force dynamics" "pertains to the linguistic representation of force interactions and causal relations occurring between certain entities within the structured situation" (Talmy 2000: 12).

e. "Cognitive state" is concerned with the speaker's knowledge status or the referent scene's status of reality, as expressed by mood, evidentials, and modal verbs (Talmy 2000: 1–18, 41, 56, 92).

The schematic system "Force dynamics" is first defined by Talmy as a fundamental semantic category in the realm of physical force and is viewed in particular as a generalization over the linguistic notion of "causative" (see Talmy 1981, 1985, 1988, 2000: 409–70). Metaphorical transfers subsequently generalize force-dynamic conceptions to the domains of internal psychological relationships and social interactions. As such, for instance, the system of English modals is analyzed in force-dynamic terms before it is shown how force dynamics also partially structures discourse and argumentation. I will largely follow this order of presentation in section 2 of this chapter. In section 3, I will turn to some of the research engendered by the notion of force dynamics, such as Jackendoff's (1990) endeavor to incorporate force dynamics in his conceptual semantics, and several studies of modal verbs in Cognitive Linguistics. In the final section, I will discuss how comparable notions, such as energy transfer, as they are introduced in Langacker (1990, 1991), can be usefully employed in the definition of grammatical categories such as 'subject' and 'object' and in the analysis of syntactic structure.

2. TALMY'S VIEW ON FORCE DYNAMICS AS A FUNDAMENTAL LINGUISTIC CATEGORY

2.1. The Fundamental Patterns

A force-dynamic pattern which underlies "all more complex force-dynamic patterns is the steady-state opposition of two forces" (Talmy 2000: 413). In language, the two participants in this fundamental scene are assigned two different semantic roles: (i) the first participant, the "Agonist," is the participant in focal attention, since the salient issue in the interaction is whether the Agonist can manifest its force tendency or not; (ii) the second participant, the "Antagonist," is considered for the effect it has on the Agonist, namely, overcoming the latter's force tendency or not. Language presents entities as possessing intrinsic force tendencies: they are held to tend intrinsically toward motion or rest, or rather toward action or inaction. Their confrontation yields a resultant, which presents the Agonist as being either in action or in inaction.

This linguistic conception of forces and their interaction results in four basic force-dynamic patterns, which are illustrated in sentences (1a)–(1d):[1]

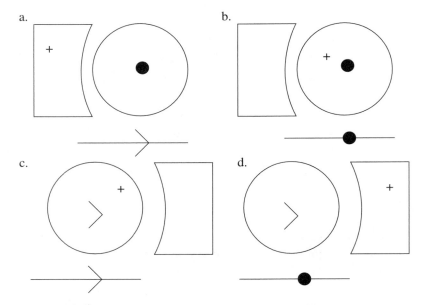

Figure 12.1. The basic steady-state force-dynamic pattern (based on Talmy 2000: 415)

    a. The Agonist's intrinsic tendency toward rest is overcome by a stronger Antagonist, which forces it to move.

    b. The Agonist's tendency toward rest is stronger than the force opposing it; consequently, the Agonist remains in place.

    c. The Agonist's inherent tendency toward motion is opposed by the Antagonist, but the Agonist is the stronger entity.

    d. The Agonist has a tendency toward motion, but the Antagonist is stronger and blocks it.

(1)   a. The ball kept rolling because of the wind blowing on it.

    b. The shed kept standing despite the gale wind blowing against it.

    c. The ball kept rolling despite the stiff grass.

    d. The log kept lying on the incline because of the ridge there.

Patterns a and d, illustrated in (1a) and (1d), where the Antagonist continuously impinges on the Agonist, are called cases of "extended causation" (see Talmy 2000: 415–16). Diagrammatically, the four basic force-dynamic patterns are represented in figure 12.1.

Adopting "force dynamics" as a semantic category enables us to integrate in a unified framework notions expressed by different grammatical categories: "honorary" auxiliaries such as *keep -ing* (as in 1a–1d); conjunctions such as *because* (1a, 1d) or *although*; prepositions such as *because of* (1a, 1d) and *despite* (1b, 1c), but also *against* (see also Schepping 1991 on French *contre*; Kristoffersen 2001 on Norwegian *mot*; and Beliën 2002 on Dutch *tegen*), German *über* (Meex 2002), or French *à travers* 'through'

(Stosic 2002); and, finally, expressions related to associated schematic models, such as STRAIGHT (Cienki 1998).

2.2. Complex Patterns

By adding supplementary factors to the four basic patterns presented above, more complex force-dynamic patterns are created.

Change over Time

The relation between the Agonist and the Antagonist can change over time, as can be seen in examples (2)–(5), where—unlike in (1a)–(1d)—the Antagonist is expressed by the subject.

(2)   The ball's hitting it made the lamp topple from the table.
(3)   The water's dripping on it made the fire die down.
(4)   The plug's coming loose let the water flow from the tank.
(5)   The stirring rod's breaking let the particles settle.

Unlike examples (1a) and (1d), these sentences exemplify 'change over time', in that they do not show steady impingement of the Antagonist on the Agonist; in (2) and (3), the Antagonist enters the state of impingement, while (4) and (5) involve cessation of impingement.

   Examples (2) and (3) are referred to by Talmy (2000: 418) as cases of "onset causation"; furthermore, (2) expresses prototypical causation, as the Antagonist's action on the Agonist reverses the latter's intrinsic tendency. Examples (4) and (5), where cessation of impingement is at stake, involve the concept of 'letting'. Here, the prototypical case is the one where the Antagonist disengages and allows the Agonist to manifest its force tendency (as in 4); in the less prototypical case (5), the Antagonist ceases to impinge on the Agonist and allows it to come to rest.

   Examples (2)–(5) show that the force-dynamic analysis allows 'causing' and 'letting' to be grouped together because these concepts are viewed as complexes of more primitive concepts that can recombine in different ways (Talmy 2000: 419, 428).[2] Force dynamics can thus be seen as a generalization over the causatives studied by Talmy (1976; 2000: 471–549).[3]

   Time can also affect the relation between the Antagonist and the Agonist in a less radical way, when the impingement of the Antagonist on the Agonist does not disappear altogether, but gradually changes the balance of forces between Agonist and Antagonist, as shown in (6):

(6)   The enemy overcame us as we stood on the border.

Finally, corresponding to examples (4) and (5), where the Antagonist moves away from the Agonist, there also exist patterns of "extended letting," where the Antagonist remains away:

(7)   The plug's staying loose let the water drain from the tank.
(8)   The fan's being broken let the smoke hang still in the chamber.

In fact, these patterns can be seen as the negation of the basic steady-state patterns:[4] whereas in the latter patterns, Agonist and Antagonist are engaged in an opposition of forces, in (7) and (8), absence of possible engagement is expressed. This is why the processes expressed in these sentences are called "secondary steady-state force-dynamic processes": they are derived from the basic steady-state patterns.

Agency

As is pointed out by Talmy (1976; 2000: 509–14), including an agent in a causative sentence makes it semantically more complex, because the intention of the agent to make something happen initiates a sequence of causally related events, from the volitional act of the agent via the moving parts of his or her body and other intermediate events to the final event (see also Croft 1991: 163–65). The resulting action sequence can be expressed by mentioning only the agent and the final event, possibly adding the penultimate event, or just its instrument (Talmy 2000: 421):

(9)   I broke the vase [(by hitting it) with a ball].

The agent can be omitted, as in (10):

(10)   The ball's hitting it broke the vase.

2.3. Alternatives of Foregrounding

While "all of the interrelated factors in any force-dynamic pattern are necessarily co-present wherever that pattern is involved" (Talmy 2000: 422), they do not all attract the same amount of attention: elements explicitly referred to, expressed earlier in the sentence, or figuring higher in some case hierarchy, tend to receive more attention. The other elements are still implicitly present, though. In (11), for instance, the Agonist is foregrounded as a result of its subject status, whereas the Antagonist is backgrounded, since it is omitted (11a) or expressed as an oblique object (11b); in (12), the distribution of attention is reversed, since now the Antagonist is in subject position and the Agonist in direct object position:

(11)   a. The ball kept rolling.
        b. The ball is rolling because of the wind.
(12)   a. The wind kept the ball rolling.
        b. The wind is making the ball roll.

2.4. Metaphorical Extensions

Talmy's analysis of the basic and complex force-dynamic patterns shows that force dynamics is a fundamental category of language. As such, it has served as a basic domain for metaphorical transfers, allowing language users to conceptualize force-dynamic patterns in domains other than the physical one.

Force Dynamics in the Psychological Domain

Utterances such as (13)–(15) present the self as divided into a desiring part (the Agonist) and a blocking part (the Antagonist), which represents a sense of responsibility or propriety and can be regarded as an internalization of social values:

(13)   He held himself back from responding.
(14)   He exerted himself in pressing against the jammed door.

These opposing elements are also present in (15), although the lexical semantics of the verb *refrain* has the effect of presenting the psyche as a whole:

(15)   He refrained from responding.

As a consequence of the conception of the self as an entity in which opposing forces are at work, the overt manifestation of force by sentient beings is generally interpreted as arising from psychological driving forces, rather than as originating in the body itself, as can be shown by comparing examples (16) and (17):

(16)   The new dam resisted the pressure of the water against it.
(17)   The man resisted the pressure of the crowd against him.

Whereas the dam is supposed to stay in place as a result of its physical properties, it is not his physical, bodily properties that make the man resist the pressure of the crowd; rather, it is his underlying psychological force dynamics, in particular a continuous expenditure of force, originating in the goal-oriented part of his psyche.

In general, the central part of the psyche is conceived as having a natural tendency toward rest, which has to be overcome by an expenditure of energy by some more peripheral part; moreover, the body is viewed as an essentially inert entity, requiring animation to be moved into action. These aspects can be combined as in example (18), which thus illustrates the "generative" capacity of force-dynamic patterns to embed and form increasingly complex patterns:

(18)   Fear kept preventing the acrobat from letting the elephant hold up his tightrope.

Force Dynamics in the Social Domain

The force-dynamic pattern can also be used to structure the social domain, as illustrated in (19):

(19)   a. He's under a lot of pressure to keep silent.
       b. Our government exerted pressure on that country to toe our line.
       c. Getting job security relieved the pressure on her to perform.
       d. The gang pushed him to do things he didn't want to do.

The metaphorical transfer underlying the examples in (19) is based on the analogy between the direct exertion of force of one object on another in order to make it move or manifest some other action, and "one sentient entity's production of stimuli, including communication, that is perceived by another sentient being, and interpreted as reason for volitionally performing a particular action" (Talmy 2000: 438).

Force Dynamics in the Psychophysical and Interpersonal Domains

Force-dynamic concepts in the physical realm also transfer easily to the psychophysical and interpersonal domains, as can be seen from the fact that the basic deontic uses of the English modals—core modals as well as honorary modals—can be defined in force-dynamic terms.[5] As such, *can* "in the context of *not* . . . indicates that the subject has a tendency toward the action expressed by the following verb, that some factor opposes that tendency, and that the latter is stronger, blocking the event" (Talmy 2000: 441); likewise, "*may not* indicates an authority's blockage to the expression of the subject's tendency" (2000: 441); and "*must* and *had better* in the context of *not* suggest an active social pressure acting against the subject to maintain him in place" (2000: 441). The subject slots of these verbs are mostly filled by the Agonist, a sentient being involved in a psychosocial, rather than a purely physical, interaction:

(20)   John *can/may/must/should/ought/would/need/dare/had better* not leave the house.

In (21) and (22), however, the same verbs allow nonsentient beings as subjects:

(21)   The cake *can/may/must/* . . . stay in the box.
(22)   The pear *could/may/must/* . . . be ripe by now.

Still these examples do not contravene the idea that the verbs refer in their basic usage to psychosocial interaction. In (21), the Agonist does not fill the subject slot, but it is implicitly present, as an Agent controlling the actions of the Patient, which fills the subject slot (Talmy 2000: 442). In (22), the modals are used with an epistemic meaning; following Sweetser (1984, 1990), Talmy (2000: 443) analyzes these epistemic uses as resulting from a metaphorical transfer from the psychosocial domain to the domain of semantic inference, from "the interpersonal impingements to the impingements of arguments on each other or on the reasoner, constraining him towards certain conclusions" (2000: 443).

Since verbs such as *make, let, have,* and *help* take a *to*-less infinitive just like the standard modal verbs (as in examples 2–5) and since these verbs can be analyzed in force-dynamic terms, Talmy (2000: 443–44) groups them in the "greater modal system," which, in English, makes up one grammatical expression of the semantic model of force dynamics. However, unlike the core and "honorary" (see note 5) modals whose subject position is occupied by the Agonist, *make, let, have,* and *help* select the Antagonist as their subject. They share this characteristic with open-class verbs such as *forbid* and *require,* whose meaning can also be defined using force-dynamic concepts:

(23)   I forbid you to leave the house.
(24)   I require you to stay in the house.

Force Dynamics in Discourse

Argumentation in discourse can be interpreted in terms of forces opposing and reinforcing particular positions or points of view, an idea that is already implicitly present in Lakoff and Johnson's (1980) description of the metaphor ARGUMENT IS WAR. A force-dynamic interpretation of this domain also permits an analysis of the meaning of "logic-gators" (Talmy 2000: 452), words and expressions such as *yes but, besides, nevertheless, moreover, granted, instead, after all*, and *on the contrary*, which can be used to direct the flow of argumentation by expressing opposition or reinforcement with respect to points argued for or against (see also Oakley 2005).

Force dynamics also operates in other discourse phenomena, such as "discourse expectation," which Talmy (2000: 453) defines as "the moment-by-moment expectations of participants in a discourse as to the direction and content of succeeding terms." "Vector reversal," for instance, refers to a situation where a discourse participant discovers that his or her assumptions about the direction of the discourse are exactly the opposite of those held by the other participant. The following dialogue on a campus e-mail system may be cited as an illustration:

(25)   A titles message: "For Chinese students only."
        B protests that it is exclusionary.
        A responds that the intent was: 'Others need not bother to look'.

Whereas B interpreted A's title as exclusionary, A signals that it was his or her assumption that others would not want to read the message and that he or she wanted to spare them the trouble.

3. Force Dynamics as a Cognitive System: Talmy and Jackendoff Compared

Talmy's work on force dynamics has been taken up, integrated, or developed further by various linguists of cognitive persuasion. In this section, I will look at Jackendoff's (1990, 1996) integration of Talmy's account of force dynamics into his system of conceptual structure and conceptual semantics formalization. Before turning to the comparison proper, I will first shortly sketch Jackendoff's views on conceptual structure.

Jackendoff (1990: 9) conceives of conceptual structure as composed of "a finite set of mental primitives and a finite set of principles of mental combination"; the combinatorial structure of the theory should allow it to explain, among other things, the "creativity" of language (in a Chomskyan sense; see Jackendoff 1990:

8–9). Each of the primitive units, called "conceptual constituents," belongs to a small set of major conceptual categories such as Thing (or Object), Event, State, Action, Place, Path, Property, and Amount (Jackendoff 1990: 22, 43). The major syntactic constituents making up a sentence map onto these conceptual constituents: the sentence *John ran toward the house*, for instance, corresponds to an Event, *John* and *the house* to Things, and *toward the house* to a Path (Jackendoff 1990: 22). The combination of these constituents into larger structures produces predicate-argument structures, following elaboration rules such as (26):

(26)   [EVENT]   [$_{Event}$ GO ([THING], [PATH])]
       [$_{Event}$ STAY ([THING], [PLACE])]

                                  (Jackendoff 1990: 43)

This rule "says that a constituent of the category Event can be elaborated as either of the two Event-functions GO or STAY, each of which takes two arguments. The arguments of GO, which denotes motion along a path, are the Thing in motion and the Path it traverses. This structure is seen most transparently in a sentence like *Bill went to New York*. The arguments of STAY, which denotes stasis over a period of time, are the Thing standing still and its location, as seen in *Bill stayed in the kitchen*, for instance" (Jackendoff 1990: 44). In representations of this kind, the thematic roles introduced by Gruber (1965) can be redefined as "shorthand" for particular structural configurations. Theme, for instance, the thematic role which Gruber defined as the object in motion or being located, now corresponds to the first argument of the functions used in (26) and (27) (Jackendoff 1990: 46):[6]

(27)   [EVENT]   [$_{State}$ BE ([THING], [PLACE])]
       [$_{State}$ ORIENT ([THING], [PATH])]
       [$_{State}$ EXT ([THING], [PATH])]

                                  (Jackendoff 1990: 43)

In these representations, the BE-function serves to specify the location of objects (*The dog is in the park*), the ORIENT-function to specify their orientation (*The sign points toward New York*), and the EXT-function to specify the spatial extension of linear objects along a path (*The road goes from New York to San Francisco*) (Jackendoff 1990: 44).

If Theme is defined as the object in motion or being located, it cannot correspond to the semantic role filled by *Fred* in sentence (28), since Fred is not an object in motion or being located:

(28)   Sue hit Fred.

Sue obviously fills the Agent role in the sentence, but *Fred* cannot constitute the Theme; rather, Fred is the Patient, the role designating the person affected. In (28), the Patient is at the same time the Goal, but this is not necessarily the case, as can be seen in (29):

(29)   Pete hit the ball into the field.

In view of the fact that being a Patient does not exclude taking up other roles, Jackendoff (1990: 126) concludes that conceptual roles fall into two tiers: a thematic tier, with Source-Theme-Goal relations, and an action tier, with Actor-Patient relations. Sentence (28), then, would be represented as (28'):

(28')   Sue   hit   Fred
         Theme   Goal
         Actor   Patient

Actor and Patient are defined respectively as the first and the second argument of a new "affect" (AFF) relation. These elements allow Jackendoff to propose the following representation of sentence (30):

(30)   Harry prevented Sam from going away.
        CAUSE ([HARRY], [NOT   GO ([SAM], [AWAY])])])
        AFF ([SAM],)
        AFF ([HARRY], [SAM])

(Jackendoff 1990: 131)

Talmy's Agonist and Antagonist can now be identified with, respectively, the Patient and the Actor on the action tier, the first and the second argument of the AFF-function; note that the notation [AFF ([SAM],)], which is part of the thematic tier, signals "Actor only" (Jackendoff 1990: 128). Jackendoff subsequently analyzes other force-dynamic structures by reformulating existing functions or adding new ones. This can be illustrated by his analysis of sentence (31):

(31)   Sam resisted Harry.
        CS^u ([HARRY], [$_{Event}$])
        $REACT^-$ ([SAM], [HARRY])

(Jackendoff 1990: 137)

The thematic tier signals that "Harry is exerting effort toward the realization of some implicit Event, with undetermined outcome" (Jackendoff 1990: 137); CS denotes a function expressing the application of force, which can have three different values (cf. Talmy's "resultant"): CS^u denotes undetermined outcome as expressed by *try* or *pressure*; CS^+ denotes successful outcome and supplants the previous CAUSE; and CS^- denotes unsuccessful outcome as expressed by *fail* or *impede*. The new function REACT on the action tier is a sort of mirror image of AFF, with the Agonist as the first argument and the Antagonist as the second. However, the REACT function entails more than a simple reversal of the linking between semantic roles and syntactic functions, since verbs of reaction assign a more active role to the Agonist than the one described by the passive Patient role (Jackendoff 1990: 138). Nevertheless, without pursuing the issue, Jackendoff suggests that AFF and REACT are to be seen as alternative realizations of a more abstract function.

Jackendoff claims to have preserved Talmy's force-dynamic generalizations, but to have adapted them to conceptual semantics through the introduction of the following system (see Jackendoff 1996: 120):

a. Distinction between two opposed force entities: Antagonist (= Agent) and Agonist (= Patient)[7]
b. Patient action desired by Antagonist
c. Success of Antagonist

However, as already pointed out above, Jackendoff's conceptual semantics is a combinatorial system, where semantic representations are built up out of atomic "building blocks" (Taylor 1996). In this respect, his theory is different from Talmy's, where all force-dynamic elements are defined with respect to a basic scene, such that the presence of one part entails that of the others (Talmy 1996b: 267, cited by Lampert and Lampert 2000: 228; see also section 2) and where all elements are always present, although some may be backgrounded. This is relevant, for instance, with respect to the use of the prepositions *from* and *to* in examples (30) and (32):

(32)   Harry forced Sam to go away.
       CAUSE ([HARRY],   GO ([SAM], [AWAY]))
                         AFF ([SAM],)
       AFF ([HARRY], [SAM])

                                                      (Jackendoff 1990: 131)

As pointed out by Deane (1996: 60), the use of the prepositions in these examples is motivated, as can be seen from a comparison of *from* and *to* in (30) and (32) with the prepositions in italics in examples (33)–(35):[8]

(33)   a. In his foolishness, Sam has turned *to* robbery.
       b. Sam has turned *(away) from* the crimes of his youth.
(34)   a. Sam is inclined *toward* going away.
       b. Sam is inclined *against* going away.
(35)   a. Harry talked Sam *into* going away.
       b. Harry talked Sam *out of* going away.

In these examples, *to*, *toward*, and *into* denote that Sam's tendency (toward action) is directed toward a particular target (expressed in the subsequent noun phrase); *(away) from*, *against*, and *out of* (and the subsequent noun phrases), on the contrary, signal a tendency of Sam's that he is no longer inclined to. Briefly, the prepositions get their meaning by referring to the direction of the Agonist's tendencies as represented within Talmy's force-dynamic scene. Jackendoff's representations, however, do not contain any such reference to these tendencies and thus seem unable to capture what is shared by both sets of prepositions. In fact, the only difference between (30) and (32) is the negative marker, which corresponds not to the difference between the individual items *to* and *from*, but to that between *force to* and *prevent from*. In other words, in Jackendoff's approach, *to* is represented as a meaningless infinitive marker, without any link to the preposition *to*; in Talmy's approach, on the contrary, as in other cognitive approaches, the use of *to* as an infinitive marker is related to its uses as a preposition.

Jackendoff can, of course, enrich his representation—whose sole aim in *Semantic Structures* was to express the correspondence between conceptual structure and syntactic argument structure. He could, for instance, bring the prepositions closer to their spatial meanings (Jackendoff 1996: 123). The question remains, however, whether he could also explain the motivated changes of interpretation these prepositions go through in context.

4. Force-Dynamic Analyses of Modals

Talmy's research on force dynamics, and his views on modals in particular, has brought about various studies developing or taking issue with Talmy's account. In sections 4.1 and 4.2, I will consider Sweetser's and Johnson's analyses of modal meaning and compare their account with Talmy's on four key issues. In section 4.3, I will pay attention to Langacker's and Achard's conception of modals as a more grammaticalized category.

4.1. Sweetser's (1990) and Johnson's (1987) Analyses of Modal Meanings

An important result that has come out of Sweetser's (1990: 28, 50) research is that there exists a general tendency among language users to speak of our internal world by employing language that normally refers to the external world. Reasoning processes, for instance, are modeled after real-world actions, as subject to compulsions, obligations, etc. (Sweetser 1990: 49–50). This metaphorical transfer explains the systematic polysemy of modal verbs in many unrelated languages,[9] whereby their "epistemic" meanings denoting necessity, probability, and possibility have been derived from their "root" meanings, denoting obligation, permission, or ability.[10] For Sweetser, modality is characterized as "basically referring to intentional, directed forces and barriers" (52), and its experientially basic level of operation is the sociophysical world; this is in contradistinction to Talmy, who holds that the physical level of force dynamics is the experientially basic one and that the sociophysical is already structured by a metaphorical projection of the basic folk model of physical force (Lampert and Lampert 2000: 221, 248, 278). Nevertheless, since Talmy also believes that the modals in their basic usage refer to psychosocial rather than to physical interaction (Talmy 2000: 441; see also Lampert and Lampert 2000: 248), Sweetser can adopt Talmy's definitions for some of the modals. *May*, for

F1

Figure 12.2. The COMPULSION schema

instance, is said to express "a potential but absent barrier" (Sweetser 1990: 52). For other modals, Sweetser prefers to change Talmy's definitions: instead of Talmy's analysis of *must* "as a barrier restricting one's domain of action to a single act" (Sweetser 1990: 52), she describes *must* as expressing a positive compulsion to do something. As pointed out by Pelyvás (1996: 124), the contrast between these two definitions could be more apparent than real, as the notion of 'compulsion' is relevant when one adopts the doer's point of view, and that of 'restricting the subject' when one adopts the speaker's point of view.

According to Sweetser (1990: 61), only the "image-schematic" properties of semantic structure are preserved in the metaphorical transfer that maps the structure of the "root" (source) domain onto the "epistemic" (target) domain (see also Lampert and Lampert 2000: 252). Image schemas have been defined by Johnson (1987: 29) as recurrent patterns, shapes, or regularities which "emerge as meaningful structures for us chiefly at the level of our bodily movements through space, our manipulations of objects, and our perceptual interactions" (see also Lakoff 1987; Gibbs and Colston 1995; Oakley, this volume, chapter 9). These patterns have Gestalt-like qualities: they are seen as unified wholes whose parts only get meaning from the unity and coherence of the whole (Johnson 1987: 41, 44).

Johnson (1987) proposes to view the notion of force in the root senses of the modal verbs as image-schematic force Gestalts. Thus, *must* is analyzed in terms of the image schema of COMPULSION, which develops from our experience of being moved by external forces. It can be summarized by the schematic representation in figure 12.2, where the dark arrow represents an actual force vector and the broken arrow a potential force vector (Johnson 1987: 45, 51):

May, on the other hand, is defined by the ABSENCE or REMOVAL OF RESTRAINT schema, which originates in our experiences of the removal of barriers and of the absence of possible restraints (e.g., door openings) and is represented by figure 12.3 (Johnson 1987: 46–47, 52).

Following Sweetser, Johnson (1987: 53–55) argues that the epistemic senses of the modals are derived by interpreting the notions of force and barrier metaphorically, the forces being the premises of an argument that "force us along a path toward some conclusion" (54). As is suggested by this formulation, argument and reasoning are also, at least partly, metaphorically structured in terms of a SOURCE-PATH-GOAL scheme: we follow a path to reach a destination, in this case, a conclusion, and various propositions can act as blockage, such that we do not reach that conclusion (54).

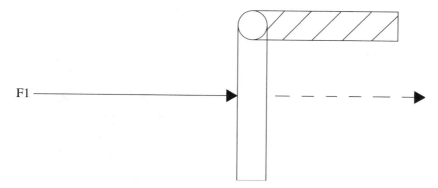

Figure 12.3. The REMOVAL OF RESTRAINT schema

4.2. A Selective Comparison

Space limitations do not allow an exhaustive comparison of the different proposals presented above (but see Mortelmans, this volume, chapter 33); we will limit ourselves to the following four key issues: (i) the basic level of force dynamics; (ii) the exact nature of the source and target domains of the metaphorical transfer; (iii) the metaphorical nature of the relation between the deontic and the epistemic meanings; and (iv) the image-schematic nature of force dynamics.

The Basic Nature of Force Dynamics

Sweetser holds that modality, conceived of in terms of intentional, directed forces and barriers, basically operates at the level of the sociophysical domain. This view is also subscribed to by Pelyvás (1996: 125, 144–46), who, like Sweetser (1990: 152, note 5), believes that we conceive the physical world in terms of basic aspects of human experience, such as actions and intentions. Despite some minor differences (see Pelyvás 1996: 135), both authors thus disagree with Talmy, who recognizes that the modals refer in their basic deontic usage to "psychosocial" interactions, and not to physical ones (Talmy 2000: 441), but sees force dynamics nevertheless as ultimately related to our kinesthetic system (2000: 467). In other words, Talmy presents the fundamental elements of force dynamics with respect to a purely physical scene (2000: 413), adding that he regards nonagentive forms of force dynamics more basic than forms containing an agent (2000: 421).[11]

The Exact Nature of the Source and Target Domains of the Metaphorical Transfer

According to Sweetser (1990: 50), the English modals developed their root meanings from nonmodal meanings (e.g., OE *magan* 'be strong, be able') before they acquired their epistemic meanings. Pelyvás (1996: 133–34), however, concludes from diachronic evidence (cf. Traugott 1989: 36, who relies on data by Bybee and Pagliuca 1985 and Bybee 1988) that both the root and the epistemic meaning of *may* are derived from a (now extinct) ability meaning and that the epistemic meaning is attested before the deontic one. This course of development could explain why the doer's intentions need to be taken into account to describe the deontic, but not the epistemic meaning (Pelyvás 1996: 134). It implies, moreover, that Sweetser's root domain conflates two meanings that would better be distinguished: sociophysical meanings implying intentionality and meanings such as 'ability', in which intentionality only plays a peripheral role (Pelyvás 1996: 125–26).[12]

The Metaphorical Nature of the Relation between the Deontic and the Epistemic Meanings

As pointed out by Pelyvás (1996: 154), the development of the epistemic meaning need not be conceived of as a metaphorical transfer. Traugott (1989) analyzes it as the conventionalization of conversational implicatures through pragmatic strengthening: for instance, "if one says *You must go* in the meaning 'You ought to go', one can implicate that one believes/concludes that it is true that you have to go" (51). The metonymic nature of the relation between deontic and epistemic meaning of *must* may also be suggested by the following observation of Lampert and Lampert (2000: 252): whereas the deontic meaning focuses on the (entire) path which the subject must follow as it is impinged upon by the Antagonist (note the infinitive *come home* in example 36), the epistemic meaning in (37) focuses rather on the path's terminal point, namely the conclusion:

(36)   You must come home by ten (Mom said so). (Sweetser 1990: 61)
(37)   You must have been home last night. (Sweetser 1990: 61)

There is, then, a difference with respect to the windowing of attention in the two meanings, which each focus on adjacent elements within the same frame (Talmy 1996b). The evolution from deontic to epistemic can also be analyzed in terms of image-schematic transformations (see Gibbs and Colston 1995: 361, cited in Lampert and Lampert 2000: 252–53).[13]

The Image-Schematic Nature of Force Dynamics

Although both Johnson and Talmy underline the schematic nature of the force-dynamic structures, their conceptions can be traced back to different origins and, consequently, are different in nature: Johnson views force dynamics in terms of image schemes that emerge out of our concrete embodied experiences, at a nonlinguistic—or prelinguistic—level; Talmy, in contrast, conceives of force dynamics as an abstract schema, common to different domains, most notably the linguistic and the kinesthetic ones (Lampert and Lampert 2000: 219–21).[14]

4.3. A More Grammatical Conception
of the Force-Dynamic Nature of Modals

Langacker (1991: 269–81) defines modals as "grounding predicates," since they specify a relationship between the process profiled by the complement clause and some element of the ground, that is, the speech event, its participants, and its immediate circumstances. As is characteristic of grounding predicates, the grounding relationship expressed by the modals remains offstage and unprofiled, and the ground is construed with a high degree of subjectivity (Langacker 2002: 7, 13, 17). Consequently, Langacker (1991) describes the development of the modal verbs, from main verbs to more grammaticalized markers, in terms of subjectification. Initially, these main verbs expressed a physical capacity to do something, with their subject denoting a "locus of some kind of potency directed at the landmark process, i.e., a physical or mental force that, when unleashed, tends to bring about the occurrence of that process" (270). When the modals are used with their root meaning, the locus of potency (corresponding here with Talmy's Antagonist) can no longer be identified with the subject; it must be associated with the speaker or some other element associated with the ground (even some "nebulous, generalized authority" [Langacker 1999: 308]), as can be seen in (38):

(38)   a. You may leave the table now!
       b. This noise must cease immediately!
       c. He absolutely will not agree with it.

Epistemic modals constitute the end point of the development. Unlike with deontic modals, the locus of potency is no longer identified with a specific individual or another element associated with the ground; the "impetus toward realization of the designated process is not provided by any specific force, but rather by the generalized force consisting in the fact that the world has a certain structure and reality is unfolding in a particular way" (Langacker 1991: 273). In Langacker's view, this generalized force can be defined using elements of a cognitive model of the way we think about the world, the "dynamic evolutionary model." In this model, the world is seen as a structured whole in which situations unfold, following an evolution that is due to an unknown force.

Because of the structured nature of the world, its evolution can to a certain extent be foreseen (for more details, see Mortelmans, this volume, chapter 33); consequently, there are (at least) two types of future paths the evolution can follow: paths which can be projected from the present with reasonable confidence, called "projected reality," and paths which reality is only not precluded from following, called "potential reality" (Langacker 1991: 277–78). These ideas allow Langacker to define the meanings of the English epistemic modals: *may* situates the designated process in potential reality, whereas *will* situates it in projected reality.

Langacker's conception differs from Sweetser's in that he presents the modals, more explicitly than Sweetser, as a grammaticalized category. Moreover, in his

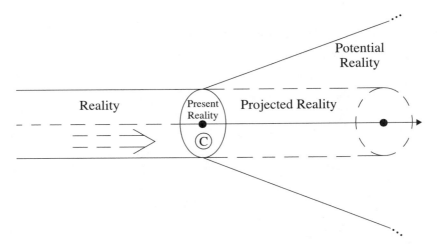

Figure 12.4. Langacker's (1991: 277) dynamic evolutionary model

view, at least in the epistemic sense, it is no longer the subject who undergoes a force and is driven along a deductive path; reality itself evolves in a structured world: "there is an essential force-dynamic element to our conception of its structure, which we can see as constraining and influencing elements that unfold within it" (Langacker 1991: 276). Langacker nevertheless holds that his account is not necessarily incompatible with Sweetser's, since the speaker is the person responsible for assessing the structure of reality and the future course of events (274).

Achard's (1996, 1998) analysis of the French modals *pouvoir* 'can' and *devoir* 'must' combines elements from both Sweetser's and Langacker's analyses. Following Sweetser, Achard (1998: 145–59) uses the terms "force" and "barrier" to define the root senses of these French modals: in (39), *pouvoir* meaning 'possibility' expresses the removal or the absence of a (potential) external barrier or obstacle, which stands between the subject and the accomplishment of the infinitival process.[15]

(39)   *Il peut venir vous voir demain.*
       'He can come and see you tomorrow.'

As such, the root meaning of *pouvoir* differs from its uses as a main verb as in (40), where it expresses ability:

(40)   *Marie est forte, elle peut soulever cent kilos.*
       'Marie is strong, she is able to lift one hundred kilos.'

Indeed, whereas in (40) the subject can be identified with the locus of potency, in (39), the locus of potency can be identified with external factors removing the barrier. Thus, as was already pointed out by Langacker, the locus of potency gets more diffused; at the same time, however, the speaker gets more and more involved, since he or she is aware of these external circumstances, whereas the subject is not.

The same holds with respect to *devoir*'s root meaning of obligation, where the locus of potency (Talmy's Antagonist) is also associated, not with the subject, but with the speaker (41) or with a more diffused source of obligation (42):

(41) *Vous devez rentrer à six heures.*
'You must come back at six o'clock.'

(42) *Les étudiants doivent respecter leurs professeurs.*
'The students must respect their teachers.'

As far as the epistemic senses are concerned, Achard (1996: 10) again follows Langacker, stating that *pouvoir* places the process in potential reality, whereas *devoir* places it in projected reality:

(43) *Je ne vois pas de lumière, il peut ne rentrer que demain.*
'I do not see any light, he may only come back tomorrow.'

(44) *Il a laissé la porte ouverte, il doit revenir bientôt.*
'He left the door open, he must be coming back soon.' (Achard 1998: 160)

Here, the locus of potency is equated with the world and its evolution, but, according to Achard (1998: 166), it is then necessarily "speaker-internal, because considerations about the world and its evolution are only accessible to the speaker by the mental operations of observation and analysis."

At the same time, Achard stresses that the speaker's control over the complement increases, as is suggested by the fact that infinitives following *savoir* and *pouvoir* in their epistemic sense can take perfect or passive markers (45), whereas this is not possible when these verbs express ability or capacity (46).

(45) a. *Il doit être enfermé, je l'entends crier.*
'He must be locked up; I can hear him scream.'
b. *Il peut ne pas avoir compris, il faudrait répéter.*
'He might not have understood, we should repeat.'

(46) a. **Il sait avoir nagé.*
*'He knows how to have swum.'
b. *?Il peut être enfermé dans le placard.*
'He can be locked up in the closet.' (Achard 1996: 3–4)

That the speaker exerts conceptual control over the complement should not come as a surprise, since the epistemic uses of *savoir* and *devoir* express the evaluation by the speaker, and not the subject, of the force of the evolutionary momentum.

5. FORCE-DYNAMICS IN SYNTAX

Langacker's (1990; 1991: 282) analysis of grammatical relations confirms the relevance of force-dynamic notions to syntax. Langacker defines clause structure with respect to two folk models, the "billiard-ball model" and the "stage model," whose combination yields the "canonical event model" (Langacker 1991: 286). In keeping with the stage model, events are conceived as observed from an external vantage point by a viewer; in accordance with the billiard-ball model, events are conceived as consisting of discrete objects moving about and interacting energetically. This model is reflected in the prototypical transitive clause, which "profiles an action chain involving the transmission of energy from the subject to the object, with the former being agentive and the latter undergoing a change of state" (Langacker 1990: 220).[16] These ideas are illustrated in examples (47)–(50):

(47)   Floyd hit/broke the glass with the hammer.
(48)   The hammer hit/broke the glass.
(49)   The glass easily broke.
(50)   Floyd hit the hammer against the glass.

The examples also show that different portions of the event expressed may receive attention: (47) focuses on the event as a whole, (48) on the interaction between the instrument and the patient, (49) on the patient's state of change, and (50) on the agent's manipulation of the instrument. Although for a full analysis of clause structure, other elements, such as the distinction between dependent and autonomous parts (Langacker 1991: 286–91), must be taken into account, the force-dynamic analysis of clause structure permits an initial characterization of central grammatical notions such as 'subject' and 'direct object'. The subject is the head of the profiled portion of the action chain or the participant that is farthest upstream with respect to the energy flow, whereas the object is the tail of the profiled portion of the action chain (Langacker 1990; 1991: 310). At first sight, these definitions are not schematic enough, since they do not seem to apply to examples with symmetric predicates such as (51) (Langacker 1991: 311):

(51)   a. Joshua resembles Jonathan.
       b. Jonathan resembles Joshua.

However, there is still some asymmetry in these sentences: in (51a), Jonathan serves as the standard of comparison for the evaluation of Joshua, whereas in (51b), this relation is reversed. Thus, in (51a), Joshua is the Figure and Jonathan is the Ground, whereas in (51b), Joshua is the Ground and Jonathan is the Figure. Consequently, Langacker (1990: 222; 1991: 313) defines the subject as the Figure of the relationship profiled by the verb and the object as the "secondary clausal Figure" (Langacker 1991: 324). At the same time, these definitions can still be held to reflect the action-chain structure, since the starting point and the end point attract more attention than the other elements (322).

Since the force-dynamic canonical event model provides a coherent basis for the prototypical notion of transitivity (Langacker 1991: 302 refers to Rice 1987 for this idea; see also Kemmer and Verhagen 1994: 126), clauses whose structure is similar to the prototypical transitive one, will, as Kemmer and Verhagen (1994: 127) argue, be based on the same force-dynamic model. Instances of such clauses are what Kemmer and Verhagen (1994) call the intransitive causative construction (52) and the transitive causative construction (53):

(52)   I made Mary cry.
(53)   I made her eat some cake.

In their view, the intransitive causative schema preserves the force-dynamic structure of transitivity and consequently shows subject and direct object marking just as in a simple transitive clause; the transitive causative schema, on the other hand, is modeled either on the structure of the ditransitive clause or on the model of clauses containing an instrumental phrase, such as *I hit it with a hammer*: in the first case, the clause contains subject, object, and indirect object marking on the three participants; in the second, it contains an instrumental participant. Causative constructions are thus again presented as ultimately based on a fundamental force-dynamic pattern.

6. CONCLUSION

Force dynamics, as proposed by Talmy, is a fundamental notion which underlies grammatical categories, such as modal verbs in English, and which structures the meanings of many lexical items. The notion has proved useful for analyzing various linguistic expressions (prepositions, conjunctions, logic-gators, etc.), as well as sentence structure and grammatical notions such as 'subject' and 'object'. Despite the fruitfulness of the notion, a lot of questions remain to be answered, especially concerning the relation of force dynamics to other linguistic and nonlinguistic systems, its use in structuring nonphysical domains (by metaphorical transfer or not?), and its exact nature (preconceptual, image-schematic or not?). Moreover, Talmy (2000, 462–67) has suggested that further research is needed on some parameters of the force-dynamic system (e.g., Is the force-exerting entity localized or distributed? Is the force exerted uniformly or does it change?). In the end, then, force dynamics is not only an essential grammatical category, but also a rich area of research.

NOTES

1. All examples in section 2 are taken from Talmy (2000: 409–70).
2. This connection between 'causing' and 'letting' is confirmed by the analysis of Dutch *laten* and *doen* as expressing indirect and direct causation, respectively (Verhagen and Kemmer 1997).

3. Earlier analyses treated causation as an atomic notion—often represented as CAUSE (McCawley 1968); and even those treatments that mentioned a more detailed set of factors (Shibatani 1973; Jackendoff 1976; and Talmy 1976, 1985) "were still founded upon an unanalyzed notion of primitive causation" (Talmy 2000: 428).

4. The idea of "negative causation" as a further type of causation is presented by Soares da Silva (1999, 2003) as the meaning unifying the different senses of the verb *deixar*.

5. Four syntactic and morphological properties define the core modal verbs (*can, may, must, shall, will, need, dare, had better*, and *ought*): "lack of *to* for the infinitive form of the following verb, lack of -*s* for the third-person singular, postposed *not*, and inversion with the subject as in questions" (Talmy 2000: 440–41). Verbs such as *have to, be supposed to, be to*, and *get to* are considered to be "honorary modals," because, although syntactically regular, their meanings and uses are comparable to those of the core modals.

6. Jackendoff (1990: 125) rejects the definition of theme as "the thing affected," an analysis which derives, in his view, "from the notion of Theme as a default case-marker, like Fillmore's (1968) Objective case."

7. It would be preferable to identify Antagonist with Actor.

8. Likewise, Boye (2001: 31–32) points out that the Danish "force modals" *burde* 'ought to', *måtte(-n)* 'must', *skulle* 'shall', and *ville* 'will'—that is, those that are defined using the notion of force and that express necessity and probability—take directional complements:

> Det   bør/må(-n)/skal/vil   frem.
> it   ought/must/shall/will out-dir
> 'It ought/must/shall/will be brought to light.'

9. The number of meanings to be distinguished in English modals varies from author to author; Sweetser (1990), for instance, also distinguishes speech act modality, whereas other authors think this is "pragmatically reducible" to one of the other kinds of modality (Boye 2001: 36); see Mortelmans (this volume, chapter 33) for more details.

10. "Root" meaning, as defined by Sweetser (1990) is broader than "deontic" modality, which is first and foremost associated "with the more narrow notion of social and moral obligation alone" (Johnson 1987: 50). Johnson himself shares Sweetser's (broader) characterization of root modality, which is also found in Langacker (1991: 246, note 4) and Achard (1998: 126), although the latter seems to regard "deontic" as a synonym to "root"; see Mortelmans, this volume, chapter 33, note 5).

11. The question is further complicated by the fact that Johnson (1987: 46), Sweetser (1990: 60), and Pelyvás (1996: 138) also describe our reasoning processes as invoking the idea of a journey through space.

12. Boye (2001: 36) calls the domain of ability the "dynamic" domain and holds it to be basic for the analysis of the Danish modals.

13. Some authors even cast doubt on the polysemy view as such; see Mortelmans, this volume, chapter 33.

14. See also Lampert and Lampert (2000: 238–39) on the different views of Talmy and Johnson concerning the shared nature of (pre)conceptual patterns.

15. The distinction between "force" and "barrier" modals is also made by Boye (2001) for Danish modal verbs.

16. For largely compatible ideas, loosely inspired by Talmy's (1972, 1976) analyses of causatives, see Croft (1991: 165–82).

REFERENCES

Achard, Michel. 1996. French modals and speaker control. In Adele E. Goldberg, ed., *Conceptual structure, discourse and language* 1–15. Stanford, CA: CSLI Publications.

Achard, Michel. 1998. *Representation of cognitive structures: Syntax and semantics of French sentential complements.* Berlin: Mouton de Gruyter.

Beliën, Maaike. 2002. Force dynamics in static prepositions: Dutch *aan, op,* and *tegen.* In Hubert Cuyckens and Günter Radden, eds., *Perspectives on prepositions* 185–209. Tübingen: Max Niemeyer Verlag.

Boye, Kasper. 2001. The force-dynamic core meaning of Danish modal verbs. *Acta Linguistica Hafniensia* 33: 19–66.

Bybee, Joan L. 1988. Semantic substance vs. contrast in the development of grammatical meaning. *Berkeley Linguistics Society* 14: 247–64.

Bybee, Joan L., and William Pagliuca. 1985. Cross-linguistic comparison and the development of grammatical meaning. In Jacek Fisiak, ed., *Historical semantics and historical word-formation* 59–83. Berlin: Mouton de Gruyter.

Cienki, Alan. 1998. STRAIGHT: An image schema and its metaphorical extensions. *Cognitive Linguistics* 9: 107–49.

Croft, William. 1991. *Syntactic categories and grammatical relation: The cognitive organization of information.* Chicago: University of Chicago Press.

Deane, Paul D. 1996. On Jackendoff's conceptual semantics. *Cognitive Linguistics* 7: 35–91.

Fillmore, Charles J. 1968. The case for case. In Emmon Bach and Robert T. Harms, eds., *Universals in linguistic theory* 1–88. New York: Holt, Rinehart and Winston.

Gibbs, Raymond W., Jr., and Herbert L. Colston. 1995. The cognitive psychological reality of image schemas and their transformations. *Cognitive Linguistics* 6: 347–78.

Gruber, Jeffrey S. 1965. Studies in lexical relations. PhD dissertation, MIT. Repr. as *Lexical structures in syntax and semantics.* Amsterdam: North-Holland, 1976.

Jackendoff, Ray. 1976. Toward an explanatory semantic representation. *Linguistic Inquiry* 7: 89–150.

Jackendoff, Ray. 1990. *Semantic structures.* Cambridge, MA: MIT Press.

Jackendoff, Ray. 1996. Conceptual semantics and cognitive linguistics. *Cognitive Linguistics* 7: 93–129.

Johnson, Mark. 1987. *The body in the mind: The bodily basis of meaning, imagination, and reason.* Chicago: University of Chicago Press.

Kemmer, Suzanne, and Arie Verhagen. 1994. The grammar of causatives and the conceptual structure of events. *Cognitive Linguistics* 5: 115–56.

Kristoffersen, Kristian-Emil. 2001. Semantic structure of the Norwegian preposition *mot. Nordic Journal of Linguistics* 24: 3–27.

Lakoff, George. 1987. *Woman, fire and dangerous things. What categories reveal about the mind.* Chicago: University of Chicago Press.

Lakoff, George, and Mark Johnson. 1980. *Metaphors we live by.* Chicago: University of Chicago Press.

Lampert, Günther, and Martina Lampert. 2000. *The conceptual structure(s) of modality: Essences and ideologies. A study in linguistic (meta-)categorization.* Frankfurt am Main: Peter Lang Verlag.

Langacker, Ronald W. 1990. Settings, participants, and grammatical relations. In Savas L. Tsohatzidis, ed., *Meanings and prototypes: Studies in linguistic categorization* 213–38. London: Routledge.

Langacker, Ronald W. 1991. *Foundations of cognitive grammar*. Vol. 2, *Descriptive application*. Stanford, CA: Stanford University Press.

Langacker, Ronald W. 1999. *Grammar and conceptualization*. Berlin: Mouton de Gruyter.

Langacker, Ronald W. 2002. Deixis and subjectivity. In Frank Brisard, ed., *Grounding: The epistemic footing of deixis and reference* 1–28. Berlin: Mouton de Gruyter.

McCawley, James. 1968. Lexical insertion in a transformational grammar without deep structure. *Chicago Linguistic Society* 4: 71–80.

Meex, Birgitta. 2002. Die Wegpreposition *über*. In Hubert Cuyckens and Günter Radden, eds., *Perspectives on prepositions* 177–94. Tübingen: Max Niemeyer Verlag.

Oakley, Todd. 2005. Force-dynamic dimensions of rhetorical effect. In Beate Hampe, ed., *From perception to meaning: Image schemas in cognitive linguistics* 443–73. Berlin: Mouton de Gruyter.

Pelyvás, Péter. 1996. *Subjectivity in English: Generative grammar versus the cognitive theory of epistemic grounding*. Frankfurt am Main: Peter Lang Verlag.

Rice, Sally. 1987. Towards a cognitive model of transitivity. PhD dissertation, University of California at San Diego.

Schepping, Marie-Therese. 1991. The lexical meaning of the French preposition *contre*. In Gisa Rauh, ed., *Approaches to prepositions*, 225–52. Tübingen: Gunter Narr Verlag.

Shibatani, Masayoshi. 1973. *A linguistic study of causative constructions*. PhD dissertation, University of California at Berkeley. Available from the Indiana University Linguistics Club, Bloomington.

Soares da Silva, Augusto. 1999. *A Semântica de DEIXAR: Uma contibuição para a abordagem cognitiva em Semântica Lexical* [The semantics of the verb *deixar*: Towards a cognitive approach in lexical semantics]. Lisbon: Fundação Calouste Gulbenkian—Ministério da Ciência e da Tecnologia. (PhD dissertation, Universidade Católica Portuguesa, Braga, 1997)

Soares da Silva, Augusto. 2003. Image schemas and coherence of the verb category: The case of the Portuguese verb *deixar*. In Hubert Cuyckens, René Dirven, and John R. Taylor, eds., *Cognitive approaches to lexical semantics* 281–322. Berlin: Mouton de Gruyter.

Stosic, Dejan. 2002. *"Par" et "à travers" dans l'expression des relations spatiales: Comparaison entre le français et le serbo-croate*. PhD dissertation, Université de Toulouse-le-Mirail.

Sweetser, Eve. 1984. Semantic structure and semantic change: A cognitive linguistic study of modality, perception, speech acts, and logical relations. PhD dissertation, University of California at Berkeley.

Sweetser, Eve. 1990. *From etymology to pragmatics: Metaphorical and cultural aspects of semantic structure*. Cambridge: Cambridge University Press.

Talmy, Leonard. 1972. Semantic structures in English and Atsugewi. PhD dissertation, University of California at Berkeley.

Talmy, Leonard. 1976. Semantic causative types. In Masayoshi Shibatani, ed., *Syntax and semantics*, vol. 6, *The grammar of causative constructions* 43–116. New York: Academic Press.

Talmy, Leonard. 1981. Force dynamics. Paper presented at the Conference on Language and Mental Imagery, University of California at Berkeley, May 1981.

Talmy, Leonard. 1985. Force dynamics in language and thought. *Chicago Linguistic Society* 21, vol. 2 (parasession): 293–337.

Talmy, Leonard. 1988. Force dynamics in language and cognition. *Cognitive Science* 12: 49–100.

Talmy, Leonard. 1996a. Fictive motion in language and "ception." In Paul Bloom, Mary Peterson, Lynn Nadel, and Merrill Garrett, eds., *Language and space* 211–76. Cambridge, MA: MIT Press.

Talmy, Leonard. 1996b. The windowing of attention in language. In Masayoshi Shibatani and Sandra Thompson, eds., *Grammatical constructions: Their form and meaning* 235–87. Oxford: Oxford University Press.

Talmy, Leonard. 2000. *Toward a Cognitive Semantics.* Vol. 1, *Concept structuring systems.* Cambridge, MA: MIT Press.

Taylor, John R. 1996. On running and jogging. *Cognitive Linguistics* 7: 21–34.

Traugott, Elisabeth Closs. 1989. On the rise of epistemic meanings in English: An example of subjectification in semantic change. *Language* 65: 31–55.

Verhagen, Arie, and Suzanne Kemmer. 1997. Interaction and Causation: Causative constructions in modern Standard Dutch. *Journal of Pragmatics* 27: 61–82.

CHAPTER 13

SPATIAL SEMANTICS

JORDAN ZLATEV

1. INTRODUCTION

This chapter presents an overview of cognitive linguistic research in spatial semantics, in other words, investigations into the meaning of spatial language that
regard language as an integrated part of human cognition. This rather broad definition is meant to cover not only the type of research that can be said to constitute "the prototype" within Cognitive Linguistics (e.g., by Lakoff, Langacker,
and Talmy), but also research that "deviates" from this prototype (e.g., by Jackendoff, Levinson, and Sinha).

Within the cognitive linguistic literature so far, there have been three substantial edited volumes (Bloom et al. 1996; Pütz and Dirven 1996; Hampe 2005),
two special issues of the journal *Cognitive Linguistics* (1995, issues 1 and 2/3), a large
number of monographs (Brugman 1981; Lindner 1981; Casad 1982; Cuyckens 1991;
Vandeloise 1991; Durst-Andersen 1992; Svorou 1994; Regier 1996; Zlatev 1997;
Takahashi 2001; Levinson 2003; Tyler and Evans 2003; Pourcel 2005), and numerous articles (e.g., Talmy 1983; Landau and Jackendoff 1993; Sinha and Kuteva 1995;
Kreitzer 1997; Cienki 1998; Pederson et al. 1998; Engberg-Pedersen 1999; Sinha and
Jensen de López 2000; Tyler and Evans 2001; Goddard 2002)—all of these dedicated largely to spatial semantics. A natural question is: why has spatial meaning
received such extensive attention?

One reason is universality. Space pertains to a central and universal aspect of
human experience, and thus constitutes a good searching ground for linguistic
universals, as exemplified in the work of, for instance, Talmy (1975, 1983, 1985, 1988,
2000). Conversely, the demonstration of language-specific patterns of semantic

and possibly conceptual categorization in this type of domain would provide a strong case for "linguistic relativity" (Whorf 1956; Pourcel 2005) or at least "linguistic mediation" (Vygotsky 1978; Bowerman 1996; Pederson et al. 1998; Levinson 2003).

The second major reason for the focus of Cognitive Linguistics on spatial semantics has to do with the supposed basic nature of space. It has long been known that there are strong parallels between space and other semantic domains, reflected in the fact that the same expressions often take spatial, temporal, and other more abstracts meanings, as seen in expressions such as *from here to there, from now to tomorrow,* and *from me to you* (Gruber 1965; Anderson 1971; Clark 1973). The standard cognitive linguistic explanation of this parallelism is *conceptual metaphor,* that is, a systematic asymmetric mapping between two experiential domains where the more abstract domain is understood in terms of the more concrete one (Lakoff and Johnson 1980; Lakoff 1987; Grady, this volume, chapter 8). Since space appears to be more concrete than the domains it maps onto, its structure is expected to be mapped onto these domains: "space is at the heart of all conceptualization" (Putz and Dirven 1996: xi); "abstract domains are consistently conceptualized in terms of spatial image schemata" (Kreitzer 1997: 317). If that is indeed the case, an understanding of spatial categorization would provide the key to human conceptual categorization in general.

However, the metaphorical interpretation of the space/nonspace analogy is not uncontroversial, other possible explanations being historical processes of grammaticalization (Heine, Claudi, and Hünnemeyer 1991) or fundamental properties of mental representation rendering space and other domains partially isomorphic (Langacker 1987; Jackendoff 1990). In both cases, it would be possible to argue that space is *not* experientially more basic than, for example, time (Engberg-Pedersen 1999; Evans 2003). At the same time, this controversy has itself sparked research into the supposed primacy of space (see section 5.4).

The overall structure of this chapter is as follows. Section 2 sets the stage by addressing two important preliminary questions, each of which allows for several answers: *What* is to be regarded as "spatial language"? and *How* can spatial semantics be studied from the nonmodular, interdisciplinary perspective of Cognitive Linguistics? Despite substantial differences between the various approaches to spatial semantics, one can discern a basic set of spatial semantic concepts within the literature, which is presented and discussed in section 3. Section 4 provides a brief review of the empirical basis for such generalizations, showing an initial focus on European languages, but a gradual movement toward non-Indo-European languages and eventually more general typological frameworks. Section 5 takes up four controversies, often discussed in connection with spatial semantics, but of more general significance for linguistic theory; reviewing these gives an idea of the "problem space" that an explanatorily adequate theory of spatial meaning would need to negotiate. The chapter concludes with a summary and some anticipations for further research in spatial semantics.

2. SPATIAL SEMANTICS: WHAT AND HOW?

2.1. What: The Scope of Spatial Semantics

Spatial semantics is the study of the meaning of spatial language, but what is to be regarded as "spatial language"? A moment's reflection suffices to show that the answer to this question is anything but trivial, since space is not a self-contained "semantic field," but rather constitutes an important part of the background for all conceptualization and meaning (Kant [1787] 1964). Furthermore, the term "space" has been used all too often in an extended, metaphorical sense in Cognitive Linguistics and cognitive science, as in "Space Grammar" (Langacker 1982), "Mental Spaces" (Fauconnier 1985), and "Conceptual Spaces" (Gärdenfors 2000). Hence, an unrestricted interpretation of the term "space" might lead us to think that "all semantics is spatial semantics," a conclusion that not even cognitive linguists would find too attractive. Therefore, the scope of spatial semantics needs to be restricted, and this can and has been done in at least three different ways: by form class, by semantic category, and by communicative function. The three definitions based on these restrictions do not coincide, however, and each leaves something to be desired.

Perhaps the most common way of defining the scope of spatial semantics is in terms of a class of expressions, or "form class," that specializes for spatial meaning, such as "spatial prepositions" (Cuyckens 1991; Landau and Jackendoff 1993), "closed-class forms" (Talmy 1983), or "spatial grams" (Svorou 1994). As Svorou has it, "To talk about space and spatial relations . . . languages make use of a relatively small number of elements. . . . I will refer to all these grammatical forms of language which express primarily spatial relations as *spatial grams*" (31). However, this way of defining spatial meaning is problematic since it lacks the appropriate means to distinguish spatial from nonspatial senses of expressions, and it aprioristically limits the domain of analysis to a class which is by no means universal (Brown 1994). Even if the class is broadened in the manner suggested by Talmy and Svorou, the definition still misses the contribution of spatial verbs, nouns, and adverbs (see section 5.2).

An alternative is to define spatial language *notionally*: spatial are those expressions which express "spatial relations" (Lakoff 1987; Sinha and Thorseng 1995; Regier 1996; Kreitzer 1997). This semantic category assumes the semantic primitives trajector (or "Figure") and landmark (or "Ground"), whereby the location or motion of the first is characterized in terms of its relationship to the second (see section 3.1 and 3.2). Again, however, this definition is not general enough because different languages may employ different strategies of locating objects in space, and not all strategies are equally relational (Levinson 1991, 1994; Kreitzer 1997). In English, we can readily characterize the meaning of (1a) in terms of a trajectory-landmark relation, and this can also be extended to (1b), where the landmark expression can be said to be "elliptic" and the landmark implicit. But to offer a similar analysis for (1c) and (1d), we would need to postulate landmarks of a different sort, possibly the sky in (1c) and the speaker in (1d).

(1)   a. The balloon passed over the house.
      b. The balloon passed over.
      c. The balloon went up.
      d. The balloon went over there.

However, treating (1a) and (1b) on a par with (1c) and (1d) would miss an important distinction: (1a) not only represents a landmark through the noun phrase *the house*, but without it there is no way to determine the spatial coordinates of the trajector. Similarly for (1b): even though the landmark is left implicit, it is still conceptually necessary to characterize the trajector's motion in space. In contrast, (1c) and (1d) not only lack an explicit landmark, as does (1b), but they *do not need* one conceptually since the trajector's position is determined not through object-like reference points, but through coordinate systems (see section 3.3). A possibility would be to exclude sentences such as (1c) and (1d) from the subject matter of spatial semantics proper. This would, however, be both arbitrary and ethnocentric considering the basically relational meaning of Indo-European adpositions.

A third way of defining spatial semantics is through *communicative function*: spatial semantics pertains to the meaning of utterances that help the addressee determine the location or trajectory of motion of a given referent in discourse (Zlatev 1997; Pederson et al. 1998; Levinson 2003). An operational definition of a spatial utterance would be one which answers a question beginning with *where* (or is such a question). This definition intuitively excludes (metaphorical) extensions such as (2), but includes the examples (1c) and (1d). This approach would be objected to by those who wish to assign spatial semantics to literal, nonspatial uses (e.g., Lakoff 1987), but it does provide a principled basis for constraining the domain of study. It may even offer a clue as to *which* extended uses can cognitively be treated as spatial: those, such as in (3b), which occur in utterances that can be given as answers to *metaphorical where*-questions (in those languages that permit such questions).

(2)   He is over his divorce.
(3)   a. Were is he now in his career?
      b. He is pretty much on the top.

However, in order to exclude from the domain of spatial semantics utterances which fulfill the locative communicative function via "conversational implicatures" (Grice 1975) (e.g., the answer *He is washing the dishes* to the question *Where is he?*, which can conversationally be inferred to mean *He is in the kitchen*), we can add the requirement that spatial utterances must express the locative function *conventionally*, similar to Grice's distinctions between conversational and conventional implicatures. Thus, we can define the object of study of spatial semantics as being (above all) *spatial expressions, that is, conventional specifications of the location or change of location (i.e., translocation) of a given entity.*

2.2. How: Methodologies for Investigating Spatial Semantics

There has been considerable debate within Cognitive Linguistics concerning the proper methodology for studying language and meaning "cognitively": Sandra and Rice (1995), Cuyckens, Sandra, and Rice (1997), and especially Sandra (1998) have expressed strong skepticism about the use of linguistic intuitions and the analyses based on them and advocate psycholinguistic experimentation. Tuggy (1999) counters that analyses based on "intersubjectively valid intuitions" can indeed provide evidence for mental representations. Geeraerts (1999) presents the controversy in the form of a Socratic dialogue between an "idealist" and an "empiricist."

This methodological debate could possibly be resolved—as suggested by Popper (1962) and Itkonen (1983, 1997)—by accepting that language exists (at least) at three different ontological levels, each with its type of data and appropriate methodology. I will therefore briefly describe an Itkonen-inspired division of linguistic levels and relate each to corresponding studies of spatial semantics. The point is to show that there is room for ontological and methodological pluralism in the study of (spatial) meaning, while at the same time emphasize that one must be aware of the limits of one's particular level and seek cross-level correspondences.[1]

The (Nonobservable) Normative Level: Language as Shared Conventions

It can be argued that ever since the time of Pânini, linguistics has always been "cognitive" in the sense that its main method has consisted in describing, in as general a way as possible, one's *intuitions* and those of informants about grammaticality and meaning. Itkonen's crucial point is that these intuitions reflect *normative* knowledge: not knowledge about how one does in fact speak, or even less about what goes on in one's head when one speaks, but intuitions about how one *should* speak. Having such intuitions of the *correctness* (often referred to with technical terms such as "grammaticality" and (semantic) "well-formedness") of locutions is a human universal. Since it is impossible to have such normative knowledge privately (Wittgenstein 1953), this level of knowledge and meaning is primarily *social*. In this sense, whether they are aware of it or not, when linguists describe linguistic structures, they describe the human mind, rather than "linguistic behavior," "a mental organ," or some Platonic realm. However, it is not the private mind of individual speakers, but the "common mind" (Pettit 1996) and the "mediated mind" (Nelson 1996), which are shared by conscious beings tapping into essentially the same set of linguistic norms or conventions, thereby avoiding the subjectivity of "idealism" pointed out by Geeraerts (1999).

The traditional and most direct way to study this level is by *explication* of these shared norms, which exist as nontheoretical knowledge, in terms of theoretical knowledge, following standard theoretical criteria such as simplicity, generality, and internal consistency. Another criterion is intuitiveness, because speakers have at least a degree of conscious access to their nontheoretical semantic knowledge (Zlatev 2007). Furthermore, this level can also be studied more indirectly, by analyzing actual performance, assuming that the underlying nonobservable knowledge guides the behavior of speakers.

It appears that so far Cognitive Linguistics has, to a large extent, failed to realize the nature and importance of the (nonobservable) normative level. This is indicated by the disparaging comments directed at it from advocates of experimentation: "purely aesthetic, that is, wholly theoretical grounds (e.g. by appeals to descriptive economy, naturalness, generality, and explanatory power), and it is that theoretic aesthetic that cognitive linguists have explicitly rejected from the beginning" (Cuyckens, Sandra, and Rice 1997: 51), as well as those who defend the use of linguistic intuitions: "So, the best you can do is stop trying to pretend that what you posit has anything to do with what is going on in people's heads, and go play hocus-pocus games with theoretical entities that correspond to nothing mentally real" (Tuggy 1999: 364). Since normative knowledge is by definition *conceptual*, it is by standard philosophical definitions neither (individual-)psychological nor empirical. It does not, however, thereby become "noncognitive," nor its description "purely aesthetic" and "hocus-pocus."

Returning to spatial semantics from this methodological digression, it becomes immediately obvious that well-known analyses such as Talmy's (1983), Jackendoff's (1983), and Lakoff's (1987), while relying on different theoretical concepts, are nothing else but explications of the authors' intuitions. A classic in the literature, the (everlasting) "Story of *Over*" (Brugman 1981), can illustrate how a cognitive semantic analysis can be criticized and improved based on the criteria downplayed in the above quotations. Lakoff (1987: 416–61) made the preposition *over* famous by reformulating Brugman's analysis into an elaborate "radial category" representation of 24 interrelated senses. However, his analysis was criticized by Vandeloise (1990) for lacking simplicity and rigor, while Vandeloise himself was attacked for failing to explain generalizations to nonspatial domains and for using "false intuitions" (Kreitzer 1997). Dewell's (1994) analysis can be said to win in terms of simplicity by positing a single central sense and deriving the others from it, but he has himself been criticized for using nonintuitive "image schema transformations," which have been argued to fail to generalize to other prepositions and languages (Keitzer 1997). Finally, Tyler and Evans (2001) criticize most of the previous analyses for lacking a systematic methodology to distinguish "senses" from "contextual interpretations," as well as deciding which sense is to be regarded as prototypical. Characteristically, the methodology they propose is based on intersubjectivity (see section 5.4).[2]

The Observable Social Level: Language as Behavior

Language can, of course, be analyzed not only on the normative level (i.e., how we think we should speak), but also as actual behavior (i.e., how we actually speak or otherwise produce instances of linguistic behavior). This actual "performance" constitutes the primary data of corpus linguists, conversation analysts, and sociolinguists. Language in this sense is still social, that is, a matter of communication, but it is not *directly* normative. Nevertheless, the two levels remain interdependent. If the "nonobservable" normative level corresponds to Saussure's *langue*, the observable social one corresponds to *parole*; and as is the case with *langue* and *parole*, the relationship between the two is dynamic: the normative level provides the system that makes language use possible, but as the latter is in constant flux, it changes the system with time. Corpus analysis is the standard method for studying language use, and it is an invaluable complement to linguistic intuitions, because it can uncover patterns and regularities, especially of a quantitative nature, which are not directly accessible to consciousness. It can also be used to corroborate or question the adequacy of particular linguistic analyses based on intuitions.

Spatial semantics has in this respect profited immensely from the cross-linguistic *Frog Story Corpus* (Berman and Slobin 1994; Strömqvist and Verhoeven 2003). For example, on the basis of Talmy's (1991, 2000) well-known typological distinction between "verb-framed" and "satellite-framed" languages, Slobin (1997) has compared the narratives of English- and Spanish-speaking children and adults and found that English and Spanish speakers systematically express motion events differently, in accordance with the type a speaker's language belongs to. Another example of how naturalistic discourse has facilitated uncovering cross-linguistic differences is provided by Pederson et al. (1998) in their investigations of the use of different "frames of reference" (see section 3.3). The authors' methodological credo is that "it is not enough to rely on descriptions of languages that are based on conventional elicitation techniques as these may not fully reflect actual socially anchored conventions" (557).

The Individual-Psychological Level: Language as Mental Representation

While Sandra (1998) is arguably misguided in claiming that linguistic analyses (and corpus studies) cannot help to elucidate the conceptual level of meaning, he is certainly right in claiming that without empirical, psycholinguistic studies, nothing particular can be said about the individual mental level of language. How, then, has this level been elucidated with respect to spatial semantics?

a. *First-language acquisition and developmental studies.* By studying the order and manner in which different spatial expressions and different senses of the same expressions are acquired by children, inferences can be made about which expressions/senses are more psychologically "basic" and about the nature of semantic primitives (Choi and Bowerman 1991; Bowerman 1996; Rice 1999; Zlatev 2003a).

b. *Second-language acquisition studies.* By studying the way second-language learners master the structures of their L2 and the mistakes they make, inferences can be drawn about the nature of their L1 categories (Frisson et al. 1996; Rice, Sandra, and Vanrespaille 1999).

c. *Off-line psycholinguistic experiments.* In a number of experiments, subjects are given stimuli sentences with different senses of the same preposition, which they are asked to reflect on and rate in terms of perceived similarity or to sort into classes. On the basis of these experiments, conclusions can be drawn concerning the perceived relatedness between, for example, spatial and nonspatial senses of prepositions (see Sandra and Rice 1995; Rice, Sandra, and Vanrespaille 1999).

d. *Online psycholinguistic experiments.* Experiments in which subjects are asked to generate sentences under time constraint (Rice, Sandra, and Vanrespaille 1999) or to perform a primed lexical decision (Sandra and Rice 1995) have attested a dominant spatial sense for the prepositions *at*, *on*, and *in*, but separate mental representations for the temporal senses.[3]

e. *Naming and description experiments.* Experiments involving a design in which the speakers' mental representation is inferred by eliciting a spatial description while varying the parameters of the described situation (e.g., Carlson-Radvansky and Irwin 1993; Levelt 1996) have shown that, for example, the Geocentric "frame of reference" (FoR) dominates over the Object-centered and the Viewpoint-centered frames (see section 3.3) in the semantics of the preposition *above*.

f. *Linguistic relativity experiments.* To determine if spatial semantic categories are used in thought and not just in language, it is necessary first to demonstrate that there are differences in the linguistic conceptualization of space, then to perform experiments involving nonlinguistic cognition and to determine if there is a *correlation* between the linguistic structure and the behavior of the speaker. Finally, alternative explanations for the correlation need to be excluded, and the direction of the causality decided. This is a difficult procedure, but it has been carried out extremely carefully by the Language and Cognition Group at the Max Planck Institute of Psycholinguistics in Nijmegen, showing that the dominant linguistic "frame of reference" (see section 3.3) does indeed appear to affect speakers' performance on various nonlinguistic spatial tasks (Levinson 1996, 2003; Pederson 1995; Pederson et al. 1998). Pourcel (2005) presents a good survey of the field and demonstrates a degree of linguistic relativity with the domain of "motion events."

The Neural Level: Language in the Brain

There is one more possible level at which (spatial) meaning may be studied—the neural level; at this level, spatial meaning is not characterized in terms of norms, behavior, or mental representation, but in terms of the neural structures supporting it. While there is much work in cognitive neuroscience on space perception and cognition, there is little that investigates spatial semantics explicitly. Landau and Jackendoff (1993) attempted to relate prepositions to the "where system" in the brain, and nouns to the "what system," but this was done without enough corroborating evidence; further, since spatial meaning is not expressed exclusively by prepositions, this proposal appears to be unsubstantiated. Another relatively early hypothesis relating space, language, and the brain was Deane's (1994) "Parietal Hypothesis," according to which spatial "image schemas" in the inferior parietal cortex may govern syntactic processing in general; the evidence for this hypothesis has, however, been called into doubt (Kemmerer 1998). More extensive attempts have been made to relate frames of reference to underlying neural analogues (Petersen et al. 1996), but these proposals, too, are not without difficulties since cognitive and linguistic reference frames are *not* the same (see section 3.3). Finally, one must mention the stimulating but preliminary attempts to explain (spatial) meaning in neural terms within the Neural Theory of Language (e.g., Feldman and Narayanan 2004; Dodge and Lakoff 2005).

In sum, one could say that despite mutual rapprochement (Rohrer 2001), Cognitive Linguistics and neuroscience have not yet converged on a joint program for dealing with language in general and spatial language in particular. However, this is likely to change in the near future. Given the potential of modern brain-imaging techniques, it should not be impossible to design an experiment in which, for instance, the neural activity of speakers of typologically different languages could be compared during performance of an identical nonlinguistic spatial task.

Computational Modeling: Which Level?

It may be tempting to interpret computational models of spatial semantics, such as Regier's (1996), as models of the neural level of organization, and indeed that is exactly how they are interpreted by Lakoff and Johnson (1999) and within the Neural Theory of Language. Regier's connectionist model is, however, only loosely inspired by neurobiology and includes elements that derive from intuition-based linguistic analysis such as Source, Path, and Goal representations. Instead, I have used Regier's original model and a minor extension of it in order to test a hypothesis concerning the *psychological* level of spatial meaning, namely that mapping situations to whole utterances, rather than to single lexical items, improves learnability and helps to explain (the mental representation of) spatial polysemy (Zlatev 1997, 1999, 2003c). Finally, computational modeling may also be interpreted as a form of explication, a theoretical re-description, of the normative level of shared conventions, as suggested by Itkonen and Haukioja (1997) for linguistic analogy and by myself (Zlatev 2000) for the ability to generalize familiar spatial descriptions to novel situations.

3. BASIC SPATIAL SEMANTIC CONCEPTS

A multitude of spatial categories have been proposed as "universals" or "primitives" in the literature, and providing a characterization for all of them would be prohibitive. However, the following seven spatial concepts are present in almost all descriptions of spatial semantics: *Trajector, Landmark, Frame of Reference, Region, Path, Direction,* and *Motion.* While authors may not agree on the terms and definitions or make different distinctions, given the large theoretical variation, the bare fact that there seems to be agreement on the essential nature of these concepts is significant. The important issue concerning their ontological status is deferred to section 5.1.

3.1. Trajector

A spatial utterance must express or profile a "trajector," the entity whose (trans) location is of relevance (Lakoff 1987; Langacker 1987; Sinha and Thorseng 1995; Regier 1996; Zlatev 1997). The trajector may be static (as in 4a) or dynamic (4b); a person or an object (4c). It can also be a whole event (4d), at least for those analyses that allow relational predicates to take proposition-size structures as arguments (e.g., Langacker 1987).

(4)   a. *She* is at school.
        b. *She* went to school.
        c. *The book* is on the table.
        d. *She is playing* in her room.

Other terms used for this concept are the Gestalt-psychological notion "Figure" (Talmy 1975, 1983, 2000; Levinson 1996, 2003) and the more general term "referent" (Miller and Johnson-Laird 1976; Levelt 1996)—though these usually apply to object-like entities and not to events as in (4d).

3.2. Landmark

The "landmark" is the reference entity in relation to which the location or the trajectory of motion of the trajector is specified. In examples (4a)–(4d), the terms *school, table,* and *room* express the corresponding landmarks. Other terms for this notion include: "Ground" (Talmy 1975, 1983, 2000; Levinson 1996, 2003) and "relatum" (Miller and Johnson-Laird 1976; Levelt 1996). Views differ, however, on whether a landmark/Ground/relatum is *always* involved in a spatial predication, as was discussed in connection with the "problematic" examples (1b) and (1c) in section 2.1. For example, is there a landmark in the commonly used English utterance (5) and, if so, what is it?

(5)   Come here!

One answer is provided by Langacker, who initiated the systematic use of the terms trajector and landmark as referring to extremely general notions which are not confined to (and need not be projections from) the spatial domain: "The trajector/landmark asymmetry is fundamental to relational predicates and underlies the universal subject/object distinction" (1987: 231). Hence, it is not surprising that in his analyses any kind of "point of reference" can serve as a landmark. Most authors (e.g., Jackendoff 1990; Sinha and Thorseng 1995; Levinson 1996) would, however, not treat the deictic center of such utterances as a landmark, and as pointed out in section 2.1, with good reasons.

3.3. Frame of Reference and Viewpoint

A spatial concept which has received considerable attention lately is that of a linguistic "frame of reference" (FoR). However, while almost all authors acknowledge its importance, no two authors define it the same way. In the most general sense, a FoR defines one or more "reference points," and possibly also a coordinate system of "axes" and "angles." Depending on the types of the reference points and coordinates, different types of FoR can be defined. A strong claim is that as far as language is concerned, "there are exactly three frames grammaticalized or lexicalized in language" (Levinson 1996: 138):

   a. *Intrinsic FoR*: The main reference point coincides with the landmark, and axes and angles are projected on the basis of its geometry (e.g., *in front of the house*).
   b. *Relative FoR*: A real or imaginary viewpoint serves as a reference point, and coordinates are projected on the basis of this viewpoint (e.g., *in front of the wall*)
   c. *Absolute FoR*: The system is anchored in fixed geo-cardinal positions (e.g., *North of the border*)

Spatial expressions defined on the basis of these frames have different logical properties: intrinsic and absolute relators are binary, while the relative one is ternary. The relative and the absolute frames support transitive and converse inferences, while the intrinsic frame does not.

Instead of "frame of reference," Levelt (1996) uses the term "perspective system" and makes a similar three-part distinction; however, he refers to the relative system as "deictic," which, without any further qualifications, is inadequate. Jackendoff (1996) distinguishes between four "intrinsic" and four "environmental" frames, but this classification is based solely on the author's own intuitions (for English) rather than on cross-linguistic generalizations and appears somewhat ad hoc. For Langacker (1987), as mentioned above, every kind of reference point is a landmark (where some may be more profiled than others); according to this model, the reference point(s) and other geometric notions constitute the "abstract domain" for the definition of a spatial expression. Thus, the notion of FoR is subsumed under that of "domain" in Cognitive Grammar. This approach is certainly general, but it does not capture what is specific about the concept "frame of reference": for example, that there appear to be only three types of FoRs in all human languages.

However, a limitation of Levinson's three-way division is that it only applies to the static projective relations on the horizontal plane. So a claim to the effect that there are languages which do not use the absolute frame would relate to the horizontal plain only and does not exclude that the absolute frame may be used for terms which refer to the vertical dimension. In earlier work (Zlatev 1997), I have made an attempt to generalize Levinson's three-way division using the terms "allocentric," "deictic," and "geocentric" frames of reference, respectively. However, this analysis is problematic since it confounds type of FoR with landmark type, while Levinson (1996: 135) correctly insists that "linguistic frames of reference cannot be defined with respect to the origin of the co-ordinate system." For example, (6a) and (6b) employ a relative frame despite different kinds of origins, while (7a) and (7b) use the different frames relative and intrinsic, respectively, despite the fact that in both cases the "origin" (O) of the frame is the speaker.

(6)   a. He is in front of the bush. (FoR: Relative, O: Speaker)
      b. He is in front of the bush from John's point of view. (FoR: Relative, O: John)
(7)   a. Sit behind the bush. (FoR: Relative, O: Speaker)
      b. Sit behind me. (FoR: Intrinsic, O: Speaker)

A generalization seems nevertheless to be possible: a *Viewpoint-centered* frame, as in (6a), (6b), and (7a), *need* not have the speaker (or the addressee) as origin, and thus need not be properly speaking "deictic." At the same time, deictic examples such as (1d) and (5) can be subsumed under this notion, with the proviso that they (i) do not involve any angles and coordinates but only a reference point and (ii) are dyadic rather than triadic. Thus, they are conceptually much simpler and, not surprisingly, are acquired earlier by children. What is common to both (dyadic and triadic) types is that the location or motion of the trajector need not be defined in relation to an explicit landmark, as it is, for instance, in (7b), but is defined in relation to a viewpoint. The *Object-centered* frame, by contrast, always involves a landmark and can be either projective (i.e., "intrinsic"), as in (7b), or nonprojective (topological), as in examples (4a)–(4d). Finally, the *Geocentric* frame involves both the horizontal and the vertical plane and, as the other two frames, can be generalized to both static (8a) and dynamic (8b) descriptions:

(8)   a. The picture is above the sofa.   FoR: GEOCENTRIC
      b. Go west!   FoR: GEOCENTRIC
      c. Go toward the setting sun!   FoR: OBJECT-CENTERED

The Geocentric frame locates the trajectory through the fixed geo-cardinal positions. As such, it differs from the Viewpoint-centered (e.g., 5 and 6) or the Object-centered frame (e.g., 7b and 8c), in that it does not rely on a viewpoint or on a landmark object, respectively.

This analysis captures Levinson's generalization that there are exactly three linguistic frames of reference and that some linguistic forms "specialize" for frame, while others may be ambiguous, and still others may "conflate" two frames.

However, it differs in predicting that all languages use all three frames, though for different expressions and to different degrees in discourse. One utterance may express all three FoRs, as in (9) which displays the power and flexibility of semantic compositionality.

(9)   He   came   up   to   the second floor.
          VIEWPOINT-C   GEOCENTRIC   OBJECT-C

3.4. Region

Even with an Object-centered FoR and a (true) landmark, languages do not relate the trajector and landmark directly, but through a "region" that can be defined as a configuration of space in relation to that landmark (Svorou 1994; Zlatev 1997). Quite recently, Talmy (2000) has used the term "conformation" for essentially the same notion. Jackendoff (1983, 1990) captures the distinction between landmark and region with the terms "thing" and "place," two of his semantic primitives, stating that, for example, spatial prepositions such as *in* express place-functions: [PLACE] → [IN ([THING])]. Figure 13.1 shows the regions lexicalized by a number of Japanese locative nouns, which apart from region also specify one (or more) frame(s) of reference (FoR).

Jackendoff holds that the set of such regions or place-functions is universal, but this is doubtful. Rather, all languages appear to make use of the concept, but they can differ substantially both as to the extension of the regions which they express and as to whether they use primarily functional ("force-dynamic") or primarily perceptual ("geometric") properties of the landmark in order to define the region (Levinson 1994). If such variation is granted, then arguments against the universal applicability of the concept "region" (see Bowerman 1996) can instead be interpreted as a characterization of its possible variation. For example, in Korean LOOSE FIT and TIGHT FIT designate basic regions, while in European languages they do not. Most, if not all, of the regions that are relevant for spatial semantics correspond to various types of "image schemas" such as CONTAINMENT and SUPPORT that have been proposed in the literature (e.g., Johnson 1987; Mandler 1996). However, despite its pivotal role within Cognitive Linguistics, the concept of "image schema" remains a controversial and ambiguous notion (Hampe 2005).

3.5. Path

The concept of "path" is used in cognitive semantic analyses in two very different ways. In its first and more common usage, which may be called "elaborated path," it refers to the trajectory of actual or imagined motion of the "trajector" with respect to the "landmark" (Talmy 1983; Lakoff 1987). This trajectory may be some-

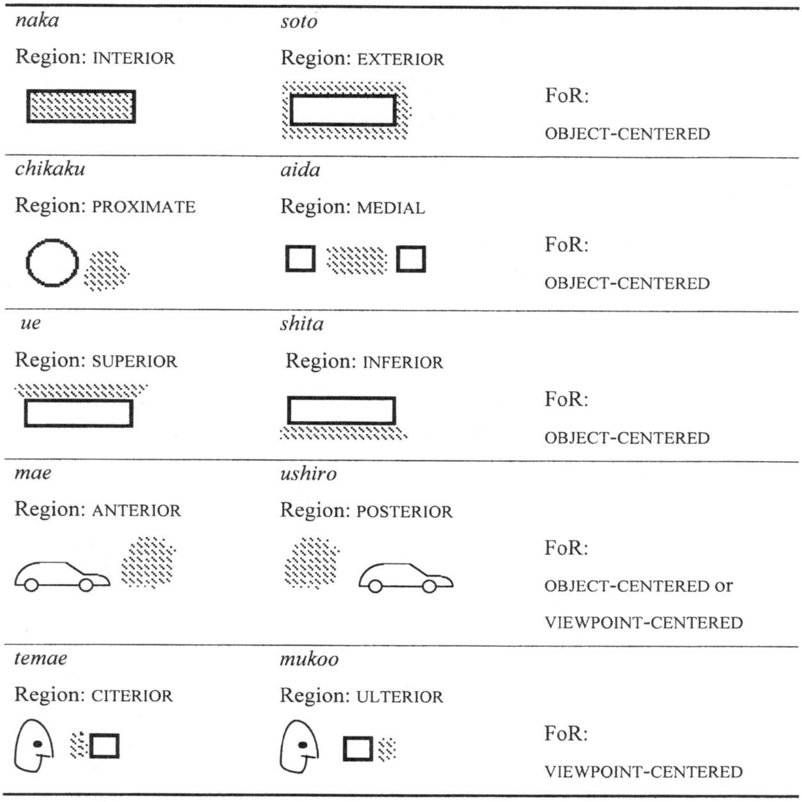

naka	soto	
Region: INTERIOR	Region: EXTERIOR	FoR: OBJECT-CENTERED
chikaku	aida	
Region: PROXIMATE	Region: MEDIAL	FoR: OBJECT-CENTERED
ue	shita	
Region: SUPERIOR	Region: INFERIOR	FoR: OBJECT-CENTERED
mae	ushiro	
Region: ANTERIOR	Region: POSTERIOR	FoR: OBJECT-CENTERED or VIEWPOINT-CENTERED
temae	mukoo	
Region: CITERIOR	Region: ULTERIOR	FoR: VIEWPOINT-CENTERED

Figure 13.1. Japanese locative nouns expressing the spatial semantic category *region*

what schematic, but it has both extension and shape. For example, in Dewell's (1994) analysis of *over*, the basic sense of the preposition profiles, in essence, a circular type of path.

The alternative usage of "path" is based on the cross-linguistic generalization that languages systematically distinguish between (at least) three components of a motion event: its beginning, middle, and end; this usage may be called the "schematic path" characterization (Jackendoff 1990; Zlatev 1997). On this view, "elaborated paths," or trajectories, are derived compositionally by combining the minimal path information (e.g., END) with the region/place information (e.g., INTERIOR) to derive the meaning of a preposition such as *into*. English (and other Indo-European languages) contain many words, mostly prepositions, which *conflate* the concepts "region" and "path," but from a broader perspective many, if not most, languages separate the two categories consistently (Heine, Claudi, and Hünnemeyer 1991; Zlatev 1997). Talmy (2000) has recently arrived at the same conclusion, and therefore currently distinguishes between the "conformation," corresponding to region as mentioned in section 3.4, and the "vector," which "comprises the three basic types of arrival, traversal and departure that a Figural schema can execute with respect to the Ground schema" (53).

Even for English, separating "region" ("conformation") and "path" ("vector") allows certain generalizations; for instance, the sentences in (10) have the same value for the category "region," but different ones for "path":

(10)   a. John went out of the room.   Region: INTERIOR   Path: BEGINNING
       b. John went through the room.   Region: INTERIOR   Path: MIDDLE
       d. John went into the room.   Region: INTERIOR   Path: END
       c. John is in the room.   Region: INTERIOR   Path: ZERO

Including ZERO (no extension) as a possible value of "path" is consistent with the structure of locative case systems in, for instance, Slavonic and Finno-Ugric languages. As shown in the Serbo-Croatian examples in (11), what distinguishes the different (schematic) paths is not expressed in the prepositions alone, but in a combination of preposition, verb-prefix, and case-marker (see also 5.2 below).

(11)   a. *On   je   u   kuć-i.*   Region: INTERIOR Path: ZERO
          he   COP   in   house-LOC
          'He is in the house.'
       b. *On   iz-lazi   iz   kuć-e.*   Region: INTERIOR Path: BEGINNING
          he   out-go   out.of   house-GEN
          'He is going out of the house.'
       c. *On   u-lazi   u   kuć-u.*   Region: INTERIOR Path: END
          he   in-go   in   house-ACC
          'He is going into the house.'

3.6. Direction

If "path" is defined minimally, then it always requires the category "region" in order to profile the trajectory, and "region" always requires a landmark. But as was suggested in section 3.3, not all reference points are of the same kind, and they should therefore not be lumped together under the cover term "landmark" (or "ground"). How, then, is the translocation of trajector defined in the Geocentric and Viewpoint-centered frames, in the cases where there are no landmarks, as in (5) and (8a)? This can be done through the concept of "direction," which is specified as a vector along one of the axes provided by a frame of reference. Consider (12):

(12)   a. The plane is flying that way.   FoR: VIEWPOINT-CENTERED
       b. The plane is flying north.   FoR: GEOCENTRIC
       c. The plane is flying toward the North pole. FoR: OBJECT-CENTERED

In most cognitive semantic analyses, particularly in those where "path" is treated in the elaborated sense (see above), the concept of direction is subsumed under the category "path" and often referred to as "imperfective path" (as in 13a) as opposed to the "perfective path" (as in 13b) (Hawkins 1984).

(13)   a. The bird flew toward its nest.
        b. The bird flew to its nest.

It is clear that at least some languages, such as English, treat the two kinds of translocative events expressed in (13) similarly, so that subsuming "direction" under "path" is not unmotivated. However, separating "path" from "direction" is motivated by other factors. For instance, when "satellite-framed" languages such as English and German (see Talmy 2000: section 4.1)—which typically do not conflate path information into their motion verbs—nevertheless seem to do so (e.g., *sink, fall, rise*), it can be argued that it is *not* "path" properly speaking, but rather "direction" that they conflate with motion (Zlatev 2003b).

3.7. Motion

Somewhat similar to the case with "path," there are (at least) two ways of characterizing the concept "motion" in spatial semantics: one that limits the notion to cases of actual perceived motion, and one which extends it to more "imaginary" scenarios. The fact that examples like (12) and (13) describe "motion events" is relatively uncontroversial, but only the second approach would also include examples of "virtual motion" (Talmy 1983), "abstract motion" (Langacker 1987), or "fictive motion" (Talmy 1996; Takahashi 2001), such as those in (14).

(14)   a. The scenery rushed past us.   ("frame-relative motion")
        b. I looked toward the valley.   ("sensory path")
        c. The road goes through the woods.   ("coverage path")
        d. The church faces toward the square. ("emanation path")
        e. The beam leans away from the wall. ("advent path")
        f. His office is through the corridor. ("access path")

The term following each example is from Talmy (1996), who presents an elaborate classification of types of "fictive motion," claiming that motion exists at different levels of "palpability" and that "every speaker experiences a sense of motion for some fictive motion constructions" (215). However, the classification is based very much on the author's introspection, rather than on linguistic evidence and (shared) intuitions (see section 2.2) and appears as somewhat ad hoc. In this respect, it is telling that Takahashi (2001), who applies Talmy's classification to Thai data, arrives at a rather different way of classifying fictive motion expressions.

On the first and more limited characterization, motion is treated as a binary category: either there is *perceived* motion or there is not. In the examples in (14), there is indeed perceived motion in (14a), but (14b)–(14f) would be analyzed from this perspective as stative (Motion: NIL). Still, they can be attributed non-ZERO values for "path": (14e) would have the value BEGINNING, (14c) and (14f) would have the value MIDDLE, while (14b) and (14d) would have the value END. This is made possible by that fact that this account of the category "motion" allows it to be *separated* from the categories "path" and "direction."

4. LINGUISTIC DESCRIPTION AND CROSS-LINGUISTIC GENERALIZATIONS

How have the theoretical concepts described above been applied to linguistic descriptions? The answer to the question is crucial for evaluating the cognitive semantic approach to spatial meaning, since it can be argued that any linguistic analysis, cognitive or not, will be judged first and foremost by its *descriptive adequacy*, not only with respect to particular languages, but also as a basis for cross-linguistic generalizations. Since it is impossible to provide a comprehensive overview of spatial semantic descriptive work here, this section only offers a schematic account of the relevant research during the past three decades.

1970–1980

The theoretical and descriptive work of Miller and Johnson-Laird (1976) and Clark (1973) is seldom acknowledged within Cognitive Linguistics, but with their focus on the relation between language and perception, with space serving as a privileged domain, these studies can properly be regarded as some of the trailblazers in cognitive linguistic research. Interestingly, this research also displayed a familiar problematic feature: a tendency to make universalistic statements on the basis of few languages, above all English. Talmy's (1975) classic analysis is also typical in this respect.

1980–1990

Seminal work in spatial semantics still largely focused on English prepositions and particles (Brugman 1981; Lindner 1981; Talmy 1983; Hawkins 1984; Herskovits 1986; Lakoff 1987; Taylor 1988). The spatial semantic systems of some typologically quite different languages were also analyzed (e.g., Casad 1982; Brugman 1983), but the analyses highlighted rather "exotic" properties such as body part terms in Mixtec and visible accessibility in Cora and did not attempt to put these in a typological perspective. One exception is Talmy's (1985) well-known typology of "lexicalization patterns" based on whether the motion verbs of a language predominantly express:

- manner/cause of motion, as in Germanic languages (e.g., *walk, crawl, roll*), while 'path' is expressed in a verb-particle or prefix, a *satellite*;

- path and direction, as in Romance languages (e.g., Spanish *salir* 'go out,' *entrar* 'go in'), while "manner" is typically expressed through an adverb;
- Figure- (trajectory-)related information, as in Atsugewi (e.g., *-lup-* 'a small shiny spherical object moving').

1990–Present

The kind of spatial semantic analyses developed earlier were extended with modifications to other European languages, including Dutch (Cuyckens 1991; Geeraerts 1992), French (Vandeloise 1991), and German (Bellavia 1996). Simultaneously, for the first time more serious attention was devoted to the spatial systems of non-Indo-European languages, including Tzeltal (Levinson 1991, 1994; Brown 1994), Cora (Casad 1993), Ewe (Ameka 1995), Zulu (Taylor 1996), Thai (Zlatev 2003b), and a whole volume on Austronesian and Papuan languages (Senft 1997). This decade also saw the *second* Talmyan typology (Talmy 1991, 2000) based on whether "path," or more generally what Talmy calls the "core schema" providing the basic semantic structure for a motion event, is predominantly lexicalized by the verb ("verb-framed" languages) or by a verb-particle or affix ("satellite-framed" languages). This distinction has proved fruitful when applied to many unrelated languages (e.g., Wienold 1995; Slobin 1997; Zlatev 1997), but when extending the database of languages and deepening the analysis, it has proved to be insufficient. For example, in Zlatev (2003b), I show that due to its *serializing* character, Thai expresses manner-of-motion and path-of-motion in different verb roots: the first and second forms in (15) respectively, and thus exemplifies a "third type." Zlatev and Yangklang (2003) provide extensive support for this claim, and Slobin (2003) generalizes this type to include even languages other than serializing languages, calling the type "equipollently-framed."

(15) *dɘɘn*   *ʔɔɔk*   *maa*   *càak*   *khâaŋ*   *nay*   *thâm*
     walk   go.out   come   from   side   in   cave
     MANNER   PATH   DEIXIS   PATH   REGION
     'walking out, (toward the deictic center) from inside the cave'

Accounting for the cross-linguistic data has given rise to more comprehensive systems of spatial primitives which try to chart out universal characteristics as well as dimensions of possible variation (Svorou 1994; Sinha et al. 1994; Sinha and Thorseng 1995; Zlatev 1997; Senft 1997). A typology based on a predominant frame of reference has been proposed (Pederson et al. 1998; Levinson 2003). Attention has also been devoted to the spatial semantics of sign languages from a typological perspective (e.g., Slobin and Hoiting 1994; Engberg-Pedersen 1999; Talmy 2001), showing more variation than previously expected and suggesting that properties that were deemed universal, such as the general nonconflation of "path" and "manner" in a single form, do not hold for sign language and, therefore, are probably in part based on the nature of the vocal modality, which displays more linearity and less iconicity than the manual-brachial one.

In sum, the recent history of descriptive work in spatial semantics can be seen as a progression from an initial focus on English, combined with a strong universalistic bias, toward an increasingly larger typological database, allowing more appropriate generalizations with substantial, though not unconstrained, linguistic variation.

5. THEORETICAL ISSUES AND CONTROVERSIES

One of the main reasons why spatial semantics has been a field of such extensive study is its intermediary position between perception, conception, and language. In this way, it constitutes a convenient field for investigating some of the basic questions concerning linguistic meaning in general. In this section, I will briefly address four such questions that have been intensely debated in the literature.

5.1. Prelinguistic or Language-based?

At least three quite diverse standpoints on this issue have been adopted within Cognitive Semantics, with the first two echoing the debates between "conceptualists" and "nominalists" from the Middle Ages (see Russell 1961) and the third being a more recent attempt to resolve the debate.

Semantic Categories as Conceptual Universals

The predominant view among cognitive linguists of the relation between semantic and conceptual spatial categories is that concepts such as "path" and (various values for) "region" constitute language-independent conceptual primitives (Talmy 1983; Lakoff 1987; Mandler 1996; Wierzbicka 1996). From this point of view, the function of language is simply to *express* (symbolize, lexicalize) largely spatial conceptual representations such as "image schemas" (Johnson 1987), which are most often considered to exist prior to and independently of language:

> In each of these cases, the metaphorical and metonymic models exist in the conceptual system independently of the given expression. . . . Similarly, the schemas for *over* exist for expressions in the spatial domain independent of the existence of *oversee, overlook,* and *look over.* What one learns when one learns these words is which of the independently existing components of their meaning are actually utilized. (Lakoff 1987: 438)

While Jackendoff's conceptual primitives differ from Lakoff's in being "digital" as opposed to "analog," and his conceptual structures "algebraic" rather than "imagistic," his semantic ontology is similar: "Conceptual structure, as developed in Jackendoff (1983, 1990) is an encoding of linguistic meaning that is independent of the particular language whose meaning it encodes" (Jackendoff 1996: 5). In Jackendoff's view of the human mind, universal "conceptual representations" (CR), defined by primitives such as PATH and PLACE, stand between an image-schematic "spatial representation" (SR) and "linguistic forms" (Lf), and the connections between the representations are established by "interface modules": SR ↔ CR ↔ LF. Given the assumptions of both types of conceptual universalism, the only way to account for language-specific semantic differences is through the *selection* of the underlying primitives and "lexicalization patterns."

There are a number of problems with this view. First, even in the universal domain of space, there is more cross-linguistic variation than predicted; consider, for example, the Korean notions of 'tight fit' and 'loose fit', which cut across English 'interior' and 'support' (Bowerman 1996). Furthermore, these are differences which are acquired early by children (Choi and Bowerman 1991), and there is no evidence that the children pass through a "universalistic phase" as predicted by Mandler (1996). An additional problem for a universal conceptual representation constituting a kind of "language of thought" is any corroboration of linguistic relativity/mediation; as pointed out, robust "Whorfian effects" have been shown in the spatial domain with respect to frame of reference (Levinson 2003). A final problem specific to Jackendoff's model, though not to the "imagistic" approach, is that actual sentences are two interfaces and one universal representation removed from Gestalt-like structures such as SR, while such "background" structures clearly play a role for interpretation.

Semantic Categories as Usage-Based

The classic alternative to regarding meaning as based on nonlinguistic concepts is to view it as immanent in the usage patterns of the language itself. With respect to spatial meaning, this view has lately been defended by Bowerman (1996) on the grounds of extensive and developmentally early cross-linguistic variation. By distinguishing semantic and conceptual structure, however, Bowerman remains noncommitted on the question whether and to what degree these differences translate into conceptual differences. However, Langacker's (1987) view of meaning as "conventional imagery" does imply a fairly strong version of linguistic relativity, though this is seldom acknowledged (see Pourcel 2005). From the premises "semantic structure is not universal; it is language-specific to a considerable degree" (Langacker 1987: 2) and "cognitive grammar equates meaning with conceptualization" (5) follows that conceptualization is language-specific. Indeed, Langacker's theory is even open to the interpretation that *perception* is language-specific, since it is claimed that "predication and perception are special instances of conceptualization" (130).

Of course, neither Bowerman nor Langacker are true "nominalists," and thus do not face antinominalist arguments based on cross-linguistic universals and similarities between linguistic and prelinguistic structures. Bowerman (1996), for example, makes it clear that spatial semantic structure should be viewed as emergent from the interaction between both linguistic and nonlinguistic categorization: "The way children initially classify space for language is the outcome of a complex interaction between their own non-linguistic recognition of similarities and differences among spatial situations, on the one hand, and the way space is classified by adult speakers of their language, on the other" (415). The problem is rather that the nature of this interaction is not analyzed, and in this way it is impossible to predict to what extent semantic and general conceptual structure would coincide.

Semantic Categories as Emergent from the Interaction of Motivation and Convention

The third possibility represents a synthesis of the preceding two in stating that spatial semantic categories are *based* on prelinguistic experience, hence broad cross-linguistic similarities are to be expected, but that they are conventionalized language-specifically, and hence that there should be differences. The spatial concepts presented in section 3 are compatible with this view, as it is embraced, for instance, by Zlatev (1997), Sinha (1999), and Talmy (2000). Regier's (1996) connectionist model of the "human semantic potential" can be seen as an explication of the idea how a constrained, though flexible initial state can result in different spatial semantic systems depending on the semantic structure of the language being acquired. From this perspective, semantic, perceptual, and conceptual structure are related but remain separate (Levinson 1996). Categories of perception *motivate* categories of language, but do not determine them. Conversely, semantic structures do not determine perception. Conceptual structures that are largely culturally mediated, such as semantic and episodic memory, are (strongly) influenced by linguistic categories. Those which are less so, such as procedural memory, are not. By way of criticism, it should be mentioned that the interactionist position is the least constrained of the three and requires considerable methodological sophistication in order to be elaborated.

5.2. Localized or Distributed?

If the first controversy concerned the "semantic pole" of language, this one concerns the "phonological pole" (Langacker 1987). As pointed out in section 2.1, it is commonly held that spatial meaning is expressed by the members of one (or more) closed classes; see, for instance, Talmy (1983, 1988), Svorou (1994), and Regier (1996). While these authors acknowledge that sometimes open classes such as nouns and verbs participate in expressing spatial meaning, they usually insist that the grammatical elements have priority: "Lexical elements do incorporate some of the same structural indications that grammatical elements express, but when the two are in association or in conflict within a sentence, it is generally always the grammatical elements' specifications of structure that are determinative" (Talmy 1988: 165).

This view, however, is objected to, among others, by Brown (1994), Ameka (1995), Sinha and Kuteva (1995), and Zlatev (1997, 2003b), on the basis of many examples from typologically different languages, such as Tzeltal, Ewe, Japanese, and Thai. As Sinha and Kuteva (1995: 168) argue, "An adequate analysis requires the abandonment of the localist approach, and the analysis of how spatial relational meaning is syntagmatically distributed over simultaneous selections from closed and open form classes." In earlier work, I have endeavored to capture these facts within the theory of Holistic Spatial Semantics (Zlatev 1997, 2003b, 2003c), assuming representations such as that in figure 13.2, which allows for a many-to-many mapping between semantic concepts, such as those presented in section 3 and form classes, without privileging the closed classes. Conflation patterns (Talmy 1985), distribution patterns (Sinha and Kuteva 1995), and patterns of compositionality (Ameka 1995) appear as special cases of this kind of mapping. A problem with this approach, however, is that it is rather unconstrained: a more adequate theory would need to explain the range of cross-linguistic variation in the values of the semantic categories as well as in the various mapping patterns.

5.3. Semantic or Pragmatic?

In contradistinction to traditional analyses (Grice 1975), which separate conventional semantic meaning from contextual and hence pragmatic interpretation, the dominant view in Cognitive Linguistics is that meaning, and hence spatial meaning, is encyclopedic and that there is no nonarbitrary boundary between semantics and pragmatics (Lakoff 1987; Langacker 1987). This view would imply a "full specification" account of the meaning of the prepositions in (16) and (17) and state that the (a) and (b) sentences embody different senses expressing different profiled regions.

(16)   a. John flew *over* the bridge.   Region: SUPERIOR
       b. John walked *over* the bridge.   Region: SURFACE
(17)   a. The room is *at the back of* the school.   Region: INTERIOR
       b. The tree is *at the back of* the school.   Region: EXTERIOR

An alternative analysis is to state that the prepositions do not express the distinction semantically, but that the relevant interpretation is derived through the Gestalt-like properties of the expressed situation (see the dashed line in figure 13.2) and the background of practices (Herzkovits 1986; Zlatev 1997). This agrees with the claims of, for instance, Levinson (1991) and Kita (1999) that in many languages, central aspects of spatial meaning are often pragmatically inferred rather than (overtly) expressed. I have argued that a separation between semantics and pragmatics along these lines can provide important cross-linguistic (typological) generalizations and is therefore to be preferred (Zlatev 2003b).

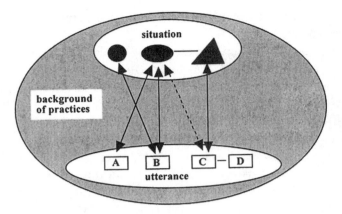

Figure 13.2. A representation of form-meaning mapping within
Holistic Spatial Semantics (from Zlatev 1997)

5.4. The Analysis of Spatial Polysemy

A claim often made in cognitive semantic analyses is that lexical items, and particularly spatial ones, are strongly polysemous, that is, characterized by a multiple set of distinct, but systematically related senses (Lakoff 1987; Langacker 1987; Deane 1988; Cuyckens 1991; Geeraerts 1993; Regier 1996; Tuggy 1999, this volume, chapter 4). These analyses are usually represented by networks of nodes standing for different senses connected via asymmetrical links. The terms for these asymmetrically linked nodes/senses may vary with the particular network model (e.g., "prototypical" vs. "extended," Langacker 1987; "central" vs. "peripheral" Lakoff 1987), but in all cases one node of the relation is seen as cognitively more basic than the other. One of the best-known applications for this kind of analysis has been precisely the semantic study of spatial expressions, where nonspatial senses are (nearly) always treated as extensions from the spatial ones.

But what exactly is the status of such polysemy networks? Are they a characterization of *psychologically real* structures and/or processes and thus relate to the individual psychological level or are they *descriptive generalizations* over the use potential of the expressions in question? Since the latter is derived on the basis of speakers' intuitions of the appropriateness (or "correctness") of a particular expression when applied to a particular situation, they obviously represent theoretical explications of the normative (nonobservable) level of language. As pointed out in section 2.2, the two kinds of linguistic reality (the individual-psychological and the collective-normative) do not coincide, and therefore it cannot be assumed that a particular analysis (of polysemy) would satisfy simultaneously the criteria of linguistic explication and psychological explanation. This pervasive mistake of equating "linguistically real" with "psychologically real" seems to be inherited by Cognitive Linguistics from the Chomskyan tradition and can be seen with respect to polysemy in the following statement: "The central member is thus the member from which all others can be most plausibly and most economically related.... Degree of centrality certainly seems to be a psychologically and linguistically real notion" (Taylor 1989: 119). What is "central" from the standpoint of analysis need not be so psychologically, and vice versa.

The question of the status of polysemy networks is raised poignantly in the title of Sandra and Rice's (1995) study: "Network Analyses of Prepositional Meaning: Mirroring Whose Mind—the Linguist's or the Language User's?" The focus of Sandra and Rice's critique is on the representational and methodological vagueness of network analyses. In particular, the authors consider "the problem of determining whether the fine distinctions are part of the mental representation (as predicted by the prepositional network approach) or the result of an interaction between monosemous mental representations and a process of contextual supplementation" (125). It is significant that the evidence adduced in a number of psycholinguistic studies, most of which are summarized in Cuyckens, Sandra, and Rice (1997), by and large does *not* support the (active) mental representation of polysemous networks with spatial prototypes and metaphorical extensions. In brief, first-language acquisition studies do not show spatially "transparent" uses to be regularly acquired before the more abstract and idiomatic ones (van Geert 1986; Rice 1999; Zlatev 2003a). In second-language acquisition, speakers tend not to transfer hypothetically polysemous L1 representations into L2 (Frisson et al. 1996; Rice, Sandra, and Vanrespaille 1999). In sentence sorting and similarity judgment tasks, subjects do not regard supposedly polysemous spatial and nonspatial senses to be more closely related than homonymous (i.e., nonrelated) controls (Sandra and Rice 1995; Rice, Sandra, and Vanrespaille 1999). Finally, and most crucially, primed lexical decision tasks (Sandra and Rice 1995) show that spatial senses of the prepositions *at, on,* and *in* do not facilitate, but rather inhibit, the recognition of examples with temporal senses, thus attesting to separate mental representations for the prepositions' spatial and temporal usages. While individually each one of these studies may not yield conclusive results, taken together, they strongly question both the existence of polysemy networks and the primacy of space—as far as the individual-psychological level of linguistic reality is concerned—thereby simultaneously going against two of the foremost tenets in Cognitive Linguistics.

At the same time, this does *not* invalidate analyses of polysemy as explications of the level of linguistic norms/conventions. Such explications do need to be made accountable to criteria of "descriptive economy, naturalness, generality and explanatory power" (Cuyckens, Sandra, and Rice 1997: 51), *pace* the comments of these authors on this issue. As pointed out in section 2.2, it is exactly these criteria which have been adduced in arguing for and against various analyses of the polysemy of *over* in the Cognitive Linguistics literature. In one of the latest contributions to this debate, Tyler and Evans (2001: 733) state the need for a "methodology ... that ... provides a rigorous and relatively consistent way of making judgments about whether a sense is distinct, and ... can be used in an intersubjective way" and propose one such methodology which they call the "principled polysemy" approach. Endeavors such as this are just as important for the analyses of polysemy on the normative level as experimentation is for the psychological one. Only with more progress in each may we hope that the two levels can be eventually meaningfully related.

6. SUMMARY AND GUIDELINES FOR FUTURE RESEARCH

The review of cognitive linguistic research in spatial semantics presented in this chapter involved a discussion of the theoretical self-understanding and methodological practices within the field (section 2); a description of basic spatial semantic concepts, showing a rather unexpected degree of cross-theoretical similarity (section 3); a brief survey of spatial semantic descriptive work (section 4); and finally an outline of four important theoretical controversies that any theory of spatial meaning would need to address (section 5). On this basis, the following generalizations concerning the present status and guidelines for future development can be suggested:

   a. *Conceptually*: The existence of different ontological levels of linguistic meaning, each with its appropriate methodology, should be more widely acknowledged, and along with that, the social normative level, accessible through "intersubjectively valid intuitions" should be rehabilitated.
   b. *Theoretically*: Further analytic work should be carried out in relating the conceptual and descriptive systems of various authors, showing where disagreements are only terminological and where they are substantial. In the latter case, one could attempt to find a theoretical synthesis, offering a resolution of the persistent theoretical controversies.
   c. *Descriptively*: The typological database should be extended with new languages, allowing even better cross-linguistic generalizations. Furthermore, *diachronic* evidence (when available) should be taken into account to a greater degree, since it is likely that language change can help to provide an explanation of patterns of polysemy and the (supposed) primacy of the spatial domain, which may or may not correspond to synchronic psychological processes.
   d. *Psychologically*: The psychological studies reviewed have provided more questions than answers: Is there a principled way to distinguish polysemy from homonymy, on the one hand, and from semantic generality (or "vagueness"), on the other? In which way does language mediate spatial thinking? and so on. The existing experimental paradigms need to be cross-checked for converging evidence, and new types of experiments should be considered. A valuable new source of evidence for uncovering parallels

between the linguistic and conceptual structures of space may be provided by gesture studies (e.g., McNeill 2000; Kita and Özyürek 2003).

e. *Computationally*: Computational simulations should be explicitly related to the appropriate level of linguistic reality they intend to model. A more adequate basis for the study of "embodied" spatial representations could possibly be found in the emerging paradigm of "epigenetic robotics" (Dautenhahn 1999; Steels 1999; Zlatev 2001; Zlatev and Balkenius 2001).

Finally, these studies will stand to profit if they can be carried out in parallel, in a collaborative nonreductionist manner—avoiding fruitless arguments concerning which level and methodology is properly entitled to the adjective "cognitive." In accordance with the interdisciplinary and nonmodular character of Cognitive Linguistics, the modifier "cognitive" would be most appropriate for the approach that manages to *integrate* the different ontological levels and methodologies most coherently.

NOTES

I am indebted to the thorough and insightful comments of the editors, which have helped improve this text considerably, and furthermore to Esa Itkonen, Chris Sinha, Tim Rohrer, Lena Ekberg, Hans Hultqvist, Lars Hermerén, and Svetlana Ozol for helpful feedback on an earlier draft.

1. This approach bears similarities to Rohrer's (1998, 2001), who proposes a framework of "levels of investigation" and applies this to the study of metaphor and frames of reference. The major difference between Rohrer's approach and mine is in the way the levels are defined: Rohrer refers to "size" and "physiological structures," while I hold that the differences are basically ontological: language exists differently at the three basic levels—as a social institution, as mental representation, and as a neural implementation.

2. A crucial point is that one should distinguish *intuitions* about the normative realm, which are in general "intersubjectively valid" from *introspection*, which is about the contents of individual minds. Notions such as "image-schema transformations" (e.g., Lakoff 1987; Ekberg 2001), deriving originally from introspection, will be useful as a tool for explicating our shared intuitions only to the extent that they help capture (cross-linguistic) generalizations.

3. Cuyckens, Sandra, and Rice (1997) provide a summary of most of the work referred to in study types (b)–(d).

REFERENCES

Ameka, Felix. 1995. The linguistic construction of space in Ewe. *Cognitive Linguistics* 6: 139–81.

Anderson, John M. 1971. *The grammar of case: Towards a localistic theory*. Cambridge: Cambridge University Press.

Bellavia, Elena. 1996. The German *über*. In Martin Pütz and René Dirven, eds., *The construal of space in language and thought* 73–107. Berlin: Mouton de Gruyter.

Berman, Ruth A., and Dan I. Slobin. 1994. *Relating events in narrative: A crosslinguistic developmental study*. Hillsdale, NJ: Lawrence Erlbaum.

Bloom, Paul, Mary A. Peterson, Lynn Nadel, and Merrill Garret, eds. 1996. *Language and space*. Cambridge, MA: MIT Press.

Bowerman, Melissa. 1996. Learning how to structure space for language—A crosslinguistic perspective. In Paul Bloom, Mary A. Peterson, Lynn Nadel, and Merrill Garret, eds., *Language and space* 385–436. Cambridge, MA: MIT Press.

Brown, Penelope. 1994. The INs and ONs of Tzeltal Locative Expressions. *Linguistics* 32: 743–90.

Brugman, Claudia. 1981. Story of *Over*. MA thesis, University of California at Berkeley. (Published as *The story of Over: Polysemy, semantics, and the structure of the lexicon*. New York: Garland, 1988)

Brugman, Claudia. 1983. The use of body-part terms as locatives in Chalcatongo Mixtec. In Alice Schlichter, Wallace L. Chafe, and Leanne Hinton, eds., *Survey of California and other Indian languages* 235–90. Studies in Mesoamerican Linguistics, report no. 4. Berkeley, CA: University of California at Berkeley.

Carlson-Radvansky, Laura A., and David A. Irwin. 1993. Frames of reference in vision and language: Where is above? *Cognition* 46: 223–44.

Casad, Eugene H. 1982. Cora locationals and structured imagery. PhD dissertation, University of California at San Diego.

Casad, Eugene H. 1993. "Locations," "Paths" and the Cora verb. In Richard A. Geiger and Brygida Rudzka-Ostyn, eds., *Conceptualizations and mental processing in language* 593–645. Berlin: Mouton de Gruyter.

Choi, Soonja, and Melissa Bowerman. 1991. Learning to express notion events in English and Korean: The influence of language-specific lexicalization patterns. *Cognition* 41: 83–121.

Cienki, Alan. 1998. STRAIGHT: An image schema and its metaphorical extensions. *Cognitive Linguistics* 9: 107–49.

Clark, Herbert H. 1973. Space, time, semantics and the child. In Timothy E. Moore, ed., *Cognitive development and the acquisition of language* 27–63. New York: Academic Press.

Cuyckens, Hubert. 1991. The semantics of spatial prepositions in Dutch: A cognitive-linguistic exercise. PhD dissertation, University of Antwerp.

Cuyckens, Hubert, Dominiek Sandra, and Sally Rice. 1997. Towards an empirical lexical semantics. In Birgit Smieja and Meike Tasch, eds., *Human contact through language and linguistics* 35–54. Frankfurt am Main: Peter Lang Verlag.

Dautenhahn, Kerstin. 1999. Embodiment and interaction in socially intelligent life-like agents. In Chrystopher L. Nehaniv, ed., *Computation for metaphors, analogy and agents*. 102–42. Heidelberg: Springer Verlag.

Deane, Paul D. 1988. Polysemy and cognition. *Lingua* 75: 325–61.

Deane, Paul D. 1994. *Grammar in mind and brain: Explorations in cognitive syntax*. Berlin: Mouton de Gruyter.

Dewell, Robert. 1994. *Over* again. Image-schema transformations in semantic analysis. *Cognitive Linguistics* 5: 351–80.

Dodge, Ellen, and George Lakoff. 2005. Image schemas: From linguistic analysis to neural grounding. In Beate Hampe, ed., *From perception to meaning: Image schemas in Cognitive Linguistics* 57–91. Berlin: Mouton de Gruyter.

Durst-Andersen, Per. 1992. *Mental grammar, Russian aspect and related issues*. Columbus, OH: Slavica Publishers.

Ekberg, Lena. 2001. Transformations on the Path-schema, and a minimal lexicon. *Studia Linguistica*: 53: 301–23.

Engberg-Pedersen, Elisabeth. 1999. Space and time. In Jens Allwood and Peter Gärdenfors, eds., *Cognitive semantics: Meaning and cognition* 131–52. Amsterdam: John Benjamins.

Evans, Vyv. 2003. *The structure of time. Language, meaning and temporal cognition*. Amsterdam: John Benjamins.

Fauconnier, Gilles. 1985. *Mental spaces: Aspects of meaning construction in natural language*. Cambridge, MA: MIT Press. (2nd ed., Cambridge: Cambridge University Press, 1994)

Feldman, Jerome, and Srini Narayanan. 2004. Embodied meaning in a neural theory of language. *Brain and Language* 89: 385–92.

Frisson, Steven, Dominiek Sandra, Frank Brisard, and Hubert Cuyckens. 1996. From one meaning to the next: The effects of polysemous relationships in lexical learning. In Martin Pütz and René Dirven, eds., *The construal of space in language and thought* 613–47. Berlin: Mouton de Gruyter.

Gärdenfors, Peter. 2000. *Conceptual spaces*. Cambridge, MA: MIT Press.

Geeraerts, Dirk. 1992. The semantic structure of Dutch *over*. *Leuvense Bijdragen* 81: 205–30.

Geeraerts, Dirk. 1993. Vagueness's puzzles, polysemy's vagaries. *Cognitive Linguistics* 4: 223–72.

Geeraerts, Dirk. 1999. Idealist and empiricist tendencies in cognitive linguistics. In Theo Janssen and Giela Redeker, eds., *Cognitive linguistics: Foundations, scope, and methodology* 163–94. Berlin: Mouton de Gruyter.

Goddard, Cliff. 2002. *On* and *on*: Verbal explications for a polysemic network. *Cognitive Linguistics* 13: 277–94.

Grice, H. Paul. 1975. Logic and conversation. In Peter Cole and Jerry Morgan, eds., *Syntax and semantics*, vol. 3, *Speech acts* 41–58. New York: Academic Press.

Gruber, Jeffrey S. 1965. Studies in lexical relations. PhD dissertation, MIT. (Published as *Lexical structures in syntax and semantics*. Amsterdam: North-Holland, 1976)

Hampe, Beate, ed. 2005. *From perception to meaning. Image schemas in Cognitive Linguistics*. Berlin: Mouton de Gruyter.

Hawkins, Bruce W. 1984. The semantics of English spatial prepositions. PhD dissertation, University of California at San Diego.

Heine, Bernd, Ulrike Claudi, and Friederike Hünnemeyer. 1991. *Grammaticalization: A conceptual framework*. Chicago: University of Chicago Press.

Herskovits, Annette. 1986. *Language and spatial cognition: An interdisciplinary study of the prepositions in English*. Cambridge: Cambridge University Press.

Itkonen, Esa. 1983. *Causality in linguistic theory: A critical investigation into the philosophical and methodological foundations of 'non-autonomous' linguistics*. Bloomington: Indiana University Press.

Itkonen, Esa. 1997. The social ontology of meaning. *SKY 1997 Yearbook of the Linguistic Association of Finland*: 49–80.

Itkonen, Esa, and Jussi Haukioja. 1997. A rehabilitation of analogy in syntax (and elsewhere). In András Kertész, ed., *Metalinguistik im Wandel: Die kognitive Wende in Wissenschaftstheorie und Linguistik* 131–77. Frankfurt am Main: Peter Lang Verlag.

Jackendoff, Ray. 1983. *Semantics and cognition*. Cambridge, MA: MIT Press.

Jackendoff, Ray. 1990. *Semantic structures*. Cambridge, MA: MIT Press.

Jackendoff, Ray. 1996. The architecture of the linguistic-spatial interface. In Paul Bloom, Mary A. Peterson, Lynn Nadel, and Merrill Garret, eds., *Language and space* 1–30. Cambridge, MA: MIT Press.

Johnson, Mark. 1987. *The body in the mind: The bodily basis of meaning, imagination and reason*. Chicago: University of Chicago Press.

Kant, Immanuel. [1787] 1964. *The critique of pure reason*. Trans. Norman Kemp Smith. London: MacMillan.

Kemmerer, David. 1998. Is syntax based on spatial image schemas in the inferior parietal cortex? Evidence against Deane's Parietal Hypothesis. *Cognitive Linguistics* 9: 180–88.

Kita, Sotaro. 1999. Japanese ENTER/EXIT verbs without motion semantics. *Studies of language* 23: 317–40.

Kita, Sotaro, and Asli Özyürek. 2003. What does cross-linguistic variation in semantic coordination of speech and gesture reveal? Evidence for an interface representation of spatial thinking and speaking. *Journal of Memory and Language* 48: 16–32.

Kreitzer, Anatol. 1997. Multiple levels of schematization: A study in the conceptualization of space. *Cognitive Linguistics* 8: 291–325.

Lakoff, George. 1987. *Women, fire, and dangerous things: What categories reveal about the mind*. Chicago: University of Chicago Press.

Lakoff, George, and Mark Johnson. 1980. *Metaphors we live by*. Chicago: University of Chicago Press.

Lakoff, George, and Mark Johnson. 1999. *Philosophy in the flesh: The embodied mind and its challenges to Western thought*. New York: Basic Books.

Landau, Barbara, and Ray Jackendoff. 1993. "What" and "Where" in spatial language and spatial cognition. *Behavioural and Brain Sciences* 16: 217–65.

Langacker, Ronald W. 1982. Space grammar, analysability, and the English passive. *Language* 58: 22–80.

Langacker, Ronald W. 1987. *Foundations of cognitive grammar*. Vol. 1, *Theoretical prerequisites*. Stanford, CA: Stanford University Press.

Levelt, Willem J. M. 1996. Perspective taking and ellipsis in spatial description. In Paul Bloom, Mary A. Peterson, Lynn Nadel, and Merrill Garret, eds., *Language and space* 77–108. Cambridge, MA: MIT Press.

Levinson, Stephen C. 1991. Relativity in spatial conception and description. Working paper no. 1, Cognitive Anthropology Research Group, Max Planck Institute for Psycholinguistics, Nijmegen, Netherlands.

Levinson, Stephen C. 1994. Vision, shape, and linguistic description: Tzeltal body-part terminology and object description. *Linguistics* 32: 791–855.

Levinson, Stephen C. 1996. Frames of reference and Molyneux's question: Crosslinguistic evidence. In Paul Bloom, Mary A. Peterson, Lynn Nadel, and Merrill Garret, eds., *Language and space* 109–70. Cambridge, MA: MIT Press.

Levinson, Stephen C. 2003. *Space in language and cognition: Explorations in cognitive diversity*. Cambridge: Cambridge University Press.

Lindner, Susan. 1981. A lexico-semantic analysis of English verb-particle constructions with OUT and UP. PhD dissertation, University of California at San Diego. (Published as A lexico-semantic analysis of English verb-particle constructions. LAUT Paper, no. 101. Trier, Germany: Linguistic Agency of the University of Trier, 1983)

Mandler, Jean, M. 1996. Preverbal representation and language. In Paul Bloom, Mary A. Peterson, Lynn Nadel, and Merrill Garret, eds., *Language and space* 365–84. Cambridge, MA: MIT Press.

McNeill, David. 2000. Analogic/analytic representations and cross-linguistic differences in thinking for speaking. *Cognitive Linguistics* 11: 43–60.

Miller, George A., and Phillip N. Johnson-Laird. 1976. *Language and perception.* Cambridge, MA: Harvard University Press.

Nelson, Katherine. 1996. *Language in cognitive development: The emergence of the mediated mind.* Cambridge: Cambridge University Press.

Pederson, Eric. 1995. Language as context, language as means: Spatial cognition and habitual language use. *Cognitive Linguistics* 6: 33–62.

Pederson, Eric, Eve Danziger, David Wilkins, Steven Levinson, Sotaro Kita, and Gunter Senft. 1998. Semantic typology and spatial conceptualization. *Language* 74: 557–89.

Petersen, Mary A., Lynn Nadel, Paul Bloom, and Merrill F Garret. 1996. Space and language. In Paul Bloom, Mary A. Peterson, Lynn Nadel, and Merrill Garret, eds., *Language and space* 555–77. Cambridge, MA: MIT Press.

Pettit, Philip. 1996. *The common mind.* 2nd ed. Oxford: Oxford University Press.

Popper, Karl. 1962. *Objective knowledge.* Oxford: Oxford University Press.

Pourcel, Stephanie S. 2005. Relativism in the linguistic representation and cognitive conceptualization of motion events across verb-framed and satellite-framed languages. PhD dissertation, University of Durham.

Pütz, Martin, and Renè Dirven, eds. 1996. *The construal of space in language and thought.* Berlin: Mouton de Gruyter.

Regier, Terry. 1996. *The human semantic potential: Spatial language and constrained connectionism.* Cambridge, MA: MIT Press.

Rice, Sally. 1999. Patterns of acquisition in the emerging mental lexicon: The case of *to* and *for* in English. *Brain and Language* 68: 268–76.

Rice, Sally, Dominiek Sandra, and Mia Vanrespaille. 1999. Prepositional semantics and the fragile link between space and time. In Masako Hiraga, Chris Sinha, and Sherman Wilcox, eds., *Cultural, typological and psycholinguistic issues in cognitive linguistics* 107–27. Amsterdam: John Benjamins.

Rohrer, Tim. 1998. When metaphors bewitch, analogies illustrate and logic fails: Controversies over the use of metaphoric reasoning in philosophy and science. PhD dissertation, University of Oregon at Eugene.

Rohrer, Tim. 2001. Pragmatism, ideology and embodiment: William James and the philosophical foundations of cognitive linguistics. In René Dirven, Bruce Hawkins, and Esra Sandikcioglu, eds., *Language and ideology*, vol 1, *Theoretical cognitive approaches* 49–81. Amsterdam: John Benjamins.

Russell, Bertrand. 1961. *History of Western philosophy.* London: George Allan and Unwin.

Sandra, Dominiek. 1998. What linguists can and can't tell you about the human mind: A reply to Croft. *Cognitive Linguistics* 9: 361–78.

Sandra, Dominiek, and Sally Rice. 1995. Network analyses of prepositional meaning: Mirroring whose mind—the linguist's or the language user's? *Cognitive Linguistics* 6: 89–130.

Senft, Gunter, ed. 1997. *Referring to space: Studies in Austronesian and Papuaan languages.* Oxford: Clarendon Press.

Sinha, Chris. 1999. Grounding, mapping and acts of meaning. In Theo Janssen and Gisela Redeker, eds., *Cognitive linguistics: Foundations, scope and methodology* 223–55. Berlin: Mouton de Gruyter.

Sinha, Chris, and Kristine Jensen de López. 2000. Language, culture and the embodiment of spatial cognition. *Cognitive Linguistics* 11: 17–41.

Sinha, Chris, and Tanya Kuteva. 1995. Distributed spatial semantics. *Nordic Journal of Linguistics* 18: 167–99.

Sinha, Chris, and Lis Thorseng. 1995. A coding system for spatial relational reference. *Cognitive Linguistics* 6: 261–309.

Sinha, Chris, Lis Thorseng, Mariko Hayashi, and Kim Plunkett. 1994. Comparative spatial semantics and language acquisition: Evidence from Danish, English and Japanese. *Journal of Semantics* 11: 253–87.

Slobin, Dan I. 1997. Two ways to travel: Verbs of motion in English and Spanish. In Masayoshi Shibatani and Sandra Thompson, eds., *Grammatical constructions: Their form and meaning* 195–220. Oxford: Oxford University Press.

Slobin, Dan I. 2003. The many ways to search for a frog: Linguistic typology and the expression of motion events. In Sven Strömqvist and Ludo Verhoeven, eds., *Relating events in narrative: Crosslinguistic and cross-contextual perspectives* 219–58. Mahwah, NJ: Lawrence Erlbaum.

Slobin, Dan I., and Nini Hoiting. 1994. Reference to movement in spoken and signed languages: Typological considerations. *Berkeley Linguistics Society* 20: 487–505.

Steels, Luc. 1999. The synthetic modeling of language origins. *Evolution of Communication Journal* 1: 1–35.

Strömqvist, Sven, and Ludo Verhoeven, eds. 2003, eds. *Relating events in narrative: Crosslinguistic and cross-contextual perspectives*. Mahwah, NJ: Lawrence Erlbaum.

Svorou, Soteria. 1994. *The grammar of space*. Amsterdam: John Benjamins.

Takahashi, Kiyoko. 2001. Expressions of emanation fictive motion in Thai. PhD dissertation, Chulalongkorn University, Thailand.

Talmy, Leonard. 1975. Semantics and syntax of motion. In John Kimball, ed., *Syntax and semantics* 4: 181–238. New York: Academic Press.

Talmy, Leonard. 1983. How language structures space. In Herbert L. Pick, Jr., and Linda Acredolo, eds., *Spatial orientation: Theory, research, and application* 225–82. New York: Plenum Press.

Talmy, Leonard. 1985. Lexicalization patterns: Semantic structure in lexical forms. In Timothy Shopen, ed., *Language typology and syntactic description*, vol. 3, *Grammatical categories and the lexicon* 57–149. Cambridge: Cambridge University Press.

Talmy, Leonard. 1988. The relation of grammar to cognition. In Brygida Rudska-Ostyn, ed., *Topics in cognitive linguistics* 165–205. Amsterdam: John Benjamins.

Talmy, Leonard. 1991. Path to realization: A typology of event conflation. *Berkeley Linguistics Society* 17: 480–519.

Talmy, Leonard. 1996. Fictive motion in language and "ception." In Paul Bloom, Mary A. Peterson, Lynn Nadel, and Merrill Garret, eds., *Language and space* 211–76. Cambridge, MA: MIT Press.

Talmy, Leonard. 2000. *Toward a cognitive semantics*. Vol 2, *Typology and process in concept structuring*. Cambridge, MA: MIT Press.

Talmy, Leonard. 2001. How spoken language and signed language structure space differently. *Lecture notes in computer science*, vol. 2205, 247–62. Heidelberg: Springer Verlag.

Taylor, John R. 1988. Contrasting prepositional categories: English and Italian. In Brygida Rudzka-Ostyn, ed., *Topics in cognitive linguistics* 299–326. Amsterdam: John Benjamins.

Taylor, John R. 1989. *Linguistic categorization: Prototypes in linguistic theory*. Oxford: Clarendon Press. (2nd ed., 1995; 3rd ed., 2003)

Taylor, John R. 1996. The syntax and semantics of locative nouns in Zulu. In Martin Pütz and René Dirven, eds., *The construal of space in language and thought* 287–306. Berlin: Mouton de Gruyter.

Tuggy, David. 1999. Linguistic evidence for polysemy in the mind: A response to William Croft and Dominiek Sandra. *Cognitive Linguistics* 10: 343–68.

Tyler, Andrea, and Vyvyan Evans. 2001. Reconsidering prepositional polysemy networks: the case of *over*. *Language* 77: 724–65.

Tyler, Andrea, and Vyvyan Evans. 2003. *The semantics of English prepositions: Spatial scenes, embodied meaning, and cognition.* Cambridge: Cambridge University Press.

van Geert, Paul. 1986. In, on, under: An essay on the modularity of infant spatial competence. *First Language* 6: 7–28.

Vandeloise, Claude. 1990. Representation, prototypes and centrality. In Savas Tsohatzidis, ed., *Meanings and prototypes: Studies in linguistic categorization* 403–37. London: Routledge.

Vandeloise, Claude. 1991. *Spatial prepositions: A case study from French.* Chicago: University of Chicago Press.

Vygotsky, Lev S. 1978. *Mind in society. The development of higher psychological processes.* Cambridge, MA: Harvard University Press.

Whorf, Benjamin L. 1956. *Language, thought and reality: Selected writings of Benjamin Lee Whorf.* Cambridge, MA: MIT Press.

Wienold, Götz. 1995. Lexical and conceptual structures in expressions for movement and space: With reference to Japanese, Korean, Thai, and Indonesian as compared to English and German. In Urs Egli, Peter Pause, Christoph Schwarze, Arnim Stechow, and Götz Wienold, eds., *Lexical knowledge in the organization of language* 301–40. Amsterdam: John Benjamins.

Wierzbicka, Anna. 1996. *Semantics: Primes and universals.* Oxford: Oxford University Press.

Wittgenstein, Ludwig. 1953. *Philosophical investigations.* Trans. G. E. M. Anscombe. Oxford: Basil Blackwell.

Zlatev, Jordan. 1997. *Situated embodiment: Studies in the emergence of spatial meaning.* Stockholm: Gotab Press.

Zlatev, Jordan. 1999. Situated embodied semantics and connectionist modeling. In Jens Allwood and Peter Gärdenfors, eds., *Cognitive semantics: Meaning and cognition* 173–94. Amsterdam: John Benjamins

Zlatev, Jordan. 2000. Connectionism and language understanding. In Dennis Burnham, Sudaporn Luksaneeyanawin, Chris Davis, and Mathieu Lafourcade, eds., *Interdisciplinary approaches to language processing* 166–92. Bangkok: NECTEC.

Zlatev, Jordan. 2001. The epigenesis of meaning in human beings, and possibly in robots. *Minds and Machines* 11: 155–95.

Zlatev, Jordan. 2003a. Beyond cognitive determination: Interactionism in the acquisition of spatial semantics. In Jonathan Leather and Jet van Dam, eds., *Ecology of language acquisition* 83–107. Amsterdam: Kluwer Academic Publishers.

Zlatev, Jordan. 2003b. Holistic spatial semantics of Thai. In Eugene H. Casad and Gene Palmer, eds., *Cognitive linguistics and non-Indo European languages* 305–36. Berlin: Mouton de Gruyter

Zlatev, Jordan. 2003c. Polysemy or generality? Mu. In Hubert Cuyckens, René Dirven, and John R. Taylor, eds., *Cognitive approaches to lexical semantics* 447–94. Berlin: Mouton de Gruyter.

Zlatev, Jordan. 2007. Embodiment, language and mimesis. In Tom Ziemke, Jordan Zlatev and Roslyn Frank, eds., *Body, language and mind*, vol. 1, *Embodiment* 297–338. Berlin: Mouton de Gruyter.

Zlatev, Jordan, and Christian Balkenius. 2001. Introduction: Why 'epigenetic robotics'? In
Christian Balkenius, Jordan Zlatev, Hideki Kozima, Kerstin Dautenhahn, and Cynthia
Breazeal, eds., *Proceedings of the First International Workshop on Epigenetic Robotics,
Modeling Cognitive Development in Robotic Systems* 1–4. Lund, Sweden: Lund
University.
Zlatev, Jordan, and Peerapat Yangklang. 2003. A third way to travel: The place of Thai in
motion event typology. In Sven Strömqvist and Ludo Verhoeven, eds., *Relating events
in narrative: Crosslinguistic and cross-contextual perspectives* 159–90. Mahwah, NJ:
Lawrence Erlbaum.

CHAPTER 14

MENTAL SPACES

GILLES FAUCONNIER

1. WHAT IS A MENTAL SPACE?

Mental spaces are very partial assemblies constructed as we think and talk for purposes of local understanding and action. They contain elements and are structured by frames and cognitive models. Mental spaces are connected to long-term schematic knowledge, such as the frame for walking along a path, and to long-term specific knowledge, such as a memory of the time you climbed Mount Rainier in 2001. The mental space that includes you, Mount Rainier, the year 2001, and your climbing the mountain can be activated in many different ways and for many different purposes. *You climbed Mount Rainier in 2001* sets up the mental space in order to report a past event. *If you had climbed Mount Rainier in 2001* sets up the same mental space in order to examine a counterfactual situation and its consequences. *Max believes that you climbed Mount Rainier in 2001* sets it up again, but now for the purpose of stating what Max believes. *Here is a picture of you climbing Mount Rainier in 2001* evokes the same mental space in order to talk about the content of the picture. *This novel has you climbing Mount Rainier in 2001* reports the author's inclusion of a perhaps fictional scene in a novel.

Mental spaces are constructed and modified as thought and discourse unfolds and are connected to each other by various kinds of mappings, in particular identity and analogy mappings. It has been hypothesized that at the neural level, mental spaces are sets of activated neuronal assemblies and that the connections between elements correspond to coactivation-bindings. On this view, mental spaces operate in working memory but are built up partly by activating structures available from long-term memory.

It is a general property of mental space configurations that identity connections link elements across spaces without implying that they have the same features or properties. When someone says, "When I was six, I weighed fifty pounds," they prompt us to build an identity connector between them now and 'them' when they were five, despite the manifest and pervasive differences.

When the elements and relations of a mental space are organized as a package we already know, we say that the mental space is *framed* and we call that organization a *frame*. So, for example, a mental space in which Julie purchases coffee at Peet's coffee shop has individual elements that are framed by COMMERCIAL TRANSACTION, and also by the subframe—highly important for Julie—of BUYING COFFEE AT PEET'S.

Spaces are built up from many sources. One of these is the set of conceptual domains we already know about (e.g., eating and drinking, buying and selling, social conversation in public places). A single mental space can be built up out of knowledge from many separate domains. The space of Julie at Peet's, for example, draws on all of the conceptual domains just mentioned. It can be structured by additional frames aside from COMMERCIAL TRANSACTION, such as TAKING A BREAK FROM WORK, GOING TO A PUBLIC PLACE FOR ENTERTAINMENT, or ADHERENCE TO A DAILY ROUTINE. Another source for building mental spaces is immediate experience: you see the person Julie purchasing coffee at Peet's and so build a mental space of Julie at Peet's. Yet another source for building mental spaces is what people say to us. *Julie went to Peet's for coffee for the first time this morning* invites us to build a new mental space, no doubt one that will be elaborated as the conversation goes on. In the unfolding of a full discourse, a rich array of mental spaces is typically set up with mutual connections and shifts of viewpoint of focus from one space to another.

Mental spaces are built up dynamically in working memory, but a mental space can become entrenched in long-term memory. For example, frames are entrenched mental spaces that we can activate all at once. Other kinds of entrenched mental spaces are 'Jesus on the Cross', 'Horatio at the bridge', and 'the rings of Saturn'. Such an entrenched mental space typically has other mental spaces attached to it, in an entrenched way, and they quickly come along with the activation. 'Jesus on the Cross' evokes the frame of 'Roman crucifixion', of 'Jesus the baby', of 'Jesus the son of God', of 'Mary and the Holy women at the foot of the Cross', of 'styles of painting the crucifixion', of 'moments of the liturgy that refer to it', and many more.

A mental space may be organized by a specific frame, such as BOXING, and a more generic frame, such as FIGHTING, and a yet more generic frame, such as COMPETITION. Each of these may have its scales, image schemas, force-dynamic patterns, and Vital Relations. One can also use finer topology in a mental space, below the level of the organizing frame. The organizing frame BOXING MATCH does not tell us the shoe sizes of the boxers or how many ounces the boxing gloves weigh or whether the boxers are wearing protective head gear, but a finer topology can include the shoe size, the weight of the gloves, and the protective head gear.

A crucial property of language, cognitive constructions, and conceptual links is the *Access Principle* (also called *Identification Principle*). This principle states that an expression which names or describes an element in one mental space can be used to *access* a counterpart of that element in another mental space.

Access Principle: If two elements a and b are linked by a connector $F(b = F(a))$, then element b can be identified by naming, describing, or pointing to its counterpart a.

2. DISCOVERING MENTAL SPACES

In the 1970s, there was an explosion of research that looked beyond the formal organization of language to its cognitive underpinnings. It became clear that grammatical and semantic structure provided evidence in nonobvious ways for general features of human conceptual systems and operations and that understanding such systems would, in turn, shed light on mysterious aspects of syntax and natural logic.

The intellectual environment remained sometimes surprisingly hostile to this enterprise. Within linguistics, the hostility was largely the result of dominant structuralist and then generative traditions during the twentieth century. Structuralist methodology relied on explicit distributional regularities that might be extracted from data. It did not view with favor indirect inferences about mental organization. Generative Linguistics, on the contrary, did promote an abstract hypothetico-deductive approach as in the natural sciences, leading to rules, constraints, and underlying structures viewed as the product of distinctly human mental capacities. But strangely enough, it applied this approach to syntax alone, with the strong bias that principles of syntax constituted an autonomous module with little connection to the more general conceptual apparatus.

Meanwhile, logical phenomena, such as quantifier scope, anaphora, opacity, and presupposition, had been largely the province of analytic philosophy. Here also, any appeal to mental constructs was anathema. Bypassing the mind/brain, semantics was framed in terms of an external theory of truth and reference, strongly inspired by the successful mathematical models of Tarski and other mathematical logicians in the Fregean tradition. To accommodate modal and intensional phenomena (including counterfactuals and *de re/de dicto* reference), possible worlds were added to the actual world as legitimate targets of reasoning and reference.

The prevailing behaviorist thinking in psychology served further to fend off the exploration of "unobservable" mental constructs.

Against this background of dogmatically antimentalistic analysis, Cognitive Linguistics embarked on a radically different course, one that placed conceptual analysis and cognitive principles squarely at the forefront of the study of mind and language. This important turn was entirely driven by results of empirical research and data observation. Scientific explanations and generalizations could be formulated within cognitively based theories. In the 1970s, the explosion of fruitful work in that direction included the development of Space Grammar (later named Cognitive Grammar) by Langacker and his students, metaphor theory by Lakoff, Johnson, Sweetser, and their students, and Talmy's work on Figure/Ground, fictive motion, and event integration.

It also included detailed work on mental spaces and mental space connections. Initially, the motivation for this work was largely that it provided simple, elegant, and general solutions to problems such as referential opacity or presupposition projection that had baffled logicians and formal linguists. For example (see section 4 below), it turned out that opacity, instead of being a logical feature of certain kind of sentences, was really the manifestation of a much more general and fundamental property of discourse—the application of the Access Principle across mental spaces as discourse unfolds. Presupposition projection, another long-standing source of logical perplexity, also turned out to be a consequence of elegant principles of mental space construction in discourse. As reported in my monograph *Mental Spaces* (Fauconnier 1985; first published in French in 1984), what emerged was a unified cognitively based approach to anaphora, presupposition, conditionals, and counterfactuals. Additionally, the gestural modality of signed languages revealed other ways in which mental spaces could be set up and operated on cognitively and physically.

Shortly thereafter, Dinsmore (1991) developed a powerful approach to tense and aspect phenomena based on mental space connections. The approach was pursued and extended in fundamental ways by Cutrer (1994) (see section 6 below), who made it possible to understand the role of grammatical markers as prompts to deploy vast networks of connected mental spaces. Further generalizations were achieved in many other areas exemplified by the diverse contributions to *Spaces, Worlds, and Grammar* (Fauconnier and Sweetser 1996). The research showcased in that volume gives a good idea of the part played by mental spaces in Cognitive Linguistics generally, for example, in Construction Grammar (Lakoff 1987; Brugman 1996), Cognitive Grammar (van Hoek 1997; Langacker 2003), metaphor theory (Lakoff 1996), pragmatics and sociolinguistics (Encrevé 1988; Rubba 1996), and narrative theory and discourse (Sanders and Redeker 1996; Turner 1996; Mushin 1998; Epstein 2001).

There is a good deal of ongoing activity today in all these areas, but at the same time there is a new wave of research focusing on the recent discovery of blended mental spaces and the integration networks that give rise to them. This exciting facet of mental space research is presented by Turner in chapter 15 of the present *Handbook*.

3. Mental Spaces in Discourse: Some Simple Examples

The following examples will help to get an idea of how mental space configurations are built up.

Romeo and Juliet

Suppose that we are engaged in a conversation about Romeo and Juliet and the following statement is made:

(1)   Maybe Romeo is in love with Juliet.

The English sentence brings in a frame from our prestructured background cultural knowledge, x IN LOVE WITH Y, with two roles highlighted (the lover x and the loved one y), and rich default information linked to the Idealized Cognitive Model tied to this frame. The word *maybe* is a space builder; it sets up a *Possibility space* relative to the discourse *Base space* at that point. The Base space contains elements a and b associated with the names *Romeo* and *Juliet*, and presumably those elements have been linked to other frames by background knowledge and previous meaning construction in the conversation. The new sentence sets up the Possibility space and creates counterparts a' and b' for a and b, which can be identified by the names *Romeo* and *Juliet*, in virtue of the Access Principle. The new space is structured internally by the frame x IN LOVE WITH Y, whose roles are filled by the elements a' and b'. Frames will be denoted here by capitalized words with some mnemonic value, for instance in the present example LOVE. And the familiar notation

LOVE a' b'

will be used to denote the internal structure added to a mental space M, namely that elements a' and b' in space M fit the frame LOVE (by filling in the grammatically specified roles of 'lover' and 'loved one').

In diagrammatic form, all this will be expressed in the following kind of representation (see figure 14.1).

The dotted line from B to M indicates that M is set up *relative* to its Parent space B (it is subordinate to B in the lattice of discourse spaces). In the present example, the Base space is the Parent space for M. I is the *connector* (in this case identity) linking a and b in space B to a' and b' in space M. The boxes represent internal structure of the spaces next to them.

Structure from a Parent space is transferred to a new space by default. In the present case, this has the effect of associating a' and b' with the names *Romeo* and *Juliet*, respectively, and also with other background structure for their counterparts

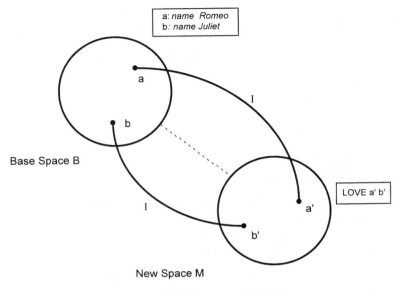

a: *name Romeo*
b: *name Juliet*

Base Space B

I

I

LOVE a' b'

New Space M

Figure 14.1. Romeo and Juliet

a and *b* in B. The default transfer, called *optimization,* will apply to the extent that it does not contradict explicit structure in the new space. For example, suppose that the conversation participants are talking about Romeo's *hostile* behavior toward Juliet. In B, this has the consequence that Romeo does not like Juliet. But this background structure will *not* transfer to the new space M, because it contradicts the *explicit* structure LOVE *a' b'*. Names will not transfer either if they are explicitly ruled out in the new space, as in (2):

(2)   Maybe, Romeo and Juliet's names are really Dick and Jane.

This example also underscores that *a'* and *b'* are accessed *from the Base,* by means of the names for *a* and *b,* in virtue of the Access Principle.

Achilles and the Tortoise

Here is another example involving more spaces:

(3)   Achilles sees a tortoise. He chases it. He thinks that the tortoise is slow
       and that he will catch it. But it is fast. If the tortoise had been slow, Achilles
       would have caught it. Maybe the tortoise is really a hare.

A cognitive construction compatible with this piece of discourse proceeds as follows.
       [First sentence] *Achilles sees a tortoise. Achilles* is a name linked to an already introduced background element *a* in the Base; the indefinite noun phrase *a tortoise* sets up a new element *b,* and ___sees___ brings in the SEE frame with *a* and *b* in the roles of seer and seen (see figure 14.2).

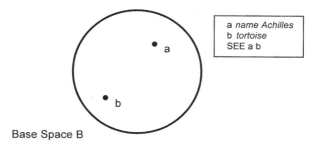

Figure 14.2. Achilles and the tortoise

[Second sentence] *He chases it.* Background information tells us that Achilles is human and the tortoise is an animal. This allows the anaphoric pronouns *he* and *it* to identify *a* and *b*, respectively, in the Base space. The second sentence simply adds more internal structure to the Base (see figure 14.3).

[Third sentence] *He thinks that the tortoise is slow and that he will catch it.* The space builder *he thinks* sets up a new space M relative to B that will partition off information about Achilles's beliefs. The complement clause *the tortoise is slow and he will catch it* will structure this new space internally. Within this complement clause, we find another space builder, the future auxiliary *will*; so a third space W appears, this time relative to M. The time reference in B has been maintained in M through the present tense; the future tense constrains event structure in W to be ordered in time after event structure in B (figure 14.4).

[Fourth sentence] *But it is fast.* This sentence returns us to the Base space, which at this stage of the discourse remains the *Viewpoint* (more on this notion below). By default, spaces are assumed nondistinct in structure (weak optimization). The word *but* is an explicit pragmatic signal to override this default: the structure of B differs from that of M with respect to the explicitly constructed structure [FAST *b*], incompatible with its counterpart [SLOW *b'*] (figure 14.5).

[Fifth sentence] *If the tortoise had been slow, Achilles would have caught it.* The conjunction *if* sets up a hypothetical mental space H. The *distal* past perfect tense *had been* indicates that H is counterfactual (with respect to the Base B). Two novel structures appear in the counterfactual space H:

slow b_1
CATCH a_1, b_1

The first (corresponding to the protasis of the conditional sentence) is a *matching condition*. It allows space H to be used for further reasoning (of the Modus Ponens variety) in later discourse: if a new space matches H with respect to this condition, it will pick up additional structure from H. The discourse up to now is in the indicative mood. In the second part of the fifth sentence of (3), we find a new mood, the conditional *would have been* (in the same past perfect tense as the matching condition protasis). This conditional mood is the grammatical sign that the

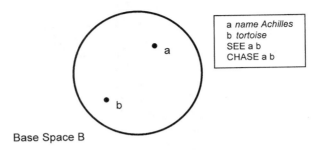

Base Space B

Figure 14.3. The chase

counterfactual space is now in *Focus*. This point will also be taken up again in more detail below. The resulting construction can be diagrammed, as in figure 14.6.

[Sixth sentence] *Maybe the tortoise is really a hare.* Viewpoint is still from the Base space. The space builder *maybe* sets up a possibility space P, in which the counterpart of the tortoise 'is a' hare. The Access Principle operates here: the counterpart b_2 in the new space P is accessed from the Base by means of the description for its trigger b (tortoise). We end up with the configuration diagrammed in figure 14.7.

4. REFERENTIAL OPACITY

The cases of referential opacity and transparency, *de re* and *de dicto* interpretations, noted by many scholars for propositional attitudes, turn out to be only special instances of the more general Access Principle. To illustrate, consider a simple situation. Suppose that James Bond, the top British spy, has just been introduced to Ursula as Earl Grey, the wealthy tea importer, and that she finds him handsome. It is equally true that *Ursula thinks the top British spy is handsome* and that *Ursula thinks the wealthy tea importer is handsome*, and both express the same belief. But in the first case, the man introduced to Ursula has been described from the point of view of the speaker, whereas in the second he is described from Ursula's point of view. Although the first description is true and the second is false, Ursula would acquiesce to *the wealthy tea importer is handsome*, but not (necessarily) to *the top British spy is handsome*. Descriptions and names given from the speaker's point of view are called *referentially transparent*, or *de re*. Descriptions and names given from the thinker's point of view are called *referentially opaque* or *de dicto*. Verbs like *think* or *hope* or *want*, which allow such descriptions in their complements, are said to create opaque contexts. Opaque contexts present a number of difficulties from a logical point of view, as noted already in medieval studies, and in modern logic by Frege, Russell, Quine, and countless others. In particular, Leibniz's Law

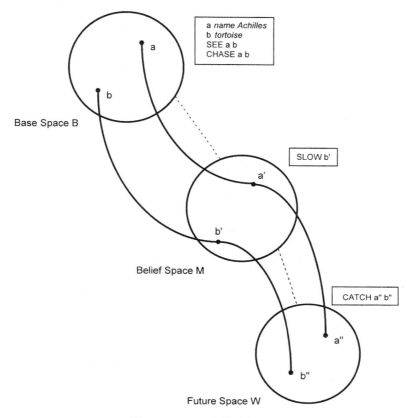

Figure 14.4. Achilles' beliefs

fails in such contexts. Leibniz's Law (substitution of identicals) allows b to be substituted for a in a formula, if $a = b$. For example, 25 can be replaced by 5^2 or by $(19 + 6)$ without changing the truth value of a mathematical statement. But in our little story, if the wealthy tea importer is actually the very ugly Lord Lipton, that is, *the wealthy tea importer = Lord Lipton*, then sentence (4a) is true, while (4b) is false:

(4) a. Ursula thinks *the wealthy tea importer* is handsome.
 b. Ursula thinks *Lord Lipton* is handsome.

Although the two names/descriptions are true of the same referent, one cannot be substituted for the other *salva veritate*. The complexity increases when several opaque contexts are embedded within one another. Consider (5):

(5) Bill said that Iris hoped that Max wanted Ursula to think that the wealthy tea importer was handsome.

And opacity shows up in a variety of grammatical constructions:

(6) Ursula thinks James is smarter than he is.

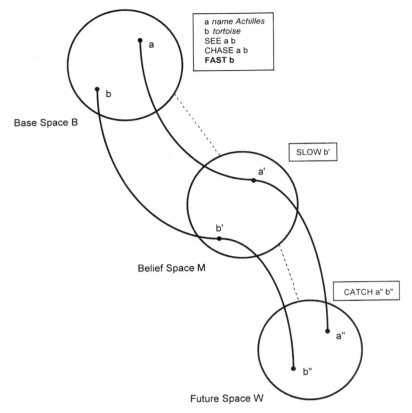

a *name Achilles*
b *tortoise*
SEE a b
CHASE a b
FAST b

Base Space B

SLOW b'

Belief Space M

CATCH a" b"

Future Space W

Figure 14.5. Back to reality

In this example, the natural interpretation is referentially transparent: *than he is* yields James's actual intelligence as measured by the speaker. A referentially opaque reading has Ursula holding the contradictory belief: *James is smarter than he is*.

Discussion of opacity in the logical and philosophical tradition has tended to view it as a property of the meaning of propositional attitudes (*think, hope, want,* etc.) and of objects of belief. But in fact, opacity follows much more generally from the Access Principle between mental spaces. According to that principle, an element in a space may be accessed by means of a description (or name) in that space or by means of a description (or name) of one of its counterparts in another space, usually a space serving as Viewpoint at that stage of the discourse construction.

So, in the case of Ursula and the spy, the following configuration might have been built by discourse participants (figure 14.8).

The next step in this discourse configuration is to structure the Belief space with the additional HANDSOME *b'* corresponding to Ursula's belief that the man she has just met is handsome. Linguistically, there are two ways to do it. The element *b'* can be accessed directly in the Belief space now in focus. With respect to that space,

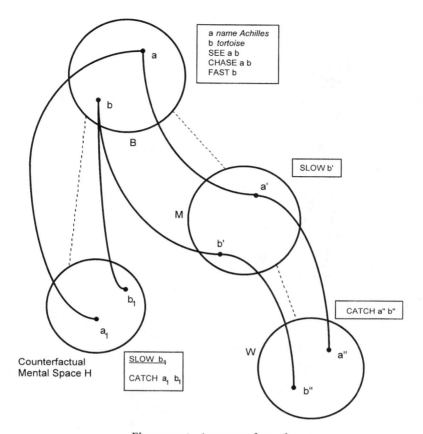

Figure 14.6. A counterfactual

the name *Grey* or the description *the wealthy tea importer* correctly identify *b'*. Sentences like the following will therefore add the proper structure:

(7) a. Ursula thinks that Grey is handsome.
  b. Ursula thinks that the wealthy tea importer is handsome.

The element *b'* can also be accessed from the Base/Viewpoint space, by means of its counterpart *b*. With respect to that space, the name *Bond* or the description *the top spy* correctly identify *b* and can therefore be used to access *b'*, according to the Access Principle. Hence, the following sentences also add the proper structure, using a different path through the space configuration:

(8) a. Ursula thinks that Bond is handsome.
  b. Ursula thinks that the top spy is handsome.

Sentences (7a) and (7b) correspond, of course, to what are traditionally called opaque readings. Sentences (8a) and (8b) correspond to transparent ones: their existence and properties follow directly from the Access Principle.

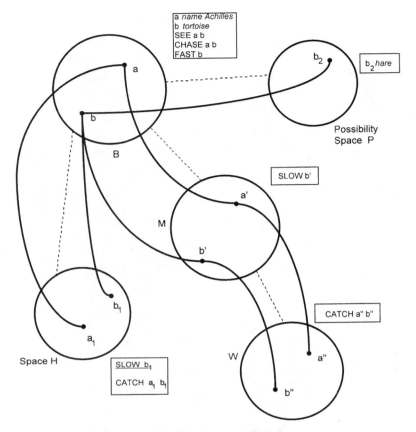

Figure 14.7. Doubting appearances

An essential point, often made in the mental space literature, is that the same ambiguities show up no matter what kind of space (belief, time, movie, counterfactual, etc.) we are dealing with. It is the multiple connecting paths available in a partitioned configuration that yield multiple understandings. It is not the content of the mental spaces (propositional attitudes, time, geographical space, images, etc.).

Also, the number of paths is not fixed for a given sentence. What matters is the spaces available in a particular discourse. The more spaces are accessible from the Focus, the more connecting paths there will be and, consequently, the more potential understandings for the sentence. For example, the sentence *If I were your father, I would help you* sets up a minimum of three spaces and has a minimum of three understandings. But if more spaces are available, there will be more readings. If the context for this sentence is the making of a movie, and the speaker is Kirk Douglas and the addressee Jane Fonda, there will be nine readings, because of the increased number of spaces and referential access paths.

The sentence itself has no fixed number of readings. It has a potential for generating connections in mental space configurations. The number of readings will

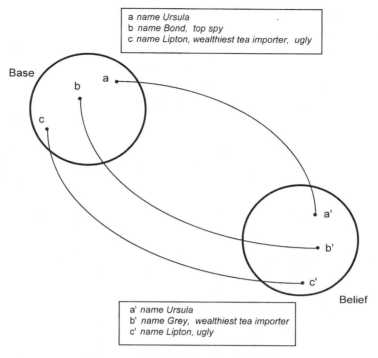

> a *name Ursula*
> b *name Bond, top spy*
> c *name Lipton, wealthiest tea importer, ugly*

Base

Belief

> a' *name Ursula*
> b' *name Grey, wealthiest tea importer*
> c' *name Lipton, ugly*

Figure 14.8. James Bond and Ursula

be a product of this potential and the spaces available (and accessible) in a particular context (Fauconnier 1990).

Elements of mental spaces can be roles linked to their values by the Access Principle and roles themselves can be values of other roles. This is a rich domain of inquiry that explains and generalizes central aspects of noun phrase reference such as distinctions between attributive, specific, and nonspecific uses (see Sakahara 1996; Fauconnier 1985, 1986, 1998).

5. Modality: The Case of Signed Languages

Spoken languages offer considerable evidence for mental space organization. But interestingly, independent evidence is also available from sign languages, such as American Sign Language (ASL), which operate in a different modality, visual-gestural rather than oral-auditory. Van Hoek (1996), Liddell (1995, 2003), and Poulin (1996) are among those who have very successfully pursued an approach initiated by Lacy in unpublished work in the late 1970s. Their research has provided extensive evidence for mental space constructions in ASL, a topic examined in more detail by Wilcox in Chapter 42 of the present *Handbook*. As Liddell demonstrates, sign languages additionally make use of grounded mental spaces in their grammars by taking advantage of the spatial modality.

The clearest example of this is the signing space set up by signers in order to perform various referential and conceptual operations. As Liddell (1996: 145–6) writes:

> Sign languages are well known for their ability to create, as part of the most ordinary discourse, elaborate conceptual representations in the space in front of the signer. Because of the importance of space in ordinary signed discourse, signed languages have come to be structured in ways, which take advantage of those spatial representations. Pronouns and some types of verbs can be produced at specific locations in space or directed towards specific areas of space to produce distinctive meanings. Signs of this type can also be directed toward things that are physically present, including the signer, the addressee, other participants, and other entities. . . . The linguistic uniqueness of the ability to make semantic distinctions by producing signs toward an apparently unlimited number of locations is beyond question.

The physical signing space with referential loci that one can point to serves to ground a corresponding mental space in which elements are being introduced and structured. Subspaces can then be set up with overt counterpart structure analogous to the mental space connections described above for our English example. Strikingly, the Access Principle operates transparently in such cases. As van Hoek (1996) shows, one can point to loci in order to access the counterparts in some space of the elements corresponding to those loci. The choice of accessing strategies is particularly interesting, since it depends on subtle distinctions having to do with focus, viewpoint, and the ultimate goals of the conversational exchange.

With examples like these and many others, van Hoek shows that the elements in one mental space may be accessed from the referential locus in the signing space appropriate for that particular mental space (e.g., past) or from a locus for its counterpart in some higher space (e.g., present/Base). The spatial modality allows the spaces to be grounded: one can actually point or direct other signs toward one or the other referential locus, as one would in pointing deictically at relevant objects, physically present in the context. Liddell (1995) shows how the manipulation of such grounded spaces (token space, surrogate space, and real space) is incorporated into the grammar of ASL to yield intricate reference mechanisms. Poulin (1996) shows how such spaces can be shifted to reflect changes in viewpoint or epistemic stance. This is typically accomplished physically by body shifts and repositioning.

Fridman-Mintz and Liddell (1998) and Liddell (2003) show in great detail the link between such referential processes incorporated into ASL grammar and general linguistic and nonlinguistic mental space building and grounding.

The relevant language universals here are the modality-independent principles of connections and access across mental spaces. The modality-specific universals are the ways in which these mental configurations can be indicated through language (spoken or signed). In both spoken and signed languages, we find grammatical devices for building spaces (adverbials, subject-verb combinations, conjunctions, etc.); in spoken language, pronominal systems and other anaphoric devices code linearly the construction or reactivation of mental space elements. In sign language, the same effect is achieved by constructing grounded spaces, which take advantage of the spatial modality.

6. Discourse Organization: Tense and Mood

Mental spaces are set up dynamically throughout an ongoing discourse on the basis of linguistic and nonlinguistic clues and information. The general scheme, as represented in figure 14.9, is one of new spaces built relative to existing ones.

A piece of discourse will start with a Base B. Space M_1 is then set up subordinate to B, then space M_{11}, subordinate to M_1, and so on. Returning to the Base B, one can open space M_2, than M_{21}, and so on, return to B a number of times, opening spaces M_i and daughter spaces M_{ij}, M_{ijk}, and so on.

At any given stage of the discourse, one of the spaces is a *base* for the system, and one of the spaces (possibly the same one) is in *focus*. Construction at the next stage will be relative either to the Base space or to the Focus space. (This is the scheme developed in Dinsmore 1991.) The discourse moves through the lattice of spaces; viewpoint and focus shift as we go from one space to the next. But at any point, the Base space remains accessible as a possible starting point for another construction.

Dinsmore (1991) and Cutrer (1994) have shown that a major function of tense in language is to establish local time ordering relations between neighboring mental spaces and to keep track of viewpoint and focus shifts. Cutrer develops a sophisticated set of principles for mental space connections guided by tense and explains, thereby, many mysterious features of the ways in which we construct time and viewpoint organization with language. We cannot, here, go into the mechanics of tense and time, but the following example, borrowed from Fauconnier (1997), will help to give an informal idea of what is going on. The example is a very short piece of discourse:

(9)   Max is 23. He has lived abroad. In 1990, he lived in Rome. In 1991, he would move to Venice. He would then have lived a year in Rome.

The space building dynamics associated with the production and/or understanding of this ministory run as follows:

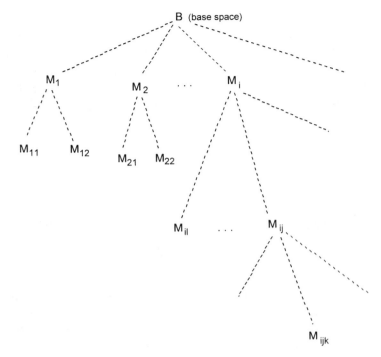

Figure 14.9. Discourse lattice

a. We start with a single space, which is the Base, and also the initial View-point and Focus. We structure that space with the information that Max is 23 years old.

b. Keeping that space in Focus, we add the (present) information that Max has lived abroad. This information is presented via a past Event space ('Max live abroad').

c. In the next sentence, *in 1990* is a space builder. It sets up a new Focus space, in which we build the content 'Max live in Rome'. This is also the new Event space, since we are considering the event/state of Max living in Rome.

d. This Focus space now becomes a Viewpoint from which to consider Max's next move. Intuitively, when we say, "In 1991, he *would* move . . . ," we are presenting 1991 as a future with respect to 1990. The 1990 space ('Max in Rome') becomes a Viewpoint from which to set up the next Focus (and Event) space, 1991, with the content 'Max move to Venice'. We could have said the "same" thing differently by using the Base (present time) as a Viewpoint: *In 1991, Max moved to Venice.*

e. The last sentence, *He would then have lived a year in Rome*, keeps 1990 as the Viewpoint and 1991 as the Focus, while using an Event space ('live a year in Rome') which is past time relative to the Focus 1991.

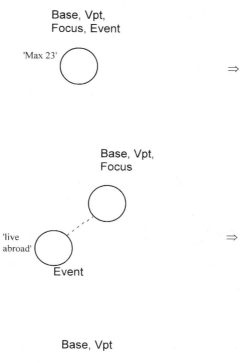

Base, Vpt,
Focus

'live
abroad'

Event

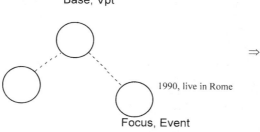

Base, Vpt

1990, live in Rome

Focus, Event

Figure 14.10. Max in Italy

Schematically, the space configuration develops as follows with successive shifts of Event, Focus, and Viewpoint (see figure 4.10. and figure 4.10. continued).

The virtue of this type of cognitive organization is to allow local manipulation of the spaces without losing sight of the entire configuration. Since time is the relevant dimension here, we need some indication of the time relationship between spaces. Typically, tense will provide us with indications of *relative* time relationship. Cutrer (1994) proposes putatively universal semantic Tense-Aspect categories, with language specific means of expressing some of their combinations. She also introduces a crucial distinction: new structure introduced into spaces may be marked as FACT or as PREDICTION, depending on the semantic tense-aspect. Much of Cutrer's work is devoted to establishing the constraints on the space configurations that are set up in this way. The (putatively universal) categories constrain the configuration in specific ways. For instance, in the case of PAST, we have:

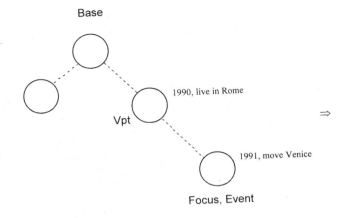

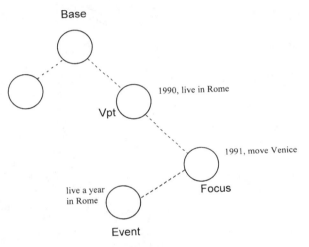

Figure 14.10. (*continued*)

PAST applied to space N indicates that:

a. N is in Focus;

b. N's parent is Viewpoint;

c. N's time is prior to Viewpoint (i.e., prior to N's parent);

d. events or properties represented in N are FACT (in relation to the parent Viewpoint space).

These general constraints are coded grammatically by languages in different ways. So what we call the grammatical "simple past," "past participle," and so on are distinguished from the semantic PAST, which specifies mental space relationships. English has the following coding system:

PAST is coded by the simple past (*lived, went, brought*) or by *have + past participle* if the verb is in infinitival position (*will have forgotten, may have left, claims to have forgotten*). Code: Verb + past or *have* + (Verb + *past participle*)

FUTURE is coded by *will* + Verb.

The construction of connected spaces, with viewpoint and focus shifts is reflected in the language code by retracing the path from the Base to the Focus space, using grammatical tenses.

In our example, when the sentence *In 1991, he would move to Venice* comes into the discourse, K is the Focus/Event space, N (1990) is the Viewpoint space, and M is the base. The grammatical coding reflects the path followed from the base to the focus:

Base space M—PAST → viewpoint Space N—FUTURE → focus Space K

The coding will appear on the verb *move*, because that verb is introducing new structure into the current focus space. The FUTURE connection of K to N will be coded in English by [*will* + Verb *move*]. The PAST connection of N to M will be coded by the simple past. The full coding from base to focus is compositional:

simple past + [*will* + Verb *move*]

⇒   (past + *will*) + *move*

⇒   would move

Languages have different ways of coding the time path, and grammar may highlight some aspects of the path, while underspecifying others. What seems to be universally available is the construction of paths and the shifts of Focus and Viewpoint within the dynamic evolving mental space configuration.

General principles govern the ways in which Focus and Viewpoint (and even Base) are allowed to shift. Cutrer (1994) proposes detailed principles of discourse organization, which include constraints like the following:

a. only one focus, one base at any given moment of the discourse interpretation;
b. new spaces are built from base or focus;
c. focus can shift to event, base, or previous focus; and
d. viewpoint can shift to focus or base.

The account of tense developed by Dinsmore (1991) and Cutrer (1994) explains why tense does not directly reflect conceptual time as one might think (and as many semantic accounts suggest). Instead, the grammar of tense specifies partial constraints on time and fact/prediction status that hold locally between mental spaces within a discourse configuration. We may obtain actual information about time by combining this with other available pragmatic information. Accordingly, the same tense may end up indicating very different objective time relations relative to the speech event. In the sentences in (10), the present tense corresponds to 'future' time; in (11), the present tense corresponds to 'past' events; in (12), the past tense corresponds to a 'present' time; in (13), the past tense corresponds to a 'future' time; and in (14), the "future" tense corresponds to a 'present' time.

(10) a. The boat *leaves* next week.
b. When he *comes* tomorrow, I'll tell him about the party.
c. If I *see* him next week, I'll ask him to call you.

(11) a. I'*m walking* down the street one day when suddenly this guy *walks* up to me . . .
b. He *catches* the ball. He *runs*. He *makes* a touchdown. (morning-after sports report)

(12) a. Do you have a minute? I *wanted* to ask you a question.
b. I wish I *lived* closer to my family, now.
c. If I *had* time now, I would help you.

(13) a. If I *had* the time next week, I would go to your party.
b. I can't go to the concert tonight. You'll have to tell me how it *was*.

(14) a. That *will be* all for now.
b. He's not on the train. He *will have* missed it.

More generally, tenses are used not just to reflect local time relations between neighboring spaces, but also to reflect epistemic distance, that is, whether a space is hypothetical or counterfactual with respect to its parent space. The coding system remains the same, and a particular tense sequence may reflect both time and epistemic distance. Here are some examples offered by Sweetser (1996: 323):

(15) a. If you have Triple-A, then if you go to a telephone, you can solve your problem.
b. If you had Triple-A, then if you went to a telephone, you could solve your problem.
c. If you had had Triple-A, then if you'd gone to a telephone, you could have solved your problem.

We can interpret all three as referring to present time but with different epistemic stances. The first is neutral as to the chances that you have Triple-A. The second suggests that maybe you do not have it. And the third is counterfactual: "you do not have Triple-A, but if you did. . . ." Alternatively, one could interpret the second sentence as referring to a past event and being neutral as to what happened and as to whether you had Triple-A, and the third sentence as referring to a past event and being counterfactual. The embedded tenses (*go, went, had gone,* and *can solve, could solve, could have solved*) reflect the full epistemic and time path from the Base, regardless of the corresponding objective time.

Mood (subjunctive vs. indicative) can serve to indicate distinctions in space accessibility. So, for example, a sentence like *Diogenes is looking for a man who is honest* opens a space in which 'Diogenes finds an honest man'. Because of the Access Principle, which was discussed earlier, the description *a man who is honest* can either access a new element directly in that space, or can identify a new element in the Base, and access its counterpart in the 'look for' space. The first accessing path corresponds to a nonspecific interpretation: any honest man will do. The second accessing path corresponds to a specific reading: there is a particular honest man that Diogenes is looking for. In French, the equivalent of the verb copula *is* can be marked as either indicative or subjunctive:

(16) a. *Diogène cherche un homme qui* **est** *honnête.* [Indicative]
      b. *Diogène cherche un homme qui* **soit** *honnête.* [Subjunctive]

Sentence (16a), with the indicative, allows both accessing paths, as in English, with perhaps a preference for access from the Base (the specific interpretation). The second sentence, on the other hand, allows only direct access to an element in the 'look for' space, the nonspecific reading. This is because the subjunctive forces the description to be satisfied in the embedded 'look for' space.

A range of intricate space accessibility phenomena linked to grammatical mood is studied in Mejías-Bikandi (1993, 1996). Rich aspectual phenomena involving spaces and viewpoint are discussed in Doiz-Bienzobas (1995). The general issue of discourse management through construction of linked spaces is addressed in Takubo (1993) and Kinsui and Takubo (1990).

7. Some Grammatical Devices for Cognitive Construction

Language has many devices to guide the construction and connection of mental spaces. Here are some of them:

a. *Space builders.* A space builder is a grammatical expression that either opens a new space or shifts focus to an existing space. Space builders take on a variety of grammatical forms, such as prepositional phrases, adverbials, subject-verb complexes, conjunctions + clause. Examples include *in 1929, in that story, actually, in reality, in Susan's opinion, Susan believes, Max hopes,* and *If it rains.* Grammatical techniques and strategies for building spaces in Japanese and English are compared in Fujii (1996). The psychological effects of using explicit space builders in discourse are examined by Traxler et al. (1997).

b. *Names and descriptions* (grammatically noun phrases). Names (*Max, Napoleon, NABISCO,* etc.), and descriptions (*the mailman, a vicious snake, some boys who were tired,* etc.) either set up new elements or point to existing elements in the discourse construction. They also associate such elements with properties (e.g., 'having the name Napoleon', 'being a boy', 'being tired', etc.).

c. *Tenses and moods.* Tenses and moods play an important role in determining what kind of space is in focus, its connection to the base space, its accessibility, and the location of counterparts used for identification.

d. *Presuppositional constructions.* Some grammatical constructions, such as definite descriptions, aspectuals, clefts and pseudo-clefts, signal that an assignment of structure within a space is introduced in the presuppositional mode; this mode allows the structure to be propagated into neighboring spaces for the counterparts of the relevant elements.

e. *Trans-spatial operators.* The copula (*be* in English) and other copulative verbs, such as *become* and *remain*, may stand for connectors between spaces. (The general function of *be* is to stand for domain mappings; connection between spaces is a special case of this general function.) Consider a grammatical structure of the form NP_1 *be* NP_2, where NP_1 and NP_2 are noun phrases and identify elements a_1 and a_2 respectively, such that a_1 is in space X and a_2 is in space Y. Suppose F is the only connector linking spaces X and Y. Then the language expression NP_1 *be* NP_2 will stipulate that a_2 in Y is the counterpart of a_1 in X via connector F:

$$a_2 = F(a_1)$$

It should be emphasized that mental spaces and their connections are pervasive in human thought and action whether or not language is directly involved (see Fauconnier and Turner 2002; Hutchins 2005). Mental spaces, then, are not directly linguistic, but a central function of language is to prompt for their construction and elaboration. As a result, there is no fixed set of ways in which mental spaces come about. The list above faithfully recapitulates some of the space-building grammatical constructions found in language after language.

It is sometimes asked what constraints there are on this powerful representational apparatus and whether space building is fully operational. The framework and the analyses within it do indeed sharply delimit what language can do and cannot do. It is useful in this regard to understand the following. A representational apparatus (e.g., a generative rule system, or a set-theoretically based formal semantics, or a Cognitive Grammar style framework) does not include *a priori* constraints other than the ones constitutive of the apparatus itself. Constraints and principles are imposed on theories formulated using the apparatus. The same is true for analysis in terms of mental spaces. The analysis is motivated by the generalizations that it affords. The principles and constraints are discovered through empirically based research. Some principles seem universal, for example, the Access Principle, presupposition projection, and the general form of the mechanisms for tense. Many other constraining principles are specific to a modality, a language, or a given construction. This is the case for the tense system in English outlined above or for the ways in which anaphoric spaces are set up by signed languages. The other crucial thing to remember is that language does not by itself set up cognitive representations operationally defined by language forms. It only prompts for cognitive constructions in context, so that the same form may give rise to widely different constructions in different circumstances. What the form provides is a mapping scheme to be used in conjunction with available contextual, cultural resources at a given stage of preexisting mental space in discourse. Universal optimality constraints and governing principles have been proposed and studied in detail for integration networks of mental spaces in chapter 16 of *The Way We Think* (Fauconnier and Turner 2002).

8. FUTURE PERSPECTIVES AND RESEARCH PROGRAMS

Mental spaces have turned out to be useful and explanatory far beyond the reference and presupposition phenomena that originally motivated them as theoretical constructs. Mappings and connections across mental spaces are used routinely in all areas of Cognitive Linguistics and also in nonlinguistic research in cognitive science. Highly sophisticated research continues to be done in all the areas where mental space theory was first applied, in particular on conditionals (see Dancygier 1998; Dancygier and Sweetser 1996, 2005), scoping phenomena on locative and temporal domains (see Huumo 1996, 1998), grammar of sign languages (see Liddell 2003), discourse (see Epstein 2001), and frame-shifting (see Coulson 2001). But at the same time, there has been an explosion of research triggered by the discovery of wide-ranging phenomena where mental spaces are assembled, connected, and constructed within networks of conceptual integration. This topic is discussed in a separate chapter of the present *Handbook*. This area of research is particularly promising in that it links linguistic and nonlinguistic phenomena in systematic ways that begin to explain how and why there can be imaginative emergent structure in human thought in its everyday manifestations as well as in its most original and singular spurts of creativity.

NOTES

This chapter uses excerpts from Fauconnier (1985, 1997) and Fauconnier and Turner (2002) to present the notion of mental spaces. In addition, it places the research in its current intellectual context within, and outside of, Cognitive Linguistics.

REFERENCES

Brugman, Claudia. 1996. Mental spaces and constructional meaning. In Gilles Fauconnier and Eve Sweetser, eds., *Spaces, worlds, and grammar* 28–56. Chicago: University of Chicago Press.

Coulson, Seana. 2001. *Semantic leaps: Frame-shifting and conceptual blending in meaning construction.* Cambridge: Cambridge University Press.

Cutrer, L. Michelle. 1994. Time and tense in narratives and in everyday language. PhD dissertation, University of California at San Diego.

Dancygier, Barbara. 1998. *Conditionals and prediction.* Cambridge: Cambridge University Press.

Dancygier, Barbara, and Eve Sweetser. 1996. Conditionals, distancing, and alternative spaces. In Adele E. Goldberg, ed., *Conceptual structure, discourse and language* 83–98. Stanford, CA: CSLI Publications.

Dancygier, Barbara, and Eve Sweetser. 2005. *Mental spaces in grammar: Conditional constructions.* Cambridge: Cambridge University Press.

Dinsmore, John. 1991. *Partitioned representations.* Dordrecht, Netherlands: Kluwer.

Doiz-Bienzobas, Aintzane. 1995. The preterite and the imperfect in Spanish: Past situation vs. Past viewpoint. PhD dissertation, University of California at San Diego.

Encrevé, Pierre. 1988. "C'est Reagan qui a coulé le billet vert". *Actes de la Recherche en Sciences Sociales* 71/72: 108–28.

Epstein, Richard. 2001. The definite article, accessibility, and the construction of discourse referents. *Cognitive Linguistics* 12: 333–78.

Fauconnier, Gilles. 1985. *Mental spaces: Aspects of meaning construction in natural language.* Cambridge, MA: MIT Press. (2nd ed., Cambridge: Cambridge University Press, 1994)

Fauconnier, Gilles. 1986. Roles and connecting paths. In Charles Travis, ed., *Meaning and interpretation* 19–44. Oxford: Oxford University Press.

Fauconnier, Gilles. 1990. Invisible meaning. *Berkeley Linguistics Society* 16: 309–404.

Fauconnier, Gilles. 1997. *Mappings in thought and language.* Cambridge: Cambridge University Press.

Fauconnier, Gilles. 1998. Mental spaces and conceptual integration. In Michael Tomasello, ed., *The new psychology of language: Cognitive and functional approaches to language structure* 1: 251–79. Mahwah, NJ: Lawrence Erlbaum.

Fauconnier, Gilles, and Eve Sweetser, eds. 1996. *Spaces, worlds, and grammar.* Chicago: University of Chicago Press.

Fauconnier, Gilles, and Mark Turner. 2002. *The way we think: Conceptual blending and the mind's hidden complexities.* New York: Basic Books.

Fridman-Mintz, Boris, and Scott Liddell. 1998. Sequencing mental spaces in an ASL Narrative. In Jean-Pierre Koenig, ed., *Discourse and cognition* 255–68. Stanford, CA: CSLI Publications.

Fujii, Seiko. 1996. English and Japanese devices for building mental spaces. In Masayoshi Shibatani and Sandra Thompson, eds., *Essays in Semantics and Pragmatics* 76–90. Amsterdam: John Benjamins.

Hutchins, E. 2005. Material anchors for conceptual blends. *Journal of Pragmatics* 37: 1555–77.

Huumo, Tuomas. 1996. A scoping hierarchy of locatives. *Cognitive Linguistics* 7: 265–99.

Huumo, Tuomas. 1998. Bound spaces, starting points, and settings. In Jean-Pierre Koenig, ed., *Discourse and cognition: Bridging the gap* 297–308. Stanford, CA: CSLI Publications.

Kinsui, Satoshi, and Yukinori Takubo. 1990. Danwakanri riron kara mita Nihongo no sijisi [A discourse management analysis of Japanese demonstrative expressions]. In *Nintikagaku no hatten* [Advances in Japanese cognitive science] 3: 85–115.

Lakoff, George. 1987. *Women, fire, and dangerous things: What categories reveal about the mind.* Chicago: University of Chicago Press.

Lakoff, George. 1996. Multiple selves. In Gilles Fauconnier and Eve Sweetser, eds., *Spaces, worlds, and grammar* 91–123. Chicago: University of Chicago Press.

Langacker, Ronald W. 2003. One *any. Korean Linguistics* 18: 65–105.

Liddell, Scott K. 1995. Real, surrogate and token space: Grammatical consequences in ASL. In Karen Emmorey and Judy S. Reilly, eds., *Language, gesture, and space* 19–41. Hillsdale, NJ: Lawrence Erlbaum.

Liddell, Scott K. 1996. Spatial representations in discourse: comparing spoken and signed language. *Lingua* 98: 145–67.

Liddell, Scott K. 2003. *Grammar, gesture, and meaning in American Sign Language.* Cambridge: Cambridge University Press.

Mejías-Bikandi, Errapel. 1993. Syntax, discourse, and acts of mind: A study of the indicative/subjunctive in Spanish. PhD dissertation, University of California at San Diego.

Mejías-Bikandi, Errapel. 1996. Space accessibility and mood in Spanish. In Gilles Fauconnier and Eve Sweetser, eds., *Spaces, worlds, and grammar* 157–78. Chicago: University of Chicago Press.

Mushin, Ilana. 1998. Viewpoint shifts in narrative. In Jean-Pierre Koenig, ed., *Discourse and cognition* 323–36. Stanford, CA: CSLI Publications.

Poulin, Christine. 1996. Manipulation of discourse spaces in American Sign Language. In Adele E. Goldberg, ed., *Conceptual structure, discourse and language* 421–33. Stanford, CA: CSLI Publications.

Rubba, Jo. 1996. Alternate grounds in the interpretation of deictic expressions. In Gilles Fauconnier and Eve Sweetser, eds., *Spaces, worlds, and grammar* 227–61. Chicago: University of Chicago Press.

Sakahara, Shigeru. 1996. Roles and identificational copular sentences. In Gilles Fauconnier and Eve Sweetser, eds., *Spaces, worlds, and grammar* 262–89. Chicago: University of Chicago Press.

Sanders, José, and Gisela Redeker. 1996. Perspective and the representation of speech and thought in narrative discourse. In Gilles Fauconnier and Eve Sweetser, eds., *Spaces, worlds, and grammar* 290–317. Chicago: University of Chicago Press.

Sweetser, Eve. 1996. Mental spaces and the grammar of conditional constructions. In Gilles Fauconnier and Eve Sweetser, eds., *Spaces, worlds, and grammar* 318–33. Chicago: University of Chicago Press.

Takubo, Yuki. 1993. Danwakanri riron kara mita Nihongo no hanjijitu jokenbun [Discourse management analysis of Japanese counterfactuals]. In T. Masuoka, ed., *Nihongo no joken hyogen* [Conditionals in Japanese] 169–83. Tokyo: Kurosio shuppan.

Traxler, Matthew, Anthony Sanford, Joy Aked, and Linda Moxey. 1997. Processing causal and diagnostic statements in discourse. *Journal of Experimental Psychology: Learning, Memory, and Cognition* 23: 88–101.

Turner, Mark. 1996. *The literary mind.* New York: Oxford University Press.

van Hoek, Karen. 1996. Conceptual locations for reference in American Sign Language. In Gilles Fauconnier and Eve Sweetser, eds., *Spaces, worlds, and grammar* 334–50. Chicago: University of Chicago Press.

van Hoek, Karen. 1997. *Anaphora and conceptual structure.* Chicago: University of Chicago Press.

CHAPTER 15

CONCEPTUAL INTEGRATION

MARK TURNER

CONCEPTUAL INTEGRATION, also called "blending," is a basic mental operation that works over mental spaces (for an introduction to mental spaces, see Fauconnier, this volume, chapter 14). Conceptual integration theory was founded jointly by Gilles Fauconnier and myself in 1993 and has been elaborated by us for more than a decade. Our research is surveyed in Fauconnier and Turner (2002); this chapter is essentially an abstract of that work. The elements introduced here are treated in much greater detail there. In the last several years, many researchers in various disciplines have advanced the basic science of blending research, as summarized at Turner (1995–2006).

As an example of blending, consider a common situation. A man is serving as a groomsman in a wedding party. He is consciously enacting a familiar mental story, with roles, participants, a plot, and a goal. But while he is fulfilling his role in the wedding story, he is remembering a different story, which took place a week before in Cabo San Lucas, in which he and his girlfriend, who is not present at the wedding, went diving in the hopes of retrieving sunken treasure. Why, cognitively, should he be able to inhabit, mentally, these two stories at the same time? There are rich possibilities for confusion, but in all the central ways, he remains unconfused. He does not mistake the bride for his girlfriend, for the treasure, for the shark, or for himself. He does not swim down the aisle, even as, in the other story, he is swimming. He speaks normally even as, in the other story, he is underwater. Everyone has had the experience of being in a moment of potential harm or achievement— a fight, an accident, a negotiation, an interview—when it would seem to be in our interest to give our complete attention to the moment, and yet even then, some other story has flitted unbidden into consciousness, without confusing us about the story we inhabit.

Human beings go beyond merely imagining stories that run counter to the present story. We can also make connections between different stories, or more generally, between different and conflicting mental spaces. The groomsman, for example, can make analogical connections between his girlfriend and the bride and between himself and the groom. We can also "blend" different mental spaces to create a third mental space with emergent structure. The groomsman, for example, can blend these analogical counterparts into a daydream in which it is he and his girlfriend who are being married right now at this exact ceremony.

This blended story is manifestly false, and he should not make the mistake, as he obediently discharges his duties at the real wedding, of thinking that he is in the process of marrying his girlfriend. But he forges the blended mental space, with potentially serious consequences: as he observes the daydream, he might come to realize that he likes it, and so formulate a plan of action to make it real. Or, in the blended scene, when the bride is invited to say, "I do," she might say, "I would never marry you!" Her fulguration might reveal to him a truth he had sensed only unconsciously, and this revelation might bring him regret or relief.

Running multiple mental spaces, or, more generally, multiple constelled networks of mental spaces, when we should be absorbed by only one, and blending them when they should be kept apart, is at the root of what makes us human. Blending, especially in its advanced forms, is creative, and it can be forced into view by pyrotechnic examples such as these. Yet it works almost entirely below the horizon of consciousness. The products of blending frequently become entrenched as units in conceptual structure, ready to be activated at a shot by someone who has learned or developed them. Grammatical constructions are such entrenched units, and the origin of human language is a byproduct of the evolution of the most advanced form of blending, known as "double-scope" blending (Fauconnier and Turner 2002: chapter 9).

Conceptual integration conforms to a set of constitutive principles: (i) A partial *cross-space mapping* connects some counterparts in the input mental spaces. For example, the girlfriend and the bride are connected in the wedding example. (ii) There is a *generic mental space*, which maps onto each of the inputs and contains what the inputs have in common. In the wedding example, the generic space has a man and a woman engaged in sustained pair bonding. (iii) There is a fourth mental space, the *blended space*, often called "the blend." It is in this space that the man is in the process of marrying his girlfriend. (iv) There is *selective projection* from the inputs to the blend. It is important to emphasize that not all elements and relations from the inputs are projected to the blend.

There are also typical features of conceptual integration networks. Chief among these, the blend develops emergent structure not in the inputs. In the wedding blend, for example, the man is marrying his girlfriend.

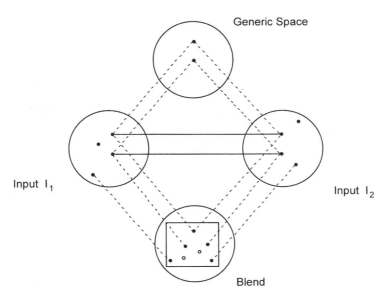

Figure 15.1. The basic diagram

The basic diagram in figure 15.1 illustrates the central features of conceptual integration.

In the Basic Diagram, the circles represent mental spaces, the solid lines indicate the matching and cross-space mapping between the inputs, and the dotted lines indicate connections between inputs and either generic or blended spaces. The solid square in the blended space stands for emergent structure. While this static way of diagramming aspects of the process is convenient, such a diagram is always a snapshot of an imaginative and complicated development that can involve deactivating previous connections, reframing previous spaces, and other actions.

Emergent structure is generated in three ways: (i) *Composition of projections from the inputs*: blending can compose elements from the input spaces to provide relations that do not exist in the separate inputs. (ii) *Completion based on independently recruited frames and scenarios*: we rarely realize the extent of background knowledge and structure that we bring into a blend unconsciously. Blends recruit great ranges of such background meaning. Pattern completion is the most basic kind of recruitment. (iii) *Elaboration*: we elaborate blends by treating them as simulations and running them imaginatively according to the principles that have been established for the blend. Some of these principles for running the blend will have been brought to the blend by completion.

Composition, completion, and elaboration lead to emergent structure in the blend; the blend contains structure that is not copied from the inputs. In the Basic Diagram, the square inside the blend represents emergent structure.

Any mental space in the integration network can be modified at any moment in its construction. In particular, the inputs can be modified by reverse mapping from the blend. In the wedding example, backward projection from the daydream blend can alter the man's sense of his actual relation to his girlfriend.

Consider a second example. The clipper ship *Northern Light* sailed in 1853 from San Francisco to Boston in 76 days, 8 hours. That time was still the fastest on record in 1993, when a modern catamaran, *Great American II,* set out on the same course. A few days before the catamaran reached Boston, observers were able to say:

(1)   At this point, *Great American II* is 4.5 days ahead of *Northern Light.*

This expression frames the two boats as sailing on the same course during the same time period in 1993. It blends the event of 1853 and the event of 1993 into a single event. In one mental space, we have the event of 1853; in a second, we have the event of 1993. These are the *input spaces* to the blend. There is a partial *cross-space mapping* that connects counterparts in the input mental spaces. It connects the two boats, the two paths, San Francisco to San Francisco, Boston to Boston, and moment of departure to moment of departure. There is a *generic mental space,* which maps onto each of the inputs and contains what the inputs have in common: an ocean voyage from San Francisco to Boston. There is *selective projection* to the blended space, which brings in the two boats, the course, their actual positions and times on the course, and so on, but not the 1853 date or the 1853 weather conditions, the fact that the clipper ship was engaged in transporting cargo, and so on. In the blend, the geographies and times of the two input spaces are fused, but the boats are not fused. They are brought in as separate elements.

The blend develops *emergent structure* not in the inputs. First, *composition* of elements from the inputs makes relations available in the blend that did not exist in the separate inputs. In the blend but in neither of the inputs, there are two boats traveling from San Francisco to Boston, instead of one. Second, *completion* brings additional structure to the blend. The scenario of two boats moving toward the same goal on the same course and having departed from San Francisco on the same day fits into an obvious and familiar frame, that of a RACE, which is automatically added to the blend by pattern *completion.* By virtue of that frame, we can now run the scenario dynamically: in the blend, the two boats are racing. Such "running of the blend" is part of *elaboration.* In this case, elaboration of the blend is constrained by projection of locations and times from the inputs. Running the blend modifies it imaginatively, delivering the actual winning and losing in the blend and the emotions associated with those relations. This is new structure: there is no relation of being "ahead" or "behind" another boat in either of the input mental spaces, even if we run them dynamically. But those two boats in the blend are projected back to the "same" boats in the two input mental spaces. Their status in the blend projects back to their counterparts in the input spaces. In this case, the expression *ahead of,* used to express the conceptual relation between the two boats, prompts for a blend in which the two boats bear close spatial and temporal relations.

The RACE frame in the blended space may be invoked more noticeably, as in (2):

(2)   At this point, *Great American II* is barely maintaining a 4.5-day lead over *Northern Light.*

Maintaining a lead is an intentional part of a race. Although in reality the catamaran is sailing alone and the clipper's run took place 140 years before, the situation is described in terms of the blended space. No one is fooled: the clipper has not magically reappeared. The blend remains solidly linked to the inputs, and inferences from the blend can be projected back to the inputs: in particular, if we know that *Great American II* is 4.5 days ahead of *Northern Light* in the blend, then we know that the corresponding location of *Northern Light* in its input is less far along the course than the corresponding location of *Great American II* in its input, and we know that it takes 4.5 days of sailing (by one of the boats) to get from the first location to the second. Another noteworthy property of the RACE frame is its emotional content. Sailors in a race are driven by emotions linked to winning, leading, losing, gaining, and so forth. This emotional value can be projected to the *Great American II* input. The solitary run of *Great American II*, conceived as a race against the nineteenth-century clipper, can be lived with corresponding emotions, which can in turn change the course of events. The crew of *Great American II* can draw courage and commitment from seeing themselves as engaged in a historic competition, or if they are daunted by *Northern Light's* performance, may be cowed into failure.

Conceptual integration networks routinely involve certain Vital Relations which can obtain between mental spaces in the network ("outer-space vital relations") or within mental spaces in the network ("inner-space vital relations") or in some cases both:

Change
Identity
Time
Space
Cause-Effect
Part-Whole
Representation
Role
Analogy
Disanalogy
Property
Similarity
Category
Intentionality
Uniqueness

In addition to the constitutive principles of conceptual blending, blending operates under a set of governing principles having much to do with Vital Relations.

   a. *Topology Principle*: other things being equal, set up the blend and the inputs
      so that inner-space relations in the blend reflect useful topology in the
      inputs and their outer-space relations.
   b. *The Pattern Completion Principle*: other things being equal, complete ele-
      ments in the blend by using existing integrated patterns as additional
      inputs. Other things being equal, use a completing frame that has relations
      that can be the compressed versions of the important outer-space vital
      relations between the inputs.
   c. *The Integration Principle*: achieve an integrated blend.
   d. *The Maximization of Vital Relations Principle*: other things being equal,
      maximize vital relations in the network. In particular, maximize the
      vital relations in the blended space and reflect them in outer-space vital
      relations.
   e. *The Intensification of Vital Relations Principle*: other things being equal,
      intensify vital relations.
   f. *The Web Principle*: other things being equal, manipulating the blend as a
      unit must maintain the web of appropriate connections to the input spaces
      easily and without additional surveillance or computation.
   g. *The Unpacking Principle*: other things being equal, the blend all by itself
      should prompt for the reconstruction of the entire network.
   h. *The Relevance Principle*: other things being equal, an element in the
      blend should have relevance, including relevance for establishing links
      to other spaces and for running the blend. Conversely, an outer-space
      relation between the inputs that is important for the purpose of the
      network should have a corresponding compression in the blend.
   i. *The Compression Principle*: achieve compressed blended spaces.

There are several routine strategies for satisfying the compression principle:
borrow compression from a compressed input; compress a vital relation (such as
time or space or change) by scaling it to human scale in the blend; compress a vital
relation by syncopating it as it is projected to the blend; compress one vital relation
into another that fits human scale better; achieve scalability of one kind of vital
relation by compressing it into a different kind of vital relation; create vital relations in the blend that are not otherwise available in the network by compressing one vital relation into another; or create compressed blends by projecting only
highlights from other mental spaces in the network that are connected by a structure of story or sequential action.

Figures 15.2 and 15.3 illustrate two of the compression hierarchies for which we
currently have evidence.

The constitutive and governing principles of conceptual integration, operating over Vital Relations, are driven by an overarching goal, *Achieve Human Scale*,
and have the effect of creating blended spaces at human scale. The most obvious
human-scale situations have direct perception and action in familiar frames that
are easily apprehended by human beings: an object falls, someone lifts an object,

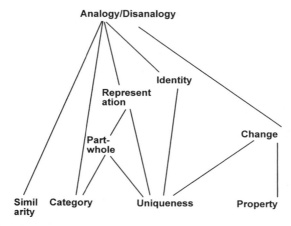

Figure 15.2. Compression hierarchy for Analogy/Disanalogy

two people converse, one person goes somewhere, and so on. They typically have direct intentionality, very few participants, and immediate bodily effect. They are immediately apprehended as coherent.

Once blending achieves a human-scale blend, the blend also counts as human-scale, and so can participate in producing other human-scale blends, in a boot-strapping pattern that characterizes much of cultural evolution.

To achieve a human-scale blend often requires imaginative transformations of elements and structure in an integration network as they are projected to the blend. There are several subgoals:

Compress what is diffuse
Obtain global insight
Strengthen vital relations
Come up with a story
Go from many to one

Conceptual integration operates indispensably in all the areas of thought and action that distinguish human beings from members of other species. Language is prominent among them and our concern here.

As we surveyed in Fauconnier and Turner (2002), even very simple constructions in language depend upon complex blending. It is natural to think that adjectives assign fixed properties to nouns, so that *The cow is brown* assigns the fixed property 'brown' to 'cow'. By the same token, there should be a fixed property associated with the adjective *safe* that is assigned to any noun it modifies. Yet consider the following unremarkable uses of *safe* in the context of a child playing at the beach with a shovel: *The child is safe, The beach is safe, The shovel is safe*. There is no fixed property that *safe* assigns to 'child', 'beach', and 'shovel'. The first statement means that the child will not be harmed, but so do the second and third—they do not mean that the beach or the shovel will not

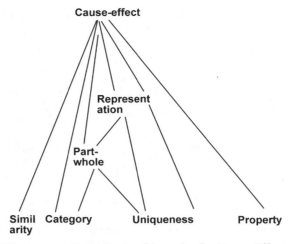

Figure 15.3. Compression hierarchy for Cause-Effect

be harmed (although they could in some other context). *Safe* does not assign a property but rather prompts us to evoke scenarios of danger appropriate for the noun and the context. We worry about whether the child will be harmed by being on the beach or by using the shovel. Technically, the word *safe* evokes an abstract frame of DANGER with roles like 'victim', 'location', and 'instrument'. Modifying the noun with the adjective prompts us to integrate that abstract frame of DANGER and the specific situation of the child on the beach into a counterfactual event of 'harm' to the child. We build a specific imaginary scenario of 'harm' in which 'child', 'beach', and 'shovel' are assigned to roles in the DANGER frame. Instead of assigning a simple property, the adjective is prompting us to blend a frame of danger with the specific situation of the child on the beach with a shovel. This blend is the imaginary scenario in which the child is harmed. The word *safe* implies a disanalogy between this counterfactual blend and the real situation, with respect to the entity designated by the noun. If the shovel is safe, it is because in the counterfactual blend it is too sharp, but in the specific situation it is too dull to cut. The disanalogy between the actual situation and the counterfactual blend is a relation between two mental spaces. One of them is already a blend. They are both inputs to yet a second blend, the one in which we have the actual situation, but now the disanalogy between the input spaces is compressed into a property of an element in the blend: in the blend, we have a *safe* child or a *safe* beach or a *safe* shovel. The word *safe* is a prompt to construct an elaborate conceptual integration network with the actual situation and a harm scenario as inputs to a counterfactual blend, and the actual situation and the counterfactual blend as inputs to a final blend in which there is an element with the property 'safe'. To understand *safe* requires constructing and using the entire network.

We can create many different blends out of the same inputs. The process is the same in all of them, but the results are different. In *The shovel is safe*, the child is the victim in the blend if we are concerned about the shovel's injuring the child, but the shovel is the victim in the blend if we are concerned about the child's breaking the shovel. Furthermore, any number of roles can be recruited for the 'danger' input. In the counterfactual blend for *The jewels are safe*, the jewels are neither victim nor instrument; they are 'possessions' and their 'owner' is the victim. If we ship the jewels in packaging, then in the counterfactual blend for *The packaging is safe*, the jewels are the 'victim', external forces are the 'cause of harm', and packaging is the 'barrier to external forces'. Other examples showing the variety of possible roles would be *Drive at a safe speed*, *Have a safe trip*, *This is a safe bet*, and *He stayed a safe distance away*.

The beach is safe shows that the "matches" between inputs are not achieved independently of blending and that there is nothing simple about "matching." The beach in the real situation is matched to the role 'doer of harm' in the 'harm' scenario because we have achieved an imaginary blend that counts as counterfactual to the real situation. That match, however, is a match between a role in a frame and a specific element that is in fact *not* an instance of the role. The real 'safe beach' is not a 'doer of harm'. That is the point of the utterance. The role 'doer of harm' in the 'harm' input is matched to a 'beach' in a blend that *is* imaginatively a 'doer of harm'. And the 'beach' in the specific situation is matched to the 'beach' in the counterfactual blend because they are opposites in the way that counts for this situation: one is a 'doer of harm', and the other is not.

Safe is not an exceptional adjective with special semantic properties that set it apart from ordinary adjectives. The principles of conceptual integration are general. Even color adjectives, which at first blush look as if they must assign fixed features, turn out to require noncompositional conceptual integration. *Red pencil* can be taken to mean a pencil whose wood has been painted red on the outside, a pencil that leaves a red mark (the lead is red, or the chemical in the pencil reacts with the paper to produce red, or . . .), a pencil used to record the activities of the team dressed in red, a pencil smeared with lipstick, or a pencil used only for recording deficits (see also Travis 1981 on *black kettle*; in addition, see the sections on "active zones" in Langacker 1987, 1990, 1991). Theories of semantics typically prefer to work with examples like *black bird* or *brown cow*, since these examples are supposed to be the principal examples of compositionality of meaning, but even these examples illustrate complicated processes of conceptual integration.

Many expressions prompt directly for blends. The exact words used in the news report in *Latitude 38* to describe *Northern Light* and *Great American II* were:

(3)   As we went to press, Rich Wilson and Bill Biewenga were barely
       maintaining a 4.5-day lead over the ghost of the clipper *Northern Light*, . . .

The word *ghost* points explicitly to the blend. Its effect is to indicate how to build connections over three separate spaces: someone in the temporally later input (in this case, the crew of *Great American II,* the reporters, and everyone following the event) remembers an element in a temporally earlier input (here, *Northern Light* in 1853); that element is not in the temporally later input, but it has a counterpart in the blend (here, the "ghost" ship).

This use of *ghost* to indicate how to build an integration network is quite conventional. It cannot be explained as just predicating a feature of a single element; it also tells us something important about the web of that element's connections. We saw a similar lexical phenomenon with *safe*, which again could not be explained as just predicating a feature of a single element; instead, it told us something important about the web of connections across spaces in an integration network involving a specific counterfactual scenario of harm. In addition, *ghost* signals that events involving the 'ghost' in the blend are constrained by the events involving its ancestor counterpart. In the *Northern Light* example, the run of the ghost must be the same as that of its ancestor. It cannot go faster than it went in 1853, benefit from 1993 weather, collide with *Great American II*, and so on. So, again, *ghost* is not telling us about specific features of the events in the two spaces, but only that those events have a particular cross-space relationship: this kind of ghost, at least, must copy its ancestor counterpart.

Nobody confuses the blend with reality. There is no inference that the sailors actually saw a ghost ship or imagined one. The construction and operation of the blend is creative, but also conventional in the sense that readers know immediately and without conscious effort how to interpret it.

Ghost is specialized as a prompt for elaborate conceptual blending that provides thorough compression to human scale. It signals various vital relations between the input spaces and also signals a category in the blend that is a compression of those vital relations. The sailors in the 1993 space know about the history of *Northern Light*. That is a link of intentionality through memory. *Ghost* prompts for the construction of that outer-space vital relation, which is often supplemented with an outer-space representation link, making the content of the memory a representation of the past event. The particular ghost in the blend compresses that outer-space representation link into a directly perceived instance of the category 'ghost'. There are three pairwise outer-space Identity links connecting that instance in the blend, an element in the input historical space, and an element in the content of the memory that is in the later input space. There is also an outer-space relation of counterfactuality between the blend and the inputs; for example, in the blend there are two boats racing, one of them a ghost, but that structure is incompatible with the structure in the inputs for 1853 and 1993. The ghost in the blend is naturally decompressed into a time link between the two inputs. These features of *ghost* are quite general. The *Northern Light* example illustrates, therefore, not only the constitutive and governing principles, the overarching goals, and the Vital Relations, but also a much more specific template of conceptual integration for *ghost* that seems to be available in every culture.

For *ghost*, one of the inputs has an element that the other input does not, and this disanalogy on existence of an element is compressed into an element in the blend that has special properties. Once this strategy of compression of disanalogy to property is recognized, we can see a vast range of similar constructions in the language. *Coming home, I drove into the wrong house and collided with a tree I don't have* is counterfactual because it depends upon the evoked but counterfactual scenario of driving into the right house and therefore not colliding with a tree. The grammatical trigger here is not *if . . . then* but rather the adjective *wrong*. In one input, the driver drives into the parking place at his or her home. In the other, he or she drives onto the property of some different house and collides with a tree. These inputs share the frame of parking a car at a house, and there are identity connectors between the cars and the drivers, but there are disanalogies between the two inputs, having to do with the value of the role 'house' and the existence of a tree at a particular location. In the blend, we have, from the space of what actually happened, the house where the driver did drive, the tree, and the collision. The disanalogy between the houses is compressed in the blend into a property of the house: it is now the 'wrong' house. And the disanalogy having to do with the tree is compressed into a property of the tree: 'a tree I don't have'. It is tempting to think that this is a property of the tree independent of the blend, but note what happens if our companion on a walk through some public woods says, pointing to a tree, "That is a tree I don't have." We are likely to interpret the speaker as meaning that he or she does not own a tree of that type. It would be quite strange if he or she actually meant to point out that he or she did not own that particular tree. In the statement we are looking at, *a tree I don't have* is not interpreted to mean that the driver does not own that particular tree, but rather that there is a counterfactual relation between the blend and the input with the driver parking his or her car at his or her home: there is no tree in the corresponding spot at his or her home, and no collision when he or she drives through that spot, either. Very generally, when disanalogy operates on existence of a value for a role, that disanalogy is a good candidate for compression into nonpossession, as in *That car does not have air conditioning, Arkansas has no coastline, Africa does not have bears,* and *My house doesn't have that porch.*

Caffeine headache, money problem, and *nicotine fit* are straightforward phrases—for a headache that comes from lack of coffee, a problem that consists of a lack of money, a fit brought on by lack of nicotine, presumably from not smoking enough—all set up an integration involving a counterfactual link between spaces. *Caffeine headache* brings up two situations, one in which you have your coffee and one in which you have a headache. There is evident identity, analogy, and disanalogy between these two situations: in both, it's late morning, and you are at work. But there is the coffee only in the first and the headache only in the second. A blended network is constructed in the following way: there are input spaces corresponding to the two contrasting situations, links of analogy, disanalogy, and identity between them, and projection of the frame of morning activities from both inputs to the blend. From the input with the headache, we project the headache.

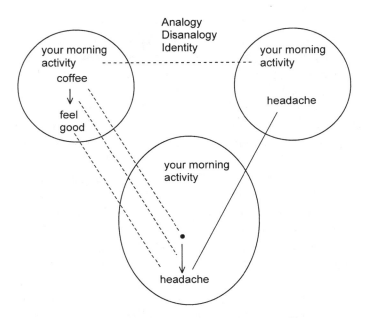

Figure 15.4. The caused headache network

From the desired input, we project the causal relation and the causal element. In the blend, the headache is now the effect of something (see figure 15.4).

The blend is the new construal of the situation. The input with coffee is counterfactual with respect to the blend. In the blend, there is a counterpart for coffee that causes the headache. It is what we refer to by means of the expression *absence of coffee*. The expression *caffeine headache* brings in the label 'caffeine' from the coffee element in the counterfactual input and applies it to its counterpart in the blended space (see figure 15.5).

In the linguistic construction shared by *caffeine headache, money problem,* and *nicotine fit,* the first noun picks out the element in the desired input whose absence in the blend is causal for the unwanted state, and the second noun picks out the bad state that obtains in one of the inputs and in the blend. So we have, for example, *security problem, arousal problem, insulin coma* and *insulin death* (in the case of hyperglycemia, which results from absence of adequate insulin), *food emergency, honesty crisis,* and *rice famine.*

These examples demonstrate the way in which blending has multiple possibilities. For example, we could read *caffeine headache* as referring to a headache 'caused' by the caffeine. For both networks, there is a cause-effect relationship in the blend, in the first case between 'absence of caffeine' and 'headache', in the second between 'presence of caffeine' and 'headache'. In both, the Cause-Effect Vital Relation is further compressed into property. There can now be *caffeine headaches, whisky headaches,* and *sex headaches.* In just the same way, we have *missing tooth, absent students,* and *a gap in the fence.*

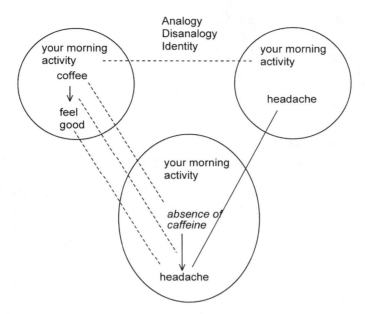

Figure 15.5. The caffeine headache network

Blending thus creates important elements that have the property of being non-things. Similarly, non-events and non-actions are nearly everywhere in our cognition. Physical reality is a material anchor for conceptual blends that typically carry many projections from counterfactual spaces. *The jar-lid won't come off*, *The stack of books has not fallen*, *The stack of books will fall*, *The jar-lid refuses to come off*, and *The stack of books wants to fall over* all present networks in which one input has nothing happening and the other input has something happening. In the blend, the nothing happening becomes an event that is contrasted with the other event: the stack of books stays upright versus the stack of books falls. *Missing a shot* evokes a blend that contains a non-event: both inputs have the shot, one input has the ball going somewhere other than into the goal, the counterfactual input has the ball going into the goal. In the blend, the ball's not going into the goal becomes a 'missed shot', a non-event.

The notion of 'absence' is not explicitly indicated by any part of the expression *caffeine headache*. It emerges from the entire network, as prompted by this grammatical construction. But there are linguistic expressions for indicating this compression explicitly: *absence of*, *lack of*, *want of*, even *no*, as in *I have a no-caffeine headache*.

These counterfactual networks are frequently very hard to notice, since we construct them so effortlessly as part of backstage cognition. Consider, for example, the report in *USA Today* for January 31, 2000, of that year's Super Bowl. In the last play of the game, the ball carrier for the Titans was tackled one yard from the goal line. We unavoidably construct the contrasting space in which the runner advances one more yard and scores. Blending these two spaces gives us a blended space in which there is now an element that is 'absence of one more yard of progress'. We might express this blend by making the negative element explicit: *The Rams won by stopping the Titans from advancing one more yard.* But the front-page headline was in fact: *Rams win by a yard.* It then becomes possible to refer to the Rams' 'one-yard win'. *One-yard win* is then identical in its integration patterns with *caffeine head-ache.* In fact, this example reveals something else. The more conventional pattern for expressions like *winning by a yard* and *winning by a nose* is, of course, that of a race where the winner crosses the finish line a yard ahead of the runner-up. This does not feel intuitively like a counterfactual expression—it seems as if we can "see" that fateful yard right there on the photograph of the finish. But if you think twice, you can see that this more standard notion of a 'one-yard win' is really also counterfactual. The crucial yard is the one that the loser failed to cover, just as the crucial yard in the Super Bowl win was the yard that separated the ball carrier from the goal line.

The central problem of language, the one that must be solved if human language is to emerge, is that relatively few linguistic patterns—such as words, syntactic patterns, and suprasegmental patterns—must be applicable to vast ranges of conceptual structure. Language must be available to be used in any and every situation. Human language has this property of being "equipotential": for any situation, real or imaginary, there is always a way to use language to express thoughts about that situation. A word like *food* or *there*, for example, must apply very widely if it is to do its job. The same is true of grammatical patterns independent of the words we put in them. Take the resultative construction in English, which has the form A—Verb—B—Adjective, where the Adjective denotes a property C (see Goldberg 1995). It means 'A do something to B with the result that B have property C', as in *Kathy painted the wall white.* We want it to prompt for conceptions of actions and results over vast ranges of human life: *She kissed him unconscious, Last night's meal made me sick, He hammered it flat, I boiled the pan dry, The earthquake shook the building apart, Roman imperialism made Latin universal,* and so on. We find it obvious that the meaning of the resultative construction could apply to all these different domains, but applying it thus requires complex cognitive operations. The events described here are in completely different domains (Roman politics versus blacksmithing) and have strikingly different time spans (the era in which a language rises versus a few seconds of earthquake), different spatial environments (most of Europe versus the stovetop), different degrees of intentionality (Roman imperialism versus a forgetful cook versus an earthquake), and very different kinds of connection between cause and effect (the hammer blow causes the immediate flatness of the object, but eating the meal one day causes sickness later through a long chain of biological events).

This very simple grammatical construction allows us to perform a complex conceptual integration which in effect compresses over Vital Relations of Time,

Space, Change, Cause-Effect, Intentionality, and Identity. The grammatical construction provides a compressed input space with a corresponding language form. It is then blended in a network with another input that typically contains an unintegrated and relatively diffuse chain of events. So, if it is our job to turn off the burner under the pan that has zucchini in boiling water, and we forget about it and all the water evaporates, we can say, confessionally, "No zucchini tonight. I boiled the pan dry. Sorry." In the diffuse input, the causal chain runs from forgetting to the invariant position of the burner knob, to the flow of gas, to the flame, to the temperature of the pan, to the temperature of the water, to the level of the water, to the dryness of the pan. The agent performs no direct or indirect action on the pan at all. But in the blend, the compressed structure associated with the grammatical construction is projected together with some selected participants from the diffuse chain of events in the diffuse input. In the blend, the agent acts directly on the pan. Moreover, although the boiling of the water is an event and its cause was something the agent did or did not do, there is cause-effect compression in the blend so that in the blend, although not in the input spaces, *boiling* is an action the agent performed on the pan.

As this example of the resultative construction in English shows, the simplest grammatical constructions require high abstraction over domains and advanced conceptual integration. The most advanced form of conceptual integration is called "double-scope" integration. Human beings are uniquely extraordinarily adept at double-scope integration. For them, it is a routine operation, and the one that makes human language possible. A double-scope conceptual integration network has inputs with different (and often clashing) organizing frames and an organizing frame for the blend that includes parts of each of those frames and has emergent structure of its own. In such networks, both organizing frames make central contributions to the blend, and their sharp differences offer the possibility of rich clashes. Far from blocking the construction of the network, such clashes offer challenges to the imagination, and the resulting blends can be highly creative. Human beings are able to blend very different conceptual inputs in a "double-scope" way and to use language attached to the inputs in order to prompt for the new blend. Language is a consequence of our ability for double-scope integration.

There is every reason to think that some species are able to operate efficiently in separate domains of, say, tool use, mating, and eating without being able to perform these abstractions and integrations. If that is so, then grammar would be of no use to them, because they cannot perform the conceptual integrations that grammar serves to prompt. But could they just have a simpler grammar? The only way they could have a simpler grammar and yet have descriptions in language for what happens would be by having separate forms and words for everything that happens in all the different domains. But the world is infinitely too rich for that to be of any use. Trying to carry around "language" of that size would be crippling. The evidence does not suggest that primates have compensated for lack of language by developing, for example, one million special-purpose words, each conveying a special scenario. On the contrary, while primate species have some specific "vocalizations" (e.g., in response to a potential predator), the best efforts to teach words to chimpanzees cannot get them past a vocabulary of about two hundred items. Having a handful of vocalizations is clearly a help, but evolution has found no use in trying to extend that strategy very far. The extraordinary evolutionary advantage of language lies in its amazing ability to be put to use in *any* situation. Double-scope conceptual integration is the key to the amazing power of the equipotentiality of language, which we take for granted and use effortlessly in all circumstances.

To date, blending analyses of specific grammatical patterns include studies of

single words like *safe*;

fixed expressions like *two-edged sword*;

clausal constructions like the resultative construction, the ditransitive construction, and the caused-motion construction in English;

Y-of networks like *Ann is the boss of the daughter of Max* and *Causation is the cement of the universe*;

nominal compounds like *boat house*, *house boat*, and *jail bait*;

adjective-noun compounds like *guilty pleasures*, *likely candidate*, and *red ball*;

morphological combinations in a single word like *Chunnel*;

grammatical forms in American Sign Language that rely on blends involving grounded mental spaces;

forms that call for blends involving counterfactual spaces;

forms with syntax that results from blending, as in double-verb causitives in French that use the verb *faire*;

morphological causatives in Hebrew; and

the mechanisms of polysemy.

The studies in this list are presented, summarized, and cited in Fauconnier and Turner (2002). Others are presented online at Turner (1995–2006).

REFERENCES

Fauconnier, Gilles, and Mark Turner. 2002. *The way we think: Conceptual blending and the mind's hidden complexities.* New York: Basic Books.

Goldberg, Adele E. 1995. *Constructions: A construction grammar approach to argument structure.* Chicago: University of Chicago Press.

Langacker, Ronald W. 1987. *Foundations of cognitive grammar.* Vol. 1, *Theoretical prerequisites.* Stanford, CA: Stanford University Press.

Langacker, Ronald W. 1990. *Concept, image, and symbol: The cognitive basis of grammar.* Berlin: Mouton de Gruyter.

Langacker, Ronald W. 1991. *Foundations of cognitive grammar*. Vol. 2, *Descriptive application*. Stanford, CA: Stanford University Press.

Travis, Charles, 1981. *The true and the false: The domain of the pragmatic*. Amsterdam: John Benjamins.

Turner, Mark. 1995–2006. Blending and Conceptual Integration (Web site). http://blending.stanford.edu.

CHAPTER 16

ICONICITY

WILLY VAN LANGENDONCK

1. INTRODUCTION

Iconicity can be contrasted with "arbitrariness," or in Peirce's terms, *iconic* is the opposite of *symbolic*. What we now call "iconicity" was until fairly recently restricted to mainly onomatopoeia. As a consequence, iconicity was largely neglected in linguistic theory, as it constituted a marginal phenomenon in the lexicon of a language. At best, the notion was expanded to encompass "sound symbolism," but at least in the Indo-European family, languages seemed to make little use of such a device. It was something to be found in music rather than in human natural language, where "arbitrariness" was thought of as being an essential feature. In its crudest formulation, Saussure's principle of the "arbitrariness of the linguistic sign" stated that there was nothing "X-like" about a word "X" in any given language. The form and meaning of a word were regarded as independent of each other (see Haiman 1985: 2). This is, of course, especially the credo of autonomous linguistics.

The principle of iconicity challenges the monopoly of arbitrariness. To be sure, this does not mean that there is more onomatopoeia or sound symbolism in the world's languages than has been commonly assumed. Accepting double articulation as an unchallengeable universal, Haiman (1985: 3) argues that there is no constant correlation between submorphemic sounds and meanings; put differently, words of similar sound will not necessarily be words of similar meaning: we should not expect, and do not find, semantic homogeneity among words like *pod*, *pot*, and *pox* (see also Bauer 1996). Admittedly, sound symbolism cannot be completely ignored, as certain languages clearly make more use of it than others. For example, sound symbolism is prominent in Yoruba and especially Japanese, where *gitaigo* is an important aspect of linguistic elements (Kakehi, Tamori, and Schourup 1996).

Still, this chapter will follow Haiman in maintaining that iconicity is not primarily to be found in the lexicon, at least not in the inventory of its roots, which are arbitrary for the most part. Rather, it should be looked for in the system of grammatical rules for combining these roots to express complex concepts. Thus, Haiman's concern—and ours—is with the grammars of languages.

1.1. Iconicity and Linguistics

Iconicity can be found not only in language but also in other domains of the world of signs. In general, there is iconicity if something in the form of a sign reflects something in the world (normally through a mental operation). For language, this means that something in the form of a linguistic sign reflects (through its meaning) something in its referent (Mayerthaler 1980, 1988).

In this respect, it is no coincidence that it was a philosopher who elaborated on different kinds of signs, among them "icons": Charles Sanders Peirce established the classic conception of iconicity.[1] In linguistics, however, "iconicity" is a relatively recent term, even though the phenomenon as such has been studied ever since the Ancient Greeks, more in particular since Plato's *Cratylus* (see for a short overview Swiggers 1993). The Stoic philosophers went particularly far in this: in order to show original insights in nature and hence the "natural" basis of language, they argued that at least the first words in a language imitated nature by means of onomatopoeia or "articulatory mimesis." For example, the liquid sound [r] imitated flowing, as in Greek *rheô* 'to flow'. Certain etymologists in the Middle Ages and even up to the eighteenth century defended similar views (e.g., C. de Brosse and Antoine Court de Gébelin). From the nineteenth century, this naive conception of iconicity has been rejected.

Modern ideas of iconicity date back only to the twentieth century and even then did not find a place either in nonfunctional structuralist or in generative theories. Thus, Saussure spent only a few pages on onomatopoeia ([1916] 1967 101–2) and the notion "motivé" (180–84). He introduced the concept of motivation to describe compound signs like the French word *dix-neuf* 'nineteen'. Although the components of this word are themselves arbitrary, the compound is, in contrast, "relatively motivated." Thus, Saussure's notion of motivation appears to coincide with Peirce's concept of "diagrammatic iconicity." Saussure also seems to link arbitrariness to the lexicon, and motivation to the grammar. Finally, he pointed to the phenomenon of analogy or isomorphism in case paradigms (221; for analogy, see Tuggy, this volume, chapter 4).

For Jakobson, as for Benveniste, Bolinger, Greenberg, and others, many linguistic universals reflect, in a rather obvious way, common perceptions about our world. For example, Jakobson (1965) pointed out that the relationship between the elements of a syntagm containing two sentences corresponds to the relationship between the events described by those sentences: after all, sentences, like events, occur in time, and the medium of language is structurally adapted to the iconic display of temporal succession. On the morphological level, Jakobson linked iconicity to the phenomenon of markedness (see below). Benveniste (1946) considered the three "persons" in verbal and pronominal paradigms and argued that the third person is in fact the nonperson since it is the person that is absent from the speech act situation. In a very large number of languages, this nonperson is iconically represented by a nondesinence in the verbal paradigm. Such is the case in Hungarian, where we find: *lát-ok* [see-1SG] 'I see', *lát-sz* [see-2SG] 'you see', *lát-Ø* [see-3SG] '(s)he sees'. A notable exception is English, where we encounter the opposite situation, at least in the present tense: *I see, you see, (s)he see-s*.

It should be remarked that iconicity is not always thought of as reflecting the external or mental world. Greenberg (1995) deals with a few cases of language-internal iconicity. These will not be gone into here.

Whether iconicity is language-external or language-internal, the statistical nature of the phenomenon would be a sufficient reason for generativists to ignore it. However, the resistance of generativists against iconicity is even more fundamental. In Noam Chomsky's opinion, the structure of the grammatical system does not reflect the properties of the world but relatively independent properties of the human mind (see especially Chomsky 1972, 1980; cf. Newmeyer 1992). The following quotation illustrates his view:

> Our interpretation of the world is based in part on representational systems that derive from the structure of the mind itself and do not mirror in any direct way the form of things in the external world. (Chomsky 1981: 3)

Haiman (1985: 7) suspects that generativists are driven to such statements not by the data they consider but by the assumption that

> the only interesting universals are those which seem to be arbitrary or pointless from a formal or functional point of view. Only these arbitrary universals can provide unambiguous evidence for a specifically human linguistic faculty which Chomsky has come to describe as an organ. (Chomsky 1976: 57; see also Chomsky 1980)

According to Haiman (1985: 8), the breakdown of iconicity into arbitrariness does not result from mysterious human genetic predispositions, but from relatively familiar principles such as economy, generalization, and association. In fact, these are the principles that are responsible for the "impairment" of iconicity in diagrams outside as well as inside language.

A theory that suits diagrammatic iconicity particularly well is Cognitive Linguistics (see Langacker 1990: 1–2). As is well known, the credo of this framework is diametrically opposed to the generativist view. Explanations in Cognitive Linguistics tend to be cognitive, functional, pragmatic, or experiential (see also Kleiber 1993; Givón 1994). The notion of iconicity fits perfectly in this view, since it assumes that a number of linguistic structures reflect the world's structure and not the brain's. Moreover, the semantic interpretation of the related concept of markedness is best interpreted from an experiential point of view, as will be argued below.[2]

According to Kleiber (1993: 105), there seems to be a curious contradiction between Langacker's promoting cognitivism in linguistics and the fact that in his main publications (1987, 1991) such terms as *iconic* and *iconicity* are absent in the glossaries and are used sparingly in the text, whereas its contrary, the word *symbolic*, is omnipresent. However, Kleiber goes on, this contradiction is only apparent. In fact, the iconicity of isomorphism is promoted to the rank of theoretical founding principle, and the iconicity of motivation shows up at regular intervals. Since both kinds of iconicity are diagrammatic in nature, let us first look at diagrams, and more generally, at icons as signs.

1.2. Icons as Signs: The Trichotomy Symbol, Index, and Icon

In Peirce's (1974: 2.249) terminology, "A Symbol is a sign which refers to the Object that it denotes by virtue of a law, usually an association of general ideas, which operates to cause the Symbol to be interpreted as referring to that Object." Most words of natural languages are symbols, or "conventional" signs, or in Saussure's terminology: "arbitrary signs." Indeed, in different, genetically unrelated languages the same sense is expressed by different forms; for example, *lion* in English corresponds to *simba* in Swahili.

The second sign distinguished by Peirce is the index: "An *Index* is a sign which refers to the Object that it denotes by virtue of being really affected by that Object" (2.248). There is a kind of causal relationship between the index and the object; for example, smoke is an index of fire, but if the fire is put out, the remaining smoke is no longer an index. In natural language, we have the indexicals *this, that, here, now,* and so on. However, insofar as they are conventional signs, these indexicals are also symbols.

The third sign is the icon, the one that interests us here: "An *Icon* is a sign which refers to the Object that it denotes merely by virtue of characters of its own, and which it possesses, just the same, whether any such Object actually exists or not" (2.247). Everything can be an icon of everything provided it resembles a certain object *and* it is used as a sign for that object.

As I have already suggested, it should be emphasized that these three kinds of signs hardly ever occur in their pure form. Most actual signs are a mixture of the three types, as is illustrated by the indexicals above, or by instances of onomatopoeia. This, eventually, is why dogs say *wafwaf* in Dutch, but *wauwau* in German (see also below).

1.3. Three Kinds of Icons: Imagic Icon, Metaphor, Diagram

Concentrating on icons, Peirce again distinguishes three subclasses: image, metaphor, and diagram. The *image* is the prototype of an icon. It is a simple sign that resembles its referent by virtue of sensory characteristics. These may be visual, as in

Figure 16.1. Representation of a face

a photograph, a statue, or a painting, but they may also be auditory, as in program music, that is, music that renders feelings or perceptions. In natural language, the obvious example of imagic iconicity is onomatopoeia, for example, in interjections like *cuckoo and cock-a-doodle-doo* (see below).

A *metaphor*, in Peirce's view, brings out the representative character of a sign by representing a parallelism in something else; for example, a lion may represent a (brave) man. It may suffice here to give metaphor its place in the classification of iconic phenomena and to refer the reader to the extensive literature on this topic, especially in Cognitive Linguistics (see Grady, this volume, chapter 8).

Our main concern in this section is with the *diagram*, or diagrammatic icon. According to Peirce (1974: 2.277), diagrammatic icons are "those which represent the relations . . . of the parts of one thing by analogous relations in their own parts." In other words, a diagram is a systematic arrangement of signs that do not necessarily resemble their referents but whose mutual relations reflect the relations between their referents. More specifically, the constellation of the object and of its diagram is similar, but the individual referents and the individual signs themselves need not resemble each other. Again, we have to point to a continuum: there is a cline from an almost pure image, for instance, a photo (with a resemblance between individual referents and individual signs) and a "pure" diagram, where there is no such resemblance, for instance, a technical diagram, a scheme, or a Gestalt such as the one in figure 16.1.

The individual signs, that is, the circle, the dash, and the dots, bear no resemblance to reality, but the constellation does, so we can still identify this picture as a 'face'.

1.4. Diagrammatic Iconicity: Isomorphism and Motivation

The linguistic importance of iconicity lies in the recognition of diagrammatic iconicity. Haiman (1985: 11) distinguishes two aspects in a diagram: isomorphism and motivation.[3] *Isomorphism* is defined as follows:

> By isomorphism, a one-to-one correspondence alone is intended, without regard for the relative position, importance, mutual relevance, or any other property

of points in a diagram. Violations of isomorphism are: many-to-one, one-to-many, one-to-zero, and zero-to-one relations between points in the diagram and points in "reality." All of these violations occur in language, and are familiar as homonymy, synonymy, polysemy, empty morphs, and "signe zéro." (11)

Isomorphism in linguistics can be seen as a variant of the higher, more general principle of "one meaning, one form," which is as old as European linguistics. It was also connected early with psychological factors that aim to eliminate purposeless variety. It is well known that young children reject such phenomena as homonymy and synonymy. Why should the word *bank* refer to a building (financial institution) as well as to a riverside? As to synonymy, its very existence is often disputed: real synonymy is claimed not to occur (Bolinger 1977). As to homonymy, it has been ascertained that when homonymy starts disturbing communication, borrowing and innovation are used to undo it.

Anttila (1972: 89) seems to have been the first to recognize isomorphism as a kind of iconicity: "Language has a general iconic tendency whereby semantic sameness is reflected also by formal sameness." Notwithstanding certain difficulties pointed out by Kleiber (1993), I will follow Anttila (1972) and Haiman (1980: 516) in their claim.

At the level of the lexicon, it was structuralism that used to posit isomorphism as an important principle. While recognizing polysemy, Goossens (1969: 98–106) provided evidence from dialect geographical data in favor of "polysemiophobia." Geeraerts (1997: chapter 4) discusses J. Goossens's arguments in the light of prototype theory. Isomorphism seems to conflict with polysemy and prototypicality, and one should at least admit that "the isomorphic principle cannot be maintained in its rigid form"; instead, it should be considered a tendency. Geeraerts (1997: 124) eventually reconciles the two phenomena by concluding:

> Prototype theory, one could say, specifies what is to be understood by 'one form, one meaning': according to the prototypical conception of categorization, the isomorphism between form and content applies to conceptual categories as a whole, that is, to prototypically organized bundles of nuances, and not to the nuances within these categories.

In the realm of syntax, the Katz-Postal hypothesis (Katz and Postal 1964) implied a rejection of isomorphism. In arguing that transformations do not change meaning, the authors had to admit that both neutralization (many deep structures, one surface structure, i.e., homonymy) and diversification (many surface structures, one deep structure, i.e., synonymy) must exist. It has become more and more apparent, however, that this thesis is untenable.

What is more, in a number of cases syntactic "homonymy" may be motivated; that is, apparent homonomy turns out to be a case of isomorphism after all. This is borne out by the fact that the "homonymous" constructions occur in unrelated languages. For example, morphological and syntactic similarity between conditional protases and polar questions is the result of a meaning common to both constructions (Haiman 1974, 1980: 518):

(1) a. I don't know if it is true.   (Question)
     b. If it is true, I'll eat my hat.   (Protasis)
(2) a. Had you known, you would have done otherwise. (Protasis)
     b. Had you known?   (Question)

The subordinate clauses in (1) can both be paraphrased as 'either it is not true or it is'; those in (2) as 'either you had not known or you had'.

According to Langacker (1987: 57; 1991), the mechanisms at work in the domain of lexical items are also applied to grammatical categories (e.g., nouns) and relations (e.g., subjects)—a view that condemns autonomous syntax since each category must then have a sense. This can be achieved by adopting the principle of schematicity,[4] whereby isomorphism is exploited to its maximum.[5] At the same time, however, motivation may play a role.

Motivation is defined by Haiman (1985: 11) as follows:

> By motivation, I have in mind the property whereby diagrams exhibit the same relationship among their parts as their referents do among their parts.

Most cases of diagrammatic iconicity are of this motivational type. For instance, the "schema," so often used in Cognitive Linguistics, is in fact an example of motivational diagrammatic iconicity in linguistics (on schematicity, see Tuggy, this volume, chapter 4).

Ideally, diagrams should show both isomorphism and motivation. However, the reason to use a diagram is precisely to simplify. As life is short and memory finite, so it is often only the essential attributes of the objects diagrams denote that are reproduced. Hence, a diagram often shows more isomorphism than motivation, or conversely, more motivation than isomorphism, even if both are always present to some degree.[6]

1.5. Iconicity and Markedness: Semantic Markedness and the Prototypical Speaker

In linguistics, motivational iconicity has mostly to do with markedness. This concept is often captured in the slogan "The more form, the more meaning."[7] The more (marked) complex the form of a sign (or of a constellation of signs), the more (marked) complex the meaning will be. This markedness principle can take the shape of a binary relation or of a cline from unmarked to most marked, a gradation gamut (Jakobson 1966). However, the question remains how to define complexity. With regard to form, complexity can be held to be a function of the number of morphemes (not of syllables). For instance, the plural *book-s* is more complex or marked than the singular *book*. Note that such oppositions do not hold in every case or in every language. Both the marked and the unmarked value may be expressed in the same way, as in *sheep*. Still, a case such as *sheep* is not considered a counterexample; it is only when the reverse holds, that is, when the unmarked form is heavier than the marked one that we have an exception, provided that semantic markedness is preserved.

More difficult to define is semantic markedness. Although in the case of number we could argue that 'more than one' (book) is more complex than just 'one', this is not possible with the overwhelming majority of categories, such as definiteness, semantic roles, and so on. What we need here is not a logical or mathematical view of meaning but rather an experiential view (Lakoff 1982).[8] More specifically, it is helpful to adduce at this point the notion of "prototypical speaker" (Mayerthaler 1980; Van Langendonck 1999). As a human being, the speaker has certain biological, psychological (perceptual), and cultural properties that can be called prototypical.[9] These prototypical properties are reflected in language as unmarked semantic categories and tend to be acquired first by children. A case in point is the spatial prepositions *in*, *on*, and *at*. Essentially, *in* refers to three dimensions (a container), *on* to two (a surface), and *at* may refer to any single dimension. Although *in* is logically the most complex, experientially it is the most "normal" case: the prototypical speaker is a container and lives in a three-dimensional space; in turn, surfaces are more important in daily life than points: for instance, as a rule we walk on a surface. Therefore, *in* is the unmarked and most frequent preposition and is acquired first; then comes *on*, and finally *at*. Logically, we would expect the reverse order, as did Clark (1973) at first when he suggested that the two-word sentence *baby highchair* meant *baby at highchair*. However, it was found later that in several languages the initial zero preposition is replaced by *in* or its equivalents: *baby in highchair*. As a consequence, the putative order of acquisition *at* < *on* < *in* was wrong and had to be reversed.

Other examples include dichotomies such as positive-negative, Agent-Patient, topic-comment, and subject-object. Since the prototypical speaker is obviously assumed to exist, it is natural that 'positive' will be semantically unmarked with respect to 'negative'. This is formally reflected in zero marking for positive statements or properties and overt marking for negative ones: *It is raining* versus *It is not raining*; *happy* versus *un-happy*. The prototypical speaker sees himself as an agent rather than a patient, and thus the notion of agent is a prominent or unmarked relation. Since the prototypical speaker is assumed to exist and is therefore topical, the topic of an utterance will be unmarked as well. From this, we can derive the idea that since the subject is the grammaticalization of the intersection of agent and topic, it will be the unmarked grammatical relation, as was, in fact, already stated by Jakobson (1966). Below (see especially section 2.2), I will discuss the iconic aspects of some morphosyntactic categories that exhibit a marked versus unmarked relationship.

1.6. Iconicity and Economy

Haiman (1985: 18, part I) argues that in languages, as in diagrams, there is an inverse correlation between iconicity and economy. The tendencies to maximize iconicity and to maximize economy are two of the most important competing motivations for linguistic forms in general. An obvious example of this is the treatment of number in Indonesian. The plural in Indonesian is iconically formed by reduplicating the word, thus while *orang* means 'human being', *orang-orang* means 'human beings'. Significantly, the latter form applies not only to 'two people', but also to more than two. For reasons of economy, the morpheme is not repeated more than once according to the real quantity, although this would in fact be more iconic if one spoke about more than two people.

By contrast, iconicity and economy can go together as well. To take number again, in many languages the singular is expressed by zero, the plural by an overt form, as with English *book* versus *book-s*. This is both economic and iconic and is in keeping with the slogan "The more form, the more meaning" (i.e., 'one' vs. 'more than one'). In fact, we are confronted here with a special case of Zipf's ([1949] 1965) principle of least effort.

2. ICONICITY ON THE PHONIC, THE MORPHOLOGICAL, AND THE SYNTACTIC LEVEL

In the following sections, I will deal with some instances of iconicity and especially of diagrammatic iconicity in the various components of grammar (in a wide sense).

2.1. Iconicity on the Phonic Level

On the phonic level, we primarily find imagic iconicity, which is well known as onomatopoeia—in fact, we should speak here of acoustic iconicity. Compared to normal vocabulary, onomatopoeia remains a marginal phenomenon in natural language, though there may be differences in the degree to which it is implemented from one language to another, as was observed above. The more onomatopoeic words get integrated in the linguistic system, the more they become symbolic and the more they lose their iconic value. For example, in its capacity of a noun, *cuckoo* can be pluralized (*cuckoo-s*); words that primarily function(ed) as interjections can become verbs like *crack*, *squeak*, *hiss*, *hush*, and so on. It is to be expected, then, that there will be certain differences between languages in rendering the same kind of interjection. Compare, in this respect, the rooster's chant as it is conventionally rendered in different languages, and notice the inevitable degree of arbitrariness: *cock-a-doodle-doo* (English), *kukeleku* (Dutch), *kikeriki* (German), *cocorico* (French), *kukareku* (Russian), and so on.

As for diagrammatic iconicity on the phonic level, it is difficult to distinguish between isomorphism and motivation. Moreover, diagrammatic iconicity is rather limited on the phonic level because it is hard to assign meanings to sounds as such (see, e.g., Birdsong 1995; Landsberg 1995). It is sometimes argued, for instance, that the sound [i] expresses smallness while [ɑ], [o], and [u] are related to big sizes. In certain expressions, this appears to be justified; note English *a wee little bit*. However, according to Hagège (1982: 25), this correlation is statistically not significant. At best, we can maintain there is something to say for this "sense" at the level of performance.

2.2. Diagrammatic Iconicity on the Morphological Level

On the morphological level, we find iconicity to various degrees in the inflectional endings of nouns, verbs, and adjectives, and, further, in the markedness relation between 'positive' and 'negative'.

Nouns usually have such features as number, definiteness, humanness, and gender. With regard to *number*, isomorphism can take a strong form, as in the above example from Indonesian, insofar as the plural *orang-orang* refers to two people. A weaker form of isomorphism is encountered in the English plural where the plural *-s* is arbitrary in itself, but isomorphic insofar as it is used consistently to indicate plural meaning. In both cases there is also some motivation: the unmarked singular has zero form while the marked plural has one more morpheme. From an experiential perspective, the singular is semantically unmarked since the prototypical speaker is a single person, not a chorus. Also, it is easier to perceive or, more generally, to deal with one object at a time than with several (see also Langacker 1991: 74–81).

With regard to *definiteness*, we may start from the fact that whereas the indefinite article or value is used to introduce a referent into the universe of discourse (e.g., *There is a girl in the garden*), the definite article or value ideally occurs when the referent is presupposed to exist and to be unique in the universe of discourse for both speaker and hearer (e.g., *The girl smiled at him*). The feature 'definite' appears to be unmarked with respect to 'indefinite' (Van Langendonck 1979; Mayerthaler 1980, 1988). From an experiential view, this squares well with the fact that prototypical speakers are "definite" in the sense that they are presupposed to exist and to be unique. This is borne out by some formal markedness phenomena. Although no argument can be drawn from the behavior of common nouns, it remains true that in inherently definite categories such as proper names and personal pronouns, this definiteness feature is mostly not expressed by an overt morpheme (e.g., *John, Mary, Paris; I, you, he, she, it*). A further reflex of the unmarked status of definiteness is that in Dutch and French, definite noun phrases are pronominalized by one morpheme while indefinite noun phrases are pronominalized by two morphemes; compare:

(3)   a. *Hij bezit een paleis.—Hij bezit **er een**.*
        'He possesses a palace.'— 'He possesses *one*.'
        *Hij bezit het paleis.—Hij bezit **het**.*
        'He possesses the palace.'—'He possesses *it*.'
    b. *Il possède un palais.—Il **en** possède **un**.*
        *Il possède le palais.—Il **le** possède.*

English does not provide further corroboration for this opposition but is not a counterexample either since both definite and indefinite pronominalization are realized by one morpheme each. The situation is not reversed, that is, definiteness is not more marked than indefiniteness.

With regard to *humanness*, we may expect that since the prototypical speaker is human by definition, the feature 'human' will be unmarked vis-à-vis 'nonhuman'. This is formally reflected by zero forms for 'human' in certain constructions. In many languages the imperative (meant for animate beings) has no ending (e.g., Swahili *come! njoo!*, Dutch *kom!*, Spanish *ven!*). Personal proper names usually have no article (e.g., English *John, Mary,* French *Jean, Marie*). Neither do names of places exhibiting some human organization, such as cities, villages, and countries. This is clearer in Germanic languages than in French, where only cities have no article (compare *London—Londres* versus *France—la France*). A final example is the impersonal passive in Dutch: in this specific construction type, the agent is always human, also if it is not expressed, as in *Er wordt gelachen* [there become.3SG laugh.PPART] 'People are laughing'.

Finally, with regard to *gender*, it is found that in most cultures the prototypical speaker is a man, not a woman. As will be clear, this is not a biological criterion but a purely cultural one, and hence subject to change. In English, there are still morphological traces of the markedness of feminine gender: compare the zero form of masculine titles with the ending *-ess* for feminine titles (e.g., *count* vs. *count-ess,* *prince* vs. *princ-ess*).

Turning from nouns to verbs, categories such as tense, aspect, and mood often manifest iconic reflexes of marked versus unmarked values. For *tense*, we know that since the prototypical speaker speaks in the present by definition (the time of the speech act), the present tense is semantically unmarked with respect to the past. This is iconically reflected by the fact that most languages have zero for the present but an overt form for the past. Compare English *I work* with *I work-ed* and French *je travaille* with *je travaill-ais.* As for *mood*, it can safely be stated that the speech act time is also the most real time. Potential or unreal events are rendered by potentialis and irrealis, which show a more marked form than the present or even the past indicative. Consider French *je travaill-er-ais* 'I would work'.

Looking at adjectives, we typically find iconicity in the expression of the degrees of comparison. In a number of languages, the comparative is more marked than the positive degree and often the superlative is more marked than the comparative. Indeed, a comparative statement can be paraphrased with a negative statement (e.g., *John is taller than Mary* = 'Mary is not so tall as John'), while the superlative would imply that nobody is as tall as John. This is reflected morphosyntactically: *tall* < *tall-er* < *tall-est.* In Latin, we find a similar gradation: *longus* < *long-ior* < *long-issimus.* In some other languages, the negation in the comparative is overtly present (see Van Langendonck, Swiggers, and Van de Velde, forthcoming), for example, in Abipon (Guaycuru):

(4) *Negetink   chik   naâ,   oagan   nihirenak   la   naâ.* (Stassen 1985: 184)
      dog   not   bad   yet   tiger   already bad
      'A tiger is more ferocious than a dog.'

Iconicity on the morphological level can, finally, also be found in the relation between positive and negative. Since the prototypical speaker is presupposed to 'exist', existence will be unmarked with respect to nonexistence; that is, 'positive' is valued higher than 'negative' (see also Hamilton and Deese 1971 for a psychological experiment). Very often, then, negation will require a special morpheme, compare:

(5)   happy vs. un-happy, animate vs. in-animate, honest vs. dis-honest, entangle vs. dis-entangle, sense vs. non-sense, etc.

It has also been argued that the first adjective in such pairs as *big—small, tall—short, long—short, thick—thin, high—low* can be explained in the same way; that is, the first element of the pair is positive, the second negative. The problem is that there is no iconic relation here nor is it even immediately obvious why the first elements should be regarded as positive. This may be right in a metaphorical sense, but then we need to know why. An explanation can be sought in relating the 'positive' meanings to properties of the prototypical speaker. For example, an expected and even desirable property of the prototypical speaker and of nature in general seems to be to grow and expand, not to shrink.

2.3. Diagrammatic Iconicity on the Syntactic Level

On the syntactic level, diagrammatic iconicity manifests itself especially as iconicity of distance (or closeness) in syntactic constructions (patterns) and as word-order iconicity.

2.3.1. *Iconicity of Distance (or Closeness) in Syntactic Patterns*

Elements that occur closely together and form a unity in experience will tend to be related to each other by the prototypical speaker on the content level as well. Conversely, what is separated will be seen as unrelated conceptually. Haiman (1983: 782) speaks about the reflection of conceptual distance or separation by physical (morphosyntactic) distance or separation. Put in a simple slogan, "The distance between expressions corresponds to the conceptual distance between the ideas they represent." In this way, we are even able to formulate universal tendencies that we can regard as constraints or meta-constraints on grammatical structures. To illustrate this, I will discuss a number of different syntactic constructions.

One relevant phenomenon is *conjunction reduction*. Originally, Generative Grammar attempted to derive a sentence like (6a) from the one in (6b):

(6)   a. We can do it quickly and well.
      b. We can do it quickly and we can do it well.

In (6b), it is possible to do something well under one set of conditions and to do it quickly under another; but grouping *quickly* and *well* together, as in (6a), implies that these are realized under the same set of circumstances (Haiman 1983: 808). Note also that this is a case where iconicity and economy are in harmony.

Another example of the iconicity of distance is found with *verbs of perception*. Usually, a distinction is made between direct perception (as in 7a) and indirect perception (as in 7b):

(7) a. I hear him sing(ing).
     b. I hear that he sings/is singing.

Generative attempts to derive (7a) from (7b) by some kind of raising appear to have failed. The reason is that different things are meant by the two constructions, which leads to different syntactic possibilities. In the *that*-clause, we have two propositions that can differ in terms of tense and modality;[10] consider in this respect also (7c) and (7d):

(7) c. I hear that he sang/was to sing.
     d. *I hear him being to sing.

Sentence (7c) encodes an indirect perception: there clearly are *two* events, iconically represented by *two* propositions. In sentence (7a), this is not the case: we have to do here with one event, one propositional Gestalt with only one tense and one modality (cf. 7d).[11]

Further, distance iconicity also appears to be at work in *causatives*. In causative constructions, we can observe a cline from direct to indirect causation. Direct causation implies a unity of action, volition, place, and time: the event is one Gestalt, and the responsibility of the causer will here be the greatest. If causation is less direct, the event seems to be spread more in time and space, and less responsibility can be invoked on the part of the causer. The continuum from direct to indirect causation is reflected in the grammar of natural languages through a continuum of lexical via morphological to syntactic causative constructions (Comrie 1981: 165; Haiman 1983: 782; Song 1992 on Korean). Partly, this is observable in one and the same language. Consider the Dutch expressions for the notion 'killing', which show a cline in formality:[12]

(8) *doden–doodmaken–doen sterven–maken dat x sterft*
     'kill–make dead–make die–make that x dies'

These alternatives require appropriate sentences, as exemplified in (9):

(9) a. *De misdadiger doodde zonder scrupules.*
         'The criminal killed unscrupulously.'

     b. *De   boer   maakte   het   dier   dood.*
         the   farmer   made   the   animal   dead
         'The farmer killed the animal'

     c. *De   zure   regen   doet   de   bomen   sterven.*
         the   acid   rain   does   the   trees   die
         'The acid rain causes the trees to die.'

     d. *Het slikken   van   een   doosje   pillen   maakte   dat   de   man   stierf.*
         the   swallowing   of   a   box   pills   made   that   the   man   died
         'The swallowing of a box of pills caused the man to die.'

We can see here that the responsibility and control in the causation of the event diminishes from left to right: for a crime only *doden* will be used, as in (9a).[13] The compound *doodmaken* in (9b) is used especially in the case of an animal patient killed by a human causer. *Doen sterven* does not require a human subject; the object is often a plant, as in (9c). In the periphrastic construction *maken dat x sterft* in (9d), the responsibility of the causer is lowest; subject and object may even be abstract propositions.

Finally, distance iconicity affects the expression of certain *grammatical relations*. By definition, prepositional objects show a greater physical distance with the verb than direct objects. This seems to correspond with greater conceptual distance. Consider the famous pair of examples in (10):

(10)   a. He smeared the wall with paint.
      b. He smeared paint on the wall.

In the so-called holistic reading of (10a), the whole wall is painted whereas this is normally not the case in (10b), where a 'partial' reading is most likely. The greater affectedness of the patient in (10a) is reflected by the fact that *the wall* in (10a), being a direct object, is closer to the verb than in (10b), where it is separated from the verb by a preposition.

2.3.2. *Word-Order Iconicity*

Several phenomena resort under word-order iconicity (see, e.g., Van Langendonck 1995; compare for English: Brinton 1987; Givón 1994; Thompson 1995; Fischer 1997).

As a first example, word-order iconicity is found in the ordering of events in narrative sequences, which tends to reflect *closeness in time*. Genette (1976: 226) points out that already in the eighteenth century, it was considered a rule that the order in discourse was a true reflection of individual thought. Greenberg (1966b: 103) formulated it as follows: "The order of elements in language parallels that in physical experience or the order of knowledge." Paraphrasing Jakobson (1965), we can state that in a narrative sequence utterance 2 follows utterance 1, just like event 2 follows event 1. There is an element of closeness here, in that the closer to each other events occur in time, the closer they are positioned in discourse. This is especially evident in asyndetic and coordinate structures, where a series of coded events is least "disturbed" by intervening linguistic elements:

(11)   *Veni, vidi, vici.*
(12)   She married and got pregnant.

Subordinating conjunctions with a particular meaning may undo the iconic order, as in (13a), whereas others are subject to a fixed iconic order, as in (13b) and (13c):

(13)   a. She got pregnant after she married.
      b. He ran too hard so (that) he fell down.
      c. *So (that) he fell down he ran too hard.

A special case of closeness in events is represented by so-called serial verbs. In certain languages, a series of closely related events that form a unity is expressed by a corresponding juxtaposition of the verbs indicating the events. Consider the following sentences in Akan (from Schachter 1974: 254): in (14), Kofi's going precedes his coming back, while in (15), the action of pouring causes the flowing to happen.

(14) *Kofi   kɔɔe   baae.*
      Kofi   went   came
      'Kofi went and came back.'
(15) *Kofi   de   aburow   gu   nsum.*
      Kofi   takes   corn   flows   water.in
      'Kofi pours corn into the water.'

At the same time, it must be pointed out that representations of events are not necessarily ordered iconically in discourse. Langacker (1991: 502) speaks of cases where the speaker scans backwards mentally through conceived time, as in the following passage:

(16) Professor Muddle died last night at the age of 75. He suffered from an inflamed ego for several years prior to his death. He taught theoretical basket weaving for almost four decades at MIT. He received his Ph.D. from that institution in 1948.

We might be inclined to think that all natural languages conform at least to the most general ordering principle as exemplified in *Veni, vidi, vici*. However, even this kind of motivation is not universal: a number of South-East Asian languages deviate. A native speaker of Burmese will understand that a series of instructions are to be followed in the order given only if the sequence is marked by extra grammatical signs. Otherwise, the instructions are to be carried out simultaneously (Haiman 1980: 533).

A second kind of iconic ordering involves the concept of *closeness to the speaker*. What is nearest to the speaker in a literal (physical) or in a metaphorical sense is mentioned first, especially again in asyndetic or in fixed coordinate structures. This principle is found to be at work in various ways. Literal closeness to the speaker is involved in spatiotemporal conjunctions like the English, Polish, and French freezes (fixed collocations, see Landsberg 1995):

(17) a. English: *here and there, this and that, now and then, sooner or later*
      b. Polish: *tu i tam* 'here and there'[14]
      c. French: *ça et là* 'here and there', *tôt ou tard* 'sooner or later'

The initial motivation for putting *here, now*, and *sooner* in first position apparently derives from the speaker's viewpoint.

Next to literal closeness, we also find metaphorical closeness to the prototypical speaker. The properties that are metaphorically "nearest" to the prototypical speaker tend to be mentioned first. Recall the unmarked features positive, human, masculine, definite, and so on mentioned above (see section 2.2). Usually, these come first in coordinate constructions, especially in freezes:

(18)   happy or unhappy, yes or no, big and small, tall and short, a man or
a mouse, husband and wife,[15] this and something else

Further, in the expression of grammatical relations, the reason for putting the
indirect object before the direct object is obviously that the former mostly refers to
a human referent but the latter to an inanimate one, as in:

(19)   John gave Mary a book.

A third example of word-order iconicity involves several formal reflections of
closeness in content. We will look at four principles where we see that elements that
are close in content in some way or other tend to be placed together. The first three
concern adjacency,[16] the last one concerns the placement of "relators" in between
their "relata."

Simple Adjacency

The first principle is that of simple adjacency of head and modifier (Hudson 1984:
98)—or, the principle of head proximity (Rijkhoff 1992: 229)—the principle
whereby a modifier is put as closely as possible to its head. One effect of this principle is the tendency for objects to accompany the verb they depend on or for
adjectives to accompany the noun by which they are governed. Of course, the
modifier may be separated from its head by other modifiers of the same head, as in
(20), where the modifiers of the noun *dolls* are as close as possible to each other.

(20)   She liked those three nice little wooden dolls.

When all modifiers precede (as in 20) or follow their head, the order of the
modifiers with respect to each other is determined by a second principle, namely,
relative adjacency.

Relative Adjacency

This principle implies that, in neutral ordering, the modifiers that are closest to the
head in content are generally placed closest to it as well. The effect of relative
adjacency is found most clearly in the noun phrase, as illustrated in (21):

(21)   those three nice little white wooden dolls

In (21), we see that the qualifying adjectives appear closer to the noun than the
quantifying modifiers. Further, absolute objective qualities like *wooden* and *white*
are closest to the noun, whereby those qualities involving substance (*wooden*) are
expressed closest to the noun. Relative objective qualities (size, e.g., *little*) are expressed farther away from the noun, and subjective qualities like *nice* are expressed
still farther. Farthest away from the noun is the determiner, since it serves only to
pick out the referent. This order appears to be widespread cross-linguistically (see
Hetzron 1978; Seiler 1978; Posner 1986). Nevertheless, Heine (1980) observed that in
some East-African languages the deictic and quantificational elements are nearer

to the noun than the true adjectives. For instance, in Rendille we find the order given in (22),

(22)   sticks-my four long white

where the opposite relative adjacency is found. To explain the difference between the two orderings, we must start from the twofold nature of common nouns. This notion derives from the logical analysis of nouns by Bach (1968), who argued that a noun is a variable combined with a predicate; for example, *a doll* means 'an x that is a doll'. In Langacker's (1991: 54) terms, a nominal displays grounding and type specification (among other things). Most languages (such as English) apparently attract first the modifiers that fit in best with the type specification, that is, the predicational content of the noun, whereas other languages (such as Rendille) highlight the grounding aspect by attracting first the deictic modifiers. At the same time, what the two language types have in common is the relative order of the nominal modifiers with respect to each other.

Adjacency of Similar Elements

A third principle involves the adjacency of similar elements, whereby similar elements are placed together. Thus, in languages with the basic orders SOV and VSO, the nominal elements subject and object are placed together. As such, for instance, in the Dutch subordinate clause in (23), the nouns (proper names) are positioned next to each other.

(23)   *dat   John   Sheila   haat*
       that   John   Sheila   hates
       'that John hates Sheila'

In Dutch, there is also a tendency for verbal elements to cluster in the so-called verbal end-group, even if this disrupts the adjacency of head and dependent, as in (24):

(24)   *dat   John   Sheila   uit   Londen   terug   **zal   brengen***
       that   John   Sheila   from   London   back   will   bring
       'that John will bring back Sheila from London'

Although *terugbrengen* 'bring back' is one verb, the nonverbal prefix *terug* can be separated from its verbal head *brengen,* as in (24), so that the verbal elements *zal* and *brengen* cluster together. However, the order *zal terugbrengen* is also possible. Again, we see two competing motivations, in this case head proximity as opposed to adjacency of similar elements.

Relator in the Middle (RIM)

A special iconic principle of adjacency is the one whereby a so-called relator is put in the middle of its two relata. One example of this principle is the typical ordering in coordination whereby a coordinator is placed between the elements it conjoins, as in *John and Mary.* There are several such constructions.

a. *Relator Constructions.* A relator can be defined as a free or bound morpheme that has basically two syntagmatic slots, or *relata*, in its semantic-syntactic structure, such that the relator defines a specific semantic-syntactic relation between the two relata. The first relatum is more general in nature, has a freer position in the sentence, and can sometimes be dropped; the second relatum is usually obligatory and has a fixed position because it has a tighter bond with the relator. As a consequence, it is normally not omitted.[17] In the following typology, the nature of the relators and their relata will be dealt with (see also Van Langendonck, Swiggers, and Van de Velde, forthcoming).

We can distinguish two major subclasses of relators: coordinative and subordinative relators, with the latter further subdividing into predicative and nonpredicative relators. Coordinative relators include coordinating conjunctions, such as *and* in (25). Predicative relators are verbs and other predicates, such as *loves* in (26); nonpredicative relators include adpositions (i.e., pre- or postpositions), subordinating conjunctions, and certain particles.[18] An example of an adpositional (prepositional) relator is *in*, as found in (27). Usually, only this third type of relator is explicitly recognized as such in the literature. However, it seems advisable to broaden the definition so as to include the three categories mentioned.

(25)   John *and* Mary
(26)   John *loves* Mary.
(27)   The girl *(is) in* the garden.

Coordinative relators are defined by the fact that their two conjuncts (relata) mostly seem to show a certain symmetry in that they are interchangeable, at least in principle. Still, even in productive coordination the first conjunct is more prominent pragmatically and often refers to the element occurring first in time or space. In freezes, where the order of the elements is fixed, the unmarked conjunct acts as the first relatum. Aside from such freezes, the second conjunct displays a tighter bond with the relator, being syntactically more essential:

(28)   a. John and Mary
       b. the king and the queen
       c. here and there
       d. She got pregnant and married.

By contrast, with *subordinative relators*, the two relata are hardly interchangeable because of the clearly asymmetric relationship between the two. Again, the first relatum is usually more prominent. According to the function of the first relatum, we can distinguish two types of subordinative relators: predicative and nonpredicative. With predicative relators, which are mostly verbs, the first relatum functions as the subject of the verb. With nonpredicative relators, the first relatum is either the relator's head or the subject of the predicate of a clause. In both types, the second relatum has again a tighter bond with its relator, functions as a kind of complement, and can hardly be omitted. Let us now consider the two types of subordinative relators more in particular. Nonpredicative relators have a complement as their second relatum: in (29a), for instance, the preposition *in* heads its object *the garden*; in (29d), the comparative particle *than* heads its object *Alice*. The first relatum is either the relator's head, as in (29a)–(29c): *girl, excitement, did*, or the subject of the clause's predicate, as in the comparative sentence (29d): *Kevin*.

(29)   a. the girl in the garden
        b. the excitement before his departure
        c. He did it before he left.
        d. Kevin is taller than Alice.

Predicative relators have the subject of the predicate as their first relatum and a complement as their second relatum. In case a verb has several complements, we have to do with more than one "second" relatum (as in 30a). The prototype of a predicative relator is a transitive verb. As is well known, in a sentence such as *John killed Bill*, the subject *John* refers to the agent of the action of killing, of which the patient, expressed by the object *Bill*, is the victim. We take predicative relators to refer here to all sorts of verbal categories (including auxiliaries and modal verbs), as well as predicative adjectives, as in *She is worth it*. As second relata of main verbs, we consider not only direct objects (as in 26 above) but, for instance, also indirect objects (as in 30a) and prepositional objects (as in 30b):

(30)   a. It cost me that.[19]
        b. She looked after him.

b. *Iconic Ordering in the Relator Construction.* As indicated by the principle formulated above, relator constructions often show iconic ordering in that relators take middle positions. Dik (1983: 274) states that "the preferred position of a Relator is in between its two relata." This syntactic order reflects the fact that the relator establishes a specific semantic connection between the relata. In the iconic ordering, the most prominent relatum takes the first position, whereas the second relatum follows the relator. Notice that it is only when the relator is a full word that it can exert any influence on order. A good example of the principle of "Relator In the Middle" (RIM) is the basic order of subject and object. As is well known, the order SVO (42%) is far more frequent than the order OVS (1%) across languages (Tomlin 1986: 22). Note that SVO competes mainly with SOV and VSO order, where we find the principle of "adjacency of similar elements."

c. *RIM Languages*. It appears to be possible to identify "RIM languages" in which relators are typically put in between their relata. Thus, in the Northern European area we have discovered a belt of languages that we can call RIM languages. These languages show the canonical order in relator constructions, but the (basic) order modifier-before-head in other constructions. As we could see above, English is such a language and forms part of this belt—as do Scandinavian, Finnish, and Russian, among others (see Van Langendonck, Swiggers, and Van de Velde, n.d.). For relator constructions, I can refer to examples (25) through (30) above. Constructions without a relator exhibit [modifier < head] as their unmarked order.[20] This is illustrated in (31).

(31)   demonstrative < noun: *that town*
        predeterminer < demonstrative: *all those*
        numeral < noun: *three plants*
        adjective < noun: *nice girl, red cap*
        proper name modifier < noun/participle: *a London shop,*
        the Everard Brothers, Italy based
        adverb < adjective: *extremely intelligent*
        adverb < adverb: *very well, not quite*
        compounds: *broomstick, furniture shop*

To conclude these paragraphs on word order, we can say that word-order iconicity appears to be constituted by one general principle of *closeness* (or, alternatively, *distance*), under which come various subprinciples. Three kinds of closeness have been reviewed: closeness of events in narrative sequence, closeness to the prototypical speaker or to the speakers as a physical entity, and finally, closeness in content. Under the latter, I subsume simple adjacency, relative adjacency, adjacency of similar elements, and the medial positioning of relators.

3. GENERAL CONCLUSION

In this survey of iconicity, I have emphasized diagrammatic iconicity in language and related it to markedness and to the prototypical speaker. It has also become clear that iconicity fits in well with the cognitive and experiential tenets of Cognitive Linguistics. Both isomorphism and motivation figure as important phenomena throughout such basic cognitivist works as Langacker (1987, 1990, 1991).

NOTES

For this overview of iconicity, I have especially benefited from the pioneering work done by John Haiman in numerous publications (e.g., 1980, 1983, 1985).

1. For comments on Peirce in relation to the linguistic sign, see, among others, Pharies (1985).

2. For overviews and reflections on iconicity, see, among others (besides Haiman's work), Bouissac, Herzfeld, and Posner (1986), Van Langendonck and de Pater (1993), Motivation et Iconicité (1993), and Simone (1994).

3. Certain authors observe that there are problems with these terms and concepts. Greenberg (1995: 57–58) finds the term "isomorphism" unfortunate. Others point out that the notion of "motivation" goes beyond that of iconicity (Motivation et Iconicité 1993).

4. According to Kleiber (1993: 120), the device of schematicity may turn out to be too powerful since there is obviously no limit to the level of abstractness that can be applied to the semantic definitions of the grammatical units in order to preserve isomorphism.

5. This generalized isomorphism paradoxically leads to the introduction of the notion *symbolic*: "Lexicon, morphology and syntax form a continuum of symbolic units" (Langacker 1990: 1).

6. In certain cases, the generalization of isomorphism generates real conflicts with motivational iconicity. Thus, Kleiber (1993: 121) contends that Langacker's (1987: 216) analysis of adjectives as relational predicates (like verbs) goes against the iconicity of motivation because the landmark of adjectives is in fact never expressed (see also note 20). I signaled a similar conflict between isomorphism and motivation with regard to proper names (Van Langendonck 2004, 2007).

7. There are several criteria for defining markedness, which may even contradict the "more form, more meaning" criterion, but we cannot go into this here. See, however, Greenberg (1966a) and, for a more recent account, Croft (2003).

8. Compare the notion of "embodiment" (see Rohrer, this volume, chapter 2).

9. Related to Mayerthaler's (1980) concept of the prototypical speaker is Langacker's (1985) notion of "subjectivity" as opposed to "objectivity." Both Mayerthaler's and Langacker's ideas lead to an explanation of the so-called animacy or empathy hierarchy, a controversial topic in linguistic typology.

10. Langacker (1991: 447) speaks of a distancing effect of the conjunction *that* even in pairs like *She knows that he likes her* versus *She knows he likes her*.

11. In the same vein, Ruwet (1984) deals with so-called equi-NP deletion: in French we have to say *je veux partir* 'I want to leave' instead of **je veux que je parte* 'I want that I leave'. However, if the volition and the action of the agent are independent of each other, two propositions are necessary and equi-NP deletion cannot apply: *je préférerais que moi je puisse faire cela* 'I would prefer I could do that' (see also Langacker 1991: 448).

12. The iconic difference between *kill* and *cause to die* was ignored by Generative Semantics, which derived *kill* from *cause to die* by a prelexical transformation. Fodor (1970) already criticized this derivation by pointing out that *cause to die*, but not *kill*, may imply a difference in time, for example in *John caused Bill to die on Sunday by stabbing him on Saturday*; see especially Wierzbicka (1975).

13. Of course, languages may differ as to the rigidity of this cline. For instance, while English may have *a car accident killed him*, the Dutch equivalent is not acceptable: **een auto-ongeval doodde hem*. This makes Dutch more iconic than English in this respect.

Apparently, the subject in English, which grammaticalizes topics rather than agents, allows for more patterns than it does in Dutch, where the subject is primarily characterized by agentivity.

14. Russian *tam i sjam* 'there and here' is an exception; here phonetic iconicity appears to have overridden the semantic principle in that stops tend to precede fricatives in such constructions: *t* before *sj* (see also Ross 1980).

15. Of course, politeness or political correctness may change this order, as in *ladies and gentlemen*.

16. In its most general form, the principle of adjacency was already formulated by Otto Behaghel (1932: 4): "Das oberste Gesetz ist dieses, dass das geistig eng Zusammengehörige auch eng zusammengestellt wird" [The primary law is that what belongs closely together semantically is also closely placed together]. Rijkhoff (1992: 214) speaks of a principle of domain integrity.

17. For example, in a sentence like *John is in London*, where *in* is the relator, *John* the first relatum, and *London* the second, *London* has a fixed position immediately after *in*, whereas *John* does not immediately precede the preposition.

18. The label "particles" also includes ad hoc morphemes that are hard to accommodate in an ordinary word class, e.g., *than*.

19. In this instance, the verbal relator has two "second relata," the direct and the indirect object.

20. That the pattern [adjective + noun] figures among the nonrelator constructions appears to contradict Langacker's claim that adjectives are "relational"; see also note 6.

REFERENCES

Anttila, Raimo. 1972. *Introduction to comparative and historical linguistics*. New York: Macmillan.

Bach, Emmon. 1968. Nouns and noun phrases. In Emmon Bach and Robert Thomas Harms, eds., *Universals in linguistic theory* 90–122. New York: Holt.

Bauer, Laurie. 1996. No phonetic iconicity in evaluative morphology: Results of tests on a genetically diverse group of 50 languages. *Studia Linguistica* 50: 189–206.

Behaghel, Otto. 1932. *Deutsche Syntax: eine geschichtliche Darstellung, Band 4. Wortstellung, Periodenbau*. Heidelberg: Winter.

Benveniste, Emile. 1946. Relations de personne dans le verbe. *Bulletin de la Société Linguistique de Paris* 43: 1–12.

Birdsong, David. 1995. Iconicity, markedness, and processing constraints in frozen locutions. In Marge E. Landsberg, ed., *Syntactic iconicity and linguistic freezes: The human dimension* 31–45. Berlin: Mouton de Gruyter.

Bolinger, Dwight. 1977. *Meaning and form*. London: Longman.

Bouissac, Paul, Michael Herzfeld, and Roland Posner, eds. 1986. *Iconicity: Essays on the nature of culture: Festschrift for Thomas A. Sebeok on his 65th birthday*. Tübingen: Stauffenburg.

Brinton, Laurel J. 1987. Diagrammatic iconicity in English syntax. *Semiotic Inquiry* 7: 55–72.

Chomsky, Noam. 1972. *Language and mind*. Enlarged ed. New York: Harcourt Brace Jovanovich.

Chomsky, Noam. 1976. On the nature of language. In Stevan Harnad, Horst Dieter Steklis and Jane B. Lancaster, eds., *The origins and evolution of language and speech* 46–57. New York: New York Academy of Sciences.

Chomsky, Noam. 1980. *Rules and representations.* New York: Columbia University Press.

Chomsky, Noam. 1981. On the representation of form and function. *Linguistic Review* 1: 3–40.

Clark, Herbert H. 1973. Space, time, semantics and the child. In Timothy E. Moore, ed., *Cognitive development and the acquisition of language* 27–63. New York: Academic Press.

Comrie, Bernard. 1981. *Language universals and linguistic typology.* Oxford: Basil Blackwell. (2nd ed., 1989)

Croft, William. 2003. *Typology and universals.* 2nd ed. Cambridge: Cambridge University Press.

Dik, Simon C. 1983. Two constraints on relators and what they can do for us. In Simon C. Dik, ed., *Advances in functional grammar* 267–98. Dordrecht, Netherlands: Foris Publications.

Dobrizhoffer, M. 1902. *Auskunft über die abiponische Sprache.* Leipzig, Germany: J. Platzmann.

Fischer, Olga. 1997. Iconicity in language and literature: Language innovation and language change. *Neuphilologische Mitteilungen* 98: 63–87.

Fodor, Jerry A. 1970. Three reasons for not deriving 'kill' from 'cause to die'. *Linguistic Inquiry* 1: 429–38.

Geeraerts, Dirk. 1997. *Diachronic prototype semantics: A contribution to historical lexicology.* Oxford: Clarendon Press.

Genette, Gérard. 1976. *Mimologiques: Voyage en Cratylie.* Paris: Seuil.

Givón, Talmy. 1994. Isomorphism in grammatical code: Cognitive and biological consideration. In Raffaele Simone, ed., *Iconicity in language* 47–76. Amsterdam: John Benjamins.

Goossens, Jan. 1969. *Strukturelle Sprachgeographie.* Heidelberg: Winter.

Greenberg, Joseph H. 1966a. Language universals. In Thomas A. Sebeok, ed., *Current Trends in Linguistics,* vol. 3, *Theoretical foundations* 61–112. The Hague: Mouton.

Greenberg, Joseph H. 1966b. Some universals of grammar with particular reference to the order of meaningful elements. In Joseph H. Greenberg, ed., *Universals of Language,* 73–113. Cambridge, MA: MIT Press.

Greenberg, Joseph H. 1995. On language internal iconicity. In Marge E. Landsberg, ed., *Syntactic iconicity and linguistic freezes: The human dimension* 57–63. Berlin: Mouton de Gruyter.

Hagège, Claude. 1982. *La structure des langues.* Paris: Presses universitaires de France.

Haiman, John. 1974. Concessives, conditionals, and verbs of volition. *Foundations of Language* 11: 341–59.

Haiman, John. 1980. The iconicity of grammar: Isomorphism and motivation. *Language* 56: 515–40.

Haiman, John. 1983. Iconic and economic motivation. *Language* 59: 781–819.

Haiman, John. 1985. *Natural syntax: Iconicity and erosion.* Cambridge: Cambridge University Press.

Hamilton, Helen W., and James Deese. 1971. Does linguistic marking have a psychological correlate? *Journal of Verbal Learning and Verbal Behavior* 10: 707–14.

Heine, Bernd. 1980. Determination in some East African languages. In Gunter Brettsch-neider and Christian Lehmann, eds., *Wege zur Universalienforschung: Sprachwis-senschaftliche Beiträge zum 60. Geburtstag von Hansjakob Seiler* 180–86. Tübingen: Gunter Narr.

Hetzron, Robert. 1978. On the relative order of adjectives. In Hansjakob Seiler, ed., *Language universals* 165–84. Tübingen: Gunter Narr.

Hudson, Richard. 1984. *Word grammar.* Oxford: Basil Blackwell.

Jakobson, Roman. 1965. Quest for the essence of language. *Diogenes* 51: 21–37.

Jakobson, Roman. 1966. Implications of language universals for linguistics. In Thomas A. Sebeok, ed., *Current Trends in Linguistics,* vol. 3, *Theoretical foundations* 263–78. The Hague: Mouton.

Kakehi, Hisao, Ikuhiro Tamori, and Lawrence Schourup. 1996. *Dictionary of iconic ex-pressions in Japanese.* In cooperation with Leslie J. Emerson. 2 vols. Berlin: Mouton de Gruyter.

Katz, Jerrold J., and Paul M. Postal. 1964. *An integrated theory of linguistic descriptions.* Cambridge, MA: MIT Press.

Kleiber, Georges. 1993. Iconicité d'isomorphisme et grammaire cognitive. *Faits de langue* 1: 105–21. (Special issue on 'Motivation et Iconité')

Lakoff, George. 1982. Categories and cognitive models. LAUT Paper, no. 96. Trier, Ger-many: Linguistic Agency of the University of Trier.

Landsberg, Marge E., ed. 1995. *Syntactic iconicity and linguistic freezes: The human dimension.* Berlin: Mouton de Gruyter.

Langacker, Ronald W. 1985. Observations and speculations on subjectivity. In John Hai-man, ed., *Iconicity in syntax* 109–50. Amsterdam: John Benjamins.

Langacker, Ronald W. 1987. *Foundations of cognitive grammar.* Vol. 1, *Theoretical prereq-uisites.* Stanford, CA: Stanford University Press.

Langacker, Ronald W. 1990. *Concept, image, and symbol: The cognitive basis of grammar.* Berlin: Mouton de Gruyter.

Langacker, Ronald W. 1991. *Foundations of cognitive grammar.* Vol. 2, *Descriptive appli-cation.* Stanford, CA: Stanford University Press.

Mayerthaler, Willy. 1980. Ikonismus in der Morphologie. *Zeitschrift für Semiotik* 2: 19–37.

Mayerthaler, Willy. 1988. *Morphological naturalness.* Ann Arbor, MI: Karoma.

Motivation et iconicité. 1993. Special issue of *Faits de Langues* 1.

Newmeyer, Frederick J. 1992. Iconicity and generative grammar. *Language* 68: 756–96.

Peirce, Charles Sanders. [1931] 1974. *Collected papers of Charles Sanders Peirce.* Ed. Charles Hartshorne and Paul Weiss. Cambridge, MA: Harvard University Press.

Pharies, David A. 1985. *Charles S. Peirce and the linguistic sign.* Amsterdam: John Benjamins.

Posner, Roland. 1986. *Iconicity in syntax: The natural order of attributes.* In Paul Bouissac, Michael Herzfeld, and Roland Posner, eds., *Iconicity: Essays on the nature of culture: Festschrift for Thomas A. Sebeok on his 65th birthday* 305–37. Tübingen: Stauffenburg.

Rijkhoff, Jan. 1992. *The noun phrase: A typological study of its form and structure.* Am-sterdam: John Benjamins.

Ross, John. 1980. Ikonismus in der Phraseologie. *Zeitschrift für Semiotik* 2: 39–56.

Ruwet, Nicolas. 1984. *Je veux partir/*Je veux que je parte*: A propos de la distribution des complétives à temps fini et des compléments à l'infinitif en français. *Cahiers de Grammaire* 7: 76–138.

Saussure, Ferdinand de. [1916] 1967. *Cours de linguistique générale.* Paris: Payot.

Schachter, Paul. 1974. A non-transformational account of serial verbs. *Studies in African Linguistics* Supplement V: 253–69.

Seiler, Hansjakob. 1978. Determination: A functional dimension for inter-language comparison. In Hansjakob Seiler, ed., *Language Universals* 301–28. Tübingen: G. Narr.

Simone, Raffaele, ed. 1994. *Iconicity in language*. Amsterdam: John Benjamins.

Song, Jae Jung. 1992. A note on iconicity in causatives. *Folia Linguistica* 26: 333–38.

Stassen, Leon. 1985. *Comparison and Universal Grammar: An essay in Universal Grammar*. Oxford: Basil Blackwell.

Swiggers, Pierre. 1993. Iconicité: Un coup d'oeil historiographique et méthodologique. *Faits de langue* 1: 21–28. (Special issue on 'Motivation et Iconité')

Thompson, Sandra A. 1995. The iconicity of 'dative shift' in English: Considerations from information flow in discourse. In Marge E. Landsberg, ed., *Syntactic iconicity and linguistic freezes: The human dimension* 155–75. Berlin: Mouton de Gruyter.

Tomlin, Russell S. 1986. *Basic word order: Functional principles*. London: Croom Helm.

Van Langendonck, Willy. 1979. Definiteness as an unmarked category. *Linguistische Berichte* 63: 33–55.

Van Langendonck, Willy. 1995. Categories of word order iconicity. In Marge E. Landsberg, ed., *Syntactic iconicity and linguistic freezes: The human dimension* 79–90. Berlin: Mouton de Gruyter.

Van Langendonck, Willy. 1999. Markedness and prototypical speaker attributes. In Leon de Stadler and Christoph Eyrich, eds., *Issues in cognitive linguistics 1993: Proceedings of the 3rd international cognitive linguistics conference* 567–76. Berlin: Mouton de Gruyter.

Van Langendonck, Willy. 2004. Proper names and forms of iconicity. *Logos and Languages: Journal of General Linguistics and Language Theory* 5: 15–30. (Special issue, Syntactic categories and parts of speech, ed. Klaas Willems)

Van Langendonck, Willy. 2007. *Theory and typology of proper names*. Berlin: Mouton de Gruyter.

Van Langendonck, Willy, and Wim de Pater. 1993. Ikonizität in natürlicher Sprache. *Kodikas* 15: 1–20.

Van Langendonck, Willy, Pierre Swiggers, and Mark Van de Velde. Forthcoming. The relator- principle as an explanatory parameter in linguistic typology: An exploratory study of comparative constructions. In Peter Lauwers and Pierre Swiggers, eds., *Linguistic concepts and currents*. Leuven, Belgium: Peeters.

Van Langendonck, Willy, Pierre Swiggers, and Mark Van de Velde. N.d. The North European belt of RIM languages. Manuscript.

Wierzbicka, Anna. 1975. Why 'kill' does not mean 'cause to die': The semantics of action sentences. *Foundations of Language* 13: 491–528.

Zipf, George K. [1949] 1965. *Human behavior and the principle of least effort: An introduction to human ecology*. New York: Hafner.

PART II

MODELS OF GRAMMAR

CHAPTER 17

COGNITIVE GRAMMAR

RONALD W. LANGACKER

1. BACKGROUND

Research leading to the formulation of Cognitive Grammar began in the spring of 1976. On the American theoretical scene, it was the era of the "linguistics wars" between Generative Semantics and Interpretive Semantics. The research was stimulated by the realization that this dispute was vacuous and sterile, that making sense of language required a wholly different way of thinking about it. Within three years, the overall architecture and basic descriptive constructs of the new framework were established. The first published descriptions, under the rubric "Space Grammar," were Langacker (1981) and (1982). Its rechristening as "Cognitive Grammar" in the first full-length presentation (Langacker 1987a) was not the result of any modification. To this very day, in fact, changes have been matters of elaboration and refinement—the basic notions remain intact.

Cognitive Grammar was not derived from any other theory, nor is it particularly close to any. While it does bear certain resemblances to numerous other frameworks, these are limited in scope and apparent only when stated in general terms. With Generative Semantics, for instance, Cognitive Grammar shares only the general vision of treating semantics, lexicon, and grammar in a unified way. The most extensive similarities are with Construction Grammar (Fillmore 1988; Goldberg 1995; Michaelis and Lambrecht 1996; Croft 2001; this volume, chapter 18). Though developed independently, the two frameworks share a number of basic ideas: that constructions (not "rules") are the primary objects of description; that lexicon and grammar are not distinct, but a continuum of constructions (form-meaning pairings); and that constructions are linked in networks of inheritance (or catego-rization). Yet their extensive differences are also quite apparent. A glance at their respective diagrams reveals radically different formats symptomatic of substantially different theoretical devices and descriptive constructs. In representing meanings, Construction Grammar largely ignores the construal factors (e.g., profiling) taken as fundamental in Cognitive Grammar. Moreover, it does not embrace the pivotal claim of Cognitive Grammar that all valid grammatical constructs have a conceptual characterization; notions like noun, verb, subject, and object are essentially treated as unanalyzable syntactic primitives.[1]

Still, Cognitive Grammar is part of the wider movement that has come to be known as Cognitive Linguistics, which, in turn, belongs to the broad and diverse functionalist tradition. The categorization of linguistic approaches as "function-alist" versus "formalist" is of course simplistic and increasingly irrelevant. While their prototypes are sharply distinct, a schematic characterization valid for the categories overall is the rather tenuous one of whether functional considerations are taken as *foundational* to an account of language structure, or merely *subsidiary* (Langacker 1995c, 1999a). By this criterion, Cognitive Grammar is strongly func-tional, granted that the two basic functions of language are *symbolic* (allowing conceptualizations to be symbolized by sounds and gestures) and *communicative/ interactive*. The symbolic function is directly manifested in the very architecture of Cognitive Grammar, which posits only symbolic structures for the description of lexicon, morphology, and syntax. A manifestation of the communicative/inter-active function is the fundamental claim that all linguistic units are abstracted from *usage events*.

What, then, is "cognitive" about Cognitive Linguistics and Cognitive Gram-mar? Within the functionalist tradition, they are distinguished by the notion that properly describing language from the communicative/interactive perspective re-quires an explicit description of the conceptual structures involved. These struc-tures include the interlocutors' apprehension of each other, of their interaction, of the context, and of the ongoing discourse itself. With respect to generative doc-trine, Cognitive Linguistics merits the label by virtue of treating language as an integral facet of cognition rather than a separate "module." Insofar as possible, language is seen as recruiting more general cognitive phenomena (e.g., attention, perception, categorization, memory) from which it cannot be dissociated.

Cognitive Grammar is envisaged as fitting into a more comprehensive theory of language structure comprising three interdependent levels. At the first level is a descriptive framework allowing the explicit characterization of the full range of linguistic structures empirically encountered. Work in Cognitive Grammar has aimed primarily at articulating such a framework. Because it needs to accommodate even the most unusual structures, the framework must be quite flexible and will thus define a very large space of structural possibilities. The appropriate restric-tiveness comes from level two, an enumeration of what kinds of structures are universal or prototypical in the world's languages and to what degree. On the basis of cross-linguistic surveys, this enumeration will specify just how the space of structural possibilities is "warped," such that certain options are exploited far more readily and frequently than others. Level three, then, consists of functional explanations for the findings at levels one and two.

A primary commitment of Cognitive Grammar is thus to provide an optimal set of constructs for explicitly describing linguistic structure. Its formulation has been guided throughout by a number of principles thought to be helpful in achieving such optimality. The first principle, already alluded to, is that functional considerations should inform the process from the outset and be reflected in the framework's architecture and descriptive apparatus. Because the functions of language involve the manipulation and symbolization of conceptual structures, a second principle is the need to characterize such structures at a reasonable level of explicit detail and technical precision. To be revealing, however, descriptions must be natural and appropriate. Thus, a third principle is that language and languages have to be described in their own terms, without the imposition of artificial boundaries or Procrustean modes of analysis based on conventional wisdom. As a corollary, formalization is not to be considered an end in itself, but must rather be assessed for its utility at a given stage of investigation. That no attempt has yet been made to formalize Cognitive Grammar reflects the judgment that the cost of the requisite simplifications and distortions would greatly outweigh any putative benefits. Finally, a fourth principle is that claims about language should be broadly compatible with secure findings of related disciplines (e.g., cognitive psychology, neuroscience, and evolutionary biology). Nevertheless, the claims and descriptions of Cognitive Grammar are all supported by specifically linguistic considerations.

Radically different when initially formulated, Cognitive Grammar seems much less so today simply because "mainstream" linguistic theory has steadily evolved in its direction. Widely contemplated today, if not generally accepted, are Cognitive Grammar notions such as the following: prototype categorization; conceptual semantics; the semantic basis of most grammaticality judgments; the inseparability of grammatical and semantic analysis; lexicon and grammar forming a continuum; constructions as the primary objects of description; inheritance networks; "rules" as schemas (or templates)—see also Tuggy this volume, chapter 4; a nonderivational ("monostratal") view; well-formedness as simultaneous constraint satisfaction; composition as "unification"; a "usage based" model. Despite these points of convergence, Cognitive Grammar remains unique (and in some eyes notorious) by virtue of certain strong and controversial claims, notably the conceptual characterization of basic grammatical notions (e.g., noun, verb, subject, object) and the full reduction of lexicon and grammar to assemblies of symbolic structures. It is further distinctive in its overall vision and at the level of specific descriptive detail.

At the same time, Cognitive Grammar is arguably quite conservative and down-to-earth. Care is taken not to invoke any cognitive phenomena that are not well known or easily demonstrable. In adopting descriptive constructs, a strategy is systematically employed of seeking converging evidence from three independent sources: in addition to being cognitively plausible, a construct must prove necessary for describing and distinguishing meanings and must further be shown to play a role in grammar (Langacker 1993b, 1999a). Moreover, the *content require-ment* imposes a kind of restrictiveness and theoretical austerity unmatched by most other theories. First, it limits the linguistic units one can posit to semantic struc-tures, phonological structures, and symbolic structures (which pair the other two). Second, the units posited must either be part of the primary data (occurring ex-pressions) or else be derivable from it via the basic psychological processes of schematization and categorization.

These conservative properties are quite desirable provided that the framework nonetheless permits an adequate characterization of language structure. Cognitive Grammar has, though, been criticized (e.g., by Huffman 1997: 331–32) as being overly conservative on another score, namely in adopting a number of traditional gram-matical notions considered problematic for a universally applicable descriptive in-ventory. Indeed, an array of traditional terms are in fact employed with something approximating their familiar values: terms like noun, verb, subject, morpheme, constituency, and subordinate clause. Attentive readers will notice, however, that in each case the notion in question has been thoroughly reconceptualized and refor-mulated in a way that avoids classic problems and makes it potentially appropriate for universal application.[2] The idea is not to stick with concepts known to be inadequate in their standard form, but to rescue what is useful with suitable mod-ification in a new overall theoretical context. In any case, Cognitive Grammar is better known for the proliferation of new concepts and terminology.

2. ARCHITECTURE

Viewed as a mental phenomenon, a language resides in organized processing ac-tivity (patterns of neural activation). The convenient use of terms like "linguistic knowledge," "linguistic system," and "internalized grammar" should not be allowed to obscure its essential dynamicity or to suggest a discretely bounded module. Knowing a language is having mastered a set of skills: a vast number of perceptual, motor, and cognitive operations that can be recruited and executed along with many others in speaking and understanding.

A language is defined in Cognitive Grammar as a structured inventory of conventional linguistic units. A *unit* is a pattern of processing activity that is thoroughly mastered and can thus be carried out more or less automatically (a "cognitive routine"). Reference to an *inventory* of units is meant to indicate the framework's nongenerative and nonconstructive nature: linguistic units do not constitute an autonomous derivational system itself responsible for constructing well-formed expressions, but are merely resources that speakers can exploit in doing so. This inventory is *structured* in the sense that, instead of being separate and discrete, units relate to one another in various ways (overlap, inclusion, symbolization, categorization, integration into higher-level units). Of course, the units recognized as part of a language must also be *linguistic* in nature and *conventional* within a speech community.

So defined, a language cannot be precisely delimited. A particular structure achieves the status of a unit through progressive psychological *entrenchment*, which is clearly a matter of degree. Also a matter of degree is *conventionality*: how widely a structure is shared among speakers (and accepted as such). Nor are there definite boundaries between "linguistic" and "extralinguistic" structures (Langacker 1987a: section 2.1.2). The delimitation of "linguistic meaning" is notoriously problematic. Hardly less so is the demarcation of "linguistic symbolization." While segmental phonology may be central, the range of conventional symbolizing structures further includes both intonational and gestural phenomena. In these domains, we observe an apparent gradation leading from established patterns to spontaneous expressivity, such that any specific boundary has to be arbitrarily imposed.

A *usage event* is defined as an actual instance of language use. It resides in the pairing of a comprehensive conceptualization, representing a full contextual understanding, with an elaborate expression, in all its phonetic and gestural detail. All linguistic units are abstracted from usage events. The abstractive process is just a matter of reinforcing whatever commonalities recur across a number of usage events, being inherent in these events at any level of granularity. Features which do not recur fail to be reinforced and are therefore filtered out. Thus, all linguistic units are selective and schematic vis-à-vis the usage events from which they arise. As entrenched processing patterns, these units are available for subsequent processing. Their activation in the context of subsequent usage events effects the latter's linguistic categorization (i.e., their interpretation with respect to the currently established system).

In principle, any facets of a usage event, or a sequence of events in a discourse, are susceptible to being abstracted and conventionalized as a unit. For analytic purposes—and with the caution that they must not be reified as separate, discretely bounded boxes—it is useful to posit a number of *sectors*, as sketched in figure 17.1 (Langacker 2001a). One sector is the *ground*, comprising the speaker (S), the hearer (H), their interaction (←→), and their immediate circumstances. Central to their linguistic interaction is the directing and focusing of attention (--→). This involves the conceptual analogue of the visual field, a subjective "space" within which a conceptualization is manifested. Called the *viewing frame*, this space delimits the general locus of viewing attention (metaphorically, it can be referred to as the "onstage region").[3] Any facet of the interlocutors' conceptual universe can appear in this frame, within which they direct their attention to a specific *focus* of attention.

All of this is embedded in a larger context, which in turn is embedded in the body of knowledge presumed to be shared by the speaker and hearer. To the extent that such factors are apprehended and mentally accessed, they figure in a usage event as part of the conceptualization constituting an expression's full contextual understanding. Of course, a crucial dimension of this understanding is apprehension of the ongoing discourse itself, comprising both previous and anticipated

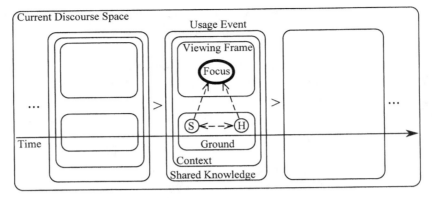

Figure 17.1. Structures relevant to discourse

usage events. This is called the *current discourse space*, that is, the mental space comprising whatever is shared by the speaker and hearer as a basis for communication at a given moment in the flow of discourse.

Hence, the overall conceptualization evoked in a usage event includes far more than what appears onstage within the viewing frame. Supporting the onstage conception is an elaborate *conceptual substrate*, which shapes it and renders it coherent. What appears onstage, moreover, is also elaborate and multifaceted. As shown in figure 17.2, the conceptualization and the expression can each be resolved into a number of *channels* (which nonetheless interact in complex ways). Two particular channels are usually most central and have the most substantial content. For conceptualization, the focused channel is the conception of the situation being discussed; as the object of discussion, this is dubbed the "objective situation." Other conceptualization channels (more peripheral to speaker awareness despite their importance) are those pertaining to information structure and speech management. On the expression side, the focused channel (in the case of spoken language) is that of "segmental" phonological content. Other major channels of expression are intonation and gesture.[4]

Since all the sectors and channels depicted in figures 17.1 and 17.2 factor into usage events, they potentially factor into the conventional linguistic units abstracted from such events. A particular unit reflects a recurring usage configuration by making specifications in certain sectors, but remains unspecified (or maximally schematic) in regard to others. At the very least, however, each unit incorporates an indication of its own conventional status: a schematized representation of interlocutors using it in speaking the language in question.[5] A unit's conventional import with respect to various factors often excluded from the scope of linguistic description (e.g., register, affect, discourse function, relative social status of the interlocutors) is also specified in sectors not focused in the viewing frame.

The two global facets of a usage event are conceptualization and expression. Corresponding to these are the two global facets of abstracted linguistic units, referred to as the *semantic pole* and the *phonological pole*. Interpreted broadly, a unit's

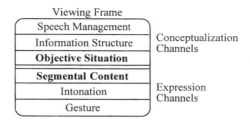

Figure 17.2. Channels

phonological pole comprises all the channels of expression. Interpreted more narrowly, the phonological pole is limited to expressive channels in which a significant specification is made.[6] A unit's semantic pole can likewise be defined either narrowly or broadly. Narrowly defined, its semantic pole consists of central and significantly specified channels of conceptualization. Conceived more broadly, however, the semantic pole includes all the sectors in figure 17.1, regardless of specificity. It is even taken as subsuming the channels of expression, on the grounds that these are also apprehended and for various purposes are advantageously treated as facets of conceptualization (Langacker 1987a: section 2.2.1).

Under the broad definitions, every linguistic unit has both a semantic and a phonological pole. Under the narrow definitions, three basic types of units can be distinguished depending on which sectors have salient and significant specifications. *Semantic units* are those that only have a semantic pole (in the narrow sense), while *phonological units* (e.g., a phoneme or a phonotactic pattern) have only a phonological pole. A *symbolic unit* has both a semantic and a phonological pole, consisting in the symbolic linkage between the two.[7] These three types of units are the minimum needed for language to fulfill its symbolic function. A central claim—embodied in the content requirement—is that *only* these are necessary. Cognitive Grammar maintains that a language is fully describable in terms of semantic structures, phonological structures, and symbolic links between them. Linguistic units are further limited to those arising from occurring expressions via schematization and categorization.

On this view, lexicon and grammar form a continuum consisting solely of symbolic structures. Lexicon is defined as the set of "fixed" expressions in a language, that is, conventional expressions with the status of units. This set is not sharply bounded, for both psychological entrenchment and conventionality in a speech community are matters of degree. Fixed expressions vary along two basic parameters: *specificity* and *symbolic complexity*. At the phonological pole, expressions are quite specific, since to be expressions they have to be overtly manifested.[8] Semantically they run the gamut from highly specific to highly schematic (e.g., *tack hammer > hammer > tool > implement > object > thing*). An expression's symbolic complexity is the number of constitutive symbolic elements it contains: *sharp < sharpen < sharpener < pencil sharpener < electric pencil sharpener*. The expressions traditionally recognized as lexical items are generally fairly specific and of limited

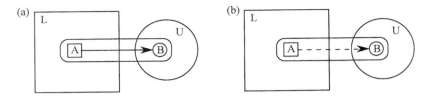

Figure 17.3. Coding

symbolic complexity. However, imposing any particular line of demarcation would be arbitrary. Thus, the highly schematic meanings of "grammatical" elements—such as the infinitival *to*, the preposition *of*, or the auxiliary verb *do*—do not prevent them from also counting as lexical items. Nor is lexicon limited to words, compounds, and short phrases. Provided that they are learned as conventional units, expressions of any size qualify as lexical items.[9]

The two parameters of specificity and symbolic complexity define a continuous field of possibilities in which particular symbolic structures can be situated. While there are no definite boundaries, various subfields roughly correspond to traditionally recognized domains. Lexical items as classically conceived occupy the subfield characterized by limited symbolic complexity and a high degree of semantic and phonological specificity. To the extent that symbolic structures are schematic rather than specific, they tend to be regarded as grammatical rather than lexical. Grammatical markers are phonologically specific, semantically schematic, and symbolically noncomplex. Basic grammatical categories (notably noun and verb) are defined abstractly by symbolically minimal structures that are highly schematic both semantically and phonologically. Corresponding to grammatical rules (combinatory patterns) are symbolic structures which are both schematic and symbolically complex.

A linguistic system is merely a vast inventory of conventional units (not a self-contained device wholly responsible for constructing or enumerating expressions). It provides an array of resources which, along with many others, can be drawn upon in speaking and understanding. Among the further resources employed are general and contextual knowledge, basic cognitive abilities (e.g., memory, attention, planning, aesthetic judgment), as well as such "imaginative" capacities as metaphor, blending, mental space construction, and the evocation of "fictive" entities (Talmy 1996; Langacker 1999d). Linguistic units themselves reflect such factors internally. These same factors figure as well in the formation of novel expressions, which thus incorporate many features not solely derivable from the linguistic units invoked.

Hence, linguistic knowledge is inextricably bound up with numerous other resources exploited in a dynamic processing system. It resides in routinized "packets" of processing activity, some of which are activated as part of the overall processing done by the system as a whole in producing or understanding a new expression. If a unit is strongly activated as part of an expression's apprehension,[10] their relationship amounts to categorization: an instantiation of the unit is immanent in the processing constituting the expression. It is through such categorization—referred

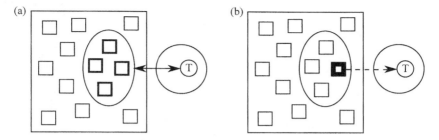

Figure 17.4. Activation of categorizing units

to as *coding* in Langacker (1987a)—that an expression is seen as manifesting a particular language and attributed a particular structure with respect to it.

An instance of coding is depicted in figure 17.3, where L represents the linguistic system, and U a usage event. It consists of unit A (from L) being activated and thus effecting the categorization of structure B (a facet of U). There are two basic possibilities, indicated by different kinds of arrows. On the one hand, A can be fully manifested in B, without distortion, though B is generally more specific. In this case the categorizing relationship is one of *elaboration*, drawn with a solid arrow. On the other hand, A might be manifested in B only partially or imperfectly. In this case the categorizing relationship is one of *extension*, drawn with a dashed arrow. But in either case, A is exploited as a resource in the processing activity constituting facet B of the usage event.

How are units selected for the categorization of usage events? At the processing phase when linguistic units are still being recruited for exploitation, a usage event is only incipient. Before the units employed are selected and fully activated, neither the conceptualization nor the vocalization has yet been fully developed and structured in accordance with their specifications. It is precisely the activation of a particular set of units that results in a full-blown usage event interpreted as manifesting a particular linguistic expression. Let T then represent a potential *target* of categorization, that is, some facet of an incipient usage event.[11] On the basis of overlapping features, T tends to activate a set of units each of which has the potential to categorize it; this *activation set* is shown as an ellipse in figure 17.4a. The set's members are all initially activated to some degree. Mutually inhibitory, they compete for the privilege of being fully activated, thereby effecting the categorization of T. A number of factors contribute to a unit's selection: degree of entrenchment (inherent ease of activation), contextual priming, and extent of overlap with the target. As shown in figure 17.4b, the competition eventually results in one unit suppressing all the others and becoming fully active as the categorizing structure.

Figures 17.3 and 17.4 show just a single categorization. However, a usage event is simultaneously categorized by many conventional units, each pertaining to a particular facet of its structure. Collectively, these categorizations constitute the event's *structural description*, that is, its interpretation with respect to the linguistic system. It is by virtue of being interpreted in a certain way that a usage event can be

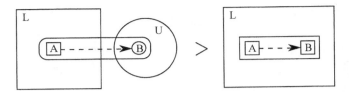

Figure 17.5. Extension

said to manifest a particular linguistic expression. Moreover, the set of categorizations provide an assessment of the expression's degree of *well-formedness* (or *conventionality*). The two kinds of categorizing relationships depicted in figure 17.3, elaboration and extension, respectively correspond to whether the target conforms to the conventional unit invoked or distorts it in some manner. If all the categorizations effected on a given occasion are elaborative, the expression is fully well-formed. Each categorization involving extension represents a measure of nonconventionality (ill-formedness). Since linguistic resources are always being stretched to accommodate new circumstances, a certain amount of nonconventionality is typical of normal language use. It is only when the distortions are drastic enough (individually or collectively) that an expression is judged as being deviant.

Figure 17.3 depicts a particular unit, A, being employed for the categorization of B in the context of a single usage event. Whether it constitutes an elaboration or an extension, B represents the contextual value assumed by A on that occasion. Suppose, now, that A is used with comparable value on a number of occasions (e.g., a lexical item might be used repeatedly with the same extended meaning). If both B and B's categorization by A occur across a series of usage events, they—like any other facet of such events—are subject to progressive entrenchment and conventionalization. The result, as shown for the case of extension in figure 17.5, is that both achieve the status of conventional linguistic units and are thus incorporated in the linguistic system (as a matter of definition). Starting from a single unit, A, successive developments of this sort can eventually yield a network of related units linked by categorizing relationships (which can themselves be recognized as units). This network is a *complex category*, with A as its *prototype* (Lakoff 1987; Langacker 1987a: chapter 10; Taylor 1995).

It is through the constant impact of usage that linguistic units maintain themselves and evolve. The activation of a unit reinforces and further entrenches it. Conversely, a unit that is not exploited tends to "decay" and may eventually be lost. Through elaboration and extension, units spawn variants which can then take on lives of their own. Schemas emerge by the reinforcing of abstract commonalities that consistently recur, and complex units arise from simpler structures that consistently co-occur. Thus, every instance of language use has some impact, however slight, on the linguistic system as currently constituted. In this *usage-based* perspective (Barlow and Kemmer 2000), synchrony and diachrony are inseparable.

3. Semantics

A central claim of Cognitive Grammar is that only symbolic structures (form-meaning pairings) need be posited for the characterization of lexicon and grammar, which form a continuum. This symbolic view of grammar implies that the elements, structures, and constructs employed in grammatical description must all be meaningful (just as lexical items are). Their meaningfulness can be recognized and accommodated only given an appropriate view of linguistic meaning, one that is strongly justified in its own terms. Required is a *conceptualist* semantics. Meaning is identified with *conceptualization*, broadly defined as encompassing any kind of mental experience: (i) both established and novel conceptions; (ii) not only abstract or intellectual "concepts" but also immediate sensory, motor, kinesthetic, and emotive experience; (iii) conceptions that are not instantaneous but change or unfold through processing time; and (iv) full apprehension of the physical, linguistic, social, and cultural context.

A conceptualist semantics has none of the dire consequences sometimes ascribed to it. There is first the doctrine, still expressed in semantics textbooks, that concepts are intrinsically mysterious, and their investigation unscientific.[12] On the contrary, cognitive semantic research (e.g., Fauconnier 1985, 1997; Lakoff and Johnson 1980, 1999; Fauconnier and Turner 1998, 2002; Talmy 2000a, 2000b) has yielded detailed, explicit, empirically grounded, and increasingly principled descriptions of conceptual structure that have greatly altered received wisdom about cognition. Within Cognitive Grammar, validity of the descriptive constructs employed is assured by requiring converging evidence from three sources (Langacker 1993b, 1999a). The basis for adopting a particular construct is to show that it is (i) necessary just for purposes of semantic description (e.g., to distinguish the meanings of semantically similar expressions), (ii) the manifestation of an independently attested cognitive ability, and (iii) critical for the explicit characterization of varied grammatical phenomena.

Nor does a conceptualist semantics imply solipsism or an inability to deal with social interaction and discourse (cf. Harder 1996). Though conceptualization takes place internally (residing in processing activity of the brain), it is not autonomous or encapsulated, and it is not itself the object of contemplation.[13] Conceptualization is always the conceptualization *of* something, a facet of either the real world we inhabit or a constructed world ultimately grounded in real world experience. Conceptualization is precisely the act of *engaging* the world, the experiential aspect of our interaction with it. Broadly understood, conceptualization includes perceptual experience, as well as the central control of motor activity and the kinesthetic sensations it induces. It further includes the interlocutors' apprehension of the discourse and the interactive context supporting it.

Also erroneous is the supposition that equating meaning with conceptualization implies the absence of any distinction between semantics and pragmatics or implies that the conceptualizations invoked for linguistic purposes are unaffected by being so employed, hence exactly equivalent to nonlinguistic conceptions.[14] Rather, semantic structures are specifically seen as representing the *adaptation* of conceptualization for expressive purposes, thus conforming to both the strictures of linguistic convention and the exigencies of language function. Cognitive Grammar's claim that the semantics/pragmatics distinction is "largely artifactual," a false dichotomy (Langacker 1987a: 154), pertains to the arbitrariness of any specific line of demarcation. It does not deny either the existence of pragmatics or the possibility of distinguishing it from semantics. It merely posits a gradation, such that notions which are indisputably semantic or pragmatic lie toward opposite extremes of a scale, the status of those in the middle being mixed or indeterminate.

This gradation is observed even in lexical semantics. At issue is whether a lexical item's meaning comprises everything speakers know about the type of entity designated (the *encyclopedic* view of linguistic semantics) or whether—as traditionally assumed—its meaning is limited to a small, strictly delimited portion of this knowledge (the *dictionary* view).[15] In adopting the encyclopedic view, Cognitive Grammar is not claiming that there are no limits or that all knowledge is equally significant. For one thing, knowledge counts as being linguistic only to the extent that it is psychologically entrenched and conventional in a speech community, both of which are matters of degree. Moreover, specifications which are familiar and widely shared vary greatly in their degree of *centrality*, that is, the likelihood of their being activated when the lexical item is used. Some specifications are so central that they can hardly be suppressed, while the activation of others is variable depending on the context, and some are so peripheral that they are activated only in very special circumstances. On the encyclopedic view, a lexical item provides a particular way of accessing associated domains of knowledge. The access it affords is flexible and subject to contextual influence, but not at all random or unconstrained.

Distinct (though not unrelated) is the issue of how many conventionally established meanings a lexical item has. As is usual in Cognitive Linguistics, Cognitive Grammar maintains that an expression used with any frequency is generally *polysemous*, having a number of different but related "senses."[16] These senses arise through usage and are linked by categorizing relationships (elaboration and extension) to form a network, usually centered on a prototype. They represent the conventional range of established usage, as well as whatever schemas are abstracted on the basis of commonalities inherent in sets of more specific senses. Since the same prototypical meaning can be extended in different directions, often forming chains of extensions, there may not be any schematic meaning that all the other senses instantiate.

This contrasts with a *monosemous* account (e.g., Ruhl 1989), which claims that only a single abstract meaning need be posited, from which all specific uses are derived by interpretive principles. While a schematic meaning should always be sought, three basic considerations argue for its insufficiency. First, the monosemous view is seemingly at odds with the privileged status of a category prototype, including its role in spawning extended and more schematic senses (both developmentally and diachronically). Second, an all-subsuming schema is often too abstract to be clearly distinct from those of other categories or to capture what seems distinctive about a particular category. Third, a single sense—either a schema or a prototype—cannot represent everything speakers know about an expression's conventional usage. Out of all the specific senses that could in principle be derived from a schema or a prototype by plausible interpretive mechanisms, only a small proportion are actually exploited and conventionally established. Knowing these is part of knowing how to speak a language. Hence they are part of the linguistic system, as defined in Cognitive Grammar.

Valid questions have been raised about the "psychological reality" of a network as the representation of a complex category (e.g., Sandra and Rice 1995; Rice 1996). Though it undeniably has a certain utility, the network model is only a metaphor, whose appropriateness cannot be taken for granted. The discreteness inherent in the metaphor—suggesting a determinate number of nodes and a particular set of links—cannot necessarily be ascribed per se to the cognitive phenomena it models. An alternative metaphor, arguably less distorting, likens an expression's range of meanings to a mountain range, which is continuous but very uneven due to rises, depressions, peaks, and valleys. Counting the senses of a lexical item is analogous to counting the peaks in a mountain range: how many there are depends on how salient they have to be before we count them; they appear discrete only if we ignore how they grade into one another at lower altitudes. The uncertainty often experienced in determining which particular sense an expression instantiates on a given occasion is thus to be expected. In terms of the metaphor, such uses correspond to points in a valley lying between two peaks. Whether we assign such points to one peak, to the other, to both, or to neither is essentially arbitrary.

How, in a conceptualist semantics, can a particular meaning (or sense) be characterized? What should be adopted as conceptual "primitives," the basic elements from which more elaborate conceptions are constructed? An essential point, too often ignored, is that something can be "basic" in many different ways, some of them mutually contradictory.[17] From the Cognitive Grammar perspective, two kinds of basicness are especially important linguistically. Basic in one respect are *conceptual archetypes*, Gestalt conceptions of some complexity representing salient aspects of our everyday experience that are highly frequent and seemingly fundamental. Here are a few examples: a physical object, an object moving through space, the human face, the human body, a physical container and its contents, a whole and its parts, seeing something, holding something, handing something to someone, exerting force to effect a desired change, speaking, a face-to-face social encounter. Basic in another respect are certain minimal and maximally schematic notions that can be manifested in any domain of experience: point versus extension, contrast, boundary, change, continuity, contact, inclusion, separation, proximity, multiplicity, group, and so on. In view of their abstractness and minimality, they can be thought of as either schematic concepts or *basic cognitive abilities*. Instead of extension, contrast, and group, for instance, one can just as well speak of mental scanning, the ability to detect a contrast, and the capacity for grouping constitutive entities.[18]

Conceptual archetypes and basic cognitive abilities have different roles in gram-mar. Being more specific and cognitively salient, the former tend to be adopted as category *prototypes*. Being highly abstract, the latter are possible candidates for the *schematic* description of a category (one valid for all instances).[19] A basic pro-posal of Cognitive Grammar is that certain fundamental and universal grammatical notions—including noun, verb, subject, object, and possessive—are semantically characterized at both levels. A noun, for example, is characterized prototypically in terms of the physical object archetype and schematically in terms of the cognitive abilities of grouping and reification (section 4). Developmentally, the abilities in question are initially manifested in prototypical instances, giving rise to the arche-type, and subsequently extended to other kinds of conceptions.

Basic in yet another way are certain realms of experience not reducible to anything more fundamental. Among these *basic domains* are space, time, and do-mains associated with the various senses, such as color space (the range of color sensations we are capable of experiencing).[20] A basic domain is not itself a concept, but rather provides the experiential potential for conceptualization to occur. Min-imal concepts exploiting this potential include such notions as line, angle, cur-vature, focal colors, and temporal precedence. These, too, are basic in the sense of being incorporated in countless other conceptions, both simple and complex.

Starting from these various sorts of basic elements, successively more elaborate conceptions can be constructed, with no upper bound on their ultimate com-plexity. A concept or conceptual complex of any size, at any level of conceptual organization, is called a *nonbasic domain*.[21] One can then make the general state-ment that a linguistic expression evokes a set of domains (basic and nonbasic) as the basis for its meaning. Collectively these domains are referred to as the expres-sion's conceptual *matrix*. A domain representing any level of organization or de-gree of complexity can be part of an expression's matrix and crucial to its semantic characterization. Thus, *red* evokes the basic domain of color space, and *arm* the archetypal conception of the human body (a nonbasic domain). For a term like *castle*, the pivotal domain consists of an elaborate body of knowledge pertaining to the rules and strategies of chess.

The domains of a matrix are often multitudinous, representing facets of speakers' encyclopedic knowledge of the entity designated. This entity (the ex-pression's *profile*) has some manifestation in all the domains, which are not dis-jointed but overlapping. Among the domains for the count noun *glass*, for exam-ple, are the following: a specification of its typical shape (presupposing the basic domain of space); the conception of its typical orientation (incorporating the shape specification); its function as a container for liquid (involving shape and orientation, as well the notions liquid, spatial inclusion, potential motion, force, and constancy through time); its role in the process of drinking (including the container function, the conception of the human body, of grasping, of motion with the arm, and ingestion); a specification of its material (usually the substance glass); its typical size (easily held in one hand); and numerous other, more peripheral conceptions (e.g., cost, washing, storage, possibility of breaking, position on a table during a meal, matching sets, method of manufacture).

Obviously, this encyclopedic knowledge cannot all be accessed on every occasion. The likelihood of particular domains being activated (their degree of centrality) is part of an expression's conventional semantic value. These default expectations can, however, be adjusted and overridden by any number of contextual factors. The specific array of domains activated, and their degree of activation, may never be exactly the same in any two usage events. In this sense, even lexical meanings are anything but fixed and determinate.

The domains activated provide an expression's conceptual content. Its meaning, however, is not just the content evoked—equally important is how that content is construed. *Construal* is our multifaceted capacity to conceive and portray the same situation in alternate ways. The construal imposed on its content is intrinsic and essential to the meaning of every expression and every symbolic unit. The many aspects of construal fall in a number of general categories: *specificity*, *prominence*, *perspective*, and *dynamicity* (see also Verhagen, this volume, chapter 3).[22]

In describing a situation, we can present it with any degree of precision and detail, depending on communicative needs and speaker objectives. Lexical items form hierarchies ranging from schematic to successively more specific characterizations, e.g., *do → act → move → run → lope*. Novel expressions of any size can likewise be arranged in such hierarchies. Naturally, an expression can be highly schematic in regard to certain facets of the situation while specifying others in fine-grained detail. Grammatical elements tend to be quite schematic in their content, their primary semantic contribution residing in the construal they impose.

Something can be *prominent* (or *salient*) in many different ways, which need to be distinguished for linguistic purposes.[23] Two particular kinds of prominence prove especially important in grammar: *profiling* and *trajector/landmark alignment*.

Within the array of content it evokes—its conceptual *base*—an expression designates (i.e., refers to) a particular substructure. This is called its *profile*. An expression's profile is thus its conceptual referent and, as such, is prominent in the sense that the expression serves to single it out and focus attention on it. Some examples are sketched in figure 17.6 (the profile is drawn in bold). The base for *hypotenuse* is the conception of a right triangle (a nonbasic domain), and its profile is the side opposite the right angle. The overall configuration of an eye functions as the base for terms like *iris* and *pupil*, which profile different portions of it. In diagram (c), the dashed arrow stands for an experiential relationship, wherein a sentient creature entertains a positive mental attitude toward some other entity. The verb *admire* profiles this relationship, while the noun *admirer* designates just the sentient individual.[24] Examples like these demonstrate that expressions with the same content can nonetheless differ in meaning by virtue of the profile they impose on it. This constitutes semantic evidence for adopting profiling as a descriptive construct.

Either a *thing* or a *relationship* can be profiled, both terms being defined quite abstractly (section 4). When a relationship is profiled, we need to recognize a

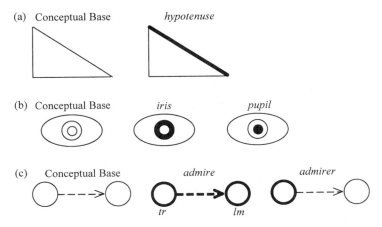

(a) Conceptual Base   *hypotenuse*

(b) Conceptual Base   *iris*   *pupil*

(c)   Conceptual Base   *admire*   *admirer*

tr   *lm*

Figure 17.6. Profiling

second kind of prominence pertaining to its participants. It is usual for one participant to be singled out as the entity conceived as being located, described, or evaluated. Called the *trajector* (*tr*), it can be characterized impressionistically as the *primary focal participant* (the primary "figure" within the profiled relationship). Often some other participant is made salient as a *secondary focal participant*, called a *landmark* (*lm*). The need for these descriptive constructs is shown by the existence of pairs of expressions that contrast semantically despite having the same conceptual base and profiling the same relationship. One example is *before* and *after*, diagrammed in figure 17.7. Each designates a relationship of temporal precedence between two events. Indeed, they profile precisely the same relation—referentially, a *before* relationship is also an *after* relationship. Their semantic contrast resides in whether the later event is invoked as a landmark for purposes of situating the earlier one, or conversely.

Turning now to perspective, the most obvious aspect of construal is *vantage point*. A simple illustration is *Come up into the attic* versus *Go up into the attic*, which presuppose different speaker locations: in the attic and down below, respectively. Of course, the vantage point adopted for a particular purpose need not be the speaker's actual one. Thus, in *Joe said to come up into the attic*, it is Joe's vantage point that is used by the speaker as the basis for choosing *come*. Nor is vantage point limited to space and vision. Consider *next year*, used as a noun phrase. As shown in figure 17.8, it profiles the year immediately following the year containing a presupposed vantage point in time. Once again, this need not be the speaker's actual temporal location (the time of speaking). In *Joe believed that next year would be full of surprises*, the vantage point adopted is the time when Joe entertained his belief.

Closely related to vantage point is the extent to which a particular entity is *subjectively* or *objectively* construed. As used in Cognitive Grammar, these terms pertain to whether the entity functions as a *subject* or *object* of conception. A tacit conceptualizing presence, a locus of consciousness that is not itself conceived, is construed with maximal subjectivity. Conversely, something explicitly singled out

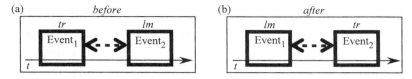

Figure 17.7. Trajector/landmark alignment

as the focus of attention is construed with maximal objectivity. In apprehending the meanings of linguistic expressions, the speaker and addressee function as subjects of conception; in that role they are subjectively construed and always remain implicit. An expression's profile—defined as the entity it directs attention to—is construed quite objectively. This basic configuration was depicted in figure 17.1, where the profile is the "onstage" focus of attention, which the speaker and hearer view from their offstage vantage point, the ground. Of course, the viewing frame can be directed at the ground itself, so that some facet of it is put onstage and profiled. When the speaker and hearer are explicitly mentioned in this fashion, by pronouns like *I* and *you*, they function as objects of conception in addition to their tacit role as conceptualizing subjects.

This ability to direct the viewing frame wherever we like, at any facet of our conceptual universe, is another aspect of perspective, referred to in Cognitive Grammar as *scope*. An expression's scope is the extent of the conceptual content it evokes as the basis for its meaning, its "coverage" in active domains. This coverage is often less than exhaustive. For example, a central domain for *next year* is the conception of one year following another, in an endless sequence. To apprehend the expression's meaning, however, the portion shown in figure 17.8 is all that needs to be considered, and is thus its scope in this domain. Within the portion evoked, moreover, a particular region often stands out from the rest as being directly relevant for the purpose at hand. In such cases, a distinction is made between the *maximal scope* and the more restricted *immediate scope*, described metaphorically as the "onstage region."[25] As the general locus of attention, the immediate scope represents the portion of the overall content evoked that is potentially available for focused viewing. An expression's profile is the specific focus of attention within its immediate scope. The conception of an eye, for instance, is the immediate scope on which *iris* and *pupil* impose alternate profiles (figure 17.6b), but since an eye is itself characterized as part of a face, their maximal scope includes the conception of a face (and more peripherally, of a head and even the body as a whole).

A final aspect of construal, dynamicity, pertains to how a conceptualization unfolds and develops through processing time. In this respect word order exerts a constant influence. Because the symbolizing elements occur in a certain sequence, the conceptual components they evoke must also be accessed in that sequence as one facet of the overall processing activity involved. Strictly speaking, semantic nonequivalence must even be recognized for pairs like *She argued about religion with her dentist* and *She argued with her dentist about religion*, reflecting the different orders in which the components symbolized by the prepositional phrases are incorporated in

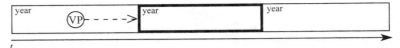

Figure 17.8. Vantage point

the overall event conception. The semantic contrast is more apparent when alternate word orders embody different global strategies for presenting a scene, as in *A dead rat lay on the counter* versus *On the counter lay a dead rat*. However, processing is not limited to a single word-by-word pass through an utterance, nor is word order always responsible for sequenced mental access. In *The roof slopes steeply upward* versus *The roof slopes steeply downward*, the contrasting directions of mental scanning are lexically induced. Such scanning occurs even in highly abstract domains, as in this example: *Forget about calculus—elementary algebra is already too difficult for him*. The domain invoked is the conception of different subjects in mathematics, arranged in order of difficulty. The mental scanning proceeds along the scale from easier subjects to harder ones, the word *already* indicating that an excessively difficult subject is encountered sooner than would be expected (see Michaelis 1991).

This last example illustrates the elaborate mental constructions we routinely create and invoke in apprehending linguistic expressions. Though traditionally neglected, "imaginative" phenomena—metaphor, metonymy, mental spaces, blending, fictivity—are not at all negligible but actually foundational for a viable linguistic semantics (Lakoff and Johnson 1980; Talmy 1996; Fauconnier 1997; Fauconnier and Turner 1998, 2002; Sweetser 1999; Langacker 1999d).[26] Research on these topics has clearly shown that the conceptualizations invoked as the meanings of expressions are not mechanically derivable from the meanings of their constitutive elements. Elaborate layers of "meaning construction" commonly intervene between lexical meanings and the complex mental constructions required for a coherent understanding of the whole expression. While rules of semantic composition are certainly part of the story (in Cognitive Grammar, they constitute the semantic pole of constructional schemas), by themselves they are not in general sufficient to compute anything recognizable as linguistic meanings. For this reason linguistic semantics is viewed in Cognitive Grammar as exhibiting only *partial compositionality*.

4. GRAMMAR

Lexicon and grammar form a continuum consisting solely of *assemblies of symbolic structures*. An assembly can exhibit any degree of symbolic complexity and any degree of specificity (or conversely, schematicity) at the semantic and phonological poles. The assemblies usually recognized as lexical items can be characterized as *fixed expressions*, "fixed" referring to their status as conventional units, and "ex-

pressions" to a substantial degree of semantic and especially phonological specificity.[27] More schematic symbolic assemblies are traditionally viewed as belonging
to grammar rather than lexicon. Grammatical markers are phonologically specific
but schematic at the semantic pole. Schematic at both poles are the symbolic assemblies representing grammatical classes and constructions. The schemas for
constructions are symbolically complex, being merely the recurring commonalities
abstracted from symbolically complex expressions. These *constructional schemas*
function as templates exploited in the formation of novel expressions.

The Cognitive Grammar claim that basic grammatical classes can be characterized semantically has to be properly understood. First, it applies to a limited set of
categories that are useful in describing many languages (if not all) and numerous phenomena in a single language. The classes in question, starting from the
positive end of a scale defined by universality and susceptibility to uniform conceptual characterization, include noun and verb, their major subclasses (e.g., count
and mass), adjective, adverb, and adposition. At the other end of the scale are idiosyncratic classes reflecting a single language-specific phenomenon (e.g., the class of
verbs instantiating a particular minor pattern of past-tense formation). Semantically
the members of such a class may be totally arbitrary.[28] Second, reference in Cognitive
Grammar to traditional parts of speech is selective and qualified (Langacker 1987a:
section 6.3.3). The traditional scheme is highly problematic, and of the standard
classes only noun and verb correspond to fundamental Cognitive Grammar categories. To some extent the others do, however, have a semantic rationale, which Cognitive Grammar notions allow one to explicate. But in each case a new conceptual
description is offered which defines the class in its own, nonstandard way.[29]

The most fundamental categories are noun and verb. Their semantic characterizations are polar opposites, at both the prototype and the schematic levels. It is
widely recognized that the respective prototypes for the noun and verb categories
are two conceptual archetypes: a physical object and a force-dynamic event (Talmy
1988), specifically an Agent-Patient interaction (Hopper and Thompson 1980; Rice
1987a). More controversial is the claim that each category has a schematic description, that is, one valid for all instances. Standard arguments against this possibility ignore some crucial factors. For one thing, an expression's grammatical
class is not determined by its overall conceptual content, but rather by the nature
of its profile. Thus, despite their identical content, *admire* is a verb and *admirer* a
noun due to the alternate profiles they impose (figure 17.6c). More generally, standard arguments presuppose an objectivist view of meaning that ignores the importance of construal. Not even considered, for instance, is the possibility that
nominalizing a verb (e.g., *arrive --→ arrival*) might involve a process of conceptual
reification so that the verb and noun are semantically distinct. Finally, the only
definitions usually contemplated are conceptual archetypes (e.g., person, object,
event, property, location), whereas a schematic characterization would have to be
considerably more abstract.

As schematic definitions, Cognitive Grammar proposes that a noun profiles a
thing, while a verb profiles a *process*.[30] These notions have only tenuous intrinsic

content, residing instead in certain basic cognitive abilities. A thing is any product of *grouping* and *reification*. The grouping of constitutive entities is ubiquitous in perception and cognition, effected (often quite automatically) on the basis of similarity or contiguity. In the following display, for instance, we automatically perceive four groups of three *x*s, not just twelve *x*s: [xxx xxx xxx xxx]. By reification is meant the manipulation of a group as a unitary entity for higher-level cognitive purposes. In the preceding display, the groups are reified when each is treated as a single entity for the purpose of counting, so that four higher-order things are observed. Many nouns profile things obviously formed from constitutive entities in this fashion: *group, set, stack, team, alphabet, orchestra, collection*, and so on. Physical objects, the category prototype, are precisely the case where grouping and reification are too low-level and automatic to be consciously accessible.[31]

A group results from conceptualizing entities together, as part of a single mental experience. A mental operation that brings entities together, an assessment that interconnects them in some fashion, constitutes the conception of a *relationship*.[32] While some relationships obtain at a single instant, others evolve (and typically change) through time. A temporally evolving relationship is most naturally accessed by *sequential scanning*, in which the component *states* (the relationships obtaining at successive points in time) are serially accessed, as in viewing a motion picture. A relationship sequentially scanned through time is called a process, used in Cognitive Grammar for the schematic definition of verbs. Verbs have a high degree of temporality, for sequential scanning reinforces the profiled relationship's temporal evolution and thereby makes it salient. Relationships with a lesser degree of temporality are said to be *atemporal*.[33] A relationship can be atemporal either because it consists of just a single state (and can thus obtain at a single instant) or because its temporal extension is viewed in *summary* fashion, with all its component states being simultaneously active and accessible, as in a multiple-exposure photograph. Adjectives, adverbs, and adpositions can be characterized as profiling different sorts of atemporal relationships. Participles and infinitives are derived from a verb by imposing a summary view on the process it designates, producing either an atemporal relation or (with reification) an abstract thing.

An expression belongs to a particular grammatical class by virtue of instantiating the schema describing it. *Admire* is thus a verb, and *admirer* a noun, because—as determined by their highest-level profiles—they respectively instantiate the verb and noun schemas: [process/ . . .] → [admire/admire]; [thing/ . . .] → [admirer/admirer].[34] Like class schemas, grammatical markers are highly schematic at the semantic pole, but phonologically they have specific content. Semantically, for instance, the auxiliary verb *do* is equivalent to the verb class schema [process/do]. When *do* combines with a full verb, as in *They do admire her*, the schematic process profiled by *do* is equated with the specific process designated by *admire*, hence the same process is symbolized twice. Being a schematic verb, *do* can also function as a clausal pro form: *They do*. The derivational suffix *-er* likewise evokes a schematic process, but only as its base; its profile is a thing (prototypically identified as the more active participant in this process), which makes it a schematic noun. It derives a specific noun from a verb stem (e.g., *admire*) by imposing its profile on the specific process designated by the latter.

Grammar consists of combinatory patterns for assembling symbolically complex expressions out of simpler ones. The traditional distinction between morphology and syntax is just a matter of whether or not the expression formed is larger than a word (e.g., *admirer* vs. *do admire*). There is otherwise no sharp distinction between them, and the same basic principles apply to both. A particular complex expression consists of an assembly of symbolic structures, each phonologically specific. The constructional schemas describing their formation consist of symbolic assemblies where some or all of the structures are both semantically and phonologically schematic. Constructional schemas categorize (and are immanent in) instantiating expressions, just as class schemas are.

Whether specific or schematic, symbolic structures are connected—and thereby form assemblies—by *correspondences* and relationships of categorization. A specific example, sketched in figure 17.9, is the nominal expression *the table near the door*.[35] Correspondences are given as dotted lines. They indicate how symbolic structures conceptually overlap by invoking entities construed as being the same. The arrows for elaboration and extension (solid and dashed, respectively) indicate that certain symbolic structures (or substructures thereof) are fully or partially immanent in others and thus contribute to their emergence. In particular, what is traditionally thought of as semantic and grammatical "composition" is viewed in Cognitive Grammar as a matter of categorization. Two levels of composition are shown in figure 17.9. At the "lower" level, two *component structures*, *near* and *the door*, categorize the *composite structure*, *near the door*. At the "higher" level, the component structures *the table* and *near the door* categorize the overall composite structure, *the table near the door*. Observe that *near* is schematic with respect to *near the door*, and *the table* with respect to *the table near the door*. On the other hand, *near the door* constitutes an extension vis-à-vis *the door*, and *the table near the door* vis-à-vis *near the door*, owing to discrepancies in the nature of their profiles.

At a given level of organization, "horizontal" correspondence lines specify which facets of the component structures conceptually overlap and thus project to the same substructure at the composite structure level. Here the landmark of *near* corresponds to the profile of *the door*, which "unify" to form the composite conception. At the higher level, the trajector of *near the door* corresponds to the profile of *the table*. It is typical for one component structure to contain a schematic element which corresponds to the profile of the other component and which is elaborated by this component. This schematic substructure is called an *elaboration site* (*e-site*), marked by hatching. The horizontal arrows thus indicate that *the door* elaborates the schematic landmark of *near*, and *the table* the schematic trajector of *near the door*. It is also typical for one component structure to impose its own profile at the composite structure level. Thus, *near* contributes its profile to *near the door* (which profiles the relationship of proximity, not the door), and *the table* to *the table near the door* (which profiles the table). Called the *profile determinant*, the prevailing component is marked with a heavy-line box.

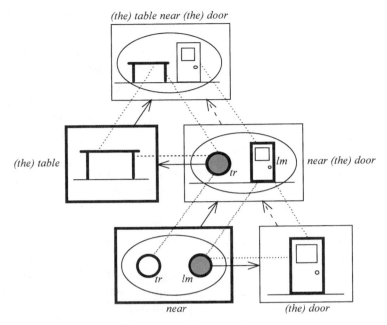

Figure 17.9. Constructions

Symbolic assemblies exhibit *constituency* when a composite structure (e.g., *near the door* in figure 17.9) also functions as component structure at another level of organization. In Cognitive Grammar, however, grammatical constituency is seen as being variable, nonessential, and nonfundamental.[36] An expression can have the same composite structure and the same grammatical relationships, with alternate orders of composition (or even a totally "flat" structure). The information essential to grammar does not reside in constituency but in the semantic characterizations of symbolic structures and how these relate to one another. A structure's grammatical class is inherently specified by the nature of its profile. Various other aspects of grammatical organization inhere in relationships of correspondence and categorization.

The *head* at a given level of organization is the profile determinant at that level, that is, the component structure whose profile corresponds to the composite structure profile. In figure 17.9, *near* is thus the head in *near the door*, and *the table* in *the table near the door*. The distinction between a *complement* and a *modifier* hinges on direction of elaboration vis-à-vis the head. A complement *elaborates* a salient e-site within the head. Hence *the door* is a complement of *near*. On the other hand, a modifier contains a salient e-site *elaborated by* the head. *Near the door* is thus a modifier with respect to *the table*. The grammatical notions *subject* and *object* are characterized in terms of the semantic constructs trajector and landmark. A subject or an object is a nominal expression whose profile corresponds, respectively, to the trajector or to the landmark of a profiled relationship. *The door* is thus the object of the preposition *near* in figure 17.9. And though it is not traditionally referred to as a subject, by this general definition *the table* bears a subject relation to *near the door*.[37]

A symbolic assembly is categorized by any number of constructional schemas corresponding to various facets of it. Representing conventional patterns of the language, the active schemas serve as templates guiding the formation of specific assemblies, in which they are fully or partially immanent. Among those immanent in the assembly of figure 17.9, for instance, are schemas for the prepositional phrase construction and for the construction in which a prepositional phrase modifies a head noun. Moreover, since the latter schema makes reference to a prepositional phrase, it incorporates the former as one component. To the extent that complex structural configurations recur, they give rise to constructional schemas of any size, incorporating any number of smaller ones as substructures. Additionally, any particular type of configuration—such as a prepositional phrase or a noun plus modifier combination—is characterized not just by a single schema, but a family of schemas representing constructional variants as well as generalizations at different levels of abstraction. Like other aspects of linguistic organization, grammatical constructions form complex categories, usually centered on a prototype. They can be modeled as networks, where each node is an entire constructional schema.

Networks of constructional schemas provide the information that determines the *distribution* of linguistic forms, that is, which elements conventionally appear in particular constructions or constructional variants. Representing varying degrees of abstraction from usage events, the schemas in a network range from highly specific structures, incorporating particular lexical items, to the maximally schematic characterization of fully general patterns. These schemas also vary in their degree of entrenchment and ease of activation for the categorization of new expressions. If high-level schemas are readily accessible, constructions are fully productive. More commonly, it is lower-level schemas that are activated, so that only the limited range of expressions they subsume (out of all those that would be sanctioned by the highest level schema) are judged acceptable. Very often the critical information resides at the lexical level. The specification that a particular lexical item in a given construction takes the form of a low-level constructional schema which incorporates that lexical item in the appropriate structural position.[38] Even the most idiosyncratic distributional information can thus be captured in properly configured networks of symbolic assemblies.

5. PHONOLOGY

In principle, Cognitive Grammar embraces phonology to the same extent as any other facet of linguistic structure. To date, however, there have been few attempts to articulate the framework's phonological pole or apply it descriptively. The theoretical discussion in Langacker (1987a, 1988b, 2000) is at best programmatic. More substantive treatments of particular problems include Farrell's (1990) usage-based account of Spanish stress, Rubba's (1993) description of discontinuous morphology in modern Aramaic, F. Kumashiro's (2000) examination of phonotactics (in comparison to the Optimality Theory approach), and Tuggy's (2003) analysis of reduplication in Nahuatl. To these, of course, must be added certain substantial and basically compatible research initiatives in the broader context of Cognitive Linguistics (Nathan, this volume, chapter 23).

A fundamental Cognitive Grammar notion is that the semantic and phonological poles of language show extensive parallelism, modulo the inherent differences between conceptualization and expression. Each pole is resolvable into a number of separate yet interacting channels (figure 17.2). At each pole, moreover, a distinction needs to be made between two sorts of elements and configurations: those intrinsic to that pole (hence "unipolar") and those determined by symbolic relationships (hence "bipolar"). Certain parallels can also be observed in the kinds of notions required for characterizing semantic and phonological structures. Beyond this, the strictures and basic theoretical concepts devised for language in general are equally applicable to phonology (e.g., the content requirement, the usage-based conception, complex categories centered on prototypes, rules as schemas).

Coexisting at either pole are two different organizational schemes, each with its own *raison d'être*. Factors internal to each pole determine its *unipolar organization*. At the phonological pole, some structures delimited in unipolar terms (representing various dimensions and levels of organization) are segments, syllables, words, moras, and feet. At the semantic pole, unipolar organization can be identified with conceptual structure viewed in its own terms, that is, independently of linguistic expression. By contrast, *bipolar organization* is that imposed by symbolic structures and assemblies. Lexical items, for instance, reside in pairings of phonological and conceptual structures that do not necessarily coincide with structures naturally delimited on unipolar grounds. It is precisely by virtue of participating in symbolic relationships that their phonological and semantic representations are recognized as linguistically significant elements.[39] More generally, each pole of a symbolic assembly consists of phonological or conceptual structures delimited in bipolar terms. The semantic and phonological structures directly referred to in grammar are those reflecting bipolar organization. Phonology, on the other hand, is primarily concerned with unipolar phonological organization

In the same way that semantic and grammatical analysis depends on the characterization of conceptual structure, phonological analysis depends on the characterization of sound structure. Although Cognitive Grammar does not yet make any specific proposals in this regard, its basic philosophy dictates an approach that straightforwardly reflects the phenomenon's intrinsic nature. In this respect, some version of "feature geometry" is closer to the mark than the representations of classical generative phonology based on unordered sets of binary features. Certain analogies (hopefully not too far-fetched) can be suggested between the descriptions of sounds and meanings. For a sound, the action of each articulator can be thought of as an "articulatory domain," analogous to the cognitive domains evoked by a lexical item as the basis for its meaning.[40] Like the domains of a matrix, articulatory domains are not disjointed but related in complex ways (e.g., voicing in the larynx creates the conditions for the shaping of vowel quality by other articulators). If articulatory domains provide phonological "content," is there something analogous to construal? At least one option seems not implausible: that accentual prominence in a word is comparable to conceptual prominence, in particular profiling.[41] More secure, perhaps, is an analogy based on *autonomy* versus *dependence* (Langacker 1987a: section 8.3). A vowel is phonologically autonomous, in the sense that it does not require the support of other sounds for its full manifestation, whereas a consonant is phonologically dependent on a vowel. In the same way, a thing is often conceptually autonomous, in that we can conceptualize it independently of any relationship involving it, but since a relationship cannot be conceived without invoking its participants, it is conceptually dependent on them.

As with lexicon and grammar, phonology is approached in Cognitive Grammar from a usage-based perspective (Langacker 1988b, 2000; Bybee 1994). It is subject to the content requirement, which limits the structures one can posit to those occurring in actual expressions and those derivable from these by means of schematization and categorization. Like lexical and grammatical units, therefore, phonological units are abstracted from usage events by the reinforcement of recurring commonalities. A multitude of units are thus abstracted, of different sizes and representing various levels and dimensions of schematization. Through relationships of categorization, they are organized in complex categories centered on prototypes.

For example, a phoneme can be viewed as a complex category and modeled as a network (Nathan 1986). Lower-level nodes in the network represent allophones, the variants occurring in particular phonological contexts; the contextually least restricted variant is the prototype ("basic allophone").[42] Higher-level nodes represent further abstractions capturing whatever is common to different sets of allophones. Various other notions of phonological theory correspond to still greater degrees of schematization. A natural class of segments is defined by an abstracted segment that is specific only in regard to certain properties, schematic in regard to others. Corresponding to phonological features are abstracted segments that are specific in regard to just a single property. A tier can be characterized as a phonological sequence that is schematic except for properties of a certain sort.

The abstraction of phonological units from usage events is not limited to structures of any particular size or nature. Among the units abstracted are schemas representing syllables, words, prosodic patterns, and intonation contours. As with segments, these are organized in complex categories comprising variants as well as the generalizations emerging at higher levels of schematicity. Inherent in these networks of abstracted units is a specification of phonological distribution and well-formedness. For example, highly schematic representations of syllables specify conventionally sanctioned syllable types (e.g., [CV], [CVC], [CCVC]), while more specific schemas (e.g., [strV . . .], [pLV . . .], [. . . VNT]) enumerate permissible consonant clusters. The phonotactic patterns of a language are thus embodied in schemas for phonologically complex structures. As part of a dynamic processing system, such units function as templates (routinized packets of processing activity) with varying degrees of accessibility for the categorization of new expressions.

In Cognitive Grammar, linguistic "rules" are simply schemas. Phonotactic rules are readily seen as schematic templates for the structures concerned. What about phonological rules classically conceived as operations deriving superficial forms from underlying representations? To the extent that these are justified, they constitute patterns of phonological extension.[43] These patterns are simply schematized representations of categorizing relationships. They conform to the content requirement because they emerge from actually occurring phonological structures through the general processes of categorization and schematization. Suppose, for instance, that a number of words ending in [d] start to manifest a variant pronunciation in which the final stop is devoiced. For each such word, usage events with [t] will be categorized as extensions from the established unit with [d]: ([Xd#]--→(Xt#)), ([Yd#]--→(Yt#)), ([Zd#]--→(Zt#)). Eventually, as shown in figure 17.5, these recurring categorizations can themselves become entrenched as conventional units, characterized at whatever level of schematization the data permits: [[. . . d#]--→[. . . t#]]. The structures related by these patterns of extension may be purely phonological, but they can also incorporate information about symbolic relationships (e.g., the specification that [d] is suffixal), making them equivalent to morphophonemic rules. Chains of extensions give the effect of rule ordering.

In a symbolic assembly (e.g., figure 17.9), each component and composite structure has both a semantic and a phonological pole. Internally, each symbolic structure's phonological pole manifests the unipolar phonological organization of the language in question: its elements, their combination, and the patterns they instantiate. External factors—the delimitation of phonological poles (by the very fact of their symbolizing function) and their relationships to one another—constitute bipolar phonological organization. In bipolar terms, the relation between component and composite phonological structures, or *phonological composition*, is the counterpart of semantic composition. Moreover, the phonological composition at each level serves to *symbolize* the semantic composition at that level. This is part of what it means to say that grammar is inherently symbolic.

Neither the phonological structures defined on a bipolar basis, nor the manner of their combination, need be natural from the standpoint of unipolar organization. It is for bipolar reasons that *picnics* is segmented into *picnic* and *-s*, whereas internally—on unipolar grounds—its basic components are *pic* and *nics*. Note further that in bipolar terms *-s* combines with *picnic* as a whole, while in unipolar terms it is incorporated in the second syllable as part of its coda. More drastically, when *-s* combines with the entire compound *picnic table*, its unipolar placement is in the coda of the final syllable of the last word: *picnic tables*. There is no "mismatch" here, for there is no reason to expect unipolar and bipolar organization to coincide in the first place. In bipolar phonological composition, the composite structure need only be some function of the component structures, with no requirement that their combination be isomorphic to unipolar composition. Hence, there are numerous ways to form a composite phonological structure other than simply juxtaposing two components. As a case in point, it is quite unproblematic for one component structure to be placed inside the other.[44]

6. COVERAGE

In assessing the empirical coverage of any linguistic theory, expectations have to be realistic. The collective and cumulative efforts of all linguists, of all theoretical persuasions, have come nowhere close to providing even minimally adequate documentation of the world's languages. For no single language have such efforts provided anything even remotely approximating an exhaustive description. Nor has any expression or phenomenon of any language been blessed with a full and definitive description that all linguists would acknowledge as such. Even the best-described and best-understood phenomena are subject to finer-grained description and characterization at deeper levels of understanding.

The limitations are of course even more severe when considering a single theory of fairly recent vintage and initially pursued by just a small group of scholars.[45] Of necessity, therefore, research in Cognitive Grammar has followed a global strategy with two main objectives. The first has been to establish the framework's viability (if not superiority) with respect to particular topics generally considered theoretically significant. To this end, a point has been made to tackle certain classic problems dealt with in Generative Grammar, especially those supposedly demonstrating the autonomy of syntax. Among such problems are passives (Langacker 1982), constraints on pronominal anaphora (van Hoek 1995, 1997), complementation (Achard 1998), so-called "raising" constructions (Langacker 1995c), and positive/negative polarity items (Israel 1996a, 1998). A special effort has been made to specify the meanings of grammatical formatives commonly taken as being semantically empty, such as *of* (Langacker 1992b), markers for case (Smith 1987) and gender (Langacker 1988a), and all the elements of the English auxiliary (Langacker 1991).

The second objective is to show that these descriptive successes are not due to a selective choice of topics, but that the theory can in principle be applied with equal success to any phenomenon in any language. Here one can point to the framework's inherent generality and flexibility (and hopefully its avoidance of blatant language bias). Still, there is no substitute for actually applying it to a large and representative sample of languages and linguistic phenomena. Cognitive Grammar is indeed being applied to more and more languages of diverse types and genetic affiliations. Branches of Indo-European where substantial work has been done include Romance (Maldonado 1988, 1992; Vandeloise 1991; Doiz Bienzobas 1995; Achard 1996; Farrell 1998), Germanic (Smith 1987, 1993, 2001; Cornelis 1997; Enger and Nesset 1999; Mortelmans 1999), Slavic (Janda 1986, 1993; Cienki 1995; Dąbrowska 1997; Nesset

1998), and modern Greek (Manney 1995, 2000). Among the growing array of non-Indo-European languages examined from a Cognitive Grammar perspective are Basque (Doiz Bienzobas 1998), Finnish (Huumo 1998), Estonian (Vainik 1995), modern Aramaic (Rubba 1993), Mandarin (Poteet 1987; Hsiao 1991; Shen 1996); Japanese (T. Kumashiro 1994, 2000; Matsumoto 1996; F. Kumashiro 2000; Nomura 2000), Korean (Lee 1999), Samoan (Cook 1988, 1993a, 1993b), and a variety of native languages of the Americas (Tuggy 1981, 1986, 1988, 1992, 2003; Casad 1982; Beck 1996; Velázquez-Castillo 1996; Ogawa and Palmer 1999).

The range of linguistic phenomena investigated from a Cognitive Grammar standpoint is likewise broad and steadily growing. On this front, a two-pronged strategy has been pursued. On the one hand, an attempt has been made to examine a wide spectrum of basic problems in preliminary terms. Here the objective is to show that the framework can in principle accommodate them, and also to provide an initial indication of what a Cognitive Grammar description might look like. An example is Langacker (1991), which considers in turn many basic aspects of nominal structure, clause structure, and complex sentences, primarily with respect to English, but with numerous references and comparisons to other languages. The papers in Casad and Palmer (2003) cover varied phenomena in non-Indo-European languages. The second prong of the strategy, complementary and clearly necessary, is to investigate particular phenomena in great depth and detail. These in-depth probes have thus far included such varied topics as Cora locatives (Casad 1982), French complementation (Achard 1998), Samoan clause structure (Cook 1988), English nominalization (Heyvaert 2003) and noun-noun compounds (Ryder 1994), dative case in Polish (Dąbrowska 1997), verb conjugation in Russian (Nesset 1998), middle voice in Spanish (Maldonado 1992) and modern Greek (Manney 2000), as well as double subject constructions (T. Kumashiro 2000; Kumashiro and Langacker 2003) and internally headed relative clauses (Nomura 2000) in Japanese.

Unavoidably, coverage of the many facets of linguistic structure has been quite uneven. While the widespread notion that Cognitive Grammar deals primarily with locative expressions is completely erroneous, this has received its share of attention (e.g., Lindner 1981, 1982; Casad 1982; Hawkins 1984; Taylor 1988; Vandeloise 1991; Cuyckens 1995; Langacker 2002d). Quite a lot has been done on nominal and clausal *grounding*, whereby a profiled thing or process is related to the speech situation (Langacker 1991, 1997c, 1999d, 2001c, 2002b, 2002c, 2003c, 2003d, 2004a, 2004d; Mortelmans 1999; Brisard 2002). Possessive constructions, which have a grounding function, have been dealt with extensively (Tuggy 1980; Langacker 1993c, 1995b, 2001d; Taylor 1994, 1996; Cienki 1995; Velázquez-Castillo 1996). Overall, the greatest concentration of effort may well have been in the general area of clause structure (Tuggy 1988; Langacker 1991, 1993a, 2001d; Cook 1993b; Smith 1993; T. Kumashiro 2000), including such topics as transitivity (Tuggy 1981; Rice 1987a, 1987b; Cook 1988), voice (Langacker 1982, 2004c, 2009: chapter 5; Maldonado 1988, 1992; Manney 1995, 2000; Cornelis 1997), and the semantics of case markers (Smith 1987; Cook 1993a; Janda 1993; T. Kumashiro 1994).

The list of topics that have not been sufficiently ir
Grammar can be as long as one cares to make it. Little has
on adverbs, comparatives, or serial verb constructions.
sion (Langacker 1991: section 11.2), coordination has not
morphology has not been ignored (Langacker 1987a,
Nesset 1998; Tuggy 2003), the full-scale description o
phological system would be quite instructive. Also, the
characterize the meanings of grammatical elements co
tention thus far devoted to lexical semantic description
1991; Farrell 1995; Shen 1996; Lee 1999; Langacker 2002a).[46] Obviously, expanding
the coverage of Cognitive Grammar into these and other areas is essential for its
continued development and empirical justification.

7. DIRECTIONS

The word 'cognitive' should not obscure the fact that Cognitive Grammar is a
linguistic theory. Its analyses, descriptive constructs, and theoretical claims are all
inspired and supported by specifically linguistic considerations. The assumptions it
makes about mind and cognitive processing are general and fairly minimal. While
it is meant to be broadly compatible with secure findings of the cognitive sciences,[47]
Cognitive Grammar does not simply adopt any extant psychological theory. Indeed,
it poses severe challenges for any processing model.

More extensive interaction with the cognitive sciences can be anticipated as
one direction in Cognitive Grammar's future development. Hinting at the potential for such interaction is a certain amount of experimental and observational
work already carried out. Studies by Harris (1998) on entrenchment and by Tomlin
(1995, 1997) on the focal prominence of subjects, illustrate experiments bearing
on particular Cognitive Grammar notions. Basic ideas of Cognitive Grammar
are incorporated in Barsalou's (1999) research on "perceptual symbol systems." Its
usage-based nature dovetails with Tomasello's (1992, 2003) observations on language acquisition. Kellogg's (1996) investigation of aphasia provides a measure of
support for its conceptual characterization of grammatical classes. In the future,
evidence from studies in psycholinguistics, neurolinguistics, language processing,
language acquisition, and aphasia ought to become increasingly important as an
empirical basis for assessing and refining Cognitive Grammar.

Though less straightforwardly empirical, applications of Cognitive Grammar are
significant as a potential source of validation. Its application to language pedagogy,
especially foreign language teaching, is starting to receive serious attention (Taylor
1993; Pütz, Niemeier, and Dirven 2001a, 2001b; Rudzka-Ostyn 2003). It offers a

f conceptual tools potentially useful for translation and literary studies
kowska 1993). For various reasons, Cognitive Grammar does not readily lend
lf to computer implementation.[48] Still, much can be learned from even partial
attempts and consideration of why the problem is so difficult (Holmqvist 1993, 1999).

Cognitive Grammar does lend itself to investigating language in its social and historical context, for it avoids the artificial disjunctures of synchrony versus diachrony and language structure versus language use (section 2). There have so far been few sociolinguistic studies specifically exploiting descriptive constructs of Cognitive Grammar (Kemmer and Israel 1994; Backus 1996; see Langacker 2003b). By contrast, diachronic issues figured prominently in the first publication on Cognitive Grammar (Langacker 1981) and have continued to receive attention (Langacker 1990b, 1992a, 1998, 1999c; Carey 1994, 1996; Rubba 1994; Israel 1996b; Doiz Bienzobas 1998—see also Bybee, this volume, chapter 36). Grammaticalization has been a special focus and is likely to remain so in view of its central importance to semantics and grammar (this volume, chapters 10, 36).

With respect to theory and description, several major themes should be pivotal to Cognitive Grammar research in the coming years. The first is *dynamicity*, pertaining to how a conceptualization unfolds through processing time (section 3). The linguistic effects of temporal sequencing are both pervasive and fundamental (Langacker 1993c, 1997b, 2001a, 2001b, 2001d, 2003c). They obtain in every dimension and at every level of organization—from discourse to sublexical semantic structure.[49] If a linguistic model is to be psychologically realistic, the inherent temporality of cognitive processing would seem to demand a dynamic account of language structure, which in any case is strongly motivated on purely linguistic grounds. The second theme is *fictivity*. Even when discussing actual individuals and occurrences, surprisingly much of what we directly refer to linguistically is "fictive" or "virtual" in nature. Fictive motion (Langacker 1986; Matsumoto 1996; Talmy 1996) is merely the tip of a virtual iceberg (Langacker 1999c, 2003d).[50] Achieving a clear understanding of the myriad kinds and levels of virtuality is crucial for advancing conceptual semantics. A final theme will be the grounding of language structure in *discourse* and *social interaction* (Langacker 2001a, 2001e, 2003b, 2004c, 2004d). While this grounding has from the outset been inherent in Cognitive Grammar's basic architecture (section 2), it has not been sufficiently emphasized in either description or theoretical formulation. In principle, Cognitive Grammar is a theory of *énonciation* (Culioli 1990). Its future development should make this increasingly more apparent in practice.

NOTES

1. These points are detailed in Langacker (2005a, 2005b). Comparison of Cognitive Grammar with two other approaches, Tesnière's Structural Syntax and the Columbia School, can be found in Langacker (1995d, 2004b). For extensive treatment of Cognitive Grammar itself, see Langacker (1987a, 1990a, 1991, 1999b) and Taylor (2002).

2. See the following references (all to Langacker): for noun and verb, 1987b; for subject, 1999a, 2001b; for morpheme, 1987a, 1995a; for constituency, 1995a, 1997a; for subordinate clause, 1991.

3. To the extent they are analogous, the term *viewing* is employed for both *perception* and *conception* in general (Langacker 1993d, 1995e; cf. Talmy 1996).

4. Also within the scope of potential linguistic concern are facial expression and even body language. Writing and gesture can be taken as alternative central channels of expression.

5. This is essentially what is shown in figure 17.1, which can be taken as a skeletal representation that all units share and that each elaborates in its own way.

6. Excluded are channels in which no specification is made (i.e., they are fully schematic), as well as those noncentral enough to be ignored for particular purposes.

7. The semantic pole of a symbolic unit is *ipso facto* a semantic unit. There can also be semantic units that are not individually symbolized (e.g., a concept that defines a category schematically but happens to represent a "lexical gap"), just as there are phonological units that do not individually serve a symbolizing function.

8. Lexical items can be partially schematic phonologically if they only occur in larger expressions where their schematic elements are specified and overtly manifested (e.g., a reduplicative morpheme of the schematic form CV-, where the schematic consonant and vowel match those of the stem). For other subtleties concerning the notion "expression," see Langacker (1987a: section 11.2.1).

9. Cognitive Grammar agrees with Construction Grammar in treating lexical items as constructions. However, it does not follow Construction Grammar in positing constructions only when there is some discernible irregularity or nonpredictability. Expressions that are semantically and grammatically regular can nonetheless be established as conventional linguistic units. Since mastery of these usual ways of saying things is essential to speaking a language fluently, it seems both arbitrary and artifactual to exclude them from linguistic knowledge just because they happen to be regular.

10. The term "apprehension" merely indicates mental occurrence. It is intended as being neutral between speaking and understanding.

11. For the speaker, this might be some aspect of the conception to be conveyed. For the listener, it might be an auditory impression and/or some aspect of the conception anticipated as representing the speaker's intent.

12. See, for example, Kempson (1977: section 2.3) and Palmer (1981: section 2.2). The word *concept* and its derivatives do not even appear in the index of Lyons (1995).

13. A common mistake is to think of conceptualization as being like an image projected on a screen inside the skull for viewing. It should instead be identified with the mental experience engendered by viewing the world "outside." Only as a special case, and to a very limited extent, can we monitor our own conceptualizing activity.

14. These egregious misinterpretations of the Cognitive Grammar view are found in Levinson (1997). The actual Cognitive Grammar position is quite close to the one Levinson espouses.

15. See Haiman (1980), Langacker (1987a: section 4.2), and Wierzbicka (1995). Reference to dictionaries and encyclopedias is metaphorical—*pace* Wierzbicka, it is not claimed, for instance, that an encyclopedic semantic characterization contains the kinds of esoteric information found in actual encyclopedias which most speakers are ignorant of.

16. In terms of encyclopedic semantics, these senses consist of different ways of accessing the same domains of knowledge, or overlapping sets of domains. Polysemy illustrates the general phenomenon of complex categories, whose formation was described

at the end of section 2. Lakoff's (1987) *radial model* of categorization is a special case of this *network model* (one that ignores the abstraction of more schematic meanings).

17. For instance, something is "basic" if it is either innately specified or first acquired. In one sense a whole is more "basic" than its parts, but also "basic," in another way, are the smallest parts out of which a whole is progressively assembled.

18. Actually, any established "concept" can equally well be described dynamically as the routinized ability to execute a certain "packet" of processing activity.

19. The examples cited by Lakoff (1987) and Johnson (1987) of "image schemas" include both sorts of basic notions, and their discussion fails to clearly distinguish them. While image schemas are supposedly abstracted from bodily experience, Cognitive Grammar is essentially agnostic on the innateness issue. However, a reasonable working hypothesis is that the basic cognitive abilities, at least, are innately provided. They make possible the structured experience required for the emergence of archetypes.

20. Other possibilities are basic domains pertaining to emotive and motor/kinesthetic experience. The irreducibility of basic domains does not preclude their being structured (e.g., color space has the dimensions of brightness, hue, and saturation) or being susceptible to metaphorical construal (e.g., *loud color*). While analysis and metaphor enhance our understanding of these domains, they do not themselves constitute the basic experience (e.g., the sensation of redness).

21. The earlier term *abstract domain* is infelicitous, since many conceptions pertain to concrete experience.

22. The term construal is preferable to *imagery*, used in earlier works, since the latter is commonly employed for other phenomena (e.g., visual imagery). Content and construal cannot be sharply distinguished; the terminological distinction is made primarily to highlight the importance of construal, which is largely ignored in traditional semantics. The classification of construal phenomena is likewise mostly for expository convenience.

23. Here, for instance, are some usual prominence asymmetries: whole > part; human > nonhuman; concrete > abstract; new > given; category prototype > noncentral members; basic-level category > subordinate/superordinate categories.

24. Because a relationship cannot be conceptualized without conceptualizing its central participants (given as circles), these are included in the relational profile.

25. In terms of figure 17.1, the immediate scope is the content appearing in the viewing frame.

26. These are unproblematic in Cognitive Grammar. For instance, metonymy consists of an alternate choice of profile within the same conceptual base. Mental space configurations and the mappings between spaces characteristic of metaphor and blending represent special cases of how the domains of a matrix can be related to one another.

27. A morpheme is a degenerate symbolic assembly consisting of just a single symbolic structure; that is, it is not analyzable into symbolic components. However, since the *analyzability* of fixed expressions is a matter of degree, morphemic status is graded as well (Langacker 1987a: section 12.1; 1995a).

28. As later discussion will show, distributional classes of this sort are readily accommodated in a usage-based model (Langacker 2000), as are the distributional properties of semantically definable categories.

29. For example, the schematic definition of a noun (an expression that profiles a thing) defines a category that includes not only the elements traditionally recognized as such, but also pronouns, articles, demonstratives, and full noun phrases. For extensive discussion of grammatical classes, see Langacker (1987a, 1987b, 1991).

30. The oft-debated issue of whether every language has a noun/verb distinction pertains to primary lexical categorization, which is just a matter of whether particular profiling options are entrenched and conventionalized. If a lexeme has no inherent profiling, the construction it appears in will nonetheless impose one, so that it functions as a noun or a verb in any given use. In claiming that nouns and verbs are universal grammatical categories, Cognitive Grammar remains agnostic as to whether they are also universal lexical categories.

31. The constitutive entities can be taken as arbitrary "splotches" of substance. As used in Cognitive Grammar, the term *entity* is maximally schematic, implying no specific properties or individual cognitive salience.

32. The entities interconnected in a relationship need not be discrete, distinct, cognitively salient, or individually mentioned. Thus, expressions that profile relationships need not have multiple (or even any) overtly specified participants.

33. A better term might be *nonprocessual*, since time is often a factor. For example, *before* and *after* (figure 17.7) are atemporal (nonprocessual) because the profiled relationship is construed as a single configuration *in* time (analogous to one in space), rather than being viewed as evolving *through* time. By contrast, the verbs *precede* and *follow* either follow this relationship through time as a stable configuration (as in *June precedes July*) or portray it as emerging through time (*Lightning preceded the storm*).

34. As abbreviations used for expository convenience, capital letters stand for semantic structures, with lower case orthography representing phonological structures. Ellipses indicate that the class schemas impose no specific phonological requirements (i.e., they are maximally schematic at the phonological pole). Although they are shown separately for analytic purposes, the schemas are actually *immanent* in their instantiations, that is, inherent in the processing activity constituting them.

35. To keep things simple, articles are omitted and only the semantic pole is shown in any detail. The pictures of a table and a door are merely mnemonic abbreviations for the full, encyclopedic meanings of *table* and *door*. An extensive treatment of grammatical constructions is offered in Langacker (2003a).

36. More fundamental are conceptual grouping, phonological grouping, symbolization, and the hierarchical organization characteristic of human behavior in general (see Langacker 1995a, 1997a).

37. A more restrictive definition reflecting traditional usage would limit the term "subject" to situations where the relationship is profiled and only at the clausal level (e.g., *The table is near the door*).

38. The schema can also be seen as one facet of the lexical item's characterization. Since a lexical item occurs in particular grammatical environments, the representation abstracted from usage events includes a set of structural frames in which it figures. If there is any representation independent of such frames, it arises by further abstraction.

39. Phonologically, for example, the word *picnics* divides into *pic* and *nics* on unipolar grounds (syllable structure), whereas bipolar considerations dictate the otherwise unmotivated segmentation into *picnic* and *-s*. Semantically, the meaning of *-s* is quite schematic and unlikely to emerge as a conceptual unit were it not for its linguistic role in forming plurals, incorporating the more specific content of the nouns it combines with.

40. Phonological representations are not just based on articulation, but also on perception, which constitutes another channel. In signed languages, the main expressive burden is shifted to the corresponding gestural channels.

41. As a facet of unipolar phonological organization, accentual prominence lacks the referential function of profiling. This follows from the inherent difference between conceptualization and expression.

42. As reflected in the history of writing, segments are psychologically less basic than syllables and words and do not occur alone except when they happen to coincide with these larger structures. Representations of segments are thus abstracted from larger structural frames, which (in schematized form) are part of their characterization. This is quite analogous to the incorporation of symbolic structural frames in the characterization of lexical items (see note 38).

43. These are analogous to patterns of semantic extension, such as the metonymic pattern [CREATOR --> CREATION] (as in *She just bought a Miró*). For some differences between derivation and categorization, see Langacker (1987a: 444).

44. For instance, a clausal subordinator might be placed in the middle of the clause as a suffix on the verb.

45. I restrict attention to research largely based on Cognitive Grammar proper (without implying any sharp distinction from work in cognitive and functional linguistics more generally). Here and in what follows, only selected citations can be given.

46. Starting with Lindner (1981, 1982), considerable attention has been devoted to polysemy and semantic networks. What I have in mind here is rather the absence of large-scale attempts at describing the conceptual semantic structure of individual meanings or senses in a systematic fashion (i.e., some analogue of Wierzbicka's 1996 lexicographic program).

47. Schönefeld (1999) offers a positive assessment of its success in this regard.

48. Among these reasons are construal, encyclopedic semantics, and the indissociability of meaning and grammar.

49. Processing at different levels occurs on different time scales. Sequentiality is quite apparent at the discourse level, owing to the large time scale involved. In the case of sublexical meanings, where the small time scale forecloses introspective observation, the evidence is substantial but indirect (Langacker 1998).

50. For instance, the cat referred to in *She doesn't have a cat* is not any actual cat but a virtual creature "conjured up" to characterize the situation whose existence is being denied. *Each protester lit a candle* does not refer directly to any actual protestor, any actual candle, or any actual event of lighting. Instead, it designates a fictive event involving fictive participants, with *each* specifying how the type of event thus characterized maps onto actuality.

REFERENCES

Achard, Michel. 1996. Two causation/perception constructions in French. *Cognitive Linguistics* 7: 315–57.

Achard, Michel. 1998. *Representation of cognitive structures: Syntax and semantics of French sentential complements*. Berlin: Mouton de Gruyter.

Backus, Ad. 1996. *Two in one: Bilingual speech of Turkish immigrants in the Netherlands*. Tilburg, Netherlands: Tilburg University Press.

Barlow, Michael, and Suzanne Kemmer, eds. 2000. *Usage-based models of language*. Stanford, CA: CSLI Publications.

Barsalou, Lawrence W. 1999. Perceptual symbol systems. *Behavioral and Brain Sciences* 22: 577–660.

Beck, David. 1996. Transitivity and causation in Lushootseed morphology. *Canadian Journal of Linguistics* 41: 109–40.

Brisard, Frank, ed. 2002. *Grounding: The epistemic footing of deixis and reference*. Berlin: Mouton de Gruyter.

Bybee, Joan L. 1994. A view of phonology from a cognitive and functional perspective. *Cognitive Linguistics* 5: 285–305.

Carey, Kathleen. 1994. Pragmatics, subjectivity and the grammaticalization of the English perfect. PhD dissertation, University of California, San Diego.

Carey, Kathleen. 1996. From resultativity to current relevance: Evidence from the history of English and modern Castilian Spanish. In Adele E. Goldberg, ed., *Conceptual structure, discourse and language* 31–48. Stanford, CA: CSLI Publications.

Casad, Eugene H. 1982. Cora locationals and structured imagery. PhD dissertation, University of California, San Diego.

Casad, Eugene H., and Gary B. Palmer, eds. 2003. *Cognitive linguistics and non-Indo-European languages*. Berlin: Mouton de Gruyter.

Cienki, Alan. 1995. The semantics of possessive and spatial constructions in Russian and Bulgarian: A comparative analysis in cognitive grammar. *Slavic and East European Journal* 39: 73–114.

Cook, Kenneth W. 1988. A cognitive analysis of grammatical relations, case, and transitivity in Samoan. PhD dissertation, University of California, San Diego.

Cook, Kenneth W. 1993a. A cognitive account of Samoan case marking and cliticization. *Studi Italiani di Linguistica Teorica e Applicata* 22: 509–30.

Cook, Kenneth W. 1993b. A cognitive account of Samoan *lavea* and *galo* verbs. In Richard A. Geiger and Brygida Rudzka-Ostyn, eds., *Conceptualizations and mental processing in language* 567–92. Berlin: Mouton de Gruyter.

Cornelis, Louise H. 1997. *Passive and perspective*. Amsterdam: Rodopi.

Croft, William. 2001. *Radical construction grammar: Syntactic theory in typological perspective*. Oxford: Oxford University Press.

Culioli, Antoine. 1990. *Pour une linguistique de l'énonciation*. Vol. 1, *Opérations et représentations*. Paris: Ophrys.

Cuyckens, Hubert. 1995. Family resemblance in the Dutch spatial prepositions *door* and *langs*. *Cognitive Linguistics* 6: 183–207.

Dąbrowska, Ewa. 1997. *Cognitive semantics and the Polish dative*. Berlin: Mouton de Gruyter.

Doiz Bienzobas, Aintzane. 1995. The preterite and the imperfect in Spanish: Past situation vs. past viewpoint. PhD dissertation, University of California, San Diego.

Doiz Bienzobas, Aintzane. 1998. La evolución diacrónica de la categoría de la modalidad deóntica en Euskera. In José Luis Cifuentes Honrubia, ed., *Estudios de lingüística cognitiva II* 559–73. Alicante, Spain: Universidad de Alicante, Departamento de Filología Española, Lingüística General y Teoría de la Literatura.

Enger, Hans-Olav, and Tore Nesset. 1999. The value of cognitive grammar in typological studies: The case of Norwegian and Russian passive, middle and reflexive. *Nordic Journal of Linguistics* 22: 27–60.

Farrell, Patrick. 1990. Spanish stress: A cognitive analysis. *Hispanic Linguistics* 4: 21–56.

Farrell, Patrick. 1995. Lexical binding. *Linguistics* 33: 939–80.

Farrell, Patrick. 1998. The conceptual basis of number marking in Brazilian Portuguese. In Jean-Pierre Koenig, ed., *Discourse and cognition: Bridging the gap* 3–16. Stanford, CA: CSLI Publications.

Fauconnier, Gilles. 1985. *Mental spaces: Aspects of meaning construction in natural language.* Cambridge, MA: MIT Press. (2nd ed., Cambridge: Cambridge University Press, 1994)

Fauconnier, Gilles. 1997. *Mappings in thought and language.* Cambridge: Cambridge University Press.

Fauconnier, Gilles, and Mark Turner. 1998. Conceptual integration networks. *Cognitive Science* 22: 133–87.

Fauconnier, Gilles, and Mark Turner. 2002. *The way we think: Conceptual blending and the mind's hidden complexities.* New York: Basic Books.

Fillmore, Charles J. 1988. The mechanisms of "construction grammar." *Berkeley Linguistics Society* 14: 35–55.

Goldberg, Adele E. 1995. *Constructions: A construction grammar approach to argument structure.* Chicago: University of Chicago Press.

Haiman, John. 1980. Dictionaries and encyclopedias. *Lingua* 50: 329–57.

Harder, Peter. 1996. *Functional semantics: A theory of meaning, structure and tense in English.* Berlin: Mouton de Gruyter.

Harris, Catherine L. 1998. Psycholinguistic studies of entrenchment. In Jean-Pierre Koenig, ed., *Discourse and cognition: Bridging the gap* 55–70. Stanford, CA: CSLI Publications.

Hawkins, Bruce W. 1984. The semantics of English spatial prepositions. PhD dissertation, University of California, San Diego.

Heyvaert, Liesbet. 2003. *A cognitive-functional approach to nominalization in English.* Berlin: Mouton de Gruyter.

Holmqvist, Kenneth. 1993. *Implementing cognitive semantics.* Lund, Sweden: Department of Cognitive Science, Lund University.

Holmqvist, Kenneth. 1999. Implementing cognitive semantics—overview of the semantic composition process and insights into the grammatical composition process. In Leon de Stadler and Christoph Eyrich, eds., *Issues in cognitive linguistics* 579–600. Berlin: Mouton de Gruyter.

Hopper, Paul J., and Sandra A. Thompson. 1980. Transitivity in grammar and discourse. *Language* 56: 251–99.

Hsiao, Yuchau E. 1991. A cognitive grammar approach to perfect aspect: Evidence from Chinese. *Berkeley Linguistics Society* 17: 390–401.

Huffman, Alan. 1997. *The categories of grammar: French* lui *and* le. Amsterdam: John Benjamins.

Huumo, Tuomas. 1998. Bound spaces, starting points, and settings. In Jean-Pierre Koenig, ed., *Discourse and cognition: Bridging the gap* 297–307. Stanford, CA: CSLI Publications.

Israel, Michael. 1996a. Polarity sensitivity as lexical semantics. *Linguistics and Philosophy* 19: 619–66.

Israel, Michael. 1996b. The *way* constructions grow. In Adele E. Goldberg, ed., *Conceptual structure, discourse and language* 217–30. Stanford, CA: CSLI Publications.

Israel, Michael. 1998. The rhetoric of grammar: Scalar reasoning and polarity sensitivity. PhD dissertation, University of California, San Diego.

Janda, Laura A. 1986. *A semantic analysis of the Russian verbal prefixes* za-, pere-, do-, *and* ot-. Munich: Verlag Otto Sagner.

Janda, Laura A. 1993. *A geography of case semantics: The Czech dative and the Russian instrumental.* Berlin: Mouton de Gruyter.

Janssen, Theo A. J. M., and Gisela Redeker, eds. 1999. *Congitive linguistics: Foundations, scope, and methodology.* Berlin: Mouton de Gruyter.

Johnson, Mark. 1987. *The body in the mind: The bodily basis of meaning, imagination, and reason.* Chicago: University of Chicago Press.

Kellogg, Margaret Kimberly. 1996. Neurolinguistic evidence of some conceptual properties of nouns and verbs. PhD dissertation, University of California, San Diego.

Kemmer, Suzanne, and Michael Israel. 1994. Variation and the usage-based model. *Chicago Linguistic Society* 30: 165–79.

Kempson, Ruth M. 1977. *Semantic theory.* Cambridge: Cambridge University Press.

Kumashiro, Fumiko. 2000. Phonotactic interactions: A non-reductionist approach to phonology. PhD dissertation, University of California, San Diego.

Kumashiro, Toshiyuki. 1994. On the conceptual definitions of adpositions and case markers: A case for the conceptual basis of syntax. *Chicago Linguistic Society* 30: 236–50.

Kumashiro, Toshiyuki. 2000. The Conceptual basis of grammar: A cognitive approach to Japanese clausal structure. PhD dissertation, University of California, San Diego.

Kumashiro, Toshiyuki, and Ronald W. Langacker. 2003. Double-subject and complex-predicate constructions. *Cognitive Linguistics* 14: 1–45.

Lakoff, George. 1987. *Women, fire, and dangerous things: What categories reveal about the mind.* Chicago: University of Chicago Press.

Lakoff, George, and Mark Johnson. 1980. *Metaphors we live by.* Chicago: University of Chicago Press.

Lakoff, George, and Mark Johnson. 1999. *Philosophy in the flesh: The embodied mind and its challenge to Western thought.* New York: Basic Books.

Langacker, Ronald W. 1981. The integration of grammar and grammatical change. *Indian Linguistics* 42: 82–135.

Langacker, Ronald W. 1982. Space grammar, analysability, and the English passive. *Language* 58: 22–80.

Langacker, Ronald W. 1986. Abstract motion. *Berkeley Linguistics Society* 12: 455–71.

Langacker, Ronald W. 1987a. *Foundations of cognitive grammar.* Vol. 1, *Theoretical prerequisites.* Stanford, CA: Stanford University Press.

Langacker, Ronald W. 1987b. Nouns and verbs. *Language* 63: 53–94.

Langacker, Ronald W. 1988a. Autonomy, agreement, and cognitive grammar. In Diane Brentari, Gary Larson, and Lynn MacLeod, eds., *Agreement in grammatical theory* 147–80. Chicago: Chicago Linguistic Society.

Langacker, Ronald W. 1988b. A usage-based model. In Brygida Rudzka-Ostyn, ed., *Topics in cognitive linguistics* 127–61. Amsterdam: John Benjamins.

Langacker, Ronald W. 1990a. *Concept, image, and symbol: The cognitive basis of grammar.* Berlin: Mouton de Gruyter.

Langacker, Ronald W. 1990b. Subjectification. *Cognitive Linguistics* 1: 5–38.

Langacker, Ronald W. 1991. *Foundations of cognitive grammar.* Vol. 2, *Descriptive application.* Stanford, CA: Stanford University Press.

Langacker, Ronald W. 1992a. Prepositions as grammatical(izing) elements. *Leuvense Bijdragen* 81: 287–309.

Langacker, Ronald W. 1992b. The symbolic nature of cognitive grammar: The meaning of *of* and of *of*-periphrasis. In Martin Pütz, ed., *Thirty years of linguistic evolution: Studies in honour of René Dirven on the occasion of his sixtieth birthday* 483–502. Amsterdam: John Benjamins.

Langacker, Ronald W. 1993a. Clause structure in cognitive grammar. *Studi Italiani di Linguistica Teorica e Applicata* 22: 465–508.

Langacker, Ronald W. 1993b. Grammatical traces of some "invisible" semantic constructs. *Language Sciences* 15: 323–55.

Langacker, Ronald W. 1993c. Reference-point constructions. *Cognitive Linguistics* 4: 1–38.

Langacker, Ronald W. 1993d. Universals of construal. *Berkeley Linguistics Society* 19: 447–63.

Langacker, Ronald W. 1995a. Conceptual grouping and constituency in cognitive grammar. In Ik-Hwan Lee, ed., *Linguistics in the morning calm 3* 149–72. Seoul: Hanshin.

Langacker, Ronald W. 1995b. Possession and possessive constructions. In John R. Taylor and Robert E. MacLaury, eds., *Language and the cognitive construal of the world* 51–79. Berlin: Mouton de Gruyter.

Langacker, Ronald W. 1995c. Raising and transparency. *Language* 71: 1–62.

Langacker, Ronald W. 1995d. Structural syntax: The view from cognitive grammar. In Françoise Madray-Lesigne and Jeannine Richard-Zappella, eds., *Lucien Tesnière aujourd'hui* 13–39. Paris: Éditions Peeters.

Langacker, Ronald W. 1995e. Viewing in cognition and grammar. In Philip W. Davis, ed., *Alternative linguistics: Descriptive and theoretical modes* 153–212. Amsterdam: John Benjamins.

Langacker, Ronald W. 1997a. Constituency, dependency, and conceptual grouping. *Cognitive Linguistics* 8: 1–32.

Langacker, Ronald W. 1997b. A dynamic account of grammatical function. In Joan L. Bybee, John Haiman, and Sandra A. Thompson, eds., *Essays on language function and language type dedicated to T. Givón* 249–73. Amsterdam: John Benjamins.

Langacker, Ronald W. 1997c. Generics and habituals. In Angeliki Athanasiadou and René Dirven, eds., *On conditionals again* 191–222. Amsterdam: John Benjamins.

Langacker, Ronald W. 1998. On subjectification and grammaticization. In Jean-Pierre Koenig, ed., *Discourse and cognition: Bridging the gap* 71–89. Stanford, CA: CSLI Publications.

Langacker, Ronald W. 1999a. Assessing the cognitive linguistic enterprise. In Theo Janssen and Gisela Redeker, eds., *Cognitive linguistics: Foundations, scope, and methodology* 13–59. Berlin: Mouton de Gruyter.

Langacker, Ronald W. 1999b. *Grammar and conceptualization*. Berlin: Mouton de Gruyter.

Langacker, Ronald W. 1999c. Losing control: Grammaticization, subjectification, and transparency. In Andreas Blank and Peter Koch, eds., *Historical semantics and cognition* 147–75. Berlin: Mouton de Gruyter.

Langacker, Ronald W. 1999d. Virtual reality. *Studies in the Linguistic Sciences* 29: 77–103.

Langacker, Ronald W. 2000. A dynamic usage-based model. In Michael Barlow and Suzanne Kemmer, eds., *Usage-based models of language* 1–63. Stanford, CA: CSLI Publications.

Langacker, Ronald W. 2001a. Discourse in cognitive grammar. *Cognitive Linguistics* 12: 143–88.

Langacker, Ronald W. 2001b. Dynamicity in grammar. *Axiomathes* 12: 7–33.

Langacker, Ronald W. 2001c. The English present tense. *English Language and Linguistics* 5: 251–71.

Langacker, Ronald W. 2001d. Topic, subject, and possessor. In Hanne Gram Simonsen and Rolf Theil Endresen, eds., *A cognitive approach to the verb: Morphological and constructional perspectives* 11–48. Berlin: Mouton de Gruyter.

Langacker, Ronald W. 2001e. Viewing and experiential reporting in cognitive grammar. In Augusto Soares da Silva, ed., *Linguagem e cognição: A perspectiva da linguística cognitiva* 19–49. Braga: Associação Portuguesa de Linguística and Universidade Católica Portuguesa, Faculdade de Filosofia de Braga.

Langacker, Ronald W. 2002a. The control cycle: Why grammar is a matter of life and death. *Proceedings of the Annual Meeting of the Japanese Cognitive Linguistics Association* 2: 193–220.

Langacker, Ronald W. 2002b. Deixis and subjectivity. In Frank Brisard, ed., *Grounding: The epistemic footing of deixis and reference* 1–28. Berlin: Mouton de Gruyter.

Langacker, Ronald W. 2002c. Remarks on the English grounding systems. In Frank Brisard, ed., *Grounding: The epistemic footing of deixis and reference* 29–38. Berlin: Mouton de Gruyter.

Langacker, Ronald W. 2002d. A study in unified diversity: English and Mixtec locatives. In Nick J. Enfield, ed., *Ethnosyntax: Explorations in grammar and culture* 138–61. Oxford: Oxford University Press.

Langacker, Ronald W. 2003a. Constructions in cognitive grammar. *English Linguistics* 20: 41–83.

Langacker, Ronald W. 2003b. Context, cognition, and semantics: A unified dynamic approach. In Ellen van Wolde, ed., *Job 28: Cognition in context* 179–230. Leiden, Netherlands: Brill.

Langacker, Ronald W. 2003c. Dynamicity, fictivity, and scanning: The imaginative basis of logic and linguistic meaning. *Korean Linguistics* 18: 1–64.

Langacker, Ronald W. 2003d. Extreme subjectification: English tense and modals. In Hubert Cuyckens, Thomas Berg, René Dirven, and Klaus-Uwe Panther, eds., *Motivation in language: Studies in honor of Günter Radden* 3–26. Amsterdam: John Benjamins.

Langacker, Ronald W. 2004a. Aspects of the grammar of finite clauses. In Michel Achard and Suzanne Kemmer, eds., *Language, culture and mind* 535–77. Stanford, CA: CSLI Publications.

Langacker, Ronald W. 2004b. Form, meaning, and behavior: The cognitive grammar analysis of double subject constructions. In Ellen Contini-Morava, Robert S. Kirsner, and Betsy Rodríguez-Bachiller, eds., *Cognitive and communicative approaches to linguistic analysis* 21–60. Amsterdam: John Benjamins.

Langacker, Ronald W. 2004c. Possession, location, and existence. In Augusto Soares da Silva, Amadeu Torres, and Miguel Gonçalves, eds., *Linguagem, cultura e cognição: Estudios de linguística cognitive* 1: 85–120. Coimbra, Portugal: Almedina.

Langacker, Ronald W. 2004d. Remarks on nominal grounding. *Functions of Language* 11: 77–113.

Langacker, Ronald W. 2005a. Construction grammars: Cognitive, radical, and less so. In Francisco J. Ruiz de Mendoza Ibáñez and Sandra Peña Cervel, eds., *Cognitive linguistics: Internal dynamics and interdisciplinary interaction* 101–59. Berlin: Mouton de Gruyter.

Langacker, Ronald W. 2005b. Integration, grammaticization, and constructional meaning. In Mirjam Fried and Hans C. Boas, eds., *Grammatical constructions: Back to the roots* 157–189. Amsterdam: John Benjamins.

Langacker, Ronald W. 2009. *Investigations in Cognitive Grammar*. Berlin: Mouton de Gruyter.

Lee, Jeong-Hwa. 1999. *A cognitive semantic analysis of manipulative motion verbs in Korean with reference to English*. Seoul: Hankuk.

Levinson, Stephen C. 1997. From outer to inner space: Linguistic categories and non-linguistic thinking. In Jan Nuyts and Eric Pederson, eds., *Language and conceptualization* 13–45. Cambridge: Cambridge University Press.

Lindner, Susan. 1981. A lexico-semantic analysis of English verb-particle constructions with OUT and UP. PhD dissertation, University of California at San Diego.

(Published as *A lexico-semantic analysis of English verb-particle constructions.* LAUT Paper, no. 101. Trier, Germany: Linguistic Agency of the University of Trier, 1983)

Lindner, Susan. 1982. What goes up doesn't necessarily come down: The ins and outs of opposites. *Chicago Linguistic Society* 18: 305–23.

Lyons, John. 1995. *Linguistic semantics: An introduction.* Cambridge: Cambridge University Press.

Maldonado, Ricardo. 1988. Energetic reflexives in Spanish. *Berkeley Linguistics Society* 14: 153–65.

Maldonado, Ricardo. 1992. Middle voice: The case of Spanish 'se'. PhD dissertation, University of California, San Diego.

Manney, Linda. 1995. Pragmatic motivation for inflectional middle voice in modern Greek. *Functions of Language* 2: 159–88.

Manney, Linda. 2000. *Middle voice in modern Greek: Meaning and function of an inflectional category.* Amsterdam: John Benjamins.

Matsumoto, Yo. 1996. Subjective motion and English and Japanese verbs. *Cognitive Linguistics* 7: 183–226.

Michaelis, Laura A. 1991. Temporal priority and pragmatic ambiguity: The case of *already*. *Berkeley Linguistics Society* 17: 426–38.

Michaelis, Laura A., and Knud Lambrecht. 1996. Toward a construction-based theory of language function: The case of nominal extraposition. *Language* 72: 215–47.

Mortelmans, Tanja. 1999. Die Modalverben *sollen* und *müssen* im heutigen Deutsch unter besonderer Berücksichtigung ihres Status als subjektivierter 'grounding predications'. PhD dissertation, University of Antwerp.

Nathan, Geoffrey S. 1986. Phonemes as mental categories. *Berkeley Linguistics Society* 12: 212–23.

Nesset, Tore. 1998. *Russian conjugation revisited: A cognitive approach to aspects of Russian verb inflection.* Oslo: Novus Press.

Nomura, Masuhiro. 2000. The internally-headed relative clause construction in Japanese: A cognitive grammar approach. PhD dissertation, University of California, San Diego.

Ogawa, Roy H., and Gary B. Palmer. 1999. Langacker semantics for three Coeur d'Alene prefixes glossed as 'on'. In Leon de Stadler and Christoph Eyrich, eds., *Issues in cognitive linguistics* 165–224. Berlin: Mouton de Gruyter.

Palmer, Frank R. 1981. *Semantics.* 2nd ed. Cambridge: Cambridge University Press.

Poteet, Stephen. 1987. Paths through different domains: A cognitive grammar analysis of Mandarin *dào*. *Berkeley Linguistics Society* 13: 408–21.

Pütz, Martin, Susanne Niemeier, and René Dirven, eds. 2001a. *Applied cognitive linguistics.* Vol. 1, *Theory and language acquisition.* Berlin: Mouton de Gruyter.

Pütz, Martin, Susanne Niemeier, and René Dirven, eds. 2001b. *Applied cognitive linguistics.* Vol. 2, *Language pedagogy.* Berlin: Mouton de Gruyter.

Rice, Sally. 1987a. Towards a cognitive model of transitivity. PhD dissertation, University of California, San Diego.

Rice, Sally. 1987b. Towards a transitive prototype: Evidence from some atypical English passives. *Berkeley Linguistics Society* 13: 422–34.

Rice, Sally. 1988. Unlikely lexical entries. *Berkeley Linguistics Society* 14: 202–12.

Rice, Sally. 1996. Prepositional prototypes. In Martin Pütz and René Dirven, eds., *The construal of space in language and thought* 135–65. Berlin: Mouton de Gruyter.

Rubba, Johanna. 1993. Discontinuous morphology in modern Aramaic. PhD dissertation, University of California, San Diego.

Rubba, Johanna. 1994. Grammaticization as semantic change: A case study of preposition development. In William Pagliuca, ed., *Perspectives on grammaticalization* 81–101. Amsterdam: John Benjamins.

Rudzka-Ostyn, Brygida, ed. 1988. *Topics in cognitive linguistics*. Amsterdam: John Benjamins.

Rudzka-Ostyn, Brygida. 2003. *Word power: Phrasal verbs and compounds (a cognitive approach)*. Berlin: Mouton de Gruyter.

Ruhl, Charles. 1989. *On monosemy: A study in linguistic semantics*. Albany: State University of New York Press.

Ryder, Mary Ellen. 1994. *Ordered chaos: The interpretation of English noun-noun compounds*. Berkeley: University of California Press.

Sandra, Dominiek, and Sally Rice. 1995. Network analyses of prepositional meaning: Mirroring whose mind—the linguist's or the language user's? *Cognitive Linguistics* 6: 89–130.

Schönefeld, Doris. 1999. Where lexicon and syntax meet: An investigation into the psychological plausibility of basic assumptions made in major linguistic models. Habilitationsschrift, Friedrich-Schiller-Universität Jena, Germany.

Shen, Ya-Ming. 1996. The semantics of the Chinese verb "come." In Eugene H. Casad, ed., *Cognitive linguistics in the redwoods: The expansion of a new paradigm in linguistics* 507–40. Berlin: Mouton de Gruyter.

Smith, Michael B. 1987. The semantics of dative and accusative in German: An investigation in cognitive grammar. PhD dissertation, University of California, San Diego.

Smith, Michael B. 1993. Aspects of German clause structure from a cognitive grammar perspective. *Studi Italiani di Linguistica Teorica e Applicata* 22: 601–38.

Smith, Michael B. 2001. Why *quirky* case really isn't quirky, or how to treat *dative sickness* in Icelandic. In Hubert Cuyckens and Britta Zawada, eds., *Polysemy in cognitive linguistics: Selected papers from the International Cognitive Linguistics Conference, Amsterdam, 1997* 115–59. Amsterdam: John Benjamins.

Sweetser, Eve. 1999. Compositionality and blending: Semantic composition in a cognitively realistic framework. In Theo Janssen and Gisela Redeker, eds., *Cognitive linguistics: Foundations, scope, and methodology* 129–62. Berlin: Mouton de Gruyter.

Tabakowska, Elzbieta. 1993. *Cognitive linguistics and poetics of translation*. Tübingen: Gunter Narr Verlag.

Talmy, Leonard. 1988. Force dynamics in language and cognition. *Cognitive Science* 12: 49–100.

Talmy, Leonard. 1996. Fictive motion in language and "ception." In Paul Bloom, Mary A. Peterson, Lynn Nadel, and Merrill F. Garrett, eds., *Language and space* 211–76. Cambridge, MA: MIT Press.

Talmy, Leonard. 2000a. *Toward a cognitive semantics*. Vol. 1, *Concept structuring systems*. Cambridge, MA: MIT Press.

Talmy, Leonard. 2000b. *Toward a cognitive semantics*. Vol. 2, *Typology and process in concept structuring*. Cambridge, MA: MIT Press.

Taylor, John R. 1988. Contrasting prepositional categories: English and Italian. In Brygida Rudzka-Ostyn, ed., *Topics in cognitive linguistics* 299–326. Amsterdam: John Benjamins.

Taylor, John R. 1993. Some pedagogical implications of cognitive linguistics. In Richard A. Geiger and Brygida Rudzka-Ostyn, eds., *Conceptualizations and mental processing in language* 201–23. Berlin: Mouton de Gruyter.

Taylor, John R. 1994. "Subjective" and "objective" readings of possessor nominals. *Cognitive Linguistics* 5: 201–42.

Taylor, John R. 1995. *Linguistic categorization: Prototypes in linguistic theory*. 2nd ed. Oxford: Clarendon Press. (3rd ed., 2003)

Taylor, John R. 1996. *Possessives in English: An exploration in cognitive grammar*. Oxford: Oxford University Press.

Taylor, John R. 2002. *Cognitive grammar*. Oxford: Oxford University Press.

Tomasello, Michael. 1992. *First verbs: A case study of early grammatical development*. Cambridge: Cambridge University Press.

Tomasello, Michael. 2003. *Constructing a language: A usage-based theory of language acquisition*. Cambridge, MA: Harvard University Press.

Tomlin, Russell S. 1995. Focal attention, voice, and word order: An experimental, cross-linguistics study. In Pamela Downing and Michael Noonan, eds., *Word order in discourse* 517–54. Amsterdam: John Benjamins.

Tomlin, Russell S. 1997. Mapping conceptual representations into linguistic representations: The role of attention in grammar. In Jan Nuyts and Eric Pederson, eds., *Language and conceptualization* 162–89. Cambridge: Cambridge University Press.

Tuggy, David. 1980. ¡Ethical dative and possessor omission sí, possessor ascension no! *Work Papers of the Summer Institute of Linguistics, University of North Dakota* 24: 97–141.

Tuggy, David. 1981. The transitivity-related morphology of Tetelcingo Nahuatl: An exploration in space grammar. PhD dissertation, University of California, San Diego.

Tuggy, David. 1986. Noun incorporations in Nahuatl. *Proceedings of the Annual Meeting of the Pacific Linguistics Conference* 2: 455–70.

Tuggy, David. 1988. Náhuatl causative/applicatives in cognitive grammar. In Brygida Rudzka-Ostyn, ed., *Topics in cognitive linguistics* 587–618. Amsterdam: John Benjamins.

Tuggy, David. 1992. The affix-stem distinction: A cognitive grammar analysis of data from Orizaba Náhuatl. *Cognitive Linguistics* 3: 237–300.

Tuggy, David. 2003. Reduplication in Nahuatl: Iconicities and paradoxes. In Eugene H. Casad and Gary B. Palmer, eds., *Cognitive linguistics and non-Indo-European languages* 91–133. Berlin: Mouton de Gruyter.

Vainik, Ene. 1995. *Eesti keele väliskohakäänete semantika (kognitiivse grammatika vaatenurgast)* [The semantics of Estonian external locative cases (from the viewpoint of cognitive grammar)]. Tallinn: Estonian Academy of Sciences, Institute of the Estonian Language.

Vandeloise, Claude. 1991. *Spatial prepositions: A case study from French*. Chicago: University of Chicago Press.

van Hoek, Karen. 1995. Conceptual reference points: A cognitive grammar account of pronominal anaphora constraints. *Language* 71: 310–40.

van Hoek, Karen. 1997. *Anaphora and conceptual structure*. Chicago: University of Chicago Press.

Velázquez-Castillo, Maura. 1996. *The grammar of possession: Inalienability, incorporation and possessor ascension in Guaraní*. Amsterdam: John Benjamins.

Wierzbicka, Anna. 1995. Dictionaries vs. encyclopaedias: How to draw the line. In Philip W. Davis, ed., *Alternative linguistics: Descriptive and theoretical modes* 289–315. Amsterdam: John Benjamins. Wierzbicka, Anna. 1996. *Semantics: Primes and universals*. Oxford: Oxford University Press.

CHAPTER 18

CONSTRUCTION GRAMMAR

WILLIAM CROFT

1. INTRODUCTION: THE REVIVAL OF CONSTRUCTIONS

Construction grammar presents a general theory of syntactic representation for Cognitive Linguistics. In this sense, construction grammar (lower case) as treated in this chapter refers to a cluster of cognitive linguistic theories of grammar, only some of which have come to be known under the name of Construction Grammar (capitalized).

The fundamental principle behind construction grammar is that the basic form of a syntactic structure is a construction—a pairing of a complex grammatical structure with its meaning—and that constructions are organized in a network. The notion of a construction, of course, goes back to the concept in traditional grammar, but it has been substantially altered in its revival. In particular, the notion of a construction has been generalized so that it is a uniform model for the representation of all grammatical knowledge—syntax, morphology, and lexicon. There are also antecedents in the 1960s and 1970s to the revival of constructions in Cognitive Linguistics and parallel proposals in other contemporary models of syntactic representation. Finally, construction grammar in contemporary Cognitive Linguistics exists in a number of variants.

In section 2, the model of syntactic representation against which construction grammarians have reacted, the componential model, is described, and the arguments for a construction-based approach to syntax, morphology, and lexicon are presented. The next two sections emphasize the commonalities among the different models of construction grammar in Cognitive Linguistics. Section 3 describes the structure of constructions, and section 4 the organization of constructions in a grammar. Section 5 discusses the major variants of construction grammar in Cognitive Linguistics, this time focusing on how they differ from one another. Section 6 discusses the relationship between construction grammar and the usage-based model, language acquisition, and language change.

2. Arguments for Construction Grammar

Construction grammar represents a reaction to the componential model of the organization of a grammar that is found in generative syntactic theories. In the componential model, different types of properties of an utterance—its sound structure, its syntax, and its meaning—are represented in separate components, each of which consists of rules operating over primitive elements of the relevant types (phonemes, syntactic units, semantic units). Each component describes one dimension of the properties of a sentence. The phonological component, for example, consists of the rules and constraints governing the sound structure of a sentence of the language. The syntactic component consists of the rules and constraints governing the syntax—the combinations of words—of a sentence. The semantic component consists of rules and constraints governing the meaning of a sentence. In other words, each component separates out each specific type of linguistic information that is contained in a sentence: phonological, syntactic, and semantic. In addition, all versions of Chomskyan Generative Grammar have broken down the syntactic component further, as levels or strata (such as "deep structure," later "D-structure," and "surface structure," later "S-structure"; Chomsky 1981) and modules or theories (such as Case theory, Binding theory, etc.; Chomsky 1981).

Further components have been proposed by other linguists. Some have argued that morphology, the internal formal structure of words, should occupy its own component (e.g., Aronoff 1993). Others have suggested that information structure, that is, certain aspects of discourse or pragmatic knowledge, should have its own component (Vallduví 1992). However many components are proposed, the general principle remains: each component governs linguistic properties of a single type—sound, word structure, syntax, meaning, and use.

The only constructs which contain information cutting across the components are words, which represent conventional associations of phonological form, syntactic category, and meaning. Words are found in their own "component," the lexicon. The lexicon differs radically from other components in that it contains information of more than one type and also in that the units in the lexicon are

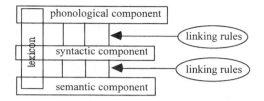

Figure 18.1. The componential model of the organization of grammar

syntactically atomic: they are the minimal syntactic units. (Words may be morphologically complex, of course.)

More recently, attention has been directed to linking rules that link complex syntactic structures to their semantic interpretation and link syntactic structures to their phonological realization. The best explored linking rules in the componential model are the rules linking semantic participant roles in the lexical semantic representation of verbs to syntactic argument positions in syntactic structure (see, e.g., Jackendoff 1990; Levin and Rappaport Hovav 1995). However, there must in principle be linking rules joining together all components of the componential model.

The componential model is illustrated in figure 18.1.
Within each component, the model of representation is essentially reductionist. That is, each component consists of atomic primitive elements and rules of combination that build complex structures out of atomic structures. Of course, the inventory of atomic primitive elements and the permissible types of rules of combination vary significantly from one componential theory to another. But the basic componential structure and the reductionist analysis of the structures in each component is common to all of the generative and formalist models of syntactic representation.

The componential model can also be interpreted as a means to represent grammatical knowledge without explicitly referring to constructions in the traditional sense of that term. The logical conclusion of the componential analysis of grammar is the hypothesis that all properties of syntactic constructions—i.e., grammatical structures larger than just a single word—can be captured with the general rules of the grammatical components and their interfaces, and thus there is no need for constructions in grammatical analysis. Chomsky makes this claim explicit:

> A central element in the work discussed here, as in recent work from which
> it evolves, is the effort to decompose such processes as "passive," "relativization,"
> etc., into more fundamental "abstract features." (Chomsky 1981: 121)

> UG [Universal Grammar] provides a fixed system of principles and a finite array
> of finitely valued parameters. The language-particular rules reduce to choice of
> values for these parameters. The notion of grammatical construction is eliminated,
> and with it, construction-particular rules. (Chomsky 1993: 4)

Chomsky's position on the generality of syntax and the irrelevance of constructions to the analysis of grammar is the complement of his view that all arbitrary and idiosyncratic aspects of grammar should be restricted to the lexicon.

Construction grammar arose out of a concern to analyze one particularly problematic phenomenon for the componential model, namely, idioms. Idioms are linguistic expressions that are syntactically and/or semantically idiosyncratic in various ways but are larger than words, and hence cannot simply be assigned to the lexicon without some special mechanism. Some idioms are lexically idiosyncratic, using lexical items found nowhere else, such as *kith and kin* 'family and friends'. Such idioms are by definition syntactically and semantically irregular, since the unfamiliar word has no independent syntactic or semantic status. Other idioms use familiar words but their syntax is idiosyncratic, as in *all of a sudden* or *in point of fact*; these are called extragrammatical idioms. Still other idioms use familiar words and familiar syntax but are semantically idiosyncratic, such as *tickle the ivories* 'play the piano'.

Idioms pose a problem for the componential model because their idiosyncrasy requires inclusion of information from multiple components, yet they are complex and often partly rule-governed and therefore appear to belong in an individual component, not the lexicon. In other words, there is no proper place in the componential model for idioms. Construction grammarians in Cognitive Linguistics were by no means the first to observe the problems that idioms pose for componential models (see, e.g., Makkai 1972; Becker 1975; Bolinger 1976).

In their seminal paper in Construction grammar, Fillmore, Kay, and O'Connor (1988) develop the argument for constructions based on the existence and pervasiveness of idioms, which they classify into three types. A theory of grammar should capture the differences among these types of idioms and their relationship to the regular lexicon and regular syntactic rules of a language. The need for a theory that can accommodate idioms is most critical for idioms which are schematic to a greater or lesser degree. Most idioms are not completely lexically specific or substantive, like the idioms given above, but instead include schematic categories admitting a wide range of possible words and phrases to instantiate those categories.

Partially schematic idioms also range over all three types described by Fillmore, Kay, and O'Connor. A schematic idiom which is lexically idiosyncratic is the Comparative Conditional construction *The X-er, the Y-er* as in *The longer you practice, the better you will become* (the form *the* is not directly related to the definite article, but is derived from the Old English instrumental demonstrative form *þy*). An example of an extragrammatical schematic idiom is the "Cousin" construction *Nth cousin (M times removed)*, as in *second cousin three times removed*, which describes different kinds of distant kin relations and has its own unique syntax. Finally, an example of a schematic idiom that is only semantically idiosyncratic is *pull NP's leg* 'joke with NP' as in *Don't pull my leg*; the NP category can be filled by any noun phrase denoting a human being.

Schematic idioms pose an even more serious challenge to the componential model than substantive idioms because schematic idioms either have regularities of their own which should be captured as regularities (the extragrammatical schematic idioms) or follow regular syntactic rules and ought to be somehow represented as doing so (the grammatical schematic idioms). Moreover, all idioms are semantically idiosyncratic, which means that they do not follow general rules of semantic interpretation. Instead, they have their own rules of semantic interpretation.

Fillmore, Kay, and O'Connor argue that the existence of idioms should be accepted as evidence for constructions. Constructions are objects of syntactic representation that also contain semantic and even phonological information (such as the individual substantive lexical items in the partially schematic idioms, or special prosodic patterns or special rules of phonological reduction as in *I wanna go too*). Constructions are like lexical items in the componential model: they link together idiosyncratic or arbitrary phonological, syntactic, and semantic information. The difference between lexical items and constructions is that lexical items are substantive and atomic (that is, minimal syntactic units), while constructions can be at least partially schematic and complex (consisting of more than one syntactic element).

Beginning with Fillmore, Kay, and O'Connor (1988) and Lakoff (1987), there have been a number of detailed studies of constructions whose grammatical properties cannot be accounted for by the general syntactic, semantic, and pragmatic rules of English; other major studies following Fillmore, Kay, and O'Connor and Lakoff's model include Goldberg (1995) and Michaelis and Lambrecht (1996). Also, the studies of syntactic structures with special pragmatic functions by Prince (1978, 1981) and Birner and Ward (1998) and the studies of syntactic structures with special semantic interpretations by Wierzbicka (1980, 1982, 1987, 1988) strengthen the case for treating those syntactic structures as constructions. Even formal syntacticians who adhere to the componential model have recognized the existence of constructions to some extent; see, for example, Akmajian (1984; cf. Lambrecht's 1990 reanalysis of the same phenomenon) and Jackendoff (1990, 1997).

All of these studies can be interpreted as merely requiring the addition of a constructional component to the componential model. But Fillmore, Kay, and O'Connor (1988: 505, note 3) observe in a footnote that there is in fact a continuum from substantive to schematic. Schematic idioms vary considerably in their chematicity. Some schematic idioms, such as the verb phrase idiom *kick the bucket* 'die', are fixed except for grammatical inflectional categories:

(1)   a. Jake kicked the bucket.
      b. Jake's gonna kick the bucket. [etc.]

Other schematic idioms have one or more open argument slots as well as inflectional flexibility, such as *give NP the lowdown* 'inform':

(2)   a. I gave/I'll give him the lowdown.
      b. He gave/He'll give Janet the lowdown. [etc.]

Still other schematic idioms have open classes for all "content" words, leaving just a salient form such as the connective *let alone* as a substantive element:

(3) a. She gave me more candy than I could carry, let alone eat.
     b. Only a linguist would buy that book, let alone read it.

Finally, a constructional analysis has been proposed for some schematic idioms in which all elements are lexically open. For example, the Resultative construction—actually one of yet another family of constructions—is analyzed as a construction by Goldberg (1995: 181):

(4) a. This nice man probably just wanted Mother to . . . kiss him unconscious.
        (D. Shields, *Dead Tongues*, 1989)
     b. I had brushed my hair very smooth. (C. Brontë, *Jane Eyre*, 1847)

Yet the Resultative construction has no lexically specific element. It can be described only by a syntactic structure, in this case [*NP Verb NP XP*], with a unique specialized semantic interpretation.

It is a short step from analyzing the Resultative construction as a construction to analyzing all the syntactic rules of a language as constructions. A syntactic rule such as *VP → V NP* describes a completely schematic construction [*V NP*], and the semantic interpretation rule that maps the syntactic structure to its corresponding semantic structure is unique to that schematic construction.

Fillmore, Kay, and O'Connor take the logical next step: regular syntactic rules and regular rules of semantic interpretation are themselves constructions. The only difference between regular syntactic rules and their rules of semantic interpretation and other constructions is that the former are wholly schematic while the latter retain some substantive elements. Likewise, Goldberg (1995: 116–19) suggests that there is a Transitive construction just as there are more specialized schematic syntactic constructions such as the Resultative construction. Reanalyzing general syntactic rules as the broadest, most schematic constructions of a language is just the other end of the substantive-schematic continuum for idioms/constructions.

Turning to semantic interpretation, one can also argue that semantically idiosyncratic constructions and compositional semantic rules differ only in degree, not in kind. Most idioms are what Nunberg, Sag, and Wasow (1994) call idiomatically combining expressions, in which the syntactic parts of the idiom (e.g., *spill* and *beans*) can be identified with parts of the idiom's semantic interpretation ('divulge' and 'information', respectively). They argue that idiomatically combining expressions are not only semantically analyzable, but also semantically compositional.

Idiomatically combining expressions are only the extreme end of a continuum of conventionality in semantic composition. The other end of the continuum is represented by selectional restrictions. Selectional restrictions are restrictions on possible combinations of words which are determined only by the semantics of the concepts denoted by the word. For example, the restrictions on the use of *mud* and *car* in (5) and (6) follow from the fact that mud is a viscous substance and a car is a machine:

(5) a. Mud oozed onto the driveway.
     b. ?*The car oozed onto the driveway.

(6) a. The car started.
　　 b. ?*Mud started.

The combinations in (5a) and (6a) are semantically compositional: the meaning of the whole can be predicted from the meaning of the parts.

Nunberg, Sag, and Wasow argue that the same analysis applies to idiomatically combining expressions. Idiomatically combining expressions are largely fixed in their words; any substitution leads to ungrammaticality, as in (7b), (7c), and (8b):

(7) a. Tom pulled strings to get the job.
　　 b. *Tom pulled ropes to get the job.
　　 c. *Tom grasped strings to get the job.
(8) a. She spilled the beans.
　　 b. *She spilled the succotash.

However, given the meanings of the words in the idiomatically combining expression, the meaning of the whole expression is compositional:

> By convention . . . *strings* [in *pull strings*] can be used metaphorically to refer to personal connections when it is the object of *pull*, and *pull* can be used metaphorically to refer to exploitation or exertion when its object is *strings*. (Nunberg, Sag, and Wasow 1994: 496)

The traditional description of idioms is that the meaning of the idiomatically combining expression is "noncompositional." But this is not the correct description. Consider the idiom *spill the beans*, illustrated in (9):

(9) spill the beans

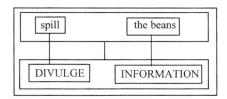

An idiomatically combining expression such as *spill the beans* is a construction. As a construction, it has unique syntax: the verb must be *spill* and its object must be *the beans*. It also has a semantic interpretation, namely 'divulge information'. All Nunberg, Sag, and Wasow are saying is that this construction has its own semantic interpretation rules, mapping *spill* onto 'divulge' and *the beans* onto 'information'. What they have done is dissociate conventionality from noncompositionality. Idiomatically combining expressions are not noncompositional. There exist truly noncompositional expressions; these are idiomatic phrases such as *saw logs* 'sleep' and *kick the bucket*. Idiomatically combining expressions differ from collocations and ordinary expressions only in that the conventional way of expressing the parts of its meaning are conventional and also relatively opaque, compared to collocations and ordinary expressions.

Constructions other than idiomatic phrases are compositional; that is, the meanings of the parts of the construction are combined to form the meaning of the whole construction. The reason that they must be represented as independent constructions is not that the construction is noncompositional, but that the semantic interpretation rules associated with the construction are unique to that construction and not derived from another more general syntactic pattern, as construction grammarians carefully note (e.g., Goldberg 1995: 13; Michaelis and Lambrecht 1996: 219).

Indeed, one can think of the general "compositional" rules of semantic interpretation as semantic rules associated with general (schematic) syntactic structures, just as specialized rules of semantic interpretation are associated with syntactically specialized extragrammatical idioms. Nunberg, Sag and Wasow's analysis of idiomatically combining expressions can easily be extended to the general rules of semantic interpretation that link syntactic and semantic structures. In other words, all syntactic expressions, whatever their degree of schematicity, have rules of semantic interpretation associated with them, although some substantive idioms appear to inherit their semantic interpretation rules from more schematic syntactic expressions such as [*Verb Object*].[1] In semantics as well as syntax, the concept of a construction can be generalized to encompass the full range of grammatical knowledge of a speaker.

Similar arguments can be applied to morphology. There are unfamiliar morphemes that exist only in single combinations, such as *cran-* in *cranberry* (cf. *kith and kin*, *pay heed*). There is also "extragrammatical" morphology, that is, morphological patterns that do not obey the general morphological rules of the language. For example, the general rule for plural formation in English is suffixation of an allomorph of *-s* to the noun stem. The ablaut plurals of English, such as *feet* and *geese*, are outside the general plural formation rule. Morphological expressions can also be placed on a continuum of schematicity. A maximally substantive morphological expression is fully specified, as in *book-s*. Partially schematic morphological expressions include *book-NUMBER* and *NOUN-s*. Fully schematic morphological expressions include *NOUN-NUMBER*. Finally, many words are what one might call "idiomatically combining words," where the meaning of a morpheme is specific to the stem it combines with (or a subclass of stems). For example, *-en* is the plural of *brother* only when *brother* refers to a member of a religious community, and *brother* refers to a member of a religious community when it is combined with *-en* (we leave aside the fact that the plural stem *brethr-* is distinct from the singular stem). All of these observations suggest that in fact morphology is very much like syntax and that a construction representation is motivated for morphology as well. The only difference between morphology and syntax is that elements in morphology are bound, whereas in syntax they are (mostly) free.

Lastly, the lexicon differs only in degree from constructions. The only difference is that constructions are complex, made up of words and phrases, while words

Table 18.1. The syntax-lexicon continuum

Construction Type	Traditional Name	Examples
Complex and (mostly) schematic	**syntax**	[SBJ *be*-TNS VERB-*en by* OBL]
Complex and (mostly) specific	**idiom**	[*pull*-TNS NP-*'s leg*]
Complex but bound	**morphology**	[NOUN-*s*] [VERB-TNS]
Atomic and schematic	**syntactic category**	[DEM], [ADJ]
Atomic and specific	**word/lexicon**	[*this*], [*green*]

are syntactically simple. Some words are morphologically complex, of course. But construction grammar would analyze morphologically complex words as constructions whose parts are morphologically bound. Morphologically simple words are atomic, that is, they cannot be further divided into meaningful parts. But a word is again just the limiting case of a construction (see Fillmore, Kay, and O'Connor 1988: 501).

The end point of this argument is one of the fundamental hypotheses of construction grammar: there is a uniform representation of all grammatical knowledge in the speaker's mind in the form of generalized constructions. The constructional tail has come to wag the syntactic dog: everything from words to the most general syntactic and semantic rules can be represented as constructions. Construction grammar has generalized the notion of a construction to apply to any grammatical structure, including both its form and its meaning. The logical consequence of accommodating idioms in syntactic theory has been to provide a uniform representation of all types of grammatical structures from words to syntactic and semantic rules. The uniform representation is referred to as the syntax-lexicon continuum (cf. Langacker 1987: 25–27, 35–36), illustrated in table 18.1.

Syntactic rules (and the accompanying rules of semantic interpretation) are schematic, complex constructions. Idioms are complex and (at least partly) substantive constructions. Morphology describes complex constructions, but constructions of bound morphemes. Words in the lexicon are atomic substantive constructions, while syntactic categories are schematic atomic constructions. In other words, grammatical knowledge represents a continuum on two dimensions, from the substantive to the schematic and from the atomic to the complex.

Construction grammar's great attraction as a theory of grammar is that it provides a uniform model of grammatical representation and at the same time captures a broader range of empirical phenomena than componential models of grammar. Langacker describes this conception of a grammar as "a structured inventory of conventional linguistic units" (Langacker 1987: 57). Constructions in the generalized sense are conventional linguistic units—more precisely, symbolic linguistic units (Langacker's formulation includes the separate representation of linguistic form and linguistic meaning).

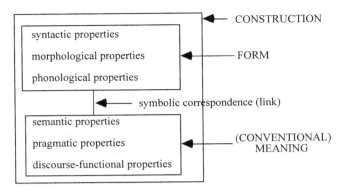

Figure 18.2. The symbolic structure of a construction

3. Syntactic and Semantic Structure: The Anatomy of a Construction

This section introduces fundamental concepts and descriptive terms for the analysis of the structure of a grammatical construction. The concepts in this section form the basis of any syntactic theory, although they are combined in different ways in different syntactic theories.

Grammatical constructions in construction grammar, like the lexicon in other syntactic theories, consist of pairings of form and meaning that are at least partially arbitrary. Even the most general syntactic constructions have corresponding general rules of semantic interpretation. Thus, constructions are fundamentally symbolic units, as represented in figure 18.2 (see Langacker 1987: 60).

The term "meaning" is intended to represent all of the conventionalized aspects of a construction's function, which may include not only properties of the situation described by the utterance but also properties of the discourse in which the utterance is found (such as the use of the definite article to indicate that the object referred to is known to both speaker and hearer) and of the pragmatic situation of the interlocutors (e.g., the use of a construction such as *What a beautiful cat!* to convey the speaker's surprise). I will use the terms "meaning" and "semantic" to refer to any conventionalized feature of a construction's function.

The central essential difference between componential syntactic theories and construction grammar is that the symbolic link between form and conventional meaning is internal to a construction in the latter, but is external to the syntactic and semantic components in the former (i.e., as linking rules). Figures 18.3 and 18.4 compare construction grammar and a componential syntactic theory on this parameter, highlighting in boldface the essential difference in the two models.

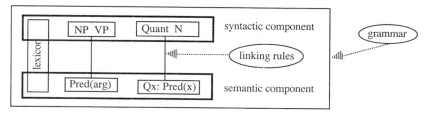

Figure 18.3. The relation between form and function in a componential syntactic theory

In the componential model, the various syntactic structures are organized independently of the corresponding semantic structures, as represented by the highlighted boxes in figure 18.3. In construction grammar, the basic linguistic units are symbolic and are organized as symbolic units, as represented by the highlighted boxes in figure 18.4. As a consequence, the internal structure of the basic (symbolic) units in construction grammar is more complex than that of basic units in the componential model.

The internal structure of a construction is the morphosyntactic structure of sentences that instantiate constructions. For example, a simple intransitive sentence like *Heather sings* is an instance of the Intransitive construction. If we compare a simplified representation of *Heather sings* in Generative Grammar to a simplified representation of the same in construction grammar (figure 18.5), we can see that they are actually rather similar except that the construction grammar representation is symbolic.

The box notation used in figure 18.5b is simply a notational variant of the bracket notation used in figure 18.5a (Langacker 1987; Kay and Fillmore 1999). Thus, we can see that both the generative grammatical representation and the construction grammar representation share the fundamental meronomic (part-whole) structure of grammatical units: the sentence *Heather sings* is made up of two parts, the Subject *Heather* and the Predicate *sings*.

The brackets in figure 18.5a are labeled with syntactic category labels, while the corresponding boxes in the syntactic structure of figure 18.5b are not labeled. This does not mean that the boxed structures in figure 18.5b are all of the same syntactic type. Construction grammarians, of course, assume that syntactic units belong to a variety of different syntactic categories. The boxes have been left unlabeled because the nature of those categories is one issue on which different theories of construction grammar diverge. That is, we may ask the following question of different construction grammar theories:

(I)   *What is the status of the categories of the syntactic elements in construction grammar given the existence of constructions?*

Beyond the meronomic structure of grammatical units, generative theories and construction grammar diverge. First, as we have already noted, construction grammar treats grammatical units as fundamentally symbolic, that is, pairings of

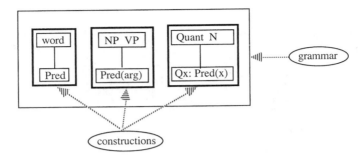

Figure 18.4. The relation between form and function in construction grammar

grammatical form and the corresponding meaning (semantic structure). As a consequence, the representation of a construction includes correspondence relations between the form and the meaning of the construction. We will call these correspondence relations symbolic links.

It will be convenient to use different names for the parts of a syntactic structure and the parts of a semantic structure. We will call the parts of the syntactic structure "elements" and parts of the semantic structure "components." Thus, a symbolic link joins an element of the syntactic structure of a construction to a component of the semantic structure of that construction. There is also a symbolic link joining the whole syntactic structure to the whole semantic structure (the middle symbolic link in figure 18.5b). This symbolic link is the construction grammar representation of the fact that the syntactic structure of the Intransitive construction symbolizes a unary-valency predicate-argument semantic structure. Each element plus corresponding component is a part of the whole construction (form + meaning) as well. We will use the term "unit" to describe a symbolic part (element + component) of a construction. That is, the construction as a symbolic whole is made up of symbolic units as parts. The symbolic units of *Heather sings* are not indicated in figure 18.5b for clarity's sake; but all three types of parts of constructions are illustrated in figure 18.6 (see Langacker 1987: 84, figure 2.8a). (Figure 18.6 suppresses links between parts of the construction for clarity.)

Figure 18.5b has two other relations apart from the symbolic relation: one joining the two syntactic elements and one joining the two semantic components. The link joining the two semantic components describes a semantic relation that holds between the two components, in this case some sort of event-participant relation. Thus, the semantic structure of a construction is assumed to be (potentially) complex, made up of semantic components among which certain semantic relations hold.

The link joining the two syntactic elements in figure 18.5b is a syntactic relation. The syntactic relation does not obviously correspond directly to anything in the Generative Grammar representation in figure 18.5a. This is because the representation of syntactic relations in most syntactic theories is more complex than

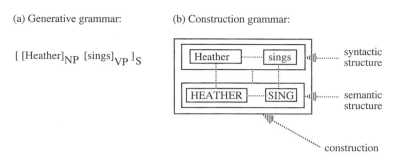

(a) Generative grammar: (b) Construction grammar:

[[Heather]$_{NP}$ [sings]$_{VP}$]$_S$

Figure 18.5. **Simplified Generative Grammar and construction grammar representations of *Heather sings***

a simple syntactic link. One layer is the syntactic relation itself, such as the Subject-Verb relation holding between *Heather* and *sings* in the construction grammar representation in figure 18.5. A second layer is the means of representing syntactic relations. Different syntactic theories use different means for representing abstract syntactic relations. For example, Generative Grammar uses constituency to represent syntactic relations, while Word Grammar (Hudson 1984; this volume, chapter 19) uses dependency. The third layer is the overt manifestation of syntactic relations, such as word order, case marking, and indexation (agreement). We strip away the latter two layers in comparing construction grammar theories.

An important theoretical distinction must be made regarding the internal structure of constructions (Kay 1997). The analysis of syntactic structure is unfortunately confounded by an ambiguity in much traditional syntactic terminology. We can illustrate this with the example of the term "Subject" in the Intransitive Clause construction in figure 18.6 illustrated once again by the sentence *Heather sings*. The term "Subject" can mean one of two things. It can describe the role of a particular element of the construction, that is, a meronomic relation between the element labeled "Subject" in the Intransitive construction and the Intransitive construction as a whole. This is the sense in which one says that *Heather* is the Subject of the Intransitive clause *Heather sings*. This part-whole relation is represented implicitly in (10) by the nesting of the box for *Heather* inside the box for the whole construction *Heather sings*.

(10)

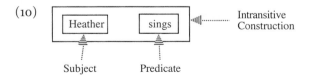

The Subject role defines a grammatical category. But the term "Subject" can also describe a syntactic relation between one element of the construction—the

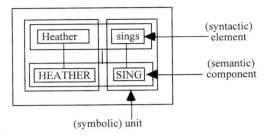

Figure 18.6. Elements, components, and units of a construction

Subject—and another element of the construction—the Verb. This is the sense in which one says that *Heather* is the Subject of the Verb *sings*. In other words, the term "Subject" confounds two different types of relations in a construction: the role of the part in the whole and the relation of one part to another part. The difference between the two is illustrated in (11):

(11)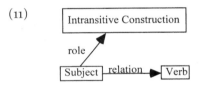

Different theories of construction grammar in Cognitive Linguistics develop rather different models of the internal relations between elements of constructions and components of constructions. These differences can be encapsulated in question (II):

(II)   *What sorts of syntactic relations are posited?*

The answers to these questions for different theories will be presented in section 5, after we have described the organization of constructions in a construction grammar.

4. The Organization of Constructions in a Construction Grammar

Constructions are not merely an unstructured list in construction grammar. Constructions form a structured inventory of a speaker's knowledge of the conventions of their language (Langacker 1987: 63–76). This structured inventory is usually represented by construction grammarians in terms of a taxonomic network of constructions. Each construction constitutes a node in the taxonomic network of constructions.

Any construction with unique idiosyncratic morphological, syntactic, lexical, semantic, pragmatic, or discourse-functional properties must be represented as an independent node in the constructional network in order to capture a speaker's knowledge of their language. That is, any quirk of a construction is sufficient to represent that construction as an independent node. For example, the substantive idiom [Sʙᴊ *kick the bucket*] must be represented as an independent node because it is semantically idiosyncratic. The more schematic but verb-specific construction [Sʙᴊ *kick* Oʙᴊ] must also be represented as an independent node in order to specify its argument linking pattern (or in older Generative Grammar terms, its subcategorization frame). Finally, the wholly schematic construction [Sʙᴊ TʀVᴇʀʙ Oʙᴊ] is represented as an independent node because this is how construction grammar represents the transitive clause that is described by phrase structure rules in Generative Grammar, such as S → NP VP and VP → V NP.

Of course, *kick the bucket* has the same argument structure pattern as ordinary transitive uses of *kick*, and ordinary transitive uses of *kick* follow the same argument structure pattern as any transitive verb phrase. Each construction is simply an instance of the more schematic construction(s) in the chain [*kick the bucket*] – [*kick* Oʙᴊ] – [TʀVᴇʀʙ oʙᴊ] (on schematicity, see Tuggy, this volume, chapter 4). Thus, these constructions can be represented in a taxonomic hierarchy, as in (12):

(12)

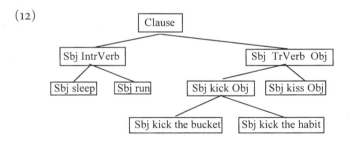

However, grammatical constructions do not form a strict taxonomic hierarchy. One of the simplifications in the hierarchy of constructions in (12) is the exclusion of Tense-Aspect-Mood-Negation marking, expressed by Auxiliaries and Verbal suffixes. If those parts of an utterance are included, then any construction in the hierarchy in (12) has multiple parents. For example, the sentence [*I didn't sleep*] is an instantiation of both the Intransitive Verb construction and the Negative construction, as illustrated in (13):

(13)

The sentence [*I didn't sleep*] thus has multiple parents in the taxonomy of constructions to which it belongs. This is a consequence of each construction being a partial specification of the grammatical structure of its daughter construction(s). For example, the Negation construction only specifies the structure associated with the Subject, Verb, and Auxiliary; it does not specify anything about a Verb's Object (if it has one), and so there is no representation of the Object in the Negation construction in (13).

A construction typically provides only a partial specification of the structure of an utterance. For example, the Ditransitive construction [SBJ DITRVERB OBJ1 OBJ2], as in *He gave her a book*, only specifies the predicate and the linkings to its arguments. It does not specify the order of elements, which can be different in, for example, the Cleft construction, as in *It was a book that he gave her*. Nor does the Ditransitive construction specify the presence or position of other elements in an utterance, such as Modal Auxiliaries or Negation, whether in a Declarative Sentence (where they are preverbal, as in 14a) or an Interrogative Sentence (where the Auxiliary precedes the Subject, as in 14b):

(14)   a. He *won't* give her the book.
       b. *Wouldn't* he give her the book?

Hence any particular utterance's structure is specified by a number of distinct schematic constructions. Conversely, a schematic construction abstracts away from the unspecified structural aspects of the class of utterances it describes. The model of construction grammar conforms to Langacker's content requirement for a grammar: the only grammatical entities that are posited in the theory are grammatical units—specifically, symbolic units—and schematizations of those units.

Constructions may be linked by relations other than taxonomic relations. A third question we may ask of different construction grammar theories is:

(III)   *What sorts of relations are found between constructions?*

The taxonomic hierarchy appears to represent the same or similar information at different levels of schematicity in the hierarchy. For example, the fact that *the bucket* is the direct object of *kick* in *kick the bucket* is, or could be, represented in the idiom construction itself [*kick the bucket*], or at any one or more of the schematic levels above the hierarchy, all the way up to [TRVERB OBJ]. Different theories of construction grammar have offered different answers to the question of how information is to be represented in the taxonomic hierarchy of constructions:

(IV)   *How is grammatical information stored in the construction taxonomy?*

In the next two sections, the answers that various theories of construction grammar give to these questions are presented.[2]

5. SOME CURRENT THEORIES
OF CONSTRUCTION GRAMMAR

This section surveys current theories of construction grammar in Cognitive Linguistics. All of the theories conform to the three essential principles of construction grammar described in sections 2–4: the independent existence of constructions as symbolic units, the uniform symbolic representation of grammatical information, and the taxonomic organization of constructions in a grammar. Of course, the exact means by which constructions and grammatical information are described in each theory, and the terminology used, varies. In each of the following subsections, the basic terminology used for the essential construction grammar features, and the approach to the four questions introduced above, will be presented for each theory. The different answers to the four questions bring out current issues of debate in construction grammar. It should be noted that the different theories tend to focus on different issues, representing their distinctive positions vis-à-vis the other theories. For example, Construction Grammar explores syntactic relations in detail; the Lakoff/Goldberg model focuses more on (nonclassical) relations between constructions; Cognitive Grammar focuses on semantic categories and relations; and Radical Construction Grammar focuses on syntactic categories in a nonreductionist model.

5.1. Construction Grammar (Fillmore, Kay, and collaborators)

Construction Grammar (in capitals) is the theory developed by Fillmore, Kay, and collaborators (Fillmore and Kay 1993; Kay and Fillmore 1999; Fillmore et al., forthcoming). Construction Grammar is the variant of construction grammar (lower case) that most closely resembles certain formalist theories, in particular Head-Driven Phrase Structure Grammar, which also calls itself a sign-based theory (i.e., a theory whose fundamental units are symbolic). Nevertheless, Construction Grammar conforms to the essential principles of construction grammar; Fillmore and Kay were among the first to articulate these principles (Fillmore, Kay, and O'Connor 1988). Construction Grammar's distinguishing features are its elaborate, and still evolving, descriptive language for the internal structure of constructions, which can only be briefly sketched here.

In Construction Grammar, all grammatical properties—phonological, syntactic, semantic, and so on—are uniformly represented as features with values, such as [cat v] (syntactic category is Verb) and [gf¬subj] (grammatical function is not Subject). The value of a feature may itself be a list of features with their own values; these are more generally called feature structures. A simple example of a feature structure is the Verb Phrase (VP) construction (Kay and Fillmore 1999: 8, figure 2).

The Verb Phrase construction may be represented by brackets around the features and feature structures, as in (15), or by an equivalent "box" notation, as in (16); we will use the box notation in the remainder of this chapter:

$$(15) \quad \begin{bmatrix} [\text{cat v}] \\ \begin{bmatrix} [\text{role head}] \\ [\text{lex +}] \end{bmatrix} \\ \begin{bmatrix} [\text{role filler}] \\ [\text{loc +}] \\ [\text{gf}\neg\text{subj}] \end{bmatrix} + \end{bmatrix}$$

(16)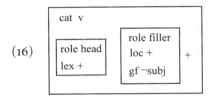

We may read the equivalent diagrams in (15) and (16) as follows. The boxes in (16) correspond to the two lower feature structures in (15). The two inner boxes/feature structures indicate the features of the verb and its complements (if any). The first box specifies that the first constituent of the VP construction is its head and that it must be lexical. For example, in *found her bracelet*, the first constituent is the head of the VP, and it is a word, not a larger constituent. The feature-value pair [cat v] above it is actually a simplification of a more complex feature structure (Kay and Fillmore 1999: 9, note 13), which specifies that the syntactic category of the head of the VP, in this case *found*, must be "Verb." The second box specifies the complements, if any, of the Verb. The + ("Kleene plus") following the second box indicates that there may be one or more complements, or zero, in the VP. In the VP *found her bracelet*, *her bracelet* is the one and only complement. In the VP construction, the complements are given the role value "filler." The feature [loc(al) +] indicates that the complement is not extracted out of the VP. An example of an extracted, [loc −], complement of *find* would be the question word *what* in the question *What did he find?*

Construction Grammar uses a number of features to indicate meronomic relations. The Construction Grammar model can be most easily understood by working from the parts to the whole. Minimal units are words (or more precisely, morphemes; we will ignore this distinction for now). Each unit has syntactic features, grouped under the feature [syn], and semantic features, grouped under the feature [sem]. Construction Grammar separates the phonological features under a feature [phon] if the construction is substantive.

The [syn] and [sem] features are themselves grouped under the feature [ss] (formerly [synsem]), which represents the symbolic structure of that part of the construction. The basic symbolic structure for Construction Grammar is given in (17):

(17)

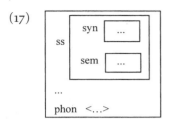

(I)   *What is the status of the categories of the syntactic elements in construction grammar given the existence of constructions?*

The elements of constructions in Construction Grammar fall into a small set of atomic category types, such as [cat v] and [gf sbj]. That is, constructions in Construction Grammar can be described in terms of complex combinations of a set of primitive atomic units. This is what I will call a reductionist model of syntactic structure: the atomic units are primitive and the complex units are derived. Why are constructions not superfluous, then, in Construction Grammar? It is because specific constructions as a whole will contain syntactic and semantic information that is not found in the units of the construction that make up its parts. For example, the *What's X doing Y?*, or WXDY construction (Kay and Fillmore 1999), illustrated by *What's this cat doing in here?*, possesses a number of syntactic and semantic properties not derivable from other constructions or the words in the construction. Its distinctive semantic property is the presupposition of incongruity of the event, which they argue cannot be derived by conversational implicature (Kay and Fillmore 1999: 4). The WXDY construction is found only with the auxiliary *be* and the main verb *do* in the progressive (yet the progressive form here can be used with stative predicates) and excludes negation of *do* or *be*, all properties not predictable from the words, related constructions, or the constructional meaning (Kay and Fillmore 1999: 4–7).

The manner in which Construction Grammar assembles the parts of a construction into a whole uses three different sets of features. The [role] feature is used to represent the role of the syntactic element in the whole. The [role] feature is associated with each part of a complex construction and defines syntactic roles such as [mod](ifier), [filler], and [head]. For instance, the Subject-Predicate construction, as in *Hannah sings*, has the roles [head] for *sings* and [filler] for *Hannah* (Kay and Fillmore 1999: 13). These roles, like the categories Verb and Subject, are defined independently of the constructions in which they occur.

(II)   *What sorts of syntactic relations are posited?*

In addition to roles, each part of a complex construction has a relation to some other part of the construction in Construction Grammar. The relations between parts of a construction are all cast in terms of predicate-argument relations. For

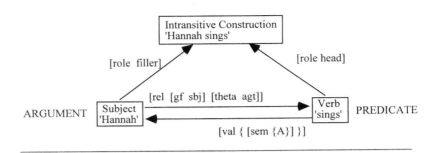

Figure 18.7. The use of [role], [val], and [rel] in Construction Grammar

example, in *Hannah sings*, *Hannah* is the argument and *sings* is the predicate. The predicate-argument relation is symbolic, that is, both syntactic and semantic. Hence, Construction Grammar posits syntactic relations (question II) as part of the symbolic predicate-argument relations. Semantically, a predicate is relational, that is, inherently relates to one or more additional concepts. In *Hannah sings*, singing inherently involves a singer. The semantic arguments of a predicate are the concepts to which the predicate relates, in this case, Hannah. Syntactically, a predicate requires a certain number of arguments in specific grammatical functions to it: *sing* requires an argument in the Subject grammatical function. And syntactically, arguments are related to the predicate by a grammatical function: in this case, *Hannah* is the subject of *sings*.

The remaining two features used to describe meronomic relations in Construction Grammar, [val] and [rel], are used on predicates and arguments, respectively. The use of [role], [val] and [rel] are illustrated in figure 18.7. The [val] feature structure is used to indicate the relation of the predicate to its argument(s), and the [rel] feature structure is used to indicate the relation of each argument to its predicate. The [val] feature is found in the predicate's representation. The value of the [val] feature will be a set, indicated by the set notation {}; the [val] feature will be a set consisting of more than one member for predicates with multiple arguments. For the predicate *sings* in figure 18.7, the [val] set consists of just one member, namely the singer argument. Construction Grammar indicates the argument of a predicate by a cross-reference to the set of semantic arguments, which is part of the [sem] feature structure. In this example, we simply indicate that the singer argument corresponds to the argument A in the [sem] feature structure for *sings*.

The [rel] feature structure in the representation of the argument phrase indicates what grammatical function the argument is found in and what semantic role it should have with respect to the predicate. The [rel] feature structure takes a syntactic feature [gf] ("grammatical function") and a semantic feature [θ] (for "thematic role," indicated as theta in 14). (Kay and Fillmore 1999: 9, note 10, also include another syntactic feature under [rel], namely [case]). In figure 18.7, the argument *Hannah*'s [rel] feature structure has a grammatical function of "Subject" and a thematic role of "Agent."

Finally, predicates and their arguments in a construction are matched with each other such that each argument's [rel] is matched up with one of the elements in the [val] list of its predicate. This is achieved through indexes on the relevant feature structures in the construction (not indicated in 15 and 16). Kay and Fillmore call this matching principle the Valence Principle (Kay and Fillmore 1999: 10).

Construction Grammar keeps distinct part-whole relations ([role]) and part-part relations ([val] and [rel]). Predicate-argument relations are independent of the role relations each predicate and argument has. For example, in both *The book is red* and *the red book*, *red* is the predicate and *(the) book* is the argument. However, in *The book is red*, *be red* is in the head role while in *the red book*, *book* is in the head role. Furthermore, Construction Grammar keeps distinct the [val] feature for predicates and the [rel] feature for arguments. The reason that [val] and [rel] are kept separate is that a single element in a construction can be a predicate taking arguments and at the same time be an argument for another predicate. For example, in *You should read this*, the element *read* is a predicate taking the argument *this*, but is itself an argument of the predicate *should* (Kay 1997).

The meronomic relations of a construction in Construction Grammar are analyzed in terms largely familiar from other syntactic theories (e.g., head, modifier, predicate, argument), although they are defined somewhat differently. In Construction Grammar, predicate-argument relations between elements are syntactic and semantic, and they are clearly distinguished from syntactic role relations between elements and the construction as a whole.

(III)   *What sorts of relations are found between constructions?*

Construction Grammar allows for meronomic as well as taxonomic relations between constructions. That is, a unit (part) of a construction may itself be another construction.

(IV)   *How is grammatical information stored in the construction taxonomy?*

We address both of these questions together because the answer to (III) is dependent on the answer to (IV).

Construction Grammar, like all construction grammars, allows taxonomic relations between constructions. In examining a construction taxonomy such as those illustrated in (12) and (13), it can be noted that what is more or less the same information is represented at multiple levels in the taxonomy. For example, the taxonomy in (12) appears to represent the fact that the object follows the verb at each of the lower three levels. Redundant representation of information need not be the case, however. One can represent the fact that the object has the grammatical function [gf obj] just once, at the highest possible level in the taxonomy—in (12), the [VERB OBJ] level. The constructions at the lower taxonomic levels will then inherit this property by virtue of being an instance of (an instance of) the

[VERB OBJ] construction. For example, the idiom *kick the habit* does not separately and redundantly represent the fact that *the habit* bears the Object grammatical function to *kick*; it inherits this feature from the [VERB OBJ] construction.

Following Goldberg (1995: 73–74), we describe a model in which information is represented nonredundantly and is inherited as a complete inheritance model. Construction Grammar is a complete inheritance model (Kay and Fillmore 1999: 7–8, 30–31). That is, Construction Grammar represents information only once in the construction taxonomy, at the highest (most schematic) level possible. One effect of a complete inheritance model is that a highly schematic construction may be posited that has only a linguistic form, since no semantic features are shared among all of the daughter constructions. An example of a construction without meaning is the Subject-Auxiliary Inversion construction as described by Fillmore (1999).

Kay and Fillmore also allow parts of a construction to inherit feature structures from another construction (Kay and Fillmore 1999: 18; see also Fillmore 1999; Kay 2002). They argue that the nonsubject *Wh*-question construction, instantiated in *Why did she leave him?*, is made up of a left-isolated (traditionally called "fronted") WH question word and an inverted clause. Thus, the nonsubject *Wh*-question construction as a whole inherits the feature structure of the schematic Left-Isolation construction, while the non-left-isolated part of the construction inherits the feature structures of the Subject-Auxiliary Inversion construction. In other words, parts of constructions can be children of other constructions, whose feature structures they inherit. Thus, Construction Grammar models meronomic relations between constructions by taxonomic relations between a parent construction and the corresponding parts of other constructions.

A related issue is the status of the information that is not partially specified in the construction. Consider again the case of argument structure constructions, which specify only the linking of participant roles in events with grammatical relations of the verbs denoting those events. They do not specify anything about the sentence's tense, aspect, mood, modality, polarity, and so on. Yet every English main clause expresses some tense, aspect, mood, modality, and polarity, in verb inflections, the presence of an auxiliary and/or negator, and in the syntax of the sentence type (declarative, interrogative, imperative). Moreover, argument structure is present in relative clauses, information ("*Wh-*") questions, the comparative, and other complex constructions in which arguments are syntactically separated from their predicate. How are the unspecified parts of a construction represented, and how are two partial specifications merged into one grammatical utterance?

Construction Grammar simply leaves unmentioned the unspecified features of a construction. Construction Grammar merges features from different constructions in a process called unification (see Shieber 1986 for a general account of unification-based grammars). We illustrate unification with a simplified example, the combination of the pronominal construction [*she*] with the construction [NP *sing-s*]. The pronominal construction [*she*] is in subject form and indicates that its referent is 3rd person, singular, and feminine. The verb in [NP *sing-s*] has a suffix indicating that the subject NP of the construction is 3rd-person singular. The features of the pronoun and the agreement inflection construction are given in (18a) and (18b):

(18)   a. *she*: [gf sbj]   b. [NP *sing-s*]: [gf sbj]
                [person 3rd]   [person 3rd]
                [number sg]   [number sg]
                [gender fem]

When [*she*] combines with [NP *sing-s*] to form [*she sing-s*], it must be specified that the features of the inflection are unified with the features of the pronoun; in Construction Grammar, the relevant sets of features are indexed in such a way that unification must apply. In unification, features match if they have the same value, as with [gf sbj], [person 3rd], and [number sg]; and if a feature is unspecified in one of the inputs, as with gender in (18b), the specified value from the other input (here, 18a) is included in the output. Hence the output of unifying the features in (18a) and (18b) is (19):

(19)   [***she*** *sing-s*]: [gf sbj]
                [person 3rd]
                [number sg]
                [gender fem]

The unification model allows one to leave the unspecified parts of the structure unrepresented if those unspecified parts can vary arbitrarily in their grammatical properties. The matching process requires matching of like parts, such that, for example, the tense inflection is placed on the verbal predicate, not the argument in the argument structure construction. This is the function of the indexes in Construction Grammar.

Finally, a unification model must somehow ensure that all the features present in an utterance get some value. For example, in an English declarative main clause utterance, the feature for Tense-Mood must have a value, and the subject element must be fully specified. Hence there must be some sort of output condition on the product of unification of constructions that partially specify an utterance so that the utterance is fully specified. This question has not been addressed in most theories of construction grammar at present.

5.2. Lakoff (1987) and Goldberg (1995)

Lakoff (1987) develops a variant of construction grammar in his important study of the *There*-construction in English. Lakoff's analysis emphasizes the complex, non-classical structure of the category of *There*-constructions, in keeping with his interest in prototypicality and radial category structure. Lakoff's student Goldberg also adopts Lakoff's emphasis in her analysis of argument structure constructions (Goldberg 1995).[3] Goldberg also addresses the other issues raised above, either explicitly or implicitly, in the context of analyzing argument structure constructions.

But the chief distinguishing characteristic of Lakoff's and Goldberg's version of construction grammar is the exploitation of principles of nonclassical categories in the analysis of relations between constructions.

(I)   *What is the status of the categories of the syntactic elements in construction grammar, given the existence of constructions?*

In her analysis of argument structure constructions, Goldberg (1995: 47–48) argues that one should analyze participant roles in complex events as derivative from the event itself. Thus, she posits participant roles for *rob/steal* as 'robber' and 'victim'. This analysis of participant roles is an example of a nonreductionist representation: the complex event or situation is treated as the primitive unit of semantic representation, and the definitions of the roles in the events are derived from the situation as a whole.

In contrast, Goldberg's analysis of syntactic roles and relations in argument structure constructions is reductionist. As in Construction Grammar, Goldberg employs a set of atomic primitive grammatical relations, such as Subject and Object, and primitive syntactic categories, such as Verb.

(II)   *What sorts of syntactic relations are posited?*

In Lakoff's (1987, 489) study of *There*-constructions, he represents constructions with the following parameters of form, which allow for relations between syntactic elements as well as relations between the elements and the construction as a whole:

   a. Syntactic elements (e.g., clause, noun phrases, verb, etc.)
   b. Lexical elements (e.g., *here, there, come, go, be*, etc.)
   c. Syntactic conditions (e.g., linear order of elements, grammatical relations such as subject and object, optionality of elements, etc.)
   d. Phonological conditions (e.g., presence or absence of stress, vowel length, etc.)

Goldberg's monograph analyzes argument structure constructions, focusing on relations between constructions (see immediately below), the semantics of argument structure, and the linking to syntactic roles. Because of the ambiguity of terms such as "Subject" between role and relation construals, Goldberg's representation of the syntactic structure of argument structure constructions (e.g., Goldberg 1995: 50–55) is compatible with either construal.

(III)   *What sorts of relations are found between constructions?*

Lakoff and Goldberg discuss a variety of relationships (links) among constructions, including taxonomic relations (Lakoff 1987, appendix 3; Goldberg 1995: 74–81). One of the links Goldberg discusses, the subpart link (78–79), corresponds to a meronomic link: "one construction is a *proper subpart* of another construction and exists independently" (78). A second type of link, the instance link (79–81), corresponds exactly to the taxonomic links described here.

Goldberg proposes a third type of construction link, the polysemy link, for subtypes of a construction that are identical in syntactic specification but different in their semantics. For example, Goldberg argues that the Ditransitive construction [Sbj Verb Obj1 Obj2] has a general meaning involving a transfer of possession of Obj2 to Obj1. However, there are semantic variations on this syntactically unified construction (Goldberg 1995: 38, figure 2.2):

(20)   *Sbj causes Obj1 to receive Obj2:*
       Joe gave Sally the ball.
(21)   *Conditions of satisfaction imply Sbj causes Obj1 to receive Obj2:*
       Joe promised Bob a car.
(22)   *Sbj enables Obj1 to receive Obj2:*
       Joe permitted Chris an apple.
(23)   *Sbj causes Obj1 not to receive Obj2:*
       Joe refused Bob a cookie.
(24)   *Sbj intends to cause Obj1 to receive Obj2:*
       Joe baked Bob a cake.
(25)   *Sbj acts to cause Obj1 to receive Obj2 at some future date:*
       Joe bequeathed Bob a fortune.

Goldberg treats the first sense (the one in example 20) as the central, prototypical sense and the other senses as extensions from the prototype. The extensions from the prototype inherit the syntactic construction schema from the prototype. The family of senses of the ditransitive construction form a radial category with the sense in (20) as the central sense.

The most important property of the polysemy analysis is that one construction sense is central and another is an extension from it. A clear case of extension from a central sense in constructions is a metaphorical extension, another type of link proposed by Goldberg, following Lakoff (1987) in his analysis of *There*-constructions.

Lakoff argues that many of the extensions of the central *There*-construction involve metaphorical extension. For example, the Perceptual Deictic *There*-construction, illustrated in (26), involves a number of metaphorical extensions from the Central Deictic *There*-construction illustrated in (27) (Lakoff 1987: 511, 509):

(26)   a. Here comes the beep.
       b. There's the beep.
(27)   There's Harry.

The Perceptual Deictic describes the impending (as in 26a) or just-realized (as in 26b) activation of a nonvisual perceptual stimulus, like an alarm clock that is about to go off. To express this meaning, the Presentational Deictic uses the metaphor of deictic motion of a physical entity in physical space. The extension of the Central Deictic to the Perceptual Deictic requires the following metaphorical mappings (Lakoff 1987: 511):

(28)   *Perceptual Deictic domain*   *Central Deictic domain*

NONVISUAL PERCEPTUAL SPACE	IS	PHYSICAL SPACE
PERCEPTS	ARE	ENTITIES
REALIZED	IS	DISTAL
SOON-TO-BE-REALIZED	IS	PROXIMAL
ACTIVATION	IS	MOTION

A metaphorical extension (or any other semantic extension, for that matter) need not establish a schema of which the basic construction and the metaphorical extension are both instantiations. Lakoff's "based on" link, like Goldberg's polysemy link, involves (normal) inheritance of both syntactic and semantic properties and so is not unlike a taxonomic link. Lakoff, however, does not posit a superordinate Deictic *There*-construction schema. On the other hand, Goldberg argues that there is a superordinate schema subsuming both a central construction and its metaphorical extension (1995: 81–89; see also 1991).

(IV)   *How is information stored in the construction taxonomy?*

Goldberg allows for the representation of information at all levels in the taxonomic hierarchy of constructions. Goldberg describes such a model as a full-entry model (Goldberg 1995: 73–74). A full-entry model may not require inheritance, but in fact many full-entry models do employ inheritance, since it is not necessarily the case that all information is stored at all levels in the grammar. An important variant on the complete inheritance model is what Goldberg calls normal inheritance (Goldberg 1995: 73; citing Flickinger, Pollard, and Wasow 1985). Normal inheritance is a method for accommodating the fact that much of what we know about a category is not true of every instance of a category. To use a much-hackneyed example from knowledge representation in Artificial Intelligence: we know that most birds fly to the point that if we hear reference to "a bird," we will assume that it can fly. Of course, if we are further informed that the bird in question is an ostrich or a penguin or that it has a broken wing or has had its wings clipped, we would cancel that assumption. One model for representing this information is to store the information 'can-fly' with the category BIRD, instead of the many instances of bird species and individual birds that can fly. The property 'can-fly' is inherited in those cases, but inheritance can be blocked if it conflicts with information in the more specific case, such as penguins, ostriches, birds with clipped or broken wings, dead birds, and so on.

Lakoff uses normal inheritance in his analysis of *There*-constructions. Normal inheritance is part of Lakoff's "based on" link between constructions (Lakoff 1987: 508); Goldberg uses normal inheritance as well (1995: 74). For example, Lakoff argues that the Presentational Deictic construction in (29) is based on the Central Deictic construction in (30) (Lakoff 1987: 520, 482):

(29)   There in the alley had gathered a large crowd of roughnecks.
(30)   There's Harry with the red jacket on.

One of the properties of the Central Deictic is that the verb must occur in the simple present tense, because the semantics of the Central Deictic is to point out a referent in the speech act situation (Lakoff 1987: 490–91). The Presentational Deictic is based on the Central Deictic but also specifies that the verb may appear in a variety of tenses as expressed in auxiliaries (Lakoff 1987: 521). This specification blocks the inheritance of the simple present-tense requirement from the Central Deictic.

It might appear to the reader that *a priori* the inheritance model (complete or normal) is to be preferred for reasons of economy. However, most cognitive linguists argue that a cognitively based grammar should not be constructed in an *a priori* fashion, because grammatical knowledge is a psychological phenomenon (see Sinha, this volume, chapter 49). Clearly, speakers do not store a representation of every utterance they have ever used or heard. Speakers form schemas that generalize over categories of utterances heard and used. But it does not necessarily follow from this observation that speakers store every piece of grammatical knowledge only once. It does not even necessarily follow that speakers form a more schematic category for every linguistic generalization that clever linguists have found (see Croft 1998).

The model of representation of grammatical knowledge cannot be separated from the processes that use it, despite our artificial separation of representation and process into separate chapters in this book. A complete inheritance model maximizes storage parsimony; that is, it minimizes the redundant storage of information. A complete inheritance model thus requires maximum online processing in order to access and use the information in the production and comprehension of utterances (see Barsalou 1992: 180–81; Goldberg 1995: 74). A full-entry model maximizes computing parsimony: as much information as possible is stored in multiple places, so that online computation is minimized during production and comprehension (Barsalou 1992: 180–81).

On the whole, the psychological evidence suggests that "concepts and properties in human knowledge are organized with little concern for elegance and [storage] parsimony" (Barsalou 1992: 180). This does not mean that a full-entry model is to be preferred in all situations, however: such a model is just as aprioristic as the inheritance model. In section 6, I will describe a model that offers predictions as to when grammatical information is stored and when it is not, the usage-based model.

5.3. Cognitive Grammar as a Construction Grammar

Cognitive Grammar is a detailed, carefully worked out theory of syntax and semantics (Langacker 1987, 1990, 1991, 1999; this volume, chapter 17). Langacker's seminal volume (Langacker 1987) gives an abstract exposition of the framework, and although the word construction rarely appears, in fact a completely different set of terms is used, Cognitive Grammar's model of syntactic representation is a construction grammar model. The distinguishing feature of Cognitive Grammar as a construction grammar is its emphasis on symbolic and semantic definitions of theoretical constructs traditionally analyzed as purely syntactic.

As noted above, Langacker defines a grammar as a structured inventory of conventional linguistic units. The conventional linguistic units are symbolic units, and their two halves, form and meaning. Cognitive Grammar emphasizes the symbolic character of the linguistic sign (to use the Saussurean term). Langacker argues that the properties of constructions, as broadly defined, fall into two categories, which we describe here as form (the signifier) and meaning or function (the signified): the formal properties are syntactic, morphological, and phonological, and the functional properties are semantic, pragmatic, and discourse-functional. A construction is thus a symbolic unit, linking form and function as a symbol or sign.

To a large extent, the division between semantics, pragmatics, and discourse is arbitrary. The important distinction is between what is conventionally associated with a construction and what is not conventionally associated with it, but instead conveyed in particular contexts of use. Hence we may group together all functional properties as part of the conventional function of the construction. Langacker describes this structure as the semantic pole of a symbolic unit.

The formal properties of a construction also appear to be disparate. Langacker groups them together under the term phonological pole. The term "phonological pole" may sound odd: syntax at least is not "phonological," particularly with respect to schematic constructions. However, Langacker argues that a schema such as Noun in the description of a construction should be thought of as phonologically as well as lexically schematic: the schema ranges over possible nouns, and those nouns are all phonologically contentful, even if their exact phonological form cannot be specified schematically. (Cognitive Grammar and Construction Grammar, like Pollard and Sag's (1993) Head-Driven Phrase Structure Grammar, eschews the use of phonologically "null" or "empty" elements.)

In the Cognitive Grammar representation of a construction, the symbolic unit itself must link the two poles of the construction. Langacker describes the link as a symbolic correspondence. Symbolic correspondences are the Cognitive Grammar equivalents to the linking rules between syntactic structures and semantic structures in the componential organization of a grammar described in section 2. There must be a symbolic correspondence that holds between the form (phonological pole) of the construction as a whole and the meaning or function (semantic pole) of the construction as a whole. Recall that a construction such as *The X-er, the Y-er* has some sort of idiosyncrasy such that its form and meaning are not predictable from more general rules (constructions). Hence, it must be an independent symbolic unit in its own right.

Cognitive Grammar also has a uniform representation of all grammatical knowledge. Langacker argues that all semantic, pragmatic, and discourse-functional properties are ultimately conceptual, a part of what he calls semantic space, which he describes as "the multifaceted field of conceptual potential within which thought and conceptualization unfold" (Langacker 1987: 76). He argues that phonological space, the space in which linguistic form is defined, is also a subset of semantic space, since in terms of the structure of grammatical knowledge, the formal structures of language are also concepts (76–81).

(I)   *What is the status of the categories of the syntactic elements in construction grammar, given the existence of constructions?*

Cognitive Grammar argues that fundamental syntactic categories such as Noun, Verb, Subject, and Object are abstract (schematic) semantic construals of the conceptual content of their denotations. Thus, fundamental syntactic categories have an essentially semantic basis, but in terms of the construal of experience, not in terms of semantic classes.

For example, the category "Noun" represents the construal of an entity as a "thing" (a technical term in Cognitive Grammar; Langacker 1987: 189). That is, the entity is construed as nonrelational and atemporal. This construal is the default one imagined with a prototypical noun in the traditional grammatical sense, such as *cat*. A cat is an individual that is (as a noun) conceptualized without presupposing reference to another entity. In this respect, *cat* contrasts with *feline* (adjective), which construes the entity as a property of another entity (e.g., *feline grace*), or *pounce* (verb), which construes the entity as an event which presupposes the existence of participants of that event. A cat (as a noun) is also construed atemporally, that is, as a single Gestalt that does not unfold over mental time (i.e., it is summarily scanned). This construal contrasts with *pounce* (verb), in which the event is construed as unfolding over mental time (sequentially scanned).

The role of conceptualization in the semantics of syntactic categories is demonstrated when applied to nonprototypical examples. The event of a *pounce* (noun) is construed nonrelationally and atemporally. The pounce (noun) profiles just the action; the participant of the action is deprofiled into the base or frame of the concept. Also, the pounce is construed atemporally, as an event that is conceived holistically in the mind, even though it takes place in an interval of external time.

Langacker has developed semantic construal analyses of a wide range of syntactic categories, including parts of speech, grammatical roles (Subject and Object), the count/mass distinction, various English Tense-Aspect inflections and auxiliaries, the English possessives -'s and *of*, ergativity, English complementizers and complement types, Cora locatives, and the Yuman auxiliary (see Langacker 1987, 1990, 1991, 1999). In the course of constructing these analyses, Langacker has developed a sophisticated analysis of conceptualization processes, including profiling, scope of predication, active zone, scanning, grounding, reference point, subjectification, the trajector-landmark opposition, and conceptual planes, as well as drawing on other cognitive linguistic conceptual constructs such as mental spaces (Fauconnier 1985), the Figure-Ground distinction, and viewing (Talmy 2000a, 2000b).

One question that can be raised about the Cognitive Grammar analysis of grammatical categories is the relationship between the abstract semantic construal definitions and the variation in both formal distribution and semantic polysemy of such categories across languages. It has been suggested that cross-linguistic variation in the universal semantic categories can be accommodated in terms of conventionalized construal (e.g., Langacker 1990: 12): the same semantic category is found everywhere, but the construal of specific experiences as belonging to the semantic category is language-specific. But it is not clear whether one can distinguish conventionalized construal from simple polysemy (that is, semantic variation across languages).

(II)   *What sorts of syntactic relations are posited?*

Cognitive Grammar takes a more radical departure from the more familiar analyses of relations among parts of a construction (Langacker 1987: chapter 8). The Cognitive Grammar concept of valence, like that of Construction Grammar, is symbolic. Unlike Construction Grammar, however, valence in Cognitive Grammar is gradient. We will begin by looking at a straightforward predicate-argument relation, where the Cognitive Grammar and Construction Grammar notions of valence coincide, and then examine the extension of valence in Cognitive Grammar to other semantic relations.

In the sentence *Hannah sings, sings* is a predicate because it is relational. The relationality of *sings* is due to the fact that singing requires a singer. Hence, the semantic structure for *sings* includes a schematic singer as a substructure. In *Hannah sings, Hannah* is an argument: it is nonrelational, and it fills the role of the singer for *sings*. *Hannah* is nonrelational because the concept of a person does not presuppose another concept. Langacker's term for an argument filling the role of a predicate is that the argument "elaborates" the relevant substructure of the predicate. The substructure that can be elaborated by an argument is an elaboration site (or e-site; Langacker 1987: 304). These relations are illustrated in (31):

(31)

As we noted above, a unit in a construction may be simultaneously a predicate and an argument, as is *read* in *You should read this*. How is this possible? It is because the event of reading elaborates a substructure of the modality expressed by *should*, and the thing read, *this*, elaborates a substructure of the event of reading. Hence, predicate and argument status—valence—is relative: they depend on what two semantic structures are being compared.

Not only is valence relative, it is gradient. In a sentence such as (32), *I* and what I am reading are traditionally analyzed as complements of *read* while *on the train* is an adjunct to *read* (we ignore the progressive *be* in this example):

(32)   I was reading this on the train.

Complements are arguments of a predicate: reading inherently involves a reader and a thing read. Adjuncts are predicates and their head is the argument: *on the train* inherently involves a Figure whose location is described by the spatial relation. Hence, *read* elaborates a substructure of *on the train*. But this description is an oversimplification. Reading is a localizable activity: reading takes place in a location, as well as involving a reader and a thing read. This is not true of all predicates; one cannot say, for instance, that *John was widowed on the train. Hence, the location of the reading event is a substructure of the semantic structure of *read*, and *on the train* also elaborates that substructure of *read*.

The solution to this apparent paradox is that the substructure of *read* that is elaborated by *on the train* in (32) is much less salient in the characterization of the reading event than the substructures of *read* elaborated by *I* and *this*. Conversely, the substructure of *on the train* that is elaborated by *read* is highly salient in the characterization of the spatial relation. *On the train* is more of an adjunct of *read* than a complement because *read* elaborates a salient substructure of *on the train*, while *on the train* elaborates a not very salient substructure of *read*. The relative strength of the two relations is illustrated in (33):

(33)

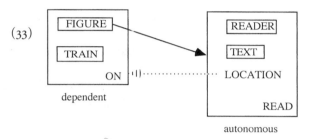

Langacker adopts the terms "autonomous" and "dependent" to describe the gradient reinterpretation of the predicate-argument distinction. The definition of autonomy and dependence is: "One structure, *D*, is dependent on the other, *A*, to the extent that *A* constitutes an elaboration of a salient substructure within *D*" (Langacker 1987: 300); and conversely *A* is autonomous relative to *D* to the extent to which it does not elaborate a salient substructure of *D*. In (33), *on the train* is dependent on *read* because *read* elaborates the highly salient figure role of the locative relation *on the train*. Conversely, *read* is autonomous relative to *on the train* because *on the train* elaborates only the not very salient substructure of the location of the reading event.

Autonomy and dependence are properties of any pair of conceptual structures. Thus, one has unipolar as well as bipolar autonomy/dependence. For example, at the phonological pole a vowel is autonomous—it can occur as the sole member of a syllable—while consonants are dependent—they must be supported by a vowel (Langacker 1987: 298–99). A bipolar autonomy/dependence relation would be the verb-prepositional phrase relation in (32): a circumstantial prepositional phrase like *on the train* is dependent on *read*.

The Cognitive Grammar analysis of "head," "modifier," and so on is both similar to and different from the analysis in Construction Grammar. In Construction Grammar, the roles represent a relation between the parts of a construction and the whole and are defined syntactically. In Cognitive Grammar, the analogous concepts also represent a relation between the parts of a construction and the whole, but they are defined semantically and symbolically.

Cognitive Grammar defines a semantic relation between part and whole as the profile determinant: the profile determinant is the part of the construction whose semantic profile the whole construction "inherits" (Langacker 1987: 289). The profile is the concept designated by the unit against the background knowledge presupposed by that concept (see Langacker 1987: chapter 2).

Langacker (1987: 309) combines the concepts of profile determinacy and autonomy/dependence to define "head," "complement," and "modifier" in the intuitively expected way: a head is a dependent predication that is a profile determinant; a complement is an autonomous predication that is not a profile determinant; and a modifier is a dependent predication that is not a profile determinant.

(III)   *What sorts of relations are found between constructions?*

Langacker advocates what he calls a unified approach to categorization (1987: chapter 10). A category has a nonclassical structure, in that there is typically a prototypical member or set of members, and nonprototypical members are categorized by extension from the prototypical members. However, it is also possible for there to exist a schema subsuming both prototype and extension, which has a classical category structure, with necessary and sufficient conditions specifying its instances:

(34)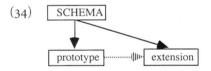

Langacker's model of categorization is of course applied also to constructions. Hence, for Langacker, as for Lakoff and Goldberg, one may have both construction schemas and also nonclassical relations between constructions, such as prototype-extension relations, including metaphorical extensions.

(IV)   *How is information stored in the construction taxonomy?*

Cognitive Grammar is neither a complete inheritance model nor a full-entry model, in the extreme sense of the latter term as storing information at all levels in the hierarchy. Cognitive Grammar is a usage-based model, in which the establishment of schematic constructions is the result of language use. In particular, one cannot automatically assume that speakers of a language have induced a highly schematic construction, even if linguists can come up with an analysis with such a schema. Nor can one assume that speakers store information only at the most schematic level in the hierarchy. In the usage-based model, the existence of a highly schematic construction is ultimately a psychological question. In this respect, Cognitive Grammar differs significantly from Construction Grammar, which does not make any claims for the psychological reality of its complete inheritance model.

The principles of the usage-based model governing the storage of grammatical information are based on research on language use, language acquisition, and language change. The usage-based model and evidence supporting it is described in section 6.

5.4. Radical Construction Grammar

Radical Construction Grammar (Croft 2001, 2005) was developed to account for typological variation in a construction grammar framework and to address certain issues of syntactic argumentation. Radical Construction Grammar adopts the nonclassical category structure of the Lakoff-Goldberg theory and of Cognitive Grammar and the usage-based model of Cognitive Grammar. The chief innovations of Radical Construction Grammar in comparison to the theories of construction grammar described above is in the analysis of syntactic categories and syntactic relations. Radical Construction Grammar differs from the preceding theories (except, possibly, Cognitive Grammar) in a thoroughly nonreductionist approach to constructions and in rejecting syntactic relations between elements in a construction.

(I)   *What is the status of the categories of the syntactic elements, given the existence of constructions?*

The standard analysis of meronomic relations between syntactic structures has been adopted by Construction Grammar. In this analysis, a construction such as the intransitive or transitive construction is made up of parts, and those parts are themselves independent constructions. For example, various clausal constructions have verbs, which are analyzed as belonging to the same part of speech, in part because they have the same inflections (present in 3rd-person singular -*s* and non-3rd-person singular zero, past in -*ed* or other allomorphs):

(35)   Present 3rd-person singular:
     a. *Intransitive:* Toni dance**s**.
     b. *Transitive:* Toni play**s** badminton.
(36)   Present non-3rd-person singular:
     a. *Intransitive:* We dance-**Ø**.
     b. *Transitive:* We play-**Ø** badminton.
(37)   Past:
     a. *Intransitive:* We danc**ed**.
     b. *Transitive:* We play**ed** badminton.

In other words, the same units occur as the parts of many different constructions. Ultimately, the decomposition of a construction will lead to a set of basic or primitive elements which cannot be analyzed further and out of which constructions are built. These atomic elements include syntactic categories such as Verb or Noun and relations such as Subject or Object, and so on. A model of grammatical structure of this type is a reductionist model: more complex structures are treated as built up out of primitive and ultimately atomic units. In the example given here, the atomic units are the basic categories and relations.[4]

The reductionist model does not capture certain empirical facts about the distribution of words. For example, while many English verbs occur in either the Transitive or Intransitive constructions, many others do not:

(38)   a. Judith danced.
        b. Judith danced a kopanica.
(39)   a. Judith slept.
        b. *Judith slept bed.
(40)   a. *Judith found.
        b. Judith found a 20-dollar bill.

One solution is to divide Verbs into Transitive Verbs and Intransitive Verbs. If so, then a decision must be made about verbs such as *dance* which occur in both constructions: Do they simultaneously belong to both subclasses? Or do they form a third distinct class? One effect of dividing verbs into transitive verbs and intransitive verbs is that one essentially defines the categories in terms of the construction(s) they occur in, Transitive or Intransitive.

One can deal with such problems in the reductionist model by adding exception features that prevent certain category members from occurring in the unacceptable constructions, as in (39b) and (40a). Again, the effect is that one is introducing a feature that specifies the category in terms of the construction it occurs in/does not occur in.

Radical Construction Grammar takes a different approach to the relations of constructions to their parts. It proposes that constructions are the basic or primitive elements of syntactic representation and defines categories in terms of the constructions they occur in. For example, the elements of the Intransitive construction are defined as Intransitive Subject and Intransitive Verb, and the categories are defined as those words or phrases that occur in the relevant role in the Intransitive construction.

Radical Construction Grammar is a nonreductionist model because it takes the whole complex structure as basic and defines the parts in terms of their occurrence in a role in the complex structure. In effect, Radical Construction Grammar takes to its logical conclusion one of the strategies for handling these problems in reductionist theories, namely the subdividing of classes and the employment of exception features which essentially specify which constructions a particular word or phrase occurs in.

Constructions are individuated like any other conceptual object, by categorization. Constructions possess formal features, including word order, patterns of contiguity, and specific morphemes (or very small classes of morphemes) in particular roles. Constructions are also symbolic units and possess often discrete meanings. Radical Construction Grammar assumes a nonclassical category model and allows for prototypes and extensions of constructions, as well as the possibility of gradience between construction types.

(II)   *What sorts of syntactic relations are posited?*

Radical Construction Grammar, like Construction Grammar and Cognitive Grammar, represents the role of a part of a construction in the whole construction. Radical Construction Grammar differs from Construction Grammar in that it defines relations between parts of a construction in purely semantic terms, that is, there are no syntactic relations in Radical Construction Grammar.

One motivation for the Radical Construction Grammar analysis is that relations between syntactic elements are not strictly necessary in a construction grammar framework from the point of view of language comprehension. Consider the phrase *the song*, illustrated in (41) with the semantic relation between [DEF] and [SONG] indicated by a link (labeled r):

(41)

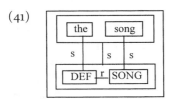

If a hearer recognizes the phrase *the song* as an instance of the construction [[DEF/ *the*] [THING/*Noun*]]—that is, can retrieve the semantic structure of the whole construction, can identify the elements of the construction (i.e., the words *the* and *song*), and can identify the corresponding components of the semantic pole (i.e., [DEF] and [THING])—then the hearer can identify the semantic relation r by virtue of the semantic relation between [DEF] and [THING] in the semantic pole of the construction. Hence, the hearer need not rely on any syntactic relation between *the* and *song*.

In Radical Construction Grammar, the various morphosyntactic properties that are taken to express syntactic relations in other theories—case marking, agreement, adpositions, word order, contiguity, and so on—are interpreted as expressing the symbolic links from the elements in the phonological pole of the construction to their corresponding components in the semantic pole of the construction. The combination of morphosyntactic properties in an utterance taken as a whole aid the hearer in identifying a construction. For example, the combination of auxiliary *be*, the past participle form of the verb, and the preposition *by*, in the proper syntactic combination with the subject phrase, the verb, and the oblique phrase, uniquely identify the passive construction, while the individual elements identify the action (verb inflection and position after auxiliary), the agent (*by* plus oblique phrase), and patient (subject position).

(III)   *What sorts of relations are found between constructions?*

In Radical Construction Grammar, each part (unit) of a construction constitutes a category whose members are defined solely by their occurrence in that role in the construction. In order to differentiate categories, we append the name of the construction to the labels for each unit in the construction. A representation of the intransitive and transitive constructions is given in (42):

(42)

Intransitive construction: Transitive construction:

The establishment of a category Verb is a linguistic generalization over the categories Intransitive Verb and Transitive Verb. This generalization is thus a taxonomic relationship, with Verb superordinate to Intransitive Verb and Transitive Verb.

    However, one cannot posit a superordinate category such as Verb, or any linguistic category, without linguistic motivation. The basis of the linguistic generalization of a superordinate category such as Verb must be its occurrence as the category in some other construction. The standard basis for positing a category Verb is the ability of its members to be inflected with the tense/agreement suffixes. In a construction grammar, this linguistic fact is essentially another construction, the morphological construction [MVerb-TnsAgr]. We use the label MVerb (Morphological Verb) to emphasize that this category is defined by a morphological construction, namely its occurrence with the Tense/Agreement suffixes (abbreviated TnsAgr). This additional fact is represented, as in (43), with the irrelevant argument elements suppressed for clarity:

(43)

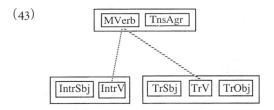

Radical Construction Grammar essentially hypothesizes that meronomic relations between a constructional whole and its parts are solely internal to the construction. In other words, Radical Construction Grammar rejects meronomic links between constructions and replaces them with taxonomic links between parts of different constructions. By using taxonomic links for parts of a construction, Radical Construction Grammar explicitly represents the process of analyzing parts of a construction as an abstraction or schematization process.

(IV)   *How is information stored in the construction taxonomy?*

In Radical Construction Grammar, as in Cognitive Grammar, it is assumed that information may be stored redundantly in the construction taxonomy and that the principles governing the level at which information is stored redundantly are determined by the usage-based model. The next section describes that model and its relationship to the dynamic aspects of language: use, acquisition, and change.

6. CONSTRUCTION GRAMMAR AND THE USAGE-BASED MODEL

The usage-based model is a model of grammatical representation in which language use determines grammatical representation. Specifically, frequency of use and similarity of form and meaning are the determining factors for the structure of grammatical knowledge in the mind. The basic principles of the dynamic usage-based model have been developed largely in the area of morphology (see Bybee 1985, 1995, 2001, and references cited therein). The basic principles may be formulated in the following four hypotheses.

> *Hypothesis 1:* The storage of a word form, regular or irregular, is a function of its token frequency.

Token frequency is the frequency of occurrence in language use of individual tokens of a grammatical type, such as the English regular past-tense forms. The usage-based model predicts that the degree of entrenchment of a form in a speaker's mind (Bybee's 1985 notion of autonomy) is a function of its token frequency, hence the concentration of irregular word forms in high-frequency items. There is also some evidence for the independent storage of high-frequency individual word forms even when those word forms are fully regular.

> *Hypothesis 2:* The productivity of a schema is a function of the type frequency of the instances of the schema.

Type frequency is the frequency of word types that conform to a schema. For example, the type frequency of the English regular past-tense inflection is the frequency of all the different verbs that use the regular past-tense inflection. Bybee (1985) argues that type frequency determines productivity. One consequence of this hypothesis is that productivity is predicted to come in degrees: schemas with a low type frequency will have a limited degree of productivity. This appears to be the case: for example, the English irregular past with [ʌ(ŋ)(g/k)] is slightly productive (compare colloquial or dialectal *sneak/snuck, bring/brung*).

> *Hypothesis 3:* In addition to source-oriented morphological rules/schemas, there also exist product-oriented schemas, which cannot be easily represented by rules.

Many traditional, structuralist and generative theories of morphology assume the existence of rules that derive one word from another, such as the past verb form from the present verb form. In those cases where such a rule is possible, Bybee (1985) speaks of a source-oriented schema, that is, a schema for a word form that can be formulated in terms of a single simple morphological operation on the alleged source form. However, there is a class of schemas which Bybee calls product-oriented schemas, in which no simple process derives the alleged product form from the alleged source form. For example, the English past schema [ʌ(ŋ)(g/k)] is a phonologically coherent and partially productive past-tense schema, but the alleged source forms, the present-tense forms, are phonologically so varied that no single rule can systematically derive the past-tense forms from the present-tense forms. The existence of product-oriented schemas argues against rules linking one form to another and supports the view that schemas are formed as taxonomic hierarchies over semantically similar forms.

> *Hypothesis 4*:   Strength of connection between word forms, and thus forces influencing their phonological shape (among other things), is a function of similarity. Similarity is measurable by comparing words to each other in both meaning and form; similarity in meaning is much stronger than similarity in form.

It was noted in section 4 that the taxonomic hierarchy is really a taxonomic web: a construction has multiple parents. The taxonomic web would be a far more complex organization of constructions than a taxonomic hierarchy. While one cannot deny the existence of the taxonomic web, it is certainly the case in morphology at least that some word forms are "closer" to each other than to other related word forms; this is the basis for the intuitive organization of forms into paradigms in traditional morphology. Bybee (1985) argues that the principle governing closeness is essentially semantic similarity, although formal similarity also plays a reinforcing role. More often, one finds analogical reformation of a paradigm so as to bring formal similarity into line with semantic similarity (i.e., paradigmatic iconicity; Croft 2003).

In principle, all four hypotheses should be supported in syntax as well as morphology, if the construction grammar model is valid. Research on the usage-based model in syntax has only begun at this point, although there is significant research in language acquisition and language change in the usage-based model, as will be seen below (see also Bybee this volume, chapter 36; Tomasello, this volume, chapter 41).

Bybee and Thompson (1997) present evidence for the role of token frequency of constructions (defined as token frequency of the substantive elements in the construction) in grammatical organization. They observe that the syntax of the English auxiliaries is conservative in that they invert with the subject in questions and precede the negator. All verbs had this possibility in Middle English, but it was lost in Modern English. Bybee and Thompson argue that the token frequency of the auxiliaries was high enough that the Subject Inversion and Postposed Negation constructions survived with auxiliaries when it was lost with other verbs. Bybee and Thompson also note that the French Subjunctive Verb construction is disappearing from the spoken language but survives in the highly frequent main clause verb *falloir* 'have to' and/or in the most frequent complement verbs.

Cruse and I argue that product-oriented syntactic schemas exist (Croft and Cruse 2004: 313–18). For example, the English Polarity Question and Declarative Negation constructions have syntactic schemas, [Aux Sbj . . . ?] and [Sbj Aux-*n't* . . .], that are more coherent than the input schemas, which may have zero, one, or more auxiliary verbs. Other product-oriented schemas include the English Declarative, which requires an overt subject even when one is semantically lacking (*It's raining*) or is extraposed (*It seems that it's never sunny in Manchester*); the so-called Extraction constructions such as the relative clause, information, and *It*-cleft constructions, in which the "extracted" element is initial no matter what position it occurs in in the simple declarative; and the Japanese Passive, in which the passive subject is initial and the verb takes the passive -*(r)are* suffix, no matter what position the subject occurs in in the active construction.

Finally, there is evidence that constructions are organized in terms of semantic similarity. For example, the historical shift of the English negative adjectival imperative from *Be not cruel!* to *Don't be cruel!* makes the negative adjectival imperative syntactically more similar to the semantically more similar negative verbal imperative *Don't jump!* than the semantically more distant negative adjectival declarative *She isn't cruel* (Croft and Cruse 2004: 320–31). Semantic similarity is also the governing principle underlying the semantic map model, used in typology and in Radical Construction Grammar (Croft 2003: 133–39; van der Auwera and Nuyts, this volume, chapter 40). The semantic map model maps the function of constructions in a conceptual space such that the functions of a single construction form a connected region in the conceptual space. If this principle is followed in cross-linguistic comparison, ideally one can construct a conceptual space such that the semantic maps of any language's constructions will form a connected region in the conceptual space. If so, then the conceptual space is structured in terms of the semantic similarity of functions as encoded in linguistic forms across languages. The organization of conceptual space allows one to arrange constructions in terms of semantic similarity; the usage-based model predicts that this arrangement will be reflected in the formal syntactic similarity of these constructions to some degree.

The usage-based model allows construction grammar to accommodate dynamic aspects of language: not simply language use, as discussed above, but also language acquisition and language change.

Research on the acquisition of syntax by Tomasello, Lieven, Pine, and others offers evidence for a usage-based, inductive model of the acquisition of syntax. Evidence from very detailed longitudinal studies of early language development demonstrates that children are in fact extremely conservative language learners (Braine 1976 is an early important study along these lines; for more recent studies, see Tomasello 2000, 2003; this volume, chapter 41). Children's earliest multiword utterances demonstrate that children use verbs and other predicates in only one construction at a time (Tomasello 1992; Lieven, Pine, and Baldwin 1997; Pine and Lieven 1997; Tomasello et al. 1997; Pine, Lieven, and Rowland 1998).

The main exception to this highly specific acquisition process is that children do substitute different object names in a single participant role in a construction from early on. Tomasello (1992) proposed the Verb Island Hypothesis, namely that verbs and other predicates form "islands" of a single verb plus a single construction, before joining together the "islands" into a construction network such as that illustrated in (12) above.

In other words, children do not utilize schematic categories such as [VERB] or schematic constructions such as the Transitive construction [SBJ VERB OBJ] in their early acquisition, whether these schematic structures are innate or not. Instead, children begin with very low level generalizations based around a single predicate and a single construction in which that predicate occurs and only later in acquisition learn more schematic categories and constructions.

Although children substitute object names or "nouns" early in acquisition, it does not appear that this implies that children acquire a schematic [NOUN] or [DETERMINER NOUN]NP category early on. Pine and Lieven (1997) found that at the earliest stage of learning nouns and determiners, children also proceed in a piecemeal fashion. In their study, Pine and Lieven found that although children use a variety of nouns with both *a* and *the*, the nouns they use with *a* and the nouns they use with *the* overlap very little at first. Instead, it appeared that children learned nouns with one determiner or that the determiner use was associated with larger structures in which the noun and determiner occur, such as [*in the* X] or [*That's a* X]. Other studies indicate that children begin with "islands" other than verbs (Pine, Lieven, and Rowland 1998), that acquisition of verbal inflections is piecemeal and sensitive to frequency (Rubino and Pine 1998, on Brazilian Portuguese; Gathercole, Sebastián, and Soto 1999 found the same in the acquisition of Spanish, but morphological complexity also played a role).

These and other language acquisition studies suggest that a careful, detailed examination of the actual course of development of children's language acquisition conforms to the predictions of the usage-based model. Children begin with very narrow construction types, even specific to individual verbs and nouns, and gradually build more schematic grammatical constructions over time. The rate of learning and generalization is influenced by the relative frequency of the constructions in the caregivers' input. The order of acquisition is also sensitive to the semantic distance between constructions.

Similar results are found in the detailed examinations of the paths of syntactic change. As many historical linguists have observed in detailed studies, the birth and growth of a construction proceeds in an incremental fashion, not terribly unlike the expansion from "islands" of highly specific constructions as in child language acquisition.

One example of a syntactic change, cast in a cognitive linguistic framework, is Israel's analysis of the development of the *way* construction, illustrated in (44) (1996: 218):

(44)   a. Rasselas dug his way out of the Happy Valley.
       b. The wounded soldiers limped their way across the field.
       c. ?Convulsed with laughter, she giggled her way up the stairs.

All of the *way*-construction examples given in (44) use a possessed direct object *way* and require a complement describing the path of motion. Example (44a) describes a means of achieving the motion along the path; (44b) describes a manner of motion along the path; and example (44c) describes an incidental activity of the subject as she travels along the path. The *way*-construction is also syntactically and semantically idiosyncratic: the verbs in the *way*-construction are normally intransitive, and their meaning does not normally entail motion.

Using data from the *Oxford English Dictionary* and the *Oxford University Press Corpus of Contemporary English*, Israel argues that the modern *way*-construction grew gradually from two different, more narrowly used *way*-constructions, the Means and Manner constructions (a third source, the acquisition or continued possession of a path, shrank rather than expanded, although it remains in certain common instances such as *find one's way*; Israel 1996: 221, note 3). The Manner construction began as a special case of the Middle English [*go one's* PATH] construction and was originally found with only the most common general motion verbs, no more than sixteen verbs before 1700 (Israel 1996: 221). The Means *way*-construction does not emerge until around 1650 and begins with verbs describing path clearing (*cut, furrow out*), road building (*pave, smooth*) and forcible motion (*force out*, Israel 1996: 223). In the nineteenth century, the Means and Manner *way*-constructions appear to merge. At the same time that the class of verbs in the *way*-construction is expanding, the overall syntactic form of the construction becomes narrower, eventually prohibiting other nouns than *way* and requiring an obligatory path expression (Israel 1996: 221, 226).

This (common) pattern in syntactic change illustrates how a new construction emerges from an often highly specific instance of an existing construction schema and then expands in its own direction. A usage-based model can account for this pattern in that it allows for the entrenchment of specific instances of construction schemas, which function as "islands" from which a new construction expands, establishing and generalizing a new construction schema with its own syntactic and semantic peculiarities.

7. PROSPECTS FOR THE FUTURE

Construction grammar is a flourishing area of grammatical theorizing, as evidenced by the range of construction grammar theories that have been proposed. On the other hand, construction grammar is also a relatively new area, and a number of aspects of constructing a model of grammatical representation need further development. Some of these aspects have been alluded to in the course of this presentation.

Any model of grammatical representation that aspires to be psychologically plausible, as construction grammar aspires to be, must also include a model of utterance comprehension and production and of grammatical acquisition and change (see also this volume, chapters 41 and 49).

Utterance comprehension involves the categorization of the utterance as an instance of the various constructions that make it up and the construction of a proper semantic interpretation of the utterance. Ideally, comprehension should be modeled by an interactive activation network model, to reflect priming and other effects that have been documented in psycholinguistic experiments.

Utterance production is a more difficult task. Construction Grammar employs a unification model (see section 5.1) for utterance production (and comprehension). But other construction grammar models allow for the novel construal of words and phrases in sentences (see Verhagen, this volume, chapter 3), which the feature-matching unification algorithm would fail to model. Construction grammars of course represent construction knowledge schematically, to a greater or lesser degree. A model of utterance production would have to specify when all that must be instantiated is in fact properly instantiated for an utterance to be produced.

Language acquisition research in a construction-based framework has made major progress in understanding the earliest stages of syntactic development. An important question which is now attracting more attention is the later development of highly schematic constructions from the more substantive structures that children begin with. Historical linguistic research, both philological and sociolinguistic, has been usage-based since long before the usage-based model evolved; but relatively few studies have taken a construction grammar approach to syntactic change.

Finally, as noted in the last section, an important desideratum for most construction grammars is the role of the usage-based model in syntactic representation. Many fundamental questions remain to be addressed: How many tokens is enough to entrench a linguistic unit? How many types are enough to give rise to some degree of productivity? What is the role of timing of exposure in facilitating entrenchment? How similar do tokens/types have to be to facilitate entrenchment of a grammatical schema? How does one measure grammatical and semantic similarity in order to compare its effect to that of token/type frequency? Substantive answers to these questions will greatly advance the grammatical theory of Cognitive Linguistics.

NOTES

1. This analysis is very similar to the rule-to-rule hypothesis of Montague Grammar (Dowty, Wall, and Peters 1981)—that for every syntactic rule, there must be an associated semantic interpretation rule—adopted by Generalized Phrase Structure Grammar (Gazdar et al. 1985) and its lineal descendant, Head-Driven Phrase Structure Grammar (Pollard and Sag 1993). The rule-to-rule hypothesis can be recast as the construction grammar generalization that every construction has associated with it a meaning and a mapping from form to meaning.

2. Other theories share some, though not all, of construction grammar's basic principles. Head-Driven Phrase Structure Grammar (HPSG; Pollard and Sag 1987, 1993), Semiotic Grammar (MacGregor 1997), and Word Grammar (Hudson 1984; this volume, chapter 19) share construction grammar's representation of grammatical units as symbolic

units and organize grammatical knowledge into a taxonomic network. However, these theories are not explicitly construction-based, although HPSG and Fillmore and Kay's (1993) version of construction grammar have converged in many respects—for example, both use attribute-value matrices combining syntactic and semantic information, both use inheritance in grammatical organization, and both use unification for combining constructions into sentences (see section 5.1). Word Grammar explicitly denies the existence of constructions as complex symbolic units: "In Construction Grammar a construction constitutes a phrase whose parts are also either words or phrases; in Word Grammar the only units are words" (Holmes and Hudson 2005: 252).

3. More recently, Lakoff and colleagues have developed Embodied Construction Grammar (Bergen and Chang 2005). Embodied Construction Grammar is distinguished by its linking of semantic representations of constructions to simulations of perceptual-motor routines in the mind. The syntactic model of Embodied Construction Grammar is largely unchanged compared to the versions of Construction Grammar described in this and the preceding sections.

4. Many contemporary syntactic theories treat categories as bundles of features, so that, for example, the category Adjective is defined as [+N, +V] (Haegeman 1994: 146). The decomposition of categories into features performs a further reduction, so that the atomic elements are features instead of categories. However, for our purposes, we may assume that the primitive elements are categories. Note that in the case of the examples given here, Construction Grammar has atomic feature values for Noun and Verb ([cat n], [cat v]) and Subject and Object ([gf subj], [gf obj]).

REFERENCES

Akmajian, Adrian. 1984. Sentence types and the form-function fit. *Natural Language and Linguistic theory* 2: 1–23.

Aronoff, Mark. 1993. *Morphology by itself: Stems and inflectional classes.* Cambridge, MA: MIT Press.

Barsalou, Lawrence W. 1992. *Cognitive psychology: An overview for cognitive scientists.* Hillsdale, NJ: Lawrence Erlbaum Associates.

Becker, Joseph D. 1975. The phrasal lexicon. In R. Schank and B. L. Nash-Webber, eds., *Theoretical issues in natural language processing* 70–73. Cambridge, MA: Association for Computational Linguistics. (Also available as Artificial Intelligence Report No. 28. Cambridge, MA: Bolt, Beranek, and Newman)

Bergen, Benjamin K., and Nancy C. Chang. 2005. Embodied construction grammar in simulation-based language understanding. In Mirjam Fried, and Jan-Ola Östman, eds., *Construction grammars: Cognitive grounding and theoretical extensions* 147–90. Amsterdam: John Benjamins.

Birner, Betty J., and Gregory Ward. 1998. *Information status and noncanonical word order in English.* Amsterdam: John Benjamins.

Bolinger, Dwight. 1976. Meaning and memory. *Forum Linguisticum* 1: 1–14.

Braine, Martin D. S. 1976. *Children's first word combinations.* Monographs of the Society for Research in Child Development 41, no. 1. Chicago: University of Chicago Press.

Bybee, Joan L. 1985. *Morphology: A study of the relation between meaning and form.* Amsterdam: John Benjamins.

Bybee, Joan L. 1995. Regular morphology and the lexicon. *Language and Cognitive Processes* 10: 425–55.

Bybee, Joan L. 2001. *Phonology and language use*. Cambridge: Cambridge University Press.

Bybee, Joan L., and Sandra A. Thompson. 1997. Three frequency effects in syntax. *Berkeley Linguistics Society* 23: 378–88.

Chomsky, Noam. 1981. *Lectures on government and binding*. Dordrecht, Netherlands: Foris.

Chomsky, Noam. 1993. A minimalist program for linguistic theory. In Kenneth Hale and Samuel Jay Keyser, eds., *The view from building 20* 1–52. Cambridge, MA: MIT Press.

Croft, William. 1998. Linguistic evidence and mental representations. *Cognitive Linguistics* 9: 151–73.

Croft, William. 2001. *Radical construction grammar: Syntactic theory in typological perspective*. Oxford: Oxford University Press.

Croft, William. 2003. *Typology and universals*. 2nd ed. Cambridge: Cambridge University Press.

Croft, William. 2005. Logical and typological arguments for Radical Construction Grammar. In Mirjam Fried, and Jan-Ola Östman, eds., *Construction grammars: Cognitive grounding and theoretical extensions* 273–314. Amsterdam: John Benjamins.

Croft, William, and D. Alan Cruse. 2004. *Cognitive linguistics*. Cambridge: Cambridge University Press.

Dowty, David R., Robert E. Wall, and Stanley Peters. 1981. *Introduction to Montague semantics*. Dordrecht, Netherlands: Reidel.

Fauconnier, Gilles. 1985. *Mental spaces: Aspects of meaning construction in natural language*. Cambridge, MA: MIT Press. (2nd ed., Cambridge: Cambridge University Press, 1994)

Fillmore, Charles J. 1999. Inversion and constructional inheritance. In Gert Webelhuth, Jean-Pierre Koenig, and Andreas Kathol, eds., *Lexical and constructional aspects of linguistic explanation* 113–28. Stanford, CA: CSLI Publications.

Fillmore, Charles J., and Paul Kay. 1993. *Construction grammar coursebook: Chapters 1 thru 11*. Berkeley: University of California at Berkeley.

Fillmore, Charles J., Paul Kay, and Mary Kay O'Connor. 1988. Regularity and idiomaticity in grammatical constructions: The case of *let alone*. *Language* 64: 501–38.

Fillmore, Charles J., Paul Kay, Laura A. Michaelis, and Ivan Sag. Forthcoming. *Construction Grammar*. Stanford, CA: CSLI Publications.

Flickinger, Daniel, Carl Pollard, and Thomas Wasow. 1985. Structure-sharing in lexical representation. In *Proceedings of the 23rd Annual Meeting of the Association for Computational Linguistics* 262–67. Chicago: Association for Computational Linguistics.

Gathercole, Virginia C. Mueller, Eugenia Sebastián, and Pilar Soto. 1999. The early acquisition of Spanish verbal morphology: Across-the-board or piecemeal knowledge? *International Journal of Bilingualism* 3: 133–82.

Gazdar, Gerald, Ewan Klein, Geoffrey Pullum, and Ivan Sag. 1985. *Generalized phrase structure grammar*. Oxford: Basil Blackwell.

Goldberg, Adele E. 1991. It can't go up the chimney down: Paths and the English resultative. *Berkeley Linguistics Society* 17: 368–78.

Goldberg, Adele E. 1995. *Constructions: A construction grammar approach to argument structure*. Chicago: University of Chicago Press.

Haegeman, Liliane. 1994. *Introduction to government and binding theory*. 2nd ed. Oxford: Basil Blackwell.

Holmes, Jasper W., and Richard Hudson. 2005. Constructions in word grammar. In Jan-Ola Östman and Mirjam Fried, eds., *Construction grammars: Cognitive grounding and theoretical extensions* 243–72. Amsterdam: John Benjamins.

Hudson, Richard. 1984. *Word grammar*. Oxford: Basil Blackwell.

Israel, Michael. 1996. The *way* constructions grow. In Adele E. Goldberg, ed., *Conceptual structure, discourse and language* 217–30. Stanford, CA: CSLI Publications.

Jackendoff, Ray. 1990. *Semantic structures*. Cambridge, MA: MIT Press.

Jackendoff, Ray. 1997. Twistin' the night away. *Language* 73: 534–59.

Kay, Paul. 1997. Berkeley construction grammar: The new feature structure decisions. Available at http://www.icsi.berkeley.edu/~kay/bcg/FSrev.html. Accessed on Dec. 10, 1999.

Kay, Paul. 2002. English subjectless tagged sentences. *Language* 78: 453–81.

Kay, Paul, and Charles J. Fillmore. 1999. Grammatical constructions and linguistic generalizations: The *What's X doing Y?* construction. *Language* 75: 1–33.

Lakoff, George. 1987. *Women, fire and dangerous things: What categories reveal about the mind*. Chicago: University of Chicago Press.

Lambrecht, Knud. 1990. "What, me worry?"—'Mad Magazine' sentences revisited. *Berkeley Linguistics Society* 16: 215–28.

Langacker, Ronald W. 1987. *Foundations of cognitive grammar*. Vol 1, *Theoretical prerequisites*. Stanford, CA: Stanford University Press.

Langacker, Ronald W. 1990. *Concept, image, and symbol: The cognitive basis of grammar*. Berlin: Mouton de Gruyter.

Langacker, Ronald W. 1991. *Foundations of cognitive grammar*. Vol 2, *Descriptive application*. Stanford, CA: Stanford University Press.

Langacker, Ronald W. 1999. *Grammar and conceptualization*. Berlin: Mouton de Gruyter.

Levin, Beth, and Malka Rappaport Hovav. 1995. *Unaccusativity: At the syntax-lexical semantics interface*. Cambridge, MA: MIT Press.

Lieven, Elena V. M., Julian M. Pine, and Gillian Baldwin. 1997. Lexically-based learning and early grammatical development. *Journal of Child Language* 24: 187–219.

MacGregor, William B. 1997. *Semiotic grammar*. Oxford: Oxford University Press.

Makkai, Adam. 1972. *Idiom structure in English*. The Hague: Mouton.

Michaelis, Laura A., and Knud Lambrecht. 1996. Toward a construction-based theory of language functions: The case of nominal extraposition. *Language* 72: 215–47.

Nunberg, Geoffrey, Ivan Sag, and Thomas Wasow. 1994. Idioms. *Language* 70: 491–538.

Pine, Julian M., and Elena V. M. Lieven. 1997. Slot and frame patterns and the development of the determiner category. *Applied Psycholinguistics* 18: 123–38.

Pine, Julian M., Elena V. M. Lieven, and Caroline F. Rowland. 1998. Comparing different models of the development of the English verb category. *Linguistics* 36: 807–30.

Pollard, Carl, and Ivan Sag. 1987. *Information-based syntax and semantics*. Vol. 1, *Fundamentals*. CSLI Lecture Notes, no. 13. Stanford, CA: CSLI Publications.

Pollard, Carl, and Ivan Sag. 1993. *Head-driven phrase structure grammar*. Stanford, CA: CSLI Publications.

Prince, Ellen F. 1978. A comparison of WH-clefts and *it*-clefts in discourse. *Language* 54: 883–906.

Prince, Ellen F. 1981. Topicalization, focus-movement and Yiddish-movement: A pragmatic differentiation. *Berkeley Linguistics Society* 7: 249–64.

Rubino, Rejane B., and Julian M. Pine. 1998. Subject-verb agreement in Brazilian Portuguese: What low error rates hide. *Journal of Child Language* 25: 35–59.

Shieber, Stuart. 1986. *An introduction to unification-based approaches to grammar*. Stanford, CA: CSLI Publications.

Talmy, Leonard. 2000a. *Toward a cognitive semantics*. Vol. 1, *Concept structuring systems*. Cambridge, MA: MIT Press.

Talmy, Leonard. 2000b. *Toward a cognitive semantics.* Vol. 2, *Typology and process in concept structuring.* Cambridge, MA: MIT Press.

Tomasello, Michael. 1992. *First verbs: A case study of early grammatical development.* Cambridge: Cambridge University Press.

Tomasello, Michael. 2000. Do young children have adult syntactic competence? *Cognition* 74: 209–53.

Tomasello, Michael. 2003. *Constructing a language: A usage-based theory of language acquisition.* Cambridge, MA: Harvard University Press.

Tomasello, Michael, Nameera Akhtar, Kelly Dodson, and Laura Rekau. 1997. Differential productivity in young children's use of nouns and verbs. *Journal of Child Language* 24: 373–87.

Vallduví, Enric. 1992. *The informational component.* New York: Garland.

Wierzbicka, Anna. 1980. *Lingua mentalis: The semantics of natural language.* New York: Academic Press.

Wierzbicka, Anna. 1982. Why can you *have a drink* when you can't **have an eat? Language* 58: 753–99.

Wierzbicka, Anna. 1987. Boys will be boys. *Language* 63: 95–114.

Wierzbicka, Anna. 1988. *The semantics of grammar.* Amsterdam: John Benjamins.

CHAPTER 19

WORD GRAMMAR

RICHARD HUDSON

1. LANGUAGE AS A CONCEPTUAL NETWORK

Word Grammar (Hudson 1984, 1990, 2007) is a theory of language which touches on almost all aspects of synchronic linguistics and unifies them all through a single very general claim (Hudson 1984: 1):

> The Network Postulate:
> Language is a conceptual network

This claim is hardly contentious in Cognitive Linguistics, where it is often taken for granted that language as a whole is a network in contrast with the more traditional view of language as a grammar plus a dictionary—a list of rules or principles and a list of lexical items. However, it is particularly central to Word Grammar, in which each of the main traditional areas of language is a subnetwork within the total network of language.

Most obviously, "the lexicon" is a network of:

a. Forms
b. Meanings
c. Lexemes

(The scare-quotes round "the lexicon" anticipate section 8, which argues that the lexicon is not an identifiable part of the total language.) This is a network rather than a simple list because the elements among the parts are in a many-to-many relation. There are lexemes which have more than one meaning (polysemy); there are meanings which are shared by more than one lexeme (synonymy); and there are lexemes which have more than one form (inherent variability).

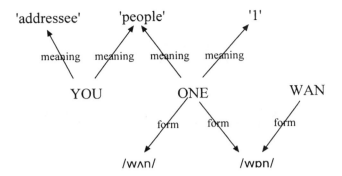

Figure 19.1. A network illustrating polysemy, homonymy, synonymy, and variability

All these mismatches can be illustrated in a single word: ONE.

a. Polysemy or homonymy: It means either '1' (contrasting with '2') or 'people' (as in *One shouldn't reveal one's feelings*).
b. Synonymy: In the second of these meanings, it is synonymous with *you*—which in turn is polysemous.
c. Inherent variability: Regardless of meaning, it has two pronunciations, which in England are /wʌn/ (in the South) and /wɒn/ (in the North). These two pronunciations compete in the speech of those (like me) who have migrated southwards. Each of these pronunciations is also available for another word: *won* or *wan*.

These relationships are most easily shown as a network, such as figure 19.1, where no one grouping takes priority as the basis for organizing the information.

Even when applied to the lexicon, the Network Postulate is controversial in comparison with the surprisingly widespread view that the lexicon is organized just like a conventional dictionary (but without the alphabetic order). In this view, the lexicon is a list of lexical items (or lexical entries) each of which combines a single meaning, a word class, and a single form (e.g., Jackendoff 1997: 109; Radford 1997: 514). The trouble with this view is that it creates a host of pseudoquestions about the boundaries between the supposed lexical items—for example, Do the two meanings of *one* belong to the same lexical item or to different items? What about the two pronunciations? It is never defended explicitly against the network view, which probably indicates a lack of interest in these questions rather than a denial of the network view. In contrast, the literature on psycholinguistics commonly presents evidence for the network view, which is now taken as uncontroversial (Aitchison 1997).

At the other end of the spectrum of views, Word Grammar claims that *all* linguistic knowledge has the same basic network architecture. The later sections of this article will show how this claim applies to other areas of language, but we must first consider what it means. What is a network (in the Word Grammar sense)? What does it contrast with?

2. Networks as Notation

At one level, the Network Postulate may be thought of simply as a claim about the notation for displaying linguistic data. Seen at that level, a network is a graph consisting of a set of nodes and a set of lines. According to Word Grammar, the formal properties of such a graph are as follows:

a. Each node must be connected by lines to at least two other nodes (otherwise it would be a mere dot, rather than a node where two lines meet).
b. There are two kinds of line (either of which may be either straight or curved):
   i. "isa" lines (showing class-member relations), with a small triangle at one end, and
   ii. arrows.
c. An "isa" line has either a node at each end or an arrow at each end.
d. An arrow points from either a node or an arrow to a node (which may be the same as the source node).
e. The nodes are all labeled as:
   i. constants (shown as a mnemonic name) or
   ii. variables (shown either as a number between 0 and 1, or simply as an unlabeled dot).
f. The lines are all labeled as constants.

As we will see in section 7, the individual labels are in fact redundant, but the distinction between variables and constants is (probably) not.

These formal characteristics of a Word Grammar network are illustrated abstractly in figure 19.2.

The notation has an unambiguous semantics:

a. A triangle-based line shows an "isa" (classification) relation in which the triangle rests on the supercategory:
   i. b isa a
   ii. d isa c
   iii. f isa e
b. An arrow points from one node to the node that has the named relation to it—in other words, it is a function from the first node to the second:
   i. the e of a is c
   ii. the f of b is d
   iii. the g of d is d

Word Grammar claims that this notation applies throughout language, from phonology through morphology and syntax to semantics and sociolinguistics. The claim that a single notation suffices for all levels of language is itself a significant part of Word Grammar theory, because it is implicitly denied by the plethora of

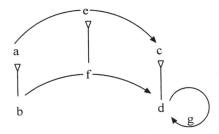

Figure 19.2. An abstract illustration of the notation of Word Grammar

different notations which are currently thought necessary for analyzing different kinds of linguistic structures. The following list is not exhaustive:

a. Trees
b. Stemmas
c. Attribute-value matrices
d. Directed acyclic graphs
e. Multitiered phonological and morphological structures
f. Linear strings of phonemes
g. Bracketed strings (of words or logical symbols), with or without labeling

3. Networks as Theory

However, the Network Postulate is not merely a matter of notation. It also implies a theory of language structure with a number of specific subtheories, which will be discussed briefly below.

a. Conceptual distance and activation
b. Entrenchment
c. Openness
d. Declarativeness

In general, the Word Grammar position on networks is typical of Cognitive Linguistics (e.g., Goldberg 1995; Langacker 1998, 2000; Barlow and Kemmer 2000), though the notation and some details differ. However, its historical roots are much earlier than the start of Cognitive Linguistics, in Stratificational Grammar (Lamb 1966, 1999) and Systemic Grammar (Halliday 1961; Hudson 1971).

3.1. Conceptual Distance and Activation

It is a commonplace of cognitive psychology that knowledge is a network and that the network supports spreading activation in which activation of one node "spills over" to neighboring nodes (Reisberg 1997: 256–303). In short, the network allows the "conceptual distance" between nodes to be represented, so that some nodes are nearer to each other than to others and the relative distances between nodes explain differences in mutual activation. There is a wealth of evidence that words activate ("prime") each other and some evidence that the same is true for more general grammatical categories—so-called "structural priming" (Bock and Griffin 2000).

The Network Postulate gives the simplest possible explanation for spreading activation in language: it happens because this is how our brains use networks and language is a network. In contrast, spreading activation would be hard to explain if language consisted of a list of unrelated lexical items plus a set of rules or principles for combining them.

Moreover, the Network Postulate generates research questions which simply do not arise otherwise; for example, why activation is directional in noun-noun compounds such as *crocodile shoes,* where *crocodile* primes *shoes,* but *shoes* does not prime *crocodile* (Harley 1995: 84; Roelofs 1996). It is not hard to think of possible explanations for this asymmetry in terms of sequential order (earlier primes later), or dependency (dependent primes head), or even the "fan" effect (the fewer links a node has, the more activation passes through each one). No doubt these alternatives can be distinguished experimentally, but the point is that the question becomes a matter of interest for linguists only if we assume that our theories of language have something to do with spreading activation. This hypothesis has recently led to a great deal of important work by cognitive linguists in areas such as language acquisition (Tomasello 2003) and diachronic change (Bybee 2001).

3.2. Entrenchment

Another closely related commonplace of cognitive psychology and psycholinguistics is that the accessibility of stored information varies from concept to concept according to how often we access this particular item of information, giving a "recency" effect and a "frequency" effect.

For example, we have variable difficulty in retrieving people's names (and other attributes), in retrieving past tenses of verbs (e.g., the past tense of *thrive* is less accessible than that of *drive*), and so on. These differences cannot be explained in terms of conceptual distance, since the distance (at least in a network analysis) is constant. Nor can they be explained in terms of accessibility of the target concept itself; for example, a name that we cannot recall may turn out to be a very common one. The explanation must lie in the link between the source (e.g., the person) and the target (their name), specifically in its degree of "entrenchment." The term is borrowed from Langacker, who generally uses it to refer to the familiarity or automaticity of a concept rather than of a link (Langacker 2000); it remains to be seen whether this difference is important (see also this volume, chapters 5 and 17).

Once again, this kind of variation can be explained in terms of a network model, since links may have different degrees of "entrenchment" reflecting differences of experience—most obviously differences of frequency: the more we use a link, the easier it is to use. In order to show entrenchment, then, we need to be able to treat entrenchment as a property of network links, which presupposes that the analysis includes the links as elements that can carry properties. Network models do include them, but others may not.

3.3. Openness

A further general characteristic of networks is their lack of natural boundaries, either internal or external. There are clear subnetworks of words which are more or less closely related to one another in terms of single criteria such as meaning, word class, morphology, or phonology, but typically the networks defined by one criterion cut across those defined in other ways. Equally, the network of language itself has no clear natural boundaries. This is most obvious where phonology fades into phonetics and where semantics fades into encyclopedic and contextual knowledge: Are the details of allophonic realization part of language (phonology) or not (phonetics)? How much of word meaning belongs to language?

The lack of clear boundaries is as expected if the Network Postulate is right, but hard to explain if language consists of a collection of linguistic rules and lexical items. The traditional rules-and-items view is closely related to the scholarly tradition in which each language is described in at least two distinct books—a grammar and a dictionary—and in which general knowledge is assigned to a third kind of book—an encyclopedia. These traditional boundaries are perpetuated in the popular idea of "modularity," according to which there is a discrete part of the mind, called a module, either for the whole of language or for each of the supposed parts of language (Fodor 1983; Chomsky 1986). This rather crude kind of modularity has always been highly contentious (Garfield 1987), but it is fundamentally incompatible with the Network Postulate. In contrast, the Network Postulate allows, and perhaps even encourages, a more subtle kind of modularity in which nodes cluster into relatively dense subnetworks, but without absolute boundaries. This is what has been called "hierarchical modularity" in recent work on the mathematics of networks (Barabási 2003: 236).

3.4. Declarative Knowledge

A final consequence of the Network Postulate is that knowledge of language is entirely declarative (rather than procedural). This must be so if the relevant knowledge consists of nothing but interconnected nodes; it is simply not possible to formulate a procedure in such terms. A network is like a map which lays out the possible routes, in contrast with a procedure for getting from one place to another. This does not of course mean that language use is irrelevant—far from it. Language use involves activation of the network and even the creation of new nodes and links (i.e., learning). But the Network Postulate distinguishes this activity conceptually from the network to which it is applied.

Of course, it is a matter of debate (and ultimately of fact) whether knowledge of language really is entirely declarative. Among those who distinguish rules and lexical items, there are many who believe that some or all of the rules are procedures of the form "If X is true, do Y" (i.e., "productions"). This is especially true in phonology (e.g., Halle and Bromberger 1989) but has been at least implicit in syntax since Chomsky's first introduction of rewrite rules. If some linguistic knowledge really does turn out to be procedural, the Network Hypothesis will have to be revised or abandoned.

4. "Isa," Default Inheritance, and Prototypes

One particularly important type of link in a Word Grammar network is the "isa" link, the relationship between a concept and a supercategory to which it belongs; for example, the link between the concepts Dog and Animal or between the word DOG and the word class Noun. This is the basis for all classification in Word Grammar, regardless of whether the classified concept is a subclass (e.g., Dog isa Animal) or an individual (e.g., Fido isa Dog) and regardless of whether it is a regular or an exceptional member. All theories in the Cognitive Linguistics tradition recognize classification relations, but the terminology varies—the term "isa," borrowed from Artificial Intelligence (Reisberg 1997: 280), is only used in Word Grammar—and Cognitive Grammar recognizes different relationships for regular and exceptional members (Langacker 2000).

"Isa" relationships are important because of their role in the basic logic of generalization: *default inheritance* (which is also recognized, with differences of terminology and some details, across Cognitive Linguistics).

Default Inheritance:
Inherit all the characteristics of a supercategory unless they are overridden.

Default logic allows generalizations to have exceptions, so in essence, if not in name, it has been the basic logic of linguistic analysis since the Greek and Sanskrit grammarians. However, it is also arguably the logic of ordinary commonsense reasoning, whereby we can recognize a three-legged cat as an exceptional cat rather than a non-cat, or a penguin as an exceptional bird.

In simple terms, if we know that A isa B, and that B has some characteristic C, then we normally assume that A too has C (i.e., A inherits C from B by default). However, there is an alternative: if we already know that A has some characteristic which is incompatible with C, this is allowed to "override" the "default" characteristic. For example, if we know that A isa Cat, and that Cat (i.e., the typical cat) has

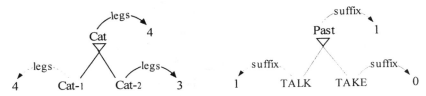

Figure 19.3. Two examples of default inheritance

four legs, we would normally inherit four-leggedness for A as well; but if we already know that A has only three legs (which is incompatible with having four), we accept this instead of the default number. Similarly, if we know that a typical past-tense verb has the suffix -ed, we inherit this pattern for any past-tense verb unless we already know that it does not contain -ed (e.g., *took*). Figure 19.3 illustrates both these cases, using the Word Grammar notation explained earlier in which the small triangle indicates an "isa" relationship. (The examples are of course simplified.) All the links shown with solid lines are stored, but those with dotted lines are inherited.

The default inheritance of Word Grammar allows multiple inheritance—simultaneous inheritance from more than one supercategory. For example, Cat isa both Mammal and Pet, so it inherits various bodily characteristics from Mammal and functional characteristics from Pet. In language, multiple inheritance applies most obviously in inflectional morphology; for example, the past tense of TALK isa both TALK and Past, inheriting its stem from TALK and its suffix from Past. This multiple inheritance is unrestricted, so in principle, it is possible to inherit conflicting characteristics from two supercategories, leading to a logical impasse. This is proposed as the explanation for the strange gap in English morphology where we expect to find *amn't* (Hudson 2000c).

Although the basic ideas of default inheritance are widely accepted in Cognitive Linguistics, they are not generally invoked in discussions of another leading idea of Cognitive Linguistics, that categories exhibit prototype effects (Barsalou 1992: 162; Lewandowska-Tomaszczyk, this volume, chaper 6). One distinctive characteristic of a prototype category is that its members have different degrees of typicality (e.g., a penguin is an untypical bird), a variation which is to be expected if we allow default characteristics to be overridden in the case of exceptional examples. The stored characteristics of penguins override some of the default bird characteristics such as flying and being about the size of a sparrow, but these exceptional characteristics do not prevent it from being classified as a bird. The advantage of invoking default inheritance as an explanation of prototype effects is that it removes the need to assume that concepts are themselves fuzzy (Sweetser 1987). Rightly or wrongly, the structure of a Word Grammar network is crystal clear and fully "digital" (except for degrees of entrenchment and activation).

5. The Best Fit Principle
and Processing

A further benefit of default inheritance is the possibility of an efficient classification in which the needs of generalization outweigh those of strict accuracy and reliability. If we know that something is a cat, we can inherit a great deal of information about it—e.g., that it enjoys being stroked and hunting small birds—even though some parts of this inherited (inferred) information may turn out to be unreliable. Most of the time, most inherited information is true, and the information flows extremely fast; we sacrifice total reliability for the sake of speed and quantity. The price we pay includes prejudice and the occasional accident.

However, there is another cost to be recognized, which is the increased difficulty of processing incoming experiences. What if the bit of experience that we are currently processing turns out to be exceptional? This is allowed by default inheritance, which allows mismatches between tokens and the types to which we assign them; and it is clearly part of our everyday experience. We are often confronted by late buses and sometimes even by three-legged cats, and in language we have to cope with misspelled words, foreign pronunciations, and poetry.

How, then, do we classify our experiences? The most plausible answer is that we apply the Best Fit Principle (Winograd 1976; Hudson 1984: 20), which favors the classification that gives the best overall "fit" between the observed characteristics of the experience and some stored category.

The Best Fit Principle:
Classify any item of experience so as to maximize the amount of
inherited information and to minimize the number of exceptions.

This principle allows us to classify a three-legged cat as a cat because all the other observable characteristics match those that we expect from a cat. It is true that we could avoid conflicting features altogether by pitching the classification at a much higher level, say at the level of Thing: although it is an exceptional cat and even an exceptional animal, it is not an exceptional thing; but classifying it merely as a thing would lose the benefits of being able to predict its behavior—for example, its reaction to being stroked.

This principle has many attractions, not least its intuitive explanatory power. It also explains another characteristic of categorization which is part of the theory of prototypes, namely, the existence of borderline categories and of categories whose borders shift from context to context. For example, is a particular person a student? It all depends on what kind of contrast we are assuming—between students and graduates, between students and prospective students, between officially registered students and others, and so on. This is as predicted by the Best Fit Principle, because relevance varies with context (Sperber and Wilson 1995).

However, this very powerful and attractive theory again has a considerable price. How does it work? Do we really compute all the possible alternative classifications and then select the winner? This cannot possibly be true, because there are so many "possible alternatives" in any full-sized network of concepts, and yet we classify our experiences almost instantaneously.

Interestingly, the theory of default inheritance also raises a similar problem. If any characteristic may be overridden, how do we know whether or not a particular characteristic actually is overridden in any given case where we might inherit it? Once again, the answer seems to involve an exhaustive search of at least a large section of the network.

Both these search problems allow the same plausible solution: *spreading activation*. As explained earlier, we already assume that this is the basis for all processing, so we can assume that at any given moment a small subset of all the nodes in the network are active (or above some threshold of activation). The solution to both the search problems is to assume that the search can be confined to the concepts that are currently active. This solution applies to the Best Fit Principle because all the relevant candidates must be active, so the problem is just to select the active node which provides the most inheritable information—which means, in effect, the most active one (e.g., Cat rather than Thing). Similarly, the solution also applies to Default Inheritance because any possible overriding node must already be active, so all other nodes in the network may safely be ignored.

6. CLASSIFIED RELATIONS

A Word Grammar network is not a mere associative network which just shows whether or not two nodes are related. Every link in the network is classified. One class of relations is the basic "isa" relation discussed above, but there are many others—'wife', 'name', 'nationality', 'meaning', 'subject', and so on. This is normal practice in Cognitive Linguistics, though Word Grammar may be the only theory which regularly uses the arrow notation illustrated in the previous diagrams.

However, Word Grammar offers a solution to a general problem that faces network analyses: how to cope with the potential proliferation of relationships (Reisberg 1997: 280). Once we start distinguishing one relationship from another, where do we stop? There are no obvious stopping points between very general relationships, such as 'part', and very specific ones, such as 'small toe on the left foot'; for example, we are clearly capable of understanding the sentence *He touched the small toe on his left foot*, which defines a unique relationship between him and the toe in question, so such specific relationships do in fact seem to be needed in a cognitive network.

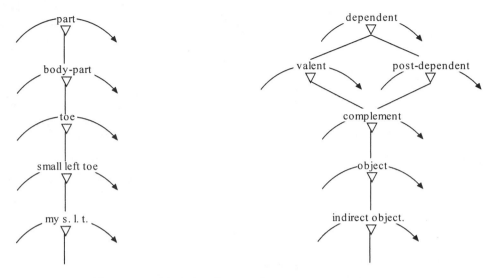

Figure 19.4. Two classification hierarchies of relationships

The Word Grammar solution is to treat relationships themselves as concepts and to allow them to be classified and subclassified just like other concepts. This produces a hierarchy of relationships linked by "isa" and interpreted by Default Inheritance, as illustrated in figure 19.4. This hierarchy naturally includes the most general relationships, such as 'part', but it may extend downwards without limit to include the most specific imaginable relationships, such as that between me and the small toe on my left foot. Since every relationship is a unique example of its supertype, this has the effect of making every relationship into a function—a relationship which has a unique value for any given argument. For example, you and I both have a unique relationship to our left small toe, but these relationships are distinct and are united only in being instances of the same more general relationship.

This hierarchical approach to relationships is most obvious in the Word Grammar treatment of grammatical relations—for example, Indirect object isa Object which isa Complement which isa Post-dependent and Valent (i.e., a non-adjunct) which isa Dependent. This classification is also shown in figure 19.4. However, similar hierarchies can be found throughout the relationships which are needed for language and (no doubt) elsewhere.

From a formal point of view, this classification of links makes Word Grammar networks very complex compared with most network models, because it defines a "second-order" network of relationships among relationships. Fortunately, the second-order relationships are all of the same kind—"isa"—so they are not likely to lead eventually to a third-order network with a danger of infinite complexity.

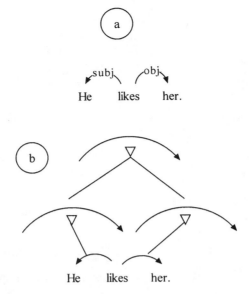

Figure 19.5. Distinguishing relationships with and without the use of labels

7. LABELS AND UNIQUENESS

This hierarchical analysis of link-types solves another problem. One of the characteristics of a network is that the nodes are defined *only* by their links to other nodes; for instance, the word CAT is the only word that is linked to the concept Cat, to the pronunciation /kæt/, to the word class Noun, and so on. No two nodes have exactly the same links to exactly the same range of other nodes, because if they did, they would by definition be the same node. As Lamb (1966, 1999: 59) points out, one consequence of this principle is that the labels on the nodes are entirely redundant, in contrast with non-network approaches, in which labels are the only way to show identity. For example, if two rules both apply to the same word class, this is shown by naming this word class in both rules; as we all know, the name chosen does not matter, but it is important to use the same name in both rules. In a network, on the other hand, labels only serve as mnemonics to help the analyst, and they could (in principle) all be removed without loss of information.

If we follow the logic of this argument by removing labels from nodes, we face a problem because the labels on *links* appear to carry information which is *not* redundant, because the links are not distinguished in any other way. This leads to a paradoxical situation in which the elements which traditionally are always labeled need not be, but those which (at least in simple associative networks) are traditionally not labeled must be labeled. The hierarchical classification of links resolves this paradox by giving links just the same status as nodes, so that they too can be distinguished by their relationships to other links—that is, by their place in the overall classification of links. By definition, every distinct link must have a unique set

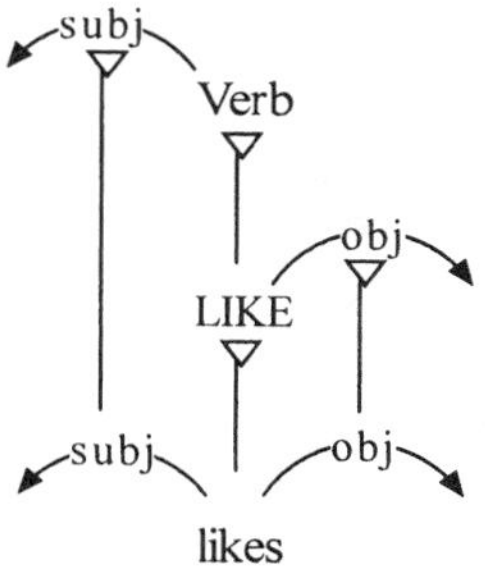

Figure 19.6. Where the subject and object of *likes* come from

of properties, so a link's properties are always sufficient to identify it, and labels are redundant. In principle, therefore, we could remove their labels too, converting a labeled diagram such as the simple syntactic structure in figure 19.5a into the unlabeled one in figure 19.5b. (The direction of the arrows in 19.5b is arbitrary and does not indicate word order, but the two intermediate arrows in this diagram must carry distinct features, such as word order, to make each one unique.)

8. "THE LEXICON," "THE GRAMMAR," AND CONSTRUCTIONS

As in other Cognitive Linguistics theories, there is no distinction in Word Grammar between the lexicon and the grammar. Instead, the "isa" hierarchy of words covers the full range of concepts and facts from the most general facts to the most specific, with no natural break in the hierarchy between "general" and "specific." As we have just seen, the same is true of dependency relationships, where the specific dependencies found in individual sentences are at the bottom of the hierarchy headed by the very general relationship 'dependent'. There is no basis, therefore, for distinguishing the lexicon from the grammar in terms of levels of generality, because generality varies continuously throughout the hierarchy.

Take the sentence *He likes her*, diagramed above in figure 19.5a. One requirement for any grammar is to predict that the verb *likes* needs both a subject and an object, but the rules concerned vary greatly in terms of generality. The subject is needed because *likes* is a verb, whereas the object is needed because it is a form of the lexeme LIKE; in traditional terms, one dependency is explained by "the grammar" while the other is a "lexical" fact, so different mechanisms are involved. In Word Grammar, however, the only difference is in the generality of the "source" concept. Figure 19.6 shows how *likes* inherits its two dependencies from the network.

This approach to lexicogrammar solves the problem of what may be called "special constructions," syntactic patterns which are fully productive but which do not fit any of the "ordinary" patterns and are tied to specific lexical items (Hudson

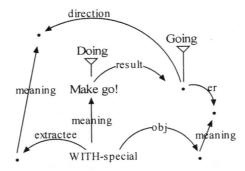

Figure 19.7. A network for the X WITH Y construction

1984: 4; Holmes and Hudson 2005). For example, the preposition WITH can be used as the root of a sentence provided that it is preceded by a direction expression and followed by a noun phrase.

(1)   Down with the government!
(2)   Off with his head!
(3)   Away with you!
(4)   Into the basket with the dirty washing!

This construction is not generated by the rules for normal sentences, but a grammar/lexicon split forces an arbitrary choice between a "grammatical" and a "lexical" analysis. In Word Grammar, there is no such boundary and no problem. The subnetwork in figure 19.7 provides the basis of an analysis.

   In words, what figure 19.7 says is that WITH-special (this special case of the lexeme WITH) means 'Do something to make Y go to X', where Y is the meaning (referent) of the object noun, and X is that of the "extracted" (front shifted) word. (The relation "er" in the semantics stands for "go-er.") Given the ordinary grammar for noun phrases and directionals, this pattern is sufficient to generate the examples in (1)–(4), but some parts of the pattern could be omitted on the grounds that they can be inherited from higher nodes which are partly "grammatical" (e.g., the word classes permitted as object) and partly "lexical" (e.g., the fact that WITH has an obligatory object).

9. MORPHOLOGY

The Word Grammar treatment of morphology separates two separate analyses:

   a. The analysis of word structure in terms of morphemes or phonological patterns
   b. The linkage between word structure and lexeme or word class

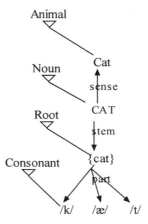

Figure 19.8. The word *cat* analyzed on four linguistic levels

For example, the recognition of a suffix in *dogs* is separate from the recognition that *dogs* is plural. The suffix and the plurality are clearly distinct—one is a morpheme, that is, a word-part, while the other is a word class, and either can exist without the other (as in the plural *geese* or the singular *news*). In this sense, therefore, Word Grammar morphology belongs firmly within the "Word-and-Paradigm" tradition in which a word's internal structure is distinguished sharply from its morphosyntactic features (Robins [1959] 2001).

The theory of morphology raises a fundamental question about the architecture of language: how many "levels of analysis" are there? This actually breaks down into two separate questions:

a. Is there a "syntactic" level, at which we recognize words?
b. Is there a "morphological" level, at which we recognize morphemes?

Word Grammar recognizes both of these levels (Creider and Hudson 1999), so the relation between semantic and phonological structure is quite indirect: meanings map to words, words to morphemes, and morphemes to phonemes (or whatever phonological patterns there are). There is a range of evidence for this view:

a. Words and morphemes are classified differently from each other and from the meanings they signal—meanings may be things or people, words may be verbs or nouns, and morphemes may be roots or affixes; and morphological "declension classes" are distinct from morphosyntactic classes.
b. Morphological patterns are different from those of syntax; for example, there is no syntactic equivalent of semitic interdigitation (whereby the plural of Arabic *kitaab* 'book' is *kutub*), nor is there a morphological equivalent of coordination or extraction; and many languages have free word order, but none have free morpheme order.

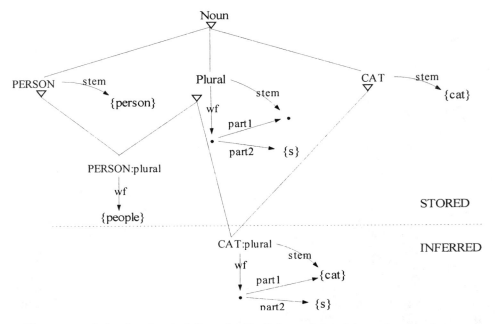

Figure 19.9. Inflectional morphology for English regular and irregular plural nouns

c. The units of morphology need not match those of syntax; for example, French syntax recognizes the two-word combination *de le* 'of the', which corresponds to a single morphological unit *du* (see figure 19.11 below).

This position is quite controversial within linguistics in general and within Cognitive Linguistics in particular. Cognitive Grammar at least appears to deny the level of syntax, since its symbolic units are merely a pairing of a semantic pole with a phonological pole (Langacker 2000: 5), so they cannot be independently categorized (e.g., in terms of nonsemantic word classes). But even if the symbolic units do define a level of syntax, there is certainly no independent level of morphology, "a basic claim of Cognitive Grammar, namely, that morphology and syntax form a continuum (fully describable as assemblies of symbolic structures)" (25). In other words, in contrast with the Word-and-Paradigm model, morphology is merely syntax within the word.

In Word Grammar, then, the word is linked to its phonological realization only via the morpheme, just as it is linked to the semantic structure only via the single concept that acts as its sense. The pattern for the word *cat* (or more precisely, the lexeme CAT) is shown in figure 19.8. We follow a fairly traditional notation for distinguishing levels: Cat is the concept of the typical cat, CAT is the lexeme, {cat} is the morpheme, and /kæt/ are the phonemes.

Morphologically complex words map onto more than one morpheme at a time, so we need to recognize a complex unit at the level of morphology, the "word

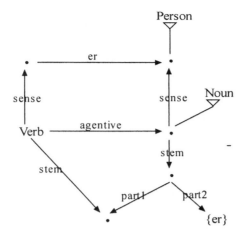

Figure 19.10. Derivational morphology for agentive nouns

form" (or "morphological word"—Rosta 1997). For example, the word form {{cat} + {s}} realizes the word CAT:plural (the plural of CAT), which isa both CAT and another word type, Plural. These two word types contribute, respectively, its stem and its suffix, so in all, there are three links between CAT:plural and its morphology:

a. The 'stem' link to the stem morpheme, inherited from CAT
b. The 'suffix' link to the suffix morpheme, inherited from Plural
c. The 'word form' link to the entire word form, also inherited from Plural

These three links are called "morphological functions"—functions from a word to specific parts of its morphological structure (Hudson 2000c). (A slightly different theory of this part of morphology is presented in Hudson, 2007; the main difference is the use of a 'variant' relation between forms instead of the 'suffix' relation from word to morpheme.)

Irregular forms can be accommodated easily thanks to default inheritance, as shown in figure 19.9. The top part of this figure (above the dotted line) represents stored information, while the bottom part is information that can be inferred by default inheritance. In words, a plural noun has a word form ("wf" in the diagram) whose first and second parts are its stem and its suffix (which is {s}). The stem of CAT is {cat}, so the word form of CAT:plural consists of {cat} followed by {s}. Exceptionally, the word form of PERSON:plural is stipulated as {people}; by default inheritance, this stipulation overrides the default. As in other areas of knowledge, we probably store some regularly inheritable information such as the plural of some very frequent nouns as well as the unpredictable irregular ones (Bybee 1995).

Derivational morphology uses the same combination of morphemes and morphological functions, but in this case, the morphology signals a relationship between

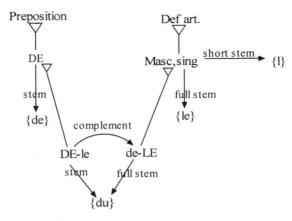

Figure 19.11. Why French *de le* is realized as *du*

two distinct lexemes, rather than between a lexeme and an inflectional category. For example, take the agentive pattern in SPEAK-SPEAKER. The relationship between these two lexemes exemplifies a more general relationship between verbs and nouns. The relevant part of the grammar, figure 19.10, shows how lexemes which are related in this way differ in terms of meaning, syntax, and morphology. In words, a verb typically has an "agentive":

a. which isa Noun,
b. whose stem consists of the verb's stem combined with the {er} suffix, and
c. whose sense is a person who is the agent ('er') of an event which isa the verb's sense.

One of the benefits mentioned earlier of the distinction between words and their morphological realization is the possibility of gross mismatches between them, as discussed extensively in Sadock (1991). Figure 19.11 illustrates the familiar case from French of *du*, a single morpheme which realizes two words:

a. the preposition *de* 'of' and
b. the masculine definite article which is written *le*.

For example, alongside *de la fille* 'of the daughter', we find *du fils* 'of the son', rather than the expected **de le fils*. One of the challenges of this construction is the interaction between morphology and phonology, since *du* is not used when *le* is reduced to *l'* before a vowel: *de l'oncle* 'of the uncle'. The analysis in figure 19.11 meets this challenge by distinguishing the 'full stem' and the 'short stem' and applying the merger with {de} only to the former. Some other rule will prevent the full stem from occurring before vowels, thereby explaining the facts just outlined. The analysis also ensures that *de le* only collapses to *du* when the *le* depends directly on the *de*, as it would in *du fils*.

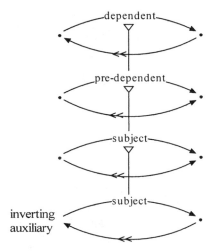

Figure 19.12. Default and exceptional word orders in English

10. SYNTAX

Syntax is the area in which Word Grammar has been applied most thoroughly (Hudson 1984, 1990, 1998, 1999, 2000a, 2000b, 2003a, 2003b, 2007), so the following discussion can be quite brief.

The most distinctive characteristic of syntax in Word Grammar is that it assumes dependency structure rather than phrase structure. The syntactic structure of a sentence is a network of nodes, in which there is a node for each word but no nodes for phrases; and the nodes are all connected by syntactic dependencies. For example, in the sentence *Small babies cry*, the noun *babies* depends on the verb *cries*, and the adjective *small* depends on *babies*, but there is no node for the noun phrase which consists of *babies* plus its dependent. It would be easy to add phrase nodes, because they can be read unambiguously off the dependencies, but there is no point in doing so because they would be entirely redundant. This way of viewing sentence structure exclusively in terms of word-word dependencies has a long history which goes back through the medieval European and Arabic grammarians to classical Greece, but it has recently been overshadowed by the phrase-structure approach (Percival 1976, 1990).

One of the advantages of the dependency approach is that grammatical functions such as 'subject' and 'object' are subdivisions of 'dependent'. Since relationships are classified in just the same way as nodes, a typical dependency inherits by default from a number of higher-level dependencies; for example, in the sentence *He likes her*, the relation between *likes* and *her* inherits from 'object', 'complement', 'valent', 'post-dependent', and 'dependent', each of which brings with it inheritable characteristics. (These relations are defined by the hierarchy shown in figure 19.4)

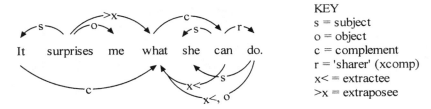

Figure 19.13. An example illustrating raising, extraction, and extraposition

Syntactic structure is primarily linear, so it is important to be able to indicate word order. A network has no inherent directionality, so linear order is shown as a separate relationship between earlier and later, by means of an arrow which points toward the earlier member of the pair; this arrow is labeled "≪." (The linear order relationship has many other applications beside word order—it orders points of time, so within language it is also used in the semantics of tense to relate the time of the verb's referent to the deictic time of its utterance.) Like any other relationships they can be overridden in the inheritance hierarchy, so it is easy to model the idea of a "basic" and "special" word order. For example, in English (a head-initial language) the basic word order puts words before their dependents, but enough dependents precede their heads to justify a general subtype 'pre-dependent', of which 'subject' is a subtype; so, exceptionally, a verb follows its subject. However, there are also exceptions to this exception: an "inverting" auxiliary verb reverts to the position before its subject.

This hierarchy is shown in figure 19.12. In words:

a. a typical dependent follows its parent (the word on which it depends): . . .
   likes her;
b. but a pre-dependent precedes its parent;
c. therefore, a subject (one kind of pre-dependent) precedes its parent:
   He likes . . . ;
d. but the subject of an inverting auxiliary follows its parent: *Does he . . . ?*

A further source of flexibility in explaining word order is the fact that syntactic structure is embedded in a network theory, which (in principle) allows unrestricted links among nodes. This flexibility is in fact limited, but some multiple links are permitted. Not only may one word have more than one dependent, but one word may also have more than one parent. This is the source of most of the well-known complications in syntax, such as raising, extraction, and extraposition. Sentence (5) below contains examples of all three and shows how they can be explained in terms of a tangle-free "surface" structure, which is displayed above the words, supplemented by extra dependencies below the words. The Word Grammar analysis is summarized in figure 19.13 (which ignores all the "isa" links to the grammar network).

(5)   It surprises me what she can do.

One of the attractions of this kind of grammar is that the structures combine concreteness (there are no word orders other than the surface one) with abstractness (the dependencies can show abstract relationships between nonadjacent words and are generally in step with semantic relationships). This makes it relatively easy to teach at an introductory level, where it is possible to teach a grammatical system which can be applied to almost every word in any text (Hudson 1998). However, at the same time, it allows relatively sophisticated analyses of most of the familiar challenges for syntactic theory such as variable word order, coordination, and Prepositional Pied-piping.

11. Lexical Semantics

According to Word Grammar, language is an area of our general conceptual network which includes words and everything that we know about them. This area has no natural boundaries, so there is no reason to distinguish between a word's "truly linguistic" meaning and the associated encyclopedic knowledge. For example, the sense of the word CAT is the concept Cat, the same concept that we use in dealing with cats in everyday life. It would be hard to justify an alternative analysis in which either there were two 'cat' concepts, one for language and one for the encyclopedia, or in which the characteristics of the Cat concept were divided into those which do belong to language and those which do not. This general philosophy has been applied in detail to the word CYCLE (Hudson and Holmes 2005).

In short, as in most other "cognitive" theories of semantics, a word's meaning is defined by a "frame of knowledge" (Fillmore 1985). In the case of Cat, the relevant frame includes the links between this concept and other concepts such as Pet, Mammal, Dog, Mouse, Fur, Milk, and Meowing. This frame of background knowledge is highly relevant to the understanding of language; for example, the idea of ownership in the concept Pet provides an easy interpretation for expressions like *our cat* in contrast with, say, *our mouse*.

Moreover, any theory of language must make some attempt to formulate linking rules which map semantic relations to syntactic relations. For instance, we must at least be able to stipulate that with the verb HEAR, the hearer is identified by the subject, in contrast with SOUND which links it to the prepositional object as in *That sounds good to me*; and it would be even better if we could make these linkages follow from more general facts. Word Grammar has the advantage of syntactic and semantic structures that have very similar formal properties, so they should be relatively easy to map onto one another. A syntactic structure consists of labeled

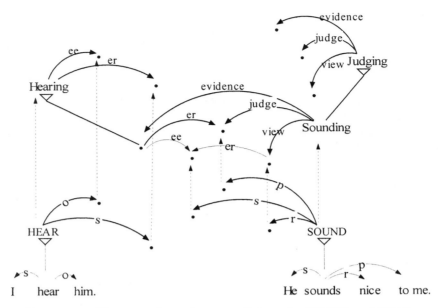

Figure 19.14. The semantics and syntax of the verbs SOUND and HEAR

dependencies between words, and a semantic structure consists of labeled dependencies between the concepts expressed by these words. Moreover, the labels reflect a hierarchical classification, so each relationship can be identified at a number of different levels of generality. For example, in syntax, 'object' isa 'complement', and similarly in semantics, 'hearer' isa 'perceiver' which isa 'experiencer', and so on. In principle, then, Word Grammar provides a good framework for exploring whatever generalizations can be made about the mapping from semantic relations to syntactic ones (Gisborne 2001; Holmes 2005).

Figure 19.14 shows subnetworks for the verbs HEAR and SOUND which illustrate this claim (Gisborne 1996). In words, the subject and object of HEAR define the hearer ('er') and hear-ee ('ee'), whereas SOUND has a more complex semantic structure. 'Sounding' is a kind of Judging, in which the evidence is an example of Hearing the individual to whom the judgment applies; for example, if John sounds nice to me, I base the judgment that John is nice on hearing John. (Another possibility is that my evidence is hearing something other than John; this meaning requires a slightly different analysis, which may be combined with the one presented here.)

The network approach allows analyses of very rich and complex areas of real-world knowledge, such as the "scenes," "scripts," or "frames" analyzed in a variety of other frameworks (Sowa 1984; Barsalou 1992: 157; Luger and Stubblefield 1993: 368–86). It has the great advantage of avoiding all boundary problems which arise in theories which assume rigid "frames" in which each item of information must be assigned to a single frame. For example, the concept Money belongs in part to the

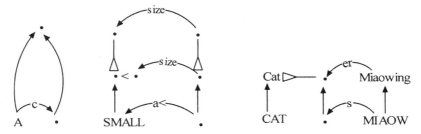

Figure 19.15. The syntax and semantics of the words A, SMALL, CAT, and MEOW

Commercial Transaction scene, but it also belongs to many other scenes—Work, Banking, Economics, Richness, and many more. In a network analysis, the one concept may be linked to all these other concepts at the same time.

12. COMPOSITIONAL SEMANTICS

Combining the meanings of individual words to make a composite "sentence meaning" is quite easy given that:

a. the words are related syntactically by word-word dependencies; and
b. some individual words have semantic structures which are linked to particular syntactic dependencies (as illustrated in figure 19.14).

However, the network architecture has interesting consequences here as well, because a word's meaning changes when it is modified by a dependent. For example, the meaning of *cat* in the phrase *a small cat* is 'Small cat' rather than simply Cat; and the particular cat is another concept again. Since these are distinct concepts, they must be represented by distinct nodes, with the consequence that the semantic structure contains a separate node for every phrase that would have been recognized in a conventional phrase structure analysis: one for *cat*, another for *small cat*, and a third for *a small cat*. This pattern is called "semantic phrasing" (Hudson 1990: 146–51). In most cases, the relation between the nodes is "isa": the particular cat isa Small cat, which in turn isa Cat. Well-known exceptions to the "isa" relationship include the effect of adding FAKE (e.g., fake diamonds are not diamonds) and NOT; metaphors also break the "isa" link. In the normal case, the word's referent (e.g., our mental representation of the particular cat) isa all its other meanings, which we may call collectively its senses.

Figure 19.15 illustrates the kinds of semantic structures which are stored permanently in the lexicogrammar and which are the building blocks out of which sentence structures are constructed. In words:

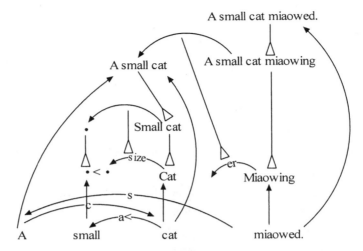

Figure 19.16. The syntactic and semantic structure of *A small cat miaowed*

a. The word A shares the same referent as its complement noun. (A complete analysis also shows that this referent is 'indefinite' and countable.)

b. SMALL, when used as a pre-adjunct ('a<') of a noun, modifies the latter's sense by specifying a value for its 'size', which is less than the default value for the relevant prototype.

c. CAT means Cat.

d. MEOW means Meowing, which has a 'meow-er' ('er') which isa Cat; this concept is shared by the words CAT and MEOW.

Given an accurate syntactic analysis, these meanings combine into the compositional semantic structure shown in figure 19.16, in which there are separate labeled nodes for the concepts 'Cat', 'Small cat', 'A small cat', 'A small cat meowing', and 'A small cat meowed' (the particular instance of meowing referred to here), each of which is a distinct semantic element corresponding to a "phrase" in the syntax. And yet this semantic structure is built in a very simple way from a completely flat syntactic structure.

Semantic phrasing also helps with some of the standard challenges of logic. For example, take a simple sentence such as *John kissed a girl*. The semantic structure contains one node which shows the modifying effect of the object and another for the subject:

(6)   a. Kissing a girl
      b. John kissing a girl

The crucial question is exactly how these are related to each other. Clearly, the second isa the first, but what about their respective 'kiss-ee' arguments? One possibility is that they too are in an "isa" relationship, rather than simple identity. This is the analysis shown in figure 19.17. The part to pay attention to here is the "isa" link between the variables *y* and *x*, showing that the girl of 'John kissing a girl' isa the one in 'Kissing a girl'.

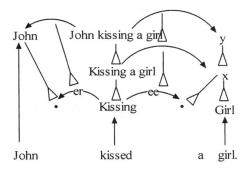

Figure 19.17. The semantic structure for *John kissed a girl*

In this sentence, the effect on the logic is exactly the same as if the same girl had been involved in both cases, because *y* has no characteristics other than those which it automatically inherits from *x*. But suppose there were several different examples of 'Kissing a girl'. In that case, the analysis in figure 19.17 would allow the girl to be either the same or different. For example, take sentence (6).

(6)   John kissed a girl, and Bill did too.

In this sentence, *did too* refers anaphorically to *kissed a girl*, but allows both interpretations: either Bill kissed the same girl as John, or he kissed a different one. Both interpretations are compatible with the analysis in which 'Bill kissing a girl' isa 'Kissing a girl', and the girl in the former isa the one in the latter. In short, the possibility of "sloppy identity" follows from the logic of default inheritance combined with semantic phrasing.

The same assumption about identity explains the ambiguity of coordinate structures such as (7).

(7)   John and Bill each kissed a girl.

Because of *each*, this has to refer to two distinct instances of 'Kissing a girl', one performed by John and the other by Bill; but if each of the girls isa the one implicated in 'Kissing a girl', the girls may be either the same or different. In other words, contrary to standard logical analyses in terms of scope, the sentence is not in fact ambiguous, but simply vague. This seems right because if we add a third male, Mike, the sentence would be compatible with a scene in which John and Bill kissed the same girl and Mike kissed a different one—an interpretation which would be hard to represent in terms of the predicate calculus. A similar analysis applies to an example such as (8).

(8)   Every boy kissed a girl.

As in the previous examples, this is vague rather than ambiguous. There is a distinct instance of 'Kissing a girl' for each boy, but the girl in each of these cases simply isa Girl and might be either the same or different.

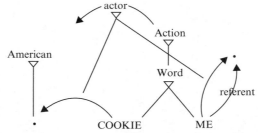

Figure 19.18. Constraints on the speaker of COOKIE and ME

Word Grammar needs a great deal more work in this area, but some foundations are already available (Hudson 1984: 131–210; 1990: 123–65; 2007).

13. SOCIOLINGUISTICS

Word Grammar is one of the few theories of language structure in which there is any provision for "sociolinguistic information"—the kind of knowledge that allows us to interpret utterances in terms of social categories such as speaker types and interaction types. Thanks to recent work in sociolinguistics, we know a great deal about the ways in which people classify speakers, in terms of geography, social class, age, sex, and so on, and in terms of speaking situations, as chatting, teaching, greeting, joking, and so on (Hudson 1996). Classification clearly presupposes knowledge ("competence"), just like the rest of language, so any cognitive theory of language must accommodate it in some way.

The Word Grammar solution is to recognize that words are actions. This is much easier to accept if we think of words as spoken rather than written and if we compare them with recurrent actions such as cleaning one's teeth, for which we have permanent stored representations. We know how and when to clean our teeth in much the same way that we know how and when to use a word, and we can distinguish the stored "type" from all of the particular "tokens" of it that we perform. The Word Grammar claim, then, is that a word type is like the action type 'Cleaning one's teeth'—a stored concept for a particular kind of action (the action of saying the relevant sounds) for a particular purpose and in a particular kind of social context.

Now, if Word isa Action, it must inherit the latter's characteristics, one of which is that it has an actor; in the case of a word, the actor of course is the speaker, so this analysis immediately allows us to represent the speaker in the analysis of a word. (This is also helpful in handling deictic semantics, such as the reference of the word ME—the referent of ME is its actor/speaker.) Furthermore, we can classify actions according to the kinds of situation in which they are socially appropriate—for example, spitting is fine when cleaning our teeth but not when eating. In the same way, we can classify words, or word combinations, according to the social situations in which they are appropriate. Figure 19.18 shows how the role 'speaker' can be exploited in the language network.

The Word Grammar work on sociolinguistics is mostly programmatic rather than thorough, but there is a small amount of Word Grammar work on quantitative sociolinguistics (Hudson 1996: 243–57; 1997a, 1997b, 2007).

14. Processing

Any theory of how we store and organize language as knowledge must also be compatible with some theory of how we use this knowledge as speakers, listeners, writers, and readers. I have already suggested various ways in which the network theory of knowledge fits what we know about these various kinds of processing. The various claims made earlier are summarized here:

  a. A network can be activated, and when one part is activated, the activation naturally spreads to neighboring parts. We know that spreading activation is a reality, as evidenced by priming in perception and by speech errors in production. It is easy to model spreading activation if the language itself is modeled as a network.
  b. A Word Grammar network is built round a number of "isa" hierarchies which allow default inheritance. This explains a number of processing effects—how we use observable word forms to derive information about unobservable meaning, how we generalize to unfamiliar cases, and how we cope with exceptions and even with deviant input.
  c. The possibility of exceptions and deviant input which follows from default inheritance explains why processing requires a global Best Fit Principle rather than more rigorous local tests for well-formedness; for example, when pushed strongly by context, we may overlook a gross misspelling or mispronunciation.
  d. Returning to spreading activation, this helps to explain how we cope with the potentially fatal problems of both default inheritance and the Best Fit Principle, both of which in principle require us to search the whole of our knowledge base for more specific overriding facts or better global fits. If we assume that all relevant nodes are already active, then the search for alternatives can focus on these and ignore the rest of the database.

15. LEARNING

Lastly, the Word Grammar theory of language structure is what would be expected according to the Cognitive Linguistics view that language is learned on the basis of usage (Barlow and Kemmer 2000). If this view is correct, then we should expect:

a. degrees of entrenchment, as recognized in section 3, whereby the more often we activate a particular link, the more deeply entrenched it is;
b. lexical detail as well as (and prior to) more schematic generalizations across lexemes; and
c. linguistic categories of all kinds (words, syntactic patterns, phonemes) which are sensitive to features of the nonverbal context.

All these characteristics are supported by a great deal of empirical evidence from studies of child language (Lieven, Pine, and Baldwin 1997; Pine, Lieven, and Rowland 1998; Tomasello 2000, 2003; Ellis 2002).

We have already shown how degrees of entrenchment can be attached to either nodes or links in a network, but the Network Postulate also helps to explain the other characteristics. If all knowledge is indeed a single integrated network, then this network must include knowledge of the tokens that we analyze as well as the stored knowledge that we apply to them. We have assumed that the relationship between the two is the "isa" relationship, so each word token isa some word type which in turn isa various more general types. If this is correct, then learning is rather simple: it involves no more than the conversion of token nodes into type nodes. That is, instead of allowing a token node to die away for lack of activation, we activate it sufficiently to keep it alive for future use as a type for classifying other tokens. Tokens are the ultimate in lexical specificity, so this process explains why children start with lexically specific patterns before inducing generalizations; and the fact that tokens are always contextualized explains why we can learn contextual ("sociolinguistic") information about linguistic items.

Finally, a rather different feature of Word Grammar turns out to be highly relevant to this account of language learning. This is the use of dependencies in syntax. Unlike phrase structure analyses, dependency analysis allows us to measure the distance between a word and the word on which it depends—the "dependency distance" (Hiranuma 1999, 2001). It turns out that in casual speech dependency distance is zero for most words—typically 70% or more of words are next to the word on which they depend (Collins 1996; Pake 1998). Moreover, every English dependency pattern may be found between adjacent words. These two facts mean that a child can learn syntax very easily by paying attention to nothing but adjacent word pairs and ignoring the 30% of patterns which do not recur.

This article has summarized the main features of Word Grammar as of late 2005, but the theory is continuously evolving. More up-to-date information may be found in Hudson (2007) or on the Word Grammar Web site, http://www.phon.ucl.ac.uk/home/dick/wg.htm.

NOTE

....

I would like to thank Joe Hilferty and the editors for helpful comments on an earlier version.

REFERENCES

....

Aitchison, Jean. 1997. *The language web.* Cambridge: Cambridge University Press.

Barabási, Albert-László. 2003. *Linked: How everything is connected to everything else and what it means for business, science and everyday life.* London: Penguin.

Barlow, Michael, and Suzanne Kemmer, eds. 2000. *Usage-based models of language.* Stanford, CA: CSLI Publications.

Barsalou, Lawrence W. 1992. *Cognitive psychology: An overview for cognitive scientists.* Hillsdale, NJ: Lawrence Erlbaum.

Bock, Kathryn, and Zenzi Griffin. 2000. The persistence of structural priming: Transient activation or implicit learning? *Journal of Experimental Psychology: General* 129: 177–92.

Bybee, Joan L. 1995. Regular morphology and the lexicon. *Language and Cognitive Processes* 10: 425–55.

Bybee, Joan L. 2001. *Phonology and language use.* Cambridge: Cambridge University Press.

Chomsky, Noam. 1986. *Knowledge of language: Its nature, origin and use.* New York: Praeger.

Collins, Michael. 1996. A new statistical parser based on bigram lexical dependencies. *Proceedings of the Association for Computational Linguistics* 34: 184–91.

Creider, Chet, and Richard Hudson. 1999. Inflectional morphology in word grammar. *Lingua* 107: 163–87.

Ellis, Nick. 2002. Frequency effects in language processing: A review with implications for theories of implicit and explicit language acquisition. *Studies in Second Language Acquisition* 24: 143–88.

Fillmore, Charles J. 1985. Frames and the semantics of understanding. *Quaderni di Semantica* 6: 223–54.

Fodor, Jerry A. 1983. *The modularity of mind.* Cambridge, MA: MIT Press.

Garfield, Jay, ed. 1987. *Modularity in knowledge representation and natural-language understanding.* Cambridge, MA: MIT Press.

Gisborne, Nikolas. 1996. English perception verbs. PhD dissertation, University of London.

Gisborne, Nikolas. 2001. The stative/dynamic contrast and argument linking. *Language Sciences* 23: 603–37.

Goldberg, Adele E. 1995. *Constructions: A construction grammar approach to argument structure.* Chicago: University of Chicago Press.

Halle, Morris, and Sylvain Bromberger. 1989. Why phonology is different. *Linguistic Inquiry* 20: 51–70.

Halliday, Michael. 1961. Categories of the theory of grammar. *Word* 17: 241–92.

Harley, Trevor. 1995. *The psychology of language.* Hove: Psychology Press.

Hiranuma, So. 1999. Syntactic difficulty in English and Japanese: A textual study. *UCL Working Papers in Linguistics* 11: 309–22.

Hiranuma, So. 2001. Measuring the syntactic difficulty of Japanese sentences. PhD dissertation, University College London.

Holmes, Jasper. 2005. Lexical properties of English verbs. PhD diss., University College London.

Holmes, Jasper W., and Richard Hudson. 2005. Constructions in word grammar. In Jan-Ola Östman and Mirjam Fried, eds., *Construction Grammars: Cognitive grounding and theoretical extensions* 243–72. Amsterdam: John Benjamins.

Hudson, Richard. 1971. *English complex sentences: An introduction to systemic grammar.* Amsterdam: North Holland.

Hudson, Richard. 1984. *Word grammar.* Oxford: Basil Blackwell.

Hudson, Richard. 1990. *English word grammar.* Oxford: Basil Blackwell.

Hudson, Richard. 1996. *Sociolinguistics.* 2nd ed. Cambridge: Cambridge University Press.

Hudson, Richard. 1997a. Inherent variability and linguistic theory. *Cognitive Linguistics* 8: 73–108.

Hudson, Richard. 1997b. The rise of auxiliary *DO*: Verb-non-raising or category-strengthening? *Transactions of the Philological Society* 95: 41–72.

Hudson, Richard. 1998. *English grammar.* London: Routledge.

Hudson, Richard. 1999. Subject-verb agreement in English. *English Language and Linguistics* 3: 173–207.

Hudson, Richard. 2000a. Discontinuity. *Traitement Automatique des Langues* 41: 15–56.

Hudson, Richard. 2000b. Grammar without functional categories. In Robert Borsley, ed., *The nature and function of syntactic categories* 7–35. New York: Academic Press.

Hudson, Richard. 2000c. *I amn't. *Language* 76: 297–323.

Hudson, Richard. 2003a. Gerunds without phrase structure. *Natural Language and Linguistic Theory* 21: 579–615.

Hudson, Richard. 2003b. Trouble on the left periphery. *Lingua* 113: 607–42.

Hudson, Richard. 2007. *Language networks: The new Word Grammar.* Oxford: Oxford University Press.

Hudson, Richard, and Jasper Holmes. 2000. Re-cycling in the Encyclopedia. In Bert Peeters, ed., *The Lexicon/Encyclopedia Interface* 259–90. Amsterdam: Elsevier.

Jackendoff, Ray. 1997. *The architecture of the language faculty.* Cambridge, MA: MIT Press.

Lamb, Sydney M. 1966. *Outline of stratificational grammar.* Washington, DC: Georgetown University Press.

Lamb, Sydney M. 1999. *Pathways of the brain: The neurocognitive basis of language.* Amsterdam: John Benjamins.

Langacker, Ronald W. 1998. Conceptualization, symbolization and grammar. In Michael Tomasello, ed., *The new psychology of language: Cognitive and functional approaches to language structure* 1–39. Mahwah, NJ: Erlbaum.

Langacker, Ronald W. 2000. A dynamic usage-based model. In Michael Barlow and Suzanne Kemmer, eds., *Usage-based models of language* 1–63. Stanford, CA: CSLI Publications.

Lieven, Elena V.M., Julian M. Pine, and Gillian Baldwin. 1997. Lexically-based learning and early grammatical development. *Journal of Child Language* 24: 187–219.

Luger, George, and William Stubblefield. 1993. *Artificial intelligence: Structures and strategies for complex problem solving.* New York: Benjamin Cummings.

Pake, James. 1998. The marker hypothesis: A constructivist theory of language acquisition. PhD dissertation, University of Edinburgh.

Percival, Keith. 1976. On the historical source of immediate constituent analysis. In James D. McCawley, ed., *Notes from the linguistic underground* 229–42. London: Academic Press.

Percival, Keith. 1990. Reflections on the history of dependency notions in linguistics. *Historiographia Linguistica* 17: 29–47.

Pine, Julian M., Elena V. M. Lieven, and Caroline F. Rowland. 1998. Comparing different models of the development of the English verb category. *Linguistics* 36: 807–30.

Radford, Andrew. 1997. *Syntactic theory and the structure of English: A minimalist approach.* Cambridge: Cambridge University Press.

Reisberg, Daniel. 1997. *Cognition: Exploring the science of mind.* New York: W. W. Norton.

Robins, Robert. [1959] 2001. In defence of WP. *Transactions of the Philological Society* 99: 114–44.

Roelofs, Ardi. 1996. Serial order in planning the production of successive morphemes of a word. *Journal of Memory and Language* 35: 854–76.

Rosta, Andrew. 1997. English syntax and word grammar theory. PhD dissertation, University of London.

Sadock, Jerrold. 1991. *Autolexical syntax: A theory of parallel grammatical representations.* Chicago: University of Chicago Press.

Sowa, John. 1984. *Conceptual structures: Information processing in mind and machine.* Reading, MA: Addison-Wesley.

Sperber, Dan, and Deirdre Wilson. 1995. *Relevance: Communication and cognition.* Oxford: Basil Blackwell.

Sweetser, Eve. 1987. The definition of *lie*: An examination of the folk models underlying a semantic prototype. In David Holland and Nigel Quinn, eds., *Cultural models in language and thought* 43–66. Cambridge: Cambridge University Press.

Tomasello, Michael. 2000. Do young children have adult syntactic competence? *Cognition* 74: 209–53.

Tomasello, Michael. 2003. *Constructing a language: A usage-based theory of language acquisition.* Cambridge, MA: Harvard University Press.

Winograd, Terry. 1976. Towards a procedural understanding of semantics. *Revue Internationale de Philosophie* 30: 260–303.

PART III

SITUATING
COGNITIVE
LINGUISTICS

CHAPTER 20

COGNITIVE LINGUISTICS AND FUNCTIONAL LINGUISTICS

JAN NUYTS

1. INTRODUCTION

This chapter is an inquiry into how Cognitive Linguistics relates to, complements, and/or differs from other approaches within the wider field of functionally oriented linguistics (of which Cognitive Linguistics is a member as well). In order to avoid terminological confusion, I will use the notion "Functional Linguistics" strictly to refer to such "other functional approaches" only, to the exclusion of Cognitive Linguistics. The notion "functionally oriented linguistics" will serve as a cover term for all functional approaches to language, including Cognitive Linguistics.

This chapter is organized as follows. In section 2, I will discuss the problem of delimiting Cognitive Linguistics on the one hand, and Functional Linguistics on the other. The subsequent sections deal with major dimensions along which one can compare Cognitive Linguistics and Functional Linguistics. Section 3 assesses the position of the two paradigms vis-à-vis the basic theoretical notions from which their names have been derived: "functionalism" and "cognition." Section 4 considers how and to what extent these two paradigms deal with major dimensions of the object domain of language (structure, meaning, discourse, etc.). Section 5 briefly addresses the methods of inquiry. Section 6, finally, turns to the views on the nature and status of (linguistic) knowledge espoused in Cognitive Linguistics and Functional Linguistics, including what may be the most significant distinctive element between them, namely, the "pattern" versus "process" issue.

2. Delimiting Cognitive Linguistics and Functional Linguistics

In order to uncover the differences and similarities between Cognitive Linguistics and Functional Linguistics, one obviously needs a clear notion of how these research fields or paradigms can be mutually delimited. It is far from easy, however, to draw an actual borderline. Cognitive Linguistics is generally considered to have a clear scientific identity, distinguishing it from other approaches in linguistics, and thus also from Functional Linguistics. The existence of the present *Handbook*, specifically devoted to Cognitive Linguistics, may testify to this point. However, when it comes to characterizing this identity, it soon turns out that there are very few criteria (if any) that are really specific or unique to Cognitive Linguistics and allow us to oppose Cognitive Linguistics to other functional approaches. Ultimately, any delimitation of Cognitive Linguistics is bound to be, to some extent, arbitrary, or inspired by nonscientific criteria, such as social ones (see below). Consequently, opinions about where to draw the line can easily diverge. The present *Handbook* can again serve as an illustration, as it features several subjects that many would consider to go well beyond Cognitive Linguistics proper, into the realm of Functional Linguistics, while others might find that the *Handbook* covers too narrow a section of the entire field of Cognitive Linguistics.

Here, then, is a brief characterization of how I will delimit the fields of Cognitive Linguistics and Functional Linguistics for the purpose of this chapter, in terms of research groups or traditions belonging to each.

Cognitive Linguistics

I define the field of Cognitive Linguistics at two "levels of extension." At the first level, I define it fairly narrowly (more narrowly than the present *Handbook*),[1] confining it to what could be considered its "core": a body of research centering around semantic analyses of the type pioneered by Talmy (1988a, 1988b, 1996, 2000a, 2000b); Lakoff (1987; Lakoff and Johnson 1980; see also Gibbs 1994); Fauconnier (in his semantic "Mental Spaces" theory; 1985, 1997); Langacker (in his model of "Cognitive Grammar"; 1987, 1991); and further found in several of the grammatical models labeled "Construction Grammar." Construction Grammar is itself a conglomerate of approaches (see Croft, this volume, chapter 18), some of which can be more or less unambiguously situated within the range of Cognitive Linguistics (e.g., the variants by Lakoff 1987; Goldberg 1995; Croft 2001). Other variants of Construction Grammar do not fall under the Cognitive Linguistics heading. This is most notably true for the version that could rightfully claim the patent on the label and the concept of Construction Grammar, namely, the version by Fillmore, Kay, and colleagues (Fillmore 1988; Fillmore, Kay, and O'Connor 1988; Fillmore et al., forthcoming), which has been "under construction" since the mid-eighties. This branch of Construction Grammar is currently clearly inclining toward a grammar model such as Head-Driven Phrase Structure Grammar (usually abbreviated to HPSG; Pollard and Sag 1994)—not the kind of model one would readily associate with Cognitive Linguistics.[2]

There is one straightforward nonscientific, geographical and thus social element which binds together Cognitive Linguistics as characterized above, namely, the fact that all the linguists mentioned have worked for at least part of their careers at Californian universities in the 1980s and 1990s, mostly at the University of California at Berkeley and at San Diego. (Of course, in the mean time, PhD students of these linguists, and even some of these linguists themselves, have spread to many other places in the United States and beyond, so that the geographical criterion has mainly become a historical one, and its validity is weakening rapidly as time goes by.) One important consequence of this social fact is that it has facilitated the dissemination of a number of basic views, notions, and research attitudes (which will be explicated in the following sections) among these scholars. This process has no doubt been stimulated considerably by the additional fact that quite a few of these linguists have gone through much of the same scientific developments: many of them had their roots in Generative Grammar, subsequently turned to Generative Semantics, and have ultimately come to completely reject the generative paradigm (Generative Semantics was a first step in their reaction to orthodox Generative Grammar and can be considered a stepping-stone to the creation of the Cognitive Linguistics movement).

Not all of these cognitive linguists have been influenced by the same ideas and notions to the same degree, however: even among the group of cognitive linguists considerable heterogeneity remains. Furthermore, (most of) the ideas characterizing this group are not exclusive to it. On the one hand, certain elements of the cognitive linguistic views and notions have developed independently in (functional) linguistic circles elsewhere, even if they have not always acquired the same central status there. What characterizes Cognitive Linguistics, then, is not any of these views or notions in particular, but rather the whole cluster of them. On the other hand, since UC Berkeley and UC San Diego have been strong attraction poles for linguists from around the world, the ideas developed there have had ample chance to influence other research paradigms

In a quite sizeable group of linguists, however, there has been such a strong mutual influence between the ideas and perspectives from Cognitive Linguistics and from other linguistic traditions—particularly, Functional Linguistics—that a blend of the two fields has emerged. Although many scholars in that situation squarely situate themselves within the field of Cognitive Linguistics (rather than within Functional Linguistics), I will call them "functional-cognitive linguists," in order to distinguish their approach from that of the cognitive linguists as defined above. These functional-cognitive linguists, then, represent the second "level of extension" in the present definition of Cognitive Linguistics. In a way, this characterization already applies to Croft's (2001) version of Construction Grammar (although it has been included in the above overview of "core" cognitive linguistic work), as it blends ideas from Cognitive Linguistics and language typology. The characterization certainly applies to scholars such as Kemmer (1993, 2003; Barlow and Kemmer 2000), Verhagen (1995, 2000; Kemmer and Verhagen 1994), or Geeraerts (1989, 1993, 1997), to name just a few (many more will be mentioned later in this chapter).[3] In fact, it applies to nearly the entire "European branch" of Cognitive Linguistics (of which Verhagen and Geeraerts are representatives, of course). After all, whereas the North American branch of Cognitive Linguistics has to a considerable extent grown out of a negative reaction against the Generative Grammar tradition that has been prevailing on that continent, the members of the European branch have mostly been trained in one of the European, functionally oriented (structuralist or post-structuralist) linguistic schools or traditions and have adopted the ideas from Californian Cognitive Linguistics in the course of their careers, while at the same time retaining many of the basic ideas and research attitudes they have been raised with. This is possible because there is usually perfect compatibility between the "old" and the "new" ideas (see below).[4]

Functional Linguistics

The field of Functional Linguistics is even harder to delimit, at least in terms of scholars or research groups belonging to it, because it is much wider and much more diverse than that of Cognitive Linguistics. In fact, the only reasonable characterization of Functional Linguistics is in terms of all research in linguistics (and directly related fields) that adopts a functional approach to the analysis of linguistic phenomena (see section 3)—this would, in principle, include Cognitive Linguistics, if it were not for the terminological conventions specified in the introduction. In other words, unlike Cognitive Linguistics, Functional Linguistics cannot be caught in terms of some specific, regional, social, or related (e.g., historical) criterion, but only in terms of a general "conceptual" criterion, namely, a single basic research attitude shared by many researchers and research groups all over the world.

Although it is nearly impossible to give an exhaustive overview, the best way to give an impression of the extension of Functional Linguistics is to present a survey of some of its major exponents.[5] This survey should obviously include a number of "schools" of functional grammar models, the most important of which are Systemic-Functional Grammar (as part of the wider field of Systemic Linguistics; Halliday 1994), Functional Grammar as developed in the Amsterdam tradition

(Dik 1997), and Role and Reference Grammar (Van Valin 1993)—see also Butler (2003). It should also cover a range of conceptual frameworks or traditions that have not really taken the shape of a (more or less formalized) model, but do formulate sets of (theoretical) principles aimed at grasping and explaining linguistic facts within different domains of the organization and functioning of language, including domains which are not covered by classical functional grammar models. These include, among many others:[6]

a. In the domain of "grammar": the discourse-oriented syntactic work by Givón (1984, 1990, 1995) and Chafe (1994), the Columbia School (e.g., Otheguy, Stern, and Reid 2002), and the strong tradition in cross-linguistic and typological research (usually more data-oriented than theoretical) in the style of Greenberg (1966, 1978; see also Comrie 1981; Croft 1990; and the typology group at the Max Planck Institute for Evolutionary Anthropology).

b. In the domain of semantics: the framework developed by Wierzbicka (1980, 1996), and also the "semantic-typological" work of the "cognitive anthropologists" at the Max Planck Institute for Psycholinguistics (Pederson et al. 1998),[7] work done in Slobin's (1996) "thinking for speaking" framework,[8] or in the Whorfian tradition (Lucy 1992a, 1992b).

c. In the domain of discourse studies: Mann and Thompson's (1988, 1992) Rhetorical Structure Theory, the linguistically oriented branches of Conversation Analysis (see Ochs, Schegloff, and Thompson 1996), Discourse Analysis (Sinclair and Coulthard 1975), and the framework developed by Halliday and Hasan (1976).[9]

d. In the domain of diachronic studies (grammatical and semantic): the body of research focusing on grammaticalization and related semantic phenomena such as subjectification[10] (Heine, Claudi, and Hünnemeyer 1991; Hopper and Traugott 1993; Bybee, Perkins, and Pagliuca 1994).[11]

Let us see, then, to what extent we can pinpoint distinctive features between Cognitive Linguistics and Functional Linguistics, both in their specific research goals and practices and in their theoretical viewpoints. In line with what has been suggested above, the following survey of potential sources of divergence will not reveal any points of radical opposition. When differences do emerge, they are rarely clean-cut, but rather involve tendencies within (one of) the two paradigms, to which there are (often numerous and important) exceptions on both sides (especially the "functional-cognitive linguists," who systematically defy any attempts at formulating oppositions). Further, differences rarely involve real incommensurability: they are mainly cases of complementarity or relatively minor differences in opinion.

3. THE BASIC PRINCIPLES: "FUNCTIONALISM" AND "COGNITION"

....

Let us start with the philosophical background and first have a look at the two foundational concepts from which Functional Linguistics and Cognitive Linguistics have taken their names: "functionalism" and "cognition." Do these stand for any real differences?

Functionalism

Functionalism in language research can be characterized as a basic method of analysis: it starts from the assumption that linguistic structure cannot be analyzed independently of the uses to which it is put (contrary to formalism, which denies the relevance of language use to understanding linguistic structure; see Nuyts 1994b). Usually, these uses are captured under the covering term of "communication," but this still includes a wide range of more specific dimensions and factors determining how language appears in actual contexts—from semantic ones, to do with the transmission of information (world knowledge), to interactive or social ones (often called "pragmatic"), to do with interpersonal relationships and with the discursive nature of language use.[12] This basic orientation characterizes Functional Linguistics. But, as mentioned in the introduction, Cognitive Linguistics, too, is an integral subpart of the wider field of functionally oriented linguistics, as its approach to language is in line with the basic premises of linguistic functionalism (see Langacker, this volume, chapter 17, section 1).

Nevertheless, there may be a difference in the way, or in the extent or intensity, to which this basic orientation is applied in both fields. Many functionalists will argue that Cognitive Linguistics only deals with certain aspects of the functionality of language: although it pays due credit to the role of purely semantic dimensions in language (specifically, dimensions pertaining to the way we conceptualize and categorize the world), it deals less extensively with the role of truly communicative dimensions (interactional and discursive features of language, the role of mutual knowledge and its effect on information structuring, interpersonal relations between speaker and hearer, etc.). Of course, even within the field of Functional Linguistics itself, this kind of contrast exists, but it usually works in the opposite direction: several functionalists pay due attention to the communicative dimensions of language but are minimally—if at all—concerned with its conceptual semantic dimension.

In sum, then, although differences in the conception of the functional dimension and its relation to language structure no doubt trigger substantial differences between specific approaches and models, such differences do not characterize the position of Cognitive Linguistics vis-à-vis Functional Linguistics per se. They rather characterize many of the differences within the field of functionally oriented language research in general.

Cognition

If the functionalist dimension is not a distinguishing factor, then maybe the cognitive dimension is. Accepting a cognitive orientation in language research means adopting a particular research goal, namely, discovering the organization and operational principles of the systems that are "implemented" (to use a dangerous word) in the human brain and are responsible for producing and interpreting linguistic behavior. There are, of course, very different views of what cognition involves more specifically, and, as a result, the cognitive orientation is found in a very heterogeneous set of approaches (at least as heterogeneous as the set of functional approaches). Anyway, while, in principle, one can distinguish between those who (in some way) do and those who do not take into consideration the problem of language and cognition, again, such a division does not coincide with the division between Cognitive Linguistics and Functional Linguistics. Obviously, cognition has at all times been a central and explicit concern to Cognitive Linguistics, but the same is true for quite a few functional linguists, including (to name some prominent examples) Givón, Chafe, Slobin, and Wierzbicka (see Chafe 1970, 1980; Givón 1979, in addition to the references given in section 2). Moreover, in the last few decades, cognition has drawn the attention of more and more members of the functional linguistic community—think only of the increasing attention for cognition in functional grammar models such as Dik's Functional Grammar and Van Valin's Role and Reference Grammar or of the renaissance of cognitive anthropology and its effect on, among others, linguistic typology. (Surely, Cognitive Linguistics has been a considerable catalyst in these.)

All in all, despite different accents in Functional Linguistics and Cognitive Linguistics concerning basic philosophical principles, there is no reason to call them substantially different research paradigms, at this level of generality.

4. DOMAINS OF LANGUAGE COVERED

A second potential source of divergences between research paradigms—and thus also between Cognitive Linguistics and Functional Linguistics—is the issue of which areas or domains of the object of inquiry are within their scope of attention. At first sight, this has more to do with practical choices (and research fashions) than with basic research orientations or positions. Yet, it is well known that, for example, taking a narrow or a broad perspective on some dimension of a research object (i.e., a perspective which either is or is not informed by the characteristics of other dimensions of the same research object) may lead to very different and often hardly reconcilable conceptions of that dimension.[13] So the matter is not without theoretical importance.

Although, arguably, there is cognitive linguistic work on practically all major domains of language (see parts IV and V of the present *Handbook*), Cognitive Linguistics as defined above is predominantly oriented to semantic phenomena (witness part I of the present *Handbook*, which almost exclusively features purely semantic notions). What is more, these semantic concerns are to a considerable extent (though certainly not exclusively) directed at phenomena such as categorization and schematization in conceptualizing the world (cognitive models, mental spaces, type-token relations, metaphorization, imagery, etc.). Cognitive Linguistics also pays serious attention to language-structural phenomena proper in Cognitive Grammar and in various Construction Grammars,[14] but research in this area is not as well represented as the semantically oriented research. Moreover, in its analysis of structure, Cognitive Grammar (much more so than the various Construction Grammars) is strongly oriented to semantics (in particular, the semantic aspects relating to human categorization) and is therefore as much a semantic model as it is a syntactic one. The level of discourse structure is practically absent in Cognitive Linguistics, except for considerations such as those in Langacker (2001a)—but see Sanders and Spooren (this volume, chapter 35) for more references from a more broadly defined field of Cognitive Linguistics. Finally, Cognitive Linguistics has a strongly synchronic orientation. Few exceptions apart (including Sweetser 1990), there is hardly any consideration of diachrony.[15] However, given a broader delimitation of the field of Cognitive Linguistics—which would then include the functional-cognitive linguists—the situation regarding diachrony is completely different: many European cognitive linguists, in particular, have always shown a very active interest in the issue of language change (again, not surprisingly, with a main focus on semantic issues; see, e.g., Geeraerts 1997; Blank and Koch 1999).

Functional Linguistics, by contrast, is mainly oriented toward an account of linguistic structure.[16] Functional Linguistics, too, has seen a few predominantly semantic approaches, such as that by Wierzbicka (which, in a way, is also about the basics of human categorization) or by the cognitive anthropologists at the Max Planck Institute for Psycholinguistics (see also several contributions in Nuyts and Pederson 1997). But, on the whole, purely semantic research, particularly of the kind predominating in Cognitive Linguistics, is rare in Functional Linguistics. Of course, meaning does play a crucial role in functional linguistic approaches to structural phenomena, as it is one of the central elements of the functionalist orientation (see also Harder 1996), and this sometimes even implies a certain concern with semantic phenomena proper. A prime example is the considerable attention in Functional Linguistics (more so than in Cognitive Linguistics) to phenomena of sentence modification and evaluation, that is, what is often called "Tense-Aspect-Modality," or "TAM," marking (despite the fact that it also involves other semantic categories, such as negation, space, and evidentiality).[17] The topic is central to very different branches of Functional Linguistics, including several of the major grammar models (see the proposals for "layered" or "hierarchical" representations of operators and adverbials/satellites in Functional Grammar and Role and Reference Grammar—see, e.g., Van Valin 1993; Van Valin and LaPolla 1997; Hengeveld 1989; Dik 1997; several contributions in Nuyts, Bolkestein, and Vet 1990; see also Nuyts 2004), the typological literature (e.g., Comrie 1976, 1985; Chafe and Nichols 1986; Willett 1988; Kahrel and van den Berg 1994; Palmer 2001; among many others), and the diachronic literature (Tense-Aspect-Modality markers are obviously crucial in both the grammaticalization and the subjectification literature—see, e.g., Traugott 1989, 1997; Bybee, Perkins, and Pagliuca 1994). However, the functional linguistic interest in these semantic categories is primarily due to the fact that their linguistic expression tends to exhibit remarkable grammatical properties that pose a challenge to many accounts of linguistic structure. Interest in the topic of Tense-Aspect-Modality markers is therefore primarily inspired by structural phenomena, and semantics are dealt with as "instrumental" to an account of the structural dimension.[18] (This strong bias toward the structural end often leads to a biased view of the semantic issues involved and to problems in handling Tense-Aspect-Modality markers in grammar; see Nuyts 2001, 2003.) The purely semantic work on space by the cognitive anthropologists obviously belongs in the same category of semantic investigations but is not biased by the structural dimension.

The attention to structure in Functional Linguistics not only pertains to the level of the sentence, but also to the level of discourse. To be sure, not all of the work in Functional Linguistics dealing with sentence structure is also explicitly concerned with discourse structure proper. For example, (traditional) Functional Grammar,[19] Role and Reference Grammar, and much typological and diachronic research shows little interest in discourse structure. But Systemic Linguistics, or the work by researchers such as Givón or Chafe (Givón 1983; see section 3 for further references), clearly does. And there is work that is even exclusively concerned with discourse structure, including, quite prominently, the frameworks of Discourse Analysis and Conversation Analysis. Still, even in the "sentence structure only" approaches, there is much attention to the way the internal structure of a sentence or clause is adjusted to its discourse environment (e.g., consider the elaborate work on information structure and its effect on word order in the clause), probably more so than in cognitive linguistic syntax. In Cognitive Grammar, for example, there is considerable attention for information structuring and perspectivization, namely, in the form of "construal" operations (where we find notions such as "trajectory" and "landmark"), but these are treated from a purely semantic perspective, in terms of how a speaker conceptualizes a situation and not in terms of how (the information in) an utterance relates to its preceding context (which would involve issues of topic continuity and topic shift, rhematicity of information and text development, contrastivity, etc.).

As already indicated, diachrony also figures prominently in Functional Linguistics; witness the flourishing of research on grammaticalization and, to a lesser extent, on subjectification.

So, on the whole, as far as the object of investigation is concerned, Cognitive Linguistics and Functional Linguistics are to a considerable extent complementary in their concerns. As a result, relating their views on different aspects of the same object may offer a wealth of new insights on both "sides". Ideally, one might even strive for a direct integration of models. But doing so is obviously only possible if these models are compatible, not only in general terms (see section 3), but also at a more concrete level. As a matter of fact, areas in which Cognitive Linguistics and Functional Linguistics have overlapping concerns (the domain of grammatical or syntactic description) demonstrate that there may be divergence in terms of their views on the nature of (linguistic and general) knowledge (see section 6 below).

5. Methods

Maybe the difference between Cognitive Linguistics and Functional Linguistics has to do with different research traditions, styles, and methods. Again, this is not the case in any principled way. Neither Cognitive Linguistics nor Functional Linguistics bar the use of any type of strategy to investigate a specific phenomenon; all methods are considered potentially valid.[20] In practice, however, they differ to some extent in terms of the default methods used in empirical research.

Systematic corpus-based analyses of phenomena are rather common in Functional Linguistics, but less so in Cognitive Linguistics. Of course, even in Functional Linguistics, corpus studies are far from general practice. Corpus investigation (including the use of quantitative methods) is, for example, almost obligatory in a framework such as Systemic Linguistics (in both its lexicogrammatical branch, i.e., Systemic-Functional Grammar, and its discourse-oriented branch); it is also popular in much other discourse-oriented work (such as that of Givón and Chafe or frameworks such as Rhetorical Structure Theory or Discourse Analysis) and in most diachronic research. By contrast, it is rather exceptional in frameworks such as Dik's Functional Grammar or Van Valin's Role and Reference Grammar. Similarly, Cognitive Linguistics shows exceptions to the general trend: corpus linguistics is very rare (if present at all) in core Cognitive Linguistics, but it is far from exceptional in the work of the functional-cognitive linguists, notably in the work of Barlow and Kemmer (see Barlow 1996; Kemmer and Barlow 2000) and of several European cognitive linguists (see, e.g., several of the contributions in Rudzka-Ostyn 1988; Geeraerts 1999).

Further, the systematic and large-scale use of cross-linguistic data is common in Functional Linguistics, but hardly so in Cognitive Linguistics (see van der Auwera and Nuyts, this volume, chapter 40). Thus, as already indicated in section 2, typology is a prominent and continuously growing branch of Functional Linguistics, and the same applies to comparative linguistics (where much smaller sets of languages are studied). In Cognitive Linguistics, the use of cross-linguistic data is far less common. Admittedly, one scholar who has been associated with Cognitive Linguistics in section 2, is also a major player in typology, namely, Croft. Then again, Croft is clearly one of those who are standing on the edge between Cognitive Linguistics and Functional Linguistics (having his roots in a functional linguistic context—the Greenbergian school). Note, incidentally, that among the versions of Construction Grammar cited above, his was the most recent to emerge. Of course, many cognitive linguistic issues are being considered from a comparative perspective to the extent that they are tested by scholars across the world on languages other than English (including non-Indo-European languages; see, e.g., Casad and Langacker 1985; Yu 1998; Casad and Palmer 2003), but this remains relatively limited in comparison to comparative research in Functional Linguistics.

One would expect cognitively oriented frameworks to develop a special interest in experimental methods. Yet this is not really true as far as Cognitive Linguistics is concerned: there is some experimental research, though mainly by language psychologists who have taken an interest in Cognitive Linguistics (e.g., Gibbs and Colston 1995; see also Sinha, this volume, chapter 49). A few more "linguistic" examples are Sandra and Rice (1995) and Brisard, Frisson, and Sandra (2001). In Functional Linguistics, a similar situation holds: in the more cognitively oriented branches, some experimental research exists, but again it is fairly limited. Interestingly, in the case of Functional Linguistics, experimental research has more often been carried out by genuine linguists, sometimes in collaboration with psychologists (e.g., Carroll and von Stutterheim 1993; Carroll 1997; Tomlin 1997; Nuyts and Vonk 1999; Dickinson and Givón 2000). Of course, much depends on what one calls an "experiment": much of the research of the cognitive anthropologists at the Max Planck Institute for Psycholinguistics is also based on "controlled data elicitation" (Pederson et al. 1998), as is the research in the context of Slobin's "thinking for speaking" project (Berman and Slobin 1994), but many experimental psychologists would consider this a marginal kind of experiment—a remark that may also apply to several of the other experiments just cited. Another issue is where to draw the disciplinary borderlines between psychology and linguistics: in addition to Slobin, there are several other psychologists who are very close to Functional Linguistics and who make systematic use of experimental techniques, including McNeill and collaborators (e.g., McNeill 1992, 1997, 2000) and Clark and collaborators (Clark 1992, 1996).

A recent development in Cognitive Linguistics, which is virtually absent in Functional Linguistics, is the attempt to use neurological or neuropsychological evidence as a means to substantiate theories. However, even within Cognitive Linguistics, this new approach has so far been mainly confined to the Lakoffian framework of Cognitive Semantics (see Lakoff and Johnson 1999).

All in all, then, Cognitive Linguistics is—more so than Functional Linguistics—inclined to draw on the linguistic practices which have become established since the generative revolution in the fifties and sixties, namely, to use artificial examples or natural examples which have occasionally or accidentally been picked from written or spoken discourse, although the way in which cognitive linguists—or functional linguists applying similar methods, for that matter—use such examples is incomparable to the way generative linguists use them.

6. Theoretical Conceptions of Language and Grammar

Last but not least, one may wonder to what extent there are systematic differences in the theoretical views in Cognitive Linguistics and Functional Linguistics regarding the nature, the organization, and the wider cognitive embedding of language and grammar at a more concrete level than the one discussed in section 3 above. Of course, the two paradigms are in themselves far from theoretically coherent. Thus, in Cognitive Linguistics, the grammatical analyses in Langacker's Cognitive Grammar are in several respects substantially different from those in Construction Grammar approaches, and they do not appear easily reconcilable. Likewise, in spite of many basic similarities, Talmy's, Lakoff's, Fauconnier's, and Langacker's views on the nature and organization of (conceptual) semantic representation are far from identical, and the differences may go well beyond placing different accents or being concerned with different facets of the issue (for example, they probably do not share the same view on the status of metaphor in semantics). In that respect, it is probably no coincidence that there is little explicit mutual discussion of views among these four scholars or their research groups. Similarly, in Functional Linguistics the major alternative grammar models often differ in substantial respects (e.g., Systemic-Functional Grammar is in many respects irreconcilable with Functional Grammar or Role and Reference Grammar), as do the various conceptions of discourse organization (recall the radical disputes between conversational analysts and discourse analysts—see, e.g., Levinson 1983: 286–94).

Still, at a sufficiently high level of generality, some patterns emerge. First of all, Cognitive Linguistics and Functional Linguistics share a few basic views regarding the status of grammar. In line with their shared functionalist orientation, they both adopt a "usage-based" concept of grammar (see Langacker 1988; Barlow and Kemmer 2000). In other words, they reject a "competence" view of grammar of the kind espoused in Chomskyan Generative Grammar, in which linguistic knowledge is considered fully independent of linguistic performance (see Nuyts 1992, 1994a). In Cognitive Linguistics and Functional Linguistics, linguistic knowledge is "knowledge for use." Correspondingly, both Cognitive Linguistics and the "cognitively conscious" branches of Functional Linguistics see the linguistic system as an integrated subpart of human cognition and reject a (strongly) modular view of the language faculty as it is adopted in the generative tradition in linguistics (or in some branches of psychology, following Fodor 1983). Thus, the principles inherent in language are assumed to be (potentially) instantiations of more general cognitive principles, and the grammar is seen as fully interconnected and tuned in with other dimensions of cognitive functioning, including the conceptual systems.

In this latter respect, there may be different tendencies in Functional Linguistics and Cognitive Linguistics with regard to the default assumptions about the nature of conceptual representation (see Pederson and Nuyts 1997 on alternative views of conceptual structure). To the extent that this issue is at stake in Functional Linguistics, there is a strong inclination to adopt a strongly language-related, or at least a propositional view. This can range from strongly language-bound views (in which conceptual structure is considered to feature linguistic or language-like structures, including the lexical material of languages), such as Dik's (1987) or the Whorfian view (Lucy 1992a, 1992b), to slightly more abstract views (which are often decompositional, i.e., assuming semantic-conceptual structure to operate in terms of semantic primitives), such as Wierzbicka's (1980), or Van Valin's (1993)—see Levinson (1997) and Nuyts (1993b, 2001) for critical discussion of some of these proposals. Many other functional linguists who take conceptual structure into consideration remain vague about its nature (see Nuyts 1996). Cognitive linguists, on the other hand, often stress the "imagery" nature of conceptualization (consider, e.g., Lakoff 1987; Langacker 1987), which might suggest that they are thinking along the lines of a vision-based view of conceptual structure. Still, closer scrutiny of their actual views reveals uncertainty regarding the issue—think, for instance, of Langacker's insistence on predicates (an essentially propositionalist notion) as the basic building blocks of conceptualization or Lakoff's openness to conceptual models of all conceivable types, including propositional ones (see Nuyts 1993a, 2001 for discussion).[21] So, even in this regard, there are probably no real incommensurabilities between Cognitive Linguistics and Functional Linguistics.

Still, there appears to be one major difference between Cognitive Linguistics and Functional Linguistics in their conception of grammar and of conceptualization, and probably of cognition in general. This difference concerns the status of structures as opposed to processes in a cognitive model. It is most conspicuous when comparing the grammatical models in the two paradigms, that is, the domain in which the two are overlapping most clearly (see section 4).

Both Cognitive Grammar and Construction Grammar stress the role of structures or "constructions" in linguistic knowledge, while they hardly consider processing, that is, the procedures or rules that might be applied by a speaker or a hearer in "building" linguistic or semantic structures (the following applies to language production and comprehension alike, but for the sake of simplicity, I will phrase the issue from the perspective of production). The point is not only that the cognitive linguistic models do not formulate the procedures or rules needed to construct utterances (many functional grammar models do not do so, either); the point is also that in models such as Cognitive Grammar or (versions of) Construction Grammar procedures are attributed only a small role: they are reduced to (probably quite simple) mechanisms combining (or "unifying") fixed, coded patterns (that are stored as such in the mind) of different degrees of complexity and schematicity—the "constructions"—in order to "assemble" a full linguistic expression. Most of the combining is presumably a matter of checking the compatibility of properties of the constructions involved. A grammar is, thus, a "structured inventory of conventional linguistic units" (Langacker 1987: 57), or, in yet other words, a network of constructions.

The functional linguistic concept of a grammar, by contrast, is essentially that of a system of rules or procedures which compose utterances.[22] To some extent, functional grammars involve coded patterns as well, such as the elements stored in the lexicon (which includes more complex idiomatic expressions that cannot be considered compositional anymore) or constructional schemata for basic word-order patterns in an utterance—such as the "constituent ordering templates" in Functional Grammar (see Dik 1997) or the "syntactic inventory" in Role and Reference Grammar (see Van Valin and LaPolla 1997). But the role of coded patterns is minimal in comparison to the role they play in the cognitive linguistic models: essentially, whatever structure is considered linguistically "productive" Functional Linguistics handles entirely in terms of productive devices (see, e.g., Dik 1997: 342–45 for a discussion of productivity in grammar).

This different conception of grammar is representative of the cognitive linguistic and functional linguistic concepts of cognition in general. Thus, it is probably no coincidence that, in semantics, cognitive linguists tend to put great emphasis on the role of metaphor (i.e., the mapping between semantic domains) when describing meaning relations or processes, whereas functional linguists in actual practice tend to think in terms of metonymy (a gradual process of contextual transfer between semantic domains) even when they are concerned with the same phenomena.[23] A case in point is the discussion about the role of metaphor as opposed to metonymy in diachronic semantic change in the range of "grammatical" or "qualificational" meanings (consider, e.g., Sweetser 1990, as opposed to Traugott 1989 and Traugott and König 1991; see Nuyts 2001: 182–83 for discussion).

There need not be incompatibility between process and representation in a cognitive model: as Barsalou and Hale (1993) argue, any viable model of linguistic (or other) behavior must be concerned with both in a balanced and integrated fashion. But the critical point is that many things that are handled by means of procedures or rules in functional linguistic models are handled in terms of constructional patterns in Cognitive Linguistics. Even so, one might claim there is no incompatibility per se: one could imagine that the mental systems for language use contain procedures that allow the productive composition of any analyzable pattern, but that frequently produced (i.e., well-entrenched) output of those systems is nevertheless stored in the form of ready-made patterns for immediate reuse (at the same time, it is not obvious whether this notion is compatible with the basic philosophy and the actual formalization of the Cognitive Grammar and Construction Grammar models).[24] However, such a concept seems to be precluded at least by Langacker (1987: 63–64; 1997), who explicitly argues against a process view of grammar (see Nuyts 1993a, 2001: 16–19 for discussion). It might seem, then, that we are facing a basic conflict between a strongly dynamic view of grammar and language in Functional Linguistics versus a static one in Cognitive Linguistics. Then again, at least in these terms, the idea of a conflict is preempted by Langacker's (1997, 2000, 2001b) argument that Cognitive Grammar does represent a dynamic, procedural view of language and cognition—a view that he reconciles with the strongly representational nature of grammar at a metatheoretical level, namely, in terms of the "phenomenological status" of a grammatical model (Langacker 1997: 239–40).

Still, this argument clearly does not preempt the apparent conflict between functional linguistic and cognitive linguistic models with regard to the actual role of processes or procedures as opposed to constructions in them. This issue definitely requires further attention in order to see to what extent we are really facing incompatibilities and in order to find out how Cognitive Linguistics and Functional Linguistics can work toward a closer integration, not only at the level of grammatical description, but also in other domains of language such as conceptual structure or discourse.

7. CONCLUSION

In sum, although there are certainly "practical" differences between Cognitive Linguistics and Functional Linguistics in terms of the domains of language they actively consider and in terms of the methods they apply, none of these appear to be clear-cut or seem to involve incommensurabilities. As to their basic philosophy, the two paradigms are essentially in agreement, and, no doubt, Cognitive Linguistics and Functional Linguistics can learn a lot from each other in many respects. But in order to find out how far the friendship can go, one critical matter needs to be resolved, namely, the "process versus pattern" view of language and mind, which, at least at first sight, holds the potential of becoming an issue of real dispute.

NOTES

Thanks to the editors of this volume, Hubert Cuyckens and Dirk Geeraerts, for useful comments on an earlier draft of this chapter. Shortcomings of the final result obviously remain my own responsibility. In this regard, let me issue an apology, right from the start, to all those who will feel mistreated in any way by the discussions to follow. Comparing research paradigms of the size and diversity of Cognitive Linguistics and Functional Linguistics in a brief chapter such as this is a very difficult enterprise. It forces one to construe opponent "strawmen" positions, cast in rather shadeless black and white terms; hence, it is bound to involve radical oversimplifications and the loss of many subtleties and nuances. This is even worsened by the fact that both paradigms (if one can call them such) are actually constantly influencing and cross-fertilizing each other (and increasingly so) and that there are numerous researchers who explicitly try to combine elements of both (many of whom are represented in the present *Handbook*). Although I have done my best to pay due credit also to the latter, in some cases they may still be the victim of the unavoidable tendency to focus on the opposition between the strawmen positions.

1. The narrow definition is used simply for the sake of the present discussion: as will be obvious from the foregoing considerations and from the discussion in the following sections, the wider one sets the margins of Cognitive Linguistics (e.g., as in the present

Handbook), the more difficult it becomes to find any distinctive features between Cognitive Linguistics and Functional Linguistics. This should definitely not be taken as a plea for maintaining a separated, narrow field of Cognitive Linguistics. Quite on the contrary: to foreshadow the conclusions of this chapter, there is every reason to consider Cognitive Linguistics a "school" within the wider field of Functional Linguistics and to strive for a stronger integration of the two.

2. Models of the HPSG style are not usually considered part of Functional Linguistics either: they are much rather considered part of the generative tradition in linguistics (see Sag and Wasow 1999). Yet they have clearly adopted a few basic ideas from syntactic approaches in European structuralism (which was, unlike its American counterpart, overwhelmingly functionalist in orientation), most notably the concept of dependency as it was originally developed by Tesnière (1959). As such, they are taking some kind of middle way between the classical formalist and functionalist traditions in the theory of grammar.

3. Determining the borderlines between the field of Cognitive Linguistics in its wider definition (including the two "levels of extension" defined above) and the field of Functional Linguistics is, even more so than for core Cognitive Linguistics, a matter of applying social criteria: one would probably have to use a criterion such as membership in the International Cognitive Linguistics Association or regular participation in its conferences to determine who is a cognitive linguist, rather than a functional linguist. On most other criteria, there will be no ground to make a clear distinction, as will appear below.

4. Incidentally, European cognitive linguists have played a major role in disseminating the ideas of Cognitive Linguistics, for example, by creating the International Cognitive Linguistics Association (of which René Dirven is the founding father) and by establishing the *Cognitive Linguistics* journal (thanks to Dirk Geeraerts) and, more recently, the *Annual Review of Cognitive Linguistics* (thanks to Francisco Ruiz de Mendoza).

5. In order to allow the reader to "objectify" the present chapter, I should mention that my own research is to be situated in the framework of Functional Linguistics, rather than Cognitive Linguistics (at least its narrowly defined "core"), even if in many respects it is fairly close to the latter (especially in its wider definition). See, for example, Nuyts (1992, 2001).

6. The borderlines between the different domains—and especially between the domains of grammar and semantics—are obviously very vague, and many of the linguists and traditions mentioned above defy straightforward classification.

7. The question is whether these "cognitive anthropologists" can be called linguists or not. This is not the place to enter into a debate regarding the demarcation of disciplines, but I include them in Functional Linguistics on the basis of the observation that the majority of scholars who have been working in this group have a linguistic background.

8. Slobin is, of course, at least as much a psychologist as a linguist. Again, limits of space prevent me from dealing with the question where to draw the disciplinary borderline, in this case between Functional Linguistics or Cognitive Linguistics on the one hand, and language psychology on the other. (See part VI of the present *Handbook*.)

9. In fact, Mann and Thompson's and Sinclair and Coulthard's frameworks are also, to a considerable extent, inspired by the work on discourse in Systemic Linguistics.

10. "Subjectification" is meant here in the sense of Traugott (1989, 1995), not in the cognitive linguistic sense as developed by Langacker (1990).

11. Because of its very wide definition of Cognitive Linguistics, some of these traditions are also represented in the present *Handbook*; for example, some of the typological literature, some of the work on discourse structure, and the grammaticalization and subjectification literature. In fact, (at least some members of) these traditions have been influenced very directly by some of the ideas developed in Cognitive Linguistics (see this volume, chapters 35, 36, and 40).

12. There is no unanimity among functionalists regarding the analysis of the functional dimension of language use (see Nuyts 1993c), nor about the question of how language structure and language function might relate. Illustrative for the latter is the difference in opinion among functionalist linguists as to whether a grammar requires separated, parallel networks to account for different functional dimensions of (different aspects or components of) linguistic structure (as is the case in Systemic-Functional Grammar; Halliday 1994), or, alternatively, whether a grammar should deal with different functional dimensions as interacting forces which jointly codetermine all dimensions and aspects of linguistic structure (as is advocated by Dik 1986).

13. This fact offers a clear argument against "methodological modularity," the approach advocated in generative linguistics to deal with one domain (syntax) to the *a priori* exclusion of any other related domains, including semantics. Whether or not modularity is maintainable as a theoretical concept can only be settled on the basis of empirical evidence, but "methodological modularity" prevents one from searching for such evidence. There is, however, not enough room to go into this issue in the present contribution.

14. I am using the notion of "language structural phenomena" as a cover term for all aspects of the structural organization of the sentence, that is, including not only the syntactic but also the morphological and the phonological levels.

15. Langacker has, of course, indicated potential links between his notion of "subjectification" (Langacker 1990) and the diachronic notion of subjectification introduced by Traugott (1989, 1995), and he also relates his concept of subjectification to aspects of grammaticalization. But this is different from active involvement with diachrony, of course.

16. Surely, not all aspects of language structure are equally well covered in Functional Linguistics. Specifically, phonology is quite underrepresented. But this is of no further interest here.

17. This is obviously not to say that these phenomena do not play a role at all in Cognitive Linguistics: see, for example, Talmy's (1988a, 2000a) and Sweetser's (1990) accounts of the meanings of the modal auxiliaries or Langacker's (1987) concept of "grounding," which pertains to the meaning of grammatical markers such as modals and tense markers. But, all in all, Cognitive Linguistics deals much less systematically and elaborately with TAM-related issues than Functional Linguistics (see also Nuyts 2002 on the relation between Langacker's notion of grounding and the functional linguistic literature on qualificational categories).

18. This is precisely how most of the functional linguistic accounts of qualificational categories differ from treatments of such categories in Cognitive Linguistics (see above): the latter clearly aim at an account of the meanings involved rather than the linguistic behavior of the expression forms.

19. At least, this was true of Functional Grammar until recently. Lately, there has been a tendency to try to expand the sentence grammar into a discourse grammar. See several contributions in Mackenzie and Gómez Gonzáles (2004) and Butler (2003).

20. This might seem obvious, but it is not. In Generative Grammar only constructed data based on intuitions of grammaticality are considered valid. On the other hand, in the (wider) margins of Cognitive Linguistics, some have argued that not all methods have equal potential in terms of what they can reveal about the cognitive organization of language (e.g., Croft 1998; Sandra 1998). One may disagree with some of these claims (as I do specifically with regards to Sandra's), but this is not the place to go into this issue.

21. These observations regarding the vagueness, implicitness, or uncertainty among cognitive and functional linguists regarding the nature of conceptualization should not be taken as a criticism. On the contrary: our current understanding of the issue is so poor that it is only fair to steer away from any radical claims in this regards.

22. The following not only applies to the established schools of grammar: it characterizes the default view of linguistic knowledge (not only syntactic, but also semantic and discursive) in Functional Linguistics in general. One of the established grammars, namely, Systemic-Functional Grammar, stands somewhat apart in a few respects: due to its systemic network formalism, it is difficult to talk about procedures or rules in this framework in other than strongly metaphorical terms. Still, the basic concept of a grammar described below, as a device which "composes" rather than "assembles" utterances, does apply to this model, as well.

23. This is, of course, again a simplified rendering of a complicated situation, since quite many cognitive linguists do not deny the role of metonymy in certain semantic relations (see below) and functional linguists do not deny the role of metaphor. Note, by the way, that this statement about the more intensive concern with metaphor versus metonymy in Cognitive versus Functional Linguistics applies at the "object level": it applies to what linguists actually do when describing semantic processes. At a metalevel, there is even more concern with the nature of metonymy (in relation to metaphor) among cognitive linguists than among functional linguists. This is, not surprisingly, again especially true for the European functional-cognitive linguists. And correspondingly, it is the latter group especially that deviates from the core cognitive linguists in tending toward a more balanced application of metonymy, next to metaphor, in the description of semantic phenomena (see, e.g., Goossens 1990; Panther and Radden 1999; Barcelona 2000).

24. Something comparable could be maintained for the metaphor versus metonymy issue: one might consider metaphor to be a macrolevel characterization of global semantic relations, which have, however, come into existence—and can in principle be reconstructed—through microlevel metonymic processes (this is, e.g., how Heine, Claudi, and Hünnemeyer 1991 and Heine 1993 reconcile metaphorical and metonymic accounts of semantic change in the range of qualificational meanings).

REFERENCES

Barcelona, Antonio, ed. 2000. *Metaphor and metonymy at the crossroads*. Berlin: Mouton de Gruyter.

Barlow, Michael. 1996. Corpora for theory and practice. *International Journal of Corpus Linguistics* 1: 1–37.

Barlow, Michael, and Suzanne Kemmer, eds. 2000. *Usage-based models of language*. Stanford, CA: CSLI Publications.

Barsalou, Lawrence W., and Christopher R. Hale. 1993. Components of conceptual representation: From feature lists to recursive frames. In Iven Van Mechelen, James Hampton, Ryszard S. Michalski, and Peter Theuns, eds., *Categories and concepts* 97–144. London: Academic Press.

Berman, Ruth A., and Dan I. Slobin. 1994. *Relating events in narrative: A crosslinguistic developmental study*. Hillsdale, NJ: Lawrence Erlbaum.

Blank, Andreas, and Peter Koch, eds. 1999. *Historical semantics and cognition*. Berlin: Mouton de Gruyter.

Brisard, Frank, Steven Frisson, and Dominiek Sandra. 2001. Processing unfamiliar metaphors in a self-paced reading task. *Metaphor and Symbol* 16: 87–108.

Butler, Chris. 2003. *Structural-functional grammars*. Amsterdam: John Benjamins.

Bybee, Joan L., Revere D. Perkins, and William Pagliuca. 1994. *The evolution of grammar: Tense, aspect, and modality in the languages of the world*. Chicago: University of Chicago Press.

Carroll, Mary. 1997. Changing place in English and German: Language-specific preferences in the conceptualization of spatial relations. In Jan Nuyts and Eric Pederson, eds., *Language and conceptualization* 137–61. Cambridge: Cambridge University Press.

Carroll, Mary, and Christiane von Stutterheim. 1993. The representation of spatial configurations in English and German and the grammatical structure of locative and anaphoric expressions. *Linguistics* 31: 1011–42.

Casad, Eugene, and Ronald Langacker. 1985. 'Inside' and 'outside' in Cora grammar. *International Journal of American Linguistics* 51: 247–81. Repr. in Ronald Langacker, *Concept, image, and symbol* 33–57. Berlin: Mouton de Gruyter, 1990.

Casad, Eugene, and Gary Palmer, eds. 2003. *Cognitive linguistics and non-Indo-European languages.* Berlin: Mouton de Gruyter.

Chafe, Wallace. 1970. *Meaning and the structure of language.* Chicago: University of Chicago Press.

Chafe, Wallace. 1980. The deployment of consciousness in the production of a narrative. In Wallace Chafe, ed., *The pear stories* 9–50. Norwood, NJ: Ablex.

Chafe, Wallace. 1994. *Discourse, consciousness, and time: The flow and displacement of conscious experience in speaking and writing.* Chicago: University of Chicago Press.

Chafe, Wallace, and Johanna Nichols, eds. 1986. *Evidentiality: The linguistic coding of epistemology.* Norwood, NJ: Ablex.

Clark, Herbert H. 1992. *Arenas of language use.* Chicago: University of Chicago Press.

Clark, Herbert H. 1996. *Using language.* Cambridge: Cambridge University Press.

Comrie, Bernard. 1976. *Aspect.* Cambridge: Cambridge University Press.

Comrie, Bernard. 1981. *Language universals and linguistic typology.* Oxford: Basil Blackwell. (2nd ed., 1989)

Comrie, Bernard. 1985. *Tense.* Cambridge: Cambridge University Press.

Croft, William. 1990. *Typology and universals.* Cambridge: Cambridge University Press.

Croft, William. 1998. Linguistic evidence and mental representations. *Cognitive Linguistics* 9: 151–73.

Croft, William. 2001. *Radical construction grammar: Syntactic theory in typological perspective.* Oxford: Oxford University Press.

Dickinson, Connie, and Talmy Givón. 2000. The effect of the interlocutor on episodic recall: An experimental study. In Michel Barlow and Suzanne Kemmer, eds., *Usage-based models of language* 151–96. Stanford, CA: CSLI Publications.

Dik, Simon C. 1986. On the notion 'functional explanation.' *Belgian Journal of Linguistics* 1: 11–52.

Dik, Simon C. 1987. Linguistically motivated knowledge representation. In Makato Nagao, ed., *Language and artificial intelligence* 145–70. Amsterdam: North-Holland.

Dik, Simon C. 1997. *The theory of functional grammar.* 2 vols. Ed. Kees Hengeveld. Berlin: Mouton de Gruyter.

Fauconnier, Gilles. 1985. *Mental spaces: Aspects of meaning construction in natural language.* Cambridge, MA: The MIT Press. (2nd ed., Cambridge: Cambridge University Press, 1994)

Fauconnier, Gilles. 1997. *Mappings in thought and language.* Cambridge: Cambridge University Press.

Fillmore, Charles J. 1988. The mechanisms of "construction grammar." *Berkeley Linguistics Society* 14: 35–55.

Fillmore, Charles J., Paul Kay, Laura A. Michaelis, and Ivan A. Sag. Forthcoming. *Construction Grammar.* Stanford, CA: CSLI Publications.

Fillmore, Charles J, Paul Kay, and Mary C. O'Connor. 1988. Regularity and idiomaticity in grammatical construction: The case of *let alone. Language* 64: 501–38.

Fodor, Jerry A. 1983. *The modularity of mind.* Cambridge, MA: MIT Press.

Geeraerts, Dirk. 1989. Prospects and problems of prototype theory. *Linguistics* 27: 587–612.

Geeraerts, Dirk. 1993. Vagueness's puzzles, polysemy's vagaries. *Cognitive Linguistics* 4: 223–72.

Geeraerts, Dirk. 1997. *Diachronic prototype semantics: A contribution to historical lexicology.* Oxford: Clarendon Press.

Geeraerts, Dirk. 1999. Idealist and empiricist tendencies in cognitive linguistics. In Theo Janssen and Gisela Redeker, eds., *Cognitive Linguistics: Foundations, scope, and methodology* 163–94. Berlin: Mouton de Gruyter.

Gibbs, Raymond W., Jr. 1994. *The poetics of mind: Figurative thought, language, and understanding.* Cambridge: Cambridge University Press.

Gibbs, Raymond W., Jr., and Herbert L. Colston. 1995. The cognitive psychological reality of image schemas and their transformations. *Cognitive Linguistics* 6: 347–78.

Givón, Talmy. 1979. *On understanding grammar.* New York: Academic Press.

Givón, Talmy, ed. 1983. *Topic continuity in discourse: A quantitative cross-language study.* Amsterdam: John Benjamins.

Givón, Talmy. 1984. *Syntax: A functional-typological introduction.* Vol. 1. Amsterdam: John Benjamins.

Givón, Talmy. 1990. *Syntax: A functional-typological introduction.* Vol. 2. Amsterdam: John Benjamins.

Givón, Talmy. 1995. *Functionalism and grammar.* Amsterdam: John Benjamins.

Goldberg, Adele E. 1995. *Constructions: A construction grammar approach to argument structure.* Chicago: University of Chicago Press.

Goossens, Louis. 1990. Metaphtonymy: The interaction of metaphor and metonymy in expressions for linguistic actions. *Cognitive Linguistics* 1: 323–40.

Greenberg, Joseph. 1966. *Language universals: With special reference to feature hierarchies.* The Hague: Mouton.

Greenberg, Joseph, ed. 1978. *Universals of human language.* 4 vols. Stanford, CA: Stanford University Press.

Halliday, Michael A.K. 1994. *An introduction to functional grammar.* 2nd ed. London: Arnold. (3rd ed., 2004)

Halliday, Michael A. K., and Ruqaiya Hasan. 1976. *Cohesion in English.* London: Longman.

Harder, Peter. 1996. *Functional semantics: A theory of meaning, structure and tense in English.* Berlin: Mouton de Gruyter.

Heine, Bernd. 1993. *Auxiliaries: Cognitive forces and grammaticalization.* New York: Oxford University Press.

Heine, Bernd, Ulrike Claudi, and Friederike Hünnemeyer. 1991. *Grammaticalization: A conceptual framework.* Chicago: University of Chicago Press.

Hengeveld, Kees. 1989. Layers and operators in functional grammar. *Journal of Linguistics* 25: 127–57.

Hopper, Paul J., and Elizabeth Closs Traugott. 1993. *Grammaticalization.* Cambridge: Cambridge University Press. (2nd ed., 2003)

Kahrel, Peter, and René van den Berg, eds. 1994. *Typological studies in negation.* Amsterdam: John Benjamins.

Kemmer, Suzanne. 1993. *The middle voice.* Amsterdam: John Benjamins.

Kemmer, Suzanne. 2003. Human cognition and the elaboration of events: Some universal conceptual categories. In Michael Tomasello, ed., *The new psychology of language: Cognitive and functional approaches to language structure* 2: 89–118. Mahwah, NJ: Lawrence Erlbaum.

Kemmer, Suzanne, and Michael Barlow. 2000. Introduction. In Michael Barlow and Suzanne Kemmer, eds., *Usage-based models of language* vii–xxviii. Stanford, CA: CSLI Publications.

Kemmer, Suzanne, and Arie Verhagen. 1994. The grammar of causatives and the conceptual structure of events. *Cognitive Linguistics* 5: 115–56.

Lakoff, George. 1987. *Women, fire, and dangerous things: What categories reveal about the mind.* Chicago: University of Chicago Press.

Lakoff, George, and Mark Johnson. 1980. *Metaphors we live by.* Chicago: University of Chicago Press.

Lakoff, George, and Mark Johnson. 1999. *Philosophy in the flesh: The embodied mind and its challenge to Western thought.* New York: Basic Books.

Langacker, Ronald W. 1987. *Foundations of cognitive grammar.* Vol. 1, *Theoretical prerequisites.* Stanford, CA: Stanford University Press.

Langacker, Ronald W. 1988. A usage-based model. In Brygida Rudzka-Ostyn, ed., *Topics in cognitive linguistics* 127–61. Amsterdam: John Benjamins.

Langacker, Ronald W. 1990. Subjectification. *Cognitive Linguistics* 1: 5–38.

Langacker, Ronald W. 1991. *Foundations of cognitive grammar.* Vol. 2, *Descriptive application.* Stanford, CA: Stanford University Press.

Langacker, Ronald W. 1997. The contextual basis of cognitive semantics. In Jan Nuyts and Eric Pederson, eds., *Language and conceptualization* 229–52. Cambridge: Cambridge University Press.

Langacker, Ronald W. 2000. A dynamic usage-based model. In Michael Barlow and Suzanne Kemmer, eds., *Usage-based models of language* 1–63. Stanford, CA: CSLI Publications.

Langacker, Ronald W. 2001a. Discourse in cognitive grammar. *Cognitive Linguistics* 12: 143–88.

Langacker, Ronald W. 2001b. Dynamicity in grammar. *Axiomathes* 12: 7–33.

Levinson, Stephen C. 1983. *Pragmatics.* Cambridge: Cambridge University Press.

Levinson, Stephen C. 1997. From outer to inner space: Linguistic categories and non-linguistic thinking. In Jan Nuyts and Eric Pederson, eds., *Language and conceptualization* 13–45. Cambridge: Cambridge University Press.

Lucy, John A. 1992a. *Grammatical categories and cognition: A case study of the linguistic relativity hypothesis.* Cambridge: Cambridge University Press.

Lucy, John A. 1992b. *Language diversity and thought: A reformulation of the linguistic relativity hypothesis.* Cambridge: Cambridge University Press.

Mackenzie, Lachlan, and María A. Gómez Gonzáles, eds. 2004. *A new architecture for functional grammar.* Berlin: Mouton de Gruyter.

Mann, William C., and Sandra Thompson. 1988. Rhetorical structure theory: Toward a functional theory of text organization. *Text* 8: 243–81.

Mann, William C., and Sandra Thompson, eds. 1992. *Discourse description.* Amsterdam: John Benjamins.

McNeill, David. 1992. *Hand and mind: What gestures reveal about thought.* Chicago: University of Chicago Press.

McNeill, David. 1997. Growth points cross-linguistically. In Jan Nuyts and Eric Pederson, eds., *Language and conceptualization* 190–212. Cambridge: Cambridge University Press.

McNeill, David, ed. 2000. *Language and gesture.* Cambridge: Cambridge University Press.

Nuyts, Jan. 1992. *Aspects of a cognitive-pragmatic theory of language.* Amsterdam: John Benjamins.

Nuyts, Jan. 1993a. Cognitive Linguistics. *Journal of Pragmatics* 20: 269–90.

Nuyts, Jan. 1993b. From language to conceptualization: The case of epistemic modality. *Chicago Linguistic Society* 29, vol. 2 (parasession): 271–86.

Nuyts, Jan. 1993c. On determining the functions of language. *Semiotica* 94: 201–32.

Nuyts, Jan. 1994a. Autonomous vs. non-autonomous syntax. In Jan Verschueren, Jan-Ola Östman, and Jan Blommaert, eds., *Handbook of pragmatics* 80–85. Amsterdam: John Benjamins.

Nuyts, Jan. 1994b. Functionalism versus formalism. In Jef Verschueren, Jan-Ola Östman, and Jan Blommaert, eds., *Handbook of pragmatics* 293–300. Amsterdam: John Benjamins.

Nuyts, Jan. 1996. Consciousness in language. *Pragmatics & Cognition* 4: 153–80.

Nuyts, Jan. 2001. *Epistemic modality, language, and conceptualization: A cognitive-pragmatic perspective*. Amsterdam: John Benjamins.

Nuyts, Jan. 2002. Grounding and the system of epistemic expressions in Dutch: A cognitive-functional view. In Frank Brisard, ed., *Grounding: The epistemic footing of deixis and reference* 433–66. Berlin: Mouton de Gruyter.

Nuyts, Jan. 2003. Layering of qualifications in a cognitive perspective. In Clara Molina Ávila, María Luisa Blanco Gómez, Juana Marín Arrese, Ana Laura Rodríguez Redondo, and Manuela Romano Mozo, eds., *Cognitive linguistics in Spain at the turn of the century* 81–101. Madrid: Universidade Autonoma de Madrid.

Nuyts, Jan. 2004. Remarks on layering in a cognitive-functional language production model. In J. Lachlan Mackenzie and Maria A. Gómez Gonzáles, eds., *A new architecture for functional grammar* 275–98 Berlin: Mouton de Gruyter.

Nuyts, Jan, A. Machtelt Bolkestein, and Co Vet, eds. 1990. *Layers and levels of representation in language theory*. Amsterdam: John Benjamins.

Nuyts, Jan, and Eric Pederson, eds. 1997. *Language and conceptualization*. Cambridge: Cambridge University Press.

Nuyts, Jan, and Wietske Vonk. 1999. Epistemic modality and focus in Dutch. *Linguistics* 37: 699–737.

Ochs, Elinor, Emanuell Schegloff, and Sandra Thompson, eds. 1996. *Interaction and grammar*. Cambridge: Cambridge University Press.

Otheguy, Ricardo, Nancy Stern, and Wallis Reid, eds. 2002. *Signal, meaning, and message*. Amsterdam: John Benjamins.

Palmer, Frank R. 2001. *Mood and modality*. 2nd ed. Cambridge: Cambridge University Press.

Panther, Klaus-Uwe, and Günter Radden, eds. 1999. *Metonymy in language and thought*. Amsterdam: John Benjamins.

Pederson, Eric, Eve Danziger, David Wilkins, Stephen Levinson, Sotaro Kita, and Gunter Senft. 1998. Semantic typology and spatial conceptualization. *Language* 74: 557–89.

Pederson, Eric, and Jan Nuyts. 1997. On the relationship between language and conceptualization. In Jan Nuyts and Eric Pederson, eds., *Language and conceptualization* 1–12. Cambridge: Cambridge University Press.

Pollard, Carl, and Ivan Sag. 1994. *Head-driven phrase structure grammar*. Chicago: University of Chicago Press.

Rudzka-Ostyn, Brigida, ed. 1988. *Topics in cognitive linguistics*. Amsterdam: John Benjamins.

Sag, Ivan, and Thomas Wasow. 1999. *Syntactic theory*. Stanford, CA: CSLI Publications.

Sandra, Dominiek. 1998. What linguists can and can't tell you about the human mind: A reply to Croft. *Cognitive Linguistics* 9: 361–78.

Sandra, Dominiek, and Sally Rice. 1995. Network analyses of prepositional meaning: Mirroring whose mind—the linguist's or the language user's? *Cognitive Linguistics* 6: 89–130.

Sinclair, John, and Malcolm Coulthard. 1975. *Towards an analysis of discourse*. Oxford: Oxford University Press.

Slobin, Dan I. 1996. From "thought and language" to "thinking for speaking." In John Gumperz and Stephen C. Levinson, eds., *Rethinking linguistic relativity* 70–96. Cambridge: Cambridge University Press.

Sweetser, Eve. 1990. *From etymology to pragmatics: Metaphorical and cultural aspects of semantic structure*. Cambridge: Cambridge University Press.

Talmy, Leonard. 1988a. Force dynamics in language and cognition. *Cognitive Science* 12: 49–100.

Talmy, Leonard. 1988b. The relation of grammar to cognition. In Brigida Rudzka-Ostyn, ed., *Topics in cognitive linguistics* 165–205. Amsterdam: John Benjamins.

Talmy, Leonard. 1996. Fictive motion in language and "caption." In Paul Bloom, Mary A. Peterson, Lynn Nadel, and Merrill F. Garrett, eds., *Language and space* 211–76. Cambridge, MA: MIT Press.

Talmy, Leonard. 2000a. *Toward a cognitive semantics*. Vol. 1, *Concept structuring systems*. Cambridge, MA: MIT Press.

Talmy, Leonard. 2000b. *Toward a cognitive semantics*. Vol. 2, *Typology and process in concept structuring*. Cambridge, MA: MIT Press.

Tesnière, Lucien. 1959. *Eléments de syntaxe structurale*. Paris: Klincksieck.

Tomlin, Russell S. 1997. Mapping conceptual representations into linguistic representations: The role of attention in grammar. In Jan Nuyts and Eric Pederson, eds., *Language and conceptualization* 162–89. Cambridge: Cambridge University Press.

Traugott, Elizabeth Closs. 1989. On the rise of epistemic meanings in English: An example of subjectification in semantic change. *Language* 65: 31–55.

Traugott, Elizabeth Closs. 1995. Subjectification in grammaticalisation. In Dieter Stein and Susan Wright, eds., *Subjectivity and subjectivisation* 31–54. Cambridge: Cambridge University Press.

Traugott, Elizabeth Closs. 1997. Subjectification and the development of epistemic meaning: The case of promise and threaten. In Toril Swan, and Olaf J. Westvik, eds., *Modality in Germanic languages: Historical and comparative perspectives* 185–210. Berlin: Mouton de Gruyter.

Traugott, Elizabeth Closs, and Ekkehard König. 1991. The semantics-pragmatics of grammaticalization revisited. In Elizabeth Closs Traugott and Bernd Heine, eds., *Approaches to grammaticalization* 1: 189–218. Amsterdam: John Benjamins.

Van Valin, Robert D. 1993. A synopsis of role and reference grammar. In Robert van Valin, ed., *Advances in role and reference grammar* 1–164. Amsterdam: John Benjamins.

Van Valin, Robert D., and Randy J. LaPolla. 1997. *Syntax: Structure, meaning and function*. Cambridge: Cambridge University Press.

Verhagen, Arie. 1995. Subjectification, syntax, and communication. In Dieter Stein and Susan Wright, eds., *Subjectivity and subjectivisation in language* 103–28. Cambridge: Cambridge University Press.

Verhagen, Arie. 2000. Interpreting usage: Construing the history of Dutch causal verbs. In Michael Barlow and Suzanne Kemmer, eds., *Usage-based models of language* 261–86. Stanford, CA: CSLI Publications.

Wierzbicka, Anna. 1980. *Lingua mentalis: The semantics of natural language*. Sydney: Academic Press.

Wierzbicka, Anna. 1996. *Semantics: Primes and universals*. Oxford: Oxford University Press.

Willett, Thomas. 1988. A cross-linguistic survey of the grammaticalization of evidentiality. *Studies in Language* 12: 51–97.

Yu, Ning. 1998. The contemporary theory of metaphor: A perspective from Chinese. Amsterdam: John Benjamins.

CHAPTER 21

COGNITIVE LINGUISTICS AND AUTONOMOUS LINGUISTICS

JOHN R. TAYLOR

1. INTRODUCTION

Anyone casting even a cursory glance over the Cognitive Linguistics literature of the past twenty years or so can hardly fail to notice a polemical streak in many of the contributions. Even when practitioners of other theoretical approaches are not being overtly taken to task, one often has the impression that Cognitive Linguistics is being "profiled" against the "base" of other linguistic theories to which it is opposed.

The object of the polemics is constituted by a cluster of trends in formalist, especially Chomskyan linguistics, trends which may conveniently be brought under the heading "autonomous linguistics." We will see in due course that "autonomy" is not a simple notion when applied to linguistic theory. It might therefore be inappropriate to characterize a theory outright as "autonomous" or "nonautonomous." Equally suspect could be the view that Cognitive Linguistics rejects autonomy in all its guises. Be that as it may, a recurring theme has been that Cognitive Linguistics differentiates itself from "autonomous linguistics" in virtue of its claim that language is embedded in more general cognitive abilities. The rejection of autonomy often takes the form of more specific claims, for example, that syntactic (and morphological) patterning is inherently meaningful, that syntax, morphology, and lexicon form a continuum, and that semantics is inherently encyclopedic in scope.

In this chapter, I explore the terms of the polemics which have been so prominent in much Cognitive Linguistics work. In section 2, I briefly substantiate the polemical nature of the Cognitive Linguistics literature. Section 3 offers a short (and necessarily patchy) account of the circumstances in which Cognitive Linguistics emerged in the 1980s as a self-conscious theoretical movement. Given these circumstances, it was perhaps inevitable that Cognitive Linguistics should have defined itself in terms of "the Other." Turning my attention in section 4 to "the Other," I review some of the theoretical and methodological issues which characterize autonomous linguistics; then, in section 5, I discuss the reaction of Cognitive Linguistics to these issues and highlight some characteristic features of this approach. In section 6, I address specifically the concept of autonomy and argue that the defining characteristic of Cognitive Linguistics may lie, not so much in its rejection of autonomy, but in its commitment to a symbolic view of language. The final section looks at some recent developments in autonomous linguistics, which testify to a certain degree of convergence on positions characteristic of Cognitive Linguistics.

2. POLEMICAL ASPECTS OF COGNITIVE LINGUISTICS

For an illustration of the underlying polemical nature of the Cognitive Linguistics literature, we can turn to the editorial statement in the first issue of the journal *Cognitive Linguistics* (Geeraerts 1990). Alongside positive statements about what Cognitive Linguistics is and how it approaches its subject matter, we also find Cognitive Linguistics characterized in terms of what it is not. Thus, in Cognitive Linguistics, language "is considered not to be isolated from the other faculties of man," and the "formal structures of language are studied not as if they were autonomous" (1). Similar sentiments are to be found in the editors' introduction to Verspoor, Lee, and Sweetser (1997). Here, two distinctive features of Cognitive Linguistics are highlighted, each of which, again, is presented in terms of opposition to other (unnamed) theoretical approaches. First, there is an emphasis on the conceptual and experiential basis of semantics, in contrast to the view that language represents "mere propositions about the world" (xi). Second, Cognitive Linguistics stands opposed to those theories "which treat grammatical constructions as meaningless" (xi).

Perhaps the only major contributor to Cognitive Linguists not to have adopted a polemical stance has been Leonard Talmy. For the others, the polemics take on different guises. Langacker, for example, introduced his Cognitive Grammar as a reaction to "current theory":

> My own dissatisfaction with the dominant trends in current theory is profound. It reaches to the deepest stratum of organizing principles: notions about what language is like and what linguistic theory should be concerned with.... Rightly or wrongly, I concluded some time ago that the conceptual foundations of linguistic theory were built on quicksand, and that the only remedy was to start over on firmer ground. (1987: v)

Indeed, Langacker offered Cognitive Grammar to the world as "an alternative to the generative tradition," which rejected "many of its underlying assumptions" (4). For the most part, however, Langacker's polemics are covert but nonetheless pervasive. I would imagine that it would have been impossible for a trained linguist to have read Langacker (1987) without having been constantly aware of allusions to positions adopted, or assumed, by contemporary scholars of other theoretical persuasions. (I have found that many of my less well read students, especially those who have not enjoyed the benefits of a grounding in Generative Grammar, often fail for this reason to grasp the full import and theoretical significance of many of the points that Langacker makes.) Consider, for example, the account of the "rule/list fallacy" (Langacker 1987: 42). It is fallacious, according to Langacker, to assume that what can be accounted for by rule needs to be separately listed. Langacker's position, instead, is that general statements (rules) and particular statements (lists) "can perfectly well coexist in the cognitive representation of linguistic phenomena." The very word "fallacy" is indicative of the underlying polemics, and most readers of the passage will surely be aware of the positions alluded to. Yet Langacker does not cite any linguist who actually proposed the rule/list dichotomy.[1]

In the case of Lakoff, the polemics are for the most part overt (see, e.g., Lakoff 1987, 1990; Lakoff and Johnson 1999). For Lakoff, the gulf separating Cognitive Linguistics and Generative Linguistics is profound and relates to the "primary commitments" which practitioners of the two approaches subscribe to. Generativists subscribe to the "generative commitment," which is "to view language in terms of systems of combinatorial mathematics" (Lakoff 1990: 43), that is, in terms of "formal grammars." For Cognitive Linguistics, the primary commitment is "to make one's account of human language accord with what is generally known about the mind and the brain, from other disciplines as well as our own" (40). According to Lakoff, these primary commitments not only lead to different analyses of data; they also determine the kinds of data that are brought under investigation and may even lead to different understandings of what linguistics is. In view of these profound differences, Lakoff finds it not at all surprising that "cognitive and generative linguists often have problems communicating with each other" (45). Indeed, what communication there is, is characterized as "bickering."[2] For other linguists, the polemics take the form of a more measured comparison and evaluation of competing approaches. In a monograph devoted to English possessive constructions

(Taylor 1996), rather than let the Cognitive Grammar analysis stand on its own merits, I felt obliged to embed the analysis in a detailed discussion and critique of alternative, largely generative accounts of the phenomena in question.

3. Some History

Cognitive Linguistics came of age in 1987, with the publication of Lakoff's *Women, Fire, and Dangerous Things* (Lakoff 1987) and the first volume of Langacker's *Foundations of Cognitive Grammar* (Langacker 1987). The movement had been in gestation for some time previously. Lakoff's 1987 monograph was foreshadowed by several earlier publications, such as Lakoff (1977, 1982), while Langacker (1991: vii) informs us that his own thinking on what was to become Cognitive Grammar began as early as 1976, with the first full-blown presentation of the model appearing in Langacker's (1982) account of the English passive. This time period was also critical for the development of autonomous linguistics. It was during the 1970s that Chomsky put paid to the Generative Semantics movement, after which he propelled the generative enterprise toward ever greater levels of abstraction and empirical restrictiveness. Landmark publications were *Lectures in Government and Binding* (Chomsky 1981) and *Knowledge of Language* (Chomsky 1986).

In order to better appreciate these developments, we need to backtrack a little and consider in general terms the state of North American linguistics up to and including the period in question.[3]

During the middle decades of the twentieth century, academic linguistics (at least in the United States) was dominated by behaviorist beliefs and methodologies, the key text being Bloomfield (1933). At that time, doing linguistics was a matter of collecting data from all manner of languages, familiar and exotic, and of dissecting and classifying it according to procedures that were becoming increasingly refined and sophisticated. No reference could be made to nonobservable entities such as meanings, intentions, or intuitions. Although it subsequently became fashionable to sneer at the behaviorist commitment of Bloomfield and his followers, it has to be remembered that much of the basic terminology of modern linguistics—notions such as "head," "complement," "constituent," "endocentric," "complementary distribution," and so on—was refined in the classificatory (or "taxonomic") workshops of the Bloomfieldians.

A major change of direction occurred in 1957, with the publication of *Syntactic Structures* (Chomsky 1957). In this short monograph, Chomsky proposed that the proper object of linguistic study was not the analysis of a corpus of observed utterances but the system of rules which accounted for, and which was able to "generate," the full set of grammatical sentences of a language, whereby the grammaticality of a sentence was determined not by the fact of its occurrence in a corpus but on the basis of native speaker intuitions. The primitive elements of the rule system were symbols such as Σ (= 'sentence'), N (= 'Noun'), NP (= 'Noun Phrase'), Aux (= 'Auxiliary'); these, like the mathematician's x and y or the logician's p and q, were variables, contentless in themselves, but which could take on as values any contentful element of the appropriate category. The rules operated over strings of such symbols, expanding them, rearranging them, and performing other kinds of transformations. Like Bloomfieldian descriptivism, the "algebraic shift" left its mark on academic linguistics by introducing a new rigor into linguistic discourse. Linguists were required to formulate rules with a degree of precision and explicitness which allowed the rules to be evaluated against counterexamples and alternative rule formulations. Within a relatively short span of time, all manner of "tests" were developed which could be applied in order to substantiate a given analysis. Many of these tests (for example, tests for confirming the status of a nominal as clausal subject, tests for diagnosing complements as opposed to adjuncts, tests for distinguishing control verbs from raising verbs) are now part of the arsenal of every practicing linguist.

It did not take long for the algebraic enterprise to be "biologized." This move was made explicit in Chomsky's next major publication, *Aspects of the Theory of Syntax* (Chomsky 1965). The system of rules which constitute the grammar had to be evaluated, not only in terms of its descriptive adequacy, but as a hypothesis about the cognitive state of a speaker (47–59). Moreover, since human beings are not born with knowledge of any particular language, the rule system pertaining to a given language had to be acquired. Attention therefore moved toward those features of the human mind which support and enable the acquisition and mental representation of language. The shift signaled the emergence of linguistics as a cognitive science.

To be sure, some linguists have ignored the "cognitive turn." They have been concerned, as was Chomsky during the earlier stages of this career, with formulating syntactic rules with maximal accuracy and precision, with little regard for the cognitive reality of the rules. Generalized Phrase Structure Grammar (Gazdar et al. 1985) belongs to this tradition. (It comes as no surprise, therefore, that it is models such as Generalized Phrase Structure Grammar, rather than the latter-day versions of Chomskyan grammar, which have been exploited for Natural Language Processing.) On the whole, however, it would be probably true to say that the majority of today's linguists would be comfortable with being described as "cognitive," on a broad understanding of the term; they would, in other words, subscribe to the view that a linguistic analysis is a hypothesis about the mental representation of language in the minds of its speakers.[4] Neither would today's linguists want to sacrifice the argumentative rigor introduced by the Chomskyans, nor the basic descriptive tools bequeathed by the Bloomfieldians. In an important sense, therefore, we witness a progressive, incremental development of the discipline, from the taxonomic phase, through the algebraic phase, to the cognitive phase. My sketch of this developmental trajectory, however, hides a number of contentious issues. It is to these that we need to turn in order to find the roots of Cognitive Linguistics, its points of contrast with Chomskyan linguistics, and its distinctive way of implementing the cognitive agenda.

Of particular relevance to our topic is the turmoil within the Chomskyan camp during the late 1960s and early 1970s. At around that time, a number of linguists closely associated with Chomsky pushed the generative enterprise in the direction of what came to be known as "Generative Semantics." As is well known, early Generative Grammar proposed a "deep" level of syntactic structure, which was converted into a "surface" structure by means of transformations. The generative semantic view was that all aspects of the meaning of a sentence, even its pragmatic force, had to be represented in the deep structure. Moreover, sentences which are (roughly) synonymous on the surface, even though they might differ in their wording, had to share the same deep structure. Regarding deep structure itself, it was usual for it to be represented in the format of predicate logic and to incorporate what were supposed to be semantic primitives. An often-cited example was the representation of *kill* in terms of the abstract elements [CAUSE] and [BECOME NOT ALIVE].[5] Such an approach, as will be evident, necessitated a vast inventory of transformational rules, many of them entirely ad hoc, which added, deleted, rearranged, and replaced material as the deep semantic structure got transformed into a surface syntactic structure. There was a time in the early 1970s when it seemed that Generative Semantics was going to conquer the field. After a particularly vicious and acrimonious period (narrated from different perspectives by Newmeyer 1980 and Harris 1993), the Generative Semantics movement collapsed, largely, it would seem, under the weight of the unconstrained transformations which it postulated. Henceforth, "orthodox" Generative Grammar would severely restrict both the kinds of transformations that were admissible and the range of data that the theory was intended to account for. In the end, only one transformation came to be recognized, that of movement, and even this became an option of "last resort" (Chomsky 1995: 150). At the same time, the empirical scope of the theory came to be restricted to "core" grammatical phenomena, to the exclusion of pragmatics and all manner of "idiosyncratic" syntactic and lexical data.

Although now largely defunct as a distinctive movement,[6] Generative Semantics is relevant to our topic because one of its main exponents, George Lakoff, was to become a leading figure in Cognitive Linguistics. Lakoff has since emphasized the line of continuity between the two movements, even going so far as to describe Cognitive Linguistics as "an updated version of generative semantics" (Lakoff 1987: 582).[7] The link between the two movements lies in the importance attached to semantic structure and to the need to study surface phenomena from the point of view of the meanings that are being conveyed. But whereas Generative Semantics had represented semantic structure in model-theoretic terms, Cognitive Linguistics construes meaning more broadly to encompass topics such as metaphorical mappings, image schemas, and mental models. And whereas Generative Semantics had proposed all manner of transformations intervening between deep and surface structure, the emerging Cognitive Linguistics proposed a more direct, symbolic relationship between aspects of form and aspects of meaning.

4. CHARACTERISTICS OF MAINSTREAM GENERATIVE LINGUISTICS

Returning now to the main line of the story, let us consider the development of "mainstream" Generative Grammar, which won out over Generative Semantics. Over the years, the Chomskyan enterprise has undergone many upheavals and transformations, from the "Standard Theory," as the approach in Chomsky (1965) came to be known, through the "Extended Standard Theory" outlined in Chomsky (1970) but more fully articulated in Jackendoff (1972), to "Government and Binding" (Chomsky 1981), "Principles and Parameters" (Chomsky 1986), and latterly "Minimalism" (Chomsky 1995).[8] The main features of the Chomskyan enterprise have, however, remained largely unchanged over the years. Some enduring characteristics are the following:

a. *The Centrality of Syntax.* The central component of a grammar was, and remains, the syntax—Jackendoff (1997: 15) refers to this aspect of the theory as its "syntactocentrism." Syntax here is construed as a computational system which operates over contentless symbols. The symbols receive phonological and semantic content only in the phonological and semantic components of the grammar after lexical material has been "inserted" into the syntactic strings. In this way, the set of grammatical sentences of a language is generated.

b. *Formalism.* Given the centrality of syntax, which is viewed as a computational mechanism, it is not surprising that Generative Linguistics has placed a high premium on formalism, that is, on precise statements of rules and the conditions under which they apply. The rules are typically presented in a quasi-mathematical format and make reference mostly to general categories, not to actual linguistic items (words, meanings, pronunciations).

c. *Grammaticality.* As a corollary of (a) and (b), the "grammaticality" of an expression comes to be defined in terms of whether the expression can be generated by the formal rules of the grammar. The likelihood of its occurrence in a corpus or even native speakers' judgments on its acceptability are secondary.

d. *Abstractness.* Especially since the 1970s, Chomskyan linguistics has become increasingly abstract, in the sense that the entities with which it deals have no overt manifestation in actual linguistic expressions. Abstract entities in this sense include traces, empty categories, pro and PRO, as well as movement operations of various kinds (which may themselves operate over "empty" categories), not to mention tree structures and the structural relations which these define, such as the c-command relation.

e. *Modularity.* The syntactic component is regarded as an encapsulated module which functions independently not only of phonology and semantics but also of more general cognitive capacities, such as perception and categorization, memory and learning, and interpersonal and rhetorical skills. The semantic and phonological components "interpret" syntactic structures (after lexical insertion) and "interface" with nonlinguistic domains, such as conceptual knowledge and processes of speech production and perception. Actual linguistic performance results from the interaction of strictly linguistic competence with nonlinguistic cognitive abilities. Not only is syntax regarded as an autonomous module, the syntactic module itself is ascribed a modular structure whose "submodules" have included the X-bar principle, the Theta principle, and the Case principle.

f. *The Neglect of Semantics.* Given the syntactocentrism of Generative Grammar, it is not surprising that semantic issues, especially lexical semantics, have been largely ignored. Indeed, it is taken as axiomatic that the syntax is structured in accordance with its own principles, which cannot be "reduced" to semantic principles nor "explained" in semantic terms. Interest in semantics has been restricted, in the main, to those topics which have an obvious reflex in syntactic organization—in particular, matters of "logical form," such as argument structure, thematic relations, quantifier scope, anaphors, reciprocals, and the like.[9]

g. *The Core and the Periphery.* The aim of the generative enterprise has been from the very start the search for high-level generalizations. In this process, the idiosyncratic, the idiomatic, and the exceptional have been sidelined. The high-level generalizations define the "core" of the language system, while the idiomatic and the peculiarities of individual constructions and lexical items were relegated to the periphery; not being amenable to high-level generalizations, the periphery was of little theoretical interest and was therefore accorded little attention. Symptomatic is the fact that the generative literature has tended to address only a very limited range of phenomena. *Wh*-movement, extraction, raising, anaphors, and reciprocals have been favorite and recurring topics.

h. *Universal Grammar and Language Acquisition.* The generative enterprise, as characterized above, brings with it a rather specific view on the mental representation of language. It is important here to bear in mind that Chomskyan linguistics developed under its own theory-internal momentum; it was not driven by independently known facts about the mind. On the contrary, it was Generative Linguistics which imposed conditions on the structure of a more general theory of cognition. The linguistic theory required a theory of cognition in which syntax could be allocated to an encapsulated computational module. Moreover, given the abstractness of the syntactic representations and the implausibility that the syntactic rules could ever be induced through exposure to linguistic data, it was necessary that the general architecture of the syntactic component, with its various interacting submodules, be genetically inherited. Acquisition thus became a matter of the "setting" of "parameters" provided by Universal

Grammar, something which, it was assumed, would be possible on only minimal exposure to data. The downside was that the parameters of Universal Grammar accounted only for the core of the language (defined, somewhat circularly, as those features of a language that could be handled by parameter setting). Everything else in a language (including such matters as the meanings and idiosyncratic behavior of individual lexical items) belonged to the periphery, which had to be learned by generalization following extensive exposure to data.

5. THE COGNITIVE LINGUISTICS REACTION

Already in the early 1970s, a number of linguists were feeling increasingly unhappy with the direction being taken by Chomsky and his followers. Some were dissatisfied with the increasing abstractness of Generative Grammar and sought to develop more surface-oriented models, such as Lexical-Functional Grammar (Bresnan 1978), Generalized Phrase Structure Grammar (Gazdar et al. 1985), and Word Grammar (Hudson 1984). Cognitive Linguistics shares with these approaches a focus on surface phenomena and a general skepticism toward constructs that are not imminent in primary linguistic data. Others deplored the encapsulation of the language system from the many uses to which language is put and argued that structural aspects of a language have been shaped by the functions it needs to perform. An early statement of the functionalist approach was Givón (1979). Finally, the self-styled cognitive linguists proposed to take seriously the claim that linguistic knowledge is a cognitive phenomenon, which needs to be studied as an integral aspect of human cognition. In practice, this has entailed framing linguistic analyses in terms of more general (i.e., not exclusively linguistic) cognitive abilities. Some, such as Lamb—who, incidentally, claims to have been the first to have used the term "cognitive linguistics" in print (1999: 381)—have gone further, insisting that linguistic theory should be consistent with what is currently known about the neuronal structure of the brain. (For this reason, Lamb prefers the designation "neurocognitive linguistics.") The neurocognitive approach has characterized Lakoff's most recent work (see the Neural Theory of Language (NLT) Web site: http://www.icsi .berkeley.edu/NTL/).

A number of chapters in this *Handbook* deal with cognitive abilities which have proved to be of crucial importance in the study of language, but which are not restricted to the domain of language. One of these is categorization, including categorization by prototype and by family resemblance (Lewandowska-Tomaszczyk, chapter 6). Categorization is most obviously relevant to lexical semantics, as well as to the structure of morphological, syntactic, and phonological categories (Taylor 1989). Categorization is also crucially involved in any act of linguistic performance, in that the unique features—phonological, structural, and semantic—of every speech act need to be assessed with a view to their categorization by existing schemas.

Several general cognitive abilities can be brought under the broad title of "construal operations" (see Verhagen, this volume, chapter 3). At issue is the fact that linguistic expressions do not, and cannot, designate a state of affairs as it "objectively" is; rather, the scene must be processed and conceptualized by the human mind. Construal operations include attentional processes (chapter 11), force-dynamic construals (chapter 12), metaphor, image schemas, and conceptual blending (chapters 8, 9, and 15). A further general ability concerns entrenchment, that is, the degree to which a cognitive representation can be strengthened through repeated activation (chapter 5). In neurocognitive terms, entrenchment is an instance of Hebb's postulate: "Cells that fire together, wire together" (Harnish 2002: 73). Highly entrenched representations can be more easily accessed and can be accessed as units, without attention being paid to their internal composition. Langacker's rejection of the rule/list fallacy, referred to earlier, was based on the view that complex expressions, even though their internal structure might be unexceptional, may nevertheless be stored and activated as wholes. Evidence that this is the case comes from the fact that frequently occurring, and therefore highly entrenched units, tend to acquire properties that are different from those of less entrenched units (Bybee 1995, 2001; Bybee and Hopper 2001; Taylor 2002: 307–18).

Perhaps the most fundamental cognitive ability, however—and the one which lends human language its distinctive properties vis-à-vis animal communication systems—is our capacity for symbolic thought (Noble and Davidson 1996; Deacon 1997). In contrast to indexical signs, which stand in a causal relation (or which are perceived to stand in a causal relation) to their designatum, the distinctive feature of a symbol is that it stands for a conceptualization and is independent of external stimuli.[10] Symbolic thought appears to be underpinned by other uniquely human cognitive abilities, such as our ability to empathize (Lieberman 1991) and our capacity for joint attention (Tomasello 1999), both of which follow from our realization that other human beings have minds and a conceptual life not unlike our own (Taylor 2002: 67–68).

Cognitive Linguistics is absolutely committed to a symbolic view of language (Lakoff 1987: 583; Langacker 1987: 11; Taylor 2002: 38–58). It is this feature which distinguishes Cognitive Linguistics not only from Chomskyan Generative Linguistics but from several other approaches which emerged in reaction to the Chomskyan agenda, such as Lexical-Functional Grammar and Phrase Structure Grammar. Thus, in Langacker's Cognitive Grammar there are only three objects of study: phonological representations (language in its "overt," perceptible form), semantic representations, and symbolic relations between phonological and semantic representations. Importantly, patterns for the combination of smaller units into larger configurations (traditionally, the province of morphology and syntax) are themselves regarded as symbolic units, albeit schematic ones, which are abstracted on the basis of encounters with their instances. As befits their symbolic nature, these "constructional schemas" or "constructions" for short, are characterized both in their formal aspects (typically, the formal characterization consists of a sequence of slots, which are able to be filled by items of the appropriate category) and with respect to their semantics (see Croft, this volume, chapter 18).

Generative Linguistics had sought to eliminate constructions from the grammar. Constructions were "epiphenomena" which emerged through the interaction of principles of Universal Grammar (Chomsky 1995: 170). In Cognitive Linguistics, on the other hand, constructions are central and perform the work that, in other theories, is handled by the syntactic component. Evidence that constructions cannot be reduced to more general syntactic principles comes from the fact that a construction may be able to contribute its schematic meaning to the meaning of an expression which instantiates it; the schematic meaning may go beyond, or even override, the meanings contributed by the component units. Thus, to take an often-cited example, it is the construction in which the word occurs which gives *sneeze* a caused-motion reading in *sneeze the napkin off the table* (Goldberg 1995: 9).

5.1. Methodological Consequences

A commitment to a symbolic view of language and attempts to ground the study of language in more general cognitive abilities have profoundly influenced the Cognitive Linguistics research program.

Thus, a distinctive feature of Cognitive Linguistics research has been a focus on what in Chomskyan linguistics would be dismissed as the theoretically uninteresting periphery. There have been a wealth of studies on the properties of individual lexical items, especially highly polysemous ones such as the prepositions, as well as on quirky grammatical constructions which have properties that cannot be predicted from general principles; see, for example, Tuggy (1996) on the double-*be* construction and Lambrecht (1990) on the incredulity response construction.

Along with an interest in the peripheral and the particular has been a general lack of enthusiasm for mathematical formalism. Rejection of formalism has not, however, meant that cognitive linguists have ignored the need for precise and detailed characterizations of the phenomena under discussion. What we witness, in fact, has been a search for alternative, especially visual, modes of representation. Pictographic representations of semantic structures are a distinctive and well-known feature of Langacker's writings. Diagrammatic representations have also been employed by Talmy (1988) in his seminal paper on force and were also an important aspect of early treatments of prepositions, such as Brugman (1981) and Lindner (1981). Network models of polysemy have also lent themselves to visual representation (e.g., Tuggy 2003), as has the notion of a construction as a linking of semantic, syntactic, and lexical specifications (Goldberg 1995).

A further notable feature of Cognitive Linguistics has been attempts to offer conceptual motivations for syntactic and morphological structures as well as for the entities over which syntax and morphology operate, such as word classes. Recall that in autonomous linguistics the syntax was a computational device which operated over contentless symbols, blind to their phonological and semantic properties. This procedure was deemed to be necessary since it was assumed that the major categories over which syntax operates—categories such as Noun, Verb, and so on—were resistant to a coherent semantic characterization, as were certain structural relations such as that of a clausal subject. Jackendoff, for whom a regular relationship between syntactic and semantic categories was indeed a "working assumption" (a position which Cognitive Linguists would certainly endorse), specifically mentions the case of nouns and subjects as evidence that syntax still needs to be accorded a certain autonomy vis-à-vis semantics (Jackendoff 1983: 14).

As a matter of fact, there is now a substantial body of literature which has addressed the functional and conceptual basis of the major word classes (Givón 1984; Wierzbicka 1986; Langacker 1987; Croft 1991; Taylor 1996). A more radical view has recently been expressed by Croft (1999, 2001). Turning on its head the generative view that constructions are mere epiphenomena, Croft argues that constructions are basic and that word classes are epiphenomenal, since they need to be defined in terms of the constructions in which they are eligible to occur. The notion of subject has also come in for intense scrutiny by Langacker (1993, 1999). Recognizing that the identification of "subject" with the semantic role "Agent" is bound to be inadequate, he proposes a highly schematic characterization in terms of the "primary figure" at the clausal level. Especially challenging for this approach are so-called expletive subjects, as in *It seems that a mistake has been made* and *There seems to have been a mistake*. On generative approaches, *it* and *there* are mere placeholders, inserted by the syntax in order to satisfy the requirement that finite clauses in English must have a grammatical subject. A symbolic view of language entails that even the so-called expletive subjects have semantic content, by virtue of which they are able to function as the primary figure.

Attempts to offer a conceptual motivation for structural aspects of a language were evident from the earliest days of Cognitive Linguistics. The earliest full-fledged presentation of Cognitive Grammar was Langacker's (1982) analysis of the English passive. His strategy was to examine each of the constituents of a passive clause—the verb *be*, the participle, the optional *by*-phrase—and to identify their contribution to a passive clause in relation to the values which these elements have elsewhere in the language. It turned out that a passive clause was not simply a compositional function of the standard values of its constituents—passive *be*, for example, has a processual value unique to the passive. Nor could a passive be regarded as the consequence of an algebraic transformation of an active. The passive turned out to be a construction in its own right whose global properties were motivated by the properties of its parts. Motivation was also a key concept in Lakoff's analysis of English *there*-constructions (1987: 462–585). Lakoff proposed a "central" construction in which *there* has a deictic, referential meaning and, radiating out from this, a large number of secondary constructions which are based on the central deictic.

Especially significant from a methodological point of view have been a number of cognitive linguistic studies which have tackled head-on the kinds of data that have been central concerns in autonomous linguistics and which are often cited as evidence, precisely, for the correctness of the autonomous approach. These include anaphoric reference (van Hoek 1997), raising (Langacker 1995), and extraction (Deane 1992). Since anaphors are discussed elsewhere in this *Handbook* (van Hoek, chapter 34), I will restrict myself to a few comments on raising. Raising has been a stock-in-trade of autonomous syntax. It was claimed that a sentence such as *Don is likely to leave* exhibits a divergence of semantic and syntactic structure. Only events are likely (to happen), not individuals. The deep structure therefore has 'be likely' predicated of the proposition '(for) Don to leave'. The divergence between the presumed semantic structure and the attested surface structure results from the "raising" of the subject of the embedded clause to be the subject of the main clause. Langacker (1995) argued against this, claiming that 'be likely' can indeed be predicated of a nominal, with the *to*-clause designating the process with respect to which the likelihood is being assessed. Statements such as *A war is likely* are fully acceptable, since the process whose likelihood is being assessed can be inferred from the semantic structure of the subject nominal ('A war is likely to occur'). In brief, Langacker claims that the overt, surface structure of the raised expression corresponds rather directly to its semantic structure; raising, as a process of rearranging elements of a presumed deep structure, is superfluous.

5.2. Acquisition

The Cognitive Linguistics enterprise offers a distinct perspective on language acquisition (Tomasello, this volume, chapter 41). There can, to be sure, be no question about humans' unique ability to acquire and to use language. To this extent, language builds on uniquely human and therefore innate, that is, genetically inherited, abilities. These abilities, however, may not be peculiar to language. I have already drawn attention to the hypothesis that language rests on the capacity for symbolic thought rather than on an innate algebraic syntax. Not to be overlooked, too, is the possibility that a number of basic grammatical categories may be grounded in cognitive abilities that emerge during the early years of life. Langacker, in this connection, speaks of "conceptual archetypes" (1999: 41). Among these are the concepts of a spatially bounded physical object and of a spatially distributed substance. These concepts underlie the emergence of the noun category and the distinction, crucial to the morphosyntax of many languages, between count and mass nouns (Soja, Carey, and Spelke 1991; Imai and Gentner 1997).

Of special significance to the cognitive linguistic view of syntax has been research on the acquisition of constructions (Tomasello 2000). On the generative view, the acquisition of a structural configuration is essentially complete once the appropriate parameters of Universal Grammar have been set. It appears to be the case, however, that constructions tend to be acquired gradually on a word-by-word basis. The two-year-old who comes out with *I kick ball* may simply have acquired an idiosyncratic property of the verb *kick* (Tomasello and Brooks 1998). Only when a number of lexically specified transitive clauses have been learned does the child apply the transitive construction productively to new verbs. A further finding (Tomasello 2000) has been that by far the greatest part of what the young child learner says consists of a collage of previously used utterances— utterances which, in the child's previous linguistic experience, have acquired the status of entrenched units. "Creativity," in the Chomskyan, generative sense, hardly features at all.

6. AUTONOMY

I now address the concept of autonomy and the extent to which the notion is relevant to the polemics between Cognitive and Generative Linguistics.

An object of study may be said to be autonomous if it cannot be "reduced" or explicated by reference to other objects of study. There are a number of ways in which the notion of autonomy can be applied to the study of language (Croft 1995; Newmeyer 1998).

a. First, we can enquire whether linguistics, that is, the academic study of language, constitutes an autonomous field of study. It is amusing to recall that as recently as 1986, Newmeyer discussed "opposition to autonomous linguistics" in precisely these terms. He defended the autonomy of linguistics as an academic discipline against three charges. These came from humanist scholars, for whom the study of language should be subsumed under the study of literary texts; from Marxist scholars, for whom language was a reflex of economic processes; and from political activists, for whom the study of language should be just one facet of the study of oppression. A concern to establish linguistics as a legitimate and "autonomous" academic discipline goes back at least to Saussure ([1916] 1967), who recognized that many disciplines have a legitimate interest in language. He argued, however, that if linguistics was to have a place in the academic curriculum, there had to be a distinctly linguistic way of studying language, and this, for Saussure, lay in recognizing the "linguistic sign" (comparable to the "symbolic unit" in Langacker's theory) as the central object of enquiry.

b. We can enquire whether knowledge of a language constitutes an autonomous object of study or whether language knowledge can be reduced to more general conceptual knowledge. While Cognitive Linguistics certainly subscribes to the view that language may be grounded in more general cognitive abilities, there is no suggestion that the study of these general abilities makes the study of linguistic structure redundant or that language is an epiphenomenal reflex of general cognitive processes. As Langacker (1999: 25) put it, "Grammar does exist."

c. Turning to linguistic structure itself, we can enquire whether the different levels of organization, such as syntax and morphology, are autonomous. To speak of the "autonomy of syntax" would mean that syntax is organized in terms of elements and relations which are unique to this level of organization—elements such as "noun phrase" and "subject of (a clause)"—and which cannot be reduced to, or fully explained in terms of, elements at other levels (such as semantics). While Cognitive Linguistics rejects the idea that syntax is autonomous in the sense described above, it also does not endorse the view that syntactic organization can be reduced to matters of conceptualization. Rather, syntactic units and their patterning are analyzed in terms of conventionalized associations between a (possibly highly schematic) phonological structure and a (possibly highly schematic) semantic structure. There is, to be sure, the expectation that syntactic structures will be motivated by their semantic aspects, and, as already noted, a major thrust of Cognitive Linguistics research has been to elucidate the nature and extent of this semantic motivation. At the same time, the approach leaves open the possibility that some associations of form and meaning may be essentially arbitrary and purely a matter of convention. This is most obviously the case with simplex morphemes. There is no reason other than convention why the phonological form [kæt] should be paired with the conceptual unit [CAT]. The allocation of items to inflection classes may also, in many cases, lack conceptual motivation. There is no conceptual motivation for the fact that the Italian noun *casa* 'house' patterns with the definite article *la*. Langacker (1991: 180–89) has suggested how facts of this nature can be accommodated within Cognitive Grammar.

d. Recall that in Langacker's Cognitive Grammar there are only three objects of linguistic study: semantic structures, phonological structures, and symbolic associations. While no special status attaches to syntax and morphology (these, as pointed out above, are analyzed in terms of assemblies of symbolic units), phonology does constitute a distinct level of organization, and to this extent it may be legitimate to regard phonology as an autonomous level of linguistic structure. (In this, of course, Cognitive Linguistics does not differ substantially from other linguistic theories.) It is evident that phonological units such as phoneme, syllable, and foot have no conceptual content in themselves and cannot therefore be reduced to matters of conceptual structure and its symbolization. This, no doubt, is one of the reasons why phonology has tended to be neglected by Cognitive Linguistics researchers. This is not to say that phonology is not a cognitive phenomenon. Sounds, classes of sounds, and schemas for the combination of sounds are subject to much the same categorization principles as symbolic and conceptual units. These issues are addressed in Nathan (this volume, chapter 23) and Taylor (2002).

While "autonomy" may be a convenient slogan for capturing some important points of contrast between Cognitive Linguistics and other approaches, a closer look at the concept suggests that a more differentiated account is called for. It is certainly not the case that Cognitive Linguistics is compatible with a wholesale rejection of autonomy in all its various applications to linguistic study. Phonological structure, for example, has to be accorded a degree of autonomy vis-à-vis semantic structure and symbolic relations. The crucial point of differentiation, I think, lies elsewhere, namely in the Cognitive Linguistics commitment to the study of language as a symbolic system. It is this commitment which has determined not only the content but also the distinctive methodology of cognitive linguistic analyses.

7. CONVERGENCES?

In recent years, practitioners from within the field of "autonomous linguistics"—in view of my above remarks on autonomy, the scare quotes around the expression are in order—have addressed topics that have been of central concern to Cognitive Linguistics and have even proposed solutions that are converging on, or at least which are not radically opposed to, positions espoused by Cognitive Linguistics.

7.1. Constraints and Rules

Generative Grammar, and indeed other formalist models, are popularly associated with algorithmic rules which perform specified operations over inputs. Needless to say, rules in this sense have no place in a theory which construes language knowledge as an inventory of units (semantic, phonological, and symbolic) which are available to speakers and hearers for the creation and interpretation of usage events. Some recent developments in Generative Grammar have, however, shifted the focus from the rules which generate an output toward the constraints which a well-formed expression has to satisfy.

Optimality Theory is a case in point. Optimality Theory (Prince and Smolensky 1993) was first developed in phonology in response to the observation that different rules of a language often seemed to "conspire" to generate outputs with certain characteristics, for example, to eliminate certain consonant clusters or to guarantee CV syllables. The idea was that competing surface forms were evaluated according to whether they satisfied constraints on acceptability. Since the satisfaction of one constraint might entail the violation of another constraint, the constraints needed to be ranked with respect to their defeasibility. Recently, attempts have been made to extend Optimality Theory principles to the study of syntactic structures (Dekkers, van der Leeuw, and van de Weijer 2000).

There are, to be sure, many aspects of Optimality Theory which are problematic from a cognitive linguistic perspective (see Nathan, this volume, chapter 23); critical voices have also been raised from other perspectives (McMahon 2000). One issue concerns the supposedly universal status of the constraints and their cognitive grounding; another concerns the processes by which the array of competing surface forms are generated and what the input to these processes might be. Nevertheless, there is an obvious affinity between the Optimality Theory notion of constraints satisfaction and the Cognitive Grammar view that "an expression's structural description resides in simultaneous categorization by numerous symbolic units, each interpretable as a constraint pertaining to some aspect of its organization" (Langacker 1991: 532). An exploration of these points of convergence, as well as the points of controversy, will likely be an important field of research in the coming years.

7.2. Idioms

There has been a growing interest from linguists of many theoretical persuasions in idioms and fixed expressions. At least since the appearance of Nunberg, Sag, and Wasow (1994), Langacker's (1987: 23–25) strictures on the treatment of idioms in mainstream linguistic theory have lost much of their polemical punch.

Jackendoff (1997), in particular, has emphasized the central role of idioms and formulaic expressions in the system of knowledge which constitutes a language. Jackendoff's approach needs to be understood against his critique of the syntactocentrism of mainstream Chomskyan theory. Jackendoff accords a central role to lexical items, which are understood as combining a phonological, semantic, and a syntactic representation. Words and morphemes combine in larger configurations through the integration of their properties at the three autonomous levels of phonology, syntax, and semantics. The approach, it will be noted, differs from the cognitive linguistic approach largely in according a degree of autonomy to syntactic organization.

Interestingly, idioms are also assimilated to the lexicon as "phrasal lexical items" (Jackendoff 1997: 153). As Jackendoff (1997: 174) notes, his treatment of "constructional idioms" (such as the *way*-construction, exemplified by *Bill belched his way out of the restaurant*) has affinities with the treatment of these expressions in Goldberg's (1995) Construction Grammar. Indeed, Jackendoff observes that the only real issue separating the two approaches concerns the treatment of "core" syntactic structures, such as the transitive clause. Jackendoff prefers to account for core phrase structures in the syntax largely, it would seen, because these are not associated with any specific semantic or lexical properties. But he also admits that core structures might also be viewed as "maximally underspecified constructional idioms." If this move were taken, the need for a level of autonomous syntax would evaporate. To all intents and purposes, Jackendoff's theory would converge on the Cognitive Linguistics position.

7.3. The Core and the Periphery

Mention must be made of a remarkable work by one of the protagonists of autonomous linguistics, Peter Culicover. Culicover (1999) offers a radical critique of Universal Grammar and the notion of acquisition through parameter setting. He argues his case by pointing out that a very great deal in a language is "idiosyncratic" and can hardly be said to fall under general, universal principles. In surveying the English determiners and quantifiers, for example, he notes that just about each of them has a unique distributional profile: "There seem to be almost as many patterns as there are elements" (64). The only plausible classification is based in semantic categories, such as "universal quantifier" and "number expression." Still, there are idiosyncrasies pertaining, for example, to partitive *of*: *all (of) the men*, *both (of) the men*, *each *(of) the men*, *all three *(of) the men*, and so on. Culicover's point is that the task of the language learner is to learn the facts as they are encountered; the learner cannot appeal to general principles of Universal Grammar: "Once the learner has identified the special properties and made the generalizations, the learner knows the relevant facts about the language in this domain, and we may say that the learner has 'acquired' this part of the language in some concrete sense" (67–68).

Culicover's account presupposes a "conservative and attentive" learner who attends to all the relevant facts about the domain and who does not generalize beyond what is justified by the facts. The conclusion, I think, is not so radically different from that reached, by a very different route, by Tomasello (2000).

Learning, in the traditional sense of the term being proposed by Culicover, was denounced by Chomsky as inadequate as a means for acquiring a language (Chomsky 1965: 54). But a traditional learning mechanism clearly must exist, given the extent of the idiosyncratic and the idiomatic in a language. But if such a learning mechanism exists for the "periphery" (which might not be so peripheral, after all), the very same mechanism can surely handle the "core." In this way, Culicover has driven a nail into some of the most central and cherished assumptions of "autonomous linguistics."

In view of these developments within the autonomous linguistics camp, many of the old polemics which defined the Cognitive Linguistics enterprise in its earlier days are losing their actuality. As Cognitive Linguistics enters the mainstream—the publication of the present *Handbook* is testimony to this—it will become increasingly anachronistic for Cognitive Linguistics to frame itself in terms of opposition to other approaches. Dialogue—and dare I suggest, integration—with other approaches may well become the order of the day.

NOTES

....

1. In the generative literature, the elimination of lists in favor to rules is often justified by the need to remove redundancy from the grammar: what can be stated as a higher-order generalization does not need to be repeated in statements of specific facts. For a representative statement of this position, see Radford (1988: 366–69).

2. Somewhat more contentiously, Lakoff (1990) distinguishes Cognitive Linguistics from Generative Linguistics in terms of the former's "generalization commitment," that is, a commitment "to characterizing the general principles governing all aspects of human language" (40); it is this commitment, Lakoff claims, which renders Cognitive Linguistics "a scientific endeavor." The corollary, presumably, is that Generative Linguistics, because it is not committed to generalizations, is not a scientific endeavor. This way of contrasting the two approaches is particularly unfortunate. In fact, one of the characteristics of Cognitive Linguistics in practice has been, precisely, a recognition of the particular, the idiosyncratic, and the quirky, in contrast to Generative Linguistics, where the search for high-level generalizations has tended to restrict the field of enquiry to "core" syntactic phenomena.

3. For a survey of twentieth-century linguistics, see Sampson (1980) (now somewhat dated, but still worth reading). For Chomskyan linguistics and its critics, see Newmeyer (1980, 1986, 1998) and Harris (1993); see Radford (1988) for a textbook presentation of the 1980s model of Generative Grammar; Culicover (1997) is a more advanced text, incorporating more recent developments.

4. In order to avoid misunderstandings on this point, it should be emphasized that a commitment to cognitive realism does not entail that speakers necessarily have conscious access to mental representations. Much of the mind's contents may well be unavailable to introspection.

5. The example is from Lakoff's 1965 PhD dissertation, published as Lakoff (1970).

6. The spirit of Generative Semantics still lives on, however; see Seuren (1997). Consider also Sadock's (1990) review of Baker (1988). In his monograph on incorporation, Baker (1988: 46) proposed that "identical thematic relations" between constituents, irrespective of their surface manifestation, had to be derived from unique representations at the level of deep structure. Sadock (himself a participant in the Generative Semantics movement) draws attention to the irony of the fact that this preeminently Generative Semantics notion is developed within the framework of orthodox Chomskyan linguistics. As Sadock (1990: 130) notes, Baker managed to write a book that "is actually more 'generative semantics' than the Generative Semantics of the late 60s and early 70s."

7. Langacker (1987: 4), however, disagrees: "Cognitive grammar is not in any significant sense an outgrowth of generative semantics."

8. For ease of presentation, I describe the development of autonomous linguistics in terms of Chomsky's publications, ignoring the numerous scholars who contributed significantly to the enterprise.

9. It is interesting, however, to note that some of Chomsky's very recent observations on semantics touch on issues which have long been of interest in Cognitive Linguistics. Noting the varying reference of the word *house* in expressions such *paint the house brown*, *be in the house*, *be near the house*, and *see the house*, Chomsky (2000: 35–36) raised the question of what the concept might be that the word *house* designates. It will be appreciated that the issues touched on by Chomsky pertain to the "active zone phenomenon," familiar to Cognitive Linguists since Langacker (1984).

10. Observe that I am using "symbol" to refer to an association of a sign with a conceptualization. Earlier in this chapter, I used the word in a very different sense, to refer to category labels such as "N" and "NP."

REFERENCES

Baker, Mark. 1988. *Incorporation: A theory of grammatical function changing.* Chicago: University of Chicago Press.

Bloomfield, Leonard. 1933. *Language.* New York: Holt, Rinehart and Winston.

Bresnan, Joan. 1978. A realistic transformational grammar. In Morris Halle, Joan Bresnan, and George A. Miller, eds., *Linguistic theory and psychological reality* 1–59. Cambridge, MA: MIT Press.

Brugman, Claudia. 1981. Story of *Over.* MA thesis, University of California at Berkeley. (Published as *The story of Over: Polysemy, semantics, and the structure of the lexicon.* New York: Garland, 1988)

Bybee, Joan L. 1995. Regular morphology and the lexicon. *Language and Cognitive processes* 10: 425–55.

Bybee, Joan L. 2001. *Phonology and language use.* Cambridge: Cambridge University Press.

Bybee, Joan L., and Paul Hopper, eds. 2001. *Frequency and the emergence of linguistic structure.* Amsterdam: John Benjamins.

Chomsky, Noam. 1957. *Syntactic structures.* The Hague: Mouton.

Chomsky, Noam. 1965. *Aspects of the theory of syntax.* Cambridge, MA: MIT Press.

Chomsky, Noam. 1970. Remarks on nominalization. In Roderick Jacobs and Peter Rosenbaum, eds., *Readings in English transformational grammar* 184–221. Waltham, MA: Ginn.

Chomsky, Noam. 1981. *Lectures on government and binding.* Dordrecht, Netherlands: Foris.

Chomsky, Noam. 1986. *Knowledge of language: Its nature, origin, and use.* New York: Praeger.

Chomsky, Noam. 1995. *The minimalist program.* Cambridge, MA: MIT Press.

Chomsky, Noam. 2000. *New horizons in the study of language and mind.* Cambridge: Cambridge University Press.

Croft, William. 1991. *Syntactic categories and grammatical relations: The cognitive organization of information.* Chicago: University of Chicago Press.

Croft, William. 1995. Autonomy and functionalist linguistics. *Language* 71: 490–532.

Croft, William. 1999. Some contributions of typology to cognitive linguistics, and vice versa. In Theo Janssen and Gisela Redeker, eds., *Cognitive linguistics: Foundations, scope, and methodology* 61–93. Berlin: Mouton de Gruyter.

Croft, William. 2001. *Radical construction grammar: Syntactic theory in typological perspective.* Oxford: Oxford University Press.

Culicover, Peter. 1997. *Principles and parameters: An introduction to syntactic theory.* Oxford: Oxford University Press.

Culicover, Peter. 1999. *Syntactic nuts: Hard cases, syntactic theory, and language acquisition.* Oxford: Oxford University Press.

Deacon, Terrence. 1997. *The symbolic species: The co-evolution of language and the human brain.* New York: W. W. Norton.

Deane, Paul D. 1992. *Grammar in mind and brain: Explorations in cognitive syntax*. Berlin: Mouton de Gruyter.

Dekkers, Joost, Frank van der Leeuw, and Jeroen van de Weijer, eds. 2000. *Optimality Theory: Phonology, syntax, and acquisition*. Oxford: Oxford University Press.

Gazdar, Gerald, Ewan Klein, Geoffrey Pullum, and Ivan Sag. 1985. *Generalized phrase structure grammar*. Oxford: Basil Blackwell.

Geeraerts, Dirk. 1990. Editorial statement. *Cognitive Linguistics* 1: 1–3.

Givón, Talmy. 1979. *On understanding grammar*. New York: Academic Press.

Givón, Talmy. 1984. *Syntax. A functional-typological introduction*. Vol. 1. Amsterdam: John Benjamins.

Goldberg, Adele E. 1995. *Constructions: A construction grammar approach to argument structure*. Chicago: University of Chicago Press.

Harnish, Robert. 2002. *Minds, brains, computers: An historical introduction to the foundations of cognitive science*. Oxford: Basil Blackwell.

Harris, Randy A. 1993. *The linguistics wars*. Oxford: Oxford University Press.

Hudson, Richard. 1984. *Word grammar*. Oxford: Basil Blackwell.

Imai, Mutsumi, and Dedre Gentner. 1997. A cross-linguistic study of early word meaning: Universal ontology and linguistic influence. *Cognition* 62: 169–200.

Jackendoff, Ray. 1972. *Semantic interpretation in generative grammar*. Cambridge, MA: MIT Press.

Jackendoff, Ray. 1983. *Semantics and cognition*. Cambridge, MA: MIT Press.

Jackendoff, Ray. 1997. *The architecture of the language faculty*. Cambridge, MA: MIT Press.

Lakoff, George. 1970. *Irregularity in syntax*. New York: Holt, Rinehart and Winston.

Lakoff, George. 1977. Linguistic gestalts. *Chicago Linguistic Society* 13: 236–87.

Lakoff, George. 1982. Categories: An essay in cognitive linguistics. In Linguistic Society of Korea, ed., *Linguistics in the morning calm* 139–93. Seoul: Hanshin.

Lakoff, George. 1987. *Women, fire, and dangerous things: What categories reveal about the mind*. Chicago: University of Chicago Press.

Lakoff, George. 1990. The invariance hypothesis: Is abstract reason based on image-schemas? *Cognitive Linguistics* 1: 39–74.

Lakoff, George, and Mark Johnson. 1999. *Philosophy in the flesh: The embodied mind and its challenge to Western thought*. New York: Basic Books.

Lamb, Sydney M. 1999. *Pathways of the brain: The neurocognitive basis of language*. Amsterdam: John Benjamins.

Lambrecht, Knud. 1990. "What, me worry?"—"Mad Magazine sentences" revisited. *Berkeley Linguistics Society* 16: 215–28.

Langacker, Ronald W. 1982. Space grammar, analysability, and the English passive. *Language* 58: 22–80.

Langacker, Ronald W. 1984. Active zones. *Berkeley Linguistics Society* 10: 172–88.

Langacker, Ronald W. 1987. *Foundations of cognitive grammar*. Vol. 1, *Theoretical prerequisites*. Stanford, CA: Stanford University Press.

Langacker, Ronald W. 1991. *Foundations of cognitive grammar*. Vol. 2, *Descriptive application*. Stanford, CA: Stanford University Press.

Langacker, Ronald W. 1993. Clause structure in cognitive grammar. *Studi Italiani di Linguistica Teorica e Applicata* 2: 465–508.

Langacker, Ronald W. 1995. Raising and transparency. *Language* 71: 1–62.

Langacker, Ronald W. 1999. Assessing the cognitive linguistic enterprise. In Theo Janssen and Gisela Redeker, eds., *Cognitive linguistics: Foundations, scope, and methodology* 13–59. Berlin: Mouton de Gruyter.

Lieberman, Philip. 1991. *Uniquely human: The evolution of speech, thought, and selfless behavior*. Cambridge, MA: Harvard University Press.

Lindner, Susan. 1981. A lexico-semantic analysis of English verb-particle constructions with OUT and UP. PhD dissertation, University of California at San Diego. (Also published as A lexico-semantic analysis of English verb-particle constructions. LAUT Paper, no. 101. Trier, Germany: Linguistic Agency of the University of Trier, 1983)

McMahon, April. 2000. *Change, chance, and optimality*. Oxford: Oxford University Press.

Newmeyer, Frederick. 1980. *Linguistic theory in America: The first quarter-century of transformational generative grammar*. New York: Academic Press.

Newmeyer, Frederick. 1986. *The politics of linguistics*. Chicago: University of Chicago Press.

Newmeyer, Frederick. 1998. *Language form and language function*. Cambridge, MA: MIT Press.

Noble, William, and Iain Davidson. 1996. *Human evolution, language and mind: A psychological and archaeological inquiry*. Cambridge: Cambridge University Press.

Nunberg, Geoffrey, Ivan Sag, and Thomas Wasow. 1994. Idioms. *Language* 70: 491–538.

Prince, Alan, and Paul Smolensky. 1993. Optimality theory: Constraint interaction in generative grammar. Rutgers University Center for Cognitive Science, Technical Report no 2. Available at http://roa.rutgers.edu/files/537-0802/537-0802-PRINCE-0-0.PDF.

Radford, Andrew. 1988. *Transformational grammar: A first course*. Cambridge: Cambridge University Press.

Sadock, Jerrold. 1990. Review of *Incorporation: A theory of grammatical function changing*, by Mark Baker. *Natural Language and Linguistic Theory* 8: 129–41.

Sampson, Geoffrey. 1980. *Schools of linguistics*. Stanford, CA: Stanford University Press.

Saussure, Ferdinand de. [1916] 1967. *Cours de linguistique générale*. Paris: Payot.

Seuren, Pieter. 1997. *Semantic syntax*. Oxford: Basil Blackwell.

Soja, Nancy, Susan Carey, and Elizabeth Spelke. 1991. Ontological categories guide children's inductions of word meaning. *Cognition* 38: 179–211.

Talmy, Leonard. 1988. Force dynamics in language and cognition. *Cognitive Science* 12: 49–100.

Taylor, John R. 1996. *Possessives in English: An exploration in cognitive grammar*. Oxford: Oxford University Press.

Taylor, John R. 2002. *Cognitive grammar*. Oxford: Oxford University Press.

Taylor, John R. 1989. *Linguistic categorization: Prototypes in linguistic theory*. Oxford: Oxford University Press. (2nd ed., 1995; 3rd ed., 2003)

Tomasello, Michael. 1999. *The cultural origins of human cognition*. Cambridge, MA: Harvard University Press.

Tomasello, Michael. 2000. First steps toward a usage-based theory of language acquisition. *Cognitive Linguistics* 11: 61–82.

Tomasello, Michael, and Patricia Brooks. 1998. Young children's earliest transitive and intransitive constructions. *Cognitive Linguistics* 9: 379–95.

Tuggy, David. 1996. The thing is is that people talk that way: The question is Why? In Eugene H. Casad, ed., *Cognitive linguistics in the Redwoods* 713–52. Berlin: Mouton de Gruyter.

Tuggy, David. 2003. The Orizaba Nawatl verb *kîsa*: A case study in polysemy. In Hubert Cuyckens, René Dirven, and John R. Taylor, eds., *Cognitive approaches to lexical semantics*. Berlin: Mouton de Gruyter.

van Hoek, Karen. 1997. *Anaphora and conceptual structure*. Chicago: University of Chicago Press.

Verspoor, Marjolijn, Dong Lee, and Eve Sweetser, eds. 1997. *Lexical and syntactical constructions and the construction of meaning: Proceedings of the Bi-annual ICLA Meeting in Albuquerque, July 1995*. Amsterdam: John Benjamins.

Wierzbicka, Anna. 1986. What's in a noun? (Or: how do nouns differ in meaning from adjectives?) *Studies in Language* 10: 353–89.

CHAPTER 22

COGNITIVE LINGUISTICS AND THE HISTORY OF LINGUISTICS

BRIGITTE NERLICH AND DAVID D. CLARKE

1. INTRODUCTION

In 1908 Friedrich Ebbinghaus stated that psychology has a long past and a short history (see Farr 1991: 371). Howard Gardener (1985: 9) has said of cognitive science that it has a very long past but a relatively short history. We have pointed out in various publications that semantics and pragmatics have short histories but long pasts (see Nerlich 1992; Nerlich and Clarke 1996). Cognitive Linguistics, too, can be said to have a long past and a short history (Nerlich and Clarke 2001). In this article, we will present a number of aspects of the long past of Cognitive Linguistics. Specifically, we will try to point out that the understanding that Cognitive Linguistics has of its own past is not in all respects optimal: on the one hand, we will point to forerunners that have hardly been recognized as such; on the other, we will make clear that some of the theoreticians that served as a negative reference point for Cognitive Linguistics were actually closer to the cognitive approach than can be derived from the discussions.

We will not, however, try to give an exhaustive overview of all relevant historical sources—actual ones or neglected ones. In particular, although the long past of Cognitive Linguistics overlaps significantly with that of philosophy, psychology, and the cognitive sciences, we will concentrate on the history of linguistics only, with an occasional excursion to the history of philosophy. (The chapters of this *Handbook* devoted to psychology, cognitive science, and philosophy include references to a number of forerunners in these fields; see Harder, chapter 48, and Sinha, chapter 49.) Section 2 of this chapter briefly describes the internal history of Cognitive Linguistics. The following sections discuss three topic areas of specific importance for Cognitive Linguistics: polysemy, metaphor, and metonymy; the embodiment of cognition; and the Gestalt nature of linguistics.

2. The Short History of Cognitive Linguistics

Cognitive Linguistics emerged from its dissatisfaction with dominant orthodoxies in twentieth-century linguistics, among them the structuralist/formalist tradition in European semantics, the generative/formalist tradition that dominated research into syntax in North America, and the formalist/computational approach to semantics that prevailed in North America and Europe during the second half of the twentieth century. Natural allies of Cognitive Linguistics by contrast are functionalists and contextualists of all persuasions from the Prague school onward: Functional Grammar (Dik), Systemic-Functional Grammar (Halliday), functional-typological theories of language (Givón), pragmatics (ordinary language philosophy, Grice), Natural Morphology and Natural Phonology (Stampe, Dressler, Donegan), as well as the Columbia School of linguistics with William Diver as its head (who himself followed in the footsteps of André Martinet). As Langacker (1998: 1) wrote, "The movement called *Cognitive Linguistics* belongs to the functionalist tradition." This means that in contrast to formalist approaches, language is no longer viewed as an autonomous system, but rather "as an integral facet of cognition (not as a separate 'module' or 'mental faculty'). Insofar as possible, linguistic structure is analyzed in terms of more basic systems and abilities (e.g., perception, attention, categorization) from which it cannot be dissociated."

The dissatisfaction with orthodoxies brought with it a questioning of various assumptions and divisions on which traditional linguistic research was based, in particular the separation of objective knowledge from subjective knowledge, of linguistic knowledge from encyclopedic knowledge, of literal language from figurative language, of conceptual/cognitive structures from linguistic structures, and finally of synchronic structures from diachronic change (see Peeters 1998). The influence of prototype theory (and also fuzzy logic) brought about a reevaluation of what had always been put into the formalist-structuralist wastebasket, namely, variability, polysemy, and diachronic semantic change. Whereas previous generations of linguists had tended to search for simplicity, monosemy, regularity, and rules, cognitive linguists revel in complexity, flexibility, and patterns, including irregular ones. "One of the reasons for the emergence of CL and one of its most significant features nowadays is a special interest in those aspects of language that were previously considered as irregular or marginal" (Bernárdez 1999: 13).

Further, the influence of a new type of cognitive science (that has been called "Second Generation Cognitive Science"; see Brockman 2000; Sinha, this volume, chapter 49) brought with it a shift from seeing the mind as a disembodied manipulation of formal symbols and of language as a syntactic arrangement of formal symbols to seeing mind, meaning, and language as embodied. Syntax, semantics, morphology, and phonology all came to be seen as exploiting universal features of human perception, bodily structure, and social interaction. This means that "cognition" and "pragmatics" are, in a sense, integral components of all aspects of language.

The beginnings of Cognitive Linguistics lie somewhere round 1975, which is the year when Lakoff appears to have used the term "Cognitive Linguistics" for the first time (see Peeters 2001). Around that period, Lakoff abandoned his earlier attempts to develop a Generative Semantics by merging Chomsky's Transformational Grammar with formal logic. As Lakoff points out in his interview with Brockman (2000), "Noam claimed then—and still does, so far as I can tell—that syntax is independent of meaning, context, background knowledge, memory, cognitive processing, communicative intent, and every aspect of the body." However, in working on his Generative Semantics, Lakoff noticed "quite a few cases where semantics, context, and other such factors entered into rules governing the syntactic occurrences of phrases and morphemes" and caused what generativists saw as "irregularities." At the same time, Lakoff realized that figures of speech, such as metaphor and metonymy, were not just linguistic decorations, or, worse still, deviations, but a part of everyday speech that affects the ways in which we perceive, think, and act. He began his collaboration with the philosopher Mark Johnson in 1979, and they published their seminal book *Metaphors We Live By* in 1980, which was the first publication to bring Cognitive Linguistics to the attention of a wider audience.

But George Lakoff was not the only one dissatisfied with transformational linguistics during the 1970s. Typically, "Cognitive Linguistics has not arisen fully-formed from a single source, it has no central guru and no crystallized formalism" (Janda 2000: 3; see also Bernárdez 1999: 11). Around 1975, in fact, Charles Fillmore was working on his theory of frame semantics, and Ronald Langacker was laying the foundations of his Cognitive Grammar (initially called "Space Grammar"). Leonard Talmy wrote his dissertation in 1972 and began to introduce principles of Gestalt psychology into linguistic analysis, especially in his study of force dynamics and event frames (see Talmy 2000a/b). Taking over some of Talmy's insights into Gestalt psychology, especially the concepts of Figure and Ground, Langacker developed his own theory of conceptual profiling, which became central to Cognitive Linguistics.

From 1980 onwards, Cognitive Linguistics began to flourish in the shape of work on metaphorical categorization (Lakoff), image schemata (Johnson), Cognitive Grammar (Langacker), mental spaces and blending (Fauconnier, Turner), and diachronic prototype semantics (Geeraerts). In the second half of the 1980s, Cognitive Linguistics became sociologically organized. In 1989, René Dirven, who was particularly instrumental in the international expansion of Cognitive

Linguistics, organized the *First International Conference on Cognitive Linguistics* in Duisburg, Germany, which became a landmark in Cognitive Linguistics. (Dirven had in fact already organized a "proto-conference" in Trier in 1985.) It was at the Duisburg conference that the International Cognitive Linguistics Association (ICLA) was founded and the journal *Cognitive Linguistics*, with Dirk Geeraerts as the first editor, and the series *Cognitive Linguistic Research*, with René Dirven and Ronald Langacker (and later also John Taylor) as editors, were launched.

During the 1990s, Cognitive Linguistics changed its status from "revolutionary" to "established." The biennial conferences of the ICLA that were successively organized in Santa Cruz (1991), Leuven (1993), Albuquerque (1995), Amsterdam (1997), Stockholm (1999), Santa Barbara (2001), Logroño (2003), and Seoul (2005) witnessed an ever-growing number of attendants, and Cognitive Linguistics may now be said to be one of the major popular frameworks within theoretical linguistics at large. There are now also various national cognitive linguistics associations all over the world.

In these years of expansion, the historical self-awareness of Cognitive Linguistics started to broaden beyond the initial contrastive stance with regard to the immediate competitors, like Generative Linguistics. Some cognitive and historical linguists began to scrutinize the novel (or allegedly novel) concepts used by cognitive linguists and discovered that most of them have hidden, forgotten, or scarcely appreciated historical roots (see Geeraerts 1988a, 1988b, 1993a, 1993b; Swiggers 1989; Nerlich 1992, 2000; Nerlich and Clarke 1997, 2000a, 2000b, 2001; Desmet, Geeraerts, and Swiggers 1997; Jákel 1999). In the course of the following pages, we will illustrate this by looking at three topic areas of specific importance for Cognitive Linguistics: polysemy, metaphor, and metonymy; the embodiment of cognition; and the Gestalt nature of linguistics. In each case, we will devote attention to linguists and philosophers who developed theories which can be compared to those developed by cognitive linguists, as well as linguists and philosophers who developed theories which directly foreshadowed and in some instances influenced the development of Cognitive Linguistics. At the same time, we will point to thinkers who developed theories in the more distant philosophical past and those who developed proto-cognitive theories of certain central concepts in the less distant past but were forgotten in the excitement of the Cognitive Linguistics revolution.

3. POLYSEMY, METAPHOR, AND METONYMY

It was noticed fairly early on that the closest relative of Cognitive Linguistics in the history of linguistics is probably the tradition of prestructuralist diachronic semantics (see Geeraerts 1988a, 1988b; Nerlich 1992). Figures of speech such as metaphor, metonymy, and synecdoche were not only of interest to philosophers exploring the relation between language and thought, they were in fact also of interest to those lexicographers and linguists who were no longer merely looking for the true, original, first, and etymological meaning of words, but came to examine how words were used to make sense by those who used them. They were interested in finding the connections between the meanings of words, in finding patterns in the evolution of meaning, and in putting order into the meanings of lexical entries. During the nineteenth century, one can observe a general shift from studying meaning as part of etymology to studying meaning as part of a new historical and psychological semantics. Michel Bréal can be regarded as epitomizing this new movement; he was, in fact, also the inventor of a new linguistic term, namely "polysemy." To get a better idea of the basis for the perceived affinity between Cognitive Linguistics and prestructuralist semantics, we will now have a closer look at Bréal's work. The ensuing two paragraphs, by contrast, focus on historical links that were misinterpreted or neglected rather than readily recognized by Cognitive Linguistics: Aristotle, and a number of twentieth-century theories of metaphor.

3.1. Bréal and Prestructuralist Semantics

From looking at multiple meanings in disembodied lexical entries, Bréal turned to polysemy as a phenomenon of language use, language acquisition, language change, and even neurolinguistics *avant la lettre*. He wanted to discover the intellectual, that is, cognitive, laws of language use and language change (see Bréal 1883). Bréal knew that, diachronically, polysemy stems from the fact that the new meanings or values that words acquire in use (through extension, restriction, metaphor, etc.) do not automatically eliminate the old ones. The new and the old meanings exist in parallel ([1897] 1924: 143–44). And yet, synchronically, or in language use, polysemy does not really exist (it is rather an artifact of lexicographers). In the context of discourse, a word always has one meaning (except in jokes and puns). The most important factor that brings about the multiplication of meanings diachronically and that helps us to "reduce" the multiplicity of meanings synchronically is the *context* of discourse ([1887] 1991: 156–57). In the constant dialectical give and take between synchrony and diachrony and between meaning and understanding, incremental changes in the meaning of words occur, insofar as hearers, having understood a word in a certain context in a slightly divergent way, become themselves speakers and might use a word in the newly understood way in yet another context, which again brings about a different type of understanding, and so on. In the long run, these slight variations in use and uptake can lead to major semantic changes and, as cognitive linguists have more recently rediscovered, to processes of grammaticalization.

More sudden shifts in meaning are brought about by the use of metaphor and metonymy. There are also shifts in meaning which have a more social than poetic root, as when the word *operation* comes to mean something different according to the social context in which it is used (by a mathematician, a general, a surgeon, and so on). Analyzing the multiplication of meanings based on the speakers' and hearers' social, poetic, and cognitive needs and activities was central to Bréal's semantics.

Bréal was fascinated by the fact that when talking to each other we neither get confused by the multiplicity of meanings that a word can have, some of which are listed in dictionaries of usage, nor are we bothered by the etymological ancestry of a word, traced by historical dictionaries. Both the usage dictionary and the historical dictionary classify the meanings of polysemous words which have been produced over time by a nation or are in use by a nation at a certain time. This is a *social* (abstract and decontextualized) classification, whereas the classification of meanings in the heads of a speaker or hearer is in each case an *individual* (cognitive, concrete, and contextual) classification. Bréal has in mind an "isosynchronic competence," a half-conscious type of user knowledge which only works inside concrete situations (see Bréal 1995: 283). It is situated semantic knowledge. Modern polysemy research still debates whether it should predominantly deal with the social or individual type of polysemy and how it should reconcile the one with the other.

Bréal observed that most of the time it is the latest, most modern meaning of the word, yesterday's or today's meaning, with which we first become familiar ([1884] 1991: 149). Hence, language understanding and language acquisition follow the opposite route of language change; that is, both in language understanding and language acquisition, it is the latest, not the first or primitive meaning of a word, which is the basic meaning. In modern parlance, one would say that the most salient, not the most "literal" meaning, is the one that we acquire first and also use and understand first (see Giora and Gur 2003).

Bréal was acutely aware of the fact that the advances made in study of the semantic, cognitive, and developmental aspects of language were not yet on a par with those made in the study of phonetics, of the more physiological side of language. In his article "How words are classified in our mind" ([1884] 1991), Bréal therefore appealed to the future to supply us with insights into the cognitive aspects of human language. With Bréal, semantics as a cognitive linguistic discipline made a first step into this future, a future in which we are still participating and to which we are still contributing at the beginning of the twenty-first century—the century of psycholinguistics, Artificial Intelligence, brain scanning, and neuropsychology. Bréal was a central figure in the new tradition of historical semantics inspired by psychology, which had started with Reisig and his interest in metaphor and metonymy as mechanisms of semantic change and ended with Stephen Ullmann's synthesis in the 1960s (see Nerlich 1992). This tradition was resurrected in the light of insights achieved by cognitive linguists in the 1980s with the work of Geeraerts, Traugott, Nerlich, Warren, Koch, Blank, Fritz, Kleparski, and others.

3.2. Aristotle

Just like Saussure and Whorf (who will be dealt with further on in this chapter), Aristotle seems to have been the misunderstood whipping-boy of many a cognitive linguist even though he "holds a position of the ubiquity of metaphor in conversation and writing which supports current views about the omnipresence of metaphor in everyday discourse and the print media" (Mahon 1999: 69). We do not want to repeat Mahon's arguments here but only support them with another quote from an early review of Lakoff and Johnson (1980). Here the reviewer, Michael Smith, argues that Aristotle in the *Rhetoric* had already remarked that "strange words simply puzzle us; ordinary words convey only what we know already; it is from metaphor that we can best get hold of something fresh" (1982: 128). It is through metaphors that we learn, that we develop our mind and our language. Further nuancing of the picture painted of Aristotle within cognitive linguistic circles can be found in Geeraerts (1989) and Kanellos (1994).

It is not this nuanced picture, however, that most cognitive linguists picked up from Aristotle. For them, Aristotle was the originator of two distorted views: an objectivist view of the relation between language and the world and a view of metaphor as simple comparison. Both Lakoff (1987: 157–95) and Johnson (1987: xxi–xxxvi) (see also Lakoff and Johnson 1999: 74–94) argue against the so-called objectivist paradigm in order to then introduce their own so-called non-Aristotelian view of language and cognition. The main tenets of the objectivist or Aristotelian paradigm of thought are that reality is structured independently of human understanding and that this structure is reflected or mirrored in human categorization, where all entities that share a given property or sets of necessary and sufficient properties belong to the same category (this is also called the Classical Theory of Categorization). By contrast, for Lakoff and Johnson, going back to Ludwig Wittgenstein (1953) and Eleanor Rosch (1978), categories are fuzzy, graded, embodied, and changeable, and therefore "subjective in a nonpejorative sense. Yet another part of the Aristotelian straw men that cognitive linguists attacked (see also Richards 1936: 90) was Aristotles' alleged view that metaphor was purely ornamental. As Mahon (1999, 77–78) has convincingly argued, "Aristotle is not claiming that metaphors *per se* are exceptional. He is only claiming that new good metaphors that are coined by tragedians and epic poets are exceptional."

3.3. Twentieth-Century Metaphor Research

At the same time that Lakoff, Johnson, Turner, Kövesces, and others were sketching their new theory of metaphor as part of the newly established Cognitive Linguistics, there were thinkers in the United States and Europe who, quite independently at first, elaborated their own new theories of metaphor and thought. Their works have parallels with the Cognitive Linguistics research program but are largely ignored by it.

First, there are a number of scholars who belong to different traditions than the linguistic one—in particular, literary theory, and philosophy. In the United States, Kenneth Burke (1945, 1969) linked the study of rhetoric (the four "mastertropes": metaphor, metonymy, synecdoche, and irony) to the study of situated symbolic actions and motives. His work is still very much appreciated by literary scholars but almost unknown among cognitive linguists (he is mentioned, however, in Turner et al. 1998). In France, the phenomenologist and hermeneutician Paul Ricoeur published his seminal book *La Métaphore Vive* in 1975, in which he discussed conceptions of metaphor from Aristotle up to ordinary language philosophy and tried to bridge the gap between continental hermeneutics and Anglo-American analytical philosophy. An article that Ricoeur wrote for a special issue on metaphor published by *Critical Inquiry* in 1978, "The Metaphorical Process as Cognition, Imagination, and Feeling," was later included in a volume edited by Mark Johnson entitled *Philosophical Perspectives on Metaphor*, which also contained articles by other major European and American philosophers of metaphor (Johnson 1981).

Second, some scholars seem to have gone unnoticed because they belong to geographically restricted traditions. In Germany, a whole line of linguists from Jost Trier onwards became interested in studying fields of metaphors, or what is now called "conceptual metaphors." Trier studied certain domains of experience which constitute major sources for metaphors (*bildspendende Felder*; cf. Trier 1934: 197–98) and major sources for making sense of the world. Taking up the notion of *Bildfeld*, Harald Weinrich then developed a theory of metaphor based on the observation of everyday language (see Jákel 1999: 23). In 1958, he made a distinction between *Bildspender* and *Bildempfänger* (Weinrich 1976: 284; see also 1967, 1980), which can be compared to that between source and target domain or, as they are sometimes called, donor domain and recipient domain. There are obvious similarities between Weinrich's theory of metaphor and that developed by Bühler and Stählin at the beginning of the twentieth century (see Nerlich and Clarke 2000a) and the interaction theory of metaphor developed by Max Black in the 1960s—a theory that cognitive linguists did not overlook in their revolutionary fervor (Black 1962; on the relation between the interaction theory of metaphor and modern metaphor studies, see Gibbs 1994).

There was one German linguist, who is even less known than Trier or Weinrich and who, in 1954, examined certain domains as sources for metaphors from an onomasiological perspective: Franz Dornseiff (see Liebert 1995: 149–51). Among many other conceptual metaphors (such as the container metaphor, the metaphor of grasping for understanding, of agitation for anger, and of verticality as an image schema projected onto social hierarchies), Dornseiff discusses what one can call in cognitive linguistic terms the projection of the image schema SOURCE-PATH-GOAL onto the domain of GOAL and GOAL-ATTAINMENT (see Dornseiff 1954: 142–43; Liebert 1995: 151).

Around the same time, the German philosopher Hans Blumenberg published his first essays on metaphor ("Light as a Metaphor for Truth," 1957; "Paradigms for a Metaphorology," 1960). He had discovered "metaphor while reconstructing the history of central philosophical and scientific concepts" (Jákel 1999: 23), such as LIFE IS A BOOK, which has reemerged as a central metaphor in modern genomic discourse (Blumenberg 1986; Nerlich, Dingwall, and Clarke 2002). He thought that the historical study of metaphor could illuminate essential aspects of human existence, culture, and society (see Blumenberg 1997; Adams 1991). As far as we know, neither Weinrich nor Dornseiff nor Blumenberg were ever read by cognitive linguists until they were rediscovered by Jákel (1999).

4. Gestalt Conceptions of Language

Ideas that were originally formulated by Gestalt play a central role in Cognitive Linguistics: foremost among these are the Figure/Ground distinction and, more generally, the idea that meanings do not exist in isolation but have to be understood in a larger context (the idea, in other words, that parts and wholes determine each other). Although Max Wertheimer is credited as the founder of Gestalt theory, the concept of Gestalt was first introduced in contemporary philosophy and psychology by Christian von Ehrenfels (see Nerlich and Clarke 1999), and Gestalt psychology developed between 1890 and about 1930. One should be able to find historical affinities between Cognitive Linguistics and earlier linguists who tried to incorporate aspects of Gestalt theory (see Nerlich and Clarke 1999).

4.1. Saussure and Structuralism

Although Ronald Langacker informed us (p.c.) that he was not influenced by Saussure's work in any way and Lakoff never mentions Saussure in his published works, there are some obvious links between Saussurean linguistics and the Cognitive Linguistics research program. In order to get a better view of these links, one first has to do away with some common misunderstandings about Saussure (see Nerlich 1999), such as described in the following quotation:

> He separates individual from society, and language from other non-linguistic sign systems. Society is an anonymous and coercive totality which is external to the individual.... The language system is a closed and static system which makes no contact with the world. Saussure is unable to explain variability and change in the linguistic and other signs that we use in social life. Language is a code by which the speaker 'encodes' and then transmits non-linguistic ideas and thoughts to the listener in the speech circuit; in turn, these are 'decoded' by the listener. The sign is not systematically shaped by its uses in concrete acts of meaning-making. (Thibault 1997: xvii–xviii)

These preconceptions or prejudices frequently serve as a backdrop for more modern, dynamic cognitive theories of language and meaning. However, as Thibault has shown, Saussure's views on language can, if interpreted in the context of sources other than the *Cours de linguistique générale* (Saussure 1916), be related to modern theories of schematicity, prototypicality, and indexicality. While this might seem rather far-fetched to some cognitive linguists, it is indisputable that at least some cognitive linguists, like Langacker, share with Saussure a concern with the linguistic sign, "even when this term is not explicitly used" (Thibault 1997: xix; see, e.g., Langacker 1987: 91).

At the same time, it must be admitted that there are also clear fault-lines that separate the post-Saussurian structuralist tradition from Cognitive Linguistics, especially insofar as the theorems of the autonomy of the language and the arbitrariness of the sign are concerned. Most interesting for further exploration into the neglected historical parentage of Cognitive Linguistics will, therefore, be those theorists that were inspired by structuralism but that went beyond a static and autonomistic conception of linguistic structure. For instance, in his "psychomechanics," Gustave Guillaume (1929, 1971) developed a new conception of the language system as a system of systems (similar to Lamb's stratificational view of language) and the act of speaking as constitutive of and dependent on the act of cognition. Karl Bühler ([1934] 1990) used Saussure's distinction between *langue* and *parole* to formulate his own pragmatic theory of language, thought, and metaphor. Roman Jakobson (1956a, 1956b) employed Saussure's distinction between syntagmatic and paradigmatic relationships to formulate a new theory of metaphor and metonymy, of myth and aphasia, and the phenomenologist Maurice Merleau-Ponty ([1945] 1962) developed the dynamic aspects of Saussurean linguistics overlooked by many structuralists. All of them were aware of the developments in Gestalt psychology and all of them anticipated various aspects of modern Cognitive Linguistics. In the following paragraphs, we will discuss the insights of these scholars in more detail; in addition, we will include a section on Whorf, who stressed (in line with Saussure and Humboldt, but, it seems, unaware of their work) that mind without language is essentially amorphous (1956).

4.2. Whorf

Lakoff devoted an entire chapter of his famous book *Women, Fire, and Dangerous Things* (1987) to a refutation of Whorf and the so-called Sapir-Whorf hypothesis, also called the relativity principle, according to which language determines thought (strong version), or, less strongly, according to which "language affects perception and memory" (weaker version) (see Gross 1999: 320). However, several scholars (Jákel 1999; Stanulewicz 1999; most importantly, Lee 1996) have shown that this "hypothesis" against which cognitive linguists mounted their attack might be nothing more than a straw man—similar to the straw man position of Saussure's view of *la langue* as an autonomous system. To arrive at a more accurate understanding of Whorf, it might be better to abandon the distinction between a weak and a strong version of the Whorf hypothesis (see Brown and Lenneberg 1958) altogether, as it leads to a misleading reduction of a multidimensional problem field in which language, thought, perception, experience, and "the world" interact in various ways. Lee (1996: 27) focuses on this interaction at the interface between language and the world when she writes:

> When we come to look in detail at the original definitions of 'the linguistic relativity principle'[,] . . . it will become evident that Whorf's notion of relativity does not in any way undermine realist acceptance of an independent world beyond our senses. What it does rely on however, is the understanding that our experiential world (which is the only reality we can say we *know*) is a function of the human perceptual interface with both the external and internal environment of the human body.
>
> Like some interesting recent work in linguistics . . . , Whorf's experientialism was grounded in insights derived from gestalt theory.

According to Whorf, our flux of experience is segmented by culturally, perceptually, and bodily grounded patterns of meaning (see Lee 1996: 144). These patterns are fluctuating networks of relationships à la Lamb: "Whorf's mature ideas effectively constitute *a field theory of mind* in which connections are paramount and entities at any analytic 'level' are both indeterminate and functions of the relationships in which they are embedded" (Lee 1996: 9). Lee and Stanulewicz point to similarities between Whorf's thinking and that of various other cognitive linguists, such as Lakoff, Johnson, Langacker, and Mark Turner (Turner et al. 1998). Stanulewicz (1999: 193) claims that, just like Whorf, Lakoff "thinks that the way people use concepts influences the way they understand experience, and believes that differences in conceptual systems significantly influence behaviour." Whorf, just like the cognitive linguists after him, recognized the importance of metaphorical thinking, used the Gestalt concepts of Figure and Ground, discussed image schemas, and saw language as embedded in a network of relations spun between mind, body, and culture. Language has influences on the mind, but language also reflects the conceptual system of the speaker.

4.3. Bühler

Gestalt psychology also had an influence on Bühler's theory of language, which he developed in the 1930s. It is fundamentally a functional field theory of language (based on the interactions between the symbolic, deictic, and practical fields of language use) which overlaps with a cognitive theory of domains and mental spaces. Unlike Saussure, Hjelmslev, or Whorf, Bühler developed an explicit theory of metaphor which has some parallels with modern theories of blending. It should be emphasized that Bühler's psychology of metaphor did not appear out of the blue. Its development was prepared by a host of nineteenth- and early-twentieth-century metaphorologists, such as Gustav Gerber, Friedrich Nietzsche, Fritz Mauthner, Gustav Stáhlin (see Nerlich and Clarke 2000a, 2001), and Hans Vaihinger, who wrote that "all cognition is the perception of one thing through another" (Vaihinger 1924: 29).

Bühler worked in the framework of the Würzburg school of *Denkpsychology*, or psychology of thought, which had close links with Gestalt psychology (see Nerlich and Clarke 1999). He was especially interested in the mysteries of language understanding, which he saw as involving the integration of new structures into already existing structures of thought. For him, meaning emerged from an integration of *symbolic* and *encyclopedic* knowledge. This is nowhere better demonstrated than in metaphor, as in metaphor production and understanding we are dealing with a mixing of spheres, *Sphärenmischung*, that is, with the *blending* of linguistic and nonlinguistic knowledge: "A duality of spheres . . . and something like a transition from one to the other can often be detected in the experience [of understanding], and this often vanishes only when idiomatically familiar constructions are involved" (Bühler [1934] 1990: 343). Bühler's favorite example of the mixing of spheres in metaphor is the following: "A boy, eight years of age, observes the motion of the long antennae of a butterfly and explains that the animal is 'knitting socks' (motion of knitting needles). This is no bad analogy, but also no great effort from a psychological point of view, merely an association by similarity" (Bühler 1930: 105; see also Bühler [1934] 1990: 395).

To conceptualize or imagine how this mixing of spheres works, Bühler tried out various analogies. The most suitable one for this procedure, which he sometimes, metaphorically, calls *Cocktailverfahren* (Bühler 1990: 343), is the comparison with binocular vision. As such, metaphorical meaning constitution is, for him, similar to visual projection passing through two filters which partially cover each other, so that only those parts of the projection can be seen that are not covered or canceled out by either one of the filters. This filtering process is both *projective* and *selective* (see Hülzer-Vogt 1989: 36). The listener creatively selects those semantic aspects in a metaphor that fit into his or her (deictical) *field* of communicative interests. The word or words used in the metaphorical speech act are drawn from "established symbol fields, but provided the listener is initiated deictically to the particular situation, new blendings of semantic spheres may be employed that give a vivid image of the intended meaning" (Musolff 1993: 268). To understand a metaphor, we have to achieve a blend between two symbolic spheres, based on our specific world or domain knowledge in that situation of discourse. In using the term "sphere," Bühler showed that we do not look at things in isolation, but that we perceive and conceptualize them inside the network of relations in which they stand to other objects, which, together, constitute a sphere or domain as an overall "Gestalt." Through the use of signs, we attribute meaning to these objects, as well as to the relations themselves, so that the emergent meanings form a new semantic or symbolic sphere.

4.4. Jakobson

Jakobson, the best known of the Prague functionalist linguists, was familiar with the work of Saussure, Whorf, and Bühler and tried to combine insights from Saussure and Bühler. From Saussure, he took the distinction between syntagmatic and paradigmatic relations, from Bühler the functional approach to language. He extended Bühler's "Organon-model" of language, based on the three functions of representation, expression, and appeal, to six functions, which included, most importantly, the poetic function of language (Jakobson 1956a). Using Saussurean oppositions, such as paradigmatic/syntagmatic, selection/combination, substitution/contexture, and similarity/contiguity, Jakobson distinguished between two poles of "human behavior": the metaphorical and the metonymic pole (Jakobson 1956a; see also 1956b). These poles characterize all types of human behavior, especially linguistic behavior: poetic language (the use of metaphor and metonymy), aphasia (dyslexia and agrammatism), and the production of literature and myths.

Jakobson's (1956a) article sparked off a wave of post-structuralist research into metaphor and metonymy in French-speaking countries. In this respect (and taking into account that Lakoff studied with Jakobson), it is surprising that in "the latest very rich literature on metaphor one finds very few references to the epoch-making short paper by Roman Jakobson" (Dirven 1993: 2)—the paper has now been republished in Dirven and Pörings (2002)—which had been so crucial to the development of what Blumenberg called a "metaphorology" in Europe.

5. EMBODIED COGNITION

The notion of embodiment in Cognitive Linguistics basically takes two different forms: a neurological one and a psychological, experientialist one (see Rohrer, this volume, chapter 2; Ziemke, Zlatev, and Frank, 2007; Frank, Dirven, and Ziemke, 2007). For each of these approaches, historical forerunners may be identified.

5.1. Lamb

Sydney Lamb wrote about Stratificational Linguistics as early as 1966 and has since then developed a neural Cognitive Linguistics of his own which runs in parallel with Lakoff's interest in the neural underpinnings of Cognitive Linguistics (Lamb 1970, 1971, 1999; see Cheng 1998).

The most important tenet of Lamb's neurocognitive linguistics, influenced by Hjelmslev and Saussure, is based on the discovery that linguistic structure is not made up of symbols or objects of any kind, but rather of relationships. For Lamb in 1964, as for Whorf and Saussure before him and neurocognitivists after him, the whole linguistic system is a network of relationships. Peeters (1999: 385–86), in his review of Lamb (1999), summarizes Lamb's conception, which can be said to project Saussure, Hjelmslev, and Whorf's ideas onto the neural level, in the following way:

> Careful examination of the available linguistic evidence from a stratificational point of view reveals that the linguistic system is a network of relationships. Between units which, under full analysis, turn out to be nothing but

interconnected nodes or nections. . . . All the information, however, is in the interconnectivity, and there is therefore no separate 'place' where 'symbols' are 'stored' and/or 'retrieved'.

5.2. Merleau-Ponty

In his book *The Body in the Mind* (1987), Johnson claimed that image schemas (such as CONTAINER-CONTENT, PATH-GOAL, etc.) structure our experience preconceptually, that this is where meaning actually comes from. Mind and meaning are therefore embodied. On the basis of these preconceptual structures, we proceed to spin out networks of meaning by metaphor and metonymy. This was a truly novel view of meaning, mind, and language, but there are obvious similarities not only with Kant and Bartlett, but also with Merleau-Ponty's phenomenology of consciousness, influenced, like Whorf's and Bühler's conceptions of language, by Gestalt psychology (see Merleau-Ponty [1945] 1962; Gill 1991; Fesmire 1994).

Merleau-Ponty, like Guillaume, Jakobson, and Ricoeur, used Husserl's phenomenology to criticize certain aspects of Saussure's linguistics, especially his division between *langue* and *parole*. He wished to see established a phenomenology of *parole* which would more openly acknowledge the dialectic process of language creation and linguistic creativity in the act of speaking, in this comparable to Guillaume. This dynamic view of language was based on a dynamic view of perception as an active process of pattern-matching and pattern-seeking. For Merleau-Ponty, perception, knowledge of the world, consciousness, and language are embodied, just as they are for modern cognitive linguists. Specifically, he stresses the crucial epistemological role of the body, in the sense that the body is "animated" and the mind "incorporated": consciousness, according to Merleau-Ponty, is experienced in and through our bodies—in short consciousness is embodied. In spite of this obvious relationship, Merleau-Ponty is not often cited in the context of Cognitive Linguistics. He is acknowledged by Lakoff (see Brockman 2000) and Johnson (1993), but an extensive treatment in a cognitive linguistic context is to be found only in Geeraerts (1985: 354–64; 1993a).

6. PAST, PRESENT, AND FUTURE
OF COGNITIVE LINGUISTICS

Cognitive Linguistics has come a long way from Aristotle, through the nineteenth-century work on diachronic semantics and the twentieth-century revival of interest in the cognitive, rhetorical, and social functions of metaphor and mind. It now covers most of the ground that general linguistics used to cover, from work on phonology to work on pragmatics, through syntax and semantics, from synchrony to diachrony and back again. It is linking up with literary studies to study the literary mind, with developmental psychology to study language acquisition, with neuropsychology to study the embodied mind, with neurobiology to study how the brain carries out the work of the mind, and with social psychology to study mind and language in social interaction. However, while the future looks bright for Cognitive Linguistics, cognitive linguists of the future should not forget that Cognitive Linguistics also has a bright past, which is worth being rediscovered.

REFERENCES

Adams, David. 1991. Metaphors for mankind: The development of Hans Blumenberg's anthropological metaphorology. *Journal of the History of Ideas* 52: 152–66.

Bernárdez, Enrique. 1999. Some reflections on the origins of cognitive linguistics. *Journal of English Studies* 1: 9–28.

Black, Max. 1962. *Models and metaphors: Studies in language and philosophy*. Ithaca, NY: Cornell University Press.

Blumenberg, Hans. 1957. Licht als Metapher der Wahrheit: Im Vorfeld der philosophischen Begriffsbildung. *Studium Generale* 10: 432–47.

Blumenberg, Hans. 1960. Paradigmen zu einer Metaphorologie. *Archiv für Begriffsgeschichte*. Vol. 6. Bonn: Bouvier.

Blumenberg, Hans. 1986. *Die Lesbarkeit der Welt*. Frankfurt am Main: Suhrkamp.

Blumenberg, Hans. 1997. *Shipwreck with spectator: Paradigm of a metaphor for existence*. Trans. Steven Rendall. Cambridge, MA: MIT Press.

Bréal, Michel. 1883. Les lois intellectuelles du langage: Fragment de sémantique. *Annuaire de l'Association pour l'encouragement des études grecques en France* 17: 132–42.

Bréal, Michel. [1884] 1991. How words are organized in the mind. In George Wolf, ed. and trans., *The beginnings of semantics: Essays, lectures and reviews* 145–51. Oxford: Duckworth.

Bréal, Michel. [1887] 1991. The history of words. In George Wolf, ed. and trans., *The beginnings of semantics: Essays, lectures and reviews* 152–75. Oxford: Duckworth.

Bréal, Michel. [1897] 1924. *Essai de sémantique: Science des significations*. Repr. of 4th ed. Paris: Gérard Monfort.

Bréal, Michel. 1995. *De la grammaire comparée à la sémantique: Textes de Michel Bréal publiés entre 1864 et 1898*. Introduction, commentaires et bibliographie par Piet Desmet et Pierre Swiggers. Leuven, Belgium: Peeters.

Brockman, John. 2000. Interview with George Lakoff after the publication of *Philosophy in the Flesh* (1999). http://www.edge.org/documents/archive/edge51.html (accessed Nov. 2000).

Brown, Roger W., and Eric H. Lenneberg. 1958. Studies in linguistic relativity. In Eleanor E. Maccoby, Theodore M. Newcomb, and Eugene L. Hartley, eds., *Readings in social psychology* 9–18. New York: Holt, Rinehart and Winston.

Bühler, Karl. 1930. *The mental development of the child: A summary of modern psychological theory*. Third impression. London: Routledge and Kegan Paul.

Bühler, Karl. [1934] 1990. *Theory of language: The representational function of language*. Trans. Donald F. Goodwin. Amsterdam: John Benjamins.

Burke, Kenneth. 1945. *A grammar of motives*. Berkeley: University of California Press.

Burke, Kenneth. 1969. *A rhetoric of motives*. Berkeley: University of California Press.

Cheng, Quilong. 1998. Interview with Sydney Lamb for *langbrain; Language and brain: Neurocognitive Linguistics*, Rice University, Houston, TX. http://www.ruf.rice.edu/%7Elngbrain/main.htm (accessed Nov. 2000). (Published in *Foreign Language Teaching and Research* 19992/2: 61–64.)

Desmet, Piet, Dirk Geeraerts, and Pierre Swiggers. 1997. L'histoire de la sémantique pré-structurale: Quatre études. Catholic University of Leuven, Department of Linguistics, Preprint no. 156.

Desmet, Piet, and Pierre Swiggers. 1995. Introduction. In Michel Bréal, *De la grammaire comparée à la sémantique* 1–34. Leuven, Belgium: Peeters.

Dirven, René. 1993. Metonymy and metaphor: Different mental strategies of conceptualisation. *Leuvense Bijdragen* 82: 1–28.

Dirven, René, and Ralf Pörings, eds. 2002. *Metaphor and metonymy in comparison and contrast*. Berlin: Mouton de Gruyter.

Dornseiff, Franz. 1954. *Bezeichnungswandel unseres Wortschatzes: Ein Blick in das Seelenleben der Sprechenden*. Lahr/Schwarzwald, Germany: Moritz Schauenburg.

Farr, Robert M. 1991. The long past and the short history of social psychology. *European Journal of Social Psychology* 21: 371–80.

Fesmire, Steven A. 1994. What is 'cognitive' about cognitive linguistics? *Metaphor and Symbolic Activity* 9: 149–54.

Frank, Roslyn, René Dirven, Tom Ziemke, and Enrique Bernárdez, eds. 2008. *Body, language, and mind*. Vol. 2, *Sociocultural situatedness*. Berlin: Mouton de Gruyter.

Gardner, Howard. 1985. *The mind's new science: A history of the cognitive revolution*. New York: Basic Books.

Geeraerts, Dirk. 1985. *Paradigm and paradox: Explorations into a paradigmatic theory of meaning and its epistemological background*. Leuven, Belgium: Leuven University Press.

Geeraerts, Dirk. 1988a. Cognitive grammar and the history of lexical semantics. In Brygida Rudzka-Ostyn, ed., *Topics in cognitive linguistics* 647–77. Amsterdam: John Benjamins.

Geeraerts, Dirk. 1988b. Katz revisited: Aspects of the history of lexical semantics. In Werner Hüllen and Rainer Schulze, eds., *Understanding the lexicon: Meaning, sense and world-knowledge in lexical semantics* 23–35. Tübingen: Max Niemeyer Verlag.

Geeraerts, Dirk. 1989. Prospects and problems of prototype theory. *Linguistics* 27: 587–612.

Geeraerts, Dirk. 1993a. Cognitive linguistics and the history of philosophical epistemology. In Richard Geiger and Brygida Rudzka-Ostyn, eds., *Conceptualizations and mental processing in language* 53–79. Berlin: Mouton de Gruyter.

Geeraerts, Dirk. 1993b. Des deux côtés de la sémantique structurale: Sémantique historique et sémantique cognitive. *Histoire Epistémologie Langage* 15: 111–30.

Gibbs, Raymond W., Jr. 1994. *The poetics of mind: Figurative thought, language, and understanding*. Cambridge: Cambridge University Press.

Gill, Jerry H. 1991. *Merleau-Ponty and metaphor*. Atlantic Highlands, NJ: Humanities Press.

Giora, Rachel, and Inbal Gur. 2003. Irony in conversation: Salience, role, and context effect. In Brigitte Nerlich, Zazie Todd, Vimala Herman, and David D. Clarke, eds., *Polysemy: Flexible patterns of meaning in mind and language* 297–316. Berlin: Mouton de Gruyter.

Gross, Richard. 1999. *Psychology: The science of mind and behaviour.* 3rd ed. London: Hodder and Stoughton.

Guillaume, Gustave. 1929. *Temps et verbe: Théorie des aspects, des modes et des temps.* Paris: Champion.

Guillaume, Gustave. 1971. *Leçons de linguistique 1948–1949.* Série A, *Structure sémiologique et structure psychique de la langue française I.* Ed. Roch Valin. Quebec: Presses de l'Université Laval.

Hülzer-Vogt, Heike. 1989. *Karl Bühler (1879–1963) und Wilhelm Stählin (1883–1975): Psychologische Fundamente der Metapherntheorie im ersten Drittel des 20. Jahrhundersts.* Münster, Germany: Nodus Publikationen.

Jákel, Olaf. 1999. Kant, Blumenberg, Weinrich: Some forgotten contributions to the cognitive theory of metaphor. In Raymond W. Gibbs, Jr., and Gerard J. Steen, eds., *Metaphor in cognitive linguistics* 9–27. Amsterdam: John Benjamins.

Jakobson, Roman. 1956a. The metaphoric and metonymic poles. In Roman Jakobson and Morris Halle, eds., *Fundamentals of language* 76–82.The Hague: Mouton.

Jakobson, Roman. 1956b. Two aspects of language and two types of aphasic disturbances. In Krystyna Pomorska and Stephen Rudi, eds., *Language in literature* 95–120. Cambridge, MA: Belknap Press of Harvard University Press.

Janda, Laura A. 2000. Cognitive linguistics. Position paper for the SLING2K workshop, Feb. 2000. http://www.indiana.edu/~slavconf/SLING2K/pospapers.html (accessed Dec. 2000).

Johnson, Mark, ed. 1981. *Philosophical perspectives on metaphor.* Minneapolis: University of Minnesota Press.

Johnson, Mark. 1987. *The body in the mind: The bodily basis of meaning, imagination, and reason.* Chicago: University of Chicago Press.

Johnson, Mark. 1993. *Moral imagination: Implications of cognitive science for ethics.* Chicago: University of Chicago Press.

Kanellos, Ioannis. 1994. Du lieu et de la nature des phénomènes de typicalité: Playdoyer pour un Aristote méconnu. *Scola* 1: 109–33.

Lakoff, George. 1987. *Women, fire, and dangerous things: What categories reveal about the mind.* Chicago: University of Chicago Press.

Lakoff, George, and Mark Johnson. 1980. *Metaphors we live by.* Chicago: University of Chicago Press.

Lakoff, George, and Mark Johnson. 1999. *Philosophy in the flesh: The embodied mind and its challenge to Western thought.* New York: Basic Books.

Lamb, Sydney M. 1970. Linguistic and cognitive networks. In Paul Garvin, ed., *Cognition: A multiple view,* 195–222. New York: Spartan Books.

Lamb, Sydney M. 1971. The crooked path of progress in cognitive linguistics. *GURT* 22: 99–123.

Lamb, Sydney M. 1999. *Pathways of the brain: The neurocognitive basis of language.* Amsterdam: John Benjamins.

Langacker, Ronald W. 1987. *Foundations of cognitive grammar.* Vol. 1, *Theoretical prerequisites.* Stanford, CA: Stanford University Press.

Langacker, Ronald W. 1998. Conceptualization, symbolization, and grammar. In Michael Tomasello, ed., *The new psychology of language: Cognitive and functional approaches to language structure* 1: 1–39. Mahwah, NJ: Lawrence Erlbaum.

Lee, Penny. 1996. *The Whorf theory complex: A critical reconstruction*. Amsterdam: John Benjamins.

Liebert, Wolf-Andreas. 1995. Metaphernbereiche der virologischen Aidsforschung. *Lexicology: An international journal on the structure of vocabulary* 1: 142–82.

Mahon, James Edwin. 1999. Getting your sources right. What Aristotle didn't *say*. In Lynne Cameron and Graham Low, eds., *Researching and applying metaphor* 69–80. Cambridge: Cambridge University Press.

Merleau-Ponty, Maurice. [1945] 1962. *The phenomenology of perception*. Trans. C. C. Smith. Atlantic Highlands, NJ: Humanities Press.

Musolff, Andreas. 1993. Karl Bühler's and Alan Gardiner's concepts of metaphor in the context of their theories of speech and language. *Beiträge zur Geschichte der Sprachwissenschaft* 3: 225–72.

Nerlich, Brigitte. 1992. *Semantic theories in Europe, 1830–1930: From etymology to contextuality*. Amsterdam: John Benjamins.

Nerlich, Brigitte. 1999. Identity, similarity and continuity: Saussure and Wittgenstein on the constitution of linguistic units. In John E. Joseph, Hans-Josef Niederehe, and Sheila Embleton, eds., *The emergence of the modern language sciences: Studies on the transition from historical-comparative to structural linguistics in honour of E. F. Konrad Koerner* 151–69. Amsterdam: John Benjamins.

Nerlich, Brigitte. 2000. Structuralism, contextualism, dialogism: Voloshinov and Bakhtin's contributions to the debate about the 'relativity' of meaning. *Historiographia Linguistica* 27: 79–102.

Nerlich, Brigitte, and David D. Clarke. 1996. *Language, action, and context: The early history of pragmatics in Europe and America, 1780–1930*. Amsterdam: John Benjamins.

Nerlich, Brigitte, and David D. Clarke. 1997. Polysemy: Patterns in meaning and patterns in history. *Historiographia Linguistica* 24: 359–85.

Nerlich, Brigitte, and David D. Clarke. 1999. Champ, Schéma, Sujet: Les contributions de Bühler, Bartlett et Benveniste à une linguistique du texte. *Langue française* 121: 36–56 (special issue on "Phrase, Texte, Discours," ed. E. S. Karabétian).

Nerlich, Brigitte, and David D. Clarke. 2000a. Blending the past and the present: Conceptual and linguistic integration, 1800–2000. *Logos and Language: Journal of General Linguistics and Language Theory* 1: 3–18.

Nerlich, Brigitte, and David D. Clarke. 2000b. Semantic fields and frames: Historical explorations of the interface between language, action and cognition. *Journal of Pragmatics* 32: 125–50.

Nerlich, Brigitte, and David D. Clarke. 2001. Mind, meaning, and metaphor: The philosophy and psychology of metaphor in nineteenth-century Germany. *History of the Human Sciences* 14: 39–61.

Nerlich, Brigitte, Robert Dingwall, and David D. Clarke. 2002. The book of life: How the human genome project was revealed to the public. *Health: An Interdisciplinary Journal for the Social Study of Health, Illness and Medicine* 6: 445–69.

Peeters, Bert. 1998. Cognitive musings. *Word* 49: 225–37.

Peeters, Bert. 1999. Review of Lamb 1999. *Cognitive Linguistics* 10: 382–91.

Peeters, Bert. 2001. Does cognitive linguistics live up to its name? In René Dirven, Bruce Hawkins, and Esra Sandikcioglu, eds., *Language and ideology: Cognitive theoretical approaches* 83–106 Amsterdam: John Benjamins.

Richards, Ivor Armstrong. 1936. *The philosophy of rhetoric*. New York: Oxford University Press.

Ricoeur, Paul. 1975. *La métaphor vive*. Paris: Seuil.

Ricoeur, Paul. 1978. The metaphorical process as cognition, imagination, and feeling. *Critical Inquiry* 5: 143–59. (Repr. in Mark Johnson, ed., *Philosophical Perspectives on Metaphor* 228–47. Minneapolis: University of Minnesota Press, 1981.)

Rosch, Eleanor. 1978. Principles of categorization. In Eleanor Rosch and Barbara B. Lloyd, eds., *Cognition and categorization* 27–48. Hillsdale, NJ: Lawrence Erlbaum.

Saussure, Ferdinand de. 1916. *Cours de linguistique générale*. Paris: Payot.

Smith, Michael K. 1982. Metaphor and mind: Review of *Metaphors we live by*, by George Lakoff and Mark Johnson. *American Speech* 57: 128–33.

Stanulewicz, Danuta. 1999. Benjamin Lee Whorf and cognitive linguistics. In Janusz Arabski, ed., *Pase papers in language studies: Proceedings of the Seventh Annual Conference of the Polish Association for the Study of English, Szczyrk, May 1998* 191–98. Katowice, Poland: Para.

Swiggers, Pierre. 1989. Le fondement cognitif et sémantique de l'étymologie chez Turgot. *Cahiers Ferdinand de Saussure* 43: 79–89.

Talmy, Leonard. 1972. Semantic structures in English and Atsugewi. Ph.D. dissertation, University of California, Berkeley.

Talmy, Leonard. 2000a. *Toward a cognitive semantics*. Vol. 1, *Concept structuring systems*. Cambridge, MA: MIT Press.

Talmy, Leonard. 2000b. *Toward a cognitive semantics*. Vol. 2, *Typology and process in concept structuring*. Cambridge, MA: MIT Press.

Thibault, Paul J. 1997. *Re-reading Saussure: The dynamics of signs in social life*. London: Routledge.

Trier, Jost. 1934. Deutsche Bedeutungsforschung. In Alfred Goetze, Wilhelm Horn, and Friedrich Maurer, eds., *Germanische Philologie: Ergebnisse und Aufgaben. Festschrift für Otto Behagel* 173–200. Heidelberg: Carl Winter Universitätsverlag.

Turner, Mark, Cristina Cacciari, Raymond W. Gibbs, Jr., and Albert Katz. 1998. *Figurative language and thought*. Oxford: Oxford University Press.

Vaihinger, Hans. 1924. *The philosophy of 'as if': A system of the theoretical, practical and religious fictions of mankind*. Trans. Charles K. Ogden. London: Routledge and Kegan Paul.

Weinrich, Harald. 1967. Semantik der Metapher. *Folia Linguistica* 1: 3–17.

Weinrich, Harald. 1976. *Sprache in Texten*. Stuttgart: Klett.

Weinrich, Harald. 1980. Metapher. In Joachim Ritter and Karlfried Gründer, eds., *Historisches Wörterbuch der Philosophie* 5: cols. 1179–86. Darmstadt, Germany: Wissenschaftliche Buchgesellschaft.

Wittgenstein, Ludwig. 1953. *Philosophical investigations*. Trans. G. E. M. Anscombe. Oxford: Basil Blackwell.

Whorf, Benjamin L. 1956. *Language, thought, and reality: Selected writings of Benjamin Lee Whorf*. Ed. John B. Carroll. Cambridge, MA: MIT Press.

Ziemke, Tom, Jordan Zlatev, and Roslyn Frank, eds. 2007. *Body, language and mind*. Vol. 1, *Embodiment*. Berlin: Mouton de Gruyter.

PART IV

LINGUISTIC STRUCTURE AND LANGUAGE USE

CHAPTER 23

PHONOLOGY

GEOFF NATHAN

1. BASIC PRINCIPLES

1.1. What a Cognitive Phonology Will Look Like

As with other levels of language, "doing" phonology within Cognitive Grammar requires a radical revision of how linguists think about their subject matter, particularly as compared with the dominant worldview of Generative Grammar. However, phonology is in a rather different position from other fields in that phonologists have not all adopted the dominant Chomskyan paradigm, with its attendant commitments to modularity, innateness, and the independence of language structure from other cognitive processes. In fact, even generative phonologists often take a strongly functional attitude, some even arguing that all phonology is either functionally motivated or conventionalized. A second difference with syntax is that there is considerable continuity within the fields of phonology from its inception in the latter part of the twentieth century to the beginnings of the twenty-first. Many of the categories and theoretical constructs that were introduced in the early development of phonology are still considered valid by virtually all theoretical bents, despite numerous theoretical revolutions. Phoneme, syllable, consonant, vowel, feature, and even process have some status in virtually all current phonological theories, both generative and functionalist. Although the Generative Grammar tradition has evolved considerably during the past fifty years, some fundamental principles would be accepted by both generative and nongenerative phonologists, as was noted by reviewers of the proceedings volume on Formal and Functional Linguistics (Carnie and Mendoza-Denton 2003).

1.2. The Phoneme as Category

Phonology can generally be defined by its practitioners' attitude toward the idea of the phone. The phoneme originated in the nineteenth century and continued into the twentieth along a number of different, often competing, lines. Some linguists over the period emphasized the autonomy of the concept (and, indeed, of all strictly linguistic concepts) from any functional motivation or explanatory aspect rooted in language use or nonlinguistic factors such as anatomy or physiology, while in contrast there is also a long tradition of functionalist phonology that is alive and forms a continuous thread back to the very beginnings of phonology. This is quite different from the current state of syntactic theory, where both the dominant theory, the Minimalist Program, and most active competitors (such as Head-Driven Phrase Structure Grammar) represent radical departures from grammatical wisdom as developed over the past hundred or more years.[1] Since Cognitive Grammar is best viewed as a kind of Functional Grammar (in the broad, generic sense), we can expect to find inspiration within the functional phonology tradition that will save cognitive grammarians from reinventing the wheel.

Over the past fifteen years, cognitive linguists have attempted to develop ways of doing phonology consistent with the assumptions of Cognitive Grammar. In part this has been a challenging task, as the theory has evolved considerably since its inception, with emphasis on the nonmodular nature of cognitive representations in the early period (and thus concern with metaphor, Idealized Cognitive Models, and Langackerian diagrams) moving to a focus on usage as a primary mechanism for acquisition and structure in recent years. Two main avenues of research have developed over that time, one continuing the emphasis on phonology as the representation of our knowledge of bodily experience (Nathan 1986, 1996, 1999, 2008) and the other expanding on the usage-based model (Bybee 1999, 2000, 2001). This chapter will explore the commonalities and differences between the two views and make some suggestions for future research.

1.3. The Phoneme's Checkered Career

A brief review of the history of the phoneme will set the stage for an understanding of the issues involved in developing a cognitive view of phonology.

Baudouin de Courtenay ([1895] 1972), the first *synchronic* phonologist, argued for a psychological, embodied view, namely that phonemes were mental images of sounds that speakers systematically deformed in the ongoing process of speech according to "physiophonetic" principles that were universally determined by the nature of the speech production and perception apparatus. Saussure ([1916] 1974), as the originator of the structuralist autonomous view, on the other hand, argued that phonemes were arbitrary contrast points in a network of sound defined one against another. He used the analogy of a chess game, where it does not matter what each piece is made of or even whether it has the right shape, as long as it has the *value* agreed upon for that piece in the game—an explicitly anti-embodiment view. Later in the twentieth century, this conflict between the phoneme as a mental construct and as an arbitrary linguistic pawn in the language game continued. Jones (1967: 7) argued that phonemes are a small "family of sounds, each family consisting of an important sound of the language together with other related sounds which, so to speak, 'represent' it in particular sequences or under particular conditions," although he was noncommittal on the question of whether there was, in addition, a single abstract image of the basic sound (217). Trubetzkoy ([1939] 1969: 36), on the other hand, argued that a phoneme is "the sum of the phonologically relevant properties of a sound [but] actual sounds are only material symbols of the phoneme." Among American structuralists, Bloomfield (1933: 79) sided with the autonomous side, stating that a phoneme was a "bundle of distinctive features," but Sapir ([1933] 1972: 23) agreed with Baudouin: "In the physical world the naïve speaker and hearer actualize and are sensitive to sounds, but what they feel themselves to be pronouncing and hearing are 'phonemes.'" Pike (1947: 145) agreed with Sapir that phonemes were psychologically real entities, arguing, for example, that the Trager-Smith phonemicization of English was probably incorrect in part because it was so hard to teach to native speakers of the language.

Within the generative tradition there has always been a claim to the psychological reality of the entities posited within the theory, but with greater and lesser degrees of seriousness. When Chomsky and Halle (1968: 259) posited the extremely abstract underlying representations for English that claimed that the underlying forms of the language had hardly changed since Chaucer's time, other generative phonologists, such as Kiparsky, took them to task for positing entities for which there was little evidence of psychological reality as evidenced by historical and other behavior. Kiparsky showed that historical changes applied to sounds at the *phonemic* level, not at the more abstract level posited by Chomsky and Halle. He also argued that native speakers treated the classical phonemic level, and not a more abstract one, as the basis for speech production. Kiparsky (1982) is the classic locus of this debate. The term "phoneme" was explicitly rejected as a label for the kinds of underlying forms that Chomsky and Halle and others were positing, but Kiparsky (1982) and Schane (1971) dissented, arguing for a level equivalent to the more traditional one.

Since the development of lexical phonology, a similar debate has taken place, with many claiming that the *output* of the lexical component constitutes the only psychologically real "underlying" forms. Postlexical rules actually apply in speech production, unlike lexical rules, which merely represent the relationships between related sets of lexical entries. At least some proponents of lexical phonology have argued that the forms generated by the output of lexical rules are essentially the units of storage—a typical discussion can be found in Gussenhoven and Jacobs (1998: 119–24).

Outside of generative phonology, two major American schools took differing tacks on this same question. Bybee, in her early work (i.e., Natural Generative Phonology, which was a highly constrained form of generative phonology; see Hooper

1976), argued that only surface forms have any psychological reality, with related forms (including most allophonic alternations) being linked by networks of connections. Bybee has modified and expanded her views within Cognitive Grammar, arguing for a usage-based theory, as discussed in Bybee (1999, 2000, 2001) and in which the concept of the phoneme as traditionally understood is rejected entirely in favor of a "usage-based" approach.[2]

The other major nongenerative phonological theory of the latter part of the twentieth century is Natural Phonology, which essentially adapted Baudouin's original insight into modern linguistic theory by arguing that phonemes were mental sound images that speakers modified in speaking and that, in perceiving others' speech, the same speakers sympathetically perceived the "deformed" output as what they would have aimed at had they said the same thing (for extensive discussion, see Donegan and Stampe 1979; Donegan 1986; Stampe 1987). The deformations were mental adaptations caused by the inherent nature and limitations of the speech tract and perceptual system and, as such, were universal but "learned" (in the same sense as a child learns to control its hands or feet).[3] I have argued (Nathan 1986, 1996, 1999, 2008) that Natural Phonology *is* Cognitive Phonology, at least in many of its basic assumptions, and I will argue for this view below.

Finally, within the past ten years a new "generative" paradigm has arisen, Optimality Theory (OT) (Prince and Smolensky 1993; Kager 1999). OT presents a radically different way of thinking about representations and rules in which crucial aspects of grammar are innate (for some theorists in the Chomskyan sense, but for others in the Stampean sense), but the grammar does not really consist of rules at all, but rather violable constraints which systematically compete with each other. For a particular language, a particular ordering of preferences wins out, and languages differ not in which constraints are active, but rather in which ones take preference in a conflict. OT does not exactly have a view on the nature of phonological representations themselves—deep, surface, or otherwise. Some discussion has centered around whether we need to construct underlying forms or whether any input at all will produce appropriate output (this is the theory of "the richness of the base"). On the other hand, without a notion of an input form the concept of "faithfulness" is not coherent, because there is nothing for the surface candidates to be faithful to.

In a sense, OT cannot claim to be a theory of interest to cognitive grammarians, because no serious claims for psychological reality have been made by many of the practitioners (however, Winters and Nathan, (2006, MS), makes a contrary suggestion). Still, there are a subset of OT theorists who have argued that all OT constraints must be grounded in properties of the human articulatory and perceptual system. Representative work has been done by Kirchner (1997), Boersma (1998), and Hayes (1999, 2004). To the extent that we believe phonology to be determined by the material out of which it is built, these functional OT phonologists are doing work that needs to be looked at, although their work is formed within a framework that is generally not of interest to Cognitive Grammar.

In attempting to formulate a theory of phonology within the general worldview entailed by Cognitive Grammar, I have argued (Nathan 1986, 1996, 1999) that the original insight of the earliest phonologists was not mistaken and that people really do perceive phonemically. That is, they hear their language as a string of basic sounds, traditionally called phonemes. They are not normally aware of the variations in those basic sounds that are induced by their position in the word or larger prosodic unit, only becoming aware of those variants if they show up in the "wrong" place (note that I use the scare quotes so as to include not only nonnative speakers producing nonnative patterns, but also the ability to recognize other dialects of one's own language—although normally without the ability to say exactly what is "wrong"). Furthermore, production processing errors that displace those basic sounds normally result in the sounds being produced with the variant appropriate to the new environment (as virtually all research on so-called Spoonerisms has found; see Fromkin 1973, 1980, 1988). Evidence from children's acquisition and perception of speech also indicates that speakers are actively constructing phonetic patterns in the process of speaking and that this processing may well produce forms that speakers (especially children) may never have produced or even heard before.

One fundamental insight that Cognitive Grammar can bring to phonology is that the identification of phonemes is simply a matter of categorization; that is, phonemes are cognitive/mental categories. As such, the principles of categorization that Cognitive Grammar crucially relies on will apply in phonology as much as in other areas of linguistic behavior. This means that all of the apparatuses that Cognitive Grammar has developed to understand the structure of categories applies also to phonemes.

1.4. Radial Sets and Processes

I will begin by establishing that the basic building block of phonological structure, the phoneme, is a psychologically real entity, the existence of which linguists need to account for, and that therefore there is some place for phonological theory within Cognitive Grammar.

This is an important point, because one of the fundamental tenets of Cognitive Grammar is the "content requirement" (Langacker 1987; Langacker 2000: 8), which holds that the only real linguistic units are semantic, phonological, or symbolic structures (i.e., there are no intermediate level units, such as D-structures, that are not either sounds or senses). In order to postulate an apparently abstract unit such as the phoneme, which in some sense is neither a sound nor a meaning, we need to justify its existence by showing that speakers and hearers behave as if they speak and hear in phonemic, not merely phonetic, surface terms.

Although much more could be said on this point (and much of this is discussed in Nathan, 2008), I will merely point out that the vast majority of languages of the world have writing systems where the basic symbols are virtually identical to phonemes—it seems to be very easy to learn such a writing system, especially compared to the more complex morphologically based ones such as Chinese and Japanese.

In order to understand how we can classify sounds into categories despite the fact that they constitute categories not associated with semantics, we need to begin by noting that individual phonemes are not semantic units at all—sounds associated with semantics are, of course, morphemes. Phonemes are abstract categories of sounds qua sounds. There is, of course, no semantics associated with sounds such as thunder or the wind blowing in the leaves (aside from the placing of the particular sound in some category), but this does not make these sounds in any way less of a category, nor does this make the assignment of individual instances to the category in any way problematic. On the other hand, it is possible that fragments of words may acquire some semantic associations—for some discussion of the possibility of semantics inherent in sounds or groups of sounds themselves, see Palmer's (1996: 279–89) discussion on sound symbolism.

The work of Lakoff (1987) established the importance of radial categories as a fundamental linguistic organizing principle. He shows how members of fairly disparate categories, such as the senses of the word *over* or classifier systems, could be unified once we give up the idea that all categories are Aristotelian in the sense that all members have to share common identifying features. This leads quite naturally to a view of phonemes that allows insightful clarification of many of the problems that had confronted classical and generative phonological theory. In the first major published work dedicated solely to the issue (Nathan 1986), I presented an analysis of the problematic (and nonproblematic) aspects of the American English phoneme /t/.

The problem with American /t/ is that the instantiations of that particular phoneme are wildly diverse and, taken as a whole, share no common point or manner of articulation. The facts are as follows:

There are at least five different variants of the /t/ phoneme in American English, as shown in (1):

(1) [tʰ]   *tall*
     [t]   *stall*
     [ʔ]   *button* (as in [bʌʔn̩])
     [t']   *What!*
     [ɾ]   *water*[4]

Notice that there is no single feature that all of these sounds share, not even [−voice] (flap is voiced); yet there is no doubt that native speakers categorize all of them as "kinds of /t/." In fact, it normally takes several months in a phonetics class before students can begin to be aware of the fact that these variants exist at all. The fact that naive speakers do not normally notice these differences constitutes what phonologists and psychologists have referred to as "phonemic perception." If speakers are asked to make judgments *about sounds as sounds*, they may well notice that things are off, or odd, but such things normally pass unremarked, unlike, say, a wrong ending or article choice. But if we assume that all of these sounds constitute "the phoneme /t/," we will be unable to adequately describe even these basic facts unless the category that we set up is non-Aristotelian (and hence, unlike any standard structuralist model).

In Nathan (1986) (see also Taylor 1995: 222–34), I argued that this sound category could be understood as a classic example of a radial set, with a prototypical central member and the other members of the phoneme radiating outwards according to well-defined phonetic principles, analogous to the extensions described by Lakoff involving such principles as metaphor, metonymy, and image schema transformation. Evidence from a number of different sources suggests that the voiceless unaspirated form [t] is the central member. For example, according to Maddieson (1984: 32), 99.7% of languages have either dental or alveolar stops, and children appear not only to acquire them early, but in most cases to acquire them by replacing their native language voiced and aspirated stops with voiceless unaspirated ones, whatever the phonemic system of the target language. Hurch (1988) argues that aspirated stops are nonprototypical compared to unaspirated ones.

From the prototypical voiceless aspirated stop it is possible to adjust the target toward alternative forms, such as the aspirated variety, the form with simultaneous glottal closure (all voiceless stops in English are produced with simultaneous glottal closure when syllable-final), and, by extension, the glottal stop.

The idea of sounds having prototype structure is not unique to Cognitive Grammar; it has been suggested by various researchers within the phonetics community. Representative work can be found in papers by Samuel (1982) and Kuhl and Iverson (1995). A clear discussion of one aspect can be seen in Lotto (2000:194), which looked at perception of vowels and found that "the best /i/ exemplars were judged to be those furthest from the /ɪ/ distribution (i.e., low F_1 and high F_2). Interestingly, these exemplars of /i/ would be very rare in natural speech because vowels are often reduced (moved away from the extremes of the $F_1 \times F_2$ space) in normal speaking contexts"[5] (194).

Each of these extensions is licensed by what Stampe called a "natural process." According to Stampe (1979: 1), a natural process is "a mental operation that applies in speech to substitute, for a class of sounds or sound sequences presenting a specific common difficulty to the speech capacity of the individual, an alternative class identical but lacking the difficult property." In Cognitive Grammar terms, this means that allophones are image schema transformations of prototypical sounds in ways that allow them to fit the particular environments (see Nathan 1996 for more extensive discussion). Let me make an analogy here to Lakoff's (1987) discussion of the word *over*. We prototypically think of this word as referring to a trajector located 'above' the landmark (i.e., oriented vertically with respect to the force of gravity), but we can certainly put some wallpaper "over" a hole in the ceiling. Just as we see the hole in the ceiling "upside down" without noticing that we have made any kind of change or extension, so we produce an aspirated /t/ without being aware that we have made it sound any different than the original target, which, as I argued above, is unaspirated.

The idea that we come pre-equipped with natural responses to motor difficulties that we need to unlearn is not mysterious, nor is it at all foreign to the basic principles of Cognitive Grammar. For example, in teaching the skills involved in karate I have observed that students are resistant to moves that require the arms to do two different activities at the same time. Even after numerous repetitions of some move, students revert (often under conditions of cognitive overload, such as standing in an unusual position or stepping backwards rather than forwards) to hand movements that I have not taught them, that they have never seen before but are more "natural" in the sense that the human body has a natural preference for limb movements to follow a pattern of bilateral symmetry. Similar "spontaneous" errors occur in learning to dance when an asymmetrical move is required. The emergence of naturally motivated patterns is a part of all human skilled motor learning, and speech production is unlikely to be exempt. Natural Phonology's "natural processes" are nothing more than the articulatory and perceptual instantiations of such "errors," and they clearly have a role in a Cognitive Phonology. Why do I argue that these changes are made "online" in the context of speech production? There are a number of reasons for making this argument—many of them assembled in Stampe (1968), a famous unpublished conference paper titled "Yes, Virginia . . ."[6] The following reasons strike me as completely persuasive, although recently Bybee and others have challenged this view. Their views will be discussed below.

We first begin by noting that speaker behavior strongly supports the idea that they do not store allophonic variants. Speakers cannot, under normal circumstances, even hear differences among allophones. It was Sapir's famous paper mentioned above that first pointed this out when he noted that his informant did not perceive the intervocalic voicing and spirantization in his language "in terms of the actual sounds, but in terms of an etymological reconstruction [we would now say, underlyingly]" ([1933] 1972: 24). Similarly, all of the early "contrastive" second-language literature pointed out that the phonemic filter of a first language prevented speakers from hearing their own allophonic variation as an instance of a phoneme in some other language (this was first discussed extensively in the classic work by Weinreich 1970). Not only can speakers not hear allophonic variation, virtually all writing systems discount it, and rhyme systems do not count as rhyme sounds that are identical if they are members of different phonemes, but do count sounds as identical if they are members of the same phoneme, even if they are different (see Stampe 1987 for discussion).

Second, there is the question of how many variants speakers store. Since each phoneme may have a number of distinct allophones, each lexical item could be pronounced differently each time it is used, depending on which words precede and follow it. This, for example, includes such allophonic variation as that discussed above, so that, for example, *hat* will come out differently as follows:

(2)   [hæɾ]   *Put your hat on your head.*
       [hæʔ]   *I can't find my hat now.*

However, not only does every obvious allophone used as an example in introductory textbooks need to be dealt with, there is in fact far more variation than those standard textbooks normally discuss. For example, all vowels are affected by the height and backness of the preceding and following vowel, even over a word boundary. Thus, each vowel will have to be sensitive to the initial vowel in the following word, as well as each final vowel in the preceding word. This fact seems to require that we attribute phonological behavior to active, online computation, since otherwise every monosyllabic word in the language would have to have a separate entry for every vowel in the language and every multisyllabic word would have to have two entries for every vowel in the language, not including the separate entries required for the initial and final consonants and variations induced by rate and formality. There would thus be an exponential increase in the size of the lexicon unless variations could be computed in the process of speech. While it is true that much more of speech is stored than is normally believed (and certainly irregular, and even some regular, morphological alternations are probably stored), it would seem likely that the computational load required to adjust the target toward the appropriate allophone for each environment would be much less than that required to select the appropriate form of each entire word relative to the surrounding words.

Additional reason to believe that allophonic variation is computed during speech comes from speech errors. Numerous researchers over the years have found that speech errors normally occur at the *phonemic* level and that the sounds moved to their new environments are always adjusted to their new positions. If words were stored in their purely surface form, we would expect displaced voiceless stops to be aspirated after /s/ and unaspirated initially, but neither change occurs. Furthermore, speech errors produce otherwise nonexistent forms that cannot possibly have been produced on the basis of existing stored forms unless those forms are "spelled" in strings of separate segments. For example, while aiming at *same time zone* I caught myself saying [tʰeɪm zaɪn], producing something which does not correspond to an existing word. Unless the segments are stored separately, in some sense, they should be unavailable to be moved in a production error such as this one.

Finally, child language acquisition indicates that children are doing online processing, reconstructing abstract phonemic representations rather than simply recording the ambient words and later reconstructing more abstract schemas from them. For example, children often produce words in ways that they have never heard them. One classic example concerns an American child who systematically referred to *mittens* as [mɪtʰənz] despite the fact that both parents always and exclusively said [mɪʔn̩z]. Numerous parallel examples can be found in such sources as Smith (1973). One striking example involves a child's pronunciation of *dog* as [gɔ] (David Stampe, p.c.). The initial velar is attributable to a commonly reported process of velar harmony, but we cannot say this child is simply repeating what he or she has heard, but rather that the child has stored the target form correctly, is processing it, with the child's production not even including the trigger of the harmony process that caused the deformation in the process. It is impossible for these children to have simply stored the surface form they heard around them, since these forms are obviously constructed on the basis of a previously stored, relatively correct version of the target.[7] If the children constructed these varying pronunciations as attempts at the same target, we can only understand what is happening if we assume that the children have stored something close to the adult *phonemic* pronunciation as some kind of privileged representation which they aim at each time they speak, and as the "ideal form" (the prototype) that they perceive when others speak.

In this respect, Cognitive Phonology is quite different from standard phonological theory. Cognitive Phonology argues that phonemes are *sounds*, that is, not underspecified lists of features, but rather real, fully specified prototypical sounds.[8] We know what a "*t*-sound" sounds like, and we can hear it in both 'two' [tʰu]*and* in 'mitten' [mɪʔn̩] even though the prototype occurs in neither. But representations are mental images of actual words, "spelled" with actual sounds. What Cognitive Phonology accepts from traditional process-oriented phonology is that the actual production normally does not match the mental image because phonemes are implemented in contexts and adjusted in real time to fit those contexts.

Here is another significant difference from the traditional structuralist view: complementary distribution and phonetic similarity are not *definitions* of the phoneme (although they may be useful tools for the linguist attempting to understand the behavior of a language he or she does not speak). As Stampe pointed out in his first works (1968, 1969), complementary distribution is a consequence of the fact that context-sensitive processes apply to underlying forms. Phonetic similarity is a direct result of the fact that processes only minimally change target sounds (although chains of processes, like chains of metaphorical extensions in semantics, may lead to very disparate instantiations of a single basic form, as in the case of glottal stop and voiced flap in American English for English /t/).

Also note that this view of the phoneme holds that it is a basic level unit, and thus a real, mental image of a sound, not a list of distinctive features. We hear phonemes in our heads (and can generally say them out loud). Otherwise we would not be able to learn to spell, a task which those with relatively phonemic writing systems find very simple. The notion that we have images in our minds has been questioned by some researchers over the years, but in a recent work, Damasio (1999) argues for a coherent view of the notion that answers the traditional questions raised by the so-called homunculus problem.

Incidentally, we should point out that this does not mean that features are not real. Donegan (2002: 8) has suggested that features "can be viewed, not as abstract categories, but as the links of motor and proprioceptive aspects of production, on the one hand, to perceptual properties (auditory, acoustic, or in acquisition, sometimes visual) on the other. Such connections may be part of an inborn, 'prewired' mechanism like that which appears to link visual stimuli to facial gestures." Phonetic features then, are not abstract classificatory devices, but rather the mind's method of unifying oral and aural impressions, a set of connections which are probably acquired during babbling. Jose Mompean (p.c.) has suggested that this is

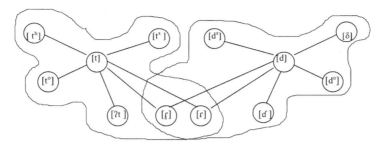

Figure 23.1. Radial set illustrating the internal structure of the English phoneme /t/

analogous to Gestalt perceptions of all kinds. Just because we see objects as unified wholes does not mean that we cannot also see that they have characteristics, but we do not see them simply as a list of those characteristics, but rather as individual *things*.

1.5. Neutralization and Overlap

Several times in the above discussion I noted that the phoneme /t/ can be pronounced in American English with a voiced alveolar flap [ɾ], as in *butter, Betty, electricity*, and *cognitive*. However, it is also the case that the phoneme /d/ can be pronounced in exactly the same way, in words such as *rider, validity*, and *grading*. That is, the categories are not completely distinct, but overlap in one area. Figure 23.1 clarifies this relationship (this diagram is based on Mompeán-González's 2004 insightful discussion of neutralization issues within the framework I am discussing).

When speakers confront such instances of category overlap, in the absence of other information, they assign the sound to the closest prototype. Thus, the flap [ɾ] "sounds like" a /d/. Classic phoneme theory denied the possibility of overlapping phonemes, but that is because classic phoneme theory relied on an Aristotelian view of categorization in which a sound could not simultaneously belong to two different categories at once. Note that the operative phrase is "in the absence of other information." Lexical access interacts with phonemic perception in complex ways. While a voiced flap sounds like a /d/ in the abstract, if it is in a word that is recognizable as containing a /t/ in the appropriate location (say, by virtue of the spelling, as in *city*, or by virtue of being related to another form of the word, such as *betting* being a form of the verb *bet*), it can also be perceived as a /t/. It is important to recognize that these perceptions are always unidirectional, however. We can think of a "*t*-sound" as occasionally sounding like a "*d*-sound" (speaking impressionistically), but no naive speaker would ever say that a "*d*-sound" sounds occasionally like a "*t*-sound."

While some phonological theories have argued that in positions of neutralization a special, more abstract (or, in Cognitive Grammar terms, more schematic) sound is stored instead, this is unlikely. It would amount to the claim that there are actually three sounds to store: /t/, /d/, and /ɾ/. But native speakers do not perceive the [ɾ] in *latter* as a third kind of sound, but rather as either a /t/ or a /d/. And again, no language has an orthography that writes morphophonemes or archiphonemes differently from the regular phonemes of the language; this can scarcely be considered a coincidence.

2. INVENTORIES AND PROTOTYPES

A further task of phonological theory is to explain why languages select the phonemes that they do. Despite the fact that there might be no limit to the possibilities for phoneme inventories in the languages of the world (after all, many American structuralists appeared to believe that languages could differ in quite extraordinary ways), if we make an inventory of inventories, we find that there is in fact a quite limited range of possibilities and that languages appear to have quite restricted possibilities for phoneme inventories. In earlier work, I suggested (Nathan 1989) that this fact was due to the universality of the human vocal tract and its acoustic consequences.

To put the argument somewhat briefly, human vocal behavior tends toward the universal because it is subject to constraints imposed by the structure of the anatomy and physiology that produces the sounds in question. For example, MacNeilage (1998) and MacNeilage and Davis (2000) have argued that syllable structure is an adaptation of chewing behavior, itself related to innate sucking behavior. The rhythmic alternation of open and closed vocal tracts provides a scaffolding on which languages have built a framework for linguistic structure in general. Principles of Gestalt psychology, which explain the organization of perception into Figure and Ground, explain why sonorants, particularly high sonority (and therefore louder) segments such as vowels, tend to be selected to serve as syllabic nuclei, while the quieter, but more perceptually discriminable consonants tend to serve as syllable margins (onsets and rhymes). A similar case can be made for the increased perceptibility of voiceless segments when contrasted with voiced vowels in the nucleus, which explains in part why Jakobson ([1941] 1968) found his implicational law that voiceless consonants are less marked (more common, earlier learned, etc.) than voiced ones.[9]

As we look at the sounds around the world, we find that their distribution follows a typical prototype category structure, with the exception of the fact that the overall categories are universal. Thus, while a prototypical bird will vary from ecosystem to ecosystem, vocal tracts are identical in human beings, and consequently stop systems will show universal prototypicality structures. And just as there are nonprototypical birds, there are nonprototypical phonemes—clicks, implosives, nasalized vowels, and so on. Each of these kinds of sound will be under some pressure to convert to a less marked one, but historical accidents will also lead to the creation of new versions of such odd sounds.

In sum, sounds are subject to prototype effects both at the individual sound level and at the "selection" level—the level of creation of inventories. It is the same set of prototypicality principles at work at both levels. At the individual level, they select one among a number of alternative sounds as the one ideal instance; at the system level, they filter out altogether those suboptimal sounds that traditionally have been labeled "marked," replacing palatal stops with palatal affricates, high back unrounded vowels with front, and so on. This is discussed in some detail in Nathan (1996).

An analogous argument, incidentally, has been made for syllable structure as a prototypical "syntactic" category, subject to similar effects (so that a preference for onsets and a dispreference for codas would behave in the same way). Discussion can be found in Taylor (1995: 234–38).

The reader will note that I have carefully limited my examples to phonological facts that traditional phonology would label "low level" processes. I have not given any examples of the more elaborate morphophonemic alternations that one normally finds in an introductory phonology textbook. The reason for this is that, following Stampe's Natural Phonology, I am not convinced that those alternations are actually *phonological*. That is, the examples I have discussed so far are all responses by the speaker to the inherent constraints on speech production dictated by the articulatory and perceptual apparatus. As Stampe (1969, 1979, 1987) has said, they are what the speaker brings to the language. The relationships among morphologically related forms, on the other hand, are not derived at all from the facts of phonetics, but are rather leftovers of earlier phonetically based processes that have lost their phonetic basis. Speakers discover them by extracting schemas from similarities among forms irrespective of the articulatory or acoustic consequences of the patterns. Within the tradition of Generative Phonology, such patterns were described by what Anderson (1981) called "crazy" rules. Within Cognitive Grammar such patterns are not rules at all, but schemas extracted from patterns that are already stored. A classic example is the English verb paradigm /ɪ : æ : ʌ/ found in such verbs as *sing, sink*, and so on. Research has shown that this pattern is so pervasive that it is somewhat productive, and speakers tend to produce new examples when presented with novel verbs such as *gring*. However, this behavior is radically different from the exceptionless insertion of aspiration on initial voiceless stops in novel words or in words borrowed from other languages. Important work on this view of relatedness of forms can be found in Bybee and Moder (1983) and Bybee (2001), also in the work of Jaeger (1980, 1984) on the psychological reality of the vowel shift rule.

This amounts to a claim for a limited version of modularity within Cognitive Grammar. It is, however, a motivated modularity. Phonology is about entrenched *motor* skills, which are quite different from entrenched patterns of similarity among forms. Phonology is about what is hard or easy for a human vocal tract to perform, while morphology is about recognition of similarities among already stored variants.

3. Usage-Based Models

3.1. The Basic Model

The original impetus for this view of phonological structure was a work by Langacker (1988),[10] which argued that the number of units of language was much greater than generative theories of linguistics claim and that the reduction in redundancy that fuels much of the theoretical apparatus of Generative Grammar is mistaken. Language is, instead, massively redundant, and much more is stored, and less generated, by rule than any current competing theory would admit.

In particular, a usage-based model argues that individual instances are stored in large numbers as well as rules. In fact, Langacker argues that rules can only arise as abstractions from overtly occurring expressions (Langacker 2000: 3). Thus, rules cannot be established by speakers without prior storage of a large enough number of individual instances to permit an extraction of the regularities in the form of a *schema* that the instances support. The abstractions from numbers of similar examples are known as schemas, and the establishment of particular schemas constitutes *schematization*.

An important psychological mechanism made use of in a usage-based theory is the notion of *entrenchment*. Entrenchment refers to the fact that some highly complex event can "coalesce into a well-rehearsed routine that is easily elicited and reliably executed. When a complex structure comes to be manipulable as a 'prepackaged' assembly, no longer requiring conscious attention to its parts or their arrangement . . . it has the status of a **unit**" (Langacker 2000: 3–4).

The result of this view of linguistic organization is "that repeated applications of such processes, occurring in different combinations at many levels of organization, result in cognitive assemblies of enormous complexity. The vision that emerges is one of massive networks in which structures with varying degrees of entrenchment, and representing different levels of abstraction, are linked together in relationships of categorization, composition and symbolization" (Langacker 2000: 5).

Further, these "linguistic categories are usually complex, and develop from prototypical structures via such processes as extension, the extraction of schemas, and the articulation of coarse-grained units into more specific ones. . . . Complex categories are **networks** in which linguistic structures of any kind and size are linked. . . . These structures—the 'nodes' or vertices of the network—might consist, for example, of the allophones of a phoneme" (Langacker, 2000: 13).

Following the general principles of usage-based grammar, Bybee (2000, 2001; this volume, chapter 36), Palmer (1996), and Langacker (2000) argue that words are stored with extensive phonetic detail, and if words are pronounced in a number of different ways, each individual pronunciation is stored separately, while commonalities (such as a possible phonemic representation) are extracted as common, underspecified schemas. Bybee says:

Phonemes, then, do not exist in the representations of words; they are not units of lexical representation. Instead phonemes are abstract patterns that emerge in the phonological organization of the lexicon (see Langacker [2000]). To the extent that abstract phonetic units are grouped together into more abstract units, this is done on the basis of the phonetic implementation schemata, and is not a strict matter of complementary distribution. (Bybee 2000: 72)

The image that I use to make this view concrete is that each instance is like a footstep in soft ground. Each successive footstep deepens the mark made, but there is never complete overlap—nonetheless a generalized pattern emerges after a sufficient number of steps.

This leads Bybee and Langacker to argue that "phonemes" do not exist as units. Instead, they claim that the phenomena that phonemes are intended to describe are relations of similarity among parts of phonetic strings. These relations of similarity can be captured by lexical connections and schemas just as other relations of similarity are. Complementary distribution, rather than a criterion for deciding on lexical status of a phone, is just a consequence of the fact that articulatory adjustments are conditioned by the surrounding environment (Bybee 1994; Bybee 2000: 82; this volume, chapter 36). From a somewhat different perspective, this is, of course, the same view I argued for above within the Natural Phonology–oriented discussion on the nature of categories.

3.2. The Nature of Online Processes in a Usage-Based Model

In her study of English /t, d/ deletion, Bybee (2000, 2001) argues that some individual past-tense forms are stored as a whole (that is, even regular past-tense forms may not be generated through online morphological rules—the more frequent verbs may have regular past-tense forms stored as wholes; Bybee 2001: 112). The deletion of /t, d/ is also not an online process; rather, individual pronunciations of past-tense forms of verbs are stored, with different versions having different (subphonemic) lengths of closure. Deletion is simply an end point on a continuum of shorter and shorter alveolar gestures, and some words are stored with zero closure as an alternative pronunciation. Consequently, variable deletion of /d/ is not deletion at all, but rather storage of widely varying forms with a wide range of implementations:

> Lexical entries containing a final coronal stop are gradually accommodating to the changing input, and will gradually restructure, losing the stop entirely. Thus there are three sources of . . . surface variation: the articulatory change is gradually reducing the gesture involved; the phonetic environment conditions whether or not the gesture can be perceived, and the lexical items themselves have different degrees of reduction. (Bybee 2000: 73)

Here a difference arises between the embodied online view I have argued for above and the usage-based model, in that Bybee (this volume, chapter 36) argues that each "derived" version created by online processing is stored and that a sufficient number of these stored versions will lead to a language change. There are means of evaluating the differences between these views and, perhaps, of attempting to reconcile them; this research is ongoing.

3.3. Morphophonemics

As discussed above, Bybee and Langacker have argued that there are no morphophonemic rules per se, but rather that speakers extract commonalities among related forms to form higher-level schemas.

Rubba (1993) has shown for Modern Aramaic, for example, that the complex patterns of alternations in a classic Semitic "triconsonantal root" language emerge out of natural processes of schematization from actual instances. For example, the words *plaxa* 'work' (infinitive), *palxa* 'work' (jussive), and *palax* 'work' (agentive) permit the extraction of the abstract schema /p ... l ... x/, abstracting away from the specific vowels.

4. SYNTHESIS—PHONOLOGY AS HUMAN ACTION

I will conclude this review by arguing that the nature of phonology as conceived of by the founders of the field, from Baudouin through Sapir to Stampe, is to account for the way that speakers of languages perceive and produce the sounds of their languages. Langacker has stated that the goal is to account for "actual distributional phenomena," but I would argue that accounting for the phenomena at hand requires a more active role for speakers in the production and perception of their speech. It is a fact that German speakers not only "don't happen to have" voiced obstruents word-finally (as is proposed in Kumashiro 2000 as well as Langacker 2000) but that they are unable to pronounce word-final obstruents, even if they try. Further, we need to explain why native speakers of Vietnamese, who have no word-final obstruents at all, *devoice* those that they do manage to say while, for example, speaking English. If phonology consists simply of patterns gathered from data already acquired, Vietnamese speakers should have no opinions at all on how to pronounce final voiced obstruents. Similarly, German speakers replace initial [ʒ] in their English (and in borrowings) with [dʒ], even though that sound does not exist in German either. Since neither sound exists, no possible schema could have been extracted to deal with it. Where does this behavior come from?

Questions like these form the next step in the development of phonology in the Cognitive Grammar framework. Although the "embodied" and "usage-based" models agree on many areas, such as the importance of viewing phonology as embodied human action and not merely the assignment of sounds and lexical items to abstract categories, the question of the extent to which phonemes are idealized mental targets shaped by natural constraints of the vocal tract and perceptual system, versus the extent to which they are built up through similarity among repeated varied instances, is not yet settled and remains an area for future research.

One of the major goals of Cognitive Grammar is to describe the nature of language as it actually occurs in speakers, accounting for all the complexity and redundancy that characterize it. The term "cognitive" implies that Cognitive Grammar's goal is to come up with a model of language that is in accord with what is known about human cognition in general and to attempt, as far as possible, to exclude from the analysis entities that appear to have no independent existence outside of other modes of cognition. Cognitive Grammar has had enormous success through its use of a few independently motivated tools, including categorization, schematization, and mechanisms of extension such as metaphor, metonymy, and image schema transformation. Lakoff and Johnson (1980) have argued that such abstract modes of mental activity as set theory are based in bodily experience with containers and small objects. Similarly, Johnson (1987) has shown that moral questions of fairness are based on our bodily experience with gravity. In short, Cognitive Grammar has achieved a tremendous amount through the recognition that human beings understand the world and its complexity through reasoning and categorizing based on basic-level categories of bodily and other reality-based experience.

Unfortunately, there has been a tendency to omit the body (and its perceptual apparatus) when discussing phonology, even though this branch of linguistics ought to be the most physically grounded part of language, consisting as it does of movements of the vocal tract that produce sounds. Phonology is more than the classification and categorization of sounds that are just "there," as if phonology were a kind of stamp collecting. Phonology comprises a description of the implementation of motor plans by speakers and the recovery of those motor plans by listeners. Motor plans are not implemented simpliciter, but are molded and modified to fit the surroundings that they find themselves in. And those modifications, while themselves motivated by facts about how the vocal tract can move in real time and by facts about what information can be retrieved by our perceptual systems, are language-specific and constitute the "phonological grammar" of a language. To do otherwise is to remove the body from the speaker and to surrender to the generative temptation of making language into an abstract manipulation of meaningless symbols. Baudouin and Sapir's original view of phonology as the implementation in real time of idealized mental images, and the sympathetic reconstruction of those language-specific images of vocal tract gestures and the sounds associated with them, stands as the best way for Cognitive Grammar to understand human phonological behavior as it is illustrated in observable behavior.

NOTES

I am grateful to Margaret Winters and José Antonio Mompean for their helpful, and at times challenging, comments and to David Stampe and Patricia Donegan for their inspiration.

1. There is another alternative view that should be mentioned, namely that phonemes are the invariant features found in the normally variable physical speech chain. As soon as acoustic phonetics became a relatively easily accessible science, however, it became obvious that there were no physical invariants available to be stored by speakers.

2. There is one additional strand of Cognitive Phonology that was begun in Lakoff (1993) but did not lead to subsequent work within the general Cognitive Grammar framework, although it did spawn a certain amount of further work within more generative-oriented frameworks and had some influence on Optimality Theory, a model that will be discussed below.

3. Donegan and Stampe (1979) used the word *innate* to describe the knowledge that native speakers have of the processes of their language, but emphasized that he did not mean the Chomskyan sense, but rather simply that the knowledge was not "learned" like the alphabet, but rather flowed from children's experience with acquiring control over their vocal tracts. Children learn that it is difficult to produce final voiced obstruents because they try to do so and fail, at least at first. It is in this sense that final devoicing is innate, according to Stampe.

4. There are actually other possible variants, such as a voiceless flap in *outhouse*, but this level of complexity should suffice. The voiced coronal flap raises other special issues that will be discussed below.

5. The $F_1 \times F_2$ space refers to the overall vowel space defined by the acoustic dimensions of the first and second formants (roughly equivalent to height and backness in traditional terms.)

6. The title of Stampe's (1968) paper is a reference to the famous newspaper article "Yes, Virginia, there is a Santa Clause." Stampe's paper was presented shortly after Generative Phonology concluded that the traditional phoneme did not exist. Although the paper was never actually published, most of the arguments appear in Stampe (1987).

7. These variations only make sense, of course, if we treat each of the variants as motivated extensions from a central prototype forming a radial prototype structure of the kind we discussed above.

8. It is important to remember that I am speaking of *mental* sounds here—auditory/articulatory images, not actual physical sounds. But they are real sounds, not abstract lists of features.

9. There is also a further reinforcing fact, namely that voiceless consonants are physiologically simpler to produce, since it is relatively more difficult to achieve airflow across the glottis if the upper portion of the vocal tract is closed; see Keating, Linker, and Huffman (1983) for discussion.

10. For a current discussion, see Langacker (2000).

REFERENCES

Anderson, Stephen R. 1981. Why phonology isn't 'natural'. *Linguistic Inquiry* 12: 493–539.

Baudouin de Courtenay, Jan. [1895] 1972. An attempt at a theory of phonetic alternations. In Edward Stankiewicz, ed. and trans., *A Baudouin de Courtenay anthology: The beginnings of structural linguistics* 144–213. Bloomington: Indiana University Press.

Bloomfield, Leonard. 1933. *Language*. New York: Holt, Rinehart and Winston.

Boersma, Paul. 1998. *Functional phonology: Formalizing the interactions between articulatory and perceptual drives*. The Hague: Holland Academic Graphics.

Bybee, Joan L. 1994. A view of phonology from a cognitive and functional perspective. *Cognitive Linguistics* 5: 285–306.

Bybee, Joan L. 1999. Usage-based phonology. In Michael Darnell, Edith Moravcsik, Frederick J. Newmeyer, Michael Noonan, and Kathleen M. Wheatley, eds., *Functionalism and formalism in linguistics*, vol. 1, *General Papers* 211–42. Amsterdam: John Benjamins.

Bybee, Joan L. 2000. The phonology of the lexicon: Evidence from lexical diffusion. In Michael Barlow and Suzanne Kemmer, eds., *Usage-based models of language* 65–86. Stanford, CA: CSLI Publications.

Bybee, Joan L. 2001. *Phonology and language use*. Cambridge: Cambridge University Press.

Bybee, Joan L., and Carol Lynn Moder. 1983. Morphological classes as natural categories. *Language* 59: 251–70.

Carnie, Andrew, and Norma Mendoza-Denton. 2003. Functionalism is/n't formalism: An interactive review of Darnell et al. (1999). Rev. of Michael Darnell, Edith Moravcsik, Frederick J. Newmeyer, Michael Noonan, and Kathleen M. Wheatley, eds., *Functionalism and Formalism in Linguistics* (Amsterdam: John Benjamins, 1999). *Journal of Linguistics* 39: 373–89.

Chomsky, Noam, and Morris Halle. 1968. *The sound pattern of English*. New York: Harper and Row.

Damasio, Antonio. 1999. *The feeling of what happens: Body and emotion in the making of consciousness*. New York: Harcourt Brace.

Donegan, Patricia J. 1986. *On the natural phonology of vowels*. New York: Garland.

Donegan, Patricia J. 2002. Normal vowel development. In Martin J. Ball and Fiona E. Gibbon, eds., *Vowel Disorders* 1–36. Boston: Butterworth-Heinemann.

Donegan, Patricia J., and David Stampe. 1979. The study of natural phonology. In Dan Dinnsen, ed., *Current approaches to phonological theory* 126—73. Bloomington: Indiana University Press.

Fromkin, Victoria A. 1973. *Speech errors as linguistic evidence*. The Hague: Mouton

Fromkin, Victoria A. 1980. *Errors in linguistic performance: Slips of the tongue, ear, pen and hand*. New York: Academic Press

Fromkin, Victoria A. 1988 The grammatical aspects of speech errors. In Frederick J. Newmeyer, ed., *Linguistics: The Cambridge survey* 2: 117–38. Cambridge: Cambridge University Press.

Gussenhoven, Carlos, and Heike Jacobs. 1998. *Understanding phonology*. London: Arnold.

Hayes, Bruce. 1999. Phonetically-driven phonology: The role of optimality theory and inductive grounding. In Michael Darnell, Edith Moravcsik, Michael Noonan, Frederick Newmeyer, and Kathleen Wheatly, eds., *Functionalism and formalism in linguistics*, vol. 1, *General papers* 243–85 Amsterdam: John Benjamins.

Hayes, Bruce. 2004. Phonological acquisition in optimality theory: The early stages. In René Kager, Joe Pater, and Wim Zonneveld, eds., *Constraints in phonological acquisition* 158–204. Cambridge: Cambridge University Press

Hooper, Joan. 1976. *An introduction to natural generative phonology.* New York: Academic Press.

Hurch, Bernhard. 1988. *Über Aspiration: Ein Kapitel aus der natürlichen Phonologie.* Tübingen: Gunter Narr Verlag.

Jaeger, Jeri. 1980. Categorization in phonology: An experimental approach. PhD dissertation, University of California at Berkeley.

Jaeger, Jeri. 1984. Assessing the psychological status of the vowel shift rule. *Journal of Psycholinguistic Research* 13: 13–36

Jakobson, Roman. [1941] 1968. *Child language, aphasia and phonological universals.* The Hague: Mouton. (Trans. of *Kindersprache, Aphasie und allgemeine Lautgesetze.* Uppsala, Sweden: Almquist and Wiksell, 1941)

Johnson, Mark. 1987. *The body in the mind: The bodily basis of meaning, imagination, and reason.* Chicago: University of Chicago Press.

Jones, Daniel. 1967. *The phoneme: Its nature and use.* Cambridge: Heffer.

Kager, René. 1999. *Optimality theory.* Cambridge: Cambridge University Press.

Keating, Patricia, Wendy Linker, and Marie Huffman. 1983. Patterns of allophone distribution for voiced and voiceless stops. *Journal of Phonetics* 11: 277–90.

Kiparsky, Paul. 1982. How abstract is phonology? In Paul Kiparsky, ed., *Explanation in phonology* 119–64. Dordrecht, Netherlands: Foris.

Kirchner, Robert. 1997. Contrastiveness and faithfulness. *Phonology* 14: 83–113.

Kuhl, Patricia. K., and Paul Iverson. 1995. Linguistic experience and the "perceptual magnet effect." In Winifred Strange, ed., *Speech perception and linguistic experience: Issues in cross-language research.* 121–54. Baltimore, MD: York Press.

Kumashiro, Fumiko. 2000. Phonotactic interactions: A non-reductionist approach to phonology. PhD dissertation, University of California at San Diego.

Lakoff, George. 1987. *Women, fire and dangerous things: What categories reveal about the mind.* Chicago: University of Chicago Press.

Lakoff, George. 1993. Cognitive phonology. In John Goldsmith, ed., *The last phonological rule* 117–45. Chicago: University of Chicago Press.

Lakoff, George, and Mark Johnson. 1980. *Metaphors we live by.* Chicago: University of Chicago Press.

Langacker, Ronald W. 1987. *Foundations of cognitive grammar.* Vol. l, *Theoretical prerequisites.* Stanford, CA: Stanford University Press.

Langacker, Ronald W. 1988. A usage-based model. In Brygida Rudzka-Ostyn, ed., *Topics in cognitive linguistics* 127–61. Amsterdam: John Benjamins.

Langacker, Ronald W. 2000. A dynamic usage-based model. In Michael Barlow and Suzanne Kemmer, eds., *Usage-based models of language* 1–64. Stanford, CA: CSLI Publications.

Lotto, Andrew J. 2000. Language acquisition as complex category formation. *Phonetica* 57: 189–96.

MacNeilage, Peter F. 1998. The frame/content theory of evolution of speech production. *Behavioral and Brain Sciences* 21: 499–548.

MacNeilage, Peter F., and Barbara L. Davis. 2000. Deriving speech from nonspeech: A view from ontogeny. *Phonetica* 57: 284–96.

Maddieson, Ian. 1984. *Patterns of sounds.* Cambridge: Cambridge University Press.

Mompeán-González, José A. 2004. Category overlap and neutralization: The importance of speakers' classifications in phonology. *Cognitive Linguistics* 15: 429–70

Nathan, Geoffrey S. 1986. Phonemes as mental categories. *Berkeley Linguistics Society* 12: 212–23.

Nathan, Geoffrey S. 1989. Preliminaries to a theory of phonological substance: The substance of sonority. In Roberta Corrigan, Fred Eckman, and Michael Noonan, eds., *Linguistic categorization* 55–68. Amsterdam: John Benjamins

Nathan, Geoffrey S. 1996. Steps towards a cognitive phonology. In Bernhard Hurch and Richard Rhodes, eds., *Natural phonology: The state of the art* 107–20. Berlin: Mouton de Gruyter.

Nathan, Geoffrey S. 1999. What functionalists can learn from formalists in phonology. In Michael Darnell, Edith Moravcsik, Michael Noonan, Frederick Newmeyer, and Kathleen Wheatley, eds., *Functionalism and formalism in linguistics*, vol. 1, *General papers* 305–27. Amsterdam: John Benjamins.

Nathan, Geoffrey S. 2008. *Phonology: A cognitive grammar account*. Amsterdam: Benjamins.

Palmer, Gary. 1996. *Toward a theory of cultural linguistics*. Austin: University of Texas Press.

Pike, Kenneth. 1947. On the phonemic status of English diphthongs. In Valerie B. Makkai, ed., *Phonological theory: Evolution and current practice* 145–51. New York: Holt, Rinehart and Winston.

Prince, Alan, and Paul Smolensky. 2004. *Optimality theory: Constraint interaction in generative grammar*. Oxford: Blackwell.

Rubba, Johanna. 1993. Discontinuous morphology in modern Aramaic. PhD dissertation, University of California at San Diego.

Samuel, A. G. 1982. Phonetic prototypes. *Perception and Psychophysics* 31: 307–14.

Sapir, Edward. [1933] 1972. The psychological reality of phonemes. In Valerie B. Makkai, ed., *Phonological theory: Evolution and current practice* 22–31. New York: Holt, Rinehart and Winston. (Trans. of La réalité pschologique des phonèmes. *Journal de Psychologie Normale et Pathologique* 30 [1933]: 247–65)

Saussure, Ferdinand de. [1916] 1974. *Cours de linguistique générale*. Edition critique préparée par Tullio de Mauro. Paris: Payot.

Schane, Sanford A. 1971. The phoneme revisited. *Language* 47: 503–21

Smith, Neilson V. 1973. *The acquisition of phonology: A case study*. Cambridge: Cambridge University Press.

Stampe, David. 1968. "Yes, Virginia..." Paper presented at the 4th regional meeting of the Chicago Linguistics Society, Chicago, Apr. 19–20.

Stampe, David. 1969. The acquisition of phonetic representation. *Chicago Linguistic Society* 5: 443–54.

Stampe, David. 1979. *A dissertation on natural phonology*. New York: Garland Press.

Stampe, David. 1987. On phonological representation. In Wolfgang Dressler, Hans C. Luschützky, Oskar Pfeiffer, and John R. Rennison, eds., *Phonologica 1984* 287–300. London: Cambridge University Press.

Taylor, John R. 1995. *Linguistic categorization: Prototypes in linguistic theory*. 2nd ed. Oxford: Clarendon Press. (3rd ed., 2003)

Trubetzkoy, Nikolaj S. [1939] 1969. *Principles of phonology*. Trans. Chistiane Baltaxe. Berkeley: University of California Press. (Trans. of *Gründzüge der Phonologie*. Prague: Travaux du cercle linguistique de Prague, 1939)

Weinreich, Uriel. 1970. *Languages in contact*. The Hague: Mouton.

Winters, Margaret E., and Geoffrey S. Nathan. 2006. Optimality theory and cognitive grammar, unpublished manuscript.

CHAPTER 24

INFLECTIONAL MORPHOLOGY

LAURA JANDA

1. INTRODUCTION

In terms of both form and meaning, inflectional morphology occupies an unusual position in language, as it teeters on the margins between lexicon and syntax in apparent defiance of definition. In most languages, inflectional morphology marks relations such as person, number, case, gender, possession, tense, aspect, and mood, serving as an essential grammatical glue holding the relationships in constructions together. Yet in some languages, inflectional morphology is minimal or may not exist at all.

From the perspective of Cognitive Linguistics, inflectional morphology presents a rich array of opportunities to apply and test core concepts, particularly those involving category structure (radial categories, prototypicality, polysemy), the grounding and organization of categories (embodiment, basic-level concepts, "ception," construal), and the means of extension and elaboration of categories (metaphor, metonymy). For example, languages with inflectional case typically present a variety of issues that must be addressed. The meanings of a given case (such as the dative case in Czech, which can express giving, taking, experiencing, subordination, competition, and domination) are at once highly abstract, yet internally complex, offering an opportunity to investigate the effects of prototypicality and polysemy within a radial category. The embodied experiences and per-/conceptions that motivate the basic-level concepts of such inflectional categories merit close analysis. The grammatical meaning of an inflectional category challenges the linguist with the various construals of meaning that it enables. The

Czech dative, for example, can be used to assert participation in an event even when this construal is contrary to reality, as in *Ten čaj ti mě zvedl* [that tea.NOM you.DAT me.ACC lifted] 'That tea picked me up (and you should care about this event)', where the referent of *ti* 'you' has no real participation in the event of picking up but is called upon to "experience" the event anyhow. Furthermore, we have only just begun to chart the behavior of metaphor and metonymy in extending the meanings of inflectional categories. For example, it appears that metaphor extends the use of the dative from concrete giving to the experiencing of benefit and harm (as the metaphorical reception of good and evil) and that metonymy is at work in motivating the use of the dative with verbs of communication (which mean 'give a message', though the direct object is not overtly expressed). Inflectional categories provide a variety of examples of linguistic expressions that do (e.g., tense and mood) and do not (e.g., case and number) deictically ground an utterance to the speaker's experience of the world (see Dirven and Verspoor 1998: 95–101).

For the purposes of this article, I will assume that there are three kinds of morphemes: lexical, derivational, and inflectional. The behavior of these three types of morphemes can best be understood within the context of constructions. If we think of a construction as a set of slots and relations among them, the lexical morpheme is what goes in a given slot. Any accompanying derivational morpheme(s) will make whatever semantic and grammatical adjustments may be necessary to fit the lexical morpheme into a given slot. The inflectional morphemes are the relations that hold the slots together. The job of an inflectional morpheme is to tell us how a given slot (regardless of what is in it) fits with the rest of the construction. I will draw primarily upon my knowledge of the highly inflected Slavic languages to illustrate this chapter and refer the reader to relevant descriptions of inflectional categories elsewhere in this *Handbook* (see particularly Boogaart and Janssen's chapter 31, Tense and Aspect).

2. WHAT IS INFLECTIONAL MORPHOLOGY?

Scholars devote much of their discussions to definitions of what inflectional morphology is, with palpable frustration. Bybee (1985: 81), for example, holds that "one of the most persistent undefinables in morphology is the distinction between derivational and inflectional morphology." As cognitive linguists, we should be able to approach this issue with the same criteria that we apply to linguistic categories: we know that categories are structured not by firm boundaries but by relationships to a prototype, and we know that categories can be language-specific. Inflectional morphology is no exception to this generalization. In keeping with our traditions as cognitive linguists, we will aim not for an airtight universal definition, but for a concatenation of the most typical characteristics and variations on that theme. This does not mean that our definition will lack any richness or rigor; it will instead be realistic and will reveal both the inner workings of inflectional morphology and its relationship to other linguistic phenomena.

In order to discover what inflectional morphology is, we must first know what a word is, or, to be more precise, what an autonomous word is. An autonomous word is one that is capable of having variants (i.e., something that is not a particle, preposition, or the like), and these variants are the stuff of inflectional morphology. The problem, of course, is that we have just defined the autonomous word by excluding everything that lacks inflectional morphology, so we have used inflectional morphology to identify the autonomous word and then used the autonomous word to define what is inflectional morphology—this is obviously a vicious circle. As the quotation from Bybee above suggests, attempts to define inflectional vis-à-vis derivational morphology are just as problematic. As a rule, a derivational morpheme is any morpheme that assigns or changes the paradigm of a word (its set of inflectional morphemes). Using this line of reasoning, the inflectional morpheme is a morpheme that does not assign or change the set of inflectional morphemes associated with a stem, and here again we are caught in a circular definition. The very existence of the ambiguous term "affix" (which refuses to draw a line between derivational and inflectional morphology) is indicative of the lack of achievable clarity; as Bybee (1985: 87) admits, "The distinction between derivational and inflectional morphology is not discrete, but rather a gradient phenomenon." Slavic aspect is an example of a category that can be interpreted as either inflectional or derivational. Because Slavic languages obligatorily mark aspect on every verb form, some researchers (particularly those who hold fast to the notion of the "aspectual pair") believe that the paradigm of a verb includes both perfective and imperfective forms, relegating aspect to the realm of inflection. Others would argue that each verb has an identity as either perfective or imperfective and that the variety of prefixes and suffixes used to derive perfectives and imperfectives are derivational morphemes. Despite the strong opinions of scholars, there is probably no definitive solution to this problem.

2.1. The Characteristics of Inflectional Morphology

Inflectional morphology highlights the relationships expressed in a language and is therefore never autonomous. I suggest we accept this lack of an autonomous role as part of the definition of inflectional morphology and move on from there. We will add to our definition characteristics frequently associated with inflectional morphology (see Bybee 1985; Talmy 1985, 2000a, 2000b; Slobin 1997; Plungian 2000), namely the observations that inflectional morphemes are typically bound, closed-class, obligatory, general, and semantically abstract. The first two characteristics (boundedness and membership in a closed class) are necessary but not sufficient features, since they are not unique to inflectional morphology. Whereas the remaining characteristics pertain more specifically to inflectional morphology, they are also considerably less concrete, reminding us again of the relative nature of this phenomenon. Collectively, these characteristics describe the linguist's Idealized Cognitive Model of inflectional morphology; the reality of actual variation is considerably more textured.

Inflectional Morphology Is Bound

A bound morpheme is fixed to a stem and cannot float off to other positions in a construction; in other words, it is part of a word (a fact which may or may not be accurately reflected orthographically). Boundedness is consistent with lack of autonomy; an inflectional morpheme is never a free agent in an utterance, for it must be attached to a lexical morpheme. When both derivational and inflectional morphemes are present in a word, the derivational morpheme(s) will generally be attached closer to the root (the lexical morpheme) than the inflectional morpheme(s). This observed hierarchy of proximity is an iconic expression of relevance (Bybee 1985: 5): inflectional morphology involves concepts that are more relevant to how the word relates to other words in a construction—viewed as a set of slots and relations—than to the lexical item itself. Indeed, whereas a derivational morpheme relates more to the identity of a word itself (in that it more directly affects the meaning of the stem), an inflectional morpheme relates the word to the rest of the construction, motivating a position on the very periphery of the word. The periphery is a precarious spot, and the grammatical categories usually associated with inflection often find themselves drawn closer in (as derivational morphemes) or spun further out (as various functor words). Both kinds of change can be documented in the Slavic languages. The possessive morpheme -*in* in Czech (e.g., *matka* 'mother' and *matčin* 'mother's') participates in derivation (as in *křovina* 'shrubbery', a collective from *křoví* 'bushes'). Bulgarian and Macedonian have lost nominal declension, but the categories of case are expressed "further out" in prepositions and resumptive pronouns. Often it is hard to tell where a lexeme ends and the inflectional morphology begins; this is particularly true in the paradigms of pronouns and demonstratives, where a very minimal stem appears fused with its affixes. Take the Czech paradigm of 'who' for example: *kdo* (nominative), *koho* (genitive/accusative), *komu* (dative), *kom* (locative), *ký m* (instrumental). Although -*o*, -*oho*, -*omu*, -*om*, and -*ým* do parallel endings in other paradigms, it seems farfetched to posit this paradigm as a stem of *k(d)-* + inflectional affixes.

Inflectional Morphology Is Closed-Class

Our three types of morphemes occupy three places on the scale of openness. Lexical morphemes are the most open, which means that new lexical morphemes can be created or borrowed and that this class of morphemes is by far the largest. Derivational morphemes are in a transitional spot, being relatively closed, admitting few borrowings, and constituting a considerably smaller class. Inflectional morphemes are extremely resistant to borrowing and are by far the smallest class of morphemes in a language. A rough count (in which the allomorphs of a given morpheme are counted as one morpheme) of morphemes listed for Czech (in Janda and

Townsend 2000) yields 50 inflectional morphemes, of which none are borrowed, but over 130 derivational morphemes, of which about 30 are foreign borrowings.

Inflectional Morphology Is Obligatory

The autonomous words in an inflected language form natural syntactic classes. Each syntactic class is associated with a set of grammatical categories, and the values of those grammatical categories constitute the paradigm. The inflectional categories associated with a given class are those that are relevant to that class; prime examples are tense, aspect, and mood, which are relevant to verbs, as opposed to case, which is relevant to nouns. Inflectional morphemes and the grammatical categories they express are productive: if a new lexical item enters a given syntactic class, it will inherit all the associated inflectional morphemes (see the principle of generality in Bybee 1985: 16–17). Inflectional morphemes are regular: every (or nearly every) member of a paradigm is instantiated for every (or nearly every) word in a given class (Plungian 2000: 125). Productivity and regularity make the associated categories obligatory for the given syntactic class of words. If, for example, a language inflects its nouns for number and case, all nouns will obligatorily express these categories. In Czech, for example, virtually all nouns (including the vast majority of borrowings) are obligatorily inflected for number and case.

Inflectional Morphology Is General

Productivity and regularity imply generality, both in terms of form and meaning. Generality of form can be examined from the perspective of the paradigm, as well as from the perspective of the construction. An inflectional morpheme is a morpheme that has been generalized to a paradigm and therefore can appear with all words associated with that paradigm. The identity of an inflectional category is determined by the constructions in which it appears (see Croft 2001); together, this set of constructions defines the meaning of the category. The meaning of an inflectional category is necessarily relative because it must be generalizable across two parameters: both the entire set of words in a syntactic class and the set of constructions built with that category. With regard to the Czech dative, this case is expressed by all nouns and collaborates in a wide variety of constructions. Below, I will further discuss how generality impacts meaning.

Inflectional Morphology Is Semantically Abstract

An inflectional morpheme does not have the capacity to change the meaning or the syntactic class of the words it is bound to and will have a predictable meaning for all such words. Thus, the present tense will mean the same thing regardless of the verb that is inflected, and the dative case will have the same value for all nouns. Semantic abstraction and relativity do not mean that there is little or simple meaning involved; inflectional categories are never merely automatic or semantically empty. The meanings of inflectional categories are certainly notoriously difficult to describe, but they exhibit all the normal behavior we expect from cognitive categories, such as grounding in embodied experience and radial structured polysemy (see Janda 1993). I prefer to think of inflectional morphology as a dynamic tension between underdetermination and overdetermination. Each value in a paradigm is semantically underdetermined, being sufficiently abstract and flexible to accommodate a wide range of words and constructions, as well as creative extensions. Collectively, the paradigm is semantically overdetermined, presenting a system with expressive means beyond the bare minimum for communication, thus allowing speaker construal to play a role in the choice of values within the paradigm.

Whereas the meaning of derivational morphemes points inward, to the word and what it means, the meaning of inflectional morphemes points away from a word. Inflectional meaning is the meaning that exists between words (the adhesive for the slots), and this fact motivates variation across languages as to whether grammatical meanings are assigned to inflection or to other parts of language.

2.2. Variations in Expressions of Inflectional Morphology

This Idealized Cognitive Model best describes synthetic languages with robust paradigms conflating the grammatical categories pertaining to each syntactic class into semantically complex inflectional morphemes. As Croft (2001) has pointed out, variation is one of the best-documented phenomena of language, and inflectional morphology is no exception. Analytic languages, such as Vietnamese, Thai, many West African languages, and most creoles (Plungian 2000: 112) are at the other end of the spectrum with virtually no inflectional morphology. Agglutinative languages occupy a transitional position, with separate inflectional morphemes for each inflectional category, usually concatenated in strings attached to stems. The agglutinative approach to inflectional morphology appears to be evolutionarily transitional as well, but this statement is not meant to imply that any one type of inflectional morphology is more evolutionarily advanced than any other. There appears to be a cycle in which autonomous analytic morphemes can be gradually modified semantically and phonologically into the role of agglutinative morphemes, further phonological and semantic forces can meld them into synthetic morphemes, and phonological erosion along with the development of new analytic morphemes can bring us back to replay the cycle (Meillet [1912] 1958; Hopper and Traugott 1993).

Different languages handle the business of relating lexical items in a construction in different ways. The semantic freight commonly associated with inflectional morphology can be shared with or shouldered by many other parts of a language, including derivational morphology, pre- and postpositions, auxiliaries, clitics, and even lexical morphemes. The exact distribution of this semantic responsibility is language-specific. In fact, the same category may even be expressed differently by different syntactic classes in the same language: in Russian, for example, gender is an inflectional category for adjectives, but a derivational category for nouns.

Each language has its own set of obligatory grammatical categories reflecting the priorities of the linguistic consciousness of its speakers. As Jakobson ([1959] 1971) observed, the difference between languages consists not so much in what each one empowers its speakers to express, as in what each one forces its speakers to express. Plungian (2000: 109) likens this to a "grammatical questionnaire" that speakers must continuously fill out and notes that automatizing this task is one of the second-language learner's greatest challenges. Finnish, for example, avoids grammatical reference to gender, whereas Polish seems by comparison grammatically obsessed with gender, particularly as it relates to the virility of male humans (Janda 1999).

The obligatory categories of a given language can be expressed in cognitive linguistic terms. These categories are experienced as entrenched mental spaces by its speakers (Fauconnier and Turner 2002: 103–6), and this conceptual entrenchment is virtually fused to perception, such that the obligatory categories are constantly processed. This fusion of perception and conception is termed "ception" (in Talmy 1996); the categories of inflectional morphology are but one example of how mental constructs interact with human perception. If we revisit the model of the three types of morphemes (lexical, derivational, and inflectional), we observe that they correlate to the three levels of conceptual organization: the superordinate, basic, and subordinate levels (Lakoff 1987). Lexical morphemes operate at the superordinate level, heading word families. Derivational morphemes work on the basic level, creating the autonomous words that belong to the word families. The subordinate level is the realm of inflectional morphemes, where specific variants for given constructions are available. Inflectional morphology resides in the basement of our linguistic consciousness, at the foundation of grammatical meaning.

3. INFLECTIONAL MORPHEMES AND THE FORM-MEANING RELATIONSHIP

Linguistic units join a phonological pole to a semantic pole (Langacker 1987), but with inflectional morphemes the substance at both poles can appear problematic. For inflection, the form-meaning relationship is abstract and complex. Inflection is also the platform for many obvious effects of markedness. We will discuss form, meaning, and markedness in turn.

3.1. The Form of Inflectional Morphemes

In comparison with what we can observe for other linguistic elements, the formal characteristics of inflectional morphemes appear disparate and diffuse. Since inflection has what might be described as a parasitic relationship with lexical items, it exercises great freedom in terms of form. The form of the lexical item can be thought of as a launching pad for the forms of associated inflectional morphemes: basically any modification to the stem will suffice. Inflectional morphemes may be concatenative, consisting of affixes applied to the stem, or they may be nonconcatenative, involving segmental modification of the stem or suprasegmental changes (e.g., to prosodic features). Both concatenative and nonconcatenative modifications can cooperate in a single morpheme. Another important, nonconcatenative option is zero morphemes, which consist of no modifications. Homophony within a paradigm (when two or more values for the inflectional categories bear the same inflectional morpheme), also known as syncresis, is quite common. So is suppletion, which involves the joining of forms from two or more (historically) unrelated stems in a single paradigm. And finally, paradigms are generally associated only with subsets of syntactic classes of words. This means that a given inflectional category will have entirely different formal realizations in different paradigms.

A typical inflected language will exhibit all of the formal options just described; here, we will use examples from Czech nominal morphology. Concatenative affixes can be illustrated by the forms for the word 'woman': *žen-a* and *žen-ou*, where the inflectional morphemes *-a* and *-ou* indicate nominative singular and instrumental singular, respectively. The forms of the word *plyn* 'gas' illustrate several phenomena: the nonconcatenative feature of length differentiates the genitive singular form *plyn-u* and the genitive plural form *plyn-ů*, which has a long final vowel. The nominative singular form *plyn* bears a zero morpheme (also evident in the genitive plural form *žen* 'women'). And the genitive singular *plyn-u* is syncretic with both the dative singular and the locative singular. Forms of the word for 'force' combine concatenative and nonconcatenative modifications: the nominative singular *síl-a* has a long stem vowel and a concatenative affix, whereas the instrumental singular *sil-ou* has a shortened stem vowel to accompany its affix. Like English, Czech exhibits suppletion in the word for 'person, people': all the singular forms are built from the stem of *člověk*, whereas all the plural forms are built from the stem of *lidé*. Each nominal paradigm has its own set of morphemes; in addition to *-ou* cited above, the instrumental singular, for instance, can be realized as *-em*, *-í*, and *-ím*.

3.2. The Meaning of Inflectional Morphemes

There is no doubt that the grammaticalizable categories available in inflection are somehow restricted. As we have seen, these categories are necessarily relative and therefore cannot indicate absolute values or specific referents. Because the number of inflectional categories even in highly inflected languages is generally quite small and because we observe similar categories across languages, scholars are tempted to construct lists of universal categories for inflection (e.g., Talmy 1985; Slobin 1997). Talmy (2000a: 37) hedges his bets by positing "a privileged inventory, albeit perhaps a partially approximate one, of grammatically expressible concepts," and suggests that at least part of this inventory may be "innate." Slobin (1997) and Plungian (2000) are more cautious, noting that only a fraction of the world's languages have been studied and that some of these languages contain unique, language-specific inflectional categories, which suggests that we do not have enough information to construct a universal list. According to Slobin (1997: 308), "Anything that is important and salient enough for people to want to refer to it routinely and automatically most of the time, and across a wide range of situations, CAN come to be grammatically marked." Given this wide semantic range, Slobin attacks the questions of innateness and universality and does so in a manner consistent with the cognitive linguistic notions of grounding and embodiment. Since inflectional categories indicate relations, they are necessarily both engendered and acquired through interactive experiences. And whereas other linguistic items might be introduced by individuals or groups, it takes an entire linguistic community to forge the categories of inflection.

In addition to being relative, the meanings of inflectional categories are necessarily participatory, for they must interact with the meanings of the lexical items they are attached to as well as with other elements in the constructions where they appear (other lexical items and functors such as pre- and postpositions). Because inflectional categories express their meanings only in the context of constructions, it can be hard to determine what portion of grammatical meaning is borne by inflectional morphemes and what part is borne by other elements in a construction. An example is the interaction between case inflection and prepositions in many Indo-European languages, where we observe both "bare" case usage (without a preposition) and prepositional usage (where a case is associated with a preposition). In the latter instance, some linguists will ask whether the meaning is in the preposition or in the morpheme that marks the case, and others will presume that if a trigger such as a preposition is present, the inflectional morpheme is semantically empty. A cognitive linguist will, however, suggest a third solution: that the meanings of the trigger element (here the preposition) and the inflectional morpheme are compatible, motivating their coexistence (see Langacker 1991: 187). This solution respects the form-meaning relationship by avoiding the positing of meaningless elements or, worse yet, elements that turn their meanings off in the presence of other elements. Of course, the problem of disentangling the meaning of the inflectional morpheme from its surroundings remains, but this is merely a more acute instance of a general problem of semantics, since nothing exists in isolation.

We have already established synthetic morphemes as the prototypical model for inflectional morphology, and clearly such morphemes present yet another issue of semantic entanglement. Synthetic morphemes conflate co-occurring categories such as case + number and tense + person + number (and, of course, the set of categories that co-occur is highly language-specific). This makes it impossible in many languages to completely separate one inflectional category from another, but then they are never separate for the purposes of those languages (or those speakers) either. Note the conflation of categories in the paradigm of the Czech verb *nést* 'carry': *nesu* 'I carry', *neseš* 'you carry', *nese* 'she/he/it carries', *neseme* 'we carry', *nesete* 'you (plural/formal) carry', *nesou* 'they carry'. The stem is of course *nes-*, and -*u* expresses present + first person + singular, -*eš* expresses present + second person + singular, and so on. The coexistence of linguistic categories in synthetic morphemes is pervasive and indicates more loaded meaning than the mere addition of categories might suggest; first-person singular has a very potent place in the imagination of speakers—it is not just the abstract notion of first person with singular tacked on. The conflated concepts presented by synthetic inflection are conventional cognitive workhorses for the languages they serve and provide considerable structure to the "grammatical questionnaires" of those languages.

The vagaries of both form and meaning endemic to inflectional morphology make it a daunting challenge for the linguist, a fact that may be responsible for the relative paucity of work on this issue. Cognitive Linguistics has taken the structuralist ideal of "one form–one meaning" a step closer to the true complexities of reality with the notion of structured polysemy, recognizing the fact that the relationship is often "one form–several (related) meanings." On the formal side of the equation, though, we have no more clarity, since there is a proliferation of forms and how they are realized. Langacker's (1987) concept of an abstract schema overarching a radial category can be invoked here: the schema is any modification to a stem associated with a given spot in a paradigm. Different paradigms are free to realize this schema differently. The prototypical modification is probably the simple addition of segments, but other modifications, including zero modification, can be used. The form-meaning relationship of inflectional morphology consists of an abstract schematic form associated with meaning that may be polysemous and/or inextricably bound to other meanings.

3.3. The Markedness of Inflectional Morphemes

Given the relativity of both form and meaning, it is logical that inflectional morphology would be a prime environment for markedness phenomena, since markedness plays upon relative values. This is indeed the case. Markedness is an organizing principle for both the values of an inflectional category and the forms that express those values. Form and meaning in inflection are (relatively) marked or unmarked, and markedness is typically aligned (such that marked forms are associated with marked meanings). As I have argued elsewhere (Janda 1995), markedness is a by-product of the structure of cognitive categories, which are inherently asymmetric, giving the prototype privileged status relative to more peripheral items. Like other phenomena associated with inflectional morphology, markedness is both language-specific and context-specific. For example, plural number tends to be marked for most nouns, but it is unmarked for nouns that are always (or nearly always) plural, and the determination of which nouns fall into which category differs from language to language (see Van Langendonck, this volume, chapter 16, on the iconic relationship between formal and semantic marking). In Russian, plural nominal inflectional morphemes tend to be at least as long as or longer than singular morphemes, as we see in a typical example such as *dom-am* [house-DAT.PL] 'houses' versus *dom-u* [house-DAT.SG] 'house', where the plural desinence -am is longer than the singular-*u*. But for some nationalities (people thought of as groups), the plural forms are shorter, because the singular forms require a singulative infix *-in*: *angličan-am* [Englishman-DAT.PL] 'Englishmen' versus *angličan-in-u* [Englishman-SGL-DAT.SG] 'Englishman'. Thus, for ethnonyms, plural is often unmarked and has a shorter form (*-am*) than the singular (*-in-u*). In these examples, we observe an iconic relationship between markedness of form (in terms of the number of segments in a morpheme) and markedness of meaning (with plural suggesting more, except in the case where individuation must be forced and the situation is reversed). Van Langendonck (this volume, chapter 16) observes parallel iconic markedness relationships among forms expressing tense and mood. Iconic relations of proximity, length, and markedness of formal features in alignment with semantic features are frequently observed in the structure of paradigms (Bybee 1985: 4; Jakobson [1958] 1971).

4. THE LINGUISTIC CATEGORIES REPRESENTED BY INFLECTIONAL MORPHEMES

Inflectional categories are based on reifications of ubiquitous embodied experiences (see section 3.2 above). As we shall see in this section, metaphor and metonymy extend the range of these categories (for some examples, see Janda 2000; Janda and Clancy 2002). What constitutes the basis of the inflectional category 'person' is the experience of self versus other, elaborated in the context of communication to include self versus interlocutor versus third party; our understanding of 'number' is based on experiences of discrete objects, groups, and masses; and a variety of canonical positions and movements motivate the meanings of many cases. The Russian genitive case, for example, is a polysemy of four major semantic nodes that connote source, goal, whole (as opposed to part), and point of reference. These meanings are related to each other via reference to an overarching schema which describes the genitive referent as a salient item that yields focus of attention to something else which exists or maneuvers in its proximity (for examples and a brief overview of this semantic network, see Janda 2000). Though the following discussion may be partially applicable to all inflected languages, it is based primarily on Russian data (for extensive analysis of the polysemies of case and their extensions, see Janda 1993; Janda and Clancy 2002).

4.1. Metaphor

By far the most important source domain for metaphorical extension of inflectional categories is space, from which we move conceptually to a variety of target domains. A frequent target domain is TIME, and SPACE > TIME mappings are commonplace in the inflection of the world's languages (Haspelmath 1997). Times before, after, and during are routinely marked with the same morphology that describes positions in front of, behind, and in; there are many parallels of this type in most languages. The relative positions of physical objects and how they occupy space probably serve as the source domain for categories of tense and aspect as well, although there are certainly other factors, and more research needs to be done. Here is a sampling of other target domains understood via spatial metaphor in the case system of Russian: MOVEMENT TOWARD > PURPOSE (prepositions *v* and *na* + accusative mean both 'to' and 'for'); PATH > INSTRUMENT (the bare instrumental case can indicate both a path and an instrument—cf. English *way*, which can be a *way to go* and a *way to do something*); PROXIMITY > POSSESSION (preposition *u* + genitive means both 'near' and 'in the possession of'); MOVEMENT FROM > CAUSATION (preposition *ot* + genitive means both 'from' and 'because of'); LOCATION IN FRONT OF > MORAL/LEGAL OBLIGATION (preposition *pered* + instrumental means 'in front of' and 'before [the law/the court/God]'); LOCATION ABOVE > CONTROL (preposition *nad* + instrumental means 'over' in both domains); LOCATION BELOW > SUBORDINATION (preposition *pod* + instrumental means 'under' in both domains); and MOVEMENT > CHANGE IN STATES OF BEING (preposition *v* + accusative means 'into' in both domains). More generally, one cannot fail to notice the fact that the accusative case routinely marks both destinations and direct objects; direct objects can be thought of as grammatical destinations if we think of a transitive clause as depicting the flow of energy from subject to object. Other (nonspatial) source domains also exist: the Russian instrumental case can be used to identify a cause, an instance of INSTRUMENT > CAUSE metaphor. Number is commonly used as a source domain for social status, where plural number is used with singular reference to indicate politeness (an instance of MORE IS UP; see Lakoff and Johnson 1980; Keown 1999).

4.2. Metonymy

Metonymies linking end points with paths are frequent in inflectional morphology, where one can sometimes have a static location (end point) marked in the same way one marks a destination (most common with the accusative and instrumental cases in Russian). Another metonymy motivates the use of the dative case with verbs of communication, benefit, and harm, since the meanings of the associated verbs absorb the referents of the missing direct objects (i.e., these verbs can be thought of as meaning 'give a message to', 'give good to', 'give evil to'). More research needs to be done on metonymy in inflectional morphology.

5. THE NATURE OF PARADIGMS

Paradigms are the aggregates of inflectional morphemes that pertain to a given syntactic class of words (or subset thereof). Like the inflectional categories they stand for, the dimensions of paradigms are language-specific. Items that might seem essential from the experience of one language will often be different or missing in others. For example, most European languages make extensive use of infinitive forms in their syntax, but an areal feature of Balkan languages is the absence of an infinitive form in verbal paradigms.

Semantically, the paradigm is a collection of mutually exclusive values for a given inflectional category (or co-occurring categories), and the forms of a paradigm are typically mutually exclusive as well (meaning that only one inflectional morpheme in the paradigm can be present at a time). The grammatical meaning of any one value of a paradigm is at least partially determined by the other values in the paradigm—no true overlaps exist, though there is opportunity for alternatives (Janda 2002). So, for example, part of the meaning of plural is a contrast with singular, and third person conveys the message that first and second person are excluded. However, speaker's construal can select various strategies, such as recognizing the object of a verb as a resource for carrying out an activity (motivating the instrumental case in Russian in *krutit' rulem* [turn.INF steering wheel.INST] 'turn using a steering wheel') or as a destination for the energy of an activity (motivating the accusative case in Russian in *krutit' rul'* [turn.INF steering wheel.ACC] 'turn a steering wheel'). Although paradigms have no independent existence, since they are realized in conjunction with a whole set of words, they do have a life of their own, and each syntactic class will usually have at least one productive paradigm to accommodate new coinages and borrowings. For example, the *-ova-* suffix in Czech provides paradigm identity so that inflectional desinences can be attached to new verbs such as Czech *spelovat* 'spell' and *mixovat* 'mix'.

In an inflected language, inflected words do not occur without their inflectional morphemes. Even if a speaker is merely listing vocabulary items, each word will instantiate a value in its paradigm. The citation form represents a privileged value in the paradigm, for "not all forms of a paradigm have the same status" (Bybee 1985: 49). Usually the citation form also performs the role of a base form, serving both as the formal prototype for the remainder of the paradigm (starting from the base form it is easiest to describe all the other inflectional forms of a word) and as the semantic prototype, since it is the most autonomous form (Bybee 1985: 127). Talmy (2000a: chapters 5 and 6) suggests that the base form is also the one that is most likely to serve as Figure (rather than Ground) in constructions, or the form which can stand alone, which explains why typical choices of base forms are values such as nominative case, first-person singular (both are Figure), and infinitive (which can stand alone because it requires no agreement). The base form serves parallel purposes in terms of both form and meaning, further justifying respect for the form-meaning relationship, despite all the qualifications we made above.

At first glance, syncretic forms may appear problematic, since they fail to make some of the distinctions that structure a paradigm. However, this is merely a case of homophony. Parallel paradigms exist where the given forms are not syncretic, and in context a syncretic form has only one meaning; it never accesses more than one value in the paradigm at one time. Thus, in constructions where a genitive case is called for, Czech *plynu* 'gas' is genitive; in constructions where a dative is expected, it is dative; and if a locative case is appropriate, it is locative.

The formal ambiguity is always resolved to yield only one semantic expression. This situation is similar to the famous line drawings of the beauty/hag and rabbit/duck. The visual form of these images is ambiguous, yet the mind insists on accepting only one interpretation at any one time—you cannot see both versions at once.

Inflected languages will frequently tolerate a few lexical items that have no paradigm at all. These are typically borrowed words that have not been nativized into the morphophonemics of the syntactic class they belong to. These words lack the appropriate stem shape that would allow them to be combined with the inflectional morphemes of the language. This situation is often resolved by giving the word a derivational morpheme that will assign an appropriate paradigm. In the meanwhile, though, a word may remain undeclinable for decades, centuries, or possibly longer. Undeclinable words exemplify complete syncresis, where every form is the same regardless of the value of the inflectional category. Undeclinable words generally do not constitute a breach in the inflectional morphology of a language, but are instead indicative of the way in which inflection interacts with other phenomena of a language. Linguistic expression is so strong and so interdependent that context can usually supply enough information if a word in a construction lacks its morphology. The power of the inflectional category persists even when the morphemes are absent. We can see the direction of development in the Czech borrowing of *fine*: in the dictionaries, it is listed as an indeclinable adjective *fajn*, but Internet searches turn up thousands of hits for forms of *fajnový*, which is a declinable adjective created by attaching the suffix *-ov-* to the borrowed root, evidence that this word is on its way toward becoming nativized to the paradigms of Czech.

Paradigms can be defective, in which case one or more forms are missing for certain words. Usually such gaps are well-motivated on logical grounds (although the details of that logic might be language-specific). So, for example, verbs denoting weather phenomena like Czech *pršet* 'rain' tend to lack first- and second-person forms, and some modal and stative verbs like Czech *moci* 'be able' and *trvat* 'last' might not have imperative forms; nouns denoting masses and abstractions sometimes lack plurals. Often the missing forms are not really absent, but merely unused; given sufficiently unusual contexts, these forms occasionally make fleeting appearances.

6. INFLECTIONAL MORPHOLOGY IN DIACHRONY

We have already mentioned (in section 2.2) the apparently cyclical process of development and decay of inflection, via grammaticalization, affixation, and phonological erosion, a process that engages the entire structure of a language. At a more local level, we can examine the behavior of paradigms and their members and observe the forces of metaphor, prototypicality, and polysemy over time.

Historical linguists are very familiar with the fact that paradigms change and that paradigm change often seems motivated by the various parallels that exist within and across paradigms. It appears that successive generations of speakers perceive and use these parallels to make the inflectional patterns of their language more regular. There is no absolute pressure to do so, of course, since irregular inflections (particularly when associated with high-frequency words) often thrive for centuries. But when change does take place, it is not chaotic and proceeds in a direction that follows the logic of the paradigms in a language, which is why this type of change is referred to as "analogy" or "leveling" (or even "analogical leveling"). Analogy unifies the inputs of inflectional form and category, creating forms that are more similar, regular, and predictable, thus clarifying and strengthening the paradigm. It is also common to speak of analogical change as an example of abductive reasoning (Andersen 1973; Janda 1996).

The Slavic locative singular shows how analogy works to eliminate stem irregularities. The nominal locative singular inflectional morpheme consisted of -ě, a segment which in Late Common Slavic conditioned the palatalization of velars ($k > c$; $g > z$ or dz; $x > š$ or s). This meant that stems ending in velars displayed an alternation of the stem-final consonant in the locative singular, but all other stems did not have such alternations. In some languages (such as Czech and Polish), the stem alternations remain to this day. In other languages (such as Slovak and Russian), this alternation has been removed, so that the inflectional morpheme is simply added without any modification of the stem. The inputs for this analogy were the inflectional forms of various nouns with and without stem-final velar consonants. Analogy produced a new form with a velar consonant that remained unpalatalized even in the presence of the locative singular morpheme, making this form more like the other forms of the same word and more like the locative singular forms of words with other stem-final consonants. Late Common Slavic had a great variety of dative plural, instrumental plural, and locative plural forms for its nominal paradigms, but Russian selected the inflectional morphemes of one paradigm (the *a*-stem) as the prototype for all paradigms. The inputs contained all the stems and the selected morphemes; in the output, the selected morphemes were generalized to all paradigms. Sometimes the effects of prototypicality and analogy produce drastic results, such as the spread of the once marginal first-person singular -*m* morpheme (belonging to a paradigm used by only five verbs) to many, and in some cases all, verbs in the lexicon of several Slavic languages. Compatibilities between the -*m* morpheme and the remainder of the verbal paradigm were palpably better than those enjoyed by the original first-person singular morpheme, motivating the recognition of -*m* (and the resulting preservation of stem shape) as prototypical; analogy then created thousands of new forms, adjusting the paradigm accordingly (for details, see Janda 1996).

Inflectional morphology experiences changes in meaning over time as well. Morphemes stranded due to paradigm or category loss are sometimes retained as semantic wild cards, providing the formal means for new semantic distinctions. In some Slavic languages the remnants of the collapsed short *u*-stem nominal paradigm were recruited to make new distinctions along the animacy hierarchy, and former dual forms also played a part in creating distinctions to signal virility (Janda 1996, 1999).

Suppletion results from the merger of forms from two or more paradigms motivated by a recognition of these items as parts of a semantic whole. For example, the suppletive Russian paradigm for *year* combines forms of the stem *god* 'year' with forms of the stem *let-* 'summer'. Inflectional splitting also occurs when the meanings of one or more forms of a paradigm become disassociated from one another. Inflectional splitting is in progress for words denoting certain time periods in Russian, where, for example, most dictionaries now list the instrumental singular form *letom* 'summer' as an adverb meaning 'in the summer time'. Czech presents an extreme split of the formally defective paradigm that should be headed by the missing infinitive **pojít*: the present-tense forms *půjdu půjdeš*, and so on mean 'depart, leave on foot'; the imperative forms *pojd'*, *pojd'te* mean 'come'; and the past-tense forms *pošel*, *pošla*, and so on are a vulgar way to express 'die'.

In diachrony we see the same forces at work that hold synchronic inflectional systems together, in particular polysemy, the structure of the radial category, and metaphor. This historical perspective gives further compelling evidence that inflectional categories are not inborn, but rather evolve in harmony with human perceptual and conceptual experience.

7. FUTURE DIRECTIONS FOR RESEARCH

In recent years, there has been strong interest in Construction Grammar (see Croft, this volume, chapter 18) and the semantics of syntax. Given the role that inflectional morphology plays in mediating the relationships between lexemes and the constructions they inhabit, this should lead to closer examination of the grammatical meanings expressed by inflectional morphemes. Talmy's (2000a, 2000b) proposed inventory of possible categories that might be expressed by closed-class morphemes amounts to a challenge: we need to verify this inventory against the data of many languages. We should also seek to prove whether a subset of these categories is universal. It is possible that universality in terms of specific categories cannot be posited, but that we should follow Croft's (2001) lead and explore the conceptual spaces that categories are mapped onto, in search of focal areas in the semantic space of grammar (a more plausible source of "universals") and the various patterns of expression that are specific to each language.

REFERENCES

Andersen, Henning. 1973. Abductive and deductive change. *Language* 49: 765–93.

Bybee, Joan L. 1985. *Morphology: A study of the relation between meaning and form*. Amsterdam: John Benjamins.

Croft, William. 2001. *Radical construction grammar: Syntactic theory in typological perspective*. Oxford: Oxford University Press.

Dirven, René, and Marjolijn Verspoor. 1998. *Cognitive exploration of language and linguistics*. Amsterdam: John Benjamins. (2nd ed., 2004)

Fauconnier, Gilles, and Mark Turner. 2002. *The way we think*: Conceptual blending and the mind's hidden complexities. New York: Basic Books.

Haspelmath, Martin. 1997. *From space to time: Temporal adverbials in the world's languages*. Munich: Lincom Europa.

Hopper, Paul J., and Elizabeth Closs Traugott. 1993. *Grammaticalization*. Cambridge: Cambridge University Press. (2nd ed., 2003)

Jakobson, Roman O. [1958] 1971. Morfologičeskie nabljudenija nad slavjanskim skloneniem [Morphological observations on Slavic declension]. In Roman O. Jakobson, *Selected writings* 2: 154–83. The Hague: Mouton.

Jakobson, Roman O. [1959] 1971. Boas' view of grammatical meaning. In Roman O. Jakobson, *Selected writings* 2: 489–96. The Hague: Mouton.

Janda, Laura A. 1993. *A geography of case semantics: The Czech dative and the Russian instrumental*. Berlin: Mouton de Gruyter.

Janda, Laura A. 1995. Unpacking markedness. In Eugene H. Casad, ed., *Linguistics in the Redwoods: The expansion of a new paradigm in linguistics* 207–33. Berlin: Mouton de Gruyter.

Janda, Laura A. 1996. *Back from the brink: A study of how relic forms in language serve as source material for analogical extension*. Munich: Lincom Europa.

Janda, Laura A. 1999. Whence virility? The rise of a new gender distinction in the history of Slavic. In Margaret H. Mills, ed., *Slavic gender linguistics* 201–28. Amsterdam: John Benjamins.

Janda, Laura A. 2000. Cognitive linguistics. Position paper for the SLING2K workshop, February 2000. http://www.indiana.edu/~slavconf/SLING2K/pospapers.html (accessed Nov. 14, 2003).

Janda, Laura A. 2002. Cognitive hot spots in the Russian case system. In Michael Shapiro, ed., *Peircean semiotics: The state of the art*. 165–88. New York: Berghahn Books.

Janda, Laura A., and Steven J. Clancy. 2002. *The case book for Russian*. Bloomington, IN: Slavica.

Janda, Laura A., and Charles E. Townsend. 2000. *Czech*. Languages of the World: Materials, no. 125. Munich: Lincom Europa.

Keown, Anne. 1999. Polite pronouns in Russian and Czech: Metaphorical motivations for their origin and usage. MA thesis, University of North Carolina, Chapel Hill.

Lakoff, George. 1987. *Women, fire, and dangerous things: What categories reveal about the mind*. Chicago: University of Chicago Press.

Lakoff, George, and Mark Johnson. 1980. *Metaphors we live by*. Chicago: University of Chicago Press.

Langacker, Ronald W. 1987. *Foundations of cognitive grammar*. Vol. 1, *Theoretical prerequisites*. Stanford, CA: Stanford University Press.

Langacker, Ronald W. 1991. *Foundations of cognitive grammar.* Vol. 2, *Descriptive application.* Stanford, CA: Stanford University Press.

Meillet, Antoine. [1912] 1958. L'évolution des formes grammaticales. In Antoine Meillet, *Linguistique historique et linguistique générale* 130–48. Paris: Champion. (First published in *Scientia (Rivista di Scienzia)* 12, no. 26, 384–400.)

Plungian, Vladimir A. 2000. *Obščaja morfologija: Vvedenie v problematiku* [General morphology: Introduction to the topic]. Moscow: Editorial URSS.

Slobin, Dan I. 1997. The origins of grammaticizable notions: Beyond the individual mind. In Dan I. Slobin, ed., *The crosslinguistic study of language acquisition*, vol. 5, *Expanding the contexts* 265–323. Mahwah, NJ: Lawrence Erlbaum.

Talmy, Leonard. 1985. Lexicalization patterns: Semantic structure in lexical forms. In Timothy Shopen, ed., *Language typology and semantic description*, vol. 3, *Grammatical categories and the lexicon* 57–149. Cambridge: Cambridge University Press.

Talmy, Leonard. 1996. Fictive motion in language and "ception." In Paul Bloom, Mary A. Peterson, Lynn Nadel, and Merril F. Garrett, eds., *Language and space* 211–76. Cambridge, MA: MIT Press.

Talmy, Leonard. 2000a. *Toward a cognitive semantics.* Vol. 1, *Concept structuring systems.* Cambridge, MA: MIT Press.

Talmy, Leonard. 2000b. *Toward a cognitive semantics.* Vol. 2, *Typology and process in concept structuring.* Cambridge, MA: MIT Press.

CHAPTER 25

WORD-FORMATION

FRIEDRICH UNGERER

1. INTRODUCTION

Word-formation is one of those linguistic terms that may be unsatisfactory on a more theoretical level, but that are immensely useful when one tries to survey processes of extending the lexicon. Loosely defined as "creating new words from existing words,"[1] word-formation ranges from prefixation and suffixation (where it overlaps with inflectional morphology in the use of bound morphemes; see Janda, this volume, chapter 24) to processes not even reflected in the phonological form of the item involved (e.g., conversion); there, word-formation borders on purely semantic processes of metaphor and metonymy (Lipka 2002: 108–9). Between these two extremes may be placed the many ways in which words can be combined, fused, and condensed (as in compounds, lexical blends, back-formations, clippings, and acronyms). Since English is one of the languages that makes use of all these processes, mostly English examples will be chosen for illustrative purposes, but it should be kept in mind that some of the processes, in particular affixation, are much more widespread and more differentiated in other languages.

However, the relative sparseness of affixal processes in English has not kept structuralist linguistics from approaching English word-formation within the framework of a morphological analysis focused on the segmentation of free and bound morphemes (with the emphasis on the latter), adding zero forms to include conversion (*dirty* adj. → *dirty* verb), back-derivation (*baby-sitt(er)* n. + Ø → *baby-sit* verb) and bahuvrihi compounds (*laptop* + Ø → *laptop computer*) and only grudgingly admitting that blends, acronyms, and other "irregular forms" did not really lend themselves to this kind of interpretation. The relationship between the constituent elements of word-formation items (i.e., the items that result from word-formation processes) was first interpreted as a hierarchy of immediate constituents based on a modifier-head relationship; later, underlying syntactic structures were used to explain derivatives, especially compounds, and when this method was found insufficient for many noun-noun compounds, semantic argument structure was introduced as an analytical tool (e.g., in Levi 1978).

Another long-standing aim of word-formation research has been the establishment of a set of rules and constraints to explain productivity of word-formation patterns (Bauer 2001); in addition, attention has been attracted by the processual aspects of institutionalization and lexicalization (Bauer 1983: chapter 3; Quirk et al. 1985: 1522–29; Lipka 2002: 6, 110–14). The "rules and constraints" approach was primarily an offspring of Transformational Grammar; but far from being restricted to formal approaches, it permeated the discussion of basic semantic patterns of composition (Levi 1978) and productive argument constellations for -er-derivations (Rappaport and Levin 1992), to name just a few examples, and reemerged in more recent onomasiological approaches (Stekauer 1998). Although the general trend over the years thus favored semantic analysis, it remained safely tied to grammatical word classes and a syntactically oriented argument structure. No wonder, it was difficult to find a place for lexical blends and acronyms in such a framework or to integrate convincing explanations for concepts such as institutionalization or lexicalization.

If this is an acceptable account of the general research situation, it should be no surprise that Cognitive Linguistics has the potential to stimulate word-formation research. Indeed, it can provide both the theoretical background and the empirical tools to complete a process that had already been set going: the semanticization of word-formation analysis. Starting from the axiom of the centrality of meaning (Langacker 1987: 12), cognitive linguists will treat all aspects of word-formation as meaningful: the concepts expressed by word-formation items and their constituents (whether they enjoy the status of morphemes or not), the structural patterns underlying derivatives and the restrictions imposed on them, and finally the processual aspects of word-formation (such as lexicalization). On the empirical level, cognitive analysis has developed ways of describing lexical concepts in terms of schemas, prototypes, and radial categories, including metonymic and metaphorical extensions, of analyzing prepositions in terms of Figure/Ground alignment, and of explaining argument structures as EVENT schemas. Linguistic processes have been described as conceptual fusion, their iconic aspects as a matter of form-meaning isomorphism. All these approaches have been used to integrate word-formation into concepts like Cognitive Grammar, Conceptual Blending, and form-meaning iconicity or, on a more specific level, to provide more comprehensive and consistent descriptions of individual word-formation phenomena.

2. General Aspects

2.1. Word-Formation in Cognitive Grammar

Since Cognitive Grammar, as developed by Langacker, does not distinguish between lexical and grammatical units in the traditional sense of the term, word-formation is regarded as part of a unified grammatical description, and this shows up with respect to categorization, Figure/Ground alignment, and accommodation.

Word-Formation as Semantic Extension

Just like additional meanings of simplex lexical items, word-formation items can be understood as encoding extensions, based on category judgments, from a profiled linguistic unit. The only difference between simplex and word-formation items is that in the latter, additional meaningful components, both lexical items and affixes, are added. This is illustrated in figure 25.1, which is based on Langacker's notation and on some of his examples (Langacker 1987: 374–83, 451) complemented by additional ones.

Figure 25.1 shows that the degree of morphological complexity is not decisive for the relationship of semantic extension from an assumed prototype unit (here TREE), but that there may be compounds that are semantically closer to the prototype than some simplex extensions, as for instance *apple tree* compared with *tree* in the metaphorical sense of 'family tree'.

Word-Formation Items and Figure/Ground Alignment

Although the Figure/Ground contrast (see Schmid, this volume, chapter 5) is employed at all levels of categorization, an important application concerns the level of words or linguistic units and their interaction with other linguistic units (Langacker's term is valence relation). Figure and Ground, here called trajector and landmark, are not only embodied in lexical items such as verbs or prepositions, but also in affixes like the *-er* suffix.[2] Figure 25.2 shows how trajector and landmark are involved in creating the prepositional phrase *above the table* and the *-er* derivation *climber*.

In figure 25.2a, the prepositional relation is characterized by the contrast between the trajector, which is positioned in the upper section, and the yet unspecified landmark, which is placed below. Combining the prepositional concept with a lexical concept like 'table' provides the specification of the landmark and establishes the composite structure, documented in the top box (see Svorou, this volume, chapter 28). The *-er* suffix (figure 25.2b) also consists of a trajector and an unspecified landmark, but the meaning of the suffix is vaguer than the prepositional meaning and the processing is complicated by the fact that lexical concepts like CLIMB already contain a complex trajector-landmark configuration spread over time (indicated by the changing position of the trajector).

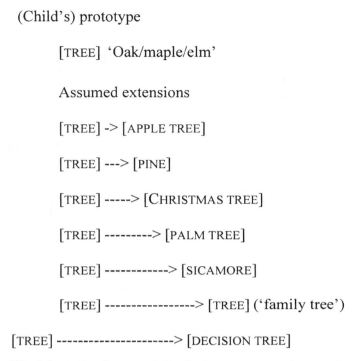

(Child's) prototype

[TREE] 'Oak/maple/elm'

Assumed extensions

[TREE] -> [APPLE TREE]

[TREE] ---> [PINE]

[TREE] -----> [CHRISTMAS TREE]

[TREE] ---------> [PALM TREE]

[TREE] ------------> [SICAMORE]

[TREE] ----------------> [TREE] ('family tree')

[TREE] --------------------> [DECISION TREE]

Figure 25.1. Word-formation items and simplex items as semantic extensions (based on Langacker's notation; length of arrows indicates relative distance from prototype)

This influences the integration of the two constituent units, which results in fusing the affix concept with the verbal concept, but does not prevent treating derivation and prepositional phrase in a parallel fashion (see figure 25.2b, top box).

Word-Formation, Composite Structures, and Accommodation

The process of *-er* derivation is just one instance of the many parallels between word-formation items and phrases emerging from Langacker's approach. Another example is compounds that can be compared with adjective-noun combinations. Figure 25.3 makes it clear that the same schema is applicable both to modifier-head phrases and compounds.

The parallels are not only a matter of structure in the more conventional sense, but include the semantic adjustment of the components and the addition of conceptual content in the composite item. This is indicated through the element X in the formula for the composite item in the schematic boxes on the left of figures 25.3a and 25.3b. The "accommodation" of the components, as Langacker (1987: 75–76) calls this semantic process, may be limited in the case of *tall tree*, where only a certain semantic adjustment of the prototypical meaning of *tall* as 'height of human beings' is required. Yet with regard to *Christmas tree*, it is obvious that a great deal of additional information, mostly of an encyclopedic kind, has to be added to permit a proper conceptualization of the item compared with the

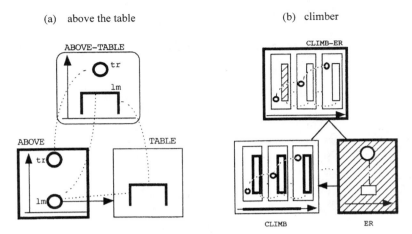

Figure 25.2. Trajector and landmark in a prepositional phrase and an -*er* derivation (from Langacker 1990: 25, figure 12a, and Langacker 1987: 311, figure 8.8, excerpt)

prototypical notion of 'tree'. Postulating the necessity of accommodation for compounding and other word-formation processes implies a rejection of full compositionality, which means that the components of word-formation items can no longer be understood as building blocks of the composite structure. Instead, Langacker (1987: 452, 461) proposes a scaffolding metaphor to indicate that the components only trigger off or motivate the compounds, supply a certain amount of conceptual assistance, but are discarded when the compound is fully entrenched by frequent activation.[3]

Compositionality and Analyzability

Yet even the partial compositionality to which Langacker admits, and which is mirrored in the scaffolding metaphor, requires a more fine-grained analysis. While compositionality can be claimed to denote an objective relationship between the composite structure and its components, analyzability introduces the psychological perspective of the hearer (or reader). Composite structures, Langacker (1987: 457) explains, may, but need not be, analyzed by the hearer in the comprehension process, and we cannot be sure to what extent this process is carried out consciously or unconsciously. For instance, *swimmer*, *mixer*, and *complainer* are derivatives suggesting a strong awareness of the constituents while, barring exceptions, the compositionality of *computer*, *propeller*, and *ruler* is not normally realized by the language user (Langacker 1987: 297).

Schematicity

So far, word-formation has been mainly approached from the angle of semantic extension and composite structures. However, Cognitive Linguistics offers an alternative, but complementary, view in terms of schematicity. As explained in detail

(a) tall tree

(b) Christmas tree

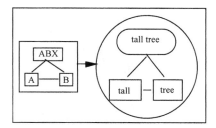
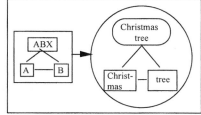

Figure 25.3. Relationship of word-formation items to semantic extension of prototypes and integration into composite structures in Langacker's system (based on Langacker's diagrammatic representation; Langacker 1987: 451, figure 12.2)

by Tuggy (this volume, chapter 4), the notion of schema (in Langacker's definition) offers a flexible way of generalization that is not understood as a fixed a priori rule, but takes account of salience based on frequency of use (see Schmid, this volume, chapter 5); "schemas are essentially routinized, or cognitively entrenched, patterns of experience" (Kemmer 2003: 78). In the lexical sphere, this is reflected in the networks in which both schematic 'superordinate' schemas and prototypes and extensions combine easily, as in figure 25.4. As shown by the boxes in bold, the salient elements of the network are not the most general schemas (ENTITY, THING), but the lower level schemas (e.g., PLANT) and the prototype (TREE).

The notion of schema becomes even more helpful when, leaving lexical networks, one looks at the "rules" (of whatever status) that have been postulated to describe compositional and derivational processes, not to mention back-formation, blending, and acronyming, and considers how all these rules are notoriously jeopardized by a host of exceptions. Understandably, then, the notion of schema has—in different ways—been applied to various word-formation phenomena, to the analysis of compounds (see section 3.4.) as well as the explanation of blends (see section 3.5.), while other phenomena still await "schematic" treatment. Furthermore, Lakoff's concept of image schemas ("basic" schemas based on bodily experience such a UP-DOWN, PART-WHOLE, CONTAINER, PATH) and EVENT schemas (first used by Talmy 1991) have been influential; image schemas have left their mark on the cognitive analysis of prefixation (see section 3.3), and EVENT schemas on the treatment of conversion (see section 3.2).

2.2. Word-Formation and Conceptual Blending

Although Tuggy (this volume, chapter 4) regards conceptual blending as still another variant of schematicity, it is preferable to treat it as a phenomenon in its own right, as the most successful cognitive attempt so far to come to terms with the online processing aspect of conceptualization. Most word-formation processes

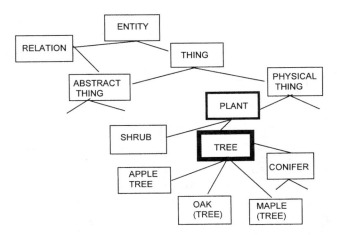

Figure 25.4. Lexical network combining schemas (ENTITY, THING, PLANT, etc.), prototype (here: TREE), and compound extensions (*apple tree*, etc.)

involve semantic combination or fusion, and this qualifies them for an analysis in terms of conceptual blending as proposed by Fauconnier and Turner (this volume, chapters 14 and 15, resp.), even if the conceptual blending analysis has taken its time to discover lexical blending and acronym formation (but see section 3.5 below)

In particular, conceptual blending seems well suited to elucidate processes like lexicalization, perhaps even more convincingly than Langacker's notion of accommodation, as shown in figure 25.5 for the compound *wheelchair*.[4]

While the two input spaces reflect the conceptual content of the two counterparts (the constituents of the compound), the blended space contains the emergent structure of the compound, which is not provided by the two input spaces alone, but which, according to Fauconnier and Turner (2002: 48–49) involves altogether three types of conceptual process: composition, completion, and elaboration. While composition refers to the contributions made by the projections from the two inputs, completion is concerned with the addition of background knowledge (here represented by the notions of 'invalid', 'hospital', 'engine'), and this permits the emergence of a new conceptual structure (indicated by the square within the blended space). Finally, elaboration may be envisaged as a test of the correctness and consistency of the conceptual content of the blended space.

2.3. Word-formation and Form-Meaning Iconicity

One aspect that is not in the foreground of Langacker's and Fauconnier's considerations is the iconic relationship between phonological form (including a form's graphic shape) and meaning (Langacker's phonological and semantic phonological poles). The link between the two is taken for granted, as in many traditional accounts, and this is probably quite acceptable for one-word (lexical) schemas, but

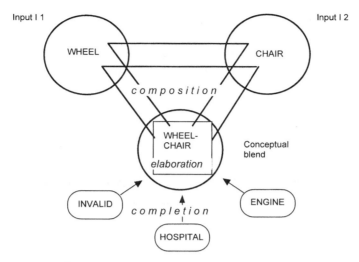

Figure 25.5. Compounding as conceptual blending process: Example *wheelchair* (based on Fauconnier 1997: 151)

not necessarily for word-formation items, in which the form-meaning relationship is systematically violated. Coupled with this item-related isomorphism is a second type of iconicity, which is process-related in the sense that an item's phonological form mirrors a particular word-formation process. While lexical blending can be seen as the word-formation enactment of conceptual blending (see section 2.2) and compounding as a clustering of two (or more) concepts, acronyming involves a reduction of conceptual content, and these processes of fusion or accumulation and reduction are duly reflected in the phonological (and graphic) shape of the items.

As I showed in Ungerer (1999), the interaction of these two types of iconicity is not always beneficial for the word-formation process. As for compounds, the parallelism of two forms and two concepts is only achieved for the minority of fairly compositional, analyzable compounds (*apple juice, silk jacket*). For compounds that have undergone conceptual accommodation and expansion, the ensuing asymmetry between two forms and multiple meanings can only be resolved if full entrenchment (or lexicalization) is achieved because the word form is no longer analyzed (as probably in *holiday*) or if the complex phonological form is reduced to a simplex form again (*paper* for *newspaper*).

The situation for word-formation blends like *skyjacking, stagflation,* or *infotainment* is the reverse, but it is not satisfactory either. Given the schematic license (see section 3.5 below), the fusion is impressively reflected in the phonological and graphic form, which thus provides an example of processual iconicity; yet one cannot be sure that a simultaneous, complete, and entrenched fusion takes place on the meaning side resulting in a new isomorphic form-meaning relationship. With regard to acronyms, the iconic reduction mirrored in chains of initial letters of words is convincing, but its effect can be devastating and cause a complete breakdown of the isomorphic form-meaning link. This is one of the reasons why acronyms are often remodeled on existing items with an identical phonological form and a related meaning; the intention is to use these "prop words" and their attested form-meaning isomorphism to promote the entrenchment of the acronym.

3. Description of Individual Word-Formation Phenomena

It is not surprising to find that more specific cognitive studies of derivation and composition have concentrated on the areas most widely discussed in traditional word-formation research: prefixation, -er suffixation, conversion or zero derivation, and noun-noun compounding. To sketch the possibilities—and hopefully the superiority—of the cognitive view, each of these domains will be represented by two different approaches. In addition, lexical blending will be discussed because its cognitive treatment opens up interesting research lines.

3.1. Prefixation, Contrast, and Diminutives

The fact that prefixation in English lends itself to an interpretation in terms of contrastivity has stimulated several differing cognitive approaches toward prefixation.

Profiling Contrast

Although English prefixes may reflect different semantic concepts, Schmid (2005: 162–65) claims that they have one thing in common: they profile contrast, and thus express a specific interpretation of the basic Figure/Ground distinction. This notion of contrast, of being 'different from X', can take on various guises depending on the semantic specification of the prefix, as shown in table 25.1, where the traditional semantic classification of prefixes is interpreted in terms of the notion 'contrast'.

The dominant role of "contrast" is supported by gaps in the productivity of prefixation. Such gaps can be observed with verbs that do not permit contrast (*unlive, *unsit, *unsleep, *unplay), as well as with most concrete nouns, which, apart from gender-sensitive pairs like man and woman, do not naturally invite semantic opposition. Adjectives, according to Schmid, are characterized by a one-dimensional semantic structure which is particularly well suited for the establishment of contrast, and they therefore feature prominently in prefixation.[5]

Table 25.1. Prefixes and types of contrast (based on Schmid 2005: 162–65)

Prefix	Type of Contrast (based on the Figure/Ground distinction)	Examples
Negative prefixes *un-, in-*	different from X	*unhappy, uneven*
Reversative prefixes *un-, dis-*	different direction from	*unwrap, disappear*
Locative prefixes *extra-, intra-*	not outside, but inside X	*extracellular, intramural*
Temporal prefixes *pre-, post-* *re-*	not during or after, but before X X again, in contrast to expectation	*prewar, postwar* *rebuild, reopen*
Prefixes of quantity (degree and number) *ultra-, sub-, super-*	more than the norm for X, less than the norm for X	*ultraright,??*
Prefixes of attitude *pro-, contra-, ounter-*	pro X, not anti X, etc.	*pro-Palestinian, counterproductive*

Contrastivity as a Complex Category

Although he is in agreement with Schmid on the significance of "contrast" for prefixation, Mettinger (1994, 1996) does not regard contrastivity as a unified cognitive principle, but as a complex category rooted in several image schemas. As for adjectives prefixed with *un-*, Mettinger holds that they involve two image schemas, the SCALE schema for the prefixation of polar adjectives (*unimportant, uncertain, unhappy*) and the CONTAINER schema for the contradictorily negated adjectives (*untrue* vs. *true*). Following Taylor's (1992) interpretation of polar adjectives, Mettinger interprets the *-un* prefix as encoding the relation between a thing serving as trajector and a scale serving as landmark scale, whereby the trajector is positioned on the landmark scale below the assumed norm (see figure 25.6a). For contradictorily negated adjectives, the container functions as landmark and the trajector is placed outside the landmark; the *un-* predication is constituted by the relation between the "extraposed" trajector and the landmark (see figure 25.6b).[6]

Prefixation, diminutives, and Underlying Idealized Cognitive Models

The reason why diminutives are treated together with prefixes is that they can best be understood if they are compared with scaling-down prefixes of degree creating a contrast, such as *maxi-* or *mini-*. As such, the difference between *kitchenette*

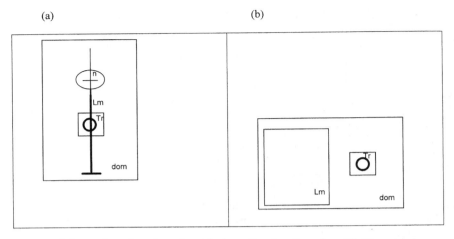

Figure 25.6. Schema-based explanation of *un*-prefixation (based on Mettinger 1994: 22, 24)

and *mini-kitchen* is that while in both cases the referents contain a scaling-down element, the diminutive *kitchenette* evokes positive emotional associations, but *mini-kitchen* does not necessarily do so (Ungerer 2002: 545–46). This evaluative quality of diminutives has been observed for a number of languages in which diminutives are more widespread than in English, for instance for Italian and German diminutives (Dressler and Barbaresi 1994), for Dutch suffixations with *-kje* and *-tje* (Bakema, Defour, and Geeraerts 1993), and for Spanish suffixations with *-ito* and *-illo* (Santibanez-Saenz 1999). The latter approach is particularly interesting from a cognitive angle as an attempt, first undertaken by Ruiz de Mendoza Ibáñez (2000) and developed by Santibanez-Saenz, to explain diminutives as an instance of conceptual fusion of three Idealized Cognitive Models (ICMs): the ICM of 'size' (which is responsible for scaling-up and scaling-down prefixation) and the ICMs of 'control' and 'cost-benefit'. This fusion yields two superficially contradictory corollaries, which can explain the existence of affectionate and pejorative meanings observed with the Spanish diminutives *-ito* and *-illo*, respectively:

a. Small entities are usually manageable; as a result, they may be perceived as likeable.
b. Small entities are usually innocuous and unimportant and may be easily ignored; as a result, they may be perceived as unpleasant.
   (Ruiz de Mendoza Ibáñez, in Santibanez-Saenz 1999: 176)

3.2. *-er* Suffixation

Of all English suffixes, *-er* has no doubt attracted most attention because of its frequency and versatility of meaning and use.

The Radial Category Approach

This approach, as pursued by Panther and Thornburg (2001), takes up the methods used successfully in describing polysemous lexical concepts in terms of protoypes, metonymic and metaphorical processes (Lindner 1981; Lakoff 1987; Rudzka-Ostyn 1985; Brugman 1981) and transfers them to *-er* derivation. In their analysis of *-er*, Panther and Thornburg start, rather than from a simple prototype concept, from a "basic EVENT schema" (or prototypical "scenario," in their terminology) and then make use of direct, metonymic, and metaphorical extensions to develop a radial category (or schematic network in Langacker's terminology); they thus explicitly transcend the word class barriers that hamper traditional accounts of *-er* derivation.

As illustrated in figure 25.7, the central sense reflects the *nomina agentis* notion of a primary participant intentionally acting on a directly affected or effected secondary participant.

The "central sense" takes "habitual occupational performance" as a starting point (as in verb-based *teacher*, *baker*, or *actor*); furthermore, it includes cases in which other elements of the prototypical scenario are metonymically expressed by nominal base concepts—for example, by the patient role (as in *hatter* 'someone who creates hats'), by the instrument role (as in *driftnetter* 'someone using a certain type of net in fishing'), or by the setting, such as that of the occupation (as in *Senator*). At varying distances from this prototypical scenario are five types of extensions, the first two sharing agentivity, but replacing habitualness by characteristic engagement (*runner*, *snorer*, or less dynamically, *owner*) or action-oriented disposition (*left-hander*, *hetero-sexer*, *hardliner*). The remaining extensions are either tied to habitualness in the sense of exhibiting an enduring attribute (*widower*, *six-footer*, *murderer*) or—somewhat more distant—try to integrate instances of context-dependent actions (*caller*, *keynoter*, *thanker*). A further metaphorical extension links animal and plant concepts (*retriever*, *creamer*) and certain object concepts (*gas-guzzler*, *sky-scraper*) to the scenario by making use of the personification metaphor (NONHUMANS ARE HUMANS).

Banking on the conceptual closenesss of instruments and agents, the prototypical scenario for nominals with human referents is complemented by an "instrument scenario," complete with verbal base and metonymic nonverbal base variants (as in *can-opener* and *freighter*, *whaler*, respectively), as well as extensions which try to integrate *-er*-formations based on lexical items denoting articles of clothing (*sweater*, *pedal-pushers*); locations (*diner* 'dining-car'), and even patients (*broiler* 'chicken', *reader* 'collection of texts').

The third large component of this radial category is made up of *-er*-formations expressing events (such as *thriller*, *stomach churner*, *brain-teaser*, etc.), which are explained as metaphorical extensions of the agent and instrument scenarios, respectively, based on the reification metaphor (EVENTS ARE OBJECTS). An interesting aspect of Panther and Thornburg's approach is that they establish an intermediate category of "*-er* Gestalts" to account for borderline cases between genuine *-er*

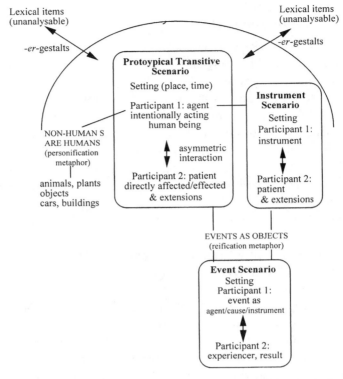

Figure 25.7. The major categories of *-er* formation (compiled from Panther and Thornburg 2001, simplified)

derivatives and unanalyzable lexicalized items (*plumber, tailor, trousers, hammer*) (2001: 189).

While Panther and Thornburg's approach is synchronic, it does make use of diachronic evidence in the selection of the central sense, and its radial extensions can be seen as possible paths along which the diversification of the *-er*-formations may have developed and should therefore be submitted to empirical diachronic verification. A weakness of this model is its limited predictive force. Although Panther and Thornburg claim that productivity decreases as one moves away from the central sense, this is no more than a rule of the thumb and is not necessarily borne out by a comparison of more central and more marginal subcategories.

The Cognitive/Pragmatic Constraints Approach

Compared with Panther and Thornburg, who introduce their basic scenarios without much reference to traditional argument-structure analysis, Ryder's (1999) study springs from detailed criticism of this approach, in particular of Rappaport and Levin's (1992) interpretation.[7] While admitting the substantial achievements of argument-structure analysis, Ryder (1999) claims that it is not comprehensive enough to cope with the multiplicity of *-er* derivations, because the only thing that an

Table 25.2. Cognitive/pragmatic constraints on the formation of -*er* derivatives (based on Ryder 1999)

RESTRICTIONS ACTING ON THE BASE CONCEPT OF -*ER* DERIVATES

1. Bases must have few, preferably only a single event schema (a condition most easily met by action verbs).
2. Event schemas must be capable of being applied to durative and habitual actions.
3. Events schemas must be specific (e.g., supported by verbs describing specific actions or nouns and adjectives providing a specific context).
4. Event schemas must be highly entrenched.

RESTRICTIONS ACTING ON THE TARGET CONCEPTS OF THE -*ER* DERIVATIVES

5. Target concepts and their referents must be salient.
6. Target concepts and their referents must be identifiable.

-*er* suffix reliably indicates in present-day English is "that the derivative is a noun" (278), without restricting the underlying word class, let alone specific argument patterns, however dominant some of them may be. While this generalization is easily captured as a high level schema in Langacker's system (see figure 25.2b), it is obviously not satisfactory as a differentiating explanation. This is why Ryder suggests two kinds of constraints: restrictions acting on the base of the -*er* items and restrictions acting on the referent of the derivative (the target concept); see table 25.2.

As far as the first two constraints of table 25.2 are concerned, Ryder's proposal is close to the traditional notion that, prototypically, -*er* forms are derived from actions verbs with agentive or instrumental subjects which are also capable of rendering the durativity required by nominalizations. Yet Ryder differs in that she does not attempt to pin down -*er* derivation to specific argument patterns (agents, certain kinds of instruments), and this permits the inclusion of -*er* forms reflecting an underlying locative, patient, or circumstantial relation (as in *diner* 'dining car', *scratcher* 'a lottery ticket that is scratched', or clothing items like *rompers* and *sleepers*; Ryder 1999: 270). The third constraint is related to Ryder's bottom-up approach to noun-noun compounds discussed below (section 3.4), in that it assigns priority to specific rather than general EVENT schemas. This restriction explains, for instance, why -*er* forms like *doer* and *maker* are rare due to the vagueness of the underlying EVENT schemas, but become quite acceptable when restricted by a noun or numeral, as in *dress-maker*, *evil-doer*, or *six-footer* (Ryder 1999: 281).

With the last three constraints, Ryder moves from the analysis of the semantic structure into the domain of psychological parameters of entrenchment (applied to base concepts), salience, and, as a kind of precondition of salience, identifiability (both applied to the target concept and its referent). While the first parameter (salience) requires little comment (although it may have to be supported by semantic frequency counts), salience and identifiability of the target concept are particularly important where a less typical underlying relationship overrides agent or instrumental relationships. In this respect, consider *roaster*, which is nowadays understood to express the patient relationship of 'roasted chicken' rather than an instrumental device used for roasting, while the agentive reading 'a person habitually engaged in roasting meat' is practically excluded (Ryder 1999: 289). Ryder's claim that her account integrates -*er* forms with nonverbal bases is not all that convincing considering that it is only supported by a few explanatory remarks (Ryder 1999: 290) and an appendix of only roughly classified material. What is missing is a systematic link between underlying nouns and adjectives and EVENT schemas that meets her own constraints of action and durativity. In this sense, Ryder does not take the issue of productivity constraints any further than Panther and Thornburg do.

3.3. Conversion

Conversion and Figure/Ground Alignment

The fact that most conversions involve a verbal processual structure (either as source or target) suggests a description in terms of Figure and Ground or trajector and landmark spread over time, an idea taken up by Twardzisz (1997). For verb-noun conversion, his interpretation is very much in line with Langacker's explanation of -*er* derivation (see figure 25.2b). The verbal concept CHEAT is combined with the schematic nominalizing morpheme NR (for nominalizer) to create the agent noun *cheat* (Twardsisz 1997: 130). The interpretation proposed for noun-verb conversions is more original. Here, Twardzisz assumes that the concept underlying the converted noun may be added, as a "secondary" landmark, to the (clausal) processual relationship between trajector and primary landmark. As illustrated in figure 25.8, the secondary landmark "interferes" with the processual relationship between trajector and primary landmark, thus affecting a change of meaning. For example, the secondary landmark 'salt' is added to the processual relationship between the trajector 'Peter' and primary landmark 'soup', as lexicalized in *Peter treated the soup in some way*, which then assumes the meaning *Peter salted the soup*.

Doubtless, Langacker's framework is ingeniously extended in Twardzisz's approach to cover an important domain of word-formation. However, there remains a gap between his fairly general and abstract application of the trajector-landmark contrast and his very concrete observations concerning examples from individual domains like food, tools, animals, and human occupations: it is only at this more specific level that Twardzisz addresses and explains questions of productivity, mainly in terms of entrenchment. What is missing is a link with the more traditional explanation based on semantic roles, as supplied by Dirven (1999) in his EVENT-schema-based approach.

Noun-Verb Conversion and EVENT Schemas

EVENT schemas are an area where the connection between Cognitive Linguistics and traditional semantic analysis is most obvious, especially if one takes Dirven's lead, who was one of the earliest adherents of Fillmore's Case Grammar. Dirven

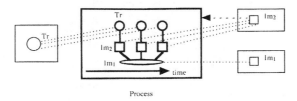

Figure 25.8. The role of "secondary" landmarks in the word-formation process of conversion (based on Twardsisz 1997: 93, 120)

(1999) develops his analysis of noun-verb conversions against the background of six major EVENT schemas, which have sprung from related configurations of predicator and semantic roles, as listed in table 25.3.

The aim is to show which of these schemas can be understood as input strategies for conversion processes. If one selects the ACTION schema 'Agent-Patient', as in *X paints a picture*, Dirven would claim that the Patient 'picture' functions as a metonymy for the painting action as a whole (or its metaphorical meaning of creating an image or representation). While this fact could have been stated within an argument-structure analysis, the explanation why this process works as it does depends on the cognitive notion of salience (see also Schmid, this volume, chapter 5). Following Langacker's approach that an EVENT schema can be seen as iconically reflecting the energy transmission in action chains, we find that the energy flow is triggered by the head of the chain (the agent) and is transmitted to the second major element, the patient, which is affected, or even changed, by the energy input. This is why the patient receives the highest degree of salience in the chain, which turns it into the "metonymic focus," as Dirven (1999: 280) calls it.

Apart from the patient, the other nonagentive roles in the ACTION schema, namely, instrument and occasionally manner, can assume the metonymic focus; thus, for the FISHING schema we find the conversions *He was harpooning fish* (< *He was catching fish with a harpoon*, focusing on the instrument) and *He was fishing pearls* (< *He was collecting them like fish*, focusing on manner). Another well-known EVENT schema is the MOTION schema, for which Dirven singles out the goal element as the metonymic focus of conversion; he stresses, however, that motion must not be understood in a literal sense, but may evoke specific scenes, such as the notion of food preservation (as in *to bottle*), of shelter (as in *to jail*), of turning something into a specific shape (as in *to slice*), or of creating a new artifact (as in the verbs *to book*, *to map*, or *to register*). The third source of verb conversion is the ESSIVE schema, which describes class membership or a special attribute of the patient, as in *He authored the book* (< *He was the author*) or *He volunteered to give blood* (< *He was a volunteer*). In addition to these basic schemas, there are combinations of the ACTION and the ESSIVE schemas (reminiscent of combining a transitive and a subject complement pattern into an object complement pattern), which elevate to salience either class membership, as in *He was knighted* (< *make someone a knight*), or, much

Table 25.3. EVENT schemas used as input for noun-verb
conversion (based on Dirven 1999)

EVENT schemas and associated semantic roles	
ACTION schema	Agent, Patient, Instrument, Manner, Result
LOCATION/MOTION schema	Place, Source, Path, Goal
ESSIVE schema	Class Membership, Attribute
EXPERIENCING schema	Experiencer, Stimulus
POSSESSION schema	Possessor, Possession
TRANSFER schema	Recipient, Beneficiary

more frequently, an attribute expressed by an adjective, as in *clean the table* (< *make the table clean*).

A further aim of Dirven's analysis, again in line with argument-structure discussions, is not just to describe verb-creating conversions, but to explain what transformational linguists would have called constraints; to that purpose, he adds three more schemas, the EXPERIENCING, POSSESSION, and TRANSFER schemas, and shows why they do not seem to be involved in verb conversion (see table 25.3). The reason they are not is that they feature human Experiencer, Recipient, or Possessor roles, which, just like the Agent role in an action schema, are the focus of attention and are thus excluded from triggering conversions. Metonymic focus, on which conversion is based, is therefore mainly reserved for nonhuman roles, unless humans are assigned to Patient roles and treated like nonhuman entities, as in *to author* or *to nurse* (Dirven 1999: 285).

What Dirven offers in his article is a consistent description, which also provides a convincing explanation of the constraints of these word-formation patterns (and in which Twardzisz's secondary landmark cases mostly reemerge as conversions based on Instrumental and Manner roles).

3.4. Noun-Noun Compounding

Multilevel Templates and the Bottom-Up Approach

Noun-noun compounding is another area of word-formation, where a long tradition of argument-structure-based analysis beckons for the use of semantic relationships (see Levi 1978).[8] The problem is that it is difficult to explain all the existing compounds in such a framework, let alone predict the meaning of novel formations. Here, Ryder (1994) offers a solution by providing a cognitive description that makes use of two of Langacker's basic tenets, the notions of multilevel schematicity and of analyzability (see section 2.1). What Ryder suggests is that the explanation of noun-noun compounds should not be tied to a single, fairly general level of semantic relationships such as favored by Levi and others, but that it should consider

	SCHEMA-BASED TEMPLATES AS ANALOGY BASES	EXAMPLES
general	– general templates, e.g. 'X has some relation to Y'	applies to most noun-noun compounds
	– constructions, e.g. 'part/whole', 'origin/entity', 'causer/result', etc. (cf . Construction Grammar)	*flower bed, state fund, hay fever*
	– several patterns linked to one core word, e.g. 'man who lives/works in X', 'man who works using X', 'man-shaped thing made of X'	*mountain man, dairy man, plowman, snowman*
specific	– construction linked to selected core words, e.g. box: 'intended to contain X'	*gift box, shoe box, snuffbox, letter box*
	– combinations containing a core word frequently used in compounds (based on the notion of entrenchment)	*billboard, keyboard, dartboard, surfboard, etc.*
	– the specific meanings of constituents (which can be understood as schemas in their own right)	*dog house, bird cage*

Figure 25.9. **Schema-based templates for the interpretation of noun-noun compounds** (based on Ryder 1994)

a range of "templates" starting from the level of simple lexical items and rising to more general levels of semantic relationship, as shown in figure 25.9.

Following Langacker's notion of analyzability, this scale of schematicity should not be seen as a systematic classification of noun-noun compounds, but as a description of the hearer's bottom-up actualization, in which the hearer attempts to link the templates with suitable encyclopedic knowledge, which Ryder conceives as organized in EVENT, ENTITY, and FEATURE schemas. This means that if hearers, upon encountering a compound, do not find the item already fully entrenched and if the context does not provide a plausible interpretation right away, they will proceed from the most specific to the most general template: from information supplied by the specific meanings of the constituents to core words, that is, words frequently occurring in compounds, and on to constructions linked to core words, and so on, until finally only the explanation contained in the general templates and the most general semantic information is left for accessing the compound—compare the bottom-up arrangements of the examples in figure 25.9. No doubt this permits a much more flexible approach than earlier attempts. To support her claims, Ryder conducted psycholinguistic tests in which participants were asked to define fabricated compounds, thus taking up a line of experimental compound analysis introduced by Downing (1977).

The Attribute-Listing and Matching Approach

Another psychological tradition that can be applied to compounding stems from the attribute-listing experiments initiated by Rosch for simplex lexical concepts (Rosch 1975). The basic idea is to collect the attributes named by participants when confronted with lexical concepts and to rank them according to frequency. Using this method for the study of compounds requires separate attribute listings for the constituents of the compound and for the compound as a whole. Comparison of these lists shows conceptual overlap and differences between the compound and its constituents and indicates where compounds attract "free" attributes from other domains.

This method may help to distinguish between different stages in the lexicalization process, as represented by the compounds *apple juice*, *wheelchair*, and *newspaper*. As illustrated in table 25.4, specifying compounds such as *apple juice* share most of their attributes with their constituents and attract only few "free" attributes. Enriched compounds like *wheelchair* draw on the attributes of their constituents to a lesser extent and mainly rely on free attributes imported from domains like 'illness' and 'hospital'; this ratio between constituent-derived and free attributes becomes even more extreme in the case of fully lexicalized compounds like *newspaper*. The findings documented in table 25.4 also support the intuition that with partonymic compounds like *coat collar*, it is the first constituent (and not the second, as suggested by the traditional modifier-head analysis) that dominates the compound conceptually. To some extent, this shift of dominance even applies to nonpartonymic compounds like *rain coat*, where largely associative attributes like 'wetness', 'bad weather', 'thunderstorm', and 'umbrella' suggest closer links with the constituent *rain* than with *coat*.

3.5. Lexical Blends: A Schematic Nonmorphemic View

Making use of a new collection of neologisms and claiming to disregard the processing aspect,[9] Kemmer (2003) finds that a crucial aspect of a satisfactory account of the huge variety of blending patterns is a schematic view of shared phonological

Table 25.4. Semantic attributes illustrating conceptual overlap and differences between compounds and their constituents (based on Ungerer and Schmid 1998; c1 = first constituent, c2 = second constituent, cpd = compound; total of attributes refers to attributes listed by at least 4 out of a sample of about 30 informants)

Type of Compound	Specifying Compound	Enriched Compound	Lexicalized Compound	Partonymic Compound	"Associative" Compound
	apple juice	wheelchair	newspaper	coat collar	raincoat
C1 + CPD + C2	4	0	0	2	1
C1 + CPD	6	2	5	7	8
CPD + C2	9	2	1	5	4
CPD ONLY	2	14	21	7	6
TOTAL OF ATTRIBUTES	13	18	27	17	17

similarities. In the case of the most frequent subgroup, overlapping blends, the overlap may involve shared segments of different size (*dumbsizing* from *dumb* and *downsizing*, *glitterati* from *glitter* and *literati*); of at least equal importance is the syllable structure the blend shares with one or both of the source lexemes (compare *dumbsizing* and *downsizing*). Substitution blends, in which one part of one source lexeme is substituted by a complete second source lexeme (as in *carjacking*; from *car* x *hijacking*), can be seen as a subgroup of overlapping blends, while "intercalative" blends (Kemmer 2003: 72), in which the two source elements are not represented contiguously in the blend (as in Lewis Caroll's famous coining *slithy*, from *slimy* and *lithe*), can be regarded as more marginal. All these variants find a place in Kemmer's account, which she summarizes as follows:

> Phonological similarity of the blend with part or whole source lexemes increases the likelihood or felicity (the 'goodness') of a blend. Similarity can range from segmental identity through segmental similarity to same or similar syllable structure; and the similarity can range from identity/similarity of the blend with both source lexemes, to one source lexeme, or to parts of these. (Kemmer 2003: 75–76)

That this phonological variation cannot be captured by a hard-and-fast rule is obvious; what is needed are generalizations which are flexible enough to cover more or less specific segmental elements as well as a syllable structure that have been repeatedly experienced by language users, and which have thus come to be accepted as sanctioning a certain type of blend. For instance, for the blend *swooshtika* (< *swoosh* 'the Nike logo' + *swastika*, with its Nazi associations), Kemmer posits a schema comprising the phonological form /swVS/ (V for vowel, S for sibilant), which is realized by *swoosh*, *SWAStika*, and *SWOOSHtika* alike; in addition, the schema includes the three-syllable structure of *swastika*, which is also taken up

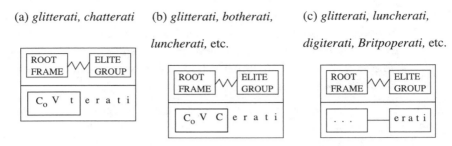

(a) *glitterati, chatterati*   (b) *glitterati, botherati,*   (c) *glitterati, luncherati,*

luncherati, etc.   *digiterati, Britpoperati*, etc.

Figure 25.10. *-erati* blends: The development from low-level to high-level schemas (excerpt from the schematic network for *-erati* blends in Kemmer 2003: 90, figure 3)

by *swooshtika*. The semantic side of the lexical blend can be captured by a three-space representation based on Fauconnier and Turner's notion of conceptual blending (see section 2.2. above). Kemmer's example for this semantic (or conceptual) description is the blend *glitterati* (< *glitter* + *literati*), an example which also enables her to show how low-level schemas can spark off higher-level schemas, as shown in figure 25.10.[10]

Figure 25.10a illustrates a relatively low-level schema whose phonological pole is applicable to the blends *glitterati*, *chatterati*, and a few others. Apart from the four-syllable structure of the second source lexeme *literati*, this schema is characterized by an overlap of an initial consonant cluster, a vowel, and the phoneme /t/. In figure 25.10b, the /t/ is replaced by the more general consonant element which admits blends like *botherati* and *luncherati*, and thus raises the schema to a somewhat higher level, while still maintaining the syllabic structure of schema (a). Finally, in figure 25.10c, phonological overlap is no longer required (but still possible), and the syllable structure, though prototypically still consisting of four syllables, may be extended to more syllables, as in *Britpoperati*. Within Kemmer's classification of blends, this marks a switch from overlap to substitution blends, and this is possible because in schema (a), the phonological string *-erati* already supports the fairly tangible meaning of 'elite group' (as indicated in the top section of the schema boxes). When the phonological overlap in the first element is dropped, as in schema (c), the second element may therefore assume the status of a derivational morpheme (traditionally called "semi-suffix"), which can freely be combined with suitable lexical morphemes. This is a good illustration of what Kemmer (2003) means when she claims that it is "the phonological strings that trigger meanings" (77). This leads her to the important conclusion (modestly hidden away in a footnote) that morphemes should be regarded as a special case of the association of sounds with meaning, "the case in which the connection of a sound string with a meaning is very well entrenched and the unit is recombinable" (note 7).

4. CONCLUSION AND
RESEARCH PROSPECTS

As this survey has shown, current cognitive research in word-formation is still very much in its initial stages. While one can be fairly certain that word-formation can smoothly be accommodated within the framework of Cognitive Grammar, the application of most empirical methods has been too selective for a proper evaluation of their usefulness and should be supported by further studies. Thus, the radial category approach could be extended beyond -*er* derivation (and, of course, phrasal verbs and prepositional compounds) to other types of suffixations, for instance, to the area of de-nominal adjectival suffixes (-*ic*, -*ical*, -*ous*, etc.); the attribute listing and matching method could be tested in a more comprehensive examination of compounds, which can be expected to yield more differentiated results.

An exciting avenue for further research would be to try to transfer Kemmer's approach of "emergent schematic networks" from lexical blends to other domains of word-formation. The obvious candidates are acronyms, both alphabetic (*UN*, *US*) and orthoepic acronyms (*ROM*, *SARS*), including those supported by prop words (*WASPS*, see also section 2.3). It might also be interesting to provide a schematic analysis of the development from letter combinations to pseudo-simplicia, which is accomplished at an ever-increasing speed (compare the development of *laser*, *AIDS*, and *SARS*), as well as a schematic network solution for the *yuppie*, *dinkie*, *taffie* series of acronyms. These analyses would probably support Kemmer's view that morphemes should be regarded as the special case of a well-entrenched and recombinable connection of a sound string with a meaning.[11] This view of word-formation would not only strengthen the position of the "ungrammatical" word-formation processes such as blending and acronyming, but would permit a refreshing glimpse at "morphemes in the making" and might well change the picture we have of this central linguistic element.[12] Finally, a cognitive approach might fuel the discussion of the question (raised in Ungerer 2002) of what the specific conceptual and communicative function of word-formation might be vis-à-vis the potential of simplex lexemes and syntactic constructions.

NOTES

1. This implies that root creations are very rare indeed in modern languages, where they are largely restricted to the creation of trade names such as *kodak*.

2. For a much wider application of the Figure/Ground contrast (and other cognitive principles) in the affix-stem morphology of incorporating languages like Nahuatl, see Tuggy (1992).

3. A still more differentiated explanation for compounds (and even more so, for idioms) is offered by Geeraerts (2002), whose "prismatic model" not only takes account

of the relationship between the composite meaning and the meaning of the constituents, but also of the metaphorical or metonymic relationship that holds between the literal and derived meanings of compounds and idioms, as in Dutch *schapenkop* (457) or English *blockhead* 'stupid person'. Within this model, the bottom-up analysis is complemented by the (less frequent) top-down analysis underlying nontransparent "semantic back-formations", as in the idiom *spekverkoper* 'boaster' (450) or the proverbial fragments *new broom* and *early bird*. In the domain of compounds, one might consider *paper* 'newspaper', *plane* 'airplane', or *car* 'motor car' as suitable candidates, even though their compound background will probably receive low analyzability ratings by language users.

4. For an application of the blending approach to nominal compounds, see Coulson (2001: 128–33); for an analysis of adjective-noun combinations, see Sweetser (1999). The representation of the compound *wheelchair* in figure 25.5 makes use of a three-space arrangement of mental spaces (i.e., dropping the representation of the fourth generic space originally suggested by Fauconnier) and has been extended to accommodate background knowledge. The subsequent description neglects the aspects of cross-mappings between input spaces, underlying vital relations and their compression in the blended space, which are important for the understanding of more complex blends.

5. Another argument mentioned by Schmid to support his theory of contrast is that word-formation items whose prefixed character is still felt by the speaker receive secondary stress on the prefix while fully lexicalized items lose the profiled contrast and receive no secondary stress (cf. ***re**-cover* 'cover again' and *recover* 'get better').

6. The domain in figure 25.6b is not represented in Mettinger (1994). It has been deduced from Mettinger (1996: 24), where a similar treatment for contrastive adjective pairs such as *male/female* is suggested.

7. Another recent analysis (Heyvaert 2003) attempts to overcome the basic assumption of an underlying agentive argument structure for verb-derived *-er* nominalizations by approaching the structure through underlying middle constructions (e.g., *This book sells best* underlying *bestseller*). The main claim is that the local and force-dynamic qualities of middle constructions have made it possible for *-er* nominalizations to develop from profiling only agents to profiling subjects in their relationship to the finite (in Halliday's terminology), complete with its interpersonal and grounding potential. Whether this "constructional approach" (which explicitly excludes nondeverbal *-er* nominalizations) is superior to the cognitive "representational" descriptions Heyvaert wants to overcome remains to be seen.

8. The fact that noun-noun compounding has been selected for closer scrutiny does not mean that other problem areas of composition have not benefited from a cognitive reanalysis as well. Among them are the so-called *scarecrow* nouns (V + O nouns whose subject is not expressed in the compound; e.g., 'Someone who scares crows'),which Tuggy (1987) explains by positing a schematic network of possessive or bahuvrihi compounds (now understood as a combination of specifying compound and metonymy; Ungerer 2002: 551).

9. Kemmer's (2003: 71) claim that she does not use a process model may be reflected in her refraining from using the input-output metaphor; however, it does not mean that she denies processual links between source and target concepts—actually, they come in automatically as she relies to a considerable extent on the model of conceptual blending. As well, her position does not exclude that it may be worth looking at the processual aspect of lexical blending and its iconic properties (see section 2.3).

10. The assignment of examples to schemas (a)–(c) in figure 25.10 also differs slightly from the assignment indicated by Kemmer's sanctioning arrows.

11. These are lexical morphemes in the case of *laser, radar, AIDS,* and *SARS* and derivational morphemes in the case of *yuppie,* where the suffix *-ie* may be understood to express 'belonging to a fashionable group'.

12. Perhaps the schematic approach could thus have a similar impact on word-formation analysis and lexicology as the study of Pidgin and Creole languages has had on sociolinguistics and linguistics in general.

REFERENCES

Bakema, Peter, Patricia Defour, and Dirk Geeraerts. 1993. De semantische structuur van het diminutief [The semantic structure of the diminutive]. *Forum der Letteren* 34: 121–37.

Bauer, Laurie. 1983. *English word-formation.* Cambridge: Cambridge University Press.

Bauer, Laurie. 2001. *Morphological productivity.* Cambridge: Cambridge University Press.

Brugman, Claudia. 1981. Story of *Over.* MA thesis, University of California at Berkeley. (Published as *The story of Over: Polysemy, semantics, and the structure of the lexicon.* New York: Garland, 1988)

Coulson, Seana. 2001. *Semantic leaps: Frame-shifting and conceptual blending in meaning construction.* Cambridge: Cambridge University Press.

Dirven, René. 1999. Conversion as a conceptual metonymy of event schemata. In Klaus-Uwe Panther and Günter Radden, eds., *Metonymy in language and thought* 273–87. Amsterdam: John Benjamins.

Downing, Pamela. 1977. On the creation and use of English compound nouns. *Language* 53: 810–42.

Dressler, Wolfgang U., and Lavinia Merlini Barbaresi. 1994. *Morphopragmatics: Diminutives and intensifiers in Italian, German and other languages.* Berlin: Mouton de Gruyter.

Fauconnier, Gilles. 1997. *Mappings in thought and language.* Cambridge: Cambridge University Press.

Fauconnier, Gilles, and Mark Turner. 2002. *The way we think: Conceptual blending and the mind's hidden complexities.* New York: Basic Books.

Geeraerts, Dirk. 2002. The interaction of metaphor and metonymy in composite expressions. In René Dirven and Ralf Pörings, eds., *Metaphor and metonymy in comparison and contrast* 435–65. Berlin: Mouton de Gruyter.

Heyvaert, Liesbet. 2003. *A cognitive-functional approach to nominalization in English.* Berlin: Mouton de Gruyter.

Kemmer, Suzanne. 2003. Schemas and lexical blends. In Hubert Cuyckens, Thomas Berg, René Dirven, and Klaus-Uwe Panther, eds., *Motivation in language: Studies in honor of Günter Radden* 69–97. Amsterdam: John Benjamins.

Lakoff, George. 1987. *Women, fire, and dangerous things: What categories reveal about the mind.* Chicago: University of Chicago Press.

Langacker, Ronald W. 1987. *Foundations of cognitive grammar.* Vol. 1, *Theoretical prerequisites.* Stanford, CA: Stanford University Press.

Langacker, Ronald W. 1990. *Concept, image and symbol: The cognitive basis of grammar.* Berlin: Mouton de Gruyter.

Levi, Judith N. 1978. *The syntax and semantics of complex nominals.* New York: Academic Press.

Lindner, Susan. 1981. A lexico-semantic analysis of English verb-particle constructions with OUT and UP. PhD dissertation, University of California at San Diego. (Also published as A lexico-semantic analysis of English verb-particle constructions, LAUT Paper, no. 101. Trier, Germany: Linguistic Agency of the University of Trier, 1983)

Lipka, Leonhard. 2002. *English lexicology: Lexical structure, word semantics and word-formation*. Tübingen: Gunter Narr.

Mettinger, Arthur. 1994. *Un*-Prefixation in English: Expectations, formats, and results. *Münstersches Logbuch der Linguistik* 5: 17–31.

Mettinger, Arthur. 1996. (Image-)Schematic properties of antonymous adjectives. *Views* 5: 12–26.

Panther, Klaus-Uwe, and Linda Thornburg. 2001. A conceptual analysis of English -*er*-nominals. In Martin Pütz, Susanne Niemeier, and René Dirven, eds., *Applied cognitive linguistics II: Language pedagogy* 149–200. Berlin: Mouton de Gruyter.

Quirk, Randolph, Sidney Greenbaum, Geoffrey Leech, and Jan Svartvik. 1985. *A comprehensive grammar of the English language*. London: Longman.

Rappaport Hovav, Malka, and Beth Levin. 1992. -*Er* nominals: Implications for the theory of argument structure. In Tim Stowell and Eric Wehrli, eds., *Syntax and semantics*, vol. 26, *Syntax and the lexicon* 127–53. New York: Academic Press.

Rosch, Eleanor. 1975. Cognitive representations of semantic categories. *Journal of Experimental Psychology: General* 104: 193–233.

Rudzka-Ostyn, Brygida. 1985. Metaphoric processes in word formation: The case of prefixed words. In Wolf Paprotté and René Dirven, eds., *The ubiquity of metaphor* 209–41. Amsterdam: John Benjamins.

Ruiz de Mendoza Ibáñez, Francisco. 1998. *El modelo cognitivo idealizado de 'tamaño' y la formación de aumentativos y diminutivos en español*. México: Instituto de Investigaciones Filológicas, Universidad Nacional Autónoma de México.

Ryder, Mary Ellen. 1994. *Ordered chaos. The interpretation of English noun-noun compounds*. Berkeley: University of California Press.

Ryder, Mary Ellen. 1999. *Bankers* and *blue-chippers*: An account of -*er* formations in present-day English. *English Language and Linguistics* 3: 269–97.

Santibanez-Saenz, Francisco. 1999. Conceptual interaction and Spanish diminutives. *Cuadernos de Investigation Filologica* 25: 173–90.

Schmid, Hans-Jörg. 2005. *Englische Morphologie und Wortbildung: Eine Einführung*. Berlin: Erich Schmidt.

Stekauer, Pavel. 1998. *An onomasiological theory of English word-formation*. Amsterdam: John Benjamins.

Sweetser, Eve. 1999. Compositionality and blending: Semantic composition in a cognitively realistic framework. In Theo Janssen and Gisela Redeker, eds., *Cognitive linguistics: Foundations, scope, and methodology* 129–62. Berlin: Mouton de Gruyter.

Talmy, Leonard. 1991. Path to realization: A typology of event conflation. *Berkeley Linguistic Society* 7: 480–519.

Taylor, John R. 1992. Old problems: Adjectives in cognitive grammar. *Cognitive Linguistics* 3: 1–46.

Tuggy, David. 1987. Scarecrow nouns, generalizations, and cognitive grammar. In Scott DeLancey and Russell S. Tomlin, eds., *Proceedings of the Third Annual Meeting of the Pacific Linguistics Conference* 307–20. Eugene: Department of Linguistics, University of Oregon.

Tuggy, David. 1992. The affix-stem distinction: A cognitive grammar analysis of data from Orizaba Nahuatl. *Cognitive Linguistics* 3: 237–300.

Twardzisz, Piotr. 1997. *Zero derivation in English: A cognitive grammar approach.* Lublin, Poland: Wydawnicto UMCS.

Ungerer, Friedrich. 1999. Iconicity in word-formation. In Max Nänny and Olga Fischer, eds., *Form miming meaning* 307–24. Amsterdam: John Benjamins.

Ungerer, Friedrich. 2002. The conceptual function of derivational word-formation in English. *Anglia* 120: 534–67.

CHAPTER 26

NOMINAL CLASSIFICATION

GUNTER SENFT

1. INTRODUCTION

The problem of "classification" is a general problem of life. That classification abilities are necessary for the survival of every organism is an important insight of biology. Human beings classify consciously, unconsciously, and even subconsciously in all situations. When we confront a scientific problem, we try to solve it by first classifying the various parts of the problem. Therefore, the history of all branches of science is also a history of how these sciences have classified their research subject. "Classification" always implies "selection," too, because, as Koestler (1983: 201) puts it, our

> minds would cease to function if we had to attend to each of the millions of stimuli which . . . constantly bombard our receptor organs. . . . The nervous system and the brain itself function as a multilevelled hierarchy of filtering and classifying devices, which eliminate a large proportion of the input as irrelevant 'noise', and assemble the relevant information into coherent patterns before it is represented to consciousness.

If we want to communicate about this perceived, classified, and filtered input, we have to classify once more: we have to transform the input into classes and categories provided by the systems that organize our communicative verbal and nonverbal faculties—thus, this second round of classification leads to categorization on the semantic level. With our systems of language and gesture, we again classify, filter, and categorize on various levels while communicating. Linguistics is the science that tries to analyze these processes of classification that are relevant for communication. Indeed, the languages of the world provide an enormous data pool for the analysis of the problem of categorization and classification—and humankind has developed a number of different linguistic techniques to apprehend our world (see Senft 1996: ix–x; 2000b: 11).

As Royen (1929: 1) points out, the philosophical discussion of nominal classification can be traced back to the Greek sophistic philosopher Protagoras (485–414 BC). Obviously, discussing the problem of "category" and "categorization," and especially the interdependences between category, categorization, and classification on the one hand, and naming, language, thought, perception, and culture on the other hand, has a long tradition, not only in philosophy (see, e.g., Foucault [1966] 1980; Rosch 1988; Vollmer 1988a, 1988b), but also in linguistics (see, e.g., Herder [1770] 1978; Humboldt [1836] 1968; Schleiermacher [1838] 1977; Whorf 1958). Even a brief glance over this literature and other literature that deals especially with nominal classification reveals that the basic problems continue to emerge in the discussion of this topic.[1]

Cognitive Linguistics is particularly interested in these problems and has devoted much attention to nominal classification and categorization. Actually, the book that undoubtedly contributed much to finally establishing Cognitive Linguistics as a subdiscipline of its own—Lakoff's (1987) influential monograph *Women, Fire, and Dangerous Things: What Categories Reveal about the Mind*—explicitly refers to categorization in its title and even mentions three (of many more) members that constitute a noun class in Dyirbal, an Australian Aboriginal language spoken in North Queensland (see Dixon 1972: 44–47, 307).

This chapter summarizes some of these problems of nominal classification in language, presents and illustrates the various systems or techniques (see Seiler 1986) of nominal classification, and points out why nominal classification is one of the most interesting topics in Cognitive Linguistics.

2. NOMINAL CLASSIFICATION

This section first discusses briefly the basic problem of how the perceived world is expressed and represented in language and how language refers to the perceived world. Then it presents and exemplifies the systems of nominal classification that can be found in the languages of the world, and finally it discusses some central problems of nominal classification.

2.1. From the World to Nouns and Systems of Nominal Classification

One of the basic questions in the study of language is how the perceived world is expressed and represented in, and through, language, and how language refers to the perceived world, to its objects, things, and living beings. Not only do we perceive the world, but we also develop concepts about what we perceive and create linguistic expressions that refer to and represent these concepts. These expressions refer—among other things—to actions, temporary states, things and objects, and persons and other living beings.

Many of these expressions are classified by linguists as "nouns"—and in many languages these "nouns" (like verbs and adjectives) constitute an open word class. Moreover, if we keep in mind Greenberg's (1978: 78) claim that as "soon as we wish to talk about an action as such, we nominalize it," we become aware (again) of the important role nouns play in our languages (at least with respect to their frequency).

As Talmy (1992: 131) points out, languages "generally subcategorize nouns grammatically along certain semantic parameters." These subcategorizations are classifications, of course. The question why most of these classifying systems apply just to the noun phrase rather than other syntactic constituents was answered by Greenberg (1978: 78) in a very convincing way:

> It is the noun par excellence which gives rise to classificational systems of syntactic relevance. It is not so much that the noun designates persisting entities as against actions or temporary states. . . . It is that nouns are continuing discourse subjects and are therefore in constant need of referential devices of identification. . . . Classification is a help in narrowing the range of possible identification.

Languages have been developing a rather broad variety of these nominal classification systems. After Royen's (1929) pioneering research, it was Seiler and his coworkers who tried to integrate the various techniques of nominal classification into an overall framework (Seiler and Lehmann 1982; Seiler and Stachowiak 1982; Seiler 1986). Recently, Grinevald (2000) and Aikhenvald (2000a) proposed new typologies for these systems of nominal classification (see also Bisang 2002). Based on these proposals, the following subsection presents an overview of nominal classification systems found in the languages of the world. The presentation of these systems follows Royen's (1929: 526) basic maxim which runs: "Von nominalen Klassen kann man erst dann reden, wenn die mentale Gruppierung der Nomina in der Sprache auf die eine oder andere Weise formal reflektiert wird" (We can speak of nominal classes only if the mental grouping of nouns is formally reflected within the language in one way or another; my translation).

2.2. Systems of Nominal Classification

Grinevald (2000) presents a typology of techniques of nominal classification that postulates a lexical-grammatical continuum of systems. " 'Lexical' here means (a) part of the lexicon and its word-building dynamics and (b) semantically compositional, while 'grammatical' means part of the morphosyntax of a language" (55). On the lexical end of this continuum, we find measure terms and class terms, and on the grammatical end of the continuum, we find gender and noun class systems. The various classifier systems "can be placed at a mid-way point" (55) on this continuum. In what follows, I will present the systems of nominal classification mentioned in Grinevald's and Aikhenvald's typologies.

Measure Terms and Class Terms

In her typology, Grinevald (2000: 58) clearly differentiates between two systems of lexical nominal classification: "Measure terms are lexical in the sense that they are semantically compositional/analytic noun phrases, and class terms are lexical in the sense that they operate on derivational or compounding morphology at word level." Measure terms express quantities; in English, for example, we find measure terms like *a glass of whisky, a slice of bread, a group of children*, and *a school of dolphins*. It should be noted here that distinguishing measure terms from numeral classifiers (see below) is a recurrent problem in numeral classifier languages, especially in isolating ones (see Aikhenvald 2000a: 98–120).

Grinevald (2000: 59) defines class terms as "classifying morphemes which participate in the lexicogenesis of a language" and differentiates three types of these terms. The plant world is probably the most common semantic domain of class terms. Thus, we find morphemes like *-berry* or *tree* that classify nouns like *strawberry, raspberry, palm tree*, and *oak tree*. In English we also find derivational morphemes like *-ist, -er*, and *-man* to designate classes of 'agents', as in *scientist, novelist, baker, writer, postman*, and *fireman*. Again, it should be noted here that distinguishing class terms from noun classifiers (see below) is a problem in many languages, such as in Australian languages or Thai (see Aikhenvald 2000a: 81–97).

Noun Class Systems and Gender

In noun class systems of nominal classification, all nouns of a language are assigned to a number of classes. These systems are typical of languages of the Niger-Congo linguistic stock, especially Bantu. They "are characterized by agreement with constituents outside the NP . . . by a higher degree of grammaticalization, evident in a closed system of a small number of classes; and by a lesser degree of semantic transparency" (Zubin 1992: 42). Noun classes in noun class systems form a "grammatical category" (Dixon 1986: 105).[2] Nineteen noun classes have been reconstructed for Proto-Bantu, for example, with the classes 1/2, 3/4, 5/6, 7/8, and 9/10 as singular/plural markers. The noun class systems of modern Bantu languages consist of 12–20 morphological classes. Demuth (2000: 273) presents the following example for a noun class system in the Bantu language Sesotho:

(1) <u>Ba</u>-shányana <u>bá</u>-ne <u>bá</u>-fúmáné   *di-perekisi*
     <u>2</u>-boys   <u>2</u>-DEM <u>2</u>-SUBJECT AGREEMENT MARKER-found   <u>10</u>-peaches
     <u>tsé</u>-monáte.
     <u>10</u>-good
     'Those boys found some tasty peaches.'

Here, the demonstrative modifying the class 2 subject noun *ba-shányana* is the class 2 demonstrative *bá-ne*. The subject marker on the verb then agrees with this nominal subject. The nominal modifier for the class 10 noun *di-perekisi* takes a class 10 relative prefix *tsé-monáte* (see also Aikhenvald 2000a: 63–65; Senft 2000b: 15).

Gender systems—which are found in Indo-European and Semitic languages, for example—are defined by Corbett (1991: 4–5) as the type of nominal classification

> which is reflected beyond the nouns themselves in modifications required of 'associated words'. . . . The determining criterion of gender is agreement; this is the way in which the genders are 'reflected in the behavior of associated words' in Hockett's definition. . . . Saying that a language has three genders implies that there are three classes of nouns which can be distinguished syntactically by the agreement they take. . . . It is not only adjectives and verbs which can show agreement in gender, but in some languages adverbs agree, in other numerals and sometimes even conjunctions agree in gender.

Taking agreement as the defining criterion for gender (see also Royen 1929: 526–27, 756–58) implies for Corbett (1991: 5) that "there are no grounds for drawing a distinction between languages in which nouns are divided into groups according to sex, and those where human/nonhuman or animate/inanimate are the criteria. Thus many languages described as having 'noun classes' fall within our study [on gender]" (see also Dixon 1986: 105–7; Senft 2000b: 15–16; Unterbeck and Rissanen 2000). Languages with gender obligatorily classify all their nouns into formal classes. Gender systems are the most limited systems of nominal classification with respect to the number of their classes. Grinevald (2000: 56) illustrates the "limited semantic motivation of assignment to classes beyond that linked to the sex of animates . . . by the different gender assignments of the name of common objects in French and Spanish":

French	Spanish	
un mur (M)	*una pared* (F)	'a wall'
la fourchette (F)	*el tenedor* (M)	'the fork'

Allan (1977: 291) even states that "by and large, European gender is semantically empty." However, more recent work on gender contradicts this statement, pointing out that gender is never semantically empty; there is always a semantic core, usually "masculine-feminine" or "human-nonhuman" (see Zubin and Köpcke 1986; Zubin 1992; see also Aikhenvald 2000a: 19–80).

Classifier Systems

Many languages use specific classifying morphemes—so-called classifiers—for the classification of their nouns (see Senft 1996: 4–11). These classifier languages are distributed all around the world, belonging to such different language families as the Malayo-Polynesian, the Austro-Asiatic, the Sino-Tibetan, the Altaic, the Dravidian, and the Indo-Aryan. Moreover, we also find classifiers in sign languages, such as American Sign Language (ASL), Egyptian Hieroglyphics, and Mesopotamian Cuneiform (see Senft: 2000b: 21). In classifier languages, nominal referents are classified according to specific characteristics of their referents. This kind of classification is based on semantic principles and results in the ordering of objects, living beings, concepts, actions, and events.[3] In other words, this classification leads to a categorization of all the nominal conceptual labels coded in such a language. The units of this classification are "semantic domains" (Berlin 1968: 34). Thus, on the basis of semantic considerations, classifiers can be grouped together and then be regarded as constituting certain semantic domains; the semantic domains constituted by these classifiers represent the semantic (sub)structures of a (classifier) language (see Friedrich 1970: 379). Moreover, Grinevald (2000: 61) rightly points out that the "characteristic of classifier systems is that they constitute grammatical systems of nominal classification in the intermediate range between lexical and morphosyntactic extremes." In what follows, I will list the various types of classifier systems.

Numeral Classifiers

Numeral classifiers represent the type of nominal classification that Allan (1977: 286) considers to be the paradigm case of classifier languages. Numeral classifier systems are found in the languages of Southeast Asia, in East Asian languages, in languages of the Americas, and in Oceanic languages. Classifier languages have a system that can be (at least in principle) an open set of classifiers. They follow the—almost—universal principle that runs as follows: "A classifier concatenates with a quantifier, locative, demonstrative or predicate to form a nexus that cannot be interrupted by the noun which it classifies" (Allan 1977: 288; but see Adams 1989: 12, 24). Languages with numeral classifiers differ from other languages primarily with respect to the following characteristic feature: in counting inanimate as well as animate referents, the numerals (obligatorily) concatenate with a certain morpheme—the so-called "classifier." This morpheme classifies or quantifies the respective nominal referent according to semantic criteria. Therefore, linguists generally differentiate between "classifiers (proper)" and "quantifiers." These classifiers and quantifiers are usually defined as follows (see Senft 1996: 6):

> *Classifiers* classify a noun inherently, i.e., they designate and specify semantic features inherent to the nominal denotatum and divide the set of nouns of a certain language into disjunct classes.

> *Quantifiers* classify a noun temporarily, i.e., they can be combined with different nouns in a rather free way and designate a specific characteristic feature of a certain noun that is not inherent to it.

Besides the terms "classifier" and "quantifier," we also find the terms "sortal classifier" and "mensural classifier" (Berlin 1968). There are a number of other terms that try to describe and specify classifiers (see Senft 1996: 7–9), but I will not discuss these terms in more detail here. This differentiation of classifiers is in itself a form of classification. It results in the claim that there are different categories of classifiers. However, with respect to this claim, I would like to maintain, with Corbett (1991: 147) "the requirement that to demonstrate the existence of a category,

evidence of distinctions in form is necessary."[4] Kilivila, the Austronesian language of the Trobriand Islanders, is a language with an inventory of probably more than 200 classifiers (Senft 1996: 16, 171–80). Kilivila does not differentiate between classifiers and quantifiers. The following examples illustrate the use of numeral classifiers for this language. The examples first present the classifier (CL) (-)na(-) in its connotation 'animals' and then illustrate a part of the noun-modifying group of classifiers that specify the noun with respect to its quantity, its order, its arrangement, and its condition or state (see Senft 1996; 2000b: 18–21):

(2)   *na-tala*   *yena*
      CL.animal-one   fish
      'one fish'

(3)   *kevala-lima*   *yena*
      CL.batch.drying-five   fish
      'five batches of smoked fish'

(4)   *oyla-lima*   *yena*
      CL.string-five   fish
      'five strings with stringed on fish'

(5)   *pwasa-lima   pwasa-tala*   *yena*
      CL.rotten-five CL.rotten-one fish
      'six rotten fish'

Like a number of other classifier languages, Kilivila also uses its classifiers for the word-formation of adjectives and demonstratives.[5]

Noun Classifiers

Contrary to numeral classifiers, noun classifiers are not a very common type of nominal classification. They are realized as "free morphemes standing in a noun phrase, next to the noun itself or within the boundaries of the noun phrase with other determiners of the noun" and "they are crucially found independently of the operation of quantification" (Grinevald 2000: 64). Aikhenvald (2000a: 81) points out that noun classifiers "are a type of non-agreeing noun categorization device" and that their choice is "determined by lexical selection." This system is found in languages of Mesoamerica, South America, and Australia; and also in Austronesian, Tai, Tibetan, and Austroasiatic languages. The following examples from the Mayan language Jakaltek illustrate the noun classifier (NCL) system (see Craig 1986b: 264; Grinevald 2000: 64–65; see also Aikhenvald 2000a: 81–97; Zavala: 2000)

(6)   *xil   naj   xuwan   no7   lab'a.*
      saw   NCL.man John   NCL.animal snake
      '(Man) John saw the (animal) snake.'

(7)   *xil   naj   no7.*
      saw   NCL.man NCL.animal
      'He (man non-kin) saw it (animal).'

Like Grinevald (2000: 65), I would like to emphasize that the label "noun classifier" should be reserved for this particular system of nominal classification—it should not be used to refer to all classifiers in general or specifically to numeral classifiers.[6]

Genitive Classifiers

In her typology of classifiers, Grinevald (2000: 66) subsumes under the label "genitive classifiers" all classifiers that are used in possessive constructions. In particular, she refers to classifiers that other researchers label as "possessed," "possessor," "possessive," "relational," and "attributive classifiers" (see Aikhenvald 2000a: 125–47). Grinevald (2000: 66) defines this type as follows:

> It is usually bound to the mark of the possessor while semantically classifying the possessed. This classifier system selects a limited set of nouns of the language for classification: they are nouns that appear to have high cultural significance and constitute a class akin to the 'alienable' nouns, to be determined for each language.

We find these classifiers in languages of the Americas, in African, Southeast Asian, and East Asian languages, and in many languages of Oceania. The following examples from the Austronesian language Ponapean (Regh 1981: 184; see also Grinevald 2000: 66) illustrate the system of genitive classifiers:

(8)   *ken-i*   *mwenge*
      CL.edible-GEN/1   food
      'my food'

(9)   *were-i*   *pwoht*
      CL.transport-GEN/1   boat
      'my boat'

Verbal Classifiers

Verbal classifiers are found inside the verb form and not—like the other classifier types mentioned so far—within the noun phrase structure. However, they do not "classify the verb itself but rather one of the nominal arguments of the verb" (Grinevald 2000: 67). Seiler (1986: 80) characterizes this system of nominal classification as follows:

> What we find in this technique is neither agreement nor selectional restriction: in both cases there would be a certain dependency of the verb vis-a-vis the noun. Instead, we find a relation of **solidarity** that emanates both from the verb and the noun. No particular relational element is needed.

Systems of verbal classifiers have been described for North American languages, and we find these classifiers also in Amazonian, Australian, and Papuan languages (see Aikhenvald 2000a: 149–71). Allan (1977: 287) refers to languages that use this type of nominal classification as "predicative classifier languages." The following subtypes of verbal classifiers can be distinguished.

a. *Classificatory noun incorporation* is a type of nominal classification that is found, for instance, in Iroquoian languages: in this system "a taxonomically superordinate (generic) noun, e.g., 'vehicle', is syntactically incorporated into the verb and cross-classifies a specific noun ('truck', 'bus') which is syntactically governed by the verb" (Zubin 1992: 41). This is illustrated in the following example from the Iroquoian language Cayuga (Mithun 1986: 388):

(10)   *Skitú*   *ake-'treht-áe'*.
        skidoo   I-vehicle-have
        'I have a skidoo.'

Grinevald (2000: 67) points out that "the classifiers of this still transparent incorporation type are akin to noun classifiers."

b. We also find verbal classifiers that are realized as *affixes*. For Grinevald (2000: 67), this "type of verbal classifier is more akin by its semantics to the numeral classifier type." In Diegueño, a Yuman language spoken in Southern California, we find, for example, the following classifying prefixes: *a-* usually indicates that the theme or the instrument of an action denoted by the verb root is a long object, the prefix *c-* indicates that the theme or the instrument of an action is an undetermined number of smaller objects, and the prefix *tu-* classifies the theme or the instrument of an action as a small, round object. This is illustrated with the following examples (see Langdon 1970: 80–87; Fedden 2002b: 410–411):

(11)   *a·mił*   'to hang (a long object)'
        a·uł   'to lay (a long object) on top of'
        a·mar   'to cover (a long object), to bury someone'
        cuł   'to put several on top'
        a·xʷił   'to put several in jail'
        tu·mił   'to hang (a small round object)'
        tu·uł   'to put on (a small round object)'
        tu·mar   'to cover over (a small round object)'

c. *Classificatory verb stems* are another type of nominal classification by verbs. Athabaskan languages, for instance, "have classificatory verbs, whose roots provide a semantically transparent classification of the intransitive subject or transitive object" (Zubin 1992: 41). Seiler (1986: 78), following Barron's (1982) analysis of Hoijer's description for Apachean languages, gives the following three criteria for the classification of nouns by verbs:

1. It must be possible to correlate the same noun classes with at least two predications.
2. It must be possible to correlate the different noun classes with one and the same predication as materialized in at least two different verb forms.

> 3. The classification of nouns is brought about by the verb forms only.... By predication is meant an invariant verbal notion.[7]

In his recent minute summary and analysis of research on classificatory verbs in North American languages, Fedden (2002a, 2002b) clearly shows that the first and second criterion mentioned by Seiler are central for this system of nominal classification, because they "determine a coherent paradigm" and therefore "serve to deliminate [this] technique from the much more general and widespread phenomenon of selectional restrictions" (Seiler 1986: 81). On the basis of these observations, Grinevald's (2000: 68) statement that "this lexical classification phenomenon can be found in any language" is falsified. One may agree with Grinevald that these classificatory verb stems should be excluded in a typology of classifiers—if we cannot identify a classifier-like form in the verb stem—however, I agree with Allan (1977), Barron (1982), Seiler (1986), Aikhenvald (2000a), and Fedden (2002b) that this subtype has to be incorporated into a general typology of systems of nominal classification. Barron (1982: 137) and Allan (1977: 287) present the following examples for the classification of nouns by classificatory verb stems in the Athapaskan language Navajo; here, the attributive use of a classificatory verb stem narrows down the meaning of the noun:

(12) *béésò   sì-ʔá.*
     money   perfect-lie (of round entity)
     'A coin is lying (there).'
(13) *béésò   sì-nìl.*
     money   perfect-lie (of collection)
     'Some money (small change) is lying (there).'
(14) *béésò   sì-X-tsòòz.*
     money   perfect-lie (of flat flexible entity)
     'A note (bill) is lying (there).'

Other Types of Classifiers

The classifier typologies of Aikhenvald (2000a: 172–83) and Grinevald (2000: 68–69) mention the following other "minor types" of classifiers.

   a. *Locative classifiers* occur in locative noun phrases. Aikhenvald (2000a: 172) points out that "their choice is determined by the semantic character of the noun involved [that is usually] the argument of a locative adposition.... Locative classifiers are 'fused' with an adposition.... The choice of adposition then depends on physical properties of the noun" (see also Broschart 1997). Locative classifiers are rather rare; we find them mainly in South American and Carib languages. Aikhenvald (2000a: 174–75) quotes the following two examples with the locative classifiers *kɛd* 'in:hollow' and *mĩ* 'in:liquid' from the Northwest Amazonian language Dâw:

(15)   *xoo-kɛd*
       canoe-in:hollow
       'in a canoe'

(16)   *nââx-pis-mĩʔ*
       water-small-in:liquid
       'in a small river'

b.   *Deictic classifiers* occur with deictic elements (see Aikhenvald 2000a: 176–83). We find them in North American, South American, and African languages, and in Eskimo. Some linguists refer to these classifiers also as "demonstrative" or "article classifiers." Goemai, a West Chadic language of Nigeria, employs five deictic classifiers that obligatorily occur in the demonstrative word. Hellwig (2003: 91, see also 192–94) provides the following example with the deictic classifier *d'yem* 'stand':

(17)   *Goe-n-d'yem-nnoe*   *a*   *lemu*
       NOMZ(sg)-ADVZ-CL:stand(sg)-DEM.PROX   FOC   orange
       goe-rok.
       NOMZ(sg)-become.sweet
       'This *standing* one is a sweet orange (tree).'

In Goemai, these classifiers grammaticalized from a form class of locative verbs, consisting of four postural verbs ('hang/move', 'sit', 'stand', 'lie') and one existential predicate. Verbs and classifiers encode information about whether or not the Figure maintains an orientation that extends beyond the Ground, and, if so, how it maintains this orientation (through a point of origin, autonomously, or through fixation). In addition, they encode classificatory information in that every physical object is associated with one default postural form, based on its canonical orientation. These defaults can be used in reference to that Figure in order to assert or negate its existence at a specific location, regardless of its transient orientation.

Finally, it should be mentioned that languages may use different systems of nominal classification at one and the same time (see Royen 1929: 266; Aikhenvald 2000a: 184–241; 2000b; Senft 2000b: 17) and that some languages employ the same set of classifiers in different environments and functions (see Senft 1996).

2.3.   Some Central Problems of Nominal Classification

Although the various types of nominal classification are, in general, well known and described in the literature, a number of open questions remain—especially from a cognitive linguistic perspective. This subsection deals with some of them and indicates how these open questions may translate into directions for future research (see also Senft 2000b).

The most obvious connection between these systems of nominal classification is their function. Besides the grouping and the subcategorization of nouns, all of them have one other major function, namely, "reference tracking" (Corbett 1991: 322). However, although all these systems of nominal classification have these basic linguistic functions in common, we do not know much about how they interact with each other. It is not clear how and why different types of nominal classification are to be found in one and the same language. And, although we can hypothesize on the basis of solid linguistic data about stages of transition that may be understood and described as stages of grammaticalization from one type of nominal classification to the other, we do not know very much about the actual processes involved in these transitions.

In section 2.2 above, I pointed out that in classifier languages nouns are classified and categorized according to their respective characteristics, and I mentioned that the criteria that structure these classifying systems are usually described by feature lists. Most, if not all, of these features represent semantic categories that are fundamental in, and for, all languages. However, a closer look at the respective classifiers which constitute the semantic domains for the individual languages on the basis of these features shows that these general and probably universal categories are defined in a culture-specific way. It is also evident that the boundaries between the individual semantic domains are rather fluid. Thus, Craig (1986a: 1)—on the basis of prototype theory—claims rightly that "categories . . . should be described as having fuzzy edges and graded membership." Therefore, the description of semantic domains within any classifier language asks for a sound analysis of how these domains are constituted, that is, which features are relevant for the definition of which semantic domain. This ethnosemantic descriptive and analytic research is rather complex and presupposes the linguist's thorough delving into the language to be described. But what do we actually do if we try to describe and analyze how these semantic domains are constituted in classifier languages? Usually we start our descriptions by characterizing and labeling certain semantic domains according to the fundamental—and probably universal—features mentioned above. This results in a number of semantic domains that we take as the semantic structures of the (classifier) language we want to describe. One of the basic and crucial mistakes we often make at this point of our analysis is that we forget that the ordering of classifiers according to semantic domains was something we ourselves did as a first methodological device to order the facts in a preanalytic way. This preanalytic ordering can only be a heuristic means for our attempts to describe the system as a whole; furthermore, it results in "static" semantic domains. The analyses proper involve looking at the actual use of the classifiers and comparing it with the criteria and features used in our preliminary definition of the semantic domains. We then have to redefine and revise these preliminary definitions of semantic domains and to give up the idea that they are "static" domains. And finally, we have to come up with a description that can cope with the dynamics—that is, with the dynamic interaction between the semantic domains—of the system of nominal classification of the language to be described.

However, more often than not, we treat the first preanalytically defined semantic domains as if they were static wholes; moreover, although they are just the result of our preanalytic classifications, we treat them as if they were actually to be found in the language. Admittedly, it is quite tempting to present a nicely ordered system of semantic classification—a system that is not messed up with the above mentioned "fuzzy edges" or with cases of "graded membership." However, these nicely ordered systems just do not represent the reality of the actual linguistic system to be described. I think more complex analyses are necessary (see Senft 1996) if we really want to get a better idea about how these systems and their dynamics function. When we know something (more) about the various functions of these systems, we will be able to come up with answers to the questions: What does a classifier actually do with respect to the linguistic system of a classifier language? What does a classifier mean?

The functions classifiers fulfill are succinctly summarized by Adams, Becker, and Conklin (1975: 2):

> Besides their function in numeral noun phrases classifiers in various lan-
> guages function as nominal substitutes, nominalizers of words in other form
> classes, markers of definiteness, relativizers, markers of possession, and as voca-
> tives; serve to disambiguate sentences; establish coherence in discourse and
> regularly mark registers and styles within a language.

However, the basic function of a classifier is to classify. But what do classifiers actually classify—extralinguistic referents (i.e., beings, objects, states, actions, etc.) or the intralinguistic category 'noun'?

In our descriptions of classifiers in the noun phrase, we usually use phrases such as "This classifier *refers to* this noun" or "This classifier *refers to* this nominal referent." Both phrases may be understood as a kind of "shorthand" for "This classifier refers to this noun, which itself is used as the expression to refer to, for example, an object in extralinguistic reality." However, the shorthand versions open up a "nice" ambiguity with respect to the notion "reference," and it is still an open question how we can resolve the ambiguity of these "shorthand versions."

Classifiers also indicate that the noun they classify must be understood as having nongeneric reference; in other words, classifiers individuate—or "unitize" (Lucy 2000: 334)—nouns in classifier languages. As I already stated, the choice of an adequate classifier to refer to a nominal referent occurs on the semantic level; it can be independent of the speech act intended and therefore attains stylistic denotation, meaning, and significance. Individual speakers use these options in their choice of classifiers—and a closer look at the actual use of a classifier system by its speakers supports Becker's (1975: 113) view that the actual "use of classifiers . . . is in part an art."

While it seems safe to conclude that all classifiers indeed "do have meaning" (Allan 1977: 290), it is still unclear how this meaning is achieved and what it does. It can be argued that when a classifier refers to a nominal referent, it individuates the noun and then highlights a special (shade of) meaning which then selects one special referent from the total set of possible extralinguistic referents of the noun when it is not specified by this classifier. If this is what classifiers do, we have to ask whether the noun with nominal classifier marking is still the same noun that is to be found in the lexicon (without classifier marking). Does a classifier only refer to an object in the extralinguistic reality, or does it also refer to the intralinguistic category 'noun' and change its meaning? Or, in other words, does the classifier refer to a 'referent' in the "real world" or to a 'noun', an entity in the lexicon of a language? We could even argue the other way around: if a noun is classified by a certain classifier, will the meaning of the noun influence the meaning of the classifier?

I will give one example that I hope will clarify the rather complex point I want to make here. Take the Kilivila noun phrase (18) and its morpheme-interlinear translation (18'):

(18)   *magudina waga*
(18')   *ma-gudi-na*   *waga*
        DEM-CL.child-DEM   canoe

Here, the noun *waga*, the Kilivila verbal sign to refer to the extralinguistic object 'canoe' is—metaphorically—classified with the classifier *gudi* in the frame of the Kilivila demonstrative pronoun. The classifier *gudi* is usually used to refer to '(a) child' or to '(an) immature adult'. The classifier that one would expect to be used with the nominal referent *waga* is *ke*; among other things, this classifier refers to '(a) tree' or to 'wooden things'—and the Trobriand Islanders' canoes are made out of wood. Now, how can we translate this phrase? A possible literal translation would be 'this child-like canoe'. However, it is obvious that this sounds funny. A look at the sentence and the situation in which this phrase was produced may help here:

(19)   *Kugisi magudina waga kekekita okopo'ula waga dimdim!*
       ku-gisi   ma-gudi-na   waga   ke-kekita
       2.-look   DEM-CL.child-DEM   canoe   CL.wooden-small
       okopo'ula   *waga*   *dimdim*
       behind   canoe   white.man

Here, the two classifiers mentioned above are used to refer to the nominal referent *waga* (note the double classification here). The sentence was uttered by a Trobriand Islander when a big motorboat with a dinghy in tow passed before the reef of Tauwema village. Now, on the basis of this background information we can translate the sentence as follows:

(19')   'Look at this small dinghy behind the motorboat!'

I cannot decide whether the meaning of the classifier has influenced or changed the meaning of the classified noun or whether the meaning of the noun has influenced or changed the meaning of the classifier or whether the co-occurence of the respective classifier with the respective noun resulted in an interactive "Sprachspiel" where both the noun and the classifier changed their meaning in and through this interaction (on the phrase level). Nor can I decide whether the act of referring with the classifier to the nominal referent here has to be understood as a verbal sign referring to a language-internal or to a language-external context.

A look at some definitions of "referent" and "act of referring" does not help very much here. Following Bußmann's (1983: 428) definition, for instance, a "referent" can be defined as an object or a fact in the extralinguistic reality to which noun phrases then as verbal signs "refer." The "act of referring" can be understood, on the one hand, as the verbal reference to language-internal and language-external contexts and, on the other hand, the relation between the verbal expression (name, word, etc.) and the object in the extralinguistic reality to which the expression refers. But this definition (like many others) does not help me to solve the ambiguity mentioned above. Given the fact, however, that I do not know what is actually going on when a classifier refers to a nominal referent, this ambiguity may not be altogether unwelcome.

To conclude, classifiers individualize nominal concepts, and they have meaning. However, the description of this meaning seems to be dependent (i) on the situation and the context in which the classifier is used; (ii) on the nominal referent to which it refers; and (iii) on the means and ends a speaker wants to achieve and express using a certain classifier (to refer to a certain noun).

Coming up with a definition of the meaning or the various meanings of a classifier is quite a difficult question. I have proposed a model for the description of the Kilivila classifier system elsewhere (Senft 1991, 1996).

To sum up, I have mentioned and tried to illustrate some problems that, at least to my mind, are typical for research on systems of nominal classification in languages. I am afraid that this has proven Royen's (1929: iv) point that the question of nominal classification raises a whole lot of other questions. However, I think this subsection has shown that it is precisely these open questions that make systems of nominal classification so interesting, especially for Cognitive Linguistics. In the last section of this chapter, I will briefly elaborate on this point.

3. Nominal Classification, Categorization, and Cognitive Linguistics

In the introduction to this chapter, it was emphasized that the survival of every organism on earth depends on its abilities to classify, filter, and categorize its perceptual input. As human beings, we heavily depend on these acts of classification when we try to make sense out of experience. The discussion and the presentation of the various systems of nominal classification in the previous section has shown that they lead to a specific categorization of the nominal conceptual labels that are coded in the languages of the world. The rise of Cognitive Linguistics in the last two decades of the twentieth century is inextricably intertwined with research on how people—and peoples—classify and categorize, that is, how they organize their knowledge. This general question for the cognitive sciences can be specified as follows for linguistics: how is the perceived world expressed, and grammatically encoded, in natural languages? In the middle of the last century, this—by no means new—question regained the importance it deserved (not only in linguistics, but also in anthropology). And it was the psycholinguistic (and cognitive anthropological) research on prototype-based forms of categorization carried out by Eleanor Rosch (see, e.g., Rosch 1977, 1978, 1988) and others that helped to establish and very much influenced Cognitive Linguistics as a new (sub)discipline. Actually, "categorization" is one of the main concerns of Cognitive Linguistics, as Geeraerts's (1995: 111; see also 1990: 1) definition reveals:

> Cognitive linguistics is an approach to the analysis of natural language that focuses on language as an instrument for organizing, processing, and conveying information. Methodologically speaking, the analysis of the conceptual and experiental basis of linguistic categories is of primary importance within cognitive linguistics: it primarily considers language as a system of categories. The formal structures of language are studied not as if they were autonomous, but as reflections of general conceptual organization, categorization principles, processing mechanisms, and experiental and environmental influences.

Given this definition of the discipline, it is obvious that systems of nominal classification are not only of special interest for, but also clearly in the focus of, cognitive linguistic research. The techniques of nominal classification provide indeed rich "sources of data that we have concerning the structure of the conceptual categories as they are revealed through language" (Lakoff 1987: 91). In what follows, I would like to illustrate this with the complex system of classifiers in Kilivila.

As mentioned in section 2.2 above, Kilivila is a classifier language with an inventory of probably more than 200 classifiers. On the basis of my field research on the Trobriands, I analyzed and described in detail 88 of these classifiers that are used by the inhabitants of Tauwema, my field-site and village of residence on Kaile'una Island (Senft: 1996).[8] Like speakers of any classifier language, a speaker of Kilivila must classify all nominal denotata—an infinite set probably—with classifiers that may, in theory, be infinite but in everyday speech constitute a finite set of formatives; thus, the statements that "classifiers are linguistic correlates to perception" (Allan 1977: 308) and "linguistic classifiers relate people to the world" (Becker 1975: 118) are plausible and convincing. The 88 classifiers produced by the inhabitants of Tauwema constitute 20 semantic domains.[9] I have shown that these semantic domains are dynamic and interact with each other. They can be understood as "program clusters," "procedures," or "scripts" that constitute a complex network (Senft 1991). Furthermore, they can be interpreted as categories that native speakers have developed (and are still developing) to order their perceived world, as it is encoded and represented in the nominal denotata of their language. This interpretation assigns to the semantic domains constituted by the classifiers the status of linguistic manifestations of Trobriand classification and categorization of their perceived world. The questions to be raised now are the following: Do the linguistic manifestations of the Trobriand perception of the world allow any kind of inferences to Trobriand cognition and to Trobriand culture? Do these categories "frame" Trobriand thought, in Goffman's (1974) sense? Do these linguistic manifestations of the Trobriand perception represent universals of human cognitive processes or do they merely represent language—or culture-specific characteristics of Trobriand thought?

My analyses of these domains have shown that most of the concepts incorporated in them are quite general and seem to be universal for human speech communities. However, the discussion of these domains has also shown that these probably universal categories are defined in a culture-specific way. As the Kilivila classifier system illustrates, the hierarchical order and the culture-specific definitions of "instantiations" of these probably universal semantic domains (or categories, or concepts) give us a good deal of information about speakers' culture, and certainly "frame" the speakers' perception, their kind of perceptive awareness, and their preferred ways of thinking, at least to a certain extent. However, this does not imply that this frame cannot be broken or changed if the speech community feels the need to do so. Thus, my analyses of the Kilivila classifier system confirm Slobin's (1991: 23) general remark that

> we can only talk and understand one another in terms of a particular language. The languages that we learn in childhood are not neutral coding systems of objective reality. Rather, each one is a subjective orientation to the world of human experience, and this orientation *affects the ways in which we think while we are speaking.*

Keeping Geeraerts's definition of Cognitive Linguistics in mind, and given this interrelationship between thinking and speaking, it is no wonder that classification and categorization as basic cognitive processes are central topics for, and in, Cognitive Linguistics. The systems of nominal classification in the languages of the world offer cognitive linguists a great empirical basis for the study of how speakers of natural languages categorize and classify their world and how they use this categorization and classification processes for the organization of their communicative needs.

NOTES

1. See, for instance, Royen (1929), Rosch (1977, 1978), Seiler and Lehmann (1982), Seiler and Stachowiak (1982), Craig (1986c), Seiler (1986), Lakoff (1987), Corbett (1991), Senft (1996, 2000a, 2000b), and Aikhenvald (2000a).

2. This basic criterion for the definition of noun class systems was emphasized by Royen (1929: 526). It may be argued—from a generalizing (and somewhat simplifying) point of view—that classifier language systems are semantically based, while noun class systems are based on formal, grammatical factors. However, this does not imply that in

noun class or gender systems there is no interplay of semantic and formal factors (see Corbett 1991: 306; see also Lakoff 1987). Allan (1977: 286) refers to languages with noun class systems as "concordial classifier languages."

3. Descriptions of the criteria that structure classifying systems generally make use of features such as "+/– human; human and social status; human and kinship relation; +/– animate; sex; shape/dimension; size; consistency; function; arrangement; habitat; number/ amount/mass/group; measure; weight; time; action; +/– visible" (Senft 1996: 9).

4. De León (1988) and Zavala (2000) have demonstrated that sortal classifiers are grammatically distinct from mensural classifiers in the Mayan languages Tzotzil and Akatek.

5. For further information and examples, see Aikhenvald (2000a: 98–124) and Senft (1996, 2000a).

6. I have complained about the lack of descriptive and terminological accuracy in the research on systems of nominal classification elsewhere (Senft 2000b: 22). I absolutely agree with Grinevald (2000: 53), who justifies the need for distinguishing the various types of classifiers by noting the confusion created by linguists who used classifier data "secondhand." She points out that "the famous discussion of Dyirbal classifiers by Lakoff (1987) actually deals . . . with noun classes" (see also Dixon 1972: 44–47, 307). Unfortunately, the title of her now classic anthology (Craig 1986c) is also somehow responsible for some such confusion within the research on nominal classification systems.

7. This can be illustrated with the Diegueño examples given above. The first two criteria are fulfilled there: the same noun class (long object) can be recognized with two predications (*hang, cover*); different noun classes (long object, round object) are realized with the same predication (*hang*) in two different verb forms; the noun class can be identified for more than one object with respect to two predications (*to put on top, to put in jail*); and the noun classes for more objects and for long objects are realized in two different forms with the predication *to put on top*. The third criterion excludes agreement phenomena between noun and verb (see Fedden 2002b: 410).

8. Malinowski (1920) describes 42 of these "Classificatory Particles," and Lawton (1980) mentions 85 classifiers; however, these classifiers were not produced by my consultants. Thus, so far 177 classifiers are known and described for this language.

9. I labeled these domains as follows: Persons/body parts; General classifiers; Animals; Trees/wooden things; Place; Quantities; Fire/oven; Names; Time; Road/journey; Qualities; Shape; Utensils; Dress/adornment; Door/entrance/window; Ritual items; Parts of a foodhouse/a canoe/a creel (containers); Measures; Yams (food); and Texts. Kilivila native speakers accept the semantic domains proposed (see Senft 1996: 295–311).

REFERENCES

Adams, Karen. L. 1989. *Systems of numeral classification in the Mon-Khmer, Nicobarese and Aslian subfamilies of Austroasiatic.* Pacific Linguistics, Series B, no. 101. Canberra: Australian National University.

Adams, Karen L., Alton L. Becker, and Nancy F. Conklin. 1975. Savoring the differences among classifier systems. Paper presented at the 8th International Conference on Sino-Tibetan Languages and Linguistics, University of California at Berkeley, October 24–26.

Aikhenvald, Alexandra Y. 2000a. *Classifiers: A typology of noun categorization devices.* Oxford: Oxford University Press.

Aikhenvald, Alexandra Y. 2000b. Unusual classifiers in Tariana. In Gunter Senft, ed., *Systems of nominal classification* 93–113. Cambridge: Cambridge University Press.

Allan, Keith. 1977. Classifiers. *Language* 53: 285–311.

Barron, Roger. 1982. Das Phänomen klassifikatorischer Verben. In Hansjakob Seiler and Christian Lehmann, eds., *Apprehension: Das sprachliche Erfassen von Gegenständen*, vol. 1, *Bereich und Ordnung der Phänomene* 133–46. Tübingen: Gunter Narr.

Becker, Alton L. 1975. A linguistic image of nature: The Burmese numerative classifier system. *Linguistics* 165: 109–21.

Berlin, Brent. 1968. *Tzeltal numeral classifiers: A study in ethnographic semantics.* The Hague: Mouton.

Bisang, Walter. 2002. Classification and the evolution of grammatical structures: A universal perspective. *Sprachtypologie und Universalienforschung* 55: 289–308.

Broschart, Jürgen. 1997. Locative classifiers in Tongan. In Gunter Senft, ed., *Referring to space: Studies in Austronesian and Papuan languages* 287–315. Oxford: Clarendon Press.

Bußmann, Hadumod. 1983. *Lexikon der Sprachwissenschaft.* Stuttgart: Kröner.

Corbett, Greville. 1991. *Gender.* Cambridge: Cambridge University Press.

Craig, Colette. 1986a. Introduction. In Colette Craig, ed., *Noun classes and categorization* 1–10. Amsterdam: John Benjamins.

Craig, Colette. 1986b. Jacaltec noun classifiers: A study in language and culture. In Colette Craig, ed., *Noun classes and categorization* 263–93. Amsterdam: John Benjamins.

Craig, Colette, ed. 1986c. *Noun classes and categorization.* Amsterdam: John Benjamins.

De León, Lourdes. 1988. Noun and numeral classifiers in Mixtec and Tzotzil: A referential view. PhD dissertation, University of Sussex.

Demuth, Katherine. 2000. Gender assignment: A typology and a model. In Gunter Senft, ed., *Systems of nominal classification* 270–92. Cambridge: Cambridge University Press.

Dixon, Robert M. W. 1972. *The Dyirbal language of North Queensland.* Cambridge: Cambridge University Press.

Dixon, Robert M. W. 1986. Noun classes and noun classification in typological perspective. In Colette Craig, ed., *Noun classes and categorization* 105–12. Amsterdam: John Benjamins.

Fedden, Sebastian. 2002a. Nominale Klassifikationssysteme: Ein Vergleich zwischen Verbalklassifikation und Nominalklassen. MA thesis, University of Bielefeld.

Fedden, Sebastian. 2002b. Verbalklassifikation in nordamerikanischen Indianersprachen. *Linguistische Berichte* 192: 395–415.

Foucault, Michel. [1966] 1980. *Die Ordnung der Dinge: Eine Archäologie der Humanwissenschaften.* Frankfurt am Main: Suhrkamp. (Translation of *Les mots et les choses.* Paris: Gallimard)

Friedrich, Paul. 1970. Shape in grammar. *Language* 46: 379–407.

Geeraerts, Dirk. 1990. Editorial statement. *Cognitive Linguistics* 1: 1–3.

Geeraerts, Dirk. 1995. Cognitive linguistics. In Jef Verschueren, Jan-Ola Östman, and Jan Blommaert, eds., *Handbook of pragmatics: Manual* 111–16. Amsterdam: John Benjamins.

Goffman, Erving. 1974. *Frame analysis. An essay on the organization of experience.* New York: Harper and Row.

Greenberg, Joseph H. 1978. How does a language acquire gender-markers? In Joseph H. Greenberg, ed., *Universals of human language*, vol. 3, *Word structure* 47–82. Stanford, CA: Stanford University Press.

Grinevald, Colette. 2000. A morphosyntactic typology of classifiers. In Gunter Senft, ed., *Systems of nominal classification* 50–92. Cambridge: Cambridge University Press.

Hellwig, Birgit. 2003. The grammatical coding of postural semantics in Goemai. PhD dissertation, Max Planck Institute and Katholieke Universiteit Nijmegen.

Herder, Johann Gottfried. [1770] 1978. Über den Ursprung der Sprache. In *Herders Werke in fünf Bänden* 2: 91–200. Berlin: Aufbau Verlag.

Humboldt, Wilhelm von. [1836] 1968. *Über die Verschiedenheit des menschlichen Sprachbaues und ihren Einfluß auf die geistige Entwicklung des Menschengeschlechts.* Bonn: Dümmler Verlag.

Koestler, Arthur. 1983. *Janus: A summing up.* London: Pan Picador.

Lakoff, George. 1987. *Women, fire, and dangerous things: What categories reveal about the mind.* Chicago: University of Chicago Press.

Langdon, Margaret. 1970. *A grammar of Diegueño: The Mesa Grande dialect.* Berkeley: University of California Press.

Lawton, Ralph. 1980. The Kiriwinan classifiers. MA thesis, Australian National University, Canberra.

Lucy, John A. 2000. Systems of nominal classification: A concluding discussion. In Gunter Senft, ed., *Systems of nominal classification* 326–41. Cambridge: Cambridge University Press.

Malinowski, Bronislaw. 1920. Classificatory particles in the language of Kiriwina. *Bulletin of the School of Oriental Studies, London Institution* 1.4: 33–78.

Mithun, Marianne. 1986. The convergence of noun classification systems. In Colette Craig, ed., *Noun classes and categorization* 379–97. Amsterdam: John Benjamins.

Regh, Kenneth L. 1981. *Ponapean reference grammar.* Honolulu: University of Hawaii Press.

Rosch, Eleanor. 1977. Human categorization. In Neil Warren, ed., *Studies in cross-cultural psychology* 1: 1–49. London: Academic Press.

Rosch, Eleanor. 1978. Principles of categorization. In Eleanor Rosch and Barbara B. Lloyd, eds., *Cognition and categorization* 27–48. Hillsdale, NJ: Lawrence Erlbaum.

Rosch, Eleanor. 1988. Coherence and categorization: A historical view. In Frank S. Kessel, ed., *The development of language and language researchers: Essays in honor of Roger Brown* 373–92. Hillsdale, NJ: Lawrence Erlbaum.

Royen, Gerlach. 1929. *Die nominalen Klassifikations-Systeme in den Sprachen der Erde: Historisch-kritische Studie, mit besonderer Berücksichtigung des Indogermanischen.* Wien: Anthropos.

Schleiermacher, Friedrich D. E. [1838] 1977. *Hermeneutik und Kritik mit besonderer Beziehung auf das neue Testament.* Aus Schleiermachers handschriftlichem Nachlasse und nachgeschriebenen Vorlesungen herausgegeben und eingeleitet von Manfred Frank [From Schleiermacher's handwritten unpublished works and from notes taken of his lectures, edited and introduced by Manfred Frank]. Frankfurt am Main: Suhrkamp.

Seiler, Hansjakob. 1986. *Apprehension: Language, object, and order.* Vol. 3, *The universal dimension of apprehension.* Tübingen: Gunter Narr.

Seiler, Hansjakob, and Christian Lehmann, eds. 1982. *Apprehension: Das sprachliche Erfassen von Gegenständen.* Vol. 1, *Bereich und Ordnung der Phänomene.* Tübingen: Gunter Narr.

Seiler, Hansjakob, and Franz-Joseph Stachowiak, eds. 1982. *Apprehension: Das sprachliche Erfassen von Gegenständen.* Vol. 2, *Die Techniken und ihr Zusammenhang in Einzelsprachen.* Tübingen: Gunter Narr.

Senft, Gunter. 1991. Network models to describe the Kilivila classifier system. *Oceanic Linguistics* 30: 131–55.

Senft, Gunter. 1996. *Classificatory particles in Kilivila.* Oxford: Oxford University Press.

Senft, Gunter, ed. 2000a. *Systems of nominal classification.* Cambridge: Cambridge University Press.

Senft, Gunter. 2000b. What do we really know about nominal classification systems? In Gunter Senft, ed., *Systems of nominal classification* 11–49. Cambridge: Cambridge University Press.

Slobin, Dan I. 1991. Learning to think for speaking: Native language, cognition, and rhetorical style. *Pragmatics* 1: 7–25.

Talmy, Leonard. 1992. Nouns. In William Bright, ed., *International encyclopedia of linguistics* 3: 130–31. Oxford: Oxford University Press.

Unterbeck, Barbara, and Matti Rissanen, eds. 2000. *Gender in grammar and cognition.* Berlin: Mouton de Gruyter.

Vollmer, Gerhard. 1988a: *Was können wir wissen?* Vol. 1, *Die Natur der Erkenntnis.* Stuttgart: Hirzel.

Vollmer, Gerhard. 1988b: *Was können wir wissen?* Vol. 2, *Die Erkenntnis der Natur.* Stuttgart: Hirzel.

Whorf, Benjamin L. 1958. Science and Linguistics. In Eleanor Maccoby, Theodore M. Newcomb, and Eugene L. Hartley, eds., *Readings in Social Psychology* 1–9. New York: Holt, Rinehart and Winston.

Zavala, Roberto. 2000. Multiple classifier systems in Akatek (Mayan). In Gunter Senft, ed., *Systems of nominal classification* 114–46. Cambridge: Cambridge University Press.

Zubin, David. A. 1992. Gender and noun classification. In William Bright, ed., *International encyclopedia of linguistics* 3: 41–43. Oxford: Oxford University Press.

Zubin, David A., and Klaus-Michael Köpcke. 1986. Gender and folk taxonomy: The indexical relation between grammatical and lexical categorization. In Colette Craig, ed., *Noun classes and categorization* 263–93. Amsterdam: John Benjamins.

CHAPTER 27

IDIOMS AND FORMULAIC LANGUAGE

RAYMOND W. GIBBS, JR.

1. INTRODUCTION

Speaking a language with any degree of fluency requires a knowledge of idioms, proverbs, slang, fixed expressions, and other speech formulas. People rarely talk using literal language exclusively. In fact, it is nearly impossible to speak of many human events and abstract ideas without employing idiomatic phrases that communicate nonliteral meaning. For example, in American English, speakers talk of revealing secrets in terms of *spilling the beans*, suddenly dying in terms of *kicking the bucket*, getting angry in terms of *blowing your stack*, taking risks as *going out on a limb*, trading gossip as *chewing the fat*, and urging others to take action by saying *the early bird catches the worm*. A traditional view of idioms and related speech formulas sees these phrases as bits and pieces of fossilized language. Under this view, speakers must learn these "dead" metaphors and speech gambits by arbitrarily pairing each phrase to some nonliteral meaning without any awareness of why these phrases mean what they do.

Yet idiomatic/proverbial phrases like the above are not mere linguistic ornaments, intended to dress up a person's speech style, but are an integral part of the language that eases social interaction, enhances textual coherence, and, quite importantly, reflect fundamental patterns of human thought. Idioms and many formulaic expressions are not simple fixed or frozen phrases. In many cases, idioms are analyzable to varying degrees and linked to enduring metaphorical and metonymic conceptual structures.

Over the past twenty-five years, cognitive linguistic research has played a significant role in advancing this new vision of idiomaticity. My aim in this chapter is to describe this revolution, of sorts, in the linguistic and psychological study of idioms and related speech formula.

2. What Is Idiomatic/ Formulaic Language?

There are major debates and numerous proposals on how best to define idiomaticity and formulaic language (Coulmas 1981; Gibbs 1994; Mel'čuk 1995; Hudson 1998; Moon 1998; Naciscione 2001, for reviews). Lexicographers and those scholars working in the linguistic tradition of phraseology have long realized that single words are not necessarily the appropriate unit for lexical description. But one working definition suggests that formulaic language is "a sequence, continuous or discontinuous, of words or other meaning elements, which is, or appears to be prefabricated: that is, stored and retrieved whole from memory at the time of use, rather than being subject to generation or analysis by the language grammar" (Wray and Perkins 2000: 1). Under this definition, formulaicity contrasts with productivity, the ability to use the structural system of language (syntax, semantics, morphology, and phonology) in a combinatory way to create and understand novel utterances.

Many scholars, following the above traditional view of formulaicity, suggest that many types of language are to a large degree formulaic, including amalgams, cliches, collocations, fixed expressions, gambits, holophrases, idioms, multiword units, noncompositional sequences, and prefabricated routines, to list just a few of the majors labels. I will not attempt to provide rigid definitions for each of these terms as each one has various useful and problematic qualities. At the very least, a rough list of the different forms of idioms and formulaic language includes the following (Gibbs 1994):

(1)   Sayings:
       a. take the bull by the horns
       b. let the cat out of the bag
(2)   Proverbs:
       a. A bird in the hand is worth two in the bush.
       b. A stitch in time saves nine.
(3)   Phrasal verbs:
       a. to give in
       b. to take off

(4)   Idioms:
    a. kick the bucket
    b. to crack the whip
(5)   Binomials:
    a. spick and span
    b. hammer and tongs
(6)   Frozen similes:
    a. as white as snow
    b. as cool as a cucumber
(7)   Phrasal compounds:
    a. red herring
    b. dead-line
(8)   Incorporating verb idioms:
    a. to babysit
    b. to sightsee
(9)   Formulaic expressions:
    a. at first sight
    b. how do you do?

My general focus will be on phraseological/idiomatic units that convey speaker meaning that cannot be determined by simply adding up the meanings of each word or morpheme. Idioms are often distinguished from metaphor, metonymy, irony, and so on. But many idioms often incorporate other kinds of figurative language (Gibbs 1994; Kövecses and Szabó 1996; especially Moon 1998, from which many of the following examples are taken). Metaphorical idioms are quite prominent. For instance, people are frequently referred to idiomatically by denoting some characteristic often equated with a specific animal (Moon 1998). Consider the following expressions in (10):

(10)   a. as blind as a bat (weak sighted)
    b. as busy as a bee (industry)
    c. treat like a dog (ill-treatment)
    d. eat like a horse (appetite)
    e. as stubborn as a mule (obstinacy)

These phrases incorporate fossilized, stereotyped beliefs, usually referring to undesirable traits in animals that are used to conceptualize of people and human actions.

Other metaphorical idioms are expressed as explicit similes which function to intensify the main adjective. Consider the following examples:

(11)   a. (as) clear as crystal
    b. dead as a doornail
    c. as good as gold

Other similes are even more institutionalized and are perhaps more frequent. These include:

(12)   a. built like a truck
       b. like getting blood out of a stone
       c. stick out like a sore thumb
       d. work like a dog

Most metonymic idioms relate to parts of the body. The particular body part mentioned represents the whole person and foregrounds the physical sense or ability which constitutes the central part of the idiom's figurative meaning. For example, *lend an ear* indicates both the person and his/her attention, and *get one's head round something* indicates a person and his/her mind or understanding. Some further examples are in (13):

(13)   a. hate someone's guts
       b. have an eye on something
       c. lend a hand
       d. lose one's nerve
       e. under someone's thumb

For the above expressions, the relationship between metonymic tenor and metonymic vehicle is often governed by physiology and the real world. Sense organs denote their respective senses, and formulaic phrases mentioning hands, for example, generally have meanings to do with holding and manipulating (Kövecses and Szabó 1996). In other cases, the relationship is culturally determined. By convention, *heart,* as in *to lose heart,* indicates emotions and depth of feeling, and *nerve,* as in *to lose one's nerve,* refers to audacity or bravery.

Other metonymic idioms involve objects and places that represent actions, activities, or results or involve other part and whole relationships. For the most part, these referents are also often culture specific. Consider the following cases:

(14)   a. at the helm/wheel
       b. from the cradle to the grave
       c. set sail
       d. take the floor
       e. without a stitch on

Hyperbolic idioms describe literally impossible processes or attributes, with the aim of intensifying our understanding of the main idea or event a speaker refers to. These include expressions like the following:

(15)   a. a storm in a teacup
       b. breathe fire
       c. jump down someone's throat
       d. shoot the breeze
       e. sweat blood
       f. tie oneself into knots
       g. raining cats and dogs

Many idioms suggest exaggerations and implausibilities, rather than actual impossibilities. Consider the following examples:

(16)   a. be paved with gold
        b. be rolling in the aisles
        c. cost an arm and an leg
        d. chilled to the bone
        e. stink to high heaven

Truisms form another group of idiomatic phrases. These expressions state the obvious, and achieve their rhetorical effect through understatement. These are completely truthful but must be interpreted in the light of what is implied in the vehicle of their metaphors. Consider the following cases:

(17)   a. cannot hear oneself think
        b. not a spring chicken
        c. not hold water
        d. not someone's cup of tea
        e. won't set the world on fire

Finally, a few formulas are always used ironically. The mismatch between surface and intended meaning can be seen as a kind of metaphoricity in which the concrete terms in the idiom are metaphorically mapped onto the situation at hand, usually with ironic effect. Consider the following examples:

(18)   a. big deal
        b. God's gift to . . .
        c. take the cake
        d. tell me about it
        e. need something like a hole in the head

The prominence of different figurative schemes in many idioms and related forms provides one source of evidence in favor of the claim that people readily conceptualize human events and abstract ideas via metaphor, metonymy, irony, and other tropes.

3. WHY SPEAK IDIOMATICALLY?

The thousands of idioms and proverbs listed in contemporary dictionaries, which do not include any other speech formulas, suggests that these phrases make up an important part of the language (for example, see the *Longman Dictionary of English Idioms* 1979, and the *Oxford Dictionary of Current Idiomatic English* 1993). But why do people speak and write idiomatically? Similar to traditional reasons for employing metaphor, people use idioms to be polite, to avoid responsibility for the import of what is communicated, to express ideas that are difficult to communicate using literal language, and to express thoughts in a compact and vivid manner (Ortony 1975; Gibbs 1994). For instance, consider the following formulaic phrases where the lexical meaning diverges from the idiomatic interpretation (adapted from Moon 1998).

(19) | | lexical reference | idiomatic reference |
|---|---|---|
| *break the ice* | action | verbal |
| *fit the bill* | action | attributive |
| *go up in smoke* | event | existential |
| *jog someone's memory* | action | cognition |
| *lose one's heart* | action | affection |
| *run out of steam* | event | attributive |
| *throw in the towel* | action | event |

In each case here, a speaker uses an idiomatic phrase to effectively communicate in an indirect manner a subjective opinion under the guise of stating a more objective physical situation. Speaking in this way communicates an interpretation and evaluation of the situation that the speaker refers to when employing an idiom.

Idiomatic language, in other cases, enables speakers to remind listeners of other related contexts to communicate relevant beliefs in the present situation. Many pithy phrases drawn from films, television, politics, and journalism become institutionalized as part of contemporary culture (e.g., American presidential candidate in 1984, Walter Mondale, asking then President Ronald Reagan with regard to his budget proposals *Where's the beef?*, which echoed a statement made in a popular hamburger-chain television commercial). This establishment of idioms in contemporary American culture is evident in still well-understood phases such as the following (Moon 1998):

(20) a. And now for something completely different
b. Go ahead, make my day
c. I'll be back
d. This could be the beginning of a beautiful friendship

More generally, formulaic language is important to social interaction for manipulating others, asserting separate identity, and asserting group identity (Wray and Perkins 2000). Thus, knowing the right familiar phrase, such as slang, to use in some situation is critical to marking a speaker as having the right status to be considered a valued member of some community.

Using idioms and other speech formulas also has important cognitive benefits, especially in providing mental shortcuts in both language production and comprehension. A speaker may easily retrieve a phrase like *John flew off the handle when he saw the messy kitchen* to express in an indirect way a very vivid image of John getting angry (Gibbs and O'Brien 1990). Listeners will readily infer the complex figurative meanings of the phrase *flew off the handle* because of their familiarity with this expression (Gibbs 1992). People readily interpret the figurative meanings of idioms faster than they do either paraphrases or literal uses of the same expressions (Gibbs 1980). For this reason, formulaic language is a means of ensuring the physical and social survival of the individual through communication, on the one hand, and a way of avoiding processing overload, on the other.

Idioms may have several organizational functions in discourse (Moon 1998). For instance, idioms are thought to be excellent ways of signaling topic transition in conversation. Consider the following excerpt from a conversation between a daughter and her mother where they talked about the death of someone they both knew (adapted from Drew and Holt 1995: 123):

(21)   Leslie: The vicar's warden, anyways, he died suddenly this week, and he was still working.

Mum: Good grace.

Leslie: He was seventy-nine.

Mum: My word.

Leslie: Yes, he was.

Mum: You've got's real workers down there.

Leslie: He was a, uh. Yes. Indeed, he was a buyer for the only horse hair factory left in England.

Mum: Good grace.

Leslie: He was their buyer. So he had a good innings, didn't he?

Mum: I should say so. Yes. Marvelous.

Leslie: Anyways, we had a very good evening on Saturday.

When Leslie says *he had a good innings* (an idiomatic allusion describing a batsman's successful performance in a cricket match), she not only summarizes the information presented in her prior turn (e.g., he was a buyer for the only horse hair factory left in England), but refers to the whole theme of the conversation up to that point (e.g., that the vicar's warden was still working at age seventy-nine when he died). Leslie's description of the vicar's warden's life metaphorically as *a good innings* refers to a more abstract, general idea than if she had simply stated that 'he had a good life' (e.g., that his life was long and very productive). Thus, the idiom acts to thematically summarize the information revealed in the conversation and allows speakers to move on to the next conversational topic. Idioms are especially useful in terminating a topic because of their distinctive manner of characterizing abstract themes in concrete ways.

Another example of how idioms provide textual coherence is seen in the following case where a speaker develops an image using the proverb *Don't put the cart before the horse* when talking about British economic problems (from *The Guardian* of July 1990, as cited in Moon 1998: 126):

To regard savings as the animating force in this scheme of things is to put the cart before the horse. The horse is the growth of national income, propelled by the level of spending, the harness linking horse and cart the financial system, and bringing up the rear is the cart of saving. The horse is larger the greater the level of investment, and the larger the horse the larger the cart of savings it can support.

The writer here uses the surface image of putting a horse before a cart to draw out various entailments of the analogy between the proverb and the financial situation in England. In this way, the author uses a common expression or parts of this phrase, with figurative meaning to provide coherence to his complex argument about an abstract topic.

Beyond these various pragmatic reasons for employing idioms and formulas in speech and writing, people speak idiomatically because they conceptualize of many ideas and events, particularly human ones, in terms of metaphor and metonymy. I will argue in a later section that the study of idioms, in fact, provides a significant source of evidence showing the fundamental figurative character of many aspects of human thought.

4. ARE IDIOMS REALLY FIXED EXPRESSIONS?

The widely held view of idioms is that these phrases are "noncompositional," or "fixed," and that their meanings must be directly stipulated in the mental lexicon in the same way that the meanings of individual words are listed in a dictionary (see Sinclair 1991). Unlike comprehension of literal language, idioms are presumably understood in one of several ways: (i) through the retrieval of their stipulated meanings from the lexicon after their literal meanings have been rejected as inappropriate (Weinreich 1969; Bobrow and Bell 1973); (ii) in parallel to processing of their literal meanings (Swinney and Cutler 1979); (iii) directly without any analysis of their literal meanings (Gibbs 1980, 1986); or (iv) when there has been significant input to recognize a configuration as an idiom (Cacciari and Tabossi 1988; Tabossi and Zardon 1993). Experimental studies show that (iii) and (iv) provide the best descriptions of how idioms are understood (Gibbs 1994). Many computational models of natural language processing include a special "phrasal" lexicon containing idiomatic and formulaic phrases that are noncompositional, but which can be quickly accessed during linguistic parsing (Becker 1975; Wilensky and Arens 1980; Gasser and Dyer 1986; see also Jackendoff 1995).

Scholars often treat idioms as "dead" metaphors. The classic case of *kick the bucket* seems to illustrate the idea that the phrase may have been at one time metaphorical but has lost its metaphoricity over time (actually, this phrase has a metonymic origin). To some extent, there are idioms that appear "dead" in this way (although even *kick the bucket* seems somewhat analyzable in that it refers to sudden, and not prolonged, death, primarily due to the influence of *kick*; see Hamblin and Gibbs 1999).

But this traditional view of idiomaticity confuses dead metaphors with conventional ones. Deciding whether an idiom is dead or just unconsciously conventional requires, among other things, a search for its systematic manifestation in the language as a whole and in our everyday reasoning patterns. For instance, consider the following list of conventional expressions:

(22) a. Look how far we've come.
      b. It's been a long, bumpy road.
      c. We're at a crossroads.
      d. We may have to go our separate ways.
      e. Our marriage is on the rocks.
      f. We're spinning our wheels.

These (and other) conventional expressions cluster together under one of the basic metaphorical system of understanding: LOVE IS A JOURNEY (Lakoff and Johnson 1980). This conceptual metaphor involves a tight mapping according to which entities in the domain of love (e.g., the lovers, their common goals, the love relationship, etc.) correspond systematically to entities in the domain of a journey (e.g., the traveler, the vehicle, destinations, etc.). Various inferences or entailments arise when we think of love as a journey. Among these are the inferences that the person in love is a traveler, the goal of ultimate love is a destination, the means for achieving love are routes, the difficulties one experiences in love are obstacles to travel, and the progress in a love relationship is the distance traveled.

Classic idioms also are systematically related. Consider the following phrases:

(23) a. blow your stack
      b. hot the ceiling
      c. flip your lid

These phrases arise from the widespread conceptual metaphor ANGER IS HEATED FLUID IN A CONTAINER, which also underlies quasi-idiomatic phrases such as *blow up* and *flipped out*. Not all idioms for anger are motivated by the conceptual metaphor ANGER IS HEATED FLUID IN A CONTAINER. Thus, *jump down someone's throat* appears to be related to ANGER IS ANIMAL BEHAVIOR. In this way, there are often several metaphorical ways of conceptualizing a single abstract concept, such as 'anger'. But the point here is that there are plenty of basic conventional metaphors that are alive, certainly enough to show that what is conventional and fixed need not be dead (Lakoff and Turner 1989). Part of the problem with the traditional view of idioms stems from its inability to account for contemporary speakers' metaphorical schemes of thought. For this reason, the traditional view simply cannot explain why so many idioms make sense to speakers in having the figurative meanings they do.

5. ANALYZABILITY OF IDIOMS

The fact that many idioms may arise from enduring conceptual metaphors provides one reason why these phrases are not simple fixed or frozen expressions whose meanings are opaque to contemporary speakers. An important extension of this idea is the fact that many idiomatic phrases appear to be decomposable or analyzable with the meanings of their parts contributing independently to their overall figurative meanings (Gibbs and Nayak 1989; Nunberg, Sag, and Wasow 1994; Titone and Connine 1999). For instance, in the phrase *pop the question*, it is easy to discern that the noun *question* refers to a marriage proposal when the verb *pop* is used to refer to the manner of uttering it. Similarly, the noun *law* in *lay down the law* refers to the rules of conduct in certain situations when the verb phrase *laying down* is used to refer to the act of invoking the law. Idioms such as *pop the question, spill the beans*, and *lay down the law* are "decomposable" because each of their components obviously contributes to their overall figurative interpretations.

Other idioms whose individual parts do not contribute individually to the figurative meaning of the idiom are semantically "nondecomposable" (e.g., *kick the bucket, shoot the breeze*) because people experience difficulty in breaking these phrases into their component parts (Gibbs and Nayak 1989; Nunberg, Sag, and Wasow 1994).

The analyzability of an idiom does not depend on that word string being literally well-formed (Gibbs and Nayak 1989). For instance, *pop the question* is literally anomalous but semantically decomposable. All that matters for an idiom to be viewed as decomposable is for its parts to have meanings, either literal or figurative, that contribute independently to the phrase's overall figurative interpretation.

The analyzability of an idiom is really a matter of degree depending on the salience of its individual parts. For instance, many speakers view the phrase *fall off the wagon* as being less decomposable than *pop the question* because the meaning that *fall* contributes to *fall off the wagon* is not as salient as the meaning that *pop* contributes to *pop the question*. When speakers judge that the idiom *let off steam* is analyzable or decomposable, they are essentially finding some relationship between the components *let off* and *steam* with their figurative referents 'release' and 'anger' (Moon 1998). It is not surprising that speakers find some relationship between the noun *steam* and the concept of 'anger' because anger is metaphorically understood in terms of heat and internal pressure (Lakoff 1987; Lakoff and Johnson 1980).

Furthermore, the parts of some idioms are more understandable than others and so their metaphoricity is not evenly spread across an entire phrase (Gibbs 1994; Moon 1998). For example, *rock the boat* is a transparent metaphor, but *rock* has an analogous metaphorical meaning 'upset' that is seen apart from idiomatic phrases. Thus, verbs such as *move, agitate, shake*, and *stir* systematically have meanings to do with physical movement and metaphorical meanings to do with emotional disturbance. Similarly, the metaphor of *spill* in *spill the beans* is simpler than that of *beans*. That is, it is easier to draw an analogy between the action of spilling some-thing physically and that of revealing a secret (compare *let slip* or *drop* as in *drop something into a conversation* and *spill one's guts*) than it is to draw an analogy be-tween beans and secret (but see Gibbs and O'Brien 1990). Thus, *beans* seems more metaphorical than *spill* and thus the idiom is asymmetrically metaphorical.

Finally, the meanings of an idiom's parts may be shaped by that phrase's overall figurative meaning. For instance, Geeraerts (1995) describes reinterpreation pro-cesses in which the parts of various Dutch idioms take on new meanings as a result of their being used in idiomatic expressions. To take an English example, the word *spill* now conventionally means 'reveal' from its participation in the idiom phrase *spill the beans*. In fact, many dictionaries now see 'reveal' as one of the primary senses of *spill*. As Geeraerts argues, semantic interpretation does not always operate in a strict bottom-up manner (going from literal to figurative meaning), but in-volves top-down processes as well (where figurative meanings shape literal ones). This possibility raises additional problems for the presumed primacy of literal meaning in linguistic interpretation (see Gibbs 1994). For the moment, though, the influence of figurative phrasal meaning on the meanings of an idiom's parts shows how idiom analyzability is not strictly grounded in lexical meaning apart from how words are actually used in idioms.

A series of psychological experiments revealed that there is reasonable consis-tency in college students' intuitions of the analyzability of idioms (Gibbs and Nayak 1989). Participants in these studies were simply asked to rate the degree to which the individual words in idioms contribute independently to these phrases' overall fig-urative interpretations. These American speakers generally see some idiomatic phrases, such as *pop the question*, *miss the boat*, and *button your lips*, as highly analyzable or decomposable, and judge other phrases as semantically nondecom-posable, such as *kick the bucket* and *shoot the breeze*. A third group of idioms was identified as being decomposable, but abnormally so, because their individual components have a different relationship to their idiomatic referents than do "normally" decomposable idioms. For example, we can identify the figurative referent in the idiom *carry a torch* only by virtue of our knowledge of torches as conventional metaphors for descriptions of warm feelings. This abnormally de-composable idiom differs from normally decomposable idioms, such as *button your lips*, whose components have a more direct relation to their figurative referents.

6. Syntactic Behavior of Idioms

The traditional noncompositional view of idioms supposedly explains why many idioms tend to be syntactically unproductive or frozen. For example, one cannot syntactically transform the phrase *John kicked the bucket* to a passive construction (i.e., *The bucket was kicked by John*) without disrupting its nonliteral meaning. Linguists have suggested a variety of formal devices that can predict the syntactic behavior of idioms (Weinreich 1969; Chafe 1970; Fraser 1970; Katz 1973; Newmeyer 1974; Bresnan 1982; Gazdar et al. 1985). For example, one proposal argued that idioms can be organized into a "frozenness hierarchy," ranging from expressions which undergo nearly all grammatical transformations without losing their figurative meanings (e.g., *lay down the law*) to those idioms that cannot undergo even the most simple transformations without losing their idiomatic interpretations (e.g., *face the music*) (Fraser 1970). According to this analysis, idioms can be marked with a single feature that assigns them to a class of those idioms which behave similarly in the operation of their syntactic rules. Another proposal suggests that some of the constituents of unproductive idioms be marked with syntactic features which block the application of transformations to strings that contain the constituent (Katz 1973). Thus, the idiomatic phrase *breathe down your neck* can be lexically marked as [−Particle Movement, −Passive, −Action Nominalization] to prevent the generation of unacceptable strings such as **I breathed your neck down the other day*. A more recent proposal suggests that idioms are subject to different grammatical principles that limit their forms. For instance, O'Grady (1998) argues in favor of the "continuity constraint," which states that an idiom's component parts must form a chain of head-to-head relations. Thus, basic idioms are phrases like *see stars* and *lose face*, which consist of a verb and the head of its theme complement (*stars* and *face*, respectively). This constraint explains why some idiom patterns do not exist (i.e., those that cannot be reduced to a continuous chain of head-to-head relations, such as verb plus genitive, subject plus object, and verb plus object of a preposition). To give one example, there should be no idioms like *A wolf in sheep's clothing V a son of a gun*, because there is no licensing relation holding between the heads of subject and a direct object.

Unfortunately, none of these syntactic accounts explains how people come to acquire the rules for knowing which transformations or constraints apply or do not apply to which idioms (Ruwet 1991; Gibbs 1994; Nunberg, Wasow, and Sag 1994). Speakers are not explicitly taught which idioms, and other formulaic phrases, are syntactically productive and which are not. Yet people somehow learn about the syntactic behavior of most idioms, including relatively rare and novel phrases. So how do speakers determine, for instance, that the noun *bucket* of the syntactically frozen phrase *kick the bucket* is understood with the feature [+Idiom] to block application of the passive transformation (we never hear **The bucket was kicked by John* as an idiom), while the noun *law* of the syntactically productive idiom *lay down the law* is not marked with such a feature? Certainly, we have never heard *The bucket was kicked by John* as an idiom, but we do not need to hear *The piper was paid by John* in order to produce *John paid the piper* or to recognize the expression as idiomatic (Gibbs 1994).

The data showing that people can differentiate between idioms based on their semantic analyzability has important implications for explaining the syntactic behavior of idioms. One hypothesis examined in several psychological studies was that people's intuitions about the syntactic versatility of idioms are affected by the analyzability or decomposability of these figurative phrases (Gibbs and Nayak 1989). In fact, the results of these studies supported this prediction. Normally decomposable idioms (e.g., *pop the question*) were found to be much more syntactically productive than semantically nondecomposable idioms (e.g., *chew the fat*). Abnormally decomposable idioms were not found to be syntactically productive because each part does not by itself refer to some component of the idiomatic referent, but only to some metaphorical relation between the individual part and the referent.

These findings suggest that the syntactic versatility of idioms is not an arbitrary phenomenon, perhaps due to unknown historical reasons (Cutler 1982), but can at least partially be explained in terms of an idiom's semantic analyzability (Nunberg, Sag, and Wasow 1994). The syntactic versatility of other formulaic language, including verb particle constructions (Bolinger 1971; Lindner 1981) and binomial expressions (Lambrecht 1984) can also be explained by appeal to the internal semantics of these phrases. For example, if the particle in verb particle constructions, such as *make up* and *put out*, has little meaning on its own, then it is difficult to move that particle to a position of semantic focus (Bolinger 1971). Thus, while it is permissible to say *Fifty states make up the United States*, it is not reasonable to say **Fifty states make the United States up* because the postposed particle *up* carries little meaning by itself and cannot be used in the sentence's final position.

Part of the reason why idioms may exhibit certain constraints on their syntactic productivity is rooted in broader generalizations about language and conceptual processes. This possibility is taken up in a later section on idiom schemas.

7. LEXICAL FLEXIBILITY OF IDIOMS

Idioms and formulaic phrases exhibit tremendous lexical variation (Gibbs et al. 1989; Moon 1998: Glucksberg 2001). For instance, the main verbs in many idioms can be changed without disrupting these phrases' figurative meanings, as seen in the following examples (see Moon 1998):

(24)   a. set/start the ball rolling
       b. throw/toss in the towel
       c. lower/let down one's guard
       d. step into/fill someone's shoes
       e. play/keep one's cards close to the chest
       f. throw/put someone off the scent

Nouns can also vary in many idioms without disrupting their figurative meanings. Consider the following pairs of expressions:

(25) a. a piece/slice of the action
      b. a skeleton in the closet/cupboard
      c. the calm/lull before the storm
      d. hold a gun/pistol to someone's head
      e. throw ones' hat/cap into the ring

Variations of adjectives are less common than those of nouns or verbs, but several examples illustrate that changing adjectives is not disruptive for many phrases' figurative meanings. Consider the following:

(26) a. a bad/rotten apple
      b. a level/even playing field
      c. close/near to the bone
      d. the best/greatest thing since sliced bread

Prepositional and adverbial participles may also exhibit little shift in meaning, as seen in the following instances:

(27) a. at/in a single sitting
      b. by/in leaps and bounds
      c. on/along the right lines
      d. out of/from thin air
      e. go round/around in circles

Finally, conjunctions may vary as seen in the following instances:

(28) a. hit and miss/hit or miss
      b. when/if push comes to shove
      c. when/while the cat's away, the mice will play

Not surprisingly, the analyzability of idioms influences people's intuitions about their lexical flexibility. A series of studies examined the role of semantic analyzability on the lexical flexibility of idioms (Gibbs et al. 1989). Participants were presented with a series of phrases that were left unchanged (e.g., *pop the question*), had their verbs substituted with relatively synonymous words (e.g., *burst the question*), had their nouns substituted with synonymous words (e.g., *pop the request*), or had both their verbs and nouns changed (e.g., *burst the request*). Accompanying each phrase was a figurative definition of the unchanged idiom (e.g., *propose marriage*). The participants' task was simply to read each phrase and judge its similarity in meaning to the paraphrase. Changing the verbs and nouns of both semantically decomposable and nondecomposable idioms was disruptive to their figurative meanings. However, changing the lexical items in semantically nondecomposable idioms was far more disruptive to these phrases' figurative interpretations than was the case for decomposable idioms. For instance, both noun and verb changes were rated as significantly less acceptable for nondecomposable idioms (e.g., *punt the pail* for *kick the bucket*) than for decomposable phrases (e.g., *burst the request* for *pop the question*). These findings suggest that the semantic analyzability of idioms provides important constraints for the lexical flexibility of idioms.

In addition, changing the individual words in an idiom may not totally disrupt that phrase's figurative meaning, at least in the sense of rendering the phrase literal. But changing some words will alter an idiom's figurative meaning in slight, but still important, ways (Glucksberg 2001). For example, the idiom *break the ice* can be altered to form *shatter the ice*, which now has the meaning of something like 'to break down an uncomfortable and stiff social situation flamboyantly in one fell swoop!' (McGlone, Glucksberg, and Cacciari 1994). *Shatter the ice* is an example, not of lexical flexibility, but of semantic productivity (McGlone, Glucksberg, and Cacciari 1994). Examples of semantically productive idiom variants appear frequently in conversation, the media, and literature. People can understand semantically productive idiom variants (e.g., *Sam didn't spill a single bean*) quite readily, and the more familiar the original idiom, the more comprehensible the variant (McGlone, Glucksberg, and Cacciari 1994). Variant idioms can also be understood as quickly as their literal paraphrases (e.g., *Sam didn't spill a single bean* versus *Sam didn't say a single word*) (Glucksberg, Glucksberg, and Cacciari 1994).

Overall, speakers tend to be significantly more creative in their use of semantically analyzable idioms, both in terms of their syntactic productivity and their lexical flexibility.

8. ANALYZABILITY IN IDIOM COMPREHENSION AND LEARNING

The analyzability of idioms also plays an important role in their immediate, "on-line" interpretations. Because the individual components in decomposable idioms contribute systematically to the figurative meanings of these phrases, people may process idioms in a compositional manner where the semantic representations of each component is accessed and combined according to the syntactic rules of the language. A series of reading-time studies showed that people took significantly less time to process the decomposable idioms than to read the nondecomposable expressions (Gibbs, Nayak, and Cutting 1989). Both normally and abnormally decomposable phrases took less time to process than their respective literal control phrases, but nondecomposable idioms actually took longer to process than their respective literal controls. These data suggest that people attempt to do some compositional analysis when understanding idiomatic phrases. When an idiom is decomposable, readers can assign independent meanings to its individual parts and will quickly recognize how these meaningful parts combine to form the overall figurative interpretation of the phrase.

Finally, children's comprehension of idioms depends on their intuitions about the internal semantics of these figurative phrases (Gibbs 1987, 1991; Nippold and Rudzinski 1993; Levorato and Cacciari 1999). Children's learning of idioms is generally thought to depend on their associating a given sequence of words with arbitrary figurative meanings (e.g., *kick the bucket* means 'to die'). However, the evidence shows that children attempt to do some compositional analysis when understanding idiomatic expressions (Gibbs 1991). Younger children (kindergartners and first graders) understood decomposable idioms much better than they did nondecomposable phrases. Older children (third and fourth graders) understood both kinds of idioms equally well in supporting contexts but were better at interpreting decomposable idioms than they were at understanding nondecomposable idioms without contextual information. Children did not understand idioms with well-formed literal meanings any better than they did ill-formed idioms. Consequently, it is unlikely that young children find analyzable or decomposable idioms easier to comprehend simply because these phrases possess well-formed literal meanings. Instead, the younger children found it easier to assign figurative meanings to the parts of decomposable idioms and did not simply analyze each expression according to its literal interpretation. There is now a vast body of work from Cognitive Linguistics and psychology showing that the traditional view of idioms as being fixed expressions is quite wrong. A comprehensive theory of idiomaticity must acknowledge the complexity of these phrasal patterns, paying detailed attention to their various lexical, semantic, syntactic, and pragmatic properties, and not assume that idioms are fixed, dead expressions.

9. IDIOM SCHEMAS

The extensive evidence reviewed in this chapter against the idea that idioms and related speech formulas are noncompositional or fixed expressions has not addressed an important issue. Any argument about the variability of idioms presupposes that the variant forms of an individual expression are to be considered as variations rather than as separate expressions with coincidentally the same meaning and with some lexis in common. Consider the idiom pairs in (29) and (30) (Moon 1998):

(29) a. champ at the bit
      b. chafe at the bit
(30) a. hit the roof
      b. hit the ceiling

Do these pairs reflect single idioms with minor variations or completely independent idioms? This question is relevant to explaining many American/British idioms pairings such as (31) and (32):

(31)   a. the shoe is on the other foot
      b. the boot is on the other foot
(32)   a. blow off steam
      b. let off steam

Most linguists and lexicographers view the examples in each pair as variations from some core phrase. But may they actually be completely different idioms in the same way that the words *gasoline/petrol* or *apartment/flat* are closely related but discrete lexical items? Moon (1998) argues that pairs like the above represent idiomatic expressions within a single idiom scheme. Under this view, variation in idiom expressions reflects further evidence of instability rather than pointing to the idea that each phrase is actually an entirely different idiom.

Although linguists have often proposed grammatical constraints on idioms, few scholars have pursued the idea that different conceptual schemes govern variation among these phrases. But how do we identify the canonical form of an idiom? Consider the phrases in (33):

(33)   a. have an axe to grind
      b. have no axe to grind
      c. with an axe to grind
      d. without an axe to grind
      e. with no axe to grind

The phrases here either represent a variable idiom cluster, where there are several possible related forms, or a frozen, unvarying idiom nucleus (i.e., *axe to grind*) that collocates with preceding *have/with/without* and *a/no*. There may be advantages to seeing the above phrases as a frozen nucleus with a collocating structure, but the core *axe to grind* is not by itself a meaningful unit. In fact, many idioms do not have fixed forms. Even the classical example *kick the bucket*, which is often cited in favor of the idea that idioms are "fixed" expressions or "frozen" phrases, can meaningfully be used in various forms such as *kick it*, *kick off*, or *kick it off*. Moreover, many traditional proverbs and sayings are truncated from their canonical or earliest forms to create lower-level grammatical units. Consider the following cases:

(34)   a. a bird in the hand (is worth two in the bush)
      b. birds of a feather (flock together)
      c. don't count your chickens (before they're hatched)
      d. make hay (while the sun shines)

In addition to idiomatic and proverbial phrases like the above, a quick look at any idiom dictionary reveals that many idiom schemes share a prominent verb or noun. Consider the word *hit* in the following clusters of expressions:

(35)   a. hit the desk
      b. hit the hay
      c. hit the sack

(36)   a. hit the beach
      b. hit the road
      c. hit the surf
(37)   a. hit the bottle
      b. hit the plum wine
      c. hit the sauce

Some linguists claim that these phrases are not individual idioms (i.e., that *hit* is polysemous), in the way that these phrases tend to be listed in idiom dictionaries. Instead, the above phrases are part of a broader pattern (Ruhl 1989). For example, *hit* is essentially monosemic, and there are principles of metonymy and analogy governing the production of these different phrases. Yet Moon (1998) suggests that rather than seeing *hit* as monosemic, there are broader patterns of idiom schemes governing the production of related idiomatic phrases. Consider the following related phrases:

(38)   a. shake in one's shoes
      b. quake in one's shoes
      c. shake in one's boot
      d. quake in one's boot
      e. quiver in one's boots
      f. quake in one's Doc Martens

The main verb in each phrase means 'shake', and this is associated with nouns meaning 'footwear' to connote fear and apprehension. Any words that convey similar meanings as do these verbs and nouns will make equally appropriate idioms. Another set of expressions reflective of an idiom scheme is the following:

(39)   a. scare the life out of someone
      b. scare the shit out of someone
      c. scare someone shitless
      d. scare the pants off someone
      e. frighten the life out of someone
      f. be frightened out of one's mind
      g. be scared out of one's wit

Once again, these formulaic phrases have several significant conceptual parts, such as scaring someone which results in the loss of something important (e.g., one's life, one's mind, one's wit, one's pants). As long as this conceptual scheme is maintained, a linguistic expression will convey idiomatic/formulaic meaning.

One more set of synonymous variations where the idiom schema is relatively clear is seen in the following list of idiomatic phrases:

(40)   a. down the chute
      b. down the drain
      c. down the pan
      d. down the plughole

    e. down the toilet

    f. down the tubes/tube

Idiom schemes like the above have some reference, a metaphor (or metonymy) or cognate words, in common, but without (necessarily) any fixed structure or specific words. The concept of idiom schemes explains several facts about the analyzability and variability in idioms and related speech formulas. As Moon (1998: 163) comments:

> Idiom schemas represent concepts embedded in the culture and associated with particular lexicalizations. They are characterized by an underlying concept (the relationship between tenor and vehicle) and an overlying preferred lexical realization, usually with connotated evaluation. The exact form of words may vary or be exploited but is still tied to the underlying concept which provides the driving or motivating force in these idiom phrases.

There has been little empirical work attempting to identify major idiom schemes or looking at people's possible use of such schemes in idiom production and understanding. But quite notably, cognitive linguists have tried to explain similar formulaic patterns in an approach known as Construction Grammar (Fillmore, Kay, and O'Connor 1988; Goldberg 1995; Kay and Fillmore 1999).

Construction grammar is a monostratal, unification-based syntactic theory that represents form-meaning complexes as construction templates, each with a specific set of morphosyntactic, semantic, and pragmatic principles, which may be combined with other templates to form more complex structures. Under this approach, grammatical constructions are not reduced to simple rewrite rules, but have specific semantic and pragmatic properties that must be captured (see also Croft, this volume, chapter 18)

Construction grammar has important implications for the study of idiomaticity in language, especially in providing a unified account of grammar and what have traditionally been viewed as peripheral aspects of language. For instance, in their analysis of the phrasal construction *let alone*, Fillmore, Kay, and O'Connor (1988, 534) argue that "it appears to us that the machinery needed for describing the so-called minor or peripheral constructions of the sort which has occupied us here will have to be powerful enough to be generalized to more familiar structures, in particular those represented by individual phrase structure rules."

For example, consider the following two sets of expressions:

(41)   a. Mary won't eat shrimp, let alone squid.

       b. I barely got up to eat lunch, let alone cook breakfast.

       c. I was too young to serve in World War Two, let alone World War One.

(42)   a. What is the scratch doing on the table?

       b. What do you think your name is doing on my book?

       c. What is it doing raining?

The phrase *let alone* allows speakers to simultaneously address a previously posed proposition and to redirect the listener to a new proposition that should be more informative. Constructions of the *What's X doing Y?* type express both a request or a demand for an explanation and the speaker's belief in the incongruity of the scene proposition. The constructional structure of these clauses is dictated by the ordinary core constructions that license familiar subject-predicate structures, verb phrases, and inverted clauses. "In grammar, the investigation of the idiomatic and of the general are the same; the study of the periphery is the study of the core—and vice versa" (Kay and Fillmore 1999: 30).

Work on formulaic phrases in construction grammar has not yet made contact with the broader empirical study of idioms in linguistics and psychology. But it seems evident that principles of idiomaticity may be governed by various constructions or idiom schemes that have more in common with more productive aspects of language than has been assumed in the past. One important possibility to explore is the idea, inherent in Construction Grammar, that construction templates are related through inheritance hierarchies, containing more and less general patterns. Thus, idiom constructions, or idiom schemes, may be organized in higher-order structures that reflect something of how people conceptualize related and less related idiomatic phrases.

One additional observation, which may relate to broader proposals on idiom schemas/constructions, is that few idioms have literally animate NPs, and there are few idiomatic phrases of the form V + Goal, such as *throw NP to the wolves* (Nunberg, Sag, and Wasow 1994). For example, English has several dozen idioms of the form *hit + NP*, as mentioned earlier, such as *hit the bottle*, *hit the road*, and *hit the sack*, where the objects denoted are inanimate. This contrasts with nonidiomatic phrases with transitive *hit* which often include objects with animate themes. What accounts for this statistical tendency?

Nunberg, Sag, and Wasow (1994) argue that the rarity of some idiom chunks arises from two general facts about meaning transfer in figurative uses of language. First, abstract situations are usually described in concrete terms. Second, inanimate concepts are mapped onto animate ones, more so than the opposite. Because animates are necessarily concrete, literally animate NPs in idiom phrases are not used to denote abstract entities. For this reason, literally animate NPs are rare in idiomatic expressions. Agents and Goals are also rare to find in idioms because they too are typically animate.

This analysis is also supported by analysis of proverbs involving NP arguments with animate literal meanings and inanimate idiomatic readings. Thus, the phrase *look a gift horse in the mouth* maps the animate *horse* onto an inanimate entity that has been freely given. This mapping illustrates the general tendency of meaning transfer where concrete things and situations (e.g., the body, spatial relations) serve as the source domains for more abstract target domains (e.g., social interactions, causal relations, etc). Under this view, it would be quite unusual to find idioms or proverbs such as *divulge the information* to mean something like 'spill the soup', as in *The waiter divulged the information all over my new suit* (Nunberg, Sag, and Wasow 1994).

It appears, then, that there are important conceptual constraints on permissible idioms and proverbs. Idiom schemas are likely constituted, at least in part, by meaning transfer processes that are grounded in nonlinguistic patterns of thought.

10. THE CONCEPTUAL BASIS
FOR IDIOMATICITY

The important empirical demonstrations on idiom analyzability suggest that the internal semantics of idioms might be correlated in systematic ways with the concepts to which idioms refer. One possibility is that the figurative meanings of idioms might very well be motivated by people's conceptual knowledge that is constituted by metaphor (and to a lesser extent metonymy) (Gibbs 1994; Kövecses and Szabó 1996). In fact, people make sense of many idioms because they tacitly recognize the metaphorical mapping of information from two domains that give rise to idioms in the first place.

Cognitive linguistic research supports this view (Lakoff 1987; Kövecses 2000). For example, the idiom *John spilled the beans* maps our knowledge of someone tipping over a container of beans onto a person revealing some previously hidden secret. English speakers understand *spill the beans* to mean 'reveal the secret' because there are underlying conceptual metaphors, such as THE MIND IS A CONTAINER and IDEAS ARE PHYSICAL ENTITIES that structure their conceptions of minds, secrets, and disclosure (Lakoff and Johnson 1980). Although the existence of these conceptual metaphors does not predict that certain idioms or conventional expressions must appear in the language, the presence of these independent conceptual metaphors by which we make sense of experience provides a partial motivation for why specific phrases (e.g., *spill the beans*) are used to refer to particular events (e.g., the revealing of secrets).

A good deal of empirical work in psycholinguistics has investigated the metaphorical motivation for idiomatic meaning. For instance, various psycholinguistic evidence supports the idea that metaphors such as ANGER IS HEATED FLUID IN A CONTAINER are really conceptual and not, more simply, generalizations of linguistic meaning. Studies have looked at people's mental imagery for idioms and proverbs (Gibbs and O'Brien 1990; Gibbs, Strom, and Spivey-Knowlton 1997), people's context-sensitive use of idioms (Nayak and Gibbs 1990) and euphemistic phrases (Pfaff, Gibbs, and Johnson 1997), people's folk understanding of how the source domains in conceptual metaphors constrain what idioms mean (Gibbs 1992), people's use of conceptual metaphors in organizing information in text processing (Allbritton, McKoon, and Gerrig 1995), and people's use of conceptual metaphors in drawing inferences when reading poetic metaphors (Gibbs and Nascimento 1996). These psycholinguistic findings support the hypothesis that different kinds of metaphorical thought partly explain why many metaphors and idioms have the meanings they do for contemporary speakers.

Let me briefly describe two sets of studies that illustrate the importance of conceptual metaphor in idiom understanding. Emphasized in this work is the idea that many conceptual metaphors are grounded in recurring patterns of embodied experience. Thus, the source domains that are mapped onto different target domains in idioms are themselves "image-schematic" structures (Johnson 1987; Gibbs and Colston 1995).

One set of psycholinguistic studies examined how people's intuitions of the bodily experience of containment, as well as several other image schemas which serve as the source domains for several important conceptual metaphors, underlie speakers' use and understanding of idioms. These studies were designed to show that the specific entailments of idioms reflect the source-to-target domain mappings of their underlying conceptual metaphors (Gibbs 1992). Most importantly, these metaphorical mappings preserve the cognitive topology of these embodied, image-schematic source domains.

Participants in a first study were questioned about their understanding of events corresponding to particular bodily experiences that were viewed as motivating specific source domains in conceptual metaphors (e.g., the experience of one's body as a container filled with fluid). For instance, participants were asked to imagine the embodied experience of a sealed container filled with fluid and then were asked something about causation (e.g., *What would cause the container to explode?*), intentionality (e.g., *Does the container explode on purpose, or does it explode through no volition of its own?*), and manner (e.g., *Does the explosion of the container occur in a gentle or a violent manner?*).

Overall, the participants were remarkably consistent in their responses to the various questions. To give one example, people responded that the cause of a sealed container exploding its contents out is the internal pressure caused by the increase in the heat of the fluid inside the container. They also reported that this explosion is unintentional because containers and fluid have no intentional agency and that the explosion occurs in a violent manner. These brief responses provide a rough image-schematic profile of people's understanding of a particular source domain concept (i.e., 'heated fluid in the bodily container').

These different image-schematic profiles about certain abstract concepts allowed me to predict something about people's understanding of idioms. For instance, people's understanding of anger should partly be structured by their folk concept for heated fluid in the bodily container as described above. Several studies showed this to be true (Gibbs 1992). Not surprisingly, when people understand anger idioms, such as *blow your stack*, *flip your lid*, or *hit the ceiling*, they inferred that the cause of anger is internal pressure, that the expression of anger is unintentional, and that it is done is an abrupt violent manner. People do not draw these same inferences about causation, intentionality, and manner when comprehending literal paraphrases of idioms, such as *get very angry*.

More interesting, though, is that people's intuitions about various source domains map onto their conceptualizations of different target domains in very predictable ways. For instance, several later experiments showed that people find idioms to be more appropriate and easier to understand when they are seen in discourse contexts that are consistent with the various entailments of these phrases. Thus, people find it easy to process the idiomatic phrase *blow your stack* when this was read in a context that accurately described the cause of the person's anger as being due to internal pressure, where the expression of anger was unintentional and violent (all entailments that are consistent with the entailments of the source-to-target domain mappings of heated fluid in a container onto anger). But readers took significantly longer to read *blow your stack* when any of these entailments were contradicted in the preceding story context.

These psycholinguistic findings show how people's metaphorical concepts underlie their understanding of what idioms mean in written texts. Moreover, they provide significant experimental evidence that people's intuitions about their embodied experiences can predict something about their use and understanding of idioms, expressions that are partly motivated by bodily based conceptual metaphors.

A different series of experiments demonstrates that people appear to compute or access metaphorical representations during their immediate understanding of idioms like *blew his stack* (Gibbs et al. 1997). In these studies, participants read stories ending with idioms and then quickly gave lexical decision responses to visually presented letter-strings that reflected either something about the conceptual metaphors underlying these idioms (e.g., 'heat' for ANGER IS HEATED FLUID IN A CONTAINER having just read *John blew his stack*) or letter-strings that were unrelated to these conceptual metaphors (e.g., 'lead').

There were two important findings from this study. First, people were faster to make these lexical decision responses to the related metaphor targets (e.g., 'heat') after having just read idioms than they were after having read either literal paraphrases of idioms (e.g., *John got very angry*) or control phrases (e.g., phrases still appropriate to the context such as *John saw many dents*). Second, people were faster in recognizing related metaphorical targets than unrelated ones after having read idioms, but not after literal paraphrases or control phrases. This pattern of results suggests that people are immediately computing or accessing at least something related to the conceptual metaphor ANGER IS HEATED FLUID IN A CONTAINER when they read idioms. In another experiment, participants were faster to make lexical decision responses to metaphor targets (e.g., 'heat') after having read an idiom motivated by a similar conceptual metaphor (e.g., *John blew his stack*) than after an idiom with roughly the same figurative meaning but motivated by a different conceptual metaphor (e.g., *John bit her head off*, which is motivated by the conceptual metaphor ANGER IS ANIMAL BEHAVIOR).

Experimental findings like these suggest that people compute or access the relevant conceptual metaphor for an idiom during some aspect of their processing of these phrases. Not all, psychologists in particular, agree with this conclusion (Glucksberg and Keysar 1990; Kreuz and Graesser 1991; Glucksberg, Brown, and McGlone 1993; Stock, Slack, and Ortony 1993; Keysar and Bly 1995; McGlone 1996). Much of the debate over whether metaphors of thought influence verbal metaphor understanding centers on the most appropriate methodology for examining linguistic understanding. One criticism about some of the above empirical research is that asking people about their intuitions as to why figurative expressions mean what they do is an unreliable way of examining the conceptual foundations for figurative meaning. This is clearly an issue that will be debated in the future.

One more important example of the conceptual basis of formulaic language is shown by cognitive linguists' studies of proverbs. The main suggestion here is that various generic-level metaphors help motivate why proverbs mean what they do (Lakoff and Turner 1989). The GENERIC IS SPECIFIC metaphor, specifically, provides a general cognitive mechanism for understanding the general in terms of the specific, one of the key features of proverbs. Once again, the mapping of source domain knowledge onto dissimilar target domains of experience preserves the cognitive structure, or topology, of the source domain. Imagine a scenario, for example, where a student is warned not to expose some cheating scandal in his/her class by the expression *It's better to let sleeping dogs lie* (Lakoff and Turner 1989; Gibbs and Beitel 1995). The "generic-level metaphor" specifies that the knowledge structures used in comprehending the case of the cheating scandal share certain things with the knowledge structures used in comprehending the literal interpretation of *let sleeping dogs lie*. To start, the generic-level schema for the source domain of *It's better to let sleeping dogs lie* has the following characteristics:

- there is an animal that is not active;
- animals can sometimes act fiercely if provoked;
- therefore, it is better to let the animal remain as it is rather than risk disturbing it and having to deal with its potential ferocity.

This information constitutes a generic-level schema. There are a variety of ways that such a schema can be instantiated. For instance, consider the following:

- there is an unpleasant situation that is dormant;
- such situations can prove difficult to handle if brought to people's attention;
- therefore, it is better to let the situation remain dormant than to risk having to deal with its negative consequences.

This very general schema characterizes an open-ended category of situations. We can think of it as a variable template that can be filled in different ways. In the case where someone utters *It's better to let sleeping dogs lie* in the context of a cheating scandal, we end up with the following specific-level metaphorical understanding of the situation:

- the dormant animal corresponds to the unpleasant situation;
- disturbing the dog corresponds to bringing the cheating scandal to people's attention;
- therefore, it is better to leave the cheating scandal left unnoticed just as it is better to sometimes let sleeping dogs remain sleeping.

These correspondences define the metaphorical interpretation of the proverb as applied to the student dealing with the cheating scandal. Moreover, the class of possible ways of filling in the slots of the generic-level schema of the problem corresponds to the class of possible interpretations for the proverb.

11. CONCLUSION

The empirical study of idioms, proverbs, and related speech formulas in Cognitive Linguistics and psycholinguistics provides considerable evidence against the idea that idioms are fixed expressions or "dead" metaphors. Many aspects of idiomatic language exhibit tremendous lexical, syntactic, and semantic flexibility, each of which are results of these phrases being, at the very least, partly analyzable or decomposable. At the same time, cognitive linguistic work suggests that many aspects of idiomaticity may be characterized in terms of broader linguistic/conceptual patterns, such as idiom schemes or grammatical constructions. Moreover, people's preexisting metaphorical understanding of many basic concepts provides part of the motivation for why people see idioms and proverbs as having the figurative meanings they do. In this way, the study of idioms and related speech formulas reveals important elements of human conceptual structures.

My review of the cognitive linguistic work on idiomaticity and the related research from psychology clearly shows that idioms and other speech formulas are not peripheral aspects of language. Many aspects of idiomaticity are closely tied to more productive grammatical patterns and enduring schemes of human thought. One reason why Cognitive Linguistics has succeeded in painting this new vision of idiomaticity is because scholars embracing this approach have explicitly looked for connections between idioms and more typical grammatical structures and between idioms and pervasive patterns of metaphorical thought. Contrary to the traditional view that ignores these possible links, Cognitive Linguistics adopts the significant methodological premise of seeking correspondences between mind and language, and not assuming that certain aspects of language are more revealing of grammatical and semantic structures than are others. The study of idioms turns out to be an ideal place to understand the rich, flexible nature of natural language and human thought.

REFERENCES

Allbritton, David, Gail McKoon, and Richard Gerrig. 1995. Metaphor-based schemas and text representations: Making connections through conceptual metaphors. *Journal of Experimental Psychology: Learning, Memory, and Cognition* 21: 612–25.

Becker, Joseph D. 1975. The phrasal lexicon. In R. Schank and B. L. Nash-Webber, eds., *Theoretical issues in natural language processing* 60–63. Cambridge, MA: Association for Computational Linguistics. (Also available as Artificial Intelligence Report No. 28. Cambridge, MA: Bolt, Beranek, and Newman.)

Bobrow, Samuel A., and Susan M. Bell. 1973. On catching on to idiomatic expressions. *Memory and Cognition* 1: 343–46.

Bolinger, Dwight. 1971. *The phrasal verb in English.* Cambridge, MA: Harvard University Press.

Bresnan, Joan, ed. 1982. *The mental representation of grammatical relations.* Cambridge, MA: MIT Press.

Cacciari, Cristina, and Patrizia Tabossi. 1988. The comprehension of idioms. *Journal of Memory and Language* 27: 668–83.

Chafe, Wallace L. 1970. *Meaning and the structure of language.* Chicago: University of Chicago Press.

Coulmas, Florian, ed. 1981. *Conversational routine: Exploration in standardized communication situations and prepatterned speech.* The Hague: Mouton.

Cutler, Anne. 1982. Idioms: The colder the older. *Linguistic Inquiry* 13: 317–20.

Drew, Paul, and Elizabeth Holt. 1995. Idiomatic expressions and their role in the organization of topic transition in conversation. In Martin Evaeaerts, Erik-Jan van der Linden, Andre Schenk, and Rob Scheuder (Eds.), *Idioms: Structural and psychological perspectives* (pp. 117-132). Hillsdale, NJ: Erlbaum.

Fillmore, Charles J., Paul Kay, and Catherine O'Connor. 1988. Regularity and idiomaticity in grammatical constructions: The case of *let alone. Language* 64: 501–38.

Fraser, Bruce. 1970. Idioms within a transformational grammar. *Foundations of Language* 6: 22–42.

Gasser, Michael, and Michael Dyer. 1986. Speak of the devil: Representing deictic and speech act knowledge in an integrated lexical memory. In *Proceedings of the Eighth Annual Meeting of the Cognitive Science Society* 388–98. Hillsdale, NJ: Lawrence Erlbaum.

Gazdar, Gerald, Ewan Klein, Geoffrey K. Pullum, and Ivan A. Sag. 1985. *Generalized phrase structure grammar.* Oxford: Basil Blackwell.

Geeraerts, Dirk. 1995. Specialization and reinterpretation in idioms. In Martin Everaert, Erik-Jan van der Linden, André Schenk, and Rob Schreuder, eds., *Idioms: Structural and psychological perspectives* 57–73. Hillsdale, NJ: Lawrence Erlbaum.

Gibbs, Raymond W., Jr. 1980. Spilling the beans on understanding and memory for idioms in conversation. *Memory and Cognition* 8: 149–56.

Gibbs, Raymond W., Jr. 1986. Skating on thin ice: Literal meaning and understanding idioms in conversation. *Discourse Processes* 9: 17–30.

Gibbs, Raymond W., Jr. 1987. Linguistic factors in children's understanding of idioms. *Journal of Child Language* 14: 569–86.

Gibbs, Raymond W., Jr. 1991. Semantic analyzability in children's understanding of idioms. *Journal of Speech and Hearing Research* 34: 613–20.

Gibbs, Raymond W., Jr. 1992. What do idioms really mean? *Journal of Memory and Language* 31: 485–506.

Gibbs, Raymond W., Jr. 1994. *The poetics of mind: Figurative thought, language, and understanding.* Cambridge: Cambridge University Press.

Gibbs, Raymond W., Jr., and Dinara Beitel. 1995. What proverb understanding reveals about how people think. *Psychological Bulletin* 118: 133–54.

Gibbs, Raymond W., Jr., Josephine M. Bogdanovich, Jeffrey R. Sykes, and Dale J. Barr. 1997. Metaphor in idiom comprehension. *Journal of Memory and Language*, 37, 141–54.

Gibbs, Raymond W., Jr., and Herbert L. Colston. 1995. The cognitive psychological reality of image schemas and their transformations. *Cognitive Linguistics* 6: 347–78.

Gibbs, Raymond W., Jr., and Solange B. Nascimento. 1996. How we talk when we talk about love: Metaphorical concepts and understanding love poetry. In Roger J. Kreuz and Mary Sue MacNealy, eds., *Empirical approaches to literature and aesthetics.* Norwood, NJ: Ablex.

Gibbs, Raymond W., Jr., and Nandini P. Nayak. 1989. Psycholinguistic studies on the syntactic behavior of idioms. *Cognitive Psychology* 21: 100–138.

Gibbs, Raymond W., Jr., Nandini P. Nayak, John L. Bolton, and Melissa E. Keppel. 1989. Speakers' assumptions about the lexical flexibility of idioms. *Memory and Cognition* 17: 58–68.

Gibbs, Raymond W., Jr., Nandini P. Nayak, and Cooper Cutting. 1989. How to kick the bucket and not decompose: Analyzability and idiom processing. *Journal of Memory and Language* 28: 576–93.

Gibbs, Raymond W., Jr., and Jennifer E. O'Brien. 1990. Idioms and mental imagery: The metaphorical motivation for idiomatic meaning. *Cognition* 36: 35–68.

Gibbs, Raymond W., Jr., Lise K. Strom, and Michael J. Spivey-Knowlton. 1997. Conceptual metaphors in mental imagery for proverbs. *Journal of Mental Imagery* 21: 83–110.

Glucksberg, Sam. 2001. *Understanding figurative language: From metaphors to idioms.* Oxford: Oxford University Press.

Glucksberg, Sam, Mary Brown, and Matthew S. McGlone. 1993. Conceptual metaphors are not automatically accessed during idiom comprehension. *Memory and Cognition* 21: 711–19.

Glucksberg, Sam, and Boaz Keysar. 1990. Understanding metaphorical comparisons: Beyond similarity. *Psychological Review* 97: 3–18.

Goldberg, Adele E. 1995. *Constructions: A construction grammar approach to argument structure.* Chicago: University of Chicago Press.

Hamblin, Jennifer L., and Raymond W. Gibbs, Jr. 1999. Why you can't kick the bucket as you die slowly: Verbs in idiom comprehension. *Journal of Psycholinguistic Research* 28: 25–39.

Hudson, Jean. 1998. *Perspectives on fixedness: Applied and theoretical.* Lund, Sweden: Lund University Press.

Jackendoff, Ray. 1995. The boundaries of the lexicon. In Martin Everaert, Erik-Jan van der Linden, André Schenk, and Rob Schreuder, eds., *Idioms: Structural and psychological perspectives* 133–66. Hillsdale, NJ: Lawrence Erlbaum.

Johnson, Mark. 1987. *The body in the mind: The bodily basis of meaning, imagination, and reason.* Chicago: University of Chicago Press.

Katz, Jerrold J. 1973. Compositionality, idiomaticity, and lexical substitution. In Stephen R. Anderson and Paul Kiparsky, eds., *A Festschrift for Morris Halle* 357–76. New York: Holt, Rinehart and Winston.

Kay, Paul, and Charles J. Fillmore. 1999. Grammatical constructions and linguistic generalizations: The *What's X doing Y?* construction. *Language* 75: 1–33.

Keysar, Boaz, and Bridget Bly. 1995. Intuitions of the transparency of idioms: Can you keep a secret by spilling the beans? *Journal of Memory and Language* 34: 89–109.

Kövecses, Zoltán. 2000. *Metaphor and emotion: Language, culture, and body in human feeling.* Cambridge: Cambridge University Press.

Kövecses, Zoltán, and Peter Szabó. 1996. Idioms: A view from cognitive semantics. *Applied Linguistics* 17: 326–55.

Kreuz, Roger J., and Arthur C. Graesser. 1991. Aspects of idiom interpretation: Comment on Nayak and Gibbs. *Journal of Experimental Psychology: General* 120: 90–92.

Lakoff, George. 1987. *Women, fire, and dangerous things: What categories reveal about the mind.* Chicago: University of Chicago Press.

Lakoff, George, and Mark Johnson. 1980. *Metaphors we live by.* Chicago: University of Chicago Press.

Lakoff, George, and Mark Turner. 1989. *More than cool reason: A field guide to poetic metaphor.* Chicago: University of Chicago Press.

Lambrecht, Knud. 1984. Formulaicity, frame semantics, and pragmatics in German binomial expressions. *Language* 60: 753–96.

Levorato, M. Chiara, and Cristina Cacciari. 1999. Idiom comprehension in children: Are effects of semantic analysability and context separable? *European Journal of Cognitive Psychology* 11: 51–66.

Lindner, Susan. 1981. A lexico-semantic analysis of English verb-particle constructions with OUT and UP. PhD dissertation, University of California at San Diego. (Also published as A lexico-semantic analysis of English verb-particle constructions, LAUT Paper, no. 101. Trier, Germany: Linguistic Agency of the University of Trier, 1983)

Longman Dictionary of English Idioms. 1979. Harlow, UK: Longman.

McGlone, Matthew S. 1996. Conceptual metaphors and figurative language interpretation: Food for thought? *Journal of Memory and Language* 35: 544–65.

McGlone, Matthew S., Sam Glucksberg, and Cristina Cacciari. 1994. Semantic productivity and idiom comprehension. *Discourse Processes* 17: 167–90.

Mel'čuk, Igor. 1995. Phrasemes in language and phraseology in linguistics. In Martin Everaert, Erik-Jan van der Linden, André Schenk, and Rob Schreuder, eds., *Idioms: Structural and psychological perspectives* 167–232. Hillsdale, NJ: Lawrence Erlbaum.

Moon, Rosamund. 1998. *Fixed expressions and idioms in English: A corpus-based approach.* Oxford: Clarendon.

Naciscione, Anita. 2001. *Phraseological units in discourse: Towards applied stylistics.* Riga: Latvian Academy of Culture.

Nayak, Nandini P., and Raymond W. Gibbs, Jr. 1990. Conceptual knowledge in the interpretation of idioms. *Journal of Experimental Psychology: General* 119: 315–30.

Newmeyer, Frederick J. 1974. The regularity of idiom behavior. *Lingua* 34: 327–42.

Nippold, Marilyn A., and Mishelle Rudzinski. 1993. Familiarity and transparency in idiom explanation: A developmental study of children and adolescents. *Journal of Speech and Hearing Research* 38: 728–35.

Nunberg, Geoffrey, Ivan A. Sag, and Thomas Wasow. 1994. Idioms. *Language* 70: 491–538.

O'Grady, William. 1998. The syntax of idioms. *Natural Language and Linguistic Theory* 16: 279–312.

Ortony, Andrew. 1975. Why metaphors are necessary and not just nice. *Educational Theory* 25: 45–53.

Oxford Dictionary of Current Idiomatic English. 1993. Oxford: Oxford University Press.

Pfaff, Kerry L., Raymond W. Gibbs, Jr., and Michael D. Johnson. 1997. Metaphor in using and understanding euphemism and dysphemism. *Applied Psycholinguistics* 18: 59–83.

Ruhl, Charles. 1989. *On monosemy: A study in linguistic semantics.* Albany: State University of New York Press.

Ruwet, Nicolas. 1991. *Syntax and human experience.* Chicago: University of Chicago Press.

Sinclair, John. 1991. *Corpus, concordance, collocation.* Oxford: Oxford University Press.

Stock, Oliviero, Jon Slack, and Andrew Ortony. 1993. Building castles in the air: Some computational and theoretical issues in idiom comprehension. In Cristina Cacciari and Patrizia Tabossi, eds., *Idioms: Processing, structure, and interpretation* 229–47. Hillsdale, NJ: Lawrence Erlbaum.

Swinney, David A., and Anne Cutler. 1979. The access and processing of idiomatic expressions. *Journal of Verbal Learning and Verbal Behavior* 18: 523–34.

Tabossi, Patrizia, and Francesco Zardon. 1993. The activation of idiomatic meaning in spoken language comprehension. In Cristina Cacciari and Patrizia Tabossi, eds., *Idioms: Processing, structure, and interpretation* 145–62. Hillsdale, NJ: Lawrence Erlbaum.

Titone, Debra, and Cynthia Connine. 1999. On the compositional and noncompositional nature of idiomatic expressions. *Journal of Pragmatics* 31: 1655–74.

Weinreich, Uriel. 1969. Problems in the analysis of idioms. In Jaan Puhvel, ed., *Substance and structure of language* 23–81. Berkeley: University of California Press.

Wilensky, Robert, and Yigal Arens. 1980. PHRAN: A knowledge-based approach to natural language analysis. Memorandum UCB/ERL M80/34. University of California, Berkeley, Electronics Research Laboratory.

Wray, Alison, and Michael R. Perkins. 2000. The functions of formulaic language: An integrated model. *Language and Communication* 20: 1–28.

CHAPTER 28

RELATIONAL CONSTRUCTIONS IN COGNITIVE LINGUISTICS

SOTERIA SVOROU

1. INTRODUCTION

The topic of adpositions is one of the most important when considering the history of Cognitive Linguistics. Some of the foundational studies of Cognitive Linguistics involved the semantics of adpositions (Talmy 1972, 1975, 1978, 1983, 1985; H. Clark 1973; E. Clark 1978; Lakoff and Johnson 1980; Brugman 1981, 1983; Lindner 1981; Herskovits 1982, 1985, 1986; Casad 1982; Casad and Langacker 1985; Hawkins 1984, 1986; Radden 1985; Lakoff 1987). These studies brought forth the experiential basis of the semantics of adpositions, accounted for their polysemous nature in terms of prototype structure and radial categories, and highlighted the metaphorical nature of their extension from the prototype. In the decades that followed, this research path proved fruitful, yielding numerous studies that strengthened some of the original findings, revising others, and it has contributed to our understanding of this aspect of language.

The term "adposition" has been used in linguistics to name free morphological forms that appear in languages primarily in a construction with noun phrases, either preposed (prepositions) or postposed (postpositions) to indicate case and case-like functions such as space, time, causality, or instrument. Such forms are also found to follow verbs, without a noun phrase. Within Cognitive Linguistics, many studies have focused on the analysis of adpositions within Indo-European languages, mainly the languages of Europe, thus exhibiting a bias toward prepositions, which represent the predominant word order pattern found in the languages of Europe.

To write about adpositions one would have to accept, first, that "adposition" is a well-defined grammatical category and, second, that this structurally defined category allows us to form hypotheses about universals of language that would account for the relationship between form and meaning (or conceptual structure). Both of these assumptions have been shown by functional and cognitive linguistic research to be problematic:

a. Accepting "adposition" as a well-defined universal category would entail ignoring facts about the nature of this category that refute its absolute universality and its clarity. Terms functionally equivalent to "adposition" such as "co-verb" and "verbid" have been proposed for Sino-Tibetan languages (Li and Thompson 1973, 1974; DeLancey 1997) as well as terms such as "relational noun" for many African languages (Heine and Reh 1984) to capture the ambivalent nature of certain grammatical forms that do not quite fulfill all the requirements for an adposition but do participate in constructions where they play the role of an adposition. Such terms reflect the developmental history of these grammatical forms, with co-verbs and verbids developing from verbs in verbal constructions and relational nouns from nouns in nominal constructions. The functional equivalence of these forms across languages forces us to adopt a view of "adposition" as a grammatical category according to which membership in the category is a matter of degree partially determined by the developmental stage of the ever-evolving form. In this view, the term "adposition" describes an evolutionary stage, a state which a grammatical form can be in for a period of time, rather than denoting a timeless category, one among many predetermined categories that are available for languages to "choose" and for children to "tune in" in their Language Acquisition Device. This view is in line with Givón's (1979) view of language as ever changing. The view of "adposition" as a stage may not always be obvious or even relevant to the analyst, especially in studies of such grammatical forms within a certain language at a particular synchronic point. It nevertheless becomes painfully obvious to anyone who attempts a comparison of languages with diverse genetic affiliations. Functionally equivalent grammatical forms may be called "co-verb," "verbid," "relational noun," "preposition," or "postposition," but transcending scholarly traditions and language families is the recognition that such forms are involved in nominal (or verbal transitive) constructions where they indicate a relation of the noun to the situation expressed by the clause in which this construction is embedded.

b. Early on in the Cognitive Linguistics enterprise, it became apparent that defining an area of study by setting selection criteria only based on restrictions of form, and not function, would present a fragmented picture of the expression of meaning within and especially across languages. Languages like Finnish, which has prepositions in addition to an elaborate system of nominal inflections, use both free and bound grammatical forms, that is, closed-class items (Talmy 1985) such as adpositions and nominal affixes, to express aspects of a semantic domain such as space or time, in addition to lexical forms, that is, open-class items such as verbs and nouns. Since Cognitive Semantics was the springboard of Cognitive Linguistics, studies were framed around semantic/functional domains and not only structural domains. Cross-language comparison proved this view productive. Since languages express similar notions, such as space, time, causality, instrument, and such, using either free (adpositions) or bound (affixes) grammatical forms, studying only free or only bound forms would yield an incomplete picture of the linguistic spectrum. Rather, a more valid distinction seemed initially to be that between open-class lexical forms versus closed-class grammatical forms. Even this distinction, however, is being challenged by scholars studying specific semantic/cognitive domains, such as space, as, for example, Stephen Levinson and the Language and Cognition Group (Levinson 2003; Levinson, Meria, and the Language and Cognition Group 2003).

To capture this similarity in function without yielding to the structural characteristics of the form, scholars have chosen to either provide a descriptive name of the domain such as "NP-based adverbial markers of time" (Haspelmath 1997) or propose terms such as "relator" and "gram" (Bybee, Perkins, and Pagliuca 1994; Svorou 1994). Here, I adopt the term "relational gram" to refer to grammatical material that expresses a relation in a nominal construction.

The nature of the relational construction and the cross-linguistic variation is discussed first in section 2. Section 3 deals with issues arising from synchronic accounts of relational grams, which are mostly semantic. Section 4 covers issues arising in the diachronic dimension of relational grams. The chapter concludes with an overview of future areas of inquiry.

2. THE RELATIONAL CONSTRUCTION

Relational grams do not operate in a vacuum; rather, they are part of a relational construction. Relational constructions have different functions within clauses: they may provide spatial or temporal information or indicate thematic relations such as instrument, recipient, agent, cause, beneficiary, and so on. In terms of dependencies, they may complement the verb, thus being an argument of the verb, or they may provide additional information involving the whole event represented by a clause. On the semantic level, a relational construction consists of a "landmark," a relational gram, and a "trajector." The landmark is a unit that profiles information against which the trajector is evaluated. The terms "landmark" and "trajector" were proposed by Langacker (1987) and are equivalent to Talmy's (1975) "Figure" and "Ground," respectively. The relational gram specifies a relation that exists between the landmark and the trajector. To illustrate the elements of the relational construction, consider the following examples:

(1)   The magazine is *in* the drawer.
(2)   They went to the Circle du Soleil performance *on* January 17.
(3)   The board gained control *by means of* extortion.
(4)   *By* trusting the people, he gained in popularity.

In (1), *the magazine* is the trajector, and it is in a locative relation of spatial containment—represented by the relational gram *in*—to the landmark, *the drawer*. In (2), the trajector is not simply a noun phrase as in (1), but rather a whole clause, *They went to the Circle du Soleil performance*; the landmark is *January 17*; and the relation is that of temporal contiguity as specified by the relational gram *on*. In (3), the landmark *extortion* profiles the instrument or means—as specified by the gram *by means of*—with which the trajector *The board gained control* is to be viewed as accomplished. In this example, the relational gram is complex and polymorphemic, as compared to the grams in (1) and (2). In (4), the landmark, *trusting the people*, is a verb phrase and the trajector, *he gained in popularity*, is a clause, while the relational gram *by* also indicates the means with which the trajector clause was accomplished.

Whereas the trajector may be a noun phrase or a clause, the landmark is most commonly a noun phrase. These units, together with the relational gram, form the relational construction. In constituent-structure-based analyses, the relational gram and the landmark are said to form a syntactic constituent. The minor variation in the form of expression of the relational gram is a mere hint of the variation that exists within and across languages as to the morphosyntactic character of relational constructions. This variation is due to general typological differences in languages, but also to semantic differences among relational grams, as well as differences in the degree of grammaticalization of various constructions.

2.1. Variation of Relational Constructions

Intralinguistic and cross-linguistic variation is observed in both the morphosyntax and the semantics of relational constructions.

The dimensions of morphosyntactic variation are:

a. *The order of relational gram and landmark.* In the languages of the world, in accordance with the Greenbergian word order correlations, relational grams either consistently precede or follow the landmark noun in the construction within a language (Greenberg 1963). Moreover, there are more languages with postposed grams than there are languages with preposed grams (Svorou 1994).

b. *The boundedness of the relational gram.* Relational grams may appear free as prepositions or postpositions or bound as prefixes and suffixes. While prepositions and postpositions exhibit low degree of fusion with the landmark noun forming a syntactic unit with it, prefixes and suffixes may be either agglutinated or fused (Bybee 1985; Svorou 1994). Agglutinated relational grams retain their formal integrity without being affected by the morphophonological environment of the host, as in the Abkhaz example in (5).

(5)   *Abkhaz* (Hewitt 1979: 130)[1]
       də-s-pə+n-gəlo-w+pʼ
       he-me-in.front-stand-STAT
       'He is standing in front of me'

Fused grams are characterized by allomorphy conditioned either phonologically or morphologically. They can be exemplified by case affixes found in inflectional languages, like Ancient Greek where the dative case suffixes /-a/, /-e:/, /-o:/, /-i/, /-oi/, /-ais/, /-ois/, /-si/ have locative uses and the accusative case suffixes /-an/, /-e:n/, /-on/, /-a/, /-e/, /-o:/, /-a:s/ have allative uses.

c. *The host of the relational gram.* Bound relational grams may be found in association with the landmark noun phrase or the verb of the sentence. Association with the landmark noun is characteristic of languages with dependent-marking morphology, whereas association with the verb is characteristic of languages with head-marking morphology (Nichols 1986).

d. *Internal structure of the relational gram.* Relational grams vary with respect to the number of morphemes that constitute them. They may be monomorphemic, as the English prepositions *in*, *from*, and *with*, or they may be complex forms consisting of a general relational morpheme and a more specific morpheme, as in the English complex prepositions *in front of*, *in back of*, and *instead of*. The internal complexity of the gram is a function of the degree of grammaticalization of the gram, as well as its semantics (Svorou 1994).

e. *The syntactic relation of governance among the elements of the relational construction.* In syntactic theory, the relational notion of "head" is an important one. A head of a construction is the most important constituent that defines the character of the construction and determines the syntactic relations of governance, modification, and agreement. Within the generative paradigm, adpositions are considered the "heads" of adpositional phrases. An adposition takes a complement noun phrase and, furthermore, governs the case marking of the noun phrase (Zwicky 1985). Within Functional Grammar (Dik 1997) and Role and Reference Grammar (Van Valin and LaPolla 1997), however, in relational constructions that encode an

argument of the verb, the noun is considered the head of a relational
construction. The status of the adposition as the head of the phrase is then
at least problematic. This is further complicated by the fact that languages
may express some relational notions with adpositions and others with
affixes bound to the noun. For example, Basque, in addition to a set of
adpositions, expresses some general locative notions with suffixes, as exemplified by the suffix -*n*:

(6)   *Basque* (Houghton 1961: 7)
       lur-e-a-n   *etch-e-a-n*
       earth-EUPH-ART-LOC   house-EUPH-ART-LOC
       'on the earth'   'in the house'

Since there is semantic equivalence of adpositions and inflectional affixes in a given domain, it only makes sense to opt for treating them
similarly. In fact, within recent versions of the generative paradigm,
inflections are taken to be the heads of adpositional phrases in languages with affixes, just like adpositions are taken to be the heads in
languages with adpositions. This approach, however, ignores, on the
one hand, the fact that in head-marking languages relational grams are
attracted to the verbal head, leaving the landmark noun phrase by itself,
and on the other, the diachronic facts, which point to a developmental
relation between adpositions and affixes.

   Relational constructions in languages with head-marking
morphosyntax defy constituency. Consider the following examples
from Navajo and Abkhaz:

(7)   *Navajo* (Young and Morgan 1980: 96)
       *ʔanʔiʔ   yi-**ghá**-ʔnaʔ*
       fence   it-through-crawled
       'He crawled through the fence.'
       (8)   *Abkhaz* (Hewitt 1979: 129)
       *a-yºnə̀   də-**dºə̀+l**-cʼə –ytʼ*
       the-house   he-out-go/come-Fin
       'He went/came out of the house.'

In both languages, the boldfaced relational gram appears as an affix
on the verbal complex with the landmark noun phrase appearing by
itself outside the verbal complex. Although the connection between
the relational gram and the landmark noun phrase exists, it does not
manifest itself in terms of syntactic constituency, at least not adjacency.
In these languages, it is rather clear that the primary information-
bearing unit (PIBU) is the landmark noun phrase and not the relational
gram (Croft 2001). Such facts point to difficulties with considering the
relational gram, be it adposition or affix, the head of the phrase.

Moreover, diachronic observations point to similar difficulties. Adpositions grammaticalize and eventually may fuse with the noun as case markers, as in the case of Hungarian, or appear as bound morphology, as in the case of Greek.

(9)   *Hungarian* (see Kahr 1976: 119)
bél- 'innards', *bel-el* 'innards-ABL'>*belöl* 'from inside' postposition
c. 1350   *(ker)ali   magzot-bele(ul)   tamadatia*
      royal   offspring-from   bring.forth
16 c.   *-ból* is the most frequent form with *belöl* still appearing
Modern   *ház-ból* 'from the inside of the house'
Kéz-böl 'from the inside of the hand'

(10)   *Greek*
Eis /es/ > /s/ (preposition)
Eis tin polin > *s-tin poli* (cliticization on the article in noun phrase initial
'To the city' position)

In the process of grammaticalization, the morphosyntactic status of the adposition changes, affecting the whole construction. Adpositions seem to behave more like heads in the earlier stages of grammaticalization, but as they grammaticalize, they may fuse with the noun, thus yielding headhood to the landmark noun. The cross-linguistic picture is characterized by morphosyntactic variation because a functionally equivalent construction, for example, the locative construction, may be in different evolutionary stages. Also, the type of locative construction may be a determinant for the degree of grammaticalization that a construction may reach even across languages. (See section 4 for a more detailed discussion of these points)

Relational constructions also express a great variety of relational notions, or of semantic variation. I have compiled a list of meaning components that feature as uses of spatial grams (Svorou 1994). They fall into the following categories:

a. Locations (e.g., interior, superior, under, lateral, middle, posterior, contiguous)
b. Directions (e.g., allative, ablative away, down, up, along, circumferential, through)
c. Distance (e.g., proximal, distal)
d. Spatiotemporal relations (e.g., anterior-order, posterior-order)
e. Temporal locations (e.g., interior-temporal, durative, end point of situation)
f. Aspectuals (e.g., continuous, inceptive, every)
g. Relations among situations (e.g., purpose, reason, concessive, reality condition)

h. Valence (e.g., benefactive, instrumental, source, recipient, comitative, dessive)

i. Manner (e.g., comparative, incremental, suddenly, punctual)

j. Predicative relations (e.g., sociative, exchange, possessive, partitive, material)

k. Conjunctive relations (e.g., inclusion, coordinative)

This list constitutes a classification of uses of relational grams that have as one of their uses a spatial one, be it the primary or not. It was created by comparing grammatical forms of the spatial domain across languages.

A different way of inquiry is to look into how a particular language expresses a certain domain, for example, location. This view has been adopted by Levinson (1991, 1994, 1996, 2003) and his colleagues of the Language and Cognition Group (Pederson et al. 1998; Levinson, Meria, and the Language and Cognition Group 2003). In studying how different languages express spatial relations, Levinson points out that some languages employ lexical means and others grammatical means for describing the same spatial scene. Such differences may be due to the means available in the language. The findings of this research have been interpreted as supporting the linguistic relativity hypothesis.

3. Semantics of Adpositions

Early studies of relational grams focused primarily on prepositions in European languages, with particular attention to English (Lindkvist 1950, 1972, 1976; Heaton 1965; Wood 1967; Hill 1968; Bennett 1972, 1975) and French (Poitier 1961, 1962), although occasional studies of relational grams in other languages exist, for example, Buck (1955) on Mongolian postpositions, Casad (1975) on Cora locationals and directionals, and Friedrich (1969a, 1969b, 1970) on Tarascan suffixes of space. Although conducted within various theoretical frameworks, a common thread to these studies is that they are concerned with providing *lists of uses* of particular relational grams, with some attempts at analyzing the uses in terms of binary semantic components (for example, Bennett 1975).[2] And while these lists of uses were a sure sign of the polysemous nature of relational grams, it was not until the advent of Cognitive Linguistics that their polysemy was seen as their most interesting and challenging semantic characteristic; witness, for instance, the introduction of polysemy networks as interrelated networks of uses around a prototype and the investigation of the relation between relational grams and context—as relational grams lend themselves to use in various contexts transforming to adapt to the semantic nuances required by the context. Furthermore, in most of these studies, the focus of analysis was on how to represent the linguistic aspects of relational grams. A few studies recognized the need to look at areas beyond the system of language for insights into the structure of linguistic categories of relational domains such as space and time. Among them, Talmy's early work (1972, 1975, 1978) as well as Miller and Johnson-Laird (1976) figure prominently. These works sketched out how language and cognition interact in the expression of relational notions involving motion, space, and time.

A seminal study for the treatment of relational categories and for Cognitive Linguistics in general is Talmy (1983). In this study, Talmy provided a sketch of how language structures spatial categories along with the levels of analysis we need to consider for understanding this mapping of language with the cognitive category of spatial orientation. Talmy's proposals are in line with the views of Herskovits (1982, 1986), Jackendoff (1983), Lakoff (1987), Langacker (1987, 1990a, 1990b, 1991), and Vandeloise (1991) in that relational grams, such as prepositions, express *construals* of the experiential situation by a conceptualizer. Speakers, as conceptualizers, use a number of mechanisms to construe a scene linguistically. Although it is not clear whether these mechanisms are processing mechanisms or mechanisms that lead to the creation of lexical and grammatical patterns in language, as Rice, Sandra, and Vanrespaille (1999) have pointed out, they can affect the linguistic encoding of a scene. Some of the proposed mechanisms are schematization, perspective, and idealization and abstraction, and are discussed below.

A fundamental consideration for the analysis of meaning is the understanding that language involves *schematization*, "a process that involves the systematic selection of certain aspects of a referent scene to represent the whole, while disregarding the remaining aspects" (Talmy 1983: 225). This process leads to the adjustment of the level of specificity employed by the conceptualizer. Compare *This is here* to *The book is in front of me*. Individual forms of language, such as relational grams, represent particular schematic abstractions called "schemas." Discussions on the nature of schemas elaborating relational grams have centered on spatial grams. Are spatial grams and the schemas that underlie them characterizable in terms of *geometric, topological properties* or in terms of *functional properties*? Earlier studies have stressed the geometric properties of language (Bennett 1975; Miller and Johnson-Laird 1976; Herskovits 1982, 1986; Talmy 1983). In this view, linguistic forms encode aspects of the geometric relations that exist between and among objects as if these relations existed in a world in which conceptualizers were only perceivers and not users of objects and experiencers of usage events. Each form is associated with a set of spatial primitives such as 'enclosure' for the representation of English *in* or 'spatial contiguity' for the representation of English *on*. Certain functional concepts, such as 'region', proposed by Miller and Johnson-Laird (1976), or 'support', which is included in Herskovits's (1986) and Miller and Johnson-Laird's (1976) accounts, appear only as secondary or in support of the more central and important geometric properties. Later studies provide evidence for the importance of functional, in addition to geometric, properties of spatial descriptions; that is, they include knowledge that is gained from our functional experience with objects (Vandeloise 1986, 1991; Talmy's 1988). Casad and Langacker (1985) provide an analysis of two Cora particles, *u* 'inside' and *a* 'outside', in terms of topological as well as functional properties such as 'accessibility'.

Vandeloise (1986) proposes that the French prepositions are best explained in terms of functional relations such as 'containment' and 'support'. Exploring the attempts to describe the French preposition *dans* as well as equivalent prepositions in English, Dutch, and German, Vandeloise (1994) points out the difficulties that these geometric or topological proposals have and instead proposes the notion of 'force' as the controlling factor in the choice of preposition to describe a spatial scene. This notion has to do with the force that the container exerts on the content and is very similar to what Garrod and Sanford (1989) and Garrod, Ferrier, and Campbell (1999) have called "location control." Coventry, Carmichael, and Garrod (1994) and Garrod, Ferrier, and Campbell (1999) provide experimental evidence for functional categories of CONTAINMENT and SUPPORT associated with the English prepositions *in, on, over,* and *beside,* according to which speakers would rely on functional information for location control in cases where the spatial scenes were less than prototypical examples of containment and support. This finding led them to the conclusion that the semantic representation of prepositions should include geometric as well as functional information. This view of schemas as rich with both geometric and functional information, put forth primarily by looking at the semantics of spatial grams in very few languages, is further corroborated by my cross-linguistic comparison of spatial grams (Svorou 1994).

Conceptualizers have the ability to view a spatial scene from different *perspectives,* thus producing different linguistic descriptions reflecting these perspectives. For example, the sentence *The apple is in the plate* presents a particular construal of an imagined or actual situation in which the apple and the plate, although both statically present in the scene, are presented asymmetrically. The apple is construed as the *trajector (Figure),* the entity to be located, and the plate as the *landmark (Ground),* the entity with respect to which the trajector is located. In the possible, but unlikely, sentence *The plate is under the apple,* the plate is construed as the trajector and the apple as the landmark. The latter construal is unlikely or rare because the larger in size plate can generally function as a better landmark than the smaller in size apple. The spatial and temporal relational domains are two of a number of other relational domains that exhibit this asymmetric organization, such as possession and causation. The meaning of relational grams can be best analyzed by considering the role of the conceptualizer and the role of the ground landmark.

In order for a reference object to be construed as a landmark, it has to undergo a process of *idealization and abstraction* by which "familiar objects, in all their bulk and physicality, are differentially 'boiled down' to match ascribed schemas" (Talmy 2000: 220). Other aspects of the objects are ignored. For example, the plate is idealized as a container in *The apple is in the plate* but as a surface in *The apple is on the plate* matching the requirements of the IN schema versus the ON schema. Moreover, encoding a spatial scene with a relational gram of containment (*in*) requires the idealization of the landmark as a container, whether it has prototypical characteristics of containers (*in the cup, in the lake*) or not (*in the rain*).

Schemas have been employed starting with Brugman (1981) to represent the multiple uses of prepositions, such as English *over*. These uses, distinguished into more or less prototypical, have been related to one another in the form of a polysemy network, a configuration of the various senses of a lexical item such as a preposition. While speakers have a good idea of what constitutes a use (Colombo and Flores D'Arcais 1984), what constitutes a use for the analyst may be controversial (Sandra and Rice 1995). Still, this particular solution to the problem of polysemy gained in popularity and led to a number of analyses of relational grams across languages in terms of polysemy networks, for example, Vandeloise (1986, 1991, 1994) and Cuyckens (1993b) for French, Cuyckens (1991, 1993a) and Geeraerts (1992) for Dutch, Rice (1996) for English, Bacz (1997) and Dancygier (2000) for Polish, Smith (1993) for German accusative and dative cases and Bellavia (1996) for German *über*, Delbecque (1996) for Spanish *para* and *por*, Schulze (1993) for English *around*, Dewell (1994) and Kreitzer (1997) for English *over*, and Kristoffersen (2001) for Norwegian *mot*. In these studies, the network consists of a central, prototypical schema and a set of related senses in a particular configuration. The granularity of analysis of networks and the level of schematization of the prototype continue to challenge cognitive linguists, as the re-telling of the story of *over* in Tyler and Evans (2001, 2003) indicates. What is generally held and argued for, on the theoretical level (among others, Brugman 1981; Lakoff 1987; Rice 1992) and shown on the experimental level (Rice, Sandra, and Vanrespaille 1999), is the validity of a polysemic approach to the representation of relational grams in contrast to a monosemic approach (Ruhl 1989).

The relations among the senses in a polysemy network are seen as a result of semantic extension from a prototypical schema. On the synchronic level, similar to the diachronic level to be discussed in section 4, the processes that lead to semantic extension are generally believed to be metaphor and pragmatic inferencing (Lakoff 1987; Schwenter and Traugott 1995, among others). Reflecting localistic accounts of cases (Anderson 1971), space is considered to be primary and the basis of semantic extension to domains such as time and causality (Radden 1985). The extension of originally spatial grams to the domain of time has been seen by many as a result of metaphor—the TIME IS SPACE metaphor (Lakoff and Johnson 1980; Claudi and Heine 1986; Lakoff 1987). Indeed, this type of extension is responsible for the development of the majority of temporal grams in many languages, as Haspelmath's (1997) detailed study on a sample of fifty languages has shown. He concluded that the TIME IS SPACE metaphor is in fact universal. Despite the alleged ubiquity of this metaphor, the question remains whether it is a live metaphor in the minds of the speakers that they use in the online construction of meaning or whether it is an epiphenomenon of historical processes that has resulted in the development of temporal grams out of spatial grams and is no longer available to the consciousness of the speakers. This question has been addressed in an experimental study by Rice, Sandra, and Vanrespaille (1999), who found that for many English and Dutch prepositions the TIME IS SPACE metaphor is fading away in the minds of the speakers. Other recent studies have shown semantic extension to be the result of pragmatic inferencing or context-induced reinterpretation of the meaning of grams on the synchronic (Tyler and Evans 2001, 2003) as well as diachronic level (Svorou 1994; Schwenter and Traugott 1995; Heine 1997). If semantic change takes place by conventionalizing inferences induced by the context in which a relational gram appears, then the same mechanism should be available for making online adjustments of meaning on the synchronic level. In this view, then, metaphor is the result of the process, and not the process itself.

The above issues on the semantics of relational grams (the mechanisms of construal, polysemy networks, and semantic extension) have been investigated in many studies, and yet many questions remain on some of the issues raised. One such issue has to do with whether to treat meaning as associated with individual forms in the lexicon or whether to treat meaning as associated with individual forms in specific constructions.

Attempts to analyze the meaning of adpositions in the 1970s have concentrated on the meaning of prepositions in languages like English and have assumed that the preposition by itself is the form that provides all the relational meaning in a relational construction such as the locative construction. For example, in *The baby is in the tub*, the preposition *in*, and nothing else, is responsible for specifying the spatial relation between the baby and the tub. The work of cognitive linguists, however, has shown that elements other than the preposition may contribute to the construal of a scene. Moreover, as discussed above, the various senses of a relational gram come from the context in which it may be found, and before they can be recognized as uses of a certain gram, these senses are emergent or latent in particular sentences. In order for the meaning of the gram to be extended, creating a polysemous structure, elements of the context have to contribute to the new meaning of the gram. In other words, the new sense of the gram is a result of rearranging semantic bits within a construction. A prerequisite for semantic extension, then, is the existence of context for the interpretation of grams and the assumption that meaning is distributed over several elements in a construction. For the locative construction, this view has been advocated by Sinha and Kuteva (1995) for English, Dutch, Japanese, and Bulgarian and by Ameka (1990, 1995) for Ewe. It finds support in studies of various languages, and it is purported to be a universal. Some examples follow.

German two-way prepositions, like *in, hinter, unter, auf*, and *an*, exhibit a variety of senses depending on whether the landmark noun carries accusative or dative marking (Smith 1988, 1993). The senses go beyond the traditional motion versus location interpretation to include senses motivated by these prototypical meanings. In all cases, the construal of the spatial situation is a function of the specific preposition used, the landmark noun, and the case marking of the landmark noun.

Similarly, Polish (Dancygier 2000) uses three interacting substems to express spatial information: (i) Direction nouns, such as *góra* 'up' and *dol* 'down' or *przód* 'front' and *tyl* 'back', describe regions in space or regions of landmarks. They combine with prepositions and appropriate case markings to indicate various spatial construals such as direction of movement, location of objects with respect to the observer, and so on. (ii) Prepositions, such as *w* 'in', which combines with the accusative or the locative, or *do* 'to' and *od* 'from', which combine with the genitive, indicate dynamic spatial construals such as path/goal or source/path. (iii) Case markings, including genitive, locative, accusative, and instrumental, usually combine with either prepositions or direction nouns to provide spatial information, except for the instrumental, which can mark landmark nouns for the expression of path and path-related notions. In any given construction, it is the interaction of all or some of these subsystems with the specific landmark noun that determines the specific construal of the situation at hand.

A relevant issue in the discussion of the interaction of preposition and case in case languages is the question of whether the preposition or the case is the primary element, the one that "governs" the other. Bacz (2000) provides a succinct discussion of this issue as far as Polish data goes. The Polish data pose a problem for any monolithic account of preposition and case because different prepositions relate to case in different ways. She proposes a solution to the problem by adopting Kuryłowicz's historical explanation whereby the role of the preposition changes throughout the history of the locative construction. That is, a preposition can be said to govern a case when that preposition can be combined with only one case. Prepositions that can be combined with a variety of cases are considered to be at an earlier historical stage where the case morpheme plays a more fundamental role in determining the semantics of a construction. The historical perspective of adpositions in general is discussed in section 4 below.

This "distributed" view of meaning constitutes a shift from previous accounts that have focused on the meaning of a single element, such as a preposition, without regard of the elements that it collocates with frequently and the influence of such elements on the meaning of the preposition. Such accounts are partly a result of analyzing languages with no significant case systems and partly of analyzing prepositions as being the *head* of the construction they participate in.

4. THE GRAMMATICALIZATION OF RELATIONAL GRAMS

In the past two decades, a cross-fertilization of functional and cognitive approaches with diachronic and cross-linguistic perspectives gave us a deeper understanding of the nature of relational grams, illuminating their semantic as well as their formal aspect. A number of language specific and cross-linguistic studies prepared the ground by providing the seed ideas.

Papers by Traugott (1975, 1978) and Kahr (1975, 1976) investigate the historical development of spatial adpositions, locationals, and case markers. Specifically, Traugott (1975, 1978) and Kahr (1975) point to body-part terms and relational nouns as the ultimate sources of spatial adpositions in many different languages. In these studies, the focus is on the description of the formal identity and semantic similarity of spatial adpositions, on the one hand, and body-part nouns and relational nouns, on the other. Kahr (1976) provides evidence for the historical processes underlying synchronic case systems in languages from five families, documenting the postpositional origin of case morphemes. A common thread in all these studies is the observation that the historically old and new forms and functions may coexist at a particular synchronic period, blurring the distinction of grammatical categories and of the lexicon and grammar.

These cross-linguistic studies complemented by some language-specific studies, such as Friedrich's (1969a, 1969b, 1970) studies on Tarascan spatial suffixes, point to the historical relation between lexical sets, such as body-part terms and spatial adpositions and affixes.

Nominal expressions are not the only source of adpositions. In a number of African and Asian languages, verbs in certain constructions, such as serial-verb constructions and participial constructions, function as "co-verbs," or "verbids," that is, as adpositions but with some verbal characteristics. Studies by Li and Thompson (1973, 1974) on Chinese, Givón (1975) on Niger-Congo, and M. Clark (1978) on Vietnamese provide evidence for a verbal source of adpositions.

As the 1980s approach, the following statements can summarize the received knowledge:

a. Prepositions and postpositions have their historical sources in two lexical categories: (i) nouns expressing body parts or relational notions and (ii) verbs of motion or existence.
b. Postpositions may be the source of case morphemes.
c. Prepositions and postpositions may coexist synchronically with their nominal or verbal sources resulting in blurring of grammatical distinctions and fuzziness of categories.

Although there was evidence for the historical relationship of adpositions to lexical sources such as nouns and verbs, there were few satisfactory ideas as to how to account for this relationship in an explanatory framework. The theoretical framework in vogue, the generative paradigm, was embracing a separatist view of grammar and lexicon and any historical connections were viewed as a result of some "radical reanalysis" (Lightfoot 1979). In the case of adpositions, this approach fails to explain why several languages could have the same form functioning as a noun and an adposition or verb and adposition at the same synchronic point, if any "radical reanalysis" were to take place. The most promising ideas were put forth by Givón's (1971, 1975) proposal of looking at the process of grammaticalization to understand the synchronic facts, as in the case of adpositions rising out of serial verbs.

Givón's proposals, corroborated by Lehmann's (1982) thoughts on grammaticalization and Heine and Reh's (1984) study on grammaticalization in African languages, were the beginning of a renewed interest in the development of grammatical material. Although grammaticalization was neither a new concept nor a new phenomenon[3]—Kuryłowicz (1975: 52) had already discussed it as "a process which involves an increase in the range of a morpheme advancing from a lexical to a grammatical or from less grammatical to more grammatical status"—the renewed interest in grammaticalization focused not only on the description of the morphosyntactic changes that morphemes underwent but also on the semantic and pragmatic changes, which, according to several scholars, precede and drive grammaticalization. A number of important publications on various grammaticalization phenomena in different languages converged in further advancing our knowledge of the process. Studies by Bybee and Pagliuca (1985), Lehmann (1985), Traugott (1982, 1988), among others, provided the theoretical and empirical foundations for a theory of grammaticalization with the following characteristics:

a. Grammaticalization is a diachronic process, although it can be interpreted synchronically.
b. Grammaticalization affects the morphosyntactic status of a lexical or grammatical form; forms/grams become phonologically eroded, their position within the sentence becomes gradually more fixed, and they lose in categoriality.
c. Grammaticalization involves semantic generalization; forms tend to assume more general meanings, losing some of their semantic specificities while retaining the basic semantic schema. Such semantic generalization is seen as a precursor to morphosyntactic changes.
d. Grammaticalization is a unidirectional process in that it leads from a "less grammatical" to a "more grammatical" unit but not vice versa.

The development of adpositions from lexical sources features prominently in most of these studies. Initially, however, the focus was on the changes that affect their morphosyntactic character. It was not until the cross-fertilization of grammaticalization theory with metaphor theory that the semantic aspect of grammaticalization started to become interesting.

The study of metaphor as a literary device is as old as literary tradition itself. The publication of Lakoff and Johnson (1980) and Lakoff (1987) provided the scholarly community with a new insight into metaphor and its ubiquity. According to them, metaphor is not simply a literary device, but a kind of conceptual manipulation that humans do, which enables the linguistic structures we call "metaphorical" (see also Grady, this volume, chapter 8). Metaphor is seen as the process responsible for creating the polysemy found in language (Brugman 1981) on the synchronic level. New uses emerge out of extensions of aspects of the meaning of a lexical item to a new context, which is unfamiliar, abstract, or difficult to comprehend. Such extensions are unidirectional going from concrete, familiar, comprehensible domains to abstract and unfamiliar domains. The process of metaphorical extension involves imposition of an image schema, which is the basis of our understanding of the meaning of a lexical item, to a new situation for the purpose of understanding the new situation. The classic example here involves the use of spatial expressions such as *before* and *after* for our understanding of time.

From the historical vantage point, the combination of grammaticalization theory and metaphor theory seemed only natural at that point: grammaticalization theorists where looking for an explanation of what drives this process, where abstract grammatical concepts emerge out of concrete lexical concepts, and why it happens, and metaphor theory involved expressing an abstract domain by making use of lexical means from a more concrete domain. Studies by Claudi and Heine (1986), Heine and Claudi (1986), Svorou (1986, 1988), Heine (1989), and Heine, Claudi, and Hünnemeyer (1991a, 1991b) employ metaphorical extension as the mechanism that operates in early stages of grammaticalization. The most straightforward argument in support of metaphorical extension taking place in grammaticalization that was offered involved the development of spatial and temporal adpositions.

Data from a wide range of languages—Claudi and Heine (1986) and Heine (1989) on data from 125 African languages, Bowden (1992) on data from 125 Oceanic languages, and Svorou (1986) on data from 26 genetically unrelated languages—provided evidence for a grammaticalization model of adpositions touching upon their semantic as well as their morphosyntactic character. Spatial adpositions involving locative orientational notions such as 'in', 'on', 'above', 'under', 'in front', 'behind', and 'between' evolve from lexical sources that involve body-part nouns (human or animal) and landmark nouns.[4] Along similar lines, Haspelmath (1997) provides evidence of the evolution of temporal grams from spatial grams.

In looking at the sources of grams with the same meaning/function, one is struck by the fact that cross-linguistically there is a relatively small set of nominal or verbal forms out of which specific grams arise. For example, 'in' grams develop from body-part terms expressing notions such as belly, abdomen, heart, mouth, liver, bowels, kidneys, tooth, torso, female sexual organs, umbilicus, tongue, stomach, throat, intestines, or landmark nouns such as meaning 'house', and in a few cases, even relational nouns such as ones meaning 'middle' (Stolz 1992; Svorou 1994). One can only speculate at this point as to what seems to be the determining factor for "selecting" one of these sources to express the locative notion of 'in'. The prevailing view is that language change is nondeterministic; therefore, predicting which language will "choose" which source to develop a gram of a certain type is deemed to be the wrong question to ask. In a nondeterministic view of language change, we would need to consider not only which source concept is similar to the type of target location, but all sorts of other factors such as cultural facts about specific body parts or landmarks as well as associated frequency of activation effects of such facts, other existing grams in the language of the same type, and possible language contact effects. This is a complex area of future inquiry in the field, which grammaticalization researchers have started to tackle by looking at language change in the making. What can be said about the relation between source and target concepts in the development of relational grams is that the same image schema configuration exists (Sweetser 1988; Heine, Claudi, and Hünnemeyer 1991b; Rubba 1994). So, for example, body-part terms such as belly, abdomen, heart, liver, bowels, stomach, intestines, umbilicus, tongue, throat, and female sexual organs are all characterized by their position relative to the human body as being in its interior. In the development of such terms into relational grams expressing containment, the relational aspect of their semantics of being contained has been retained. The container is no longer the human body but rather a generalized landmark notion which can accommodate a host of concrete as well as abstract entities construed as containers, as, for example, in *in the building, in the water, in my thoughts.*

The role of metaphor in language change, and specifically the development of relational grams, would not be as compelling if it were not for ample evidence for the synchronic deployment of this process. In many languages, nominal sources and their relational gram targets exist at the same synchronic period. Brugman (1983) and Brugman and Macaulay (1986), for example, among several other studies, provide such evidence for spatial grams of Chalcatongo Mixtec. The synchronic existence of such forms create the preconditions for potential grammaticalization and license the assumption that similar synchronic stages have existed even in cases where no such direct evidence can be documented.

While a number of scholars have attributed the historical development of ad-positions to metaphor and metaphorical processes (Heine, Claudi, and Hünnemeyer 1991a, 1991b, and others), others argue that metaphor as a process is too static and stiff to account for small meaning adjustments that take place when a particular con-struction gets fine-tuned to the current context. Schwenter and Traugott (1995: 264), for example, in discussing the development of English *instead of/in place of/in lieu of*, building on discussion presented in Traugott and König (1991), Heine, Claudi, and Hünnemeyer (1991b), and Hopper and Traugott (1993), propose "that a metaphor is predominantly a product where meaning change as opposed to individual, often creative innovations, is concerned. By contrast, metonymy, being associative and pragmatically involving context-induced inferencing, is an ongoing process which results in a new product (Heine's 'context-induced reinterpretation') but is poten-tially present in all language use.". The product of historical change may look like metaphor but has resulted from the process of context-induced reinterpretation.

The small meaning adjustments induced by context that take place constantly in language use result in observable changes which are the result of high frequency use of a set of meaning adjustments. Such changes have been represented by evo-lutionary chains or continua with identifiable stages linking sets of sources and targets. Heine (1997: 44), summarizing analyses of cross-linguistic data presented in Heine, Claudi, and Hünnemeyer (1991b) and Svorou (1994), presents a four-stage scenario of conceptual shift from body-part to spatial concept as follows:

    a. Stage 1: a region of the human body
    b. Stage 2: a region of an (inanimate object)
    c. Stage 3: a region in contact with an object
    d. Stage 4: a region detached from the object

These conceptual shifts involve the development of one type of relational grams that have their source in body-part terms. This type of grams constitutes a large part of spatial grams, but they are not the only sources of relational grams. Others develop from landmark nouns, such as *earth, ground, sky, trace,* and *footprint,* and relational nouns, such as *front, middle, back, interior,* and so on. Sources other than nominal include adverbs, such as *up* and *down,* and verbs, such as *ascend, descend, fall, enter, exit,* and so on. The above studies, as well as Heine and Kuteva (2002), provide detailed discussions and data in support of these developments.

Conceptual shifts are accompanied by, or even trigger, changes in the morphosyntactic status of the forms undergoing grammaticalization. The above stages of conceptual shift are paralleled by the following morphosyntactic changes:

a. Stage 1: head noun in genitive inalienable construction (the *front* 'forehead' of my father) (< Latin *frons* 'forehead')
b. Stage 2: head noun in genitive construction (the *front* of the house)
c. Stage 3: head noun embedded in relational construction (in the *front* of the house)
d. Stage 4: relational gram with genitive NP complement (*in front* of the house)

The grammaticalization does not stop with stage 4. Once a form becomes grammatical, semantic generalization may lead to other changes in the morphosyntactic form. One such change expands the possibilities of the case of the complement that the relational gram may take to include an accusative NP (*before* him). As many studies have shown, relational grams of adpositional nature may become bound in the form of affixes, as case markers (Reh 1986). Alternatively, adpositions may become subordinators of various adverbial clauses (Genetti 1986, 1991). This is what is expected by the broadening of the types of contexts that a relational gram is used in: phrasal relations and clausal relations are conceived of as being analogous to nominal relations.

One determinant of the degree of grammaticalization that a construction may reach may be the type of language. Bybee (1997) has argued that some languages generalize grammatical meaning to a greater extent than others do, and consequently, we observe differences in the level of grammaticalization of forms in functionally equivalent constructions. Another determinant is the particular semantics of a construction. As I have argued (Svorou 2002b), across languages, interior region grams are more likely to reach high levels of grammaticalization as compared to top or bottom region grams and the latter more likely than front or back region grams. It is conjectured that this asymmetry is due to the semantic and cognitive complexity of front and back region grams as compared to interior region grams.

In the process of grammaticalization, which does not stop with a gram reaching a point clearly recognizable as an adposition, relational grams change in terms of their semantics. The process of change has been described as *semantic bleaching* (Givón 1979), *generalization* (Bybee, Perkins, and Pagliuca 1994), or *semantic attenuation* (Langacker 1990b), in contrast to earlier accounts which hold that grammatical material may become practically meaningless. One of the aspects of semantic change of relational grams involves a shift from describing an objective situation to representing a *construal* of the situation from the point of view of a conceptualizer, therefore, providing a *subjective* view of it. For example, compare (8) and (9), which illustrate an objective and a subjective point of view of a scene.

(8)   The squirrel jumped over the fence.
(9)   The squirrel is over the fence.

In (8), the squirrel occupied a series of positions sequentially leading from one side of the fence to the other, thus representing an objective sequence of events. In (9), however, the squirrel may be in the same position with respect to the fence and the observer but occupying this position did not necessarily involve moving to the other side of the fence; yet, the conceptualizer in (9) construes the relation subjectively, as if the squirrel had in fact moved. This phenomenon has also been observed by Matsumoto (1996), who terms it *subjective motion*, and has been explored extensively by Talmy (1996, 2000), who talks about *fictive motion*. Talmy also observes that there is an asymmetry in that the process of conceptualizing static events in terms of dynamic is more common than the process of conceptualizing dynamic events as static.

While these aspects of grammaticalization are generally supported by research and accepted, other aspects still remain controversial or unresolved. One such aspect involves the claim that grammaticalization is a unidirectional process, which creates grams out of lexical items (Heine, Claudi, and Hünnemeyer 1991a; Traugott and Heine 1991; Hopper and Traugott 1993; Haspelmath 1999). Recent studies, however, point to a reversal of the process, degrammaticalization, where a gram gets to be used as a lexical item (Ramat 1992; Campbell 2001; Janda 2001; Norde 2001). Given that lexicon and grammar form a continuum, some fluency might be expected, but such a process may also depend on the kind of grammatical element at issue; a spatial gram may give rise to a noun (*the ups and downs*), but for a verbal perfective affix this would be more difficult. Another question involves the distinction of degrammaticalization from conversion or functional shift. When the English preposition *up* is used as a verb *to up*, I would argue that this is an example of conversion rather than degrammaticalization, since this shift can happen instantaneously and takes place outside the construction in which *up* functions as a grammatical element. Moreover, using *up* as a verb immediately creates all the paradigm of *to up*, making past-tense and participial forms available (*upped, upping*). In contrast, the process of degrammaticalization would involve the reversal of the process of grammaticalization of an element within its construction and would be a gradual process (Svorou 2002a). It still remains to be resolved in cases where an adposition is also used as an adverb whether it is an example of degrammaticalization, conversion, or simply a common situation in grammaticalization where forms from consecutive diachronic stages may also exist at the same synchronic stage.

5. Looking Ahead: Themes for the Next Decade

Despite the progress that was made within Cognitive Linguistics toward a deeper understanding of relational constructions in the last two decades, many issues remain unresolved, unaddressed, or controversial.

One such issue has to do with the definition of a domain of investigation. Given what we have learned, is cross-language comparison more fruitful by focusing on structural or on functional equivalence? In other words, do we compare the grammatical inventory of languages as far as a certain semantic domain is concerned, or do we compare languages as to how they express a certain domain, regardless of whether they employ lexical or grammatical means? The former view involves developing a grammatical typology of a specific domain. The latter view is what Levinson and his colleagues have argued for. Both views are indispensable since comparing results from these different perspectives would be most revealing about human language and conceptualization.

Another point of future investigation remains the description of relational constructions in the languages of the world. Most studies have focused on English or European languages, resulting in a biased view of the area of inquiry. Expansion of the inventory of languages under investigation would enrich our understanding of the domain.

NOTES

1. Abkhaz is a head-marking language. Hewitt (1979) uses "+" to indicate boundaries between morphological elements that bear derivational relations and "−"to separate morphemes that bear clausal-level relations.

2. A comprehensive bibliography on prepositions up to the late 1970s is Guimier (1981).

3. For an account of the history of grammaticalization, see Hopper and Traugott (1993).

4. In cases where explicit historical information was not available, given the pervasiveness of the formal similarity of adpositions with body-part nouns in language after language, it was argued that the observed similarity was a result of evolution of such nouns into adpositions.

REFERENCES

Ameka, Felix. 1990. The grammatical packaging of experiences in Ewe: A study in the semantics of syntax. *Australian Journal of Linguistics* 10: 139–81.

Ameka, Felix. 1995. The linguistic construction of space in Ewe. *Cognitive Linguistics* 6: 139–81.

Anderson, John M. 1971. *The grammar of case: Towards a localistic theory.* Cambridge: Cambridge University Press.

Bacz, Barbara. 1997. On the meaning and the prototype of the locative case: A semantic study of the Polish locative with the preposition *przy. Langues et Linguistique* 23: 1–18.

Bacz, Barbara. 2000. On the status of preposition in case languages: Does preposition govern case? *Langues et Linguistique* 26: 1–22.

Bellavia, Ellena. 1996. The German *über*. In Martin Pütz and René Dirven, eds, *The construal of space in language and thought* 73–107. Berlin: Mouton de Gruyter.

Bennett, David C. 1972. Some considerations concerning the locative-directional distinction. *Semiotica* 5: 58–88.

Bennett, David C. 1975. *Spatial and temporal uses of English prepositions: An essay in stratificational semantics*. London: Longman.

Bowden, John. 1992. *Behind the prepositions: Grammaticalization of locatives in oceanic languages*. Canberra: Australian National University.

Brugman, Claudia. 1981. Story of *Over*. MA thesis, University of California at Berkeley. (Published as *The story of Over: Polysemy, semantics, and the structure of the lexicon.* New York: Garland, 1988)

Brugman, Claudia. 1983. The use of body-part terms as locatives in Chalcatongo Mixtec. In Alice Schlichter, Wallace L. Chafe, and Leanne Hinton, eds., *Survey of California and other Indian languages* 235–90. Studies in Mesoamerican Linguistics. Report no. 4. Berkeley: University of California at Berkeley.

Brugman, Claudia, and Monica Macaulay. 1986. Interacting semantic systems: Mixtec expressions of location. *Berkeley Linguistics Society* 12: 315–27.

Buck, Frederick H. 1955. *Comparative study of postpositions in Mongolian dialects and the written language*. Cambridge, MA: Harvard University Press.

Bybee, Joan L. 1985. *Morphology: A study of the relation between meaning and form*. Amsterdam: John Benjamins.

Bybee, Joan L. 1997. Semantic aspects of morphological typology. In Joan L. Bybee, John Haiman, and Sandra Thompson, eds., *Essays on language function and language type* 25–37. Amsterdam: John Benjamins.

Bybee, Joan L., and William Pagliuca. 1985. Cross-linguistic comparison and the development of grammatical meaning. In Jacek Fisiak, ed., *Historical semantics and historical word-formation* 59–83. Berlin: Mouton de Gruyter.

Bybee, Joan L., Revere D. Perkins, and William Pagliuca. 1994. *The evolution of grammar: Tense, aspect, and modality in the languages of the world*. Chicago: University of Chicago Press.

Campbell, Lyle. 2001. What's wrong with grammaticalization? *Language Sciences* 23: 113–61.

Casad, Eugene. 1975. Location and direction in Cora discourse. *Anthropological Linguistics* 19: 216–41.

Casad, Eugene. 1982. Cora locationals and structured imagery. PhD dissertation, University of California at San Diego.

Casad, Eugene, and Ronald Langacker. 1985. 'Inside' and 'outside' in Cora grammar. *International Journal of American Linguistics* 51: 247–81. Reprinted in Ronald Langacker, *Concept, image, and symbol* 33–57. Berlin: Mouton de Gruyter, 1990.

Clark, Eve. 1978. Locationals: Existential, locative, and possessive constructions. In Joseph Greenberg, Charles Ferguson, and Edith Moravcsik, eds., *Universals of human language* 1: 85–126. Stanford, CA: Stanford University Press.

Clark, Herbert H. 1973. Space, time, semantics and the child. In Timothy E. Moore, ed., *Cognitive development and the acquisition of language* 28–63. New York: Academic Press.

Clark, Marybeth. 1978. *Coverbs and case in Vietnamese*. Pacific Linguistics Series B, no. 48. Canberra: Australian National University.

Claudi, Ulrike, and Bernd Heine. 1986. On the metaphorical base of grammar. *Studies in Language* 10: 297–335.

Colombo, Lucia, and Giovanni B. Flores D'Arcais. 1984. The meaning of Dutch prepositions: A psycholinguistic study of polysemy. *Linguistics* 22: 51–98.

Coventry, Kenny R., Richard Carmichael, and Simon C. Garrod. 1994. Spatial prepositions, object-specific function, and task requirements. *Journal of Semantics* 11: 289–309.

Croft, William. 2001. *Radical construction grammar: Syntactic theory in typological perspective*. Oxford: Oxford University Press.

Cuyckens, Hubert. 1991. The semantics of spatial prepositions in Dutch: A cognitive-linguistic exercise. PhD dissertation, University of Antwerp.

Cuyckens, Hubert. 1993a. The Dutch spatial preposition *in*: A cognitive-semantic analysis. In Cornelia Zelinsky-Wibbelt, ed., *The semantics of prepositions: From mental processing to natural language* 27–71. Berlin: Mouton de Gruyter.

Cuyckens, Hubert. 1993b. Spatial prepositions in French revisited. *Cognitive Linguistics* 4: 291–310.

Dancygier, Barbara. 2000. How Polish structures space: Prepositions, direction nouns, case, and metaphor. In Ad Foolen and Frederike van der Leek, eds., *Constructions in cognitive linguistics: Selected papers from the Fifth International Cognitive Linguistics Conference* 27–45. Amsterdam: John Benjamins.

DeLancey, Scott. 1997. Grammaticalization and the gradience of categories: Relator nouns and postpositions in Tibetan and Burmese. In Joan L. Bybee, John Haiman, and Sandra A. Thompson, eds., *Essays on language function and language type* 51–69. Amsterdam: John Benjamins.

Delbecque, Nicole. 1996. Towards a cognitive account of the use of the prepositions *por* and *para* in Spanish. In Eugene H. Casad, ed., *Cognitive linguistics in the Redwoods: The expansion of a new paradigm in linguistics* 249–318. Berlin: Mouton de Gruyter.

Dewell, Robert. 1994. *Over* again: Image-schema transformations in semantic analysis. *Cognitive Linguistics* 5: 351–80.

Dik, Simon C. 1997. *The theory of functional grammar*. Ed. Kees Hengeveld. 2 vols. Berlin: Mouton de Gruyter.

Friedrich, Paul. 1969a. Metaphor-like relations between referential subsets. *Lingua* 24: 1–10.

Friedrich, Paul. 1969b. On the meaning of the Tarascan suffixes of space. *International Journal of American Linguistics* 35: 5–48.

Friedrich, Paul. 1970. Shape in grammar. *Language* 46: 379–407.

Garrod, Simon, Gillian Ferrier, and Siobhan Campbell. 1999. *In* and *on*: Investigating the functional geometry of spatial prepositions. *Cognition* 72: 167–89.

Garrod, Simon C., and Anthony J. Sanford. 1989. Discourse models as interfaces between language and the spatial world. *Journal of Semantics* 6: 147–60.

Geeraerts, Dirk. 1992. The semantic structure of Dutch *over*. *Leuvense Bijdragen* 81: 205–30.

Genetti, Carol. 1986. The development of subordinators from postpositions in Bodic languages. *Berkeley Linguistics Society* 12: 387–400.

Genetti, Carol. 1991. From postposition to subordinator in Newari. In Elizabeth Closs Traugott and Bernd Heine, eds., *Approaches to grammaticalization*, vol. 2, *Focus on types of grammatical markers* 227–56. Amsterdam: John Benjamins.

Givón, Talmy. 1971. Historical syntax and synchronic morphology: An archaeologist's field trip. *Chicago Linguistic Society* 7: 394–415.

Givón, Talmy. 1975. Serial verbs and syntactic change: Niger-Congo. In Charles Li, ed., *Word order and word order change* 47–117. Austin: University of Texas Press.

Givón, Talmy. 1979. *On understanding grammar*. New York: Academic Press.

Greenberg, Joseph. 1963. Some universals of grammar with particular reference to the order of meaningful elements. In Joseph H. Greenberg, ed., *Universals of language: Report of a conference held at Dobbs Ferry, New York, April 13–15, 1961* 73–113. Cambridge, MA: MIT Press.

Guimier, Claude. 1981. *Prepositions: An analytical bibliography*. Amsterdam: John Benjamins.

Haspelmath, Martin. 1997. *From space to time: Temporal adverbials in the world's languages*. Munich: Lincom Europa.

Haspelmath, Martin. 1999. Why is grammaticalization irreversible? *Linguistics* 37: 1043–68.

Hawkins, Bruce W. 1984. The semantics of English spatial prepositions. PhD dissertation, University of California at San Diego. (Also published as LAUT Paper no. 142, Trier, Germany: Linguistic Agency of the University of Trier, 1985)

Hawkins, Bruce W. 1986. The preposition 'out': A case of semantic elision. LAUD Paper no. 169. Essen: Linguistic Agency of the University of Duisburg-Essen.

Heaton, J. B. 1965. *Prepositions and adverbial particles*. Essex: Longman.

Heine, Bernd. 1989. Adpositions in African languages. *Linguistique Africaine* 2: 77–127.

Heine, Bernd. 1997. *Cognitive foundations of grammar*. New York: Oxford University Press.

Heine, Bernd, and Ulrike Claudi. 1986. *On the rise of grammatical categories: Some examples from Maa*. (Kölner Beiträge zur Afrikanistik, 13.) Berlin: Reimer

Heine, Bernd, Ulrike Claudi, and Friederike Hünnemeyer. 1991a. From cognition to grammar: Evidence from African languages. In Elizabeth Closs Traugott and Bernd Heine, eds., *Approaches to grammaticalization* 1: 149–88. Amsterdam: John Benjamins.

Heine, Bernd, Ulrike Claudi, and Friederike Hünnemeyer. 1991b. *Grammaticalization: A conceptual framework*. Chicago: University of Chicago Press.

Heine, Bernd, and Tania Kuteva. 2002. *World lexicon of grammaticalization*. Cambridge: Cambridge University Press.

Heine, Bernd, and Mechthild Reh. 1984. *Grammaticalization and reanalysis in African languages*. Hamburg: Helmut Buske Verlag.

Herskovits, Annette. 1982. Space and the prepositions in English: Regularities and irregularities in a complex domain. PhD dissertation, Stanford University.

Herskovits, Annette. 1985. Semantics and pragmatics of locative expressions. *Cognitive Science* 9: 341–78.

Herskovits, Annette. 1986. *Language and spatial cognition: An interdisciplinary study of the prepositions in English*. Cambridge: Cambridge University Press.

Hewitt, B. G. 1979. *Abkhaz*. Lingua Descriptive Studies, no. 2. Amsterdam: North Holland.

Hill, L. A. 1968. *Prepositions and adverbial particles: An interim classification, semantic, structural and graded*. London: Oxford University Press.

Hopper, Paul J., and Elizabeth Closs Traugott. 1993. *Grammaticalization*. Cambridge: Cambridge University Press. (2nd ed., 2003)

Houghton, Herbert P. 1961. *An introduction to the Basque language: Labourdin dialect*. Leiden, Netherlands: E. J. Brill.

Jackendoff, Ray. 1983. *Semantics and cognition*. Cambridge, MA: MIT Press.

Janda, Richard D. 2001. Beyond "pathways" and "unidirectionality": On the discontinuity of language transmission and the counterability of grammaticalization. *Language Sciences* 23: 265–340.

Kahr, Joan Casper. 1975. Adpositions and locationals: Typology and diachronic development. *Working Papers on Language Universals* 19: 21–54.

Kahr, Joan Casper. 1976. The renewal of case morphology: Sources and constraints. *Working Papers on Language Universals* 20: 107–51.

Kreitzer, Anatol. 1997. Multiple levels of schematization: A study in the conceptualization of space. *Cognitive Linguistics* 8: 291–326.

Kristoffersen, Kristian Emil. 2001. Semantic structure of the Norwegian preposition *mot*. *Nordic Journal of Linguistics* 24: 3–27.

Kuryłowicz, Jerzy. 1975. The evolution of grammatical categories. In Jerzy Kuryłowicz, *Esquisses linguistiques* 2: 38–54. Munich: Wilhelm Fink Verlag.

Lakoff, George. 1987. *Women, fire, and dangerous things: What categories reveal about the mind.* Chicago: University of Chicago Press.

Lakoff, George, and Mark Johnson. 1980. *Metaphors we live by.* Chicago: University of Chicago Press.

Langacker, Ronald W. 1987. *Foundations of cognitive grammar.* Vol. 1, *Theoretical prerequisites.* Stanford, CA: Stanford University Press.

Langacker, Ronald W. 1990a. *Concept, image, and symbol: The cognitive basis of grammar.* Berlin: Mouton de Gruyter.

Langacker, Ronald W. 1990b. Subjectification. *Cognitive Linguistics* 1: 5–38.

Langacker, Ronald W. 1991. *Foundations of cognitive grammar.* Vol. 2, *Descriptive application.* Stanford, CA: Stanford University Press.

Lehmann, Christian. 1982. *Thoughts on grammaticalization: A programmatic sketch.* Vol. 1. Cologne: Institut für Sprachwissenschaft der Universität.

Lehmann, Christian. 1985. Grammaticalization: Synchronic variation and diachronic change. *Lingua e Stile* 20: 303–18.

Levinson, Stephen C. 1991. Relativity in spatial conception and description. Working paper no. 1, Cognitive Anthropology Research Group, Max Planck Institute for Psycholinguistics, Nijmegen, Netherlands.

Levinson, Stephen C. 1994. Vision, shape, and linguistic description: Tzeltal body-part terminology and object description. *Linguistics* 32: 791–856.

Levinson, Stephen C. 1996. Frames of reference and Molyneux's question: Crosslinguistic evidence. In Paul Bloom, Mary A. Peterson, Lynn Nadel, and Merrill F. Garrett, eds., *Language and space* 109–69. Cambridge, MA: MIT Press.

Levinson, Stephen C. 2003. *Space in language and cognition: Explorations in cognitive diversity.* Cambridge: Cambridge University Press.

Levinson, Stephen C., Sérgio Meria, and The Language and Cognition Group. 2003. Natural concepts in the spatial topological domain: Adpositional meanings in crosslinguistic perspective: An exercise in semantic typology. *Language* 79: 485–516.

Li, Charles, and Sandra Thompson. 1973. Serial verb constructions in Mandarin Chinese. In Claudia Corum, T. Cendric Smith-Stark, and Ann Wieser, eds., *You take the high node and I'll take the low node: Papers from the Comparative Syntax Festival.* Chicago: Chicago Linguistic Society.

Li, Charles, and Sandra Thompson. 1974. Co-verbs in Mandarin Chinese: Verbs or prepositions? *Journal of Chinese Linguistics* 2: 257–78.

Lightfoot, David. 1979. *Principles of diachronic syntax.* Cambridge: Cambridge University Press.

Lindkvist, Karl-Gunnar. 1950. *Studies on the local sense of the prepositions 'in', 'at', 'on' and 'to' in Modern English.* Lund: Lund University Press.

Lindkvist, Karl-Gunnar. 1972. *The local sense of the prepositions 'over', 'above', and 'across' studied in present-day English.* Stockholm: Almqvist and Wiksell.

Lindkvist, Karl-Gunnar. 1976. *A comprehensive study of conceptions of locality in which English prepositions occur.* Stockholm: Almqvist and Wiksell

Lindner, Susan. 1981. A lexico-semantic analysis of English verb-particle constructions with OUT and UP. PhD dissertation, University of California at San Diego. (Also published as A lexico-semantic analysis of English verb-particle constructions. LAUT Paper, no. 101. Trier, Germany: Linguistic Agency of the University of Trier, 1983)

Matsumoto, Yo. 1996. Subjective motion and English and Japanese verbs. *Cognitive Linguistics* 7: 183–226.

Miller, George A., and Philip N. Johnson-Laird. 1976. *Language and perception*. Cambridge, MA: Harvard University Press.

Nichols, Johanna. 1986. Head-marking and dependent-marking grammar. *Language* 62: 56–119.

Norde, Muriel. 2001. Deflexion as a counterdirectional factor in grammatical change. *Language Sciences* 23: 231–64.

Pederson, Eric, Eve Danziger, David Wilkins, Stephen Levinson, Sotaro Kita, and Gunter Senft. 1998. Semantic typology and spatial conceptualization. *Language* 74: 557–89.v

Poitier, Bernard. 1961. Sur le système des prépositions. *Le français moderne* 29: 1–6.

Poitier, Bernard. 1962. *Systématique des élements de relation: Etude de morphosyntaxe structurale romane*. Paris: Klincksieck.

Radden, Günter. 1985. Spatial metaphors underlying prepositions of causality. In Wolf Paprotté and René Dirven, eds., *The ubiquity of metaphor: Metaphor in language and thought* 177–207. Amsterdam: John Benjamins.

Ramat, Paolo. 1992. Thoughts on degrammaticalization. *Linguistics* 30: 549–60.

Reh, Mechthild. 1986. Where have all the case prefixes gone? *Afrikanistische Arbeitspapiere* 5: 121–34.

Rice, Sally. 1992. Polysemy and lexical representation: The case of three English prepositions. In *Proceedings of the Fourteenth Annual Conference of the Cognitive Science Society* 89–94. Hillsdale, NJ: Lawrence Erlbaum.

Rice, Sally. 1996. Prepositional prototypes. In Martin Pütz and René Dirven, eds., *The construal of space in language and thought* 135–65. Berlin: Mouton de Gruyter.

Rice, Sally, Dominiek Sandra, and Mia Vanrespaille. 1999. Prepositional semantics and the fragile link between space and time. In Masako Hiraga, Chris Sinha, and Sherman Wilcox, eds., *Cultural, psychological and typological issues in cognitive linguistics* 107–27. Amsterdam: John Benjamins.

Rubba, Jo. 1994. Grammmaticization as semantic change: A case study of preposition development. In William Pagliuca, ed., *Perspectives on grammaticalization* 81–101. Amsterdam: John Benjamins.

Ruhl, Charles. 1989. *On monosemy: A study in linguistic semantics*. Albany: State University of New York Press.

Sandra, Dominiek, and Sally Rice. 1995. Network analyses of prepositional meaning: Mirroring whose mind—the linguist's or the language user's? *Cognitive Linguistics* 6: 89–130.

Schulze, Rainer. 1993. The meaning of *(a)round*: A study of an English preposition. In Richard A. Geiger and Brygida Rudzka-Ostyn, eds., *Conceptualizations and mental processing in language* 399–431. Berlin: Mouton de Gruyter.

Schwenter, Scott A., and Elizabeth Closs Traugott. 1995. The semantic and pragmatic development of substitutive complex prepositions in English. In Andreas H Jucker, ed., *Historical pragmatics: Pragmatic developments in the history of English* 243–73. Amsterdam: John Benjamins.

Sinha, Chris, and Tania Kuteva. 1995. Distributed spatial semantics. *Nordic Journal of Linguistics* 18: 167–99.

Smith, Michael B. 1988. The semantics of case assignment by two-way prepositions in German: Toward an empirically more adequate account. In Elmer H. Antonsen and Hans Henrich Hock, eds., *Germanic linguistics II: Papers from the second symposium on Germanic linguistics* 123–32. Bloomington: Indiana University Linguistics Club.

Smith, Michael B. 1993. Cases as conceptual categories: Evidence from German. In Richard A. Geiger and Brygida Rudzka-Ostyn, eds., *Conceptualization and mental processing in language* 531–65. Berlin: Mouton de Gruyter.

Stolz, Thomas. 1992. On turning bellies into locatives: Mesoamerican, universal or both? *Papiere zur Linguistik* 47: 165–89.

Svorou, Soteria. 1986. On the evolutionary paths of locative expressions. *Berkeley Linguistics Society* 12: 515–27.

Svorou, Soteria. 1988. The experiential basis of the grammar of space: Evidence from the languages of the world. PhD dissertation, State University of New York at Buffalo.

Svorou, Soteria. 1994. *The grammar of space*. Amsterdam: John Benjamins.

Svorou, Soteria. 2002a. The lexicalization of locative grams and the uni-directionality hypothesis. Paper presented at the New Reflections on Grammaticalization 2 Conference, Amsterdam, April 2–4.

Svorou, Soteria. 2002b. Semantic constraints in the grammaticalization of locative constructions. In Ilse Wischer and Gabrielle Diewald, eds., *New reflections on grammaticalization* 121–42. Amsterdam: John Benjamins.

Sweetser, Eve. 1988. Grammaticalization and semantic bleaching. *Berkeley Linguistics Society* 14: 389–405.

Talmy, Leonard. 1972. Semantic structures in English and Atsugewi. PhD dissertation, University of California at Berkeley.

Talmy, Leonard. 1975. Semantics and syntax of motion. In John Kimball, ed., *Syntax and Semantics* 4: 181–238. New York: Academic Press.

Talmy, Leonard. 1978. Figure and ground in complex sentences. In Joseph Greenberg, ed., *Universals of human language*, vol. 4, *Syntax* 625–49. Stanford, CA: Stanford University Press.

Talmy, Leonard. 1983. How language structures space. In Herbert L. Pick, Jr., and Linda P. Acredolo, eds., *Spatial orientation: Theory, research, and application* 225–82. New York: Plenum Press.

Talmy, Leonard. 1985. Lexicalization patterns: Semantic structure in lexical forms. In Timothy Shopen, ed., *Language typology and syntactic description*, vol. 3, *Grammatical categories and the lexicon* 57–149. Cambridge: Cambridge University Press.

Talmy, Leonard. 1988a. Force dynamics in language and cognition. *Cognitive Science* 12: 49–100.

Talmy, Leonard. 1996. Fictive motion in language and "ception." In Paul Bloom, Mary Peterson, Lynn Nadel, and Merrill Garrett, eds., *Language and space* 211–76. Cambridge, MA: MIT Press.

Talmy, Leonard. 2000. *Toward a cognitive semantics*. Vol. 1, *Concept structuring systems*. Cambridge: MIT Press.

Traugott, Elizabeth Closs. 1975. Spatial expressions of tense and temporal sequencing: A contribution to the study of semantic fields. *Semiotica* 15: 207–30.

Traugott, Elizabeth Closs. 1978. On the expression of spatio-temporal relations in language. In Joseph Greenberg, Charles Ferguson, and Edith Moravcsik, eds., *Universals of human language* 3: 369–400. Stanford, CA: Stanford University Press.

Traugott, Elizabeth Closs. 1982. From propositional to textual and expressive meanings: Some semantic-pragmatic aspects of grammaticalization. In Winfred P. Lehmann and Yakove Malkiel, eds., *Perspectives on historical linguistics* 245–71. Amsterdam: John Benjamins.

Traugott, Elizabeth Closs. 1988. Pragmatic strengthening and grammaticalization. *Berkeley Linguistics Society* 14: 406–16.

Traugott, Elizabeth Closs, and Bernd Heine, eds. 1991. *Grammaticalization*. 2 vols. Amsterdam: John Benjamins.

Traugott, Elizabeth Closs, and Ekkehard König. 1991. The semantics-pragmatics of grammaticalization revisited. In Elizabeth Closs Traugott and Bernd Heine, eds., *Approaches to grammaticalization* 1: 189–218. Amsterdam: John Benjamins.

Tyler, Andrea, and Vyvyan Evans. 2001. Reconsidering prepositional polysemy networks: The case of *over*. *Language* 77: 724–65.

Tyler, Andrea, and Vyvyan Evans. 2003. *The semantics of English prepositions: Spatial scenes, embodied meaning and cognition*. Cambridge: Cambridge University Press.

Vandeloise, Claude. 1986. *L'espace en francais*. Paris: Editions Du Seuil.

Vandeloise, Claude. 1991. *Spatial preposition: A case study from French*. Chicago: University of Chicago Press.

Vandeloise, Claude. 1994. Methodology and analyses of the preposition *in*. *Cognitive Linguistics* 5: 157–84.

Van Valin, Robert D., Jr., and Randy J. LaPolla. 1997. *Syntax: Structure, meaning and function*. Cambridge: Cambridge University Press.

Wood, Frederick T. 1967. *English preposition idioms*. New York: St. Martin's Press.

Young, Robert W., and William Morgan. 1980. *The Navajo language: A grammar and colloquial dictionary*. Albuquerque: University of New Mexico Press.

Zwicky, Arnold M. Heads. *Journal of Linguistics* 21: 1–29.

CHAPTER 29

CLAUSE STRUCTURE AND TRANSITIVITY

JOSÉ M. GARCÍA-MIGUEL

1. INTRODUCTION

Clause structure is one of the central issues for most theories in contemporary linguistics. This chapter will present an overview of clause structure and transitivity from a cognitive and constructional approach. The starting point will be the concept of construction: every aspect of clause structure must be interpreted in terms of the construction in which it appears. More specifically, constructions are symbolic units, that is, conventional associations between meaning and form. The meaning pole includes semantic, pragmatic, and discourse-functional properties. On the formal pole, we have to consider phonological and morphosyntactic properties of constructions. This chapter will cover clause structures as particular types of syntactic constructions, our main concern being the correspondences between meaning and form.

A fundamental claim of Cognitive Linguistics is that grammatical structures and categories have an experiential and conceptual basis. Let me start by saying that the conceptual basis of clause structures is found in the conceptualizations of actions and events. According to Langacker (1990: 209–11; 1991: 13–14; 2000: 24), our conceptions of actions and events combine in a complex archetypal notion defining a "canonical event," comprising at least two cognitive models. One of them is the "billiard-ball model," the conception of our world "as being populated by discrete objects...capable of moving about and interacting with others....Energy is transmitted from the mover to the impacted object; this may cause the latter to move also" (1990: 209). In relation to the second archetype, the "stage model," "we tend to organize the scenes we observe in terms of distinct 'participants' who interact within an inclusive and reasonable stable 'setting'" (210). Therefore, a canonical event implies an energetic interaction between participants within a setting. But how does the canonical event model correspond to elements of clause constructions?

This chapter focuses more on the symbolic links between meaning and form than on the nature of our conceptualizations of actions and events. The following section includes a short review of the basis of syntactic roles and an introduction to the interaction between verbs and clausal constructional schemas. In section 3, I pay attention to the conceptualization of events and move from event types toward a more general account in terms of force dynamics, action chains, and salience. The remaining sections are devoted to the semantic motivations of some more basic or more common clausal constructions and grammatical relations.

2. CLAUSE CONSTRUCTIONS

2.1. Syntactic Roles

From a syntactic point of view, a constructional schema "can be thought of as a kind of formula consisting of an ordered sequence of slots" (Taylor 1995: 198). In clauses—viewed as constructional schemas—these slots are typically filled by:

  a. a finite verb, symbolizing a type of interaction (a type of event) and locating this event relative to the ground, i.e., the speech situation (through the categories of tense, modality, etc.)—this verb is the head (that is, the profile determinant) of the entire clause;
  b. one or more nominals, symbolizing the main participants in the event; and
  c. other optional elements, symbolizing secondary participants or some aspects of the setting.

Among other things, clauses differ in the number of explicit participants. Latin and English examples of one-participant, two-participant, and three-participant events can be found in (1):

(1)   a. *Claudia legit.*
         'Claudia is reading.'
      b. *Claudia Octavium amat.*
         'Claudia loves Octavius.'
      c. *Claudia Octavio epistulas dat.*
         'Claudia gives Octavius the letters.'

Complex expressions like these evoke events that are globally understood (as Gestalts) and that in actual usage involve much more than what is explicitly designated

Table 29.1. A first account of clause structure strata

Participant roles	<P1	P2	Event-type>
Syntactic roles	SUBJ	OBJ	PRED
Syntactic categories	N-NOM	N-ACC	V-3SG
Lexis	*Claudi-a*	*Octavi-um*	*ama-t*

by their component units. By abstracting the recurring commonalities from symbolically complex expressions such as these, we can set up constructional schemas (much in the same way as grammatical categories can be abstracted from specific units). As such, constructional schemas can be expressed as combinations of syntactic categories (e.g., NP–V–NP or Nominative Noun–Accusative Noun–Verb). Another commonly used and convenient way to formulate the structure of a construction is by identifying its slots by the names of different syntactic functions or roles (e.g., Predicate–Subject–Object). In so doing, we can describe a clausal construction in terms of several structural strata, each of them resulting from an abstraction process from concrete expressions: (i) the participants in the scene, each associated with a role which we can simply label as P1, P2, and so on; (ii) syntactic roles, or grammatical relations, such as subject and object; and (iii) categorization relations, such as that existing between the word *Claudia* and the category nominative noun. These clause structure strata are represented in table 29.1.

While almost any aspect of clausal constructions may be subject to debate, one of the most complex questions is the nature and relevance of syntactic roles. Langacker's Cognitive Grammar (Langacker 1987, 1991, this volume, chapter 17) makes the claim that grammar consists only of semantic structures, phonological structures, and symbolic links between them, together with categorizing relationships. This view of grammar rules out a purely syntactic definition of subject and object; it does not rule out, however, a conceptual characterization or the existence of formal reflexes of these basic concepts.

The main problem in defining and identifying grammatical relations is that there exist no formal criteria that are cross-linguistically valid for any such relation. From Keenan (1976) onward, it has become a common practice to distinguish between coding properties (order, case marking, agreement) and behavior and control properties (deletion, passivization, control of co-reference, etc.). While traditionally the notion of subject has been taken for granted, Keenan's proposal allows a prototype approach to grammatical relations as universal notions, so that the nominal in a particular language can be considered the subject if it bears more coding and control properties than others. This approach is followed, among others, by Givón (2001: 173–97) but has been challenged within the functionalist tradition by Dryer (1997) and by Radical Construction Grammar (Croft 2001). The main problems for a formal characterization of the notion 'subject' (or any other grammatical relation) as a universal are (i) that different coding devices are used in different languages and (ii) that coding properties vary in their distribution across constructions from language to language; as such, for instance, there is no formal category in, say, Dyirbal that matches the English subject. In Dyirbal, the English subject corresponds to the absolutive in intransitive clauses and to the ergative in transitive clauses. In language-specific constructions, similar problems occur, since the different coding devices do not show homogeneous behavior across different constructions.

In this regard, Croft (2001) has come to the conclusion that syntactic roles are not only language-specific but also construction-specific, so that, for example, the subject of a transitive clause in English is different from that of an intransitive clause in the same language (see Croft 2001: 54). From that perspective, 'subject' is at most a convenient label for a slot in a particular construction, but it is not a primitive concept that can be used as one of the atomic building blocks of constructions. Nevertheless, slots may show correspondences across constructions. These generalizations, in Croft's view (2001: 55–57), are represented as taxonomic generalizations, that is, as taxonomic relations between constructions; as such, transitive and intransitive clauses, for instance, share enough grammatical properties to warrant setting up the category 'clause'. As Croft puts it, "the existence of the Clause construction allows us to establish the superordinate categories SbjArg ('subject as an argument') and Pred" (57).

In what follows, I will assume that constructions are the basic units of grammar, that syntactic roles must be characterized relative to the constructions in which they appear, and that elements belonging to different constructions in the same language (for instance, subject in a transitive clause and subject in an intransitive clause) share the same syntactic role (subject) to the extent that they share formal encoding mechanisms (order, agreement, case, control of co-reference, etc). A significant consequence of this approach is the fact that these correspondences can simply be partial; for example, syntactic roles across constructions may share agreement, but not case. Conversely, the same morphological property, namely case, can correspond to different syntactic roles, reflecting some schematic commonality between them or some semantic relatedness. For example, the accusative case in Latin or German and the preposition *a* in Spanish are polysemic elements allowing a complex range of syntactic and semantic relations. That means that each element of an expression can be simultaneously characterized by a cluster of relational categories. For example, in sentences (1b) and (1c), *Claudia* is simultaneously the subject of a transitive clause, the initial component in such a construction, a name in nominative case, and the nominal that specifies the number and person expressed morphologically in the verb. Each of these "formal" properties has its own meaning, whereby a single constituent, *Claudia*, enters a complex network of semantic relations.

2.2. The Interaction between Verbs and Constructions

Constructions are arranged at different levels of schematicity, so that they form a structured inventory that can be represented in terms of a taxonomic network (Croft, this volume, chapter 18; Tuggy, this volume, chapter 4). Knowledge of a language includes knowledge of its schematic constructions, such as the transitive construction in English or Spanish, and knowledge of its more substantive constructions, such as *kick the bucket*. As a matter of fact, a construction may combine substantive and schematic elements to different degrees (Croft 2001: 17; this volume, chapter 18). The variable combination of schematic and substantive elements is indicative of the syntax-lexicon continuum and of the impossibility of establishing fixed limits between lexicon and grammar; furthermore, the existence of levels of schematicity is a demonstration of such continuity: the verb *see*, whose constructional characterization must allow combining with subject and object, gives rise to a constructional schema which can be instantiated by an expression such as *John sees Mary* and, at the same time, instantiates the more general transitive constructional schema. A nonreductionist, nonderivational grammatical model such as Cognitive Grammar incorporates both constructional schemas (at different levels of schematicity) and substantive constructions.

(2)

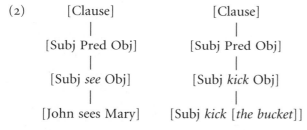

The continuity of lexicon and grammar also applies to idiomatic expressions. The idiom *kick the bucket* is also an instantiation of the construction [Subj *kick* Obj] as well as of the higher-level transitive construction, even though most of the meaning of the idiom cannot be normally derived from either that of the verb or that of the transitive construction.

In setting up syntactic schemas and subschemas, one might want to make use of the meaning of lexical items and their distributional patterns. As such, some lexicalist accounts (e.g., Rappaport and Levin 1998) assume that the syntactic frame of a verb is determined by the verb's lexical semantics. However, this approach has an important drawback: given that most verbs enter in more than one constructional schema, the same verb would have to belong to more than one (sub)class. Put differently, as meaning differences between syntactic configurations must, on the lexicalist approach, be attributed to differences in the semantic representation of the main verb, a new verb sense needs to be posited for each verb construction, even when there is no need to posit independent verb senses (as for *send* in 3a and 3b).

(3)   a. Joe sent Chicago a letter.
      b. Joe sent a letter to Chicago.

Against this lexical approach, Goldberg (1995) has proposed a constructional approach where the meaning of an expression results from the integration or fusion of the meaning of the verb with the meaning associated specifically with the constructional schema, provided that both meanings are compatible ("semantic

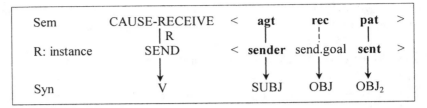

Figure 29.1. Composite fused structure: Ditransitive + *send* (Goldberg 1995: 55) (Sem = semantics; agt = agent; rec = recipient; pat = patient ; R = relation [way in which the verb is integrated into the construction]; Syn = syntax)

coherence principle"). For example, the verb *send* can fuse its meaning with the ditransitive construction or with the caused-motion construction. As shown in figure 29.1 and figure 29.2, the verb provides the specific roles of the participants, whereas the ditransitive construction [*Subj V Obj Obj₂*] provides the meaning of an Agent causing a Receiver to receive a Patient, and the caused-motion construction [*Subj V Obj Obl*] provides the meaning of a Cause causing a Theme to move to a Goal.

An important advantage of Goldberg's proposal is that in those frequent cases in which a verb is registered in more than one syntactic schema the differences of meaning are attributed to surface formal differences, that is, to differences in the construction, with no need to suggest independent verb senses that are hard to justify. An additional advantage of attributing a meaning to the construction itself is the easy accommodation of novel uses. In Goldberg's popular example (4),

(4)   He sneezed the napkin off the table.

the verb *sneeze* does not need to be assigned a caused-motion sense in addition to that of the intransitive construction, which is the more frequent and basic one with this verb. According to Goldberg, the sense of caused motion is provided by the construction, not by the verb.

Still, Goldberg's proposal about the nature of the meaning of constructions and the relation between constructional meaning and verb meaning is not beyond controversy.[1] For one, Goldberg reduces verbal polysemy by increasing constructional polysemy, with polysemic constructions being viewed as units with extended meanings radiating out from a central constructional meaning. With regard to the ditransitive constructions, the central sense is 'X CAUSES Y to RECEIVE Z' (or 'Agent successfully causes Recipient to receive Patient') and is instantiated by verbs such as *give, pass, throw, bring*, and so on. Extended senses include 'X INTENDS to CAUSE Y to RECEIVE Z' (*leave, grant*), 'X ENABLES Y TO RECEIVE Z' (*permit, allow*), and 'X CAUSES Y not to RECEIVE Z' (*deny, refuse*) (Goldberg 1995: 37–39).

The idea that constructions are polysemic units with extended meanings originating from one or more central senses does not need to be not rejected. The problem at issue is that if the meaning of an expression is understood as the integration/fusion of the meaning of the verb and the meaning of the construction, as in figure

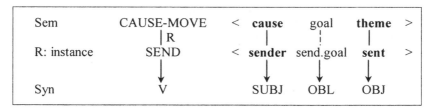

Figure 29.2. Composite fused structure: Caused-motion + *send* (based on Goldberg 1995)

29.1, it can be argued that its extended senses are simply the result of semantic differences among the verbs *give, leave, permit, deny*, and so on. This leads us to reconsider to what extent one can detach the meaning of the construction from the meaning of the verb, and, concomitantly, which level of schematicity is required in order to describe the meaning of the constructions.

It could be argued that (some of) Goldberg's characterizations of grammatical constructions are not schematic enough, in that they best apply to prototypical cases and that they only include components and semantic roles which seem to derive from the verb, not from the construction itself. As such, a more abstract or schematic meaning would have to be set up for each construction, which accounts for all its instantiations.[2] Goldberg maintains that an abstractionist account cannot capture the intuition that the construction has a more basic, central sense, "since by virtue of positing only a single very abstract sense, *all* instances instantiate the construction equally" (1995: 35). However, Langacker (1987: 369–86) has shown that an abstractionist account is not incompatible with a semantic network consisting of prototypical instances and extensions from central cases. Let us look in this respect at Langacker's view of the interaction between verbs and constructions in the continuum lexicon-grammar, as illustrated in figure 29.3.

Send NP NP is both an instantiation of the ditransitive construction and an instantiation of the verb *send*. In particular, *send* can be described as a network of related senses. Given that the verb profiles a relation, each meaning (schematic or specific) must include a more or less schematic characterization of the entities making up that relation. As such, "a lexical item's characterization includes a set of 'structural frames' in which it conventionally occurs" (Langacker 2000: 124). For a verb such as *send*, these structural frames make up "a network of constructional schemas describing its grammatical behavior" (123). At the most abstract level, the verb *send* can be characterized schematically without reference to particular constructions, even if some construction is prototypical for it.

Likewise, the ditransitive construction can be schematically characterized without reference to particular verbs instantiating it, even though some verbs (*give, send, throw, bring*, etc.) are more typical in this construction than others (for example, *cry* as in *cry me a river*; see Goldberg 1995: 150). The ditransitive construction can also be described as a network of related senses, the more central sense being "that of a successful transfer between a volitional agent and a willing recipient" (151)

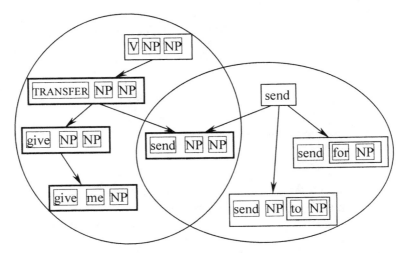

Figure 29.3. Partial networks for ditransitive construction and *send* (Langacker 2000: 123)

In sum, the differences between the meaning of verbs and the meaning of constructional schemas arise only at the more abstract or schematic levels. At more concrete levels, we find more specific constructional schemas such as *send NP NP*, which instantiate simultaneously the ditransitive construction and the verb *send*, and those two aspects are indistinguishable (see also Croft 2003; Langacker 2005: 147–55). At any rate, it seems clear that verb and construction interact semantically selecting and elaborating each other's meaning and that new uses are based both on an abstract schema that provides a template and on concrete uses that serve as a model.

3. The Meaning of the Clause

3.1. Event Types and Semantic Roles

A basic insight of Cognitive Linguistics is that meanings are described relative to frames or cognitive models (Cienki, this volume, chapter 7), that is, "specific unified frameworks of knowledge, or coherent schematizations of experience" (Fillmore 1985: 223). As such, the meaning of verbs and clauses includes reference to a rich background of world and cultural knowledge. A typical example of frame, provided by Fillmore, is that of a commercial transaction event, involving such concepts as possession, change of possession, exchange, and money and including as basic frame elements the money, the goods, the buyer, and the seller.

Fillmore's conception of a frame, as applied to an event, is close to Talmy's notion of event frame, which is defined as follows: "A set of conceptual elements and interrelationships that are evoked together or co-evoke each other can be said to lie within or constitute an *event frame*, while the elements that are conceived of as incidental—whether evoked weakly or not at all—lie outside the event frame" (Talmy 1996: 238). Talmy (1996: 238) points to some differences between his concept of event frame and that of Fillmore: (i) whereas Fillmore emphasizes the co-presence of certain interrelated conceptual elements, Talmy's notion of event frame "is intended to stress as well the exclusion of other conceptual elements from the privileged core" (Talmy 2000: 260); (ii) while Fillmore "seems to represent a concept or phenomenon that may be specific to a particular language or set of languages," Talmy's event frame "is generally understood as a more generic category that is quite likely universal across languages" (260); for example, a commercial event might be a particular form of generic universal event type consisting of an interchange of entities. This latter point about the universality or cultural-boundness of event frames does not concern us specifically in this chapter, although it affects some aspects of the classification of event types to be treated below.

In Langacker's studies, a common (and universal) cognitive model for viewing events is called the "stage model":

> Just as actors move about the stage and handle various props, we tend to organize the scenes we observe in terms of distinct "participants" who interact within an inclusive and reasonable stable "setting". We further impose structure along the temporal axis, by chunking clusters of temporally contiguous interactions (particularly those involving common participants) into discrete "events".
> (1990: 210)

Furthermore, each participant plays some role in such an event—usually expressed in grammatical theories in terms of "thematic" or "semantic" roles (such as Agent, Patient, Instrument, Experiencer, etc.). There is, however, no definitive list of roles because the roles of participants are specific to particular scenes, although they can be generalized across different events:

> An inventory of semantic roles can always be refined and articulated into more specific types on the basis of further data or a finer-grained analysis—at the extreme, every verb defines a distinct set of participant roles that reflect its own unique semantic properties (e.g., the subject of *bite* is a slightly different kind of agent from the subject of *chew*). (Langacker 1991: 284)

When abstracting away from the peculiarities of individual examples, we arrive at event types and role archetypes. The "standard" semantic roles are prelinguistic concepts which, to some extent, reflect a commonsense interpretation of extralinguistic knowledge. However, their descriptive function is only to provide the prototypical values of cases and grammatical relations (Langacker 1990: 236). They do not match all the roles participants can play in actual events, and their formal reflexes may vary from language to language.[3]

Event types are schematic conceptualizations of actual events and are hierarchically organized. "Basic event types" which correlate with basic sentences types are very general categories of events ('doing', 'moving', 'giving', etc.). In addition to these schematic superordinate categories, we need more concrete "basic-level categories" (e.g., 'painting'), and less schematic subordinate level categories ('daubing') (see Tuggy, this volume, chapter 4; Schmid, this volume, chapter 5). This event type categorization is reflected linguistically in lexis, and more specifically in the hierarchical structure of the verbal vocabulary. At the higher levels, we find a reduced (although difficult to limit) set of maximally general verbs categorizing possible events, such as *be, happen, do*, or *move, say, know*, and so on. Most verbs are not so general and denote less schematic events such as *paint* and *daub*.

The idea that languages have a network of related verb senses has a practical application in "FrameNet," a lexicographic project led by Fillmore (Fillmore, Johnson, and Petruck 2003; Ruppenhofer et al. 2005). In FrameNet, roles are defined in relation with specific frames; as such, the roles associated with, for example, the verb *tell* (Speaker, Addressee, Message) are very different from roles associated with the verb *throw* (Agent, Theme, Source, Path, Goal). Some frames are quite general, while others are specific to a small family of lexical items. More specific frames can inherit the syntactic and semantic characteristics of the more general ones. Each frame can account for diverse clause patterns, and it can be applied to different related verbs. For example:

(5)   *Frame*: Communication statement
      Frame elements: Speaker [S], Addressee [A], Message [M], Topic [T]
      [$_S$ Leslie] **stated** [$_M$ that she could not participate in this event]
      [$_S$ Leslie] **told** [$_A$ me] [$_M$ that she could not participate in this event]
      [$_S$ Leslie] **informed** [$_A$ us] all [$_T$ about her unwillingness in this matter]
      [$_S$ The teacher] **discussed** [$_T$ the recent campus incidents]

FrameNet classification does not always presuppose a hierarchical structure. The most general frames ("Inherited frames") can cross-cut the main domains and the frames included in them. There are also cases of "frame blending" (for example, 'conversation' + 'fighting': *argue, dispute, quarrel*) and "frame composition" (complex frames are made of parts that are also frames and which designate sequences of states of affairs and transitions between them).

The main advantages of the FrameNet approach is that it does away with the problems of a list of semantic roles, common to all events types, and that it groups together just the roles that are found in a single event type and does not mix roles from incompatible event types in a unified hierarchy of case roles. On the other hand, FrameNet does not provide a unified basis for an explanation of syntactic structure and grammatical relations. For this, we will need to state generalizations over frames (see Croft 1998: 29–30). This generalization can be carried out only in terms of a more generic and schematic universal characterization of event types and event structure, in terms of force dynamics and causal chains.

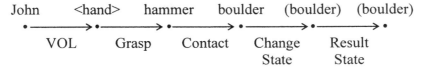

Figure 29.4. The causal chain of *John broke the boulder with a hammer*

3.2. Causal Chains and the Verbal Profile

As mentioned earlier, what Langacker calls the "billiard-ball model" is one of the basic models of our conception of events. This model of causal structure is based on force-dynamic relations (Talmy 1988; De Mulder, this volume, chapter 12) and has also been used by Croft (1991, 1998) in a way very similar to Langacker's. According to Croft (1991: 159–63), the basic difference with respect to other models of causal structure is that relevant causal relations are not established between events or between individuals and events, but between individuals, in such a way that an individual A acts upon individual B, which may act upon a third individual C, and so on. Figure 29.4 portrays in a simplified way the causal chain symbolized by *John broke the boulder with a hammer* (Croft 1991: 166), parentheses being used for force-dynamic relations involving facets of the same participant.[4]

In actual situations, there is an indefinite number of force-dynamic relations between entities participating in a complex interactive network. Within that network, a causal chain—Langacker (1990: 215; 1991: 283) uses the term "action chain"—is a unidirectional asymmetrical series of transmission of force. A verb profiles a segment of a causal chain; this is called the "verbal segment" by Croft (1991: 173). Subject and object delimit the verbal segment, so that "the subject is consistently the 'head' of the PROFILED portion of the action chain," whereas "the object is the 'tail' of the profiled portion of the action chain" (Langacker 1990: 217).

The characterization of subject and object as head and tail of the profiled action chain is a more schematic definition than Agent and Patient and allows us to understand better that the selection of subject and object is above all a matter of construal. Many constructional differences can be accounted for as a result of profiling action chains of different lengths. For example, *break* can profile a segment whose head is either the Agent, or the Instrument, or the Patient (the symbols # indicate here, in Croft 1991's style, the head and tail of the profiled action chain)

	F	H	G	(G)
(6) a. *Floyd broke the glass (with the hammer)*	###			###
b. *The hammer (easily) broke the glass*		###		###
c. *The glass (easily) broke*			###	###

Similarly, the verbs *speak*, *say*, and *tell* differ with regard to the segment of the (metaphorical) chain of communication each profiles, and, as a consequence, these verbs differ in object selection.

(7)   speaker   utterance   hearer

　　　•　　　──────▶　　(•)　　──────▶　　•　　──────▶　　•

　　　###　　　*speak*　　###

　　　###　　　*say*　　　　　　###

　　　###　　　　　　　　*tell*　　　　　　　　　　###

Other examples of alternative subject and object selection, according to which focal participants are selected from the base frame, include the inversion *give/receive* (Langacker 1990: 226–27) and alternative verbs for the commercial frame: *buy/sell/ spend/charge/pay/cost* . . . (Fillmore 1977: 102–9).

4. TRANSITIVITY

Like any other conceptual or linguistic category, constructions tend to be structured as radial categories around some central or prototypical member(s) (Lakoff 1987; Taylor 1995, 1998). From a semantic as well as from a formal point of view, transitivity is a multifactorial and gradual notion (Lakoff 1977; Hopper and Thompson 1980; Taylor 1995: 197–221). The central sense of the transitive construction in any language can roughly be characterized as that of an Agent carrying out an action affecting a concrete, individuated Patient and modifying it. This semantic characterization involves several elements that vary independently and tries to summarize the cluster of properties listed by Lakoff (1977: 244) and the grammatical parameters of cardinal transitivity proposed by Hopper and Thompson (1980). Nevertheless, Rice (1987) observes that a coherent prototype of transitivity must depart from conceptual models of action and interaction. According to Rice, the transitive prototype must be conceptualized in terms of the "billiard-ball model," as it involves two participants asymmetrically related and involved in some activity. The interaction is unidirectional typically from Agent to Patient; because there is movement and affect, there must be contact with the second participant being directly affected. In sum, her characterization of transitive clauses relies on force-dynamics chains. A canonical transitive event implies an asymmetric energetic interaction between two participants.

However, the transitive construction can be extended from canonical transitive events (the prototype) to the symbolization of other cognitive domains that do not necessarily imply force dynamics. A transitive clause prototypically designates a concrete, perceptible action, symbolized by verbs such as *kill*, *break*, *move*, or *kick*.

Some volitional verbs (*want*) are also common in the transitive construction. More marginal instantiations are expressions with verbs of perception (*see, watch*), mental state (*like, forgot, regret*), or static relation (*resemble*). Nevertheless, even marginal cases of the transitive construction show some kind of asymmetry between participants, which justifies the use of the transitive construction and subject and object syntactic roles (Langacker 1990: 219–24; Croft 1991: 212–25). For example, perception and other mental verbs do not denote a physical causation event and "we have no reason to posit any kind of energy transfer from the experiencer to the other participant," but "their interaction is obviously asymmetrical, and the experiencer's role is energetic to the extent that we think of energy as being required for mental activity" (Langacker 1990: 222):

(8)   a. Several witnesses saw the accident.
      b. She likes classical music.

Still, since the two participants in mental processes do not differ to the same extent as the Agent and the Patient in a dynamic physical event, such processes can easily give rise to alternative construals. For instance, an Experiencer may direct his or her attention to the stimulus, thus assuming the subject role; as in (8). Alternatively, the stimulus may cause a particular mental state in the Experiencer, thus motivating a reverse construal, with the stimulus as subject (as in *Classical music pleases her*).

A similar situation occurs with predicates expressing symmetrical relations, which allow reverse construals in the languages that admit transitive (or alike) constructions for this kind of predicates:[5]

(9)   a. Marsha resembles Hilda.
      b. Hilda resembles Marsha

In a definition of transitivity involving energy transfer, an intrinsic orientation is imposed between subject and object participants from the head to the tail of the action chain. But the existence of transitive constructions such as (9) forces us to look for more abstract definitions of subject and object. Langacker proposes a schematic definition of the subject as "trajector" (primary figure) and the object as "landmark" (secondary figure) of the relation profiled by the verb. Therefore, in (9) the construction imposes an asymmetric construal of subject and object based only on the selection of the primary figure. The definition of subject as the trajector at clausal level subsumes other well-known characterizations; among them are Givón's (1984) definition as the grammaticalization of "primary clausal topic," Chafe's (1994) notion of "starting point," and the relation between subject and empathy, as defined by Kuno (1987). Langacker's definitions place the characterization of subject and object at a more general level and emphasize the role of construal in the linguistic coding of events. The close affinity between topics and subjects is explained by Langacker (1998) in that a topic construction expresses a reference-point relationship between a thing and a proposition, whereas the subject-trajector and the object-landmark can be described as first and second elements in a reference point chain, giving mental access to the relation provided by the verb. There is also a close affinity between subjects and possessors: in a possessive construction, the possessor can be described schematically as a reference point, and the possessed, as a target found in its dominion. In (10a) the child, as subject, is a reference point in the mental access to the resemblance relation, and, as possessor (*his*), it is a reference point with respect to the father. The oddity of (10b) can be justified because of conflicting reference points: the father is a reference point by the fact that it is coded as the subject; at the same time, the child, as a possessor, is a reference point with respect to the father.

(10)   a. The child resembles his father.
        b. ?His father resembles the child

It is interesting as well that across languages, instantiations of the transitive construction range over a variety of central and less central cases (Taylor 1995: 218–20). For example, the English language uses the transitive construction for many event types for which German (or Spanish) uses dative/indirect object plus nominative/subject:

(11)   I like Mary.
(12)   *Mir gefällt Mary.*
        'To me [DATIVE] pleases Mary [NOMINATIVE]'
(13)   *A ella le gusta la música clásica.*[6]
        'She [IO] likes classical music [SUBJ]'

By considering the integration of components in the construction and the symbolic correspondences between form and meaning, one can determine where prototypicality comes from and where it is manifested in transitivity. First of all, prototype effects in a construction normally come from prototype effects in the components of the construction: "Because words, as a rule, do not cluster in internally homogeneous categories, the instantiations of syntactic constructions also tend to exhibit prototype effects" (Taylor 1998: 185). In transitive constructions, prototypicality correlates with the degree to which subject and object are filled by nouns. For example, (14a), with a concrete specific noun phrase as object, is a better example of a transitive construction than (14b), with a complement clause:

(14)   a. John broke the window.
        b. John believes that they will arrive on time.

On the other hand, the syntactic roles subject and object admit some range of formal variation, which can be corroborated by the coding devices (variable marking of subject and/or object) and by the behavioral properties (e.g., passivizability) of the syntactic functions. For example, in English, $V + Prep + NP$ constructions can be passivized to the extent that they approach the semantic prototype of transitivity. For example, "[15a] specifies something about a single participant acting within a setting, whereas [16a] specifies something about a participant acting on and affecting an entity which we might otherwise construe as a setting" (Rice 1987: 95–96):[7]

(15)   a. Mary exercises in the living room.
       b. *The living room is exercised in by Mary.
(16)   a. That flea-bitten dog has slept in this bed again.
       b. This bed has been slept in again by that flea-bitten dog.

The variable behavior of these examples is symptomatic of another relevant property of syntactic prototypes, namely, the "merging of constructions at boundaries" (Taylor 1998: 196). In English, the sequence *V + Prep + NP* may correspond to three different constructions in a continuum with no clear boundaries (Rice 1987: 144): the verb particle construction, the prepositional verb construction, and the verb plus prepositional phrase construction.

Languages also vary according to the set of constructions they have available for encoding events with two participants (see the overview by Onishi 2001). For example, Finnish objects use accusative case if the action is complete (telic) and partitive case if it is incomplete (atelic), the latter implying a lesser degree of transitivity:

(17)   a. *Lapsi   luki   kirja-n.*
          boy.NOM   read.PST.3SG book-ACC
          'The boy read a book [ACCUSATIVE].'
       b. *Lapsi   luki   kirja-a.*
          boy.NOM   read.PST.3SG book-PART
          'The boy read a book [PARTITIVE].'

In Spanish, inanimate direct objects are usually coded without prepositions, whereas personal direct objects are usually preceded by the preposition *a*.[8]

(18)   a. *Andrés   encontró   a   María.*
          Andres   met   TO   Maria
          'Andres met Mary.'
       b. *Andrés encontró un tesoro.*
          'Andres found a treasure.'

Most objects in Spanish transitive clauses are not animate and are not preceded by the preposition *a*. Frequency of usage generates particular expectations about the elements that fill the slots constituting a schema: an asymmetric interaction is typically instantiated by a human NP as subject and a concrete, mostly nonhuman, NP as object. While zero-coding of the object is associated with the more frequent cases and a broader asymmetric relation between participants, overt coding is reserved for less frequent cases and the reversibility of the subject-object asymmetry. All this suggests a correlation between prototypicality, high frequency, and nonovert coding. Anyway, these are independent parameters, and it remains an empirically open question in what measure they correlate.

5. Ergative and Accusative Systems

We have seen that Langacker defines subject and object as, respectively, trajector and landmark of the relation profiled by the verb. He also states that "subject and object relations are universal and non-primitive" (Langacker 2000: 28; also Langacker 2005: 128–36). Croft (2001), however, argues that syntactic roles are language-specific and construction-specific. How can these contradictory views, both of them cognitive linguistic, be reconciled? Note that this is a different problem from that of the nature of transitive constructions. When questioning the universality of subjects, we are dealing with what kind of formal marking (particularly, case, as well as word order and agreement) is employed in which constructions and with the semantic motivations for this distribution. The central issue here is that a specific pattern of formal marking is language- and construction-specific, whereas its semantic motivation is universal. The classic phenomenon that has been discussed in this context is that of ergativity, that is, the system where a grammatical property (case, agreement, order, etc.) is applicable to "intransitive subjects" and "transitive objects," but not "transitive subjects."

It is commonly assumed that all languages have syntactic constructions encoding the asymmetric interaction between the participants prototypically associated with the roles Agent (A) and Patient (P), that is, constructions whose semantic prototype is the canonical transitive event; in other words, with the distinction between A and P correlates a syntactic distinction. It is also accepted that every language has constructions with only one core participant (S). Syntactically, this sole participant may be encoded similarly to the encoding of A (accusative system) or to the encoding of P (ergative system). In Cognitive Grammar, the existence of these and other alignment systems is assumed to have a semantic motivation: the fact that S is encoded similarly to the encoding of A or to the encoding of P involves any of three different parameters to a greater or lesser extent:

a. The role archetypes Agent and Patient
b. Focal prominence
c. The autonomous-dependent distinction (Langacker 1991: 378–96)[9]

With regard to the first parameter, we would expect the encoding of S as A if it is possible to categorize S as an Agent or as a semantic extension of an Agent, and we would expect the encoding of S as P if S can be categorized as a Patient or a semantic extension of a Patient. However, it should be noted that intransitive clauses, given their focus on a single participant, neutralize the asymmetric contrast between participants. In terms of action chains, the only participant of an intransitive clause is both at the beginning and at the end of the event profiled by the verb. As a consequence, intransitive subjects can be semantically more similar to agents (19b) or more similar to patients (19c):

Table 29.2. Hierarchy of Agent-like to Patient-like marking of
the intransitive argument

controlled activities	< inactive actions	< bodily actions, uncontrolled activities, dispositions/properties, inchoatives	< temporary states

(19) a. Mark is cooking potatoes.
      b. Mark is cooking.
      c. Potatoes are cooking.

This similarity is a gradient, depending on the type of event. Mithun (1991) has shown that there is a considerable amount of cross-linguistic variation in the case marking of "intransitive subjects." This cross-linguistic variation in the encoding of participants in different event types (where some are more A-like and some more P-like) has led Croft (1998: 53) to posit the following implicational hierarchy (table 29.2).

This table suggests that the unique participant of controlled activities is more likely to be marked in the same manner as A and that the unique participant of temporary states is more likely to be marked in the same manner as P. Languages with accusative systems generalize A-like marking to every intransitive clause, and languages with ergative systems generalize P-like marking. In between, some languages choose the marking of the intransitive subject according to event type (so-called "active systems") or in correlation with aspect or some other categories akin to the event type. The rationale is that "transitive agent and volitional intransitive subject constitute a unified semantic category" (DeLancey 1990: 289) and so do transitive Patient and nonvolitional intransitive subjects.

In relation to the focal prominence, it seems logical that the sole participant (S) in intransitive constructions must be considered the "trajector," the primary figure. In transitive constructions, either one of the two participants could be the protagonist and that might justify the existence of two of the most common systems in the world's languages, namely, the accusative system, where A's marking is identical to that of S, and the ergative system, where P's marking is identical to that of S. Langacker considers grammatical behavior as being merely symptomatic of the conceptual import of subject, whose definition as primary focal participant is proposed to be universal. He also states that "it need not be the case in every language that trajector status is prototypically associated with agents. I believe, in fact, that in some languages (Tagalog perhaps being one) the default situation is for primary focal prominence to fall instead on what I call the theme" (Langacker 2005: 136). Nevertheless, in most languages grammatical behavior gives some evidence in favor of participant A as the primary clausal figure and in favor of the grouping of S + A as subject. Indeed, some properties of grammatical relations

Table 29.3. Ranking of all properties of grammatical
relations according to universality and
functional transparency

Most Universal (Most Transparent)

---

a. Functional reference-and-topically properties

b. Behavior-and-control properties

c. Word-order

d. Grammatical agreement

e. Nominal case-marking

   Least Universal (Least Transparent)

(such as control of co-reference across clause boundaries) tend to treat A and S in the same way, even in languages whose case system is ergative.[10] Givón (1995: 253; 2001: 196) has ordered the grammatical properties according to their "universality," as shown in table 29.3.

Here the use of the terms "universal" and "transparency" is controversial, because it takes for granted the universality of categories that can be checked formally in English and in other European languages, but that are hardly detected in other systems. However, their functional basis is correct. If we seek grammatical correlates of the notion "primary clausal topic" (Givón) or of "clausal trajector," the first element on a scale of prominence (Langacker), cross-linguistic evidence shows that there exists a clear tendency toward assigning such prominence to A (or the grouping A + S defining accusative systems), rather than to P (or the grouping P+S defining ergative systems). Such evidence comes from the tendency for the subjects (A+S) to convey accessible information (Chafe 1994: 82–92), from the tendency against the lexical instantiation of A and, to a lesser degree, S (Du Bois 1987), and from the preference for subjects to serve as reference points in accessing the relation profiled by the verb (Langacker 1998). What table 29.3 means is that behavior and control properties of grammatical relations (passivization, reflexivization, relativization, etc.) "are transparently linked to topicality and referential continuity" and that "of the three overt coding properties of [grammatical relations], both word-order and pronominal agreement are transparently associated with the coding of topicality" (Givón 2001: 196).[11] And properties more associated with topicality are also more associated with the grouping of S + A as subject. In a similar vein, Croft (2001) scales the properties and the constructions which characterize syntactic functions on a hierarchy which he labels as the subject construction hierarchy (figure 29.5): if a construction patterns accusatively (that is, grouping A + S as 'subject'), the left constructions on the scale will also pattern accusatively.

Finally, the semantic distinction "autonomous-dependent" plays a role in the behavior of verbs such as English *break* and *open*. Such verbs may express a relation with a single participant affected by the process denoted by the verb. Importantly, coordination < purposive < relativization < verb agreement < case marking

Figure 29.5. The Subject Construction Hierarchy (Croft 2001: 155)

this "core" relation can be conceptualized autonomously (see 20a), and to this nuclear relation, different components may be added whose conceptualization is 'dependent' on it (such as an entity supplying energy, as in 20b).

(20)   a. (The door opened)
      b. (Sam (opened the door))

This alignment, which can also be observed in other areas of linguistic structure is, according to Langacker (1991: 386–89), the basis of ergativity—the formal alignment of intransitive S and transitive P as absolutive versus the transitive A as ergative. In this system, the absolutive is normally unmarked and corresponds consistently to the most involved participant in the event (Mithun and Chafe 1999: 583–84). Mithun and Chafe note, however, that speakers have choices concerning which the most involved participant is. In Yup'ik, for example, with a verb meaning 'to eat', the absolutive may be the eater, as the sole relevant participant (21a), or the eaten, as in (21b):

(21)   a. *ner-u-q*
        eat-INTR-3SG.ABS
        'She [ABSOLUTIVE] is eating.'
      b. *luqruuyak   ner-a-a*
        pike.**ABS**   eat-TR-3SG.ERG/3SG.ABS
        'She is eating the pike [ABSOLUTIVE].'

The semantic basis of ergativity finds further corroboration in noun-verb compounding, incorporation, verb-phrase idioms, and in general in the dependency of the meaning of the predicate of the nature of the absolutive referent (Keenan 1984: 201). Ergativity also has a discourse basis: Du Bois (1987) notes that new referents tend to be introduced either in S or in P slots, but not in A position. In fact, about half of the entities in S-slots introduce new referents either in accusative or in ergative languages (García-Miguel 1999a), so that ergativity can be seen to imply a generalization and grammaticalization of this partial similarity between S and P.

In sum, we have seen that across languages, intransitive clauses can be subdivided according to whether their unique participant aligns with the Agent (A) or Patient (P) role of canonical transitive events. There is no clear dividing line between these two categories, but rather a continuum, whereby the unique participant of controlled activities tends to form a semantic category with the transitive Agent A (accusative system) and the unique participant of temporary states tends to group with the transitive Patient P (ergative system). Second, we have seen that the trajector-landmark asymmetry motivates the grouping of S and A as the primary figure (even in some morphologically ergative languages). Finally, ergative systems are motivated by the involvement of participants and the conceptual autonomy of this involvement motivate the ergative systems.

Considering that in accusative systems the subject is the unmarked role and that in ergative systems the absolutive is the unmarked role (the other role being absent in intransitive clauses and usually morphologically marked in transitive clauses), in selecting an accusative or an ergative system, languages grammaticalize either one of two possible orientations in the conceptualization of events with two participants: starting from subject and eventually extending to an object or starting from the nuclear relation with an absolutive and eventually extending to an ergative. But it is important to bear in mind that in a language some facts and constructions may behave "accusatively" and others may behave "ergatively."

6. DITRANSITIVE CLAUSES, INDIRECT OBJECTS, AND DATIVES

So far, we have focused mainly on transitive constructions, subject and object grammatical relations, and ergative-absolutive alignment. However, we have seen that a clause may have more than two participants and that some two-participant clauses exhibit a special marking, indicating that they are less transitive. These two facts lead us to posit core grammatical relations different from subject and direct object.

The conceptual structuring of three-participant situations, and in particular that of transfer events, can be seen as an extension of the Agent-Patient model, with two entities competing for the status of primary landmark, as represented in figure 29.6.

The most common constructions for transfer and other three-participant events differ, then, in the selection of the primary landmark but also in the construal of the third participant (see Newman 1996: 61–132). One common option is to code the third entity in an oblique form, for example, construing the Recipient as a Goal, as in Finnish (22), or construing a transferred thing as an Instrument, as in the Latin example (23):

(22) *Annan*   *kirja-n*   *tei-lle.*
      give.1SG   book-ACC   you-ALL
      'I (will) give the book to you.' (Finnish)

(23) *Octavi-us*   *Claudia-m*   *coron-a*   *donav-it.*
      Octavius-NOM   Claudia-ACC   corona-ABL   presented-3SG
      'Octavius presented Claudia (with) a crown' (Latin)

Constructions with Subject + Object + Oblique, independently of which entity is selected as Object (primary landmark), are closest to monotransitive constructions as far as they present only two core participants. According to Tuggy (1998), the construal of the Giver as Agent/subject and the Thing as Patient/object employs

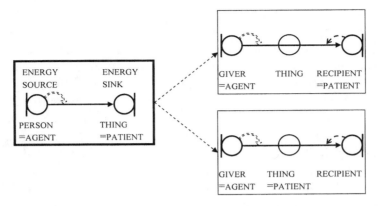

Figure 29.6. The Agent-Patient model extended to GIVE (Newman 1996: 67)

the Manipulation archetype in the conceptualization of the event; then again, if the Recipient is made Patient/object, the situation is construed according to the Human Interaction archetype. In addition, the oblique phrase may add construals such as 'motion of the Patient toward a Goal' (in the allative) or 'transferred thing as an Instrument used in human interaction'.

Even so, the more typical constructions for three-participant events involve two arguments showing object properties to a variable degree. Also in that case, languages tend to exploit either of the following possibilities:

a. Double object construction, as in English, with the Recipient as first object (or primary object as proposed by Dryer 1986) and two noun phrases showing some object properties (Hudson 1992; Newman 1996: 74–80), as in (24)
b. Direct Object plus Dative/Indirect Object construction, as in (25)

(24)   She gave Harry the book.
(25)   *Ya   dal   knig-u   uchital-yu.*
         I   gave   book-ACC   teacher-DAT
         'I gave the book to the teacher.' (Russian)

Both these constructions are labeled ditransitive. Their semantic properties have been dealt with in Cognitive Linguistics either by considering the construction as a whole (Goldberg 1992, 1995; van der Leek 1996) or by specifically considering indirect objects and datives (Smith 1985, 1993; Langacker 1991; Janda 1993; Maldonado 2002). In either case, 'transfer' serves as the prototype from which several extensions emerge. Goldberg, for instance, defines the central meaning of the ditransitive construction as 'an Agent successfully causes Recipient to receive Patient' (see section 2.2); furthermore, she views constructions as radial categories, extending from the central sense to other senses such as 'permission', 'intention', 'future transfer', 'refusal', and 'promises'. Geeraerts's definition of indirect object also starts from the transfer prototype: "active recipient (with controlling power) of a benefactive transfer of material entities" (1998: 203); but he shows the necessity of a multidimensional structure to indicate how nonprototypical readings are linked. The main paths of extension include the metaphorical extension toward a communicative transfer instead of a benefactive transfer or toward an abstract entity instead of a material entity and generalization toward an Experiencer instead of an active Recipient.

Langacker (1991: 327), then again, looks for a more schematic characterization and defines the indirect object in terms of force dynamics and action chains as an "active experiencer in the target domain." This definition accommodates some observations by Smith (1985) about German to the effect that the dative generally encodes participants in an event who are affected entities (i.e., in the target domain) and at the same time affectors (i.e., potentially active), whereas the accusative encodes entities who are affected only. Langacker's characterization includes both Recipients with *give* and other verbs of transfer and Experiencers with verbs of mental experience (*seem, please, be hungry, frighten, bother*, etc.).[12] Nevertheless, it constitutes the base for more complex elaborations and extensions. For example, Maldonado (2002) has shown how the Spanish dative extends from encoding the Recipient of a transfer ("indirect object") to designating some participant in the setting not directly involved in the event ("setting dative") or even a participant in the viewer's space ("sympathetic dative") added to an indirect object:

(26) *Le   envié   el   paquete   a   María.* [receiver of transfer]
      3SG.DAT send.1SG the   package   to   María
      'I sent the package to María.'

(27) *Le   castigaron   al   niño.* [setting dative]
      3SG.DAT punish.3PL   to.the   kid
      'They punished his child.' (literally: 'They punished the kid on him.')

(28) *Me   le   pusieron un cuatro al   niño.* [sympathetic dative]
      1SG.DAT 3SG.DAT put.3PL   a   four   to.the   kid
      'They flunked my son.' (literally: 'They gave a four to the kid on me.')

The point is that the dative could play a crucial role in the construal of events, bringing onstage additional participants that do not fit exactly as subject or object, construing them as central participants.[13] This leads us to the last point in this chapter, the contrast between center and periphery in the structure of the clause.

7. ARGUMENTS AND ADJUNCTS

A clause can be viewed as consisting of a head (the verb) and two types of dependent elements, namely, arguments and adjuncts; what distinguishes arguments and adjuncts is the (relative) obligatoriness of the former and the (relative) optionality of the latter. This distinction is similar, even though not equivalent, to that operating in many languages between the core and oblique elements in a clause. The latter distinction relies on more formal grounds: in some languages, such as English, core elements are instantiated by bare NPs, whereas obliques are instantiated by adpositional phrases. In other languages, it is agreement or cross-reference that accounts for the distinction: for example, in Basque, the auxiliary verb agrees with absolutive, ergative, and dative arguments. Be that as it may, adjuncts largely correspond to oblique elements (coded by an oblique form) and arguments to core elements. For example, in *She broke the window in the kitchen*, subject and object are the core arguments, and *in the kitchen* is an adjunct in an oblique form.

The "obligatory-optional" as well as the "core-oblique" distinctions have a similar semantic basis. In the canonical event model involving distinct "participants" who interact within an inclusive and reasonable stable "setting," arguments basically correspond to the participants in the scene and adjuncts to some facet of the setting. The setting of the event needs to be distinguished from its location(s), that is, a fragment of the setting that locates a participant and that may be required by the verb (as in *put the book on the table*). Finally, participants in the event may have a "central" role (primarily, subject and object) or may be considered secondary or peripheral. Adjuncts are usually reserved for secondary or peripheral participants (e.g., Instruments, Beneficiaries, and so on).

Even though the explanation just offered accounts for the prototypical cases, the distinction between arguments and adjuncts has, in Langacker's view, a more general basis, which is related to the opposition "autonomous-dependent" and to the way in which correspondences between elements are established in the assembly of complex structures. An argument elaborates a salient substructure (the e-site) of the predicate. For example, the verb *break* includes in its meaning a relation between the breaker and the broken thing. In the transitive construction, these salient substructures are elaborated by the subject NP and the object argument(s), respectively. An adjunct or modifier does not elaborate a salient substructure of the head (the verb) but, rather, a substructure of the adjunct is elaborated by the predicate. For example, the preposition *in* of *in the kitchen* establishes a static relation between a setting (the kitchen) and some other entity, which can, for instance, be elaborated by the predication *She broke the window*.

Note that the distinction between argument and adjunct relies on the saliency of substructures and that saliency is a gradient. Some participants—above all, the theme or the absolutive—are inherent to the meaning of a verb, some others are less inherent, still others such as a location are usually not salient in the characterization of an event, although localizability is a relatively inherent property of some (not all) predicates (Croft 2001: 274). Therefore, argument and adjuncts range along a continuum according to the relative salience of the semantic substructures they elaborate.

Besides being a gradient, saliency is also subject to alternative construals. The very same participant in an objective scene may, in various construals, be conceptualized as more or less salient and coded accordingly. Even a setting, which is normally assigned adjunct function, can be construed as subject, the primary figure in the conceptualization of an event (Langacker 1991: 345–48). Determining the relative salience of the elements in a scene is not just based on the selection of the subject but rather on the core-oblique distinction, which distinguishes central participants from marginal elements.

We have observed two sources of salience in clause structure. On the one hand, the verb's meaning implies which elements of the frame-semantic knowledge are obligatorily accessed; these are the "arguments" implied lexically by the verb. On the other hand, core grammatical functions "profile particular roles as being semantically salient or as having some kind of discourse prominence" (Goldberg 1995: 49). Goldberg uses the term *participants* for 'lexically profiled roles', and the term *arguments* for 'constructionally profiled roles'.[14] The important point at issue is that in a particular clause there must be coherent links between arguments and participants. Take the verb *send* as in figures 29.1 and 29.2 above. The verb selects three roles: the Sender, the Sent, and the Goal. The DITRANSITIVE construction gives prominence to all three roles (matching constructional roles Agent, Receiver, and Theme), whereas the CAUSED-MOTION construction just gives prominence to the sender and the sent (as Causer and Theme, respectively), coded with the core grammatical functions subject and object.

Note that neither "lexical profiling" nor "constructional profiling," as used by Goldberg, are equivalent to the concept of profiling in Cognitive Grammar (Langacker 2005: 129). According to Langacker (1987: 118), the profile is the part of the conceptual base designated by an expression. A clause (and a verb) profiles a temporal relation, where subject and object act as trajector and landmark, respectively; that is, the clausal profile concerns the relation itself, more than the participants. Nevertheless, there is some affinity between Langacker's profiling and Goldberg's constructional profiling: subject and object are central participants, the entities delimiting the event and defining the "verbal segment." For this reason, such entities are especially salient in the construal of the event. In other cases—and this may differ across languages—prominence is given to additional participants not directly involved in the event (often as a result of particular construals and depending on the grammatical routines established in a particular language).

8. CONCLUSION

This chapter has provided a brief and necessarily incomplete survey of basic problems in clause structure. The guiding assumption has been that the units of grammar (constructions) are symbolic units and thus that grammatical structures must be understood in terms of their meaning, rooted in cognition and language use. This chapter has focused on schematic and prototypical characterizations of basic syntactic constructs, such as the subject or the transitive clause. It has dealt with issues such as the relations of categorization between clausal constructions and specific linguistic expressions, the interaction between verbs and constructions, and conceptual schemas underlying transitive constructions and accusative and ergative systems. Among the basic concepts that have shown to be particularly useful for the understanding of clausal structure, I have dealt with the notion of prototype, schema, construal, and saliency. On several occasions, I have observed that minor formal differences may give rise to alternate construals, which give more or less prominence to different aspects of a frame.

Many problems have not been covered in this chapter. I have left for further research the study of the way in which the meanings of the different elements in a construction are integrated, not only the meaning of the verb and of the constructional schema but also that of agreement, case, and other morphemes.

NOTES

1. It is worth comparing Goldberg's approach with Fauconnier and Turner's (1996) concept of *blending* (see also Turner, this volume, chapter 15). A blend does not integrate a constructional schema with a verb, but a prototypical instance of a construction and an unintegrated novel conceived event sequence.

2. A more schematic or abstract view of the meaning of constructions leads to question the appropriateness of cause, receive, move, and so on (or the semantic roles Agent, Patient, etc.) as components of the constructional meaning (van der Leek 1996, 2000).

3. See, for example, Nishimura (1993: 506–8) for the differences between the notion of Agent in English and Japanese. Davidse (1998) has argued that semantic roles can be defined formally, by bringing in paradigmatically related constructions (such as passives, alternative adpositional phrases, etc.). Such paradigmatic alternatives are alternate construals of the same scene, each with its own meaning; and, in my opinion, they are merely symptomatic of semantic roles, as far as alternate construals are semantically coherent with some event types and not others.

4. In his latest work, Croft uses a three-dimensional representation, which is detailed in Croft (forthcoming).

5. I am assuming here that the main criterion for the identification of a transitive construction in English is the occurrence of a postverbal NP. This is, of course, a simplification. Verbs such as *resemble* do not admit other commonly recognized criteria such as passivization, which may be a signal of its deviation from the prototype of transitivity.

6. Similar constructions have been interpreted in some languages as having a "dative subject." In these languages, however, the grammatical properties of the subject do not cluster on a single participant. In Spanish, for example, the Experiencer appears in first position, but the verb agrees with the postverbal Stimulus. More generally, it appears that across languages, subject and/or object properties are spread to variable degrees over core participants in less transitive clauses.

7. Rice (1987) relies on passivizability as the main formal test for transitivity, but this criterion is subject to controversy: "If one takes passivizability as the criterion for Direct Object in English, then one's conclusions will tell us something about the passive, not about some allegedly global category Direct Object" (Croft 2001: 46). No doubt, the use of passive overlaps to a large extent with the conceptual space of transitivity, but in the final

analysis the grammaticality of (15b) and (16b) only depends on the construal made by the passive construction, not the transitive construction (see Langacker 1990 on the English passive).

8. 'Humanness' is just one of the main factors correlating with the use of "personal" *a*. Another important factor is 'individuation'. Actually, the explanation for the use of *a* must be stated at clause-level (see Delbecque 1998, 2002) and has to do with the potential reversibility of subject and object roles, that is, with a weakening of subject-object asymmetry.

9. These three parameters correspond with those proposed by Mithun and Chafe (1999): "semantic role," "starting point," and "immediately involved," respectively.

10. This fact has been alleged since Anderson (1976) suggested a distinction between "syntactic" ergativity, based on behavior and control properties, and morphological ergativity, based on case marking, and suggested the universality of "deep" subject, defined with syntactic criteria. However, besides the fact that the terms "syntactic" and "morphological" in this context are misleading, "behavior-and-control" properties do not behave uniformly across languages either.

11. "Topicality is fundamentally a cognitive dimension, having to do with the focus of attention on one or two important events-or-state participants during the processing of multi-participant clauses." (Givón 2001: 198)

12. I have mentioned above the use of dative case in less transitive two-participant clauses.

13. The status of indirect objects as core participants (in Spanish) is stressed by Vázquez Rozas (1995) and García-Miguel (1999b).

14. In previous work (García-Miguel 1995a: 41–46; 1995b: 27–52), I have used the terms *arguments* or *actants* for lexically determined prominent roles and *central participants* for grammatically salient roles, the distinction being equivalent to that of Goldberg.

REFERENCES

Anderson, Stephen R. 1976. On the notion of subject in ergative languages. In Charles Li, ed., *Subject and topic* 1–23. New York: Academic Press.

Chafe, Wallace. 1994. *Discourse, consciousness, and time: The flow and displacement of conscious experience in speaking and writing.* Chicago: University of Chicago Press.

Croft, William. 1991. *Syntactic categories and grammatical relations: The cognitive organization of information.* Chicago: University of Chicago Press.

Croft, William. 1998. Event structure in argument linking. In Miriam Butt and Wilhelm Geuder, eds., *The projection of arguments: Lexical and compositional factors* 21–63. Stanford, CA: CSLI Publications.

Croft, William. 2001. *Radical construction grammar: Syntactic theory in typological perspective.* Oxford: Oxford University Press.

Croft, William. 2003. Lexical rules vs constructions: a false dichotomy. In Hubert Cuyckens, Thomas Berg, René Dirven, and Klaus-Uwe Panther, eds., *Motivation in Language: Studies in honor of Günter Radden* 49–68. Amsterdam: John Benjamins.

Croft, William. Forthcoming. Verbs: Aspect and argument structure (Seven chapters on causal-aspectual representation). Draft, August 2000. http://www.unm.edu/~wcroft/WACpubs.html.

Davidse, Kristin. 1998. The dative as participant role versus the indirect object: On the need to distinguish two layers of organization. In Willy Van Langendonck and William Van Belle, eds., *The dative*, vol. 2, *Theoretical and contrastive studies* 143–84. Amsterdam: John Benjamins.

DeLancey, Scott. 1990. Ergativity and the Cognitive Model of Event Structure in Lhasa Tibetan. *Cognitive Linguistics* 1: 289–321.

Delbecque, Nicole. 1998. Why Spanish has two transitive construction frames. *Leuvense Bijdragen* 87: 387–415.

Delbecque, Nicole. 2002. A construction grammar approach to transitivity in Spanish. In Kristin Davidse and Béatrice Lamiroy, eds., *The nominative and accusative and their counterparts* 81–131. Amsterdam: John Benjamins.

Dryer, Matthew. 1986. Primary objects, secondary objects and antidative. *Language* 62: 808–45.

Dryer, Matthew. 1997. Are grammatical relations universal? In Joan L. Bybee, John Haiman, and Sandra A. Thompson, eds., *Essays on language function and language type* 343–66. Amsterdam: John Benjamins.

Du Bois, John. 1987. The discourse basis of ergativity. *Language* 63: 805–55.

Fauconnier, Gilles, and Mark Turner. 1996. Blending as a central process of grammar. In Adele E. Goldberg, ed., *Conceptual structure, discourse and language* 113–29. Stanford, CA: CSLI Publications

Fillmore, Charles J. 1977. Topics in lexical semantics. In Roger Cole, ed., *Current issues in linguistic theory* 76–138. Bloomington: Indiana University Press.

Fillmore, Charles J. 1985. Frames and the semantics of understanding. *Quaderni di Semantica* 6: 222–54.

Fillmore, Charles J., Christopher R. Johnson, and Miriam R. L. Petruck. 2003. Background to FrameNet. *International Journal of Lexicography* 16: 235–50.

García-Miguel, José M. 1995a. *Las relaciones gramaticales entre predicado y participantes*. Santiago de Compostela: Servicio de Publicacións da Universidade de Santiago de Compostela.

García-Miguel, José M. 1995b. *Transitividad y complementación preposicional en español*. Santiago de Compostela: Servicio de Publicacións da Universidade de Santiago de Compostela.

García-Miguel, José M. 1999a. La expresión de actantes centrales en español (romance) y bribri (chibcha): Tipología, discurso y cognición. In Mário Vilela and Fátima Silva, eds., *Actas do 1° Encontro de Lingüística Cognitiva* 101–21. Porto: Faculdade de Letras.

García-Miguel, José M. 1999b. Grammatical relations in Spanish triactant clauses. In Leon G. de Stadler and Christoff Eyrich, eds., *Issues in cognitive linguistics* 447–70. Berlin: Mouton de Gruyter.

Geeraerts, Dirk. 1998. The semantic structure of the indirect object in Dutch. In Willy Van Langendonck and William Van Belle, eds., *The dative*, vol. 2, *Theoretical and contrastive studies* 185–210. Amsterdam: John Benjamins.

Givón, Talmy. 1984. *Syntax: A functional-typological introduction*. Vol. 1. Amsterdam: John Benjamins.

Givón, Talmy. 1995. *Functionalism and grammar*. Amsterdam: John Benjamins.

Givón, Talmy. 2001. *Syntax: An introduction*. 2 vols. Amsterdam: John Benjamins.

Goldberg, Adele E. 1992. The inherent semantics of argument structure: The case of the English ditransitive construction. *Cognitive Linguistics* 3: 37–74

Goldberg, Adele E. 1995. *Constructions: A construction grammar approach to argument structure*. Chicago: University of Chicago Press.

Hopper, Paul J., and Sandra A. Thompson. 1980. Transitivity in grammar and discourse. *Language* 56: 251–99.

Hudson, Richard. 1992. So-called 'double objects' and grammatical relations. *Language* 68: 251–76.

Janda, Laura A. 1993. *A geography of case semantics: The Czech dative and the Russian instrumental.* Berlin: Mouton de Gruyter.

Keenan, Edward L. 1976. Toward a universal definition of 'subject.' In Charles Li, ed., *Subject and topic* 303–33. New York: Academic Press.

Keenan, Edward L. 1984. Semantic correlates of the ergative/absolutive distinction. *Linguistics* 22: 197–223.

Kuno, Susumu. 1987. *Functional syntax: Anaphora, discourse and empathy.* Chicago: University of Chicago Press.

Lakoff, George. 1977. Linguistic gestalts. *Chicago Linguistic Society* 13: 236–87.

Lakoff, George. 1987. *Women, fire, and dangerous things: What categories reveal about the mind.* Chicago: University of Chicago Press.

Langacker, Ronald W. 1987. *Foundations of cognitive grammar.* Vol. 1, *Theoretical prerequisites.* Stanford, CA: Stanford University Press.

Langacker, Ronald W. 1990. *Concept, image, and symbol: The cognitive basis of grammar.* Berlin: Mouton de Gruyter.

Langacker, Ronald W. 1991. *Foundations of cognitive grammar.* Vol. 2, *Descriptive application.* Stanford, CA: Stanford University Press.

Langacker, Ronald W. 1998. Topic, subject, and possessor. *Linguistic notes from La Jolla* 19: 1–28. (Revised version in Hanne Gramm Simonsen and Rolf Theil Endresen, eds., *A cognitive approach to the verb: Morphological and constructional perspectives* 11–48. Berlin: Mouton de Gruyter, 2000)

Langacker, Ronald W. 2000. *Grammar and conceptualization.* Berlin: Mouton de Gruyter.

Langacker, Ronald W. 2005. Construction Grammars: cognitive, radical and less so. In Francisco J. Ruiz de Mendoza Ibáñez, and M. Sandra Peña Cervel, eds., *Cognitive Linguistics: Internal dynamics and interdisciplinary interaction* 101–59. Berlin: Mouton de Gruyter.

Maldonado, Ricardo. 2002. Objective and subjective datives. *Cognitive Linguistics* 13: 1–65.

Mithun, Marianne. 1991. Active/agentive case marking and its motivations. *Language* 67: 510–46.

Mithun, Marianne, and Wallace Chafe. 1999. What are S, A, and O? *Studies in Language* 23: 569–96

Newman, John. 1996. *Give: A cognitive linguistic study.* Berlin: Mouton de Gruyter.

Nishimura, Yoshiki. 1993. Agentivity in cognitive grammar. In Richard A. Geiger and Brygida Rudzka-Ostyn, eds., *Conceptualizations and mental processing in language* 487–530. Berlin: Mouton de Gruyter.

Onishi, Masayuki. 2001. Non-canonically marked subjects and objects: Parameters and properties. In Alexandra Y. Aikhenvald, Robert M. W. Dixon, and Masayuki Onishi, eds., *Non-canonical marking of subjects and objects* 1–51. Amsterdam: John Benjamins.

Rappaport Hovav, Malka, and Beth Levin. 1998. Building verb meanings. In Miriam Butt and Wilhelm Geuder, eds, *The projection of arguments: Lexical and compositional factors* 97–134. Standford, CA: CSLI Publications.

Rice, Sally A. 1987. Towards a cognitive model of transitivity. PhD dissertation, University of California at San Diego.

Ruppenhofer, Josef, Michael Ellwood, Miriam R. L. Petruck, and Christopher R. Johnson. 2005. FrameNet: Theory and Practice. http://framenet.icsi.berkeley.edu/book/book.html.

Smith, Michael B. 1985. Event chains, grammatical relations, and the semantics of case in German. *Chicago Linguistic Society* 21: 388–407.

Smith, Michael B. 1993. Cases as conceptual categories: Evidence from German. In Richard A. Geiger and Brygida Rudzka-Ostyn, eds., *Conceptualizations and mental processing in language* 531–65. Berlin: Mouton de Gruyter.

Talmy, Leonard. 1988. Force dynamics in language and cognition. *Cognitive Science* 12: 49–100.

Talmy, Leonard. 1996. The windowing of attention in language. In Masayoshi Shibatani and Sandra A. Thompson, eds., *Grammatical constructions: Their form and meaning* 235–87. Oxford: Clarendon Press.

Talmy, Leonard. 2000. *Toward a cognitive semantics*. Vol. 1, *Concept structuring systems*. Cambridge, MA: MIT Press.

Taylor, John R. 1995. *Linguistic categorization: Prototypes in linguistic theory*. 2nd ed. Oxford: Clarendon Press. (3rd ed., 2003)

Taylor, John R. 1998. Syntactic constructions as prototype categories. In Michael Tomasello, ed., *The new psychology of language: Cognitive and functional approaches to language structure* 1: 177–202. Mahwah, NJ: Lawrence Erlbaum.

Tuggy, David. 1998. Giving in Nawatl. In John Newman, ed., *The linguistics of giving* 35–66. Amsterdam: John Benjamins.

van der Leek, Frederike. 1996. Rigid syntax and flexible meaning: The case of the English ditransitive. In Adele E. Goldberg, ed., *Conceptual structure, discourse and language* 321–32. Stanford, CA: CSLI Publications.

van der Leek, Frederike. 2000. Caused-motion and the 'bottom-up' role of grammar. In Ad Foolen and Frederike van der Leek, eds., *Constructions in cognitive linguistics* 301–31. Amsterdam: John Benjamins.

Vázquez Rozas, Victoria. 1995. *El complemento indirecto en español*. Santiago de Compostela: Servicio de Publicacións da Universidade de Santiago de Compostela.

CHAPTER 30

COMPLEMENTATION

MICHEL ACHARD

1. THE COMPLEMENT RELATION

The term "complement" has a very general interpretation in Cognitive Linguistics. For example, in Langacker's Cognitive Grammar (Langacker 1987, 1991), a complement structure corresponds to and elaborates a salient subpart of the relation evoked by the head. For example, in the phrase *under the table*, the nominal *the table* stands in a complement relation to the preposition *under* (the head), because it corresponds to and elaborates its landmark. In that sense, complements contrast with modifiers. In a modifier relation, the head elaborates a salient substructure of the entity that modifies it. For example, in the phrase *big tree*, the head *tree* corresponds to the trajector of *big* and gets elaborated by it. *Big* therefore stands in a modifying relation with respect to the head *tree*.

The amount of space allotted to this chapter makes it impossible to treat complementation in this general sense. Consequently, we will be exclusively concerned with clausal complements. For our purposes, a complement is a clause that functions as an argument with respect to the main verb. For example, in *I believe she came back*, the subordinate clause *she came back* elaborates the landmark of the main verb *believe*.

In a way congruent with the overall cognitive linguistic goals and methods, the main focus of the research on complementation has consisted of exploring the semantic import of the complement constructions and investigating the isomorphism that exists between the form of those constructions and their semantic-conceptual organization both language-internally and cross-linguistically (Givón 1980, 1990; Haiman 1985). A nonexhaustive list of the languages whose complementation systems have been insightfully analyzed includes: Bella Coola and Lushootseed (Beck 2000),

English (Wierzbicka 1988; Dirven 1989; Langacker 1991; Verspoor 1999, 2000), French (Ruwet 1984, 1991; Achard 1996, 1998, 2002a, 2002b), Korean (Horie 2000), Japanese (Suzuki 1996, 2000; Horie 2000), Spanish (Delbeque 2000), and Tsez (Polinsky 2000). Across languages, the research has mostly focused on the cross-linguistic definition of subordination (Cristofaro 1998, 2003) or the typological dimension of the morphosyntactic form of the complements (Givón 1980, 1990, 1995; Noonan 1985; Horie 1993).

The purpose of this chapter is to present an overview of this research. While it is clear that space limitations preclude an exhaustive presentation of any one of the issues introduced, the examples chosen aim to provide the reader with a basic understanding of the issues raised by cognitive linguists about complementation, as well as the methods they have designed to answer them. Section 2 introduces the crucial concept of "conceptual subordination." Section 3 presents some of the semantic contrasts that complement constructions code in English, Japanese, and French. Section 4 considers the Cognitive Grammar account of raising construc-tions in order to show that a semantically based framework can provide a satis-factory account of phenomena traditionally regarded as purely syntactic. Section 5 summarizes and concludes this chapter.

2. Conceptual Subordination

2.1. General Issues

Because the topic of this chapter is clausal complements, we first need to briefly introduce some basic concepts pertaining to the structure of a clause before turning our attention to more complex constructions. Langacker (1991: 13–95) argues that the internal organization of a clause closely parallels that of a noun phrase and that, like the noun phrase, it exhibits a layering of semantic functions. Just as a noun represents a noun type, a verb stem represents a process type. Both types need to be instantiated, that is to say, considered with respect to a particular location in their domain of instantiation before being quantified. For verbs, the nonfinite markers (aspect and voice, for example) provide the quantification function. The quantified instances are finally grounded, that is, considered with respect to the speech situa-tion. In this analysis, an infinitival complement profiles a type specification, whereas an indicative clause profiles a grounded instance of a process type.

Independent or main clauses are usually fully grounded (finite). Complement clauses, on the other hand, exhibit all levels of semantic elaboration. For example, in *I know that she left*, the subordinate clause profiles a grounded instance of the process of leaving. By comparison, in *I want to leave*, the complement clause pres-ents leaving as a mere type. The eclecticism of its possible forms indicates that the definition of a complement clause needs to remain independent from any specific morphosyntactic realization. Langacker (1991: 436) suggests that a complement clause is a clause whose profile is superseded by that of another (main) clause:

> A **main clause** is the *head* at a particular level of organization, i.e. the clause that lends its profile to the composite structure of a multiclausal expression. A **subordinate clause** is then describable as one whose profile is overridden by that of a main clause.... In a typical complement clause construction, the two clauses combine directly and the main clause is clearly the profile determinant: *I know* **she left** designates the process of knowing, not of leaving.[1]

This overriding of the profile of the complement clause reflects the conceptual subordination of the event coded by that clause on the event profiled by the main clause. Langacker (1991: 440) expresses conceptual subordination in the following fashion: "By the very nature of a complement clause, the process it describes undergoes a kind of conceptual subordination: rather than being viewed in its own terms as an independent object of thought, it is primarily considered for the role it plays within the subordinate relationship expressed by the main clause."

Because of the iconic properties of grammatical structures (Haiman 1985), there is a high degree of correlation between the level of semantic elaboration of the complement clause (reflected in its morphosyntactic shape) and the degree of independence of the subordinate event with respect to the main event. Consequently, the level of conceptual integration of the subordinate event into the main event can be evaluated. Givón (1980: 338) provides three parameters to determine the degree of independence of the subordinate event with respect to the main event:

> i) The degree to which the agent/subject/topic marking of the embedded clause reflects the markings in independent/main clauses; ii) The degree to which independent-clause tense-aspect-modality marking of the verb is preserved in the embedded clause; iii) The presence or degree-of-presence of predicate-raising of the complement clause verb onto the main verb; i.e., the degree to which the complement verb is lexicalized as one word with the main verb.

For example, in *I know that she came*, the subordinate clause *she came* is identical in form to an independent clause. The logical subject of *come* is marked in the nominative, as it would be in an independent clause. Furthermore, the subordinate verb retains its own Tense-Aspect-Modality markings. In fact, the presence of the complementizer *that* alone formally reflects the conceptual dependence of the subordinate clause by introducing a distancing effect that provides a quasi-nominal construal of that clause (Langacker 1991). By comparison, in *She wants me to come back*, the form of the complement *me to come back* indicates that the event it codes has a lesser degree of independence with respect to the main verb *want*. The logical subject of the subordinate verb is in the accusative instead of the expected nominative in an independent clause, and there are no Tense-Aspect-Modality markings on that verb. Givón's criteria clearly show that increasing dependence on the main event is reflected in the increasing loss of specifically verbal markings on the form that codes the subordinate event. This decrease in verbal specificity is fully congruent with the fact that complementation is often treated syntactically as nominalization in different languages (Beck 2000; Horie 2000; Polinsky 2000).

2.2. The Semantic Basis of Conceptual Subordination

One of the most important tasks in complementation research consists of motivating the distribution of particular complement forms with the main verbs they occur with. Givón (1980, 1990) shows that the semantics of the main verb go a long way toward determining that distribution. His binding hierarchy explores "the systematic isomorphism that exists between the semantics of the complement-taking verbs, and the syntax of the verb-plus-complement constructions" (Givón 1990: 515). Givón's analysis considers the form of the complement as the result of the "binding force" of the main verb, that is, the influence of the main clause subject over the complement scene. The top of the scale is composed of the manipulative verbs, such as *cause, make,* and *force,* and the bottom consists of cognition utterance verbs, such as *know.*

The "emotional factor" involved in certain verbs provides an additional dimension to the hierarchy, and yields opposite results if applied at the top or at the bottom of the scale. "The more the subject/agent of a manipulative verb is emotionally committed to the outcome encoded in the complement clause, the higher the verb will be on the binding scale. The more emotionally committed the subject/agent of a manipulative verb is with the outcome encoded in the complement clause, the lower the manipulative verb will be on the binding scale" (Givón 1980: 337). The two dimensions yield the following scale: the manipulative implicative verbs (*make, have, cause*) occupy the top, followed by the nonimplicative and increasingly emotion-encoding verbs, such as *tell, ask,* and *want.* Emotion-encoding cognition verbs, such as *regret,* occupy a lower position, just above the nonemotive cognition verbs, such as *know,* which constitute the lowest point of the scale.

The interest of Givón's hierarchy resides in the prediction it makes for the type of complement structure that follows each verb type.

> The main purpose of this study is to show that the syntactic nature (coding) of the complement clauses of verbs which take verbal/sentential complements is largely predictable from their position on the scale. Not altogether unexpectedly, the binding force of a verb roughly correlates to the degree to which its complement appears syntactically like an independent/main clause. The relation is, however, inverse. The higher a verb is on the binding scale, the less would its complement tend to be syntactically coded as an independent/main clause. (Givón 1980: 337)

One example will suffice to illustrate Givón's hierarchy. A verb at the top of the scale, such as *make,* occurs with the logical subject of the subordinate verb raised in the position of object of the main verb and a subordinate predicate in the infinitive as in *Chris made Pat cry,* for example. It cannot occur with a finite complement because the subordinate event lacks the independence required to be coded that way (*Chris made that Pat cried*). On the other hand, a lower verb, such as *know*, is perfectly felicitous with a finite complement, the form that best approximates an independent clause (*I know that she came yesterday*).

Givón's hierarchy represents one of the most useful typologies of complement-taking verbs because it allows us to relate seemingly very diverse constructions in different languages. However, it cannot fully account for complement distribution, because it is exclusively concerned with the meaning of the main verb. In particular, if it can predict the range of constructions a given verb can take, it cannot motivate the choice of a specific construction within that range. A thorough account of complement distribution also needs to pay careful attention to the meaning of the complement constructions themselves. This is extremely difficult to do cross-linguistically, because the necessary generality of the analysis overlooks the semantic subtlety of the contrasts different constructions express in individual languages. Typological research therefore needs to be complemented by in-depth language-specific investigations that bring to light the different kinds of semantic contrasts various complement constructions code.

3. SEMANTIC CONTRASTS

The most efficient way to present these language-specific investigations is to consider each language separately. Two main reasons explain this strategy. First, specific constructions code different contrasts in different languages, and these contrasts are consistent with the global ecology of the language considered (i.e., other contrasts coded elsewhere in the grammar). Secondly, the morphosyntactic means by which these constraints are expressed also obviously depend on the lexical and structural apparatus available in the language. Consequently, the constructs that most conveniently describe complementation systems vary substantially across languages, and each one is best introduced in the context of the language for which it is relevant. For this reason, this section presents an overview of the research on the complement systems of English, Japanese, and French. Here again, the purpose of this section is not to be exhaustive, but merely to provide the reader with an illustration of the results obtained in those languages.

3.1. English

It is fitting to start this overview with the English situation for several reasons. First, English has a rich system with a highly complex distribution of complements and verb types. Secondly, the syntactic aspects of that distribution make the area of English complementation "one of the greatest challenges to a theory of syntax based on semantic foundations" (Wierzbicka 1988: 23). Finally, most of the original research on complementation was done with respect to English, and the results obtained sparked semantic interest in complement constructions in other languages. Most of those early works (Jespersen 1909–42; Wood 1956; Bolinger 1968, 1972, 1974; Kiparsky and Kiparsky 1970; Karttunen 1971; Borkin 1973; Hooper 1975; Ney 1981; Dixon 1984; among others) could not be called cognitive in the strictest sense, because they predate the establishment of Cognitive Linguistics as a unified theoretical approach. However, they are crucial in illustrating the basic tenet that will be formulated as one of the guiding assumptions of the Cognitive Linguistics movement, namely that "a difference in syntactic form always spells a difference in meaning" (Bolinger 1968: 127).

It is a well-known fact that in English most verbs can only take specific complements. For instance, certain verbs can only take gerund (-*ing*) complements while others can only be followed by *to* + -*ing* structures, as illustrated in (1) and (2):

(1)   a. We all wanted to stay at home.
      b. *We all wanted staying at home.
(2)   a. *We all kept to play.
      b. We all kept playing.

The main thrust of the research on English complementation has consisted of providing a semantic definition for the four complement types commonly found in the language, namely, -*ing*-, *to*-, *for . . . to*-, and *that*-complements. Once these complement types are recognized as specific constructions with their own semantic import, their syntactic behavior, that is, their distribution with the relevant verb classes, is primarily a matter of semantic compatibility between meaningful elements. It is simply impossible to do justice to all the solutions proposed in the literature. Consequently, I will primarily base this overview on Wierzbicka's (1988) solution and refer the reader to the aforementioned works, as well as Dirven (1989), Duffley (1999), Verspoor (1999, 2000), and Smith and Escobedo (2001) for additional information. Wierzbicka's analysis has been chosen because it represents perhaps the most complete and best-articulated account of the semantic base of the English complementation system. It provides a thorough semantic analysis of -*ing*-, *to*-, *for . . . to*-, and *that*-complements and convincingly argues that the distribution of these four forms is directly predictable from their meanings.

There are two kinds of -*ing*-complements: temporal and nontemporal. Temporal complements originate in situations where -*ing* combines with the temporal semantic verb types of events, processes, or actions, entities for which time is relevant. Nontemporal complements arise when -*ing* combines with the semantic verb types of facts and possibilities, entities for which time is irrelevant. For the temporal complements, the presence of -*ing* indicates some element of 'sameness of time' between the main and subordinate verb. This constraint is obviously irrelevant with the nontemporal complements. This contrast is illustrated in (3) and (4). The sentence in (4) is adapted from Wierzbicka (1988: 69).

(3)   She enjoyed watching the movie.

(4)   John regretted (yesterday) quarreling with Jane (last month).

In (3), the complement refers to the action of watching the movie. Consequently, because actions are time-sensitive, the enjoying and the watching must occur at the same time. In (4), on the other hand, the complement refers to the nontemporal fact of quarreling with Jane. The sameness of time constraint is therefore irrelevant, and the quarreling is rightfully construed as preceding the regretting.

To-complements are particularly sensitive to two semantic notions. First, they are associated with the "first-person mode," that is, they uniquely describe what the conceptualizer himself or herself knows, thinks, or wants, as opposed to the experience of other conceptualizers. Secondly, they always contain some form of "future orientation."[2]

The future orientation of the *to*-complements makes them obviously different from the *-ing*-forms, which accounts for the following contrast (from Wierzbicka 1988: 64):

(5)   He tried frying the mushrooms.

(6)   He tried to fry the mushrooms.

Because of the sameness-of-time constraint imposed by the *-ing*-complement in (5), the trying and the frying are construed as occurring at the same time. In (6), because of the future orientation of the *to*-complement, the trying necessarily precedes the frying. The choice between the two constructions is obviously determined by the speaker's evaluation of which one best structures the scene he or she wants to describe (Duffley 1999; Smith and Escobedo 2001).

For...to-complements conflict with *to*-complements in two important respects. The first is the level of confidence with which the accomplishment of the process in the complement is envisaged. This is illustrated in (7) and (8) (from Wierzbicka 1988: 167):

(7)   a. She expected him to come.
       b. *She expected for him to come.

(8)   a. *She waited him to come.
       b. She waited for him to come.

The verb *expect* in (7) indicates more confidence in the realization of the coming process than *wait* in (8). Consequently, *expect* is possible with *to-*, but infelicitous with *for...to*-complements. *Wait* conversely occurs with *for...to* but not with *to*.

The second area where the *for...to-* and *to*-complements contrast concerns their 'self' versus 'other' orientation. Whereas *to*-complements describe the speaker's self experience, *for...to*-complements usually express the experience of other conceptualizers.[3] The 'other' orientation of *for...to* is often expressed by the presence of different subjects for the main and subordinate verbs. The respective orientations of *to-* and *for...to*-complements toward the self and others accounts for the contrast in (9) and (10) (from Wierzbicka 1988: 167):

(9)   She was keen to go.
(10)   a. She was keen for him to go.
         b. *She was keen for herself to go.

While it is felicitous to describe the speaker's experience in (9), *to* is infelicitous to describe another conceptualizer's experience in (10), even if the self is construed like an other. Finally, the *for . . . to*-complements have an "anti-assertive" value that emphasizes its connection with the subjunctive mood found in other languages.

   That-complements basically pertain to knowledge and the intellectual apprehension of a given entity. This yields the well-documented contrast illustrated in (11) and (12):

(11)   I saw him coming.
(12)   I saw that he had come.

The presence of *-ing* in (11) indicates that the main and subordinate processes occur at the same time and that the process of coming was directly perceived. The presence of the *that*-clause in (12) indicates a more mental act that did not necessarily result from direct perception (Bolinger 1968; Borkin 1973).[4]

3.2. Japanese

In Japanese, complementation essentially reduces to the kind of complementizer used and to whether or not that complementizer functions as a nominalizer. The language has several different complementizers, the most frequent of which are *no*, *koto*, and *to*.[5] The use of these three complementizers is illustrated in (13)–(15). The examples are from Horie (2000):

(13)   *Mary-wa*   [*John-ga*   *toori-o*   *wataru*]   *no-o*   *mi-ta*.
         M.-TOP   J.-NOM   street-ACC   cross   NR-ACC   see-PST
         'Mary saw John cross the street.'
(14)   *Mary-wa*   [*John-ga*   *toori-o*   *watat-ta*]   *koto-o*   *sit-ta*.
         M.-TOP   J.-NOM   street-ACC   cross-PST   NR-ACC   know-PST
         'Mary learned that John had crossed the street.'
(15)   "*Asita-wa*   *ko-nai*   *yo*,"   *to*   (**o*)   *it-ta*.
         tomorrow-TOP   come-NEG   SFP   COMP   ACC   say-PST
         'He said: "won't come tomorrow".'

Suzuki (2000: 34) characterizes the main structural difference between the three complementizers in the following way. "While *no* and *koto* are nominalizers and thus incorporate their complement as the object of the matrix verb, *to* does not nominalize the complement and thus does not incorporate the complement into the rest of the sentence as well as the nominalizers do." The impossibility for *to* to be a nominalizer is illustrated in (15) by the infelicity of the accusative marker *-o*.[6]

   The research on Japanese complementation constructions has mostly centered on precisely establishing the nature of the contrast between the constructions introduced by the three complementizers. It seems clear that *no, koto*, and *to* code some sort of scale relative to the directness with which the scene profiled in the complement clause is construed. However, the structural difference between *no* and *koto*, on the one hand, and *to*, on the other hand, needs to be recognized.

The contrast between *no* and *koto* has been expressed in different terms over the years. Kuno (1973) explains it in terms of a concrete-abstract distinction. Josephs (1976) analyzes it in terms of directness versus indirectness. More recently, Horie (2000) argues that the semantic category coded by the *no-koto* contrast is most judiciously expressed in terms of event versus proposition. His account is certainly compatible with the earlier ones. The perception of an event is more direct and, in that sense, more concrete than the conception of a proposition, an object of thought remote from the immediacy of perception. Horie's analysis explains why *no* can sometimes encode a proposition if the main verb is a cognitive one, such as *siru* 'learn', but *koto* does not usually code events, as illustrated in (16):

(16) **Mary-wa* [*John-ga   toori-o   wataru*] *koto-o   mi-ta.*
      M.-TOP   J.-NOM   street-ACC cross   NR-ACC   see-PST
      'Mary saw John cross the street.'

The distinction between the nominalizing *no* and *koto* and the nonnormalizing *to* has also been investigated. In Kuno (1973), it is expressed in terms of factivity-nonfactivity. Suzuki (1996) argues that *no, koto*, and *to* form a continuum in relation to the extent to which the speaker accepts the information presented to him or her. In later work, however, she claims that the structural difference between *to* and the nominalizing complementizers is best expressed in terms of Frajzyngier's (1991) terminology of *de re* versus *de dicto*. The entities coded by *koto* and *no* (events or propositions) belong to the domain of reality (*de re*), whereas the complements introduced by *to* belong to the domain of speech (*de dicto*) (Suzuki 2000: 34). Suzuki claims that "the framework of *de re* vs. *de dicto* was chosen because the notion of domain of speech fits well with the character of *to*, which was originally used only for reporting another speaker's statement and later became a complementizer with a wider application" (34).

As a *de dicto* complementizer, *to*'s main function is to mark "the speaker's psychological distance from the information expressed in the complement clause" (Suzuki 2000: 37). This function is clearly visible in the minimal pairs in (17) and (18), where *to* contrasts with *no* (from Suzuki 2000: 36):

(17) *Watashi-wa   kare-ga   nemutte-iru   to   mi-ta.*
      I-TOP   he-NOM   is-sleeping   COMP   see-PST
      'I saw (judged) that he was sleeping.'
(18) *Watashi-wa   kare-ga   nemutte-iru   no-o   mi-ta.*
      I-TOP   he-NOM   is-sleeping   NR-ACC see-PST
      'I saw him sleeping.'

With verbs of perception, the presence of *no* indicates a directly perceived event, whereas *to* indicates that the information in the complement is inferred, that is, obtained in a less direct manner. This contrast directly parallels the one illustrated in (11) and (12) for English.

3.3. French

In French also, events are usually coded with infinitival complements, whereas propositions are marked with finite clauses, as illustrated in (19) and (20):

(19) *Jean   a   vu   sortir   Marie.*
      John   has   see.PP   go.out   Mary
      'John saw Mary go out.'

(20) *Jean   a   vu   que   Marie   était   sortie.*
      John   has   see.PP   COMP   Mary   is.IMPF   go.out.PP
      'John saw that Mary had left.'

In a way consistent with the English and Japanese systems, the less verbal infinitive form in (19) codes a directly perceived event, whereas the proposition in (20) is marked with a finite clause.

However, French differs from both English and Japanese in two major respects. First, the distinction between infinitival and finite constructions often pertains to whether or not the main and subordinate verbs have similar or different subjects. The second one concerns the presence of an indicative-subjunctive distinction when the complement form is finite. The infinitival-finite contrast is presented in (21) and (22):

(21) *Marie   aime   aller   au   cinéma.*
      Mary   likes   go.INF   to.the   cinema
      'Mary likes to go to the cinema.'

(22) *Marie   aime que   son frère   aille   au   cinéma avec elle.*
      Mary   likes COMP   her brother   go.SUBJ   to.the   cinema with her
      'Mary likes her brother to go to the cinema with her'

In (21), the co-reference of the subjects of the verbs *aimer* and *aller* yields an infinitival complement. In (22), the complement verb has a conjugated form (subjunctive), because the main and subordinate verbs have different subjects.[7]

With respect to the second contrast, the verbs of perception, declaration, and propositional attitude are most often followed by complements in the indicative, whereas the verbs of volition and emotional reaction are followed by complements in the subjunctive. This distinction is illustrated in (23) and (24):

(23) *Jean   sait   que   vous   avez   déménagé.*
      John   knows   COMP   you   have.IND   move.out.PP
      'John knows that you moved out.'

(24) *Jean   veut   que   vous   ayez   déménagé   avant   dimanche.*
      John   wants   COMP   you   hav.SUBJ   move.out.PP   before   Sunday
      'John wants you to have moved out before Sunday.'

Although they are obviously related, the two contrasts illustrated in (21)–(24) are relatively independent from each other and are therefore analyzed separately. Building on Ruwet's (1984) original insight that certain verbs semantically treat a self-to-self relation in a way similar to a self-to-other relation whereas other verbs treat them differently, I provide an account based on the viewing arrangement that exists between the conceptualizer and the scene conceptualized (Achard 1996, 1998). The notion of viewing arrangement needs to be understood in the sense of Langacker (1985, 1990, 1991); it refers to the vantage point from which the scene coded by a particular expression is conceptualized, as well as the precise nature of the relation that exists between the subject and object of conceptualization.

I argue that the presence of a finite complement (indicative or subjunctive) reflects an objective construal on the scene coded in the complement from the vantage point of the main clause conceptualizer. Because the vantage point from which it is construed is external to its scope of predication (Langacker 1985, 1990), the whole scene, including the subject of the subordinate process, is part of the objective scene and thus profiled. The presence of an infinitival complement reflects the subjective construal of the scene coded in the complement. More precisely, that scene is conceptualized from the internal vantage point of the subordinate subject. Because the subordinate subject is construed subjectively, it is not specifically mentioned. The subordinate process alone is profiled. This configuration increases the involvement of the main subject in the scene coded in the complement, because he or she construes the latter from the vantage point of someone already involved in that process. This kind of analysis accounts for the fact that an infinitival complement can only occur in cases where the main and subordinate subjects are co-referential.[8]

The objective-subjective construal of the scene coded in the complement is primarily a matter of speaker choice. However, as part of their semantic organization, certain verbs tend to impose an inherently objective or subjective construal on their complement. The perception verbs, for example, impose an objective construal on their complement scene regardless of whether the main and subordinate subjects are co-referential or not (Ruwet 1984). Consequently, they are usually not found with infinitival complements, as illustrated in (25) and (26):

(25)   *Je   remarque   avoir   les   cheveux   frisés.
       I   notice   have.INF   the   hairs   curly
       'I notice to have curly hair.'

(26)   Je   remarque   que   j'   ai   les   cheveux   frisés.
       I   notice   COMP I   have.IND the   hairs   curly
       'I notice that I have curly hair.'

Conversely, the volition verbs impose an inherently subjective construal on the complement scene, which is why a finite clause in cases of co-referentiality between the main and subordinate subjects is usually infelicitous. The examples in (27) and (28) from Ruwet (1984: 75) illustrate the well-documented phenomenon of obviation (Ruwet 1984; Farkas 1992):

(27) *Je   veux   partir.*
      I   want   leave.INF
      'I want to leave.'
(28) **Je   veux   que   je   parte.*
      I   want   COMP I   leave.SUBJ
      'I want that I leave.'

With the verbs that do not impose any inherent construal on their complement scene, an objective or subjective construal reflected by the presence of a finite or infinitival complement depends on the discourse context.

The indicative-subjunctive distinction has some measure of independence from the infinitive-finite distinction. It essentially pertains to grounding, described by Langacker (1991: 440) as follows: "Grounding locates the event with respect to the speaker's conception of reality." Consequently, the base relative to which the meaning of the two inflections needs to be characterized is composed of the different Idealized Cognitive Models that articulate our conceptions of reality and possession. I argue that the propositions a given conceptualizer considers true can be manipulated just like concrete objects (Achard 2002b). Consequently, the conceptual control he or she exercises over those propositions can be understood in terms of abstract possession. Just as the set of objects a person owns defines his or her dominion, the set of propositions he or she considers true (i.e., his or her conception of elaborated reality) represents his or her dominion.

The indicative inflection codes "the epistemic effort required to establish the conceptualized event's putative location in elaborated reality. . . . Importantly, this definition applies to any kind of epistemic effort that aims to establish control over the population" (Achard 2002b: 212; Langacker 2002). Crucially, the indicative is the only mood that can appropriately serve to describe the elements of a conceptualizer's dominion, because it is the only one that can provide events with their necessary putative address in elaborated reality. Subjunctive complements do not describe an element of a conceptualizer's dominion because they do not make the necessary reference to elaborated reality. The complement content is merely considered with respect to a specific local mental space. For example, in *Jean veut que vous partiez* 'John wants you to leave', the complement content is merely considered with respect to the mental space of John's desires.

Viewed in this way, the meaning of the indicative and subjunctive inflections emphasize the parallel between nominal phrases and clauses. Langacker (1991) argues that a finite (indicative) clause represents a grounded instance of a process type, that is, a unique element of some conceptualizer's dominion. In that sense, it is similar to a definite nominal. I argue that a subjunctive clause represents an arbitrary instance of a process type, that is, an instance specifically conjured up for a specific purpose (Achard 1998, 2002b). The value of an arbitrary instance is independently motivated to account for the behavior of the English indefinite article *a* in opaque contexts (*John wants to marry a dancer*) and the generic use of the indefinite article (*A cat is a mammal*).

3.4. Overall Results

The results obtained with respect to the meaning of the complement forms in individual languages present an interest both at the cross-linguistic and language-internal levels. Cross-linguistically, the complement systems of English, French, and Japanese are remarkably similar. First, they are all consistent with Givón's prediction that the forms that code more independent events resemble main/independent clauses more closely. In the three languages considered, we witnessed a striking isomorphism between the level of independence of the event in the complement and the form by which it is expressed. Second, the same kinds of events get coded as more or less independent in different languages. For example, directly perceived events are consistently coded by whatever morphosyntactic means indicate the highest possible level of conceptual integration in the language considered.

The similarities are even more striking if one overlooks the specific descriptive constructs invoked in a given language because of their particular relevance to that language. To give just one example, the notion of perspective is treated systematically in French, but it is also relevant to English. We have seen that both French and English code the way in which certain verbs code the self-to-self relation as similar or different from the self-to-other relation. However, in English, this contrast is quite restricted because it is only manifested in the choice between *to* and *for . . . to*. In French, it is more general and systematic because it is manifested by a language-wide constraint on same-different subject distribution, as well as decisions that pertain to indicative versus subjunctive mood selection and obviation. The important point, however, is that both languages code the same contrast at different levels of generality.

Language-internally, the most interesting result of Cognitive Linguistics research is the way in which it relates the meanings of the complement forms to the global ecology of individual languages. For example, in English the sameness of time constraint the *-ing*-form exhibits between the main and subordinate verbs is closely related to the meaning of *-ing* in participial clauses (*He came into the room screaming*), where simultaneity between the events expressed in the verb and the participle is also implied (Wierzbicka 1988). In a similar fashion, the future orientation of the complementizer *to* is directly related to the meaning of *to* as a preposition, namely, to express motion toward a goal (Duffley 1999; Smith and Escobedo 2001). Finally, in Japanese, the meaning of *to* as expressing the speaker's psychological distance is motivated by the expression's semantic characterization as representing remote, detached knowledge in other constructions (Suzuki 2000). This precise evaluation of the semantic role of the complement constructions in the global ecology of a given language cuts to the very core of the meaning of complement systems, because it may explain why certain languages code specific contrasts as opposed to other possible ones. For example, Horie (2000) shows that two languages as closely related as Korean and Japanese code different contrasts in their complement systems because of the importance those contrasts hold elsewhere in the language. He shows that Korean codes the realis-irrealis contrast as opposed to the event-proposition contrast relevant to Japanese because of a global tendency to code the realis-irrealis contrast throughout the language.

4. RAISING

In addition to issues pertaining to the overall structure of complementation systems, certain constructions have received individual attention in the literature because they clearly illustrate relevant theoretical concerns. For example, the syntactic behavior of the raising verbs figures prominently in the argumentation in favor of different levels of representation in different models of Generative Grammar (Chomsky 1965; Rosenbaum 1967). Because of their heightened theoretical status, these constructions deserve to be treated separately. This section presents raising constructions as an example to show that Cognitive Grammar can provide a satisfactory account of phenomena usually regarded as strictly structural.

4.1. Description of Raising

The facts about raising are well known. They are illustrated in (29)–(31).

(29) Mary seems to understand.
(30) Mary wants to understand.
(31) It seems that Mary understands.

Despite their similar surface form, the sentences in (29) and (30) are structurally quite different. First, *seem* imposes no restrictions on its subject, but *want* is usually only felicitous with animate subjects. Second, several structural tests were designed to show that while Mary is the real subject of *want*, it is not the real subject of *seem*, but rather that of *understand*. In order to capture this structural difference, generative linguists posited two separate underlying representations for raising (*seem*) and control (*want*) verbs. The raising verbs were assigned the underlying structure in (32), the control verbs the one in (33):[9]

(32) [$_{NP}$ e] seem [$_{S'}$ COMP [$_S$ Mary INFL [to understand]]]
(33) Mary want [$_{S'}$ COMP [$_S$ PRO INFL to understand]]

The underlying form in (32) yields the surface form in (29). *Mary* is moved to the position of subject of *seem*. If the move does not occur, the empty subject position is filled by the dummy *it* to satisfy the structural need for a surface subject, as illustrated in (31).

4.2. A Cognitive Grammar Solution

The Cognitive Grammar solution differs from the generative account on two major points. First, it argues that the relation that exists between the raised and unraised constructions is not a structural one, but one of construal (Langacker 1991, 1995). Second, it shows that the syntactic behavior of the raising verbs directly results from their semantic organization, which directly challenges the need to assign them a specific underlying representation.

Several researchers have pointed out that pairs of sentences such as (29) and (31) are not semantically equivalent (Newman 1981; Ruwet 1983). Raising verbs are therefore considered polysemous, each with a raised and an unraised variant. Each variant profiles the conceptualized scene in a different way. With the unraised variant in (31), the impersonal *it* represents an abstract setting within which the proposition in the complement can be located (Smith 1985; Langacker 1991, 1995; Achard 1998). That setting is given focal prominence and therefore marked as the subject. The event or proposition as a whole is the landmark of the main relation. In the raised variant in (29), the main participant in the located event is chosen as the trajector of the main relation. Reality remains off profile, as part of the base. The raised variant of *seem* therefore profiles the apparent participation of an entity in a given process.

In order for this analysis to be satisfying, we need to show that *Mary* can indeed be the subject of *seem* even though the latter is usually an event. This difficulty disappears, however, if we recognize Langacker's concept of active zones. The active zones of an entity are "those facets of an entity capable of interacting directly with a given domain or relation" (Langacker 1987: 485). With the raised variant, the complement process (*understand*) represents the subject's (*Mary*) active zone with respect to its participation in the main relation (*seem*). It is with respect to *understand* that *Mary* can be considered the subject of *seem*.

The choice of subject in both variants is a direct result of the raising verb's semantic structure.[10] Verbs such as *seem* code the way in which specific facets of reality reveal themselves to some conceptualizers, without any epistemic effort on their part. The only entities available for subject selection are therefore part of the conceptualized scene. If no participant is particularly salient, the abstract location within which the scene can be observed (i.e., the relevant part of reality) is chosen. This configuration corresponds to the unraised variant. Any participant in the complement scene can be chosen as the main subject because of its salience, and that choice corresponds to the raised variant. The selection of the raised or unraised variant therefore depends on the specific way in which the speaker chooses to structure his or her conceptualization for expressive purposes.

This analysis makes an interesting prediction concerning the discourse distribution of the raised and unraised variants:[11]

> It is claimed that, in *Don is likely to leave*, *Don* functions as a reference point with respect to the process of his leaving: the notion of leaving is accessed via the conception of *Don* and conceived in relation to that individual. The reference-point relationship is absent in the corresponding sentence *That Don will leave*

is likely, which consequently has a slightly different meaning. The 'raised' NP can be thought of as a kind of local topic, i.e. a topic for purposes of ascertaining the actual (or direct) participant in the profiled main-clause relationship (*Don* calls to mind a process involving *Don*, and such a process can be accessed for likelihood). It makes the prediction that raised NPs should tend to exhibit greater 'topicality' than their unraised counterparts. (Langacker 1995: 37–38)

I argue that this prediction is indeed borne out for French subject-to-subject raising constructions (Achard 2000). Using a corpus of journalistic prose, I show that the overwhelming majority of the subjects of the raised variant of *sembler* 'seem' are indeed cognitively accessible (topical or inferable), while the subjects of the unraised variant tend to be less accessible.

The semantic structure of the raising verbs directly accounts for the absence of restrictions placed on their subjects. It also explains their other syntactic behaviors. For example, in French, the distribution of the clitic *en* 'of it' is different with raising and control verbs.[12] This difference is illustrated in (35) and (36) (from Ruwet 1983: 17):

(35) a. *L'* *auteur* *de* *ce* *livre* *semble* *être* *génial.*
          the   author   of   this book   seems   be.INF brilliant
          'The author of this book seems to be brilliant.'

      b. *L'* *auteur* *de* *ce* *livre* *prétend* *être* *génial.*
          the   author   of   this book   pretends be. INF brilliant
          'The author of this book pretends to be brilliant.'

(36) a. *L'* *auteur* *semble* *en* *être* *génial.*
          the   author   seems   of.it be.INF brilliant
          'The author of it seems to be brilliant.'

      b. *L'* *auteur* *prétend* *en* *être* *génial.*
          the   author   pretends of.it be.INF brilliant
          'The author of it pretends to be brilliant.'

The examples in (35) and (36) show that the clitic *en* 'of it', replacing the prepositional phrase *de*-NP (*de ce livre*), part of the subject NP, can only be cliticized on the subordinate verbs when the main verb is a raising verb. In the case of a control verb such as (36b), the cliticization of *en* on the subordinate verb is impossible. I show that the distribution of *en* results from the interplay between the respective semantics of the raising and control verbs and that of the clitic *en* in the specific context of the test situation (Achard 2001).

5. CONCLUSION

This chapter has provided an overview of Cognitive Linguistics research on complementation. It presented the notion of conceptual subordination and showed the strong correlation that exists between the form of the complement and the level of independence of the event it codes. Several contrasts were introduced, coded by different constructions in English, Japanese, and French. These contrasts were shown to be relevant both language-internally and cross-linguistically. Finally, the Cognitive Grammar analysis of raising constructions was presented in order to illustrate the fact that a semantically based account can explain complex syntactic behavior in a satisfactory fashion. This overview is far from being exhaustive, but it should suffice to show that the area of complementation perfectly illustrates the isomorphism between form and function that stands at the core of Cognitive Linguistics.

Despite its promising beginning, however, cognitive research on complementation is far from being completed. In particular, the notion of conceptual subordination needs to be defined more specifically. The broad range of phenomena it covers has raised questions as to the legitimacy of considering the grammar of complementation as a single category. For example, Thompson (2002, 155) argues that in everyday English conversation, the grammar of complementation "may be better understood as a combination of an epistemic/evidential phrase together with a declarative or interrogative clause" (see also Englebretson 2003). This alternative analysis raises interesting issues. For example, is conceptual subordination as it was presented in this chapter predominantly a written-language phenomenon? Or is it more strongly relevant in particular languages? In order to precisely delineate the scope of complement research, we need to precisely describe constructions from a larger number of languages. Furthermore, the diachronic evolution of these constructions needs to be carefully investigated, both language-specifically and cross-linguistically.

NOTES

1. This definition is also valid for other subordinate structures, such as adverbial constructions and relative clauses (Langacker 1991; Cristofaro 1998, 2003).

2. Other researchers argue that *to*'s future orientation only represents one instance of a more abstract meaning of the complementizer, namely, to code the conceptual distance that exists between the main and subordinate clauses (Smith and Escobedo 2001).

3. These two contrasts are obviously related. The speaker can reasonably be more confident in the outcome of a process he or she is experiencing than in some other conceptualizer's experience.

4. In a compatible analysis, *that*-complements are characterized as belonging to the domain of discourse (*de dicto*), as opposed to the domain of reality (*de re*) in Frajzyngier and Jasperson (1991).

5. Other complementizers include *tokoro*, used to present a visually witnessed event (Horie 2000), *tte*, *toka*, and *nante*, which are argued to belong to the domain of discourse (*de dicto*) in Suzuki (2000).

6. This structural difference explains the glossing differences between *no* and *koto* on the one hand, and *to* on the other hand.

7. In certain cases, the infinitive is preceded by the prepositions *à* 'to' or *de* 'of'. The preposition obviously lends its own semantic import to the construction in which it occurs. Kemmer and Bat-Zeev Shyldkrot (1995) provide a semantic analysis of these prepositions. Achard (2002a) illustrates how their semantics contribute to the meaning of causative constructions.

8. The only case where the complement is an infinitive clause and the main and subordinate subjects are different is the perception/causation constructions illustrated in (19). These structures have their own individual history, and they are often considered separately in the literature. For a cognitive account of those constructions, see Talmy (1975, 1976, 1983, 1988), Kemmer and Verhagen (1994), Achard (1998), and Stefanowitsch (2001).

9. The rules in (32) and (33) are presented in the spirit of Chomsky's (1981) Government and Binding theory. They are simply intended to capture the spirit of the generative tradition, still very much alive in the current, more sophisticated models.

10. The difference in the semantic structure of raising and control verbs has received a fair amount of attention in the literature. Langacker (1995: 41) argues that a control predicate, such as *persuade*, designates "a complex DIRECT interaction between the trajector and the landmark." Conversely, the trajector of a raising predicate, such as *expect*, "does not directly interact with the landmark per se." In a compatible analysis, I argue that the subjects of French control verbs have a conceptualizing role with respect to the scene profiled in the complement whereas the subjects of the raising verbs do not (Achard 1998, 2001).

11. For an in-depth discussion of the notion of reference point, see Langacker (1993).

12. Among the battery of structural tests designed to differentiate between the raising and control verbs, the one based on *en*'s behavior represents in the words of Ruwet (1991: 56) "the most spectacular and most strictly syntactic."

REFERENCES

Achard, Michel. 1996. Perspective and syntactic realization. *Linguistics* 34: 1159–98.

Achard, Michel. 1998. *Representation of cognitive structures: Syntax and semantics of French complements*. Berlin: Mouton de Gruyter.

Achard, Michel. 2000. The distribution of French raising constructions. *Berkeley Linguistics Society* 26: 1–15.

Achard, Michel. 2001. The syntax of French raising verbs. In Alan Cienki, Barbara Luka, and Michael B. Smith, eds., *Conceptual and discourse factors in linguistic structure* 1–26. Stanford, CA: CSLI Publications.

Achard, Michel. 2002a. Causation, constructions, and language ecology: An example from French. In Masayoshi Shibatani, ed., *The grammar of causation and interpersonal manipulation* 127–55. Amsterdam: John Benjamins.

Achard, Michel. 2002b. The meaning and distribution of French mood inflections. In Frank Brisard, ed., *Grounding: The epistemic footing of deixis and reference* 197–249. Berlin: Mouton de Gruyter.

Beck, David. 2000. Nominalization as complementation in Bella Coola and Lushootseed. In Kaoru Horie, ed., *Complementation: Cognitive and functional perspectives* 121–47. Amsterdam: John Benjamins.

Bolinger, Dwight. 1968. Entailment and the meaning of structures. *Glossa* 2: 119–27.

Bolinger, Dwight. 1972. *That's that.* The Hague: Mouton.

Bolinger, Dwight. 1974. Concept and percept, two infinitive constructions and their vicissitudes. In *Working papers in phonetics: Festschrift for Dr. Onishi's Kiju* 65–91. Tokyo: Phonetic Society of Japan.

Borkin, Ann. 1973. *To be* or not *to be. Chicago Linguistic Society* 9: 44–56.

Chomsky, Noam. 1965. *Aspects of the theory of syntax.* Cambridge, MA: MIT Press.

Chomsky, Noam. 1981. *Lectures on government and binding.* Dordrecht: Foris.

Cristofaro, Sonia. 1998. Subordination strategies: A typological study. PhD dissertation, University of Pavia.

Cristofaro, Sonia. 2003. *Subordination.* Oxford: Oxford University Press.

Delbecque, Nicole. 2000. Cognitive constraints on complement clause cliticization in Spanish. In Kaoru Horie, ed., *Complementation: Cognitive and functional perspectives* 149–97. Amsterdam: John Benjamins.

Dirven, René. 1989. A cognitive perspective on complementation. In Dany Jaspers, Yvan Putseys, Wim Klooster, and Pieter Seuren, eds., *Sentential complementation and the lexicon: Studies in honor of Wim de Geest* 113–39. Dordrecht: Foris.

Dixon, Robert M. W. 1984. The semantic basis of syntactic properties. *Berkeley Linguistics Society* 10: 583–95.

Duffley, Patrick. 1999. The use of the infinitive and the *-ing* after verbs denoting the beginning, middle and end of an event. *Folia Linguistica* 33: 295–331.

Englebretson, Robert. 2003. *Searching for structure: The problem of complementation in colloquial Indonesian Conversation.* Amsterdam: John Benjamins.

Farkas, Donka. 1992. On obviation. In Ivan Sag and Anna Szabolcsi, eds., *Lexical matters* 85–109. Stanford, CA: CSLI Publications.

Frajzyngier, Zygmunt. 1991. The *de dicto* domain in language. In Elizabeth Closs Traugott and Bernd Heine, eds., *Approaches to grammaticalization*, vol. 1, *Focus on theoretical and methodological issues* 219–51. Amsterdam: John Benjamins.

Frajzyngier, Zygmunt, and Robert Jasperson. 1991. *That*-clauses and other complements. *Lingua* 83: 133–53.

Givón, Talmy. 1980. The binding hierarchy and the typology of complements. *Studies in Language* 4: 333–77.

Givón, Talmy. 1990. *Syntax: A functional-typological introduction.* Vol. 2. Amsterdam: John Benjamins.

Givón, Talmy. 1995. *Functionalism and grammar.* Amsterdam: John Benjamins.

Haiman, John. 1985. *Natural syntax: Iconicity and erosion.* Cambridge: Cambridge University Press.

Hooper, Joan. 1975. On assertive predicates. In John Kimball, ed., *Syntax and Semantics* 4: 91–124. New York: Academic Press.

Horie, Kaoru. 1993. A cross-linguistic study of perception and cognition verb complements: A cognitive perspective. PhD dissertation, University of Southern California.

Horie, Kaoru. 2000. Complementation in Japanese and Korean. In Kaoru Horie, ed., *Complementation: Cognitive and functional perspectives* 11–31. Amsterdam: John Benjamins.

Jespersen, Otto. 1909–42. *A modern English grammar on historical principles.* 6 vols. London: George Allen and Unwin.

Josephs, Lewis. 1976. Complementation. In Masayoshi Shibatani, ed., *Syntax and semantics*, vol. 3, *Japanese generative grammar* 307–70. New York: Academic Press.

Karttunen, Lauri. 1971. Implicative verbs. *Language* 47: 340–58.

Kemmer, Suzanne, and Hava Bat-Zeev Shyldkrot. 1995. The semantics of "empty prepositions" in French. In Eugene H. Casad, ed., *Cognitive linguistics in the Redwoods* 347–88. Berlin: Mouton de Gruyter.

Kemmer, Suzanne, and Arie Verhagen. 1994. The grammar of causatives and the conceptual structure of events. *Cognitive Linguistics* 5: 115–56.

Kiparsky, Paul, and Carol Kiparsky. 1970. Fact. In Manfred Bierwisch and Karl E. Heidolph, eds., *Progress in linguistics* 143–73. The Hague: Mouton.

Kuno, Susumu. 1973. *The structure of the Japanese language*. Cambridge, MA: MIT Press.

Langacker, Ronald W. 1985. Observations and speculations on subjectivity. In John Haiman, ed., *Iconicity in syntax* 109–50. Amsterdam: John Benjamins.

Langacker, Ronald W. 1987. *Foundations of cognitive grammar*. Vol. l, *Theoretical prerequisites*. Stanford, CA: Stanford University Press.

Langacker, Ronald W. 1990. Subjectification. *Cognitive Linguistics* 1: 5–38.

Langacker, Ronald W. 1991. *Foundations of cognitive grammar*. Vol. 2, *Descriptive application*. Stanford, CA: Stanford University Press.

Langacker, Ronald W. 1993. Reference-point constructions. *Cognitive Linguistics* 4: 1–38.

Langacker, Ronald W. 1995. Raising and transparency. *Language* 71: 1–62.

Langacker, Ronald W. 2002. The control cycle: Why grammar is a matter of life and death. *Proceedings of the Annual Meeting of the Japanese Cognitive Linguistics Association* 2: 193–220.

Newman, John. 1981. The semantics of raising constructions. PhD dissertation, University of California at San Diego.

Ney, James. 1981. *Semantic structures for the syntax of complements and auxiliaries in English*. The Hague: Mouton.

Noonan, Michael. 1985. Complementation. In Timothy Shopen, ed., *Language typology and syntactic description* 2: 42–140. Cambridge: Cambridge University Press.

Polinsky, Maria. 2000. Variation in complementation constructions: Long-distance agreement in Tsez. In Kaoru Horie, ed., *Complementation: Cognitive and functional perspectives* 59–90. Amsterdam: John Benjamins.

Rosenbaum, Peter. 1967. *The grammar of English predicate complement constructions*. Cambridge, MA: MIT Press.

Ruwet, Nicolas. 1983. Montée et contrôle: Une question à revoir? In Michael Herslund, Ole Mørdrup, and Finn Sørensen, eds., *Analyses Grammaticales du Français: Études publiées à l'occasion du 50e anniversaire de Carl Vikner* 17–37. Copenhagen: I kommission hos Akademisk forlag.

Ruwet, Nicolas. 1984. Je veux partir/*Je veux que je parte. A propos de la distribution des complétives à temps fini et des compléments à l'infinitif en Français. *Cahiers de Grammaire* 7 : 75–138.

Ruwet, Nicolas. 1991. *Syntax and human experience*. Chicago: University of Chicago Press.

Smith, Michael B. 1985. An analysis of German dummy subject construction in cognitive grammar. In Scott DeLancey and Russell S. Tomlin, eds., *Proceedings of the First Annual Meeting of the Pacific Linguistics Conference* 412–25. Eugene: University of Oregon, Department of Linguistics.

Smith, Michael B., and Joyce Escobedo. 2001. The semantics of English *to*-infinitival vs. -*ing* verb complement constructions. *Chicago Linguistic Society* 37: 549–63.

Stefanowitsch, Anatol. 2001. Constructing causation: A construction grammar approach to analytic causatives. PhD dissertation, Rice University.

Suzuki, Satoko. 1996. Incorporation of information and complementizers in Japanese. *Pragmatics* 6: 511–51.

Suzuki, Satoko. 2000. *De dicto* complementation in Japanese. In Kaoru Horie, ed., *Complementation: Cognitive and functional perspectives* 33–57. Amsterdam: John Benjamins.

Talmy, Leonard. 1975. Semantics and syntax of motion. In John P. Kimball, ed., *Syntax and semantics* 4: 181–238. New York: Academic Press.

Talmy, Leonard. 1976. Semantic causative types. In Masayoshi Shibatani, ed., *Syntax and semantics*, vol. 6, *The grammar of causative constructions* 43–116. New York: Academic Press.

Talmy, Leonard. 1983. How language structures space. In Herbert L. Pick, Jr., and Linda Acredolo, eds., *Spatial orientation: Theory, research and application* 225–82. New York: Plenum Press.

Talmy, Leonard. 1988. Force dynamics in language and cognition. *Cognitive Science* 12: 49–100.

Thompson, Sandra A. 2002. "Objects complements" and conversation towards a realistic account. *Studies in Language* 26: 125–64.

Verspoor, Marjolijn. 1999. *To* infinitives. In Leon de Stadler, ed., *Issues in cognitive linguistics* 505–26. Berlin: Mouton de Gruyter.

Verspoor, Marjolijn. 2000. Iconicity in English complement constructions. In Kaoru Horie, ed., *Complementation: Cognitive and functional perspectives* 199–225. Amsterdam: John Benjamins.

Wierzbicka, Anna. 1988. *The semantics of grammar*. Amsterdam: John Benjamins.

Wood, Frederick. 1956. Gerund versus infinitive. *English Language Teaching* 11: 11–16.

CHAPTER 31

TENSE AND ASPECT

RONNY BOOGAART
AND THEO JANSSEN

1. INTRODUCTION

When using a *tensed* clause, the speaker indicates that the situation[1] described in the clause relates to an evaluative situation (usually the speech situation)[2] and how the situation described relates to the evaluative situation. By indicating the relationship between the situation described and the evaluative situation, the speaker contextualizes the situation described into the current discourse.[3] In view of its contextualizing function, tense is called a deictic or grounding category. The evaluative situation functions as the deictic center, vantage point, or ground (defined by Langacker as the speech event, its participants, and its setting; Langacker 1987, 1994) to which the situation described is related.

The *aspectual* information in a clause provides information on how the language user conceives of the *internal* temporal constituency of the situation described in that clause (Comrie 1976). In using aspect, the language user indicates whether this situation is construed as either bounded or unbounded. Since aspect does not serve to link the situation externally to the evaluative situation, aspect is not considered a deictic or grounding category. In the absence of tense marking, however, aspect can have a deictic effect (see section 3.1).

This chapter will address the description of tense (section 2) and aspect (section 3) separately, with the relation between tense and aspect being discussed in section 3.1. In sections 2 and 3, we will present the principal issues of tense and aspect as they are discussed in the traditional literature. We will then consider the specific contribution of Cognitive Linguistics in these areas. General cognitive linguistic

Table 31.1. Tense forms according to Reichenbach's tense analysis (x—y stands for 'x precedes y' x = y stands for 'x and y coincide')

	Anterior (E−R)	*Simple (E=R)*	*Posterior (R−E)*
PAST (R−S)	ANTERIOR PAST *had left*	SIMPLE PAST *left*	POSTERIOR PAST *would leave*
PRESENT (S=R)	ANTERIOR PRESENT *has left*	SIMPLE PRESENT *leaves*	POSTERIOR PRESENT *will leave*
FUTURE (S−R)	ANTERIOR FUTURE *will have left*	SIMPLE FUTURE *will leave*	POSTERIOR FUTURE *will be going to leave*

issues addressed here in particular are the symbolic nature of tense and aspect, that is, as representing pairings of form and meaning, and the idea that meaning can be identified with conceptualization.

The chapter will conclude with some remarks on future research into tense and aspect phenomena (section 4).

2. TENSE

First, we will deal with the question of which elements can be considered to be tense forms (section 2.1) and subsequently what meaning these forms signal and how they do it (section 2.2).

2.1. Form

Tense forms, which are usually understood as denoting temporal relations involving the referential categories of past, present, and future, are formally different across languages. Some tense forms belong to a morphological category comprising single, finite verb forms; other tense forms are clusters of finite, auxiliary verb forms and one or more nonfinite verb forms. It is only due to their notional and functional coherence that formally different categories can be assumed to constitute a single linguistic system.

The most influential account of a time-based morphosyntactic system of tenses is the analysis proposed by Reichenbach (1947). Reichenbach proposed a system of nine tenses, each encoding a temporal relation of the time of the event (E) with respect to the point of reference (R) *and* a temporal relation of the point of reference (R) with respect to the time of speech (S). Both E and R and R and S may enter into relations of coincidence and precedence, as is shown in table 31.1.

The temporal relations in table 31.1 can be illustrated with Reichenbach's (1947: 293) examples (1) and (2).

(1)   I did not know that you would be here.

Clause$_1$:   *I did not know* $E_1 = R_1 - \quad\quad S$

Clause$_2$:   *(that) you would be here* $R_2 - E_2 = S$

The characterization of clause$_1$, expressed as E=R–S, and the characterization of clause$_2$, expressed as R–E=S, indicate that both clauses share the time of speech as well as the point of reference; furthermore, the time of the event in clause$_1$ precedes the time of the event in clause$_2$.

Reichenbach's example (2) illustrates the temporal relation between a clause in the anterior past and two clauses in the simple past.

(2)   I had mailed the letter when John came and told me the news.

Clause$_1$:   *I had mailed the letter* $E_1 - R_1 - S$

Clause$_2$:   *John came* $E_2 = R_2 - S$

Clause$_3$:   *[John] told me the news* $E_3 = R_3 - S$

Clause$_1$ shares s and R with clause$_2$ and clause$_3$. As the diagram of sentence (2) shows, the situations of clause$_2$ and clause$_3$ occur when the situation in clause$_1$ has ended. However, sentence (2) can be interpreted in two ways: in one interpretation, there is an interval of time between the time at which the speaker finished mailing the letter (E_1) and the time at which John came (E_2); in the more likely interpretation, there is also a time interval between the time at which John came ($E_2 = R_2$) and the time at which he told the speaker the news ($E_3 = R_3$). Because of the time gap between R_2 and R_3, R cannot represent a temporal *point*; however, if R represents a *stretch* of time, another problem arises, since R_2 and R_3 in (2) do not share one single stretch of time. Regardless of how it is defined, the notion of "point of reference," or rather "time of reference," is the most controversial issue of Reichenbach's tense analysis.[4]

Two of Reichenbach's tense characterizations allow for more than one temporal structure. The posterior past, as exemplified in clause$_2$ in (1), is characterized as R–E=s, but it can also be characterized as R–E–s (*[I did not know that] you would be there yesterday*) or as R–s–E (*[I did not know that] you would be there tomorrow*). The anterior future (*will have left*) can be characterized as E–s–R, E=s–R, and s–E–R. Furthermore, Reichenbach does not provide a characterization of the conditional perfect (past future perfect), such as *would have left*. Possible combinations are $E-R_1$ (the *left* time relates to the *have* time), R_1-R_2 (the *have* time relates to the *would* time), and R_2-s (the *would* time relates to the speech time) (Comrie 1981: 27; 1985: 76–77).

Form/meaning-oriented approaches to the English tenses only assume two types of tense form: the present-tense forms (e.g., *leaves*) and the past-tense forms (e.g., *left*). Since the so-called complex tenses are understood as sponging on their finite auxiliaries, they are not considered tense forms as such.[5]

In the next section, we will see that Reichenbach's two temporal dimensions (the relation of E with R and the relation of R with S), in which R is the cardinal point, also serve in most of the analyses in which the tense system is reduced to the present and past tense. And even those tense analyses which are not based on the notion of time can be assumed to have a two-dimensional quality in order for us to understand the role of tense in the contextualization of the situation described. We will now turn to the two-dimensionality of tense within Cognitive Linguistics, and discuss the status of the various notions proposed as alternates for the Reichenbachian time of reference.

2.2 Meaning

In Cognitive Linguistics, some scholars analyze tense as based on time (Paprotté 1988; Taylor 1989; Dinsmore 1991; Cutrer 1994; Harder 1996; Michaelis 1998; Langacker 2001b; Wada 2001), whereas others consider time to be epiphenomenal in the analysis of tense (Langacker 1978; Janssen 1987; Brisard 1999).[6] We will first discuss the time-based analyses by Cutrer (1994) and Harder (1996) and then turn to a number of analyses that reject time as a necessary notion for the analysis of tense. With regard to both types of tense analysis, we will focus on the notions proposed as alternatives to Reichenbach's R.

2.2.1. *Tense Analyses Based on Time*

Cutrer (1994) analyzes tense within the framework of mental space theory: as such, she uses the descriptive concepts of "Base space" (Fauconnier 1985), "Viewpoint space" (Sweetser and Fauconnier 1996: 12–16), "Focus space" (Dinsmore 1991), "Event space" (Cutrer 1994: 71–75), and the distinction between FACT and PREDICTION (Cutrer 1994: 22, 156, 171; see also King 1983: 115). She proposes "characterizations of a set of putatively universal tense-aspect categories: {PRESENT, PAST, FUTURE, PERFECT, PROGRESSIVE, IMPERFECTIVE, PERFECTIVE}," whereby "each tense-aspect category is a universal type of discourse link between spaces" (Cutrer 1994: 22). The way she describes, for instance, the categories PRESENT and PAST is shown in (3) and (4) and graphically represented in figures 31.1 and 31.2 (Cutrer 1994: 88–89; Fauconnier 1997: 75–76).[7]

(3)   PRESENT applied to space M indicates that:
    a. M is in FOCUS,
    b. M or M's parent space is viewpoint,
    c. the time frame represented in M is *not* prior to viewpoint/base, and
    d. events or properties represented in M are FACTS.

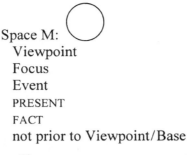

Space M:
   Viewpoint
   Focus
   Event
   PRESENT
   FACT
   not prior to Viewpoint/Base

Figure 31.1. PRESENT TENSE

(4)   PAST applied to space N indicates that:
   a. N is in focus,
   b. N's parent space is viewpoint,
   c. N's time is prior to viewpoint, and
   d. events or properties represented in N are FACT (from viewpoint).

In figure 31.1, space M (not prior to the base space) comprises the Viewpoint space, the Focus space, and the Event space. In figure 31.2, space N comprises the Focus space and the Event space.

The concepts of Viewpoint space, Focus space, and Event space resemble Reichenbach's S, R, and E, respectively. The FACT-PREDICTION dichotomy serves to distinguish between posterior events, which are presented as (scheduled) facts, and posterior events, which are presented as being predictions (Cutrer 1994: 22, 156–62, 171–79).

Harder's (1996: 326) time-based analysis assumes two deictic tenses, the present and past, and six relational tenses inside the scope of the present and past, as is illustrated in the structure in (5).

(5)   'past'/'present' (+/–'future' (+/–'perfect' (state-of-affairs)))

Within the framework of his functional-interactive semantics, Harder describes the meanings of the present and past tense as in (6) and (7), where the "points-of-application" S and P "denote directions-of-pointing, not actual times" (Harder 1996: 327–28).

(6)   The meaning of the present tense is to direct the addressee to identify a point-of-application S (a situation as it is at the time S of speech) as that which the state-of-affairs in its scope applies to.

(7)   The meaning of the past tense is to direct the addressee to identify a point-of-application P (a situation as it is at time P (such that P lies before S)) as that which the state-of-affairs in its scope applies to.

Harder (1996: 328) adds to these characterizations, stating that "both deictic tenses point from the 'basis time', i.e., utterance time, toward a 'function time,'" that is, a point-of-application. Thus, both points-of-application can be considered

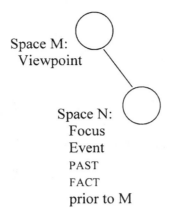

Space M:
Viewpoint

Space N:
Focus
Event
PAST
FACT
prior to M

Figure 31.2. PAST TENSE

to be analogical to the Reichenbachian time of reference (see also Harder 1996: 342, 404). In order to account for various modal uses of the past tense, Harder (1996: 344) characterizes P as "a non-actual point of application P*."

2.2.2.   Tense Analyses Not Based on Time

The relevance of a nontemporal approach to tense arises from a series of descriptive problems which cannot be accounted for by an analysis based on the notion of time. First, there are problems such as the temporal relation between the RS in Reichenbach's sentence (2). Second, in many languages the past-tense forms apply to nonpast situations. And third, present-tense forms may apply to past or future situations.

Reichenbach's sentence (2), *I had mailed the letter when John came and told me the news,* can be interpreted as follows: there is an interval of time between the time at which the speaker finished the mailing of the letter and the time at which John came and also between the time at which John came and the time at which he told the speaker the news. Since the RS of the situations involved do not share one single point or stretch of time, the question is how the obvious connection of the situations involved can adequately be accounted for within a time-based framework.[8]

In many (non-)Indo-European languages, past-tense forms can be used to indicate nonpast situations; witness (8)–(15).[9]

(8)   It is time we had a holiday. (Leech 1987: 14)
(9)   Would you like some peas? (Leech 1987: 119)
(10) If I had time, I would write to you. (Fleischman 1989: 5)
(11) *Si   j'   avais   le   temps, je t'   écrirais.*
      If   I   have.PST   the   time   I   you write.FUTPST
      'If I had time, I would write to you.' (Fleischman 1989: 5)
(12) *Si   tuviera   tiempo, te   escribiría.*
      If   I have.PSTSUBJ time   you   write.FUTPST
      'If I had time, I would write to you.' (Fleischman 1989: 5)

(13)   *Desiderava?*
       wanted.you
       'What did you want?' (/'May I help you?')

                                              (Bazanella 1990: 444)

(14)   *Ik   vertrok   graag   morgen.*
       I   left   with.pleasure   tomorrow
       'I would like to leave tomorrow.'

                                              (Janssen 1994: 122)

(15)   *Nou,   maar   ik   vertrok   morgen!*
       Well   but   I   left   tomorrow
       'Well, but I left (was supposed to leave) tomorrow!'

                                              (Janssen 1994: 122)

Furthermore, present-tense forms can be used to indicate nonpresent situations.[10]
Let us first consider past situations encoded by present-tense form, as in (16)–(20).

(16)   Ex-champ dies. (headline reporting the death of a former boxer; Leech
       1987: 12)

(17)   A man holds portraits of his relatives Saturday at Babi Yar. (photo-
       graphic caption, *Washington Post*, 7 October 1991; see also Leech 1987: 12;
       Langacker 2001a: 270)[11]

(18)   John tells me you're getting a new car. (Leech 1987: 11)

(19)   Fred,   iemand   vraagt   naar   je.   Kom   je   even?
       Fred   someone   ask.PRS   for   you   come   you   just
       'Fred, somebody is asking for you. Will you come here for a minute?'

(20)   Paul: Huh! [Pause] Huh! [Pause] Huh! [Jamie grabs the paper and reads it]
       Jamie: Huh!
       Paul: That's all I'm saying.
       (in a sitcom, Paul is reading a paper and Jamie is working nearby)

(21)   *Gisteravond   vertrok   je   morgen   en   nu   vertrek   je*
       last.night   left   you   tomorrow   and   now   leave.PRS   you
       overmorgen!   Wat   moet ik   nu   geloven?
       the.day.after.tomorrow   what   must I   now   believe
       'Last night you were leaving tomorrow and now you are leaving the day after
         tomorrow! What am I supposed to believe?' (Janssen 1994: 122; also
         Huddleston 1969: 787)

Example (17) is noteworthy in that it shows seemingly opposite deictics: the
present-tense form goes together with an adverbial indicating a past interval of
time. In (18)–(20), the telling, asking, and saying (which are in the past) do not even
partly overlap with the (present) time of speech. Here, the use of the present tense
can be explained by the fact that it indicates a past action with an ongoing effect in
the current communicative situation (Leech 1987: 11). Still, this does not alter the
fact that the action took place in the past. Such discrepancies cannot be accounted
for coherently in exclusively temporal terms. From a time-based tense perspective,
the situations referred to must be temporally related to the time of speech. From a

linguistic perspective (i.e., on the basis of purely linguistic indications), however, a temporal link can be conceived of as being merely epiphenomenal. In the first conjunct of example (21), the past-tense form *vertrok* 'left, was leaving' co-occurs with both the past time adverb *gisteravond* 'last night' and the future time adverb *morgen* 'tomorrow'. This relationship contrasts with the relationship between the time adverb and tense form in the second conjunct, which we turn to now.

In the second conjunct of (21) and in (22), the situations referred to are situated in the future.

(22)   Tomorrow is Sunday.

In the second conjunct of (21), the present-tense form *vertrek* 'leave, are leaving' co-occurs with both the present time adverb *nu* 'now' and the future time adverb *overmorgen* 'the day after tomorrow'. In English, present-tense forms can be used for future situations if "the constitution, order, schedule, habit of things is such that the occurrence can be expected to take place" (Calver 1946: 323; see also Langacker 1991: 263–66; 2001b), as is the case in (22). In Dutch, the present-tense form has a somewhat wider range of uses: it signals that the situation in question is (considered to be) on the agenda.

Let us now consider the non-time-based tense analyses of Langacker (1978, 1991), Brisard (1999), and Janssen (1989, 1991, 1993, 2002).

Langacker (1991: 242–46) holds that present and past tense are grounding predications which relate a situation to an "epistemic" domain. Since the situation is regarded as directly accessible to the language users, they accept it as old information. Langacker relates this acceptance of a directly accessible situation as old information to the definiteness (mental contact with a referent) of demonstratives. In particular, he relates the proximal/distal contrast in demonstratives to the present/ past distinction. In other words, in his view, the English present- and past-tense forms signal a proximal/distal distinction, whereby the present/pasttime interpretation is merely one possible instantiation of this distinction, albeit the prototypical one. The proximal form indicates that the situation described is actual and immediate to the ground (in particular the time of speaking). The distal form indicates the nonimmediacy of the situation described: "Distance within reality normally amounts to 'past tense'" (Langacker 1994: 141). The term "distal" suggests distance from the ground "not in a temporal but in an epistemic sense" (Langacker 1978: 869).

Brisard (1999, 2002), elaborating on Langacker's idea of the epistemic status of tenses, defines the present tense in terms of givenness and presence (immediacy) (1999: 367) and the past tense in terms of givenness and nonpresence (absence/ nonimmediacy) (1999: 353). He explicitly rejects Langacker's distinctive terms "proximal" and "distal" in order to avoid "a metaphorical interpretation of 'distance', in which temporal distance ('pastness') is shifted to the domain of epistemic reasoning ('hypotheticalness')" (Brisard 1999: 235). The notion of givenness is the function that is assigned to the notion "time of reference" in other analyses.

Janssen (1987, 2002) relates tense to other types of deixis, such as demonstratives.[12] He examines how a situation to be described is contextualized by means of a deictic element, whereby he assumes a vantage point from which the language user, and possibly the addressee, surveys a mental field of vision. In the case of tense, the mental field of vision is divided into two contexts-of-situation, such that a verb in the present-tense form signals 'VERB-in-THIS-context-of-situation', whereas a verb in the past-tense form signals 'VERB-in-THAT-context-of-situation'.

The Reichenbachian relation between s and r is, in Janssen's analysis, accounted for by the relation of the speaker's, and possibly the addressee's, vantage point (usually the speech situation) with either THIS-context-of-situation (the current mental field's region of focal concern) or THAT-context-of-situation (the current mental field's region of disfocal concern). The situation described by means of a tensed clause is assumed to occupy the relevant context-of-situation. Thus, the relevant context-of-situation is considered the situation's direct frame of reference.

Since Janssen replaces r by a situational frame of reference, his approach to the three situations of sentence (2), which are temporally different but situationally related, allows for a meaningful coherent connection between the situations involved. This connection follows from the situated interpretation by the addressee. The three situations in sentence (2) can be conceived of as related to one single situational frame of reference, namely the one indicated by means of the relative temporal adverb *when* (Janssen 1998).

The postulation of the reference point, or frame, in the semantics of tense is not undisputed. The notion serves primarily to explain why situations presented by means of a finite, or tensed, form are conceived of as definite: there has to be a unique relationship with the time or frame of reference given by the context or situation. In this view, the notion can be used to distinguish, for instance, between the interpretation of the simple past and the present perfect in languages like English and Dutch. In the present perfect construction, the main verb is a nonfinite form (past participle); therefore, the construction can be used to present situations that are *not* linked to an already given time or frame of reference, but that are 'all new'. However, some tensed forms, such as the simple past tense in English, may also signal 'indefinite past'. See (23) and (24).

(23) Cicero was executed by Marcus Antonius. (Michaelis 1998: 225)
(24) What happened to your sister? She bought a gold-mine. (adapted from
      Heny 1982: 134)

In order for (23) and (24) to be felicitous, no time or frame has to be given beforehand. For such sentences, therefore, a one-dimensional analysis of the past tense (whereby the situation precedes the evaluative situation) seems to be sufficient. Given such cases, in which no r seems to be needed, it is questionable whether "definiteness" and the notion of r can be considered to be present in the semantics of tense or whether, as Michaelis (1998: 226) argues, the English simple past tense is unmarked with respect to this feature. Boogaart (1999) has argued that the presence or absence of r, as well as the "definiteness" of tense, is a matter of aspect rather than tense. The imperfective past requires a previously given, or inferable, reference time, whereas the perfective past—which, in Boogaart's view, includes eventive clauses in English such as (23) and (24)—is compatible with such a definite reading, but does not require it.

3. Aspect

Whereas tense locates a situation with respect to the evaluative situation (usually the time of speech), aspect does not serve any such deictic, or grounding, function. Rather than linking the situation externally to the discourse's ground, aspect concerns the internal temporal structure of situations (Comrie 1976). More specifically, aspect indicates whether a situation is conceptualized as unbounded (imperfective aspect) or as bounded (perfective aspect).[13]

Before addressing the form (section 3.2) and meaning (section 3.3) of aspect, we will first make some remarks on the interaction between aspect and tense (section 3.1).

3.1. Aspect and Tense

In order to determine whether a situation is either "in progress" or "completed" (aspect), some evaluative situation is arguably needed, just as it is the case for the category of tense. However, the evaluative situation needed for the interpretation of aspect does not necessarily consist of the ground of the discourse (the point of speech). For instance, a situation may be ongoing at a point in time preceding the point of speech (imperfective past), at the point of speech itself (imperfective present), or at a point in time which is future with respect to the point of speech (imperfective future): *I was reading a book, I am reading a book, I will be reading a book*. Therefore, aspect is not considered a deictic category and is, in principle, independent of tense. In terms of Cognitive Grammar, both tense and aspect delimit what counts as the profiled part of a situation, but they do so at different levels. For instance, the English progressive (aspect) imposes an "immediate scope" that excludes the end point of a situation; tense marking, as either present or past, imposes its own "immediate scope" which is located with respect to the time of speaking (Langacker 2001b: 259–61).

In spite of this, the categories of aspect and tense do interact. This is most clearly illustrated by the incompatibility of present tense and perfective aspect: a situation cannot be simultaneously complete (perfective aspect) and valid at the moment of speech (present tense). In English, events (as opposed to states) presented by means of a simple tense get a perfective reading. The event is interpreted as a completed whole. If the tense is past, as in (25a), the tense-aspect combination does not constitute a problem. But if the tense is present, as in (25b), the sense of completion (aspect) clashes with the semantic contribution of the present tense. Therefore, (25b) is infelicitous, unless it receives a habitual reading.[14]

(25)   a. He learnt the poem.
        b. He learns the poem.

(Langacker 1999: 223)

Similarly, perfective forms are usually interpreted as referring to the past if tense marking is lacking (see Moore 2000).[15] In their large-scale typological research,

Dahl (1985) and Bybee, Perkins, and Pagliuca (1994) likewise found that perfective forms typically describe events that are in the past. Thus, even though aspect is not a deictic category, aspectual information sometimes enables one to infer temporal location with respect to the ground.

3.2. Form

Information about the internal temporal structure of situations, that is, aspectual information, can be expressed in different ways. The traditional literature on aspect often makes a distinction between aspectual information present in lexical items, most notably verbs, and aspectual information as expressed by language-specific grammatical means, such as the perfective-imperfective morphology in Slavic languages. The first type of aspectual information is referred to as *lexical aspect* or *Aktionsart*. The second type is labeled as *grammatical aspect* or simply *aspect* (see Binnick 1991: 135–214 on the history of the terms). The distinction between lexical aspect and grammatical aspect raises interesting questions: Is it necessary to make the distinction at all? If one does make the distinction, then how do the two sub-systems of aspect interact? And where do constructions like the English progressive fit in the picture?

Vendler (1967) made an influential contribution to the study of lexical aspect when he proposed his "four time schemata implied by the use of English verbs" (144). He divided the verbs of English into four classes depending on (i) whether or not the situation as expressed by the verb has duration, (ii) whether the situation involves change, and (iii) whether the situation is telic, that is, has an "inherent end point." This results in the four so-called Vendler classes, given in (26) with some of Vendler's own examples.

(26) a. STATE (durative, no change, atelic), e.g., *have, possess, know, love, hate*
      b. ACTIVITY (durative, change, atelic), e.g., *walk, swim, push, pull*
      c. ACCOMPLISHMENT (durative, change, telic), e.g., *paint a picture, build a house*
      d. ACHIEVEMENT (nondurative, change, telic), e.g., *recognize, stop, start*

The class to which a given verb belongs can be detected by "diagnostic tests," such as its compatibility with the progressive—which distinguishes states from nonstates—or with adverbial phrases as *in/for x hours* (see Dowty 1979). The latter is illustrated in (27) and (28).

(27) a. He walked *for two hours.*
      b. ?He walked a mile *for two hours.*
(28) a. ?He walked *in two hours.*
      b. He walked a mile *in two hours.*

Atelic predicates like *walk* in (27a) can be combined with *for*-adverbials, whereas telic predicates such as *walk a mile* in (27b) cannot, unless they receive an iterative reading. The reverse is true for adverbials of the *in x hours* kind: they are fine with telic predicates, as in (28b), but marked with telic predicates, as in (28a), which can only get a kind of inceptive reading.

Even though Vendler's classes are referred to as *verb classes*, it should be apparent that in order to determine *Aktionsart*, looking at verbs alone does not suffice. According to the test in (27)–(28), the verb *walk* by itself is atelic, whereas the predicate *walk a mile* is telic. But if other elements in the clause co-determine "lexical" aspect, this raises questions as to the usefulness of classifying verbs as such. The problem is all the more urgent since the influence of other elements in the clause is not restricted to the direct object. The nature of the subject should equally be taken into account (e.g., *Lotsa people walked a mile for two hours*). This suggests that *Aktionsart* is a property of complete clauses rather than a property of verbs or predicates. Verkuyl (1993) has shown that it can be built up compositionally out of the temporal information given by the verb and the nontemporal information provided by its arguments, in other words, whether or not they designate a "specified quantity."

Independently of the Vendler-Dowty tradition, which dealt with lexical aspect, there was a long-standing tradition of studies into the perfective/imperfective distinction as expressed in, for instance, Slavic languages and in the past tenses of the Romance languages. Early on, Garey (1957) made clear that, semantically, the grammatical distinction between perfective and imperfective aspect cannot be equated with the telic/atelic distinction assumed by the lexical tradition. More specifically, a telic situation has an inherent end point, independently of whether it is presented by means of a perfective past, like the French *passé simple* and *passé composé*, or by means of an imperfective past, such as the French *imparfait*. The independence of *Aktionsart* and aspect is shown in (29) (Garey 1957: 106).[16]

(29)   Imperfective   Perfective
     Telic   *Pierre arrivait*   *Pierre est arrivé*
     Atelic   *Pierre jouait*   *Pierre a joué*

The situation described by the French verb *arriver* 'to arrive' is telic, but it may be presented by either the imperfective past *imparfait* (*arrivait*) or the perfective past *passé composé* (*est arrivé*). Whereas a perfective past sets up a telic situation as a complete whole, an imperfective past presents a situation from an internal viewpoint, as being in progress at a particular point in time, and it does not necessarily imply that the inherent end point of the telic situation was actually reached. (However, in the case of nondurative situation types, such as expressed by *arriver*, the begin point and the end point of the situation more or less coincide so it is hard to imagine a context for *Pierre arrivait* in which Pierre did not actually arrive.) Likewise, the verb *jouer* 'to play' presents an atelic situation, but such a situation may still be presented either imperfectively (*jouait*) or perfectively (*a joué*). Atelic situation types do not, at the level of *Aktionsart*, have a natural end point, but when such a state of affairs is presented by means of a perfective form, it is understood to have ended at some, relatively arbitrary, point in time. The distinction between telicity and perfectivity, and thus between lexical aspect and grammatical aspect, is well known in the aspect literature. Morphological expression by means of affixes, such as in Slavic languages, is not considered a precondition for talking about (grammatical) aspect: the term is used also for periphrastic constructions like the French *passé composé* in (29) and the English progressive. The latter construction is usually regarded as a subcategory, or a restricted application, of the category imperfective aspect (Comrie 1976), the main restriction being that it cannot be used with most stative predicates (?*He is having blond hair*).

In the cognitive linguistic literature, the distinction between lexical and grammatical aspect is usually not made at all, and traditional labels are used to denote different concepts. We will briefly discuss the approaches to aspect advocated by Langacker, Croft, and Michaelis.

According to Langacker (1999: 223), "English verbs divide into two broad aspectual classes, my terms for which are *perfective* and *imperfective*." The distinction is of a "primal character," since it is related to the basic cognitive capacity of perceiving change (perfective) or the lack thereof (imperfective) (Langacker 1987: 258). As a diagnostic for classifying a verb as either perfective or imperfective, Langacker uses its compatibility with the progressive form: only perfectives occur in the progressive. The same test was used by Vendler to distinguish states from nonstates. Consequently, Langacker's perfective processes cannot be equated with the telic situation types from the traditional literature discussed above. More specifically, Vendler's atelic activity verbs (*walk, swim, sleep*) denote perfective processes in Langacker's approach (see Kochanska 2000: 144).

While the "grammatical" terminology of perfective/imperfective aspect is applied here to a Vendler-like lexical classification of verbs, Langacker does warn against treating these classes as a rigid lexical partitioning: verbs may have a default value, but the aspectual interpretation of a given expression is "flexibly and globally determined" (1999: 390, note 14). This is illustrated in (30).

(30)   a. The road winds through the mountains.
       b. The road is winding through the mountains.

The verb *wind* in (30a) is imperfective; the sentence does not express change. The verb *wind* in (30b), however, is considered by Langacker to be a perfective verb since it is used in the progressive form. These sentences, therefore, nicely illustrate the crucial role of construal in the domain of aspect: one and the same situation may be construed as either perfective or imperfective. To complicate matters, the progressive itself, providing an internal perspective on a perfective process, is called an "imperfectivizing device," making the process expressed by the sentence (30b) as a whole imperfective. As the discussion of (30) shows, Langacker does not make a fundamental distinction between lexical and grammatical aspect but rather subsumes both under the common concept of "perfectivity," which is applied to verbs, constructions, as well as to complete expressions.

Croft (1998) refers to Langacker's perfective and imperfective processes as *actions* (involving change) and *states* (involving no change), respectively. Actions are subdivided into *processes* (extended in time) and *achievements* (not extended in time). In addition, Croft introduces the notion of *point state* (no change, not extended in time) for such things as *It is eight o'clock* and *The train is on time*. Croft addresses the complex interplay between the temporal structure of events as named by verbs and "aspectual grammatical constructions," such as the simple/progressive distinction in English. On the one hand, lexical aspect seems to determine certain grammatical patterns. This is evidenced, for instance, in the constraint on the use of the simple present tense in English demonstrated in (24b). On the other hand, aspectual constructions themselves provide a conceptualization of the temporal structure of the event, and language users are flexible in adjusting the temporal structure to fit the construction. This is illustrated in (31) (Croft 1998: 71).

(31)   a. ?I am loving her.
        b. I am loving her more and more, the better I get to know her.

The verb *love* is one of Vendler's examples of states (see 26a), and, accordingly, it does not easily appear in the progressive form (see 31a). However, a shift in "temporal scale" leads to a shift in acceptability. In (31b), the state of loving turns out to involve change, and thus the progressive can be used. Examples such as these (and the sentences in 30) lead Croft to conclude that verbs cannot be divided into word classes on the basis of the grammatical constructions in which they occur. (He makes a similar point for the test involving adverbials as in 27 and 28). Croft, therefore, seriously questions the value of "distributional analysis": words do not have a fixed distribution across constructions; the interaction between lexicon and grammar is "mediated by conceptualization processes" (1998: 79).

Contrary to Langacker and Croft, Michaelis (1998) sharply distinguishes between lexical and grammatical aspect, as *situation aspect* and *viewpoint aspect*, respectively (following the terminology of Smith 1991). As for the former, she regards the distinction between events and states as a universal cognitive distinction, independent of its specific manifestation in a given language. Viewpoint aspect, the perfective/imperfective distinction, concerns the grammatical encoding of the event/state distinction using language-specific resources. There is no one-to-one mapping between situation aspect and viewpoint aspect, since viewpoint aspect may override "the canonical representation" of situations, as was exemplified in (31) (see Smith's 1991 marked and unmarked aspect choice). English, in Michaelis's view, does not grammatically encode the event/state distinction at all, which makes viewpoint aspect a covert category of English.

Michaelis departs from a long-standing tradition in the aspect literature by not treating the progressive as an expression of imperfective aspect, but introducing a third category in addition to situation aspect and viewpoint aspect, namely the category of *phasal aspect*. This is a cover term for (i) inceptive aspect (*start, begin*), (ii) the progressive, and (iii) the perfect. In Michaelis's view, the progressive does not directly encode the event/state distinction, but rather presupposes it and accomplishes a perspectival shift from an event predication to a state predication. Michaelis, therefore, calls the progressive an "override construction." The same intuition was captured by Langacker in his treatment of the progressive as an "imperfectivizing" device. And, in his discussion of (31), Croft as well assumes that the "default" semantic class of a verb may be altered by the grammatical environment it occurs in (cf. the notions of "coercion" and "shift" discussed by Moens & Steedman 1988 and Hayase 1997).

3.3. Meaning

The cognitive linguistic literature on the semantics of aspect departs from traditional accounts in two ways. First, rather than defining aspectual categories by single semantic contrasts (e.g., complete/noncomplete, durative/nondurative), the semantics of aspectual categories is assumed to be organized around a prototype with many language-particular extensions, including extensions in other domains (tense, modality). Such an approach to aspect can already be found in the work of Hopper (1979) and has received wide support from large-scale typological studies (Dahl 1985) and from the grammaticalization literature (Bybee, Perkins, and Pagliuca 1994; Carey 1994). Case studies within Cognitive Grammar are offered by Midgette's (1995) analysis of the progressive in Navajo, by Kochanska's (2000) work on the semantics of aspect in Polish, and by Dickey's (2000) comparative analysis of aspect in the Slavic languages generally.

Second, in the cognitive linguistic literature on aspect, the focus of attention has shifted from defining aspect in terms of "the internal temporal constituency of a situation" (Comrie 1976: 3) to describing the function of aspectual distinctions at the discourse level. In particular, aspect is said to indicate viewpoint and to play a role in establishing relations across clauses.

3.3.1. Aspect and Viewpoint

To describe the difference between the French perfective past *passé simple* and the imperfective past *imparfait*, Cutrer (1994) uses the descriptive tools from mental space theory outlined in section 2.2. She defines the difference between perfective and imperfective aspect as a difference in perspective: the imperfective past indicates that the Focus space is also Viewpoint space, whereas the perfective past does not indicate viewpoint. The way Cutrer describes IMPERFECTIVE and PERFECTIVE is shown in (32) and (33) and graphically represented in figures 31.3 and 31.4 (Cutrer 1994: 193–95).

(32)   The IMPERFECTIVE identifies a FOCUS space N and indicates that N is viewpoint.

(33)   The PERFECTIVE identifies a FOCUS space N and indicates that N is not viewpoint.

As was explained in 2.2.1, the past tense sets up a past Focus space in relation to a parent Viewpoint space. In fact, the representation for PERFECTIVE PAST in figure 31.4 is identical to the one for PAST in figure 31.2; the PERFECTIVE PAST does not indicate Viewpoint. The situation is thus construed from an external Viewpoint (in the parent space M). The IMPERFECTIVE PAST, however, indicates that the past

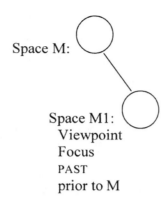

Space M:

Space M1:
Viewpoint
Focus
PAST
prior to M

Figure 31.3. PAST IMPERFECTIVE

Focus space is also a Viewpoint. Thus, imperfective aspect establishes a shift from an "external" Viewpoint position to an "internal" one. (The "external" Viewpoint in space M, however, may still be available. Space M may, for instance, be a speech or thought space, carrying its own Viewpoint role, as in indirect speech.) Cutrer's analysis of the perfective/imperfective distinction in terms of perspective is supported by many observations regarding the use of imperfective forms in discourse representing the thought or speech of an individual other than the speaker, as in indirect speech and free indirect speech (Ehrlich 1987; Caenepeel 1989).

3.3.2.   *Aspect and Discourse Relations*

Aspectual information also turns out to be relevant for determining relations beyond clausal boundaries. In fact, according to Hopper (1982: 5), "The fundamental notion of aspect is not a local-semantic one, but is discourse pragmatic." Hopper argues that the distinction between perfective and imperfective aspect primarily serves to indicate *foreground* and *background* in discourse:

> The perfective aspect is found mainly in kinetic, sequential events which are central to the unfolding of the narrative.... Imperfective aspect is used typically for backgrounding: situations, descriptions and actions which are simultaneous or overlapping with a perfective event. (Hopper 1979: 58)

Thus, aspect is said to convey information on the temporal ordering of situations presented in consecutive sentences: perfective forms present sequential situations, making up a narrative chain of events; imperfective forms present situations that are "going on" in the background (see Fleischman 1985). Reinhart (1984) has shown that the distinction between foreground and background is analogous to the distinction between Figure and Ground in visual perception, "neutral ... and clearly unavoidable organization systems" (790); this analogy was already noted in the writings of Talmy (1978) (see also Hayase 1997).

While Hopper restricts his discussion to grammatical forms of (perfective/ imperfective) aspect in various languages, a highly similar approach has been

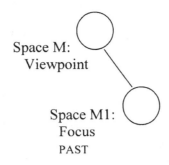

Figure 31.4. PAST PERFECTIVE

proposed for English within Discourse Representation Theory in terms of the distinction between events and states (Kamp and Reyle 1993). In this framework, the Reichenbachian notion of reference point (see section 2) is used to formalize the intuition expressed above by Hopper. Tenses in discourse are always interpreted with respect to a reference point provided by a preceding sentence, but while events follow their reference point, states are said to include their reference point (Kamp and Reyle 1993: 528). Thus, the situation of John walking to the bookcase in (34a) is correctly predicted to follow the situation of John opening the door, which serves as reference time. Together they form an iconically ordered sequence of events (i.e., Hopper's "foreground").

(34)   a. John opened the door and walked to the bookcase.
        b. John opened the door. It was pitch dark in the room.

The second sentence of (34b), however, presents a state, which includes the reference point provided by the previous sentence: it was dark both before and after John opened the door (i.e., Hopper's "background").

While it seems clear that aspectual information has a role to play in the process of interpreting temporal relations in discourse, it is not possible to maintain that aspect alone determines temporal relations. It should be noted, for instance, that the linguistic information provided by (34b) does not exclude the possibility that the room was not dark at all before John opened the door. In fact, the preferred interpretation of (35) is one in which the state of the room being dark follows but does not precede the event of the first sentence.

(35)   John switched off the light. It was pitch dark in the room because
        the Venetian blinds were closed.

(Hinrichs 1986: 68)

Interestingly, Cutrer's "perspective approach" to aspect, mentioned in section 3.3.1, does seem applicable to both (34b) and (35): the second sentence describes the state of the room being dark from John's perspective, in other words, as the first thing he noticed after opening the door or switching off the light. To explain the *temporal* ordering of such cases, it will be clear that, in addition to (or perhaps even *instead of*) aspect, a considerable amount of world knowledge and pragmatic reasoning must be invoked.[17]

4. DIRECTIONS FOR FUTURE RESEARCH

A number of tense/aspect domains deserve serious attention and further investigation.

4.1. Comparative Analysis of Tense and Aspect

Given the general, cognitive linguistic tool for the analysis of tense and aspect developed in the literature, there is at present a need for comparative analyses of tense and aspect systems in the languages of the world using these analytic tools—Dickey's (2000) comparative analysis of aspect in the Slavic languages can be mentioned as an exemplary study in this respect. So far, the primary focus in the cognitive linguistic literature has been on the general concepts underlying tense and aspect rather than on the formal manifestation of these categories and their use in particular languages (with the possible exception of English). However, it is well known that tense and aspect categories show a great deal of variation across languages (see Dahl 1985, 2000; Thieroff and Ballweg 1994; Thieroff 1995; Hewson and Bubenik 1997; Stassen 1997). Thus, in order to test the validity of the proposals and, if necessary, to refine them, more languages should be examined, including those languages that are claimed to lack the category of tense altogether (see Bohnemeyer 1998 on Yucatec Maya). A promising perspective for describing and explaining such cross-linguistic differences in the domain of tense and aspect is offered by the framework of grammaticalization (Bybee, Perkins, and Pagliuca 1994). But here as well, detailed diachronic studies of language-specific developments are, for the most part, still lacking.

4.2. Interaction Tense/Aspect and Modality

It should have become clear from the preceding sections that the categories of tense and aspect interact in interesting ways. Within the domain of aspectuality, a similar kind of interaction was noted for "grammatical" and "lexical" aspect. However, not all possible interactions were addressed in this chapter. In particular, the category of modality and its interaction with both tense and aspect deserves more attention (see Sasse 2002: 266).

4.2.1. *Tense and Modality*

As was discussed in section 2.2.2, the past tense can be used to express epistemic (nontemporal) distance with respect to the ground, such as in the *irrealis*. In addition, the future tense "more often than not fails to express pure futurity and is instead bound up with modality and the expression of belief and possibility" (Frawley 1992: 356). And in many languages, the present tense is not exclusively used to express a temporal relationship either (e.g., Janssen 1998; Cook-Gumperz and Kyratzis 2001; Langacker 2001a; Brisard 2002; for the present perfective, see Asic 2000). The precise relationship between tense and modality is as yet an unsolved problem (Foley 1986: 158–66).

4.2.2. *Aspect and Modality*

The connection between tense and modality has often been noted but the interaction between aspect and modality has largely been ignored. However, there is a host of data in the literature suggesting a cross-linguistic relationship between perfective aspect and "objective" or "factive" information on the one hand, and between imperfective aspect and "subjective," "perspectivized," or "counterfactual" information on the other (Fleischman 1995) (see section 3.2 on aspect and perspective). Whereas the nontemporal use of tense forms has been related to the overall nontemporal meaning of tense (see section 2.2.2), there has been no satisfactory account of aspect in which the widely divergent "modal" interpretations of, in particular, imperfective aspect are related to the overall meaning of aspect. What is the exact relationship between the domains of aspectuality and modality? Why do so many languages use one and the same form to present incomplete as well as "perspectivized" and "counterfactual" situations?

4.3. Aspect/Aktionsart

In the noncognitivist literature on aspect, some effort has been made to distinguish between lexical aspect, or *Aktionsart* (telicity), and grammatical aspect (perfectivity). As was noted in section 3.2., Cognitive Linguistics does not always make that distinction, which should come as no surprise since it is impossible to make a clear-cut, principled distinction between grammar and lexicon. However, defining all aspectual categories—verb aspect, grammatical aspect, and the aspect of entire expressions—in the same terms blurs the distinction between aspect and Aktionsart, as well as interesting interactions among them (Boogaart 2004). Therefore, it remains necessary to investigate in more detail what Croft (1998) calls the "conceptualization processes" mediating between Aktionsart and aspect.

In the fields of language acquisition and signed languages, thorough studies on tense and aspect from the cognitive linguistic perspective are still lacking. (An exception is constituted by the papers on language acquisition collected by Li and Shirai 2000.)

NOTES

1. The term *situation* will be used to refer to various types of situations. Although a number of linguists use the term *event* as the cover term (see some quotes in this chapter), the term *event* easily leads to the misunderstanding that the *Aktionsart* involved is a nonstate (see section 3.2).

2. Usually the speaker and the addressee(s) share the evaluative situation. However, when reading a sentence such as *I'm writing this letter on the balcony of my hotel in Debrecen* (Fillmore 1997: 82), the addressee has to project his or her mind into a past situation, namely the writer's situation of writing.

3. For the notion of contextualization, see Dinsmore (1991: 193–94, 221–25), Fillmore (1981), and Gumperz (1982: 160–71), who introduces the notion in a more general communicative sense.

4. Critical overviews of the status of the Reichenbachian notion of reference in various tense analyses are presented by Hamann (1987), Harder (1996: 320–23, 398–404), Michaelis (1998: 29–34, 43–51), Brisard (1999: 375–94), and Boogaart (1999: 36–38, 57–77). Binnick (1991: 37–43) surveys related ideas of analysts predating Reichenbach's "time of reference" notion. An elaborated alternative to Reichenbachian analyses is presented by Declerck (e.g., 1991, 1995, 1997, 1999); for comments, see, e.g., Janssen (1995, 1996b, 1998) and Salkie and Reed (1997).

5. A tense system featuring more than two types of simple tense form is, for instance, (modern) Greek (Paprotté 1988; Binnick 1991); more generally, see Thieroff and Ballweg (1994), Thieroff (1995), Hewson and Bubenik (1997), Dahl (2000), and Squartini (2003).

6. Older two-tense analyses are Paardekooper (1957), Burger (1961), Joos (1964), Weinreich (1964), Huddleston (1969), Casparis (1975), and King (1983).

7. Cutrer's (1994: 88–89) and Fauconnier's (1997: 75–76) notations show slight differences.

8. As for the temporal relation between the situations of clauses like *John came* and *[John] told me the news* in (2), Kamp and Reyle (1993: 497) allow the tense of *told* to refer to some time in the vicinity of the time of *came*. This vicinity solution is a spurious element in their time-based analysis. The distance between the times of the situations involved is merely delimited by a functional coherence between the situations (Boogaart 1999: 68–70).

9. See also Steele (1975), James (1982, 1991), and Tyler and Evans (2001). Past-tense forms such as the French *passé simple* in contrast to the *imparfait* (De Mulder and Vetters 2002), the Spanish *pretérito indefinido* in contrast to the *pretérito imperfecto* (Doiz-Bienzobas 2002), and the Polish perfective past-tense forms in contrast to the imperfective past-tense forms (Kochanska 2002) cannot be used to indicate nonpast situations. However, Polish perfective non-past-tense forms in contrast to imperfective non-past-tense forms (Kochanska 2002) can serve to indicate situations other than strictly present or future ones.

10. Langacker (2001b: 268) claims: "The key to understanding 'non-present' uses of the present tense is to recognize the special viewing arrangements they presuppose"; see also Langacker (2003).

11. Various languages show this type of use (Janssen 1996a).

12. Janssen (1993, 1996a, 2002)—see also Kirsner (1993) and Harder (1996: 273)—rejects the distinction "proximal/distal" for the analysis of this and that (as made by, e.g., Langacker 1991, 1994).

13. It should be noted that the term *perfective*, as used in traditional aspect studies, does not refer to the semantics of the perfect construction. The perfective/imperfective distinction is manifested, for instance, in the semantic difference between *He read a book* (perfective past) and *He was reading a book* (imperfective past). The construction used in *He has read a book* may be called *perfect*, but not *perfective*. It should be noted that Langacker's Cognitive Grammar uses the terms *perfective* and *imperfective* in a way that departs from traditional aspect studies (see section 3.2).

14. Not all languages solve the conceptual clash between perfective aspect and present tense in the same way. In Russian, for instance, present perfective forms are not ungrammatical, but they are interpreted as referring to the future (Binnick 1991: 138).

15. "Tense as such is not marked in Wolof, but the time of occurrence of an event or state relative to the speech act is inferred from the type of predicator in a sentence and the presence or absence of aspectual marking" (Moore 2000: 313).

16. Even though the categories of perfect and perfective should be carefully distinguished (see note 8), Garey exemplifies the category perfective aspect by means of the French perfect (*passé composé*). He can do so because the perfect has taken over the function of the perfective past *passé simple* in French spoken discourse. The diachronic development of perfect forms acquiring perfective, or general past, uses has been documented for many languages (Bybee, Perkins, and Pagliuca 1994: 51–105).

17. On the importance of pragmatic reasoning for the temporal interpretation of discourse, see Paprotté (1988), Lascarides and Asher (1993), Moeschler (1993), Wilson and Sperber (1993), Michaelis (1998: 29–40), Bohnemeyer (1998: 641–73), and Boogaart (1999: 110–27).

REFERENCES

Asic, Tijana. 2000. Le présent perfectif en serbe: Temps, mode ou puzzle? *Cahiers de Linguistique Française* 22: 275–94.

Bazanella, Carla. 1990. 'Modal' uses of the Italian *indicativo imperfetto* in a pragmatic perspective. *Journal of Pragmatics* 14: 439–57.

Binnick, Robert I. 1991. *Time and the verb: A guide to tense and aspect.* New York: Oxford University Press.

Bohnemeyer, Jürgen. 1998. Time relations in discourse: Evidence from a comparative approach to Yucatec Maya. PhD dissertation, Katholieke Universiteit Brabant, Netherlands.

Boogaart, Ronny. 1999. *Aspect and temporal ordering: A contrastive analysis of Dutch and English.* The Hague: Holland Academic Graphics.

Boogaart, Ronny. 2004. Aspect and Aktionsart. In Geert Booij, Christian Lehmann, and Joachim Mugdan, eds., *Morphology: An international handbook on inflection and word formation* 2: 1165–80. Berlin: Mouton de Gruyter.

Brisard, Frank. 1999. A critique of localism in and about tense theory. PhD dissertation, University of Antwerp, Belgium.

Brisard, Frank. 2002. The English present. In Frank Brisard, ed., *Grounding: The epistemic footing of deixis and reference* 251–97. Berlin: Mouton de Gruyter.

Burger, André. 1961. Significations et valeur du suffixe verbal français '-ę-'. *Cahiers Ferdinand de Saussure* 18: 5–15.

Bybee, Joan L., Revere D. Perkins, and William Pagliuca. 1994. *The evolution of grammar: Tense, aspect and modality in the languages of the world.* Chicago: University of Chicago Press.

Caenepeel, Mimo. 1989. Aspect, temporal ordering and perspective in narrative fiction. PhD dissertation, University of Edinburgh.

Calver, Edward. 1946. The uses of the present tense form in English. *Language* 22: 317–25.

Carey, Kathleen. 1994. Pragmatics, subjectivity and the grammaticalization of the English perfect. PhD dissertation, University of California at San Diego.

Casparis, Christian P. 1975. *Tense without time: The present tense in narration.* Bern, Switzerland: Francke.

Comrie, Bernard. 1976. *Aspect.* Cambridge: Cambridge University Press.

Comrie, Bernard. 1981. On Reichenbach's approach to tense. In Roberta A. Hendrick, Carrie S. Masek, and Mary Frances Miller, eds., *Chicago Linguistic Society* 7: 24–30.

Comrie, Bernard. 1985. *Tense.* Cambridge: Cambridge University Press.

Cook-Gumperz, Jenny, and Amy Kyratzis. 2001. Pretend play: Trial ground for the simple present. In Martin Pütz, Susanne Niemeier, and René Dirven, eds., *Applied Cognitive Linguistics* 1: 41–62. Berlin: Mouton de Gruyter.

Croft, William. 1998. The structure of events and the structure of language. In Michael Tomasello, ed., *The new psychology of language: Cognitive and functional approaches to language structure* 1: 67–92. Mahwah, N.J.: Lawrence Erlbaum.

Cutrer, L. Michelle. 1994. Time and tense in narrative and in everyday language. PhD dissertation, University of California at San Diego.

Dahl, Östen. 1985. *Tense and aspect systems.* Oxford: Basil Blackwell.

Dahl, Östen, ed. 2000. *Tense and aspect in the languages of Europe.* Berlin: Mouton de Gruyter.

Declerck, Renaat. 1991. *Tense in English: Its structure and use in discourse.* London: Routledge.

Declerck, Renaat. 1995. Is there a relative past tense in English? *Lingua* 97: 1–36.

Declerck, Renaat. 1997. *When-clauses and temporal structure.* London: Routledge.

Declerck, Renaat. 1999. Remarks on Salkie and Reed's (1997) 'pragmatic hypothesis' of tense in reported speech. *English Language and Linguistics* 3: 83–116.

De Mulder, Walter, and Carl Vetters. 2002. The French imparfait, determiners and grounding. In Frank Brisard, ed., *Grounding: The epistemic footing of deixis and reference* 113–49. Berlin: Mouton de Gruyter.

Dickey, Stephen M. 2000. *Parameters of Slavic aspect: A cognitive approach.* Stanford, CA: CSLI Publications.

Dinsmore, John. 1991. *Partitioned representations.* Dordrecht, Netherlands: Kluwer.

Doiz Bienzobas, Aintzane. 2002. The preterit and the imperfect as grounding predications. In Frank Brisard, ed., *Grounding. The epistemic footing of deixis and reference* 299–347. Berlin: Mouton de Gruyter.

Dowty, David R. 1979. *Word meaning and Montague Grammar.* Dordrecht, Netherlands: Reidel.

Ehrlich, Susan. 1987. *Point of view: A linguistic analysis of literary style.* London: Routledge.

Fauconnier, Gilles. 1985. *Mental spaces: Aspects of meaning construction in natural language.* Cambridge, MA: MIT Press. (2nd ed., Cambridge: Cambridge University Press, 1994)

Fauconnier, Gilles. 1997. *Mappings in thought and language.* Cambridge: Cambridge University Press.

Fillmore, Charles J. 1981. Pragmatics and the description of discourse. In Peter Cole, ed., *Radical pragmatics* 143–66. New York: Academic Press.

Fillmore, Charles J. 1997. *Lectures on deixis*. Stanford: CSLI Publications. (First published as *Santa Cruz Lectures on Deixis*. Bloomington: Indiana University Linguistics Club, 1975)

Fleischman, Suzanne. 1985. Discourse function of tense-aspect oppositions in narrative: Toward a theory of grounding. *Linguistics* 23: 851–82.

Fleischman, Suzanne. 1989. Temporal distance: A basic linguistic metaphor. *Studies in Language* 13: 1–50.

Fleischman, Suzanne. 1995. Imperfective and irrealis. In Joan L. Bybee and Suzanne Fleischman, eds., *Modality in grammar and discourse* 519–51. Amsterdam: John Benjamins.

Foley, William A. 1986. *The Papuan languages of New Guinea*. Cambridge: Cambridge University Press.

Frawley, William. 1992. *Linguistic semantics*. Hillsdale, NJ: Lawrence Erlbaum.

Garey, Howard B. 1957. Verbal aspect in French. *Language* 33: 91–110.

Gumperz, John J. 1982. *Discourse strategies*. Cambridge: Cambridge University Press.

Hamann, Cornelia. 1987. The awesome seeds of reference time. In Alfred Schopf, ed., *Essays on tensing in English*, vol. 1, *Reference time, tense and adverbs* 27–69. Tübingen: Max Niemeyer Verlag.

Harder, Peter. 1996. *Functional semantics: A theory of meaning, structure and tense in English*. Berlin: Mouton de Gruyter.

Hayase, Naoko. 1997. The role of Figure, Ground, and coercion in aspectual interpretation. In Marjolijn Verspoor, Kee Dong Lee, and Eve Sweetser, eds., *Lexical and syntactical constructions and the construction of meaning* 33–50. Amsterdam: John Benjamins.

Heny, Frank. 1982. Tense, aspect and time adverbials. Part 2. *Linguistics and Philosophy* 5: 109–54.

Hewson, John, and Vit Bubenik, eds. 1997. *Tense and aspect in Indo-European Languages: Theory, typology, diachrony*. Amsterdam: John Benjamins.

Hinrichs, Erhard. 1986. Temporal anaphora in discourses of English. *Linguistics and Philosophy* 9: 63–82.

Hopper, Paul J. 1979. Some observations on the typology of focus and aspect in narrative language. *Studies in Language* 3: 37–64.

Hopper, Paul J. 1982. Aspect between discourse and grammar: An introductory essay for the volume. In Paul Hopper, ed., *Tense-aspect between semantics and pragmatics* 3–18. Amsterdam: John Benjamins.

Huddleston, Rodney. 1969. Some observations on tense and deixis in English. *Language* 45: 777–806.

James, Deborah. 1982. Past tense and the hypothetical: A cross-linguistic study. *Studies in Language* 6: 375–403.

James, Deborah. 1991. Preterit forms in Moose Cree as markers of tense, aspect, and modality. *International Journal of American Linguistics* 57: 281–97.

Janssen, Theo A. J. M. 1987. Acht, zes of twee tempora? [Eight, six, or two tenses?]. *Forum der Letteren* 28: 89–93.

Janssen, Theo A.J.M. 1989. Tempus: interpretatie en betekenis [Tense: interpretation and meaning]. *De nieuwe taalgids* 82: 305–329.

Janssen, Theo A. J. M. 1991. Preterit as definite description. In Jadranka Gvozdanović and Theo A. J. M. Janssen, eds., *The function of tense in texts* 157–81. Amsterdam: North-Holland.

Janssen, Theo A. J. M. 1993. Tenses and demonstratives: Conspecific categories. In Richard Geiger and Brygida Rudzka-Ostyn, eds., *Conceptualizations and mental processing in language* 741–83. Berlin: Mouton de Gruyter.

Janssen, Theo A. J. M. 1994. Preterit and perfect in Dutch. In Co Vet and Carl Vetters, eds., *Tense and aspect in discourse* 115–46. Berlin: Mouton de Gruyter.

Janssen, Theo A. J. M. 1995. The preterit enabled by the pluperfect. In Pier Marco Bertinetto, Valentina Bianchi, Östen Dahl, and Mario Squartini, eds., *Temporal reference, aspect and actionality*, vol. 2, *Typological perspectives* 239–54. Torino, Italy: Rosenberg and Sellier.

Janssen, Theo A. J. M. 1996a. Deictic and anaphoric referencing of tenses. In Walter De Mulder, Liliane Tasmowski-De Ryck, and Carl Vetters, eds., *Anaphores temporelles et (in-)coherence* 79–107. Amsterdam: Rodopi.

Janssen, Theo A. J. M. 1996b. Tense in reported speech and its frame of reference. In Theo A. J. M. Janssen and Wim van der Wurff, eds., *Reported speech: Forms and functions of the verb* 237–59. Amsterdam: John Benjamins.

Janssen, Theo A. J. M. 1998. The referentiality of tenses. *Belgian Journal of Linguistics* 12: 209–26.

Janssen, Theo A. J. M. 2002. Deictic principles of pronominals, demonstratives and tenses. In Frank Brisard, ed., *Grounding. The epistemic footing of deixis and reference* 151–93. Berlin: Mouton de Gruyter.

Joos, Martin. 1964. *The English verb: Form and meaning*. Madison: University of Wisconsin Press.

Kamp, Hans, and Uwe Reyle. 1993. *From discourse to logic: Introduction to modeltheoretic semantics of natural language, formal logic and discourse representation theory*. Dordrecht, Netherlands: Kluwer Academic Publishers.

King, Larry D. 1983. The semantics of tense, orientation, and aspect in English. *Lingua* 59: 101–54.

Kirsner, Robert S. 1993. From meaning to message in two theories: Cognitive and Saussurean views of the modern Dutch demonstratives. In Richard Geiger and Brygida Rudzka-Ostyn, eds., *Conceptualizations and mental processing in language* 83–114. Berlin: Mouton de Gruyter.

Kochanska, Agata. 2000. Verbal aspect and construal. In Ad Foolen and Frederike van der Leek, eds., *Constructions in cognitive linguistics* 141–66. Amsterdam: John Benjamins.

Kochanska, Agata. 2002. A cognitive grammar analysis of Polish non-past perfectives and imperfectives: How virtual events differ from actual ones. In Frank Brisard, ed., *Grounding: The epistemic footing of deixis and reference* 349–90. Berlin: Mouton de Gruyter.

Langacker, Ronald W. 1978. The form and meaning of the English auxiliary. *Language* 54: 853–82.

Langacker, Ronald W. 1987. *Foundations of cognitive grammar*. Vol. 1, *Theoretical prerequisites*. Stanford, CA: Stanford University Press.

Langacker, Ronald W. 1991. *Foundations of cognitive grammar*. Vol. 2. *Descriptive application*. Stanford, CA: Stanford University Press.

Langacker, Ronald W. 1994. Remarks on the English grounding systems. In Ronny Boogaart and Jan Noordegraaf, eds., *Nauwe Betrekkingen* 137–44. Münster, Germany: Nodus Publikationen. (Repr. in Frank Brisard, ed., *Grounding: The epistemic footing of deixis and reference* 29–38. Berlin: Mouton de Gruyter, 2002)

Langacker, Ronald W. 1999. *Grammar and conceptualization*. Berlin: Mouton de Gruyter.

Langacker, Ronald W. 2001a. Cognitive linguistics, language pedagogy, and the English present tense. In Martin Pütz, Susanne Niemeier, and René Dirven, eds., *Applied cognitive linguistics*, vol. 1, *Theory and language acquisition* 3–39. Berlin: Mouton de Gruyter.

Langacker, Ronald W. 2001b. The English present tense. *English Language and Linguistics* 5: 251–72.

Langacker, Ronald W. 2003. Extreme subjectification: English tense and modals. In Hubert Cuyckens, Thomas Berg, René Dirven, and Klaus-Uwe Panther, eds., *Motivation in language: Studies in honor of Günter Radden* 3–26. Amsterdam: John Benjamins.

Lascarides, Alex, and Nicolas Asher. 1993. Temporal interpretation, discourse relations and commonsense entailment. *Linguistics and Philosophy* 16: 437–93.

Leech, Geoffrey N. 1987. *Meaning and the English verb*. 2nd ed. London: Longman.

Li, Ping, and Yasuhiro Shirai, eds. 2000. *The acquisition of lexical and grammatical aspect*. Berlin: Mouton de Gruyter.

Michaelis, Laura A. 1998. *Aspectual grammar and past time reference*. London: Routledge.

Midgette, Sally. 1995. *The Navajo progressive in discourse*. New York: Peter Lang Verlag.

Moens, Marc, and Marc Steedman. 1988. Temporal ontology and temporal reference. *Computational Linguistics* 14: 15–28.

Moeschler, Jacques. 1993. Aspects pragmatiques de la référence temporelle: Indétermination, ordre temporel et inférence. *Langages* 112: 39–54.

Moore, Kevin E. 2000. Spatial experience and temporal metaphors in Wolof: Point of view, conceptual mapping, and linguistic practice. PhD dissertation, University of California at Berkeley.

Paardekooper, Piet C. 1957. De 'tijd' als spraakkunstgroep in het ABN ['Time' seen as a linguistic element in standard Dutch]. *De Nieuwe Taalgids* 50: 38–45.

Paprotté, Wolf. 1988. A discourse perspective on tense and aspect in standard modern Greek and English. In Brygida Rudzka-Ostyn, ed., *Topics in cognitive linguistics* 447–505. Amsterdam: John Benjamins.

Reichenbach, Hans. 1947. *Elements of symbolic logic*. New York: Free Press.

Reinhart, Tanya. 1984. Principles of Gestalt perception in the temporal organization of narrative texts. *Linguistics* 22: 779–809.

Salkie, Raphael, and Susan Reed. 1997. Time reference in reported speech. *English Language and Linguistics* 1: 319–48.

Sasse, Hans-Jürgen. 2002. Recent activity in the theory of aspect: Accomplishments, achievements, or just non-progressive state? *Linguistic Typology* 6: 199–271.

Smith, Carlota. 1991. *The parameter of aspect*. Dordrecht, Netherlands: Kluwer.

Squartini, Mario. 2003. Sequence of tenses in Old Italian (Comrie vs. Declerck). *Folia Linguistica* 37: 319–45.

Stassen, Leon. 1997. *Intransitive predication*. Oxford: Clarendon.

Steele, Susan. 1975. Past and irrealis: Just what does it all mean? *International Journal of American Linguistics* 41: 200–217.

Sweetser, Eve, and Gilles Fauconnier. 1996. Cognitive links and domains: Basic aspects of mental space theory. In Gilles Fauconnier and Eve Sweetser, eds., *Spaces worlds and grammar* 1–28. Chicago: University of Chicago Press.

Taylor, John R. 1989. *Linguistic Categorization. Prototypes in Linguistic Theory*. Oxford: Clarendon Press.

Talmy, Leonard. 1978. Figure and ground in complex sentences. In Joseph Greenberg, ed., *Universals of human language*, vol. 4, *Syntax* 625–49. Stanford, CA: Stanford University Press.

Thieroff, Rolf, ed. 1995. *Tense systems in European languages II*. Tübingen: Max Niemeyer Verlag.

Thieroff, Rolf, and Joachim Ballweg, eds. 1994. *Tense systems in European languages*. Tübingen: Max Niemeyer Verlag.

Tyler, Andrea, and Vyvyan Evans. 2001. The relation between experience, conceptual structure and meaning: Non-temporal uses of tense and language teaching. In Martin Pütz, Susanne Niemeier, and René Dirven, eds., *Applied cognitive linguistics*, vol. 1, *Theory and language acquisition* 63–105. Berlin: Mouton de Gruyter.

Vendler, Zeno. 1967. *Linguistics in philosophy*. Ithaca, NY: Cornell University Press.

Verkuyl, Henk J. 1993. *A theory of aspectuality: The interaction between temporal and atemporal structure*. Cambridge: Cambridge University Press.

Wada, Naoaki. 2001. Interpreting English tenses: A compositional approach. Tokyo: Kaitakusha.

Weinrich, Harald. 1964. *Tempus, besprochene und erzählte Welt*. Stuttgart: Kohlhammer.

Wilson, Deirde, and Dan Sperber. 1993. Pragmatique et temps. *Langages* 112: 8–25.

CHAPTER 32

GRAMMATICAL VOICE IN COGNITIVE GRAMMAR

RICARDO MALDONADO

1. INTRODUCTION: BASIC VOICE NOTIONS

Voice or diathesis, as first termed by Dionysius, is the grammatical category by which the arguments of the verb receive different prominence status in the sentence through a variety of semantic-syntactic and even pragmatic coding patterns. In verbs involving at least two arguments, the arrangement is always asymmetrical, with one argument being more prominent than the other. For all languages, there seems to be a canonical unmarked voice pattern, most commonly the *active*, where the Agent is more prominent than the Patient (but see section 7 on Middle voice). Active voice contrasts with a variety of marked voice patterns: *passive*, *antipassive*, *inverse*, and *middle*. Each voice pattern designates alternative views of an event as Agent and Patient receive different degrees of prominence. A wider view of voice, that is, diathesis proper, will include *causative* and *applicative* constructions, since they also involve adjusting subject and object prominence. Yet these constructions involve a wide variety of force-dynamic phenomena as well as different degrees of event complexity, which require an independent paper.

Table 32.1. Cooreman's four basic pragmatic voices

Active direct	Ag	>	Pat
Inverse	Pat	>	Ag
Passive	Pat	≫	Ag
Antipassive	Ag	≫	Pat

Functional and typological approaches to voice phenomena have provided the basis for defining these profiling strategies (Keenan 1976, 1985; Dixon 1980; Givón 1990; Klaiman 1991; Cooreman 1994; Zavala 1997; Givón and Yang 1998). This chapter has grown from those analyses, with a view to providing a Cognitive Grammar approach (Langacker 1987a, 1990, 1991, 2000 and many other publications) that motivates the emergence of a variety of voice marking systems as corresponding to alternative conceptualization strategies.

While middle voice refers to actions or states remaining in the subject's dominion, the other four voice marking strategies refer to alternative prominence adjustments between Agent (Ag) and Patient/Theme (pat/Th). Cooreman (1987) has provided this four-way voice contrast in terms of topicality:

a. *Active direct*: Both Agent and Patient are topical, yet the Agent is more topical than the Patient;

b. *Inverse*: Both Agent and Patient are topical, yet the Patient is more topical than the Agent;

c. *Passive*: The Patient is topical and the Agent is completely nontopical; and

d. *Antipassive*: The Agent is topical and the Patient is completely nontopical.

Cooreman's proposal is schematically represented in table 32.1.

I consider Cooreman's four-way distinction to be a solid basis for further evaluation of the cognitive import of each voice type with respect to the basic patterns of event construction in the languages of the world.

In line with Langacker (1990, 1991) and Schulze (2000), I will assume that languages are not ergative or absolutive *per se* (so that one should not speak about accusative *versus* ergative languages), but instead have dominant accusative or ergative strategies to construe events. Thus, so-called "ergative languages" largely employ ergative patterns (scenarios in Schulze's terms) in most situations, yet they may employ accusative patterns to conceptualize alternative event types. On the other hand, so-called "accusative languages" may have dominant accusative patterns while also exhibiting some ergative strategies to conceptualize specific marked situations. The fundamental difference between ergative and accusative tendencies, then, is determined by the basic strategies of event representation in each language, namely, whether the event is scanned (i) from the core of the event, that is, from the change of state out to the energy input, the CORE > OUT strategy, or (ii) from the energy

Table 32.2. Absolutive/Ergative strategies

	Accusative			Ergative	
Intransitive	S (nom)				S (abs)
Transitive	S (nom)	O (accus)	S	(erg)	O (abs)

input into the change of state, the OUT > IN strategy (Langacker 1990). It is these basic strategies to construe an event in a language type that determine its dominant voice patterns. More restricted voice patterns encode situations that are cognitively marked for that language.

Crucial to event construction is the notion of *starting point*, defined as the specific part of the event from which we begin construing a scene. There are three levels at which starting points operate:

a. *Prominence*: The hierarchy of participant prominence: subject > object > other;
b. *Inductivity*: The hierarchy of participants organized according to their capacity to initiate the event as determined by the conceptual content of the verb: Agent > Instrument > Patient; Causer > Causee; Experiencer > Theme; and
c. *Case marking*: The association between prominence and inductivity.

The starting point for case marking is what determines the contrast between so-called "accusative" and "ergative" languages. The two general patterns are tradi-tionally represented in table 32.2.

In accusative strategies, prominence and inductivity coincide, as the most en-ergetic participant at the "inductivity" level is chosen as the trajector of the event, in other words, the subject at the "prominence" level.[1] The event is scanned starting from the Agent as event-initiating participant to the core of the event (OUT > IN). This, then, makes the object/Patient the marked element. In contrast, ergative lan-guages start from "the thematic relationship that constitutes the essential nucleus for the conception of the complex event or situation" (Langacker 1990: 247). The event is calculated from the CORE > OUT; as such, the absolutive subject—commonly marked by a zero morpheme—encodes the Theme as the naturally most prominent par-ticipant, while the Agent in many cases is either not encoded at all or is marked as an oblique. Thus, the unmarked sentence is commonly intransitive. Transitive clauses—with ergative Agent and absolutive Patient—certainly exist in these languages; how-ever, they are used to designate less natural situations where the Agent needs to be profiled for a variety of discourse purposes, such as emphasis or contrast.

The notion of starting point also explains why antipassive constructions are more commonly found in languages where the dominant pattern is ergative, while passive constructions are more common in accusative-dominant languages. In both cases, the (anti)passive voice constitutes an operation which diminishes the degree of salience of the default most prominent participant in the event. Thus, the absolutive is downplayed in ergative-dominant languages, while it is the nominative Agent that is downplayed in accusative-dominant languages. The notion of starting point furthermore accounts for active and stative languages: actives calculate the event from the perspective of the (event-)initiating force, while stative languages focus on the core. Thus, in active languages, nonactive construal is marked and commonly applies to a restricted class of verbs. Likewise, in stative languages nonstative construal is marked.

In the following sections, each of the voice patterns will be presented, starting with active voice.

2. ACTIVE-DIRECT

We may define the active-direct voice as a construction whose most prominent participant is at the same time the most energetic one; that is, the starting point of the event encoded by the active-direct construction is constituted by the highest element in the PROMINENCE and INDUCTIVITY hierarchies. The event is calculated from the initiating input of the Agent, and the energy thus transmitted is traced down until some change is imposed on the Patient. In the abstract analogue of this construal, the subject—most commonly an Experiencer—establishes mental contact with a thematic element lying "downstream" from him or her. Thus, the event is calculated in much the same manner, in that it is initiated by the Experiencer. And although the thematic object does not change *per se*, the Experiencer's mental representation of the object undergoes the transformations determined by the specific context in which the mental contact is established.

In languages with a dominant accusative strategy—such as the Romance and Germanic languages, Finnish, and Japanese, to name a few—the active-direct is the default; passive, antipassive, and inverse code marked situations.

In languages with ergative dominance there are two basic tendencies. For some languages the basic construction is active. Thus, the starting point of the event is the Agent, very much like accusative-dominant languages. The second tendency involves languages in which the starting point is the core of the event. Representing the first group are languages like Chamorro and Akatec. According to Cooreman's (1994) and Zavala's (1997) respective text counts in these ergative languages, active voice ranks at 72% against the other voice strategies (inverse, passive, and antipassive). The second group is represented by languages like Newari (Tibeto-Burman) where the starting point is the Theme. Thus, examples such as (1a)—with a zero-marked Theme participant—constitute the default case, rather than sentences such as (1b)—where the Agent participant with ergative marking is in focus.

(1)   a. *Wa   manu   jaa   thuyaa   cona.*
         the   man   rice   cooking   be
         'The man *is cooking the rice*'

b. *Wa   manu-nan   jaa   thuyaa   cona.*
the   man-ERG   rice   cooking   be
'*The man* is cooking the rice.'

While (1a) is used in response to the question "What is the man doing?" (1b) is an adequate answer to "Who is cooking the rice?" Under normal circumstances, Newari traces the event from the CORE > OUT. The Theme in (1a) is more prominent than the Agent, as is underscored by the fact that the Theme participant, that is, the absolutive nominal (zero-marked), occurs adjacent to the verb and that the Agent participant takes up the second position from the verb (after the thematic subject) (see section 5 on the Inverse). The active direct, involving an Agent participant with ergative marking, seems to have a specific interpretation, whereby the Agent participant is in focus (see Cook 1988; Langacker 1990).

As will be shown in the following section, the passive provides an alternative event construal from the active.

3. PASSIVE

Despite the amount of attention it has received in contemporary analyses, the passive construction is rather restricted in everyday discourse. It is a marked construction where the prominent participant is not the expected one. In languages where the unmarked construction is the active, the passive corresponds to marked situations where the focus of attention shifts from the Agent to the Patient/Theme while the Agent is downgraded either as an oblique or as an implicit force, as in (2).

(2)   It wasn't until dusk that the song was played (by Valeria).

The passive construction is represented in figure 32.2 and can be contrasted with the representation of the active in figure 32.1.

3.1. Putting the Theme in Focus

Given that in the active voice transitive constructions involve two profiled participants, the passive construction may be obtained through two types of operation: (i) by profiling the Theme, thus relegating the Agent to the background, and (ii) by downgrading the Agent, thus giving the Theme maximal prominence. While the two strategies select the Theme as primary figure, they have reverse effects: in the first, the initiating properties of the Agent are preserved; in the second, those properties are drastically reduced.

The first strategy tends to be chosen in most formal and functional-cognitive analyses either as a mechanical device of promotion (Perlmutter and Postal 1983, 1984;

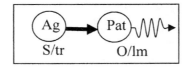

Figure 32.1. Active

Aissen 1987) or as a change in conceptualization (Langacker 1982, 1987b). Putting the Theme in focus is by no means mechanical, as differences in coding correspond with deeper and meaningful contrasts—a view exemplified in various cognitive linguistic analyses. As such, the change to passive represents a strategy where a participant with secondary profiling status is selected as the primary figure in the event, and it involves an attention shift from the initiator to the core of the event.

Langacker (1982) has proposed that, in languages like English, the passive emerges from the symbolic structure of the perfective participle "perf₃." The general representation of the perfective participle "perf" involves a shift of attention by which the change of state imposed on the Theme is put in profile (to the detriment of the Agent). This representation can be elaborated in at least three different ways: (i) the perfective participle "perf" may designate a state characterized as the final state in a process, "perf₁"; (ii) it may take a resultative meaning, "perf₂"; or, while in "perf₁" and "perf₂" the process itself remains in the base of the predication, (iii) "perf₃" profiles both the Theme and the process by which the change of state comes about. The contrast between the three types of perfective is illustrated in the examples in (3) taken from Langacker (1987b):

(3)   a. My wrist is all swollen.   'perf₁' = STATE
      b. The town was already destroyed (when we got there).   'perf₂' = RESULT
      c. The town was destroyed (house by house).   'perf₃' = PASSIVE

The content of the perf₃ passive fully coincides with the representation in figure 32.2, where a solid line is used for the Theme but not for the Agent. Notice that the energy-transfer process is represented by a boldface arrow—which in the state and resultative constructions, perf₁ and perf₂, respectively, would not be in boldface. The perfective participle perf₃ imposes a processual view, yet it is the verb *be* that re-temporalizes the whole event to obtain a complete passive construction. The passive construction may then be defined as an event construal where the Theme is chosen as the trajector of a process. Note that passive construals may also exist without the presence of the verb *be*, as in *He ordered the town destroyed by a bomber squadron.* As such, the verb *be* is not mechanically inserted, as is claimed by several formal analyses, but it profiles a temporal view of a passive process.

Not surprisingly, the content of perf₃ will be encoded in different ways in other languages. Passive markers, for instance, can be said to accomplish a function parallel to perf₃, since they designate a view of the event as profiling its terminal part; in other words, just like Romance, Germanic, and many other languages employ the passive structure to encode this type of construal, Indonesian (4b) and Nepali (5b) make use of a passive marker.

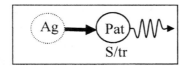

Figure 32.2. Passive

(4) Indonesian
   a. *Dokter   itu   me-meriksa   saya.*
      doctor   the   TRNS-examine   I
      'The doctor examined me.'
   b. *Saya   di-periksa   oleh   dokter   itu.*
      I   PASS-examine   by   doctor   the
      'I was examined by the doctor.'

(5) Nepali
   a. *Raj-le   Ram-lay   mar-yo.*
      Raj-ERG   Ram-OBJ   kill-PST.3SG.M
      'Raj killed Ram.'
   b. *Raj-dwara   Ram-lay   mar-I-yo.*
      Raj-OBL   Ram-OBJ   kill-PASS-PST.3SG.M
      'Ram was killed by Raj.'

As already mentioned, the second strategy for passive formation is one where the Agent is somehow downgraded. Shibatani (1984) convincingly shows that passives relate in many languages not only to reflexives and reciprocals, but crucially to potential, honorific, and spontaneous constructions, as exemplified by Japanese and Ainu. The following are examples from Japanese (Shibatani 1984), where *-are* marks passive, potential, honorific, and spontaneous constructions:

(6) Japanese
   a. *Taroo   wa   sikar-are-ta.*
      Taroo   TOP   scold-PASS-PST
      'Taro was scolded.'
   b. *Boku   wa   nemur-are-nakat-ta.*
      I   TOP   sleep-POT-NEG-PST
      'I could not sleep.'
   c. *Sensei   ga   waraw-are-ta.*
      Teacher   NOM   laugh-HON-PST
      'The teacher laughed (honorific).'
   d. *Mukasi   ga   sinob-are-ru.*
      old.time   NOM   think.about-SPON-PRS
      'An old time comes (spontaneously) to mind.'

According to Shibatani's survey, the use of the same form for passive and potential constructions is also found in Hindi, Turkish, Russian, and Nahuatl.

Similarly, passives and honorifics take the same marker in Chamorro, Mojave, Nahuatl, Guarijio, Quechua, and Indonesian. probably the most common coincidence is the use of the same marker for middle passives and spontaneous events, as attested in Romance languages as well as, for instance, in Russian, Chamorro, Guarijio, and Nahuatl. On the basis of this typological investigation, Shibatani has been able to show, thus confirming Jespersen (1924), that the primary pragmatic function of the passive is to defocus the Agent; as a result, the Agent is not syntactically encoded, and the patient becomes the subject.

Shibatani's proposal nicely accounts for a variety of pragmatically driven phenomena. As he points out, what passives and honorifics have in common is Agent defocusing; indeed, in conveying indirectness (6c), honorifics avoid singling out an Agent—be it the addressee, the speaker, or other actor, commonly marking the noun as plural (Shibatani 1984). Even more obvious is the association between passives and spontaneous (6d) and potential constructions (6b), both of which involve Agent defocusing in that they exclude the control of an Agent. As can be seen from (6d), if an event is dissociated from its Agent driving force, it will be construed as spontaneous. It is only a short step, then, from spontaneous to potential construals: both event types involve propensity for an event to happen, yet its actual occurring remains uncertain. This explains the fact that it is quite common for potential constructions to correlate with negative readings, as coded by-*nakat* in (6b). Finally, Shibatani accounts for the correlation between passive, stative, and resultative (perfect) constructions as a consequence of the inactive nature of the passive subject.

The merit of Shibatani's Agent defocusing strategy lies in the fact that it draws attention to a variety of pragmatic factors that had been left unnoticed in functional and formal analyses. Yet, his passive prototype excludes an overt Agent and is therefore, to some extent, insufficient in that it fails to account for overt Agent passives as deviations (from the prototype) involving incomplete defocusing of the Agent. As is well known, there are many languages whose passives permit an Agent coded in an oblique phrase.

As well, many languages commonly have more than one passive construction: one excluding the Agent (7c) and one strongly implying a specific Agent which may or may not be overtly coded (7b). As such, the contrastive examples from Spanish in (7b) and (7c) not only represent passive constructions as they are found in Romance languages, but in a variety of unrelated languages:

(7)   a. ACTIVE
        El   cerrajero   abri-ó la   puerta.
        DET.M   locksmith   open-PST.3SG   DET.F door
        'The locksmith opened the door.'

    b. PERIPHRASTIC PASSIVE
        La   puerta fue   adierta (por el   cerrajero).
        DET.F   door   be-PST.3SG   open-PP (by   DET.M   locksmith)
        'The door was opened (by the locksmith).'

c. REFLEXIVE/MIDDLE PASSIVE

La   puerta   se   abri-ó   (*por   el   cerrajero).
DET.F   door   mid   open-PST.3SG   (*by   DET.M   locksmith.M).
'The door opened/got opened (*by the locksmith).'

The Spanish data argues for two independent, though related, constructions encoding different conceptualizations. The periphrastic passive (7b) focuses on the process imposed on the Theme. Agent demotion is thus conditioned by the Theme focusing strategy. Whether the demoted implied Agent is elaborated or not is of secondary importance for the more process-oriented conceptualization of the periphrastic construction. In contrast, the reflexive/middle passive responds to Shibatani's Agent defocusing construction. It is my contention, then, that the two alternative conceptualizations complement each other. As such, the languages of the world may either have one of the two construction types, or they can develop both constructions for separate discourse purposes, as is the case for Spanish. This ties in with Langacker's (2000) approach to constituency, that in an event construal not only the actual construction is at play but that equally informative are the constituent steps building that event. Figures 32.3 and 32.4 represent the two alternative construals. In the periphrastic construction (figure 32.3), the conceptualizer's (C) operation consists of focusing on the thematic core of the event. Although the Agent is demoted to oblique, it is strongly implied in the event and can, but needs not, be made specific. In the reflexive/middle passive (figure 32.4), the operation involves defocusing the Agent, who in turn can only be represented in highly schematic terms as an initiating driving force. It is this type of construal that allows the defocusing passive (see 6) to correlate with spontaneous, honorific, and potential markers.

We have seen that the Indonesian, Achenese, and Nepali examples in (4) and (5), the Spanish periphrastic passive, and the English *be*-passive correspond to the "Theme in focus" strategy, while the Japanese example in (6), the spontaneous Spanish passive in (7c), and the impersonal middle (e.g., *Se resolvieron los problemas entre los candidatos* 'The problems among the candidates were solved') correspond to the "Agent-defocusing" strategy.

The construals in figures 32.3 and 32.4 constitute the basis for a variety of aspectual contrasts in passive constructions. For one, the Dutch auxiliary passive with *worden* 'to become' shows a contrast parallel to that in figures 32.3 and 32.4 with the passive with *zijn* 'to be'. Verhagen (1992) has shown that *worden* construes the concept designated by the stem of the participle as a process coming about. Consequently, it presents the situation from the perspective of a participant other than the Agent. This produces the pragmatic effect of deliberate backgrounding of the Agent, which can then be used for ironic purposes and similar pragmatic inferences. On the other hand, the *zijn*-passive is more stative and does not invite the inference that the Agent is present in the situation, thus no special effects obtain as a result of leaving the Agent's viewpoint aside. The contrast can be observed below:

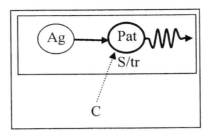

Figure 32.3. Passive: Theme in focus

(8) *Er   wordt   gehold en   gerold en   iemand   roept:...*
     There be(comes) run   and rolled and somebody   calls:...
     'There is running and rolling and somebody calls:...'
(9) *Er   is jarenlang verbazend hard gewerkt.*
     There is years.long amazingly hard worked
     'For years, there has been some amazingly hard working.'

Verhagen claims that the irony in (8) comes from the fact that while *hollen* 'running' and *rollen* 'rolling' invokes a process with agentive participants, with *worden* these processes are presented as if they did not originate from any specific source. Since the *zijn*-passive (9) implies no Agent, there is no expectations conflict and no ironic reading is invoked. While *worden* encodes the "Theme in focus" construal, *zijn* corresponds to Shibatani's "Agent-defocused" construction.

The English *get*-construction seems to be a blend of the "Theme in focus" and the "defocused Agent" construal. To begin with, it should be pointed out that, following Langacker (2000: 312–14), I regard *get*-constructions—lexical as well as grammatical ones—as consisting of a finite verb (plus Agent) and a passive participial complement (comprising an Agent and a Patient), whereby the Agent of *get* and the Patient of the verb in the complement crucially denote the same participant (see figure 32.5). The development from a full verb to a grammatical passive marker involves defocusing the Agent of *get*, allowing the Patient complement to become most prominent. Illustrating this development are the following examples from Langacker (2000: 312):

(10) a. Sue got (herself) appointed to the governing board.
      b. Ralph got fired again.
      c. All my books got stolen.
      d. Another bank got robbed last night.

In all the examples in (10), the "Theme in focus" strategy has applied in the (passive) participial complement. Thus, the patient is profiled as the trajector of the complement. Now, the defocused Agent strategy is also applied to the trajector of *get*. In (10a), Sue is still construed as a volitional subject that brings about the event designated by the participle, for her benefit. The high degree of subject self-

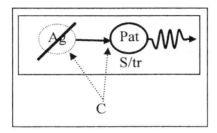

Figure 32.4. Passive: Defocused agent

involvement triggers the use of the reflexive pronoun. Sentence (10b), then, illustrates the most common form of the *get* passive, where the subject may still be responsible in some way for the participial complement, but where his control has substantially decreased in that he does not volitionally control its occurrence (Lakoff 1971; Givón 1990; Givón and Yang 1998; Langacker 2000). Control is gradually reduced to zero from (10c) to (10d). Here, the complement trajector cannot be responsible since in both cases it is inanimate. And while the possessor in (10c) may be vaguely responsible for having left the books unattended, in (10d) no participant is to blame for the robbery. In the following diagrams, slightly modified from Langacker (2000), the "Theme in focus" strategy can be observed in the smaller rectangle, as the Patient is the complement trajector and the Agent is backgrounded. The defocusing Agent strategy in (10b)–(10d) is schematically represented in the change from the double arrow in figure 32.5a (where the Agent still has control) via a dashed arrow in figure 32.5b (depicting the Agent losing control) to the nonbold circle in figure 32.5c (the most grammaticized case where the subject of *get* is no longer in profile).

Finally, let us turn to the issue of passives in intransitive stems. As can be seen from Shibatani's (1984) Latin, Welsh, and German examples in (11)–(13), the main operation is one of Agent defocusing, as claimed by Shibatani.

(11) Latin
      pugn-aba-tur.
      fight-IMPERF-3SG.PASS
      'It was fought. (i.e., There was some fighting).'

(12) German
      Hier   wurde   ganzen   Abend   getanzt.
      here   become.PST   all.ACC   evening   danced
      'There was dancing here all night.'

(13) Welsh
      Dannsywyd   gan   y   plant.
      danced   with   DET   children
      'It was danced by the children.'

Notice that in the case of Welsh in (13), the oblique Agent is interpreted as defocused since the verb is intransitive and there is no focused thematic argument

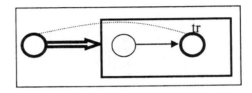

Figure 32.5a. *Get*

downplaying *the children*. Now the important restriction about intransitives is that Agent defocusing only obtains with agentive subjects as attested by the ungrammaticality of examples in Welsh (14) and Spanish (16), both of which involve a non-active subject:

(14) **Tyfwud   gan   y   plant   yn   sydyn.*
      grown   with   DET   children   PRED   suddenly
      'There was growing by the children suddenly.' (Perlmutter and Postal 1984: 145)

(15) *Se   bailó   en   grande   toda   la   noche.*
      IMPERS/MID   dance-PST.3SG   in   great   all.F   DET.F   night
      '(They) danced a great deal all night.'

(16) **Se   creció   mucho.*
      IMPERS/MID   grow-PST.3SG   much
      '(They) grew a lot.'

Yet the question is whether all of these constructions involving an intransitive stem are actually passive. Let us therefore consider sentence (12) from German and sentences (11) and (15) from Latin and Spanish in somewhat more detail: (12) exemplifies the presentative construction and (11) and (15) the impersonal active construction (Cennamo 1993; Maldonado 1999). For one, while these constructions show overlap with the passive in that their Agent is made schematic, no passive meaning is put forward. Indeed, crucial to passive constructions (and passive meaning) is the fact that the change-of-state undergone by a thematic subject is made most prominent, and this is not the case in the examples under discussion. What is put in profile is an action being performed, not its terminal point. Note that impersonal constructions are in clear contrast with medio-passive and spontaneous constructions whose subject can be thematic:

(17) *Se   abrieron   las   puertas.*
      MID   open.PST.3PL   DET.F.PL   doors
      'The doors opened.'

Second, the fact that the passive marker extends to impersonal constructions is in itself not sufficient evidence to view them as passive. The impersonal *se* pronoun, not the passive, can be translated by the English impersonal *they* or by the French impersonal pronoun *on* as in *On a dancé beaucoup* 'They danced a lot'. Moreover, *se* impersonal constructions designate generic situations where people

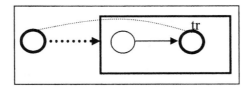

Figure 32.5b. *Get'*

in general tend to do different actions. Again, the focus is on the action, not on the result or on the end point of the event. Notice from (18) that the Agent is schematically encoded by the clitic *se*, and *lugares* 'places' cannot be interpreted as the subject since there is no number agreement with the verb:

(18) *En lugar-es como ese se crec-e/bail-a bien.*
in place-PL like DEM MID grow-PRS.3SG/dance PRS.3SG well
'In places like that one grows/dances well.'

Finally in current Mexican Spanish, it is also possible to have impersonal past constructions referring to specific actions developed by unidentified people, as in the dialogue in (19):

(19) *Qué tal estuvo la fiesta?* 'How was the party?'
Genial, se bebió y se bailó en grande. 'Great, people drunk and danced a great deal.'

No passive reading is attainable here, and no passive interpretation can be obtained in all dialects of Spanish when the clitic *se* designates an arbitrary interpretation of the Agent equivalent to 'one' or 'we', as in (20):

(20) *No contamos con los recursos necesarios, así que se hizo lo que se pudo.* 'We did not have the funds needed, so we (one) did what we (one) could.'

These data suggest that the "Agent-defocused" strategy may be a source for passive formation in languages that do not have the option of profiling the Theme, while for languages having the two options, the "Agent-defocused" strategy leads to impersonal constructions that need not be interpreted as passive.

3.2. Oblique Agent

So far, we have seen that the various strategies to profile the Theme are crucial to the passive construction. Yet the way the Agent is encoded must also be taken into consideration.

The way the oblique Agent is linguistically encoded provides crucial information about the basic strategies to construct a passive. Figures 32.3 and 32.4 represent two ways in which the prominence of the Agent in the active clause can be

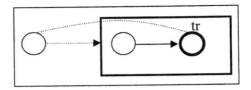

Figure 32.5c. *Get"*

downplayed in the passive construction. In the "Theme-in-focus" construal, there is always an Agent as driving force—with different degrees of prominence. When the Agent is not expressed, it remains in the base; when it is overtly expressed as an oblique phrase, the Agent's driving force is downplayed with respect to the main change-of-state designated by the passive. The presence of an oblique phrase is not just the result of mechanical demotion, but it is meaningful. In the case of English, the *by*-phrase lexicalizes the source of energy bringing about actions (21b) as well as effected objects (21a):

(21)   a. The sculpture is by Zúñiga
        b. Bragging by officers will not be allowed. (examples taken from
           Langacker 1982: 69)

Both *sculpture* and *bragging* constitute the trajector of the clause; they only differ in that the former is nominal and the former processual.

As the *by*-phrase may be the source of energy bringing about a new object or an action, it constitutes the natural choice for coding a downplayed Agent. Its input in a passive construction in (22) is the same as in the nominal and the processual examples in (21a) and (21b):

(22)   The keynote was delivered by Talmy.

This characterization allows us to differentiate passive and stative constructions. Consider (23):

(23)   a. His antics amuse me.
        b. I am amused at his antics.
        c. I am amused by his antics.

As observed by Langacker (after Postal 1971), (23c) is a passive, but (23b) is not. The latter conforms to the stative, adjectival value of perf$_2$. The prepositional phrase *at* simply designates a location always accessible for contact. The experiencer can either receive some impulse from, or have access to, *antics* for the sensation of amusement to come about. In contrast, in (23c), the *by*-phrase designates the source of energy effectuating a change-of-state in the Experiencer, as coded by perf$_3$. To the extent that the oblique phrase depicts an initiating cause, a perf$_3$ construal obtains, resulting in a passive construction.

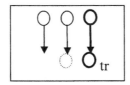

Figure 32.6a. *by* nominal

The contrast between initiating source and noninitiative location is of course gradual. Inanimate entities can be construed as agentive if conceptualized as literally extending from an animate Agent (e.g., a stone can be viewed as agentive if it is construed as extending from the stone thrower). As such, the polish Agent/ Instrumental contrast from Słoń (2000) is thus common in Romance languages, English, and many other languages:

(24) a. *Okno*   *zostało*   *stłuczone*
        window.NOM   become.PST:PERF:3SG   break.PST PART:PERF:SG
        przez   *kamień.*
        by   stone.ACC
        'The window was broken by a stone.'
     b. *Okno*   *zostalo*   *stłuczone*
        window.NOM   become.PST.PERF.3SG   break-PST PART.PERF.SG
        kamieniem.
        stone.INST
        'The window was broken with a stone.'

Inanimate elements may become "sources of energy" (and thus assume the properties of an Agent), while the opposite transformation—Agents becoming Instruments—is quite uncommon (Słoń 2000). Thus, across languages (24a) tends to be acceptable, but *The window was broken with John* tends to be rejected, as can be expected from a general tendency to humans as Agents not as Instruments of some other initiating force.

Common to all situations rendered by the passive construction is that the second most prominent participant of its active counterpart is coded as the trajector of the event in the passive. This situation is typical of accusative-dominant languages, which basically trace an event using an OUT > IN strategy. In languages using the alternative IN > OUT strategy, we would expect antipassives, which render the reverse type of construal, to be quite productive. This phenomenon is addressed in the following section.

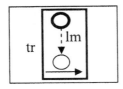

Figure 32.6b. *by* processual

4. ANTIPASSIVES

Antipassives are best conceived as the mirror image of passive constructions. While in the passive the Theme becomes most prominent, in antipassives the Theme is downplayed giving the Agent maximal prominence. Antipassives are commonly, but not exclusively, found in ergative-dominant systems, where, as I have suggested previously, the event is naturally traced from the CORE > OUT, that is, from the change-of-state undergone by the Theme to its event-initiating driving force. Thus, under normal circumstances the Theme is first accessed to trace the event and as such it receives special prominence. While in accusative-dominant systems the passive construction attributes secondary status to the Agent, in ergative-dominant systems the antipassive construction gives less prominence to the Theme, resulting in decreased accessibility to the energy transmission from the event-initiating driving force and, correspondingly, increased difficulty to fully complete the intended event. In other words, the antipassive indicates that the action is not fully carried out since there is a certain degree of difficulty for the Agent to have the intended effect on the object (Dixon 1980; Cooreman 1994). In the following examples, the degree of affectedness of the object decreases in the antipassive construction:

(25)   Chamorro
    a. *Un-patek   i   ga'lago.*
       ERG.2SG-kick   the   dog
       'You kicked the dog.'
    b. *Mamatek   hao   gi   ga'lago.*
       AP-kick   2SG.ABS   LOC   dog
       'You kicked at the dog.' (Cooreman 1988: 578)
(26)   Samoan
    a. *Sa   'ai   e   le   tiene   le   i'a.*
       PST   eat   ERG   DET   girl   DET   fish
       'The girl ate (all of) the fish.'
    b. *Sa   'ai   le   tiene   i   le   i'a.*
       PST   eat   DET   girl   LOC   DET   fish
       'The girl ate some of the fish (lit.: at the fish).' (Mosel 1989; cited in Cooreman 1994: 61)

The ergative-absolutive behavior of these examples is evidenced by the change of the ergative marking on the Agent in the transitive samples (23a) and (24a) to its absolutive marking in the antipassive construction in (25b) and (26b). Note that in Samoan, as in many other ergative languages, the absolutive is zero-marked. Alternatively, in (25b) and (26b), *fish* and *dog* are oblique. In languages that do not have an antipassive marker *per se*, locative, dative, and genitive are common antipassive markers.

The inability rendered by antipassive constructions to fully carry the intended effect on the object can be viewed as conceptual distance. While in the active the subject makes contact with, and imposes some change in the object, in the antipassive, the downplayed object, now an oblique, is at a relative distance from the subject's action and is not available for contact. This contrast between active direct and antipassive can be represented as in figures 32.1 and 32.7.

Since in the antipassive construction the downplayed object is not available for contact, energy transmission is not totally projected onto the object (the dotted arrow), and as such no affectedness is predicated (no squiggly arrow).

The notion of "conceptual distance" provides a natural way to account for a variety of meanings normally associated with the antipassive construction. Example (23b) is the prototypical case of an antipassive whose object is not as affected as the direct object would be in an active-direct construction. In this example, the subject may not have been lucky enough to hit the dog when kicking it, or he or she may have not have affected the dog as much as he or she would have expected. Example (26b) represents another common use of the antipassive: the partitive reading. While the active involves eating the whole fish, the antipassive involves eating only a portion. We can see, then, that conceptual distance may operate at two levels: (i) it may diminish the degree of affectedness of the oblique object, or (ii) the event may not be taken to full completion. The partitive reading in Samoan (26b), in fact, contains both: the complex object is not totally affected, and the event is not fully completed. Yet either reading may occur independently: according to Bittner (1987), in Greenlandic Eskimo the antipassive may depict noncompleted events:

(27)   Greenlandic Eskimo (Bittner 1987)
    a. *Jaaku-p   illu   taa-nna   sana-pa-a.*
       Jacob-ERG house this.SG-ABS build-TRNS.IND-3SG.ERG/3SG:ABS
       'Jacob built/was building this house (may but need not have finished).'
    b. *Jaaku   illu-mik   taa-ssuinnga   sana-Ø-pu-p.*
       Jacob   house-INST   this-SG.INST   build-AP-INT.IND-3SG:ABS
       'Jacob was/is building this house (has not finished yet).'

In other languages, it designates low degree of individuation/identification of the oblique object, such that the Patient is not accessible for the Agent to interact with. Thus, the antipassive designates a low degree of affectedness on the Theme. In Chamorro, the antipassive is obligatory when the object is indefinite (Cooreman 1987); as such, the antipassive in (28a) contrasts with the ergative construction in (28b), which contains a definite object (examples taken from Cooreman 1994: 54):

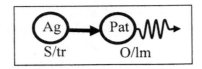

Figure 32.1'. Active

(28)   a. *Mgnonne'   (guihan)   i   peskadot.*
          AP.catch   (fish)   DET   fisherman
          'The fisherman caught a fish.'
       b. *Ha   -kone'   i   peskadot   i   guihan.*
          ERG.3SG -catch   DET   fisherman   DET   fish
          'The fisherman caught the fish.'

Furthermore, in Greenlandic Eskimo the antipassive may be employed when the speaker has a nonspecific referent in mind or some specific referent that he or she does not want to specify (see Bittner 1987):

(29)   a. *atuartut   ilaat   ikiur-tariaqar-pa-ra.*
          of.students one.of.them.ABS   help-must-TRNS.IND-1SG.ERG/3SG.ABS
          'I must help one of the students.'
       b. *atuartut   ilaannik   ikiu-i-sariaqar-pu-nga.*
          of.students one.of.them.INST   help-AP-must-INTR.IND-1SG.ABS
          'I must help one of the students.' (any student will do)

The extreme case of low individuation/identification occurs where the object is not expressed at all. The antipassive is commonly used when the object is not identified. In the case of Mam (Mayan), for instance, the antipassive construction does not allow for the unknown or unspecified object to be explicitly encoded (example taken from Cooreman 1994: 53; as cited in England 1988: 533):

(30)   a. *ma   Ø-   -w   -aq'na-7n-a.*
          PERF   ABS.3SG -ERG.1SG -work-DS-1SG
          'I worked on it.' (something)
       b. *ma   chin   aq'naa-n-a.*
          PERF   ABS.1SG work-AP-1SG
          'I worked.' (no implication of what was worked on)

The lack of an overt object is represented in figure 32.8 by the dotted circle, which means that the object remains implicit in the base; the downplayed object construal is represented in figure 32.7'; here, the object is a regular part of the base.

We can see that the object may be left implicit for a wide variety of pragmatic reasons, most notably to designate general tendencies and routine actions. It may also be left implicit when the object is easily recoverable from context or when the speaker wants to keep the object unspecified although it may be definite. One may

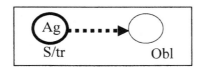

Figure 32.7. Antipassive

be tempted to suggest a grammaticalization continuum where the object first is downgraded to oblique and then is deleted; however, Cooreman (1994) points out that no language in her survey uses the antipassive to downplay the oblique object without also allowing optional or obligatory object deletion. It seems reasonable to suggest, then, that the conceptual path of antipassive object demotion goes from implicit to oblique rather than the other way around:

(31) ANTIPASSIVE OBJECT DEMOTION:
      object > implicit > oblique

In other words, there seem to be two general pragmatic motivations for the object's absence. Either it is recoverable from the verb's meaning or the action is generic. In contrast, when the antipassive downgrades the object to oblique, it does so to designate more specific situations where the object is not totally affected or the event is not totally completed.

Given these meanings, we may expect important aspectual correlates. While passives are most commonly associated with perfective aspect (perfect, resultative, and stative),[2] antipassives tend to take imperfective aspect (durative, continuative, repetitive, and habitual) (Tsunoda 1988). Imperfective antipassives tend to depict general tendencies for things to happen as well as habitual and repetitive actions. The habitual is represented by the Tsutsujil (Maya) example (from Dayley 1985: 346), and the repetitive is from Chamorro. Both examples have been taken from Cooreman (1994: 57–58):

(32) Tsutsujil
      Ja   nuutee7   b'aráata   nk'ayin   wi7.
      the   my.mother   cheaply   3SG.ABS.sell.AP   EMPH
      'My mother sells cheaply (at low prices).'
(33) Chamorro
      Mang-galuti   gue'   ni   ga'lago.
      AP-hit   ABS   OBL   dog
      'He pounded on/repeatedly hit the dog.'

The passive and the antipassive correspond to construals where the default most prominent participant or trajector is downplayed to profile a landmark. There is an alternative strategy where a secondary participant may gain prominence without downgrading the trajector to oblique. Inverse constructions, as introduced in the next section, accomplish that purpose.

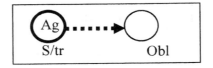

Figure 32.7'. Antipassive

5. INVERSE

Inverse voice involves coding a secondary participant as the most prominent element in an event without downgrading the participant naturally chosen as event trajector. The construction involves the presence of a marker indicating that the default representation of an event has been reversed in favor of a secondary participant. Crucially, grammatical relations—subject and object—remain unchanged. In Olutec, a Mixe-Zoquean language from Mexico, first person is the default prominent element, in that it usually is more prominent than third person; as such, when the default event representation is reversed, with the subject as third person and the object as first, the inverse marker is used:

(34)   Olutec (Zavala 2003)
    a. DIRECT 1:3
       Tan-tze:k-küx-u   *ja7.*
       ERG1.scold-3PL-COMPL   3PRO
       'I scolded them.'
    b. INVERSE 3:1
       *Ta-tze:k-küx-**ü**-w-a7.*
       ABS1-scold-3PL-**INV**-COMPL-3PRO
       'They scolded me.'

Likewise, in the classical Algonquian voice system (Dahlstrom 1986), the third-person arguments Agent and Patient contrast in terms of topicality: the more topical is case-marked as proximate, and the less topical as obviate. In the active direct clause, the Agent is the proximate and the Patient is the obviate. The inverse is used when there is a topicality switch; that is, the Patient becomes the proximate, and the Agent is the obviate, as in (35b) (from Givón 1994: 20; citing Dahlstrom 1986), where the young man is more prominent than his father—note that the Agent is still the grammatical subject and that the verb remains active:

(35)   a. DIRECT
       *Aya.hcinniw-**ah*** *nisto* *e.h-npaha.t*   *awa* *na.pe.sis*
       Blackfoot-**OBV** there kill/**DIR-3/OBV** this boy/**PROX**
       'The boy [PROX] killed the Blackfoot (men) [OBV]'

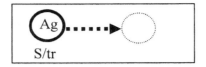

Figure 32.8. Antipassive implicit object

b. INVERSE

*osa.m   e.-sa.khikot   ohta.wiy-**ah**   wa   o.skini.kiw*
much   love/INV/OBV-3   his/father-OBV   this   young.man/PROX
'(For) his father [OBV] loved this young man [PROX] too'

In general, the obviate can be said to mark a participant conceptualized as distant from the norm (Langacker 1990: 248): a participant may be physically, socially, or temporally distant from the speaker; or he or she may be distant in the sense of being dissimilar—in terms of individuation, animacy, agentivity, and so forth—from the prototypical representation in a given domain. As such, in (35b), where the Patient is more prominent than the Agent, the inverse construction signals dissimilarity from a prototypical situation where the Patient participant would be *less* prominent than the Agent.

In a similar vein, Givón (1994: 23) has proposed tentatively that the inverse signals "a norm reversal vis-à-vis the expected relative topicality of event participants," and Cook (1997) has extended that definition of the inverse as a system marking norm reversal to various other domains. A crucial case is that of Samoan, in which the inverse suffix *-ina* (and its allomorph *-a*) covers a wide array of domains. One relevant domain is certainly animacy. In particular, entities which score high on the animacy scale are prototypically marked by the ergative. In contrast with humans, then, an animal marked for ergative is distant from the expected norm; thus, it takes the inverse marker, as in (36b):

(36)   a. *Na   opo   e   le   tama   le   tiene.*
          PAST   hug   ERG   the   boy   the   girl
          'The boy hugged the girl.'
       b. *'Ua   etoeto-ina   lona   lima   e   le   pusi.*
          PERF   lick-INV   his   hand   ERG   the   cat
          'The cat licked his [a person's] hand.'

Inverse marking is determined by an animacy scale where humans score higher than animals. This pattern is also found in Mayan languages and is also expected in other languages with an inverse system.

Cook shows, following Chung (1978), that the use of the inverse suffix *-ina* does not signal a change in grammatical relations. In an inverse construction, the participant marked for ergative remains the trajector of the clause. This can be tested in at least two evident situations. In an EQUI-construction, it is the ergative subject of the embedded transitive clause, as in (37a), which can be deleted under coreference with the main-clause subject. The ungrammaticality of (37b) comes from deleting the absolute instead of the ergative subject:

(37)   a. E   *alu*   *le*   *fili*   *e*   *fa'aleaga(-ina)*   *le*   *nu'u.*
          IMPERF   go   the   enemy   INF   destroy(-ina)   the   village
          'The enemy is going (literally moving through space) to destroy
          the village.'

       b. *E   *alu*   *le*   *tiene e*   *opo(-ina)*   *e*   *le*   *tama.*
          IMPERF   go   the   girl INF   liug-itia   ERG   the   boy
          'The girl is going [literally moving through space] to be hugged
          by the boy.'

Likewise, only the ergative subject, as in (38a)—not the absolute object, as in (38b)—of an embedded clause can raise to be the main clause subject:

(38)   a. *E*   *mafia*   *e*   *le*   *tama*   *ona*   *fululu(-ina)*   *le*   *ta'avale.*
          IMPERF   able   ERG   the   boy   COMP   wash-ina   the   car
          'The boy can wash the car'

       b. *E*   *mafia*   *le*   *ta'avale*   *ona*   *fulufu(-ina)*   *e*   *le*   *tlama.*
          IMPERF   able   the   car   COMP   wash(-ina)   ERG   the   boy
          'The car can be washed by the boy.'

In support of the claim that the inverse marks events involving reversal of a norm in different domains, Cook shows that the inverse also selects as trajector socially remote roles, such as doctors, the government, an enemy, or an institution, as in (39) and (40), and, above all, the Christian God, as in (41):

(39)   *Sá*   *'ve' 'ese-ina*   *e*   *leoleo*   *le*   *pâgotâ.*
       PST   take.away-INV   ERG   police   the   prisoner
       'The police took the prisoner away.' (Milner 1966: 38)

(40)   *'Ua*   *tâofi-a*   *lona*   *'alauni*   *e*   *le*   *Mâlo.*
       PERF   stop-INV   his   allowance   ERG   the   Government
       'The Government has stopped his allowance.' (Milner 1966: 241)

(41)   *'Ua*   *sâuni-a*   *e*   *Iesû*   *le*   *fa'olataga.*
       PST   prepare-INV   ERG   Jesus   the   salvation
       'Jesus has prepared the salvation.' (Milner 1966: 220)

Further extensions of this pattern of reversal apply to cases of negativity. Since affirmative events are expected to take place, negative ones are deviations from the norm. While the negative meaning takes -ina, the affirmative does not:

(42)   a. *Fufulu*   *le*   *ta'avale.*
          wash   the   car
          'Wash the car.'

       b. *'Aua*   *le*   *fufulu-ina*   *le*   *ta'avale.*
          don't   the   wash-INV   the   car
          'Don't wash the car.'

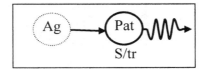

Figure 32.3'. Passive

As well, the pattern applies to the contrast between actions and states. Since verbs predominantly designate actions, states are conceived as deviations from the norm. They are thus marked by *-ina*, signaling an inverse construction. Example (43a) constitutes the norm, while the inverse in (43b) reverses the expected norm:

(43) a. *'O   le'âfa'aitiiti   lana   tologi.*
        FUT   reduce   his   salary
        'His salary will be reduced.' (Milner 1966: 88)
    b. *'Ua   fa'aitiiti-a   le   âiga.*
        PERF   reduce-INV   the   family
        'The family has been reduced in numbers.' (Milner 1966: 88)

Finally, word-order changes in Samoan also take the inverse *-ina* marker. This is the case of Agent-fronting in a relative clause (44b), question formation about the Agent (44c), and a cleft sentence (44d). All these cases contrast with the un-marked direct sentence where the Agent takes ergative marking, as in (44a):

(44) a. *Na   fufulu   e   le   tama   le   ta'avale.*
        PST   wash   ERG   the   boy   the   car
        'The boy washed the car.'
    b. *'O   fea   le   tama   na   fufulu-ina   le   ta'avale?*
        PRED   where   the   boy   PST   wash-INV   the   car
        'Where is the boy who washed the car?'
    c. *'O   ai   na   fufulu-ina   le   fa'avale?*
        PRED   who   PST   wash-INV   the   car
        'Who washed the car? (Who is it that washed the car)'
    d. *'O   le   tama   na   fululu-ina   le   ta'avale.*
        PRED   the   boy   PST   wash-INV   the   car
        'It is the boy who washed the car.'

While there are important parallels between the passive and the inverse in that they give special prominence to the default secondary figure, these voice patterns also show a clear contrast: the inverse does not downgrade the original primary figure of the event, while the passive does. Diagrams 32.3' and 32.9 represent this contrast.

Figure 32.9 shows that in the inverse construction, as in the active-direct construction, both the grammatical relations subject/object and the asymmetry between trajector and landmark are preserved. Yet, the import of the inverse construction is to focus on the landmark letting the trajector remain the primary

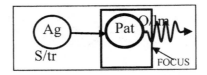

Figure 32.9. Inverse

figure. Inverse constructions iconically represent the default cultural values of a social group being linguistically coded and being reversed for specific communicative purposes. The inverse construction simultaneously shows the default interpretation and the way the norm has been reversed.

In all the languages considered so far, there exists some type of asymmetry between participants—most notably between Agent and Patient—for which different profiling adjustments can take place. The case of Philippine languages poses a different set of voice alternations; they are briefly discussed in the following section.

6. PHILIPPINE LANGUAGES

Philippine languages constitute a knotty problem for voice systems. Unlike in most languages, in the Philippine family the verb does not impose a clear asymmetry between trajector and landmark. Thus, a verb of action does not designate the Agent as the obvious default trajector. In fact, the most common pattern is one where the Patient/Theme is the trajector—which, for Givón (1990) and Payne (1982), suggests that these languages are ergative. Against that view, Shibatani (1988) has offered an approach in terms of prototypicality and prominence, according to which the Agent-actor is preferred over the Theme in "long distance" phenomena such as gapping in coordinate structures. While the most general pattern is that the topic nominal, be it the goal or the actor, controls the subordinate gap, in coordinate constructions the actor can be the controller, regardless of whether it is a topic or not (Shibatani 1988: 121)

At present, the data are far from conclusive. In the Philippine languages, any participant (locative, instrumental, benefactive, etc.) may be selected as the most prominent participant in the event (Bell 1983); furthermore, voice alternations are determined by the element chosen as event trajector. By way of illustration, consider the Tagalog examples in (45a)–(45d), which have been extracted from Schachter (1976): (i) the marker *ang* denotes the selected trajector; this role is variously filled by the Agent in (45a), the Theme (goal) in (45b), the Locative in (45c), and the Beneficiary in (45d); (ii) the verb receives an affix indicating the voice type of the clause, which, in turn, is determined by the element chosen as event trajector, or clause focus).

(45)   a. AGENT IN FOCUS (AF)

   Mag-*salis*   **ang** babae   ng   bigas   sa   sako   para sa bata.
   AF-will.take.out   TR   woman   DET   rice   LOC   sack   BEN   child
   'The woman will take some rice out of a/the sack for {a/the} child.'

   b. THEME IN FOCUS (TF)

   *Aalis-**in***   ng   babae   **ang**   bigas   sa   sako para sa bata.
   will.take.out-TF   DET   woman   TR   rice   LOC   sack   BEN   child
   '{A/the} woman will take the rice out of {a/the} sack for the child.'

   c. LOCATION IN FOCUS (LF)

   *Aalis-**an***   ng   babae   ng   bigas   **ang** sako   para sa   bata.
   will.take.out-LF   DET   woman   DET   rice   TR   sack   BEN   child
   '{A/the} woman will take the rice out of the sack for {a/the} child.'

   d. BENEFICIARY IN FOCUS (BF)

   Ipag-*salis*   ng   babae   ng   bigas   sa   sako   **ang**   bata.
   BF-will.take.out   DET   woman   DET   rice   LOC   sack   TR   child
   '{A/the} woman will take the rice out of {a/the}sack for the child.'

Notice that choosing one participant as the trajector does not imply defocusing or demoting any other element in the clause. In light of these facts, Langacker (2003) suggests that the verb in these languages is unspecified for trajector. Thus, *ang* is best analyzed as a marker imposing an element in focus and determining a particular voice structure. (See Reid 2002 for a compatible analysis of the problem).

While the voice phenomena discussed in sections 2–5 represent profile adjustments in which the event default object can be either profiled or downplayed in contrast with the default event trajector, in the Philippine languages, one element is selected as the main figure without downplaying any other participant in the event. The fact that Agent and Patient are most commonly chosen as event trajectors is attributable to the basic configuration of the languages of the world, where participants are by default more prominent than the setting.

The last profiling strategy to be considered is precisely opposite to the Philippine system. Middle voice, as introduced in the next section, is a construal which involves focusing on, and selecting, the subject in detriment of all other event participants.

7. MIDDLE VOICE

7.1. Middle Voice as a Signal of Change-of-State Affecting the Subject Only

Middle voice depicts actions, events, or states pertaining to the subject's own sphere. It contrasts with active-direct voice in that the action or change-of-state remains focused on the subject instead of being directed to another participant. In other words, "the 'action' or 'state' affects the subject of the verb or his interests" (Lyons 1968: 373). Further, in light of Kemmer's (1993b, 1994) claim that voice patterns reflect situation types, the transitive active corresponds to situations where two participants (most commonly Agent/Patient) interact; middle voice marking, in contrast, signals situation types implying only the subject, or as I previously stated it (Maldonado 1992, 1999), the middle construction focuses on the subject's dominion. As such, middles easily overlap with intransitive constructions since both construction types involve one participant: what in some languages is expressed with an intransitive verb takes a middle marker in others. Consider, for instance, the well-known contrast between such intransitive verbs in English as exemplified in (46) and their middle-marked equivalents in other languages (middle marking is in bold):

(46)   English   *wash*
       Latin   *lavo-**r***
       Spanish   *lavar-**se***

In languages having an intransitive/middle contrast, the middle designates an extra feature, a semantic specification not present in the plain intransitive. One obvious example is the aspectual contrast in Spanish verbs of motion:

(47)   a. *Valeria   subi-ó   el   Popocatepetl   in   dos   días.*
          Valeria   went.up-3SG   the   Popocatepetl   in   two   days
          'Valeria went/climbed up the Popocatepetl Mountain in two days.'
       b. *Al ver al   ratón   Valeria   **se**   subi-ó   a   la   mesa de un   salto.*
          As see the   mouse   Valeria   MID   go.up-PST   to   the   table of one   jump
          'As Valeria saw the mouse, she got on the table in one jump.'

In contrast with the (long) imperfective path depicted by the plain intransitive in (47a), the middle in (47b) involves an abrupt change of location. Languages, of course, need not have an intransitive/middle contrast. Tarascan, a Mesoamerican language from Mexico, employs several middle markers to designate a wide variety of situations remaining in the subject's dominion (Nava and Maldonado 2004). In (48a), the middle marker *-pi* refers to a subject's physical feature, while in (48b) the middle marker *-ku* 'angle' designates the subject's change of position:

(48)   a. *Siranta   ch'era-**pi**-s-Ø-ti.*
          paper   wrinkle-PRED.MID-PERF-PRS-IND.3
          'The paper got/is wrinkled.'
       b. *Dora   ke-nti-**ku**-s-Ø-ti.*
          Dora   move-angle-MID-PERF-PRS-IND.3
          'Dora hid in the corner [of the room].'

Kemmer (1994) identifies a relatively small number of situations expected to be middle-marked translinguistically and illustrates them with examples from assorted languages of the world. The following is a small sample from Kemmer (1994):

a. Grooming or body care
   Latin   *lavo-r* 'wash'
   Indonesian   **ber**-*dandan* 'get dressed'
b. Non translational motion
   Kanuri   tàn-**t**-în 'stretch one's body'
   Latin   *reverto-r* 'turn'
c. Change in body posture
   Indonesian   **ber**-*lutut* 'kneel-down'
   Guugu Yimidhir   d*aga*-**adhi** 'sit down'
d. Translational motion
   Pangwa   **i**-nu-xa 'climb up'
   Indonesian   **ber**-*djalan* 'go away'
e. Naturally reciprocal events
   Latin   *amplecto-r* 'embrace'
   Sanskrit   *amvadat-e* 'speak together'
f. Indirect middle
   Turkish   *ed-**in*** 'acquire'
   Classical Greek   *kta-**sthai*** 'acquire for oneself'
g. Emotion middle
   Mohave   **mat** iθa:v 'be angry'
   Hungarian   *bán-**kod**-* 'grieve, mourn'
h. Emotive speech actions
   Latin   . *quero-r* 'complain'
   Cl. Greek   *olophyre-**sthai*** 'lament'
   Turkish   döv-**ün** 'lament'
i. Cognition middle
   Indonesian   **ber**-*pikir* 'be cogitating'
   pangwa   -**i**-*sala* 'think over, consider'
j. Spontaneous events
   French   *s'evatiouir* 'vanish'
   Hungarian   *kelet-**kez**-* 'originate, occur'

Spanish is particularly interesting in that it has middle verbs for all categories suggested by Kemmer. For space restrictions, I will simply provide the most representative ones from Spanish:

a. Interaction limited to body part or inalienable possession ~ grooming or body care: *lavarse* 'wash', *peinarse* 'comb'
b. Self benefit actions ~ benefactive middle: *conseguirse* 'get', *allegarse* 'obtain'
c. Nontranslational motion ~ change in body posture: *pararse* 'stand up', *sentarse* 'sit', *voletarse* 'turn', *estirarse* 'strech out'

d. Change in location ~ translational motion: *irse* 'leave', *subirse* 'get on top of something', *meterse* 'go in'

e. Interaction among two or more participants ~ naturally reciprocal events:[3] *abrazarse* 'hug, embrace', *pelearse* 'fight'

f. Internal change (emotional) ~ emotion middle: *alegrarse* 'gladden', *entristecerse* 'sadden', *enojarse* 'become angry'

g. Verbal actions manifesting emotions ~ emotive speech actions: *quejarse* 'complain', *lamentarse* 'lament'

h. Internal change (mental) ~ cognition middle: *acordarse* 'remember', *imaginarse* 'imagine'

i. Changes of state whose energetic source is not identified ~ spontaneous events: *romperse* 'break', *quebrarse* 'crack'

All these situations naturally motivate the use of a middle marker. Most of them refer to actions involving internal energy transmission resulting in the subject's change in body posture (*sit*, *turn*) or change in location ("translational motion"; e.g., *leave*). Some situations involve an internal change, be it mental ("cognition middles"; e.g., *ponder*) or emotional ("emotion middles"; e.g., *be angry*). Some other situations imply external input; however, they are restricted to elements conceived within the subject's dominion, such as body parts and inalienable possessions ("grooming or body care"; e.g., *wash*) or elements brought into the subject's dominion ("self-benefactive"; e.g., *get*, *obtain*). Finally, some situations may involve two participants, yet each participant keeps the other within his or her dominion such that they are conceptualized as making up one unit ("reciprocal middles"; e.g., *embrace*).

Kemmer has rightly suggested that the fact that the event remains centered on one participant results in a low degree of event elaboration. Since the subject's action does not need to be distinguished from the object's affectedness, as it is, for instance, in the direct-active voice pattern, the event can be simplified. The lack of differentiation between the two participants in a middle construction provides an obvious, general characterization of that construction. However, the middle can be captured in terms of a more basic schema: its core function is to focus on the change-of-state undergone by the subject (Maldonado 1992, 1999). In other words, since the middle marker imposes a conceptualization centered on the subject, it crucially profiles the observable change-of-state. Its focus may be, even more specifically, on the crucial moment of change. Spontaneous events, as in (47b), are thus expected middles: instead of scanning the development of an event step by step, what the middle depicts is the pivotal moment of change.

The middle's focusing function also crucially involves designating inchoative events, as in (49b) and (50b), which contrast with the events designated by transitive and intransitive verbs, as in (49a) and (50a):

(49) a. *Victor/   la   tormenta   rompi-ó   la   ventana.*
      Victor/   the   storm   break-PST.3SG   DET   window
      'Victor broke the window.'

b. *La   ventana   se   rompi-ó.*
DET   window   MID   break-PST.3SG
'The window broke.'

(50) a. *Adrián   fue   al   cine.*
Adrian   go.PST.3SG   to.DET   movies
'Adrian went to the movies.'

b. *Adrián   se   fue.*
Adrian   MID   go.PST.3SG
'Adrian left.'

From the focusing function of the middle, as exemplified in (49b), actually two types of information can be inferred: (i) aspectual information regarding the inchoative nature of the event and (ii) pragmatic information to the effect that no agentive subject—as it occurs in the transitive correlate in (49a)—is necessary. It follows that the clitic *se* and the agentive subject are mutually exclusive, thus **Adrián se rompió la copa* 'Adrian broke-MID the cup' is ungrammatical with the spontaneous-inchoative reading.[4] In other words, the use of the middle obviates the need for an Agent responsible for the event.

We have seen that by focusing on the core of the event, the middle marker either eliminates the participant driving the force of the event (47b) or the force itself that brings it about (49b). This type of construal has two obvious consequences. First, inchoative middles may further develop to mark events designating abrupt or sudden changes, as is the case in the examples (51b) and (52b) from Spanish:

(51) a. *El   presidente   volte-ó   para   saludar   a   la   gente.*
The   president   turn-PST.3SG   for   greet   to   the   people
'The president turned to greet the audience.'

b. *El   presidente   se   volte-ó   para   que   las   piedra-s*
The   president   MID   turn-PST.3SG   for   that   the.PL   stone-PL
no   le   dieran   en   la   cara.
not   DAT   give-PST.3PL   in   the   face
'The president turned (away) to avoid the stones being thrown at his face.'

(52) a. *El   humo   desapareci-ó   poco   a   poco.*
The   smoke   disappear-PST.3SG   bit   by   bit
'The smoke disappeared bit by bit.'

b. *El   fantasma   se   desapareci-ó   de   pronto.*
The   smoke   MID   disappear-PST.3SG   of   sudden
'The ghost disappeared all of a sudden.'

Second, as is partially evidenced by (52b), middles may also encompass event construals, whereby the event is not only abrupt but also unexpected (Maldonado 1988, 1993). As such, in the absence of further information, the event in (52b) can be construed as running counter to normal expectations. This construal is best explained in terms of force-dynamics (Talmy 1985, 2000; this volume, chapter 11). In the physical realm, animate objects, from a force-dynamic perspective, normally resist the influence of gravity. In a falling situation, then, nonresisting inanimate objects simply fall in a nonenergetic manner, constituting an absolute construal (Langacker 1990); energetic resisting objects, however, establish a force-dynamic interaction, which is marked by a middle. At an abstract level, a corresponding resisting force may be distinguished, which consist in the conceptualizer viewing the event as running counter to normal expectations.

Examples such as (52b) are not isolated: they also account for a wide range of Spanish examples, as in (53) and (54), that have so far not received a convincing explanation. Examples (53) and (54), again, show a contrast between an absolute, intransitive construal profiling no energy at all (53a, 54a) and an energetic construal depicting a force-dynamic situation (53b, 54a, 54c). The examples in (53) belong to the physical realm; those in (54) involve a more abstract conceptualization:

(53) a. *La   lluvia(*se)   cae.*
          the   rain(*MID)   fall.3SG
          'Rain falls.'
      b. *La   taza   se   cay-ó   de   la   mesa.*
          The   cup   MID   fall-PST.3SG   of   the   table
          'The cup fell down from the table.'

(54) a. *Mi   padre   muri-ó   en   1988.*
          my   father   die-PST.3SG   in   1988
          'My father died in 1988.'
      b. *Mi   padre   se   muri-ó   en   un   accidente.*
          my   father   MID   die-PST.3SG   in   an   accident
          'My father died in a car accident.'
      c. *Mi   padre   se (*Ø)   me   murió   en   los   brazos.*
          my   father   MID   DAT.1SG   die-PST. 3SG   in   the.PL   arms
          'My father died in my arms.'

In (53b) and (54b), the use of the middle marker *se* is obligatory with the unexpected reading. Notice that in (54b) the event is subjectively construed from the conceptualizer's viewpoint (Langacker 1985). Now the conceptualizer can be overtly expressed with a dative clitic, such as the first person clitic *me* in (54c). The dative clitic designates an abstract setting for the event—that is, the event happens in the conceptualizer's dominion (Maldonado 2002)—thus the dative participant is affected by the result of the event. Since the use of the dative clitic puts conceptualizer's expectations in profile, the use of *se* is obligatory, as can be seen from (54c).

Without *se*, the examples in (54) depict an objective construal in which the conceptualizer's view is totally excluded from the event. This is the case for newspaper headlines where the cold and objective report of an event rules out the use of *se*. Although an accident is reported in (55), the event is reported with no speaker's involvement:

(55) *Choque de tren-es en Turkía. Muere-n más de 250 pasajero-s.*
      crash of train-PL in Turkey die-3PL more of 250 passenger-PL
      'Trains crash in Turkey. More than 250 passengers die.'

Summing up, we have seen that the middle signals 'change-of-state affecting only the subject'; in other words, many of these changes-of-state are restricted to the subject domain, be it the physical, the relational, or the emotional sphere. To the extent that the middle focuses on the change undergone by the subject, the event tends to be inchoative and tends to focus on the crucial moment of change. The rapid, abrupt, and unexpected readings are predictable from this semantic core of the middle. The following section attempts to motivate the cognitive paths for the middle construction.

7.2. Middle Conceptual Paths

There has been a general tendency in linguistics to interpret the emergence of the middle construction as evolving from the reflexive construction. A motivating explanation comes from Kemmer's "distinguishability hypothesis" (1994), according to which there exists a cline from the transitive two-participant event to the intransitive one-participant event; I offer figure 32.10 as a representation of a gradual reduction of participant differentiation, with the transitive construction as a first step.

While in the transitive construction there are two different participants in the reflexive construction, there is a split representation of the self. Subject and object are distinguishable as two coreferential participants, which interact with each other much in the same way as they would with other participants. In contrast, the middle involves an event (self-action or state) implying no participant division, as the event only happens within the realm of the subject. Haiman's (1983: 796) now classic Russian example shows that the middle/reflexive contrast may also be reflected iconically:

(56) a. REFLEXIVE EVENT
          On utomil sebja.
          he exhausted REFL
          'He exhausted himself.'
      b. MIDDLE EVENT
          On utomil-sja.
          he exhausted-MID
          'He grew weary.'

The long form *sebja* codes the more complex reflexive event, while the short form -*sja* signals the simpler middle construal (see Kemmer's lower degree of elaboration). More generally, an occurrence of the light/heavy contrast seems to consistently signal a contrast whereby the longer, reflexive form designates events involving the

Two participant event	Reflexive	Middle	One participant event
+	---		-
	Degree of Distinguishability		

Figure 32.10. Kemmer's distinguishability hypothesis

subject exerting a high degree of (mental) control and the shorter, middle form marks spontaneous situations involving the subject acting as an undergoer or experiencer. This contrast is common in Dutch (pronoun *zichzelf* vs. the light pronoun *zich*), Hungarian (pronoun *magat* vs. the verbal suffix *-kod-* or *-koz*), Turkish (pronoun *kendi* vs. affix *-in-*), Latin (clitic *se* vs. suffix *-r*), Greek (reflexive pronoun *afto* vs. inflected middle), and many other languages. An eloquent example from Dutch illustrates the lower degree of subject control in the middle construction (57b):

(57)   a. *Jan   zag   zichzelf   naast   zijn   ouders   staan   op   de   foto.*
        Jan   saw   HRM   next   his   parents   stand   on   the   picture
        'Jan saw himself [i.e., he conjured up a picture of himself] standing next to his parents in the picture.'
       b. *In   gedachten   zag   Jan   zich   in   de   gevangenis   belanden*
        in   thoughts   saw   Jan   LRM   in   the   prison   land
        'Jan saw himself [i.e., had a mental picture of himself] ending up in prison.' (based on van der Leek 1991: 455)

Given the previous contrasts, the idea that the middle develops from the reflexive has commonly been accepted (Faltz 1985; Fagan 1988; Givón 1990; Kemmer 1993b, 1994). On that view, the middle occupies a position one stage down the cline from the position occupied by reflexives; in other words, just like reflexives reduce transitive subject/object differentiation by having subject and object co-refer, middles further reduce the split representation to the point where the two co-referring participants are no longer distinguishable.

Now, the commonly accepted assumption that middles necessarily develop from reflexives has been misguided by the idea that all languages have the transitive action-chain model as their base line. According to cognitive analyses, however, languages may start construing an event from the dominion of the subject such that interaction with another participant and action involving no other participant are simply two alternative, equally natural conceptualizations (Manney 1998, 2000; Maldonado 1999; Nava and Maldonado 2004; Nava 2005). As pointed out by Tuggy (1981) in reference to Nahuatl reflexives, the way we interact with ourselves differs a great deal from the way we interact with others. While routine self-care, mental or emotional interactions may be natural, what is really awkward is to have a participant interacting with the "self" as if it where a different participant. Reflexives are thus conceptually marked in opposition to middle and transitive constructions.[5]

The nature of the middle construction as independent from the reflexive is also observable in other languages. As Manney (2000) has shown, in Modern Greek the middle is separate and distinct, both synchronically and diachronically, from the reflexive. While the (inflected) middle depicts one-participant events with a high degree of affect and a low degree of volition, the use of the reflexive involves marked situations with a higher degree of volition. In a typical agentless middle situation (the case of hitting oneself unintentionally, as when bumping against the edge of a table), the middle construction constitutes the unmarked coding (57a); when the action is intentional, the reflexive prefix *afto-* is added (57b), while the use of the periphrastic reflexive (57c) is either marginal or ungrammatical:

(57)   a. *Travmatís-tike.*
          injure-3SG.MID.PST
          'He injured himself /was injured.'
       b. *Afto-travmatís-tike.*
          self-injure-3SG.MID.PST
          'He injured himself (intentionally).'
       c. ?/**Travmá-tise   ton   eaftó   tu.*
          injure-3SG.ACT   the.ACC   self.ACC   GEN.3SG
          'He injured himself.' (strange or unacceptable)

In Modern Greek as well, there are many basic contrasts between the middle and the active without implying the reflexive construction:

(58)   a. *Stenaxori-éme   me   tin   iyía   tu.*
          Worry-1SG.MID.PRS   with   the.ACC   health   3SG.POSS
          'I am worried about his health.' (I am very worried)
       b. *i   iyía   tu   me   stenaxorí.*
          the.NOM   health   3SG.POSS   1SG.ACC   worry.3SG.PRS.ACT
          'His health worries me.' (I am less worried)

Other unrelated languages illustrate the basic nature of the middle in even more dramatic terms. In Tarascan (Mesoamerican), middles and reflexives contrast iconically in the way pointed out by Haiman for Russian (see example 56): the short form in (59) designates the middle, which is the unmarked situation, while the long, reflexive form in (59b) conveys the emphatic meaning:

(59)   a. *Dora   kwata-**ra**-s-Ø-ti.*
          Dora   soft-MID-PERF-PRS-IND.3
          'Dora is/got tired.'
       b. *Dora   kwata-**kurhi**-s-Ø-ti.*
          Dora   soft-REFL-PERF-PRS-IND.3
          'Dora is fed up (tired herself of doing something).'

In Tarascan middles, two patterns can be distinguished: (i) the middles either show up in equipollent contrast with active transitive constructions, or (ii) they simply constitute the base form for deriving active transitive constructions (Nava 2005)—the reflexive is a marked construction deriving either from a transitive or from a middle construction. In the second case, the reflexive is in contrast with the transitive as will be shown below (Nava and Maldonado 2004). With regard to the first pattern, Tarascan has a number of middle/active duplets that designate the trajector's location/position or a variety of the trajector's properties. The complex stem *ké-nti* 'move angle' must take either the middle *-ku* or the transitive *-ta*, whereby no form is more basic than the other:

(60) a. *Dora   ké-nti-**ku**-s-Ø-ti.*
          Dora   move-angle-MID.angle-PERF-PRS-IND.3
          'Dora hid in the corner.'

      b. *Marcosï   Dora-ni   ké-nti-**ta**-s-Ø-ti.*
          Marcos   Dora-OBJ   move-MID.angle-ACT-PERF-PRS-IND.3
          'Marcos made Dora hide in the corner.'

In the second pattern, a causative morpheme must be added to the middle-marked stem to obtain an active-transitive construction. The middle marker *-pi* designates attributes such as color, texture, shape, and consistency. The active-transitive preserves the middle marker as it is derived by means of a causative *-ra*, as in (61). The same is true for locative situations, change of body posture, and spontaneous events.

(61) *Itsï   sïranta-ni   ch'era-**pe-ra**-s-Ø-ti.*
       water   paper-OBJ   wrinkle-MID-CAUS-PERF-PRS-IND.3
       'The water wrinkled the paper.'

Crucially, if a reflexive marker is used, it will take up the slot of the transitive marker. Even more significantly, the reflexive may appear for emphatic purposes after the middle, as in (62), thus contrasting with the basic middle construction in (60a):

(62) *Dora   ké-nti-**ku-kurhi**-s-Ø-ti.*
       Dora   move-angle-MID-REFL-PERF-PRS-IND.3
       'Dora hid herself in the corner.'

While the reflexive *-kurhi* constitutes a marked construction contrasting with the middle and the transitive, the middle constitutes a basic voice pattern. The basic nature of the middle and the marked status of the reflexive can be attested in a variety of unrelated languages: Balinese (Artawa 1994), Amharic (Shibatani 2001), Otomí (Palancar 2004), and Toba (Messineo 2002). For all of them, there are middle stems which contrast with transitive constructions. The reflexive may come as a marked construction deriving either from the middle or from the transitive stem. There are also languages like Otomi in which there is no reflexive construction at all. In order to achieve a reflexive meaning, Otomi exploits the genitive construction.

We may conclude that, while the middle may evolve from the reflexive in some languages whose base form is the transitive construction, in other languages it constitutes a category in its own right, for it corresponds to a basic conceptualization of

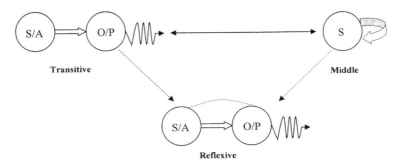

Figure 32.11. Nonderived middle

a vast variety of actions developing within the subject's dominion and may in fact be the source not only for reflexive but also for transitive constructions. This conceptual pattern is represented in figure 32.11, where transitive and middle contrast while the reflexive construction derives from the transitive having two coreferential participants.

The last point to consider for the proper understanding of middle voice systems is the fact that in languages with middle voice there is always a list of deponent verbs, that is, verbs that only occur as middles (e.g., Latin: *oblivisco-r* 'forget', *vereo-r* 'tear'; Gugu Yimidhirr: *daga-**adhi*** 'sit down'; Spanish: *jactarse* 'brag', *quejarse* 'complain'). Little needs to be said about deponent verbs given the approach suggested here. Deponent middles correspond to situations that naturally fall in the subject's dominion. Most situations refer to internal mental, psychological, or physical changes or states for which the middle is the natural form. In principle there is nothing in these situations to imply any type of interaction with another participant. To the degree that the middle encodes 'events in the subject's dominion', corresponding to situations that involve only the subject, the middle may be as basic as a transitive action-chain situation involving two participants.

8. CONCLUSIONS

Syntactic Voice has been defined as a complex category by which the arguments of the verb may receive different prominence status in the clause. While I accept in general terms Cooreman's four-way voice contrast in terms of topicality, Cognitive Grammar affords us further insights into the problem. I have proposed that voice alternations depend crucially on the starting point from which languages construe basic events. Accusative languages take the active as the base form and use the passive to allow the Theme to become the event trajector. Ergative languages diminish the natural prominence of the absolute Theme to afford primary figure status to the Agent. The inverse construction can have more than one starting point since there are different realms in which the natural organization of a social community and its conceptualization of the world can be reversed. For languages having verbs unspecified for trajector, as is the case for the languages of the Philippines, voice is very productive and flexible. Indeed, the selection of a particular participant as the trajector determines the voice pattern in which the event is construed. In these languages, the selection of a participant as the trajector of the clause implies no demotion of other participants. In this respect, Philippine languages behave in a way precisely opposite to languages having middle voice. In middle constructions, only one participant is chosen for maximal prominence to the detriment of all other nominal forms. From a cognitive perspective, then, syntactic voice can be defined as the set of grammaticized patterns emerging from the speaker's ability to construe events in ways that differ from a language's prototypical coding strategy.

NOTES

I would like to thank Enrique Palancar and Maura Velázquez for invaluable comments on different versions of this chapter. I am also very thankful to Ken Cook and Matt Shibatani for very fruitful discussions on different matters of voice.

1. With nonenergetic intransitive verbs, the rule applies by default since the subject will be the only participant in the event. However, in languages with intransitive splits (Guaraní, Dakota, and Seneca), the energetic participant tends to align with A (the agentive subject in Dixon's 1980 notation) while the nonenergetic with O (the thematic subject).

2. The term "perfective" as referred to aspect contrasts with the term "imperfect" and denotes a situation seen as concluded. The event is conceptualized as a whole without considering the internal temporal composition of the verb (Comrie 1976).

3. Reciprocals have been the attention of recent analyses (Kemmer 1993a; Evans 2004). Reciprocals show differences parallel to the ones found between reflexives and middles. In simplex reciprocals the interaction between two participants is seen as one. Complex reciprocals designate situations where separate actions by each participant can be observed.

4. The example may be grammatical with an emphatic self-benefactive reading; for further analysis, see Maldonado (2000).

5. Evidence from language acquisition of Spanish middle-reflexive *se* (Jackson, Maldonado, and Thal 1998) reveals that by 28 months of age children have mastered transitive, intransitive, and middle constructions—the reflexive, however, is not available yet. The use of the middle is distributed as follows: motion middles (*se fue* 'he left'), 32%; sudden or unexpected changes (*se cayó* 'it fell down', *se mojó* 'it got wet'), 30%; change of state (*se va a dormir* 'she is going to sleep'), 10%; and impersonal standard procedures (*se corta así* 'It is cut in this way'), 9%. These facts suggest that the middle is a basic, not a dependent construal.

REFERENCES

Aissen, Judith. 1987. *The Tzotzil clause structure.* Dordrecht, Netherlands: Reidel.

Artawa, K. 1994. Ergativity in Balinese syntax. PhD dissertation, La Trobe University, Australia.

Bell, Sarah. 1983. Advancements and ascensions in Cebuano. In David Perlmutter, ed., *Studies in relational grammar* 1: 143–218. Chicago: University of Chicago press.

Bittner, Maria. 1987. On the semantics of the Greenlandic antipassive and related constructions. *International Journal of American Linguistics* 53: 194–231.

Cennamo, Michela. 1993. *The reanalysis of reflexives: A diachronic perspective.* Naples, Italy: Liguori Editore.

Chung, Sandra. 1978. *Case marking and grammatical relations in Polynesian.* Austin: University of Texas Press.

Comrie, Bernard. 1976. *Aspect.* Cambridge: Cambridge University press.

Cook, Kenneth. 1988. The semantics of Newari case-marking distinctions. *Linguistic Notes from La Jolla* 14: 42–56.

Cook, Kenneth. 1997. The Samoan transitive suffix as an inverse marker. In Marjolijn Vespoor, Kee Dong Lee, and Eve Sweetser, eds., *Lexical and syntactical constructions and the construction of meaning* 347–61. Amsterdam: John Benjamins.

Cooreman, Ann. 1987. *Transitivity and discourse continuity in Chamorro narratives.* Berlin: Mouton de Gruyter.

Cooreman, Ann. 1988. Variations on the Theme of transitivity. In Masayoshi Shibatani, ed., *Passive and voice* 561–93. Amsterdam: John Benjamins.

Cooreman, Ann. 1994. A functional typology of antipassives. In Barbara Fox and Paul Hopper, eds., *Voice: Form and function* 49–87. Amsterdam: John Benjamins.

Dahlstrom, Amy. 1986. Plains Cree morphosyntax. PhD dissertation, University of California at Berkeley.

Dayley, John. 1985. *Tsutsujil grammar.* Berkeley: University of California Press.

Dixon, R. M. W. 1980. *The languages of Australia.* Cambridge: Cambridge University Press.

England, Nora. 1988. Mam Voice. In Masayoshi Shibatani, ed., *Passive and Voice* 525–45. Amsterdam: John Benjamins.

Evans, Nicholas. 2004. Complex events, predicate overlay and the special status of reciprocal clauses. Plenary lecture, Conceptual Structure Discourse and Language Conference, University of Alberta, October 8–10.

Fagan, Sarah. 1988. The English middle. *Linguistic Inquiry* 19: 181–203.

Faltz, Leonard. 1985. *Reflexivization: A study in Universal Syntax.* New York: Garland.

Givón, Talmy. 1990. *Syntax: A functional typological introduction.* Vol 2. Amsterdam: John Benjamins.

Givón, Talmy. 1994. The pragmatics of de-transitive voice: Functional and typological aspects of inversion. In Talmy Givón, ed., *Voice and inversion* 3–46. Amsterdam: John Benjamins.

Givón, Talmy, and Lynne Yang. 1998. The rise of the English *get*-passive. In Masayoshi Shibatani, ed., *Passive and Voice* 119–49. Amsterdam: John Benjamins.

Haiman, John. 1983. Iconic and economic motivation. *Language* 59: 781–819.

Jackson-Maldonado, Donna, Ricardo Maldonado, and Donna J. Thal. 1998. Reflexive and middle markers in early child language acquisition: Evidence from Mexican Spanish. *First Language* 18: 403–29.

Jespersen, Otto. 1924. *The philosophy of grammar*. London: Allen and Unwin.

Kemmer, Suzanne. 1993a. Marking oppositions in verbal and nominal collectives. *Faits de Langues: Revue de Linguistique* 2: 85–95.

Kemmer, Suzanne. 1993b. *The middle voice*. Amsterdam: John Benjamins.

Kemmer, Suzanne. 1994. Middle voice, transitivity and events. In Barbara Fox and Paul Hopper, eds., *Voice: Form and Function* 179–230. Amsterdam: John Benjamins.

Keenan, Edward L. 1976. Toward a universal definition of "subject." In Charles Li, ed., *Subject and topic* 247–302. New York: Academic Press.

Keenan, Edward L. 1985. Passive in the world's languages. In Timothy Shopen, ed., *Language typology and syntactic description* 1: 243–81. Cambridge: Cambridge University Press.

Klaiman, M. H. 1991. *Grammatical voice*. Cambridge: Cambridge University Press.

Lakoff, Robin. 1971. Passive resistance. *Chicago Linguistic Society* 7: 149–62.

Langacker, Ronald W. 1982. Space grammar, analysability and the English passive. *Language* 58: 22–80.

Langacker, Ronald W. 1985. Observations and speculations on subjectivity. In John Haiman, ed., *Iconicity in syntax* 109–50. Amsterdam: John Benjamins.

Langacker, Ronald W. 1987a. *Foundations of cognitive grammar*. Vol. 1, *Theoretical prerequisites*. Stanford, CA: Stanford University Press.

Langacker, Ronald W. 1987b. Nouns and verbs. *Language* 63: 53–94.

Langacker, Ronald W. 1990. *Concept, image, and symbol: The cognitive basis of grammar*. Berlin: Mouton de Gruyter.

Langacker, Ronald W. 1991. *Foundations of cognitive grammar*. Vol. 2, *Descriptive application*. Stanford, CA: Stanford University Press.

Langacker, Ronald W. 2000. *Grammar and conceptualization*. Berlin: Mouton de Gruyter.

Langacker, Ronald W. 2003. Grammar as image: The case of voice. Paper presented at the Imagery in Language Conference, Łódź University, September 28–30.

Lyons, John. 1968. *Introduction to theoretical linguistics*. Cambridge: Cambridge University Press.

Maldonado, Ricardo. 1988. Energetic reflexives in Spanish. *Berkeley Linguistics Society* 14: 153–65.

Maldonado, Ricardo. 1992. Middle voice: The case of Spanish 'se'. PhD dissertation, University of California at San Diego.

Maldonado, Ricardo. 1993. Dynamic construals in Spanish. *Studi italiani di linguistica teorica e applicata* 22: 531–66.

Maldonado, Ricardo. 1999. *A media voz: problemas conceptuales del clítico SE en español*. Mexico: Instituto de Investigaciones Filológicas, Universidad Nacional Autónoma de México.

Maldonado, Ricardo. 2000. Conceptual distance and transitivity increase in Spanish reflexives. In Zygmunt Frajzyngier and Traci S. Curl, eds., *Reflexives: Forms and functions* 153–86. Amsterdam: John Benjamins.

Maldonado, Ricardo. 2002. Objective and subjective datives. *Cognitive Linguistics* 13: 1–65.

Manney, Linda Joyce. 1998. The reflexive archetype and its various realizations in Modern Greek. *Studies in Language* 22: 1–48.

Manney, Linda Joyce. 2000. *Middle voice in Modern Greek: Meaning and function of a morphosyntactic category*. Amsterdam: John Benjamins.

Messineo, Cristina. 2002. La marcación verbal activa/inactiva en toba (guaycurú) y sus motivaciones. *Línguas Indígenas Americanas* 2: 49–62.

Milner, George. 1966. *Samoan dictionary*. London: Oxford University Press.

Mosel, Ulrike. 1989. On the classification of verbs and verbal clauses in Samoan. In Ray Harlow and Robin Hooper, eds., *Vical 1: Oceanic languages: papers from the Fifth International Conference on Austronesian Linguistics, Auckland, New Zealand, January 1988* 377–98. Auckland: Linguistic Society of New Zealand.

Nava, Fernando. 2005. Voz media en tarasco. PhD dissertation, Universidad Nacional Auntónoma de México.

Nava, Fernando, and Ricardo Maldonado. 2004. Basic voice patterns in Tarascan (P'orhepecha). In Michel Achard and Suzanne Kemmer, eds., *Language, culture, and mind* 461–78. Stanford, CA: CSLI publications.

Palancar, Enrique. 2004. Middle voice in Otomi. *International Journal of American Linguistics* 70: 52–85.

Payne, Thomas. 1982. Role and reference related subject properties and ergativity in Yup'ik Eskimo and Tagalog. *Studies in Language* 6: 75–106.

Perlmutter, David, and Paul Postal. 1983. Toward a universal characterization of passivization. In David Perlmutter, ed., *Studies in relational grammar* 1: 3–29. Chicago: Chicago University Press.

Perlmutter, David, and Paul Postal. 1984. Impersonal passives and some relational laws. In David Perlmutter and Carol Rosen, eds., *Studies in relational grammar* 2: 126–70. Chicago: Chicago University Press.

Postal, Paul. 1971. *Cross-over phenomena.* New York: Holt.

Reid, Lawrence. 2002. Philippine languages in focus and out of focus. Paper presented at the Institute for the Study of Languages and Cultures of Asia and Africa Linguistics Seminar, University of Hawaii. October 4.

Schachter, Paul. 1976. The subject in Philippine languages: Topic, actor, actor-topic, or none of the above. In Charles Li, ed., *Subject and topic* 491–518. New York: Academic Press.

Schulze, Wolfgang. 2000. Towards a typology of the accusative-ergative continuum. *General Linguistics* 37: 71–155.

Shibatani, Masayoshi. 1984. Passive and related constructions: A prototype analysis. *Language* 61: 821–48.

Shibatani, Masayoshi. 1988. Voice in Philippine languages. In Masayoshi Shibatani, ed., *Passive and voice* 85–142. Amsterdam: John Benjamins.

Shibatani, Masayoshi. 2001. Syntactic voice lectures. Departamento de Lingüística, Universidad Autónoma de Querétaro, Mexico. November 19–23.

Słoń, Anna. 2000. Coding a demoted initiator in Polish and English passive constructions: A Cognitive grammar analysis. In Bozena Rozwadowska, ed., *Papers in language studies: Proceedings of the 8th annual conference of the Polish association for the study of English* 259–69. Wrocław: Uniwersytet Wrocławski.

Talmy, Leonard. 1985. Force dynamics in language and thought. *Chicago Linguistic Society* 21, vol. 2 (parasession): 293–337.

Talmy, Leonard. 2000. *Toward a cognitive semantics.* Vol. 1, *Concept structuring systems.* Cambridge, MA: MIT Press.

Tsunoda, Tasaku. 1988. Antipassives in Warrungu and other Australian languages. In Masayoshi Shibatani, ed., *Passive and voice* 595–650. Amsterdam: John Benjamins.

Tuggy, David. 1981. The transitivity-related morphology of Tetelcingo Nahuatl: An exploration in space grammar. PhD dissertation, University of California at San Diego.

van der Leek, Frederike. 1991. Iconicity and two-form reflexive systems. *Chicago Linguistics Society* 27: 447–63.

Verhagen, Arie. 1992. Praxis of linguistics: Passives in Dutch. *Cognitive Linguistics* 3: 301–42.

Zavala, Roberto. 1997. Functional analysis of Akatek voice constructions. *International Journal of American Linguistics* 63: 439–74.

Zavala, Roberto. 2003. Verb classes, semantic roles and inverse in Olutec. In Paulette Levy, ed., *Del Cora al Maya Yucateco: Estudios lingüísticos sobre lenguas indígenas mexicanas* 179–268. Mexico: Instituto de Investigaciones Filológicas, Universidad Nacional Autónoma de México.

CHAPTER 33

MODALITY IN COGNITIVE LINGUISTICS

TANJA MORTELMANS

1. THE NOTION OF MODALITY AND SOME OF THE QUESTIONS IT RAISES

It is well known that the semantic category of modality is not as easily defined as tense or aspect (Bybee, Perkins, and Pagliuca 1994: 176). Van der Auwera and Plungian (1998: 80) hold that "modality and its types can be defined and named in various ways," and that "there is no one correct way." Some linguists even question the status of modality as an independent category. According to Lampert and Lampert (2000: 296), for instance, modality "as a cognitively valid category . . . is simply gratuitous"; the only incentive, they claim, to entertain a separate category of modality is the fact that it provides a unitary semantic label for the formal category of modal verbs.

Much of the research on modality within a cognitive linguistic framework has indeed focused on modals, more specifically, on the English modals, and this language bias has undoubtedly shaped the typical understanding of modality as the cognitive semantic category roughly corresponding to the meanings expressed by modal verbs. Cognitive linguistic studies of other "modal" expression types— moods (e.g., Achard 1998, 2002; Mejías-Bikandi 1996; Mortelmans 2001, 2002,

2003), modal adjectives and adverbs (e.g., Nuyts 1994, 2001, 2002), mental state predicates (e.g., Nuyts 1994, 2001, 2002; Pelyvás 2001), evidential markers (e.g., Floyd 1999; Matlock 1989; Casad 1992; Lee 1993), lexical verbs acquiring epistemic meanings (e.g., Verhagen 1995, 1996; Cornillie 2005a)—which venture into languages other than English do exist, but often lack a common core: they are like scattered pieces of a highly complex puzzle. The main focus in this chapter on modality within Cognitive Linguistics will therefore also lie on modals; at the same time, however, I will try to capture some of the basic insights that have arisen from research on other modal expression types in languages other than English and try to sketch possible future lines of research.

Let us take up the initial question again: what is modality? A traditional extensional characterization is provided in Bybee, Perkins, and Pagliuca (1994: 176), in which a distinction is made between "grams with uses that are traditionally associated with modality—for instance, those indicating obligation, probability, and possibility—and those traditionally associated with mood—imperative, optative, conditional, and subordinate verb forms."[1] More schematically, modality can be taken to signal "the speaker's attitude toward the proposition" (Givón 1994: 266), whereby "attitude" subsumes both epistemic (relating to issues of truth, belief, certainty, evidence, and the like) and valuative (dealing with desirability, preference, intent, ability, obligation, and manipulation) attitudes. Givón's distinction between valuative and epistemic attitudes is reflected in the well-known polysemy of the modal verbs, which carry (at least) two kinds of related meanings: a basic root meaning and an epistemic meaning—both of which are taken, within Cognitive Linguistics, to involve some element of force (see section 2.2). The link between root and epistemic modality is usually regarded as metaphorical, whereby the real-world, sociophysical force associated with root modality is mapped onto the epistemic domain of reasoning; this issue is, however, not uncontroversial, as section 2.3 will show.

From a diachronic perspective, the evolution of the English modals has been described in terms of progressive subjectification (Langacker 1990, 1991a, 1999, 2003), whereby they are claimed to have acquired the status of (highly grammaticalized) "grounding predications," which, together with tense and person inflections, relate the complement to the speech situation (the ground). This process of subjectification can also be witnessed in other modal expressions (as in the French, Spanish, and German modal verbs or in the lexical verbs *threaten* and *promise* and their German, Spanish, and Dutch equivalents), without them acquiring the status of grounding predications, however. In languages such as French and German, which still have a highly functional mood paradigm, it is the highly grammaticalized moods which are normally attributed the function of grounding a finite clause (see section 3).

In their epistemic use, the English modals are mainly concerned with the degree of likelihood or the degree of personal commitment of the speaker toward the truth of the proposition. Evidential qualifications,[2] pertaining to the (type of) information source through which the speaker has accessed the proposition, do not seem to play an important role in the (grammaticalized) system of English modality—although the inferential meaning carried by verbs like *must* and *should* has been considered as evidential rather than genuinely epistemic by a number of scholars (van der Auwera and Plungian 1998; Nuyts 2001: 173).[3] More generally, there does not seem to be a consensus regarding the relationship between epistemic modality (in terms of speaker commitment) and evidentiality (information source). Are they to be seen as separate qualificational categories (van der Auwera and Plungian 1998; Nuyts 2001)? Or, do they both pertain to a broadly defined domain of epistemic modality which would also include the grammatical coding of speaker attitudes like surprise (Floyd 1999) or of the evaluation of a state of affairs in terms of its accordance with background expectations (Lee 1993)? The fact that there appears to be a strong cross-linguistic connection between speaker commitment and information source to the extent that direct evidence generally evokes strong commitment, whereas indirect evidence (reported or inferred) pairs with weaker degrees of commitment (Givón 1982; see also Sanders and Spooren 1996), would support the latter position. In view of the relatively small amount of cognitive linguistic studies of evidential categories (see Floyd 1999 for a notable exception),[4] we will not elaborate this issue any further.

One of the main merits of a cognitive linguistic analysis of modality is its focus on semantics, which has resulted in a considerable number of fine-grained semantic (network) analyses of modal markers, both from a diachronic and a synchronic point of view. Moreover, Talmy's force dynamics (see, e.g., Talmy 1985) has provided a schematic conceptual background, against which a number of different, but related, models of modal meaning (see, e.g., Johnson 1987; Sweetser 1990; and Langacker 1990, 1991a) have been developed.

2. THE MODAL VERBS IN COGNITIVE LINGUISTICS

2.1. Polysemy versus Monosemy

A recurrent theme in the study of modal verbs is their semantic ambiguity; that is, modals display a wide array of senses, among which two stand out: the diachronically more basic root meaning,[5] on the one hand, and the epistemic meaning, on the other.[6]

> A modal is regarded as epistemic, when its sole import is to indicate the likelihood of the designated process. In a root modal, there is additionally some conception of potency directed toward the realization of that process, i.e. some notion of obligation, permission, desire, ability, etc. (Langacker 1991a: 272)

It is generally agreed upon to treat the semantic ambiguity in modals as a case of polysemy; that is, the modals are taken to code a variety of *interrelated* meanings.

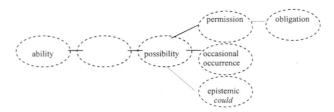

Figure 33.1. Present-day English *can* as a radial category (based on Goossens 1992: 389)

However, there is less agreement when it comes to the exact number and the theoretical status of these various senses. Goossens (1992), for instance, provides a semantic analysis of the multiple meanings of English *can* in terms of a radial category organized around a number of prototypical cores (see figure 33.1). These cores correspond to a number of salient uses, established on the basis of frequency, centrality in the network of uses, and onomasiological contrasts with other modals (Goossens 1992: 377). These prototypical usages have acquired some degree of entrenchment, they are—to some extent—conventionalized.

Sweetser (1990), on the other hand, allows for a greater indeterminacy by proposing only three different meanings or senses, which correspond with conventionalized metaphorical mappings of the modals to three domains of human experience: (i) to the sociophysical world (in their root sense; see 1a); (ii) to the world of reasoning (in their epistemic sense; see 1b); or (iii) to the conversational world (so-called speech act modality; see 1c).

(1)   a. John may go.
       b. John may be there.
       c. He may be a university professor, but he sure is dumb.

Whereas this threefold ambiguity belongs to the conventionalized semantics of the modals, any other specification (e.g., the identification of the imposer and imposee of the modality) is a matter of pragmatics and should therefore not be included in a modal's semantics (Sweetser 1990: 65–68).

The polysemy of modals is even more downplayed by Langacker (1990, 1991a). For the present-day English modals, he presents a schematic semantics that focuses more on the strength and existence of the directed potency than on its exact nature. The potency associated with *must*, for instance, is vaguely referred to as "a kind of necessity"; as a grounding predication (see below), *must* is claimed to designate (or profile) the process deemed necessary in the complement (Langacker 1990: 27).

Whereas Langacker still distinguishes between root and epistemic senses, though, Wierzbicka (1987: 38) advocates a purely monosemic approach, claiming that the different interpretations of *can* (and of every other modal, for that matter) "have more to do with the context, either explicit or implicit, than with the meaning of the modal as such." Such an account, however, does not seem to be able to offer an explanation for the semantic restrictions of the modals. English *can*, for instance, does not allow an epistemic meaning, which cannot easily be accounted for based on Wierzbicka's very general semantic description.

2.2. The Modals as a Force-Dynamic Category

The notion of "force" has been highly influential in the way modality is conceptualized in Cognitive Linguistics (Sweetser 1982, 1984, 1990; Talmy 1985, 1988, 2000; Johnson 1987; Langacker 1990, 1991a, 1999; Pelyvás 1996, 2000; Achard 1998). Most prominent in this respect has been Talmy's force-dynamic framework (see Talmy 1985, 1988, 2000), which was originally developed to provide a generalization over the traditional semantic category "causation" (Talmy 1976). According to Talmy, force dynamics involves four crucial parameters (see also De Mulder, this volume, chapter 12):

a. A *force opposition* between an *Agonist*—the focal force entity—and an *Antagonist*, opposing the former;
b. An *intrinsic force tendency* (either toward action or toward rest);
c. The *relative strengths* of the opposed forces, whereby a stronger entity will be able to manifest its tendency at the expense of the weaker one; and
d. The *resultant* of the force interaction—either action or rest, assessed only for the Agonist.

The English modals, then, are viewed as constituting the grammatical category that corresponds to the semantic category of force dynamics; that is, the modals are the grammaticalized encodings of the various ways in which entities interact with respect to forces and barriers. In the case of *cannot*,[7] for instance, a typically sentient subject (the Agonist) is inclined toward the action expressed by the infinitive, but some opposing factor (force) blocks the realization of the event. With *must*, the Agonist is exposed to "an active social pressure" (Talmy 1988: 79) that tries to keep him or her in place.[8] Talmy does not restrict his force-dynamic analysis to the traditional modal verbs, but also accords "honorary" modal status to the less grammaticalized verbs *have to*, *be supposed to*, *be to*, and *get to*. Moreover, a number of lexical verbs (*make*, *let*, *have*, *help*) are integrated into the so-called "greater modal system" (Talmy 1988: 81): syntactically, these verbs are on a par with the core modals insofar as they take a *to*-less infinitive complement; semantically, they are shown to have force-dynamic reference, but they differ from the more grammaticalized modals in coding the Antagonist as subject (*I made him push the car to the garage* vs. *He must push the car to the garage*).[9]

In their root usage, the modals are taken to refer mostly to psychosocial (rather than physical) interaction involving a sentient Agonist as subject (Talmy 1988: 79).[10] There are two notable exceptions to this basic pattern. In the case of Agonist demotion, the Agonist is backgrounded in favor of a promoted (typically nonsentient) Patient (as in *The cake must stay in the box*). Second, nonsentient subjects also occur in the epistemic usage, which is regarded as "the application of modality to the domain of our reasoning processes about various propositions" (Talmy 1988: 80). The use of modals in epistemic contexts has been elaborated by Sweetser (1984, 1990): in the epistemic realm, the sociophysical forces and barriers are said to be metaphorically mapped onto premises in the world of reasoning.[11]

> In the real world . . . *must* is taken as indicating a *real-world force* imposed by the *speaker* (and/or some other agent) which compels the *subject* of the sentence (or someone else) to *do the action* (or bring about its doing) expressed in the sentence. . . . Here [i.e. in the epistemic world] *must* is taken as indicating an *epistemic force* applied by some *body of premises* (the only thing that can apply epistemic force), which compels the *speaker* (or people in general) to reach the *conclusion* embodied in the sentence. (Sweetser 1990: 64)

Sweetser's approach is not unproblematic, as she herself admits. For one thing, she is unable to explain why some metaphorical mappings are better than others. For instance, why does positive *can* hardly allow an epistemic reading, unlike *can't*, *could*, or *can* in interrogatives? The same holds for *need*, whose epistemic potential only arises in negative or interrogative environments. And why is an epistemic meaning ruled out altogether for *shall*? In his review of Sweetser (1990), Foolen (1992) argues that a purely monosemic account à la Wierzbicka, which views the different senses of the modals as pragmatic ambiguities, cannot account for these restrictions. It is difficult to see, though, how Sweetser's approach could (as Sweetser herself admits).[12]

Langacker (1990, 1991a, 1999) also takes a force-dynamic stance in his characterization of the English modals, both for their root and epistemic uses. Langacker's account of force dynamics in epistemic modals differs considerably from Sweetser's, though. In his view, it is not so much the force of evidence which pushes the speaker toward a certain conclusion, but rather the highly abstract force residing in reality's evolutionary momentum, that is, reality's constant evolution based on (the speaker's conception of) its structure. Note, however, that the notion of evolutionary momentum remains to some extent speaker-related as well, because "the speaker is involved in any case as the primary conceptualizer and the person responsible for assessing the likelihood of reality evolving in a certain way" (Langacker 1991a: 274).

An analysis in force-dynamic terms is also presented by Achard (1996b, 1998) for the French modals *savoir*, *pouvoir*, and *devoir*.[13] Achard divides the French modals into three usage groups (main-verb constructions, root senses, and epistemic senses),[14] which correspond to the three subjectification stages presented by Langacker (1990, 1991a) to capture the diachronic evolution of the English modals (see below). The French modal *pouvoir* in its 'ability' sense, which represents the main-verb construction, is said to exhibit the following force-dynamic configuration: "The force stored in the locus of potency allows the latter to overcome the resistance (or force) coming from the activity profiled in the landmark, and therefore perform an occurrence of that process" (Achard 1998: 143). Note, furthermore, that in the 'ability' sense the locus of potency—that is, "the origin of the force responsible for the potential realization of the landmark process" (142)—is located in the subject. At the same time, the speaker's role is limited to that of a mere conceptualizer: the speaker does not participate in the force-dynamic configuration. In its root sense of 'possibility', *pouvoir* focuses on the presence (in the case of negated possibility) or absence of a barrier between the subject and the infinitival process. *Pouvoir*'s root sense of 'possibility' differs from its 'ability' sense in two respects. First, the locus of potency is no longer equated solely with the subject, but becomes more diffuse, as it may also refer to the circumstances in general preventing or enabling the realization of the infinitival process (compare *Il peut venir vous voir demain* 'It is possible for him to come and see you tomorrow' with *Marie peut soulever cent kilos* 'Marie is able to lift one hundred kilos').[15] Second, the speaker's role gains more prominence, as it is the speaker who points to the absence or presence of a barrier, that is, to the circumstances surrounding the modal situation. The speaker can therefore be taken to partake, albeit minimally, in the force-dynamic configuration, as he or she has mental access to the locus of potency. If the speaker removes the obstacle by himself or herself, the speaker's involvement becomes stronger. This is particularly clear in the social domain, in which case the removal of a social barrier equates with granting permission (*Tu peux aller au cinema* 'You can go to the movies'). The 'obligation' sense of *devoir* can be described along the same lines: the speaker's role is "strong" when the speaker associates himself or herself with the locus of potency (the source of obligation); a weaker role is attributed to the speaker when he or she only conveys the source of obligation.

It should be noted that Achard's distinction between a weaker and a stronger speaker role in the root domain considerably deviates from Langacker's description, who—in view of the fact that the evolution of modal verbs can be described in terms of the locus of potency becoming progressively less salient and well defined— explicitly states that the identification of the source of potency (the locus of obligation or permission) is not a crucial matter: "An analysis of the modals ought to focus more on the existence and strength of the directed potency than on pinning it down to a specific source and type" (Langacker 1991a: 272). In fact, Achard's ideas on weaker and stronger speaker roles seem to be more in line with Traugott's (1989) more pragmatic interpretation of the subjectification process (see section 2.5).

2.3 From Root to Epistemic Modality: Metaphor, Metonymy, Minimal Shifts/Partial Sanctioning?

Whether the development of epistemic modality out of root modality is indeed an instance of metaphorization (Johnson 1987: 48–61; Sweetser 1990; Pelyvás 1996, 2000) is a matter of considerable debate (for an overview, see, e.g., Heine 1992: 37– 46; Nuyts 2001: 182–83). For one thing, it remains rather unclear how the source domain for the metaphorical mapping has to be established, that is, which aspects of the image-schematic structure of the root modal are to be mapped onto the epistemic world. For *may*, for instance, Sweetser, following Talmy, takes the 'permission' meaning of the verb as a starting point, with *may* denoting a potential, but absent barrier: "*May* denotes lack of restriction on the part of someone else" (Sweetser 1990: 53). Pelyvás (1996, 2000), however, correctly remarks that the epistemic meaning has not developed out of the 'permission' meaning (as is shown, for instance, in Bybee, Perkins, and Pagliuca 1994: 199), but rather out of a prior 'possibility' sense of the verb.[16]

A number of authors, mainly working within grammaticalization theory (Traugott and König 1991; Hopper and Traugott 1993; Diewald 1999), reject the metaphorical analysis, since the conceptual leap evoked by a metaphorical mapping from one discrete conceptual domain onto another is not in line with the gradual character of the actual development of the epistemic meaning. They regard the extension from root to epistemic meanings as a metonymic process based on contiguity.

> *Must* in the epistemic sense of 'I conclude that' derived from the obligative sense of 'ought to' by strengthening of conversational inferences and subjectification. If I say *She must be married* in the obligation sense, I invite the inference that she will indeed get married. This inference is of course epistemic, pertaining to a state of affairs that is anticipated to be true at some later time. (Traugott and König 1991: 209)

Bybee, Perkins, and Pagliuca (1994: 196) in general advocate the metonymy position as well, whereby "inferences that can be made from the meaning of a particular modal become part of the meaning of that modal." They do not accept this view for English *must*, however, arguing that "the epistemic use of *must* arises in contexts with aspectual interpretations distinct from the obligation uses" (201); the appropriate conversational implicatures, therefore, do not arise.

Goossens (1999, 2000) takes yet another stance, as he rejects both metaphor and metonymy as the basic patterns of meaning extension in the development of epistemic out of root modality. On the basis of corpus material, Goossens describes the development from root to epistemic *must* as a concatenation of minimal and very gradual shifts of uses, which are only partially sanctioned with respect to the conventionalized uses of the verb. Genuinely metonymic uses in which a deontic and an inferential (epistemic) reading are simultaneously possible do occur (albeit less frequently than expected) and have supported the development of the subjective epistemic meaning. These semantic developments are to be seen against the background of a more global shift: it is the process of "subjectification in the participant-external, more specifically the deontic, area [which] paved the way for the development of the (subjectified) epistemic sense" (Goossens 2000: 167).

2.4. Subjectification and "Grounding Predications"

Subjectification, defined as the "shift from a relatively objective construal of some entity to a more subjective one" (Langacker 1999: 297), not only plays a crucial role in our understanding of the diachronic evolution of the English modals, but also helps to clarify their grammatical status vis-à-vis the (less grammaticalized) modals in other languages like German, Spanish, or French. The distinction between objective and subjective construal (see also Verhagen, this volume, chapter 3) is based on the perspective taken by the conceptualizer on a particular scene; it is thus a matter of viewing. In Langacker's definition, an entity is objectively construed insofar as it is the explicit focus of attention, whereas it is subjectively construed to the extent that it remains offstage and unmentioned. Langacker draws explicit attention to the fact that his technical use of the terms "subjective" and "subjectification" differs from Traugott's (1989, 1995) definition. For Traugott, subjectification refers to the diachronic process whereby "meanings become increasingly based in the speaker's subjective belief state/attitude toward the proposition" (1995: 31). Whereas Langacker's subjectification is a matter of perspective and vantage point, subjectification à la Traugott pertains to the "domain in which a relation or property is manifested" (Langacker 1999: 393).

In the case of the English modals, Langacker argues that subjectification can be witnessed to the extent that the locus of potency, which in the original main verb stage can be identified with the (onstage) subject,[17] has come to be gradually construed in a more implicit and diffuse manner. With root modality (exemplified in 2), the source of potency (Talmy's Antagonist) "may be the speaker but need not be.... It is not necessarily any specific individual, but may instead be some nebulous, generalized authority" (Langacker 1999: 308).

(2)   a. You must go home right away—your wife insists.
      b. Passengers should arrive at the airport two hours before their flight.

The same holds for the target of the potency (Talmy's Agonist), which may be a specific individual, but again, which need not be. In (3), for instance, the force is "simply directed toward realization of the target event, to be apprehended by anyone who might be in a position to respond to it" (Langacker 1999: 308).[18]

(3)   There may not be any alcohol served at the party.

Epistemic modals, then, show a maximally diffuse source and target of potency, "inhering in the evolutionary momentum of reality itself as assessed by the speaker/conceptualizer" (Langacker 1999: 309).

In the case of the English modals, the process of subjectification is accompanied by formal grammaticalization to the extent that the English modals are claimed to function as "grounding predications." Together with tense and person inflections, the English modals are said to ground a finite clause, that is, to locate the process designated by the content verb in a particular epistemic region vis-à-vis the ground (the speech event, its participants, and its immediate circumstances).

The subjectification of the English modals has proceeded in two phases: a first phase involves the realignment of the potency relation from the subject (as an objective participant) to a more subjectively construed participant (the default case being the ground itself).[19] This reoriented relationship, typically anchored in the ground, remains in profile, however; that is, it is construed with a considerable degree of objectivity (this situation, as Langacker claims, can still be observed for the German modals, which, being less grammaticalized than the English modals, are still grounded by tense and mood; for a more qualified assessment of the grounding status of the German modals, however, see Mortelmans 2000, 2001). For modals to function as genuine grounding predications, the potency relationship itself must be construed subjectively. The modal thus does not profile the potency relationship (anymore), but the complement process at which the potency is directed.[20] The typical formal characteristics of the English modals are interpreted as reflecting their grounding function. As grounding predications, the English modals are auxiliaries that necessarily precede the clausal head and cannot occur within it. They lack participial and infinitival forms (unlike the German and French modals), whose atemporal character would be inconsistent with the function of grounding a finite clause. The modals lack a third-person singular marker -s, since the latter is viewed as a grounding predication in its own right, situating the state of affairs within immediate reality.[21]

The semantic import of the English modals is characterized with respect to a number of Idealized Cognitive Models, the most essential of which is the so-called "basic epistemic model" (which is also inherent in Achard's "basic reality"; see below). This model is made up of "known reality" (comprising those situations that are accepted by a conceptualizer as being real), "immediate reality" (reality at its latest stage of evolution functioning as the vantage point from which the conceptualizer views things), and "irreality" (everything other than known reality).

Note that Langacker adheres to a dynamic view on reality, which is conceptualized as "an ever-evolving entity whose evolution through time continuously augments the complexity of the structure defined by its previous history" (1994: 139). Roughly, then, the absence of a modal is said to indicate that "the speaker accepts the designated process as part of known reality" (1991a: 245)—the unmarked option. A modal, by contrast, locates the process somewhere within irreality.

In order to arrive at a finer characterization of the semantic contribution of modals, especially in their epistemic usage, Langacker introduces the "dynamic evolutionary model" (reflected in Achard's 1998, 2002 conception of "elaborated reality"; see below), which integrates the notion "structured world" with force dynamics. The notion "structured world" recognizes the fact that we conceive of the world as being structured in a particular way, that we do not feel surrounded by mere chaos. It tries to capture the difference between (i) incidental events (which simply occur, but cannot be predicted or anticipated) and (ii) those events that are "direct manifestations of the world's structure" and as such exhibit a degree of regularity and predictability (Langacker 1991a: 264). Future events of the latter kind can be projected, confidently anticipated, as "present circumstances include those under which the world is biased toward the occurrence of particular sequences of events" (277). It is this bias toward certain developmental paths, "this tendency for reality, having evolved to its present state, to continue its evolution along certain

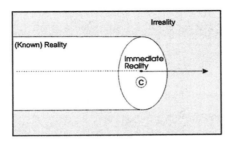

Figure 33.2. Langacker's basic epistemic model

paths in preference to others" (277) that can be regarded in force-dynamic terms, namely as the force inherent in reality's evolutionary momentum. The locus of potency can therefore be said to be maximally vague und undifferentiated.[22] The cases in which this force is conceived as strong enough to push reality toward certain future events (which can be confidently anticipated) are referred to as "projected reality"; the term "potential reality" is used for those future paths which are not excluded from being followed. The epistemic modals *may* and *will*,[23] then, are said to place the designated processes in the realm of potential and projected reality, respectively.

A similar analysis is put forward by Achard (1996b, 1998) for the epistemic uses of the French modals *devoir* and *pouvoir* and by myself (Mortelmans 2001) for the German modals *müssen* and *können*. In particular, *devoir* and *müssen* are said to situate the infinitival process within projected reality, while *pouvoir* and *können* situate it within potential reality.[24] Achard describes the evolution of the French modals from main-verb constructions to epistemic senses in terms of a subjective realignment of their modal force; that is, "the modal force anchored by the subject becomes progressively more and more aligned onto the conceptualization relation anchored by the speaker" (1998: 163). This process of subjectification is mirrored in a number of formal properties: to the extent that the subject's intentionality is less at stake (and its role as a locus of potency is therefore minimal), there are fewer grammatical constraints imposed by the modal on the complement process; that is, the infinitive can be marked for voice (passive) or perfect aspect. In other words, to the extent that the speaker becomes more clearly associated with the locus of potency, possible constraints on the infinitival complement are loosened, since "the speaker gains independent access to the complement process" (Achard 1998: 169). Markers of aspect and voice—both instances of conceptual manipulation of the complement process—are interpreted as signals that the speaker (instead of the subject) has gained conceptual control over the infinitival process.[25] In spite of the fact that the epistemic usage is strongly subjectified, Achard does not take the possible grounding status of the epistemic French modals into consideration. Following Achard, clausal grounding in French is effected by the tense and mood operators only (for the latter, see section 3).

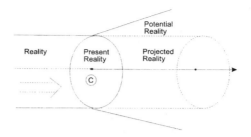

Figure 33.3. Langacker's dynamic evolutionary model

2.5. Subjectification: Langacker versus Traugott

Langacker (1990, 1991a, 1999, 2003) views the English modals as "grounding predications," irrespective of whether they have a root or an epistemic meaning. As
such, the distinction between these types of modality can be said to be independent
of the status of the English modals as grounding predications. Goossens (1996),
however, criticizes Langacker's uniform characterization of the English modals as
grounding predications; he shows, among other things, that in the case of root
modality the potency relation is not always as subjectively construed as Langacker
would have it.[26] Goossens therefore accepts the inherent grounding status of the
epistemic modals, whose semantics by necessity involves the speaker (conceptualizer) as an implicit reference point, but he considers root modals to be grounding
only "in the case of *deontic* modalities where the authority for the permission or
obligation is clearly in the ground, as a rule, when the speaker has or assumes
authority" (Goossens 1996: 28). This distinction between the speaker (implicitly)
assuming authority or not can be linked to Achard's notion of a stronger speaker
role, which Achard also links to a "subjective realignment of the modal force"
(Achard 1998: 154)—and hence to subjectification. This use of the notion subjectification, however, seems to be more in line with Traugott's use of the term
than with Langacker's (for further discussion of the notion subjectification, see also
Verhagen, this volume, chapter 3, and Athanasiadou, Canakis, and Cornillie 2006).

3. Mood in Cognitive Linguistics

As was already mentioned, cognitive accounts of modality have to a large extent
concentrated on the modal verbs, whereby the (typically highly grammaticalized)
category of mood has largely been neglected.[27] Still, a number of cognitive solutions
for the interpretation of mood phenomena in languages such as French, German,
and Spanish have been proposed, which unfortunately lack a common core.

Probably the most elaborated model dealing with the semantics of mood from a cognitive linguistic perspective is the one proposed by Achard (1996a, 1998, 2002) for the French moods indicative, subjunctive, and conditional.[28] These three moods are all taken to contribute to the grounding of a finite clause, their selection being "determined by the evaluation of the status of the conceptualized event with respect to reality" (Achard 2002: 197). In Achard's view, only an indicative clause presents a *fully* grounded instance of a process type, whereby the conceptualized process is precisely located with respect to reality—by means of the tense morphemes (present, past, and future). The conditional and subjunctive, on the other hand, each locate the state of affairs outside reality (and thus lack tense predications), but in different ways. The conditional, whose main territory seems to be the apodosis of (hypothetical and counterfactual) conditionals,[29] is taken to impose restrictions on the conditions of occurrence of the event it is attached to, to the extent that the event is construed as an *alternative to reality*. The conditional thus marks a prediction of the speaker, based on the speaker's knowledge of the structure of reality and his or her conception of its evolutionary momentum (with the speaker assuming that the evolutionary momentum of reality will take another course than the one marked by the conditional). This characterization of the meaning of the French conditional is compatible with my analysis (Mortelmans 2000) of the semantics of the German past subjunctive (or *Konjunktiv II*), which in its prototypical use is taken to signal a speaker's negative epistemic stance so that the state of affairs is typically located within irreality (the German *Konjunktiv II* shares the French conditional's preference for conditional constructions).

(4)   French: *Si je la connaissais, j'irais lui parler tout de suite.*
       German: *Wenn ich sie kennen würde, würde ich gleich zu ihr gehen und mit ihr reden.*
                 'If I knew her, I would go and talk to her right away.'

The French subjunctive, which most often occurs in subordinate clauses following verbs of volition and emotional reaction, is taken to signal that the event is only considered with respect to a very local and specific mental space (the subject's desires, for instance, in the case of verbs of volition) and not with respect to reality as such.[30]

(5)   a.   *Le patron veut que vous reveniez tout de suite.*
            'The boss wants you to come back right away.'
       b.   *Je suis heureux que vous soyez sorti de ce piège.*
            'I am happy that you got out of that trap.'
            (examples and glosses are taken from Achard 2002)

The subjunctive is said to represent an *arbitrary* instance of a process type, conjured up for a specific purpose, but not represented as part of reality.

The prototypical function of the German present subjunctive (*Konjunktiv I*), on the other hand, resides in the marking of indirect speech.[31] It can therefore be taken to signal a shift in vantage point, as it is not the original speaker, but the reported one who has assessed the reported state of affairs as factual (Diewald 1999: 182). It should be noted that the aforementioned past subjunctive in German can also take up this function without the speaker necessarily distancing himself or herself from the content of the reported utterance (*pace* Wierzbicka 1988). In the latter case, the meaning of the past subjunctive merges with that of the present subjunctive.

(6)   *"Der Kinderarzt sagte, er **hätte** [KonjunktivII] selten ein so prächtiges Baby gesehen," sagte Delia stolz.*
        ' "The pediatrician said that only rarely had he seen such a beautiful baby," Delia said with pride.'

In terms of the level of reality that is addressed, the French subjunctive can be said to attach to events which are conceptualized with respect to basic reality, whereas the indicative situates an event with respect to elaborated reality.[32] With the latter level, the event is construed as a proposition and as such provided with a putative address in reality (by means of the tense morphemes). The observation that the subjunctive in Spanish has a slightly different distribution—verbs of thought and belief (which in French typically take the indicative) allow both indicative and subjunctive, whereas verbs of emotional reaction (taking subjunctive complements in French, as in *avoir peur* 'to be afraid', *être content* 'to be glad', and *détester* 'to hate') are also compatible with indicative marking—does not pose any problems for Achard's analysis: this distribution is explained in terms of construal flexibility (Achard 1998: 264), whereby Spanish speakers simply have the choice to construe the complement as either a proposition or an arbitrary instance.

4. CONCLUSION AND OUTLOOK

In order to arrive at a better understanding of modality, modal markers in languages other than English ought to be thoroughly analyzed, and in a next step, new empirical findings should be confronted with the main theoretical models that have been established up to now. For one thing, the observation that the root-epistemic polysemy in modal verbs is a typical trait of languages in Europe, but is less common in other languages (see van der Auwera and Ammann 2005), points to important conceptual differences between root and epistemic meanings which tend to be downplayed by their similar coding in familiar languages such as English, German, Spanish, or French. Other interesting areas for further research include the status of modal verbs and moods in terms of grounding predications and the possible inclusion of other markers (e.g., mental-state predicates like *I believe* or evidential markers) in this category. This question crucially involves an assessment of the degree of subjectification of particular meaning elements, which, in its turn, makes a proper understanding of the notion of subjectification (on which Langacker and Traugott clearly have different views—see especially Traugott and Dasher 2002: 89–99) unavoidable.

Overall, however, the cognitive linguistic concepts of force dynamics, on the one hand, and of subjectification (and grounding, which is related, but not identical, to it), on the other, have proved to be highly powerful tools to discover common cores in a wide variety of modal expression types.

NOTES

1. This characterization of modality reflects to a certain extent the long-standing, traditional view on modality as a logical category, at the core of which are the notions of possibility and obligation/necessity (for similar definitions of modality, see van der Auwera and Plungian 1998; Achard 1998). This "logical" bias partly accounts for the fact that *must* denoting necessity and *may/can* denoting possibility (and their counterparts in other languages) are the most recurrent objects of study in modality research (Sweetser 1990: 52). For criticism, see Diewald (1999: 156) or Wierzbicka (1987).

2. An excellent survey of evidentiality and the relevant literature is given in Floyd (1999: 13–39). Compare also Wierzbicka (1994), where the data from Chafe and Nichols's (1986) volume on evidentiality are reanalyzed in terms of universal semantic primitives.

3. Note that the German paradigm of modal verbs codes both epistemic and evidential distinctions—the modals *sollen* and *wollen* in their nonroot sense present the complement as 'reported': e.g., *Er soll krank sein* 'He is said to be ill' (Diewald 1999).

4. Lee (1993) mainly offers a discourse-pragmatic (in terms of informativeness, immediacy, and factuality) analysis of factors influencing the use of three evidential markers in Korean, which all mark newly perceived information. Although these markers are termed "epistemic" by the author, they mainly pertain to evidential qualifications.

5. The term root modality is used by Sweetser (1990), Langacker (1990, 1991a, 1991b), and Achard (1998) to refer to the obligation, permission, ability, and volition meanings of the modals. The traditional term "deontic" as a cover term for the full range of nonepistemic meanings has been criticized as being too narrow and even misleading (see, e.g., Sweetser 1990: 152; Diewald 1999: 74). Other terms (agent-oriented modality, participant internal/participant external modality, nondeictic modality) will not be used here, as they are liable to criticism as well or presuppose a particular theoretical stance.

6. The use of the same items to express both root and epistemic meanings can be observed in a large set of languages (Palmer 1986; Sweetser 1990: 49, 152). The findings in van der Auwera and Ammann (2005), however, caution against overgeneralizing this tendency. In fact, high or (near-)total overlap between expressions of root and epistemic modality is found to be almost (but not exclusively) confined to Europe. Outside Europe, languages with no overlap seem to dominate quantitatively.

7. It should be noted that Talmy only seems to regard negated *can* as expressing a force-dynamic configuration. At first sight, the use of *can* expressing positive ability is problematic in an analysis that is based on forces and counterforces (compare also Lampert and Lampert 2000: 243). Achard (1998: 143) and Johnson (1987: 52), however, do not have any problems incorporating positive ability (enablement) in a force-dynamic account.

8. Talmy (1988) views the modality expressed by *must, have to, need,* and *ought to* in terms of barriers, restricting the Agonist's scope of action, whereas Sweetser prefers an analysis of these verbs in terms of positive forces ("positive compulsion rather than negative restriction"; Sweetser 1990: 52). Sweetser's view is also adopted by Johnson (1987: 51), who regards the root sense of *must* as "denoting a compelling force that moves a subject towards an act."

9. This integration of lexical expressions into a discussion of modality is rather unique: Sweetser, Achard, Langacker, and Johnson, for instance, all restrict themselves to the (English or French) core modals. For a cognitive-pragmatic account of other (epistemic) markers, see Nuyts (2001).

10. It should be noted that force dynamics is generally conceptualized as primarily pertaining to physical interaction; as far as modality is concerned, however, Talmy (1988: 79) contends that reference to the psychosocial/interpersonal domain is basic.

11. For a radically different view, see Heine (1992), who claims that the distinction between root and epistemic modality is based on the presence versus absence of a modal force. Heine equates the notion of force with an element of will, exerted by an entity who has an interest in the event either occurring or not occurring.

12. Another problem for Sweetser is the "pure future" meaning of *will* indicating "a completed path to an action or intention" (Sweetser 1990: 55); this meaning hardly fits into a force-dynamic analysis. This might be due to the fact that Sweetser takes the pure future meaning of *will* as the source domain for the metaphorical mapping (*John will come*, glossed as 'The present state of affairs will proceed to the future event of John's arrival'). Langacker's example of root *will (not)*, however, features elements of volition and resolve (as in *He absolutely will not agree to it*). Here, the force dynamic nature is clear: the sentient subject *he* opposes some kind of force which tries to make him agree. Langacker treats the pure future use of *will* as a limiting case of epistemic *will*, in which the notion of evolutionary momentum—the "force" in the epistemic use of *will*—has faded away (Langacker 1991a: 278).

13. Note that the French modal class is not as easily delimited as the English one (Achard 1998: 124–31).

14. It should be stressed that in their root and epistemic usages, too, the French modals behave like main (lexical) verbs: they have not acquired the same degree of formal grammaticalization as their English counterparts (Achard 1996b: 5).

15. The modal force remains primarily associated with the subject, however, because of the subject's inherent intentionality.

16. In fact, Pelyvás (1996: 146) links the epistemic meaning to the original (but now extinct) 'ability' sense of *may*. However, there seems to be an intermediary root possibility stage, out of which the epistemic meaning has developed.

17. As main verbs, the predecessors of the present-day English modals are said to profile the potency relation between a trajector (the subject) and a landmark process—an option still available for *can* (*Can she lift it?*), as is remarked by Langacker (1991a: 273).

18. Note, however, that with root modality the subject can still function as a target of potency—a possibility ruled out for epistemic modals.

19. Langacker (1999) introduces a slightly adapted characterization of the process of subjectification, which views subjectification in terms of the objective component fading away and leaving only a subjectively construed relationship behind: "the subjective relationship was immanent in the objective one." (299). This alteration, however, does not seem to affect the "grounding" analysis in a crucial way.

20. The fact that Langacker refrains from a detailed description of the meaning of the English modals should be understood in this vein: "Grounding expressions tend to be abstract and schematic semantically." Moreover, their characterization pertains to fundamental cognitive notions whose import is not unreasonably described as "epistemic" (Langacker 1993: 48).

21. Interestingly, Langacker assumes that the verb following a modal is not an (atemporal) infinitive, but an uninflected simple verb representing the same semantic class as the modal (Langacker 1991a: 248).

22. Equating the locus of potency with evidence driving the speaker metaphorically along a deductive path would, in Langacker's (1991a: 274) view, violate the request of maximal subjectivity.

23. Unlike Sweetser, Langacker is able to integrate future *will* rather easily in a force-dynamic account: "If not rerouted by an unforeseen input of energy, reality is compelled by its evolutionary momentum to pursue a course such that the process does take place" (Langacker 1991a: 278).

24. It should be stressed that in spite of the semantic similarities between the English and French modals—especially with regard to their epistemic meanings—Achard does not consider the French modals as grounding predications. On the other hand, I assess the grounding status of the German modals in a more qualified way, depending on the degree of grammaticalization of the respective modals (Mortelmans 2001). A similar stance is taken by Cornillie (2005a, 2005b) with regard to the Spanish modals, which in their epistemic readings are taken to function as grounding predications as well.

25. It should be noted that passive and aspect markings are also possible with the 'obligation' and 'possibility' senses of *devoir* and *pouvoir*, respectively. Even in the case of a weak speaker role (with *devoir* expressing obligation, for instance), the subject of *devoir* lacks the initial impulse or initiative toward the complement process. Voice and aspect markers are ruled out, however, for *pouvoir* expressing ability and *savoir* (Achard 1998: 139).

26. In the case of the "remote" forms *would* and *could*, Goossens (1996) points out that they can still express past volition and past ability/possibility, which implies that the modal relationship itself is grounded—by tense, and hence is not maximally subjective.

27. For a more general introduction to the subjunctive, see Bybee, Perkins, and Pagliuca (1994: 212–36) and Givón (1994).

28. It should be noted that Achard (1998) only considers the use of indicative and subjunctive in finite complements. A more general approach, which also takes main clause and other uses into account, can be found in Achard (2002).

29. In independent sentences, the conditional is found to have an attenuating effect, often making the utterance more polite. Note that Achard does not discuss the use of the conditional as a marker of indirect speech (cf. Dendale 1993).

30. Compare also Mejías-Bikandi (1996), who offers a compatible account of the meaning of the Spanish subjunctive, which is said to close a particular mental space M, "so that information contained in it cannot flow to higher spaces" (Mejías-Bikandi 1996: 175).

31. See also Wierzbicka (1988: 140–61), who claims that, from a cross-linguistic perspective, the subjunctive not only has an anticognitive ('I don't say: I know this'), but also an antiassertive component ('I don't say: I say this'). The scope of the anticognitive component in German seems to be much smaller than in French: in German, the use of the

present subjunctive (and to some extent even that of the past subjunctive) is mainly governed by the antiassertive aspect of the subjunctive.

32. I put forward a similar claim for the German moods *Konjunktiv I* and *II* (Mortelmans 2003).

REFERENCES

Achard, Michel. 1996a. Complement construal in French: A cognitive perspective. In Eugene H. Casad, ed., *Cognitive linguistics in the Redwoods: The expansion of a new paradigm in linguistics* 569–607. Berlin: Mouton de Gruyter.

Achard, Michel. 1996b. French modals and speaker control. In Adele E. Goldberg, ed., *Conceptual structure, discourse and language* 1–15. Stanford, CA: CSLI Publications.

Achard, Michel. 1998. *Representation of cognitive structures: Syntax and semantics of French sentential complements*. Berlin: Mouton de Gruyter.

Achard, Michel. 2002. The meaning and distribution of French mood inflections. In Frank Brisard, ed., *Grounding: The epistemic footing of deixis and reference* 197–249. Berlin: Mouton de Gruyter.

Athanasiadou, Angeliki, Costas Canakis, and Bert Cornillie, eds. 2006. *Subjectification: Various paths to subjectivity*. Berlin: Mouton de Gruyter.

Bybee, Joan L., Revere D. Perkins, and William Pagliuca. 1994. *The evolution of grammar: Tense, aspect, and modality in the languages of the world*. Chicago: University of Chicago Press.

Casad, Eugene H. 1992. Cognition, history, and Cora *yee*. *Cognitive Linguistics* 3: 151–86.

Chafe, Wallace, and Johanna Nichols, eds. 1986. *Evidentiality: The linguistic coding of epistemology*. Norwood, NJ: Ablex.

Cornillie, Bert. 2005a. Agentivity and subjectivity with Spanish *prometer* 'to promise' and *amenazar* 'to threaten': A study of constructional and diatopical variation. *Revista Internacional de Lingüística Iberoamericana* 3: 171–96.

Cornillie, Bert. 2005b. Reference point and subjectification in grounding predications: The case of the Spanish modals. *Annual Review of Cognitive Linguistics* 3: 56–77.

Dendale, Patrick. 1993. Le conditionnel de l'information incertaine: Marqueur modal ou marqueur évidentiel? In Gerold Hilty, ed., *Actes du XXe Congrès International de Linguistique et Philologie Romanes, Université de Zurich* 164–75. Tübingen: A. Francke Verlag.

Diewald, Gabriele. 1999. *Die Modalverben im Deutschen: Grammatikalisierung und Polyfunktionalität*. Tübingen: Max Niemeyer Verlag.

Floyd, Rick. 1999. *The structure of evidential categories in Wanka Quechua*. Dallas, TX: Summer Institute of Linguistics.

Foolen, Ad. 1992. Review *From etymology to pragmatics*, by Eve Sweetser. *Lingua* 88: 76–86.

Givón, Talmy. 1982. Evidentiality and epistemic space. *Studies in Language* 6: 23–49.

Givón, Talmy. 1994. Irrealis and the subjunctive. *Studies in Language* 18: 265–337.

Goossens, Louis. 1992. CUNNAN, CONNE(N), CAN: The development of a radial category. In Günter Kellermann and Michael D. Morrissey, eds., *Diachrony within synchrony— Language history and cognition: Papers from the international symposium at the University of Duisburg, 26–28 March 1990* 377–94. Frankfurt am Main: Peter Lang Verlag.

Goossens, Louis. 1996. *English modals and functional models: A confrontation.* Antwerp Papers in Linguistics (APiL), no. 86. Antwerpen: University of Antwerp. http://webhost.ua.ac.be/apil/list.html.

Goossens, Louis. 1999. Metonymic bridges in modal shifts. In Klaus-Uwe Panther and Günter Radden, eds., *Metonymy in language and thought* 193–210. Amsterdam: John Benjamins.

Goossens, Louis. 2000. Patterns of meaning extension, "parallel chaining," subjectification, and modal shifts. In Antonio Barcelona, ed., *Metaphor and metonymy at the crossroads: A cognitive perspective* 149–70. Berlin: Mouton de Gruyter.

Heine, Bernd. 1992. Agent-oriented vs. epistemic modality: Some observations on German modals. In Joan L. Bybee and Suzanne Fleischman, eds., *Modality in grammar and discourse* 17–53. Amsterdam: John Benjamins.

Hopper, Paul J., and Elizabeth Closs Traugott. 1993. *Grammaticalization.* Cambridge: Cambridge University Press. (2nd ed., 2003)

Johnson, Mark. 1987. *The body in the mind: The bodily basis of meaning, imagination, and reason.* Chicago: University of Chicago Press.

Lampert, Günther, and Martina Lampert. 2000. *The conceptual structure(s) of modality: Essences and ideologies. A study in linguistic (meta-)categorization.* Frankfurt am Main: Peter Lang Verlag.

Langacker, Ronald W. 1990. Subjectification. *Cognitive Linguistics* 1: 5–38.

Langacker, Ronald W. 1991a. *Foundations of cognitive grammar.* Vol. 2, *Descriptive application.* Stanford, CA: Stanford University Press.

Langacker, Ronald W. 1991b. *Concept, image, and symbol: The cognitive basis of grammar.* Berlin: Mouton de Gruyter.

Langacker, Ronald W. 1993. Deixis and subjectivity. In S. K. Verma and V. Prakasam, eds., *New horizons in functional linguistics* 43–58. Hyderabad, India: Booklinks Corporation.

Langacker, Ronald W. 1994. Remarks on the English grounding systems. In Ronny Boogaart and Jan Noordegraaf, eds., *Nauwe betrekkingen: Voor Theo Janssen bij zijn vijftigste verjaardag* 137–44. Amsterdam: Stichting Neerlandistiek.

Langacker, Ronald W. 1999. *Grammar and conceptualization.* Berlin: Mouton de Gruyter.

Langacker, Ronald W. 2003. Extreme subjectification: English tense and modals. In Hubert Cuyckens, Thomas Berg, René Dirven, and Klaus-Uwe Panther, eds., *Motivation in Language: Studies in honor of Günter Radden* 3–26. Amsterdam: John Benjamins.

Lee, Hyo Sang. 1993. Cognitive constraints on expressing newly perceived information, with reference to epistemic modal suffixes in Korean. *Cognitive Linguistics* 4: 135–67.

Matlock, Teenie. 1989. Metaphor and the grammaticalization of evidentials. *Berkeley Linguistics Society* 15: 215–25.

Mejías-Bikandi, Errapel. 1996. Space accessibility and mood in Spanish. In Gilles Fauconnier and Eve Sweetser, eds., *Spaces, worlds, and grammar* 157–78. Chicago: University of Chicago Press.

Mortelmans, Tanja. 2000. Konjunktiv II and epistemic modals in German: A division of labour. In Ad Foolen and Frederike van der Leek, eds., *Constructions in cognitive linguistics* 191–215. Amsterdam: John Benjamins.

Mortelmans, Tanja. 2001. An introduction to Langacker's grounding predications: Mood and modal verbs in German. In Heinz Vater and Ole Letnes, eds., *Modalität und mehr / Modality and more* 3–26. Trier, Germany: Wissenschaftlicher Verlag.

Mortelmans, Tanja. 2002. 'Wieso sollte ich dich küssen, du hässlicher Mensch!': A study of the German modals *sollen* and *müssen* as 'grounding predications' in interrogatives. In Frank Brisard, ed., *Grounding: The epistemic footing of deixis and reference* 391–432. Berlin: Mouton de Gruyter.

Mortelmans, Tanja. 2003. The 'subjective' effects of negation and past subjunctive on deontic modals: The case of German *dürfen* and *sollen*. In Friedrich Lenz, ed., *Deictic conceptualisation of space, time and person* 153–82. Amsterdam: John Benjamins.

Nuyts, Jan. 1994. *Epistemic modal qualifications: On their linguistic and conceptual structure.* Antwerp Papers in Linguistics (APiL), no. 81. Antwerpen: University of Antwerp. http://webhost.ua.ac.be/apil/list.html.

Nuyts, Jan. 2001. *Epistemic modality, language and conceptualization: A cognitive-pragmatic perspective.* Amsterdam: John Benjamins.

Nuyts, Jan. 2002. Grounding and the system of epistemic expressions in Dutch: A cognitive-functional view. In Frank Brisard, ed., *Grounding. The epistemic footing of deixis and reference* 433–66. Berlin: Mouton de Gruyter.

Palmer, Frank R. 1986. *Mood and modality.* Cambridge: Cambridge University Press.

Pelyvás, Péter. 1996. *Subjectivity in English: Generative grammar versus the cognitive theory of epistemic grounding.* Frankfurt am Main: Peter Lang Verlag.

Pelyvás, Péter. 2000. Metaphorical extension of *may* and *must* into the epistemic domain. In Antonio Barcelona, ed., *Metaphor and metonymy at the crossroads: A cognitive perspective* 233–50. Berlin: Mouton de Gruyter.

Pelyvás, Péter. 2001. The development of the grounding predication: Epistemic modals and cognitive predicates. In Enikö Németh and Károly Bibok, eds., *Pragmatics and the flexibility of word meaning* 151–74. Amsterdam: Elsevier.

Sanders, José, and Wilbert Spooren 1996. Subjectivity and certainty in epistemic modality: A study of Dutch epistemic modifiers. *Cognitive Linguistics* 7: 241–64.

Sweetser, Eve. 1982. Root and epistemic modals: Causality in two worlds. *Berkeley Linguistics Society* 8: 484–507.

Sweetser, Eve. 1984. Semantic structure and semantic change: A cognitive linguistics study of modality, perception, speech acts, and logical relations. PhD dissertation, University of California at Berkeley.

Sweetser, Eve. 1990. *From etymology to pragmatics: Metaphorical and cultural aspects of semantic structure.* Cambridge: Cambridge University Press.

Talmy, Leonard. 1976. Semantic causative types. In Masayoshi Shibatani, ed., *Syntax and semantics*, vol. 6, *The grammar of causative constructions* 43–116. New York: Academic Press.

Talmy, Leonard. 1985. Force dynamics in language and thought. *Chicago Linguistic Society* 21, vol. 2 (parasession): 293–337.

Talmy, Leonard. 1988. Force dynamics in language and cognition. *Cognitive Science* 12: 49–100.

Talmy, Leonard. 2000. *Toward a cognitive semantics.* Vol. 1, *Concept structuring systems.* Cambridge, MA: MIT Press.

Traugott, Elizabeth Closs. 1989. On the rise of epistemic meanings in English: An example of subjectification in semantic change. *Language* 65: 31–55.

Traugott, Elizabeth Closs. 1995. Subjectification in grammaticalisation. In Dieter Stein and Susan Wright, eds., *Subjectivity and subjectivisation: Linguistic perspectives* 31–54. Cambridge: Cambridge University Press.

Traugott, Elizabeth Closs, and Richard B. Dasher. 2002. *Regularity in semantic change.* Cambridge: Cambridge University Press.

Traugott, Elizabeth Closs, and Ekkehard König. 1991. The semantics-pragmatics of grammaticalization revisited. In Elizabeth Closs Traugott and Bernd Heine, eds., *Approaches to grammaticalization* 189–218. Amsterdam: John Benjamins.

van der Auwera, Johan, and Andreas Ammann. 2005. Overlap between situational and epistemic modal marking. In Matthew Dryer, David Gil, Martin Haspelmath, and Bernard Comrie, eds., *World atlas of language structures* 310–13. Oxford: Oxford University Press.

van der Auwera, Johan, and Vladimir A. Plungian. 1998. Modality's semantic map. *Linguistic Typology* 2: 79–124.

Verhagen, Arie. 1995. Subjectification, syntax, and communication. In Dieter Stein and Susan Wright, eds., *Subjectivity and subjectivisation in language* 103–28. Cambridge: Cambridge University Press.

Verhagen, Arie. 1996. Sequential conceptualization and linear order. In Eugene H. Casad, ed., *Cognitive linguistics in the Redwoods: The expansion of a new paradigm in linguistics* 793–817. Berlin: Mouton de Gruyter.

Wierzbicka, Anna. 1987. The semantics of modality. *Folia Linguistica* 21: 25–43.

Wierzbicka, Anna. 1988. *The semantics of grammar.* Amsterdam: John Benjamins.

Wierzbicka, Anna. 1994. Semantics and epistemology: The meaning of 'evidentials' in a cross-linguistic perspective. *Language Sciences* 16: 81–137.

CHAPTER 34

PRONOMINAL ANAPHORA

KAREN VAN HOEK

1. INTRODUCTION

One of the fundamental beliefs guiding the cognitive linguistic enterprise is that grammar is meaningful. Rather than being conceived as a separate module or sub-theory of language, grammar is viewed as the conventionalized patterns by which complex meanings are expressed. Grammatical phenomena should therefore be fully characterizable in terms of meaningful linguistic units, rather than requiring that we posit special theoretical constructs for their explication.

The theory of Cognitive Grammar developed by Langacker (1987, 1991), arguably the most fully developed grammatical theory within the field of Cognitive Linguistics, assumes that there are in fact only three kinds of linguistic units: semantic, phonological, and symbolic, where a symbolic unit is a bipolar unit consisting of a semantic unit paired with a phonological unit, similar to a Saussurean "sign." Cognitive Grammar takes the position that syntactic phenomena can be fully characterized using only these three kinds of units, without requiring a special vocabulary or special constructs for the description of syntax.

An ideal test case for these claims is the classic problem of pronominal anaphora: the principles governing the circumstances under which a pronoun (such as *he*, *she*, *it*) and a name or descriptive noun phrase (*Sally*, *the green car*, *that guy over there*) can be interpreted as referring to the same person or thing. The principles of pronominal coreference have been the focus of intensive study in Generative Linguistics since the late 1960s. The most widely accepted models within the generative tradition are based on the notion of *c-command*, a theoretical construct which does not satisfy the criteria for inclusion in a cognitive linguistic approach, for reasons explained below.

The mystery of pronominal anaphora can be illustrated quite simply. The sentences in (1a) and (1b) allow for an interpretation in which the pronoun corefers with the name. (I use the term *corefer* to mean 'picks out the conception of the same person or thing', without any implication that there must be a real-world referent with which the nominal is associated.) Though they differ only slightly from the first pair, the sentences in (1c) and (1d) require a different interpretation, in which the pronoun refers to someone else. Italics are used to indicate coreference; the asterisk indicates that the sentence is unacceptable under the relevant reading (under a noncoreferential interpretation, each of the sentences is perfectly fine).

(1)   a. Near *him, Luke* saw a skunk.
      b. *His* mother says *John* is a wonderful human being.
      c. *Near *Luke, he* saw a skunk.
      d. *He* says *John*'s mother is a wonderful human being.

The common-sense idea that the name should be mentioned before a pronoun can be used to "refer back" will obviously not explain these facts. In (1a) and (1b), the pronoun precedes the name, and in (1c) it does not.

Observations such as these have led generativists to develop explanations based on constructs of autonomous syntax, such as c-command. Greatly simplified, the c-command analysis (Reinhart 1983) states that certain geometric configurations of nominals—as defined on syntactic tree structures—rule out coreference. If the first branching node above the pronoun in the tree structure also dominates the full noun phrase (the name or descriptive phrase), then the pronoun is said to "c-command" the full noun phrase, and coreference is ruled out. As illustrated in figure 34.1—a highly simplified tree structure for (1c)—the branching node S dominating the pronoun *he* also dominates the prepositional phrase *near Luke*. Coreference between the pronoun and name is therefore ruled out.

From a cognitive linguistic standpoint, there are numerous problems with the c-command approach. The theory of Cognitive Grammar takes as one of its guiding principles the Content Requirement, which effectively rules out any analysis analogous to c-command.

(2)   *The Content Requirement*
      The only structures permitted in the grammar of a language are (1)
      phonological, semantic, or symbolic structures that actually occur in
      linguistic expressions; (2) schemas for such structures; and (3) categorizing
      relationships involving the elements in (1) and (2). (Langacker 1987: 488)

The Content Requirement essentially says that only linguistic structures which have either meaning or sound, or both, are permitted in a grammar. Schemas are

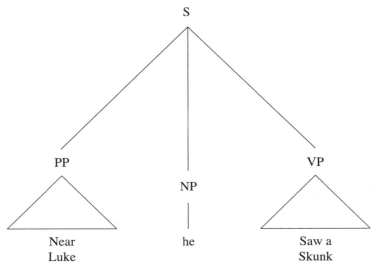

Figure 34.1. Tree structure for *Near Luke, he saw a skunk*

templates or patterns which generalize across more specific exemplars and which speakers can use as templates for the construction of new expressions. They also constitute semantic, phonological, or symbolic units, but are more schematic, that is, less detailed than individual specific expressions.

As the tree structures on which the c-command relationship is defined represent neither meaning nor pronunciation—they are instead purely syntactic constructs—they are not allowable in a Cognitive Grammar analysis. It should also be noted that c-command does not offer a grounded explanation for the facts—that is, it does not explain the coreference patterns in terms of more general notions, but merely stipulates that certain geometric configurations are ruled out. It also offers no account of the observable similarities between sentence-internal and cross-sentential coreference patterns, nor does it provide any way of dealing with the effects of phenomena, such as *point of view*, that are not represented on generative syntactic tree structures. Instead, it offers a rule which governs only a small range of the relevant data and which cannot be modified to apply more generally, given that it is defined on tree structures which are posited to exist only within the "syntax module" of a speaker's linguistic knowledge.

The goal of a Cognitive Grammar analysis is to provide a grounded explanation of the facts: one which explicates grammatical patterns in terms of the meanings which they convey and which is built on more general properties and principles of language and, ideally, of cognition in general. We can begin by briefly looking at facets of meaning which provide the basis for an explanation.

2. Nominal Semantics

A number of researchers have noted that full noun phrases and pronouns simply do not convey the same nuances, even when they refer to the same person or thing. Accessibility Theory (Givón 1989; Ariel 1990) posits that different nominal forms signal different degrees of "accessibility" of a referent, where accessibility means something like 'the ease with which the conception can be brought into conscious awareness'.

A full noun phrase indicates that the person or thing it refers to requires relatively more effort to access, either because the addressee is not currently thinking about the person or because the person is entirely unfamiliar. A pronoun accesses a notion that is relatively easily retrieved, such as the conception of a person already under discussion or physically present. (There are finer gradations among the different nominal forms and crosslinguistic variation; see Givón 1989; Ariel 1990.)

Accessibility Theory provides a way of grounding the coreference facts in the mental experience of the speaker (or conceptualizer, as the same principles apply to private thoughts) and addressee. The issue is thus not a matter of abstract geometric relationships between nodes and nominals, but of the mental models the speakers construct and the cues they give to indicate the status of a referent relative to the current context.

The notion of accessibility can also be thought of in terms of the corollary notion of conceptual distance. Something which is more accessible is conceptually closer to the speaker and addressee than something which is less accessible. This idea may be made clearer if we think about a typical discourse in terms of Langacker's (1985) metaphor of the Stage Model. The speaker and addressee are analogous to an audience watching a play; the conceptions which the speaker places in the center of awareness are, metaphorically speaking, put on "stage" to be viewed by the "audience." In Langacker's terms, the audience is construed *subjectively*, meaning that they are the viewers, rather than that-which-is-viewed. The "onstage" conceptions are viewed *objectively*, as the center of attention.

Some forms of reference mark a clear distinction between the offstage, subjective viewers and the onstage focus of attention. A full noun phrase (such as *Jim* or *the three-legged dog*) focuses the speaker and addressee's attention on a conception and renders it fully objective. It thereby portrays the referent as relatively distant from the speaker and addressee. This can be contrasted with the way a pronoun portrays its referent. A pronoun places onstage a conception that is identifiable only through its association with an offstage participant. The pronouns *I* and *you*, for example, focus attention on conceptions identified as the discourse participants themselves. This is indicated in figure 34.2a by the dotted line—indicating correspondence—between the onstage conception (represented by a circle) and the speaker (represented by the circle labeled *S*). The person described by the pronoun *I* plays a dual role as both the viewer and the object of viewing.

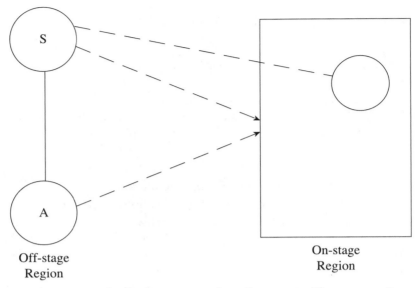

Figure 34.2a. Semantic representation of pronouns: The pronoun *I*

The pronoun blurs the distinction between the onstage and offstage, or objective and subjective, regions, thereby portraying its referent as conceptually closer to the speaker and addressee than does a full noun phrase. This is especially clear in the case of first-person reference. Under most circumstances, it is anomalous for the speaker to refer to himself or herself by name. The name *Joe Smith* places the conception of Joe Smith fully onstage. If Joe Smith is actually the speaker, referring to Joe Smith by name is usually bizarre, inasmuch as it implies that he can see himself 'from the outside', as he would see another person. Only a shift in point of view can make sense of such usage. For this reason, reference to the speaker via a name may be used as a signal of a point of view shift. In (3), from an interview with Oliver North, North's use of his own name implies that he is taking an external perspective and thus underscores the fact that he is describing "Ollie North" within the reporters' conception of reality, not his own self-perception.

(3)   While reporters were talking about how Ollie North sodomized goats on the south lawn of the White House, or how Ollie North was selling White House china to fund the Contras.... (Oliver North, interview in *TV Guide*, December 28, 1991)

There are similar restrictions on the use of a name to refer to the addressee. Generally, using a name rather than *you* is permissible only when the speaker wants to get the person's attention (since the addressee is not yet paying attention to what the speaker is saying, the addressee is presumably not considered part of the offstage "audience"). A name may also be used to reassure the addressee that she or he has the speaker's full attention or sympathy (as in *I know how you must feel,*

Bob). In the latter case, the addressee's role as coviewer of the onstage conception is de-emphasized to give prominence to the addressee's role as object of the speaker's attention.

In the absence of one of these specialized contexts, reference to the speaker or addressee via a name or descriptive phrase, rather than a pronoun, will be judged as bizarre and inappropriate. Full noun phrases imply that the referent is construed as distant, "held at arm's length" from the offstage audience. Except in the special circumstances described above, the speaker and addressee cannot be construed that way. The judgments in such cases will easily be as strong as the judgments of unacceptability for (1c) and (1d), yet in such cases there is no way to explain speakers' judgments in terms of prohibited relationships between nominals or illegal geometric configurations within tree structures.

Although third-person pronouns such as *he, she, they,* and so forth do not refer to participants in the discourse, they nevertheless place onstage a conception which is identified by its relationship with a central offstage element. In this case, the offstage element is the conception of a person or thing which is physically present or has already been discussed and thus is established as part of the shared discourse world of the speaker and addressee. Thus, even a third-person pronoun portrays its referent as conceptually close to the discourse participants by being shared knowledge understood by both. This is represented in figure 34.2b, where the person the speaker and addressee are discussing is indicated by the circle labeled *X*, which corresponds to the onstage profile of the pronoun (indicated by the dotted line).

In the case of third-person reference, use of a name is not as highly restricted as it is in the case of first- and second-person reference. Since the person or thing being talked about is not a coviewer of the onstage conception, there is more flexibility with regards to construing him, her, or it as part of the shared offstage world. Nevertheless, the difference in implied conceptual distance between pronouns and full noun phrases is robust enough that speakers frequently choose forms of reference to convey their attitude toward the person being spoken of. Speakers frequently use full names when they wish to express ridicule or disapproval of a person, even in contexts in which a pronoun could have been used with no loss of clarity (see van Hoek 1997a: 39–42). Full names or noun phrases are also used when the speaker disagrees with something that another speaker has just said about the referent (as in *Wasn't that Tom I saw going out the back door? – No, Tom hasn't been here in weeks*) (see Fox 1987b). The conceptual distancing implied by the name signals that the speaker is holding the other person's idea "at arm's length" rather than accepting it and building on it.

Conceptual distance is merely a different way of thinking about accessibility. If a conception is construed as highly accessible, it means that it is known to both speaker and addressee, that it is part of the shared world of things which both are aware of and can easily call into the center of attention. It is therefore conceptually closer than something which is less accessible and thus farther away from the shared offstage world. The twin concepts of accessibility and conceptual distance

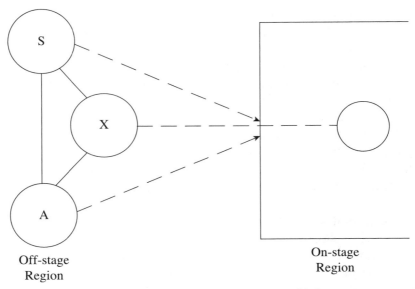

Figure 34.2b. Semantic representation of pronouns: A third-person pronoun *I*

are simply two sides of the same coin. Both ways of thinking about it are useful, however, for they help us to understand the ways that speakers actually use the distinctions between different nominal forms to convey nuances.

In addition to its role in conveying nuances of the speaker's attitude, the accessibility distinction between pronouns and noun phrases is the basis for the patterns of acceptable and anomalous coreference. A full noun phrase is appropriately used only in a context in which its referent is not highly accessible. If a pronoun is used, thereby establishing that the referent is highly accessible, a full noun phrase placed in the immediate context defined by the pronoun would be anomalous. The juxtaposition of the pronoun and full noun phrase would result in contradictory signals concerning the accessibility of the referent; one way for speakers to resolve the conflict is to assume that the pronoun must refer to someone else. A simple example is given in (4).

(4)   *He* loves *John*'s mother.

The pronoun *he* indicates that its referent is accessible; the name indicates the opposite. If speakers are required to read the two as coreferential, they judge the sentence to be anomalous (i.e., unacceptable). Thinking of it in terms of conceptual distance, the placement of the pronoun and name here is roughly equivalent to portraying the person as very close to the speaker and addressee (via the pronoun) and then portraying the same person as simultaneously distant (via the name). The two views of the referent are incoherent.

Note that this is not because an autonomous principle of pronominal distribution, such as c-command, has been violated. The judgment of anomaly comes directly from the meanings of the pronoun and the name and the way that they are juxtaposed in the sentence. No additional principles are needed.

We do, however, need to know how to tell which nominal is construed as part of the context within which the other one must be interpreted, or in other words, how do we know which vantage point to "look from" in order to decide whether the views of the referent are congruent. The examples in (1) made it clear that linear order alone will not be sufficient. In fact, while linear order does play a role, its contribution is relatively weak compared to the more central factors described in the next section.

3. CONCEPTUAL REFERENCE POINTS

The relevant notion of context is defined in terms of the notion of a conceptual reference point, a notion first introduced in Langacker's (1991) analysis of possessive constructions. A reference point is any element which is taken as a starting point from which to access other conceptions. It is similar to an abstract point of view. An element may be selected as a reference point because it is especially prominent (the relevant notions of prominence are defined below) or because it comes before other elements in the linear string.

The conceptions which are accessed from the perspective of the reference point and construed in relationship to it are said to be in its dominion. Relative to the elements in its dominion, the reference point functions as a central but subjectively construed part of the background: it is a key part of the conceptual "lens" through which the conceptualizer "views" the dominion. It is not itself in the center of attention. The reference point/dominion configuration thus has a dynamic quality to it: On one level, the reference point is selected because it stands out as prominent relative to the surrounding context (even if only by virtue of coming earlier in the phonological string). Within the dominion, however, the reference point "fades into the background," exerting a critical influence on the construal of the conceptions in the center of attention but not itself occupying the center of attention.

A sentence or stretch of discourse may have any number of reference point/dominion configurations, such that the conceptualizer—the speaker or addressee—mentally moves through the conceptions, shifting attention from reference point to dominion and on to other reference points and their associated dominions. Common configurations of reference points and dominions may become established as conventional, entrenched facets of the meaning of certain grammatical patterns. For example, the status of the subject of a clause as a reference point (relative to the predicate) is no doubt entrenched as part of the subject-predicate relationship.

The principles governing coreference can thus be stated very simply:

a. A pronoun must appear in the dominion of a corresponding reference point (i.e., a conception of the person or thing the pronoun refers to). This is simply part of the meaning of a pronoun—correspondence between the conception it places onstage and an offstage conception which is highly accessible, i.e., functioning as a reference point.

b. A full nominal—a name or descriptive phrase—cannot appear in the dominion of a corresponding reference point, as this would result in a semantic conflict between the meaning of a full nominal (which includes low accessibility and conceptual distance from the referent) and the context in which the full nominal appears.

Note that these are not special principles which must be independently stated as abstract grammatical rules; rather, they are simply part of the meanings of nouns and pronouns.

3.1. Factors Determining Reference Point Selection

The factors determining reference point selection are intuitively plausible: an element tends to be selected as a reference point if it is prominent and/or if it comes earlier in the linear string. That is, speakers tend to begin with those elements which stand out or which they encounter earlier in the string, and they interpret other parts of the phrase, sentence, or discourse within the contexts set up by those prominent or prior elements. Once a reference point has been selected, its dominion does not extend forever, but generally encompasses only those conceptions which are felt to be connected with it, in a sense to be made clearer below. Thus, there are three facets of the reference point/dominion configuration which we need to explore in more detail:

a. *Prominence.* The most important factor in reference point selection is prominence. Cognitive Grammar posits two different dimensions or facets of prominence: the profile/base distinction and Figure/Ground alignment. Both of these play important roles in determining reference point organization.

b. *Linear Order.* Linear precedence is a kind of prominence in its own right, but here I treat it as separate from the notions of prominence mentioned above, as linear order seems to be a weaker factor. Its effects are most visible only when other factors do not clearly determine a particular construal vis- à-vis reference point selection and the extent of a dominion.

c. *Connectivity.* The dominion of a reference point extends to include those elements with which it is conceptually connected, as for example when there is a verb or preposition describing a relationship between the elements. When there is no such overt connectivity—as for example when two

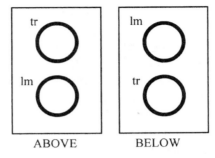

Figure 34.3. Two relations differing only in Figure/Ground alignment

nominals are contained in the same paragraph, or even in the same sentence, but with no overtly specified connection between them—speakers tend to construe the two nominals as relatively independent from one another and may therefore not assume that one nominal must be in the dominion of the other.

3.2. Prominence

The notions of prominence which are of central importance in the reference point model were not developed specially to explain the pronominal anaphora facts; rather, they are long-established constructs of Cognitive Grammar (see Langacker 1987, 1991, 1998; this volume, chapter 17). These are *Figure/Ground asymmetry* and the *profile/base* distinction.

Figure/Ground Asymmetry

In keeping with its central goal of grounding linguistic phenomena in more widely attested cognitive facilities, Cognitive Grammar characterizes grammatical relations in terms of the well-known distinction between Figure and Ground. Every relational expression—be it a verb, an adjective, or a preposition—imposes an asymmetric construal on the participants in the relation. One of the participants stands out as the Figure, while the rest of the relational conception—including any other participants—is construed as the Ground.

The distinction between *above* and *below*, for example, is a matter of Figure/Ground alignment. Both describe a configuration involving two things in vertically oriented space. *Above* picks out the upper element as Figure, as in *The lamp is above the table*, while *below* picks out the lower element, as in *The table is below the lamp*. The technical term for the Figure is *trajector*, while the other participant in the relation (if there is one) is termed the *landmark*. These are labeled *tr* and *lm* in the diagrams, respectively.

The trajector/landmark distinction manifests at the clausal level in the familiar subject/object distinction. The subject is the Figure within the conception described by the clause. The direct object, if there is one, is the primary landmark—the second most prominent nominal in the clause. If there are two objects, there is a distinction in prominence between the direct object (the primary landmark) and the other object, the secondary landmark.

The subject's status as Figure means that—with certain exceptions discussed in section 4—other nominals within the sentence are construed within its dominion, regardless of linear word order. The subject serves as a starting point or vantage point from which to mentally enter or view the rest of the clause. This explains facts such as (1a), (1c), and (1d), repeated here as (5).

(5)   a. Near *him*, *Luke* saw a skunk.
      b. *Near *Luke*, *he* saw a skunk.
      c. *He* says *John*'s mother is a wonderful human being.

In (5a), the name *Luke* is the subject, hence it serves as a reference point relative to the rest of the clause, including the pronoun *him*. The sentence is therefore acceptable, as the pronoun appears in the dominion of a corresponding reference point and the name does not. Sentence (5b) reverses the configuration, resulting in a semantic conflict—the name appears in the dominion of the reference point *he*. Sentence (5c) involves the same kind of conflict; the embedded clause which contains the name *John* serves as the object of the higher verb *says*, thus the entire clause, including the notion of John, is construed within the dominion of the subject *he*.

The subject's status as Figure is so unambiguous that even placing the name before the pronoun, as in (5b), is not sufficient to remove the name from the subject's dominion. The entire clause is interpreted in relation to the subject, in other words, even if part of it comes before the subject in the linear string. (Some kinds of modifiers can "escape" the subject's dominion if they are placed in sentence-initial position; this is discussed in section 4.)

The subject's role as primary reference point within the clause means that it also tends to be a locus of empathy or point of view, in the sense that speakers sometimes view the imagined scene through the eyes of the subject. Even when they do not, however, the subject still functions as a reference point. A reference point is almost identical to what is commonly called a point of view, except that a reference point need not involve any salient sense that one is seeing through the eyes of the individual or experiencing his or her thoughts.

The direct object serves as the secondary figure in the clause; as such, it is more prominent than other nominals except the subject and functions as a reference point with other nominals in its dominion. This explains facts such as (6).

(6)   a. I gave *John his* book.
      b. *I gave *him John*'s book.
      c. Sally saw *John* at *his* sister's house.

    d. *Sally saw *him* at *John's* sister's house.

    e. Ralph showed *Samantha* a picture of *her* cat.

    f. *Ralph showed *her* a picture of *Samantha's* cat.

Profile and Base

Thus far, our attention has been focused on nominals that play central roles within the clause: subjects and objects. There we found that certain nominals are invariably construed as belonging to the dominions of the more prominent nominals, so that the possibilities for coreference between full noun phrases and pronouns is rigidly circumscribed.

When we turn our attention to the more peripheral nominals—those that are participants in modifying relations, rather than serving as complements of the verb—we find that there is, at least sometimes, a rather striking flexibility concerning the placement of names and pronouns. This is illustrated by (7). (Example 7c is the title of a newspaper article; 7e is the inscription on the wall of the Lincoln Memorial in Washington, DC.)

(7)   a. The people who know *him* worship *Al Gore*.

      b. The people who know *Al Gore* worship *him*.

      c. Even *his* admirers admit *Mandela* is no miracle worker.

      d. Even *Mandela's* admirers admit *he's* no miracle worker.

      e. In this temple, as in the hearts of the people for whom *he* saved the Union, the memory of *Abraham Lincoln* is enshrined forever.

      f. In this temple, as in the hearts of the people for whom *Abraham Lincoln* saved the Union, *his* memory is enshrined forever.

Even in those examples in which the pronoun comes before the name in the linear string (what is termed "backwards anaphora"—backwards in the sense that it is assumed that normally the name will precede the pronoun), speakers do not automatically interpret the pronoun as a reference point with the name in its dominion. The key factor in each of the backwards anaphora examples is that the pronoun is contained within a modifier.

To discuss modifiers from a Cognitive Grammar perspective, we first need to understand that Cognitive Grammar posits that every linguistically encoded conception (i.e., every semantic representation) consists of a *profile* imposed on a *base*. The base for an expression is all the conceptions which are accessed or activated by that expression, both elements that are central to its meaning and those that are relatively peripheral. Within the base, the profile is the portion which receives special prominence (or is especially highly activated) as that which the expression designates. It seems likely that the profile is something like a focus of attention, though Langacker (1987) refrains from explicitly defining the notion of profile in terms of attentional mechanisms.

The profile/base distinction can be illustrated with a few simple examples. The noun *roof* invokes as its base the conception of a house (or building) and profiles

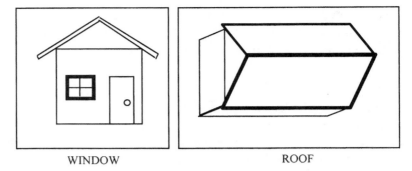

WINDOW   ROOF

Figure 34.4. Profile and base

one part of that conception. (Even if one is talking about a detached roof—blown off by a tornado, perhaps—it is still part of the meaning of roof that it is canonically part of a house, so the conception of a house still functions as a crucial part of the base.) The noun *window* also invokes the conception of a house or building as a central part of its base, but profiles a different subpart.

Even expressions whose meanings do not lend themselves to pictorial illustration involve a profile imposed on a base. The expression *U.S. President* invokes as its base the conception of the United States, with particular focus on its political system, and profiles an individual who plays a particular role within it. Relational conceptions—those described by verbs, prepositions, and adjectives—also invoke a base and profile certain participants and interconnections between them. The expressions *above* and *below*, previously discussed, invoke as their base the conception of vertically oriented space and profile two participants and the spatial relationship between them (see Langacker 1987 for more detailed explanation of the profiles of relational conceptions.)

When individual words are combined to form more complex expressions, they form a composite profile which includes some of the profiles of the individual words. However, some of the elements which are profiled at the level of the individual words become merely part of the unprofiled base within the composite conception.

The expression *a hole in the roof*, for example, describes a conception whose composition is indicated in figure 34.5. The noun *hole* invokes as its base the conception of some thing (represented by a circle) and profiles a perforation of indeterminate shape (represented by the irregular shape in bold). The *g* enclosed in a circle stands for grounding and indicates that the nominal conception is associated with an article (i.e., *a*). The relational expression *in* profiles two things, one located inside the other.

In this example, the landmark of *in* corresponds to the profile of *roof*, as indicated by the dotted lines. The crosshatching and arrow indicate that *roof*

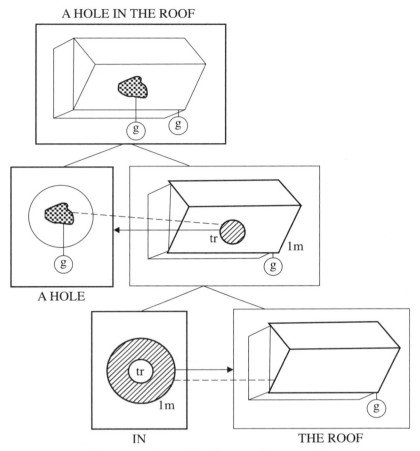

Figure 34.5. Assembly of a complex expression

"elaborates" (i.e., provides further specifications for) the schematic notion of the landmark in the relation *in*. The two conceptions—*in* and *roof*—are combined by superimposing the corresponding substructures to produce a composite conception. This occurs at multiple levels of organization within a complex (multipart) expression. At each level of conceptual organization, one element functions as the *profile determinant*, the conception which contributes its profile to the composite conception (the profile determinant is what is termed the "head" in many syntactic frameworks). In this case, the profile determinant is *in*, as indicated by the bold box enclosing that conception. The profile of *roof* is included in the composite conception profiled by *in-the-roof*. Another way to say it is that *roof* functions as a complement of *in*.

At the next level of organization, the profile determinant is *hole*. Its profile corresponds to the trajector of the relation *in-the-roof*. When these are combined, the composite conception (which is, like the profile determinant, marked by

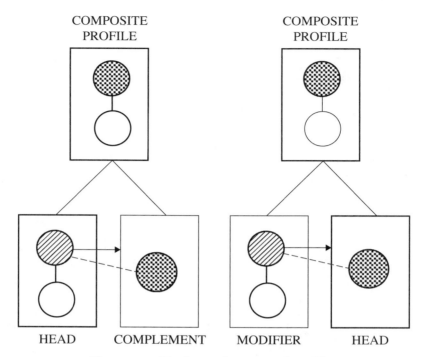

Figure 34.6. Head, complement, and modifier

bolding of the surrounding box) profiles only *hole*, while *in-the-roof* becomes an unprofiled part of the base. In short, *in-the-roof* functions as a modifier.

The complement/modifier distinction is thus captured in Cognitive Grammar in terms of inclusion or exclusion from the composite profile. An element whose profile is included in the composite profile is a complement; one whose profile is excluded from the composite is a modifier. This is illustrated very schematically in figure 34.6.

The fact that modifiers describe conceptions which are not included in the composite profile, but are instead relegated to the unprofiled base, offers an immediate explanation for the behavior of pronouns contained within modifying phrases, as exemplified in (7) above. Unlike the situation with the subject and direct object of the verb—the two most prominent nominals in the sentence—a nominal within a modifier is quite peripheral, excluded from the "window of prominence" defined by the composite profile. Even when a pronoun within a modifier comes very early in the linear string, speakers can, so to speak, "ignore" it—that is, not take it as a reference point—and wait to interpret the pronoun until the referent is identified by a name or other full noun phrase in a more prominent position within the sentence. The more prominent nominal can then function as a reference point in relationship to the less prominent pronoun which precedes it in the linear string, producing a backwards anaphora construction (a construction in which the pronoun precedes its antecedent).

In van Hoek (1997b), I present evidence that backwards anaphora typically involves a clear prominence asymmetry between the pronoun and the antecedent. The pronoun tends overwhelmingly to be contained in a preposed modifying phrase, and within that phrase it is usually a possessor (i.e., it is itself an unprofiled modifier of another nominal), while the antecedent tends overwhelmingly to be the subject of the main clause. This specific description accounts for 61% of a corpus of 600 examples of backwards anaphora collected from texts. In other words, almost two-thirds of the cases of backwards anaphora found in actual usage in that study fit the pattern exemplified in (8).

(8) a. In *its* tireless pursuit of tax cheats, the *IRS* threatened to seek a court order allowing it to exhume the body of a man who died owing the feds money. (*NOLO* Newsletter, Winter 1990)
   b. Even with a hatchet in *his* head, *the patient* wasn't docile. (*San Diego Union* 2, February 1991)

Even those backwards anaphora examples which do not fit precisely into the narrow template described above nevertheless exhibit the same general characteristics: the pronoun is in a peripheral position, thus unlikely to be construed as a reference point, while the antecedent is highly prominent. The prominence of the antecedent may be due to its role as a central participant in the clausal profile (as in 9a), its placement in the focus of the sentence (as in 9b, repeated from 7e), or typographical cues (as in 9c, where the antecedent appears in enlarged, boldface type while the pronoun is in much smaller italics).

(9) a. Once *it*'s built in Simi Valley, California, scholars will flock to *the Ronald Reagan* Presidential *Library* to sift through state papers. (*Time*, January 16, 1989)
   b. In this temple, as in the hearts of the people for whom he saved the Union, the memory of Abraham Lincoln is enshrined forever
   c. *With some in his own party skeptical and the whole GOP gleeful, is California ready for . . .* **The Rebirth of Jerry Brown**? (*Los Angeles Herald Examiner*, June 2, 1989)

The fact that backwards anaphora examples overwhelmingly include a marked asymmetry of prominence between the pronoun and the full noun phrase is readily explained in terms of reference point selection. Given that a reference point normally precedes the material in its dominion, backwards anaphora constructions could easily be misconstrued as configurations in which the pronoun is to be interpreted as a reference point with the name in its dominion. The extreme asymmetries of prominence typical of backwards anaphora serve to override the contribution of linear order and provide a clear signal that in fact the name is intended to be the reference point, with the backgrounded pronoun interpreted within its dominion.

In van Hoek (1997b), I compare backwards anaphora with near-equivalent examples of both forward anaphora and "repeat identification" (i.e., examples in which the antecedent appears in an earlier sentence, so that the name which follows the pronoun merely renames the referent but is not needed to function as the actual antecedent for the pronoun) and show that only backwards anaphora comes with such strong requirements of prominence asymmetry between the pronoun and full noun phrase. In both forward anaphora and repeat identification, where there is no need to overcome the misleading contribution of linear order to arrive at the right construal of the reference point relationship, there is much greater variability with respect to the relative prominence of the pronoun and the name.

4. Conceptual Connectivity and Linear Order

As mentioned in section 3.2 above, some modifying phrases, when placed in sentence-initial position, seem to "escape" the dominion of the subject. Others cannot. The crucial factor is the strength of conceptual connectivity between the elements in the sentence. Where connectivity is strong, linear order is a relatively weak factor; changes in word order are insufficient to change the construal of the reference point/dominion configuration. The effects of linear order become evident where connectivity is weakest.

Conceptual connectivity is a matter of degree. It is convenient for purposes of exposition to divide the continuum into three major subdivisions (but it should be borne in mind that it is a continuum): (i) the strongest connectivity is that created by a profiled relational conception explicitly connecting two participants; (ii) weaker connectivity is seen when two nominals are contained within the same larger linguistic unit—a sentence or a discourse unit—but are not explicitly interconnected; and (iii) the weakest connectivity—perhaps better termed lack of connectivity—is found when there is a conceptual discontinuity or attentional shift separating the two nominals. Each of these is discussed in turn below.

4.1. Strong Connectivity: Complements and Process-Internal Modifiers

The strongest connectivity is based on prominence in the form of profiling. A relational expression which profiles an explicit interconnection between two nominals binds them together so tightly that it is inevitable that one nominal will be construed as belonging to the dominion of the other. This is the case in (10).

(10) a. *John* put a handkerchief in *his* pocket.
      b. In *his* pocket, *John* put a handkerchief.
      c. **He* put a handkerchief in *John's* pocket.
      d. **In *John's* pocket, *he* put a handkerchief.

The nominal *John's pocket* describes one of the complements of the verb *put*, thus the conceptual connection between it and the subject of the sentence is too strong to permit the nominal to escape the subject's dominion, even in (10d) where it appears at the beginning of the sentence.

Note that in these examples, the possessive nominal (*his* or *John's*) is a modifier and therefore does not itself correspond directly to one of the participants profiled by the verb. The entire nominal (*his pocket* or *John's pocket*) is, however, interpreted within the dominion of the subject.

The notion of strong connectivity explains the fact that the judgments for sentences such as those in (10) or (1) above are typically so reliable across speakers. If we think of the profile of the verb as a window of prominence which includes its complements, we can imagine attention spreading automatically from the trajector (the figure) to the landmark and thence to any embedded complements within the object. The nominals within an embedded clause, for example, will be strongly interconnected with both the subject and the object of the verb within the uppermost clause, as in (11).

(11) a. *Sally* thought Sam said *she* was right.
      b. **She* thought Sam said *Sally* was right.
      c. Sam told *Sally* that *she* deserved a better job.
      d. **Sam told *her* that *Sally* deserved a better job.

The complements of a head (and the complements of their complements, etc.) form a tightly interconnected sequence of reference points and dominions. In van Hoek (1992, 1997a), I term this sequence the *complement chain*. Langacker (1998) points out that at the sentential level the complement chain forms an abstract "line of sight" through the sentence, in which each reference point serves as the vantage point for "viewing" the conceptions farther down in the complement chain (see Langacker 1995 for further development of this notion).

As it happens, the nominals which are prominent within the complement chain are precisely those which generative theorists such as Reinhart (1983) describe as c-commanding much of the rest of the clause. Generative syntactic tree structures are drawn so that the subject c-commands most of the clause and so that the object of the verb c-commands everything in the verb phrase, but not the subject. C-command works to the extent that it does because the tree structures provide a very rough sketch of the relative prominence of nominals and the connectivity between them.

While modifiers of the clause do not (by definition) correspond to part of the composite profile of the clause, they may—depending on their meaning—

nevertheless be strongly connected with the clausal profile (and hence with the subject and object(s)), though not quite to the same degree as complements. These are modifiers which correspond to some internal part of the unprofiled base of the conception described by the clause.

To be more specific, we can briefly consider a simple clause such as (12).

(12)   John broke the bottle.

While the verb *break* profiles only two participants, the imagined scene may include additional elements: an instrument (e.g., *with a hammer*), a setting (e.g., *in the park at five o'clock*), peripheral participants (e.g., *in front of five witnesses, while Sally looked on in horror*, etc.), and so forth. Modifiers describing these elements elaborate significant, albeit unprofiled, portions of the conception described by the verb, and thus behave similarly to complements.

Such modifiers, which may be termed *process*-internal, typically describe:

a. participants in the scene which do not correspond to direct (i.e., profiled) participants in the relation profiled by the verb;
b. the spatial or temporal setting; and
c. additional characteristics of the central participants, such as their appearance, intentions, or feelings.

Process-internal modifiers are construed within the dominion of the subject, whether or not they precede the subject in the linear string. This explains data such as (13).

(13)   a. *John* breeds tarantulas in *his* apartment.
       b. **He* breeds tarantulas in *John's* apartment.
       c. **In *John's* apartment, *he* breeds tarantulas.
       d. *Mr. Green* printed an entire book on *his* printer.
       e. **He* printed an entire book on *Mr. Green's* printer.
       f. **On *Mr. Green's* printer, *he* printed an entire book.

Thus far, we have been looking only at elements which are strongly connected with other participants in the clause. Weaker connectivity is found when the modifier does not elaborate any part of the conception invoked by the clause. In these cases, the connection between the modifier and the other elements in the clause is quite loose, and there is no automatic flow of attention from the clausal profile to the modifier. This is the situation with *process-external modifiers*.

4.2. Weaker Connectivity: Process-External Modifiers

Process-external modifiers are those which provide an overall comment on the content of the clause or which set up a conceived context—such as an imagined world—within which the clause is to be understood. Typical process-external modifiers include:

a. mental space builders (Fauconnier 1985) —modifiers which define an imaginary world or point of view within which the entire clause is contextualized;

b. phrases which relate the clause as a whole to the larger discourse; and

c. comments and afterthoughts (Bolinger 1979).

The construal of process-external modifiers is much more sensitive to the effects of linear word order than is the case with process-internal modifiers. Process-external modifiers are construed within the dominion of the subject so long as they follow the clause in the linear string without a sharp intonation break. This explains the judgments in (14) (examples 14c and 14d are from Reinhart 1983).

(14) a. *Tom Cruise* gets framed for murder in *his* latest movie.
      b. **He* gets framed for murder in *Tom Cruise's* latest movie.
      c. *Rosa* is riding a horse in Ben's picture of *her*.
      d. **She* is riding a horse in Ben's picture of *Rosa*.
      e. *John* is described as mild-mannered in *his* biography.
      f. **He* is described as mild-mannered in *John's* biography.

In the unacceptable sentences, the modifier contains a name which is construed within the dominion of the subject, which is marked with a pronoun; the name is construed within the dominion of the pronoun not because there is a strong conceptual connection between the two, but simply because the subject is highly prominent and the modifier follows it without an intonation break. Speakers assume that a prominent reference point remains relevant throughout the sentence, unless an intonation break signals an attentional shift that can bring "closure" to the subject's dominion. The latter possibility is illustrated by the examples in (15) (examples 15a and 15b are from Bolinger 1979; 15c is from Bosch 1983).

(15) a. *He* lied to me—something that *John* was rather fond of doing.
      b. *He* was quite a guy, if *John* doesn't mind my saying so.
      c. *He* lied to me, and *John* was my friend!

The looseness of the connection between the subject and the process-external modifier manifests further in the fact that placing the modifier at the beginning of the sentence is sufficient to remove it from the subject's dominion. This explains the data in (16).

(16) a. In *Tom Cruise's* latest movie, *he* gets framed for murder
      b. In Ben's picture of *Rosa*, *she* is riding a horse.
      c. So far as *Sally* knows, *she* is well liked.

Thus, we find that, unlike process-internal modifiers, process-external modifiers are obligatorily construed within the subject's dominion only if they follow the clause without an intonation break. They may *optionally* be construed within the subject's dominion, of course, as in the backwards anaphora examples in (17).

(17)   a. In *his* latest movie, *Tom Cruise* gets framed for murder.
    b. In Ben's picture of *her*, *Rosa* is riding a horse.
    c. So far as *she* knows, *Sally* is well-liked.

Relative to the object, process-*internal* modifiers behave in the same way that process-external modifiers behave relative to the subject. That is, they are automatically construed within the object's dominion so long as they follow it in the linear string, as in (18a) and (18b). Unlike the subject, which is the figure for the entire clause, the object is a more local figure, prominent only in relation to elements with which it is more directly interconnected, that is, participants in the core interaction described by the verb (see van Hoek 1997a: 92–94 for a more detailed account). When process-internal modifiers are preposed, they therefore escape the object's dominion, as in (18c) and (18d) (examples 18b and 18d are from Reinhart 1983).

(18)   a. *I handed *him* the contract outside *Ralph's* office.
    b. *Rosa tickled *him* with *Ben's* peacock feather.
    c. Outside *Ralph's* office, I handed *him* the contract.
    d. Rosa tickled *Ben* with *his* peacock feather.

Only one type of modifier seems to straddle the two categories: temporal modifiers which take the form of a subordinate clause. As (19) illustrates, they are construed within the dominion of the object when they follow the object.

(19)   a. I saw *John* after *he* came back from work.
    b. *I saw *him* after *John* came back from work.
    c. Alex called *Sue* when *she* was in Chicago.
    d. *Alex called *her* when *Sue* was in Chicago.

As Bolinger (1979) puts it, the temporal modifiers are "captured" by the verb phrase when they follow the verb. However, when they are preposed, they behave as process-external modifiers, escaping even the dominion of the subject. It is therefore possible to have a name in the preposed modifier which corresponds to a pronominal subject of the main clause, as in (20).

(20)   a. After *John* came home from work, *he* took a shower.
    b. When *Sue* was in Chicago, *she* visited the museum.

We can assume that it is the ambiguous status of the first clause vis-à-vis the second that allows it to behave as a process-external modifier. On the one hand, a temporal modifier describes the temporal setting for the main clause; on the other hand, these are separate clauses with their own tensed verbs, describing events distinct from those described by the main clause, and may therefore be construed almost as separate sentences in the discourse. In a similar vein, Matthiesen and Thompson (1988) propose that the first clause be thought of as an independent "satellite" describing an event which is related to the "nucleus" provided by the second clause.

4.3. Discontinuity at the Discourse Level

The last point on the connectivity continuum is the point at which two nominals are separated by an attentional shift, in which case neither nominal is in the dominion of the other. In that case, speakers reidentify the referent with a full nominal.

The nature of the relevant discontinuity varies depending on the spoken or textual genre. Fox (1987b) points out that in popular narrative a new narrative unit begins at the point at which a character takes action. Authors typically then re-identify the character, as in Fox's example in (21).

(21)   She [Ripley] did not see the massive hand reaching out for her from the concealment of deep shadow. But Jones did. He yowled.
Ripley spun, found herself facing the creature. [*Alien*, p. 267]

Fox (1987a) further identifies textual unit boundaries in other genres and points out that the beginning of a new textual unit coincides with reestablishing the referent by name. Tomlin (1987) has found similar patterns in spoken narratives.

The continuum of conceptual connectivity thus spans the range from con-figurations in which the coreference possibilities are rigidly determined to con-figurations at the sentential and discourse level at which there is more flexibility. Under this approach, there is no need for a distinction between "syntactic" anaphora facts and "discourse" facts with separate principles for each, as in the traditional generative c-command account (see Reinhart 1983). Rather, there is a single set of considerations—prominence (including the kind of prominence contributed by precedence in the linear string) and conceptual connectivity—determining the organization of reference points and dominions, at all levels of linguistic organization.

5. POINT OF VIEW EFFECTS

Traditional generative accounts give short shrift to the effects of point of view in anaphora, for several reasons. Point of view is difficult or impossible to represent in syntactic tree structures. Moreover, the judgments of point of view effects are notoriously slippery and variable. It is thus tempting to ignore them or at least relegate them to some other domain of study, outside the realm of pronominal anaphora proper.

I would argue, however, that it is misguided to dismiss point of view effects. First of all, they cannot be fully separated from the "core" anaphora facts. As noted in section 2, restrictions on the use of names for first- and second-person reference are essentially a matter of point of view: it is anomalous for the speaker to portray himself or herself or the addressee as anything other than a coviewer of the conceptions placed onstage in the discourse.

Moreover, third-person coreference restrictions, even in the domain of "core" anaphora facts, frequently involve point of view considerations as well. As noted, the complement chain is a metaphorical "line of sight" through the clause, and a reference point is essentially a schematic viewpoint. The only thing needed to make a reference point a full-fledged point of view is a vivid sense that one is empathizing with a particular person or seeing through his or her eyes. Empathy is however a matter of degree. Many (though not all) speakers report that their understanding of such "core" disjoint reference examples as *Near Luke, he saw a skunk* involves a vivid sense that they are seeing through the subject's eyes and are disconcerted by then seeing the same person at some distance away. Others report that they are looking over the subject's shoulder. Still others have no vivid visual imagery at all. The extent to which the subject is merely a schematic reference point or a full-fledged point of view is thus a matter of degree and varies across speakers (and no doubt across contexts, as well).

However, it is true that for the anaphora facts which have traditionally been considered significant, viewpoint does not have to be taken into account if one merely wishes to make the right predictions concerning coreference. Point of view needs to be considered in such cases only if one wishes to fully explicate a native speaker's experience of the constructions. In other cases, point of view is a critical factor which must be considered in order to explain why coreference is impossible. Such data often involve slippery or variable judgments, but this is not always the case. Sentence pair (22) provides very clear judgments concerning coreference, in which the only relevant factor is point of view.

(22)　a. *John's* worst fear is that *he* might have to sing in public.
　　　b. **His* worst fear is that *John* might have to sing in public.

The unacceptability of coreference in (22b) is explained very simply: *his worst fear* sets up the expectation that the clause which follows it will be construed as a representation of John's thoughts. It is therefore 'viewed' from John's viewpoint, thus the name is anomalous. Note that c-command cannot explain (22), as the pronoun does not c-command the name.

An example which gives more variable judgments is (23).

(23)　a. That *he* might have AIDS worries *John*.
　　　b. %That *John* might have AIDS worried *him*.

Speakers' judgments are about evenly split as to whether coreference is acceptable in (23b), although even those who find it unacceptable find it less so than (22b). The reason for the ambiguity is that, unlike in (22b) where the phrase *his worst fear* explicitly sets up the idea of John's point of view as a reference point from the beginning of the sentence, in (23b) the embedded clause *that John might have AIDS* comes first in the linear string. Some speakers therefore construe the full noun phrase from the point of view of the speaker and judge coreference to be acceptable. Others take John's implied point of view as a reference point with the embedded clause in its dominion, even though it comes later in the linear string—similar to the different interpretation possibilities seen for the sentences in (16) and (17) above, where speakers may take either prominence or linear order as their primary cue for determining reference point organization. In this case, some speakers feel that both (23a) and (23b) are acceptable, while some feel that the point of view effect in (23b) is too strong to allow for coreference.

The fact that perspective effects are more variable than the effects of prominence and connectivity should not come as any surprise, nor is it a reason to relegate point of view effects to a separate domain of study. We have already seen that the strongest, clearest judgments of coreference possibilities are found where prominence and conceptual connectivity combine to produce a clear, unequivocal reference point/dominion configuration. Where the cues are more subtle, there is more flexibility in interpretation, and other factors have more influence. The very fact that a full noun phrase is used in a particular position, such as the embedded clause in (23b), may in fact be construed as a signal that the embedded clause is not to be construed from the viewpoint of the experiencer *him*. In the core complement chain examples, such as *He loves John's mother*, the use of the name *John* would not be sufficient to signal that one should not construe the clause within the dominion of the subject; the subject is too firmly established as a reference point to be overridden in that way.

In some cases, however, point of view effects can interfere with even the somewhat more established anaphora patterns. As explained in section 4.1, a modifier of a nominal is construed within the same dominions as the nominal it modifies. When the modifier is complex, however, such as a relative clause, and has an explicit marker of a perspective shift, it is sometimes possible to construe it as independent of the dominions to which it would otherwise belong. The perspective shift serves as a conceptual discontinuity, in other words. This explains contrasts such as (24).

(24)   a. *She* joined a new organization, which paid *Sally* a lot more money.
       b. *She* joined a new organization, whose members all found *Sally* to be absolutely delightful.
       c. *He* found a new insurance company, which promised *Mark* excellent benefits.
       d. *He* married a former dental hygienist, who clearly thinks *Mark* is the greatest guy on earth.

A c-command account would claim that all the examples in (24) should be equally unacceptable. In fact, the shift in perspective in (24b) and (24d) changes the coreference possibilities by interrupting the flow of attention from the subject of the main clause to the modifier of the nominal. (Not all speakers find 24b and 24d fully acceptable, but the majority consulted do, and the others report that they are markedly improved as compared with 24a and 24c.)

Far from being irrelevant to the "core" anaphora model, viewpoint is a significant factor, albeit one which is often difficult to isolate from the others.

Nevertheless, these examples show that it can interact with other factors to change coreference possibilities. Although it is discussed here as a separate subsection, the contribution of viewpoint effects should be considered an integral element in the reference point model of anaphora.

6. Conclusion

The model briefly summarized here shows the potential of Cognitive Linguistic constructs to provide insightful analyses of phenomena which have traditionally been considered strong evidence for the necessity of autonomous syntax. Moreover, it illustrates several of the key principles of Cognitive Linguistics: the search for syntactic analyses that are grounded in meaning; the goal of unifying domains of data (such as sentence-internal and discourse-level coreference facts, as well as point of view effects) which would be subjected to piecemeal treatment under a modular account; and the goal of not only predicting grammaticality judgments but explaining why variability exists in some cases but not in others and how different ways of saying "the same thing" reflect different construals of meaning.

The domain of pronominal anaphora is a particularly rich area for exploring some of the subtle yet significant facets of sentential and cross-sentential semantics in the form of reference point organization. The reference point model also has potential for explaining phenomena outside of pronominal anaphora, such as quantifier scope and constraints on the formation of *Wh*-questions. It is particularly noteworthy that the central factors in reference point organization are prominence, conceptual connectivity, temporal sequence, and empathy or point of view—all factors which are arguably grounded in more general, nonlinguistic dimensions of cognition. Thus, the analysis of pronominal anaphora and the true nature of so-called "c-command effects," which have traditionally been among the centerpieces of autonomous syntactic theory, points toward cognitive bases of grammar which are not unique to language. The study of pronominal anaphora, and of reference point effects more generally, thus have deeper and broader implications for the understanding of the nature of language itself.

REFERENCES

Ariel, Mira. 1990. *Accessing noun-phrase antecedents*. London: Routledge.
Bolinger, Dwight. 1979. Pronouns in discourse. In Talmy Givón, ed., *Syntax and semantics*, vol. 12, *Syntax and discourse* 289–309. New York: Academic Press.
Bosch, Peter. 1983. *Agreement and anaphora*. New York: Academic Press.

Fauconnier, Gilles. 1985. *Mental spaces: Aspects of meaning construction in natural language*. Cambridge, MA: MIT Press. (2nd ed., Cambridge: Cambridge University Press, 1994)

Fox, Barbara. 1987a. Anaphora in popular written English narratives. In Russell S. Tomlin, ed., *Coherence and grounding in discourse* 157–74. Amsterdam: John Benjamins.

Fox, Barbara. 1987b. *Discourse structure and anaphora*. Cambridge: Cambridge University Press.

Givón, Talmy. 1989. The grammar of referential coherence as mental processing instructions. Technical Report No. 89–7. Eugene: University of Oregon.

Langacker, Ronald W. 1985. Observations and speculations on subjectivity. In John Haiman, ed., *Iconicity in syntax* 109–50. Amsterdam: John Benjamins.

Langacker, Ronald W. 1987. *Foundations of cognitive grammar*. Vol. 1, *Theoretical prerequisites*. Stanford, CA: Stanford University Press.

Langacker, Ronald W. 1991. *Foundations of cognitive grammar*. Vol. 2, *Descriptive application*. Stanford, CA: Stanford University Press.

Langacker, Ronald W. 1995. Viewing in cognition and grammar. In Philip W. Davis, ed., *Alternative linguistics: Descriptive and theoretical models* 153–212. Amsterdam: John Benjamins.

Langacker, Ronald W. 1998. Conceptualization, symbolization, and grammar. In Michael Tomasello, ed., *The new psychology of language: Cognitive and functional approaches to language structure* 1: 1–39. Mahwah, NJ: Lawrence Erlbaum.

Matthiesen, Christian, and Sandra A. Thompson. 1988. The structure of discourse and "subordination." In John Haiman and Sandra A. Thompson, eds., *Clause combining in grammar and discourse* 275–330. Amsterdam: John Benjamins.

Reinhart, Tanya. 1983. *Anaphora and semantic interpretation*. Chicago: University of Chicago Press.

Tomlin, Russell S. 1987. Linguistic reflections of cognitive events. In Russell S. Tomlin, ed., *Coherence and grounding in discourse*. Amsterdam: John Benjamins.

van Hoek, Karen. 1997a. *Anaphora and conceptual structure*. Chicago: University of Chicago Press.

van Hoek, Karen. 1997b. Backwards anaphora as a constructional category. *Functions of Language* 4: 47–82.

van Hoek, Karen. 1992. Paths Through Conceptual Structure: Constraints on Pronominal Anaphora. Ph.D. dissertation, University of California at San Diego

CHAPTER 35

DISCOURSE AND TEXT STRUCTURE

TED SANDERS
AND WILBERT SPOOREN

1. DISCOURSE, TEXT STRUCTURE, AND COGNITIVE LINGUISTICS

The alliance between Cognitive Linguistics and the study of discourse has become stronger in the recent past. This is a natural development. On the one hand, Cognitive Linguistics focuses on language as an instrument for organizing, processing, and conveying information; on the other, language users communicate through discourse rather than through isolated sentences. Nevertheless, at the moment, the cognitive linguistic study of discourse is still more of a promising challenge to linguists and students of discourse, rather than a well-established part of everyday cognitive linguistic practice. We start this chapter from the assumption that the grounding of language in discourse is central to any functional account of language (Langacker 2001). Discourse is often considered a crucial notion for understanding human communication, or, as Graesser, Millis, and Zwaan (1997, 164) put it, "Discourse is what makes us human."

Consider the following example from a Dutch electronic newspaper, which we have segmented into (1a) and (1b).

(1)   a. *Greenpeace heeft in het Zuid-Duitse Beieren een nucleair transport verstoord.*
        'Greenpeace has obstructed a nuclear transport in the South German state of Bavaria.'

      b. *Demonstranten ketenden zich vast aan de rails.* (*Telegraaf*, April 10, 2001)
        'Demonstrators chained themselves to the rails.'

This short electronic news item does not create any interpretation difficulties. Nevertheless, in order to understand the fragment correctly, a massive amount of inferencing has to take place. For instance, we have to infer that the nuclear transport was not disturbed by the *organization* Greenpeace, but by members of that organization; that the protesters are members of the organization; that the nuclear transport took place by train; that the place where the protesters chained themselves to the rails is on the route that the train took; that the time at which the protesters chained themselves to the rails coincided with the time of the transport; and that the obstruction of the transport was *caused* by the protesters chaining themselves to the rails.

Some of these inferences are based on world knowledge, for instance that organizations consist of people and that people, but not organizations, can carry out physical actions. Others are based on discourse structural characteristics. Here are two examples: (i) The phrase *the rails* is a definite noun phrase that functions as an anaphor with a presupposed antecedent. Since there is no explicit candidate to fulfill the role of antecedent, the noun phrase necessarily invites the inference of a referential link with *transport*, the most plausible interpretation being that the transport took place by a vehicle on rails, a train. (ii) People reading news texts expect to get explanations for the phenomena described. When one event in the text can be interpreted as an explanation for another, readers will infer a causal link between them.[1]

In this chapter, we will focus on discourse-structural characteristics like these, which, we believe, can account for the connectedness that discourse shows when compared to a random set of sentences. Given the limited space of a chapter like this, there are many specific issues that we cannot discuss, despite the fact that they are of great interest.

Thus, we will not discuss the structure of spoken discourse. Obviously, there are fundamental differences between written and spoken discourse. For instance, many connectives in written language function to express the meaning relationships—*coherence relations*—between segments, such as *but* in example (2), which expresses a relation of *denial of expectation*. Connectives fulfill the same function in conversation, but often they simultaneously function as *sequential markers*: for instance, they signal the move from a digression back to the main line of the conversation. This type of marker is commonly referred to by the term discourse marker (see Schiffrin 2001, who is the source of example 3).

(2)   The murder suspect—described by Hampshire police as "very dangerous"— had been spotted by a British tourist on Saturday, but she only informed New York police on Tuesday afternoon after returning home and seeing his photo in the British media. (*The Guardian*, June 6, 2002)

(3)   Jack: [The rabbis preach,   ["Don't intermarry"
       Freda: [But I did—   [But I *did* say those intermarriages that we
       have in this country are healthy.

According to Schiffrin, *but* in (3) performs multiple functions, including the function of displaying nonalignment with Jack, realizing an action of rebuttal during an argument, and attempting to establish Freda as the current speaker.

Clearly, connectives have multiple functions, and, clearly, these functions are related. It is an interesting research question under which conditions a connective that expresses a coherence relation can also be used as sequential marker. This type of question is under investigation in the grammaticalization literature (see Hopper and Traugott 1993: chapter 7; Traugott 1995). In this chapter we confine ourselves to the coherence relation function of connectives.

Other aspects of discourse structure that are specific to spoken language include prosody and the occurrence of so-called *adjacency pairs*, minimal pairs such as *Question-Answer* and *Summons-Response* (Sacks, Schegloff, and Jefferson 1974). These topics, too, are subject to ongoing research (see the overview in Ford, Fox, and Thompson 2002) and can be considered especially important, as they cut across linguistic subdisciplines such as grammar and the study of conversation. Still, however important and promising this research may be, we will for reasons of space not go further into it.

Instead, we want to focus on the crucial characteristics spoken and written discourse have in common. After all, these characteristics are central to the linguistic study of the level at stake here, namely, that of discourse. We will use the term "discourse" as the more general term to refer to both spoken and written language, and we will only use "text" to refer to phenomena restricted to written language.

Over the years, the notion of "discourse" has become increasingly important in linguistics—a remarkable development, considering that linguistics used to deal almost exclusively with sentences in isolation. Nowadays, the discipline includes the study of form and meaning of utterances in context, and there exist formal, functional, and cognitive approaches that consider the discourse level as the core object of study. There seems to be a consensus that what makes a set of utterances into genuine discourse is (primarily) their meaning rather than their form. More specifically, there is a shared belief that "discoursehood" is based on the possibility to relate discourse segments to form a coherent message. As a result, the dividing line between cognitive linguistic approaches and more formal approaches seems to be less clear-cut than at the sentence level (Knott, Sanders, and Oberlander 2001). Still, there are large differences between formal and cognitive or functional accounts of discourse. In formal linguistics, discourse-oriented work centers on the semantic theories of Kamp (e.g., Kamp and Reyle 1993) and Heim (1982). Here, issues like anaphora and presupposition are studied in short stretches of discourses usually consisting of constructed sets of sentences. In formal computational linguistics, however, attention is increasingly turning to the interpretation and production of extended pieces of text (Lascarides and Asher 1993). This type of approach is gradually moving in the direction of cognitively and functionally inspired work, which focuses on the discourse structure of naturally occurring language (Mann and Thompson 1986; Polanyi 1988) and on the cognitive representation of discourse in the mind of the language user (Sanders, Spooren, and Noordman 1992, 1993).

The central claim of this chapter is that the connectedness of discourse is a mental phenomenon. When confronted with a stretch of discourse, language users make a coherent representation of it. At the same time, discourse itself contains (more or less) overt signals that direct this interpretation process, which is in line with views of grammar as a processing instructor (Givón 1995; Kintsch 1995). Thus, our view of discourse revolves around two central notions: "mental representation" and "overt linguistic signals." The latter goes back to the Hallidayan work on cohesion (Halliday and Hasan 1976), which describes text connectedness in terms of cohesive ties such as conjunction and ellipsis. The problem with this approach is that sequences like *John was happy. It was a Saturday* can be coherent, even though they do not have any cohesive ties. The notion of "mental representation" relates to approaches like Hobbs's (1979), who coined the phrase *coherence relation* for interclausal relationships. What we inherit from this work is what we consider the best of both worlds: the attention for linguistic detail in the cohesion approach is combined with the basic insight that coherence is a cognitive phenomenon.

Considering coherence as a *mental* phenomenon implies that it is not an inherent property of a *text* under consideration. Language users establish coherence by relating the different information units in the text. The notion of coherence has a prominent place in both (text-)linguistic and psycholinguistic theories of text and discourse. Although this is not a particularly new view of coherence (see, among many others, van Dijk and Kintsch 1983; Hobbs 1990; Garnham and Oakhill 1992; Sanders, Spooren, and Noordman 1992; Gernsbacher and Givón 1995; Noordman and Vonk 1997), it *is* a crucial starting point for theories that aim at describing the link between the structure of a text as a linguistic object, its cognitive representations, and the processes of text production and understanding. In our view, it is this type of theory, located at the intersection of linguistics and psycholinguistics, that could lead to significant progress in the field of discourse studies (T. Sanders and Spooren 2001b). Cognitive linguists have already made substantial contributions to the study of discourse. At the same time, Cognitive Linguistics can benefit from insights in discourse to further develop itself as the study of language in use (Barlow and Kemmer 2000).

In the remainder of this chapter, we will discuss two types of coherence and their textual signals: (i) Referential coherence: how does reference to individuals create continuity and (as a result) coherence? The signals that we will be considering involve reference to objects and concepts; more specifically, we will consider the ways in which reference is realized: through full NPs, pronouns, zero anaphora, and so on. (ii) Relational coherence: how do coherence relations like causals and contrastives constitute connectedness? The signals that we will be considering are connectives and lexical cue phrases. At the end of this chapter, we will reach some conclusions about the relationship between discourse/text structure and Cognitive Linguistics, and on the basis of our analysis of the state of the art, we will suggest some challenging issues for future research.

2. REFERENTIAL COHERENCE

Text (4) illustrates how referential coherence structures discourse.

(4)   The heaviest human in medical history was Jon Brower Minnoch (b. 29
       Sep 1941) of Bainbridge Island, WA, who had suffered from obesity since
       childhood. The 6-ft-1-in-tall former taxi driver was 392 lb in 1963, 700 lb in
       1966, and 975 lb in September 1976. In March 1978, Minnoch was rushed
       to University Hospital, Seattle, Ø saturated with fluid and Ø suffering from
       heart and respiratory failure. It took a dozen firemen and an improvised
       stretcher to move him from his home to a ferryboat. When he arrived at the
       hospital he was put in two beds lashed together. It took 13 people just to
       roll him over. (*The Guinness book of records 1994*: 151)

The discourse topic Jon Brower Minnoch is identified in the first sentence and is
referred to throughout this fragment in each sentence. Here are the referential forms
used in the text:

Jon Brower Minnoch (b. 29 Sep 1941) of Bainbridge Island, WA
The 6-ft-1-in-tall former taxi driver
Minnoch
Ø
Ø
him
he
he
him

First of all, this list shows that the linguistic indicators for referential coherence
can be lexical NPs, pronouns, and other devices for anaphoric reference. Second, it
appears that the longest referential forms are used in the beginning of the fragment,
and once the referent has been identified, the pronominal forms suffice. This is not
a coincidence. Many linguists have noted this regularity and have related it to the
cognitive status of the referents. Ariel (1990, 2001), for instance, has argued that this
type of pattern in grammatical coding should be understood to guide processing.
She has developed an *Accessibility Theory* in which high accessibility markers consist
of less linguistic material and signal the default choice of continued activation. By
contrast, low accessibility markers consist of much linguistic material and signal
termination of activation of the current (topical) referent and the (re)introduction
of a different referent. Ariel has also developed an Accessibility Marking Scale (Ariel
1990), from low to high accessibility markers:

(5)   Full name > long definite description > short definite description > last
       name > first name > distal demonstrative > proximate demonstrative
       > NP > stressed pronoun > unstressed pronoun > cliticized pronoun
       > zero.

For examples such as our text in (4), Ariel has convincingly shown that zero anaphora and unstressed pronouns co-occur with high accessibility of referents, whereas stressed pronouns and full lexical nouns signal low accessibility. This co-occurrence can easily be understood in terms of cognitive processes of activation: High accessibility markers signal the *default* choice of continued activation of the current topical referent. Low accessibility anaphoric devices, such as full NPs or indefinite articles, signal termination of activation of the current topical referent and the activation of another topic. Ariel (1990) has even argued that the framework has consequences for the binding conditions of Chomsky's Government and Binding Theory on the distribution and interpretation of pronominal and anaphoric expressions: these conditions are actually the "grammaticalized versions" of cognitive states of attention and of the accessibility of concepts that are referred to linguistically. This Accessibility Theory is based on earlier work by Chafe and Givón: "Chafe (1976, 1994) was the first to argue for a direct connection between referential forms and cognitive statuses. Accessibility Theory can be seen as an extension of his (and later Givón's 1983) basic insight" (Ariel 2001: 60).

Many functional and cognitive linguists have argued that the grammar of referential coherence plays an important role in the mental operations of connecting incoming information to existing mental representations. This cognitive interpretation of referential phenomena is supported by a growing body of empirical data from corpus studies along the lines set out by functional linguists like Du Bois (1980). In a distributional study, Givón (1995), for instance, shows that in English the indefinite article *a(n)* is typically used to introduce nontopical referents, whereas topical referents are introduced by *this*. In addition, there is a clear interaction between grammatical subjecthood and the demonstrative *this*: most *this*-marked NPs also appear as grammatical subjects in a sentence, while a majority of *a(n)*-marked NPs occur as nonsubjects. Across languages, there appears to be a topic persistence of referents: in active-transitive clauses the topic persistence of subject NPs is systematically higher than that of object NPs.

In experimental research on text processing, quite some work has been done which can be taken to demonstrate the "psychological reality" of linguistic indicators of referential coherence. For instance, it is easier to resolve a pronoun with only one possible referent than one with ambiguous reference, and it is easier to resolve a pronoun with a proximal referent than one with a distant referent. As for the time course, eye fixation studies have repeatedly shown that anaphoric expressions are resolved immediately (e.g., Carpenter and Just 1977; Ehrlich and Rayner 1983).

(6)   a. The guard mocked one of the prisoners in the machine shop.
        b. He had been at the prison for only one week.

When readers came upon ambiguous pronouns, such as *he* in (6b), the data showed many regressions; that is, readers frequently looked back in the text. More than 50% of these regressive fixations were to one of the two nouns in the text preceding the pronoun, suggesting that readers attempted to resolve the pronoun immediately. As for meaning representation, it has been shown that readers have difficulty understanding the text correctly when the antecedent and referent are too far apart and reference takes the form of a pronoun.

On a more global text level, rather less research has been done into the exact working of accessibility markers as processing instructions. Well researched, however, is the influence of typical discourse phenomena such as prominence of a referent in the discourse context. Garrod and Sanford (1985) used a spelling error detection procedure, and on the basis of that earlier experiment, Garrod, Freudenthal, and Boyle (1993) did an eye-tracking study with texts such as the one rendered (in a simplified version) in (7).

(7)   *A dangerous incident at the pool*
      Elizabeth was an inexperienced swimmer and wouldn't have gone in if the male lifeguard hadn't been standing by the pool. But as soon as she got out of her depth she started to panic and wave her hands about in a frenzy.
      Target:
      Within seconds she sank into the pool. (**Thematic, Consistent**)
      Within seconds she jumped into the pool. (**Thematic, Inconsistent**)
      (a simplified version of experimental texts used by Garrod, Freudenthal, and Boyle 1993)

The eye-tracking data show strong evidence for very early detection of inconsistency, as is apparent from longer fixations (in this case on the verb), but only when the pronoun maintains reference to the focused thematic subject of the passage, in other words, in the thematic conditions. In nonthematic conditions, that is, when the pronoun does not refer to the subject in focus, there is no evidence for early detection of inconsistency.

In recent approaches to discourse anaphora, the modeling of this type of discourse focusing is pivotal. This is especially true for *Centering Theory* (Walker, Joshi, and Prince 1998), which aims at modeling the center of attention in discourse in terms of the relationship of attentional state, inferential complexity, and the form of referring expressions in a given discourse segment. Centering Theory makes explicit predictions about the referent that is "in focus" at a certain moment in a discourse. It is even predicted that the degree of coherence exhibited by a textual sequence is determined by the extent to which that sequence conforms to the "centering constraints." These constraints suggest that topic continuity is the default discourse situation, because frequent topic-shifting results in less local coherence. Without going into much detail, we discuss two examples of "centering rules" (based on Grosz, Weinstein, and Joshi 1995; Walker, Joshi, and Prince 1998). These rules concern the transition from one discourse segment to another and are illustrated by the following short text, adapted from Grosz, Weinstein, and Joshi (1995).

(8)   a. Susan gave Betsy a pet hamster.
      b. She reminded Betsy that such hamsters were quite shy.

   c. Betsy told her that she really liked the gift.

   d. She said she loved these little animals.

There are two referents present in this discourse, both referred to with proper names in (8a) and with pronouns later on. Centering Theory predicts that, given its grammatical role of subject, Susan is the center of (8a).[2] Centering Theory further predicts that the most likely continuation in (8b) is a zero anaphor or a third-person pronoun (*she*) referring back to the center, Susan. This, then, is a case of *center continuation*. In (8c), Betsy is pronominalized (*she*) as well. In (8d), then, there is a *smooth shift* to Betsy as the center. Sequence (9) is an example of a *rough shift* from Susan to Betsy from (9b) to (9c).

(9)   a. Susan gave Betsy a pet hamster.

     b. She reminded her that such hamsters were quite shy.

     c. She told her that she really liked the gift.

The shift in (9) is rough because of the grammatical role and the expression types used to encode both Betsy and Susan in (9b) and (9c): Betsy has been pronominalized in (9b), and in (9c) Betsy is referred to with a pronoun in subject position, whereas Susan is referred to with a pronoun in object position. This shift is so rough that the sequence could even be judged incoherent (as Cornish 1999: 171 does)—or at least hard to process. Indeed, several processing studies have shown the cognitive relevance of the referential factors identified in Centering Theory (see especially Gordon, Grosz, and Gilliom 1993). The precise predictions of Centering Theory not only show how linguistic expressions of referential coherence can function as processing instructions, they also suggest that there is a referential linguistic system at the discourse level, which is a challenging topic for further investigation (see Cornish 1999).

Vonk, Hustinx, and Simons (1992) also showed the relevance of discourse context for the interpretation of referential expressions. Sometimes anaphors are more specific than is necessary for their identificational function (for instance, full NPs are used rather than pronominal expressions). Vonk, Hustinx, and Simons convincingly argue that this phenomenon can be explained in terms of the thematic development of discourse: if a discourse participant is referred to by a proper name after a series of pronominal referential expressions, this serves to indicate that a shift in topic is occurring. As is apparent from reading times, readers process the referential expressions differently.

Where anaphoric reference modulates the availability of previously mentioned concepts, cataphoric devices change the availability of concepts for the text that follows. Gernsbacher (1990) and her colleagues have demonstrated readers' sensitivity to this type of linguistic indicator of reference. They contrasted cataphoric reference by means of indefinite *a(n)* as opposed to definite *this*, both used to introduce a new referent in a story. For example, the new referent *egg* was introduced either as *an egg* or as *this egg*. It was hypothesized that the cataphor *this* would signal that a concept is likely to be mentioned again in the following story and that the *this*-cataphor therefore results in higher activation. Subjects listened to texts and were then asked to continue the text after the critical concept. They appeared to refer sooner and more often to a concept introduced by *this* than to a concept introduced by *an*. These and other results show that concepts that were marked as a potential discourse topic by *this* are more strongly activated, more resistant to being suppressed in activation, and more effective in suppressing the activation of other concepts (Gernsbacher 1990). It is this type of findings that provide the psycholinguistic underpinning for the idea of "grammar as a processing instructor."

By now, the results of online studies of pronominal reference make it possible to formulate cognitive parsing principles for anaphoric reference (see Garrod and Sanford 1994 for an overview; also Sanford and Garrod 1994; Gernsbacher 1990; Sanders and Gernsbacher 2004). Person, number, and gender obviously guide pronominal resolution. More interestingly, data from reading time, eye-tracking, and priming studies show that it takes less processing time

    a. to resolve pronouns with only one possible referent than several;
    b. to resolve pronouns with proximal referents than distant ones; and
    c. to resolve reference to topical concepts than to less topical ones.

One obvious explanation for these findings lies in the notion of accessibility: anaphoric expressions are instructions to connect incoming information with referents mentioned earlier, and the referent nodes can be more accessible or less accessible. As a result, it takes less or more processing time, respectively, to understand anaphoric expressions (Gernsbacher 1990).

3. RELATIONAL COHERENCE

So far, we have discussed examples of the way in which linguistic signals of *referential coherence* affect text processing. We now move to signals of *relational coherence*. In many approaches to discourse connectedness, coherence relations are taken to account for the coherence in readers' cognitive text representation (see Hobbs 1979; Mann and Thompson 1986; Sanders, Spooren, and Noordman 1992). Coherence relations are meaning relations that connect two text segments (minimally consisting of clauses). Examples are relations such as CAUSE-CONSEQUENCE, LIST, and PROBLEM-SOLUTION. These relations are conceptual and they can, but need not, be made explicit by linguistic markers: so-called connectives (*because, so, however, although*) and lexical cue phrases (*for that reason, as a result, on the other hand*).

Ever since Ducrot (1980) and Lang (1984), there have been linguistic accounts of connectives as operating instructions. The basic idea is that a connective serves to relate the content of connected segments in a specific type of relationship. Anscombre and Ducrot (1977), for instance, analyze *but* as setting up an argumentative scale (for instance, the desirability of John as a marriage candidate in 10), with one segment tending toward the negative side of the scale and the other toward the positive side:

(10)   John is rich, but dumb.

In his influential work on *Mental Spaces*, Fauconnier (1994) treats connectives as one of the so-called *space builders*, that is, linguistic expressions that typically establish new *Mental Spaces*. Mental spaces are mental constructs set up to interpret utterances, "structured, incremental sets . . . and relations holding between them . . . , such that new elements can be added to them and new relations established between their elements" (Fauconnier 1994: 16). An example of a connective acting as a space builder is the *if-then* conditional, as in *If I were a millionaire, my VW would be a Rolls*. An expression like *if p then q* sets up a new mental space *H* in which *q* holds. In other words, *if I were a millionaire* is the space builder and in this new space my VW from the initial space is identified with the Rolls in the new space (for the detailed analyses see Fauconnier 1994, chapters 3–4; Sweetser 1996).

Is there any psycholinguistic work showing the relevance if these ideas of connectives as processing instructors? Various online processing studies have examined the function of linguistic markers. These studies have primarily investigated the processing role of the signals per se, rather than the more sophisticated issues such as the exact working of "space building." The experimental work typically involves the comparison of reading times of identical textual fragments with different linguistic signals preceding them. Recent studies on the role of connectives and signaling phrases show that these linguistic signals affect the construction of the text representation (see Millis and Just 1994; Noordman and Vonk 1998; Cozijn 2000; Sanders and Noordman 2000).

Millis and Just (1994), for instance, investigated the influence of connectives such as *because* immediately after reading a sentence. After participants had read two clauses that were either linked or not linked by a connective, they had to judge whether a probe word had been mentioned in one of the clauses. The recognition time to probes from the first clause was consistently faster when the clauses were linked by a connective. The presence of the connective also led to faster and more accurate responses to comprehension questions. These results suggest that the connective *does* influence the representation immediately after reading.

Using eye-movement techniques, Cozijn (2000) studied the exact location of the various effects of using *because*. Using *because* implies a causal link between the related segments. Comparing reading times in segments linked by a connective to segments not linked by a connective, Cozijn found that, in clauses with a connective, words immediately following the connective were read faster, but reading slowed down toward the end of the clause. This suggests that connectives help to integrate linguistic material (thus leading to faster reading when the connective is present), whereas at the same time they instruct the reader to draw a causal inference (thus slowing down clause-final reading).

In sum, several studies show the influence of linguistic markers on text *processing*. However, studies of the influence on text *representation* show a much less consistent pattern (see Degand, Lefèvre, and Bestgen 1999; Sanders and Noordman 2000; Degand and Sanders 2002 for an overview). On the one hand, some results show that linguistic marking of coherence relations improves mental text representation. This becomes apparent from better recall performance, faster and more accurate responses to prompted recall tasks, faster responses to verification tasks, and better answers on comprehension questions. On the other hand, there are a number of studies indicating that linguistic markers do *not* have this facilitating role, as shown by a lack of effect on the amount of information recalled or a lack of better answers on multiple-choice comprehension questions. Some authors even claim a negative impact of connectives on text comprehension.

There are several plausible explanations for the reported contradictions (Degand and Sanders 2002). One is that the category of linguistic markers under investigation is not well defined. For instance, in the signaling literature different types of *signals* seem to be conflated. A second explanation is that some experimental methods, such as the recall task, are simply too global to measure the effect of relational markers. Other methods such as recognition, question answering, or sorting (Kintsch 1998) might be more sensitive in this respect. Indeed, Degand, Lefèvre, and Bestgen (1999) and Degand and Sanders (2002) provide evidence for the claim that under average conditions (i.e., in natural texts of normal text length and with a moderate number of connectives) causal connectives do contribute significantly to the comprehension of the text. In sum, connectives and cue phrases seem to affect both the construction process and the representation once the text has been processed, but the effects are rather subtle and specific measurement techniques are needed to actually assess them.

Thus far, we have discussed the role of connectives and signaling phrases in discourse processing. A preliminary conclusion might be that they can be treated as linguistic markers that instruct readers how to connect a new discourse segment with a previous one (Britton 1994). In the absence of such instructions, readers have to determine for themselves what coherence relation connects the incoming segment to the previous discourse. Such an inference process requires additional cognitive energy and results in longer processing times. If this idea has any validity, it implies that the coherence relations themselves should have a major influence on discourse processing as well. One might expect that the type of relation that connects two discourse segments, be it causal, additive, contrastive, or the like, affects discourse representation.

Here we move into another area where the combination of text linguistic and discourse psychological insights has lead to significant progress: the discussion about the types or categorization of coherence relations. In the last decade, a significant part of the research on coherence relations has focused on the question how the many different sets of relations should be organized (Hovy 1990; Redeker 1990; Knott and Dale 1994; T. Sanders 1997; Pander Maat 1998). Sanders, Spooren, and Noordman (1992) have started from the properties common to all relations, in order to define the "relations among the relations," relying on the intuition that some coherence relations are more alike than others. For instance, the relations in (11), (12), and (13) all express (a certain type of) causality, whereas the ones in (14) and (15) do not. Furthermore, a negative relation is expressed in (14), as opposed to all other examples. Finally, (15) expresses a relation of enumeration or addition.

(11)   The buzzard was looking for prey. The bird was soaring in the air for hours.
(12)   The bird has been soaring in the air for hours now. It must be a buzzard.
(13)   The buzzard has been soaring in the air for hours now. Let's finally go home!
(14)   The buzzard was soaring in the air for hours. Yesterday we did not see it all day.
(15)   The buzzard was soaring in the air for hours. There was a peregrine falcon in the area, too.

Sweetser (1990) introduced a distinction dominant in many existing classification proposals, namely that between content relations (sometimes also called ideational, external, or semantic relations), epistemic relations, and speech-act relations. In the first type of relation, segments are related because of their propositional content, that is, the locutionary meaning of the segments. They describe events that cohere in the world. The relation in (16) can be interpreted as a content relation, because it connects two events in the world; our knowledge allows us to relate the segments as coherent in the world. Similarly, the relation in (16) could be paraphrased as 'the neighbors suddenly having left for Paris last Friday leads to the fact that they are not at home' (T. Sanders 1997).

(16)   The neighbors suddenly left for Paris last Friday. As a consequence they are not at home.
(17)   The lights in their living room are out. So the neighbors are not at home.
(18)   Why don't you turn up the radio? The neighbors are not at home.

In (17), however, the two discourse segments are related not because there is a causal relation between two states of affairs in the world, but because we understand the second part as a conclusion from evidence in the first: it is *not* the case that the neighbors are not at home because the lights are out. The causal relation in (17) could be paraphrased as 'I observe that the lights in their living room are out. I conclude from that that the neighbors are not at home'. This is an example of an epistemic relation. Example (18) is a speech-act relation: its paraphrase is 'I invite you to turn up the radio'. The basis for that invitation is that the neighbors are not at home.

If this distinction is applied to the set of examples above, the causal relation (11) is a content relation, whereas (12) is an epistemic relation and (13) a speech-act relation. This systematic difference between types of relation has been noted by many students of discourse coherence. Still, there is quite a lot of discussion about the exact definition of a distinction like this (see, e.g., Hovy 1990; Martin 1992; Moore and Pollack 1992; Knott and Dale 1994; Knott 1996; Bateman and Rondhuis 1997; Oversteegen 1997; T. Sanders 1997; Knott and Sanders 1998; Pander Maat 1998; T. Sanders and Spooren 1999; Degand 2001). At the same time, several researchers have come up with highly similar distinctions, and there seems to be basic agreement on the characteristics of the prototypical relations (T. Sanders 1997).

If categorizations of coherence relations have real cognitive significance, they should prove relevant in areas such as discourse processing and language development, both synchronically (language acquisition) and diachronically (language change). In all three areas, much suggestive evidence already exists in the literature and additional, substantial studies are under way.

Experimental studies on the processing of coherence relations have especially dealt with causal relations. For instance, causally related events are recalled better (Black and Bern 1981; Trabasso and van den Broek 1985), and at the same time they are processed faster (Haberlandt and Bingham 1978; Sanders and Noordman 2000). These results possibly imply that causality has a special status. In Zwaan's (1996) Event Indexing Model, readers construct coherent representations of a narrative text by integrating the events in the text on five different dimensions: time, space, causation, motivation, and protagonist. By default, readers assume inertia: discontinuities on any of these dimensions (leaps in time, space, etc.) lead to processing problems. That explains why temporal inversion increases processing time (Zwaan 1996), why noncausally related events are more difficult to process than causally related events (Singer et al. 1992), and why causally related sentences which follow the order *cause-consequence* take less processing time than sentences presented in the reversed order *consequence-cause* (Noordman 2001).

Using both reading-time and eye-tracking data, Louwerse (2001) investigated the cognitive reality of several conceptual dimensions underlying coherence relations and found some suggestive evidence. For instance, the more complex relations, CAUSAL rather than ADDITIVE and NEGATIVE rather than POSITIVE, took longer to process and triggered more regressions: readers looked back more often. Longer reading times and regressions are generally considered as indicators of processing difficulty.

Research on first-language acquisition suggests that the order in which children acquire connectives reflects increasing complexity, which can be accounted for in terms of the relational categories mentioned above: ADDITIVES (*and*) before CAUSALS (*because*), POSITIVES (*and, because*) before NEGATIVES (*but, although*) (Bloom 1991; Spooren 1997; Evers-Vermeul 2005; Spooren and Sanders 2003). In a corpus of naturalistic data, Kyratzis, Guo, and Ervin-Tripp (1990) found that speech-act causal relations are frequent even at a very early age, whereas epistemic causal relations are acquired very late (they hardly occur, even in the oldest age group studied by Kyratzis, Guo, and Ervin-Tripp, of 6;7–12;0 years). It remains to be seen how these issues of cognitive complexity of coherence relations relate to so-called usage-based or input-based accounts of language acquisition (Tomassello 2000; see also Evers-Vermeul 2005).

In research on diachronic development, too, the classification categories of connectives show to be relevant. Sweetser (1990) originally introduced her three-domain distinction to cover the semantics of a number of related phenomena involving verbs of perception, modal elements, and connectives. She argues that, from their original content meanings, these linguistic elements have diachronically developed new meanings in the more subjective epistemic and speech-act domains. Examples of such developments in the realm of connectives have been presented by König and Traugott (1988) and Traugott (1995). Thus, *still* originally meant 'now as formerly' but has changed from an expression of simultaneity to one of denial of expectation. Similarly, *while* developed from a marker exclusively expressing simultaneity ('at the time that') to a marker used to express contrast and concession (see 19); German *weil* had the same root meaning, but developed into a causal connective. Traugott (1995: 31) considers this a case of "subjectification: meanings become increasingly based in the speaker's subjective belief state/attitude toward the proposition."

(19)   a. Mary read while Bill sang.
     b. Mary liked oysters while Bill hated them. (Traugott 1995: 31)

Traugott shows how subjectification plays a significant role in the grammaticalization processes on the sentence level. However, subjectivity and subjectification are also valid at the discourse level, as becomes apparent from the study of coherence relations and connectives. Some have claimed that distinctions between content relations, epistemic relations, and speech act relations should be replaced by a subjectivity scale of *speaker involvement* (Pander Maat and Degand 2001). This scale is a continuum on which content relations such as CAUSE-CONSEQUENCE are maximally objective, whereas epistemic relations are very subjective. Volitional causal relations such as the REASON-relation in *John wanted to leave. He was tired* hold an intermediate position. Some corpus evidence may be found in the distribution of Dutch and French connectives, since the notion of subjectivity, that is, the amount of speaker involvement—to what extent is the speaker responsible for the utterance?—seems to provide an explanation for differences in meaning and use of causal connectives like Dutch *daardoor* 'as a result', *daarom* 'that is why', and *dus* 'so' (Pander Maat and Sanders 2000, 2001). In the case of the nonvolitional *daardoor* (see 20), for instance, the causality is located outside of the speaker as a subject-of-consciousness. There is a minimal amount of speaker involvement. In the epistemic use of *dus* in (22) and the volitional use of *daarom* in (21), a subject-of-consciousness *can* be identified, either the current speaker or the actor.

(20)   *Er was een lawine geweest op Roger's pass. Daardoor was de weg geblokkeerd.*
     'There had been an avalanche at Roger's pass. As a result, the road was blocked.'

(21)   *Daan wilde op tijd thuis zijn. Daarom vertrok hij om 5 uur.*
     'Daan wanted to be home in time. That is why he left at 5 o'clock.'

(22)   *Het waren grote grijze vogels, die veel lawaai maakten. Dus het moeten wel kraanvogels geweest zijn.*
     'They were large grey birds that made a lot of noise. So it must have been cranes.'

Proposals such as these illustrate the unmistakable tendency in recent text-linguistic work to use the notions of subjectification and perspective. This tendency goes back on Ducrot (1980), who already stressed the diaphonic nature of discourse. Even in monologic texts traces can be found of other "voices," information that is not presented as fact-like, but as coming from a particular point-of-view, either the current speaker's (subjectified information, in the terminology of J. Sanders and Spooren 1997) or another cognizer's (perspectivized information). Cognitive Linguistics has a large role to play in the development of this line of work, because of the key role it attributes to processes of subjectification in natural language, but also because it allows for a dynamic approach to connectives "as processing instructors." Fauconnier's Mental Space framework is very suitable to model this type of phenomena, as has been suggested by Dancygier and Sweetser (2000), Verhagen (2000, 2005), and T. Sanders and Spooren (2001a). As an example, consider Verhagen's (2005) use of the Mental Space framework to analyze differences between epistemic and content uses of *because* and *although*. In a content use of *because* such as (23), the only mental space involved is the speaker's space, containing the facts that 'John passed his exams' and 'John worked hard', as well as the general rule 'Normally, working hard increases your chances of passing your exam'.

(23)   John passed his exams because he worked hard.
(24)   John must have worked hard, because he passed his exams.

In epistemic uses of *because* as in (24) the first segment functions as a claim, for which the second is an argument. This use of *because* requires the construction of a more complex Mental Space configuration. The speaker's space contains the general rule that 'Normally, working hard increases your chances of passing your exam'. It also contains the fact that John passed his exams, and it contains the (abductive) inference that John worked hard. In addition to this speaker's space, a mental space is created that contains a nonpositive epistemic stance, probably uttered by a conversational partner, regarding the issue of whether or not John has been working hard. Together, the configuration captures the interpretation that epistemic *because* reaffirms a possible inference from another cognizer, as may be clear from the paraphrase 'The inference is correct that John may have been working hard considering that he has passed his exams'.

Verhagen proceeds by analyzing content and epistemic uses of *although*, which are based on the same pattern of Mental Space configurations. Especially the allusion to other cognizers' interpretation is a clear example of how the polyphonic, perspectivizing nature of epistemic *because* and *although* can be analyzed. Fauconnier's Mental Space framework seems adequate in capturing perspective, which remains an elusive notion for linguistics and psycholinguistics alike (J. Sanders 1994).

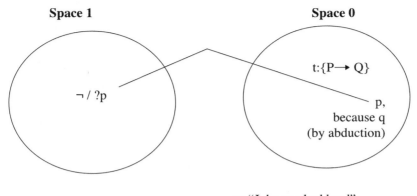

p: "John worked hard"
q: "he passed his exams"

Figure 35.1. Verhagen's (2005) Mental Space analysis of epistemic *because*

4. COGNITIVE LINGUISTICS
AT THE DISCOURSE LEVEL

What is the place of a chapter on discourse structure in a handbook of Cognitive Linguistics?

We have presented an overview of current research in the field of discourse and text structure, focusing on issues of referential and relational coherence. It can be concluded that the study of discourse provides us with important insights in the relationship between language, on the one hand, and the cognitive representation that language users have or make of discourse, on the other. Highly attractive, in this context, is the idea that linguistic expressions are instructions for the construction of such a representation. Even if the research that we have discussed is not cognitive linguistic "by nature," it can be concluded that many of its results can and should be incorporated in Cognitive Linguistics. Reasons are the following:

a. Cognitive Linguistics is a source of inspiration for the modeling of discourse structure. Major contributions, such as those by Fauconnier (Mental Spaces), Langacker (Subjectivity), and Sweetser (Domains of Use), offer the terminology and theoretical framework to consider linguistic phenomena as structure-building devices.

b. Cognitive Linguistics provides theoretical insights that can be—and partly have been—extended to the discourse level. An example is the classic cognitive linguistic work on categorization. Human beings categorize the world around them. As Lakoff (1987) and Lakoff and Johnson (1999) have shown, the linguistic categories apparent in people's everyday language use provide us with many interesting insights in the working of the mind.

Over the last decade, the categorization of coherence relations and the linguistic devices expressing them have played a major role in text-linguistic and cognitive linguistic approaches to discourse. For instance, the way in which speakers categorize related events by expressing them with one connective (*because*) rather than another (*since*) can be treated as an act of categorization that reveals language users' ways of thinking.

c. Cognitive Linguistics is the study of language in use; it seeks to develop so-called usage-based models (Barlow and Kemmer 2000) and in doing so increasingly relies on corpora of naturally occurring discourse that make it possible to adduce cognitively plausible theories to empirical testing.

d. Cognitive Linguistics typically appreciates the methodological strategy of converging evidence. In principle, linguistic analyses are to be corroborated by evidence from areas other than linguistics, such as psychological (Gibbs 1996) and neurological processing studies.

5. Looking into the Future: Integration of Different Approaches

At the end of this chapter, we have reached the point where we can stop and ask about the avenues that lie ahead of us. We see several interesting developments that may set the research agenda for the coming years. We focus on issues that follow from our analysis of the state of the art in the preceding sections. A first and very basic issue is the question of discourse segmentation: What are the building blocks of discourse? To what extent do they correspond to traditional units of analysis such as the clause, sentence, and—in the spoken mode—the turn? Are discourse units in spoken and written language comparable? To what extent are grammatical and discourse structure isomorphic? (See Verhagen 2001 for a discussion of similar topics.)

A second important issue is the linguistics–text linguistics interface. As noted in section 1, we see a growing exchange or sharing of ideas between grammarians, (formal) semanticists, and pragmaticists on the one hand, and text linguists on the other. Questions that can be asked are: What is the relationship between information structuring at the sentence level and at the discourse level? And, how do factors such as tense and aspect influence discourse connections (Lascarides and Asher 1993; Oversteegen 1997)? For instance, discourse segments denoting events that have taken place in the past (*The duke fell of his horse. He died.*) will be typically connected by coherence relations linking their content, whereas segments whose events take place in the present or future typically contain many evaluations or other subjective elements (*I am sure I saw the duke fall of his horse just now. He may die.*) and are prototypically connected by epistemic relations.

Another promising topic related to the sentence-discourse interface is that of intraclausal and interclausal relationships: Are the types of causality found at the intraclausal level (*John made him pay the bill* vs. *John let him pay the bill*; Verhagen and Kemmer 1997) similar to the types of causality found at the discourse level (Stukker 2005)? For instance, can *The headache caused the soprano to cancel the concert* be (insightfully) compared to *Because she had a headache the soprano cancelled the concert*?

A final topic related to the linguistics–text linguistics interface is the relationship between discourse and grammar. In the more functionally oriented literature, there is a rich tradition of corpus studies of linguistic structures in a discourse context. A good example is the work on the discourse function of subordinated clauses (Tomlin 1985), more specifically *if/when*-clauses (Haiman 1978; Ramsay 1987) and purpose clauses (Thompson 1985; Matthiessen and Thompson 1988). Thus, the discourse function of purpose clauses appears to depend on their placement in relation to the main clause. In medial or final position, their role is one of local elaboration, but in initial position, their role becomes one of foregrounding information. They signal how to interpret the following clause and how to relate it to the preceding text. Hopefully, such studies will inspire more (cognitive) linguists to look at linguistic structures as vehicles built by language producers to enable interpreters to understand what they have in mind. Recently, Langacker (2001) has presented a framework for the further integration of discourse and Cognitive Grammar.

A third, obvious issue is the relationship between the principles of relational and referential coherence. Clearly, both types of principles provide language users with signals during discourse interpretation. Readers and listeners interpret these signals as instructions for how to construct coherence. Therefore, the principles will operate in parallel, and they will influence each other. The question is: how do they interact? This issue can be illustrated with the simple example in (25).

(25)   John congratulated Pete on his excellent play.
    a. He had scored a goal.
    b. He scored a goal.

At least two factors are relevant in resolving the anaphoric expression *he* in (25a) and (25b): the aspectual value of the verb in the sentence and the coherence relations that can be inferred between the sentences. At sentence level, the verb in (25a) is in the perfect tense; at the discourse level, there is one straightforward interpretation of coherence relation available, namely, the backward causal relation CONSEQUENCE-CAUSE. In (25b), the verb is in the imperfect tense, and, at the discourse level several coherence relations can exist, such as TEMPORAL SEQUENCE (of events) or ENUMERATION/LIST (of events in the game). The resolution of the anaphor-antecedent relation is related to these two factors. In (25a); *he* must refer to Pete, while in (25b), several antecedents are possible: John, Pete, or even an actor mentioned earlier. Interestingly, the interrelationship of sentence and discourse levels turns up again: How does the sentence-internal property of aspect interact with the discourse property of coherence relations in the process of anaphor resolution? Is the anaphor resolved as a consequence of the interpretation of the coherence relation? Questions of this kind have already been addressed in the seminal work of Hobbs (1979) and have recently been taken up again in a challenging way by Kehler (2002).

A fourth specific issue is the refinement of the relationship between the central concepts of subjectivity, perspectivization, and the typology of coherence relations, which needs to be explored in much greater detail (T. Sanders and Spooren 2001a). The starting point for these studies consists of corpus-based accounts of connectives in terms of subjectivity and speaker involvement (Pander Maat and Degand 2001; Pander Maat and Sanders 2001), discussions of perspective and subjectivity (J. Sanders and Spooren 1997; Pit 2003), and Mental Space analyses of perspective (Sanders and Redeker 1996) and connectives (Dancygier and Sweetser 2000; Verhagen 2005).

A fifth issue and area for further research is the interrelationship between spoken and written discourse. Results from text-linguistic and psycholinguistic studies presented here are largely based on the study of written discourse. To what extent can they be generalized to spoken discourse? And what will the specific insights from the linguistic analysis of spoken discourse add to the picture we have so far? These questions become especially important when claims concerning *cognitive reality* are at stake. After all, our most natural and spontaneous way to communicate is not simply in discourse, but in *spoken* discourse.

Finally, there is an important methodological issue on the road ahead. A traditional *forte* of Cognitive Linguistics is its determination to provide cognitively plausible analyses of linguistic phenomena. A less well developed aspect of Cognitive Linguistics is the empirical study of language in use, aiming either to find regular patterns that feed the theories or to actually test theories against language use. Plausible theoretical ideas regularly have to be revised after serious empirical testing. And even though there are more and more examples of studies combining linguistic theorizing with some kind of testing—either in corpus examinations or in language processing experiments—these studies do not dominate the field.

Still, to balance the picture of the actual situation, we are happy to find that there is indeed a growing tendency toward quantitative, usage-based studies in Cognitive Linguistics in general. We will mention three fields where we see this tendency. First, there is the field of lexical studies where Geeraerts, Grondelaers, and Bakema (1994) have shown how lexical salience can be operationalized on a corpus of actual language use and can then be employed to explain the actual choices of lexical construal that language users make. More recently, the same quantitative approach has been extended to more grammatical fields of research. Bybee (2001) epitomizes the use of the quantitative analysis of salience in the phonological (and to some extent morphological) domain; specifically, she uses type and token frequencies to explain diachronic phonological changes (see also this volume, chapter 36). Second, in the field of syntax, Grondelaers's (2000) work on Dutch *er* is an excellent illustration of how the work by Ariel can be extended and incorporated into quantitative studies of syntactic variation. Building on corpus data and experimental findings, Grondelaers extends Ariel's Accessibility Theory of definite reference to indefinite reference, to explain and predict the distribution of *er* 'there' in sentences like *Op de hoek van de straat is (er) een bakker* 'At the corner of the street (there) is a bakery'. Grondelaers's work is especially interesting in that it uses offline corpus data to generate hypotheses that are subsequently tested in a psychoexperimental design. Third, in the area of language acquisition, the work of Tomasello (2000) and his coworkers generates many new insights *and* further questions: Do we want to explain the acquisition order of connectives only in terms of the input provided by the parents? How would such a usage-based account relate to theories of increasing cognitive complexity (see section 3 and Evers-Vermeul and Sanders 2001)?

In conclusion, it seems that, especially on the level of discourse, the integration of cognitively plausible theories with empirical testing is the ultimate aim, rather than a situation that has already been realized. Therefore, we consider the level of discourse a "new frontier" for Cognitive Linguistics.

NOTES

1. Another, less preferred reading of this fragment is that the second sentence gives an elaboration of the first sentence. Such a reading does not disprove our central point here that the reader has to link the second sentence to the first sentence.

2. Because we only want to illustrate the transition principles of Centering Theory, we simplified things here. In fact, Centering Theory distinguishes between a forward and a backward looking center for each segment.

REFERENCES

Anscombre, Jean-Claude, and Oswald Ducrot. 1977. Deux MAIS en Français? *Lingua* 43: 23–40.

Ariel, Mira. 1990. *Accessing noun-phrase antecedents*. London: Routledge.

Ariel, Mira. 2001. Accessibility theory: An overview. In Ted Sanders, Joost Schilperoord, and Wilbert Spooren, eds., *Text representation: Linguistic and psycholinguistic aspects* 29–87. Amsterdam: John Benjamins.

Barlow, Michael, and Suzanne Kemmer, eds. 2000. *Usage-based models of language*. Stanford, CA: CSLI Publications.

Bateman, John A., and Klaas Jan Rondhuis. 1997. Coherence relations: Towards a general specification. *Discourse Processes* 24: 3–49.

Black, John B., and Hyman Bern. 1981. Causal coherence and memory for events in narratives. *Journal of Verbal Learning and Verbal Behavior* 20: 267–75.

Bloom, Lois. 1991. *Language development from two to three*. Cambridge: Cambridge University Press.

Britton, Bruce K. 1994. Understanding expository text: Building mental structures to induce insights. In Morton Ann Gernsbacher, ed., *Handbook of psycholinguistics* 640–74. New York: Academic Press.

Bybee, Joan L. 2001. *Phonology and language use*. Cambridge: Cambridge University Press.

Carpenter, Patricia Ann, and Marcel Adam Just. 1977. Reading comprehension as eyes see it. In Marcel Just and Patricia Carpenter, eds., *Cognitive processes in comprehension* 109–39. Hillsdale, NJ: Lawrence Erlbaum.

Chafe, Wallace L. 1976. Givenness, contrastiveness, definiteness, subjects, topics and point of view. In Charles N. Li, ed., *Subject and topic* 25–55. New York: Academic Press.

Chafe, Wallace L. 1994. *Discourse, consciousness, and time: The flow and displacement of conscious experience in speaking and writing*. Chicago: University of Chicago Press.

Cornish, Francis. 1999. *Anaphora, discourse and understanding: Evidence from English and French*. Oxford: Oxford University Press.

Cozijn, Reinier. 2000. Integration and inference in understanding causal sentences. PhD dissertation, Tilburg University.

Dancygier, Barbara, and Eve Sweetser. 2000. Constructions with *if*, *since*, and *because*: Causality, epistemic stance, and clause order. In Elisabeth Couper-Kuhlen and Bernd Kortmann, eds., *Cause, condition, concession and contrast: Cognitive and discourse perspectives* 111–42. Berlin: Mouton de Gruyter.

Degand, Liesbeth. 2001. *Form and function of causation: A theoretical and empirical investigation of causal constructions in Dutch*. Leuven, Belgium: Peeters.

Degand, Liesbeth, Nathalie Lefèvre, and Yves Bestgen. 1999. The impact of connectives and anaphoric expressions on expository discourse comprehension. *Document Design* 1: 39–51.

Degand, Liesbeth, and Ted Sanders. 2002. The impact of relational markers on expository text comprehension in L1 and L2. *Reading and Writing* 15: 739–57.

Du Bois, John W. 1980. Beyond definiteness: The trace of identity in discourse. In Wallace L. Chafe, ed., *The Pear Stories: Cognitive, cultural and linguistic aspects of narrative production*. Norwood, NJ: Ablex.

Ducrot, Oswald. 1980. Essai d'application: MAIS – les allusions à l'énonciation – délocutifs, performatifs, discours indirect. In Herman Parret, ed., *Le langage en context: Etudes philosophiques et linguistiques de pragmatique* 487–575. Amsterdam: John Benjamins.

Ehrlich, Kate, and Keith Rayner. 1983. Pronoun assignment and semantic integration during reading: Eye movements and immediacy of processing. *Journal of Verbal Learning and Verbal Behavior* 22: 75–87.

Evers-Vermeul, Jacqueline. 2005. The development of Dutch connectives: Change and acquisition as windows on form-function relations. PhD dissertation, Utrecht University, Netherlands.

Evers-Vermeul, Jacqueline, and Ted Sanders. 2001. 'Usage-based' versus 'Cognitive complexity'? The acquisition order of Dutch connectives explained. Paper presented at the 7th International Cognitive Linguistics Conference, Santa Barbara, CA, July 22–27.

Fauconnier, Gilles. 1994. *Mental spaces: Aspects of meaning construction in natural language*. 2nd edition. Cambridge: Cambridge University Press. (1st edition, Cambridge, MA: MIT Press, 1985)

Ford, Cecilia E., Barbara A. Fox, and Sandra A. Thompson, eds. 2002. *The language of turn and sequence*. Oxford: Oxford University Press.

Garnham, Alan, and Jane Oakhill, eds. 1992. Discourse representation and text processing. Special issue of *Language and Cognitive processes* 7.3/4.

Garrod, Simon C., David Freudenthal, and Elizabeth Boyle. 1993. The role of different types of anaphor in the on-line resolution of sentences in a discourse. *Journal of Memory and Language* 32: 1–30.

Garrod, Simon C., and Anthony J. Sanford. 1985. On the real-time character of interpretation during reading. *Language and Cognitive Processes* 1: 43–61.

Garrod, Simon C., and Anthony J. Sanford. 1994. Resolving sentences in a discourse context: How discourse representation affects language understanding. In Morton Ann Gernsbacher, ed., *Handbook of psycholinguistics* 675–98. San Diego, CA: Academic Press.

Geeraerts, Dirk, Stefan Grondelaers, and Peter Bakema. 1994. *The structure of lexical variation: Meaning, naming, and context.* Berlin: Mouton de Gruyter.

Gernsbacher, Morton Ann. 1990. *Language comprehension as structure-building.* Hillsdale, NJ: Lawrence Erlbaum.

Gernsbacher, Morton Ann, and Talmy Givón, eds. 1995. *Coherence in spontaneous text.* Amsterdam: John Benjamins.

Gibbs, Raymond W., Jr. 1996. What's cognitive about cognitive linguistics? In Eugene H. Casad, ed., *Cognitive linguistics in the Redwoods* 27–54. Berlin: Mouton de Gruyter.

Givón, Talmy, ed. 1983. *Topic continuity in discourse: A quantitative cross-language study.* Amsterdam: John Benjamins.

Givón, Talmy. 1995. Coherence in text vs. coherence in mind. In Morton Ann Gernsbacher and Talmy Givón, eds., *Coherence in spontaneous text* 59–115. Amsterdam: John Benjamins.

Gordon, Peter, Barbara Grosz, and Laura Gilliom. 1993. Pronouns, names and the centering of attention in discourse. *Cognitive Science* 17: 311–47.

Graesser, Arthur C., Keith K. Millis, and Rolf A. Zwaan. 1997. Discourse comprehension. In Janet Spence, John Darley, and Donald Foss, eds., *Annual Review of Psychology* 48: 163–89. Palo Alto, CA: Annual Reviews.

Grondelaers, Stefan. 2000. De distributie van niet-anaforisch *er* buiten de eerste zinsplaats: Sociolexicologische, functionele en psycholinguïstische aspecten van *er*'s status als presentatief signaal [The distribution of non-anaphoric *er* in non-sentence-initial position: Sociolexcicological, functional and psychological aspects of the status of *er* as a presentative marker]. PhD dissertation, University of Leuven, Belgium.

Grosz, Barbara, Scott Weinstein, and Aravind K. Joshi. 1995. Centering: A framework for modeling the local coherence of discourse. *Computational Linguistics* 21: 203–25.

Haberlandt, Karl, and George Bingham. 1978. Verbs contribute to the coherence of brief narratives: Reading related and unrelated sentence triples. *Journal of Verbal Learning and Verbal Behavior* 17: 419–25.

Haiman, John. 1978. Conditionals are topics. *Language* 54: 564–89.

Halliday, Michael A. K., and Ruqaiya Hasan. 1976. *Cohesion in English.* London: Longman.

Heim, Irene. 1982. The semantics of definite and indefinite noun phrases. MA thesis, University of Massachusetts at Amherst.

Hobbs, Jerry R. 1979. Coherence and coreference. *Cognitive Science* 3: 67–90.

Hobbs, Jerry R. 1990. *Literature and cognition.* Stanford, CA: CSLI Publications.

Hopper, Paul J., and Elizabeth Closs Traugott. 1993. *Grammaticalization.* Cambridge: Cambridge University Press.

Hovy, Eduard H. 1990. Parsimonious and profligate approaches to the question of discourse structure relations. In *Proceedings of the Fifth International Workshop on*

Natural Language Generation 128–36. Pittsburgh, PA. Also available at http://acl
.ldc.upenn.edu/W/W90/W90-0117.pdf.

Kamp, Hans, and Uwe Reyle. 1993. *From discourse to logic: Introduction to modeltheoretic semantics of natural language, formal logic and discourse representation theory.* Dordrecht, Netherlands: Kluwer.

Kehler, Andrew. 2002. *Coherence, reference and the theory of grammar.* Chicago: University of Chicago Press.

Kintsch, Walter. 1995. How readers construct situation models for stories: The role of syntactic cues and causal inferences. In Morton Ann Gernsbacher and Talmy Givón, eds., *Coherence in spontaneous text* 139–60. Amsterdam: John Benjamins.

Kintsch, Walter. 1998. *Comprehension: A paradigm for cognition.* Cambridge: Cambridge University Press.

Knott, Alistair. 1996. A data-driven methodology for motivating a set of coherence relations. PhD dissertation, University of Edinburgh, UK.

Knott, Alistair, and Robert Dale. 1994. Using linguistic phenomena to motivate a set of coherence relations. *Discourse Processes* 18: 35–62.

Knott, Alistair, and Ted Sanders. 1998. The classification of coherence relations and their linguistic markers: An exploration of two languages. *Journal of Pragmatics* 30: 135–75.

Knott, Alistair, Ted Sanders, and Jon Oberlander. 2001. Levels of representation in discourse. *Cognitive Linguistics* 12: 197–209.

König, Ekkehard, and Elizabeth Closs Traugott. 1988. Pragmatic strengthening and semantic change: The conventionalizing of conversational implicature. In Werner Hüllen and Rainer Schulze, eds., *Understanding the lexicon: Meaning, sense and world knowledge in lexical semantics* 110–24. Tübingen: Max Niemeyer Verlag.

Kyratzis, Amy, Jiansheng Guo, and Susan Ervin-Tripp. 1990. Pragmatic conventions influencing children's use of causal constructions in natural discourse. *Berkeley Linguistics Society* 16: 205–14.

Lakoff, George. 1987. *Women, fire and dangerous things: What categories reveal about the mind.* Chicago: University of Chicago Press.

Lakoff, George, and Mark Johnson. 1999. *Philosophy in the flesh: The embodied mind and its challenge to Western thought.* New York: Basic Books.

Lang, Ewald. 1984. *The semantics of coordination.* Amsterdam: John Benjamins.

Langacker, Ronald W. 2001. Discourse in cognitive grammar. *Cognitive Linguistics* 12: 143–88.

Lascarides, Alex, and Nicholas Asher. 1993. Temporal interpretation, discourse relations and common sense entailment. *Linguistics and Philosophy* 16: 437–93.

Louwerse, Max. 2001. An analytic and cognitive parameterization of coherence relations. *Cognitive Linguistics* 21: 291–315.

Mann, William C., and Sandra A. Thompson. 1986. Relational propositions in discourse. *Discourse Processes* 9: 57–90.

Martin, James R. 1992. *English text: System and structure.* Amsterdam: John Benjamins.

Matthiessen, Cristian, and Sandra A. Thompson. 1988. The structure of discourse and "subordination." In John R. Haiman and Sandra A. Thompson, eds., *Clause combining in grammar and discourse* 275–330. Amsterdam: John Benjamins.

Millis, Keith K., and Marcel Adam Just. 1994. The influence of connectives on sentence comprehension. *Journal of Memory and Language* 33: 128–47.

Moore, Joanna D., and Martha E. Pollack. 1992. A problem for RST: The need for multi-level discourse analysis. *Computational Linguistics* 18: 537–44.

Noordman, Leo. 2001. On the production of causal-contrastive although-sentences in context. In Ted Sanders, Joost Schilperoord, and Wilbert Spooren, eds., *Text representation: Linguistic and psycholinguistics aspects* 153–80. Amsterdam: John Benjamins.

Noordman, Leo, and Wietske Vonk. 1997. The different functions of a conjunction in constructing a representation of the discourse. In Michel Fayol and Jean Costermans, eds., *Processing interclausal relationships in production and comprehension of text* 75–93. Hillsdale, NJ: Lawrence Erlbaum.

Noordman, Leo, and Wietske Vonk. 1998. Memory-based processing in understanding causal information. *Discourse Processes* 26: 191–212.

Oversteegen, Leonoor. 1997. On the pragmatic nature of causal and contrastive connectives. *Discourse Processes* 24: 51–85.

Pander Maat, Henk. 1998. The classification of negative coherence relations and connectives. *Journal of Pragmatics* 30: 177–204.

Pander Maat, Henk, and Liesbeth Degand. 2001. Scaling causal relations and connectives in terms of speaker involvement. *Cognitive Linguistics* 12: 211–45.

Pander Maat, Henk, and Ted Sanders. 2000. Domains of use or subjectivity? The distribution of three Dutch causal connectives explained. In Elisabeth Couper-Kuhlen and Bernd Kortmann, eds., *Cause, condition, concession and contrast: Cognitive and discourse perspectives* 57–81. Berlin: Mouton de Gruyter.

Pander Maat, Henk, and Ted Sanders. 2001. Subjectivity in causal connectives: An empirical study of language in use. *Cognitive Linguistics* 12: 247–73.

Pit, Mirna. 2003. How to express yourself with a causal connective: Subjectivity and causal connectives in Dutch, German and French. PhD dissertation, Utrecht University, Netherlands.

Polanyi, Livia. 1988. A formal model of the structure of discourse. *Journal of Pragmatics* 12: 601–38.

Ramsay, Violetta. 1987. The functional distribution of preposed and postposed 'if' and 'when' clauses in written discourse. In Russell S. Tomlin, ed., *Coherence and grounding in discourse* 383–408. Amsterdam: John Benjamins.

Redeker, Gisela. 1990. Ideational and pragmatic markers of discourse structure. *Journal of Pragmatics* 14: 305–19.

Sacks, Harvey, Emmanuel A. Schegloff, and Gail Jefferson. 1974. A simplest systematics for the organization of turn-taking for conversation. *Language* 50: 696–735.

Sanders, José M. 1994. Perspective in narrative discourse. PhD dissertation, Tilburg University, Netherlands.

Sanders, José, and Gisela Redeker.1996. Perspective and the representation of speech and thought in narrative discourse. In Gilles Fauconnier and Eve Sweetser, eds., *Spaces, worlds and grammars* 290–317. Chicago: University of Chicago Press.

Sanders, José, and Wilbert Spooren. 1997. Perspective, subjectivity and modality from a cognitive linguistic point of view. In Wolf-Andreas Liebert, Gisela Redeker, and Linda Waugh, eds., *Discourse and perspective in cognitive linguistics* 85–112. Amsterdam: John Benjamins.

Sanders, Ted. 1997. Semantic and pragmatic sources of coherence: On the categorization of coherence relations in context. *Discourse Processes* 24: 119–47.

Sanders, Ted, and Morton Ann Gernsbacher. 2004. Accessibility in discourse and text processing. *Discourse Processes* 37: 79–89.

Sanders, Ted, and Leo Noordman. 2000. The role of coherence relations and their linguistic markers in text processing. *Discourse Processes* 29: 37–60.

Sanders, Ted, and Wilbert Spooren. 1999. Communicative intentions and coherence relations. In Wolfgang Bublitz, Uta Lenk, and Eija Ventola, eds., *Coherence in text and
discourse* 235–50. Amsterdam: John Benjamins.

Sanders, Ted, and Wilbert Spooren. 2001a. Modeling causal and contrastive connectives:
On domains, subjectivity and mental spaces. Paper presented at the 7th International
Cognitive Linguistics Conference, Santa Barbara, CA, July 22–27.

Sanders, Ted, and Wilbert Spooren. 2001b. Text representation as an interface between
language and its users. In Ted Sanders, Joost Schilperoord, and Wilbert Spooren, eds.,
Text representation: Linguistic and psycholinguistic aspects 1–25. Amsterdam: John
Benjamins.

Sanders, Ted, Wilbert Spooren, and Leo Noordman. 1992. Toward a taxonomy of coherence relations. *Discourse Processes* 15: 1–35.

Sanders, Ted, Wilbert Spooren, and Leo Noordman. 1993. Coherence relations in a cognitive theory of discourse representation. *Cognitive Linguistics* 4: 93–133.

Sanford, Anthony J., and Simon C. Garrod. 1994. Selective processes in text understanding.
In Morton Ann Gernsbacher, ed., *Handbook of Psycholinguistics* 699–720. New York:
Academic Press.

Schiffrin, Deborah. 2001. Discourse markers: Language, meaning, and context. In Deborah
Schiffrin, Deborah Tannen, and Heidi Hamilton, eds., *The handbook of discourse
analysis* 54–75. Oxford: Basil Blackwell.

Singer, Murray, Michael Halldorson, Jeffrey C. Lear, and Peter Andrusiak. 1992. Validation
of causal bridging inferences. *Journal of Memory and Language* 31: 507–24.

Spooren, Wilbert. 1997. The processing of underspecified coherence relations. *Discourse
Processes* 24: 149–68.

Spooren, Wilbert, and Ted Sanders. 2003. What does children's discourse tell us about the
nature of coherence relations? Unpublished manuscript, VU Amsterdam / UiL OTS
Utrecht.

Stukker, Ninke. 2005. Causality marking across levels of language structure: A cognitive
semantic analysis of causal verbs and causal connectives in Dutch. PhD dissertation,
Utrecht University, Netherlands.

Sweetser, Eve. 1990. *From etymology to pragmatics: Metaphorical and cultural aspects of
semantic structure.* Cambridge: Cambridge University Press.

Sweetser, Eve. 1996. Mental spaces and the grammar of conditional constructions. In Gilles
Fauconnier and Eve Sweetser, eds., *Spaces, worlds and grammar* 318–33. Chicago:
University of Chicago Press.

Thompson, Sandra A. 1985. Grammar and written discourse: Initial and final purpose
clauses in English. *Text* 5: 55–84.

Tomasello, Michael. 2000. First steps toward a usage-based theory of language acquisition.
Cognitive Linguistics 11: 61–82.

Tomlin, Russell S. 1985. Foreground and background information and the syntax of
subordination. *Text* 5: 85–122.

Trabasso, Tom, and Paul van den Broek. 1985. Causal thinking and the representation of
narrative events. *Journal of Memory and Language* 24: 612–30.

Traugott, Elizabeth Closs. 1995. Subjectification in grammaticalization. In Dieter Stein and
Susan Wight, eds., *Subjectivity and subjectivisation: Linguistic perspectives* 31–54.
Cambridge: Cambridge University Press.

van Dijk, Teun A., and Walter Kintsch. 1983. *Strategies of discourse comprehension.* New
York: Academic Press.

Verhagen, Arie. 2000. Concession implies causality, though in some other space. In Elisabeth Couper-Kuhlen and Bernd Kortmann, eds., *Cause – condition – concession – contrast: Cognitive and discourse perspectives* 361–80. Berlin: Mouton de Gruyter.

Verhagen, Arie. 2001. Subordination and discourse segmentation revisited; or, Why matrix clauses may be more dependent than complements. In Ted Sanders, Joost Schilperoord, and Wilbert Spooren, eds., *Text representation: Linguistic and psycholinguistic aspects* 337–57. Amsterdam: John Benjamins.

Verhagen, Arie. 2005. *Constructions of intersubjectivity: Discourse, syntax, and cognition.* Oxford: Oxford University Press.

Verhagen, Arie, and Suzanne Kemmer. 1997. Interaction and causation: Causative constructions in modern standard Dutch. *Journal of Pragmatics* 27: 61–82.

Vonk, Wietske, Lettica Hustinx, and Wim Simons. 1992. The use of referential expressions in structuring discourse. *Language and Cognitive Processes* 7: 301–33.

Walker, Marilyn, Aravind Joshi, and Ellen Prince, eds. 1998. *Centering theory in discourse.* Oxford: Clarendon Press.

Zwaan, Rolf. 1996. Processing narrative time shifts. *Journal of Experimental Psychology: Learning, Memory, and Cognition* 22: 1196–1207.

PART V

LINGUISTIC VARIATION AND CHANGE

CHAPTER 36

DIACHRONIC LINGUISTICS

JOAN BYBEE

1. INTRODUCTION

This chapter deals with recent advances in the understanding of linguistic change as these derive from or relate to the new perspectives afforded by Cognitive Linguistics. Traditionally, the study of language change has been divided into the areas of sound change, analogy, morphosyntactic change, and semantic change. This organization will be followed in the present chapter, since significant recent developments have occurred in all of these areas. In particular, the last two areas, which have traditionally been less studied, have come under close scrutiny in recent years (as part of grammaticalization research) and are considered an important part of the development of Cognitive Linguistics. Comparative and internal reconstruction will not be dealt with, though the consequences of the findings discussed here for reconstruction are considerable. In particular, the unidirectionality of change in various domains places strong constraints on reconstruction.

As language is viewed less as a structured, tight-knit system and more as a variable, negotiated set of social and cognitive behaviors, the importance of the study of language change increases. Language change provides evidence for the nature of linguistic representation and processing, and thus provides a window on synchronic mental representation and the forces that create grammar. Moreover, since all synchronic states are the result of a long chain of diachronic developments, the construction of complete explanations for linguistic structures requires attention to the diachronic dimension.

Recent developments in cognitive and usage-based linguistics have afforded new perspectives on language change at all levels. In particular, the view that language is embodied (See Rohrer, this volume, chapter 2) supports the view that change in articulatory gestures is a prominent basis of sound change; the discovery that many of the lexical sources for grammaticization of relational terms such as adpositions are body-part terms also contributes to the notion of embodiment. The rejection of the rule/list fallacy in favor of usage-based exemplar storage as proposed in the work of Langacker provides a grammar that is more compatible with the lexical and phonetic gradualness of change, including not just sound change, but also analogical change, grammaticization, and syntactic change. Taking into account frequency of use also provides explanations for the direction of the lexical diffusion of change, again, not just sound change, but analogical change and morphosyntactic change. With regard to semantic change, prototypicality turns out to be important in the understanding of change in lexical semantics and also in the creation of constructions. Finally, the role of metaphor and metonymy in the semantic changes found in grammaticization has been brought to light in the cognitive framework.

2. A Usage-Based Approach to Sound Change

Phonological production is a neuromotor procedure that becomes more highly automated and more fluent with repetition. As with other highly practiced neuromotor behaviors, there is a tendency toward the greater compression and reduction of the gestures involved. It is this tendency that accounts for the fact that sound change occurs so frequently in the history of languages. In this view, then, sound change is a natural outcome of language use and the embodied nature of language. It is possible, furthermore, that given a greater understanding of the effects of repetition on neuromotor behavior, a theory could eventually be developed to predict the class of possible sound changes. The view that sound change results from the natural effects that repetition has on neuromotor behavior is supported by the fact that in the lexical diffusion of a sound change, high-frequency words are affected before low-frequency words in most cases.

2.1. Specifying the Class of Sound Changes

A theory of sound change requires first a typology of changes involving phonology, since not all changes that involve sounds are technically "sound changes." Mowrey and Pagliuca (1995) propose a set of restrictions that delineates a class of changes that constitute sound changes. First, these have to be actually attested and not reconstructed changes. Second, they must affect the core vocabulary, including frequent lexical material. Third, they are most easily observed in relatively unmonitored speech, and fourth, the changes take place in a phonetically gradual manner. (Note that these last two criteria are those that determine the natural processes of Stampe's 1973 Natural Phonology.) Excluded are changes due to language contact, analogical changes, and hypercorrections. Of course, some problems exist for maintaining this distinction; it is sometimes a matter of dispute whether the origin of a change is physical or social, whether a change is purely internal or due to contact. Nevertheless, an attempt must be made to delimit the set of changes that constitute sound change.

2.2. Gestures and the Nature of Sound Change

While the usual alphabetic notation makes it appear as though one segment is changing into another—for example, [p]>[f] or [u] > [ü]—it is important to remember that this is just a shorthand and the speech stream is a continuous flow of muscular activity, with some gestures overlapping others. Even distinctive features are usually associated with specific segments, which further encourages us to think of the speech stream as a sequence of consonants and vowels. In dealing with sound change, the fluid and continuous nature of the speech stream must be borne in mind.

It is thus useful in trying to explain sound change to consider the articulatory gesture as the basic unit for phonological description. According to the theory being developed by Browman and Goldstein (1990, 1992, 1995), "Gestures are events that unfold during speech production and whose consequences can be observed in the movement of the speech articulators" (1992: 156). A typical utterance is composed of multiple gestures overlapping or sequenced with respect to one another. An individual gesture is produced by groups of muscles that act in concert, sometimes ranging over more than one articulator: for instance, constricting lip aperture involves the action of the upper lip, the lower lip, and the jaw, but such a constriction is considered one gesture.

In sound change, then, gestures are changed. Given that the great majority of sound changes, as defined by Mowrey and Pagliuca (1995), are assimilatory or reductive in nature, there is some hope of developing a predictive theory of sound change with reference to the gesture. Pagliuca and Mowrey (1987) and Mowrey and Pagliuca (1995) propose that sound change is due to either substantive reduction or temporal reduction, and in most cases, both. Substantive reduction refers to the reduction in the magnitude of a muscular gesture, such as occurs in the change of a stop to a fricative ([d] > [ð]) or the centralization of a vowel to [ə]. Temporal reduction refers to the compression of gestures, either by a single articulator, as when [si] changes to [ʃi], or by multiple independent articulators, as when VN [vowel + nasal consonant] becomes ṼN. The term "temporal reduction" entails a reduction in the duration of the whole sequence of gestures. Pagliuca and Mowrey (1987) and Mowrey and Pagliuca (1995) claim that constellations of gestures in a linguistic string tend to get shorter over time, as well as reduced in the amount of articulatory energy required for the production of the individual gestures.

Browman and Goldstein (1990, 1992) put forward a very similar proposal. They hypothesize that all examples of casual speech alterations are the result of gestures having decreased magnitudes (both in space and in time) and increased temporal overlap. Browman and Goldstein restrict their hypothesis to casual speech alterations. This restriction has the advantage of defining an empirically verifiable sample of alterations. Mowrey and Pagliuca (1995) wish to address all sound change but with the restrictions stated above. Given these definitions, it is not controversial to claim that the great majority of attested sound changes have an articulatory etiology and in particular involve assimilation (retiming) or reduction. The controversial issue is whether or not it is accurate to take the further step of proposing that *all* sound changes are reductions and retimings and further that all changes are articulatory in their motivation and gradual in their implementation, a question I will return to in sections 2.7 and 2.10.

One goal of gestural research, then, is to demonstrate that attested changes are better explained in a gestural model than in a model using binary features, segments, or acoustic features. In addition, it is important to demonstrate that apparent strengthenings (such as the addition of a segment) and apparent acoustically motivated changes can be seen in gestural terms as instances of substantive or temporal reduction (see also Pagliuca 1982). Let us now consider how some common sound changes would be described in a gestural model.

2.3. Assimilation

Consider first the traditional conceptualization of assimilation, perhaps the most common of all phonological processes. As an illustration of a gestural rather than a segmental approach, Pagliuca and Mowrey (1987) discuss the palatalization of [s] before [i], as, for example, occurs in Japanese. A segmental characterization that represents the change as gradual might be given as (1).

(1)   [si]   >   [sʲi]   >   [ʃi]

The segmental representation which shows the [s] as first palatalized and then transformed into an alveopalatal would be described in distinctive features by saying that the [s] first changes the value of [high] from minus to plus. This would be explained on the basis of the [+high] specification for [i] spreading to the preceding segment. In the next step, the value for [anterior] will be changed from plus to minus. The first step changes one feature of [s] to be the same as one feature of [i]. The second step has no clear assimilatory explanation.

Many problems with this form of description could be pointed out, such as the fact that there is nothing to predict that it would be the feature [high] that would change its value rather than some other feature that differs between the two segments, such as [syllabic]. Nor is there any natural way to explain or predict the change in the feature [anterior]. Related to this lack of predictability is the more fundamental fact that this feature-and-segment analysis does not give a very accurate picture of what is really happening in a language with this process.

Pagliuca and Mowrey (1987) argue that it is not a feature or property of [s] that has changed to be more like [i], but rather the formerly sequential gestures producing the [s] and the [i] have gradually been compressed so that first the transition between the [s] and the [i] is highly affected by the position of the tongue for [i]. A further and later development is that the two gestures come to overlap to such an extent that the whole articulation of the fricative is affected by the domed-tongue gesture of the [i], increasing the area of the point of constriction. This analysis is confirmed in Zsiga (1995), whose electropalatographic data show that in productive palatalization of [s + j] across word boundaries (as in *miss you*), the contact of the tongue with the palate is just what one would expect if the [s] and the [j] were articulated at the same time.

A consequence of this analysis is the view that this assimilation process is actually a temporal reduction: two previously sequential gestures are now simultaneous for at least part of their articulation. Other examples of assimilation that can be explained in this way include vowel nasalization, which takes place preferentially when a vowel is followed by a nasal consonant in the same syllable. In this case, the gesture that opens the velum for nasalization is anticipated; it is retimed to occur during the articulation of the vowel. The view of this change as a modification in timing makes it possible to relate articulatory processes of speech to modifications made in other well-rehearsed motor events, where repetition increases efficiency or fluency because sequences of events can be anticipated and one event can begin before the preceding one is totally completed.

2.4. Other Retiming Changes

Temporal factors are also involved in what has previously been viewed as the insertion and deletion of segments. Insertion of consonants is not very common, and when it does occur, it is clear that the articulatory gestures that compose the consonant were all present before the consonant appeared. An interesting diachronic example occurred in a set of future tense verbs of Spanish, when the grammaticalizing auxiliary *haber* suffixed to the infinitive form of the verb with which it formed a construction. Subsequently, some high frequency second and third conjugation verbs lost the vowel preceding the stressed suffix and developed an excrescent [d] between the [n] of the root and the [r] of the erstwhile infinitive:

(2) *venir + he > veniré > venré > vendré*   'I will come'
     tener + he > teneré > tenré > tender   'I will have'
     poner + he > poneré > ponré > pondré   'I will put'

Note first that it is a coronal stop that develops here, in other words, one at the same point of articulation as surrounding consonants, rather than a labial or velar.

Secondly, it is voiced, as are the surrounding consonants. To explain [nr] developing into [ndr], a straightforward gestural analysis is possible. The velic opening corresponding to the [n] is retimed such that the velum is reclosed before the stop gesture at the alveolar ridge is complete. The result is a period of stop closure without nasality, or, in other words, a [d]. Note that the loss of the vowel in the auxiliary *haberé* > *habré* does not lead to an "excrescent" [d], but the loss of the vowel in *saliré* > *saldré*, where alveolar gestures are present, does.

2.5. Reductive Processes

Besides changes in the relative timing of gestures, there can also be reduction in the magnitude of the gestures in casual speech or in sound change. Such reduction in consonants will usually fall into the class of lenitions or weakenings. The reduction of a consonant, such as [p], along a path which is cross-linguistically common, that is, [p] > [Φ]/[f] > [h] > φ is characterized as a successive decrease and loss of muscular activity. The production of [p] requires muscular activity of both the upper and lower lips, which act to bring them together, as well as the activity required to open the glottis. The production of [f] requires less or no activity in the muscles of the upper lip, but continued activity in the lower lip and glottis. The sound [h] is produced with no activity in the labial muscles at all, but requires the opening of the glottis. Total deletion involves the loss of all the muscular events that were associated with the original consonant (Mowrey and Pagliuca 1995: 81–83).

In addition to the reduction of a consonant to zero, another path of reduction for consonants yields a more sonorous or vowel-like consonant. Such changes are most notable in syllable-final position or postvocalic position. For example, the change of a syllable-final [l] to a back unrounded glide [ɯ] involves the loss of the tongue tip gesture. This change occurs in American English pronunciations of words such as *milk* as [mɪɯk].

Temporal reduction of a stop is another possibility. The English alveolar flap found in words such as *latter* and *ladder* is significantly shorter than the [t] or [d] that occurs preceding a stressed vowel (Zue and Laferriere 1979). The medial stops in *upper* and *trucker* are also shorter than their counterparts preceding the stress, but this difference is not as salient (Hoard 1971).

Vowels reduce by lessening the magnitude of the gesture as well. In unstressed syllables, reduction can be manifest in various changes in the gestures, some of which may co-occur. Laxing of vowels usually refers to a decrease in muscular activity involving a lowered articulation for high vowels and more central articulation for peripheral vowels, and even a shortening compared to vowels in stressed syllables. Centralization is the result of a lessening of the magnitude of gestures that move the articulators to peripheral positions. Shortening involves a loss of temporal duration of muscular activity. When reduction leads to complete deletion, both temporal and substantive reduction have occurred.

2.6. Acoustic-Perceptual Aspects of Phonological Processes and Change

Analyzing phonological processes in terms of gestures does not imply that there is not also an acoustic-perceptual component to these processes. Any change in gestures or their timing produces an acoustic-perceptual change. In fact, for a gestural change to proceed and become conventionalized as part of the language, its perceptual effects must be registered in storage.

The remarkable degree to which speakers of the same dialect achieve similarity in the details of their phonetic output attests to the exquisite attunement of the perceptual system to fine detail. Therefore, it is unlikely that a hearer who has already acquired the phonetics of his or her dialect would misperceive already acquired words to the extent that that might cause a sound change. However, there are two roles for perception in change. First, it is likely that in certain cases a change can occur because children fail to perceive and acquire a relatively difficult phonetic configuration (such as front rounded vowels, see section 2.10 for an example and discussion). Second, where contextual change has already occurred for articulatory reasons, a perceptual reanalysis could extend a change that has already begun (Ohala 1981). For instance, in a situation in which the vowel in a VN sequence is nasalized, if the nasal consonant is also weakening, then the nasalization could be attributed to the vowel rather than to the consonant, thereby contributing to the continuation of the change toward having just a nasalized vowel with a deleted consonant. Ohala (2003) refers to this as a change in the normalization process.

2.7. Strengthenings

Two types of counterexamples to the strong claims about sound change made by Mowrey and Pagliuca (1995) need to be noted and discussed. First, I will discuss some cases of apparent strengthenings which appear to be well attested; in the next section, I will discuss the possibility of perceptually based changes and a proposal for distinguishing them from articulatorily based changes.

Recall that some apparent strengthenings, such as the insertion of an obstruent into certain sequences of consonants, have already been dealt with in section 2.4. Diphthongization, which is viewed by some as a strengthening, can also be analyzed as a retiming since one can hypothesize that diphthongs are produced by sequencing vowel gestures that were formerly simultaneous. The crucial question would be whether or not the resulting diphthong has a greater temporal duration than the simple vowel from which it arose. Similarly, vowel lengthening needs to be studied in this context to determine whether over time a vowel can increase its length, and it needs to be determined whether or not consonant "insertions" such as shown in (2) above affect the overall length of the consonant cluster. Finally, vowel insertions that break consonant clusters (e.g., Dutch *melk* [melək] 'milk', *Delft* [deləft] 'Delft (place name)') are potential counterexamples as well. They could be considered

retiming changes, but they need to be studied to see if the change results in an overall lengthening of the word.

In addition, Pagliuca and Mowrey (1987: 462) suggest that affrication of voiceless stops, as occurred in the High German Consonant Shift ([p] > [pf] > [f], [t] > [ts] > [s], [k] > [kx] > [x]), is due to "the erosion of stop closure integrity, which has, as an aerodynamic consequence, an increase in acoustic energy" and not a fortition as some assume. Evidence that the general path of change which includes the stop-to-affricate step is a general lenition, or weakening, is that the subsequent step that yields a fricative is uncontroversially a weakening.

However, at least some major challenges to the reduction theory remain: the well-attested case in Spanish of the strengthening of a glide in syllable-initial position to a fricative, stop, or affricate. This change has occurred in several dialects of Latin America, yielding voiced or even voiceless fricatives or affricates in words such as *yo* 'I', *oye* 'listen', and *hielo* 'ice' (Lipski 1994). Such cases need to be examined in detail to determine their implications for the reduction theory.

2.8. Lexical Diffusion of Sound Change

Lexical diffusion refers to the way a sound change affects the lexicon: if sound change is lexically abrupt, all the words of a language are affected by the sound change at the same rate. If a sound change is lexically gradual, individual words undergo the change at different rates or different times. Whether sound changes exhibit gradual or abrupt lexical diffusion is a topic of some recent concern (see references below). One early contribution to this debate by Schuchardt (1885) is the observation that high-frequency words are affected by sound change earlier and to a greater extent than low-frequency words.

William Labov (1981, 1994) also deals with the issue, availing himself of the data from his numerous studies of sound change in progress. His proposal is that there are two types of sound change: "regular sound change," which is gradual, phonetically motivated, and occurs without lexical or grammatical conditioning or social awareness, and "lexical diffusion change" such as those studied by Wang (1969, 1977), which are "the result of the abrupt substitution of one phoneme for another in words that contain that phoneme" (Labov 1994: 542). He observes this type of change most often in "the late stages of internal change that has been differentiated by lexical and grammatical conditioning" (542). Labov even goes so far as to propose that certain changes, such as the deletion of glides and schwa, will be regular changes, while the deletion of obstruents will show lexical diffusion.

A number of researchers have challenged this position. Phillips (1984) has presented evidence that even low-level sound changes exhibit gradual lexical diffusion. Oliveira (1991) argues also that it is likely that gradual lexical diffusion occurs even in changes that turn out to be regular. Krishnamurti (1998) demonstrates that the change of [s] > [h] > Ø in Gondi exhibits gradual lexical diffusion but still goes through to completion in some dialects.

Table 36.1. Rate of [t]/[d]-deletion for entire corpus
by word frequency

	Deletion	Nondeletion	% deletion
High frequency	898	752	54.4%
Low frequency	137	262	34.3%

Chi-squared = 41.67; $p < .001$; df = 1

In many of these case studies, high-frequency words are affected earlier and to a greater extent than low-frequency words (Hooper 1976b). In Bybee (2000b) I show that American English [t]/[d]-deletion occurs more often in words of high frequency than in words of low frequency. In a corpus of some 2,000 tokens divided somewhat arbitrarily into two groups according to their frequency in the Francis and Kucera (1982) word count (with words of a frequency of 35 or less classified as low frequency and words with a frequency of more than 35 classified as high), a significant difference in the rate of deletion was found, as shown in table 36.1.

Similarly, in Bybee (2002b) I report that the rate of deletion of Spanish intervocalic [ð] in New Mexican Spanish is significantly affected by word frequency. As table 36.2 shows, higher-frequency words are more likely to undergo deletion of [ð] than lower-frequency words. The frequency count used in this case is the 1.1-million-word *Corpus oral de referencia del Español contemporáneo* (*COREC* 1992). (The figures in table 36.2 exclude the past participle morpheme because it is known to have a higher rate of deletion than average.)

In addition to consonant reduction, another type of change that shows robust word frequency effects is vowel reduction and deletion. Fidelholtz (1975) demonstrates that the essential difference between words that do reduce a prestress vowel, such as *astronomy, mistake*, and *abstain*, and phonetically similar words that do not, such as *gastronomy, mistook*, and *abstemious*, is word frequency. Van Bergem (1995) finds that reduction of a prestress vowel in Dutch also is highly conditioned by frequency. The high-frequency words *minuut* 'minute', *vakantie* 'vacation', and *patat* 'chips/French fries' are more likely to have a schwa in the first syllable than the phonetically similar low-frequency words, *miniem* 'marginal', *vacante* 'vacant', and *patent* 'patent'.

Table 36.2. Rate of deletion of [ð] according to token frequency for all
non past participle tokens in the New Mexican corpus
using the COREC as a measure of frequency

	Low (0–99)	High (100+)	Total
Retention	243 (91.4%)	287 (78.6%)	530 (84.0%)
Deletion	23 (8.6%)	78 (21.4%)	101 (16.0%)
Total	266	365	631

Chi-square = 17.3; $p < .001$; $N = 631$; df = 1

It is not quite clear whether the same pattern can be found in vowel shift changes. Labov searches for, but does not find, robust evidence for lexical diffusion in his data. The cases he does note are the raising of short [æ], which affects the adjectives ending in [d] *mad, glad,* and *bad,* but not *sad.* In this same shift, some evidence for lexical diffusion by frequency is cited: Labov (1994: 506) notes that when word-initial short [æ] "occurs before a voiceless fricative, only the more common, monosyllabic words are tensed: tense *ass* and *ask;* lax *ascot, aspirin, astronauts, aspect, athletic, after, African, Afghan.*"

In Moonwomon's (1992) study of the centralization of /æ/ in San Francisco English, she finds that in the environment before a fricative this vowel is more centralized than before a nonfricative; it is also more centralized after [l]. The most commonly used word with this pair of phonetic environments is *class. Class* shows more centralization than the other words with these two environments, such as *glass, laugh,* and so on.

Moonwomon also studies the fronting of /ɔ/ in the same speakers. Here a following /t/ or /d/ conditions more fronting than other consonants. Of the words in the corpus ending in final /t/, *got* is the most frequently occurring. Moonwomon also shows that the fronting in *got* is significantly more advanced than in other words ending in alveolars, such as *not, god, body, forgot, pot,* and so on.

It appears, then, that some evidence that high-frequency words undergo vowel shifts before low-frequency words can be found. The lack of stronger evidence may be due to a greater difficulty in discerning frequency effects in vowel shifts because of the effects of the preceding and following environments, which narrow each phonetic class to a small number of words.

2.9. Theoretical Consequences of Lexically and Phonetically Gradual Sound Change

Both Wang's and Labov's views of lexical diffusion assume that a change that diffuses gradually through the lexicon must be phonetically abrupt. This is a necessary assumption if one accepts a synchronic phonological theory that has phonemic underlying representations. Words can change one by one only if the change is a substitution of phonemes in such a theory. The discovery that sound change can be both phonetically gradual and lexically gradual forces a different view of the mental representation of the phonology of words (Hooper 1981; Bybee 2000b). If subphonemic detail or ranges of variation can be associated with particular words, an accurate model of phonological representation must allow phonetic detail in the cognitive representation of words.

A recent proposal is that the cognitive representation of a word can be made up of the set of exemplars of that word that have been experienced by the speaker/hearer. Thus, all phonetic variants of a word are stored in memory and organized into a cluster in which exemplars that are more similar are closer to one another than the ones that are dissimilar, and moreover, exemplars that are frequently occurring are stronger than less frequent ones (Johnson 1997; Bybee 2000a, 2001; Pierrehumbert 2001). These exemplar clusters change as experience with language changes: repeated exemplars grow stronger, and less used ones may fade over time, as other memories do.

Changes in the phonetic range of the exemplar cluster may also take place as language is used and new tokens of words are experienced. Thus, the range of phonetic variation of a word can gradually change over time, allowing a phonetically gradual sound change to affect different words at different rates. Given a tendency for online reduction, the phonetic representation of a word will gradually accrue more exemplars that are reduced, and these exemplars will become more likely to be chosen for production where they may undergo further reduction, gradually moving the words of the language in a consistent direction. The more frequent words will have more chances to undergo online reduction and thus will change more rapidly. Words that are more predictable in context (which are often also the more frequent ones) will have a greater chance of having their reduced version chosen, given an appropriate context, and thus will also advance the reductive change more rapidly.

The exemplar model in principle allows every word of a language to have a distinct set of phonetic gestures and an unlimited range of variation. The reason languages do not avail themselves of this possibility is because categorization of the components of words into a small set of gestural constellations is necessary given the size of the vocabulary of natural languages. In order to organize the lexicon and automate production and perception, it is necessary to reuse the same gestures in large numbers of lexical items. Evidence from sound change also shows that the range of variation for a single word tends to narrow as change goes to completion and that this narrowing tends to be consistent across lexical items, with very high frequency items being the only exceptions (Bybee 2000b, 2001). The sets of gestures that are reused across the lexicon are roughly equivalent to phonemes.

2.10. Perceptually Motivated Change

Less commonly, sound change may be motivated by misperceptions, especially on the part of learners (Ohala 1992), or reanalysis. In these cases, the pattern of lexical diffusion should proceed from low-frequency words to high-frequency words. Thus, patterns of lexical diffusion can be used as diagnostics of the motivations for sound change (Bybee 2001). For instance, as we will see in section 3.1, analogical leveling affects low-frequency words before high-frequency words.

Phillips (1984) found a similar pattern of diffusion for some sound changes. For instance, the Old English diphthong <eo> monophthongized to a mid front rounded vowel /ö/, with both a long and a short version in the eleventh to twelfth centuries. In some dialects, these front rounded vowels were maintained into the fourteenth century, but in Lincolnshire, they quickly unrounded and merged with /e(:)/. A text written around 1200 AD, the *Ormulum*, captures this change in progress. The author was interested in spelling reform, and so, rather than regularizing the spelling, he represented the variation, using two spellings for the same word in many cases (e.g., *deop*, *dep* 'deep'). Phillips found that within the class of nouns and verbs, the low-frequency words are more likely to have the spelling that represents the unrounded vowel.

If this were a phonetically motivated reduction that facilitates production, we would expect the high-frequency words to change first. Indeed, the frequent adverbs and function words have changed, suggesting they might be yielding to production pressures, but the fact that nouns and verbs show more change in low-frequency items suggests a different motivation for the change. Phillips proposes that a constraint against front rounded vowels is operating to remove these vowels, but how would such a constraint manifest itself, and why would it allow front rounded vowels for a time, only to obliterate them later? In Bybee (2001) I argue that, like other changes affecting low-frequency items first, this change might be caused by imperfect learning. Front rounded vowels are difficult to discriminate perceptually, and children acquire them later than unrounded vowels. Gilbert and Wyman (1975) found that French children confused [ö] and [ɛ] more often than any other nonnasal vowels they tested. A possible explanation for the Middle English change is that children correctly acquired the front rounded vowels in high-frequency words that were highly available in the input but tended toward merger with the unrounded version in words that were less familiar.

2.11. Suprasegmental Changes

Changes in stress patterns are not like the segmental changes discussed so far, as they seem to be based on generalizations that speakers have made over existing forms and are perhaps more like analogy, which I will treat in section 3. For instance, stress changes in Spanish verb forms indicate a change from a system in which stress is reckoned from the end of the word (as in Latin) to a system in which, for verbs at least, stress is a morphological marker. Thus, indicative and subjunctive imperfective verb forms shifted stress away from the penultimate syllable in first- and second-person plural to the antepenultimate. The result is a consistent stress pattern for this aspect: the stress falls on the first syllable of the suffix.

(3)		Old Spanish		Modern Spanish	
	Indicative	Subjunctive		Indicative	Subjunctive
1SG	*cantába*	*cantára*		*cantába*	*cantára*
2SG	*cantábas*	*cantáras*		*cantábas*	*cantáras*
3SG	*cantába*	*cantára*		*cantába*	*cantára*
1PL	*cantabámos*	*cantarámos*		*cantábamos*	*cantáramos*
2PL	*cantabáis*	*cantaráis*		*cantábais*	*cantárais*
3PL	*cantában*	*cantáran*		*cantában*	*cantáran*

Stress shifts also exhibit lexical diffusion. Phillips (1984, 1998) has studied the lexical diffusion of an English stress shift that moves the stress to the first syllable of nouns, creating diatones, that is, noun/verb pairs that differ only in stress placement, such as *pérmit* (noun) and *permít* (verb). This shift affects low-frequency words earlier than high-frequency words. Thus, while *ánnex* and *annéx* are diatones, *amóunt* is not; compare also *cómpress/compréss* and *commánd*, and so on. The stress shift appears to affect the noun, by giving it initial stress, and thus seems to be based on a generalization about the lexicon that nouns tend to have initial stress, while verbs have no such restriction. The more frequent nouns with aberrant stress can resist the tendency to change, while the less frequent ones bow to the more general schema. This type of change, then, resembles analogical change, which I discuss in section 3.

2.12. Life Cycle of Phonological Alternations

As sound change produces permanent effects on the words of a language, in cases of morphological complexity, there is a potential for the development of alterna-tions in paradigms. These alternations become morphologized, that is, they lose their phonetic conditioning and take on morphological or lexical conditioning. The diachronic trajectory shown in (4) is both universal and unidirectional (Kiparsky 1971; Vennemann 1972; Hooper 1976a; Dressler 1977, 1985; Bybee 2001).

(4)   phonetic process > morpholexical alternation

Thus, for example, a phonetic process of voicing of intervocalic fricatives in Old English produced the alternating pairs *wife/wives*; *leaf/leaves*; *house/hou*[z]*es*; *bath/ba*[ðz]. Today, however, the alternation is morphologized, in the sense that it applies only in the plural of nouns (not in possessive form, e.g., *wife's*), and it is lexicalized in the sense that it applies only to a certain set of nouns (not, e.g., to *chief* or *class*). Once an alternation becomes morphologized or lexicalized, it is then sub-ject to further changes which are generally designated as analogical changes. These will be treated in section 3.

2.13. Conclusions about Sound Change

The view presented here is that sound change is largely the result of the automa-tization of articulatory gestures with the reduction and temporal compression of gestures accounting for most changes. It is a usage-based phenomenon and as such affects high-frequency words and phrases in advance of the lower-frequency items. Being both lexically and phonetically gradual, sound change shows lexical effects, which suggest that phonetic detail is stored in the lexicon.

Often it is difficult to establish the causes and mechanisms of phonologi-cal changes, but I have argued here that recent findings on lexical diffusion are promising resources for diagnostics of the cause of change. Sound change due to automatization will proceed from high-frequency words to low-frequency words, but phonological changes based on analogy to existing patterns will proceed in the opposite direction. Thus, where lexical diffusion data are available, we have evidence for the mechanism involved.

3. Analogical Change

Analogical change has traditionally referred to morphophonological change, in particular the loss or leveling of paradigm-internal alternations or the extension of alternations from one paradigm to another. Analogy is usually treated as if it were of secondary importance to sound change, as little more than a way of accounting for exceptions to sound changes. Indeed, analogy has been regarded as irregular and thus possibly unpredictable, as in Sturtevant's famous paradox: sound change is regular and creates irregularities (in the morphology); analogy is irregular and creates regularity.

In the last few decades, great strides have been made in our understanding of the mechanisms and the pathways of analogical change and their psycholinguistic basis. In this section, I will present these findings as they relate to analogical leveling or regularization in sections 3.1 to 3.3 and to analogical extension in section 3.4.

One popular model of analogy introduced in textbooks is the proportional model in which it is claimed that analogical change occurs as a result of the comparison of surface forms on the model of 'X is to X_1 as Y is to Y_1'. I will argue that while this model produces a description of what may be obtained in this type of change in some cases, it does not work in all cases and does not represent the actual psycholinguistic mechanism that applies in creating analogical changes.

3.1. Analogical Leveling

In analogical leveling, a paradigm that exhibits an alternation loses that alternation and thus becomes regularized. Examples in English are the changes of *weep/wept* to *weep/weeped*, *hou[s]e/hou[z]es* to *hou[s]e/hou[s]es*, *roof/rooves* to *roof/roofs*. Three important tendencies in analogical leveling help us understand the mechanism involved.

  a. Leveling affects the least frequent paradigms first, leaving alternations in the more frequent paradigms.
  b. The alternate that survives after leveling is the alternate of the more basic, unmarked, or more frequent member of the category.
  c. Leveling is more likely among forms that are more closely related to one another.

Given the robust experimental finding that high-frequency forms are easier to access than low-frequency forms, we assume that high frequency adds to the strength of the lexical representation of a form (Bybee 1985). Leveling occurs when a lower-frequency form is difficult to access, but a related higher-frequency form is accessible. The latter form is used to create a new form on the basis of a productive pattern or one that applies to a larger number of forms. Thus, if *weep* is easier to access than *wept*, a speaker searching for a past may use *weep* and the regular past suffix to create the new form *weeped*. Thus, analogical leveling is not change in an old form, but the creation of a new form. This explains why alternate forms, such as *wept* and *weeped*, can coexist in a language.

The greater accessibility or strength of forms with high token frequency also explains why low-frequency forms are more prone to leveling than high-frequency forms. High-frequency forms resist leveling because of their greater availability in the experience of the speaker, which affords them a greater lexical strength (Bybee 1985). Thus, it is normal for irregularities among nouns, verbs, and adjectives to be found primarily in the most frequent paradigms (those whose words have high token frequency), such as, *man/men, child/children; go/went, have/had; good/better/ best*. Of course, it should be added that some languages maintain multiple patterns or irregularities throughout their systems, for example, Greek verb paradigms, Hausa noun pluralization, so there is no necessity to have only one productive pattern or to level alternations.

3.2. The Direction of Analogical Leveling

A question that has generated some interest in the study of historical linguistics is the question of which alternate survives when leveling occurs. Or, to put the question in the terms of the discussion above, which form serves as the base for the creation of the new form. I have already stated above that it is the more accessible or the more frequent form, but given that other proposals have been made, it is important to examine the evidence for this claim.

Kuryłowicz (1949) proposed that morphologically related pairs consist of base forms (*formes de fondation*) and derived forms (*formes fondées*) and that the analogy proceeds from the base form to the derived one. This would mean that the variant found in the base form would survive in the leveling process, as the new form is constructed from it. Kuryłowicz further explains that the base form is the one with the more general distribution; the one that can be used when no contrast is needed. The base form, then, seems equivalent to the unmarked form in Jakobson's (1957) theory of markedness. Indeed, Kuryłowicz uses the same type of examples as Jakobson, saying that the masculine adjective in French is basic because the feminine is constructed from it and the masculine can be used in cases where both genders are included. Kuryłowicz also hastens to add that it is not a matter of frequency, but rather of distribution.

Kiparsky (1988) and others have taken Kuryłowicz's reference to basic and derived forms as similar to underlying and surface forms. In this formulation, leveling would occur when the underlying form surfaces unchanged, without the application of a phonological rule. Thus, leveling would be represented formally as rule loss, or in some cases, rule reordering (Kiparsky 1971, 1988). Of course, the embarrassment for this theory is the fact that leveling occurs item-by-item, with some paradigms "losing" the rule while others retain it. Since rules by their very nature should apply equally to all items, the gradual lexical diffusion of leveling

suggests that the alternations in question are not rule-governed after all, a conclusion that connectionist research supports (Rumelhart and McClelland 1986).

Mańczak (1958a, 1958b) replied to Kuryłowicz's principles for predicting analogy
with hypotheses of his own that made reference not to theoretical constructs such as
"base form," but to specific features of words, such as their length or their grammatical category. Thus, he noted that the indicative triggered changes in other moods
more than vice versa and that the present triggered changes in other tenses more than
vice versa. In Mańczak (1978, 1980), he pulled together a set of such predictions under
the generalization that more frequent forms were more likely to be maintained in the
language than less frequent forms, more likely to retain an archaic character, more
likely to trigger changes in less frequent forms, and more likely to replace them.

These predictions fit well with the approach to markedness introduced in
Greenberg's (1966) monograph *Language Universals*, where it is demonstrated that
unmarked members of categories have a higher token frequency than marked
members. Then the question arises as to whether it is the higher token frequency
that makes inflected forms less susceptible to change and more likely to serve as the
basis of change, or whether it is the more abstract notion of conceptual markedness.

Tiersma (1982) contributes to this debate by showing that analogical leveling
does not always cause the reformation of the marked member on the basis of the
unmarked one, but rather in certain cases of singular/plural pairs where the plural is
more frequent because the noun refers to entities that occur more often in pairs or
groups (such as horns, tears, arms, stockings, teeth), a reformation of the singular is
possible in analogical leveling. Thus, it is not the abstract marking relations of the
grammatical category that determine the direction of leveling, but the local patterns
of frequency of use. This constitutes, then, another case in which the way language
is used determines the direction of change.

3.3. The Domain of Analogical Leveling

A paradigm (the set of inflected forms sharing the same stem) can be highly complex in languages that have inflections for person and number, tense, mood, and
aspect. In such languages, some alternations are more likely to level than others. In
Bybee (1985) I present the hypothesis that some inflectional categories create greater
meaning differences than others. For instance, the difference in aspect between
perfective and imperfective creates a greater semantic distinction than the difference between forms such as first person versus third person. It is also more common
cross-linguistically to find formal variants corresponding to aspectual differences
across person/number lines than to person/number differences across aspectual
lines. Thus, Spanish has perfective/imperfective forms with stem changes, such as
supe/sabía and *quise/quería*, but no stem allomorphy within these aspects that
corresponds to person/number distinctions. We can thus predict that analogical
leveling of alternations across closely related forms, such as first-person singular
and plural within perfective or within imperfective, would be more common than

a leveling across aspectual lines, with the result that, for example, the first-person singular always has the same stem.

Thus, leveling occurs within subparadigms of closely related forms where the more frequent form serves as the basis for the creation of a new form that replaces the less frequent form. For instance, consider the changes in the paradigm for *to do* in Old and Middle English (Moore and Marckwardt 1960):

(5)			*Old English*	*Middle English*
PRS. IND	1SG		dō	do
	2SG		dēst	dest
	3SG		dēþ	doth
	PL		dōþ	do
PRET. IND	1SG		dyde	dide, dude [dyde]
	2SG		dydest	didest, dudest
	3SG		dyde	dide, dude

Old English had an alternation in the singular present between first person and second and third. There was also an alternation between present and preterite. In the preterite, there is a vowel change (from the present) and also an added consonant [d]. Given some leveling, there are theoretically two possibilities: the one that occurs, in which the vowel alternations among the present forms are lost, leaving only a vowel alternation between present and preterite. In this case, the vowel alternation now coincides with the major semantic distinction in the paradigm, the tense distinction. The other alternative would be to view the alternations marking the distinction between first person, on the one hand, and second and third, on the other, as the major distinction. In that case, leveling would mean eliminating the distinction between present and preterite in the first person, giving preterite *dode* for first person. Second- and third-person preterite might also become *dedest, dede*. Then the paradigm would be organized as follows:

(6)	1SG	PRS. IND.	*do*
		PRET. IND.	*dode*
	2SG	PRS. IND.	*dest*
		PRET. IND.	*dedest*
	3SG	PRS. IND.	*deth*
		PRET. IND.	*dede*

Such changes apparently do not occur because the person/number forms within tenses or aspects (or moods, for that matter) are more closely related to one another than they are to the same person/number forms in other tenses, aspects, or moods. It is notable that the traditional presentation of a verbal paradigm groups person/number forms together according to tense, aspect, and mood, as in (5), and does not group tense/aspect forms together according to person/number. Also, in the languages of the world, alternations often correspond to tense, aspect, or mood and rarely to person/number distinctions across tense, aspect, or mood (Hooper 1979; Bybee 1985).

To summarize, then, research into the structure and representation of morphological categories and forms has yielded predictions about analogical leveling. There are two usage effects related to the frequency of paradigms and forms within them. First, the low-frequency paradigms tend to level earlier and more readily than high-frequency paradigms, which tend to maintain their irregularities. Second, the higher-frequency forms with a paradigm or subparadigm tend to retain a more conservative form and serve as the basis of the reformation of the forms of lesser frequency. Note further that the fact that paradigms tend to undergo leveling one by one and not as a group indicates that morphophonological alternations are not generated by rule, but rather that each alternation is represented in memory in the forms of the paradigm. The fact that the more frequent forms resist change and serve as the basis of change for lower-frequency forms means that all of these forms are represented in memory, but that the higher-frequency forms have a stronger representation than the lower-frequency forms.

3.4. Analogical Extension

An alternation is said to have undergone extension if a paradigm that previously had no alternation acquires one or changes from one alternation to a different one. For instance, while *cling/clung* and *fling/flung* have had a vowel alternation since the Old English period, the verb *string* which was formed from the noun has only had a vowel alternation, *string/strung*, since about 1590. Similarly, the past of *strike* has had a variety of forms, but most recently, in the sixteenth century, the past was *stroke*, which was replaced by *struck* in the seventeenth century.

As mentioned above, it is popular to describe extensions as if they arose through proportional analogies, such as '*fling* is to *flung* as *string* is to X', where the result of the analogy is of course *strung*. However, there are examples that are very difficult to describe with such formulas. For instance, the original set of verbs that constitute the class to which *string* belongs all had nasal consonants in their codas: *swim, begin, sing, drink*. In the sixteenth and seventeenth centuries, however, *stick/stuck* and *strike/struck* were added to this class. A little later, the past of regular *dig* became *dug*. More recent nonstandard formations are also problematic: *sneak/snuck* and *drag/drug* (both used in my native dialect) present dual problems. First, all of the mentioned items require a stretching of the phonological definition of the class, since originally verbs ending in [k] or [g] without a nasal would not have belonged to the class. Second, *strike, sneak,* and *drag* do not have the vowel [ɪ] in the base form as other members of the class do. The question for proportional analogy would be: what are the first two terms of the proportion that allow *strike/struck* to be the second two terms? Perhaps, *string/strung* is the most similar pair existing at the time, but *strike* has both the wrong vowel and the wrong coda to pair up with *string*.

One solution is to suppose that the requisite categorization is of the past/past participle form, not the base form, nor the relation between the base and the past form. Thus, a schema is formed over the past forms, which have similar phonological shape and similar meaning (Bybee 1985, 1988; Langacker 1987). There is no particular operation specified as to how to derive the past from the base, such as [ɪ] → [ʌ], as such a derivation would not apply to *strike*, *sneak*, or *drag*; rather, there is only the specification of the schema for the past form. Modifications that make a verb fit this schema could be different in different cases (Bybee and Moder 1983). Also, the schema is stated in terms of natural categories; that is, the phonological parameters are not categorical, but rather define family resemblance relations. Since so many members of the class have velar nasals originally, it appears that the feature velar was considered enough of a defining feature of the class that it could appear without the feature nasal, opening the door to extensions to verbs ending in [k], such as *stick* or *strike*, and eventually verbs ending in [ɡ], such as *dig*. A schema defined over a morphologically complex word, such as a past, is a product-oriented schema (Zager 1980; Bybee and Slobin 1982; Bybee and Moder 1983).

All researchers agree that analogical extension is less common than analogical leveling. As with leveling, it is informative to observe the conditions under which extension occurs. Since extension is not very common, the historical record does not provide enough information about the parameters that guide its application. However, recently, experimentation with nonce probe tasks and computer simulations of the acquisition of morphological patterns have provided evidence to supplement the diachronic record. (An example is the experiment of Bybee and Moder 1983, cited above.) These sources of evidence indicate that extension relies on a group of items with at least six members having a strong phonological resemblance to one another. Such a group of words has been called a "gang," and the attraction of new members to the group has been called a "gang effect." Another constraint is that most members of the group should have sufficient frequency to maintain their irregularity, but items of extreme high frequency do not contribute to the gang effect, as they are in general more autonomous, or less connected to other items (Moder 1992). In general, the productivity of a class or gang depends upon the interaction of two factors: the phonological definition of the class and the number of members in the class.

Phonological similarity and type frequency play off one another in the following way: if a class has a high type frequency, then the innovative form does not have to be so similar to the other members of the class; if it has a low type frequency, then the innovative form must be highly similar (Bybee 1995; Hare and Elman 1992, 1995). Note that these parameters predict, correctly, that analogy based on only one form would be quite uncommon. This is another reason that the proportional analogy model is incorrect: proportional analogy requires only one form as the basis of the analogy and thus would predict many extensions that never occur.

Hare and Elman (1995) apply some of these principles to the changes in the English past-tense verb system from the Old English period to the modern period using connectionist modeling. One of their models accounts for the collapse of the subclasses of weak verbs into a single class. The connectionist model is "taught" the weak verb system, but with some "errors" remaining. The resulting not-quite-perfect system then provides input to the next learning epoch. At each epoch, the number of errors or changes in the system increases. Given the factors of type frequency and phonological similarity, the result is the collapse of the four-way distinction among weak verbs in favor of a two-way distinction, which parallels the actual developments at the end of the Old English period through the beginning of the Middle English period. A simulation of the generational transmission of the entire system—both weak and strong verbs—yields similar results. In each case, classes of verbs that are less common and less well defined phonologically tend to be lost.

In the Hare and Elman simulations, the analogical changes come about through imperfect learning, but this does not necessarily imply that children are responsible for initiating and propagating these changes. The simulations merely point out the weak or variable points in the system, and over successive transmissions these points become even weaker. The actual changes in the forms produced could occur in either adults or children.

3.5. Conclusions Concerning Analogy

Analogical changes may be sporadic and appear to be random, but they provide us with a valuable window on the cognitive representation of morphologically complex forms. Since analogy works word by word, we have evidence of the stored representation of morphologically complex words organized into an associative network, rather than a rule-based model. Since frequent words are less subject to analogical leveling, we have evidence for the varying strength of representations. In addition, the workings of analogical extension point to a prototypical organization for classes of words that behave the same.

4. GRAMMATICALIZATION

This section focuses on the importance of grammaticalization for general linguistics, emphasizing the universality of paths of grammaticalization, its unidirectionality, parallel development of form and meaning, and the dramatic increases in frequency of use accompanying grammaticalization.[1]

4.1. Properties of Grammaticalization

Grammaticalization is usually defined as the process by which a lexical item or a sequence of items becomes a grammatical morpheme, changing its distribution and function in the process (Meillet [1912] 1958; Givón 1979; Lehmann 1982; Heine and Reh 1984; Heine, Claudi, and Hünnemeyer 1991a, 1991b; Hopper and Traugott

1993). Thus, English *going to* (with a finite form of *be)* becomes the intention/future marker *gonna.* However, more recently it has been observed that it is important to add that grammaticalization of lexical items takes place within *particular constructions* (Bybee, Perkins, and Pagliuca 1994; Traugott 2003) and further that grammaticalization is the creation of new constructions (Bybee 2003). Thus, *be going to* does not grammaticalize in the construction exemplified by *I'm going to the store* but only in the construction in which a verb follows *to*, as in *I'm going to buy a car.* If grammaticalization is the creation of new constructions (and their further development), then it also can include cases of change that do not involve specific morphemes, such as the creation of word-order patterns.

The canonical type of grammaticalization is that in which a lexical item becomes a grammatical morpheme within a particular construction. Some characteristics of the grammaticalization process are the following:

a. Words and phrases undergoing grammaticalization are phonetically reduced, with reductions, assimilations, and deletions of consonants and vowels producing sequences that require less muscular effort (see sections 2.3–2.5). For example, *going to* [goiŋtʰuw] becomes *gonna* [gənə] and even reduces further in some contexts to [ənə], as in *I'm (g)onna* [aimənə].

b. Specific, concrete meanings entering into the process become generalized and more abstract and, as a result, become appropriate in a growing range of contexts, as in the uses of *be going to* in sentences (7) through (9) below. The literal meaning in (7) was the only possible interpretation in Shakespeare's English, but now uses such as those shown in (8) and (9) are common.

   (7)   MOVEMENT: We are going to Windsor to see the King.
   (8)   INTENTION: We are going to get married in June.
   (9)   FUTURE: These trees are going to lose their leaves.

c. A grammaticalizing construction's frequency of use increases dramatically as it develops. One source of the increased frequency is an increase in the types of contexts in which the new construction is possible. Thus, when *be going to* had only its literal meaning (as in 7), it could only be used in contexts where movement was to take place, with subjects that were volitional and mobile. Now it can be used even in (9), where no movement in space on the part of the subject is implied, or indeed possible. As the *gonna* construction becomes appropriate with more types of subjects and verbs, it occurs more frequently in texts.

d. Changes in grammaticalization take place very gradually and are accompanied by much variation in both form and function. Variation in form is evident in *be going to* and *gonna*. Variation in function can be seen in the three examples above, of 'movement', 'intention', and 'future', all of which are still possible uses in Modern English.

4.2. General Patterns of Grammaticalization

One of the most important consequences of recent research into grammaticalization is the discovery of the universality of the mechanisms of change as well as the particular paths of change that lead to the development of grammatical morphemes and constructions. It is now well documented that in all languages and at all points in history, grammaticalization occurs in very much the same way (Bybee, Perkins, and Pagliuca 1994; Heine and Kuteva 2002). Some well-documented examples follow.

In many European languages, an indefinite article has developed out of the numeral 'one': English *a/an*, German *ein*, French *un/une*, Spanish *un/una*, and Modern Greek *ena*. While these are all Indo-European languages, in each case this development occurred after these languages had differentiated from one another and speakers were no longer in contact. Furthermore, the numeral 'one' is used as an indefinite article in colloquial Hebrew (Semitic) and in the Dravidian languages Tamil and Kannada (Heine 1997). Examples of demonstratives becoming definite articles are also common: English *that* became *the*; Latin *ille*, *illa* 'that' became French definite articles *le*, *la* and Spanish *el*, *la*; in Vai (a Mande language of Liberia and Sierra Leone) the demonstrative *mε* 'this' becomes a suffixed definite article (Heine and Kuteva 2002).

Parallel to English *will*, a verb meaning 'want' becomes a future marker in Bulgarian, Rumanian, and Serbo-Croatian, as well as in the Bantu languages of Africa—Mabiha, Kibundu, and Swahili (Bybee and Pagliuca 1987; Heine and Kuteva 2002). Parallel to English *can* from 'to know', Baluchi (Indo-Iranian), Danish (Germanic), Motu (Papua Austronesian), Mwera (Bantu), and Nung (Tibeto-Burman) use a verb meaning 'know' for the expression of ability (Bybee, Perkins, and Pagliuca 1994). Tok Pisin, a creole language of New Guinea, uses *ken* (from English *can*) for ability and also *savi* from the Portuguese *save* 'he knows' for ability. Latin *potere or *possum* 'to be able' gives French *pouvoir* and Spanish *poder*, both meaning 'can' as auxiliaries and 'power' as nouns. These words parallel English *may* (and past tense *might*), which earlier meant 'have the physical power to do something'. Verbs or phrases indicating movement toward a goal (comparable to English *be going to*) frequently become future markers around the world, found in languages such as French and Spanish, but also in languages spoken in Africa, the Americas, Asia, and the Pacific (Bybee and Pagliuca 1987; Bybee, Perkins, and Pagliuca 1994).

Of course, not all grammaticalization paths can be illustrated with English or European examples. There are also common developments that do not happen to occur in Europe. For instance, a completive or perfect marker—meaning 'have (just) done'—develops from a verb meaning 'finish' in Bantu languages, as well as in languages as diverse as Cocama and Tucano (both Andean-Equatorial), Koho (Mon-Khmer), Buli (Malayo-Polynesian), Tem and Engenni (both Niger-Congo), Lao (Kam-Tai), Haka and Lahu (Tibeto-Burman), Cantonese, and Tok Pisin (Heine and Reh 1984; Bybee, Perkins, and Pagliuca 1994). In addition, the same development from the verb 'finish' has been recorded for American Sign Language, showing that grammaticalization takes place in signed languages the same way as it does in spoken languages (Janzen 1995).

For several of these developments, I have cited the creole language, Tok Pisin, a variety of Melanesian Pidgin English, which is now the official language of Papua New Guinea. Pidgin languages are originally trade or plantation languages that develop in situations where speakers of several different languages must interact, though they share no common language. At first, pidgins have no grammatical constructions or categories, but as they are used in wider contexts and by more people more often, they begin to develop grammar. Once such languages come to be used by children as their first language and thus are designated as creole languages, the development of grammar flowers even more. The fact that the grammars of pidgin and creole languages are very similar in form, even among pidgins that developed in geographically distant places by speakers of diverse languages, has been taken by Bickerton (1981) to be strong evidence for innate language universals. However, studies of the way in which grammar develops in such languages reveals that the process is the same as the grammaticalization process in more established languages (Sankoff 1990; Romaine 1995).

4.3. Paths of Change and Synchronic Patterns

The picture that emerges from the examination of these and the numerous other documented cases of grammaticalization is that there are several highly constrained and specifiable *grammaticalization paths* that lead to the development of new grammatical constructions. Such paths are universal in the sense that development along them occurs independently in unrelated languages. They are also unidirectional in that they always proceed in one direction and can never proceed in the reverse direction. As an example, the following are the two most common paths for the development of future tense morphemes in the languages of the world:

(10) THE MOVEMENT PATH
      movement toward a goal > intention > future
(11) THE VOLITION PATH
      volition or desire > intention > future

The first path is exemplified by the development of *be going to* and the second by *will*.

New developments along such paths may begin at any time in a language's history. In any language we look at, we find old constructions that are near the end of such a path, as well as new constructions that are just beginning their evolution and constructions midway along. Grammar is constantly being created and lost along such specifiable and universal trajectories.

Development along the MOVEMENT PATH begins when a verb or phrase meaning 'movement toward a goal' comes to be used with a verb, as in *They are going to Windsor to see the King.* At first, the meaning is primarily spatial, but a strong inference of intention is also present: *Why are they going to Windsor? To see the King.* The intention meaning can become primary, and from that, one can infer future actions: *He's going to (gonna) buy a house* can state an intention or make a prediction about future actions (see section 6.3).

Such developments are slow and gradual, and a grammaticalizing construction on such a path will span a portion of it at any given time. Thus, English *be going to* in Shakespeare's time could express both the 'change of location' sense and the 'intention' sense. In Modern English, the intention sense is still present, but the future sense is also possible, with no intention or movement implied (*That tree is going to lose its leaves*). As a result of the gradualness of change and the fact that in any particular language a future morpheme might be anywhere on one of these paths, there is considerable cross-linguistic variation in the meaning and range of use of a future morpheme at any particular synchronic period. For this reason, it is very difficult to formulate synchronic universals for grammatical categories such as tense and aspect. It appears instead that the diachronic universals in terms of the paths of change such as (10) and (11) constitute much stronger universals than any possible synchronic statements.

4.4. Conceptual Sources for Grammatical Material

The examples discussed in the preceding sections showed lexical items entering into the grammaticalization process. One of the major cross-linguistic similarities noted in the previous section is that the same or very similar lexical meanings tend to grammaticalize in unrelated languages. Of all the tens of thousands of words in a language, only a small set provides candidates for participation in the grammaticalization process. Are there any generalizations that could be made concerning the members of this set?

Researchers in this area have made some interesting observations about the lexical items that are candidates for grammaticalization. Heine, Claudi, and Hünnemeyer (1991b) have observed that the terms in this set are largely culturally independent, that is, universal to human experience. Furthermore, they represent concrete and basic aspects of human relations with the environment, with a strong emphasis on the spatial environment, including parts of the human body. Thus, we find terms for movement in space, such as 'come' and 'go' in future constructions, and postures, such as 'sit', 'stand', and 'lie' in progressive constructions. The relationship in space between one object and another is frequently expressed in terms of a human body part's relation to the rest of the body. Thus, the noun for 'head' evolves into a preposition meaning 'on top of', 'top', or 'on'. 'Back' is used for 'in back of' (English provides an example of this derivation), 'face' for 'in front of', 'buttock' or 'anus' for 'under', and 'belly' or 'stomach' for 'in' (Heine, Claudi, and Hünnemeyer 1991b: 126–31). In a survey of such relational terms in 125 African languages, Heine and his collaborators found that more than three-quarters of the terms whose etymology was known were derived from human body parts. Svorou (1994), using a sample representative of all the language families of the world, also finds human body parts to be the most frequent sources of relational terms.[2] Less concrete, but nonetheless basic and culturally independent, notions such as volition, obligation, and having knowledge or power also enter into the grammaticalization process.

The relation between locational terms and abstract grammatical concepts has been recognized for several decades. Anderson (1971) proposes a theory of grammatical cases (nominative, accusative, dative, etc.) based on spatial relations. Thus, a relational term meaning 'toward' further develops to mean 'to' whence it can become a dative marker (*I gave the book **to** John*) or can even further develop into an accusative (as in Spanish: *Vi **a** Juan* 'I saw John'). Or, with a verb, 'to' can signal purpose and eventually generalize to an infinitive marker (Haspelmath 1989; see section 7). In this way, even the most abstract of grammatical notions can be traced back to a very concrete, often physical or locational concept involving the movement and orientation of the human body in space.

The claim here is not that the abstract concepts are forever linked to the more concrete, only that they have their diachronic source in the very concrete physical experience. Grammatical constructions and the concepts they represent become emancipated from the concrete and come to express purely abstract notions, such as tense, case relations, definiteness, and so on. It is important to note, however, that the sources for grammar are concepts and words drawn from the most concrete and basic aspects of human experience.

4.5. Grammaticalization as Automatization

Some recent studies of grammaticalization have emphasized the point that grammaticalization is the process of automatization of frequently occurring sequences of linguistic elements (Haiman 1994; Boyland 1996; Bybee 2003). Boyland (1996) points out that the changes in form that occur in the grammaticalization process closely resemble changes that occur as nonlinguistic skills are practiced and become automatized. With repetition, sequences of units that were previously independent come to be processed as a single unit or chunk. This repackaging has two consequences: the identity of the component units is gradually lost, and the whole chunk begins to reduce in form. These basic principles of automatization apply to all kinds of motor activities: playing a musical instrument, playing a sport, stirring pancake batter. They also apply to grammaticalization. A phrase such as *(I'm) going to (VERB)*, which has been frequently used over the last couple of centuries, has been repackaged as a single processing unit. The identity of the component parts is lost (children are often surprised to see that *gonna* is actually spelled *going to*), and the form is substantially reduced. The same applies to all cases of grammaticalization.[3]

5. MORPHOSYNTACTIC CHANGE

5.1. Development of New Constructions

Grammaticalization occurs when a specific instance of a more general construction increases in frequency and takes on new functions. For instance, several movement verbs are appropriate to fit into the following constructional schema of English:

(12) [[MOVEMENT VERB + PROGRESSIVE] + PURPOSE CLAUSE (*TO* + INFINITIVE)]
   a. I am going to see the king.
   b. I am traveling to see the king.
   c. I am riding to see the king.

However, the only instance of this construction that has grammaticalized is the one with *go* in it. The particular example of this construction with *go* in it has undergone phonological, morphosyntactic, semantic, and pragmatic changes that have the effect of splitting the particular grammaticalizing phrase off not only from other instances of *go* but also from other instances of this general construction.

Israel (1996) discusses the development of the *way* constructions (e.g., *Joan made her way home*) out of a more general construction in which an intransitive verb could have an object indicating the path or way, as in *wente he his ride, wente he his strete* ('road, path'), *I ran my way* (examples from Israel 1996: 221). The object in the construction is now restricted to *way*, but the nature of the verb has changed gradually over time. Starting with verbs that indicate the manner of motion (*sweep, creep, winged, speed*, etc.), the construction extended to verbs that indicate the means by which the path is built (*hew out, sheer, plough, dig*, etc.), then also to less direct means to achieving a goal (*fight, battle, write*), and further to incidental activities accompanying the movement whether figurative or literal (*whistle, hum and haw*). The changes are gradual and very local, occurring one verb at a time. Israel (1996: 223) writes, "Long strings of analogical extensions lead to discrete clusters of usage, which then license the extraction of more abstract schemas for the construction."

In other cases of grammaticalization, similar extensions can be observed. The development of *can* as an auxiliary shows it is first used with main verbs indicating understanding, communicating, and some skills. Each of these classes of main verbs expands gradually to encompass a wider range of meaning until all verbs are possible in this construction (Bybee 2003).

5.2. Lexical Diffusion of Constructions

Apparently, all constructions extend their categories gradually, producing an effect that could be called lexical diffusion. The direction of the diffusion resembles that of analogical change in that it proceeds from the least frequent to the most frequent.

In some cases the most frequent instances of a construction retain archaic characteristics so that two means of expressing the same thing exist in a language (Tottie 1991; Ogura 1993). A case studied by Tottie (1991) involves the development of negation expressed by *not* in English. Synonymous pairs of sentences exist in English using two constructions, of which the one with *not* is the more recent and now more productive:

(13) a. He did not see any books.
      b. He saw no books.
(14) a. He did not see anything.
      b. He saw nothing.
(15) a. He did not see it any longer.
      b. He saw it no longer.

Tottie examines a large number of spoken and written texts and finds that the older construction is still used only with very frequent verbs, that is, existential and copular *be*, stative *have*, and the lexical verbs *do, know, give,* and *make*:

(16) At last she got up in desperation. There was no fire and she was out of aspirins.
(17) The Fellowship had no funds.
(18) I've done nothing, except, you know, bring up this family since I left school.
(19) . . . I know nothing about his first wife.

The resistance of particular verb-plus-negative combinations to replacement by the more productive constructions suggests a strong representation of these particular sequences in memory. Even though they are instances of more general constructions, these particular local sequences have a representation that allows them to maintain the more conservative construction. In this case, an understanding of diachrony helps us explain why there are two alternate, synonymous constructions and why they are distributed as they are. It also provides evidence for a strong connection between lexicon and grammar.

5.3. Decategorialization

Decategorialization is the term applied to the set of processes by which a noun or verb loses its morphosyntactic properties in the process of becoming a grammatical element (Heine, Claudi, and Hünnemeyer 1991a; Hopper 1991). In some cases, the lexical item from which a grammatical morpheme arose will remain in the language (*go* retains many lexical uses, despite the grammaticalization of *be going to*), and in other cases, the lexical item disappears and only the grammatical element remains (*can* is grammaticalized, and the main verb from which it developed, *cunnan* 'to know', has disappeared). In both cases, the grammaticalizing element ceases to behave like a regular noun or verb.

Grammatical morphemes typically have more restricted distributions than lexical morphemes. Thus, the process of decategorialization is the result of the freezing of items into specific constructions and their split from other instances of the same item that occur more freely.

Verbs lose canonical verbal properties when they become auxiliaries. Consider the auxiliary *can*, which derives from the Old English main verb *cunnan* 'to know'. In Old English, *cunnan* could be used with a noun phrase object, but today *can* occurs only with a verb complement: **I can that* and **I can her* are ungrammatical. The English modal auxiliaries have lost all their inflected or derived forms and are invariable. There is no infinitive **to can*, no progressive or gerund form **canning*, and the past form of *can*, which is *could*, is developing nonpast uses (*I could do it tomorrow*) and will perhaps lose its function as the past of *can*, just as *should* no longer expresses the past of *shall*. The auxiliaries rarely modify one another. While the use of *shall can* was possible in Middle English, such constructions have disappeared from Modern English. In other words, *can* has no main verb uses.

An example of an erstwhile noun that has lost much of its categoriality is the conjunction *while*, which was previously a noun meaning a length of time. Today it is very limited in its use as a noun. When it is clause-initial and functioning as a conjunction, it has no noun properties. Thus, it does not take articles, nor can it be modified as in (20) (Hopper and Traugott 1993).

(20)   *I was there the same while you were.

In other contexts, its use as a noun is restricted to set phrases such as *all the while*, *a long while*. It cannot be freely used as a noun; thus (21)–(23) are unacceptable.

(21)   *I've been there many whiles.
(22)   *I waited a boring while.
(23)   *The while was very long.

Examples such as these that show the gradual loss of lexical categorial status point to the importance of viewing grammar as organized in gradient categories rather than in discrete ones. This issue is further discussed in section 5.5.

5.4. Loss of Constituent Structure in Grammaticalization

The elements in constructions that are grammaticalizing become more tightly fused together, and the internal constituent structure of the construction tends to reduce. This is a direct result of the chunking process that is associated with automatization of frequently repeated sequences. In this process, two clauses become one, two verb phrases become one, and so on. Two illustrative examples follow.

Heine, Claudi, and Hünnemeyer (1991a) report that in Teso (a Nilo-Saharan language of western Kenya and eastern Uganda) the negative construction (24) derived from a construction with a main clause and subordinate clause, as in (25).

(24)   *mam   petero   e-koto   ekiŋok.*
        not   Peter   3SG-want   dog
        'Peter does not want a dog.'

(25) *e-mam   petero   e-koto   ekiŋok.*
      3SG-is.not   Peter (who) 3SG-want   dog
      'It is not Peter who wants a dog.'

The sentence in (25) consists of the main verb -*mam*, which originally meant 'not to be', with Peter as its object, and a relative clause modifying Peter. In the current construction, as in (24), the verb is grammaticalized to a negative particle and the negative sentence consists of one clause rather than two.

Another interesting case of the reduction of two verb phrases to one occurs in languages that allow serial verb constructions. The following example from Yoruba illustrates this nicely (Stahlke 1970; Givón 1975; Heine and Reh 1984). In (26), there are two verbs that each have direct objects and approximately equal status:

(26) *mo   fi   àdé   gé   igi*
      I   took machete cut tree

This can either be interpreted as 'I took the machete and cut the tree', or, since *fi* is grammaticalizing as an instrumental preposition, it is more likely to be interpreted as 'I cut the tree with the machete'. The fact that the serial verb construction has become a single verb phrase with the grammaticalization of *fi* is underscored by examples such as (27):

(27) *mo   fi   ọgbọ   gé   igi.*
      I   took/with cleverness cut tree
      'I cut the tree cleverly.'

Almost every case of grammaticalization involves such a change in constituent structure. When viewed in terms of a structural analysis of the successive synchronic states, it is tempting to say that a reanalysis has taken place. For example, in the two cases just examined, what was a verb is reanalyzed as an auxiliary in one case and a preposition in the other. In the next section, we discuss reanalysis as a type of linguistic change in grammaticalization and independent of it.

5.5. Reanalysis

In the preceding examples of grammaticalization, one could say that a syntactic reanalysis has taken place since the constituent structure or category labels have changed. But it is important to note that even these reanalyses take place gradually, which means that when grammaticalization is occurring, it may not be possible to uniquely assign elements to particular grammatical categories or structures. Heine (1993) argues that the reason there is so much controversy surrounding the category of auxiliary verb, in that some linguists argue that they are verbs and others argue that they are a separate category, is that auxiliaries derive gradually from verbs and have not always lost all their verbal properties even though they have become grammaticalized. Haspelmath (1998) argues that the gradual changes in category labels that occur in grammaticalization show not so much that reanalysis has taken place, but more that the categories postulated for grammar must be more flexible. If a verb can gradually change into a preposition (as in 26 and 27), then the categories verb and preposition must themselves allow gradience. Thus, the attempt by some researchers (e.g., Harris and Campbell 1995) to reduce grammaticalization to reanalysis denies the importance of usage-based factors and emphasizes the view of grammar as a discrete entity.

Haspelmath (1998) also notes that most examples of reanalysis cited in the literature (including the many cases discussed in Langacker 1977) are also cases of grammaticalization, in that they involve greater fusion of the whole construction, the change from a lexical to a grammatical category, and a change that is irreversible. Thus, it could be said that the main impetus for reanalysis is grammaticalization.

The few cases of reanalysis that seem independent of grammaticalization involve a resegmentation, such as the change of the assignment of the [n] of the English indefinite article in *an ewt* and *an ekename* to the noun, yielding *a newt* and *a nickname*. As is typical of reanalysis, the opposite change also occurred (however, mostly in loan words); for example, *a naperon* became *an apron*. Even a case such as this is not totally independent of grammaticalization, however, since the development of the alternation in the indefinite article was related to its increased grammaticalization. Similarly, the case of the colloquial French interrogative marker *ti*, which developed from the third-person verbal suffix *-t* plus the inverted third singular masculine pronoun *il*, might also be considered a case of grammaticalization since, as Campbell (1999: 233–34) notes, it involves greater cohesion in the phrase.

(28)   *Votre père part-il?*   'Does your father leave?'
(29)   *Votre père par ti?*

The evidence for the reanalysis (since both 28 and 29 are pronounced the same) is the extension of *ti* to contexts where it was not previously appropriate, as in these examples from Campbell (1999: 234):

(30)   *Les filles sont ti en train de dîner?*   'Are the children eating dinner?'
(31)   *Tu vas ti?*   'Are you going?'

Other cases of reanalysis without grammaticalization mentioned in Haspelmath (1998) include the change of prepositions to complementizers, which could also be viewed as a step in the grammaticalization process.

From the point of view of cognitive and functional theory, the whole notion of reanalysis must be considered suspect because it assumes a grammar that allows only one analysis of a structure at any given synchronic stage. However, if the cognitive system allows redundancy and multiple coexisting analyses, then reanalysis is accomplished by adding an alternate analysis to an existing one. This alternate analysis might in successive generations become the only surviving analysis. Thus, *part-il* and other verbs plus *il* might be units of representation highly associated with interrogative, and if the *il* (which reduces to [i]) gradually loses its association with the third-person singular masculine pronoun but retains its association with interrogative, then the change is accomplished without an abrupt change in structure suggested by the term "reanalysis."

6. Semantic Change
in Grammaticalization

....

This section discusses semantic change that accompanies grammaticalization and emphasizes the mechanisms of change that have been proposed to explain semantic change. These mechanisms help us explain why grammatical meaning is abstract and relational as well as highly dependent on context.

6.1. Bleaching or Generalization

As grammatical morphemes develop, they lose specific features of meaning and thus are applicable in a wider range of environments. Haiman's (1994) study of ritualization in language strongly suggests that frequency increases in themselves lead to bleaching through the habituation process (see also Bybee 2003). Just as swear words lose their sting with repetition, so grammaticalizing constructions come to express less meaning as they are used more. As a result, they become applicable in more contexts, and this further depletes their meaning.

It is important to note that bleaching may describe the result of change even when it is not a mechanism in itself. For instance, in the case cited above of the grammaticalization of English *be going to*, the meaning of movement in space is completely lost, and this loss can be described as bleaching. However, the mechanism by which that meaning comes to be lost has been described by some as metaphorical extension (Fleischman 1982; Sweetser 1988) and by others as pragmatic inference. Thus, many of the mechanisms of change in grammaticalization lead to bleaching or generalization of meaning.

6.2. Metaphor as a Mechanism of Change

Many changes of lexical meaning to grammatical meaning involve a metaphorical process (Sweetser 1990). Such a process is identifiable as the transfer of reference from one semantic domain to another while preserving aspects of the structural relations present in the original meaning. Body-part terms used as relational adpositions make excellent examples (Heine, Claudi, and Hünnemeyer 1991b). For instance, the phrase *the head of X* expresses a relation (with reference to humans) between a part of an object that is at the top in relation to the whole object. When this schematic relation is extended to objects other than humans, a metaphorical extension has occurred. Now the meaning of *the head of X* is generalized or bleached, since it is no longer restricted to the domain of the human body.

Typically metaphors express abstract relations in terms of more concrete relations. Thus, the direction of semantic change where metaphor is the mechanism is from concrete to abstract. Metaphorical extension then explains part of the pervasive unidirectionality that characterizes grammaticalization.

Heine, Claudi, and Hünnemeyer (1991a, 1991b) have proposed that metaphorical extensions go through a predictable sequence of domains of conceptualization, as represented in the metaphorical chain in (32). In this chain, any of the domains may serve to conceptualize any other category to its right.

(32)   PERSON > OBJECT > PROCESS > SPACE > TIME > QUALITY

It is possible to document some of these sequences of domains in a single grammaticalization chain, but not all. For instance, OBJECT > SPACE > TIME is a well-documented chain. The English preposition *before*, if we assume that *fore* was once a noun designating the front of an object, came to express the front space and, with the preposition *bi-*, came to express 'space in front of', and later, 'time before'. One problem with this proposal is that it is not certain that the shift from SPACE to TIME takes place by the mechanism of metaphor, since, as we see in the next section, proposals that such shifts are inferential in nature are quite convincing. A second problem is that the last stage of the chain, TIME to QUALITY is not documented in grammaticalization, but rather appears only in lexical shifts, as in the example (33).

(33)   *é   tsí   megbé.* QUALITY
         3SG   remain   behind
         'He is backward/mentally retarded.'

In fact, it appears that metaphorical extension is a more important mechanism of change in lexical semantics than in grammaticalization. The case could be made that pragmatic inferencing, which leads to the conventionalization of implicature, is the primary mechanism for the development of grammatical meaning.

6.3. Inference or Pragmatic Strengthening

A model of grammaticalization in which the only change is that lexical meaning is lost or bleached cannot account for all the changes that are documented. Clear cases exist in which meaning is added into grammaticalizing constructions through pragmatic inferencing. The ability to infer meaning is an important part of the communication process. The speaker is able to say less than he or she means because the addressee is able to infer the part of the meaning that is omitted (Grice 1975). Thus, the addressee is always asking, "Why is she telling me this?" and inferring the speaker's attitude and motivation. When a particular inference is frequently made in connection with a particular construction, that inference can become conventionalized and thus part of the meaning of the construction. Thus, the source of the new meanings that can be accrued in the grammaticalization process is inference-based on the context. Traugott and König (1991) use the following example to illustrate how inferencing can change meaning. In example

(34a), the conjunction *since*, which originally meant 'from the time that', is used in a temporal sense. However, since events described in temporal relation often also have a causal relation, that is, the first event causes the second (as in 34b), and since speakers and addressees are usually less interested in pure temporal sequence and more interested in causes, a causal inference becomes conventionalized as part of the meaning of *since*. As a result, a sentence such as (34b) can have either or both interpretations. In fact, the previously inferred sense can even become independent, leading to sentences such as (34c), which has a purely causal interpretation.

(34)   a. I have done quite a bit of writing since we last met. TEMPORAL
       b. John has been very miserable since Susan left him. TEMPORAL/CAUSAL
       c. I'll have to go alone since you're not coming with me. CAUSAL

This particular change, from temporal to causal, can be documented across languages (Traugott and König 1991), which means that this particular inference, from temporal to causal, may be culturally independent. Thus, some of the unidirectionality and predictability found in paths of grammaticalization may be due to predictable patterns of inferencing.

Traugott (1982, 1989) and Traugott and Dasher (2002) have proposed a general direction for meaning change in grammaticalization from "meanings grounded in more or less objectively identifiable extralinguistic situations to meanings grounded in text-making (for example connectives, anaphoric markers, etc.) to meanings grounded in the speaker's attitude to or belief about what is said" (Traugott and König 1991: 189). This pattern, roughly specifiable as propositional > textual > expressive, represents increased subjectivization in meaning. That is, while linguistic elements and constructions begin by expressing more objective meaning about the world and events, the addressee's tendency to infer textual relations, such as causation, concession, and so on, and the speaker's attitudes or beliefs, leads to the conventionalization of inferences of an increasingly nonobjective nature. Commonly occurring examples are changes from spatial to temporal meaning, changes from demonstratives to personal pronouns, and changes from agent-oriented to epistemic modality.

6.4. Metaphor or Metonymy?

Change from pragmatic inference is considered a metonymic process, since a meaning (from the inference) that is often associated with a construction becomes one of the meanings of the construction. It must be emphasized that the association of the inference with the construction must be frequent enough in use for it to become conventionalized. This type of change, then, is highly dependent upon language use.

The grammaticalization literature of the 1980s and 1990s discusses the relative merits of viewing metaphor or inference as the mechanism in change in grammaticalization. It seems that an important role for metaphor was originally assumed

(Bybee and Pagliuca 1985; Sweetser 1990; Heine, Claudi, and Hünnemeyer 1991a, 1991b), due to the fact that many changes preserve the image-schematic structure of the original meaning. However, once Traugott presented the case for inference or metonymic change, many proposals had to be reexamined.

One problem addressed by Heine, Claudi, and Hünnemeyer (1991b) is that metaphorical extension should be abrupt since it involves a move across domains, while change by inference can be gradual, as the inference gains in frequency and eventually becomes the central meaning of the construction. Heine and his colleagues argue that the gradualness of change points to a major role of context in change and that metonymy may be the gradual mechanism that promotes change, but the result can be described as a metaphorical transfer. It appears, then, that the actual mechanism of change proposed by Heine and his colleagues is change by metonymy or inference.

Note also that some changes cannot be due to metaphorical extension because they do not preserve the image-schematic structure of the original meaning. For instance, a common change involving perfect or anterior marking is that with an inchoative or change of state verb, or a stative verb, the perfect construction takes on present meaning. Thus, in Island Carib, certain stative verbs in the perfective denote a present state. For instance, *lamaali* 'he is hungry' is a perfective form. Similarly, the stative *funatu* 'it is red' becomes the perfective *funaali* 'it has turned red', with inchoative meaning, which, in turn, when said of fruit gives the stative sense 'it is ripe'. Such inferential changes are not restricted to inherently stative predicates, but also apply to the resultative reading of change of state verbs. Thus, for example, *hilaali* 'he has died' can also mean 'he is dead' (Taylor 1956: 24). Similar examples are found in Kanuri, where the perfect suffix *-na* with certain verbs has a present stative interpretation (Lukas [1937] 1967: 43; see also Hutchison 1981: 121–22):

(35) *nŏŋîn*   'I learn, I shall know'
      nŏŋə́nà   'I know (I have learnt)'
      nâmŋĭn   'I (shall) sit down'
      námŋə́nà   'I am seated (I have sat down)'
      ragə́skĭn   'I am getting fond of, I shall like'
      raggskə̀nà 'I like (I have got fond of)'

The change to present meaning from perfect is clearly a result of inference: it would only be relevant to say that he has become hungry if he is still hungry; if the fruit has become ripe, then the implication is that it is now ripe; what I have learned, I now know, and so on. A metaphorical analysis will not apply in this case: the image-schematic structure of entering into a state in no way resembles that of being in a state.

Note also that many changes that appear to result in metaphorical extension probably took place by the conventionalization of implicature. These include changes from the spatial domain to the temporal as well as changes from agent-oriented modality to epistemic.

A change of a *BE GOING TO* construction from spatial to temporal might also be regarded as metaphorical (Fleischman 1982; Sweetser 1988), were it not for clear examples in which the spatial interpretation has an inference of intention, as in this example from Shakespeare (Hopper and Traugott 1993):

(36)   *Duke.* Sir Valentine, whither away so fast?
       Val.   Please it your grace, there is a messenger
               That stays in to bear my letters to my friends,
               And *I am going to deliver them.*
       (1595, Shakespeare, *Two Gentlemen of Verona* III.i.51)

In this example, the explicit meaning of the question is clearly spatial but the implied message of the answer states intention rather than specific location. This answer is quite appropriate, however, because what the Duke really wants to know is Valentine's intention. Thus, rather than a switch directly from a spatial or a temporal meaning, we have a move from the expression of movement in space to the expression of intention. Later, an inferential change can take intention to prediction, that is, future, as in the following example from Coates (1983: 203), which is ambiguous between an intention and a prediction reading. Note that even if intention is what is meant, prediction is implied.

(37)   The National Enterprise Board, which is going to operate in Scotland . . .

Other changes which appear to have metaphorical structure, such as the change from the ability or root possibility reading of *may* to an epistemic reading (Sweetser 1990), can be shown in texts to result from a frequently made inference in clauses without a specific agent (Bybee 1988).

It appears, then, that the most powerful force in creating semantic change in grammaticalization is the conventionalization of implicature, or pragmatic strengthening. The role of metaphor seems to be restricted to lexical change and early stages of grammaticalization, as when body-part terms are used for general spatial relations. Change by inference comes about through the strategies used by speaker and addressee in communicating and is directly related to the extra information that the addressee reads into the utterance. Of course, change by inference only occurs when the same inferences are frequently associated with a particular construction.

7. CONCLUSIONS

The developing view of language change inspired by cognitive and functional considerations is that usage gradually changes with a concomitant change in cognitive representation, which can also be gradual. This contrasts sharply with the view within Generative Grammar that language change is change in the grammar, with change in usage being only incidental (Lightfoot 1979). Croft (2000) presents a theory of language change that is in accord with recent findings in cognitive and functional studies of change. Croft's evolutionary theory of change suggests an analogy with genetic change in which it is the utterance that is replicated in communicative acts. This replication can be "normal" in the sense that exact utterances are replicated, or more commonly, replication is altered. Altered replication leads to the development of contextual variants and the gradual rearrangement of the relation between the conventional structures and their functions. The mechanisms by which utterances undergo altered replication are precisely the mechanisms of change that have been discussed in this chapter. All of the mechanisms discussed here—automatization, gestural reduction, analogical reformation, categorization, metaphorical extension, pragmatic inferencing, generalization—are processes that occur in individual communicative acts. Their frequent repetition and thus cumulative effect is language change, but none of these processes is undertaken with the goal of changing the language. These processes operate like an "invisible hand" (Keller 1994). The audience for the juggler in the plaza does not plan to make a perfect circle; the individuals each have the goal of trying to see better and the circle emerges from these individual acts. Similarly, language users do not plan to change language, but by using language in a multitude of communicative acts, given the processes natural to human beings, language change occurs.

Recent studies in phonology, morphology, and syntax all point to a deep intermixing of grammar and lexicon. Lexical diffusion is shown to operate in all areas; change does not occur in a rule-like fashion in which all items submit to the rule at one time. Rather, change gradually diffuses across the mental representations of language. Here also, usage is important, as shown by the frequency effects that turn up in all domains. High-frequency items and constructions undergo reductive changes quickly, including phonological reduction, syntactic reduction (loss of constituent structure), and semantic change (generalization, etc.). But in the presence of competition from analogy of newer constructions, high-frequency instances hold out: high-frequency verbs resist regularization, and high-frequency instances of constructions (e.g., *I know nothing...*) resist reformulation in the new pattern (*I don't know anything...*). Thus, diachrony provides us with evidence for the interrelation of lexicon and grammar and also with evidence for the nature of the cognitive representation of phonological and grammatical form. In particular, it points to highly specific (though categorized) representations that are constantly changing to reflect details of language use, such as gradual phonological reduction, new inferential meanings, or new contexts of use. These representations also reflect frequency of use in their strength and accessibility as evidenced by resistance to change.

All the changes discussed here have been shown, when viewed up close, to be gradual. This means that all the categories of grammar must be gradient, as gradual change belies the structuralist conceptions of grammar as a closed system consisting of discrete structures. Cognitive Grammar, with gradient categories and immediate responsiveness to changes in usage, provides a model in which change is not only possible, but inevitable.

It is important to remember that grammar is always being created and re-created by language use. Mechanisms of change that create grammar are built into the language ability; they occur synchronically, as language is used. Thus, explanations for linguistic structures must make crucial reference to diachronic change and the mechanisms that propel that change. Moreover, because the mechanisms of change are universal, paths of change are highly similar cross-linguistically and change is typically unidirectional.

8. FUTURE DIRECTIONS

Advances in cognitive and usage-based linguistics have opened up a bright future for the study of language change. For the first time since philology dominated the field of historical linguistics, we have a framework that allows change to be gradual and specific on various dimensions, such as the lexical, phonetic, and morphosyntactic, while at the same time providing general principles of linguistic organization that explain why change moves in certain directions and not others. Future work will surely serve to further clarify the relation between the very specific and the very general in language change largely through the study of the process of lexical diffusion of various types of changes.

At the same time, cognitive views of change need to seek a better integration with the social factors in change, both at the general level of groups of speakers and at the interpersonal level. The latter study is just beginning to come into its own with the rapid development of a new field of historical pragmatics (Traugott and Dasher 2002), but more work needs to be directed toward general social factors in change and their interaction with cognitive factors.

Clearly, reference to cognitive factors brings us closer to explanation in both the diachronic and synchronic realms. In diachrony, it is of utmost importance to emphasize not just the motivation for change, but also the mechanism; that is, in order to establish why changes occur in a certain direction, we also have to understand how changes occur.

NOTES

Parts of section 2 are taken from Bybee (2001) and Bybee (2002b). Parts of sections 4 and 5 are taken from Bybee (2002a).

   1. The terms "grammaticalization" and "grammaticization" will be used interchangeably.

2. The other frequent sources for relational terms are the body parts of livestock and landmarks.

3. Bybee, Pagliuca, and Perkins (1991) and Bybee, Perkins, and Pagliuca (1994) demonstrate for a large cross-linguistic sample a significant relationship between degree of grammaticalization in semantic terms and formal reduction.

REFERENCES

Anderson, John M. 1971. *The grammar of case: Towards a localistic theory.* Cambridge: Cambridge University Press.

Bickerton, Derek. 1981. *Roots of language.* Ann Arbor, MI: Karoma.

Boyland, Joyce Tang. 1996. Morphosyntactic change in progress: A psycholinguistic approach. PhD dissertation, University of California at Berkeley.

Browman, Catherine P., and Louis M. Goldstein. 1990. Tiers in articulatory phonology, with some implications for casual speech. In John Kingston and Mary E. Beckman, eds., *Papers in laboratory phonology I: Between the grammar and physics of speech* 341–76. Cambridge: Cambridge University Press.

Browman, Catherine P., and Louis M. Goldstein. 1992. Articulatory phonology: An overview. *Phonetica* 49: 155–80.

Browman, Catherine P., and Louis M. Goldstein. 1995. Dynamics and articulatory phonology. In Timothy van Gelder and Robert F. Port, eds., *Mind as motion* 175–93. Cambridge, MA: MIT Press.

Bybee, Joan L. 1985. *Morphology: A study of the relation between meaning and form.* Amsterdam: John Benjamins.

Bybee, Joan L. 1988. Semantic substance vs. contrast in the development of grammatical meaning. *Berkeley Linguistics Society* 14: 247–64.

Bybee, Joan L. 1995. Regular morphology and the lexicon. *Language and Cognitive Processes* 10: 425–55.

Bybee, Joan L. 2000a. Lexicalization of sound change and alternating environments. In Michael Broe and Janet Pierrehumbert, eds., *Papers in laboratory phonology*, vol. 5, *Language acquisition and the lexicon* 250–68. Cambridge: Cambridge University Press.

Bybee, Joan L. 2000b. The phonology of the lexicon: Evidence from lexical diffusion. In Michael Barlow and Suzanne Kemmer, eds., *Usage-based models of language* 65–85. Stanford, CA: CSLI Publications.

Bybee, Joan L. 2001. *Phonology and language use.* Cambridge: Cambridge University Press.

Bybee, Joan L. 2002a. Cognitive processes in grammaticalization. In Michael Tomasello, ed., *The new psychology of language: Cognitive and functional approaches to language structure* 2: 145–67. Mahwah, NJ: Lawrence Erlbaum.

Bybee, Joan L. 2002b. Word frequency and context of use in the lexical diffusion of phonetically-conditioned sound change. *Language variation and change* 14: 261–90.

Bybee, Joan L. 2003. Mechanisms of change in grammaticization: The role of repetition. In Richard Janda and Brian Joseph, eds., *Handbook of historical linguistics* 602–23. Oxford: Blackwell.

Bybee, Joan L., and Carol Lynn Moder. 1983. Morphological classes as natural categories. *Language* 59: 251–70.

Bybee, Joan L., and William Pagliuca. 1985. Cross-linguistic comparison and the development of grammatical meaning. In Jacek Fisiak, ed., *Historical semantics, historical word formation* 59–83. The Hague: Mouton.

Bybee, Joan L., and William Pagliuca. 1987. The evolution of future meaning. In Anna Giacolone Ramat, Onofrio Carruba, and Giuliano Bernini, eds., *Papers from the 7th International Conference on Historical Linguistics* 109–22. Amsterdam: John Benjamins.

Bybee, Joan L., William Pagliuca, and Revere D. Perkins. 1991. Back to the future. In Elizabeth Closs Traugott and Bernd Heine, eds., *Approaches to grammaticalization* 1: 17–58. Amsterdam: John Benjamins.

Bybee, Joan L., Revere D. Perkins, and William Pagliuca. 1994. *The evolution of grammar: Tense, aspect, and modality in the languages of the world.* Chicago: University of Chicago Press.

Bybee, Joan L., and Dan I. Slobin. 1982. Rules and schemas in the development and use of the English past tense. *Language* 58: 265–89.

Campbell, Lyle. 1999. *Historical linguistics: An introduction.* Cambridge, MA: MIT Press.

Coates, Jennifer. 1983. *The semantics of the modal auxiliaries.* London: Croom Helm.

COREC. *Corpus oral de referencia del Español contemporáneo.* 1992. Director, Francisco Marcos-Marín. Textual corpus. Universidad Autónoma de Madrid. Online available: http://www.lllf.uam.es/corpus/corpus_lee.html#A.

Croft, William. 2000. *Explaining language change: An evolutionary approach.* London: Longman.

Dressler, Wolfgang. 1977. Morphologization of phonological processes. In Alfonse Juilland, ed., *Linguistic studies offered to Joseph Greenberg* 313–37. Saratoga, CA: Anma Libri.

Dressler, Wolfgang. 1985. *Morphonology: The dynamics of derivation.* Ann Arbor, MI: Karoma.

Fidelholtz, James. 1975. Word frequency and vowel reduction in English. *Chicago Linguistic Society* 11: 200–213.

Fleischman, Suzanne. 1982. *The future in thought and language.* Cambridge: Cambridge University Press.

Francis, W. Nelson, and Henry Kucera. 1982. *Frequency analysis of English usage.* Boston: Houghton Mifflin.

Gilbert, John H., and Virginia J. Wyman. 1975. Discrimination learning of nasalized and non-nasalized vowels by five-, six-, and seven-year old children. *Phonetica* 31: 65–80.

Givón, Talmy. 1975. Serial verbs and syntactic change: Niger-Congo. In Charles N. Li, ed., *Word order and word order change* 47–112. Austin: University of Texas Press.

Givón, Talmy. 1979. *On understanding grammar.* New York: Academic Press.

Greenberg, Joseph. 1966. *Language universals: With special reference to feature hierarchies.* The Hague: Mouton.

Grice, H. Paul. 1975. Logic and conversation. In Peter Cole and Jerry Morgan, eds., *Syntax and semantics*, vol. 3, *Speech acts* 41–58. New York: Academic Press.

Haiman, John. 1994. Ritualization and the development of language. In William Pagliuca, ed., *Perspectives on grammaticalization* 3–28. Amsterdam: John Benjamins.

Hare, Mary, and Jeffrey L. Elman. 1992. A connectionist account of English inflectional morphology: Evidence from language change. *Annual Conference of the Cognitive Science Society* 14: 265–70.

Hare, Mary, and Jeffrey L. Elman. 1995. Learning and morphological change. *Cognition* 56: 61–98.

Harris, Alice, and Lyle Campbell. 1995. *Historical syntax in cross-linguistic perspective.* Cambridge: Cambridge University Press.

Haspelmath, Martin. 1989. From purposive to infinitive: A universal path of grammaticization. *Folia Linguistica Historica* 10: 287–310.

Haspelmath, Martin. 1998. Does grammaticalization need reanalysis? *Studies in Language* 22: 315–51.

Heine, Bernd. 1993. *Auxiliaries: Cognitive forces and grammaticalization.* New York: Oxford University Press.

Heine, Bernd. 1997. *Cognitive foundations of grammar.* New York: Oxford University Press.

Heine, Bernd, Ulrike Claudi, and Friederike Hünnemeyer. 1991a. From cognition to grammar: Evidence from African languages. In Elizabeth Closs Traugott and Bernd Heine, eds., *Approaches to grammaticalization* 1: 149–87. Amsterdam: John Benjamins.

Heine, Bernd, Ulrike Claudi, and Friederike Hünnemeyer. 1991b. *Grammaticalization: A conceptual framework.* Chicago: University of Chicago Press.

Heine, Bernd, and Tania Kuteva. 2002. *World lexicon of grammaticalization.* Cambridge: Cambridge University Press.

Heine, Bernd, and Mechtild Reh. 1984. *Grammaticalization and reanalysis in African languages.* Hamburg: Helmut Buske.

Hoard, James E. 1971. Aspiration, tenseness and syllabiation in English. *Language* 47.133–40.

Hooper, Joan B. 1976a. *Introduction to natural generative phonology.* New York: Academic Press.

Hooper, Joan B. 1976b. Word frequency in lexical diffusion and the source of morphophonological change. In W. Christie, ed., *Current progress in historical linguistics* 96–105. Amsterdam: North Holland.

Hooper, Joan B. 1979. Child morphology and morphophonemic change. *Linguistics* 17: 21–50.

Hooper, Joan B. 1981. The empirical determination of phonological representations. In Terry Myers, John Laver, and John M. Anderson, eds., *The cognitive representation of speech* 347–57. Amsterdam: North Holland.

Hopper, Paul J. 1991. On some principles of grammaticization. In Elizabeth Closs Traugott and Bernd Heine, eds., *Approaches to grammaticalization* 1: 17–35. Amsterdam: John Benjamins.

Hopper, Paul J., and Elizabeth Closs Traugott. 1993. *Grammaticalization.* Cambridge: Cambridge University Press. (2nd ed., 2003)

Hutchison, John. 1981. *The Kanuri language: A reference grammar.* Madison: African Studies Program, The University of Wisconsin.

Israel, Michael. 1996. The *way* constructions grow. In Adele E. Goldberg, ed., *Conceptual structure, discourse and language* 217–30. Stanford, CA: CSLI Publications.

Jakobson, Roman. 1957. *Shifters, verbal categories, and the Russian verb.* Cambridge, MA: Harvard University Russian Language Project.

Janzen, Terry. 1995. The polygrammaticalization of FINISH in ASL. MS, University of Manitoba.

Johnson, Keith. 1997. Speech perception without speaker normalization. In Keith Johnson and John W. Mullennix, eds., *Talker variability in speech processing* 145–65. San Diego, CA: Academic Press.

Keller, Rudi. 1994. *On language change: The invisible hand in language.* London: Routledge.

Kiparsky, Paul. 1971. Historical linguistics. In William Orr Dingwall, ed., *A survey of linguistic science* 576–635. College Park: Linguistics Program, University of Maryland.

Kiparsky, Paul. 1988. Phonological change. In F. Newmeyer, ed., *Linguistics: The Cambridge survey*, Vol. II, 363–415. Cambridge: Cambridge University Press.

Krishnamurti, Bh. 1998. Regularity of sound change through lexical diffusion: A study of s > h > Ø in Gondi dialects. *Language Variation and Change* 10: 193–220.

Kuryłowicz, Jerzy. 1949. La nature des procès dits 'analogiques'. *Acta Linguistica* 5: 15–37.

Labov, William. 1981. Resolving the Neogrammarian controversy. *Language* 57: 267–308.

Labov, William. 1994. *Principles of linguistic change: Internal factors*. Oxford: Basil Blackwell.

Langacker, Ronald W. 1977. Syntactic reanalysis. In Charles Li, ed., *Mechanisms of syntactic change* 59–139. Austin: University of Texas Press.

Langacker, Ronald W. 1987. *Foundations of cognitive grammar*. Vol. 1: *Theoretical prerequisites*. Stanford, CA: Stanford University Press.

Lehmann, Christian. 1982. *Thoughts on grammaticalization: A programmatic sketch*. Arbeiten des Kölner Universalien-Projekt, no. 48. Cologne: Universität zu Köln. (Repr. as *Thoughts on grammaticalization*. Munich: LINCOM, 1995)

Lightfoot, David. 1979. *Principles of diachronic syntax*. Cambridge: Cambridge University Press.

Lipski, John M. 1994. *Latin American Spanish*. London: Longman.

Lukas, Johannes. [1937] 1967. *A study of the Kanuri language: Grammar and vocabulary*. London: Dawsons of Pall Mall, for the International African Institute.

Mańczak, Witold. 1958a. Tendances générales des changements analogiques. *Lingua* 7: 299–325.

Mańczak, Witold. 1958b. Tendances générales des changements analogiques II. *Lingua* 7: 387–420.

Mańczak, Witold. 1978. Les lois du développement analogique. *Linguistics* 205: 53–60.

Mańczak, Witold. 1980. Laws of analogy. In Jacek Fisiak, ed., *Historical morphology* 283–88. Berlin: Mouton de Gruyter.

Meillet, Antoine. [1912] 1958. L'évolution des formes grammaticales. In Antoine Meillet, *Linguistique historique et linguistique générale* 130–48. Paris: Champion. (First published in *Scientia (Rivista di Scienzia)* 12, no. 26, 6)

Moder, Carol Lynn. 1992. Productivity and categorization in morphological classes. PhD dissertation, SUNY at Buffalo.

Moonwomon, Birch. 1992. The mechanism of lexical diffusion. Paper presented at the annual meeting of the Linguistic Society of America, Philadelphia, January 9–12, 1992.

Moore, Samuel, and Albert H. Marckwardt. 1960. *Historical outline of English sounds and inflections*. Ann Arbor, MI: George Wahr.

Mowrey, Richard, and William Pagliuca. 1995. The reductive character of articulatory evolution. *Rivista di Linguistica* 7: 37–124.

Ogura, Meiko. 1993. The development of periphrastic *do* in English: A case of lexical diffusion in syntax. *Diachronica* 10: 51–85.

Ohala, John J. 1981. The listener as a source of sound change. *Chicago Linguistic Society* 17 (parasession): 178–203.

Ohala, John J. 1992. What's cognitive, what's not, in sound change. *Lingua e stile* 28: 321–62.

Ohala, John J. 2003. Phonetics and historical phonology. In Brian D. Joseph and Richard D. Janda, eds., *Handbook of Historical Linguistics* 669–86. Oxford: Blackwell.

Oliveira, Marco Antonio de. 1991. The Neogrammarian controversy revisited. *International Journal of the Sociology of Language* 89: 93–105.

Pagliuca, William. 1982. Prolegomena to a theory of articulatory evolution. PhD dissertation, SUNY at Buffalo.

Pagliuca, William, and Richard Mowrey. 1987. Articulatory evolution. In Anna Giacolone Ramat, Onofrio Carruba and Giuliano Bernini, eds., *Papers from the 7th International Conference on Historical Linguistics* 459–72. Amsterdam: John Benjamins.

Phillips, Betty S. 1984. Word frequency and the actuation of sound change. *Language* 60: 320–42.

Phillips, Betty S. 1998. Word frequency and lexical diffusion in English stress shifts. In Richard M. Hogg and Linda van Bergen, eds., *Historical linguistics 1995*, vol. 2, *Germanic linguistics* 223–32. Amsterdam: John Benjamins.

Pierrehumbert, Janet. 2001. Exemplar dynamics: Word frequency, lenition and contrast. In Joan L. Bybee and Paul Hopper, eds., *Frequency and the emergence of linguistic structure* 137–57. Amsterdam: John Benjamins.

Romaine, Susan. 1995. The grammaticalization of irrealis in Tok Pisin. In Joan L. Bybee and Suzanne Fleischman, eds., *Modality in grammar and discourse* 389–427. Amsterdam: John Benjamins.

Rumelhart, David, and James. L. McClelland. 1986. On learning the past tenses of English verbs: Implicit rules or parallel distributed processing? In James L. McClelland, David Rumelhart, and the PDP Research Group, eds., *Parallel distributed processing: Explorations in the microstructure of cognition*, vol. 2, *Psychological and biological models* 216–71. Cambridge, MA: MIT Press.

Sankoff, Gillian. 1990. The grammaticalization of tense and aspect in Tok Pisin and Sranan. *Language Variation and Change* 2: 295–312.

Schuchardt, Hugo. 1885. *Über die lautgesetze*. Berlin: Verlag von Robert Oppenheim. (Translated by Theo Venneman and Terence H. Wilbur as *On sound laws: Against the Neogrammarians* 1–114. Frankfurt: Athenäum, 1972)

Stahlke, H. 1970. Serial verbs. *Studies in African Linguistics* 1: 60–99.

Stampe, David. 1973. A dissertation on natural phonology. PhD dissertation, University of Chicago.

Svorou, Soteria. 1994. *The grammar of space*. Amsterdam: John Benjamins.

Sweetser, Eve. 1988. Grammaticalization and semantic bleaching. *Berkeley Linguistics Society* 14: 389–405.

Sweetser, Eve. 1990. *From etymology to pragmatics: Metaphorical and cultural aspects of semantic structure*. Cambridge: Cambridge University Press.

Taylor, Douglas. 1956. Island Carib II: Word-classes, affixes, nouns, and verbs. *International Journal of American Linguistics* 22: 1–44.

Tottie, Gunnel. 1991. Lexical diffusion in syntactic change: Frequency as a determinant of linguistic conservatism in the development of negation in English. In Dieter Kastovsky, ed., *Historical English syntax* 439–67. Berlin: Mouton de Gruyter.

Tiersma, Peter. 1982. Local and general markedness. *Language* 58: 832–49.

Traugott, Elizabeth Closs. 1982. From propositional to textual to expressive meanings: Some semantic-pragmatic aspects of grammaticalization. In Winfred. P. Lehmann and Yakov Malkiel, eds., *Perspectives on historical linguistics* 245–71. Amsterdam: John Benjamins.

Traugott, Elizabeth Closs. 1989. On the rise of epistemic meaning in English: An example of subjectification in semantic change. *Language* 65: 31–55.

Traugott, Elizabeth Closs. 2003. Constructions in grammaticalization. In Brian D. Joseph and Richard D. Janda, eds., *Handbook of Historical Linguistics* 624–47. Oxford: Blackwell.

Traugott, Elizabeth Closs, and Richard B. Dasher. 2002. *Regularity in semantic change*. Cambridge: Cambridge University Press.

Traugott, Elizabeth Closs, and Ekkehard König. 1991. The semantics-pragmatics of grammaticalization revisited. In Elizabeth Closs Traugott and Bernd Heine, eds., *Approaches to grammaticalization* 1: 189–218. Amsterdam: John Benjamins.

Van Bergem, Dick. 1995. *Acoustic and lexical vowel reduction.* Studies in language and language use, no. 16. Amsterdam: IFOTT (Instituut voor functioneel onderzoek van taal en taalgebruik).

Vennemann, Theo. 1972. Rule inversion. *Lingua* 29: 209–42.

Wang, William S.-Y. 1969. Competing changes as a cause of residue. *Language* 45: 9–25.

Wang, William S.-Y., ed. 1977. *The lexicon in phonological change.* The Hague: Mouton.

Zager, David. 1980. A real time process model of morphological change. PhD dissertation, SUNY at Buffalo.

Zsiga, Elizabeth Closs 1995. An acoustic and electropalatographic study of lexical and post-lexical palatalization in American English. In Bruce Connell and Amalia Arvaniti, eds., *Phonology and phonetic evidence: Papers in laboratory phonology IV* 282–302. Cambridge: Cambridge University Press. (Also published in Haskins Laboratories Status Report on Speech Research. SR 117/118: 1–14)

Zue, Victor W., and Martha Laferriere. 1979. An acoustic study of medial /t, d/ in American English. *Journal of the Acoustical Society of America* 66: 1039–50.

CHAPTER 37

LEXICAL VARIATION AND CHANGE

STEFAN GRONDELAERS, DIRK SPEELMAN, AND DIRK GEERAERTS

1. INTRODUCTION

The present chapter has a double purpose. First, it introduces the contribution made by Cognitive Linguistics to diachronic lexicology. In doing so, it is complementary to Bybee's chapter 36 of the present *Handbook*, which covers the field of historical linguistics, largely with the exception of lexical and lexicosemantic change. Second, this chapter describes how lexical studies within Cognitive Linguistics are gradually and naturally evolving toward a sociolexicological approach that links up with sociolinguistics. As will be shown, this sociolexicological perspective opens up toward studies of intralinguistic social variation in areas of Cognitive Linguistics other than the lexicon.

This chapter takes the distinction between semasiology and onomasiology as its basic organizing principle. Although it is not fully accepted in canonical (Anglo-Saxon) linguistic terminology, the distinction is traditionally employed in Continental Structural Semantics and the Eastern European tradition of lexicological research. The following quotation from Baldinger (one of the important linguists within European structuralism) illustrates the distinction quite nicely: "Semasiology . . . considers the isolated word and the way its meanings are manifested, while onomasiology looks at the designations of a particular concept, that is, at a multiplicity of expressions which form a whole" (1980: 278). The distinction between semasiology and onomasiology, then, equals the distinction between *meaning* and *naming*: semasiology takes its starting-point in the word as a form and charts the meanings that the word can occur with; onomasiology takes its starting point in a concept or referent and investigates by which different expressions the concept or referent can be designated, or named.

Making use of this distinction, we will first have a look at the contribution made by Cognitive Linguistics to the study of semasiological change—diachronic (lexical) semantics in the narrow sense. We will then chart the field of onomasiology (probably the lesser known of the two subfields of lexicology) and describe the contribution of Cognitive Linguistics to that field. The importance of a sociolexicological approach for the study of onomasiological variation and change is illustrated in the final section, which includes references to sociolinguistic studies at large within Cognitive Linguistics.

2. THE CONTRIBUTION OF COGNITIVE LINGUISTICS TO DIACHRONIC SEMASIOLOGY

There are two ways in which Cognitive Linguistics contributes to diachronic semasiology: by employing such mechanisms of semantic change as metaphor and metonymy, which Cognitive Linguistics has shed new light on, and by exploiting the prototype-based structure of polysemy. For the contribution of metaphor and metonymy, we refer to chapters 8 and 10 of the present *Handbook*. For the importance of the prototypical view on diachronic semasiology, we will present the gist of Geeraerts (1997), which is the most elaborate treatment of the topic so far. (For a broad overview of diachronic semantics, including cognitive approaches next to structuralist and traditional ones, see Blank 1997.)

If a prototypical view is accepted as an adequate model for the description of synchronic categories, specific characteristics of semantic change can be explained as predictions following from that view. It is useful to think of that synchronic prototype structure in terms of the following four features. First, prototypical categories exhibit degrees of typicality; not every member is equally representative of a category. Second, prototypical categories exhibit a family resemblance structure, or more generally, their semantic structure takes the form of a radial set of clustered and overlapping readings concentrating around one or more salient readings. Third, prototypical categories are blurred at the edges; there may be entities whose membership of the category is uncertain, or at least less clear-cut than that of the bona fide members. And fourth, prototypical categories cannot be defined by means of a single set of criterial (necessary and sufficient) attributes.

Although these four characteristics do not necessarily co-occur, they are systematically related. The first and third are extensional in nature and involve category membership, whereas the second and fourth represent an intensional perspective and involve definitions rather than members. Characteristics one and two refer to salience effects and differences of structural weight, whereas three and four focus on flexibility and demarcation problems. (In what follows, we will sometimes use the notion *nonequality* with regard to features one and two and *nondiscreteness* with three and four.) There is obviously much more to be said about the status of the four features and their relations (see Geeraerts, Grondelaers, and Bakema 1994), but for present purposes, this brief overview will suffice. Turning to historical semantics, we can now convert each of the four characteristics of prototypicality into a statement about the structure of semantic change.

Modulations of Core Cases

By stressing the extensional nonequality of lexical semantic structure, prototype theory highlights the fact that changes in the referential range of one specific word meaning may take the form of modulations on the core cases within that referential range. In other words, changes in the extension of a single sense of a lexical item are likely to take the form of an expansion of the prototypical center of that extension. If the referents in the range of application of a particular lexical meaning do not have equal status, the more salient members will probably be more stable (diachronically speaking) than the less salient ones. Changes will then take the form of modulations on the central cases: if a particular meaning starts off as a name for referents exhibiting the features *ABCDE*, the subsequent expansion of the category will consist of variations on that type of referent. The further the expansion extends, the fewer features the peripheral cases will have in common with the prototypical center. A first layer of extensions, for instance, might consist of referents exhibiting features *ABCD*, *BCDE*, or *ACDE*. A further growth of the peripheral area could then involve feature sets *ABC*, *BCD*, *CDE*, or *ACD* (to name just a few).

The Development of Radial Sets

By stressing the intensional nonequality of lexical semantic structure, prototype theory highlights the clustered-set structure of changes of word meaning. This hypothesis shifts the attention from the extensional structure of an individual meaning of a lexical category to the intensional structure of the lexical item as a whole, that is, to the overall configuration of the various readings of the word. The hypothesis suggests that the structure of semasiological change mirrors the synchronic semantic structure of lexical categories, given that the latter involves family resemblances, radial sets, and the distinction between central and peripheral readings. Semasiological change, then, involves the change of prototypically clustered concepts. This general statement can be broken down into two more specific ones. First, the structure of semasiological change as a whole is one of overlapping and interlocking readings; specifically, a novel use may have its starting point in several existing meanings at the same time. Second, there are differences in structural weight among the readings of an item; specifically, there are peripheral meanings that do not survive for very long next to more important meanings that subsist through time.

Semantic Polygenesis

By stressing the extensional nondiscreteness of lexical semantic structure, prototype theory highlights the phenomenon of incidental, transient changes of word meaning. That is to say, the synchronic uncertainties regarding the delimitation of a category have a diachronic counterpart in the form of fluctuations at the boundaries of the item. In Geeraerts (1997: 62–68), a specifically striking example of such fluctuations is discussed under the heading "semantic polygenesis." Semantic polygenesis involves the phenomenon that one and the same reading of a particular lexical item may come into existence more than once in the history of a word, each time on an independent basis. Such a situation involves what may be called extremely peripheral instances of a lexical item: readings that are so marginal that they seem to crop up only incidentally and disappear as fast as they have come into existence. Specifically, when the same marginal meaning occurs at several points in time that are separated by a considerable period, we can conclude that the discontinuous presence of that meaning is not due to accidental gaps in the available textual sources, but that the meaning in question must actually have come into existence independently at the two moments.

Semantic Change from Subsets

By stressing the intensional nondiscreteness of lexical semantic structure, prototype theory highlights the encyclopedic nature of changes in word meaning. That is to say, diachronic semantics has little use for a strict theoretical distinction between the level of senses and the level of encyclopedic knowledge pertaining to the entities that fall within the referential range of such senses. In semantic change, the encyclopedic information is potentially just as important as the purely semantic senses (to the extent, that is, that the distinction is to be maintained at all). This view follows from a prototype-theoretical conception in general, and from the fourth feature mentioned above in particular, in the following way. If the meaning of a lexical item (or a specific meaning within a polysemous item) cannot be defined by means of a single set of necessary features that are jointly sufficient to distinguish the category from others, the definition necessarily takes the form of a disjunction of clustered subsets. If, for instance, there is no feature or set of features covering *ABCDE* in its entirety, the category may be disjunctively defined as the overlapping cluster of, for instance, the sets *ABC*, *BCD*, and *CDE* (and, in fact, others). Similarly (turning from a description based on an extensional perspective to a description undertaken from an intensional perspective), if no single combination of features yields a classical definition of a category, it can only be properly defined as a disjunction of various groupings of the features in question.

From a diachronic point of view, this means that semantic changes may take their starting point on the extensional level just as well as on the intensional level, or in the domain of encyclopedic information just as well as in the realm of semantic information. Even where a classical definition *is* possible, extensional subsets or intensional features with an "encyclopedic" rather than a "semantic" status may play a crucial role in processes of semantic change. That is to say, semantic extensions may start from a typical or otherwise salient example of a category, rather than from a "meaning" in the traditional sense.

To round off the overview, it should be stressed that the aspects of semantic change enumerated here were not necessarily brought to diachronic semantics by prototype theory or Cognitive Linguistics alone. What is indubitably new, however, is the fact that these known aspects of change can now be incorporated into a global model of lexical semantic structure. That is to say, from a descriptive point of view the importance of prototype theory probably resides less in the novelty of its observations, taken separately, than in the fact that it brings them together in an overall model of the structure of lexical meaning.

Further, of the four prototype-based mechanisms of change, the second has enjoyed most theoretical attention. Detailed examples of all types may be found in Geeraerts (1997). The radial set structure of semantic change is acknowledged and exemplified in Dirven (1985), Lewandowska-Tomaszczyk (1985), Casad (1992), Evans (1992), Goossens (1992), Nerlich and Clarke (1992), Rudzka-Ostyn (1992), Anstatt (1995), Dekeyser (1996), Kronenberg (1996), Maffi (1996), Cuyckens (1999), Soares da Silva (1999), De Mulder and Vanderheyden (2001), Eckardt (2001), Tissari (2001), Koivisto-Alanko (2002), and many other studies. The application of the model to the evolution of grammatical rather than lexical categories is illustrated, among others, by Winters (1989, 1992a, 1992b), Melis (1990), Nikiforidou (1991), Kemmer (1992), Luraghi (1995), Cook (1996), and Aski (2001); see also De Mulder (2001).

3. FROM SEMASIOLOGY
TO ONOMASIOLOGY

Given that Cognitive Linguistics is strongly involved with categorization as a basic cognitive function, a shift from the semasiological to an onomasiological perspective is a natural one: from the point of view of the speaker, the basic act of categorization is, after all, the onomasiological choice of a category to express a certain idea. So, what are the contributions of Cognitive Linguistics to onomasiological research? Before we can answer that question, we first have to chart the field of onomasiological research. Apart from the distinction between synchrony and diachrony, the conceptual map of onomasiology should be based on at least the following four distinctions: the distinction between *structural and pragmatic onomasiology*, the distinction between *the qualitative and the quantitative aspects* of lexical structures, the distinction between *referential and nonreferential types of meaning*, and the distinction between *lexicogenetic mechanisms and sociolexicological mechanisms*.

Structural and Pragmatic Onomasiology

The two elements that make up Baldinger's description of onomasiology (see the quotation at the beginning of this chapter) are not equivalent. On the one hand, studying "a multiplicity of expressions which form a whole" (1980: 278) leads directly to the *traditional, structuralist conception of onomasiology*, that is, to the study of semantically related expressions (as in lexical field theory or the study of the lexicon as a relational network of words interconnected by links of a hyponymical, antonymical, synonymous nature, etc.). On the other hand, studying "the designations of a particular concept" (1980: 278) opens the way for a *contextualized, pragmatic conception of onomasiology*, involving the actual choices made for a particular name as a designation of a particular concept or a particular referent. This distinction can be further equated with the distinction between an investigation of *structure* and an investigation of *use*, or between an investigation of *langue* and an investigation of *parole*.

Qualitative and Quantitative Aspects

The distinction between what may roughly be described as the *qualitative* versus the *quantitative* aspects of linguistic semantic structure may be introduced by considering semasiological structures first. Qualitative aspects of semasiological structure involve the following questions: which meanings does a word have, and how are they semantically related? The outcome is an investigation into polysemy, and the relationships of metonymy, metaphor, and the like that hold between the various readings of an item. Quantitative aspects of lexical structure, on the other hand, involve the question whether all the readings of an item carry the same *structural weight*. The semasiological outcome of a quantitative approach is an investigation into prototypicality effects of various kinds, as described above.

The distinction between qualitative and quantitative aspects of semantic structure transfers easily into the realm of onomasiology. The qualitative question then takes the following form: what kinds of (semantic) relations hold between the lexical items in a lexicon (or a subset of the lexicon)? The outcome is an investigation into various kinds of lexical structuring: field relationships, taxonomies, lexical relations such as antonymy, and so on. The quantitative question takes the following onomasiological form: Are some categories cognitively more salient than others; that is, are particular categories more likely to be chosen for designating things out in the world than others? Are certain lexical categories more obvious names than others? This type of "quantitative" research is relatively new. The best-known example to date is Berlin and Kay's basic-level model (Berlin and Kay 1969; Berlin 1978), which involves the claim that there exists a particular taxonomic level which constitutes a preferred, default level of categorization. The basic level in a taxonomy is the level that is (in a given culture) most naturally chosen as the level where categorization takes place; it has, in a sense, more structural weight than the other levels (see also Schmid, this volume, chapter 5).

The relationship between this type of "quantitative" onomasiology and the pragmatic perspective mentioned in the previous distinction probably does not need further clarification. A particular onomasiological structure (like a level in taxonomy) can be identified as a preferred level of categorization only by taking into account the pragmatic perspective, that is, the actual choices language users make from among a set of alternative possibilities.

Referential and Nonreferential Types of Meaning

The distinction between *referential* (denotational) and *nonreferential* (connotational) aspects of meaning will be clear enough in itself. It involves the distinction between the descriptive aspects of lexical expressions (the contribution they can make to the propositional content of sentences) and their *emotive, stylistic,* or *discursive* value. Although there is a general bias in lexical semantics toward the study of referential rather than nonreferential meanings, this relative lack of attention is to be specifically regretted from an onomasiological perspective, because the ties between nonreferential meaning and onomasiology are perhaps even stronger than those between nonreferential meaning and semasiology.

In fact, the very definition of nonreferential meaning involves the concept of onomasiological alternatives. Indeed, we invoke the notion of nonreferential meaning precisely when a word's communicative value differs from that of a referential synonym or when its communicative value cannot be defined in referential terms. The latter case involves the meaning of expressions like *Hello!* What this expression does (i.e., to perform the speech act of greeting) cannot be defined in purely referential terms; the expression does not describe a state of affairs or a process, but it performs an action. In the same way, the word *yuck* does not describe aversion, but expresses it. In cases such as these, we say that *hello* has a discursive meaning or that *yuck* has an emotive meaning. The words *dead* and *deceased* or *departed*, on the other hand, do have an identifiable referential value. At the same time, their communicative value is not identical: *deceased* and *departed* are less straightforward and slightly more euphemistic than *dead*—that is to say, although their referential values are equivalent, they differ in nonreferential value.

Crucially, the distinction between referential and nonreferential meaning leads to the identification of the sociostylistic value of words. For instance, the introduction of the loan word *Computer* into German initially involves the spread of the concept 'computer'. What lies behind this simultaneous introduction of a conceptual and a lexical innovation is a common expressive need on the part of the language users; that is, the driving force behind the spread of the concept 'computer' and the word *Computer* is basically just the growing familiarity of language users with this new piece of equipment. However, when the word *Rechner* is introduced as an alternative term for *Computer*, the concept 'computer' is already in place. Now, in order to get a grip on the factors behind the competition between *Computer* and *Rechner*, we have to take into account their nonreferential values as well, that is, the differences they exhibit in terms of their stylistic value, which may determine the preference for one or the other term. These values will necessarily have to include the sociolinguistic distribution of *Computer* and *Rechner*: if it turns out that one or the other is preferred because it belongs to a prestigious variety of the language, then this sociolinguistic characterization of the item will go into its nonreferential meaning. Note that sociolinguistics as referred to here is to be taken in the broadest possible sense: whether a word is typical of a learned register, of a rural dialect, of an expert jargon, of a trendy youth culture, or of an upper-class sociolect are all aspects of its sociolinguistic character, and this sociolinguistic character is part and parcel of its nonreferential meaning. This implies, in other words, that the nonreferential value of lexical items involves not just their emotive, stylistic, or discursive value, as mentioned above, but their variational value at large, including all possible kinds of sociolinguistic characteristics.

Lexicogenetic and Sociolexicological Mechanisms

In light of the foregoing, it is now a relatively straightforward matter to explain the difference between lexicogenesis and sociolexicology. *Lexicogenesis* involves the mechanisms for introducing new "word form–word meaning" pairs—all the traditional mechanisms, in other words, such as word-formation, word creation (the creation of entirely new roots), borrowing, blending, truncation, ellipsis, folk etymology, and others, which introduce new items into the onomasiological inventory of a language. Crucially, the semasiological extension of the range of meanings of an existing word is itself one of the major mechanisms of onomasiological change—one of the mechanisms, that is, through which a concept gets encoded by a lexical expression. In this sense, the study of onomasiological changes is more comprehensive than the study of semasiological changes, since the former encompasses the latter.

Traditionally, lexicogenetic mechanisms are sometimes discussed as if triggered by language as such. We might say, for instance, that German borrows *Computer* from English. But the language as such is obviously not an anthropomorphic agent: what happens is that individual language users act in a specific way (say, by using a loan word) and that these individual acts lead to changes at the level of the language as a whole—that is, at the level of the speech community. This phenomenon has revealingly been described by Keller (1990), who suggests that linguistic change may be characterized as an "invisible hand" process—a notion he borrowed from economics. As such, changes spread through a linguistic community as if guided by an invisible force, whereas the actual process involves a multitude of communicative acts.[1] The invisible hand metaphor, however, stops short of indicating precisely how the transition from the individual level to the global level occurs. What exactly are the mechanisms that enable the cumulative effects? Logically speaking, two situations may occur: either the changes work in parallel, or they take place serially. The first situation occurs when members of a speech community are confronted with the same communicative, expressive problem and independently choose the same solution. The introduction of *Computer* as a loan from English into German (and many other languages) may at least to some extent have proceeded in this way. More or less simultaneously, a number of people face the problem of giving a name to the new thing in their native language; independently of each other, they then adopt the original name that comes with the newly introduced object. The second type occurs when the members of a speech community imitate each other. For instance, when one person introduces a loan word, a few others may imitate him or her, and they in turn may be imitated by others, and so on. In the same way, the overall picture of a traffic jam is one in which a great number of cars appear to be halted by an invisible hand, while what actually happens is a cumulative process of individual actions: when the first car brakes to avoid a dog running over the highway, the car behind it has to slow down to avoid an accident, and so on.

Studying how onomasiological changes spread through a speech community is typically an aspect of *sociolexicology*, as it is meant here: in addition to identifying onomasiological mechanisms along traditional lexicogenetic lines, we need to study how these mechanisms are put to work and how they may lead to overall changes in the habits of the language community. In short, classifications of lexicogenetic mechanisms merely identify the space of *possible* or *virtual* onomasiological changes; sociolexicology studies the *actual* realization of the changes. Needless to say, the latter approach coincides with the pragmatic perspective (it concentrates on the actual onomasiological choices made by language users), and it crucially involves all the nonreferential values mentioned above (as factors that may influence these choices).

4. The Contribution of Cognitive Linguistics to Onomasiology

Various approaches in lexical semantics have contributed in different ways to the study of onomasiology. *Prestructuralist semantics*—apart from coining the term *onomasiology* itself (Zauner 1903)—has introduced some of the basic terminology for describing lexicogenetic mechanisms. Although basically concerned with semasiological changes, the major semasiological treatises from Bréal (1897) and Paul (1880) to Stern (1931) and Carnoy (1927) do not restrict themselves to strictly semasiological mechanisms like metaphor and metonymy, but also devote attention to mechanisms of onomasiological change like borrowing or folk etymology. Characteristically, there is a certain degree of overlap among the overviews given by Kronasser (1952) and Quadri (1952) of semasiological and onomasiological research, respectively. Attempts to classify lexicogenetic mechanisms continue to the present day. Different proposals may be found in the work of, among others, Dornseiff (1966), Tournier (1985), Zgusta (1990), and Grzega (2002). It lies beyond the scope of the present chapter to systematically compare these proposals, but it may be noted that there is no single, universally accepted classification.

Structuralist semantics makes two important contributions to onomasiology. First, it insists, in the wake of Saussure himself, on the distinction between semasiology and onomasiology. In the realm of diachronic linguistics, this shows up in Ullmann's (1951, 1962) classification of semantic changes and in Baldinger's (1964) argumentation for studying the interplay between semasiological and onomasiological changes. More importantly, the bulk of (synchronic) structuralist semantics is devoted to the identification and description of different onomasiological structures in the lexicon, such as lexical fields, taxonomical hierarchies, lexical relations like antonymy and synonymy, and syntagmatic relationships. From the point of view of the classification presented above, structuralist semantics is mainly situated within the field of "qualitative" synchronic onomasiology: it concentrates on onomasiological structures within the (synchronic) lexicon. Second, structuralist semantics has identified one of the possible explanatory factors for onomasiological change, namely, homonymic clashes (Gilliéron and Roques 1912). Gilliéron claims that homonymy is a pathological situation that calls for curative devices, namely, the therapeutic elimination of one of the homonyms. The principle of avoidance of homonymy derives from the idea that there exists an isomorphism between the form and the content of natural languages, a principle that is summarized in the maxim "one form, one meaning." Although this isomorphic principle is presented as a structural cause for change, the most realistic way of interpreting it is to accept that it ultimately relies on communicative mechanisms: in some communicative situations, homonymy may lead to difficulties of understanding, and such homonyms may eventually be avoided by the language users. In this respect, avoidance of homonymy may be considered a first example of a pragmatic perspective in onomasiology.

There are at least four important contributions that *Cognitive Semantics* has made to onomasiological research:

a. Cognitive Semantics has drawn the attention to a number of "qualitative" onomasiological structures that did not come to the fore in the structuralist tradition. This holds true, on the one hand, for the development of the Fillmorean frame model of semantic analysis (Fillmore 1977, 1985; Fillmore and Atkins 1992; Cienki, this volume, chapter 7). On the other hand, the seminal introduction of conceptual metaphor research in the line of Lakoff and Johnson (1980) (see also Grady, this volume, chapter 8) can be seen as the identification of figurative lexical fields: the ensembles of near-synonymous metaphors studied as conceptual metaphors constitute fields of related metaphorical expressions (just like ordinary semantic fields consist of ensembles of near-synonymous lexical items).

b. Cognitive Semantics introduces a "quantitative" perspective into the study of onomasiological structures. As mentioned above, basic-level research in the line of Berlin and Kay introduces the notion of salience (which is well known in Cognitive Semantics through the semasiological research into prototypicality) into the description of taxonomical structures: basic levels are preferred, default levels of categorization. Further research (Geeraerts, Grondelaers, and Bakema 1994) has established that the concept of onomasiological salience may be further refined: their notion of entrenchment, defined over individual concepts rather than taxonomic levels, is a generalization of the notion of onomasiological salience as represented by the notion of basic level (see Schmid, this volume, chapter 5).

c. Cognitive Semantics introduces a "quantitative" perspective into the study of lexicogenetic mechanisms. Within the set of lexicogenetic mechanisms, some could be more salient (i.e., might be used more often) than others. Superficially, this could involve, for instance, an overall preference for borrowing rather than morphological productivity as mechanisms for introducing new words, but from a cognitive semantic perspective, there are other, more subtle questions to ask: do the way in which novel words and expressions are being coined reveal specific (and possibly preferred) ways of conceptualizing the onomasiological targets? An example of this type of research (though not specifically situated within a cognitive semantic framework) is Alinei's work (e.g., 1996) into the etymological patterns underlying the European dialects: he argues, for instance, that taboo words in the European dialects may be motivated either by Christian or Islamic motifs or by pre-Christian, pre-Islamic heathen motifs; the quantitative perspective then involves the question whether one of these motifs is dominant or not. Within Cognitive Semantics properly speaking,

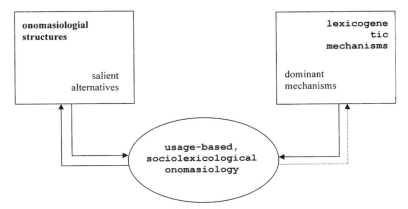

Figure 37.1. The central position of usage-based onomasiology

this type of approach is represented by the search for dominant (or even universal) conceptual metaphors for a given domain of experience. A case in point is the work of Kövecses (1990; 2000). On a broader scale, the etymological research project described by Koch and Blank (Koch 1997; Blank and Koch 1999) intends to systematically explore motivational preferences in the etymological inventory of the Romance languages. In comparison with much of the metaphor-based research, the approach put forward by Blank and Koch takes into account all possible pathways of lexicalization (and not just metaphor).

d. Cognitive Semantics highlights the crucial role of a usage-based socio-lexicological approach to the study of lexical change. Onomasiological change cannot be understood unless we take into account pragmatic onomasiology: changes are always mediated through the onomasiological choices made at the level of usage. Words die out because speakers refuse to choose them, and words are added to the lexical inventory of a language because some speakers introduce them and others imitate these speakers; similarly, words change their value within the language because people start using them in different circumstances. Lexical change, in other words, is the output of processes that are properly studied in the context of pragmatic onomasiology. To repeat a point made earlier, this pragmatic, usage-based perspective automatically takes the form of a socio-lexicological investigation: in choosing among existing alternatives, the individual language user takes into account their sociolinguistic, nonreferential value, and conversely, the expansion of a change over a language community is the cumulative effect of individual choices. In this sense, it is only through an investigation into factors determining these individual choices that we can get a grasp on the mechanisms behind the invisible hand of lexical change.

The overall structure, then, of onomasiological research within Cognitive Linguistics looks as in figure 37.1.

Within each box, the boldface captions identify the "qualitative" aspects, whereas the other captions identify the "quantitative" approaches. The arrows pointing away from the boxes indicate that both boxes constitute input for the processes that play at the pragmatic level: an act of naming may draw from the potential provided by the lexicogenetic mechanisms, or it may consist of choosing among alternatives that are already there. The arrows pointing toward the boxes indicate how the pragmatic choices may lead to change. These processes will primarily affect the actual synchronic structures, through the addition or removal of senses or items, shifts in the variational value of expressions, or changes in the salience of certain options. Secondarily (hence the dotted arrow), a change may affect the lexicogenetic mechanisms, for instance, when a particular lexicalization pattern becomes more popular.

Onomasiological research at the usage level, in other words, is central to the whole onomasiological enterprise: it mediates between what is virtual and what is actual; it combines the traditional qualitative approaches and the recent quantitative innovations; it naturally includes an interest in the nonreferential, variational values of lexical items; and it makes the invisible hand visible. So how could we make the usage-based sociolexicological approach more concrete?

5. SOCIOLEXICOLOGY AND BEYOND

Central to a sociolexicological approach is the distinction between "conceptual" and "formal" onomasiological variation. Whereas conceptual onomasiological variation involves the choice of different conceptual categories, formal onomasiological variation merely involves the use of different names for the same conceptual category. The names *jeans* and *trousers* for denim leisure wear trousers—to give an example—constitute an instance of conceptual name variation, because they represent different categories; *jeans* and *blue jeans*, however, represent no more than different (but synonymous) names for the same category. In what follows, we will briefly present two case studies of what a quantitative, usage-based sociolexicological approach might look like. We will first present an example of contextual influence on conceptual onomasiological variation. The second case study not only concentrates on formal onomasiological variation, it also introduces the diachronic perspective. The studies presented here concentrate on synchronic variation and short-term lexical changes. Similar studies, starting from cognitive semantic models or taking a sociolexicological perspective, have been devoted to long-term onomasiological changes: Dekeyser (1990, 1991, 1995, 1998), Geeraerts (1999), and Molina (2000).

Table 37.1. Hyperonymy ratios in the naming of cancer in
Knack 1991–94 and *De Volkskrant* 1994

	−*medical*	+*medical*	*Total*
+personal	0.878	0	0.837
	(36/41)	(0/2)	(36/43)
−personal	0.296	0.127	0.147
	(8/27)	(26/204)	(34/231)
Total	0.647	0.126	0.255
	(44/68)	(26/206)	(70/274)

5.1. A Case Study of Conceptual Onomasiological Variation

Grondelaers and Geeraerts (1998) investigate how avoidance strategies influence the choice of cancer designations. More particularly, they are interested in finding out how the emotive value of, on the one hand, generic or specific cancer terms such as *cancer* or *breast cancer* and, on the other, vague terms such as *disease* or *illness* influence lexical choice; it is indeed to be expected that in some contexts the vaguer terms will be preferred for euphemistic reasons. To that effect, they investigated a CD-ROM text corpus consisting of the 1991–94 volumes of the Belgian weekly *Knack* and the 1994 edition of the Dutch quality newspaper *De Volkskrant*. In particular, they looked for quantitative support for the hypothesis that vague terms for cancer are favored in nonscientific contexts, namely, articles which do not or do not primarily report on medical topics, and in personalized contexts, that is, contexts in which the effects of cancer on individual patients are depicted (in contrast with generic contexts, in which cancer is referred to in general). The dependent variable in this study is lexical specificity in the naming of cancer, which is quantified as the ratio between the frequency of hyperonymous designations for cancer (such as *disease* or *illness*) and the overall frequency with which the disease cancer is mentioned (by means of various lexical items) in the sources.

Table 37.1 contains the hyperonym ratios in the naming of cancer in the Belgian weekly *Knack* and the Dutch newspaper *De Volkskrant*. This table distinguishes vertically between personalized contexts and generic contexts and horizontally between medical and nonmedical texts. As predicted, average hyperonym ratios are indeed significantly higher in nonmedical contexts (0.647 > 0.126) and personalized contexts (0.837 > 0.147), which seems to confirm the hypothesis.

A methodological problem which complicates the identification of avoidance factors—and contextual factors in general—is the fact that the same variational pattern may be caused by more than one factor. In the cancer example, the predominance of vague designations in nonmedical contexts could just as well be due

Table 37.2. Absolute and relative frequency of different
taxonomical ranks in the naming of specific
types of cancer in *Knack* 1991–94 and
De Volkskrant 1994

	−medical	+medical
Unique beginner	22	23
	(61.12%)	(13.45%)
Generic	2	16
	(5.5%)	(9.36%)
Specific	12	132
	(33.33%)	(77.19%)

to an upward shift of the taxonomical basic level as a result of the irrelevance of medical detail in articles which are not primarily concerned with scientific progress.

Table 37.2, however, constitutes additional evidence in favor of a taboo-related explanation of the asymmetrical distribution of hyperonymy in table 37.1. Table 37.2 charts absolute and relative frequencies of different taxonomical ranks in the designation of specific types of cancer, such as breast cancer or lung cancer. On the vertical axis, unique beginners such as *disease* or *disorder* are contrasted with the generic item *cancer* and specific terms like *breast cancer* or *lung cancer*. Now, if it is the absence of technicality which engenders an increased use of hyperonymy in nonmedical contexts, this increase would affect both the generic level and the unique beginner level in roughly the same way. In other words, unlike the medical context, the nonmedical context would show an increase of hyperonymy, but this increase would be comparable on both the generic and the unique beginner level. The table, however, shows that the generic level and the unique beginner level are affected differently, in that increased hyperonymy almost exclusively affects the unique beginner level. There is, in other words, a tendency to "jump over" the generic level. This avoidance of the generic term can best be explained in light of the fact that the generic term *cancer* is still specific enough to cause offense; it would be difficult to explain as the result of decreased technicality alone.

5.2. A Case Study in Formal Onomasiological Variation

Dutch basically comes in two varieties: Dutch as used in the Netherlands and Dutch as used in the Flanders region of Belgium (sometimes referred to as Flemish). The situation of the standard language in both countries is somewhat different. In Flanders, the standardization process that started off (as in most European countries) in the Early Modern Period was slowed down as a result of Flanders's political separation from the Netherlands during the Eighty Years' War. Standard Dutch developed in the Netherlands in the course of the seventeenth century, but as Flanders was politically separated from the Netherlands, remaining under foreign (Spanish or Austrian) rule, it did not link up with this process of standardization. Rather, French was used more and more as the language of government and high culture, a practice that received an important impulse after the birth of the Belgian state in 1830. Dutch then survived basically in the form of a variety of Flemish dialects. However, as a result of a social and political struggle for the emancipation of Flanders and the Flemish-speaking part of the Belgian population, Dutch again gained ground as a standard language (the language of learning, government, and high culture) in Flanders. This process started somewhat hesitantly in the late nineteenth century as a typically romantic movement, gained momentum during the first half of the twentieth century, and finally made a major leap after World War II and during the booming 1960s. Still, most linguists agree that the standardization process has not yet reached its final point, or at least, that the level of standardization has not reached the same height as in the Netherlands.

The latter observation is the starting point for the research reported on in Geeraerts, Grondelaers, and Speelman (1999): Can we quantify the relationship between Belgian Dutch and Netherlandic Dutch (and the internal stratification of both varieties)? Can we calculate how close or how distant both varieties of Dutch are with regard to each other? In Geeraerts, Grondelaers, and Speelman (1999), a measure of lexical overlap was developed, based on the notions *onomasiological profile* and *uniformity*.

The *onomasiological profile* of a concept in a particular source is the set of synonymous names for that concept in that particular source, differentiated by relative frequency. Table 37.3 contains the onomasiological profiles for the concept "*overhemd*" 'shirt' in the Belgian and the Netherlandic 1990-database:

Uniformity is a measure for the correspondence between two onomasiological profiles. Our computation of uniformity has its starting point in the idea that a common language norm triggers uniform linguistic behavior. In its most extreme form, lexical uniformity in the naming of a concept obtains when two language varieties have an identical name for that concept, or several names with identical frequencies in the two varieties. Much more frequent than these examples of "ideal" uniformity, however, are such partial correspondences as illustrated in table 37.3. Let us, for the sake of illustration, assume that the relative frequencies in table 37.3

Table 37.3. Onomasiological profiles for the concept '*overhemd*' 'shirt' in the Belgian and Netherlandic data (1990)

	B90	*N90*
hemd	31 %	17 %
overhemd	69 %	46 %
shirt	0 %	37 %

represent 100 actual naming instances in each of both profiles, rather than percentages. The partial overlap between the profiles in table 37.3 is quantified by counting the naming instances for which there is a counterpart in the other profile. In the ideal scenario outlined above, each of the 100 naming events in each of both profiles has its counterpart in the other profile, yielding a maximal uniformity of 100%. In table 37.3, however, 14 instances of *hemd* in B90 have no counterpart in N90; 23 Belgian *overhemden* have no Netherlandic counterpart; and there are no Belgian counterparts for the 37 Netherlandic *shirts*. On the grand total of 200 naming events in the two profiles, only $200 - (14 + 23 + 37) = 126$ instances have counterparts in the other profile, which yields a uniformity of $126/2 = 63\%$. For the sake of quantitative convenience, it should be noticed that this percentage equates the sum of the smallest relative frequency for each alternative term, that is, $17 + 46 + 0 = 63\%$. If more than one concept is investigated, a uniformity index U is defined as the average of the uniformity indexes of the separate concepts, whereas uniformity index U' is defined as a *weighted average*, in which the relative frequency of each concept in the investigated samples is taken into account. In the present context, we will focus exclusively on the weighted uniformity U', in which high frequency concepts have a more outspoken impact on the overall uniformity.

The empirical foundation of the research project consisted of 40,000 observations of language use. We collected the different names (and their frequencies) used to denote 30 concepts, 15 from the field of clothing terminology and 15 from the field of football (i.e., soccer) terminology. The resulting database allows us, for instance, to calculate the proportion in Belgian and Netherlandic sources of the term *buitenspel* 'offside' and the loanword *offside* for the concept '*offside*'; in the case of the concept '*jurk*' 'dress', we can determine whether the lexical choices involve a preference for either *jurk*, *japon*, or *kleed*. The core of the observed material consisted of magazine and newspaper materials recorded in 1990.

This core was extended in two ways. In the first place, similar material was collected for 1950 and 1970, which enabled us to carry out a real-time investigation of lexical convergence or divergence processes. In addition, the stratification of language use was taken into account. Between standard and dialect, there are a number of strata on which register differences may co-occur with an increasing geographic specialization. For an investigation of the relationship between Belgian and Netherlandic Dutch, these strata—namely, the regionally colored informal variants of the standard language—are extremely relevant: it can be expected that the linguistic differences between Belgium and the Netherlands will increase on this regiolectic level. This intermediate level between dialect and written standard language was represented by the clothing terms we collected from labels and price tags in shop windows in two Belgian (Leuven and Kortrijk) and two Netherlandic towns (Leiden and Maastricht). The intended audience of this form of communication is more restricted than the national or binational audience which is the target of the magazines from which the core material was selected. The fact that we are dealing with written language in a semiformal situation, on the other hand, ensures that we steer clear of the purely dialectal pole of the stratificational continuum.

Given this database, what can we expect to find with regard to the relationship between the various language varieties? With respect to the status and the development of Belgian Dutch, two uncontroversial hypotheses can be found in the linguistic literature. First, there is an expectation of *diachronic convergence* between Belgian and Netherlandic Dutch. The standardization process in Flanders is characterized by an explicit normative orientation toward Netherlandic Dutch: the standardization of Belgian Dutch took the form of an adoption of the Dutch standard language that existed already in the Netherlands. In addition, the unfinished character of the standardization of Belgian Dutch is believed to manifest itself in a larger *synchronic distance* between local and national language in Belgium than in the Netherlands. Even to the untrained observer, it is obvious that the differences between regional and supraregional registers are much larger in Belgium than in the Netherlands.

The diachronic and the synchronic hypothesis may now be made operational in terms of uniformity values as defined above. Diachronically, convergence and divergence can be quantified as increasing or decreasing uniformity. Synchronically, the larger distance between national and local language we expect in Belgian Dutch will manifest itself in a smaller uniformity between magazine and shop window materials in Belgian Dutch than in Netherlandic Dutch. Table 37.4 contains the relevant results. B50 stands for 'Belgian data from 1950', N50 stands for 'Netherlandic data from 1950'. $B_{sw}90$ refers to the shop window materials in Belgium, in contrast with B90, which stands for the data taken from magazines and newspapers.

The data in table 37.4 unambiguously confirm the diachronic as well as the synchronic hypothesis. Diachronically, the increase in uniformity between Belgian and Netherlandic Dutch suggests an evident lexical convergence between both varieties:

$$U'(B50,N50) \; < \; U'(B70,N70) \; < \; U'(B90,N90)$$

$$69.84 \quad < \quad 74.59 \quad < \quad 81.70$$

Table 37.4. U' values comparing Belgium and the Netherlands (1950–1970–1990) and comparing written data from magazines and newspapers with local shop window data (1990)

B50/N50:	69,84
B70/N70:	74,59
B90/N90:	81,70
B90/B_{sw}90:	45,90
N90/N_{sw}90:	67,75

Synchronically, the delayed or unfinished standardization of Belgian Dutch manifests itself in a distinctly lower uniformity between the Belgian magazine and shop window data than between the Netherlandic magazine and shop window materials:

$$U'(B90, B_{sw}90) \; < \; U'(N90, N_{sw}90)$$

$$45.90 \quad\quad < \quad\quad 67.75$$

For further extensions of this type of usage-based sociolexicological research, see Grondelaers et al. (2001) and Speelman, Grondelaers, and Geeraerts (2003).

5.3. Beyond Sociolexicology

Sociolexicological research of the type just illustrated links up naturally with sociolinguistics at large, if only because a quantitative sociolinguistics of the lexicon resumes the thread of the lexicological work done by Labov in the 1970s (1973, 1978). It has to be admitted, though, that language-internal variation has been much less studied in Cognitive Linguistics than variation across languages (for the latter, see Pederson, Palmer, and van der Auwera and Nuyts, this volume, chapters 38, 39, and 40, respectively). Still, we may note a number of developments within Cognitive Linguistics that are likely to contribute to an increased interest in sociolinguistic research.

First, there is the interest in cultural models and the way in which they may compete within a community (see this volume, chapters 46 and 47, for an introduction to this particular type of socially determined semantic variation). It has recently been pointed out (Geeraerts 2003) that such models may also characterize the beliefs that language users entertain regarding language and language varieties. In this way, Cognitive Linguistics may link up with existing sociolinguistic research about language attitudes.

Second, a number of researchers have started to investigate social variation outside the lexical realm: see, for instance, the work by Kristiansen (2003) on phonetic variation and the studies carried out by Berthele (2005) on differences in syntactic construal between dialects. Recent work by Grondelaers (Grondelaers 2000; Grondelaers et al. 2002) focuses on grammatical phenomena whose distribution is determined by a combination of internal (structural or semantic) and external (contextual or sociolinguistic) factors. Methodologically speaking, the latter type of research ties in with the plea of Gries (2003) for a more sophisticated use of corpus materials in Cognitive Linguistics. Although Gries hardly includes sociolinguistic variation in his analyses, the multifactorial quantitative approach that he advocates exemplifies a type of statistical analysis that can easily be extended toward sociolinguistic factors.

And third, there is a growing tendency in the theoretical conception of language entertained by Cognitive Linguistics to stress the social nature of language.

Researchers like Tomasello, Sinha, and Zlatev (see this volume, chapters 41, 49, and 13, respectively) emphasize that the experientialist nature of Cognitive Linguistics does not only refer to material factors (taking embodiment in a physical and physiological sense) but that the cultural environment and the socially interactive nature of language should be recognized as primary elements of a cognitive approach.

In short, while the sociolexicological examples show that the extension of Cognitive Linguistics toward language-internal variation of a social, geographic, stylistic nature can be achieved in a fruitful and methodologically rigorous way, the interest in the social nature of language appears to be growing in Cognitive Linguistics at large.

NOTES

1. As applied to economics, the invisible hand metaphor involves two levels of analysis. On the microlevel, the economic life of a community consists of countless individual actions and transactions. Macroeconomically, however, these individual actions result in global phenomena, such as inflation or an economic boom. Crucially, the individuals who engage in the basic transactions do not have the conscious private intention of, for instance, changing the rate of inflation. Nor do they act in accordance with a collective decision. Rather, phenomena like inflation are a cumulative consequence on the macrolevel of a myriad of individual acts on the microlevel.

REFERENCES

Alinei, Mario. 1996. Aspetti teoretici della motivazione. *Quaderni di Semantica* 17: 7–17.

Anstatt, Tania. 1995. *'Zeit': Motivierungen und Strukturen der Bedeutungen von Zeitbezeichnungen in slavischen und anderen Sprachen*. Munich: Otto Sagner.

Aski, Janice. 2001. Prototype categorization and phonological split. *Diachronica* 18: 205–39.

Baldinger, Kurt. 1964. Sémasiologie et onomasiologie. *Revue de linguistique romane* 28: 249–72.

Baldinger, Kurt. 1980. *Semantic Theory*. Oxford: Basil Blackwell. (Translation of *Teoría semántica: Hacia una semántica moderna*. Madrid: Ediciones Alcalá, 1977)

Berlin, Brent. 1978. Ethnobiological classification. In Eleanor Rosch and Barbara B. Lloyd, eds., *Cognition and categorization* 9–26. Hillsdale, NJ: Lawrence Erlbaum.

Berlin, Brent, and Paul Kay. 1969. *Basic color terms: Their universality and evolution*. Berkeley: University of California Press.

Berthele, Raphael. 2005. Static spatial relations in German and Romance: Towards a cognitive dialectology of posture verbs and locative adverbials. Markku Filppula, Juhani Klemola, Manjatta Palander, and Esa Penttilä, eds. In *Dialects across borders: Selected papers from the 11th International Conference on Methods in Dialectology (Methods XI)*, Joensuu 2002 31–50. Amsterdam: Benjamins.

Blank, Andreas. 1997. *Prinzipien des lexikalischen Bedeutungswandels am Beispiel der romanischen Sprachen*. Tübingen: Max Niemeyer Verlag.

Blank, Andreas, and Peter Koch. 1999. Onomasiologie et étymologie cognitive: L'exemple de la tête. In Mario Vilela and Fatima Silva, eds., *Actas do 1° Encontro Internacional de Linguística Cognitiva* 49–72. Porto, Portugal: Faculdade de Letras.

Bréal, Michel. 1897. *Essai de sémantique.* Paris: Hachette.

Carnoy, Alfred. 1927. *La science du mot: Traité de sémantique: Science des significations.* Leuven, Belgium: Editions Universitas.

Casad, Eugene. 1992. Cognition, history, and Cora *yee. Cognitive Linguistics* 3: 151–86.

Cook, Kenneth. 1996. The *cia* suffix as a passive marker in Samoan Oceanic. *Linguistics* 35: 57–76.

Cuyckens, Hubert. 1999. Historical evidence in prepositional semantics: The case of English *by.* In Guy A. J. Tops, Betty Devriendt, and Steven Geukens, eds., *Thinking English grammar: To honour Xavier Dekeyser* 15–32. Leuven, Belgium: Peeters.

Dekeyser, Xavier. 1990. The prepositions *with, mid* and *again(st)* in Old and Middle English: A case study of historical lexical semantics. In Dirk Geeraerts, ed., *Diachronic Semantics* 35–48. Brussels: Editions de l'Université de Bruxelles.

Dekeyser, Xavier. 1991. Romance loans in Late Middle English: A case study. In Sylviane Granger, ed., *Perspectives on the English lexicon. A tribute to Jacques van Roey* 153–62. Louvain-la-Neuve, Belgium: Cabay.

Dekeyser, Xavier. 1995. Travel, journey and voyage: An exploration into the realm of Middle English lexico-semantics. *North-Western European Language Evolution* 25: 127–36.

Dekeyser, Xavier. 1996. Loss of prototypical meanings in the history of English semantics or semantic redeployment. *Leuvense Bijdragen* 85: 283–91.

Dekeyser, Xavier. 1998. *Alway(s)* and *algate(s)* in Middle and Early Modern English: From space to time and beyond. *Leuvense Bijdragen* 87: 37–45.

De Mulder, Walter. 2001. La linguistique diachronique, les études sur la grammaticalisation et la sémantique du prototype: présentation. *Langue Française* 130: 8–32.

De Mulder, Walter, and Anne Vanderheyden. 2001. L'histoire de *contre* et la sémantique prototypique. *Langue Française* 130: 108–25.

Dirven, René. 1985. Metaphor as a basic means for extending the lexicon. In Wolf Paprotté and René Dirven, eds., *The ubiquity of metaphor: Metaphor in language and thought* 85–119. Amsterdam: John Benjamins.

Dornseiff, Franz. 1966. *Bezeichnungswandel unseres Wortschatzes: Ein Blick in das Seelenleben der Sprechenden.* Lahr/Schwarzwald, Germany: Moritz Schauenburg Verlag.

Eckardt, Regine. 2001. On the underlying mechanics of certain types of meaning change. *Linguistische Berichte* 185: 31–74.

Evans, Nicholas. 1992. Multiple semiotic systems, hyperpolysemy, and the reconstruction of semantic change in Australian languages. In Günter Kellermann and Michael D. Morrissey, eds., *Diachrony within synchrony: Language, history, and cognition* 475–508. Frankfurt am Main: Peter Lang Verlag.

Fillmore, Charles J. 1977. Scenes-and-frames semantics. In Antonio Zampolli, ed., *Linguistic structures processing* 55–81. Amsterdam: North Holland.

Fillmore, Charles J. 1985. Frames and the semantics of understanding. *Quaderni di Semantica* 6: 222–54.

Fillmore, Charles J., and Beryl T. Atkins 1992. Towards a frame-based lexicon: The semantics of RISK and its neighbors. In Adrienne Lehrer and Eva Feder Kittay, eds., *Frames, fields, and contrasts: New essays in semantic and lexical organization* 75–102. Hillsdale, NJ: Lawrence Erlbaum.

Geeraerts, Dirk. 1997. *Diachronic prototype semantics: A contribution to historical lexicology*. Oxford: Clarendon Press.

Geeraerts, Dirk 1999. Vleeshouwers, beenhouwers en slagers: Het WNT als bron voor onomasiologisch onderzoek [Vleeshouwers, beenhouwers en slagers: The *Woordenboek der Nederlandsche Taal* as a source for onomasiological investigation]. *Nederlandse Taalkunde* 4: 34–46.

Geeraerts, Dirk. 2003. Cultural models of linguistic standardization. In René Dirven, Roslyn Frank, and Martin Pütz, eds., *Cognitive models in language and thought: Ideology, metaphors and meanings* 25–68. Berlin: Mouton de Gruyter.

Geeraerts, Dirk, Stefan Grondelaers, and Peter Bakema. 1994. *The structure of lexical variation: Meaning, naming, and context*. Berlin: Mouton de Gruyter.

Geeraerts, Dirk, Stefan Grondelaers, and Dirk Speelman. 1999. *Convergentie en divergentie in de Nederlandse woordenschat: Een onderzoek naar kleding -en voetbaltermen* [Convergence and divergence in the Dutch lexicon: An investigation into clothing and football terms]. Amsterdam: Meertens Instituut.

Gilliéron, Jules, and Mario Roques. 1912. *Etudes de géographie linguistique*. Paris: Champion.

Goossens, Louis. 1992. CUNNAN, CONNE(N), CAN: The development of a radial category. In Günter Kellermann and Michael D. Morrissey, eds., *Diachrony within synchrony: Language history and cognition—Papers from the international symposium at the University of Duisburg, 26–28 March 1990* 377–94. Frankfurt am Main: Peter Lang Verlag.

Gries, Stefan Thomas. 2003. *Multifactorial analysis in corpus linguistics: A study of particle placement*. New York: Continuum Press.

Grondelaers, Stefan. 2000. De distributie van niet-anaforisch *er* buiten de eerste zinsplaats: Sociolexicologische, functionele en psycholinguïstische aspecten van *er*'s status als presentatief signaal [The distribution of non-anaphoric *er* in non-sentence-initial position: Sociolexcicological, functional and psychological aspects of the status of *er* as a presentative marker]. PhD dissertation, University of Leuven, Belgium.

Grondelaers, Stefan, Marc Brysbaert, Dirk Speelman, and Dirk Geeraerts. 2002. *Er als accessibility marker: On- en offline evidentie voor een procedurele interpretatie van presentatieve zinnen [Er* as an accessibility marker: On- and offline evidence for a procedural interpretation of presentative sentences]. *Gramma/TTT* 9: 1–22.

Grondelaers, Stefan, and Dirk Geeraerts. 1998. Vagueness as a euphemistic strategy. In Angeliki Athanasiadou and Elzbieta Tabakowska, eds., *Speaking of emotions: Conceptualisation and expression* 357–74. Berlin: Mouton de Gruyter.

Grondelaers, Stefan, Hilde Van Aken, Dirk Speelman, and Dirk Geeraerts. 2001. Inhoudswoorden en preposities als standaardiseringsindicatoren. De diachrone en synchrone status van het Belgische Nederlands. *Nederlandse Taalkunde* 6: 179–202.

Grzega, Joachim. 2002. Some aspects of modern diachronic onomasiology. *Linguistics* 40: 1021–45.

Keller, Rudi. 1990. *Sprachwandel. Von der unsichtbaren Hand in der Sprache*. Tübingen: Francke Verlag.

Kemmer, Suzanne. 1992. Grammatical prototypes and competing motivations in a theory of linguistic change. In Garry Davis and Gregory Iverson, eds., *Explanation in historical linguistics*, 145–66. Amsterdam: John Benjamins.

Koch, Peter. 1997. La diacronica quale campo empirico della semantica cognitiva. In Marco Carapezza, Daniele Gambarara, and Franco Lo Piparo, eds., *Linguaggio e cognizione*:

Atti del XXVIII Congresso Internazionale della Società di Linguistica Italiana 225–46. Rome: Bulzoni.

Koivisto-Alanko, Paivi. 2002. Abstract words in abstract worlds: Directionality and prototypical structure in the semantic change in English nouns of cognition. PhD dissertation, University of Helsinki.

Kövecses, Zoltán. 1990. *Emotion concepts*. New York: Springer Verlag.

Kövecses, Zoltán. 2000. *Metaphor and emotion: Language, culture, and body in human feeling*. Cambridge: Cambridge University Press.

Kristiansen, Gitte. 2003. How to do things with allophones: Linguistic stereotypes as cognitive reference points in social cognition. In René Dirven, Roslyn Frank, and Martin Pütz, eds., *Cognitive models in language and thought: Ideology, metaphors, and meanings* 69–120. Berlin: Mouton de Gruyter.

Kronasser, Heinz. 1952. *Handbuch der Semasiologie: Kurze Einführung in die Geschichte, Problematik und Terminologie der Bedeutungslehre*. Heidelberg: Carl Winter Universitätsverlag.

Kronenberg, David B. 1996. *Plastic glasses and church fathers: Semantic extension from the ethnoscience tradition*. Oxford: Oxford University Press.

Labov, William. 1973. The boundaries of words and their meanings. In Charles-James Bailey and Roger Shuy, eds., *New ways of analyzing variation in English* 340–73. Washington, DC: Georgetown University Press.

Labov, William. 1978. Denotational structure. *Chicago Linguistic Society* 14.2 (parasession): 220–60.

Lakoff, George, and Mark Johnson. 1980. *Metaphors we live by*. Chicago: University of Chicago Press.

Lewandowska-Tomaszczyk, Barbara. 1985. On semantic change in a dynamic model of language. In Jacek Fisiak, ed., *Historical semantics—historical word formation* 297–323. Berlin: Mouton de Gruyter.

Luraghi, Silvia. 1995. Prototypicality and agenthood in Indo-European. In Henning Andersen, ed., *Historical linguistics* 254–68. Amsterdam: John Benjamins.

Maffi, Luisa. 1996. Liquor and medicine: A Mayan case study in diachronic semantics. *Journal of Linguistic Anthropology* 6: 27–46.

Melis, Ludo. 1990. *La voie pronominale: La systématique des tours pronominaux en français moderne*. Paris: Duculot.

Molina, Clara. 2000. "Give sorrow words": Reflexiones semanticas y lexicologicas en torno al dolor en la lengua inglesa desde la diacronia cognitiva. PhD dissertation, Universidad Complutense de Madrid.

Nerlich, Brigitte, and David D. Clarke. 1992. Semantic change: Case studies based on traditional and cognitive semantics. *Journal of Literary Semantics* 21: 204–25.

Nikiforidou, Kiki. 1991. The meanings of the genitive: A case study in semantic structure and semantic change. *Cognitive Linguistics* 2: 149–205.

Paul, Hermann. 1880. *Prinzipien der Sprachgeschichte*. Halle, Germany: M. Niemeyer.

Quadri, Bruno. 1952. *Aufgaben und Methoden der onomasiologischen Forschung: Eine entwicklungsgeschichtliche Darstellung*. Tübingen: A. Francke Verlag.

Rudzka-Ostyn, Brygida. 1992. Prototypes, schemas, and cross-category correspondences: The case of ask. *Linguistics* 27: 613–61.

Soares da Silva, Augusto. 1999. *A Semântica de DEIXAR: Uma contibuição para a abordagem cognitiva em Semântica Lexical* [The semantics of the verb *deixar*: Towards a cognitive approach in lexical semantics]. Lisbon: Fundação Calouste Gulbenkian,

Ministério da Ciência e da Tecnologia. (PhD dissertation, Universidade Católica Portuguesa, Braga, 1997)

Speelman, Dirk, Stefan Grondelaers, and Dirk Geeraerts. 2003. Profile-based linguistic uniformity as a generic method for comparing language varieties. *Computers and the Humanities* 37: 317–37.

Stern, Gustaf. 1931. *Meaning and change of meaning*. Gothenburg, Sweden: Elanders.

Tissari, Heli. 2001. Affection, friendship, passion and charity: A history of four "love lexemes" since the fifteenth century. *Neuphilologische Mitteilungen* 102: 49–76.

Tournier, Jean. 1985. *Introduction à la lexicogénétique de l'anglais contemporain*. Paris: Champion.

Ullmann, Stephen. 1951. *The principles of semantics*. Oxford: Basil Blackwell.

Ullmann, Stephen. 1962. *Semantics: An introduction to the science of meaning*. Oxford: Basil Blackwell.

Winters, Margaret E. 1989. Diachronic prototype theory: On the evolution of the French subjunctive. *Linguistics* 27: 703–30.

Winters, Margaret E. 1992a. Diachrony within synchrony: The challenge of cognitive grammar. In Martin Pütz, ed., *Thirty years of linguistic evolution: Studies in honour of René Dirven on the occasion of his sixtieth birthday* 503–12. Amsterdam: John Benjamins.

Winters, Margaret E. 1992b. Schemas and prototypes: Remarks on syntax change. In Günter Kellermann and Michael D. Morrissey, eds., *Diachrony within synchrony: Language history and cognition* 265–80. Frankfurt am Main: Peter Lang Verlag.

Zauner, Adolf. 1903. Die romanischen Namen der Körperteile: Eine onomasiologische Studie. *Romanische Forschungen* 14: 339–530.

Zgusta, Ladislav. 1990. Onomasiological change. In Edgar C. Polomé, ed., *Research guide on language change* 389–98. Berlin: Mouton de Gruyter.

CHAPTER 38

COGNITIVE LINGUISTICS AND LINGUISTIC RELATIVITY

ERIC PEDERSON

1. INTRODUCTION

Linguistic relativity (also known as *the Sapir-Whorf Hypothesis*) is a general cover term for the conjunction of two basic notions. The first notion is that languages are *relative*, that is, that they vary in their expression of concepts in noteworthy ways. What constitutes "noteworthy" is, of course, a matter of some interpretation. Cognitive scientists interested in human universals will often describe some particular linguistic variation as essentially minor, while others, for example, some anthropological linguists, may describe the same variation as significant.

The second component notion to linguistic relativity is that the linguistic expression of concepts has some degree of influence over conceptualization in cognitive domains, which need not necessarily be linguistically mediated. In textbooks, this notion of language affecting conceptualization is typically divided into "strong" and "weak" hypotheses. The "strong" hypothesis (also known as *linguistic determinism*) is that the variable categories of language essentially control the available categories of general cognition. As thus stated, this "strong" hypothesis is typically dismissed as untenable. The "weak" hypothesis states that the linguistic categories may influence the categories of thought but are not fundamentally restrictive. As thus stated, this "weak" hypothesis is typically considered trivially true.

Arguably, this simplification of the broad issue of the relationship between linguistic and cognitive categorization into two simple ("strong" vs. "weak") statements has impeded development of genuinely testable hypotheses and has helped lead studies of linguistic relativity into academic ill-repute. Modern research into the general question of linguistic relativity has focused on more narrowly stated hypotheses for testing, that is, investigating the specific relationships between particular linguistic categories (e.g., the categories of number, color, or spatial direction) and more exactly specified cognitive operations (e.g., encoding into long-term memory or deductive reasoning).

This chapter is organized as (i) a brief history of the research question (section 2); (ii) a discussion of the challenges in designing research into linguistic relativity (section 3); (iii) the treatment of linguistic relativity within works generally representative of Cognitive Linguistics (section 4); and (iv) a survey of classic and more modern (pre- and post-1980s) research within linguistics, anthropology, and psychology (section 5).

In addition to this chapter, several other surveys of linguistic relativity may be consulted. Lucy (1997a) gives a broad overview of different approaches which have investigated linguistic relativity, while Lucy (1992b) elaborates on a particular empirical approach and provides detailed critiques of previous empirical work. Lee (1996) provides historical documentation to the often poorly understood work of Benjamin Lee Whorf (see also Lee 2000). Hill and Mannheim (1992) trace the history of the notion of world view with respect to language through twentieth-century anthropology, from Boas through Cognitive Linguistics of the 1980s to the work of John Lucy. Hill and Mannheim also provides a useful overview of the anthropological cum semiotic approach to culturally embedded language use—see especially Hanks (1990) and Silverstein (1985, 1987).

Smith (1996) also discusses the writings of Sapir and Whorf to clarify that most popular accounts of the Sapir-Whorf Hypothesis are not directly derivative of their work. She is also concerned that the relatively large-scale dismissal of the Sapir-Whorf Hypothesis in academic culture has been at the expense of serious research into the relationships between language and thought. Similar discussion of the "demise" of the "Whorf Hypothesis" and the misconstrual of Whorf's actual writings can be found in Alford (1978).[1]

Koerner (2000) also provides a survey of the "pedigree" of linguistic relativity "from Locke to Lucy," that is, from the seventeenth through the twentieth century. Chapters 10–12 of Foley (1997) as well provide historical coverage of the notion, with summaries of fairly recent work with spatial language and classifiers. Duranti (1997) similarly provides historical coverage with particular emphasis on the American anthropology traditions.

Hunt and Agnoli (1991) revisit linguistic relativity from the perspective of cognitive psychology, which had largely rejected the notion as either false or uninteresting during the 1970s. Within canonical Cognitive Linguistics, Lakoff (1987) dedicates chapter 18 of *Women, Fire, and Dangerous Things* to discussions of evidence for and types of linguistic relativity. Many of the principles from that chapter have informed the remainder of his work.

2. Historical Speculation and Modern Formulations

Given the wealth of historical surveys of linguistic relativity, this chapter will focus more on modern work and methodological issues. However, a brief overview of the history of linguistic relativity theorizing will help to situate the modern research questions.

2.1. From Humboldt through Whorf

The most widely cited intellectual antecedent for linguistic relativity is the work of Humboldt. Later, the work of Boas is widely seen as the inheritor of the Humboldtian notions and through him, the concern with linguistic relativity was taken up in the writings of Sapir, who developed the vital notion of the "patterns" or structural systematicity of language as being particularly relevant to the relationship between language, mind, and culture.

Humboldt's principal work addressing linguistic relativity is *Über die Verschiedenheit des menschlichen Sprachbaues und ihren Einfluss auf die geistige Entwicklung des Menschengeschlecht* [On the diversity of human language construction and its influence on the mental development of the human species]. There are many editions and translations of this work; for a recent edition of Peter Heath's English translation, see Losonsky (1999). The philosophical precursors to Humboldt, as well as linguistic relativity in general, is discussed in Manchester (1985), and an overview of Humboldt's notion of language and *Weltansicht* ('world view') is provided in Brown (1967).

The writings of Benjamin Lee Whorf are best known through Carroll's edited collection Whorf (1956). This collection helped to popularize the notion that the categories of language may influence the categories of thought. However, Lee (1996) argues—especially in light of the previously unpublished "Yale report" (see Whorf and Trager [1938] 1996)—that Whorf was concerned with the interpenetration of language and thought; that is, the two words *language* and *thought* refer to aspects of a single system, and it is a misapprehension to ask in what way one affects the other. This is quite distinct from the more modular view of language processing dominant in current psychology and linguistics.

2.2. Literacy

While modern linguistics places considerable emphasis on *spoken* language—which means that this chapter will focus on the potential cognitive impact of the categories found in spoken or signed languages—the role of *literacy* to cognitive and cultural development has long been a subject of debate.

Early twentieth-century experiments on the relationship between literacy and cognitive development were conducted by Aleksandr Luria and colleagues (for an overview in English, see Luria 1976). This classic work investigated the effects of previously established, Soviet-era adult literacy programs on the development of various cognitive skills. There were a number of methodological problems with that work—perhaps the most significant one being the confounding of formal schooling with the acquisition of literacy (or conversely, the lack of formal schooling with nonliterate populations). The largest single effort to overcome this common confound is reported by Scribner and Cole (1981), who investigated effects of literacy acquisition in the absence of formal schooling. The designs and subject pools were still not completely free of confounding factors and the results, while fascinating, give a largely mixed picture of the effects of literacy as an independent factor on cognition.

"The literacy hypothesis," namely that various cultural features can be traced to the development of literacy in the history of a given culture, has been subject to considerable debate. Goody and Watt (1962), one of the better known works, extolled the effects of specifically *alphabetic* literacy as critical in the development of early Greek and later European culture. This view came under considerable criticism, and Goody himself later backed away from the specific claims about alphabetic literacy.[2] However, on a more general level, the claim that literacy engenders certain cognitive changes—especially enhanced metalinguistic awareness—continues to be argued. Readers interested in the effects of literacy on cognition could also consult Scinto (1986), Graff (1987), Olson (1991, 2002), Ong (1992), and references therein.

Rather than studying the general effects of reading and writing on cognition, one line of research has been concerned with the effects of learning particular writing systems. Morais et al. (1979) investigate the effects of child-acquired literacy on phonemic awareness, and Read et al. (1986) present evidence arguing that alphabetic literacy, but not logographic and syllabic literacy, leads to phonemic awareness. In Danziger and Pederson (1998) and Pederson (2003), I argue that familiarity with specific graphemic qualities can lead to differences in visual categorization in nonwriting/nonreading tasks.

2.3. Folk Classification

Anthropologists have long been concerned with *folk classification*, that is, the culturally specific ways in which linguistic and other categories are organized into coherent systems. Perhaps the richest body of work is in the area of taxonomies of natural kinds (plants, animals, etc.). This research is conveniently served by having a scientific standard for comparison. While there is abundant anecdotal evidence that people interact with natural kinds according to their taxonomical relations to other natural kinds (e.g., *X* is a pet, so treat it like other pets), there has not been much in the way of psychological-style testing of specific linguistic relativity hypotheses in this domain. For an introduction to folk classification, see Hunn (1977, 1982), Berlin, Breedlove, and Raven (1973), Berlin (1978), and Blount (1993).

2.4. Formulations of Linguistic Relativity

There are many semantic domains one could search for linguistic relativity effects— that is, domains in which one might find linguistic categories conditioning non-linguistic categorization. For example, cultures and languages are notorious for having varying kinship terms, which group into major types with various subtypes. Importantly, the categories of allowable behaviors with kin tend to correspond to the grouping by kinship terminology. For example, South Indian (Dravidian) languages systematically distinguish between cross-cousins and parallel cousins, with marriage allowed between cross-cousins and incest taboo applying to parallel cousins. In contrast, North Indian languages typically classify all cousins with siblings and incest taboo applies to all (see Carter 1973).

However important sexual reproduction may be to our species, the standards of marriage are clearly the result of cultural convention overlaid on biological predispositions. Accordingly, finding linguistic variation corresponding to categories of human behavior in such a domain is not generally taken as a particularly revealing demonstration of linguistic relativity. Likewise, elaborated vocabulary sets in expert domains and impoverished sets where there is little experience, however interesting, are also not taken as particularly revealing. While a tropical language speaker may lack the broad vocabulary of English for discussing frozen precipitation, that same speaker may be quite particular in distinguishing what English speakers lump together as 'cousins'.

In other words, cases of categorization which are dependent on environmentally or culturally variable experience are generally considered uninteresting domains for the study of linguistic relativity. This corresponds to the late twentieth-century bias toward universalism in the cognitive sciences; namely, for variation to be noteworthy, it should be in a domain where variation was not previously thought to be possible. That is to say, for linguistic relativity to be broadly interesting, it must apply within cognitive domains which operate on "basic" and universal human experience.

3. CHALLENGES IN RESEARCHING LINGUISTIC RELATIVITY

3.1. Intralinguistic Variation

Speakers may use language differently across different contexts, and this difference may be indicative of shifting conceptual representations. One of the few studies within Cognitive Linguistics to empirically address intralinguistic variation is Geeraerts, Grondelaers, and Bakema (1994, especially chapter 4: "Onomasiological Variation"), which explores alternative expressions as the representation of different construals and perspectivization.

Of course, some of these alternative expressions may be confined to some subcommunities and dialects. While linguistic relativity is typically discussed as the difference across speakers of distinct languages, there is every reason to wonder about parallels with differences in conceptualization that may exist within a single language community. Speakers of different dialects may have different linguistic patterns which might be hypothesized to correspond to different habitual conceptualizations. In Pederson (1993, 1995), I investigate communities of Tamil speakers who systematically vary in their preference for terms of spatial reference, but who otherwise speak essentially the same dialect.

The work of Loftus (1975) has demonstrated that the choice of particular linguistic expressions at the time of encoding or recall may well influence nonlinguistic representation of events. Extrapolating from Loftus's work, we might wonder to what extent language generally can prime specific nonlinguistic representations—I call this the *language as prime* model. The fact that social humans are surrounded by linguistic input suggests that there might be a cumulative effect of this language priming. Indeed, if a particular linguistic encoding presented before a certain perception influences the nonlinguistic encoding or recall of that perception, what then might be the cumulative effect of one type of linguistic encoding rather than another being used throughout a speaker's personal history? If, for example, the classifiers of a speaker's habitual language force categorization of certain objects as 'long and thin', it seems reasonable that such objects may be remembered as potentially longer or thinner than they actually were.

Of course, if there were no consistent pattern to the linguistic priming, then we would not expect any single representation to become dominant. Indeed, Kay (1996) has argued that there is considerable flexibility within any language for alternative representations, and speakers may well alternate from one representation to another. This suggests that rather than a single and simple "world-view" necessary for a cleanly testable hypothesis, speakers may draw on complex "repertoires" of representations. While this does not preclude the possibility of systematic differences across languages having different repertoires, it certainly argues that the differences are far less obvious.

Given flexibility within a single language, a linguistic relativity hypothesis to be tested may need to compare patterns which are pervasive in one language and underexpressed in another language. This can be difficult to compensate for in an experimental design. A balanced design might seek opposing, but functionally equivalent systems, which are dominant in each language community. Each community may have both systems in common, but not to the same level of default familiarity. Of course, the experimental measure needs to be sufficiently non-priming itself so as to allow each subject population to rely on their default mode of representation.

3.2. Selecting a Domain

Universals in categorization may be of more than one type. Most relevantly, some categories may be essentially innate, that is, an internal predisposition of the organism. Other universal categories may be the result of commonalities of all human environments in conjunction with our innately driven mechanisms. Even assuming that we can reliably presume that certain categories are universal, determining which are purely innate and which derive from interaction with universal properties of the environment is not a trivial task.

Variation in innate properties is impossible—except inasmuch as the variation is within innately proscribed limits—so we cannot look for linguistic relativity effects in these domains. For linguistic relativity effects to be both interesting to cognitive scientists and robust in their operations, they must apply in a domain which is generally presumed universal by virtue of the common environment, but which can be hypothesized to be nonuniversal. As discussed above, demonstrating effects from language type in cognitive domains with wide variation is unexciting. It follows that the researcher interested in testing linguistic relativity best seeks a domain which is hypothesized to be fairly basic to cognition, but just shy of exhibiting a universal pattern.

This motivates modern linguistic relativity studies to examine categorization in domains presumed to derive somewhat immediately from basic perceptual stimuli or fundamental mechanisms of reasoning. The majority of such empirical studies concern categorization of visual or spatial properties of objects or the environment. A few studies have examined purported differences in reasoning, but these are inherently more difficult to pursue. Object properties and the environment can be experimentally controlled, but processes of reasoning—especially in cross-cultural work—are notoriously difficult to measure while maintaining adequate control of subject variables.

3.3. Independent Evidence for Language and Cognition

Linguists—especially cognitive linguists—frequently claim that a particular linguistic form represents a particular underlying conceptualization. Obviously, however, any substantial claim of a relationship between language and cognition needs independent assessment of each and a correlation established between the two.

Perhaps surprisingly, most work on linguistic relativity spends remarkably little effort demonstrating the linguistic facts prior to seeking the hypothesized cognitive variable. Some of the most severe criticisms of linguistic relativity studies have worried about this insufficient linguistic description. Lucy (1992b) is especially clear in his call for more careful linguistic analysis preparatory to linguistic relativity experimentation.

Given the relative accessibility of the linguistic facts compared with the difficulty inferring cognitive behavior from behavioral measures, one could argue that the often minimal characterization of language is of unacceptable sloppiness. More charitably, linguistic facts are typically quite complex, and in an effort to seek a testable hypothesis, a certain amount of simplification becomes inevitable. Unfortunately, there is no standard to use in evaluating the adequacy of a linguistic description for linguistic relativity work other than using the general standards of descriptive linguistics. Descriptive linguistics tends to be as exhaustive as is practically possible and does not necessarily foster the creation of simple hypotheses about linguistic and conceptual categorization. On the other hand, it is difficult to argue that studies in linguistic relativity should hold their linguistic descriptions to a lower standard.

A related problem is the variability of language. Since many different varieties of language exist depending on communicative and descriptive context, it can be quite misleading to speak of Hopi or English as having a specific characteristic, unless one can argue that this characteristic is true and uniquely true (e.g., there are no competitive constructions) in all contexts. This is, needless to say, a difficult endeavor, but failing to argue the general applicability of the pattern invites the next linguist with expertise in the language to pull forth numerous counterexamples. Studies most closely following the approaches advocated by Whorf have tended to focus on basic grammatical features of the language which are presumed to be fairly context independent. However, this may overlook other linguistic features which may well be relevant to a particular hypothesis of linguistic and conceptual categorization.

One way to partially circumvent this problem was followed in Pederson et al. (1998), which seeks to describe language characteristics typically used for, in this case, table-top spatial reference. There is no attempt to include or exclude information on the basis of whether or not the relevant language elements were grammaticized or lexicalized. Rather, if the information was present in the language used for a particular context, these linguistic categories are presumed to be available conceptual categories within same or similar contexts. This approach leaves unanswered the question of how broadly the linguistic description (or for that matter the cognitive description as well) applies to the subject population in a variety of other contexts, but it does help ensure that the linguistic description is the most exact match for the cognitive enquiry.

3.4. Subvocalization or What Is Nonlinguistic?

If independent measures are to be taken of both language use and cognitive processes, then great care is necessary to ensure that the behavioral measure for the nonlinguistic cognitive process is not covertly measuring linguistically mediated behavior.

Ideally, the entire cognitive task would be nonlinguistic, but as a practical minimum, the instructions and training for the task must be couched in language which is neutral with respect to the current hypothesis. This is particularly difficult to manage when a language has grammatically obligatory encoding. How do we interpret an effect which may be due to obligatory encoding in the instructions? Is this just an effect of the instructions, or can we interpret this as a general language effect because the instructions only exemplify the continual linguistic context the subjects live within?

There is a general presumption that instructions to the subjects should be in the subjects' native language. One might be tempted to use a shared second language as a type of neutral metalanguage for task instructions, but this introduces unexplored variables. If there is the possibility of a cognitive effect from the regular use of one's native language, then there is also the possibility of an effect from the immediate use of the language of instruction. Additionally, it is more difficult to be certain that all subjects understand the second-language instructions in exactly the same way as the experimenter. Finally, it is unclear how one would guarantee that the language of instruction is neutral with respect to anticipated behavioral outcomes. The very fact that it may mark different categories from the native language may influence the outcome in unpredictable ways.

It is safest therefore to minimize any language-based instruction. General instructions (e.g., "Sit here") cannot be excluded, but critical information is best presented through neutral examples with minimal accompanying language. Since a dearth of talking makes it more difficult to monitor subject comprehension, it is imperative that the experimental design include a built-in check (e.g., *control trials*) to ensure that each subject understands the task in the same way—except, of course, for the variation for which the task was designed to test. An account of the effects of subtle changes in instruction with children in explorations with base ten number systems can be found in Saxton and Towse (1998).

Another concern is that subjects involved in an ostensibly nonlanguage measure actually choose to use language as part of the means of determining their behavior. For example, the subjects may subvocalize their reasoning in a complex problem and then any patterning of behavior along the lines of the linguistic categories is scarcely surprising. In Pederson (1995), I address this concern by arguing that if subjects have distinct levels of linguistic and conceptual representations, they should only choose to approach a nonlinguistic task using linguistic means if there were a sufficiently close match between these two levels with respect to the experiment. In effect, a subject's unforced decision to rely on linguistic categories can be understood as validation of at least one sort of linguistic relativity hypothesis.

3.5. Finding Behavioral Consequences of Linguistically Determined Cognitive Variation

Variation in categorization of spatial or perceptual features can be of relatively minor consequence. Whether one thinks of pencils more fundamentally as tools or as long skinny objects has probably little effect on their employment.

The most basic features of humans and their environment are stable across linguistic communities. Gravity pulls in a constant direction, visual perception is roughly comparable, and so forth. If there are cognitive differences across communities with respect to universal features, then these different cognitive patterns must have *functional equivalence*; that is, different ways of thinking about the same thing must largely allow the same behavioral responses. For example, whether a line of objects is understood as proceeding from left to right or from north to south makes little difference under most circumstances. If the objects are removed and the subject must rebuild them, either understanding of the array will give the same rebuilt line with no effect on accuracy. Accordingly, any experimental task must select an uncommon condition where the principle of functional equivalence fails to hold (see especially Levinson 1996). To continue this example, if the subject is rotated by 90 or 180 degrees before being asked to rebuild an array, the underlying representation (left-right or north-south) should result in a different direction for the rebuilding.

Without a context which effectively disambiguates the possible underlying representations from behavioral responses, a researcher must demonstrate that one subject population has a deficient or improved performance on a task and that this differential performance corresponds to a difference in (default) linguistic encoding. There is a long and sordid history of attributing deficiencies to populations that the investigator does not belong to. Accordingly, it is entirely appropriate that the burden of proof fall particularly hard on the researcher claiming that a studied population is somehow impaired on a given task as a result of their pattern of linguistic encoding. Even if the population is claimed to have an ability which is *augmented* by linguistic encoding, it is difficult to demonstrate that any difference in ability derives specifically from linguistic differences and not from any of a myriad of environmental (perhaps even nutritional) conditions.

Related to this is the concern for the *ecological validity* of the experimental task. A task may fail to measure subject ability or preferences owing to unfamiliarity of the materials, instructions, or testing context. Further, it is difficult to decide on the basis of just a few experiments which effects can be generalized to hold for nonexperimental contexts—to wit, the complexity of daily life. This is not, however, an argument against experimentation as the inherently interpretive nature of simple observational data ultimately requires experimentally controlled measures.

3.6. Types of Experimental Design

Various types of experimental tasks have been used for investigating the cognitive side of linguistic relativity. Whatever research methods are used, reliability of the results is far more likely if there is triangulation from a number of observational and experimental methods.

Sorting and Triads Tasks

Perhaps the most common design used in linguistic relativity studies is a sorting task. Quite simply, the subject is presented with a number of stimuli and is asked to group them into categories. These categories may be ad hoc (subject determined) or preselected (researcher determined). Multiple strategies may be used for the sorting task, giving different sorting results. The most common variant of the sorting task is the triads task which presents a single stimulus to the subjects and asks them to group it with either of two other stimuli or stimuli sets; that is, does stimulus X group better with A or with B? (hence, the term *AXB test* in some research paradigms). For an archetypal example of a triads task, see Davies et al. (1998).

This task is easy to administer as long as the stimuli are reasonably tangible, interpretable, and able to be considered in a nearly simultaneous manner. One consideration of sorting designs is that subjects often report awareness of multiple strategies which might be employed. Of course, the researcher cannot indicate which is a preferred strategy and can only instruct the subject to sort according to "first impression," "whatever seems most natural," or other such instructions. The interpretation of these instructions may add an uncontrolled variable. Further, sorting tasks inherently invite the subjects to respond according to their beliefs about the researcher's expectations, which may not in fact be what would be the normal sorting decision outside of this task.

Discrimination Tasks

Other tasks seek to find different discriminations across populations. As a practical consequence, differences usually boil down to one population making finer or more distinctions than another population; see, for example, much of the work on color discrimination and linguistic labeling discussed in the debates in Hardin and Maffi (1997). However, it is at least theoretically possible that one population might be more sensitive to certain features at the expense of other features and that a contrasting population would show the reverse pattern.

A limitation of discrimination tasks is that for them to be interpretable, one must be able to assume that beyond the independent variable of different linguistic systems, all subjects brought the same degree of attention, general task satisfying abilities, and so on to the experimental task. Should, for example, one population be less likely to be attentionally engaged, then this reduces the possibility of isolating a linguistic effect on cognition.

Problem Solving Tasks

Problem solving tasks are readily used in many types of research. In linguistic relativity studies, they are typically of two design types: difficult solution or alternative solution.

The first type involves a task which provides some difficulty in finding the solution. Some subjects are anticipated to be better or worse than others at solving the task. As with reduced discrimination just discussed, it is extremely difficult to argue that it is specifically the categories of language which lead to differential performance. The counterfactual reasoning task employed by Bloom (1981) was such a task, and the difficulty in interpreting its results was part of much of the controversy surrounding that work.

The second type of problem solving tasks allow for alternative solutions each of which should be indicative of a different underlying representation. As such, these are similar to triads tasks in that they allow each subject to find the most "natural" solution for them (at least within the given experimental context). For example, in Pederson (1995) I describe a transitivity task in which subjects know how each of two objects are spatially related to a third object. They must then decide which side of the second object the first/test object must be placed. Depending on how these relationships are encoded, the test object will be placed on a different side of the second object. Like triads tasks, there is the potential problem that the subjects may be aware of the possibility of multiple solutions, prompting responses derived from any number of uncontrolled factors.

Embedded Tasks

Within psychological research, there is a common solution to the problem of subject awareness of multiple possible responses. Namely, the actual measure of the task is *embedded* within another task for which the subject is more consciously aware. For example, subjects may be asked to respond as to whether a figure is masculine or feminine, but the researcher is really measuring the distribution of attention to the figures. While the embedded task may still be influenced by subject expectations, it is an indirect and presumably nonreflected influence. As such, one can argue that the responses measured by the embedded task are more likely to correspond to default behaviors used outside of this exact experimental context. The "Animals in a Row" task discussed in Pederson et al. (1998) was one such task, where subjects understood the task as one to recreate a *sequence* of toy animals, but the critical dependent measure was the *direction* the animals were facing when subjects placed them on the tabletop before them.

Variable Responses

The researcher must also be careful in coding fixed response types from the subjects. It may be that subject preference is for a response type not allowed by the forced choice, and when pigeonholed into a different response type, subjects may not be responding in a manner reflecting their typical underlying representations. Also, certain patterns (or lack of patterns) of responses may actually indicate a preference for a response type not anticipated by the experimental design. For example, in the "Animals in a Row" task just discussed, some populations—and not others—appear on the scoring sheets as preserving the orientation of the original stimuli roughly half the time. On closer inspection, many of these subjects were actually entirely consistent in giving the animals the same orientation (e.g., always facing left) regardless of the original orientation of the stimuli. Since the task appeared to be about the order and not the orientation of the animals, this is a perfectly reasonable response. Unfortunately, there was no hypothesis anticipating this response, and no claims could be made as to why some subjects and not others gave this response pattern.

3.7. Controlling Extraneous Variables

Work such as Kay and Kempton (1984) demonstrates that the effects of native language on nonlinguistic categorization tasks can vary with even slightly varied task demands. This is commonly interpreted as an indication that "relativity effects" are "weak." A more conservative interpretation is that there are many factors (of undetermined "strength") which can effect results and that language may be only one of many possible factors. The exact total effect of language will depend on what other nonlinguistic factors are in effect. This requires that an experimental design for linguistic relativity effects carefully control all foreseeable linguistic and nonlinguistic variables.

Linguistic Variables

Since they are most directly related to the tested hypothesis, language variables are perhaps the most critical to control in one's design.

Of fundamental importance is that one must be certain that the base language of the subjects is consistent with respect to whatever features have led to the specific hypothesis. This may seem trivial, but dialectal (and even idiolectal) variation may well have the effect that some speakers do not share certain critical linguistic features even though they ostensibly speak the same language.

Perhaps even more problematic is the issue of bilingualism. Unless all subjects are totally monolingual, this is a potential problem for the design. Generally, linguistic relativity tests presume that one's "native" language capacity is the most relevant, but this cannot preclude effects from other known languages. Age of acquisition of second languages may also vary widely; there is certainly no established model of the effects of age of acquisition on nonlinguistic category formation.

If nonnative categories have been learned, how can we assume that they are not also brought to bear on the experimental task—clouding the results in unpredictable ways? This is perhaps most insidious when the language of instruction differs from the native language. Suitably, then, serious work in linguistic relativity needs to use the native language for instruction, but even this is not necessarily a straightforward task. For example, how does one ensure that instructions to multiple populations are both exactly and suitably translated?

How to Control for Exact Translations in a Comparative Work?

Work in linguistic relativity has had an impact in translation theory. Indeed, belief in a sufficiently strong model of insurmountable language differences would suggest that complete translations would be difficult to attain. House (2000) presents an overview of the challenges of translation and suggests a solution to the problem of linguistic relativity and translation. Chafe (2000) also discusses translation issues with respect to linguistic relativity, and Slobin (1991, 1996) uses translations in his discussions of how languages most suitably express motion events (see the section on space, below). The work of Bloom and his critics (see the discussion below) is particularly relevant for this issue because the ability to translate the experimental task from English to Chinese was central to his research question of counterfactual reasoning. Indeed, one might be skeptical of any attempt to investigate linguistic relativity in which the nonlinguistic experimental design is essentially a language-based task.

Of immediate practical concern is the translation of instructions for any research instrument itself. It is difficult enough to be confident that two subjects speaking the same language have the same understanding of a task's instructions. How, then, can the researcher be confident that translations of instructions are understood identically by speakers of different languages especially in the context of an experiment which seeks to confirm that speakers of these different languages in fact do understand the world in different ways?

The most obvious solution is to avoid linguistic instruction entirely. This does not remove the possibility that subjects understand the task differently, but it does ensure that any different understanding is not the direct result of immediate linguistic context. However, there are severe restrictions on what can be reliably and efficiently instructed without language. Understandably, then, most research relies on language-based instruction. In such cases, one must seek to phrase instructions in such a way that one sample is not more influenced by the particular choice of phrasing than the other sample.

To invent an example, imagine we are interested in the effect of evidential marking (linguistic markings which indicate how information is known to the speaker) on the salience of sources of even nonlinguistic information to speakers of a language which obligatorily marks evidentiality. This population would contrast with speakers of a language which essentially lacks routine marking. How, then, might we word our instructions? Do we use expressions typical for each language such that one set of instructions contains evidential marking and the other not? Alternatively, do we provide evidential information for both languages? In the case of the language which does not typically mark evidentials, providing this information would obviously be more "marked" in usage than for the other language. This greater markedness of the information might make the evidential information *more* salient for those subjects who normally do not concern themselves with any language expression of evidentiality, which in turn could make issues of evidentiality more salient than they would be under average conditions—countering the entire design of the experiment!

Recent Language Use

Another potential language factor affecting results might be preexperimental, but recent, language use. If the language of instruction can influence results, could not language use immediately prior to instruction also influence the results? Indeed, if we assume that linguistic categories prime access to parallel nonlinguistic categories, then how do we control for language use outside of the experimental setting? On the one hand, one could argue that language use outside of the experiment is exactly the independent variable under consideration, and this is controlled simply through subject selection. On the other hand, if a language has multiple ways of representing categories, what is the potential effect if a subject has most recently been using one of the less typical linguistic categories for his or her language? Once again, the cleanest solution to this risk is to test categories for which there is minimal linguistic variation within each of the examined languages.[3]

Conversation during Task

The last of the language variables to consider is language use during the experiment itself. Lucy and Shwedder (1988) found that forbidding subjects to have conversations between exposure and recall in a memory task allowed a greater recall of focal color terms than of nonfocal color terms (see the subsection on color below). Subjects who had (unrelated) conversations remembered focal and nonfocal colors about equally well. While Lucy and Shwedder do not provide a model for why this might be the case, it clearly suggests that even incidental language use during and perhaps around a task can have significant influences on performance. Other work (see Gennari et al. 2002) has suggested that even in cases where there might normally be no particular relation between habitual language use and performance on a nonlinguistic task, language used during exposure or memorization to stimuli can lead to nonlinguistic responses in alignment with language use.

Nonlinguistic Subject Variables

Even more heterogonous to a subject sample than the linguistic variables are the cultural, educational, and other experiential variables. Subject questionnaires are the usual ways to try to control these variables in post hoc analysis, but this control is limited by the foresight to collect adequate information.

One of the more obvious variables to control or record is the amount of schooling and literacy. Unfortunately, while schooling is easily represented on an ordinal scale (first to postsecondary grades), there is little guarantee that this represents the same education especially across, but even within, two population samples. For example, literacy is also not as simple a variable as it might appear. Subjects may be literate in different languages (and scripts) and may have very different literacy practices. Coding subjects who only read the Bible in their nonnative language and other subjects who read a variety of materials in their native language as both simply "literate" clearly glosses over potentially significant differences in experience.

Expertise may also vary considerably across samples. One of the most thorny obstacles in cross-cultural psychology is comparing testing results across two populations, one of which habitually engages with experiment-like settings and the other of which does not. This may have effects beyond simple difficulty in performance, but may affect the way in which subjects understand instructions, second-guess the intentions of the experimenter, and so on.[4]

Sex or gender, age, and the more physiologically based experiences are also difficult to compare. Being a woman in different societies means very different daily experiences beyond the variables of amount of schooling and the like. To what extent are subjects in their thirties the same across two populations. In one society but not another, a 35-year-old might typically be a grandparent in declining health with uncorrected vision or hearing loss.

Testing Environment

Lastly, variation in the testing environment is often difficult to control. The more broadly cross-cultural the samplings, the greater the dependence on local conditions. One might think of the ideal as an identical laboratory setup for each population sampled. However, since different subjects might react differently within such an environment, this is not necessarily a panacea (in addition to the obvious practical difficulty in implementation).

The best approach is to carefully examine the environmental features needed for the task at hand. If an experiment is about color categorization, lighting obviously needs to be controlled; if an experiment is about spatial arrays, adjacent landmarks and handedness need to be controlled; and so on. For example, in the basic experiment reported in Pederson et al. (1998), the use of table tops was not considered essential for tasks testing "table-top space," but the use of two delimited testing surfaces and the geometrical relationship and distances between these surfaces was critical to the design. This allowed the individual experimenters to set up tables or mats on the ground/floor as was more appropriate for the broader material culture.[5]

3.8. Establishing Causal Directionality

Once a correlation between a language pattern and a behavioral response has been experimentally established, the problem of establishing causal directionality remains. While this is a problem for any correlational design, it is particularly vexing for studies of linguistic relativity. Quite simply, it is difficult to rule out the possibility that subjects habitually speak the way they do as a consequence of their culture (and environment) as opposed to the possibility that the culture thinks the way it does because of their language. For discussions of the role of culture vis-à-vis language in linguistic relativity studies, see Bickel (2000), Enfield (2000), and the fairly standard reference of Hanks (1990).

In specific response to work on spatial cognition, Li and Gleitman (2002) argue that behavioral response patterns are not causally attributable to community language preferences, but rather that language use reflects cultural practice and concerns, for example, the many words for snow used by skiers—however, see also Levinson et al. (2002) for an extensive response. To the extent that the language features under investigation are roughly as changeable as the culture, this is certainly a likely possibility. On the other hand, when the language features are essentially fossilized in the grammatical system, they cannot be understood as the consequences of current cultural conditions. If anything, the pattern of grammaticized distinctions reflects the fossilized conceptualizations of one's ancestors.

4. Work within Cognitive Linguistics

Some of the earliest cognitive linguistic work (1970s) explicitly tying grammatical structure to cognition is found in studies by Talmy (see especially Talmy 1977, 1978). This work largely focuses on the universal (or at least broadly found) patterns of language and has been revised and expanded in Talmy (2000a, 2000b). Talmy treats language as one of many "cognitive systems" which has the "set of grammatically specified notions [constitute] the fundamental conceptual structuring system of language. . . . Thus, grammar broadly conceived, is the determinant of conceptual structure within one cognitive system, language" (2000a: 21–22). However, the relationship between this cognitive system (language) and others (i.e., nonlinguistic cognition) is relatively unspecified in his work. Structural commonalities between the various cognitive systems are suggested—most specifically between visual perception and language—but, importantly, Talmy avoids claims that there is any causal effect from linguistic categories to nonlinguistic categories.[6]

Langacker is bolder in the relationship between grammar and cognition: in Cognitive Grammar's "view of linguistic semantics. Meaning is equated with conceptualization (in the broadest sense)" (Langacker 1987: 55). Langacker (1991) further argues that the cognitive models underlying clause structure have prototypes which are rooted in (variable) cultural understanding. To the extent that we find interesting cross-linguistic variation, we can see the work of Talmy and Langacker as sources for linguistic relativity hypotheses to test—as, for example, Slobin (1996, 2000) has begun with the motion event typology of Talmy (1985).

As mentioned above, Lakoff (1987: chapter 18) directly addresses linguistic relativity. Within this chapter on linguistic relativity, there is a discussion of different ways in which two cross-linguistic systems might be "commensurate." They might be *translatable, understandable* (though this is vaguely defined), *commensurate* in usage, share the same *framing*, and/or use the same *organization* of the various underlying concepts. In addition to a summary of the now classic Kay and Kempton (1984), there is an elaborate extension to linguistic relativity of semantics work in Mixtec and English by Brugman (1981) and Brugman and Macaulay (1986).

Metaphor is an obvious area of interest to many cognitive linguists (see Grady, this volume, chapter 8, and references therein). The nature of metaphor is to consider conceptualizations in terms of other linguistically expressed domains. To the extent that source domains can vary cross-linguistically or cross-culturally (or different features of these source domains are mapped), this is an area ripe for linguistic relativity studies. To date, however, linguistic relativity studies—that is to say, work with behavioral data—have largely limited themselves to the study of elemental and literal language. One exception to this is linguistic relativity research on time, which almost necessarily is metaphorically expressed (see section 5.6 below).

5. RESEARCH BY TOPIC AREA

This section gives a brief overview of modern linguistic relativity work organized by topic area. While some comments are given, it is impossible in this space to summarize the findings of the entire body of work. Further, the empirical details of each study are essential to critical evaluation of the findings, so the original sources must be consulted.

5.1. Color

Perhaps the greatest debate in linguistic relativity has been in the domain of color. Historically, linguists and anthropologists had been struck by the seemingly boundless diversity in color nomenclature. Given the obvious biological underpinnings of color perception, this made "color" a domain of choice to seek language-specific effects overriding biological prerequisites.

Lenneberg and Roberts (1956) is one of the earliest attempts to empirically test linguistic relativity, and as such this study spends considerable space defining the intellectual concerns before it reports on a relatively small study involving Zuni versus English color categorization. Brown and Lenneberg (1958) report on various work and develop the notion of *codability*: that is, the use of language as a way to more efficient coding of categories for the purposes not only of communication, but also of augmenting personal memory.

Berlin and Kay (1969) and the updated methodology in Kay and McDaniel (1978) have laid the groundwork of considerable research in color terminology. Central to the method is the use of Munsell color chips as a reference standard which can be carried to various field sites. Universal patterns were found to establish a typology of different color systems which appeared to be built out of a small set of universal principles. Research continues to be robust in this area and the interested reader may wish to consult the conference proceedings published as Hardin and Maffi (1997) for more current perspectives.

Eleanor Rosch (under her previous name: Heider 1971, 1972) found that focal colors (or Hering primaries from Hering's theory of light and color, see Hering 1964) were better remembered even by young children and were also more perceptually salient for them. Further, Heider and Olivier (1972) and Rosch (1973) found that, even for members of a community (the Dani of Papua New Guinea) who had little color terminology at all, certain color examples were better remembered. She argues that these "natural" categories are generally favored in human learning and cognition. This work is often taken as support for universals of color perception, though since the Dani had no linguistic categories to sway them away from biologically primary colors, this cannot be taken as evidence against a potential linguistic influence on color perception.

The effects of language on color categorization could be seen in Kay and Kempton (1984), but any effects of language-specific color terms only surfaced under specific conditions, and the effects were not as robust as earlier researchers had hoped. Various proposals have been made to revise the Berlin and Kay approach in ways which accommodate linguistic relativity effects within a basically universally constrained system. Most notable of these is Vantage Theory, which seeks to explain multiple points of view—even within the putative universals of color perception—and how points of view may be linguistically mediated; see especially MacLaury (1991, 1995, 2000).

Work by Davies and colleagues has also expanded upon the work of Kay and Kempton (1984) by examining a variety of linguistic systems for denoting colors. They then test participants from these speech communities using various categorization tasks. For Turkish, see Oezgen and Davies (1998); for Setswana, English, and Russian, see Davies (1998), Davies and Corbett (1997), and Davies et al. (1998); see also Corbett and Davies (1997) for a discussion of method in language sampling for color terminology.

Especially within anthropology, there has been concern about the fundamental adequacy of the empirical method followed by Berlin and Kay (and later modifications). Jameson and D'Andrade (1997) address the adequacy of the theory of color perception inherent in the use of the Munsell color system. Lucy (1997b) criticizes most work on color terminology as insufficiently descriptive of the actual linguistic properties of the color terms themselves: without an adequate investigation into these properties, it is unclear what the effects may be of forcing reference with these terms into the Munsell system. The worry is that the Munsell system will not only standardize the coding of the responses, but actually create standardized and unnatural responses rather than allowing the terms to refer to their actual reference.

For a survey of recent work exploring color naming and its relationship to nonlinguistic cognition, see Kay and Regier (2006).

5.2. Shape Classification

In determining whether or not the Navajo shape classification system influenced sorting behavior, Carroll and Casagrande (1958) attempted to balance cultural factors across samples by using English-speaking and Navajo-speaking ethnic Navajo children. As a control group, English-speaking, middle-class American children were used. The results from triad classification (by either shape/function or color) were largely consistent with the Navajo verb classification, in that the Navajo-speaking Navajo children demonstrated a greater preference for shape sorting than English-speaking Navajo children. Note, however, that English-speaking middle-class children also patterned like Navajo-speaking children, suggesting to Carroll and Casagrande that cultural factors beyond language play an important role in such classification.

Lucy and Gaskins (2001) also use triad-type methods to compare Yucatecan children and adults with English-speaking Americans. Again, a broad consistency with each language's classification system is found, but interestingly, this only becomes prominent after age nine (see section 5.6)

5.3. Conditional Reasoning

With basic reasoning processes, variation is more likely to be viewed as directly advantageous or disadvantageous, that is, essentially correct or incorrect. Whether the hypothesized cause is linguistic or otherwise, in modern academia, the burden of proof appropriately falls most heavily on the researcher hoping to demonstrate any potential absence (or "deficiency") within a particular community.

The work of Alfred Bloom and his many detractors falls fully into this predicament. Bloom (1981) proposed that Chinese (unlike English) lacks a specific counterfactual construction and that this has led to reduced ability to engage in counterfactual reasoning. The debate was carried across several volumes of *Cognition*: Au (1983, 1984), Bloom (1984), Liu (1985), Takano (1989); making use of different samples, these studies did not generally replicate Bloom's findings.[7] Unfortunately, there has been a tendency to interpret the various results (or lack thereof) as disconfirming linguistic relativity more generally rather than demonstrating a failure of a particular experimental design. Takano used Japanese speakers, who like Chinese speakers, lack a *dedicated* counterfactual construction, but found that their reasoning patterned like English speakers. More recently, Lardiere (1992) investigated Arabic speakers. Arabic patterns like English in that there is an explicit counterfactual construction, yet the Arabic participants performed like Bloom's original Chinese subjects on counterfactual reasoning. From these studies, both Takano and Lardiere conclude that the principal effect on counterfactual reasoning is traceable not to linguistic habit, but to cultural practices of reasoning, testing conventions, and the like.

Another conclusion one might draw from these studies is that we cannot automatically assume that either linguistic or nonlinguistic habit will be discernable from the presence or absence of specialized linguistic constructions. Obviously, those Chinese and Japanese speakers trained in formal counterfactual reasoning must have found some means of expression. Conversely, the Arabic speakers need not have used their counterfactual construction in ways analogous to the ways of formally educated English speakers.

5.4. Number

Cardinal Numbers

One clear way in which languages vary is in their cardinal number systems. In addition to the obvious lack of larger numbers in many languages (at least as native vocabulary), languages also vary in their organization of these numbers. Various languages partially use a base twenty counting system and other languages appear to have relics of base five systems. But even within primarily base ten systems, there is variation of consistency and expression.

Miura (1987) argues that the generally superior mathematical abilities of school children in or from some cultures (especially East Asian) result at least in part from the transparency and exception-free nature of the base ten numerals used for counting, which children generally control prior to beginning formal education— see also the follow-up cross-linguistic studies: Miura and Okamoto (1989), Miura et al. (1988), Miura et al. (1993), Miura et al. (1994), Miura et al. (1999).

Saxton and Towse (1998) provide a more cautious conclusion, suggesting that the influence of native language on the task of learning place values is less than argued for by Miura and colleagues. Many other differences in performance were found across groups which were better accounted for as resulting from general cultural attitudes toward education and so on, than as the result of the linguistic number system.

Grammatical Number

On a grammatical level, languages vary in terms of their grammatical encoding of the number of entities in an event or scene. While this topic has not been widely taken up, the work of Lucy (1992a) is noteworthy for its extensive consideration of attention to number in Mayan and English speakers. An extensive typological discussion of grammatical number, though without focus on issues of linguistic relativity, is provided by Corbett (2000). Lastly, Hill and Hill (1998) discuss the effects of culture on language (rather than linguistic relativity) for number marking (plurals), and in particular the "anti-Whorfian effect" they find in Uto-Aztecan.

5.5. Space

Reference Frames

Currently, the primary area of linguistic relativity research in spatial domains is with reference frames (however, there is also the important developmental work on topological relations by Choi and Bowerman 1991, see below).

Reference frames are the psychological or linguistic representation of relationships between entities in space. They require fixed points of reference, such as the speaker, a landmark, or an established direction. Within linguistics, the typology of reference frames is complicated, but most accounts include something like an intrinsic reference frame (whereby an object is located only with respect to an immediate point, e.g., *The ball is next to the chair*) and various flavors of reference frames which make use of additional orientation (e.g., *The ball is to my right of the chair* or *The ball is to the north of the chair*). Languages vary in terms of their habitually selected reference frames, and following the linguistic relativity hypothesis, speakers should also vary in their encoding spatial memories, making locational calculations, and so forth. For extensive work measuring event-related potential data (recordings at the scalp of electrical charges from brain activity during specific tasks), see the work of Taylor and colleagues: Taylor et al. (1999) and Taylor et al. (2001). These works compare the viewer/speaker-relative (or *egocentric*) reference frame with the intrinsic.

Of note for being broadly comparative across diverse linguistic and cultural communities is the work reported in Pederson et al. (1998), which found correlations between habitual linguistic selection of reference frames and cognitive performance on spatial memory (and other) tasks. There were many studies within this same general project. Perhaps the most important to consult for the theoretical underpinnings for the project are Brown and Levinson (1993) and Levinson (1996). As pointed out by Li and Gleitman (2002), the populations reported as using an absolute/geocardinal (*north of ...*) reference frame were largely rural populations, and the populations using a speaker-relative/egocentric reference frame are largely urban, so there is a potential confound in the population samples between language and culture/environment. For a rebuttal to these concerns and Li and Gleitman's similar experiments, see Levinson et al. (2002); see also Pederson (1998) for a discussion of this urban/rural cultural split.

Motion Events

Talmy (1985, 2000b) identifies a typological contrast in the ways that languages encode basic motion events. To simplify, some languages such as the Romance languages commonly encode the fact of motion and the basic path with the main verb (e.g., *to enter, to ascend*, etc.). In contrast, Germanic and many other languages most commonly encode the fact of motion along with the manner of motion in the verb (e.g., *to wiggle*), and the path is expressed elsewhere.

Slobin (1991, 1996) considers the cognitive consequences of these linguistic patterns for English and Spanish speakers. Slobin (2000) extends this approach to French, Hebrew, Russian, and Turkish. Gennari et al. (2002) and Malt, Sloman, and Gennari (2003) examine these contrasts experimentally and argue for some effects of one's native language pattern on certain nonlinguistic tasks.

5.6. Time

While spatial relationships have been extensively studied for linguistic relativity effects, the effects of different temporal encoding have received much less attention. In part, this may be attributed to the relative difficulty of developing research instruments. An obvious difference cross-linguistically is whether or not a language grammatically encodes tense. Bohnemeyer (1998) discusses the lack of tense-denoting constructions in Yucatec Mayan and contrasts this with German speakers observing the same video stimuli; nonetheless, both samples appeared to have encoded similar event orderings in memory. Languages also have some variation in preferred metaphors for talking about time. Boroditsky (2000, 2001) argues that Mandarin Chinese speakers have a different metaphor for time (vertical) and this appears to influence their nonlinguistic encoding as well.

5.7. Developmental Studies

Ultimately, any linguistic relativity effects must be explained in terms of the acquisition of linguistic categories and the effects on cognitive development.

Choi and Bowerman (1991) and Bowerman and Choi (2001) contrast early lexical acquisition of Korean and English spatial terms, principally those expressing contact, closure, and similar concepts. Korean-speaking adults use spatial terms to categorize subtypes of these different relationships in very different ways from English-speaking adults. Perhaps surprisingly, Choi and Bowerman report that Korean-speaking children as young as two demonstrate linguistic patterning more like the Korean-speaking adults than like the English-speaking children (and vice versa). This suggests that even in fairly early lexical acquisition, children show remarkable sensitivity to the specific language input rather than relying on purportedly universal cognitive categorizations and fitting the language categories onto these.

Lowenstein and Gentner (1998), Gentner and Loewenstein (2002), and Gentner and Boroditsky (2001) argue that metaphor and analogical reasoning are key parts of concept development and early word meaning. To the extent that these are cross-linguistically variable, it can be argued that linguistic relativity effects may be present especially for abstract reasoning which most depends on relational terminology and analogy.

As mentioned in the section on shape classification, Lucy and Gaskins (2001) look at the age of development of language-particular patterns in shape versus material sorting tasks. Assuming one can extrapolate from their data, the critical age at which language helps to direct nonlinguistic behavior (for these sorts of tasks) is around ages 7–9. This suggests that the acquisition of language categories need not immediately manifest cognitive effects in nonlinguistic domains, but rather that there may be a period in which the linguistic categories are initially more solely linguistic and then eventually the analogy from language to other types of categorization is drawn. It may also reflect a greater dependence on linguistically mediated internal thought, à la Vygotsky.

Susan Goldin-Meadow and colleagues have examined the interplay of gesture, home sign, and conventional language use and their relationships to underlying (and developing) cognitive representations. A good recent summary may be found in Goldin-Meadow (2002) and the references within. Zheng and Goldin-Meadow (2002) examine the similarities across cultures in home sign despite notable differences in the adult spoken languages. These commonalities suggest what the underlying conceptual categories may be in children prior to acquiring the "filter" provided by the model of a specific language.

Working with English-speaking children and language acquisition delayed deaf children, de Villiers and de Villiers (2000) argue that language has a vital role in the development of understandings of false beliefs—at least insofar as demonstrated in unseen displacement. (For example, the puppet doesn't see that I replaced the crayons in the crayon box with a key; what does the puppet think is in the crayon box?) Language is eminently suited for the representation of counterfactual and alternative beliefs, so it is unclear whether it is the specifics of language acquisition or just general exposure to alternatives that happen to come through the medium of language which might be driving this development. For a summary of the work by Gopnik and colleagues on the potential interactions of language and cognitive development, especially around ages 1–2, see Gopnik (2001).

5.8. Sign Language versus Spoken Language

Lastly, what of the medium of the language itself? Might the mechanical constraints of spoken language versus sign language have their own influences? Working with native ASL signers and English speakers on mental rotation tasks,

Emmorey, Klima, and Hickok (1998) show evidence that the vast experience of signers in understanding their interlocutors' spatial perspective during signing has given them some advantage in nonlinguistic rotation tasks compared with nonsigners.

6. Future Directions

As can be seen from the above discussion, the issue of linguistic relativity is as open a question as it is broad. However, as empirically driven models of human cognition become increasingly detailed, work within linguistic relativity (and Cognitive Linguistics generally) becomes increasingly specific in its description of cognitive mechanisms.

The question "Does language influence thought?" is being replaced by a battery of questions about whether a given feature of a specific language influences particular cognitive operations, what the exact cognitive mechanisms are which give rise to this influence, and how we can most precisely characterize the nature of this influence? Rather than this being a step away from the "big picture" of human cognition, this general trend toward increasingly precise definitions and, ideally, more falsifiable hypotheses leads us to a simply more reliable understanding of cognition and the role of language within it.

As we discover more of the specific interactions between language and the rest of the cognitive systems, there is a need to understand the time course of this development. Except for Lucy and Gaskins (2001) and some of the home sign studies, there has been virtually no attempt to determine the time course of any linguistic relativity effects. If language influences a particular cognitive operation or conceptualization, does it do so upon acquisition of the language model, shortly subsequent to this acquisition, or is there a gradual "internalization" (in Vygotskian terms) of the linguistic structure as something more than a learned code?

One must also wonder whether certain linguistic construals more readily have influences beyond language than others. For example, is spatial categorization more likely to be influenced by language than color categorization is, or vice versa? If some domains are more linguistically sensitive, what do these domains have in common?

These are all broad questions and are unlikely to be resolved in the immediate future. However, as research in linguistic relativity becomes increasingly mainstream within psychology and linguistics, it seems certain that we will understand ever more of the complexities between language and thought.

NOTES

1. Many more recent writings by Alford on Whorf, linguistic relativity, and related topics can be found on Alford's Web site: http://www.enformy.com/alford.htm.

2. This idea was apparently insufficiently discredited as it has more recently resurfaced in the popular press with Shlain (1998)—where it is now associated with the demise of polytheism and the claimed consequent surge of misogyny in European history.

3. Anecdotally, I can report that subjects in spatial reference frame experiments would use their linguistically dominant frame of reference in nonlinguistic tasks but would switch when they heard an alternate frame of reference used immediately before the task. (Specifically, when an assistant erroneously used nonneutral language in an example.) In subsequent tasks, with no reference frame language repeated, the subjects could switch over to what might well have been a more default reference frame for such tasks. Of course, these subject results are not coded with other subjects, and this dictated extreme care in controlling the immediately preceding linguistic environment during experimental sessions.

4. College students (especially those participating for credit in an introductory psychology class!) are infamous for trying to second guess the "hidden" purpose of an experiment. Surely, such subjects are less directly comparable with the perhaps experimentally less savvy subjects drawn from other populations.

5. Li and Gleitman (2002) changed "small procedural details" (see their footnote 5) in this experiment—notably they eliminated the distance between the tables—and report different results. Although they do not attribute the different results to these changes, but rather to other uncontrolled variables in the original study, the control of the experimental setup clearly can be critical for evaluating the results.

6. The linguistic parallels with basic operations in visual perception imply a bias favoring the building of linguistic categories from more fundamental cognitive categories rather than any particular influence from language to cognition.

7. Cara and Politzer (1993) also found no correspondence of language to reasoning with Chinese and English speakers on counterfactual reasoning tasks, though the design seems uninfluenced by the debate in *Cognition*.

REFERENCES

Alford, Dan K. H. 1978. The demise of the Whorf hypothesis. *Berkeley Linguistics Society* 14: 485–99.

Au, Terry Kit-Fong. 1983. Chinese and English counterfactuals: The Sapir-Whorf hypothesis revisited. *Cognition* 15: 155–87.

Au, Terry Kit-Fong. 1984. Counterfactuals: In reply to Alfred Bloom. *Cognition* 17: 289–302.

Berlin, Brent. 1978. Ethnobiological classification. In Eleanor Rosch and Barbara B. Lloyd, eds., *Cognition and categorization* 9–26. Hillsdale, NJ: Lawrence Erlbaum.

Berlin, Brent, Dennis E. Breedlove, and Peter H. Raven. 1973. General principles of classification and nomenclature in folk biology. *American Anthropologist* 75: 214–42.

Berlin, Brent, and Paul Kay. 1969. *Basic color terms: Their universality and evolution*. Berkeley: University of California Press.

Bickel, Balthasar. 2000. Grammar and social practice: On the role of 'culture' in linguistic relativity. In Susanne Niemeier and René Dirven, eds., *Evidence for linguistic relativity* 161–91. Amsterdam: John Benjamins.

Bloom, Alfred H. 1981. *The linguistic shaping of thought: A study in the impact of language on thinking in China and the West.* Hillsdale, NJ: Lawrence Erlbaum.

Bloom, Alfred H. 1984. Caution—the words you use may affect what you say: A response to Au. *Cognition* 17: 275–87.

Blount, Ben G. 1993. Cultural bases of folk classification systems. In Jeanette Altarriba, ed., *Cognition and culture: A cross-cultural approach to psychology* 3–22. Amsterdam: Elsevier.

Bohnemeyer, Jürgen. 1998. Time relations in discourse: Evidence from a comparative approach to Yukatek Maya. PhD dissertation, Katholieke Universiteit Brabant, Netherlands.

Boroditsky, Lera. 2000. Metaphoric structuring: Understanding time through spatial metaphors. *Cognition* 75: 1–28.

Boroditsky, Lera. 2001. Does language shape thought? Mandarin and English speakers' conceptions of time. *Cognitive Psychology* 43: 1–22.

Bowerman, Melissa, and Soonja Choi. 2001. Shaping meanings for language: Universal and language-specific in the acquisition of spatial semantic categories. In Melissa Bowerman and Stephen C. Levinson, eds., *Language acquisition and conceptual development* 475–511. Cambridge: Cambridge University Press.

Brown, Penelope, and Stephen C. Levinson. 1993. "Uphill" and "downhill" in Tzeltal. *Journal of Linguistic Anthropology* 3: 46–74.

Brown, Roger Langham. 1967. *Wilhelm von Humboldt's conception of linguistic relativity: Janua linguarum.* The Hague: Mouton.

Brown, Roger W., and Eric. H. Lenneberg. 1958. Studies in linguistic relativity. In Eleanor E. Maccoby, Theodore M. Newcomb, and Eugene L. Hartley, eds., *Readings in social psychology* 9–18. New York: Holt, Rinehart and Winston.

Brugman, Claudia. 1981. Story of *Over.* MA thesis, University of California at Berkeley. (Published as *The story of Over: Polysemy, semantics, and the structure of the lexicon.* New York: Garland, 1988)

Brugman, Claudia, and Monica Macaulay. 1986. Interacting semantic systems: Mixtec expressions of location. *Berkeley Linguistics Society* 12: 315–27.

Cara, Francesco, and Guy Politzer. 1993. A comparison of conditional reasoning in English and Chinese. In Jeanette Altarriba, ed., *Cognition and culture: A cross-cultural approach to psychology* 283–97. Amsterdam: Elsevier.

Carroll, John B., and Joseph B. Casagrande. 1958. The function of language classifications in behavior. In Eleanor. E. Maccoby, Theodore M. Newcomb, and Eugene L. Hartley, eds., *Readings in social psychology* 18–31. New York: Holt, Rinehart and Winston.

Carter, Anthony T. 1973. A comparative analysis of systems of kinship and marriage in South Asia. *Proceedings of the Royal Anthropological Institute of Great Britain and Ireland*: 29–54.

Chafe, Wallace. 2000. Loci of diversity and convergence in thought and language. In Martin Pütz and Marjolijn Verspoor, eds., *Explorations in linguistic relativity* 101–23. Amsterdam: John Benjamins.

Choi, Soonja, and Melissa Bowerman. 1991. Learning to express motion events in English and Korean: The influence of language-specific lexicalization patterns. *Cognition* 41: 83–121.

Corbett, Greville G. 2000. *Number.* Cambridge: Cambridge University Press.

Corbett, Greville G., and Ian R. L. Davies. 1997. Establishing basic color terms: Measures and techniques. In C. L. Hardin and Luisa Maffi, eds., *Color categories in thought and language* 197–223. Cambridge: Cambridge University Press.

Danziger, Eve, and Eric Pederson. 1998. Through the looking glass: Literacy, writing systems and mirror image discrimination. *Written Language and Literacy* 1: 153–64.

Davies, Ian R. L. 1998. A study of colour grouping in three languages: A test of the linguistic relativity hypothesis. *British Journal of Psychology* 89: 433–52.

Davies, Ian R. L., and Greville G. Corbett. 1997. A cross-cultural study of colour grouping: Evidence for weak linguistic relativity. *British Journal of Psychology* 88: 493–517.

Davies, Ian R. L., Paul T. Sowden, David T. Jerrett, Tiny Jerrett, and Greville G. Corbett. 1998. A cross-cultural study of English and Setswana speakers on a colour triads task: A test of the Sapir-Whorf hypothesis. *British Journal of Psychology* 89: 1–15.

de Villiers, Jill G., and Peter A. de Villiers. 2000. Linguistic determinism and the understanding of false beliefs. In Peter Mitchell and Kevin John Riggs, eds., *Children's reasoning and the mind* 191–228. East Sussex: Psychology Press.

Duranti, Alessandro. 1997. *Linguistic anthropology*. Cambridge: Cambridge University Press.

Emmorey, Karen, Edward Klima, and Gregory Hickok. 1998. Mental rotation within linguistic and non-linguistic domains in users of American sign language. *Cognition* 68: 221–46.

Enfield, Nick J. 2000. On linguocentrism. In Martin Pütz and Marjolijn Verspoor, eds., *Explorations in linguistic relativity* 125–57. Amsterdam: John Benjamins.

Foley, William A. 1997. *Anthropological linguistics: An introduction*. Oxford: Basil Blackwell.

Geeraerts, Dirk, Stefan Grondelaers, and Peter Bakema. 1994. *The structure of lexical variation: Meaning, naming, and context*. Berlin: Mouton de Gruyter.

Gennari, Silvia P., Steven A. Sloman, Barbara C. Malt, and W. Tecumseh Fitch. 2002. Motion events in language and cognition. *Cognition* 83: 49–79.

Gentner, Dedre, and Lera Boroditsky. 2001. Individuation, relativity, and early word learning. In Melissa Bowerman and Stephen C. Levinson, eds., *Language acquisition and conceptual development* 215–56. Cambridge: Cambridge University Press.

Gentner, Dedre, and Jeffrey Loewenstein. 2002. Relational language and relational thought: Language, literacy, and cognitive development. In Eric Amsel and James P. Byrnes, eds., *The development and consequences of symbolic communication* 87–120. Mahwah, NJ: Lawrence Erlbaum.

Goldin-Meadow, Susan. 2002. From thought to hand: Structured and unstructured communication outside of conventional language. In Eric Amsel and James P. Byrnes, eds., *Language, literacy, and cognitive development: The development and consequences of symbolic communication* 121–50. Mahwah, NJ: Lawrence Erlbaum.

Goody, Jack, and Ian Watt. 1962. The consequences of literacy. *Comparative Studies in Sociology and History* 5: 304–45.

Gopnik, Alison. 2001. Theories, language and culture: Whorf without wincing. In Melissa Bowerman and Stephen C. Levinson, eds., *Language acquisition and conceptual development* 45–69. Cambridge: Cambridge University Press.

Graff, Harvey J. 1987. *The legacies of literacy*. Bloomington: Indiana University Press.

Hanks, William F. 1990. *Referential practice: Language and lived space among the Maya*. Chicago: University of Chicago Press.

Hardin, C. L., and Luisa Maffi. 1997. *Color categories in thought and language*. Cambridge: Cambridge University Press.

Heider, Eleanor R. 1971. "Focal" color areas and the development of color names. *Developmental Psychology* 4: 447–55.

Heider, Eleanor R. 1972. Universals in color naming and memory. *Journal of Experimental Psychology* 93: 10–20.

Heider, Eleanor R., and Donald C. Olivier. 1972. The structure of the color space in naming and memory in two languages. *Cognitive Psychology* 3: 337–54.

Hering, Ewald. 1964. *Outlines of a theory of the light sense.* Cambridge, MA: Harvard University Press.

Hill, Jane H., and Kenneth C. Hill. 1998. Culture influencing language: Plurals of Hopi kin terms in comparative Uto-Aztecan perspective. *Journal of Linguistic Anthropology* 7: 166–80.

Hill, Jane H., and Bruce Mannheim. 1992. Language and world view. *Annual Review of Anthropology* 21: 381–406.

House, Juliane. 2000. Linguistic relativity and translation. In Martin Pütz and Marjolijn Verspoor, eds., *Explorations in linguistic relativity* 69–88. Amsterdam: John Benjamins.

Hunn, Eugene S. 1977. *Tzeltal folk zoology: The classification of discontinuities in nature.* New York: Academic Press.

Hunn, Eugene S. 1982. The utilitarian factor in folk biological classification. *American Anthropologist* 84: 830–47.

Hunt, Earl, and Franca Agnoli. 1991. The Whorfian hypothesis: A cognitive psychology perspective. *Psychological Review* 98: 377–89.

Jameson, Kimberly, and Roy G. D'Andrade. 1997. It's not really red, green, yellow, blue: An inquiry into perceptual color space. In C. L. Hardin and Luisa Maffi, eds., *Color categories in thought and language* 295–319. Cambridge: Cambridge University Press.

Kay, Paul. 1996. Intra-speaker relativity. In John J. Gumperz and Stephen C. Levinson, eds., *Rethinking linguistic relativity* 97–114. Cambridge: Cambridge University Press.

Kay, Paul, and Willett Kempton. 1984. What is the Sapir-Whorf hypothesis? *American Anthropologist* 86: 65–79.

Kay, Paul, and Chad K. McDaniel. 1978. The linguistic significance of the meanings of basic color terms. *Language* 54: 610–46.

Kay, Paul, and Terry Regier. 2006. Language, thought and color: Recent developments. *Trends in Cognitive Sciences* 10: 51–54.

Koerner, Konrad E. F. 2000. Towards a 'full pedigree' of the 'Sapir-Whorf Hypothesis': From Locke to Lucy. In Martin Pütz and Marjolijn Verspoor, eds., *Explorations in linguistic relativity* 1–23. Amsterdam: John Benjamins.

Lakoff, George. 1987. *Women, fire, and dangerous things: What categories reveal about the mind.* Chicago: University of Chicago Press.

Langacker, Ronald W. 1987. Nouns and verbs. *Language* 63: 53–94.

Langacker, Ronald W. 1991. *Foundations of cognitive grammar.* Vol. 2, *Descriptive application.* Stanford, CA: Stanford University Press.

Lardiere, Donna. 1992. On the linguistic shaping of thought: Another response to Alfred Bloom. *Language in Society* 21: 231–51.

Lee, Penny. 1996. *The Whorf theory complex: A critical reconstruction.* Amsterdam: John Benjamins.

Lee, Penny. 2000. When is 'linguistic relativity' Whorf's linguistic relativity? In Martin Pütz and Marjolijn Verspoor, eds., *Explorations in linguistic relativity* 45–68. Amsterdam: John Benjamins.

Lenneberg, Eric H., and John M. Roberts. 1956. *The language of experience: A study in methodology.* International Journal of American Linguistics Memoir, no. 13. Baltimore, MD: Waverly Press.

Levinson, Stephen C. 1996. Frames of references and Molyneux's question: Crosslinguistic evidence. In Paul Bloom, Mary A. Peterson, Lynn Nadel, and Merrill Garrett, eds., *Language and space* 109–69. Cambridge, MA: MIT Press.

Levinson, Stephen C., Sotaro Kita, Daniel B. M. Hauna, and Björn H. Rasch. 2002. Returning the tables: Language affects spatial reasoning. *Cognition* 84: 155–88.

Li, Peggy, and Lila Gleitman. 2002. Turning the tables: Language and spatial reasoning. *Cognition* 83: 265–94.

Liu, Lisa Gabern. 1985. Reasoning counterfactually in Chinese: Are there any obstacles? *Cognition* 21: 239–70.

Loftus, Elizabeth F. 1975. Leading questions and the eyewitness report. *Cognitive Psychology* 7: 560–72.

Losonsky, Michael, ed. 1999. *Wilhelm von Humboldt: On language: On the diversity of human language construction and its influence on the mental development of the human species.* Cambridge: Cambridge University Press.

Lowenstein, Jeffrey, and Dedre Gentner. 1998. Relational language facilitates analogy in children. *Proceedings of the Twentieth Annual Conference of the Cognitive Science Society* 615–20. Mahwah, NJ.: Lawrence Erlbaum.

Lucy, John A. 1992a. *Grammatical categories and cognition: A case study of the linguistic relativity hypothesis.* Cambridge: Cambridge University Press.

Lucy, John A. 1992b. *Language diversity and thought: A reformulation of the linguistic relativity hypothesis.* Cambridge: Cambridge University Press.

Lucy, John A. 1997a. Linguistic relativity. *Annual Review of Anthropology* 26: 291–312.

Lucy, John A. 1997b. The linguistics of "color." In C. L. Hardin and Luisa Maffi, eds., *Color categories in thought and language* 320–46. Cambridge: Cambridge University Press.

Lucy, John A., and Suzanne Gaskins. 2001. Grammatical categories and the development of classification preferences: A comparative approach. In Melissa Bowerman and Stephen C. Levinson, eds., *Language acquisition and conceptual development* 257–83. Cambridge: Cambridge University Press.

Lucy, John A., and Richard A. Shwedder. 1988. The effect of incidental conversation on memory for focal colors. *American Anthropologist* 90: 923–31.

Luria, Aleksandr Romanovich. 1976. *Cognitive development, its cultural and social foundations.* Cambridge, MA: Harvard University Press.

MacLaury, Robert E. 1991. Exotic color categories: Linguistic relativity to what extent? *Journal of Linguistic Anthropology* 1: 26–51.

MacLaury, Robert E. 1995. Vantage theory. In John R. Taylor and Robert E. MacLaury, eds., *Language and the cognitive construal of the world* 231–76. Berlin: Mouton de Gruyter.

MacLaury, Robert E. 2000. Linguistic relativity and the plasticity of categorization: Universalism in a new key. In Martin Pütz and Marjolijn H. Verspoor, eds., *Explorations in linguistic relativity* 251–93. Amsterdam: John Benjamins.

Malt, Barbara C., Steven A. Sloman, and Silvia P. Gennari. 2003. Speaking versus thinking about objects and actions. In Dedre Gentner and Susan Goldin-Meadow, eds., *Language in mind: Advances in the study of language and thought* 81–111. Cambridge, MA: MIT Press.

Manchester, Martin L. 1985. *The philosophical foundations of Humboldt's linguistic doctrines.* Amsterdam: John Benjamins.

Miura, Irene T. 1987. Mathematics achievement as a function of language. *Journal of Educational Psychology* 79: 79–82.

Miura, Irene T., Chungsoon C. Kim, Chih-mei Chang, and Yukari Okamoto. 1988. Effects of language characteristics on children's cognitive representation of number: Cross-national comparisons. *Child Development* 59: 1445–50.

Miura, Irene T., and Yukari Okamoto. 1989. Comparisons of U.S. and Japanese first graders' cognitive representation of number and understanding of place value. *Journal of Educational Psychology* 81: 109–14.

Miura, Irene T., Yukari Okamoto, Chungsoon C. Kim, Chih-Mei Chang, Marcia Steere, and Michel Fayol. 1994. Comparisons of children's cognitive representation of number: China, France, Japan, Korea, Sweden, and the United States. *International Journal of Behavioral Development* 17: 401–11.

Miura, Irene T., Yukari Okamoto, Chungsoon C. Kim, Marcia Steere, and Michel Fayol. 1993. First graders' cognitive representation of number and understanding of place value: Cross-national comparisons: France, Japan, Korea, Sweden, and the United States. *Journal of Educational Psychology* 85: 24–30.

Miura, Irene T., Yukari Okamoto, Vesna Vlahovic-Stetic, Chungsoon C. Kim, and Jong Hye Han. 1999. Language supports for children's understanding of numerical fractions: Cross-national comparisons. *Journal of Experimental Child Psychology* 74: 356–65.

Morais, José, Luz Cary, Jésus Alegria, and Paul Bertelson. 1979. Does awareness of speech as a sequence of phones arise spontaneously? *Cognition* 7: 323–31.

Oezgen, Emre, and Ian R. L. Davies. 1998. Turkish color terms: Tests of Berlin and Kay's theory of color universals and linguistic relativity. *Linguistics* 36: 919–56.

Olson, David R. 1991. Literacy as metalinguistic activity. In David R. Olson and Nancy Torrance, eds., *Literacy and orality* 251–70. Cambridge: Cambridge University Press.

Olson, David R. 2002. What writing does to the mind. In Eric Amsel and James P. Byrnes, eds., *Language, literacy, and cognitive development: The development and consequences of symbolic communication* 153–65. Mahwah, NJ: Lawrence Erlbaum.

Ong, Walter J. 1992. Writing is a technology that restructures thought. In Pam Downing, Susan D. Lima, and Michael Noonan, eds., *The linguistics of literacy* 293–319. Amsterdam: John Benjamins.

Pederson, Eric. 1993. Geographic and manipulable space in two Tamil linguistic systems. In Andrew U. Frank and Irene Campari, eds., *Spatial information theory* 294–311. Berlin: Springer Verlag.

Pederson, Eric. 1995. Language as context, language as means: Spatial cognition and habitual language use. *Cognitive Linguistics* 6: 33–62.

Pederson, Eric. 1998. Spatial language, reasoning, and variation across Tamil communities. In Petr Zima and Vladimír Tax, eds., *Language and location in space and time* 111–19. Munich: Lincom Europa.

Pederson, Eric. 2003. Mirror-image discrimination among nonliterate, monoliterate, and biliterate Tamil speakers. *Written Language and Literacy* 6: 71–91.

Pederson, Eric, Eve Danziger, David Wilkins, Stephen Levinson, Sotaro Kita, and Gunter Senft. 1998. Semantic typology and spatial conceptualization. *Language* 74: 557–89.

Read, Charles, Yun-Fei Zhang, Hong-Yin Nie, and Bao-Qing Ding. 1986. The ability to manipulate speech sounds depends on knowing alphabetic writing. *Cognition* 24: 31–44.

Rosch, Eleanor. 1973. Natural categories. *Cognitive Psychology* 4: 328–50.

Saxton, Matthew, and John N. Towse. 1998. Linguistic relativity: The case of place value in multi-digit numbers. *Journal of Experimental Child Psychology* 69: 66–79.

Scinto, Leonard F. M. 1986. *Written language and psychological development*. New York: Academic Press.

Scribner, Sylvia, and Michael Cole. 1981. *The psychology of literacy*. Cambridge, MA: Harvard University Press.

Shlain, Leonard. 1998. *The alphabet versus the goddess: The conflict between word and image*. New York: Viking.

Silverstein, Michael. 1985. Language and the culture of gender: At the intersection of structure, usage, and ideology. In Elizabeth Mertz and Richard J. Parmentier, eds., *Semiotic mediation: Sociocultural and psychological perspectives* 219–59. Orlando, FL: Academic Press.

Silverstein, Michael. 1987. Cognitive implications of a referential hierarchy. In Maya Hickmann, ed., *Social and functional approaches to language* 125–64. Orlando, FL: Academic Press.

Slobin, Dan I. 1991. Learning to think for speaking: Native language, cognition, and rhetorical style. *Pragmatics* 1: 7–25.

Slobin, Dan I. 1996. Two ways to travel: Verbs of motion in English and Spanish. In Masayoshi Shibatani and Sandra A. Thompson, eds., *Grammatical constructions: Their form and meaning* 195–219. Oxford: Oxford University Press.

Slobin, Dan I. 2000. Verbalized events: A dynamic approach to linguistic relativity and determinism. In Susanne Niemeier and René Dirven, eds., *Evidence for linguistic relativity* 107–38. Amsterdam: John Benjamins.

Smith, Marion V. 1996. Linguistic relativity: On hypotheses and confusions. *Communication & Cognition* 29: 65–90.

Takano, Yohtaro. 1989. Methodological problems in cross-cultural studies of linguistic relativity. *Cognition* 31: 141–62.

Talmy, Leonard. 1977. Rubber-sheet cognition in language. *Chicago Linguistic Society* 13: 612–28.

Talmy, Leonard. 1978. The relation of grammar to cognition—a synopsis. In David Waltz ed., *Proceedings of TINLAP-2* 14–24. New York: Association for Computing Machinery.

Talmy, Leonard. 1985. Lexicalization patterns: Semantic structure in lexical form. In Timothy Shopen, ed., *Language typology and syntactic description*, vol. 3, *Grammatical categories and the lexicon* 57–149. Cambridge: Cambridge University Press.

Talmy, Leonard. 2000a. *Toward a cognitive semantics*. Vol. 1, *Concept structuring systems*. Cambridge, MA: MIT Press.

Talmy, Leonard. 2000b. *Toward a cognitive semantics*. Vol. 2, *Typology and process in concept structuring*. Cambridge, MA: MIT Press.

Taylor, Holly A., Robert R. Faust, Tatiana Sitnikova, Susan J. Naylor, and Phillip J. Holcomb. 2001. Is the donut in front of the car? An electrophysiological study examining spatial reference frame processing. *Canadian Journal of Experimental Psychology* 55: 175–84.

Taylor, Holly A., Susan J. Naylor, Robert R. Faust, and Phillip J. Holcomb. 1999. "Could you hand me those keys on the right?" Disentangling spatial reference frames using different methodologies. *Spatial Cognition and Computation* 1: 381–97.

Whorf, Benjamin L. 1956. *Language, thought, and reality: Selected writings of Benjamin Lee Whorf*. Cambridge, MA: MIT Press.

Whorf, Benjamin L., and George L. Trager. [1938] 1996. Report on linguistic research in the department of Anthropology of Yale University for the term Sept. 1937–June 1938. In Penny Lee, *The Whorf theory complex: A critical reconstruction* 251–80. Amsterdam: John Benjamins.

Zheng, Mingyu, and Susan Goldin-Meadow. 2002. Thought before language: How deaf and hearing children express motion events across cultures. *Cognition* 85: 145–74.

CHAPTER 39

COGNITIVE LINGUISTICS AND ANTHROPOLOGICAL LINGUISTICS

....

GARY B. PALMER

1. INTRODUCTION

....

Coming from opposite directions on the cognitive-cultural spectrum, linguists are approaching a theory of grammar in which meaning originates not only in biologically driven cognitive processes and embodied categories of physical and social experience, but also in cultural traditions. Each of these sources of meaning provides schemas and more elaborate cognitive models that constitute semantic categories. Culture takes on heightened significance in this equation when we consider that even embodied categories such as that of 'container' may be shaped by living within dwellings of various architectures or by the sight, feel, and characteristic usage of household cups, bowls, saucers, and baskets (Sinha and Jensen de López 2000). This perspective has been called *Cultural Linguistics* (Palmer 1996), but it is entirely consistent with Cognitive Linguistics as defined by Langacker (1999a: 16), who has stated that "language is an essential instrument and component of culture, whose reflection in linguistic structure is pervasive and quite significant." Similarly, Lakoff has argued that metaphorical idioms involve cultural knowledge in the form of conventional images and that links in radial semantic categories are structured by experiential domains, which may be culture-specific

(Lakoff 1987: 95; Lakoff and Johnson 1999: 69).[1] Making the point even more directly, Geeraerts and Grondelaers (1995: 177) claimed, "If cognitive models are cultural models, they are also cultural institutions." Thus, it is clear that Cognitive Linguistics must keep one eye on culture. It is the shift of focus to culture as a source of lexicon, grammar, and metaphor that takes us into the realm of Anthropological Linguistics.

This chapter focuses on the intersection of cultural knowledge with the semantic component of Cognitive Grammar. In the theory of Cognitive Grammar, the semantic component includes Idealized Cognitive Models and maps, domains of experience, image schemas, conceptual metaphors and metonymies, prototypes, complex categories, radial categories, and encyclopedic knowledge (Lakoff and Johnson 1980; Lakoff 1987; Langacker 1987, 1990, 1991, 2000). These elements almost always present important cultural components, in that they take specific forms which speakers learn in the course of socialization and enculturation. Cognitive models that are culturally specific may be termed *cultural models*. Though we may think of cultural models as primarily structuring social interaction and cultural artifacts, they may also provide specific conceptual structure for *cognitive maps* of salient physical domains of nature, such as geography or anatomy (Hallowell 1955; Wallace 1965; Bickel 1997; Basso 1990; Palmer 1998a). Cultural models of social action may be termed *scenarios* (Lakoff 1987; Palmer 1996) or *cultural scripts* (Schank and Abelson 1977; Frake 1981; van Dijk 1987; Wierzbicka 1994a, 1994b), depending on whether one wishes to highlight contingencies and expectations (scenarios) or fixed sequences with slots for paradigmatic alternatives (scripts).[2] Others simply refer to them as *schemas* (Malcolm and Sharifian 2002; Sharifian 2001, 2002) or *scenes* (Grady and Johnson 1997). The conceptual content of scenarios may pertain to any social institutions or domains of discourse, from the mythical and ritual to the economic and domestic. Lakoff (1987) based his famous interpretation of Dyirbal noun classifiers on the domain of myth. In Palmer and Woodman (1999) and Palmer (2006), we centered our analysis of Shona noun classifiers on the domestic activity of pounding grain. Wierzbicka (1994b) presented scripts of discourse on various topics in Japanese and in American Black and White English.

Examples of cultural structuring of scenes with schemas, scenarios, or scripts are myriad; but a few examples will make the point. In English, we commonly conceptualize the future as lying ahead of us on the horizontal plane. When the speaker of Cora, a Uto-Aztecan language of Mexico, talks about the future, we find that time marches uphill, curving around the side of the hill on a path leading to the top (Eugene Casad, p.c.). In southwest Australia, Aboriginal English *half* refers to any degree of partiality (Malcolm and Sharifian 2002; also see Sharifian 2001), which suggests that these speakers apply a different cultural schema than that of non-Aboriginal English *half*. In Zapotec, the schemas that in English must be termed *in* or *under* are both referenced by one term whose prototype meaning is 'stomach' (Sinha and Jensen de López 2000). Examples such as these, revealing conceptualizations that are simultaneously semantic and cultural, could be multiplied into the thousands. Scholars have been aware of cross-linguistic differences in construal and categorization of common experiences since at least the early nineteenth century (Humboldt [1836] 1972).

If we subscribe to Langacker's (1987: 63) assertion that semantic knowledge is encyclopedic, then semantic schemas may be discovered and recorded by systematic ethnographic research. Linguistics that aspires to explain grammatical structure requires ethnographic methods aimed at discovering and verifying those cultural models, maps, and scenarios that govern and motivate linguistic usages, where *usage* refers not only to grammar, but also to the pragmatic dimension of language—the uses of language to accomplish social goals (Duranti 1997).

This chapter examines research in two broad semantic domains: (i) agency and emotion and (ii) spatial orientation. There is no presumption that these categories have folk or emic status in other languages; their status is merely analytic. In actual case studies, one seeks to discover how speakers themselves delineate their semantic domains. One can think of other semantic domains that linguists and anthropologists have studied—color, kinship, illness, firewood, botany, anatomy, geography, and the earmarkings of reindeer come to mind. The two discussed in this chapter are less well publicized than the research on color terms and kinship, but they are prominent in contemporary research.[3] My purpose is to discuss new approaches and findings in each of the selected domains that offer promise for Anthropological Linguistics. I focus on studies demonstrating strong interdependencies between grammar and culture, but I will show that the findings do not support a strong Whorfian position on the determination of perception by grammar.

2. Agency and Emotion

Emotion language has been the object of intensive study in recent years, both in Cognitive Linguistics and in anthropology (see, e.g., Niemeier and Dirven 1997; Palmer and Occhi 1999; Wierzbicka 1999; Kövecses 2000). Much of this research has focused on the search for universals in emotion language and the debate over whether any universals can be demonstrated (see, e.g., Geeraerts and Grondelaers 1995 vs. Kövecses 1995; Kövecses and Palmer 1999; Kövecses, Palmer, and Dirven 2002). In this section, I will first show that many verbal expressions of emotion are governed by conceptual scenarios in which emotions are evoked and lead to subsequent actions and thoughts (see also Dirven, Wolf, and Polzenhagen, this volume, chapter 46). These scenarios of emotion presume agents and patients who possess various qualities and degrees of agency that are specific to languages and cultures. The topic of agency is one that has received much attention in contemporary anthropology, especially among critical theorists who study social inequalities pertaining to race, ethnicity, gender, or class (Ortner 1996; Ahearn 1999). In linguistics, topics pertinent to agency include voice, ergativity, transitivity, and hierarchies of animacy or empathy, all of which have received extensive study.[4] Thus, it seems worthwhile to explore connections between the anthropological notion of agency and the grammatical topic of voice. I propose that morphemes of voice predicate and profile highly abstract scenarios of agency. To illustrate, I will describe the usage of grammatical voice in the emotion language of a Tagalog melodrama in which agency is very much at stake. Emotion language is not the only domain exhibiting connections between voice and agency, but emotional scenes often highlight the links.

2.1. Agency and Grammatical Voice

The grammar of voice should be of high interest to linguistic anthropologists as well as to linguists, because it provides vehicles for the communication of agency. Linguistic anthropologists take it as axiomatic that agency is not only expressed by language, but also constructed and maintained by it (Duranti 1997; Ahearn 1999). Agency is the capacity of an intentional being or social group to make choices, to perform actions that have intended consequences, to effect results, or to control situations. It is conferred by political and economic power, which are central to theories of self, gender, race, ethnicity, and class. Grammatical voice refers to how linguistic forms and constructions predicate relationships between nominal participants in a clause, particularly the degree of influence of active Agents on the objects of action or attention. *Voice* covers such phenomena as the English active and passive voice, the "middle" voice of Greek and Interior Salish languages, reflexive verbs, noncontrol verbal affixes (which may be misleadingly called "causatives"), experiential verb forms, "impersonal" constructions, and antipassives (Crystal 1991; Langacker 1991). Ergative markers and active transitive constructions signal relatively high agency in a clausal subject or focal participant. Passive constructions, absolutive markers, and noncontrol or stative verb forms signal relatively low agency in subjects and focal participants. Thus, these voicing constructions are crucial to discourses involving the assertion, denial, and negotiation of agency.

But agency is not one-dimensional. Prototypically, it involves an Agent who applies mechanical force to an object or a Patient, but it could also mean applying social influence or controlling the actions of a secondary active participant. Or it may involve nothing more than active attention and perception as contrasted with experience over which one lacks control. Thus, it would appear that there is no simple semantic model of agency that can be applied cross-linguistically and cross-culturally. Most probably, the grammar of agency is constructed more or less uniquely in each language. Here I propose that grammatical morphemes and constructions of voice predicate highly schematic scenarios that characterize either the influence of agents on other participants, the degree of control over events affecting the agent or patient, or the degree of direct involvement of agents in predicated events or processes. These semantic qualities are independent of, but interact with, related potentials in the verb or verb stem. Some of these possibilities are diagrammed for Tagalog voice constructions in Palmer (2006).

To the extent that expressions signaling voice are based either directly or met-aphorically on scenes involving mechanical forces, their semantics may be repre-sented by Talmy's (1988) model of force dynamics (see also De Mulder, this vol-ume, chapter 12). A well-known feature of Navajo verb morphology demonstrates that each culture arrives at its own conventional construals of the force dynamics of events. Navajo can mark a transitive verb construction with one or the other of the prefixes *yi-* or *bi-*. It was formerly thought that the *yi-* marked transitive objects and *bi-* marked passive subjects, but Witherspoon (1977) has shown this to be an oversimplification. The *bi-* is best understood as marking a scenario in which a controlling subject allows him-/her-/itself to be acted upon by a noncon-trolling agent. Relative control is defined by a cultural schema that ranks intelli-gent "talking" beings (mostly people) above less intelligent "calling" beings (mostly animals), large beings above small ones, and animate beings above inanimate ob-jects. Infants are ranked with "calling" beings. Thus, Navajo grammar is not simply marking Agonists and Antagonists as Agents and objects; it is also marking the Navajo construal of the mental efforts that control events (Palmer 1996: 158), a lin-guistic development whose appearance in some language or other would have been predictable from Talmy's (1988) theory of force dynamics.

In many languages, it is uncommon to explicitly mention agents of transitive constructions, so that sentence subjects are often Experiencers or objects of tran-sitive actions. In some of these languages, such as Samoan, a transitive Agent may require explicit ergative marking, while in others, such as Tagalog, transitive Agents are given no special marking,[5] but absolutives (objects, Patients, and Experiencers) are focused. In a study of village council meetings in Western Samoa, Duranti (1994: 114–43) has shown how the study of grammar in context can reveal estab-lished patterns of agency as well as bids and concessions thereof. During the be-ginnings of meetings, participants use few constructions with ergative Agents, re-vealing a reluctance to assign agency. As meetings progress, ergative constructions are used only where participants are receiving credit or blame or where the power of actors is acknowledged. This is most evident in talk about actions of the Al-mighty, which place the Lord in the ergative case (126). Duranti pointed out that speaking with ergative Agents constructs relations of power as much as it reflects them. The powerful may use ergative constructions to frame the situation, but the less powerful use them at their own risk. Section 2.2 will demonstrate how voice morphology expresses qualities of agency in Tagalog by predicating scenarios in-volving direct and indirect agency and noncontrol.

2.2. Agency and Emotion Language

In linguistics, emotion is often regarded as a kind of basic experience that is expressed or predicated by particular lexemes and constructions, but in linguistic anthropology, emotion language is more likely to be treated as a kind of discourse with pragmatic consequences (Rosaldo 1984; Lutz 1988; Palmer and Brown 1998).

Such discourses are culturally specific, as are the emotionally evocative and reactive scenarios. In fact, in some languages one discusses the evocations and reactions rather than the focal emotional experience (Rosaldo 1984, 1990; Palmer and Brown 1998).

The importance of emotion scenarios is recognized by both linguistic relativists and universalists. For example, Catherine Lutz, a relativist, said in her study of Ifaluk emotion words that "to understand the meaning of an emotion word is to be able to envisage (and perhaps to find oneself able to participate in) a complicated scene with actors, actions, interpersonal relationships in a particular state of repair, moral points of view, facial expressions, personal and social goals, and sequences of events" (1988: 10). Lutz used the terms *scene* and *scenario* interchangeably. Wierzbicka (1994c; 1996: 183; 1999) defines each emotion term by listing a culturally specific set of scripts (see also Harkins and Wierzbicka 2001). Each emotion script is constructed using items from a small set of proposed universal semantic primitives, such as BAD, DO, FEEL, THINK, WANT, and so on.

Kövecses (1988), a universalist, proposed that the English model of TRUE LOVE begins with the ideas 'true love comes along', 'the other attracts me irresistibly', and 'the attraction reaches a limit point on the intensity scale at once'. Using the terms *scene* and *scenario* interchangeably, Kövecses found that emotion metaphors of English are susceptible to analysis in terms of force dynamics. At the heart of the system is a scenario that forms the basis of "the most pervasive folk theory of emotion coded into English" (Kövecses 2000: 85):

> (1) cause of emotion—force tendency of the cause of emotion => (2) self has emotion—force tendency of emotion => (3) self's force tendency ↔ emotion's force tendency => (4) resultant effect.

Thus, we find that several prominent researchers with diverse perspectives on emotion language have found useful the notions of scenario and script. Such scenarios may involve the self or groups undergoing experiences over which they lack control, being impelled to action, or undertaking volitional actions. In the remainder of this section, it will be shown that grammatical voice provides vehicles for the expression of force dynamics in scenarios of emotion, and thereby provides linguistic anthropologists with an entry to the topic of agency.

Using the approach outlined above, I studied a Tagalog video melodrama, *Sana'y Maulit Muli* 'I Hope It Will Be Repeated Again', which depicts two young Filipino middle-class lovers, Agnes and Jerry (Palmer 1998b). Agnes's mother, who lives in San Francisco, urges her to come to the United States. She complies, and Jerry arrives later. In the course of the film, the couple experiences the anguish of separation from family and one another, onerous social demands imposed by the market economy, and victimization by callous employers and immigration officials. Their emotional conversations appear to be largely about the loss and recapture of personal agency. Alice and Jerry are not from the world's downtrodden classes, but they belong to an age group and social class for whom agency is problematic; and therefore, their use of grammatical voice is of interest.

In Tagalog, several voice affixes predicate the agency or nonagency of the focal participant in a clause. In their conversations, Agnes and Jerry most often present themselves as grammatical Experiencers or Patients. In those instances when they represent themselves as actors, they are seldom placed in grammatical focus, so their agency is de-emphasized. Focus is marked by the referential preposition *ang* (e.g., *ang babae* 'the woman'), by the use of a referential pronoun (e.g., *ako* 'I'), or by the use of a referential personal name marker (e.g., *si Adelfa*). The focus construction in Tagalog is here interpreted as a marker of salience, a means of *profiling* participants and processes (Langacker 1999a: 27). Grammatical focus on an actor marks the actor's agency as salient. If an experiencer in a noncontrol construction or undergoer in a transitive construction has grammatical focus, it indicates lack of agency on the part of that participant. The examples which follow will illustrate use of focus in emotional expressions. Very typical of the emotional language in this melodrama is a construction with a noncontrol affix (*ma-* ~ *na-* ~ *pa-*) and focus on the patient or experiencer, as in Agnes's complaint of boredom in (1). Focus is indicated by the referential first-person pronoun *ako*, which contrasts with genitive *ko* and directional *akin*.

(1) **na**-ba-bato   **ako**
     NC.RLS-R-stone   1SG.SPC
     'I am stoned [turned to stone].'

At the climax of the story, Jerry appears to examine his own motivations and uses more active language. His one clearly agentive utterance is that in (2), in which his use of the active prefix *nag-*, although it is not a highly transitive prefix, placed him in focus as the actor, as shown by the referential prefix *ako*.

(2) *dahil*   ***nag**-ba-baka-sakali*   ***ako**-ng*   *ma-ulit*   *yun-ng*
     because RLS.AF-R-perhaps-COND 1SG.SPC-LG NC.IRR-repeat REM.SPC-LG
     dati
     former
     'because I am hoping the past will be repeated'

Sentence (3), from a pop song not in the film, shows that emotional language can be strongly agentive, in the sense of invoking mental effort and choice, even where transitivity is weak. Once again, the active verbal prefix *nag-* occurs in a construction with the referential first-person pronoun *ako*, which here appears twice, once in the inverse position before the verbs. The English expression "I love you" is used as a verb stem.

(3) *Ngayon **ako**-ay*   ***nag**-si-sisi*   *kung bakit **ako***   ***nag**-"I love you"!!!*[6]
     now   1SG.SPC-PM AF.RLS-R-regret COND why 1SG.SPC AF.RLS-"I love you"
     'Now I am regretting ever saying "I love you"!!!'

How do these expressions relate to scenarios of emotion, such as the English scenario outlined by Kövecses (2000)? Many of the emotional expressions in the film are like (1), expressions of emotion with noncontrol morphology. These are clear examples of Kövecses's step 2, *self has emotion—force tendency of emotion*, but the causes (step 1) may only be recoverable from an understanding of the preceding events. Sentence (3), with active voice, corresponds to Kövecses's step 3, the struggle between self and emotion: *self's force tendency ↔ emotion's force tendency*. Thus, the voice morphology of Tagalog does not in itself predicate all the force dynamics of emotion scenarios, but it supplies elements of force-dynamic constructions.

Close analyses of ergativity and voice, such as those of Witherspoon (1977), Duranti (1994), Palmer (1998b, 2006), and Siiroinen (2003), can reveal much about the construal of discourse situations by the participants, especially the construal of scenarios involving force dynamics. It is thus an indispensable tool in Anthropological Linguistics, where human agency is a central interest. Conversely, constructions involving ergativity and voice can best be studied by examining their uses in discourses where agency is at issue. Such discourses are always defined and structured by culture. The same issues that structure research on emotion language—universals, voice, agency, scenarios, and metaphor/metonymy—also surface in the domain of thinking (D'Andrade 1995; Fortescue 2001; Palmer, Goddard, and Lee 2003).

3. Spatiocultural Orientation

Spatial orientation has commonly been investigated as a semantic domain with absolute or intrinsic frames of reference. My purpose in this section is to relativize this domain and unify the theory of spatial domains with that of other semantic domains. Unification is possible if spatial maps are treated as subtypes of cultural models and if it is acknowledged that in all cultures some spatial maps are tightly integrated with other kinds of cultural maps and models, such as those of gender, ethnicity, ethics, and cosmology. This perspective, developed within a general framework of cognitive processes, should find many sites of application in Anthropological Linguistics.

3.1. Spatial Orientation

Spatial language holds great fascination for both cognitive and anthropological linguists, perhaps because spatial contexts can be more readily controlled and described than is possible for domains such as emotion. Perhaps we all feel that we understand our three-dimensional environment intuitively and that cross-linguistic studies will readily sort out languages into a few logical types in their partitioning of space. If that is the case, it is not evident in recent research results, which favor a relativistic view of spatial language. If the topic of how people talk about space, spatial relations, and orientations in space appears at first to be straightforward, it soon leads on into unexpected complexities. Subtopics include image schemas and their transformations (Brugman 1981; Talmy 1983; Lakoff 1987; Zlatev, this volume, chapter 13), deixis and orientation (Casad and Langacker 1985; Casad 1988, 2001; Brown 1991; Levinson 1992, 1996; Haviland 1993, 1996; Bickel 1997; Heine 1997; Senft 1997a, 1997b; Zlatev, this volume, chapter 13), folk topographical and navigational models (Hutchins 1995; Hill 1997; Wassmann 1997), metonymy and compositionality of spatial terms (Langacker 1999b), and spatial metaphors (Casad 2003).

In this study, I will concentrate on studies of particular interest to linguistic anthropology; but in order to treat them systematically, it is first necessary to present a more relativistic theoretical framework for the discussion of spatial orientation than Levinson's (1996) popular framework, which begins with classical mathematical coordinate systems. The framework developed here differs in focusing on the culturally defined cognitive maps of speakers and listeners. It builds on the approach to spatial language developed in Casad and Langacker (1985), Casad (1988, 1993), and Langacker (1999b). The approach enables the analysis of deictic orientations that are discounted in Levinson's framework, and it more easily achieves a fine-grained analysis of complex spatial predications. Furthermore, since cognitive maps of spatial relations are cultural models in this approach, it is readily apparent how spatial maps can be semantically integrated with other kinds of cultural models, such as those of gender, history, and supernatural belief systems.

Levinson (1996) distinguished "frames of reference" on three dimensions: (i) whether their coordinates are intrinsic or relative, (ii) whether the origin of their coordinates is speaker, addressee, third person, or object, and (iii) whether their "relatum" (Ground in a Figure/Ground relation) is the same as or different from the origin. But since we are dealing with cognitive maps of spatial relations, an intrinsic coordinate need only be intrinsic to a cognitive model, not to an object in the world. Since we are concerned with orientation and topography, I will use the term *map* for cognitive models that include orientational frames (Bickel 1997). Therefore, in place of *intrinsic*, I suggest the alternative term *object map* to evoke a topographical cognitive model of an object, an environment, or some other entity. Levinson arrived at three linguistic frames of reference: *intrinsic*, *relative*, and *absolute*. My framework will include only two—*object maps* and *view maps*—with deictic orientation being a property of some view maps. In place of Levinson's absolute frame, I propose the term *macro-map*, which I take to be a subtype of object map.

Levinson discounted deictic orientations because the usual classification (deictic-intrinsic-extrinsic) does not adequately account for expressions such as *For John, the ball is in front of the tree*, which uses a relative frame that is not grounded in the discourse situation. His framework describes this example easily as having relative coordinates with third-person origin (John) and an object relatum (tree).

Yet the grounding situation is clearly salient in many, if not all, languages, as evidenced, for example, by first- and second-person pronouns and in demonstratives by distinctions of proximal (by speaker or interlocutors) and medial (by addressee) locations. Therefore, it seems reasonable to retain the term *deictic* as one that cross-cuts Levinson's framework (cf. Zlatev, this volume, chapter 13). "Deictic" here refers to orientations that are based on cognitive maps of the ground or on view maps deployed by persons in the ground. The *ground* is defined by Langacker (1987: 489) as "the speech event, its participants, and its setting. (Distinct from the sense of ground that contrasts with figure.)." Even Levinson (1996: 142) conceded that "there can be little doubt that the deictic uses of this system [of frames of reference] are basic (prototypical), conceptually prior, and so on."

My proposal departs from Levinson's in another way. Like Zlatev (this volume, chapter 13), I begin with Langacker's (1987) relational structure of *trajector* and *landmark*. These terms stand for Figure and Ground at the level of the clause. The task of orientational expressions is to locate a trajector with respect to a landmark. Thus, trajector, relation, and landmark are always found in the base of an orientational predication.[7] A predication may profile any of these in any combination, but often it is only the relation and the entity representing new information that is specified, as the other entity is understood, having been mentioned in the preceding discourse or assumed by convention. This means that every orientational predication specifies a relation, so it is misleading to distinguish, as Levinson does, between "relational frameworks" and other types (typically "intrinsic" and "absolute"). All orientations are relative to one or more landmarks.

There are two fundamental kinds of maps that serve as the conceptual base for relations and landmarks, and therefore provide orientational frameworks. These are *object maps* and *view maps* (i.e., speaker or hearer's map of a viewer's field of view). View maps are like object maps—in that persons and other sorts of observers are also objects—except that they include a field of view as part of their conceptualization. Thus, if we use Levinson's (1996: 137) example, *The ball is to the right of the lamp, from your point of view*, we have in mind an image of a second-person viewer and field of view (see figure 39.1).

Levinson would refer to the observer as the "origin" of the line-of-sight coordinate and treat the orientation as "ternary" (Figure, Ground, and origin). But the expression is actually too complex to characterize as "ternary." The phrase *to the right* contains a relation *to* that profiles directing of attention to a subregion (*the right*) of the field of view (figure 39.1).[8] The subregion constitutes the primary landmark—the one most directly linked to the trajector. An abstract trajector, here instantiated by the phrase *the ball*, is located within this subregion. The full scope of predication of the complex relation *to the right* includes the abstract trajector, the map of the viewer and field of view with its right and left subregions on either side of a line of sight, and an abstract secondary landmark located on the line of sight. The secondary landmark is instantiated by *the lamp*. The preposition *of* predicates a relation between the primary and secondary landmarks.[9] In this

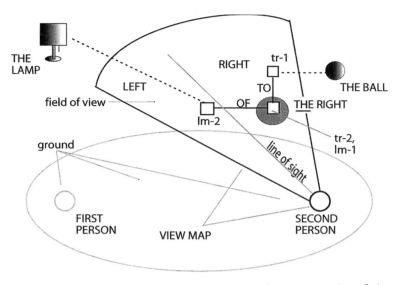

Figure 39.1. The ball is to the right of the lamp from your point of view

second relation, the primary landmark functions as a trajector. Thus, the expression describes a *focus chain* with five elements, not three (Langacker 2000). The five elements are shown in the left column of the table.

concept	instantiation	symbol
tr-1	SPECIFIC BALL	*the ball*
rel-1	TO	*to*
lm-1=tr-2	SPECIFIC RIGHT	*the right*
rel-2	OF	*of*
lm-2	SPECIFIC TREE	*the tree*

Three of the elements—SPECIFIC RIGHT, OF, and the secondary landmark lm-2—belong to the view map. The remaining elements appear to be more independent of the view map. One might regard *to the right of* as a complex relation in the view map and see the whole structure as ternary, but contrasting phrases such as *from the right* or *on the right* argue for a more complex analysis. All the elements within the bold lines constitute the view map, which in this instance is instantiated by second person. The relation *to* is given only an abstract representation rather than an iconic one. Since orienting expressions can be compounded recursively, it does not seem useful to characterize them as profiling merely ternary relations. The classification that I propose distinguishes orienting expressions by the type of map in the conceptual base (scope of predication) of the relation or the landmark. The main distinction is between *view maps* and *object maps* (including the subtype *macro-maps*).

View Maps

In this type, a Figure or trajector is located relative to a conceptual landmark located within or attached to a view map. The view map may be instantiated by speaker, addressee, third person, or some other entity construed to be animate and possessing a field of view. The field of view is the crucial component of the map, but knowledge of the orientation of the observer may also be necessary to an interpretation. A profiled relation, such as *right* or *away*, is a component of the view map. If the view map is instantiated by first or second person, the expression is deictic. Orientations based on observer models in (4) and (5) are deictic, at least on a default reading, but (6) is not. The examples are from Levinson (1996: 137).

(4)   The ball is in front of the tree.
(5)   The ball is to the right of the lamp, from your point of view.
(6)   John noticed the ball to the right of the lamp.

An expression such as *the car moved away* presupposes a view map, but its landmark and the instantiation of observer as first person or other must be disambiguated from context, with different consequences for the construal of relations in the map. The landmark may be construed as the observer himself or herself or as an entity lying on the line of sight. A similar problem is posed by demonstratives, such as the medial demonstratives in Tagalog *iyán* or Coeur d'Alene *ʔuʔ* both meaning 'that one, by addressee'.[10] These deictics do not always presuppose an observer's field of view, per se, but they do presuppose a model of the discourse ground. One can verify that field of view is not at issue by mentally rotating first person in any direction. The meaning does not change. Yet it seems likely that the prototype or default construal is one in which interlocutors face one another, so that second person lies within first person's field of view.

Object Maps

In this type, a Figure or trajector is located relative to a conceptual entity that has orientational values by virtue of its shape or other qualities. An observer's field of view need not be invoked for an interpretation. Object maps are the more-or-less stable orientations in the cultural models imposed upon viewable objects such as the human body, animal bodies, plants, cars, houses, and culturally significant landforms. The front of a car or a house does not ordinarily change with the speaker's vantage point, though people may disagree over what they construe to be the front or back of a truck bed or a building. Orientation frames based on object maps are frequently termed *intrinsic* (Levinson 1996; Bickel 1997; Zlatev, this volume, chapter 13). They are often based on maps of human or animal bodies (MacLaury 1989). For example, as with many other languages, in Tagalog, the top part or front of anything may be referred to as the 'head' (*ulo*).

Macro-Maps

Macro-maps constitute a subtype of object maps lying toward the high end on a gradient of geological or cosmological scale, permanence, and fixed location. This refers to the large-scale and permanent orientations inherent in cultural models of the environment and cosmos, involving movements of the sun, the direction of prevailing winds, the tracks of stars and planets, and the orientations of large-scale landmarks or landforms such as major rivers and mountain ranges, regardless of a viewer's vantage point. Macro-map orientation is often termed *absolute* or *cardinal* orientation (Levinson 1996; Bickel 1997; Heine 1997). Terms such as *up* and *down*, *east* and *west*, *upriver* and *downriver* are based on macroschemas. In Tagalog, for example, *Silangan* is the direction of the sun's rising, *Kanluran*, the direction of the sun's drowning in the sea. When we say that something lies to the/our north, the figure is located relative to a known landmark (location of first or second person in the default construal) on the macromodel of cardinal directions as defined in Western cultures.[11] An expression such as *the arctic is in the north* requires that the arctic region be conceptualized relative to a subregion of the macromodel of the earth and its cardinal directions.

Thus, macro-orientation is very much like basic object map orientation in that both locate a figure relative to cognitive maps having subregions. They differ only in the scale and mobility of the map referents. The orientation of the macro-map is fixed, but that of a smaller object may change. For example, I might say that a deer is downslope from a particular mountain peak, which would be structurally analogous to saying that the deer is in front of a car. The only real difference in the mental calculations is that the macro-map of geological slope has a fixed orientation, but the orientation of the car must be determined in order that the subregion of the object map predicated by the phrase *front* can be calculated. But, under certain disorienting conditions, it might be necessary for a speaker to make a similar redetermination of the lay of the land in the macro-map, especially where slope is not locally obvious, but must, by convention, be specified.

It may be more surprising that there is little difference between the use of object maps versus view maps instantiated by third persons. After all, persons are objects and their cultural modeling involves dimensions like front-back, left-right, and top-bottom. Charles Fillmore (1982: 39) observed the similarity, saying, "In the uses I refer to as 'deictic by default' [e.g., *They're up front.*] the reference object is the speaker's body." He also asserted that such categories as up-down, front-back, and left-right are basically nondeictic. Field of view is not a part of an object map, but the location and orientation of an object may still have to be considered much as one would have to determine the location and orientation of an observer.

For example, to say that a deer is in front of a car requires a mental calculation analogous to that posed by saying that the deer is in front of a third person.[12] Thus, all three ideal types of orientation, whether based on view maps, object maps, or macro-maps, involve the same basic mental calculations. A trajector is located in relation to a landmark which is either a part of a topographical map or coincident with the map. Relations may also be features of the map. The orientation of the map itself is known, either through long experience and cultural tradition in the case of macro-maps or, most often, through online calculations and context-based conventions in the case of observer and object maps.

Levinson (1996: 134) reviewed a number of experiments that demonstrate that many languages use "an 'absolute' [i.e., macro-map] frame of reference . . . where European languages would use a 'relative' or viewpoint-centered one."[13] Many languages fail to provide an observer-based frame of description (1996: 144, 156). For example, in Tzeltal Mayan, in any scale, one speaks not in terms of 'left', 'right', 'front', or 'back', but in terms of 'downhill', 'uphill', and 'across'. Orientations are clearly cultural choices, as Levinson (1996: 145) implied:

> No simple ecological determinism will explain the occurrence of such systems, which can be found alternating with, for example, relative [view map] systems, across neighboring ethnic groups in similar environments, and which occur in environments of contrastive kinds (e.g., wide open deserts and closed jungle terrain). [brackets added]

Vertical orientation appears to conflate or alternate between two conceptual bases. To the extent that the category is emergent from the bodily experience of gravity, it belongs to the view map, which is anchored to the person. But to the extent that it is located in the primal scene (Alverson 1991) of earth, horizon, and sky, it is also a macromodel. I will assume as a working hypothesis that all cultures allow for the conceptualization of verticality using both maps, either separately or combined.

Typically, orienting expressions are constructions which combine or superimpose multiple maps. The sentence *Las Vegas is west of here* combines the macromap of cardinal directions (*west*) with a deictic view map (*of here*). If I describe myself as *looking up* at a building, the expression combines viewer based *looking* with the macro-map-based subregion *up*. Fillmore's famous expression, something like *Get back down from out of up in that tree*, makes use of the object map of the container (*out of . . . in*), the macro-map of verticality (*down . . . up*), and a view map (*back . . . from*). In Cora, the combining of spatial frames in a series of prefixes is a typical form of construction, as in the initial word of (7) from Casad (1988: 365). The morphemes that predicate shape and path schemas function as constructors in building complex path maps.

(7) ***a-hu-ku-rá'a-****raa*   *áh-ka'i*   *irí*   *hece*
     outside-slope-around-corner-go   slope-overhill   hill   at
     OBSVR-OBJ-PATH-OBJ-go
     'He went off over the edge of the hill.'

3.2. Cultural Models of Space and Orientation Theory

All orientations are relative to cultural models of spatial structure. Often, languages provide grammatical instantiations of salient spatial schemas. For example, compact objects, long thin objects, flat objects, containers, and fluid substances (including sand, etc.) are marked in both Bantu and Apache noun classifier systems (Palmer 1996). Models of human and animal bodies vary widely and terms for body parts such as *face*, *belly*, *back*, *head*, and *buttocks* are often metonymically extended to terms for orientations, as in the terms *facing* and *back of* (Friedrich 1979; Brugman 1983; Heine 1997; Zlatev, this volume, chapter 13). Spaces have structure, too. They may, for example, be straight or curved, wide or narrow, small or voluminous, open, enclosed, empty, partly full, full, or interrupted. Processes also have spatial orientation and structure: there is orientation in 'coming' and 'going'; there is both structure and orientation in 'crossing', 'climbing' and 'falling', 'entering' and 'leaving', and in 'sifting' and 'sowing' (see Bybee 1985: 14). Orientations and spatial structures may be predicated by all sorts of linguistic devices: prepositions; affixes; reduplications; nominal, stative, and verbal roots; and constructed lexemes, phrases, and sentences (Senft 1997a; Zlatev, this volume, chapter 13).

Recent studies demonstrate the importance of culture in structuring space and spatial orientations. The dependence of Tzeltal orientational language on a macro-map of slope plus the view map implied by *across* was mentioned above. It can be shown that the same map governs nonlinguistic spatial orientation. When Tzeltal subjects are shown an arrangement of items and are then rotated 180 degrees and asked to reproduce the arrangement, they preserve the fixed, macro-map bearings, placing items to the east if they were originally on the east. By contrast, Dutch speakers preserve observer-based left or right orientation (Levinson 1996). Levinson (1997: 37) argued that it is the linguistic system which forces speakers to compute absolute or relative locations, because the coordinate systems "could only be shared throughout a community through the agency of a shared public language." This is probably largely correct, especially if we include gestural systems within the category of linguistic system, but perhaps we should not forget that other symbolic representations, such as diagrams and dwellings, also inscribe and communicate orientational structure. For example, the opening of the Pawnee earth lodge faced east to admit the morning rays of the sun and the altar to the Evening Star goddess was in the west sector of the lodge (Weltfish 1965).

There is abundant evidence that culture plays a large role in orientation. Bickel (1997) presented a detailed ethnography of spatial orientation in Belhare, a language spoken by a subgroup of about 2,000 of the Kiranti of Eastern Nepal. He defined four different "mapping operations" in Belhare orientations, three of which are object maps and one of which is observer based:

a. *ecomorphic* (including above, below, and horizontal)
b. *geomorphic* (in large scale based on the orientation of the Himalayas)

    c. *person-morphic* (including further from, nearer to, and lateral to a person)
    d. *physiomorphic* (as in upper teeth, lower teeth, and across teeth, i.e., molars)

Bickel's ecomorphic, geomorphic, and physiomorphic mappings are object maps. Furthermore, the ecomorphic and geomorphic mappings are macro-maps. Physiomorphic orientation may be regarded as based on a micro-model. Only his person-morphic category is a view map.

    Symbolic spatial arrangements in Belhare psychology and religion are positioned on the ecomorphic schema. Belhare have a "ubiquitous fear of stumbling and falling." If one dies as a result of falling, "the corpse is turned face down . . . and the soul is believed to enter a dark world of small humanoids below the surface of the earth" (Bickel 1997: 76). He concluded that spatial schemas are fundamental to the culture. By the same token, we can say that the culture, developed within the potentials and constraints of its geomorphic environment, heightens the salience of selected spatial schemas. Comparable reviews of orientation terms in the Mayan languages Tzeltal and Tzoltzil and the Austronesian languages Tolei and Giman appear in Senft (1997a).

    Cross-cultural differences in the conceptualization of spatial tasks can be truly astounding, even between two languages in the Indo-European family. Carroll (1997) compared the structuring of space in English and German "when describing entities such as the layout of a town or village or when giving instructions on how to assemble the parts of an object" (137). She showed that in such tasks, speakers of English orient with object maps while speakers of German use deictic models. Speakers of English were "object-centered" on both tasks, dividing rooms into sections and delimiting a toy truck by the shape of its parts. By contrast, speakers of German bind spatial structures to persons and associated "deictic viewpoints" that are encoded in the forms *hin* 'thither' and *r-* 'hither'. In other words, one might also say that the German speakers were placing the real objects within their view maps of the scene. Where the speaker of English might say *Slide it so the button type of object on the bottom slides into the track on the grey piece*, the German would say something like *Okay, from in front to the black (piece) thither is it to be hither-in pushed* (Carroll 1997: 150).

    The role of culture is revealed most clearly in the experiments of Sinha and Jensen de López (2000), who studied the acquisition of spatial linguistic categories in Zapotec (an Otomanguean body part locative language) and Danish (Indo-European). They found no evidence that early usage was governed by categories based on a child's experience of his or her own body as a prototype: "Utterances in which the speaker's body, or part of it, is either landmark or trajector do not seem to systematically precede utterances in which both landmark and trajector are other objects" (22). Furthermore, "Spatial schemas implicate 'non-self' objects and events at least as much as they implicate the developing child's own body." If this is the case, then the development of spatial categories must be largely cultural, since most of the objects that would serve as trajectors and landmarks are cultural creations that are encountered and presented in orientations and perspectives that are culturally (and linguistically) structured. Based on experiments too detailed to discuss here, Sinha and Jensen de López concluded that at least some semantic categories are acquired by reinforcing prelinguistic or allo-linguistic cultural categories. Their results argue against the strong Whorfian position of Lucy (1992) that it is grammatical categories that cause speakers to habitually attend to certain qualities of objects in their environment (see also Palmer 1996: 16–18, 159–63). They also argue against the notion of Johnson (1987) that spatial categories such as CONTAINER are exclusively emergent from basic bodily experiences.

3.3. Fictive Spaces, Transpositions of Ground, and Post-Whorfian Relativity

Perhaps the most amazing human cognitive ability is that of shifting a conceptualized discourse ground or landmark, or as Bühler ([1934] 1982: 22) put it, "deixis at the phantasma." Because of this ability, speakers can alternately take the positions of other speakers in a discourse and say what they said or might say and be understood by addressees as representing the fictive speaker. If the topic of discussion is spatial orientation, speakers can describe situations with a fictive field of view far removed from the actual discourse ground.[14] Such descriptions are normally accomplished with a combination of orientational language and gestures.

Haviland (1993) described just such a narrative in which a speaker of Guugu Yimithirr, a language of Queensland, Australia, described the direction taken by swimmers after a boat capsized. Facing west, the narrator gestured to the southwest, as though the place where he was sitting was actually located some (unspecified) distance to the northeast where the event took place. On another occasion, he retold the story while facing north, so his gestures pointed "behind him, over his shoulder" (1993: 13), simultaneously maintaining the translocated landmark (i.e., origin) and the relative movement away from speaker within the framework of the macro-map. Haviland concluded that the *interactional space* (i.e., the deictic ground *à la* Langacker 1987: 489) "comes equipped with cardinal directions conceptually attached" (1993: 26). *Narrative spaces* are "laminated over the immediate interactional space" (26).

Narrators construct other sorts of transposed fictive spaces. The same narrator described the fin of a shark that surfaced during the capsize event as though it were located directly in front of him (in the ground) and oriented independently from the macro-map. Narrators also construct *narrative interactional spaces* in which remembered or fictive narrators are removed in time and place from the actual ground. Narrative interactional spaces may or may not be anchored to a known location. Haviland (1993: 37) concluded that "it is this multiplicity of 'gesture spaces' . . . and the evanescent shifting between them, that belies the alleged simplicity of pointing gestures as primitive referential devices." In Haviland (1996), the approach is generalized to transpositions other than spatial ones, including those involved in indexical projections, perspective, and construals of resolution or level of schematization. He also discussed types of transposition "triggers," including quotation, narration, and various "generic brackets," such as paralinguistic quotation marks or shifts in register or genre, as with the use of ritual speech.

The production and comprehension of orientational language and gestures depends not only on the ability of narrators and audiences to follow the shifting grounds and narrative spaces, but also on their historical and cultural knowledge, such as their knowledge of locations, actors, and events. It depends additionally on knowledge of gesture etiquette in various social contexts. As an example, McKenzie (1997) reported that local speakers of Aralle-Tabulahan, an Austronesian language of Sulawesi, use a directional referring to upstream when heading from Tabulahan near the west coast to Polopo, which lies directly east on the other side of an impassable highland jungle. Since Polopo lies on the coast of the Bay of Bone, it cannot be regarded as upstream in any direct sense. The usage may derive from a former time when it was still possible to travel east through the jungle. Similarly, Haugen (1969: 334), trying to understand contradictory usages of cardinal terms in Iceland, distinguished between *proximate orientation*, based on celestial observations, and *ultimate orientation*, "based on social practices developed in land travel in Iceland."

3.4. Cultural-Spatial Models

Important as it is, orientation theory covers only part of the terrain of spatial language. There remain many questions of how shapes and the shape of movements through space are conceptualized cross-linguistically. One path on this quest could lead us back to classifiers, which may predicate shapes and textures that are characteristic of culturally salient domestic or ritual activities, as mentioned above. Another could lead to languages whose verbal predicates include specifications of shapes (Whorf 1956: 169; Talmy 1985), including those of sign languages (Emmorey 1996). There is also the large realm of spatial metaphors (see Grady, this volume, chapter 8) and their uses in emotional expression and social orientation (Lakoff and Johnson 1980). When several salient cultural linguistic domains are linked with space in pervasive symbolic complexes, almost any orientational expression takes on metaphorical or metonymic values. For example, consider the following passage from Keesing (1997: 134):

> Vertical axes are extensively developed in Kwaio ritual and mythology, in relation to gender polarity and to purity and pollution, sacralization, and desacralization.... A Kwaio settlement expresses a cosmological design where men's sacred area is up, women's polluted area is down, and the zone of the mundane is in the middle. The men's house in the upper part of the clearing and the shrine above are symbolic mirror images of the menstrual hut in the lower part of the clearing, and the childbirth hut in the forest below. To **fane** 'ascend' is, for men, to pass from the mundane to the sanctified, and for women, to pass from the polluted to the mundane. [emphasis added]

Similarly, Shore (1996: 269) reported a fundamental distinction in the Samaon village of Matavai, Safune, between *tai* 'seaward' and *uta* 'inland'. *Tai* is the realm of women, light, clean, and formal, where there is civil life, social control, and good speaking. *Uta* is the realm of men, dark and dirty, but intimate, where it is uncivilized, village laws are inoperative, and there is bad speaking. Clearly, one would need to understand these associations in order to make proper use of Samoan orientational language in Matavai.

The topic of orientation merges almost imperceptibly with that of ethnogeography. Among the Kaluli of Papua New Guinea, every waterway is named, and places in the forest are named after local streams. Schieffelin (1976: 30) reported that "the name of a locality carries, in effect, its own geographical coordinates, which place it in determinate relation to the brooks and streams that flow through the forest." Long narrative songs navigate localities, so that each mentioned place evokes fond memories of shared experiences with deceased relatives. In the 1970s, the Kaluli identified with their home territories to the extent that they yelled place-names as war cries.

Ethnogeography is a source of metonymies. Basso (1990: 109) characterized Apache place-names as "thoroughly descriptive," "pointedly specific in the physical details they pick out." Part of this detail consists of orientational predicates, as example (8) illustrates. In Palmer (1996: 261–62), I used a cognitive linguistic approach to compare the structure of Apache place-names to those of the Salishan language Coeur d'Alene.

(8) tse   biká'   tú   ya-   -hi- -líí
     rock   on.top.of.it   water   downward   REP   it.flows
     'Water flows down on top of a regular succession of white rocks.'

But our concern here is with the moral schemas that attach to places. In Apache, the mere mention of a place-name known as the location of an event having moral significance can "shoot" a victim, identifying him or her as having committed a certain type of transgression. Basso (1984, 1990) referred to this practice as "stalking with stories." The process by which a name comes to stand for a moral transgression is both metonymic and metaphorical: PLACE FOR MORAL STORY; TARGET PARTICIPANT IS STORY CHARACTER.

In Coeur d'Alene, there is a correspondence between the topological naming of the body and the naming of landforms and bodies of water (Palmer and Nicodemus 1985, 1998a). Surface features on the body are named with complex terms that contain orientational morphology, as in (9), which contains two relational predicates: the spatial orientational prefix *hn* 'in' and the relational body part suffix *ič'ņ* 'back ~ back of' (see also Casad 1988). The orientational prefixes, such as *hn* in (9), are highly polysemous, a topic that has been explored in Occhi, Palmer, and Ogawa (1993), Palmer (1996, 1998a), and Ogawa and Palmer (1999).

(9) s-   hṇ   č'em   -ič'ņ   -"čt
     NOM   in   surface   back   hand
     'surface in the back of the hand' (palm)

(10)   *hṇ   č'em   -qiλn   -kʷiʔ*
in   surface   head   water
'Surface at the Head (of the Water)'

Understanding this polysemy is necessary to comprehending fine discriminations in the nomenclatural semantics of Coeur d'Alene. But again, it is not the orientational structure of the terms that primarily concerns us here; it is the comparison of such terms to place-names. Of the 135 known place-names in Coeur d'Alene, nearly half have the relational structure rel–tr–lm with body-part suffixes that restrict the landmark as in (9). Item (10), which has parallel structure to (9), is the name of a traditional village on Lake Coeur d'Alene at the outlet of the Spokane River at the metaphorical top of the lake, which also has a named bottom.

If we now compare the grammatical structure of Coeur d'Alene place-names to those of Apache, we find that by contrast, the structure of the Apache term in (8) is rel–tr–lm. The postposition *biká'* 'on top of it' serves as a landmark restrictor much like the Coeur d'Alene anatomic suffix. The approach of Cognitive Grammar very clearly reveals parallels and contrasts in the semantic structure of the complex terms for places and body parts precisely because it provides a conceptual structure for relational predications.

3.5. General Orientation Semantics

Given that we now possess a useful body of observations and theoretical perspectives on spatial orientation, it appears that a general theory of orientation language must conform to the following propositions:

a. Orientational maps are highly schematic, language-specific, topographical maps of shapes, directions, and affordances (e.g., consider *into, around, cross, climb*).

b. Orientational maps may be based on an observer or an object. Deictic orientation, based on a conceptualization of the discourse ground, seems to presuppose a view map (of the speaker) as part of its base of predication, at least in prototypical usages. Macro-maps are a subtype of object maps having fixed orientations and geological or cosmological scales. Macro-orientation is relative rather than absolute.

c. Every orientational expression necessarily contains in its base of predication a trajector, a relation, and a landmark. An orienting expression may profile any one or a combination of these. In view maps, the relation of trajector to landmark is situated within the construed field of view.

d. Orientational maps are often combined in the predications of constructions or conflated in the predications of single terms.

e. Interlocutors reconstrue perspectives and fictive orientations by translocating or rotating maps, by zooming in and out, and perhaps even by shrinking or expanding maps. Alternative construals provide a basis for orientational polysemy.

f. Spatial maps conflate with image schemas of movement (e.g., consider *towards, away from, cross, climb*).

g. Spatial maps are often, if not always, superimposed or "laminated" onto social, cultural, and historical schemas, which provide or enrich conceptual landmarks. The matrix of imbricated spatial maps, movement schemas, and sociocultural and historical models presents a rich semantic field requiring ethnographic as well as linguistic methods for an adequate grammatical description of orientation language. It follows that orientation terms will normally be polysemous across these types of models.

The studies reviewed in this chapter reveal a shift away from the strong Whorfian notion of language as the determiner of spatial perception to the notion of language as a set of cognitive abilities and acquired verbal and gestural skills operating on cultural-experiential models within social and historical contexts. As Senft (1997a: 22) put it, "The analysis of space concepts and spatial reference in various cultures and languages must consider not only the linguistic context of an utterance but also the paramount cultural context in which such an utterance is produced and adequately understood." Similarly, Foley (1997: 229) asserted that spatial language is at least partly a product of "our history of engaging with our spatial environment and sedimented in our linguistic practices." But Foley (1997: 215–29) reached this relativist position from within the relative-absolute spatial framework that is critiqued here.

4. Summary, Conclusions, and Suggestions for Further Research

Cognitive and anthropological linguists are struggling to parse out the influences of heredity, basic experience, and culture on semantics. Some basic experiences are universal because they are motivated by biological and environmental universals, but others are constrained by architecture, material culture, and socially constructed patterns of discourse. Grammar emerges as a community of speakers negotiates conventional construals of verbal and signed forms and constructions within the constraints set by innate cognitive processes.

These considerations establish that grammar is pervasively, though not entirely, a cultural phenomenon. As such, it should be studied in culturally defined contexts, such as the Tagalog melodrama examined in this paper. The emotion of melodrama is communicated by means of constructions in which grammatical voice is profiled, because agency is often at stake. The grammar of voice is a grammar of agency because it predicates abstract scenarios of transitive action and degrees of actor control and involvement. In this melodrama, the Tagalog morphology of voice evokes a force-dynamic model of emotions that partially constitutes a model of agency.

In the realm of spatial language, I propose that all orientational predications presuppose spatial maps in their conceptual bases. A general and relativistic theory of orientation leads us into connections with sacred language and other cultural frames, such as ethnoanatomy, ethnogeography, gender, and ethics. Culturally motivated semantic distinctions are fine-grained, influenced by the conventional and prelinguistic uses of containers, the arrangement of objects, and the repertoire of orientational schemas and maps. These and other findings weaken the case for the strong Whorfian hypothesis but lead to a better understanding of linguistic relativity.

Cognitive Linguistics has provided new conceptual tools for the study of cultural-semantic domains. These new tools, which transcend the ethnoscience of the 1960s and 1970s, could be viewed as the elaboration of the paradigm of linguistic relativity developed over a century and a half by scholars such as Wilhelm von Humboldt, Wilhelm Wundt, Franz Boas, Edward Sapir, and Benjamin Whorf and then largely neglected for thirty years after 1950 (Lee 1996; Palmer 1996; Sinha, this volume, chapter 49). Other antecedents are the prestructuralists who worked in the tradition of diachronic semantics (Geeraerts 1988; Nerlich and Clarke, this volume, chapter 22). In my experience, the concepts of Cognitive Linguistics have yielded new insights in every conceptual domain to which they have been applied. These encouraging results argue for an enthusiastic cross-linguistic research program, which should include ethnography that is focused on semantic categories, including the semantics of signing and of the temporal coupling of gestures with speech (McNeil 1992, 1997; Stokoe 2001). The goal is a discipline of Anthropological Linguistics that is well grounded in cognitive theory and equally well suited to the study of discourse as it is to the study of semantic domains.

NOTES

I wish to thank my research assistant Jennifer Hansen for meticulous and insightful copy editing. Any remaining mistakes are my own.

1. Lakoff actually used the phrase "characterized by," rather than "structured by."

2. Lakoff (1987) treated a scenario as a kind of Idealized Cognitive Model (see 1987: 78) and equivalent to a script (284). He regarded it as metaphorically structured by a SOURCE-PATH-GOAL schema in the time domain (285) and having a "purpose structure, which specifies the purposes of people in the scenario" (286). My usage is more general.

3. For a review of the work on kinship and color terms, see Foley (1997). The research on color terms is also discussed in Palmer (1996), where I reached similar conclusions regarding the need to consider both universalist and relativist positions.

4. See Dixon (1979) on ergativity, Comrie (1981) and Croft (1990) on animacy, Langacker (1990, 1991, 2000) and Croft (1990) on voice, and Hopper and Thompson (1982) on transitivity.

5. In Tagalog, transitive agents are typically preceded by a genitive marker or realized as a genitive pronoun. In some constructions, transitive objects are in genitive case, so the genitive itself is not a transitive or ergative marker, though it is commonly regarded as such.

6. *Maniwala Ka Sana* 'Your Belief Is Hope' by Parokya Ni Edgar, *KHANGKHUN GKHERRNITZ THE ALBUM*, Parokya Ni Edgar: Backbeat. Pasig, Metro Manila (audiotape).

7. But see Zlatev (this volume, chapter 13) for an alternative view.

8. On regions, see also, Zlatev (this volume, chapter 13).

9. Langacker (2000) theorized that *of* predicates an intrinsic relationship between two entities. This can only be true if the two entities are the subregion *the right* and the abstract landmark of the view map, not the instantiated landmark *the lamp*, which normally would have no intrinsic 'right' side. One could say that the abstract landmark's instantiation inherits the intrinsic relation of the view map.

10. Coeur d'Alene is known more properly, but less widely, as *Snchítsu'umshtsn*.

11. But compare Zlatev (this volume, chapter 13) for an alternative view.

12. Let us leave aside the question of whether the object model of the car derives content from that of an animate observer, whether by metaphor or metonymy.

13. Levinson (1996: 149) showed that absolute frames of reference differ from intrinsic ones in that rotating an array consisting of a Figure and Ground requires a new description in the absolute frame, but not in the intrinsic. However, it is possible to conceptually rotate an array consisting of Figure, Ground, and the macromodel itself, in which case the original description is still valid. For example, if we conceptually rotate north to south, an object described as 'north' of a landmark is still north. The fact that this is not normally done is a practical matter rather than a cognitive constraint. In fact, Levinson observes that "in certain respects, absolute and intrinsic viewpoints are fundamentally similar—they are binary relations that are viewpoint independent" (1996: 151).

14. See Talmy (1996) on general fictivity.

REFERENCES

Ahearn, Laura M. 1999. Agency. *Journal of Linguistic Anthropology* 9: 12–15.

Alverson, Hoyt. 1991. Metaphor and experience: Looking over the notion of image schema. In James W. Fernandez, ed., *Beyond metaphor: The theory of tropes in anthropology* 94–117. Stanford, CA: Stanford University Press.

Basso, Keith H. 1984. "Stalking with stories": Names, places and moral narratives among the Western Apache. In Edward M. Bruner, ed., *Text, play and story* 19–55. Washington, DC: American Ethnological Society.

Basso, Keith H. 1990. *Western Apache language and culture: Essays in linguistic anthropology.* Tucson: University of Arizona.

Bickel, Balthasar. 1997. Spatial operations in deixis, cognition, and culture: Where to orient oneself in Belhare. In Jan Nuyts and Eric Pederson, eds., *Language and conceptualization* 46–83. Cambridge: Cambridge University Press.

Brown, Penelope. 1991. Spatial conceptualizations in Tzeltal. Working paper no. 6, Cognitive Anthropology Research Group. Nijmegen, Netherlands: Max Planck Institute for Psycholinguistics.

Brugman, Claudia. 1981. Story of *Over*. MA thesis, University of California at Berkeley. (Published as *The story of Over: Polysemy, semantics, and the structure of the lexicon*. New York: Garland, 1988)

Brugman, Claudia. 1983. The use of body-part terms as locatives in Chalcatongo Mixtec. In Alice Schlichter, Wallace Chafe, and Leanne Hinton, eds., *Survey of California and other Indian languages* 235–90. Studies in Mesoamerican Linguistics, report no. 4. Berkeley: University of California at Berkeley.

Bühler, K. [1934] 1982. The deictic field of language and deictic words. In Robert J. Jarvella and Wolfgang Klein, eds., *Speech, place, and action: Studies in deixis and related topics* 9–30. Chichester, UK: John Wiley.

Bybee, Joan L. 1985. *Morphology: A study of the relation between meaning and form*. Amsterdam: John Benjamins.

Carroll, Mary. 1997. Changing places in English and German: Language-specific preferences in the conceptualization of spatial relations. In Jan Nuyts and Eric Pederson, eds., *Language and conceptualization* 137–61. Cambridge: Cambridge University Press.

Casad, Eugene. 1988. Conventionalization of Cora locationals. In Brygida Rudzka-Ostyn, ed., *Topics in cognitive linguistics* 345–78. Amsterdam: John Benjamins.

Casad, Eugene. 1993. "Locations," "paths," and the Cora verb. In Richard A. Geiger and Brygida Rudzka-Ostyn, eds., *Conceptualizations and mental processing in language* 593–645. Berlin: Mouton de Gruyter.

Casad, Eugene. 2001. Subjectivity and Cora spatial language. Paper presented at the 7th International Conference of the International Cognitive Linguistic Association, University of California, Santa Barbara, July 22–27.

Casad, Eugene. 2003. Context, speaker intuition and Cora conceptual metaphors. In Eugene H. Casad and Gary B. Palmer, *Cognitive linguistics and non-Indo-European languages*. 65–89. Berlin: Mouton de Gruyter.

Casad, Eugene, and Ronald Langacker. 1985. 'Inside' and 'outside' in Cora grammar. *International Journal of American Linguistics* 51: 247–81. Repr. in Ronald Langacker, *Concept, image, and symbol* 33–57. Berlin: Mouton de Gruyter, 1990.

Comrie, Bernard. 1981. *Language universals and linguistic typology*. Oxford: Basil Blackwell. (2nd ed., 1989)

Croft, William. 1990. *Typology and universals*. Cambridge: Cambridge University Press.

Crystal, David. 1991. *A dictionary of linguistics and phonetics*. 3rd ed. Oxford: Basil Blackwell.

D'Andrade, Roy. 1995. *The development of cognitive anthropology*. Cambridge: Cambridge University Press.

Dixon, Robert M. W. 1979. Ergativity. *Language* 55: 59–138.

Duranti, Alessandro. 1994. *From grammar to politics: Linguistic anthropology in a Western Samoan village*. Berkeley: University of California Press.

Duranti, Alessandro. 1997. *Linguistic anthropology*. Cambridge: Cambridge University Press.

Emmorey, Karen. 1996. The confluence of space and language in signed languages. In Paul Bloom, Mary A. Peterson, Lynn Nadel, and Merril F. Garrett, eds., *Language and space* 171–209. Cambridge, MA: MIT Press.

Fillmore, Charles J. 1982. Towards a descriptive framework for spatial deixis. In Robert J. Jarvella and Wolfgang Klein, eds., *Speech, place, and action: Studies in deixis and related topics*. 31–59. Chichester, UK: John Wiley.

Foley, William A. 1997. *Anthropological linguistics: An introduction*. Oxford: Basil Blackwell.

Fortescue, Michael. 2001. Thoughts about thought. *Cognitive Linguistics* 12: 15–39.

Frake, Charles O. 1981. Plying frames can be dangerous: Some reflections on methodology in cognitive anthropology. In Ronald W. Casson, ed., *Language, culture, and cognition* 366–77. Houndmills, UK: Macmillan.

Friedrich, Paul. 1979. *Language, context, and the imagination: Essays by Paul Friedrich*. Stanford, CA: Stanford University Press.

Geeraerts, Dirk. 1988. Cognitive grammar and the history of lexical semantics. In Brygida Rudzka-Ostyn, ed., *Topics in cognitive linguistics* 647–77. Amsterdam: John Benjamins.

Geeraerts, Dirk, and Stefan Grondelaers. 1995. Looking back at anger: Cultural traditions and metaphorical patterns. In John R. Taylor and Robert E. MacLaury, eds., *Language and the cognitive construal of the world* 153–79. Berlin: Mouton de Gruyter.

Grady, Joseph, and Christopher Johnson. 1997. Converging evidence for the notions of subscene and primary scene. *Berkeley Linguistics Society* 23: 123–36.

Hallowell, A. Irving. 1955. Cultural factors in spatial orientation. In A. Irving Hallowell, *Culture and experience* 184–202. New York: Schocken Books.

Harkins, Jean, and Anna Wierzbicka, eds. 2001. *Emotions in crosslinguistic perspective*. Berlin: Mouton de Gruyter.

Haugen, Einar. 1969. The semantics of Icelandic orientation. In Stephen A. Tyler, ed., *Cognitive anthropology* 330–42. New York: Holt, Rinehart, and Winston.

Haviland, John C. 1993. Anchoring, iconicity, and orientation in Guugu Yimithirr pointing gestures. *Journal of Linguistic Anthropology* 3: 3–45.

Haviland, John C. 1996. Projections, transpositions, and relativity. In John J. Gumperz and Stephen C. Levinson, eds., *Rethinking linguistic relativity* 271–323. Cambridge: Cambridge University Press.

Heine, Bernd. 1997. *Cognitive foundations of grammar*. New York: Oxford University Press.

Hill, Deborah. 1997. Finding your way in Longgu: Geographical reference in a Solomon Islands language. In Gunter Senft, ed., *Referring to space: Studies in Austronesian and Papuan languages* 101–26. Oxford: Clarendon Press.

Hopper, Paul J., and Sandra A. Thompson. 1982. *Studies in transitivity*. New York: Academic Press.

Humboldt, Wilhelm von. [1836] 1972. *Linguistic variability and intellectual development*. Philadelphia: University of Pennsylvania Press.

Hutchins, Edwin. 1995. *Cognition in the wild*. Cambridge, MA: MIT Press.

Johnson, Mark. 1987. *The body in the mind: The bodily basis of meaning, imagination, and reason*. Chicago: University of Chicago Press.

Keesing, Roger. 1997. Constructing space in Kwaio (Solomon Islands). In Gunter Senft, ed., *Referring to space: Studies in Austronesian and Papuan languages* 127–41. Oxford: Clarendon Press.

Kövecses, Zoltán. 1988. *The language of love: The semantics of passion in conversational English*. Lewisburg, PA: Bucknell University Press.

Kövecses, Zoltán. 1995. Anger: Its language, conceptualization, and physiology in the light of cross-cultural evidence. In John R. Taylor and Robert E. MacLaury, eds., *Language and the cognitive construal of the world* 181–96. Berlin: Mouton de Gruyter.

Kövecses, Zoltán. 2000. *Metaphor and emotion: Language, culture, and body in human feeling*. Cambridge: Cambridge University Press.

Kövecses, Zoltán, and Gary B. Palmer. 1999. Language and emotion concepts: What experientialists and social constructionists have in common. In Gary B. Palmer and

Debra J. Occhi, eds., *Languages of sentiment: Cultural constructions of emotional substrates* 237–62. Amsterdam: John Benjamins.

Kövecses, Zoltán, Gary B. Palmer, and René Dirven. 2002. Language and emotion: The interplay of conceptualizations with physiology and culture. In René Dirven and Ralf Pörings, eds., *Metaphor and metonymy in comparison and contrast* 133–59. Berlin: Mouton de Gruyter.

Lakoff, George. 1987. *Women, fire and dangerous things: What categories reveal about the mind*. Chicago: University of Chicago Press.

Lakoff, George, and Mark Johnson. 1980. *Metaphors we live by*. Chicago: University of Chicago Press.

Lakoff, George, and Mark Johnson. 1999. *Philosophy in the flesh: The embodied mind and its challenge to Western thought*. New York: Basic Books.

Langacker, Ronald W. 1987. *Foundations of cognitive linguistics*. Vol. 1, *Theoretical prerequisites*. Stanford, CA: Stanford University Press.

Langacker, Ronald W. 1990. *Concept, image, and symbol: The cognitive basis of grammar*. Berlin: Mouton de Gruyter.

Langacker, Ronald W. 1991. *Foundations of cognitive linguistics*. Vol. 2, *Descriptive application*. Stanford, CA: Stanford University Press.

Langacker, Ronald W. 1999a. Assessing the cognitive linguistic enterprise. In Theo Janssen and Gisela Redeker, eds., *Cognitive linguistics: Foundations, scope, and methodology* 13–59. Berlin: Mouton de Gruyter.

Langacker, Ronald W. 1999b. A study in unified diversity: English and Mixtec locatives. *Rask* 9: 215–56.

Langacker, Ronald W. 2000. *Grammar and conceptualization*. Berlin: Mouton de Gruyter.

Lee, Penny. 1996. *The Whorf theory complex: A critical reconstruction*. Amsterdam: John Benjamins.

Levinson, Stephen C. 1992. Vision, shape, and linguistic description: Tzeltal body-part terminology and object descriptions. Working paper no. 12, Cognitive Anthropology Research Group. Nijmegen, Netherlands: Max Planck Institute for Psycholinguistics.

Levinson, Stephen C. 1996. Frames of reference and Molyneux's question: Crosslinguistic evidence. In Paul Bloom, Mary A. Peterson, Lynn Nadel, and Merril F. Garrett, eds., *Language and space* 109–70. Cambridge, MA: MIT Press.

Levinson, Stephen C. 1997. From outer to inner space: Linguistic categories and non-linguistic thinking. In Jan Nuyts and Eric Peterson, eds., *Language and conceptualization* 13–45. Cambridge: Cambridge University Press.

Lucy, John A. 1992. *Grammatical categories and cognition: A case study of the linguistic relativity hypothesis*. Cambridge: Cambridge University Press.

Lutz, Catherine A. 1988. *Unnatural emotions: Everyday sentiments on a Micronesian atoll and their challenge to Western theory*. Chicago: University of Chicago Press.

MacLaury, Robert E. 1989. Zapotec body-part locatives: Prototypes and metaphoric extensions. *International Journal of American Linguistics* 55: 119–54.

Malcolm, Ian, and Farzad Sharifian. 2002. Aspects of Aboriginal English oral discourse: An application of cultural schema theory. *Discourse Studies* 4: 169–81.

McKenzie, Robin. 1997. Downstream to here: Geographically determined spatial deictics in Arelle-Tabulahan (Sulawesi). In Gunter Senft, ed., *Referring to space: Studies in Austronesian and Papuan languages* 221–50. Oxford: Clarendon Press.

McNeill, David. 1992. *Hand and mind: What gestures reveal about thought*. Chicago: University of Chicago Press.

McNeill, David. 1997. Growth points cross-linguistically. In Jan Nuyts and Eric Pederson, eds., *Language and conceptualization* 190–212. Cambridge: Cambridge University Press.

Niemeier, Susanne, and René Dirven, eds. 1997. *The language of emotions: Conceptualization, expression, and theoretical foundation.* Amsterdam: Benjamins.

Occhi, Debra, Gary B. Palmer, and Roy H. Ogawa. 1993. Like hair or trees: Semantic analysis of the Coeur d'Alene prefix ne' 'amidst'. In Margaret Langdon, ed., *Proceedings of the Meeting of the Society for the Study of the Indigenous Languages of the Americas and the Hokan-Penutian Workshop* 40–58. Survey of California and other Indian languages, report no. 8. Berkeley: Linguistics Department, University of California at Berkeley.

Ogawa, Roy H., and Gary B. Palmer. 1999. Langacker semantics for three Coeur d'Alene prefixes glossed as 'on'. In Leon de Stadler and Christoph Eyrich, eds., *Issues in cognitive linguistics* 165–224. Berlin: Mouton de Gruyter.

Ortner, Sherry B. 1996. *Making gender: The politics and erotics of culture.* Boston: Beacon Press.

Palmer, Gary B. 1996. *Toward a theory of cultural linguistics.* Austin: University of Texas Press.

Palmer, Gary B. 1998a. Foraging for patterns in interior Salish semantic domains. In Ewa Czaykowska-Higgins and M. Dale Kinkade, eds., *Studies in Salish linguistics: Current perspectives* 349–86. Berlin: Mouton de Gruyter.

Palmer, Gary B. 1998b. *Sana'y Maulit Muli*: Emotion, denial of agency, and grammatical voice in a Tagalog video melodrama. Paper presented to the Annual Meeting of the American Anthropological Association, Philadelphia, December 2–8, 1998, and to the Linguistics Colloquium, University of the Philippines, Diliman Campus, February 11, 1999.

Palmer, Gary B. 2006. When does cognitive linguistics become cultural? Case studies in Tagalog voice and Shona noun classifiers. In June Luchjenbroers, ed., *Cognitive linguistics investigations across languages, fields, and philosophical boundaries* 13–45. Amsterdam: John Benjamins.

Palmer, Gary B., and Rick Brown. 1998. The ideology of honor, respect, and emotion in Tagalog. In Angeliki Athanasiadou and Elzbieta Tabakowska, eds., *Speaking of emotions: Conceptualization and expression* 331–55. Berlin: Mouton de Gruyter.

Palmer, Gary B., Cliff Goddard, and Penny Lee, eds. 2003. Talking about thinking across languages. Special issue of *Cognitive Linguistics* 14.2/3.

Palmer, Gary B., and Lawrence G. Nicodemus. 1985. Coeur d'Alene exceptions to proposed universals of anatomical nomenclature. *American Ethnologist* 12: 341–59.

Palmer, Gary B., and Debra J. Occhi. 1999. *Languages of sentiment: Cultural constructions of emotional substrates.* Amsterdam: John Benjamins.

Palmer, Gary B., and Claudia Woodman. 1999. Ontological classifiers as polycentric categories, as seen in Shona class 3 nouns. In Martin Puetz and Marjolijn Verspoor, eds., *Explorations in linguistic relativity* 225–49. Amsterdam: John Benjamins.

Rosaldo, Michelle. 1984. Toward an anthropology of self and feeling. In Richard A. Shweder and Robert A. LeVine, eds., *Culture theory: Essays on mind, self, and emotion* 137–57. Cambridge: Cambridge University Press.

Rosaldo, Michelle. 1990. The things we do with words: Ilongot speech acts and speech act theory in philosophy. In Donald Carbaugh, ed., *Cultural communication and intercultural contact* 373–407. Hillsdale, NJ: Lawrence Erlbaum.

Schank, Roger C., and Robert P. Abelson. 1977. *Scripts, plans, goals, and understanding.* Hillsdale, NJ: Lawrence Erlbaum.

Schieffelin, Edward L. 1976. *The sorrow of the lonely and the burning of the dancers*. New York: St. Martins Press.

Senft, Gunter. 1997a. Introduction. In Gunter Senft, ed., *Referring to space: Studies in Austronesian and Papuan languages* 1–38. Oxford: Clarendon Press.

Senft, Gunter, ed. 1997b. *Referring to space: Studies in Austronesian and Papuan languages*. Oxford: Clarendon Press.

Sharifian, Farzad. 2001. Schema-based processing in Australian speakers of Aboriginal English. *Language and Intercultural Communication* 1: 120–34.

Sharifian, Farzad. 2002. Chaos in Aboriginal English discourse. In Andy Kirkpatrick, ed., *Englishes in Asia: Communication, identity, power and education* 125–41. Melbourne: Language Australia.

Shore, Bradd. 1996. *Culture in Mind: Cognition, culture, and the problem of meaning*. Oxford: Oxford University Press.

Siiroinen, Mari. 2003. Subjectivity and the use of Finnish emotive verbs. In Eugene H. Casad and Gary B. Palmer, eds., *Cognitive linguistics and non-Indo-European languages* 405–17. Berlin: Mouton de Gruyter.

Sinha, Chris, and Kristine Jensen de López. 2000. Language, culture and the embodiment of spatial cognition. *Cognitive Linguistics* 11: 17–41.

Stokoe, William C. 2001. *Language in hand: Why sign came before speech*. Washington, DC: Gallaudet University Press.

Talmy, Leonard. 1983. How language structures space. In Herbert L. Pick, Jr., and Linda P. Acredolo, eds., *Spatial orientation: Theory, research, and application* 225–82. New York: Plenum Press.

Talmy, Leonard. 1985. Lexicalization patterns: Semantic structure in lexical forms. In Timothy Shopen, ed., *Language typology and syntactic description*, vol. 3, *Grammatical categories and the lexicon* 57–149. Cambridge: Cambridge University Press.

Talmy, Leonard. 1988. Force dynamics in language and cognition. *Cognitive Science* 12: 49–100.

Talmy, Leonard. 1996. Fictive motion in language and "ception." In Paul Bloom, Mary Peterson, Lynn Nadel, and Merrill Garrett, eds., *Language and space* 211–76. Cambridge, MA: MIT Press.

van Dijk, Teun A. 1987. *Communicating racism: Ethnic prejudice in thought and talk*. Newbury Park, CA: Sage Publications.

Wallace, Anthony F. C. 1965. Driving to work. In Melford E. Spiro, ed., *Context and meaning in cultural anthropology: In honor of A. Irving Hallowell* 277–92. London: Macmillan.

Wassmann, Jürg. 1997. Finding the right path: The route knowledge of the Yupno of Papua New Guinea. In Gunter Senft, ed., *Referring to space: Studies in Austronesian and Papuan languages* 143–74. Oxford: Clarendon Press.

Weltfish, Gene. 1965. *The lost universe: The way of life of the Pawnee*. New York: Ballantine Books.

Whorf, Benjamin. 1956. *Language, thought and reality: Selected writings of Benjamin Lee Whorf*. Ed. John B. Carroll. Cambridge, MA: MIT Press.

Wierzbicka, Anna. 1994a. 'Cultural scripts': A new approach to the study of cross-cultural communication. In Martin Pütz, ed., *Language contact and language conflict* 69–87. Amsterdam: John Benjamins.

Wierzbicka, Anna. 1994b. 'Cultural scripts': A semantic approach to cultural analysis and cross-cultural communication. *Pragmatics and Language Learning Monograph Series* 5: 1–24.

Wierzbicka, Anna. 1994c. Emotion, language, and cultural scripts. In Shinobu Kitayama and Hazel Rose Markus, eds., *Emotion and culture: Empirical studies of mutual influence* 133–96. Washington, DC: American Psychological Association.

Wierzbicka, Anna. 1996. *Semantics: Primes and universals.* Oxford: Oxford University Press.

Wierzbicka, Anna. 1999. *Emotions across languages and cultures: Diversity and universals.* Cambridge: Cambridge University Press.

Witherspoon, Gary. 1977. *Language and art in the Navajo universe.* Ann Arbor: University of Michigan Press.

CHAPTER 40

COGNITIVE LINGUISTICS AND LINGUISTIC TYPOLOGY

JOHAN VAN DER AUWERA AND JAN NUYTS

1. INTRODUCTION

This chapter looks into the relations between Cognitive Linguistics and linguistic typology. The first half of the chapter offers a "neutral" characterization of the field of linguistic typology. Linguistic typology is defined as a cross-linguistic, descriptive as well as explanatory enterprise devoted to the unity and diversity of language with respect to linguistic form or the relation between linguistic form and meaning or function. Section 3 is devoted to an exploration of the relations between linguistic typology and Cognitive Linguistics. It is argued that the two strands are eminently compatible, that there is work that illustrates this, but also that most cognitive linguists and typologists nevertheless work in different spheres. In section 3.1, we discuss the difficulty of applying typology's sampling method in Cognitive Linguistics. In section 3.2, we focus on the typologists' prime orientation on grammar and their hesitation to relate their strictly speaking linguistic generalizations to wider cognitive concerns.

2. WHAT IS LINGUISTIC TYPOLOGY?

....

The term "linguistic typology" is rather general. It could be taken to mean no more than the investigation of linguistic types. Linguistic types appear when the linguist has classified linguistic entities in virtue of a similarity. In this sense, any linguistic discipline counts as typology. In morphology, for instance, prefixes and suffixes can be said to be entities of the same type, called "affixes"; and affixes and roots or stems are also entities of the same type, called "morphemes." In sociolinguistics, most Australian languages and most native American languages are of the same type: they are all threatened languages. Or in historical linguistics, one can say that Norwegian and Danish are languages of the Germanic type. In reality, however, the term "linguistic typology" is used in a narrower way. Although, in part as a result of the generality of the literal meaning just described, there are various controversies as to its exact nature, the definition in (1) captures at least its most central concerns.

(1)   Linguistic typology is a cross-linguistic (a) description (b) and explanation (c) of the unity and diversity of languages (d) with respect to linguistic form (e) or the relation between linguistic form and meaning/function (f).

In the above definition, six features are singled out. We will discuss them in some detail.

Saying that linguistic typology should be *cross-linguistic*—feature (a)—means that observations should be based on a wide variety of languages. In principle, one cannot do typology on the basis of one language, not even if the language is a conglomerate of divergent dialects. Also, in studies of only a handful of languages one does not usually speak about "typology," but about "contrastive linguistics." The languages selected should furthermore constitute a sample. The size of the sample (which can vary considerably—cf. the 22 languages of Xrakovskij 2001 on imperatives to the 272 of Siewierska 1999 on verbal agreement) is geared toward being representative of the variation in the totality of the world's language. Of course, representativeness is not solely a matter of sample size. Typologists now have increasingly better methods to control for genetic or areal bias, that is, the danger of taking too many languages of (respectively) the same family or the same area, and even for typological bias, that is, the danger of taking too many languages of which it is already known that they are typologically similar (see Dryer 1989; Rijkhoff and Bakker 1998; Croft 2003: 19–28).

As to feature (b), typologists first of all need to *describe* the facts. This is less obvious than it may sound, however. Descriptions are based on analytic concepts, which are unavoidably inspired by theories. Hence, no description can be fully theory-independent. This is a matter of degree, however. In extreme cases, descriptions can vary tremendously, to the point even of being incomprehensible to any but linguists of the same theoretical persuasion. Since typological descriptions should be useful to linguists of diverse theoretical orientations, however, it is essential to reduce their theory dependence as much as possible. A version of this aim for neutrality coupled with an aversion to the current proliferation of linguistic theories has been called "basic linguistic theory" by Dixon (1997: 128–35).

Before we turn to feature (c), concerning explanation, let us clarify what it is that should be described. Feature (d) states that typologists are looking for the *unity and diversity* of languages. Typologists describe how languages differ, but at the same time also how they are similar or even identical, relative to one or more parameters. Features characterizing all languages are called "universals." There are what may be called "absolute universals," which apply to all languages, as illustrated in (2), and there are nonabsolute or "statistical" universals, which hold true of most languages, as illustrated in (3).

(2)   a. All languages have nouns and verbs. (Whaley 1997: 59)
       b. All languages have stops. (Maddieson 1984: 39)
(3)   Most languages have either an SOV or an SVO basic word order.
       (Tomlin 1986: 22)

The universals in (2) and (3) make a claim about a property that does not depend on any other property of language, that is, they are not "conditional" or—the preferred term—not "implicational." But there are also implicational universals, and it is these that have been most prominent in the last few decades. They, too, can be absolute or statistical. Examples of absolute implicational universals are given in (4).

(4)   a. If a language has a dominant VSO word order, it will have preposi-
          tions. (Greenberg 1963: 78)
       b. If a language has NP-internal agreement, then the agreement features
          may include case, but not person. (Lehmann 1988: 57)

Particularly interesting about an implicational universal is that it does not only tell us about unity but also about diversity. The implicational universal in (4a), for instance, implies three subsets of possible languages:

(5)   a. Dominant VSO order and prepositions
       b. No dominant VSO order and prepositions
       c. No dominant VSO order and no prepositions

In logical terms, this kind of universal is a material implication. There are three situations that make it true: antecedent true and consequent true; antecedent false and consequent true; antecedent false and consequent false. Hence, postulating this kind of universal goes hand in hand with a classification of languages. An implicational universal does rule out one situation, of course, namely that of a true antecedent and a false consequent. Thus, (4a) rules out the combination in (5).

(5)   d. dominant VSO order and no prepositions

Actually, typologists now believe that languages of type (5d) do exist after all (see Song 2001: 46). This means that the universal in (4a) is statistical only and, in fact, that the more typical universal has now become the statistical one (Dryer 1998). Of course, this observation in no way diminishes the value of the universal. On the contrary, typologists must now explain both the very strong tendency to rule out (5d), as well as the fact that some languages can nevertheless withstand this tendency.

This takes us to feature (c) of the definition in (1), namely *explanation*. Do typologists also attempt to explain the regularities they observe? They do, but in some corners of linguistics their explanations are taken to be of negligible or insufficient quality. The reason is that explanation requires a theory, and not all theories are compatible. As stated before, most typological descriptions aim to be relatively theory-neutral and to offer "descriptive" or "empirical" observations, of the kind in (2)–(4). These generalizations can then serve as input for various theories. In a simple world, then, the typologists could be deliverers of data, and it would be up to theoreticians to explain these. But in the actual world, the division of labor is not that simple. In modern typology, most typologists attempt to explain the data themselves, and this part of the work is not theory-neutral at all. In terms of the current sharp division in linguistics between formalist and functionalist paradigms, typologists tend to be functionalists.[1] As a consequence, the nontypological theoretician of the functionalist brand will usually not only appreciate the data from the typologist, but also his or her theoretical considerations. But the formalist nontypological theoretician will usually at best be grateful for the data but feel free to neglect the typologist's theory.

What can a "typological explanation" be, then? Let us first discuss two features that it should *not* have, at least not according to many typologists: it cannot rely on "genetic inheritance," and it cannot be "areal." Both elements require some elaboration.

First, saying that typological explanation cannot rely on "genetic inheritance" means that a similarity between languages cannot be accounted for by simply referring to the hypothesis that they inherited it from a common ancestor language. (Note that this only concerns genetic inheritance per se, and not genetic/ diachronic explanation in general; see below.) For example, part of the reason why both modern Danish and modern Dutch have two types of preterit—with a dental suffix or with a stem vowel change—is that the parent language had them too. Or, most Tibeto-Burman languages are verb-final and postpositional, and they may have inherited this from Proto-Sino-Tibetan (DeLancey 1987: 806). But, of course, these observations as such cannot be the whole story, for languages do also easily discard part of their inheritance, namely through language change. The essential question is: why do languages (ancestors and inheritors) have such features, and why did they keep or not keep them in diachronic change?

We are touching here upon the issue of the borderline between linguistic typology and historical linguistics. Languages obviously change in a relatively orderly fashion; thus, one can study types of language change. Does this fall within the purview of typology, or should one keep this as part of the subject matter of historical linguistics? Both views are represented in the literature. The main spokesman for "diachronic typology" is Croft (1990: 203–45; 2003: 212–79). Most typologists, however, do not use this terminology. Instead, they see typology as relevant to historical linguistics, but prefer to talk in terms of an application of typology to the concerns of the historical linguist (e.g., Comrie 1981: 194–218; Song 2001: 297–317). And they also accept the relevance of historical linguistics to the concerns of the typologist. In particular, they allow regularities of linguistic change as explanatory of synchronic universals. Heine (1997b), for instance, in a typological study of the expression of possession, explains much of the synchronic variation in his data diachronically: the attested expression types are stages of universal grammaticalization chains (see also Svorou 1994; this volume, chapter 28).[2]

Second, at least according to many typologists, typological explanation should not be "areal." In an areal explanation, a similarity between languages is hypothesized to be due to contact between them, often through bilingualism. In the Balkans, Romanian, Bulgarian, Macedonian, Albanian, and Greek either have no infinitives at all or do not make much use of them. This feature is not due to inheritance, but probably results from contact convergence. There are several other features of this kind that characterize the Balkan languages, such as the postposed definite article or the pronominal doubling of objects. One could say that these features define a "Balkan language type," and since Trubetzkoy (1930) the name for this kind of clustering is *Sprachbund*. Now, since a *Sprachbund* can be said to define a type of language, it is no surprise that one finds the term "areal typology" employed in this connection. But not everybody favors this term, the reason being that linguistic typology in general is definitionally devoted to the study of all the languages of the world. Nevertheless, the employment of the term "areal typology" is on the increase, no doubt because typologists are becoming increasingly aware of the importance of contact as a source of explaining similarity (see Dryer 1989; Nichols 1992; witness also the resurrection of Whorf's 1941 "Standard Average European," Haspelmath 2001).

If genetic inheritance and contact interference may be excluded as typological explanations, what factors can be used then to explain similarities and differences and be considered typological? We can distinguish two types: internal and external ones. An internal explanation accounts for linguistic properties with reference to other linguistic properties. For instance, if a language has "object-verb" (OV) as its unmarked word order, one may want to explain this with the following set of assumptions: (i) many elements of grammar are either heads or dependents, (ii) in the relation between a verb and its objects, the objects are dependents and the verb is the head, and (iii) in that language, heads generally or always follow dependents, that is, it has a dependent-head order.

Any explanation may itself be in need of explanation, however, and that is where external explanation comes in, that is, explanation in terms of nonlinguistic factors. For example, assuming that the above internal explanation is correct, one should ask why languages would prefer dependent-head orders or, the opposite, head-dependent orders. Two types of answers have been offered in this connection. A first type refers to our genetic makeup—the approach defended by generative linguists. Thus, Kayne (1994) takes the VO order to be innate. This explanation is external since the genetic makeup of human beings is not itself a linguistic property. In the second type of answer, a preference for dependent-head or head-dependent ordering is related to language processing: consistency in this ordering pattern may be argued to make the language easier to produce and to comprehend (e.g., Dryer 1992; Hawkins 1994). Again, one can push the explanation further and ask why word-order consistency should be easier from a processing point of view. Ultimately, the reference must again be to genes, the ones that are responsible for the human language processor, but these genes are typically not taken to be inherently linguistic.[3]

Typology describes and explains unity and diversity of languages, but unity and diversity in what? Features (e) and (f) of our definition in (1) characterize two possible answers. One possibility is that the typologist only studies form—feature (e). The typologist can thus study the phonetic inventories of languages. The description and explanation of nasal vowels, for instance, may well go on in complete abstraction from issues of meaning or function. The other possibility is that the typologist studies both form and meaning/function—feature (f). Quantitatively, this orientation characterizes the bulk of modern typology. Relative clauses, Tense-Aspect-Modality marking, comparatives, or number, to name just a few examples, are topics which have engaged typologists in both matters of meaning/function and of form (see, e.g., Lehmann 1984; Dahl 1985; Corbett 2000). In this kind of study, it is typically the (grammatical) meaning or function that defines the topic of investigation. For example, one first describes the role of relative clauses, and one then tries to find out what the strategies are which languages employ to realize this meaning/function in their grammar. But to some extent the alternative perspective is possible, too. One can, for instance, define the verb-initial sentence format and then go on to study its semantic/functional potential across languages. The problem is that the formal definition of verb-initial sentences presupposes that one knows what a verb is, and this problem must ultimately bring in semantic/functional considerations again (see Croft 2003: 17–18 on the distinction between what he calls "external" and "derived structural" definitions).

At this point, it is useful to come full circle and return to the notion of "type," which we started out with. Many people will associate linguistic typology with an attempt to classify languages. In fact, historically, linguistic typology started as a discipline about "language types," more specifically morphological types, aiming to classify languages as fusional, agglutinative, or isolating. Yet the foregoing exposition has been, and current linguistic typology generally is, about "types" of strategies or expressive devices which languages use to realize certain grammatical functions: types of relativization strategies, types of Tense-Aspect-Modality systems, types of expressions of comparison, and so on. Did typology change its agenda? Not really. For any one grammatical function, languages may use more than one "type" of strategy. Thus, a language may have both prenominal and postnominal relative clauses, for instance. Or, in terms of basic word orders, a language may exhibit both an SVO and an SOV pattern. But it is, of course, also possible that a language only allows one type of strategy or that there is a reason for considering one type as the unmarked one. To that extent, the language as such can be said to be of a certain type, say the prenominal relative type or the SVO type. This demonstrates how easy it is to go from statements about strategies or expression types to statements about language types (see also Whaley 1997: 8).

3. Linguistic Typology and Cognitive Linguistics

As explained in detail in chapter 20 of the present *Handbook*, Cognitive Linguistics (in the narrow sense, as a specific part of the wider field of cognitively oriented linguistics) can be characterized as a (conglomerate of) theoretical perspective(s) on language, which is/are essentially functionally oriented and which aim(s) to discover the cognitive principles and systems behind language use, both regarding language structure and semantic/conceptual structure (with a focus on the latter). If one compares this characterization with the description of the field of linguistic typology in section 2 above, it is clear that these two branches of linguistics are, in principle, highly compatible. Still, to a considerable extent the two "live their own lives," which is, at least in part, due to practical circumstances and/or differences in research agendas. Correspondences and divergences between them can be considered at two levels: the methodological level and the theoretical level.

3.1. The Methodological Level: The Use of Typological Data

As appears from section 2, linguistic typology involves a method of sample-based data collection. Nothing in Cognitive Linguistics bars the use of such data. On the contrary, since a considerable portion of what cognitive linguists are investigating concerns notions and principles which are hypothesized to be essential parts of our conceptual and/or linguistic apparatus (metaphor, mental spaces, frames, constructions, etc.), it is crucial to test their universality and variability against the facts of a representative sample of the world's languages (or rather, against the facts of the linguistic behavior of users of a representative sample of languages from all over the world). In practice, however, the use of truly typological data by cognitive linguists is rare (exceptions aside, see below). Surely, some of the notions figuring centrally in Cognitive Linguistics have been applied to individual languages other than English, including typologically unrelated ones—see, e.g., Alverson (1994), Emanatian (1995), Goddard (1996), and Yu (1998) on (aspects of) metaphor theory; or Casad and Langacker (1985), Poteet (1987), Tuggy (1988), and Langacker (1998) on aspects of Langacker's (1987, 1991) Cognitive Grammar; see also some contributions in Hiraga, Sinha, and Wilcox (1999) and in Casad and Palmer (2003). But, according to the norms of current typological linguistics, to the extent that these studies involve the comparison of languages, they typically count as cross-linguistic rather than as typological.

But some work in Cognitive Linguistics does count as typology. A prime example is Talmy's research over the past three decades, as it has been brought together in his 2000 monograph. Throughout his work, Talmy has made frequent reference to different languages. (His PhD thesis, Talmy 1972, already involved a detailed comparison of semantic notions in English and Atsugewi, an Indian language of Northern California.) As such, his work has been taken very seriously by typologists, witness among others his contributions (Talmy 1978a, 1978b) to the seminal series *Universals of Human Language*, edited by Greenberg. For typologists, Talmy's best-known research concerns his distinction between two "types" of languages in terms of how they express event structure, namely, "verb-framed" versus "satellite-framed" languages (Talmy 1985, 1991). This distinction, originally developed to account for differences in the expression of motion events, has been extended later to cover other types of events as well. But, for the sake of simplicity, let us confine the presentation to motion events here. In strongly simplified terms,[4] if (a path of) motion is expressed jointly with a further specification of its circumstances or properties, such as its cause or manner, then languages can do two things. Verb-framed languages express the motion itself in the main verb and express the additional property in a satellite (or what others would call an adverbial constituent) attached to the clause; satellite-framed languages, in contrast, will express the motion itself in a satellite (often with the help of an adposition expressing motion) and will express the additional property in the main verb. Consider Talmy's (2000: 223–24) original example in (6), comparing English as a moderate example of a satellite-framed language and Spanish as a good example of a verb-framed language.

(6)   a. *The bottle floated out.* (English)
       b. *La botella salió flotando.* (Spanish)

In the English example, the satellite *out* expresses the motion (the path), and the main verb expresses the manner of the motion; in Spanish, it is the main verb which expresses the motion (again the path), and the manner is expressed in a satellite (here a gerund). Talmy himself illustrated this difference by means of several languages, and its typological relevance has been worked out further by other researchers, especially by Slobin (1996a, 1996b, 2004)—see also Pederson (this volume, chapter 38) on implications for the linguistic relativity hypothesis.[5]

One of the reasons why typological research in Cognitive Linguistics is rare is no doubt the fact that existing grammars and grammatical descriptions of languages, which constitute an important source of information for current typological research, do not offer a great deal of information on the conceptual semantic notions central to cognitive linguistic theorizing. Consequently, a typological investigation of these notions has to start with the bare essentials of collecting first-hand information on the languages in one's sample. This would be an enormous undertaking, even if this sample was fairly limited, let alone if it consisted, as is common in current typological linguistic practice, of up to several hundred languages. So it appears unavoidable to first have an intensive phase of systematic comparative or cross-linguistic research, in which the primary data for different individual languages are collected, before a truly typological study of the notions at stake will be feasible.[6]

3.2. The Theoretical Level: The Presence of Explicit Cognitive Concerns

Since cognitive linguists as well as (most) typologists take a functionalist perspective on their subject matter, there is no principled incompatibility between them at this level either. There is a difference between them, however, in terms of their "cognitive concerns." Few typologists will deny that the notions they use in their accounts of the typological data—especially the semantic or functional ones—are relevant to cognitive theorizing and are at least potentially cognitively plausible. They would furthermore accept that an external explanation referring to language processing or language acquisition can be called "cognitive" as well. The point is, though, that most typologists are interested only in the linguistic aspects of their findings and do not wish or dare to make explicit claims about, or present arguments for, how their findings ought to be incorporated in a cognitive theory, nor do they try to relate them to nonlinguistic dimensions of human cognition.

This "cognitive modesty" of most typologists no doubt has to do with the fact that they have their roots in "traditional" functionalist theories of grammar, for example, in various streams of the functionalist "underground" in the North American linguistics of the mid- to late twentieth century or in traditional schools in European functionalism—neither of which (at least originally) had cognitive ambitions. Surely, some cognitive linguistic notions, and the corresponding cognitive linguistic way of thinking about the phenomena involved, have made their entrance in the theoretical considerations of certain typologists, but on the whole, typologists do not often draw on cognitive linguistic theories. And this, in turn, is related to the "topical orientation" of current typological research. As indicated in section 2, current typology is predominantly concerned with describing and explaining structural (grammatical) phenomena in languages, such as word order, relativization strategies, or morphosyntactic or morphological phenomena such as Tense-Aspect-Modality marking, and these are issues which are much more central to traditional functionalist theories than to (most) theories of the cognitive linguistic brand. Or at least, such phenomena have received much more attention in the former than in the latter: in principle, of course, the more grammar-oriented branches of Cognitive Linguistics—such as Langacker's Cognitive Grammar, or (the cognitively oriented versions of) Construction Grammar—offer a framework in which all these phenomena can be described and explained as well. Maybe, these more grammar-oriented branches are simply too "young" to have thus far been able to substantially influence linguistic typology—and this may obviously change in the future. In fact, in the recent literature there are already signs of developments in that direction, among others in the work by Heine (1993, 1997a, 1997b), and even more so in Croft's (2001) Radical Construction Grammar (see also Helmbrecht 1997).

As such, Heine has adopted the cognitive linguistic notion of "EVENT schemas" and has developed it into an influential "explanatory tool" for typological analysis. Perhaps the best illustration is his work on possession (Heine 1997b). One cross-linguistically frequent strategy to express that 'X possesses Y' is to say that 'Y is at X's place' or to use a construction that historically derives from the latter. Russian is a case in point.

(7)   *U   menja   kniga.*
       at   me   book
       'I have a book.'

'Y is at X's place' is the EVENT schema. For Heine (1997b: 225), EVENT schemas "are part of the universal inventory of cognitive options to humans." As such, they assume a wider relevance than just a linguistic one: "They appear to be but one manifestation of a more general cognitive mechanism that is recruited for understanding and transmitting experience" (Heine 1997b: 222).

One of the notions central to Croft's Radical Construction Grammar is that of the "semantic map." The idea comes from typology, but as the title of the introductory chapter to the present *Handbook* suggests, it appeals to cognitive linguists other than Croft as well. A brief discussion of the notion "semantic map" will allow us to clarify the difference between an innocuous and an outspoken cognitive perspective on typology.

Semantic maps have become an increasingly important tool for representing essential typological facts, in particular cross-linguistic similarity and difference. The essential idea underlying the semantic map model is that linguistic elements are similar because the meanings or functions they encode are similar. Consider the sentences in (8), and more particularly the meanings of the modal verb *must*.

(8)   a. To get to the garden you *must* go through the kitchen.
       b. Mary *must* be home now.

Sentence (8a) expresses a "situational necessity": there is something in the situation, that is, the design of the house, that necessitates going through the kitchen in order to reach the garden. Sentence (8b) expresses a strong inference or (near) certainty. "Situational necessity" and strong inference or (near) certainty are by no means the same concepts, yet they are related. Indeed, a strong inference or (near) certainty is also a kind of necessity, even if it is situated in a different sphere, namely, an "epistemic" or "inferential" (or "evidential") one: there is evidence which necessitates the speaker of (8b) to believe that Mary is home now (in "logical" terms: the premises are sufficient relative to the conclusion, and the conclusion is necessary relative to the premises).[7] Clearly, in English the auxiliary *must* can be used for both kinds or dimensions of necessity. In the Tungusic language Evenki, however, this is not the case: Evenki has a marker for situational necessity, namely, the suffix *-mAchin*, and another one for epistemic necessity, namely, the suffix *-nA*.

(9)   a. *Minggi girki-v*   *ilan-duli   chas-tuli   suru-mechin-in.*
         my   friend-1SG.POSS   three-PROL   hour-PROL   go.away-SITNEC-3SG
         'My friend must go/leave in three hours.'
      b. *Su   tar   asatkan-me   sa:-na-s.*
         you   that   girl-ACC.DEF   know-EPISTNEC-2PL
         'You must know that girl.' (Nedjalkov 1997: 264, 265, 269)

We now have a mini-typology of languages, consisting of two types: (i) languages which have a grammatical form that can express both situational and epistemic necessity, and (ii) languages that do not have such a form. We also have a mini-map, as represented in (10).

(10)   situational necessity ——— epistemic necessity

Situational and epistemic necessity occupy two distinct points in what could be called a "semantic space." But these points are related; hence the connecting line. On this map, we can plot the meanings of English *must* and of Evenki *-mAchin* and *-nA*.

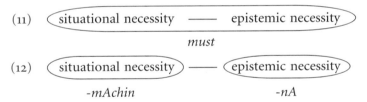

The criterion for assigning a separate position to situational and epistemic necessity on the map is inherently cross-linguistic. If all modal necessity markers in all languages were like English *must*, the semantic map would feature only 'necessity' as such. It is only because there is at least one language that has separate grammatical forms for situational and epistemic necessity that the two deserve separate positions. Of course, even for English *must*, linguists may be convinced that situational and epistemic necessity describe two different meanings of *must* and that English *must* is polysemous (e.g., Palmer 1979). But there are also linguists that claim that English *must* has the same meaning in (8a) and in (8b) and that the difference is only pragmatic and concerns different functions or uses (e.g., Perkins 1983). For semantic map making, polysemy versus monosemy decisions are irrelevant: the polysemist will consider the map in (10) as showing two separate meanings, and the monosemist as showing two uses of the same meaning, yet they can collaborate in their typology.

The field of modality is, of course, much more complex than shown in (10) to (12). The more complete map has to relate necessity to possibility, it has to introduce additional types of modality and/or distinguish subtypes of situational and epistemic modality (e.g., the 'obligation' use of English *must*), it has to account for intermediary values in some of the modality types (e.g., degrees of epistemic probability), and it also has to relate the modal concepts to nonmodal ones (a more complete map is proposed in van der Auwera and Plungian 1998). Whatever the complexity of the resulting map, however, the strategies that languages use to encode the meanings or uses have to cover contiguous portions of the map. This has been called the "adjacency requirement" (van der Auwera and Plungian 1998: 111–14) or "connectivity hypothesis' (Croft 2001: 96). Consider the abstract maps in (13).

(13) a. (meaning/use 1   meaning/use 2)   meaning/use 3

  b. meaning/use 1 (meaning/use 2   meaning/use 3)

  c. (meaning/use 1)   meaning/use 2   (meaning/use 3)

The constellations in (13a) and (13b) are predicted to be possible, and the one in (13c) is taken to be impossible. If a marker can be employed for two meanings or uses that are not contiguous, it must also apply to any intermediate meaning or use. It is in part because of the strong predictive power and falsifiability of semantic maps that typologists have grown to like them.[8]

Despite the success of the semantic map idea, it is of interest to note that their ontological status is not quite clear. Strikingly, the maps are not always simply called "semantic" (as in Kemmer 1993, 2003; Stassen 1997; van der Auwera and Plungian 1998; Haspelmath 2003). In Haspelmath (1997), they are called "implicational,"[9] in Kortmann (1997) "cognitive," in Anderson (1986) "mental," and in Croft (2001, 2003) "conceptual" (in the latter case, with the further complication that Croft calls "spaces" what are here called "maps" and that he reserves the term "map" for any construction-specific region of the map). For some linguists, the choice of a more cognitive rather than a more linguistic label does not matter much. For instance, Kortmann's "cognitive maps" lie within "semantic space," and he would not mind the term "polysemy chains" (Kortmann 1997: 177) either. Conversely, the use of the more linguistic terminology may go hand in hand with a cognitive perspective. Kemmer (2003: 90), for instance, who sticks to the label "semantic map," proposes to call the kind of linguistics which gives pride of place to semantic maps "cognitive typology," and the categories which she proposes are supposed to be fundamental to linguistic semantics and also to pertain to "deeper levels of conceptualization." For this reason, she is also interested in nonlinguistic evidence, such as found in the behavior of prelinguistic infants (Kemmer 2003: 98). The same perspective is embraced by Croft (2001: 105): "Conceptual space [i.e., the totality of semantic maps] presents a universal structure of conceptual knowledge for communication in human beings," or again, "a geography of the human mind, which can be read in the facts of the world's languages in a way that the most advanced brain scanning techniques cannot ever offer us" (364). But, in line with our earlier characterization of their position, most typologists would not go that far.[10] From their point of view, a semantic map pictures the universal space that linguistic forms move around in, subject to certain rules. And while it cannot be excluded that these semantic maps may be necessary for characterizing (aspects of) human cognition, hypothesizing a semantic map neither requires evidence to that effect nor needs to be relevant to modeling cognition. An excellent illustration is Stassen's (1997: 578) position on his semantic map of intransitive predication: in Stassen's view, this map is "a general semantic 'topography' or 'layout', which is universal, and *somehow* anchored in human cognition" (emphasis ours). Another, more specific illustration concerns the semantic map of a modal auxiliary such as *must*. Recall that we mentioned above that the semantic map of modal *must* expressing 'necessity' is indifferent as to whether *must* is monosemous or polysemous. For cognitive modeling, however, this issue—and the related one of the mental status for the speaking subject of the meanings featured on the map—is very relevant. But the semantic map of modality does not offer any arguments to resolve this dispute, nor is it affected by its outcome.

4. CONCLUSION

It is beyond any doubt that Cognitive Linguistics and linguistic typology are mutually compatible fields of inquiry, both with respect to method and theoretical assumptions. Still, to a considerable extent they remain separated strands on the linguistic scene. On the one hand, Cognitive Linguistics rarely uses the "typological method," largely because of the unavailability of the relevant types of data and the difficulties involved in getting at them. On the other hand, linguistic typologists are often "cognitive agnosticists," possibly because of typology's focus on grammar and because it is hard enough to achieve valid generalizations over the enormous range of facts from the languages of the world. As recent developments demonstrate, however, there is every reason to expect a closer collaboration between the two fields in the future.

NOTES

1. This is the perspective from which to understand the phrase "the functional-typological approach," advocated by among others Croft (1990: 2; 2003: 2).

2. The one process that will be most relevant to typology is grammaticalization, as in the study of Heine (1997b) just cited, and the recent upsurge of interest in this

phenomenon is at least as much due to typologists, starting with Lehmann (1982), as to historical linguists (especially Hopper and Traugott 1993). In particular, semantic maps, which have an independent *raison d'être* in typology (see section 3.2), can be the ideal background for drawing grammaticalization paths (see van der Auwera and Plungian 1998).

3. Linguistic change, in particular, grammaticalization, has been identified already as an important explanatory factor, but it is not clear whether it should be considered external or internal. Heine (1997b: 7) considers it to be external, because the process of change is *outside* of the states of the language prior and posterior to the change. But the change is still linguistic, and from this point of view, internal, and hence in need of further explanation, such as the need for expressiveness (Haspelmath 1999) and habituation (Bybee 2003).

4. In Talmy's conceptual semantic analysis, this actually involves a complex "macro-event" consisting of a framing event—i.e., the motion—plus a secondary "co-event" which supports the framing event by specifying further elements of it—e.g., its manner, cause, etc.

5. In this respect, one can also refer to Berlin and Kay's (1969) work on color terms. Interestingly, this work arose in the context of anthropology. While it predates the rise of Cognitive Linguistics, it is now considered an integral part of it, not least because it offers a beautiful illustration of the prototype notion (Ungerer and Schmid 1996: 2–19). The study was also deemed highly important by Comrie (1981: 34) for typology, yet it has not become a classic in this field, largely because of the focus in typology on grammatical meaning.

6. This is, for example, also the kind of approach taken by Levinson (2003) and his colleagues at the Max Planck Institute for Psycholinguistics (see also Pederson et al. 1998) in their semantic-typological investigation of the conceptualization of space. For lack of reliable existing sources of information, this research is conducted through careful collection of (often very subtle) first-hand semantic and linguistic data, for instance, by means of experimental techniques, through intensive fieldwork on a number of individual languages across the globe. This research group would not generally be characterized as part of Cognitive Linguistics, nor as part of linguistic typology, but their research does offer an excellent illustration of how to bridge the gap between the kinds of concerns of the two fields (see also Palmer, this volume, chapter 39).

7. The question whether *must* is epistemic or inferential is a matter of dispute, of course. For the sake of simplicity, we will henceforth label the meaning involved "epistemic." This does not signal that we are taking sides in this dispute, however—we are not, but a discussion of the matter would lead us astray.

8. Semantic maps have now been proposed for a large variety of linguistic topics. We single out the perfect, as the topic of the earliest influential study in this connection (Anderson 1982), and indefinite pronouns, as the typologically most detailed application of the semantic map model (Haspelmath 1997).

9. The term "implicational" is motivated as follows: the adjacency requirement triggers implications—if two meanings or uses are encoded by a strategy, then any intermediate meaning or use will get the same strategy—and since the maps are taken to be universal, we can talk about "implicational universals."

10. Haspelmath (2003: 233) is attracted by the strong cognitive perspective, and quotes Croft approvingly. He is, however, aware of the danger that these ambitions may not be appropriate (219, 239).

REFERENCES

Alverson, Hoyt. 1994. *Semantics and experience: Universal metaphors of time in English, Mandarin, Hindi, and Sesotho*. Baltimore, MD: John Hopkins University Press.

Anderson, Lloyd B. 1982. The 'perfect' as a universal and as a language-particular category. In Paul J. Hopper, ed., *Tense-aspect: Between semantics and pragmatics* 227–64. Amsterdam: John Benjamins.

Anderson, Lloyd B. 1986. Evidentials, paths of change, and mental maps: Typologically regular asymmetries. In Wallace Chafe and Johanna Nichols, eds., *Evidentiality: The linguistic coding of epistemology* 273–312. Norwood, NJ: Ablex.

Berlin, Brent, and Paul Kay. 1969. *Basic color terms: Their universality and evolution*. Berkeley: University of California Press.

Bybee, Joan L. 2003. Cognitive processes in habituation. In Michael Tomasello, ed., *The new psychology of language: Cognitive and functional approaches to language structure* 2: 145–67. Mahwah, NJ: Lawrence Erlbaum.

Casad, Eugene, and Ronald Langacker. 1985. 'Inside' and 'outside' in Cora grammar. *International Journal of American Linguistics* 51: 247–81. (Repr. in Ronald Langacker, *Concept, image, and symbol* 33–57. Berlin: Mouton de Gruyter, 1990)

Casad, Eugene H., and Gary B. Palmer, eds. 2003. *Cognitive linguistics and non-Indo-European languages*. Berlin: Mouton de Gruyter.

Comrie, Bernard. 1981. *Language universals and linguistic typology*. Oxford: Basil Blackwell. (2nd ed., 1989)

Corbett, Greville G. 2000. *Number*. Cambridge: Cambridge University Press.

Croft, William. 1990. *Typology and universals*. Cambridge: Cambridge University Press.

Croft, William. 2001. *Radical construction grammar: Syntactic theory in typological perspective*. Oxford: Oxford University Press.

Croft, William. 2003. *Typology and universals*. 2nd ed. Cambridge: Cambridge University Press.

Dahl, Östen. 1985. *Tense and aspect systems*. Oxford: Basil Blackwell.

DeLancey, Scott. 1987. Sino-Tibetan languages. In Bernard Comrie, ed., *The world's major languages* 797–810. London: Routledge.

Dixon, Robert M. W. 1997. *The rise and fall of languages*. Cambridge: Cambridge University Press.

Dryer, Matthew. 1989. Large linguistic areas and language sampling. *Studies in Language* 13: 257–92.

Dryer, Matthew. 1992. The Greenbergian word order correlations. *Language* 68: 81–138.

Dryer, Matthew S. 1998. Why statistical universals are better than absolute universals. *Chicago Linguistic Society* 33: 123–45.

Emanatian, Michele. 1995. Metaphor and the expression of emotion: The value of cross-cultural perspectives. *Metaphor and Symbolic Activity* 10: 163–82.

Goddard, Cliff. 1996. Cross-linguistic research on metaphor. *Language and Communication* 16: 145–51.

Greenberg, Joseph H. 1963. Some universals of grammar with special reference to the order of meaningful elements. In Joseph H. Greenberg, ed., *Universals of language* 58–90. Cambridge, MA: MIT Press.

Haspelmath, Martin. 1997. *Indefinite pronouns*. Oxford: Clarendon Press.

Haspelmath, Martin. 1999. Why is grammaticalization irreversible? *Linguistics* 37: 1043–68.

Haspelmath, Martin. 2001. The European linguistic area: Standard Average European. In Martin Haspelmath, Ekkehard König, Wulf Oesterreicher, and Wolfgang Raible, eds., *Language typology and language universals/Sprachtypologie und sprachliche Universalien/La typologie des langues et les universaux linguistiques* 2: 1492–1510. Berlin: Mouton de Gruyter.

Haspelmath, Martin. 2003. The geometry of grammatical meaning: Semantic maps and cross-linguistic comparison. In Michael Tomasello, ed., *The new psychology of language: Cognitive and functional approaches to language structure* 2: 211–42. Mahwah, NJ: Lawrence Erlbaum.

Hawkins, John A. 1994. *A performance theory of order and constituency.* Cambridge: Cambridge University Press.

Heine, Bernd. 1993. *Auxiliaries: Cognitive forces and grammaticalization.* New York: Oxford University Press.

Heine, Bernd. 1997a. *Cognitive foundations of grammar.* New York: Oxford University Press.

Heine, Bernd. 1997b. *Possession: Cognitive sources, forces, and grammaticalization.* Cambridge: Cambridge University Press.

Helmbrecht, Johannes. 1997. *Universalität und Vagheit semantischer Funktionen: Untersuchungen zum funktionalen Zusammenhang morphosyntaktischer und kognitiver Kategorien der Sprache.* Munich: LINCOM.

Hiraga, Masako, Chris Sinha, and Sherman Wilcox, eds. 1999. *Cultural, psychological and typological issues in cognitive linguistics.* Amsterdam: John Benjamins.

Hopper, Paul J., and Elizabeth Closs Traugott. 1993. *Grammaticalization.* Cambridge: Cambridge University Press. (2nd ed., 2003)

Kayne, Richard. 1994. *The antisymmetry of syntax.* Cambridge, MA: MIT Press.

Kemmer, Suzanne. 1993. *The middle voice.* Amsterdam: John Benjamins.

Kemmer, Suzanne. 2003. Human cognition and the elaboration of events: Some universal conceptual categories. In Michael Tomasello, ed., *The new psychology of language: Cognitive and functional approaches to language structure* 2: 89–118. Mahwah, NJ: Lawrence Erlbaum.

Kortmann, Bernd. 1997. *Adverbial subordination: A typology and history of adverbial subordinators based on European languages.* Berlin: Mouton de Gruyter.

Langacker, Ronald W. 1987. *Foundations of cognitive grammar.* Vol. 1, *Theoretical prerequisites.* Stanford, CA: Stanford University Press.

Langacker, Ronald W. 1991. *Foundations of cognitive grammar.* Vol. 2, *Descriptive application.* Stanford, CA: Stanford University Press.

Langacker, Ronald W. 1998. Cognitive Grammar meets the Yuman auxiliary. In Leanne Hinton and Pamela Munro, eds., *Studies in American Indian languages: Description and theory* 41–48. Berkeley: University of California Press.

Lehmann, Christian. 1982. *Thoughts on grammaticalization: A programmatic sketch.* Arbeiten des Kölner Universalien-Projekt, no. 48. Cologne: Universität Köln (Repr. as *Thoughts on grammaticalization.* Munich: LINCOM, 1995)

Lehmann, Christian. 1984. *Der Relativsatz: Typologie seiner Stukturen, Theorie seiner Funktionen, Kompendium seiner Grammatik.* Tübingen: Gunter Narr.

Lehmann, Christian. 1988. On the function of agreement. In Michael Barlow and Charles A. Ferguson, eds., *Agreement in natural language: Approaches, theories, descriptions* 55–66. Stanford, CA: CSLI Publications.

Levinson, Stephen C. 2003. *Space in language and cognition: Explorations in cognitive diversity.* Cambridge: Cambridge University Press.

Maddieson, Ian. 1984. *Patterns of sounds*. Cambridge: Cambridge University Press.

Nedjalkov, Igor. 1997. *Evenki*. Routledge Descriptive Grammars, no. 42. London: Routledge.

Nichols, Johanna. 1992. *Linguistic diversity in space and time*. Chicago: University of Chicago Press.

Palmer, Frank R. 1979. *Modality and the English modals*. London: Longman.

Pederson, Eric, Eve Danziger, David Wilkins, Stephen Levinson, Sotaro Kita, and Gunter Senft. 1998. Semantic typology and spatial conceptualization. *Language* 74: 557–89.

Perkins, Michael R. 1983. *Modal expressions in English*. London: Pinter.

Poteet, Stephen. 1987. Paths through different domains: A cognitive grammar analysis of Mandarin *dào*. *Berkeley Linguistics Society* 13: 408–21.

Rijkhoff, Jan, and Dik Bakker. 1998. Language sampling. *Linguistic Typology* 2: 263–314.

Siewierska, Anna. 1999. From anaphoric pronoun to grammatical agreement marker: Why objects don't make it. *Folia Linguistica* 33: 225–51.

Slobin, Dan I. 1996a. From "thought and language" to "thinking for speaking." In John J. Gumperz and Stephen C. Levinson, eds., *Rethinking linguistic relativity* 70–96. Cambridge: Cambridge University Press.

Slobin, Dan I. 1996b. Two ways to travel: Verbs of motion in English and Spanish. In Masayoshi Shibatani and Sandra A. Thompson, eds., *Grammatical constructions: Their form and meaning* 195–219. Oxford: Oxford University Press.

Slobin, Dan I. 2004. The many ways to search for a frog: Linguistic typology and the expression of motion events. In S. Strömqvist and L. Verhoeven, eds., *Relating events in narrative: Typological and contextual perspectives* 219–57. Mahwah, NJ: Lawrence Erlbaum.

Song, Jae Jung. 2001. Linguistic typology: Morphology and syntax. Harlow, UK: Longman.

Stassen, Leon. 1997. *Intransitive predication*. Oxford: Clarendon Press.

Svorou, Soteria. 1994. *The grammar of space*. Amsterdam: John Benjamins.

Talmy, Leonard. 1972. Semantic structures in English and Atsugewi. PhD dissertation, University of California at Berkeley.

Talmy, Leonard. 1978a. Figure and ground in complex sentences. In Joseph Greenberg, ed., *Universals of human language*, vol. 4, *Syntax* 625–49. Stanford, CA: Stanford University Press.

Talmy, Leonard. 1978b. Relations between subordination and coordination. In Joseph H. Greenberg, ed., *Universals of human language*, vol. 4, *Syntax* 487–513. Stanford, CA: Stanford University Press.

Talmy, Leonard. 1985. Lexicalization patterns: Semantic structure in lexical forms. In Timothy Shopen, ed., *Language typology and syntactic description*, vol. 3, *Grammatical categories and the lexicon* 57–149. Cambridge: Cambridge University Press.

Talmy, Leonard. 1991. Path to realization: A typology of event conflation. *Berkeley Linguistics Society* 17: 480–519.

Talmy, Leonard. 2000. *Toward a cognitive semantics*. Vol. 2, *Typology and process in concept structuring*. Cambridge, MA: MIT Press.

Tomlin, Russel. 1986. *Basic word order: Functional principles*. London: Croom Helm.

Trubetzkoy, Nikolai, S. 1930. Proposition 16. In *Actes du premier congrès international de linguistes à La Haye* 17–18. Leiden, Netherlands: Brill.

Tuggy, David. 1988. Náhuatl causative/applicatives in cognitive grammar. In Brygida Rudzka-Ostyn, ed., *Topics in cognitive linguistics* 587–618. Amsterdam: John Benjamins.

Ungerer, Friedrich, and Hans-Jörg Schmid. 1996. *An introduction to cognitive linguistics*. London: Longman.

van der Auwera, Johan, and Vladimir A. 1998. Plungian. Modality's semantic map. *Linguistic Typology* 2: 79–124.

Whaley, Lindsay J. 1997. *Introduction to typology: The unity and diversity of language*. Thousand Oaks, CA: Sage.

Whorf, Benjamin L. 1941. The relation between habitual thought and behavior to language. In L. Spier, ed., *Language, culture and personality: Essays in memory of Edward Sapir 75–93*. Menasha, WI: Sapir Memorial Publication Fund. (Repr. in John B. Carroll, ed., *Language, thought and reality: Selected writings of Benjamin Lee Whorf*, 134–59. Cambridge, MA: MIT Press, 1956)

Xrakovskij, Victor S., ed. 2001. *Typology of imperative constructions*. Munich: LINCOM. (Revised and expanded translation of Victor S. Xrakovskij, ed., *Tipologija imperativnyx konstrukcij*. St. Petersburg: Nauka, 1992)

Yu, Ning. 1998. *The contemporary theory of metaphor: A perspective from Chinese*. Amsterdam: John Benjamins.

CHAPTER 41

COGNITIVE LINGUISTICS AND FIRST LANGUAGE ACQUISITION

MICHAEL TOMASELLO

1. INTRODUCTION

Human beings are the only organisms on planet Earth who actively attempt to direct and share the attention of conspecifics to outside entities. In human ontogeny this begins nonlinguistically, as human infants employ a variety of nonlinguistic means of attention-directing and attention-sharing, including such things as pointing to interesting events and holding up objects to show them to other people. These species-unique communicative behaviors set the stage for language acquisition by establishing the "referential triangle" (me-you-it, or alternatively, speaker-listener-topic) within which all future linguistic communication will take place.

Some time after their first birthday, infants begin to make their first serious attempts to acquire and use pieces of a conventional language. These attempts are not aimed at learning words, quite simply because infants at this age do not know what words are (see Wittgenstein's 1953 critique of the assumption that the young child "already knows a language, just not this one"). They are aimed at learning the communicative behaviors by means of which adults attempt to manipulate other persons' attention, namely, utterances. Children thus learn first to comprehend and produce whole utterances they have heard other people using, although they may do this initially in child-like form (e.g., they may learn just one part of the adult's utterance to express the entire communicative intention—a so-called holophrase). Over time, children then learn to extract from these utterances words and other functionally significant pieces of language for future use as constituents in other utterances. In addition, as in all areas of their cognitive and social development, children gradually begin to construct abstract categories and schemas—out of both whole utterances and utterance constituents such as words and phrases—for comprehending and producing linguistic creations that they have never before heard. This process operates differently for different languages, of course, although with some universal features across languages as well.

To investigate the acquisition process in more detail, what is needed most urgently is an adequate description of precisely what it is children are attempting to acquire—that is, a description of both language in general and the specific language being acquired by a given child in particular. Generative Grammar, with its abstract, essentialistic, quasi-mathematical categories that cannot change ontogenetically, is obviously of no help. The most useful descriptions for developmental researchers come from Functional and Cognitive Linguistics, because these approaches allow researchers to talk explicitly about the symbols, conceptualizations, and communicative functions that constitute human linguistic competence, and they allow them to do this in a way that can be adapted flexibly to changes that occur over developmental time.

In this chapter, I review some of the best-known and most interesting work on language acquisition from within the framework of Functional-Cognitive Linguistics, broadly construed. This includes most importantly work on (i) meaning and conceptualization and (ii) usage and grammar (grammatical constructions). Although the term is often used more narrowly, I will call this general theoretical approach "usage-based" to emphasize the assumption common to all functional and cognitive approaches that linguistic structure emerges from use, both historically and ontogenetically. This is as opposed to the dominant view in the field of language acquisition today in which "core" grammatical competence is innately given, and all that develops is peripheral skills involving the lexicon, pragmatics, information processing, and the like (e.g., Pinker 1994).

2. MEANING AND CONCEPTUALIZATION IN CHILD LANGUAGE

Lakoff (1990) argues that what distinguishes Cognitive Linguistics most clearly from other approaches to human language is the cognitive commitment, which enjoins linguists to perform their analyses in theoretical terms compatible with other research in the cognitive sciences. Similarly, Langacker (1987a) argues that languages are best described and explained *exclusively* in terms of more basic processes of human cognition and communication. This foundational role for general cognition does not preclude the possibility, of course, that acquiring a particular language may lead the people of a particular cultural group to construe the world to some extent in their own individual way. Developmental research has approached the issue from both of these perspectives, that is, in terms of the cognitive foundations of language acquisition and in terms of the role of language acquisition in shaping cognitive development.

2.1. Image Schemas and Word Meanings

Mandler (1992) attempted to specify some of the most important conceptualizations that enable human infants to acquire a language. Along with the conceptualization of objects, infants must also conceptualize the dynamic and relational aspects of their experience such as animacy, containment, support, and the like. Mandler posited that these more dynamic aspects of infant condition are best characterized in terms of image schemas as investigated by Johnson (1987), Lakoff (1987), Langacker (1987a), and Talmy (1988). For example, Mandler proposed that to account for the cognitive dimensions of early language we must posit that young children understand a number of different kinds of motion, both inanimate and animate (illustrated in figure 41.1). These image schemas are based in children's perception of the world, but they are more general and abstract than any particular perceptual experience; they are conceptualizations that result from a process of "perceptual analysis" in which the commonalities across a number of specific experiences are extracted. Mandler (1992: 587) thus proposes that "image schemas provide a level of representation intermediate between perception and language that facilitates the process of language acquisition." Other image schemas she discusses are well-known examples from the Cognitive Linguistics literature, such as CONTAINMENT, FORCE, PART-WHOLE, LINK, PATH, and so on. Following cognitive linguists still further, she also hypothesizes that such logical relations as *if-then* derive from these concrete, perceptually based image schemas.

Focusing on the earliest stages of language acquisition, Gentner (1982) and Gentner and Boroditsky (2001) provided a plausible explanation for why many children acquiring many different languages typically learn nouns earlier than verbs. In brief, her answer was that the nouns children learn early in development are prototypically used to refer to concrete objects, and concrete objects are more easily individuated from their environmental surroundings than are states, actions, and processes. Gentner's hypothesis may be seen as providing developmental support for Langacker's (1987b) analysis in which nouns are seen as words used to construe some experience as a "bounded entity" whereas verbs are used to construe some experience as a state or process (e.g., *explosion* vs. *explode*), with nouns being autonomous and verbs being dependent (in the sense of only being comprehensible

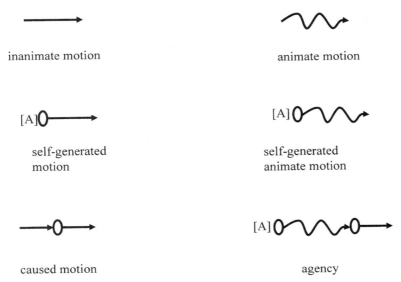

Figure 41.1. Mandler's (1992) analysis of some important dynamic image schemas underlying early language development ([A] represents a source of self-generated motion)

as the state or activity of a preexisting participant of some type). Gentner's analysis and data thus show that words for autonomous entities, that is, nominals, are generally learned first and that the prototype of a nominal referent is a spatially discrete individual object—with the noun category later extending from this prototype to less concrete bounded entities.

In the case of verbs, I attempted to specify—using Langacker-like image-schema diagrams—the particular conceptualizations underlying one English-speaking child's early use of verbs (Tomasello 1992). I began with the premise that young children do not conceptualize the world in the same way as adults. Therefore, in providing descriptions of the conceptualizations underlying children's language, it was necessary to invoke a specific theory of the nature of those cognitive structures at a particular period of ontogeny. Invoking Piaget's ([1935] 1952, [1937] 1954) theory of infant cognition, I proposed that the meanings of particular verbs could be specified in terms of four basic conceptual elements: space, time, causality, and objects. That is, following Langacker (1987b), a verb was seen as depicting a process that unfolded in a series of discrete sequential steps, typically with an object changing location or state across this time (with perhaps the causal source of that motion integrally involved as well). The hypothesized conceptualizations underlying this child's early language thus had the virtue of being things that, insofar as Piaget's cognitive theory is correct, he or she could potentially have constructed from his or her own experience as the child attempted to comprehend and use these words in communicating with adults. Figure 41.2 provides for some examples. The diagram for *get* indicates that some person [P] acts as an agent to bring an object [o] from Location X to himself or herself. The diagram for *back* indicates that an object left the child's sphere of influence (to Locations X) and that he or she now wants it to return (manner unspecified). The

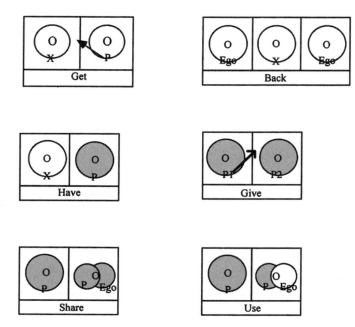

Figure 41.2. Hypothesized conceptualizations underlying one child's early use of some verbs of possession

diagrams for *have* and *give* indicate possession (shaded circles), with the main difference being that *give* is more specific about where the object is now (P1's possession) and how P2 comes to possess it (P1 causes). Finally, the diagram for share indicates that the child wishes to possess an object simultaneously with another person for some time, whereas the diagram for use indicates that he or she wants for the moment exclusive control but not possession—the child will return it later. As development proceeded, more complex conceptualizations were constructed on the basis of both nonlinguistic and linguistic experience.

Budwig (1989) explicitly investigated the causality and agency underlying some of children's earliest utterances. Specifically, she investigated how young English-speaking children refer to the self. It turns out that in the second and third years of life, children say such non-adult-like things as *Me jump* and *My build tower*, along with some adult-like things such as *I like peas*. In a detailed analysis of how the children used these different words, Budwig determined that the words *me* and *my* were used most often for prototypical agency, whereas *I* was used most often for references to self as experiencer. Invoking prototype theory, Budwig claimed that agent and experiencer are two different ways to construe the role of the self in various activities. Essentially, the agent is a causal source—in terms of Talmy's (1988) "force-dynamic schema"—in a way that experiencer is not.

There has been no systematic work on the metaphorical dimensions of young children's early language. Although there are some studies of young children's understanding of explicit metaphors (Winner 1988) and a few theoretical speculations about "primary metaphors" that might apply to children (Grady and Taub 1996), there is basically nothing like a systematic study of how young children relate, for example, concrete uses of prepositions as in *out of the box* to less concrete uses as in *out of her mind*—and indeed there is very little research on children's understanding of abstract words and expressions in general. The one main exception is Johnson's (1999) "constructional grounding" hypothesis, in which young children are aided in the acquisition of, for example, the epistemic meaning of *see* (e.g., *I see your point*) by first being exposed to uses of *see* that are ambiguous between the perceptual and epistemic meanings (e.g., *Let's see what's in the box*). There are good reasons for the relative neglect of these issues, as in all cases it is very difficult to determine the extent to which children are understanding an expression as metaphorical rather than as straightforwardly conventional. But there should be ways using experimental methods to make such determinations, and so this would seem to be an area of developmental research wide open for exploration by cognitive linguists.

2.2. Social Cognition, Perspective-Taking, and Culture

The acquisition of language also has important foundations in children's social cognition. Most importantly, the ability to understand linguistic symbols as devices for directing attention emerges out of young children's broader nonlinguistic skills for participating with adults in joint attentional interactions (Bruner 1983). These may be different to some degree in different cultures.

In Tomasello (1999), I argue that the very same social cognitive skills that enable children to follow into and direct adult attention nonlinguistically are also responsible for children's ability to understand the different perspectives and construals that linguistic symbols embody. In general, all of the different kinds of construals outlined by Langacker (1987a), Fillmore (1988b), Talmy (1996), and others, are part and parcel of language acquisition practically from the beginning. Clark (1997), in particular, has documented the myriad different ways that young children may indicate different perspectives linguistically. In general, children learn quite early to make distinctions based on granularity-specificity (chair, furniture, thing), perspective (chase-flee, buy-sell), function (father, lawyer, guest), spatial perspective (here-there, come-go), and many other of the categories of linguistic construal outlined by cognitive linguists. Clark (1997: 1) concludes: "The many-perspectives account of lexical acquisition proposes that children learn to take alternative perspectives along with the words they acquire, and, therefore, from the first, readily apply multiple terms to the same objects or events."

Clancy (2003) demonstrated that young children use some of these same social-pragmatic skills in more extended discourse. In particular, she showed that young Korean-speaking children make many of the same kinds of referential choices as adults in verb-argument constructions, and thus they create the same kinds of "preferred argument structure" configurations in which new information as embodied in lexical nouns occurs mostly in intransitive subjects and transitive objects (S and O), not in transitive subjects (A). However, as Berman and Slobin (1994) showed in their large-scale study, there is still much work to be done. In a cross-linguistic investigation of preschool children's ability to narrate a relatively complex story with multiple interrelated events, they found that young children have great difficulties in using their fledgling perspective-taking abilities in more complex discourse interactions and narratives. In documenting the greater skills of school-age children as compared with preschool children, they note that "younger children take fewer expressive options because: (a) cognitively, they cannot conceive of the full range of encodable perspectives; (b) communicatively, they cannot fully assess the listener's viewpoint; and (c) linguistically, they do not command the full range of formal devices" (Berman and Slobin: 1994: 15). The overall conclusion of their mammoth study is that children's perspective-taking skills in language result from a complex interaction of their cognitive and communicative skills and the symbolic resources provided by the particular language they are learning.

Recent research has also demonstrated that particular languages play an instrumental role in leading young children to conceptualize and perspectivize the world in particular ways. Of special importance empirically is the work of Choi and Bowerman (1991). They showed that very young children, still in their second year of life, conceptualize spatial relationships differently depending on the language they are learning. Thus, young English-speaking and Korean-speaking children conceptualize differently basic spatial relations of containment and support because English encodes these with prepositions such as *in* and *on*, whereas Korean uses verbs that indicate such different kinds of things as 'tight fitting' and 'loose fitting'. Also of interest is the empirical work of Brown (2000) and de León (2000), who have shown that Gentner's (1982) hypothesis of the developmental primacy of nouns over verbs may not hold for some Mayan languages in which verbs play a much more important communicative role than nouns in child-adult discourse. Recent theoretical and empirical work by Sinha and Jensen de López (2000; reviewed in chapter 49 of this volume) extends this same perspective to a varied array of other basic spatial concepts. Sinha (this volume, chapter 49) argues that just as language may be said to emerge from cognition embodied in the human body, it may also be said to emerge from cognition embodied in the culture at large.

3. Usage and Grammar in Child Language

Perhaps the central problem in the study of child language acquisition from a functional-cognitive point of view is the problem of how children create complex and abstract linguistic constructions in the language they are learning. Of most direct application are the ideas of Langacker (1987a) on constructional schemas, Fillmore (1988a) and Goldberg (1995) on constructions, and Bybee (1995) on the role of frequency-based processes such as token frequency (entrenchment) and type frequency. Also important is cross-linguistic work demonstrating the great variety of grammatical constructions that human beings can create and learn (e.g., Dryer 1997; Croft 2000).

3.1. Cognitive and Functional Bases

In a major statement on the cognitive bases of children's early grammatical development, Slobin (1985–97) proposed that young children's prelinguistic cognition was organized into a small number of basic experiential scenes. Following the lead of Fillmore's (1977a, 1977b) ideas on the everyday interactional scenes and frames that structure human language, Slobin proposed that much of children's early language was structured by (i) the Manipulative Activity Scene, in which an animate agent causes a change of state in an inanimate patient, and (ii) the Figure/Ground scene, in which a person or object moves along some spatial path. Following the lead of Talmy (e.g., 1985, 1988), Slobin further proposed that certain of the concepts in these scenes were designated universally and *a priori* to be especially conducive to grammatical rather than to lexical expression. Grammatical development then consisted of children learning how their particular language encoded these privileged concepts, with the acquisition process taking place in the context of a number of cognitive operating principles that reflected general cognition—which played a role in determining such things as order of acquisition, ease of acquisition, and so forth.

In one of the most important papers in the modern study of child language acquisition, Slobin (1997) modified his views significantly. As a result of the decade of cross-linguistic work that he has conducted or collected together in his series of edited volumes (e.g., Slobin 1985–97, 1997) and taking into account typological work in general, Slobin's revised view is that there is much too much variation across languages (and much too rapid changes within languages) for any set of privileged grammaticalizable notions to be designated by Mother Nature ahead of time. In this view, universals of language structure emerge from the simultaneous interaction of universals of human cognition, communication, and vocal-auditory processing. The particularities of particular languages—as embodied in historically constituted constructions of various types—then present children with a problem space within which these universal abilities operate and create grammatical structure. The importance of Slobin's new view—solidly grounded in the largest body of cross-linguistic work collected to date—is its demonstration that language acquisition is a complex constructive process, requiring virtually all of the child's cognitive resources.

The more cognitive side of this view is elaborated in Tomasello and Brooks (1999), which characterizes children's early linguistic productions holistically in terms of Fillmorean scenes and Goldbergean constructions. We argue that children do not proceed by first learning words and then learning how to glue them together with grammar, but rather from the beginning they are attempting to learn whole adult utterances/constructions to express whole communicative intentions—which they must later decompose into constituent elements (see also Tomasello 1998, and commentaries). The more functional side of this view is elaborated by researchers such as Bates and MacWhinney (1982, 1989), who have focused on the cues (including their validity and reliability) that particular grammatical constructions present to young children. They propose that languages are shaped both historically and ontogenetically by a "competition" among various linguistic cues, with the only constructions that can survive being those that present their speakers with clear, reliable, and efficient symbolizations. In their cross-linguistic work, Bates and MacWhinney have been able to identify the grammatical markers that children learning specific languages find to be most valid and reliable, for example, word order for English speakers' marking of grammatical relations and case for German speakers' marking of grammatical relations.

3.2. Constructional Schemas

It is standard practice in Generative Grammar approaches to child language acquisition to observe a child utterance and assume that it instantiates the same abstract constructional schema for the child as it does for the adult (as described in Generative Grammar terms, of course). This is basically equivalent to observing a Tagalog utterance and analyzing it within the framework of Latin or English grammar. The proper procedure, if we are interested in the actual psychological processes underlying a particular child's use of a particular piece of language, is to look systematically at all of this child's uses of that piece of language and, from this more systematic distributional evidence, to make hypotheses about underlying structure.

Using this more systematic method, it has now been demonstrated beyond a reasonable doubt that young children's early syntactic constructions are highly concrete, that is to say, organized around individual lexical items or phrases. For example, in Tomasello (1992), I investigated my English-speaking daughter's early use of verbs. I found that during exactly the same developmental period some verbs were used in only one type of constructional schema and that schema was quite simple (e.g., *Cut X*), whereas other semantically similar verbs were used in more complex schemas of several different types (e.g., *Draw X, Draw on Y, Draw X for Y, Z draw on Q*). In addition, morphological marking (e.g., for past tense) was also very uneven across verbs. Within a given verb's development, however, there was great continuity, with new uses almost always replicating previous uses with only one small addition or modification (e.g., the marking of tense or the adding of a new participant role); there appeared to be no transfer of structure across verbs. The hypothesis was thus that children have an early period in which each of their verbs forms its own island of organization in an otherwise unorganized language system (the Verb Island hypothesis), thereby serving to define lexically specific syntactic categories such as 'hitter', 'thing hit', and 'thing used to hit with' (as opposed to subject, object, and instrument) (see also Lieven, Pine, and Baldwin 1997).

A number of systematic studies of children learning languages other than English have also found early item-based organization. For example, in a study of young Italian-speaking children, Pizzuto and Caselli (1992, 1994) found that of the six possible person-number forms for each verb in the present tense, about half of all verbs were used in one form only, and an additional forty percent were used with two or three forms. Of the ten percent of verbs that appeared in four or more forms, approximately half were highly frequent, highly irregular forms that could only have been learned by rote—not by application of an abstract schema or rule. In a similar study of one child learning to speak Brazilian Portuguese, Rubino and Pine (1998) found adult-like subject-verb agreement patterns only for the parts of the verb paradigm that appeared with high frequency for particular verbs (and not for others). The clear implication of these findings is that Romance-speaking children do not master the whole verb paradigm for all their verbs at once, but rather they only master some endings with some verbs—and often different ones with different verbs. (For additional findings of this same type, see Berman and Armon-Lotem 1995 for Hebrew; Allen 1996 for Inuktitut; Serrat 1997 for Catalan; Behrens 1998 for Dutch; Stoll 1998 for Russian; and Gathercole, Sebastián, and Soto 1999 for Spanish). It should also be noted that syntactic overgeneralization errors such as *Don't fall me down*—which might be seen as evidence of more general and categorical syntactic knowledge—are almost never produced before about 2.5 to 3 years of age (see Pinker 1989).

Experiments using novel verbs have also found that young children's early productivity with syntactic constructions is highly constrained. Thus, when 2- to 3-year-old children are taught a novel verb in one construction (e.g., intransitive, passive) and are then encouraged in various ways to use it in another construction (e.g., transitive), they have great difficulties. They can use a novel verb in a transitive construction if that is the way they hear it used; it is just that children this young do not seem to have an abstract and verb-general transitive construction that readily assimilates verbs that have not been heard in that construction (Akhtar and Tomasello 1997; Tomasello and Brooks 1998; see Tomasello 2000, for a review). As they get older, children become quite skillful in experiments such as these, demonstrating that once they have acquired more abstract linguistic skills children are perfectly capable of demonstrating their productivity with novel verbs (Maratsos et al. 1987; Pinker, Lebeaux, and Frost 1987). In a similar set of studies demonstrating a similar developmental progression, Akhtar (1999) found that if 2.5- to 3.5-year-old children heard such things as *The bird the bus meeked*, when given new toys they quite often repeated the pattern and said such things as *The bear the cow meeked*—only consistently correcting to canonical English word order at 4.5 years of age. This behavior is consistent with the view from the other kinds of nonce-verb studies that when 2- to 3-year-olds are learning about *meeking* they are just learning about *meeking*; they do not assimilate this newly learned verb to some more abstract, verb-general linguistic category or construction that would license a canonical English transitive utterance.

The general conclusion is clear. In the early stages, children mostly use language the way they have heard adults using it; they learn via imitation, where imitation is characterized not as blind mimicking but as reproducing the same behavior for the same purpose as someone else (one form of "cultural learning"; Tomasello, Kruger, and Ratner 1993). This leads to an inventory of item-based utterance schemas, with perhaps some slots in them built up through observed type variation in that utterance position (see below). The reason that children do not operate with more abstract linguistic categories and schemas is quite simply because they have not yet had sufficient linguistic experience in particular usage events to construct these adult-like linguistic abstractions.

Interestingly, and perhaps surprisingly, this same item-based approach is also quite revealing in the case of many of children's more complex constructions as well. For example, Dąbrowska (2000) looked in detail at one child's earliest uses of *Wh*-questions in English. Her most general finding was that eighty-three percent of this child's questions during her third year of life came from one of just twenty formulas such as *Where's* THING? *Where* THING *go? Can I* PROCESS? *Is it* PROPERTY? and so forth. Relatedly, Rowland and Pine (2000) attempted to explain why English-speaking children sometimes invert the subject and auxiliary in *Wh*-questions and sometimes not—leading to errors such as *Why they're not going?* What they found was that the child they studied from age 2 to 4 consistently inverted or failed to invert particular *Wh*-word–auxiliary combinations. She thus consistently said such incorrect things as *Why I can . . . ? What she will . . . ? What you can . . . ?*, but at the same time she also said such correct things as *How did . . . ? How do . . . ? What do . . . ?* In all, of the fifty particular *Wh*-word–auxiliary pairs this child produced, forty-seven of them were produced either a hundred percent correctly or a hundred percent incorrectly. Both of these studies of children's questions thus show again the item-based nature of children's early constructions, in this case for a set of constructions that develop well into the preschool years.

Children's use of passive constructions in English also shows some item-based effects. Thus, Budwig (1990) found that young children use both *be*-passives and *get*-passives relatively early in development (mostly without the *by*-phrase). However, they use these two constructions for two different functions. *Get*-passives are mostly used to indicate negative things happening to animate agents (e.g., *It got smashed*), whereas *be*-passives are most often used adjectivally or in cases where the agent is simply not important (e.g., *It was tied up*). Because of this difference of function, the two constructions are used with two completely different sets of verbs. (This finding is thus reminiscent of the findings of Pine and Lieven 1997, that young children's earliest use of the English articles *a* and *the* is with almost completely nonoverlapping sets of nouns—because these two articles occur in different constructions and have very different functions in them.) Israel, Johnson, and Brooks

(2000) also analyzed the development of English passives, with particular attention to the passive participle. They found evidence for a version of Johnson's constructional grounding hypothesis (see above) as children tended to begin with stative participles (e.g., *Pumpkin stuck*), then use some participles ambiguously between stative and active readings (e.g., *Do you want yours cut?*), then finally use the active participles characteristic of the full passive (e.g., *The spinach was cooked by Mommy*).

Finally, Diessel and Tomasello (2000) investigated young English-speaking children's earliest relative clauses. Surprisingly, these did not turn out to be what are often thought of as prototypical relative clauses used to restrict referents with all kinds of nominals. Instead, virtually all of children's earliest relative clauses had as the main clause a presentational construction with a copular verb, for example, *It's a . . .*, *There's a . . .*, *Where's the . . .?*, *Here are the . . .*, and so on. The relative clause then served to provide new information about the predicate nominal (object) (see Lambrecht 1988 and Fox and Thompson 1990 for some similar analyses of many adult relative clauses in informal adult conversation). This led to such utterances as *That's the toy I found*, *Here's the one that's empty*, and so forth. Unlike in adult written discourse and most experiments with young children, there were virtually no relative clauses modifying subjects. The main point in the current context is that even this very complex construction is firmly based in a set of simpler constructions (copular presentationals) that children have mastered as item-based constructions some time before relative clauses are first acquired and produced.

3.3. Usage-Based Syntax

The imitative learning of particular linguistic forms cannot be the whole story of language acquisition, however, since children do at some point go beyond what they have heard from adults and create novel yet canonical utterances. They do this first by creating "slots" in otherwise item-based schemas (Tomasello et al. 1997), leading to verb-island and related constructions. It is not known precisely how they create such slots, but one possibility is that they observe variation in that utterance position in the speech they hear around them, and so induce the slot on the basis of "type frequency." In general, in usage-based models the token frequency of an expression in the language learner's experience tends to entrench the constituent items as a unit, enabling the user to access and fluently use the expression as a whole, for example, the common English discourse reply *I-dunno* (Langacker 1988; Krug 1998; Bybee and Scheibman 1999). On the other hand, the type frequency of an expression, that is, the number of different forms (items) in which the language learner experiences the expression or some element of the expression, determines the creative possibilities, or productivity, of the construction (Bybee 1985, 1995). Together, these two types of frequency—along with the corresponding child learning processes—may explain the ways in which young children acquire the use of specific linguistic expressions in specific communicative contexts and then generalize these expressions to new contexts based on the various kinds of type variations they hear—including everything from type variation in a single slot to type variation in all of the constituents of a complex construction.

Another possibility—not mutually exclusive but rather complementary to this process—is that abstract constructions are created by a relational mapping across different verb island constructions (Gentner and Markman 1997). For example, in English the several verb island constructions that children have with the verbs *give*, *tell*, *show*, *send*, and so forth, all share a 'transfer' meaning, and they all appear in a structure: $NP + V + NP + NP$. The specific hypothesis is thus that children make constructional analogies based on similarities of both form and function: two utterances or constructions are analogous if a "good" structure mapping is found both on the level of linguistic form and on the level of communicative function. Precisely how this might be done is not known at this time, but there are some proposals that a key element in the process might be some kind of "critical mass" of exemplars, to give children sufficient raw material from which to construct their abstractions (Marchman and Bates 1994). From another perspective, Goldberg, Casenhiser, and Sethuraman (2004) propose that all of the most basic verb-argument constructions of English have one or more basic verbs, usually a "light verb," as their central sense (e.g., *give* for the ditransitive), and they provide some evidence that many children learn their first verb-argument constructions with this central verb for this central sense (see Ninio 1999 for a similar proposal).

The only experimental study of children's construction of an abstract constructional schema is Childers and Tomasello (2001). We investigated the linguistic skills and representations underlying English-speaking 2.5-year-olds' production of transitive utterances such as *He's kicking it*. The main study was a training study in which children heard several hundred transitive utterances in three separate sessions. Half the children learned new English verbs (and so increased their transitive verb vocabularies during training), whereas the other half heard only verbs they already knew. Within these groups, some children heard all of the utterances with full nouns as agent and patient, whereas others heard utterances with both pronouns (i.e., *He's VERB-ing it*) and full nouns as agent and patient. They were then tested to see if they could creatively produce a transitive utterance with a nonce verb. Children were best at generalizing the transitive construction to the nonce verb if they had been trained with pronouns and nouns, regardless of the familiarity of the trained verbs. That is, the consistent pronoun frame *He's VERB-ing it* seemed to facilitate children's formation of a verb-general transitive schema to a greater degree than the learning of additional transitive verbs alone, in the absence of such a stabilizing frame. This suggests that children construct their early abstract constructions out of both (i) particular lexical or morphological items and patterns and (ii) observed type variation (with some functional consistency) in particular utterance constituents. A possible graphic depiction of the process may be seen in figure 41.3 (based on Dąbrowska 2000, who based hers on Langacker 1987a).

As constructions become more abstract, their generalizing tendencies must also be constrained; all verbs cannot be used in all constructions (see Pinker 1989). One

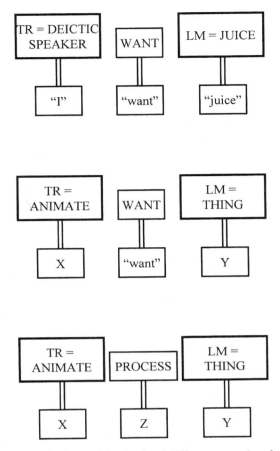

Figure 41.3. Three levels of schematicity in the child's constructional schemas
(TR = trajector; LM = landmark)

hypothesis is that they do this by becoming more entrenched and resistant to flex-ible use (see Bybee 1995). In the only experimental investigation of this process, Brooks et al. (1999) modeled the use of a number of fixed-transitivity English verbs for children from 3.5 to 8 years—verbs such as *disappear* that are exclusively in-transitive and verbs such as *hit* that are exclusively transitive. There were four pairs of verbs, one member of each pair typically learned early by children and used often by adults (and so presumably more entrenched) and one member of each pair typically learned later by children and used less frequently by adults (less en-trenched). The four pairs were: *come-arrive, take-remove, hit-strike, disappear-vanish* (the first member of each pair being more entrenched). The finding was that, in the face of adult questions attempting to induce them to overgeneralize, children of all ages were less likely to overgeneralize the strongly entrenched verbs than the weakly entrenched verbs; that is, they were more likely to produce *I vanished it* than *I disappeared it*. This finding suggests not only that children say what they hear, but that the more they hear it, the more it seems to them that this is the only way it can be said. Brooks and Tomasello (1999) demonstrated that the alternative constructions children have available to meet discourse demands (e.g., in the above example, the availability of *I made it disappear*) also play an important role in constraining abstract constructions. After four years of age, children also rely on generalizations about which semantic classes of verbs (as identified by Pinker 1989) participate in which abstract constructions.

Given that children are acquiring linguistic constructions of various shapes and sizes and degrees of abstraction throughout early development (i.e., building their linguistic inventories), we may now ask about their ability to put these constructions together creatively in order to adapt to the exigencies of particular usage events. Lieven et al. (2003) addressed this issue in a naturalistic study of one 2-year-old child learning English. The novelty was that this child's language was recorded using extremely dense taping intervals—five hours per week for six weeks, roughly five to ten times denser than most existing databases of child language and accounting for approximately eight to ten percent of all of the child's utterances during this period. In order to investigate this child's constructional creativity, all of her 500+ utterances produced during the last one-hour taping session at the end of the six-week period were designated as target utterances. Then, for each target utterance, there was a search for "similar" utterances produced by the child (not the mother) in the previous six weeks of taping. The main goal was thus to determine for each utterance recorded on the final day of the study what kinds of syntactic operations were necessary for its production, that is to say, in what ways did the child have to modify things she had previously said (her "stored linguistic experience") to produce the thing she was now saying. We may call these operations "usage-based syntactic operations" since they explicitly assume that the child does not put together each of her utterances from scratch, morpheme by morpheme, but rather, she puts together her utterances from a motley assortment of different kinds of preexisting psycholinguistic units.

And so, following the usage-based models of Bybee (1995), Croft (2000), and Langacker (2000), the question was how this child was able to "cut and paste" together her previously mastered linguistic constructions (mostly item-based in one way or another) in order to create a novel utterance in a specific usage event. What was found by this procedure was that:

- over 3/4 of the utterances the child produced on this day were things she had previously said before (some of these being conversational routines such as *Bye-bye*, but others were less formulaic utterances);
- of the creative utterances, almost 3/4 consisted of repetitions of an established utterance schema plus other linguistic material "filled in" to slots or "added on" to the beginning or end; for example, the child had said many scores of times previously *Where's the X?*, but on the target tape she said creatively *Where's the butter?*;
- a small minority of utterances (5% of the total utterances) differed from things she had said before in more than one way; these mostly involved the combination of "filling in" and "adding on" to an established utterance schema.

It is also important that there was almost perfect functional consistency across different uses of this child's utterance schemas; the child filled the slot with the same kind of linguistic items or phrases across the six-week period of study. The overall picture is thus that the young child's linguistic creativity occurs in the context of her already well-established item-based constructions.

This "cut-and-paste" approach is also used by young children to construct some of their more complex utterances a bit later in their development. For example, in Diessel and Tomasello (2001), we looked at young English-speaking children's earliest utterances with sentential complements from 2 to 5 years of age. We found that virtually all of them were composed of a simple sentence schema that the child had already mastered, combined with one of a delimited set of matrix verbs (see also Bloom 1991). These matrix verbs were of two types. First were epistemic verbs such as *think* and *know*. In almost all cases, children used *I think* to indicate their own uncertainty about something, and they basically never used the verb *think* in anything but this first-person present-tense form; that is, there were virtually no examples of *He thinks* . . . , *She thinks* . . . , or the like, virtually no examples of *I don't think* . . . , *I can't think* . . . , or the like, and virtually no examples of *I thought* . . . , *I didn't think* . . . , or the like. And there were almost no uses with a complementizer (virtually no examples of *I think that* . . .). It thus appears that for many young children *I think* is a relatively fixed phrase meaning something like 'maybe'. The child then pieces together this fixed phrase with a full proposition as a sort of evidential marker, but not as a "sentence embedding" as it is typically portrayed in more formal analyses. The second kind of matrix verbs were attention-getting verbs like *Look* and *See*, used in conjunction with full finite clauses. In this case, children used these "matrix" verbs almost exclusively in imperative form (again almost no negations, no nonpresent tenses, no complementizers), suggesting again an item-based approach not involving syntactic embedding. Thus, when examined closely, children's earliest complex sentences look much less like adult sentential complements (which are used most often in written discourse) and much more like various kinds of "pastiches" of various kinds of established item-based constructions (see Hopper 1998).

4. CONCLUSION

From the beginning, the study of language acquisition has been a central component in the Generative Grammar paradigm, and even today issues of "learnability" play a central role in the theory. This is ironic, of course, because in Generative Grammar nothing essential is really acquired; the "core" aspects of grammar are biologically given and only the "peripheral" aspects of linguistic competence are actually learned. Equally ironic, however, is the fact that the study of language acquisition—as exemplified in the many studies reviewed here—has not played a central role in the Cognitive Linguistics paradigm. The irony in this case derives from the fact that Cognitive Linguistics stresses language use, entrenchment, constructional schema formation, and other usage-based processes that obviously have their origins in childhood, but empirical studies of how these things actually take place have traditionally not been considered of direct relevance for theory.

But things are beginning to change. The study of language acquisition is becoming more prominent both in the publications and in the meetings of cognitive linguists, as developmentalists see that they need a workable theory of adult linguistic competence and cognitive linguists see that there is something to be gained from studying simpler forms of linguistic competence and how they evolve into more complex forms ontogenetically. Hopefully, this convergence will accrue to the benefit of people who are mainly concerned with linguistic theory, of people who are mainly concerned with language history, and of people who are mainly concerned with children's development. Future research should concentrate on the usage-based mechanisms by means of which both children and adults both acquire and creatively modify the linguistic constructions they have inherited historically from previous users of their language.

REFERENCES

Akhtar, Nameera. 1999. Acquiring basic word order: Evidence for data-driven learning of syntactic structure. *Journal of Child Language* 26: 339–56.

Akhtar, Nameera, and Michael Tomasello. 1997. Young children's productivity with word order and verb morphology. *Developmental Psychology* 33: 952–65.

Allen, Shanley. 1996. *Aspects of argument structure acquisition in Inuktitut.* Amsterdam: John Benjamins.

Bates, Elizabeth, and Brian MacWhinney. 1982. Functionalist approaches to grammar. In Eric Wanner and Lila Gleitman, eds., *Language acquisition: State of the art* 112–50. Cambridge: Cambridge University Press.

Bates, Elizabeth, and Brian MacWhinney. 1989. Functionalism and the competition model. In Brian MacWhinney and Elizabeth Bates, eds., *The cross-linguistic study of sentence processing* 1–43. Cambridge: Cambridge University Press.

Behrens, Heike. 1998. Where does the information go? Paper presented at the Workshop on Cross-linguistic Perspectives on Argument Structure: Implications for Learnability, Max Planck Institute for Psycholinguistics, Nijmegen, Netherlands, June 26–29.

Berman, Ruth A., and Sharon Armon-Lotem. 1995. How grammatical are early verbs? Paper presented at the *Colloque International de Besançon sur l'Acquisition de la Syntaxe en langue maternelle et en langue étrangère*, Besançon, France, November 24–25.

Berman, Ruth A., and Dan I. Slobin. 1994. *Relating events in narrative: A crosslinguistic developmental study.* Hillsdale, NJ: Lawrence Erlbaum.

Bloom, Lois. 1991. *Language development from two to three.* Cambridge: Cambridge University Press.

Brooks, Patricia, and Michael Tomasello. 1999. How young children constrain their argument structure constructions. *Language* 75: 720–38.

Brooks, Patricia, Michael Tomasello, Lawrence Lewis, and Kelly Dodson. 1999. How children avoid argument structure errors: The entrenchment hypothesis. *Child Development* 70: 1325–37.

Brown, Penelope. 2000. The conversational context for language acquisition: A Tzeltal (Mayan) case study. In Melissa Bowerman and Stephen C. Levinson, eds., *Language acquisition and conceptual development*, 512–43. Cambridge: Cambridge University Press.

Bruner, Jerome. 1983. *Child's talk.* New York: Norton.

Budwig, Nancy. 1989. The linguistic marking of agentivity and control in child language. *Journal of Child Language* 16: 263–84.

Budwig, Nancy. 1990. The linguistic marking of nonprototypical agency: An exploration into children's use of passives. *Linguistics* 28: 1221–52.

Bybee, Joan L. 1985. *Morphology: A study of the relation between meaning and form.* Amsterdam: John Benjamins.

Bybee, Joan L. 1995. Regular morphology and the lexicon. *Language and Cognitive Processes* 10: 425–55.

Bybee, Joan L., and Joanne Scheibman. 1999. The effect of usage on degrees of constituency: The reduction of *don't* in English. *Linguistics* 37: 575–96.

Childers, Jane, and Michael Tomasello. 2001. The role of pronouns in young children's acquisition of the English transitive construction. *Developmental Psychology* 37: 739–48.

Choi, Sonja, and Melissa Bowerman. 1991. Learning to express motion events in English and Korean: The influence of language-specific lexicalization patterns. *Cognition* 41: 83–121.

Clancy, Patricia. 2003. The lexicon in interaction: Developmental origins of preferred argument structure in Korean. In John W. Du Bois, Lorraine E. Kumpf, and William J. Ashby, eds., *Preferred argument structure: Grammar as architecture for function* 78–111. Amsterdam: John Benjamins.

Clark, Eve. 1997. Conceptual perspective and lexical choice in acquisition. *Cognition* 64: 1–37.

Croft, William. 2000. *Explaining language change: An evolutionary approach.* London: Longman.

Dąbrowska, Eva. 2000. From formula to schema: The acquisition of English questions. *Cognitive Linguistics* 11: 1–20.

de León, Lourdes. 2000. The emergent participant: Interactive patterns in the socialization of Tzotzil (Mayan) infants. *Journal of Linguistic Anthropology* 8: 131–61.

Diessel, Holger, and Michael Tomasello. 2000. The development of relative constructions in early child speech. *Cognitive Linguistics* 11: 131–52.

Diessel, Holger, and Michael Tomasello. 2001. The acquisition of finite complement clauses in English: A corpus-based analysis. *Cognitive Linguistics* 12: 97–141.

Dryer, Matthew. 1997. Are grammatical relations universal? In Joan L. Bybee, John Haiman, and Sandra Thompson, eds., *Essays on language function and language type* 324–51. Amsterdam: John Benjamins.

Fillmore, Charles J. 1977a. The case for case reopened. In Peter Cole and Jerrold M. Sadock, eds., *Syntax and semantics*, vol. 8, *Grammatical relations* 59–81. New York: Academic Press.

Fillmore, Charles J. 1977b. Topics in lexical semantics. In Peter Cole, ed., *Current issues in linguistic theory* 76–138. Bloomington: Indiana University Press.

Fillmore, Charles J. 1988a. The mechanisms of "construction grammar". *Berkeley Linguistics Society* 14: 35–55.

Fillmore, Charles J. 1988b. Toward a frame-based lexicon. In Adrienne Lehrer and Elaine Kittay, eds., *Frames, fields, and contrast* 203–34. Hillsdale, NJ: Lawrence Erlbaum.

Fox, Barbara, and Sandra Thompson. 1990. A discourse explanation of 'The Grammar' of relative clauses in English conversation. *Language* 66: 297–316.

Gathercole, Virginia C. Mueller, Eugenia Sebastián, and Pilar Soto. 1999. The early acquisition of Spanish verbal morphology: Across-the-board or piecemeal knowledge? *International Journal of Bilingualism* 3: 133–82.

Gentner, Dedre. 1982. Why nouns are learned before verbs: Linguistic relativity versus natural partitioning. In Stan Kuczaj, ed., *Language development* 2: 98–131. Hillsdale, NJ: Lawrence Erlbaum.

Gentner, Dedre, and Lera Boroditsky. 2001. Individuation, relativity and early word learning. In Melissa Bowerman and Stephen C. Levinson, eds., *Language acquisition and conceptual development* 215–56. Cambridge: Cambridge University Press.

Gentner, Dedre, and Arthur Markman. 1997. Structure mapping in analogy and similarity. *American Psychologist* 52: 45–56.

Goldberg, Adele E. 1995. *Constructions: A construction grammar approach to argument structure.* Chicago: University of Chicago Press.

Goldberg, Adele, Devin Casenhiser, and Nitya Sethuraman. 2004. Learning argument structure generalizations. *Cognitive Linguistics* 15: 289–316.

Grady, Joseph, and Sarah Taub. 1996. Primitive and compound metaphors. In Adele E. Goldberg, ed., *Conceptual structure, discourse and language* 56–91. Stanford, CA: CSLI Publications.

Hopper, Paul. 1998. Emergent grammar. In Michael Tomasello, ed., *The new psychology of language: Cognitive and functional approaches to language structure* 1: 233–56. Mahwah, NJ: Lawrence Erlbaum.

Israel, Michael, Christopher Johnson, and Patricia Brooks. 2000. From states to events: The acquisition of English passive participles. *Cognitive Linguistics* 11: 1–27.

Johnson, Christopher. 1999. Constructional grounding. PhD dissertation, University of California at Berkeley.

Johnson, Mark. 1987. *The body in the mind: The bodily basis of meaning, imagination, and reason.* Chicago: University of Chicago Press.

Krug, Manfred. 1998. String frequency: A cognitive motivating factor in coalescence, language processing, and language change. *Journal of English Linguistics* 26: 286–320.

Lakoff, George. 1987. *Women, fire, and dangerous things: What categories reveal about the mind.* Chicago: University of Chicago Press.

Lakoff, George. 1990. The invariance hypothesis: Is abstract reason based on image-schemas? *Cognitive Linguistics* 1: 39–74.

Lambrecht, Knud. 1988. There was a farmer had a dog: Syntactic amalgams revisited. *Berkeley Linguistics Society* 14: 319–39.

Langacker, Ronald W. 1987a. *Foundations of cognitive grammar.* Vol. 1, *Theoretical prerequisites.* Stanford, CA: Stanford University Press.

Langacker, Ronald W. 1987b. Nouns and verbs. *Language* 63: 53–94.

Langacker, Ronald W. 1988. A usage-based model. In Brygida Rudzka-Ostyn, ed., *Topics in cognitive linguistics* 134–78. Amsterdam: John Benjamins.

Langacker, Ronald W. 2000. A dynamic usage-based model. In Michael Barlow and Suzanne Kemmer, eds., *Usage-based models of language* 1–37. Stanford, CA: CSLI Publications.

Lieven, Elena V. M., Heike Behrens, Jennifer Speares, and Michael Tomasello. 2003. Early syntactic creativity: A usage-based approach. *Journal of Child Language* 30: 333–70.

Lieven, Elena V. M., Julian M. Pine, and Gillian Baldwin. 1997. Lexically-based learning and early grammatical development. *Journal of Child Language* 24: 187–219.

Mandler, Jean. 1992. How to build a baby: II. Conceptual primitives. *Psychological Review,* 99: 587–604.

Maratsos, Michael, Roxane Gudeman, Poldi Gerard-Ngo, and Ganie DeHart. 1987. A study in novel word learning: The productivity of the causative. In Brian MacWhinney, ed., *Mechanisms of language acquisition* 278–301. Hillsdale, NJ: Lawrence Erlbaum.

Marchman, Virginia A., and Elizabeth Bates. 1994. Continuity in lexical and morphological development: A test of the critical mass hypothesis. *Journal of Child Language* 21: 339–66.

Ninio, Anat. 1999. Pathbreaking verbs in syntactic development and the question of prototypical transitivity. *Journal of Child Language* 26: 619–54.

Piaget, Jean [1935] 1952. *The origin of intelligence in children.* New York: W.W. Norton.

Piaget, Jean [1937] 1954. *The construction of reality in the child.* New York: Basic Books.

Pine, Julian M., and Elena V. M. Lieven. 1997. Slot and frame patterns and the development of the determiner category. *Applied Psycholinguistics* 18: 123–38.

Pinker, Steven. 1989. *Learnability and cognition: The acquisition of verb-argument structure.* Cambridge MA: Harvard University Press.

Pinker, Steven. 1994. *The language instinct: How the mind creates language.* New York: Morrow.

Pinker, Steven, David Lebeaux, and Laura Frost. 1987. Productivity and constraints in the acquisition of the passive. *Cognition* 26: 195–267.

Pizzuto, Elena, and Christina Caselli. 1992. The acquisition of Italian morphology. *Journal of Child Language* 19: 491–557.

Pizzuto, Elena, and Christina Caselli. 1994. The acquisition of Italian verb morphology in a cross-linguistic perspective. In Yonata Levy, ed., *Other children. other languages* 98–123. Hillsdale, NJ: Lawrence Erlbaum.

Rowland, Caroline, and Julian M. Pine. 2000. Subject-auxiliary inversion errors and wh- question acquisition: What do children know? *Journal of Child Language* 27: 157–82.

Rubino, Rejane B., and Julian M. Pine. 1998. Subject-verb agreement in Brazilian Portuguese: What low error rates hide. *Journal of Child Language* 25: 35–59.

Serrat, Elisabeth. 1997. Acquisition of verb category in Catalan. PhD dissertation, University of Barcelona.

Sinha, Chris, and Kristine Jensen de López. 2000. Language, culture, and the embodiment of spatial cognition. *Cognitive Linguistics* 11: 17–41.

Slobin, Dan Isaac. 1985–97. *The crosslinguistic study of language acquisition.* 5 vols. Hillsdale, NJ: Lawrence Erlbaum.

Slobin, Dan Isaac. 1997. On the origin of grammaticalizable notions: Beyond the individual mind. In Dan Isaac Slobin, ed., *The crosslinguistic study of language acquisition,* vol. 5, *Expanding the contexts* 3–64. Hillsdale, NJ: Lawrence Erlbaum.

Stoll, Sabine. 1998. The acquisition of Russian aspect. *First Language* 18: 351–78.

Talmy, Leonard. 1985. Lexicalization patterns: Semantic structure in lexical forms. In Timothy Shopen, ed., *Language typology and syntactic description,* vol. 3, *Grammatical categories and the lexicon* 57–149. Cambridge: Cambridge University Press.

Talmy, Leonard. 1988. The relation of grammar to cognition. In Brygida Rudzka-Ostyn, ed., *Topics in cognitive linguistics* 165–205. Amsterdam: John Benjamins.

Talmy, Leonard. 1996. The windowing of attention in language. In Masayoshi Shibatani and Sandra Thompson, eds., *Grammatical constructions: Their form and meaning* 235–87. Oxford: Oxford University Press.

Tomasello, Michael. 1992. *First verbs: A case study of early grammatical development.* Cambridge: Cambridge University Press.

Tomasello, Michael. 1998. The return of constructions. *Journal of Child Language* 75: 431–47.

Tomasello, Michael. 1999. *The cultural origins of human cognition.* Cambridge, MA: Harvard University Press.

Tomasello, Michael. 2000. Do young children have adult syntactic competence? *Cognition* 74: 209–53.

Tomasello, Michael, Nameera Akhtar, Kelly Dodson, and Lauren Rekau. 1997. Differential productivity in young children's use of nouns and verbs. *Journal of Child Language* 24: 373–87.

Tomasello, Michael, and Patricia Brooks. 1998. Young children's earliest transitive and intransitive constructions. *Cognitive Linguistics* 9: 379–95.

Tomasello, Michael, and Patricia Brooks. 1999. Early syntactic development. In Martyn Barrett, ed., *The development of language* 76–111. London: Psychology Press.

Tomasello, Michael, Ann Kruger, and Hilary Ratner. 1993. Cultural learning. *Behavioral and Brain Sciences* 16: 495–552.

Winner, Ellen. 1988. *The point of words: Children's understanding of metaphor and irony.* Cambridge, MA: Harvard University Press.

Wittgenstein, Ludwig. 1953. *Philosophical investigations.* Oxford: Basil Blackwell.

CHAPTER 42

SIGNED LANGUAGES

SHERMAN WILCOX

1. DEAFNESS AS A CULTURAL IDENTITY

Deaf people are commonly identified as a group by their disability or handicap. This pathological perspective regards deaf people as having a medical condition, the inability to hear. This perspective also denies the linguistic status of signed languages, regarding them as defective forms of spoken language. Such respected scholars as Edward Sapir (1921) dismissed signed languages as mere substitutes for speech. Perhaps the most egregious case of misrepresenting the nature of signed languages comes from Helmer Myklebust (1957: 241–42):

> The manual language used by the deaf is an ideographic language. . . . It is more pictorial, less symbolic. . . . Ideographic language systems, in comparison with verbal systems, lack precision, subtlety, and flexibility. It is likely that Man cannot achieve his ultimate potential through an Ideographic language. . . . The manual sign language must be viewed as inferior to the verbal as a language.

A more appropriate way to understand deaf people is as members of a linguistic and cultural minority (Charrow and Wilbur 1989; S. Wilcox 1989; Lane, Hoffmeister, and Bahan 1996). The linguistic-cultural perspective view recognizes that deaf people are members of a language community who share a set of cultural beliefs and practices (Padden and Humphries 1988). It also recognizes that the deaf community is multilingual and that signed languages are minority languages.

Scholars now use the terms "deaf" and "Deaf" to distinguish the audiological condition of deafness from the cultural and linguistic identity, respectively.

2. THE WORLD'S SIGNED LANGUAGES

Although no formal survey of the world's signed languages has ever been conducted, it is generally recognized that they number in the hundreds. The thirteenth edition of the Summer Institute of Linguistics *Ethnologue* of the world's languages lists 103 signed languages (Grimes 1996). This surely is a quite conservative number.

Like spoken languages, signed languages may be classified into genetic or family groups. These genetic relations follow the historical development of signed languages, and so do not reflect the same relations as those for spoken languages. French Sign Language, for example, is the parent language of American Sign Language (ASL) and Russian Sign Language.

3. LINGUISTIC RESEARCH ON SIGNED LANGUAGES

Over the past forty years, linguists have demonstrated that signed languages may be described using the same analytic units as spoken languages. While differences in structure attributable to modality (spoken vs. signed) have been noted (Klima and Bellugi 1979), the overwhelming conclusion is that signed languages share important characteristics with spoken languages (Meier, Cormier, and Quinto-Pozos 2002).

The modern era of linguistic research on signed language began in the late 1960s with the pioneering work of William C. Stokoe. As a professor of English at Gallaudet College (now Gallaudet University), Stokoe (1960) began to apply linguistic techniques from the structuralist tradition prevalent at the time to study the language that he saw deaf students using.

3.1. Phonology

One of the pioneering discoveries made by Stokoe was that signed languages can be described phonologically. Before this, it was assumed that the signs, or the words, of signed languages were unanalyzable. Stokoe demonstrated that signs consist of analyzable units of structure. Stokoe coined the term "chereme" for these units, the structural equivalent of the phonemes of spoken languages.

Stokoe analyzed the phonology of signs into three major classes: handshape (the configuration that the hand makes when producing the sign), location (the place where the sign is produced, for example, on the head or in the neutral space in front of the signer's body), and movement (the motion made by the signer in producing the sign, for example, upward or toward the signer's body). Stokoe called these three *aspects* of a sign, recognizing that, unlike the sequential ordering of phonemes in spoken languages, cheremes occur simultaneously and cannot be produced independently: it is not possible to articulate a movement without also articulating that which moves (the handshape).

Linguists later called these aspects the parameters of a sign. Battison (1978) added a fourth parameter, orientation (the direction the hand faces when producing the sign). The psychological reality of parameters is demonstrated by minimal pairs, signs differing only in one parameter which have different meanings (Klima and Bellugi 1979). Linguists now rely on a variety of theoretical models to study the phonology of signed languages, and analyses of phonetics, intonation, prosody, and stress are common in the literature (Liddell 1984a; Sandler 1986; Padden and Perlmutter 1987; Liddell and Johnson 1989; Wilbur 1990, 1999b; Goldsmith 1991; Greftegreff 1992; Brentari 1998).

3.2. Morphology

The morphology of signed languages reflects their expression in the gestural-visual modality. Signed languages make extensive use of space in their morphology, for example, by incorporating spatial locations to indicate verbal arguments; in addition to the hands, the face plays a critical role in signed language morphology, expressing a range of grammatical information such as questions, topic, adverbials, and so forth.

ASL, like many signed languages, is highly synthetic with tendencies toward polysynthesis (Wallin 1990; Engberg-Pedersen 1993). ASL allows morphemes indicating action, person agreement, aspect, and adverbial information to be combined into a single, multimorphemic ASL word; for example, 'I very carefully gave [one] to each person' would be expressed with a single sign in ASL.

Signed languages commonly have complex verb morphology (Klima and Bellugi 1979; Liddell 1984b; Meir 2002). ASL exhibits extensive morphology for representing iterative, habitual, continuative, inceptive, and other verb aspects. Aspect is indicated by changes to the temporal profile of the root's lexical movement.

Supalla and Newport (1978) first described noun-verb derivational morphology in ASL. Pizzuto and Corazza (1996) report on noun morphology in Italian Sign Language. Johnston (2001) argues that Auslan (Australian Sign Language) noun-verb derivational morphology is only partially grammaticalized, remaining closely linked to an iconic base.

Signed languages rely on facial markers to signal intonation and prosody (Sandler 1999); to mark interrogatives, imperatives, and other utterance types (Wilbur 1999a; Reilly, McIntire, and Bellugi 1990); and to indicate various types of adverbial information such as intensity of action (Anderson and Reilly 1998). Facial markers also commonly signal speaker subjectivity (Janzen, Shaffer, and Wilcox 2000).

3.3. Syntax

Research on the syntax of signed languages has examined issues of word class, word order, and relations among constituents such as relative clauses (Coulter 1983; Bouchard 1996; Senghas et al. 1997; Wilbur 1997); question formation (Celo 1996); topic-comment structure and the flow of information in discourse (Janzen 1997, 1999); the interaction of morphology and syntax (Aarons and Morgan 2000); and the grammatical use of space (van Hoek 1992; Engberg-Pedersen 1993; Emmorey and Riley 1995).

Discourse in signed languages is characterized by a prevalence of topic-comment structure. In ASL, topics are marked grammatically, with the topic phrase accompanied by raised eyebrows, a slightly backward head tilt, and a pause between the topic and comment phrases. Topic-comment structure has been described as a kind of ASL sentence type along with questions, imperatives, assertions, and others (Baker and Cokely 1980).

ASL distinguishes two types of interrogatives: *Wh*-questions and *yes-no* questions. *Yes-no* questions are typically statements with the addition of facial markers including raised eyebrows and head tilted forward. *Wh*-questions are indicated with a question word and facial markers including brow furrow, eye squint, and head tilted backward or to one side (Baker and Cokely 1980).

3.4. Fingerspelling

Fingerspelling is a system of manually representing the letters of a written language. ASL, for example, uses fingerspelling to represent the twenty-six letters of the English alphabet. Fingerspelling is often used for proper names or technical terms and is a source of loan words from spoken languages (Battison 1978; Sutton Spence 1999; Brentari and Padden 2001). A variety of fingerspelling systems are used in the world's signed languages. ASL and many other signed languages use a one-handed system; British Sign Language (BSL) and related languages use a two-handed fingerspelling system (Sutton Spence, Woll, and Allsop 1990).

Studies of fingerspelling have examined its acquisition (Padden and Le Master 1985), relation to reading (Hanson, Liberman, and Shankweiler 1983; Padden and Ramsey 1998), and phonetic structure (S. Wilcox 1992; Ann 1993).

4. Signed Languages and Cognitive Linguistics

4.1. Iconicity

Iconicity is clearly a feature of signed languages, so much so that before the scientific study of these languages the overriding belief was that signs were merely pictorial representations without linguistic structure. As linguists turned their attention to signed languages, they faced two obstacles in their efforts to demonstrate that these were, in fact, natural human languages: Saussure's claim that a defining characteristic of language is the arbitrary relation of *signifiant* to *signifié* and Hockett's (1966) proposal of a set of design features universally characteristic of human language. According to Hockett, these defining features of language included arbitrariness (the relation between a meaningful element in language and its denotation is independent of any physical or geometrical resemblance between the two), discreteness (the possible messages in any language constitute a discrete repertory rather than a continuous one), and vocal/auditory channel (the channel for all linguistic communication is vocal/auditory).

Within the signed language literature, iconicity has typically been viewed as a direct relation between linguistic form and reality. Wilbur (1987: 162) defines iconicity as "a reflection in language of the actual state of affairs in the real world." Valli and Lucas (1995: 6) regard the iconic relation to be one in which "the form of the symbol is an icon or picture of some aspect of the thing or activity being symbolized."

Mandel (1977) defined iconicity in a way more compatible with the cognitive perspective. According to Mandel, an iconic sign consisted of a gesture (any movement of the body or a part of the body that is used meaningfully in ASL discourse) "perceived by signers, or potentially perceived by them, as visually related to its referent" (94). Mandel described a number of iconic devices in ASL and argued that the lexicon and the grammar of ASL are motivated by these devices. Iconic devices fall into two major classes: (i) presentation, in which the signer presents a token of action (mime) or points to a token of an object type (indexical presentation), and (ii) depiction, in which the articulator takes on the shape of an object (substitutive or substantive depiction) or in which the moving articulator leaves a trace in the shape of the object (virtual depiction). Mandel also noted that iconicity and conventionality are distinct parameters of language that are, nevertheless, implicationally related. Thus, while it is common to find signs which are highly iconic and highly conventional, it is impossible for signed language to include signs that are entirely arbitrary *and* completely ad hoc.

DeMatteo (1977) explored the continuous as opposed to discrete nature of ASL's coding system, arguing that visual imagery and analogical representations of real-world scenes are integral to the grammar.

This early research on the iconic and analogical properties of signed languages was highly controversial. While signed language scholars recognized the ubiquity of iconicity, the predominant reaction was to deny any role to iconicity in the grammars of signed languages. Ironically, this occurred at a time when cognitive and functional linguists were exploring iconicity for the insights it could provide onto the structure of language and the mind (Haiman 1985; Givón 1989; Croft 1990).

Frishberg (1975) demonstrated that historical change acts to erode iconicity and heighten the arbitrary nature of ASL. Frishberg's data came primarily from morphologically simple forms as represented in dictionaries or word lists, which left open the question of what role iconicity plays in grammar. Klima and Bellugi (1979) expanded the scope of investigation to include morphological data. Although they consistently recognized what they called the "two faces" of sign, its iconicity as well as its arbitrariness, Klima and Bellugi stressed that the grammars of signed languages act to submerge any inherent iconic properties of individual lexical signs: "One of the most striking effects of regular morphological operations on signs is the distortion of form so that iconic aspects of the signs are overridden and submerged" (1979: 30).

One example given by Klima and Bellugi is the morphological change marking intensification on certain statives in ASL. Phonologically, this change consists of a slight initial hold on the movement of a sign followed by a rapid movement. When this grammatical morpheme is applied to the ASL stem SLOW, the resulting sign means 'very slow'. Klima and Bellugi point out that the sign VERY-SLOW is made with a fast movement, faster than that used in the base sign SLOW: "Thus the form of 'very slow' is incongruent with the meaning of the basic sign" (1979: 30).

Echoing this position, Valli and Lucas (1995: 7) claim that while iconicity may be present in individual noun and verb forms, it plays no role in the grammatical relation between noun and verb forms:

> It is probably true that the form of the sign SIT is an iconic representation of human legs sitting. . . . [However,] focusing on its iconicity will not provide much insight into the interesting relationship between SIT and the noun CHAIR, and other noun-verb pairs.

Stokoe (1986: 179), on the other hand, recognized a near-universal diagrammatic iconicity in noun-verb morphology:

> If a hand (or both of them) plays a role in the sign's formation, it is quite possible, given the testimony of all of the world's signed languages so far studied, that the hand's configuration signifies the actor more than it signifies the action, and that the hand's action or movement signifies more the signified action than the actor.

Valli and Lucas (1995: 7) also claim that iconicity is not present in verb aspect morphology: "Nor will [iconicity] help explain how the movement of SIT can be modified to mean SIT FOR A LONG TIME (slow, circular movement) or SIT ABRUPTLY (short, sharp movement)."

If iconicity is seen as a direct mapping of linguistic form to an objective real-ity, clearly iconicity will be easiest to find in more concrete lexical items such as CHAIR, less so in abstract, bound morphology such as intensification, and virtually impossible to locate in the highly abstract grammatical areas of the language such as verb aspect or grammatical class distinctions. It is here that Cognitive Linguistics has the most to contribute to the study of iconicity.

4.2. Cognitive Iconicity

In S. Wilcox (2002b), I propose a cognitive linguistic framework for understanding iconicity in signed languages. Cognitive iconicity builds on the claim made by cog-nitive linguists that phonological and semantic space are subregions of conceptual space (Langacker 1987). For signed languages, the import of cognitive iconicity is that the articulators, hands and their motions, are to be regarded conceptually; cognitive iconicity consists in mappings across phonological and semantic spaces. Taub (2001: 19), also working within the cognitive linguistic framework, makes the same claim: "Iconicity is not an objective relationship between image and referent; rather, it is a relationship between our mental models of image and referent."

Conceptual features of objects and motions are captured in the billiard ball Idealized Cognitive Model (Langacker 1991: 13). When applied to the phonological pole of signs, the billiard-ball model recognizes that hands are physical objects instantiated in space and their movements are instantiated in time. Further, hands as objects instantiated in material substance have certain qualities: basic qualities such as shape, size, and location, as well as derived qualities such as function.

Newport and Meier (1985: 885) report the following formational patterns in ASL classifier predicates:

> The handshape is a classifier for the semantic category (e.g. human vs. animate nonhuman vs. vehicle) or size and shape of the moving object; the movement path (one of a small number of discretely different movements, e.g. straight vs. cir-cular vs. arc) is a morpheme representing the path of motion of the moving object; the manner of movement is a morpheme for the manner of motion along the path (e.g. bounce vs. roll vs. random); a second handshape (typically produced on the left hand) is a classifier for a secondary object, with respect to which the primary object moves; and the placement of the second handshape along the path is a morpheme for the spatial relationship of the movement path with respect to this secondary object (e.g. from vs. to vs. past).

Across all of these forms, we see that handshapes represent objects and their features; secondary handshapes represent secondary objects and their features; the spatial relationship of hands represents the spatial relationship of referents; hand movements represent actions; and manner of motion of the articulator re-presents manner of motion of the referent. Classifier predicates thus exhibit a systematic pattern of iconic relations in which conceptual objects and actions are mapped onto handshapes and their movements.

Consider once again the VERY-SLOW example. VERY-SLOW is multimorphemic, consisting of the base morpheme SLOW and a bound, grammatical morpheme marking intensification. This bound morpheme is realized as a change in the movement of the base morpheme: an initial hold is followed by the sudden release into a rapid motion. The same morpheme appears on other lexical roots, such as VERY-SMART and VERY-FAST. While it is true, as Klima and Bellugi noted, that the form of VERY-SLOW is incongruent with the meaning of the lexical stem SLOW, it is not true that the form of the intensifier morpheme is incongruent with its meaning.

Intensity is a conceptually dependent notion, relying on a prior conception of what is being intensified: something is 'very *slow*' or 'very *hot*' or 'very *big*' but not simply 'very' *tout court*. In addition, the abstract notion of intensity is often understood metaphorically by reference to more grounded concepts such as the sudden release of pent up pressure. A cognitive analysis shows that the construction VERY-SLOW is iconic in two ways. First, it is iconic because the articulators directly represent the metaphorical conceptualization of intensity as a sudden release of pent up pressure. Second, the nature of intensity as a conceptually dependent notion is also iconically represented: change in *how* a movement is articulated relies on a prior conception of *what* movement was produced.

The derivational morphology data is likewise iconic. The basis for nouns and verbs within Cognitive Linguistics lies in the conceptual distinction of objects and their interactions, captured by the billiard-ball model. Nouns are regions in some domain; Cognitive Grammar uses the term "thing" for the class of nouns. Verbs comprise a series of stative relations (a stative relation being a single, internally consistent configuration) distributed continuously through conceived time, the component states being scanned sequentially by the conceptualizer. This relation is said to comprise a "process." At the semantic pole, every noun profiles a thing, while every verb profiles a process.

Klima and Bellugi (1979: 295–96) describe the formal characteristics of noun-verb pairs in ASL:

> Both continuous and hold manner occur in the verb signs (a continuous sweep as opposed to a noticeable stop at the end of the movement); the related noun forms show a consistently restricted pattern: they are the same as the verb forms except that they have reduplicated movement and a restrained manner (that is, the muscles are tightened in performing the movement). As a result of the restrained manner the nouns are typically made with smaller movements than their related verbs.

The articulation of ASL noun forms in a restricted region of space motivates their construal as things at the phonological pole. Verb forms make salient in their articulation motion through space; they are thus construed as processes at their phonological pole. The mapping of phonological thing and process onto semantic thing (noun) and process (verb), respectively, makes these noun-verb forms highly iconic, not for the specific meanings of the nouns and verbs they represent but for the grammatical class of noun and verb.

Turning to verb aspect, signed languages exhibit a general type of iconic mapping. The semantic pole of aspectual markers designate situation-internal temporal features such as inception, duration, or completion of an event (Langacker 1972). Aspect is coded phonologically in many signed languages by modifying the sign's lexical movement. This need not be so; we could logically envision a signed language in which verb aspect is marked by changing the handshape or the location parameter. In fact, no known signed language marks verb aspect in this way. Instead, event-internal features of the phonological pole (changes to the temporal profile of the sign's movement parameter) are mapped onto event-internal temporal features of the event encoded in the semantic pole.

As Mandel pointed out, it is important to recognize that iconicity and conventionality interact. One consequence of this is that iconicity does not imply predictability of form. Within the cognitive iconicity framework, this fact is captured by noting that iconic mappings are not between objective forms and scenes. Rather, they are bipolar mappings of construals. As Langacker (1991: 294) notes:

> Conceptually, there are countless ways of construing a given event, and a particular event conception might deviate from the canon in any manner or to any degree.... An event's objective properties are consequently insufficient to predict the grammatical structure of a clause describing it.

This observation also applies to the conception of signed language articulatory events. There are countless ways of construing a moving hand: as movement (of an object), as an object (moving), as an instrument (an object performing some functional action such as cutting), as a tracing device (performing virtual depiction), and so forth. Just as an event's objective properties are insufficient to predict the grammatical structure of a clause describing it, the objective properties of visible articulators are insufficient to predict how they may be construed.

Because of the bipolar construal of symbolic structures, even highly iconic signs may also exhibit a high degree of arbitrariness. This fact has been documented by Pietrandrea (2002) in the Italian Sign Language (LIS) lexicon. In a study of 1,944 signs, it was found that 50 percent of handshape occurrences and 67 percent of body location occurrences have an iconic motivation. Along with this pervasive iconicity, Pietrandrea found a deep arbitrariness in the LIS lexicon due to the fact that iconic signs exhibit arbitrary selection of different aspects of articulators and referents to convey different meanings.

Russo and his colleagues (Russo 1999; Russo, Giurana, and Pizzuto 2001) studied iconic aspects of LIS in poetic, prose, and lecture genres. Russo distinguished two types of iconicity in these texts: (i) frozen iconicity, that is, those iconic features of signs which appear irrespective of discourse context, and (ii) dynamic iconicity, that is, those iconic features of signs or their sublexical components "that arise from the meaning they assume in discourse and/or from the relationship they entertain with the other signs with which they co-occur" (90). Russo found that while frozen iconicity appeared in the lecture data, it was present in poetic texts to a markedly higher degree than in lectures (77 percent vs. 47 percent). Dynamic iconicity was a distinctive and productively used device in the poems, occurring in 53 percent of the constructions analyzed. In contrast, dynamic iconicity played only a minor role in the lecture data, appearing in only 13 percent of the constructions.

4.3. Metaphor

Metaphor plays a significant role in the phonology, morphology, and discourse of signed languages. Wilbur (1987) identified several spatialization, ontological, and structural metaphors in ASL. For example, the metaphor HAPPY IS UP is seen in ASL signs such as CHEERFUL, HAPPY, and EXCITED; NEGATIVE VALUE IS DOWN is present in signs such as LOUSY, IGNORE, and FAIL. Wilbur also described the ontological metaphor THE MIND IS A CONTAINER using the size-and-shape specifier handshape C, commonly used for containers such as cup or glass; when the C-handshape is made on the signer's forehead, the sign means 'knowledgeable'.

P. Wilcox (2000) demonstrated the complexity of metaphorical mappings in ASL by examining a number of ontological and structural metaphors in detail. The MIND IS A CONTAINER metaphor, for example, sanctions a number of extensions including a front-back mapping: consciously known or remembered information is in the front of the head, unconsciously known or remembered information is situated in the back of the head.

ASL exhibits a network of metaphorical mappings based on the IDEAS ARE OBJECTS ontological metaphor (P. Wilcox 2000). The metaphor IDEAS ARE OBJECTS SUBJECT TO PHYSICAL FORCE is seen in signs for 'forget' (ideas falling out of the mind-as-container). IDEAS ARE OBJECTS TO BE MANIPULATED OR PLACED appears in signs produced with the flat-O handshape, used to manipulate or place physical objects (e.g., 'put', 'give') and metaphorical objects ('learn', 'move ideas around', 'put knowledge into an unconscious thinking area', and the ASL compound 'remember; I'll mark that in my memory' signed as PUT-STAY on the forehead).

The metaphor IDEAS ARE OBJECTS TO BE GRASPED is seen in a number of spoken languages for concepts related to understanding, as in *I get what you mean* or *I didn't fully grasp his argument*. Although this metaphor does not map onto understanding in ASL, it is used to motivate expressions in which ideas are remembered (grasping near the forehead) or ideas which were once held firmly in place are released. In the latter, a sign made with the closed fist near the forehead is rapidly opened into an open-5 handshape while simultaneously moving downwards. This sign may be used in a context in which an author who has, over the course of many years, collected a store of Deaf folklore, in a brief period of time documents them in a book.

IDEAS ARE OBJECTS TO BE GRASPED is mapped onto understanding in other signed languages. Catalan Sign Language exhibits the metaphor in the sign meaning

'I understand you': an open-5 handshape moves from a position away from the signer to one near the signer's head while simultaneously closing into a fist handshape. Italian Sign Language has a similar sign, also based on the IDEAS ARE OBJECTS TO BE GRASPED metaphor.

The metaphor IDEAS ARE OBJECTS TO BE CAREFULLY SELECTED uses an F-handshape (index and thumb touching, other fingers extended). This handshape is used for small physical objects such pins or seeds which require special care and attention in their manipulation. In ASL, the sign meaning 'to carefully select an idea' is made with this handshape at the forehead, 'selecting' one idea from the mind-as-container's store of ideas (P. Wilcox 2000).

A number of signed languages use a TIME IS SPACE metaphor to represent time concepts (S. Wilcox 2002b). Signed languages incorporate space as time in at least two ways: time may be conceptualized as an entity residing at a certain point in space (LOCATION IN TIME IS LOCATION IN SPACE), or the continuous flow of time may be conceived as movement through space (FLOW OF TIME IS MOVEMENT IN SPACE). In the first case, ASL and several other signed languages (Klima and Bellugi 1979; Engberg-Pedersen 1993) use various time lines, setting spatial locations along a line to represent points in time. In the latter case, the spatial movement of certain lexical items such as the ASL signs PROGRESS and PROCEED represents movement through time (S. Wilcox 2002b).

The close relation between language, cognition, and culture is vividly revealed in the metaphorical mappings that occur in signed language poetry. P. Wilcox (2000) analyzes one ASL poem, "The Dogs" by Deaf poet Ella Mae Lentz. In this poem, Lentz describes two dogs, a grizzled mutt and a sophisticated Doberman, tied together by a chain. P. Wilcox found a number of manifestations of the SOCIAL RELATIONS ARE SPATIAL RELATIONS metaphor for describing relations among different classes of deaf people (those who use ASL, those who prefer a signed representation of English, those who are culturally Deaf versus those who are only audiologically deaf, and so forth), including:

- social identity = physical closeness
- social constraint = physical constraint
- involuntary social unity = involuntary physical connectedness
- shared social identity = chain linking two dogs

When this poem was shown to Deaf people in other countries with different cultural and historical backgrounds, differing interpretations of the metaphors emerged. Deaf people in Switzerland often saw the two dogs in the poem not as different cultural and linguistic groups within the deaf community but as deaf (the "mutt") and hearing people (the Doberman). Some interpreted the two protagonists as different aspects of a single deaf person: one dog represented that part of the self that felt hearing, while the other represented their deaf identity. Deaf people in Rome, Italy, interpreted neither of the two dogs as deaf; instead, they saw the poem as a metaphor for different races fighting each other.

4.4. Metonymy

Metonymy is widespread in the lexicons of signed languages. In ASL and Catalan Sign Language, the metonymy PROTOTYPICAL CHARACTERISTIC FOR WHOLE ENTITY is seen in BIRD (a sign representing the beak) and CAT (representing the whiskers), and SPECIFIC INTERACTION WITH PROTOTYPICAL ELEMENT FOR WHOLE ACTIVITY is seen in several Catalan Sign Language forms of DRINK representing the ways different types of drink are consumed (e.g., 'drink beer' vs. 'drink brandy').

Metonymy is commonly seen in name signs. In one type of name sign, a prominent physical characteristic may be used as the name for a person, as in 'person with bandage on arm'. Fingerspelling may interact metonymically with name signs: the ASL signs for Chicago, Texas, and Philadelphia are made with a movement resembling the number '7' traced in the air, but are distinguished by using a handshape representing a single letter from the written word: C for Chicago, X for Texas, and P for Philadelphia. Some name signs incorporate a more complex blend of metonymies in which a single handshape representing the first letter of the person's written name combines with the location and movement of a sign identifying a distinctive quality of the person: Phyllis, for example, might have the name sign combining the handshape 'P' with the location and movement of the sign for 'music' to indicate that she loves music.

Catalan Sign Language uses a set of metonymies to represent PHYSICAL CONSEQUENCE FOR DEGREE OF THE PERCEPTUAL QUALITY: CRAZY-EYES for 'really good', OPEN-MOUTH for 'astonishment', and SEIZURE for 'incredible'. Italian Sign Language uses a similar metonymy in the sign JAW-STRAIN meaning 'make an effort'.

Metonymy is often found in morphologically related noun-verb pairs in ASL. For example, metonymy relates the verb PUT-OBJECT-IN-MOUTH 'eat' to the noun 'food'; ACTIVITY FOR INSTRUMENT metonymy relates the verb MOVE-FINGERS 'type' to its noun form 'typewriter'.

P. Wilcox (2000) describes a cumulative metaphonymy in ASL in the sign THINK-HEARING, a derogatory sign referring to a person who is audiologically deaf but accepts uncritically the ideology of the hearing world (Padden and Humphries 1988). The sign HEARING is normally produced at the mouth, metonymically representing the activity of speaking ('hearing people' are thus conceptualized as 'those who speak'). In THINK-HEARING, this sign is moved upward and signed at the forehead, indicating that the person is 'hearing in the mind'.

4.5. Summary

The picture that emerges from the study of iconicity, metaphor, and metonymy in signed languages is that these tropes interact in quite complex ways, whether we examine spontaneous discourse or artistic genres. The overriding presence of iconicity is undeniable. Metaphor and iconicity are often simultaneously present, but analysis reveals that in many of these cases, iconicity depends on a logically prior metaphorical mapping.

4.6. Mental Space and Blends

Liddell (2000) has explored the concept of blended mental spaces (Fauconnier and Turner 1996) at it applies to ASL. Liddell argues that signed language discourse makes use of spontaneous gestures, distinguishable from lexical signs, that convey meanings such as are conveyed by gesture in spoken language discourse. He goes on to suggest that signed languages differ from spoken languages in having developed mechanisms that allow the gestural component to combine with linguistic aspects of signs.

Liddell (1998) describes grounded blends in ASL resulting from the blending of elements from a mental space with elements of the signer's immediate physical environment. Liddell demonstrates that grounded blends often incorporate the conceptual scene from a nongrounded space, projecting that onto the current physical setting. In ASL discourse, for example, if the signer is one of the blended elements, first-person pronouns no longer refer to the speaker but to the conceptual element blended with the speaker.

5. GESTURE

Until recently, the prevailing view among linguists has been that language and gesture are categorically distinct systems. For example, Chomsky (1972: 70) claims that while it may be possible to find a direct link between human gesture and animal communication, human language is based on principles entirely different from either. Recent research on gesture does not support such a claim. Scholars such as Kendon (1972, 1980), Calbris (1985, 1990), McNeill (1985, 1992, 2000), and Duncan (2002) have explored the deep links between gesture and language. On the basis of this work, McNeill (1992: 23) has concluded that "gestures and speech should be viewed within a unified conceptual framework as aspects of a single underlying process."

5.1. Definitions

A number of definitions of gesture have been offered in the literature. Kendon (2000) uses the term "gesture" to refer to a range of visible bodily actions produced as part of a person's willing expression. This definition excludes from gesture unintentional expressions of affect and behaviors such as posture, postural shifting, and direction of gaze, which Kendon sees as part of the way in which participants in interaction establish and maintain their orientations to each other. Kendon (1988) described an ordering of gestures, which McNeill (1992) has dubbed "Kendon's continuum":

Gesticulation → Language-like Gestures → Pantomimes → Emblems
→ Sign Languages

McNeill (1992: 37) notes that as we move from left to right along this gestural continuum, (i) the obligatory presence of speech declines, (ii) the presence of language properties increases, and (iii) idiosyncratic gestures are replaced by socially regulated signs. McNeill limits his use of the term "gestures" to the gesticulation end of the continuum. In his view, gestures are "idiosyncratic spontaneous movements of the hands and arms accompanying speech" (1992: 37). In distinguishing the visible movements of a speaker into gesture and nongesture, McNeill notes that the latter comprise self-touching (e.g., stroking the hair) and object manipulation.

Armstrong, Stokoe, and Wilcox (1995) take a broader view of gesture, defining it, after Studdert-Kennedy (1987: 77), as a functional unit, "an equivalence class of coordinated movements that achieve some end (Armstrong, Stokoe, and Wilcox 1995: 43). There are three motivations for this more inclusive definition of gesture. First, it permits us to categorize together the movements that psychologists and phoneticians regard as the components of speech (Neisser 1967; Browman and Goldstein 1989) with cospeech gestures and signed languages. Second, by not specifying that gestures must be intentionally produced or communicative, it allows the study of how unintentional, noncommunicative movements which happen to be informative about future actions come to have communicative significance (Krebs and Davies 1993). Third, researchers such as King (2004) report that such an approach to gesture permits the discovery of how gestural communication emerges in the nonvocal social communication of African great apes.

5.2. Types of Gesture

One type of gesture that is widely recognized across cultures has come to be called the emblem. According to McNeill (1992: 56), emblems are part of a social code but are not fully structured as language. They have names or standard paraphrases, are learned as specific gestural symbols, and can be used to substitute for spoken words or phrases. An example of an emblem is the so-called Hand Purse, produced by holding the hand upright with the fingers and thumb pressed together at the tips. The Hand Purse has several meanings, including 'query' (in Italy, Sardinia, and Sicily), 'good' (Portugal, Greece, and Turkey), 'fear' (Belgium and France), and 'emphasis' (Holland and Germany). Morris et al. (1979) describe 20 emblems in use across Europe. Kendon (1981) notes that although emblems are complete speech acts, they are limited in their function: they regulate and comment on behavior, reveal one's emotional state, make promises, swear oaths, and function to command, request, reply to a challenge, insult, threaten, or express fear. They do not, however, function referentially to signify objects or events.

McNeill (1992) identifies four basic types of gestures: iconic, metaphorical, deictic, and beat. Iconic gestures bear a close formal relationship to the semantic content of speech, depicting in their form and manner of production some aspect of the same scene that is expressed in the co-occurring speech. McNeill (1992: 78) offers the example of a gesture that accompanies the utterance *He tries going up inside the pipe this time* in which the hand rises upward.

Metaphorical gestures also depict an image, but the image is of an abstract concept such as knowledge or language. An example is a gesture presenting the concept of a question as a cupped hand. As McNeill points out, metaphorical gestures are related to iconic gestures, in that they both present images.

Deictic gestures are pointing movements. They are typically made with a pointing finger, but any extensible body part can be used, such as the chin or lips, as well as nonbody objects such as a pencil. McNeill notes that deictic gestures produced during spoken narrative rarely point to concrete entities. Rather, they select a part of the gesture space, and their meaning depends on a prior referential value that has been attached to this space.

McNeill defines beats as movements that do not present a discernible meaning. Beats typically are composed of two movement components consisting of small, low energy, rapid movements of the fingers or hand. The meaning of a beat gesture lies not in its referential value, but merely in indicating that something is significant because of its relation to the overall discourse. For example, a beat may accompany the first mention of an important character in a narrative discourse.

Calbris (1990) takes a more semiotic approach to the study of gesture. Although the focus of her work is coverbal gestures, she does not limit the range of gesture quite as much as do Kendon or McNeill. For Calbris, coverbal gesturing may include "expressive gestures" as well as facial expressions. Calbris describes her work as "more semantic than pragmatic, addressing the significance of gestures more than their interactive role" (xv). Her focus is more on the internal symbolic analysis of gestures, which allows her to discover and describe subtle nuances of the semantic field of gestures. For example, Calbris explores the inherent conceptual symbolism of circular, straight-line, and curved movements; combinations of movements such as forward loops, hands turning around each other, or a circle repeated on itself in a horizontal plane; and several cases of complex gestures such as movement and configuration (e.g., fist forward, palm outward, or thumb and forefinger joined in pincers).

Because of her careful study of gestural semantics, Calbris is able to discover a range of polysemy in her data. This leads her to propose two types of polysemy in the French gestural system:

> In the first [type] (a), the link between the signifier and the signified is unique, while the signified is subject to semantic shifts: there is no single motivation. In the second type (b), there are multiple links associating one or more of the signifying elements of the gesture with one or more signifieds: the motivation is plural. (1990: 207)

Calbris suggests that the polysemy of a singly motivated gesture, her type (a), is explained by semantic shifting: "The gesture takes on new meanings as the meaning of the signified passes from literal to figurative, from concrete to abstract, from the

Figure 42.1. American Sign Language sign MUST (Humphries, Padden, and O'Rourke 1980)

spatial to the temporal world, from the physical to the psychological level, from a particular domain to everyday life" (1990: 207). Plural motivation is explained by the rich symbolism in the physical signifier.

Along with the prevailing view that gestures and language are distinct systems is the assumption that gestures are merely "nonverbal" accompaniments to speech, adding little or no distinct information of their own to the overall utterance. The evidence from research on gesture refutes this assumption. Calbris also concludes that it would be erroneous to regard gesture as merely illustrating or substituting for speech. Instead, she suggests that gesture adds complementary information to that given in the spoken utterance. In this way, she suggests, speech and gesture together function in a type of topic-comment relation: "Gestures comment on utterance" (1990: 209).

6. GESTURE AND GRAMMATICIZATION IN SIGNED LANGUAGES

Grammaticization operates in signed languages as it does in spoken languages. The source for the agentive suffix in ASL, for example, was the lexical form meaning 'body' signed by touching the torso with two open hands, first on the chest and then on the abdomen. At the turn of the twentieth century, the sign meaning 'teacher' appears to have been a compound of TEACH+BODY. Over time, the form became phonetically reduced. The contemporary sign for teacher consists of the sign TEACH, made by moving two flat-O handshapes outward from the head (metaphorically 'transfer ideas from me to you'), and the agentive suffix, made by slightly opening and dropping the hands. The unreduced, older form BODY remains in the ASL lexicon.

In the case of signed languages, grammaticization may be extended to account for the development of lexical and grammatical material, both manual and facial,

Figure 42.2. Contemporary French Sign Language sign IL FAUT (Girod 1997)

from gestural sources. Wilcox and Wilcox (1995) described a set of modal forms in ASL that trace a path from gesture to lexicon to grammar. The modal form CAN indicating possibility and ability had as its source the lexical morpheme STRONG. The ASL evidential forms SEEM, FEEL, and OBVIOUS grammaticized from lexical morphemes MIRROR, FEEL (used in the physical sense), and BRIGHT, respectively. Each of these lexical morphemes can be traced in turn to a gestural source. Thus, the full developmental path for these forms is:

- [gesture enacting upper body strength] → STRONG → CAN
- [gesture enacting looking in a mirror] → MIRROR → SEEM
- [gesture enacting physically sensing with finger] → FEEL (physical) → FEEL (evidential)
- [metaphorical gesture indicating rays of light] → BRIGHT → OBVIOUS

Shaffer (2002) notes that the ASL deontic modal MUST (figure 42.1) is related to the French Sign Language IL FAUT 'it is necessary' (figure 42.2). IL FAUT is also attested in mid-nineteenth-century French Sign Language (figure 42.3). It appears likely that these forms derive from a gesture used as early as Roman times to signal obligation. Dodwell (2000: 36) discusses a gesture (figure 42.4) that he classifies an imperative: "It consists of directing the extended index finger towards the ground." The gesture was described by Quintilian in the first century AD: "when directed towards the ground, this finger insists" (Dodwell 2000: 36).

Janzen and Shaffer (2002) identify the source of the ASL future morpheme as an ancient, pan-Mediterranean gesture (de Jorio 2000). The gesture is still in use among hearing people in the Mediterranean region to signal departure-demand and departure-description (Morris et al. 1979). The gesture also appears in the 1855 lexicon of French Sign Language (Brouland 1855) as the lexical morpheme PARTIR 'depart'.

Grammaticization also accounts for the emergence of modal and evidential forms from gestural sources in Catalan Sign Language (S. Wilcox 2002a). The Catalan Sign Language forms EVIDENT 'obvious', CLAR 'clear', PRESENTIR 'have a feeling, have a premonition', and SEMBLAR 'seem', which have physical

Figure 42.3. 1855 French Sign Language sign IL FAUT (Brouland 1855)

meanings in their lexical uses (visual perception, bright light, smell, and physical resemblance, respectively), have developed more subjective senses, one indication that a form has become more grammatical. For example, the Catalan Sign Language grammatical morpheme PRESENTIR expresses the speaker's inferences about actions or intentions:

(1)   PRO.3 DIR ANAR HOLANDA NO [pause] PRESENTIR CANVI.IDEA
      [pause] MARXAR SEGUR
      She said she wouldn't go to Holland, but I feel she'll change her mind. I'm sure she'll go.

These Catalan Sign Language forms have sources in metaphorical or enacting gestures indicating the eyes and visual perception, bright light, the nose and the sense of smell, and facial appearance. Once again, the full grammaticization path is from gesture to lexical morpheme to grammatical morpheme.

7. FUTURE DIRECTIONS

Although we have learned much in the past fifty years about the structure of signed languages, especially those in more developed countries, linguists have only begun to investigate the world's signed languages. For the cognitive linguist, signed languages provide an ideal source of data for studying the influence of perception on cognition and the grammatical structure of languages; usage-based models of language; the relation between form and structure; the complex interactions among metaphor, metonymy, and iconicity; and the evolution of language from embodied, gestural sources.

Figure 42.4. Roman gesture meaning 'insistence'

REFERENCES

Aarons, Debra, and Robert Morgan. 2000. The interaction of classifiers and syntax in South African Sign Language. *Stellenbosch Papers in Linguistics* 33: 1–20.

Anderson, Diane E., and Judy S. Reilly. 1998. Pah! The acquisition of adverbials in ASL. *Sign Language and Linguistics* 1: 117–42.

Ann, Jean. 1993. The phonetics of fingerspelling. *Language and Speech* 36: 471–75.

Armstrong, David E., William C. Stokoe, and Sherman Wilcox. 1995. *Gesture and the nature of language*. Cambridge: Cambridge University Press.

Baker, Charlotte, and Dennis Cokely. 1980. *American Sign Language: A teacher's resource text on grammar and culture*. Silver Spring, MD: T. J. Publishers.

Battison, Robbin. 1978. *Lexical borrowing in American Sign Language*. Silver Spring, MD: Linkstok Press.

Bouchard, Denis. 1996. Sign languages and language universals: The status of order and position in grammar. *Sign Language Studies* 91: 101–60.

Brentari, Diane. 1998. *A prosodic model of sign language phonology*. Cambridge, MA: MIT Press.

Brentari, Diane, and Carol Padden. 2001. A lexicon with multiple origins: Native and foreign vocabulary in American Sign Language. In Diane Brentari, ed., *Foreign vocabulary in sign languages: A cross-linguistic investigation of word formation* 87–119. Mahwah, NJ: Lawrence Erlbaum.

Brouland, Josephíne. 1855. *Langage mimique: Spécimen d'un dictionaire des signes*. Washington, DC: Gallaudet Archives.

Browman, Catherine P., and Louis M. Goldstein. 1989. Articulatory gestures as phonological units. *Phonology* 6: 201–51.

Calbris, Geneviève. 1985. Espace-temps: Expression gestuelle du temps. *Semiotica* 55: 43–73.

Calbris, Geneviève. 1990. *The semiotics of French gestures*. Bloomington: Indiana University Press.

Celo, Pietro. 1996. Linguistic and pragmatic aspects of the interrogative form in Italian Sign Language. In Ceil Lucas, ed., *Multicultural aspects of sociolinguistics in deaf communities* 132–51. Washington, DC: Gallaudet University Press.

Charrow, Veda R., and Ronnie B. Wilbur. 1989. The deaf child as a linguistic minority. In Sherman Wilcox, ed., *American Deaf culture: An anthology* 103–15. Burtonsville, MD: Linstok Press.

Chomsky, Noam. 1972. *Language and mind*. Enlarged ed. New York: Harcourt Brace Jovanovich.

Coulter, Geoffrey R. 1983. A conjoined analysis of American Sign Language relative clauses. *Discourse Processes* 6: 305–18.

Croft, William. 1990. *Typology and universals*. Cambridge: Cambridge University Press.

de Jorio, Andrea. 2000. *Gesture in Naples and gesture in classical antiquity* [La mimica degli antichi investigata nel gestire napoletano]. Bloomington: Indiana University Press.

DeMatteo, Asa. 1977. Visual imagery and visual analogues. In Lynn Friedman, ed., *On the other hand: New perspectives on American Sign Language* 109–36. New York: Academic Press.

Dodwell, C. Reginald. 2000. *Anglo-Saxon gestures and the Roman stage*. Cambridge: Cambridge University Press.

Duncan, Susan D. 2002. Gesture, verb aspect, and the nature of iconic imagery in natural discourse. *Gesture* 2: 183–206.

Emmorey, Karen, and Judy Riley, eds. 1995. *Sign, gesture, and space*. Hillsdale, NJ: Lawrence Erlbaum.

Engberg-Pedersen, Elisabeth. 1993. *Space in Danish Sign Language: The semantics and morphosyntax of the use of space in a visual language*. Hamburg: SIGNUM-Verlag.

Fauconnier, Gilles, and Mark Turner. 1996. Blending as a central process of grammar. In Adele E. Goldberg, ed., *Conceptual structure, discourse and language* 113–30. Stanford, CA: CSLI Publications.

Frishberg, Nancy. 1975. Arbitrariness and iconicity: Historical change in American Sign Language. *Language* 51: 676–710.

Girod, Michel. 1997. *La langue des signes*. Vol. 2. Paris: Edition Marketing.

Givón, Talmy. 1989. *Mind, code and context: Essays in pragmatics*. Hillsdale, NJ: Lawrence Erlbaum.

Goldsmith, John. 1991. Qu'est-ce qu'une phonologie d'une langue des signes? *Revue que-becoise de linguistique theorique et appliquee* 10: 11–20.

Greftegreff, Irene. 1992. Orientation in indexical signs in Norwegian Sign Language. *Nordic Journal of Linguistics* 15: 159–82.

Grimes, Bernard. 1996. *Ethnologue*. Dallas, TX: Summer Institute of Linguistics.

Haiman, John, ed. 1985. *Iconicity in syntax*. Amsterdam: John Benjamins.

Hanson, Vicky L., Isabelle Y. Liberman, and Donald Shankweiler. 1983. Linguistic coding by deaf children in relation to beginning reading success. *Haskins Laboratories Status Report on Speech Research* 73: 141–56.

Hockett, Charles. 1966. The problem of universals in language. In Joseph Greenberg, ed., *Universals of language*. Cambridge, MA: MIT Press.

Humphries, Tom, Carol Padden, and Terence O'Rourke. 1980. *A basic course in American Sign Language*. Silver Spring, MD: T. J. Publishers.

Janzen, Terry. 1997. Pragmatic and syntactic features of topics in American Sign Language. *Meta* 42: 502–14.

Janzen, Terry. 1999. The grammaticization of topics in American Sign Language. *Studies in Language* 23: 271–306.

Janzen, Terry, and Barbara Shaffer. 2002. Gesture as the substrate in the process of ASL grammaticization. In Richard Meier, Kelly Cormier, and David Quinto-Pozos, eds., *Modality and structure in signed and spoken languages* 199–223. Cambridge: Cambridge University Press.

Janzen, Terry, Barbara Shaffer, and Sherman Wilcox. 2000. Signed language pragmatics. In Jef Verschueren, Jan-Ola Östman, Jan Blommaert, and Chris Bulcaen, eds., *Handbook of pragmatics* 1–20. Amsterdam: John Benjamins.

Johnston, Trevor. 2001. Nouns and verbs in Australian Sign Language: An open and shut case? *Journal of Deaf Studies and Deaf Education* 6: 235–57.

Kendon, Adam. 1972. Some relationships between body motion and speech. In Aron Sigman and Benjamin Pope, eds., *Studies in dyadic communication* 177–210. New York: Permamon Press.

Kendon, Adam. 1980. Gesticulation and speech: Two aspects of the process of utter-ance. In M. R. Kay, ed., *The relation between verbal and nonverbal communication* 206–27. The Hague: Mouton.

Kendon, Adam. 1981. Geography of gesture. *Semiotica* 37: 129–63.

Kendon, Adam. 1988. How gestures can become like words. In Fernando Poyatos, ed., *Cross-cultural perspectives in nonverbal communication* 131–41. Toronto: Hogrefe.

Kendon, Adam. 2000. Language and gesture: Unity or duality? In David McNeill, ed., *Language and gesture* 47–63. Cambridge: Cambridge University Press.

King, Barbara. 2004. *The dynamic dance: Nonvocal social communication in African great apes*. Cambridge, MA: Harvard University Press.

Klima, Edward, and Ursula Bellugi. 1979. *The signs of language*. Cambridge, MA: Harvard University Press.

Krebs, John R., and Nicholas B. Davies. 1993. *An introduction to behavioural ecology*. Oxford: Basil Blackwell.

Lane, Harlan, Robert Hoffmeister, and Ben Bahan. 1996. *A journey into the deaf-world*. San Diego, CA: DawnSignPress.

Langacker, Ronald W. 1972. *Fundamentals of linguistic analysis*. New York: Harcourt Brace Jovanovich.

Langacker, Ronald W. 1987. *Foundations of cognitive grammar*. Vol. 1, *Theoretical prereq-uisites*. Stanford, CA: Stanford University Press.

Langacker, Ronald W. 1991. *Foundations of cognitive grammar*. Vol. 2, *Descriptive application*. Stanford, CA: Stanford University Press.

Liddell, Scott K. 1984a. THINK and BELIEVE: Sequentiality in American Sign Language. *Language* 60: 372–99.

Liddell, Scott K. 1984b. Unrealized-inceptive aspect in American Sign Language: Feature insertion in syllabic frames. *Chicago Linguistic Society* 20: 257–70.

Liddell, Scott K. 1998. Grounded blends, gestures, and conceptual shifts. *Cognitive Linguistics* 9: 283–314.

Liddell, Scott K. 2000. Blended spaces and deixis in sign language discourse. In David McNeill, ed., *Language and gesture* 331–57. Cambridge: Cambridge University Press.

Liddell, Scott K., and Robert Johnson. 1989. American Sign Language: The phonological base. *Sign Language Studies* 64: 195–278.

Mandel, Mark A. 1977. Iconic devices in American Sign Language. In Lynn Friedman, ed., *On the other hand: New perspectives on American Sign Language* 57–108. New York: Academic Press.

McNeill, David. 1985. So you think gestures are nonverbal? *Psychological Review* 92: 350–71.

McNeill, David. 1992. *Hand and mind: What gestures reveal about thought*. Chicago: University of Chicago Press.

McNeill, David, ed. 2000. *Language and gesture*. Cambridge: Cambridge University Press.

Meier, Richard, Kelly Cormier, and David Quinto-Pozos, eds. 2002. *Modality and structure in signed and spoken languages*. Cambridge: Cambridge University Press.

Meir, Irit. 2002. A cross-modality perspective on verb agreement. *Natural Language and Linguistic Theory* 20: 413–50.

Morris, Desmond, Peter Collett, Peter Marsh, and Marie O'Shaughnessy. 1979. *Gestures: Their origin and distribution*. New York: Stein and Day.

Myklebust, Helmer. 1957. *The psychology of deafness*. New York: Grune and Stratton.

Neisser, Ulrich. 1967. *Cognitive psychology*. New York: Appleton-Century-Crofts.

Newport, Elisa L., and Richard Meier. 1985. The acquisition of American Sign Language. In Dan I. Slobin, ed., *The crosslinguistic study of language acquisition*, vol. 1, *The data* 881–938. Hillsdale, NJ: Lawrence Erlbaum.

Padden, Carol, and Tom Humphries. 1988. *Deaf in America: Voices from a culture*. Cambridge, MA: Harvard University Press.

Padden, Carol A., and Barbara Le Master. 1985. An alphabet on hand: The acquisition of fingerspelling in deaf children. *Sign Language Studies* 47: 161–72.

Padden, Carol A., and David M. Perlmutter. 1987. American Sign Language and the architecture of phonological theory. *Natural Language and Linguistic Theory* 5: 335–75.

Padden, Carol, and Claire Ramsey. 1998. Reading ability in signing deaf children. *Topics in Language Disorders* 18: 30–46.

Pietrandrea, Paola. 2002. Iconicity and arbitrariness in Italian Sign Language. *Sign Language Studies* 2: 296–321.

Pizzuto, Elena, and Serena Corazza. 1996. Noun morphology in Italian Sign Language (LIS). *Lingua* 98: 169–96.

Reilly, Judy S., Marina McIntire, and Ursula Bellugi. 1990. The acquisition of conditionals in American Sign Language: Grammaticized facial expressions. *Applied Psycholinguistics* 11: 369–92.

Russo, Tommaso. 1999. Immagini e metafore nelle parlate e segnate: Modelli semiotici e applicazioni alla LIS (Lingua Italiana dei Segni). PhD dissertation, Universities of Palermo, Calabria, and Rome 3.

Russo, Tommaso, Rosaria Giurana, and Elena Pizzuto. 2001. Italian sign language (LIS) poetry. *Sign Language Studies* 2: 85–112.

Sandler, Wendy. 1986. The spreading hand autosegment of American Sign Language. *Sign Language Studies* 50: 1–28.

Sandler, Wendy. 1999. Prosody in two natural language modalities. *Language and Speech* 42: 127–42.

Sapir, Edward. 1921. *Language: An introduction to the study of speech.* New York: Harcourt, Brace, and World.

Senghas, Ann, Marie Coppola, Elisa Newport, and Ted Supalla. 1997. Argument structure in Nicaraguan Sign Language: The emergence of grammatical devices. *Proceedings of the Annual Boston University Conference on Language Development* 21: 550–61.

Shaffer, Barbara. 2002. CAN'T: The negation of modal notions in ASL. *Sign Language Studies* 3: 34–53.

Stokoe, William C. 1960. *Sign language structure.* Silver Spring, MD: Linstok Press.

Stokoe, William C. 1986. Where should we look for language? *Sign Language Studies* 51: 171–81.

Studdert-Kennedy, Michael. 1987. The phoneme as a perceptuomotor structure. In David A. Allport, ed., *Language perception and production: Relationships between listening, speaking, reading, and writing* 67–84. New York: Academic Press.

Supalla, Ted, and Elisa L. Newport. 1978. How many seats in a chair? In Patrica Siple, ed., *Understanding language through sign language research* 91–132. New York: Academic Press.

Sutton Spence, Rachel. 1999. The influence of English on British Sign Language. *International Journal of Bilingualism* 3: 363–94.

Sutton Spence, Rachel, Bencie Woll, and Lorna Allsop. 1990. Variation and recent change in fingerspelling in British Sign Language. *Language Variation and Change* 2: 313–30.

Taub, Sarah. 2001. *Language in the body: Iconicity and metaphor in American Sign Language.* Cambridge: Cambridge University Press.

Valli, Clayton, and Ceil Lucas. 1995. *Linguistics of American Sign Language: An introduction.* Washington, DC: Gallaudet University Press.

van Hoek, Karen. 1992. Conceptual spaces and pronominal reference in American Sign Language. *Nordic Journal of Linguistics* 15: 183–99.

Wallin, Lars. 1990. Polymorphemic predicates in Swedish Sign Language. In Ceil Lucas, ed., *Sign language research: Theoretical issues* 133–48. Washington, DC: Gallaudet University Press.

Wilbur, Ronnie B. 1987. *American Sign Language: Linguistic and applied dimensions.* Boston: College-Hill Press.

Wilbur, Ronnie B. 1990. Why syllables? What the notion means for ASL research. In Susan D. Fischer and Patricia Siple, eds., *Theoretical issues in sign language research*, vol. 1, *Linguistics* 81–108. Chicago: University of Chicago Press.

Wilbur, Ronnie B. 1997. A prosodic/pragmatic explanation for word order variation in ASL with typological implications. In Marjolijn Verspoor, Kee Dong Lee, and Eve Sweetser, eds., *Lexical and syntactical constructions and the construction of meaning* 89–104. Amsterdam: John Benjamins.

Wilbur, Ronnie B. 1999a. A functional journey with a formal ending: What do brow raises do in American Sign Language? In Michael Darnell, Edith Moravcsik, Frederick Newmeyer, Michael Noonan, and Kathleen Wheatley, eds., *Functionalism and formalism in linguistics*, vol. 2, *Case studies* 294–314. Amsterdam: John Benjamins.

Wilbur, Ronnie B. 1999b. Stress in ASL: Empirical evidence and linguistic issues. *Language and Speech* 42: 229–50.

Wilcox, Phyllis P. 2000. *Metaphor in American Sign Language.* Washington, DC: Gallaudet University Press.

Wilcox, Phyllis P., and Sherman Wilcox. 1995. The gestural expression of modality in American Sign Language. In Joan L. Bybee and Suzanne Fleischman, eds., *Modality in grammar and discourse* 125–62. Amsterdam: John Benjamins.

Wilcox, Sherman. 1989. *American Deaf Culture: An anthology.* Silver Spring, MD: Linstok Press.

Wilcox, Sherman. 1992. *The phonetics of fingerspelling.* Amsterdam: John Benjamins.

Wilcox, Sherman. 2002a. The gesture-language interface: Evidence from signed languages. In Rolf Schulmeister and Heimo Reinitzer, eds., *Progress in sign language research: In honor of Siegmund Prillwitz / Fortschritte in der Gebärdensprachforschung: Festschrift für Siegmund Prillwitz* 63–81. Hamburg: SIGNUM-Verlag.

Wilcox, Sherman. 2002b. The iconic mapping of space and time in signed languages. In Liliana Albertazzi, ed., *Unfolding perceptual continua* 255–81. Amsterdam: John Benjamins.

PART VI

....

APPLIED AND INTERDISCIPLINARY PERSPECTIVES

....

CHAPTER 43

COGNITIVE LINGUISTICS AND APPLIED LINGUISTICS

MARTIN PÜTZ

1. INTRODUCTION: DEFINITION AND OUTLINE

The term "applied linguistics" as defined in *The Encyclopedic Dictionary of Applied Linguistics* refers "somewhat exclusively to the field of language teaching and learning, rather than to any field where language is a relevant consideration" (Johnson and Johnson 1998: 9). Likewise, for the purpose of the present chapter, Applied Cognitive Linguistics is concerned with the acquisitional and pedagogical implications of Cognitive Linguistics in Second and Foreign Language Teaching/ Learning. Some broader applied topics are dealt with in other chapters of the section "Applied and Interdisciplinary Perspectives" of the present *Handbook*.

Recently, Langacker (2001a) has recognized the importance of the applied and didactic implications of cognitive linguistic theory. Generally he sees "the effectiveness of pedagogical applications as an important empirical test for linguistic theories," and self-assuredly he expects that "in the long run, *cognitive grammar* will not fare badly in this regard" (3). In the past, there have been several fruitful attempts to integrate Cognitive Linguistics into the realm of applied linguistic knowledge. However, it must equally be stated that, as yet, the application of cognitive linguistic theory to language use in the foreign language classroom is restricted to very few theoretically sound studies. Some of these will be discussed in more detail in section 3.

The chapter is organized in the following fashion: Section 2 discusses some of the main tenets of Second Language Acquisition in the light of linguistic theories and relates them to the Cognitive Linguistics enterprise. Section 3 gives a brief overview of studies which so far have dealt with pedagogical considerations in light of the theory of Cognitive Linguistics. Section 4 outlines in detail the major mental principles or operations, such as iconicity, construal, and prototypicality, which are relevant for a didactic application of cognitive linguistic theory to practical fields such as organized language learning. Section 5 presents the main ideas, methodologies, and results of some of these studies in more detail by briefly exploring the teaching and learning strategies of specific grammatical and lexical constructions such as phrasal verbs and phraseology. In conclusion, section 6 offers an outlook on future research.

2. Cognitive Linguistics and Second Language Acquisition

Before outlining a Cognitive Linguistics inspired approach to language pedagogy, I will briefly describe and evaluate, from a cognitive linguistic perspective, earlier accounts of foreign-language instruction and methods of grammar teaching which were formulated in the wake of successive approaches to linguistic theory.

Historically, it has always been a hotly debated question as to whether grammar should be taught deductively or inductively (Johnson and Johnson 1998: 146–48). On the deductive approach, learners are supposed to consciously learn the rules of grammar, and they should possess an explicit, metalinguistic knowledge of these rules. The rationale is based on the traditional approach to the teaching of Latin and is commonly described by its detractors as the grammar-translation method. Sets of grammatical rules and long lists of words have to be memorized, and the written language rather than the spoken language is emphasized. Cognitive Linguistics, likewise, offers the learner so-called rules for correct usage, but the Cognitive Grammar conception of a grammatical rule takes the form of a constructional schema, a generalization over a set of linguistic expressions (Achard 1997: 164). Furthermore, Cognitive Linguistics does not focus on the violation of some arbitrary rule of syntax; rather, it assumes that syntactic structures are subject to a semantic explanation, as forms which symbolize meanings (Taylor 1993).

The inductive approach, however, argues that the rules of foreign languages may be induced by learners if language input is organized and offered in a systematic way. This view developed as a result of the structural approach to linguistics, which was geared toward analyzing human language in terms of minimally contrasting units. The structural syllabus was mainly associated with the method of audiolingualism in the 1950s, which focused on sentence patterns as the unit of analysis. In the behaviorist climate of Bloomfieldian Structuralism, the discovery of sentence patterns was coupled with pattern drills. In the wake of Cognitive Linguistics, it has become clear that patterns (now called "constructions") are linguistic realities indeed governing a large amount of language use. This does not mean, however, that the process of sentence construction is largely determined by the grammatical properties of linguistic units, such as words—as has traditionally been held in formal linguistics (e.g., Harris 1964). From a cognitive linguistic perspective, meaning, rather than grammar, is unarguably the primary determinant of whether linguistic units can combine with each other (Lee 2001: 70).

The audiolingual approach was soon called into question in the 1960s following Chomsky's (1959) devastating criticism of Skinner's Behaviorism and his view of learning. Chomsky proposed a mentalist approach to acquisition, whereby sentences are not learned by stimulus-response drills on patterns but generated from the learner's underlying competence. Chomsky's generative theory of grammar and language acquisition involving an autonomous Language Acquisition Device only led to a didactic oversimplification, equating first and second language, with no rule formulation and mainly rich learning environments for the Language Acquisition Device to operate.[1] Chomsky's narrowing down of linguistic competence to grammatical competence and its intuitive strategies of acquisition provoked a reaction from functionalist and sociolinguistic approaches to language, synthesized by Hymes (1974) in terms of the notion "communicative competence" and in terms of his "ethnography of communication." Following the rise of sociolinguistics and of functionalism in theoretical linguistics (Halliday 1985), a great deal of attention was indeed being paid to the social and functional aspects of language use. In the area of language teaching, this, in turn, led to the "communicative approach"—a largely British innovation. It opposes the view that consciously learning the grammar of a language will result in an ability to use that language in social interaction. More specifically, its focus is on a functional account of language use which places emphasis on language as an instrument for conveying meanings in social situations. In other words, the functional and communicative potential of language should be emphasized (e.g., 'requests', 'denials', 'offers', 'complaints', etc.), rather than the mere mastery of formal structures (e.g., phonological, grammatical). Communicative competence, the ability to use the linguistic system effectively and appropriately, is the desired goal. These characteristics of the communicative view of language are in line with Richards and Rodgers's (1986: 71) assumptions that (i) the primary function of language is for interaction and communication and (ii) the structure of language reflects its functional and communicative uses.

This last point raises the need to bridge the gap between, on the one hand, the structural aspects of Second Language Acquisition and, on the other hand, its functional and sociolinguistic aspects. In other words, a linguistic theory is needed which stresses the conceptual link between the form and the function of language. Clearly, nothing is to be expected here from Generative Grammar, where Second Language Acquisition research has been mainly syntactic in nature, abstracted from social and functional considerations. Achard (1997) illustrates the issue by means of a syntactic analysis of English modals: the generative paradigm simply claims the existence of an innate universal grammar providing the possible parameters for language and uses a parameter-setting approach depending on which specific language is involved; it views acquisition as complete "once the appropriate parameters have been set properly" (162). Given the belief in an autonomous language module, functional considerations of the conventional and social usage of modals by the young child are not taken into account. Generativists adhere to the theorem that the use or function of language is something analytically distinct from the structure of language.

As such, a model is needed which emphasizes that language relates to our conceptual world and our human experience in such a way that every grammatical construction reflects its conceptual experiential value. It is precisely the theoretical model of Cognitive Grammar which represents a valid framework within which Second Language Acquisition research may take place, especially "because it affords a satisfying conceptual integration of the structural and social aspects of L2 acquisition" (Achard 1997: 159). Apprehension of the physical, social, cultural, and linguistic context is implicitly acknowledged in Langacker's dynamic usage-based model (see section 4.2 in more detail), which focuses on the actual use of the linguistic system and a speaker's knowledge of this use. Basically, the model claims that linguistic units are abstracted from usage events, that is, the actual instances of language use, and that such events consist of "a comprehensive conceptualization, comprising an expression's full contextual understanding, paired with an elaborate vocalization, in all its phonetic detail" (Langacker 2001b: 144). The contextual facets of Cognitive Linguistics including the social, cultural, and discourse ingredients of language can therefore be exploited for a communicative and usage-based approach to language teaching in the classroom.

Independently of Cognitive Linguistics, another trend opposing Chomsky's views developed, the so-called cognitive-code learning theory, which allows for a conscious focus on grammar and a recognition of the role of abstract mental processing in language learning. This view implies that learners should be made aware of the correspondences between varying structures and that grammar can be taught and learned deductively (Johnson and Johnson 1998: 149). Although there has been considerable interest in the implication of the cognitive-code theory for language teaching, no particular method incorporating this view of learning has emerged (Richards and Rodgers 1986: 60).

3. OVERVIEW OF APPLIED COGNITIVE LINGUISTICS ORIENTED STUDIES

Having positioned Cognitive Linguistics within the context of a number of models and methods of Second Language Acquisition, I will now present a selection of studies which are viewed as instances of the cognitive linguistic approach to language pedagogy. Given the duality in early Cognitive Linguistics between Langacker's concentration on grammar and Lakoff's conception of the world of thought via metaphor research, we can expect these two trends to emerge in Applied Cognitive Linguistics, too.

One of the first linguists to discuss in detail the cognitive-didactic approach to English grammar is Dirven (1989a), who investigated where Cognitive Linguistics can make a contribution to the general process of facilitating language learning. More specifically, the following four major tenets of Cognitive Linguistics were dealt with in the light of one learning problem, namely that of the English modality system: (i) the unity of linguistic levels (i.e., morphology, syntax, and semantics); (ii) the role of context for a linguistic expression; (iii) the concepts of profile and base in the characterization of linguistic expressions; and (iv) the concepts of prototypes and schematicity, the former covering the more frequent senses of expressions and the latter representing the commonality between all senses. The analysis shows that in general a pedagogical grammar of English is bound to analyze language-specific forms from a categorizing perspective, that is, to uncover the conceptualizations encoded in linguistic expressions. With respect to the issue of Foreign Language Learning, this means that cross-linguistic contrasts between conceptualizations must be identified in order to facilitate the learning process (see section 4.5).

The first systematic and principled account of the application of cognitive linguistic insights in the teaching and learning of grammar is provided by Taylor (1993). He starts from the process of "consciousness raising," which, in the wake of the contrastive linguistics approach of the 1960s and 1970s, had been developed as a new insight in foreign language pedagogy, particularly as a counterbalance against purely intuitive communicative learning. Given its view of meaning as largely identical to conceptualization, Cognitive Linguistics can only strongly support the role of consciousness in language learning, at the same time emphasizing other cognitive linguistic principles such as the notion of imagery and rules in Cognitive Grammar. Central to Taylor's account is the general cognitive assumption that syntax is motivated by semantics and that therefore the perceived arbitrariness of the foreign language system must be reduced and its motivated structures explained to the language learner. In a less didactic contribution, but intended as a fragment of a pedagogical grammar of English, Dirven and Taylor (1994) are concerned with the basic conceptualizations of modal auxiliaries such as *can, may,* and *must/have to.* On the basis of the schematic meanings of modal auxiliaries, the different domains of modality (e.g., potentiality, necessity, desirability) and the forms that are used in each domain, for example *can/could* (ability), *may* (permission), *may have/might have* (potentiality), are identified. Although the didactic aspect is not explicitly outlined in this paper, we may conclude from the analysis that a schematic account of the basic meanings of the modal auxiliaries provides cognitive insight in the rule complexes of English modality, thus facilitating the language learning process.

Given the immediate impact of Lakoff and Johnson's *Metaphors We Live By* (1980), it is no wonder that by far the bulk of applied cognitive linguistic studies concentrates on the issue of metaphors and, as a corollary, on the area of vocabulary acquisition without, however, exploiting the didactic and methodological tools of Cognitive Linguistics in a systematic way. The results from the numerous studies on metaphor can obviously not be ignored and will have to find their way into new strategies and methods of language teaching and learning.

Most studies on metaphor provide predominantly theoretical accounts of the cognitive underpinnings to language teaching (e.g., Low 1988; MacLennan 1994; Radden 1994; Barcelona 2001) or engage in experimental studies to demonstrate the usefulness of the cognitive approach in foreign language pedagogy (e.g., Lazar 1996; Deignan, Gabryś, and Solska 1997; Verspoor 1997; Boers and Demecheleer 1998; Boers 2000a, 2000b). Methodological approaches to figurative language and metaphor are proposed by Lazar (1996) and Lindstromberg (1996), who suggest appropriate teaching techniques and sample procedures. One of the first studies to give metaphor a more prominent place in language teaching from a cognitive linguistic perspective is Low (1988), which looks at the functions of metaphor in language use and the pedagogical implications for devising teaching and reference materials. Low argues quite convincingly that the systematicity of metaphor requires a discussion of methodological problems, such as constraints on the design of teaching materials and the development of effective types of exercise (e.g., multi-text and multitask activities). A more theoretical account of the implications of cognitive insights to Foreign Language Learning is provided by Radden (1994), who discusses the importance of image schemas and conceptual metaphors in order to make explicit to the learner the systematic coherence of metaphorical expressions in language use. Central to his claim is the idea that a considerable part of the lexicon is iconically motivated and therefore cognitively easier to grasp for the language learner (see section 4.1). Boers (2000b), then, introduces Cognitive Semantics into the field of "English for Specific Purposes" and explores the potential benefits of an enhanced metaphorical awareness on the part of the language learner. Such an enhanced metaphorical awareness may be achieved by drawing students' attention to the source domain or the origin of the figurative expressions (for instance, in socioeconomic discourse). As the results of a small-scale experiment show, enhanced metaphorical awareness may indeed help learners to better retain unfamiliar figurative expressions.

From a cross-linguistic perspective, Deignan, Gabryś, and Solska (1997) suggest awareness-raising activities for Polish learners of English and develop strategies for comprehending and creating metaphors in the second language (see also section 4.5).

Another important area of applied cognitive linguistic research includes work on phrasal verbs and verb particles. In this respect, Rudzka-Ostyn (2003) worked out materials stimulating learners to develop strategies in order to grasp the meaning of English phrasal verbs and particles that are used metaphorically (see especially section 5). More general discussions on the importance of the cognitive linguistic approach to phrasal verbs and phraseological expressions can be found in Dirven (2001), Kurtyka (2001), and Queller (2001). Finally, the more general study of idiomaticity is dealt with in Kövecses and Szabó (1996), Cornell (1999), and Kövecses (2001).

4. Conceptual Frameworks
and Acquisition

Having outlined the relevance of some major studies for Applied Cognitive Linguistics, I will now examine some specific tenets of Cognitive Linguistics and relate them to pedagogical implications and Second Language Acquisition research.

4.1. Learning through Insight in Motivation: Iconicity and Language Awareness

According to Ungerer and Schmid (1996: 273), "The liberation from the form/content division is probably the most important contribution that cognitive linguistics has made to pedagogical grammar and language teaching." In other words, natural language is not just a system consisting of arbitrary signs, as assumed in the Saussurean paradigm; instead, large areas of language structure also turn out to be motivated as part of our conceptual system. The cognitive claim is that, beyond the single lexeme, language shows a strong tendency for a structural or formal correspondence between a symbol's form and its meaning. In this regard, Radden (1992) refers to Haiman's (1985) notion of "iconicity," which is said to provide an excellent case against the "dogma of arbitrariness" and which may explain a great deal of motivation in language use.

Uncovering the iconic structure of language is closely linked with the concept of consciousness raising or language awareness, defined by Rutherford and Sharwood Smith (1985: 274) as a "deliberate attempt to draw the learner's attention specifically to the formal properties of the target language." Although the terms "consciousness raising" and "language awareness" may be used interchangeably, the latter has a wider connotation in that it refers to knowledge about language not simply in the second language learning context, but also in the framework of first language learning and teacher education (Johnson and Johnson 1998: 85). It is the latter concept of language awareness which is particularly relevant for the purposes of Applied Cognitive Linguistics oriented language pedagogy. It not only includes recognition of second language structures but also an awareness of equivalent structures in the first language, thus allowing insight into the conceptual differences of the target system and the first language or mother tongue.

From a cognitive linguistic perspective, language awareness involves making the learner aware of the semantic impact of so-called symbolic units. These include not only morphosyntactic and lexical categories, but also metaphors, idioms, and formulaic phrases. The principle of language awareness and the recognition of form-meaning pairings has especially been emphasized in applied cognitive linguistic studies on figurative expressions and language teaching. In particular, students should not be geared toward random blind memorization of symbolic units, but should rather be offered explanations of the systematicity and schematic nature of idiomatic language and metaphorical expressions. When linguistic expressions are paired with their underlying conceptual metaphors, they will become more transparent to the language learner; in other words, the motivation behind their idiomatic meaning will become obvious.

Furthermore, it will be a central instructional principle to take into account cross-cultural differences in metaphorical themes, and in conceptual metaphors in particular (see section 4.5). Lazar (1996), for instance, refers to the figurative meaning of different colors which may vary from one language community to another. Idiomatic expressions like *to be green* and *to have green fingers* may evoke certain associations in some cultures which may be different from what we find in British English, where the color 'green' is conventionally, though not uniquely (e.g., *green-eyed* 'jealous'; *greenhorn* 'inexperienced') associated with nature and innocence. Obviously, students should be made aware of these cross-cultural differences by comparing the two language systems—first language and second language— in a principled way, thereby enhancing their metaphor awareness (Boers 2000b). More instances of linguo-cultural features and their underlying metaphorical sources are discussed by MacLennan (1994: 102) and Deignan, Gabryś, and Solska (1997: 354).

4.2. Context- and Usage-Based Language Learning

The present subsection discusses the contextual basis of Cognitive Semantics and its implications for language pedagogy. Traditionally, from the perspective of the methodology of language teaching, three major theoretical views of language and language proficiency may be distinguished (Richards and Rodgers 1986: 16).

a. *The structural view.* It refers to language as a system of structurally related elements for the encoding of meaning; the mastery of the elements of this system (phonological, grammatical, lexical) is seen as the target of language learning.

b. *The functional view.* It suggests that language is a means for the expression of functional meaning. The focus is on the semantic and communicative dimension rather than on the structural and grammatical characteristics of language.

c. *The interactional view.* It sees language as a vehicle for the expression of interpersonal relations and the creation and maintenance of social relations. Language teaching is then organized around linguistic exchanges and conversational analysis.

Clearly, the functional and, to a certain extent, the interactional approach to language learning, both of which focus on the communicative function of language, seem to be most compatible with the tenets and insights of Cognitive Linguistics. The structural view is obviously the least compatible as it is in conflict with the cognitive linguistic tenet that semantics determines syntax. Recently, Langacker (2001b: 143) stated that "the grounding of language in discourse and social interaction is a central if not a defining notion within the functionalist tradition" and furthermore "this is no less true for cognitive linguistics." Langacker (1994, 1997, 2000, 2001b) explicitly states that the study of language in its social, cultural, and discourse context is fully compatible with his claim that a conceptual and encyclopedic view of meaning must be contextually grounded. He even goes so far as to say that "despite its mental focus, cognitive linguistics can also be described as social, cultural, and contextual linguistics" (Langacker 1997: 240). Langacker identifies language and culture as facets of cognition and, at the same time, recognizes the role of context and of social interaction in language use and situated discourse. In this regard, the anthropological notion of schema (see also Ungerer and Schmid's 1996: 45–52 discussion of cognitive and cultural models)—which implies an interdependence of language, culture, and cognition—turns out to be useful as well. Consider, for instance, Sharifian's (2001: 125) study of Aboriginal English texts. By identifying major schemas in these texts, such as the TRAVEL schema, the HUNTING schema, and the OBSERVING schema, Sharifian is able to show that cultural knowledge and schemas may shape or influence the conceptualizations underlying discursive structures in Aboriginal speech; in other words, schemas are cognitive structures that can be determined by cultural experiences; they are thus reflected in linguistic expressions or discourse patterns.

From a language teaching perspective, then, differences in cultural practices and conceptualizations may therefore lead to miscommunication between indigenous students and the representatives of the mainstream schooling system.

The functional and interactional approaches are compatible with a learner-centered and experience-based view of second language pedagogy (Richards and Rodgers 1986: 69). This experiential view is likewise inherent in the framework of Cognitive Linguistics, where it is suggested that the world is not something merely objectively given, but that it is something *construed* by human perception; this construal is, in turn, guided by cultural cognition, that is, by the associations and impressions which people make as part of their personal and sociocultural experiences. The notion of "construal" and its implications for language pedagogy will be discussed in the next section.

4.3. The Learner as Conceptualizer: Construal and Linguistic Choices

According to Langacker (2000: 5), the meaning of an expression consists not only of the conceptual content it evokes; equally significant is how that content is construed. Speakers are able to construe the same content in alternate ways, which may then result in substantially different meanings; in other words, construal refers to a speaker's choice between various alternatives. As such, linguistic production is in particular to be seen as an instance of the individual speaker's choice or construal. These construals or linguistic alternatives may be determined by (i) the specificity or precision with which a scene is portrayed; (ii) the speaker's perspective, which includes the Figure/Ground organization and the related aspect of viewpoint; and (iii) background assumptions which the use of a linguistic form may evoke. From a cognitive point of view, this suggests that in choosing one way of expression over the other the speaker encodes certain meanings in a specific way.

The notion of "construal" certainly has an impact on the teaching of grammar, as appears from Achard (n.d.), in which an account is given of a construal-based approach. In particular, Achard considers two causative constructions in French that differ from each other in their word order:

(1) *Marie a laissé partir Jean.*
    Mary has let leave John.
    'Mary let John leave' (Achard n.d.: 8)

(2) *Marie a laissé Jean partir.*
    Mary has let John leave.
    'Mary let John leave'

In (1), the causee (John) is represented as the initiator of the leaving event, which results in the choice of a V-V-O order; in (2), John is not presented as the source of energy initiating the process, making V-O-V the favored choice. It can be seen, then, that the two different word orders reflect the speaker's selection of a linguistic expression more than the grammatical rules of the system per se. These different perspectives must be taken into account by the language instructor. Certainly, more research on construal-based approaches to lexical and grammatical constructions is needed.

4.4. Frequent Uses (Prototypes) and General Meaning (Schematicity) in Language Learning

The cognitive notions of "prototype" and "schematicity" can be helpful in spelling out the semantic content of a word or a grammatical construction and can thereby facilitate the language learning process. Recall that, in Langacker's terms, a prototype is "a typical instance of a category (and) there are degrees of membership based on degrees of similarity" (1987: 371), which means that some members of a category appear to be more typical and more salient than others. When considering the category 'furniture', we think immediately of 'tables' and 'chairs' as best examples, not of 'mirrors' and 'clocks', which suggests that membership in a category is a matter of gradience. The internal structure of categories in terms of prototypical or central members and noncentral or peripheral members is likewise reflected in the semantics of grammatical categories. Taylor (1993: 211), for example, proposes as the prototype of 'count noun' a three-dimensional, concrete 'thing' and as the prototype of 'mass noun' an internally homogenous, divisible 'substance' (e.g., 'bottle' vs. 'beer'). This distinction between 'thing' and 'substance' may then be transferred to the domain of time and events, which can be seen as things, and to the domain of emotional states and activities, which can bee seen as a substance.

In contrast to the notion of prototype, which is a typical instance of a category, a schema is "an abstract characterization that is fully compatible with all the members of the category it defines" (Langacker 1987: 371); in other words, the schema embodies the commonality of its members. The importance of schematic characterizations for language pedagogy has been shown by a study on English complementation carried out by Dirven (1989b). Each of the complement clauses (e.g., *to*-infinitive, gerund, *that*-clause, etc.) has a very distinct schematic value of its own, which may be given different values and meanings in concrete contexts. Consider the following example (taken from Dirven 1989b: 116):

(3)   a.   It's easy to park your car here.
       b.   Parking the car is a problem.

The *to*-infinitive in (3a) denotes a bounded single occurrence of the event (of parking one's car) while the predicate *a problem* in (3b) is a more abstract notion which requires a nonspecified, unbounded construal of the event. In structural grammar, the learner has no choice but to learn by rote the many verbs, adjectives, or nouns that govern a specific complement pattern. From the perspective of Cognitive Linguistics, however, it will be possible to formulate a schematic characterization of each complement pattern—which entails various contextual senses—thus facilitating the language learning process.

Let us now return to the notion of prototype and focus more closely on its function in the construal of prepositional meanings. In Lakoff's (1987) cognitive semantic framework, prepositions may be described as radial categories or networks which are built around central or prototypical senses and from which various senses radiate outward and are linked to the central sense by such meaning-extension processes as metaphor and metonymy. Prepositions are thus polysemous items which have different, yet related senses, and are described by various relations in English. Such locative relations as the UP-DOWN and FRONT-BACK orientations, for instance, reflect basic experiences and are regarded as "image schemas," simple and basic cognitive structures which are derived from our everyday interaction with the external world (see Oakley, this volume, chapter 9).[2] Making use of work by Brugman (1981) and Lakoff (1987), Lindstromberg (1996) was one of the first to apply the findings of prototype semantics to prepositional meaning, thereby indicating pedagogical applications of prepositional semantics in the field of English Language Teaching. According to the author, current English Language Teaching methods and material are not satisfactory on the grounds that only a very small set of meanings for any one preposition is presented, thus neglecting that prepositional semantics is to a large extent systematically structured. With regard to the preposition *on*, for instance, Lindstromberg presents a set of learning points that identify a sense of the preposition "which is worth bringing to the attention of individual students at some point in their learning career" (Lindstromberg 1996: 228). In particular, exploiting the notion "prototypicality," he attempts to demonstrate that a wide range of nonspatial meanings of the preposition *on* can be regarded as special instances or metaphorical extensions of its spatial meanings. Just like *on* in its concrete meaning denotes 'contact' (e.g., *The pencil is on the book*) and, we may add, 'support' (e.g., *The man is sitting on the chair*), in its metaphorical extensions it also means mental contact (e.g., *I spoke to her on the phone*) or mental support (e.g., *You can rely on me*). All in all, Lindstromberg's study provides one of the first attempts to consider the applied cognitive linguistic aspects of prepositional meaning (see also his more comprehensive volume on explaining prepositions, Lindstromberg 1998).

The prototype perspective is also employed by Ungerer (2001), who is concerned with the notion of basic-level terms and their application in vocabulary acquisition. Ungerer holds that superordinate and subordinate concepts in First Language Acquisition are acquired later than basic ones and that this order should also serve as a model in context of Second Language Acquisition, especially in the teaching of vocabulary. Traditionally, frequency lists or pedagogical vocabularies have been devised without any semantic principles underlying the composition of basic vocabulary lists. Ungerer attempts to show that a more systematic ordering of vocabulary is possible when basic terms are discussed and taught in light of their intrinsic connection with the superordinate and subordinate terms. On the basis of a corpus study comprising German textbooks of English and several newspapers, he demonstrates that vocabulary selection, for example, would benefit mostly from the basic/nonbasic distinction if basic-level terms were preferred as entry points, "where the respective superordinate concepts involve less tangible taxonomic notions" (2001: 216), rather than being introduced at a later stage.

To conclude this section, let us consider a different view of radial categories put forward by Tyler and Evans (2001). Their approach is likely to have an impact on the way English tenses may be taught in the classroom setting. Tyler and Evans's comprehensive and detailed discussion is centered around the analysis of a schematic account of tense phenomena in English. The central thesis of their paper is that the so-called exceptional, nontemporal uses of tense are related to its time-reference function in a motivated way. A number of distinct and fundamentally nontemporal meanings associated with tense can be distinguished, such as intimacy (between speakers), salience (foregrounding vs. backgrounding), actuality (realis vs. irrealis), and attenuation (linguistic politeness), all of which are shown to be related to each other in a systematic principled way. However, unlike Lakoff, Tyler and Evans do not consider "metaphorical extensions" an all-revealing explanation. Rather, they assume that the exceptional meanings associated with tense are grounded in experience, by virtue of so-called experiential correlations, that is, "independently motivated and recurring correspondences in experience" (2001: 68). All in all, Tyler and Evans's approach to language seems to be particularly helpful for teachers as well as learners. The traditional view, treating nontemporal uses as exceptions or ignoring them altogether, often led to difficulties for language learners as they tended to be discussed in terms of arbitrary meaning patterns to be memorized. Tyler and Evans's unified approach offers a systematic, motivated account of how English tense usage works.

4.5. Cross-Cultural Learning: Different Conceptualizations

Contrastive Analysis, the comparison of the linguistic systems of two languages, was developed and practiced in the 1950s and 1960s as an application of Structural Linguistics to language teaching. The Contrastive Analysis Hypothesis broadly claims that difficulties in second language learning derive from the differences between the target language and the learner's first language and are mainly caused by interference from the first language. As Taylor (1993) points out, Contrastive Analysis is compatible with a cognitive approach to grammar as well; however, this cognitive approach will focus on semantic content and conceptualization rather than on merely formal entities. In other words, target language structures will be difficult to learn to the extent that they symbolize conceptual categories which are not found in the learner's first language (e.g., for learners of English, the distinction between simple and progressive tense forms). Specific conceptualizations may thus exhibit, for a learner, a high or low degree of cognitive naturalness, depending on the similarity or the differences between conceptual categories found in the source and target language. In this respect, a fine-grained comparison between the ways a conceptual metaphor is linguistically construed in two languages has been provided by Barcelona (2001), who compares English and Spanish conceptual metaphors for emotional domains such as 'sadness'/'happiness', 'anger', and 'romantic love'. For instance, speakers of English and Spanish conceptualize the domain of anger differently in that English invokes the CONTAINER image while Spanish is not CONTAINER-oriented (e.g., *The news threw him into a terrible rage* vs. *Su conducta me puso furioso* [His behavior me put furious] 'His behavior made me furious'). Such an analysis may uncover the differences in metaphorical themes and ultimately predict a number of errors a learner may engage in. Similarly, Soffritti and Dirven (1998) make a strong claim that Second Language Acquisition research must take into consideration any previously acquired linguistic structure (first language) and linguistic categories. This generally means, from the perspective of Cognitive Linguistics, that the learners' task must be to revise first language categories, schemas, and prototypes at all levels of language and that the revision means "adapting an old mental situation to specific data from a foreign language" (1998: 268). These similarities and dissimilarities in conceptualization should be made explicit to the foreign language learner.

A theoretically interesting, contrastive analysis is provided by Boers and Demecheleer (1998), who investigate prepositional semantics from an applied cognitive linguistic perspective. They discuss the pedagogical importance of drawing learners' attention to the links between a preposition's spatial sense and its metaphorical extensions. From a cross-linguistic perspective, obviously, the factor of first language interference plays a vital role in the conceptualization of linguistic expressions or metaphors. For French learners of English, one of the spatial senses of the English preposition *behind* in which the trajector pushes the landmark forward (e.g., *the man behind the wheelbarrow*) is absent from its French equivalent *derrière* (*l'homme à la brouette*). Since French *derrière* does not have this spatial sense, it also lacks its extension; that is, the figurative, causal sense of *behind* also appears to be absent from French *derrière*, as in *What's the motive behind this crime?* versus *Quel est le motif (à l'origine) du crime?* (1998: 200). Boers and Demecheleer hypothesize that the lack of the causal sense of the French *derrière* causes more comprehension problems than may be evident in regard to the other figurative senses of *behind*. They suggest that it may be pedagogically fruitful to draw learners' attention to the spatial sense behind an unfamiliar figurative sense. In particular, they suggest highlighting the conceptual links between the spatial sense and its figurative extension by offering to the language learner similar examples which involve different levels of abstraction such as (i) *the man behind the wheelbarrow*, (ii) *the man behind the wheel of the company*, and (iii) *the people behind the strike* (1998: 200).

Obviously, drawing learners' attention to the contrastive uses of figurative senses refers to the important dimension of metaphor awareness in Foreign Language Teaching (already discussed in section 4.1). In several language learning experiments, Boers (2000b) has shown that unfamiliar figurative expressions can systematically be traced back to a limited number of metaphorical themes or conceptual metaphors. Raising metaphor awareness in language learners constitutes a motivating factor and makes it possible to enhance in-depth comprehension and to facilitate the acquisition of vocabulary. In a similar vein, Deignan, Gabryś, and Solska (1997) discuss the need for students to develop "metaphorical competence" and to teach metaphors to them using awareness-raising activities. Their cross-linguistic comparison between the English and Polish metaphor system revealed similarities and differences between the two languages both in terms of conceptual metaphor and linguistic expressions. From the perspective of language transfer, it turned out that some types of metaphor were particularly difficult for Polish learners of English. For example, due to the lack of an identical metaphor in the two languages, linguistic expressions such as *bring something (a fact, situation) home to someone* and *drive a message/idea home* do not have semantically similar equivalents in the students' first language (Polish) (Deignan, Gabryś, and Solska 1997: 355). In order to encourage students to explore and discuss the ways in which metaphorical use varies across two languages, the authors designed a series of awareness exercises focusing mainly on the cultural aspects of metaphors. As a result, students experienced less difficulty in learning English metaphors if they were asked to think about conceptual metaphors and their linguistic expressions in their first language (Polish) and to compare them to equivalents in the target language English.

5. Cognitive Linguistics Inspired Language Instruction: Phrasal Verbs

Having referred to central tenets of the cognitive framework and their implications for Second Language Acquisition, I will now discuss in more detail the application of these cognitive tenets to the teaching and learning of concrete linguistic expressions, and of phrasal verbs and phraseology in particular. According to Biber et al.'s (1999) corpus-based grammar of spoken and written English, there are four major kinds of multiword combinations (403–8): (i) phrasal verbs, (ii) prepositional verbs, (iii) phrasal-prepositional verbs and (iv) other multiword verb constructions. Both phrasal verbs and prepositional verbs represent single semantic units which cannot be derived from the individual meanings of the two parts. What makes phrasal and prepositional verbs even more difficult for the language learner is the fact that especially activity verbs often have secondary meanings in some other domain. The phrasal verbs *make up, make out, sort out,* and *take in* can all refer to either physical or mental activities, as in *I find myself obliged to make up ground* versus *I used to make up stories for him* (Biber et al. 1999: 408). In general, phrasal verbs are predominantly used in fiction and conversation and therefore constitute an important linguistic means of expression for the language learner, especially in the context of a communicative approach to language teaching/learning. Given the importance of the domain of space for Cognitive Linguistics (Langacker's Cognitive Grammar was first called Space Grammar; see also Zlatev, this volume, chapter 13), it should not come as a surprise that much work has been on the conceptualization of space, especially on its expression by prepositions and particles in combination with verbs.

The textbook *Word Power: Phrasal Verbs and Compounds—A Cognitive Approach*, designed by the late Rudzka-Ostyn (2003), is a didactic application of Cognitive Linguistics, largely based on the concepts of trajector and landmark and involving the extension of prototypical literal senses into metaphorized, more abstract senses represented in radial networks. The aim is "to discover which semantic features are conveyed by the particle or by the phrasal verb as a whole" (ix), that is, to make the learner acquainted with the nonspatial or figurative meanings inherent in the particle and/or prepositional system. Moreover, it adheres to one of the principles of a pedagogical grammar—that it should be based on an, at least implicitly, contrastive approach (Dirven 2001: 18)—in that it provides the students with cognitive insights and tools to analyze the ways in which their native language expresses similar relations with the world.

Unlike traditional, nonsemantic ways of grouping particles around one specific verb, this textbook groups verbs around particles/prepositions. In this way, the figurative meanings of the particles/prepositions can become transparent, and this transparency is said to lead to more meaningful learning. While traditional

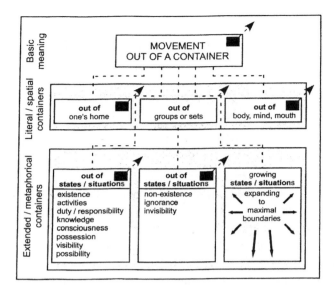

Figure 43.1. Graphic synthesis of the related meanings of *out*

approaches to teaching phrasal verbs largely concentrate on the formal (syntactic) aspects of their use or on those aspects in which the semantic content of specific verbs is emphasized (Kurtyka 2001: 30), *Word Power* examines the various senses of the particles/prepositions, their internal coherence, and their gradual buildup from the concrete prototype to the peripheral abstract meanings. This process can be illustrated, for instance, by the semantic network of the particle *out*. The basic spatial meaning of *out* involves the CONTAINER concept and an object which moves out of the container. In general, the container may be whatever surrounds a given entity that moves *out of* it.

In this regard, 'one's home', 'groups'/'sets', and 'body'/'mind'/'mouth' can be seen as literal/spatial containers while 'states'/'situations' may represent extended/ metaphorical containers (Rudzka-Ostyn 2003: 41).

Generally, visualization in terms of abstract drawings plays an important role in a cognitive approach to language and even more so in a didactic presentation. Figure 43.2, taken from *Word Power* (Rudzka-Ostyn 2003: 41), refers to the spatial, prototypical meaning of the most frequent particles/prepositions.

Such visual representations of meaning alongside verbal explanations and example sentences seem to facilitate language learning considerably, as could be demonstrated by Kurtyka (2001) in a small-class experiment. While understanding the different senses of a particle is considered to be the first important step in the learning process, full command of the verbs is only guaranteed through repetition and dynamic use. Therefore, so-called exetests (a combination of an exercise and a test) give students an opportunity to go through a succession of small steps of learning as often as necessary before testing their knowledge of the phrasal verbs in question.

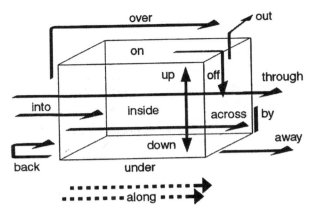

Figure 43.2. Metaphorical or extended meanings of the particles

Although Dirven (2001: 17) recognizes Rudzka-Ostyn's work as a "unique milestone on the road to a full-fledged Pedagogical Grammar of English," he still sees the necessity to consult in detail the descriptive work done in the area of phrasal verbs and phraseology.

6. Outlook on Future Research: Programs

This chapter has attempted to show how the various strands of Cognitive Linguistics can provide a framework of starting points that may be used to systematically investigate the pedagogical implications of the interplay between language, experience, and cognition. The application of cognitive linguistic theory to Foreign Language Teaching and Learning is still in its infancy, and more substantial work on Applied Cognitive Linguistics from different perspectives seems necessary and desirable. In this regard, it has been advocated that the metaphorical structure of language should be presented to foreign language learners as an integral part of language that is nonarbitrary in nature and that allows systematic treatment.

Not much research is available on the concrete application of applied cognitive linguistic material in the foreign language classroom. The use of authentic and appropriate speech is certainly one of the prerequisites in order to make the cognitive enterprise in the classroom a success. A first step in the right direction is reflected in the set of exercises or teaching aids propagated by Lennon (1998), which are intended as guidelines for the teacher to stimulate cognitive activity in the learner's mind (see also Deignan, Gabryś, and Solska 1997). In addition to language material representing actual usage, we must consider the necessity of taking into account large corpora of authentic speech. These may provide an extremely useful resource for investigating, for instance, idioms and metaphors (see especially Aston 2001) and their situated use in communication. A field which has hardly been researched involves the multicultural classroom, in which the status and use of the underlying contrastive metaphor systems in two or more languages could be systematically explored (Lennon 1998: 21). In this regard, more work should be done on the role of interference, which can give an account of the learner's cognitive strategies and provide an understanding of the social range of linguistic expressions in the target language (Achard 1997).

Although research has focused on various grammatical and lexical aspects of linguistic structure, there is still a need to provide further substantial studies from an applied cognitive linguistic perspective in order to show the all-embracing embodied nature of human language, in other words, a holistic understanding of the way language works. In order to demonstrate that, for example, grammar has an experiential and interactional grounding and to allow young learners "'to grasp', 'feel' or 'see' the syntax of English" (Lapaire 2002: 624), it will be necessary to understand grammar as fundamentally embodied and imaginative, through metaphor and image schemas. From this, it also follows that more emphasis should be given to visualization within the applied cognitive framework, that is, the ability to form mental representations of verbal and nonverbal input (Kurtyka 2001). Pictures, drawings, and diagrams, and especially so-called KineGrams (Lapaire 2002: 624) as conceptualizing gestures, may illustrate the schematic nature of grammatical meaning.

We may conclude that the theory of Cognitive Linguistics, as applied to the domain of language teaching/learning, provides fascinating insights into the relationship between language, cognition, and foreign language teaching/learning; at the same time, these interrelationships deserve further investigation.

NOTES

I wish to thank René Dirven for his valuable suggestions and criticisms of an earlier draft of this chapter and Hubert Cuyckens for his careful editing of this chapter.

1. Independently of Cognitive Linguistics, another trend opposing Chomsky's views developed, the so-called cognitive-code learning theory, which allows for a conscious focus on grammar and a recognition of the role of abstract mental processing in language learning. This view implies that learners should be made aware of the correspondences between varying structures and that grammar can be taught and learned deductively (Johnson and Johnson 1998: 149). Although there has been considerable interest in the implication of the cognitive-code theory for language teaching, no particular method incorporating this view of learning has emerged (Richards and Rodgers 1986: 60).

2. Image schemas are structures which are grounded in physical, bodily experience and which organize our perception and understanding of physical space. It is worth mentioning that these schemas are not to be regarded as fixed pictures, but rather should

be seen as less stable structures which are applied in a flexible way. For example, Boers (1996: 12) in this regard refers to the CONTAINER schema which is applied to both three-dimensional entities (a box) and two-dimensional ones (e.g., a bounded area). (For further information on image schemas, see Oakley, this volume, chapter 9).

REFERENCES

Achard, Michel. 1997. Cognitive grammar and SLA investigation. *Journal of Intensive English Studies* 11: 157–76.

Achard, Michel. n.d. Grammatical instruction in the natural approach: A cognitive grammar view. Manuscript.

Aston, Guy, ed. 2001. *Learning with corpora*. Houston, TX: Athelstan.

Barcelona, Antonio. 2001. On the systematic contrastive analysis of conceptual metaphors: Case studies and proposed methodology. In Martin Pütz, Susanne Niemeier, and René Dirven, eds., *Applied cognitive linguistics*, vol. 2, *Language pedagogy* 117–46. Berlin: Mouton de Gruyter.

Biber, Douglas, Stig Johansson, Geoffrey Leech, Susan Conrad, and Edward Finegan. 1999. *Longman grammar of spoken and written English*. Harlow, UK: Pearson Educated.

Boers, Frank. 1996. *Spatial prepositions and metaphor: A cognitive semantic journey along the UP-DOWN and the FRONT-BACK dimensions*. Tübingen, Germany: Gunter Narr Verlag.

Boers, Frank. 2000a. Enhancing metaphoric awareness in specialised reading. *English for Specific Purposes* 19: 137–47.

Boers, Frank. 2000b. Metaphor awareness and vocabulary retention. *Applied Linguistics* 21: 553–71.

Boers, Frank, and Murielle Demecheleer. 1998. A cognitive semantic approach to teaching prepositions. *ELT Journal* 52: 197–203.

Brugman, Claudia. 1981. Story of Over. MA thesis, University of California at Berkeley. (Published as *The story of Over: Polysemy, semantics, and the structure of the lexicon*. New York: Garland, 1988)

Chomsky, Noam. 1959. Review of *Verbal Behavior*, by B.F. Skinner. *Language* 35: 26–58. (Repr. in Jerry A. Fodor and Jerrold J. Katz, eds., *The structure of language: Readings in the philosophy of language* 547–78. Englewood Cliffs: Prentice-Hall, 1964)

Cornell, Alan. 1999. Idioms: An approach to identifying major pitfalls for learners. *International Review of Applied Linguistics* 37: 1–22.

Deignan, Alice, Danuta Gabryś, and Agnieszka Solska. 1997. Teaching English metaphors using cross-linguistic awareness-raising activities. *ELT Journal* 51: 352–60.

Dirven, René. 1989a. Cognitive linguistics and pedagogic grammar. In Gottfried Graustein and Gerhard Leitner, eds., *Reference grammars and modern linguistic theory* 56–75. Tübingen, Germany: Max Niemeyer Verlag.

Dirven, René. 1989b. A cognitive perspective on complementation. In Dany Jaspers, Yvan Putseys, Wim Klooster, and Pieter Seuren, eds., *Sentential complementation and the lexicon: Studies in honor of Wim de Geest.* 113–39. Dordrecht, Netherlands: Foris.

Dirven, René. 2001. English phrasal verbs: Theory and didactic application. In Martin Pütz, Susanne Niemeier, and René Dirven, eds., *Applied cognitive linguistics*, vol. 2, *Language pedagogy* 3–27. Berlin: Mouton de Gruyter.

Dirven, René, and John R. Taylor. 1994. English modality: A cognitive-didactic approach. In Keith Carlon, Kristin Davidse, and Brygida Rudzka-Ostyn, eds., *Perspectives on English: Studies in honour of Professor Emma Vorlat* 542–56. Leuven, Belgium: Peeters.

Haiman, John. 1985. *Iconicity in syntax*. Amsterdam: John Benjamins.

Halliday, Michael A. K. 1985. *Introduction to functional grammar*. London: Arnold.

Harris, Zellig S. 1964. *String analysis of sentence structure*. The Hague: Mouton.

Hymes, Dell. 1974. *Foundations of sociolinguistics: An ethnographic approach*. Philadelphia: University of Pennsylvania Press.

Johnson, Keith, and Helen Johnson, eds. 1998. *Encyclopedic dictionary of applied linguistics: A handbook for language teaching*. Oxford: Basil Blackwell.

Kövecses, Zoltán. 2001. A cognitive linguistic view of learning idioms in an FLT context. In Martin Pütz, Susanne Niemeier, and René Dirven, eds., *Applied cognitive linguistics*, vol. 2, *Language pedagogy* 87–115. Berlin: Mouton de Gruyter.

Kövecses, Zoltán, and Péter Szabó. 1996. Idioms: A view from cognitive semantics. *Applied Linguistics* 17: 326–55.

Kurtyka, Andrzej. 2001. Teaching English phrasal verbs: A cognitive approach. In Martin Pütz, Susanne Niemeier, and René Dirven, eds., *Applied cognitive linguistics*, vol. 2, *Language pedagogy* 29–54. Berlin: Mouton de Gruyter.

Lakoff, George. 1987. *Women, fire and dangerous things: What categories reveal about the mind*. Chicago: University of Chicago Press.

Lakoff, George, and Mark Johnson. 1980. *Metaphors we live by*. Chicago: University of Chicago Press.

Langacker, Ronald W. 1987. *Foundations of cognitive grammar*. Vol. 1, *Theoretical prerequisites*. Stanford, CA: Stanford University Press.

Langacker, Ronald W. 1994. Culture, cognition and grammar. In Martin Pütz, ed., *Language contact and language conflict* 25–53. Amsterdam: John Benjamins.

Langacker, Ronald W. 1997. The contextual basis of cognitive semantics. In Jan Nuyts and Eric Pederson, eds., *Language and conceptualization* 229–52. Cambridge: Cambridge University Press.

Langacker, Ronald W. 2000. *Grammar and conceptualization*. Berlin: Mouton de Gruyter.

Langacker, Ronald W. 2001a. Cognitive linguistics, language pedagogy, and the English present tense. In Martin Pütz, Susanne Niemeier, and René Dirven, eds., *Applied cognitive linguistics*, vol. 1, *Theory and language acquisition* 3–39. Berlin: Mouton de Gruyter.

Langacker, Ronald W. 2001b. Discourse in cognitive grammar. *Cognitive Linguistics* 12: 143–88.

Lapaire, Jean-Remi. 2002. Imaginative grammar. In Barbara Lewandowska and Kamila Turewicz, eds., *Cognitive linguistics today* 623–42. Frankfurt am Main: Peter Lang Verlag.

Lazar, Gillian. 1996. Using figurative language to expand students' vocabulary. *ELT Journal* 50: 43–51.

Lee, David. 2001. *Cognitive linguistics: An introduction*. Oxford: Oxford University Press.

Lennon, Paul. 1998. Approaches to the teaching of idiomatic language. *International Review of Applied Linguistics* 32: 11–30.

Lindstromberg, Seth. 1996. Prepositions: Meaning and method. *ELT Journal* 50: 225–36.

Lindstromberg, Seth. 1998. *English prepositions explained*. Amsterdam: John Benjamins.

Low, Graham D. 1988. On teaching metaphor. *Applied Linguistics* 9: 125–47.

MacLennan, Carol H. G. 1994. Metaphors and prototypes in the learning and teaching of grammar and vocabulary. *International Review of Applied Linguistics* 32: 97–110.

Queller, Kurt. 2001. A usage-based approach to modeling and teaching the phrasal lexicon. In Martin Pütz, Susanne Niemeier, and René Dirven, eds., *Applied cognitive linguistics*, vol. 2, *Language pedagogy* 55–83. Berlin: Mouton de Gruyter.

Radden, Günter. 1992. The cognitive approach to natural language. In Martin Pütz, ed., *Thirty years of linguistic evolution: Studies in honour of René Dirven on the occasion of his sixtieth birthday* 513–41. Amsterdam: John Benjamins.

Radden, Günter. 1994. Konzeptuelle Metaphern in der kognitiven Semantik. In Wolfgang Börner and Klaus Vogel, eds., *Kognitive Linguistik und Fremdsprachenerwerb: Das mentale Lexikon* 69–87. Tübingen, Germany: Gunter Narr Verlag.

Richards, Jack C., and Theodore S. Rodgers. 1986. *Approaches and methods in language teaching: A description and analysis*. Cambridge: Cambridge University Press.

Rudzka-Ostyn, Brygida. 2003. *Word power: Phrasal verbs and compounds: A cognitive approach*. Berlin: Mouton de Gruyter.

Rutherford, William, and Michael Sharwood Smith. 1985. Consciousness raising and universal grammar. *Applied Linguistics* 6: 274–282.

Sharifian, Farzad. 2001. Schema-based processing in Australian speakers of Aboriginal English. *Language and Intercultural Communication* 1: 120–34.

Soffritti, Marcello, and René Dirven. 1998. Language comparison: Sociology of language, language typology and contrastive linguistics. In René Dirven and Marjolijn Verspoor, eds., *Cognitive exploration of language and linguistics* 247–77. Amsterdam: John Benjamins.

Taylor, John R. 1993. Some pedagogical implications of cognitive linguistics. In Richard A. Geiger and Brygida Rudzka-Ostyn, eds., *Conceptualizations and mental processing in language* 201–23. Berlin: Mouton de Gruyter.

Tyler, Andrea, and Vyvyan Evans. 2001. The relation between experience, conceptual structure and meaning: Non-temporal uses of tense and language teaching. In Martin Pütz, Susanne Niemeier, and René Dirven, eds., *Applied cognitive linguistics*, vol. 1, *Theory and language acquisition* 63–105. Berlin: Mouton de Gruyter.

Ungerer, Friedrich. 2001. Basicness and conceptual hierarchies in foreign language learning: A corpus-based study. In Martin Pütz, Susanne Niemeier, and René Dirven, eds., *Applied cognitive linguistics*, vol. 2, *Language pedagogy* 201–22. Berlin: Mouton de Gruyter.

Ungerer, Friedrich, and Hans-Jörg Schmid. 1996. *An introduction to cognitive linguistics*. London: Longman.

Verspoor, Marjolijn. 1997. True blue: A cognitive approach to vocabulary acquisition. In Birgit Smieja and Meike Tasch, eds., *Human contact through language and linguistics* 203–17. Frankfurt am Main: Peter Lang Verlag.

CHAPTER 44

LEXICOGRAPHY

DIRK GEERAERTS

1. INTRODUCTION

Cognitive Linguistics has had a major impact on lexical studies: more than any other recent theory, it has in the last twenty years led to a renewed interest in lexical research. But what about lexicography? What is the relationship between Cognitive Linguistics and lexicography, the applied linguistic sister discipline of lexicology and lexical semantics? In what follows, I will try to answer that question in two steps. In line with earlier metalexicographical discussions of the relationship between Cognitive Linguistics and lexicography (such as Geeraerts 1990; Swanepoel 1992; Hanks 1994), I will first indicate how the views of lexical semantics developed within Cognitive Linguistics provide a theoretical framework that is highly congenial to the actual practice of dictionaries—more so, in fact, than the structuralist theories that are sometimes found in the metalexicographical literature. As a second step, I will present an overview of suggestions made and initiatives taken to extend lexicographical practices on the basis of ideas linking up with Cognitive Linguistics. In this second step, specific attention will be devoted to the FrameNet project.

2. VINDICATIONS OF CURRENT PRACTICES

A number of existing definitional and descriptive practices in the dictionary that are somewhat suspect from an older theoretical point of view receive a natural interpretation and legitimacy in the theoretical framework offered by Cognitive

Linguistics. More specifically, there are three aspects of the Cognitive conception of lexical semantic structure that have to be discussed: (i) the importance of prototypicality effects for lexical structure, (ii) the intractability of polysemy, and (iii) the structured nature of polysemy. It can be argued that each of these points inspires a specific conclusion for lexicographical practice, or at least, that it vindicates existing aspects of lexicographical practice. (Because the relevant structural features are discussed in some detail elsewhere in this *Handbook*, they are presented here without further illustration or analysis.)

a. The *importance of prototypicality effects for lexical structure* (see chapters 5 and 6 of the present *Handbook*) blurs the distinction between semantic information and encyclopedic information. This does not entail that there is no distinction between dictionaries and encyclopedias as types of reference works, but rather that references to typical examples and characteristic features are a natural thing to expect in dictionaries.

b. The *intractability of polysemy* (see chapter 6 of the present *Handbook*) involves the absence of a coherent set of criteria for establishing polysemy; a more charitable way of wording things would be to say that distinctiveness between senses of a lexical item is to some extent a flexible and context-based phenomenon. Dictionaries, then, will use various definitional techniques to accommodate the flexibility of meaning.

c. The *structured nature of polysemy* (see chapters 6, 8, and 10 of the present *Handbook*) involves, basically, the radial set structure of polysemy. While lexicography has certainly never denied the existence of links between the various readings of a lexical item, Cognitive Linguistics has added a number of new insights: the clustered nature of polysemic structures is now being analyzed in more detail than ever. For lexicography, this implies a recognition of the linearization problem that traditional dictionaries have to face.

In the following pages, I will identify the specific expectations with regard to lexicographical practice that may be deduced from this theoretical analysis and then proceed to show that these predicted features are indeed part and parcel of actual lexicographical practice—in spite of what might be expected on the basis of other theoretical approaches to semantics. In particular, it is important to see that the specific conception of lexical structure advocated by Cognitive Linguistics differs crucially from a structuralist conception, which exerted a considerable influence on Continental metalexicographical theorizing through studies such as Rey-Debove (1971). First, while the cognitive linguistic approach includes both the semantic (intensional) and the referential (extensional) level in the semantic description, a structuralist view of lexicology tends to suggest that only the semantic level (the level of senses) is worthy of linguistic analysis. Second, while structuralist approaches to semantics tend to be reluctant to take into account differences of structural weight and demarcational fuzziness, Cognitive Linguistics readily accepts these phenomena as relevant aspects of semantic structure. And third, linking up with prestructuralist semantics (see Nerlich and Clarke, chapter 22 of this Handbook), Cognitive Semantics puts a new emphasis on the multidimensional, clustered nature of semasiological structures.

Now, what would be the consequences for lexicographical practice? Or rather, if the cognitive linguistic conception of semantic structure is by and large correct, what could we expect to find in actual dictionaries? The three characteristics highlighted above lead to the following hypotheses:

a. If it is correct that the referential level of semantic structure is part and parcel of a proper semantic description, we may expect dictionaries to include references to that level—despite the traditional, strict distinction between the semantic and the encyclopedic level of description. In particular, we may expect dictionaries to refer to prototype instances of categories or to typical (rather than general) features of the members of those categories.

b. If it is correct that the description of meaning has to come to terms with fuzziness, demarcation problems, and nonuniqueness, we expect dictionary definitions to use definitional methods that take into account these characteristics. Instead of definitions that rigidly take the form of separately general and mutually distinctive features, we expect the intrusion of unorthodox definitional methods such as enumerations, disjunctions, and the cumulation of near-synonyms.

c. If it is correct that semantic structures predominantly take the form of a multidimensional radial set structure, we may expect dictionaries to face a linearization problem: how can the multidimensional nature of the semantic structures be mapped onto the linear order of the dictionary?

In the following subsections, these expectations will be confronted with actual examples. It will be shown that the expectations are basically correct.

2.1. Prototypicality Effects in Lexical Structure

Consider the following definitions (of separate meanings or idiomatic expressions) from the *New Shorter Oxford English Dictionary* (CD-ROM version, 1997):

abiogenesis The production of organic matter or compounds, other than by the agency of living organisms; esp. the supposed spontaneous generation of living organisms.

baritone *A 1* The male voice between tenor and bass, ranging typically from lower A in the bass clef to lower F in the treble clef; a singer having such a voice; a part written for such a voice.

cup *b* An ornamental vessel, typically of silver and comprising a bowl with a stem and base, that is offered as a prize in a competitive event.

defoliate Remove the leaves from; cause the defoliation of, esp. as a military tactic.

dwarf *A 1 b* Any of a mythical race of diminutive beings, typically skilled in mining and metalworking and often possessing magical powers, figuring esp. in Scandinavian folklore.

hear! hear! An exclam. calling attention to a speaker's words, e.g. in the House of Commons, and now usu. expressing enthusiastic assent, occas. ironical derision.

heart *5* A central part of distinct conformation or character, e.g. the white tender centre of a cabbage, lettuce, etc.

honours of war Privileges granted to a capitulating force, e.g. that of marching out with colours flying.

model *2 a (fig.)* A person or thing resembling another, esp. on a smaller scale.

tea *5* A meal or social gathering at which tea is served. Now esp. (a) a light afternoon meal, usu. consisting of tea, cakes, sandwiches, etc. (also more fully afternoon tea, five o'clock tea); (b) (in parts of the UK, and in Australia and NZ) a main meal in the evening that usually includes a cooked dish, bread and butter, and tea (also more fully high tea)

tee A conical metallic structure, usually hung with bells, surmounting the pagodas of Myanmar (Burma) and adjacent countries.

thimblerig A sleight-of-hand game or trick usually played with three inverted thimbles and a pea, the thimbles being moved about and bystanders encouraged to place bets or to guess as to which thimble the pea is under.

In each of these definitions, words such as *especially*, *typically*, *usually*, and *often* introduce descriptive features that are not general but that rather identify typical (prototypical, if one likes) characteristics or instances of the category. Within a structuralist conception of semantics, this would be inadmissible, because these elements belong to the "encyclopedic" level rather than the semantic level. In actual practice, however, this prototype-oriented definitional technique can hardly be called exceptional in the context of the dictionary as a whole. The expression *esp.*, for instance, is used no less than 28,335 times in 18,274 entries in the dictionary as a whole.

Does this mean, by the way, that the difference between dictionaries and encyclopedias is a spurious one? The question asks for a brief excursion. An early discussion of the question between Haiman (1980) and Frawley (1981), with a further reply by Haiman (1982), provides a good starting point for delimiting the Cognitive point of view (for a more recent discussion of the theoretical question, see the contributions in Peeters 2000). On the one hand, the theoretical basis for a distinction between dictionaries and encyclopedias cannot be provided by the structuralist approach (as in Lara 1989): it is a crucial aspect of Cognitive Linguistics that the distinction between the two levels of description is not as strict as presupposed by the structuralist doctrine. On the other hand, there is a practical difference between dictionaries and encyclopedias that need not be abolished: there is a difference in scope and content between, say, the *Encarta* and the *New Shorter Oxford English Dictionary* or between the *Encyclopaedia Britanica* and the *Oxford English Dictionary*, and no cognitive linguist would argue against the distinction.

This distinction basically resides in two features. Macrostructurally, the encyclopedia focuses on proper names, nouns, and maybe a number of other elements from open word classes, whereas the dictionary includes all word classes (typically excluding all or most proper names). Microstructurally, the encyclopedia focuses on expert information as provided by scientific, technical, or professional experts, whereas that information is only one of the types of semantic description that the dictionary may include, together with the more everyday uses of the words.

But if Cognitive Linguistics accepts this distinction, how can it justify it? As a theoretical background for the distinction between the type of information typically included in encyclopedias and that included in dictionaries, we need a "sociosemantic" theory: a theory about the distribution of semantic knowledge within a linguistic community. Scientific, technical, professional information is, in fact, primarily information that is produced and certified by a specific group of people—the experts, who are recognized by the community as such and on whom the community relies when expert knowledge is at stake. Although no such "sociosemantic" theory is as yet available with any reasonable degree of comprehensiveness, a starting point is provided by Putnam's (1975) theory of the "division of linguistic labor," which explicitly distinguishes between *extensional concepts* (the expert's knowledge) and *stereotypes* (the basic semantic knowledge that language users are supposed to possess if they are to count as full-grown members of the linguistic community). A combination of Putnam's approach with prototype theory is not impossible (see Geeraerts 1985, 1987): if a prototypically organized concept combines all the various nuances with which a lexical item may be used within a linguistic community, then extensional and stereotypical concepts are particular members of the full prototypical set of applications of an item. Extensional concepts are characterized by their expert nature, whereas stereotypes represent the minimal amount of semantic knowledge that the language user is supposed to possess if he or she is to count as mastering the language. Roughly speaking, stereotypes are likely to coincide with the most common, most central senses within a prototypical cluster: what people are primarily supposed to know are the central readings of the cluster.

This recognition of a possible theoretical combination of prototype theory and a theory of the division of linguistic labor yields a theoretical framework for reference works that naturally provides a place for both the encyclopedia and the dictionary (see Geeraerts 1985, 1987). In fact, three basic types may be distinguished.

a. Technical, professional, scientific expert knowledge is treated in encyclopedias and terminological dictionaries.
b. The full prototypically organized set of senses of a lexical item, including nuances and less frequent or more specialized readings, is treated by

large-scale dictionaries, of the size represented by (to name just a few) the *New Oxford Dictionary of English* or *Merriam Webster's Collegiate Dictionary*, and any dictionary beyond that size.

c. Standard desk dictionaries can be related to the notion of stereotype: they make a selection from the full prototypical set by presenting only the most central, most frequent senses.

Closing the excursion, we may conclude that a cognitive linguistic conception of the relationship between semantic and encyclopedic knowledge does not preclude a theoretical justification for the distinction between dictionaries and encyclopedias as different types of reference works.

2.2. The Intractability of Polysemy

Definitional demarcation problems show up in the fact that dictionaries appear to use definitional techniques that are "unorthodox" from the point of view of a traditional conception of meaning. Consider the following set of entries, again from the *New Shorter Oxford English Dictionary*. (The entries are rendered in a reduced form: etymologies, quotations, dates, and a number of labels have been left out.)

primer I
1 A prayer-book or devotional manual for the laity.
2 An elementary textbook (orig. a small prayer-book) used in teaching children to read. b A small introductory book on any subject; *fig.* something introducing or providing initial instruction in a particular subject, practice, etc. c (A child in) an elementary class in a primary school.
3 A size of type. Chiefly & now only in *great primer, long primer*.

primer II
1 a = *priming-wire*. b A cap, cylinder, etc., containing a compound which responds to friction, electrical impulse, etc., and ignites the charge in a cartridge etc.
2 A substance used as a preparatory coat on previously unpainted wood, metal, canvas, etc., esp. to prevent the absorption of subsequent layers of paint or the development of rust.
3 A person who primes something.
4 *Aeronaut.* A small pump in an aircraft for pumping fuel to prime the engine.
5 a *Biochem.* A molecule that serves as a starting material for a polymerization. b *Zool. & Physiol.* A pheromone that acts initially on the endocrine system, and is thus more general in effect than a releaser.

primer III
1 First in order of time or occurrence; early; primitive.
2 First in rank or importance; principal, chief.

In almost half of the fourteen senses or subsenses presented here, we find definitional techniques that would seem to be inadmissible if one assumes that meanings have to be defined in terms of necessary and sufficient, general and distinctive characteristics. To begin with, we find disjunctions in I 1 ("A prayer-book *or* devotional manual for the laity"), in I 2b ("something introducing *or* providing initial instruction in a particular subject, practice, etc."), in II 2 ("A substance used as a preparatory coat on previously unpainted wood, metal, canvas, etc., esp. to prevent the absorption of subsequent layers of paint *or* the development of rust"), in III 1 ("First in order of time *or* occurrence"), and in III 2 ("First in rank *or* importance"). From a traditional point of view, disjunctions are barred from definitions, because they fail to capture the common aspects of the category to be defined.

In a similar way, open-ended enumerations should be avoided: they may illustrate or partially demarcate a category, but they do not define it, if one assumes a rigid conception of definitions. In the examples, however, quite a number of open-ended enumerations appear: in I 2b ("something introducing or providing initial instruction in a particular subject, practice, *etc.*"), in II 1 a ("A cap, cylinder, *etc.*, containing a compound which responds to friction, electrical impulse, *etc.*, and ignites the charge in a cartridge *etc.*"), and in II 2 ("A substance used as a preparatory coat on previously unpainted wood, metal, canvas, *etc.*").

Finally, we may note that the juxtaposition of near-synonyms is yet another way of loosening up the definitions. In example III 1, the near-synonyms *early* and *primitive* do not have exactly the same meaning (what is early is not necessarily primitive, and vice versa). At the same time, they add something to the analytic definition; in particular, the near-synonym *primitive* adds a nuance of lack of sophistication that is not explicit in the definition "First in order of time or occurrence."

Lexicographical practice, in short, appears to be in accordance with the lexicological observation that the distinction between meanings need not be clear-cut. This fact has not escaped the lexicographers themselves, to be sure: among others, see Ayto (1983), Stock (1983), and Hanks (1994). In the neighboring field of computational lexicography, similar voices may be heard: Kilgarriff (1997).

2.3. The Structured Nature of Polysemy

Let us consider the first seven senses of the adjective *fresh* in the *Oxford English Dictionary*, 2nd edition. (In the overview below, the definitions are sometimes rendered only partially. Some meaning nuances have been left out.)

I New, recent
 1. a. New, novel; not previously known, used, met with, introduced, etc.
  b. In weaker sense: Additional, another, other, different, further.
 2. Recent; newly made, recently arrived, received, or taken in.
 3. Making one's first acquaintance with a position, society, etc.; raw, inexperienced; unsophisticated, 'green'.

II. Having the signs of newness.

4. Of perishable articles of food, etc.: New, in contradistinction to being artificially preserved; (of meat) not salted, pickled, or smoked; (of butter) without salt; (of fruits, etc.) not dried or preserved in sugar or the like

5. Of water: Not salt or bitter; fit for drinking.

6. Untainted, pure; hence, possessed of active properties; invigorating, refreshing. Said *esp.* of air.

7. Retaining its original qualities; not deteriorated or changed by lapse of time; not stale, musty, or vapid.

The article exhibits a linear ordering of the meanings, with a higher-order, taxonomic structure of three levels. Even a cursory inspection of the definitions reveals that the hierarchical ordering does not make explicit all the relations that exist among the different senses.

a. The senses 1–3 within group I are related by similarity, with sense 1 probably as the prototypical center of the group. Roughly, sense 1 can be paraphrased as 'new according to the perspective of a beholder'. Sense 2 is 'new as such, newly produced'. Sense 3 may receive the paraphrase 'new in a specific context, new in a given position or function'. The senses within group II are likewise related by similarity, but 7 seems to be a more encompassing one than the others: if 7 is paraphrased as 'retaining its originally optimal character', then both the 'pure and strong' reading of 6 and the 'optimal for consumption, still in possession of all its nutritional value' reading of 4 are specializations of 7. Sense 5 'fit for drinking', on the other hand, belongs in the same group, as a nuance of 4. In short, the linear order within group I and within group II does not have an identical value, or at least, the semantic relations within each group are more specific than can be expressed by a mere linear ordering.

b. The relationship between group I and group II is a metonymic one: having the features of newness is a causal result of being new, in whatever sense. However, such a metonymic relationship also appears within group I. The nuance 'raw, inexperienced, unsophisticated' that appears after the colon in definition 3 is as much a 'sign of newness' in sense 3 as the meanings 4–7 are signs of newness in the sense defined by 2. We see, in other words, that the same type of relationship is not always treated in the same way. This also holds for the relationship of semantic specialization that links 7 to 4, 5, and 6. Notice, in fact, that reading 1b is a semantic specialization of 1a. The things that are fresh in 1b are not just novel from the point of view of the beholder, they are novel in comparison with a set or series of similar things.

All in all then, the semantic structure of the item is a multidimensional one. A further, more detailed analysis would undoubtedly reveal more dimensions, but at this point, it may be sufficient to take into account the three dimensions that came to the fore in our cursory analysis: the relationship of similarity between 1, 2, and 3; the relationship of specialization that exists between 7 and 4, 5, 6 on the one hand and between 1a and 1b on the other; and the metonymic relationship between 2 and 7, and between 3 and 3' (where 3' refers to the reading 'raw, inexperienced, unsophisticated'). The overall picture can be graphically represented as in figure 44.1. (The vertical line represents the similarity relationship, the horizontal line the metonymic relationship, and the diagonal line the relationship of specialization.)

The point, to be sure, is not that the linear order in the *Oxford English Dictionary* should be condemned as an inadequate rendering of the underlying semantic structure. The point is rather that *any* traditional form of linear ordering cannot do full justice to the multidimensional nature of semantic structures. In Geeraerts (1990), I dubbed this phenomenon the *lexicographical linearization problem*: the fact that lexicographers compiling traditional dictionaries have to project a multidimensional, clustered semantic structure onto the linear order of the dictionary. That article contained a detailed analysis of the word *vers* (the Dutch counterpart of English *fresh*) and its treatment in the *Woordenboek der Nederlandsche Taal* (the Dutch counterpart of the *Oxford English Dictionary*), plus a description of the various mechanisms (like hierarchical groupings, labels, and cross-references) that lexicographers may employ to circumvent the problem. The main point then, as now, was not a practical but a theoretical one: if the linearization problem is indeed a recurrent problem for practical lexicography, then a lexicographical metatheory had better start from a linguistic theory that explicitly recognizes the underlying semantic multidimensionality.

3. Extensions of Current Practices

The discussion in the previous pages suggests that the conception that Cognitive Linguistics has of polysemy and semantic structure is consonant with the actual practice of dictionaries. As such, what Cognitive Linguistics seems to offer to lexicography is a conception of semantic structure that is perhaps in a number of respects more realistic than what many other semantic theories (in particular, theories of a structuralist persuasion) can provide. This recognition does not, however, exhaust the interaction between Cognitive Linguistics and lexicography. There are at least two further points that should be mentioned to put the matter in a wider context.

To begin with, the previous discussion was restricted to the way in which Cognitive Linguistics encompasses a theoretical perspective that so to speak vindicates

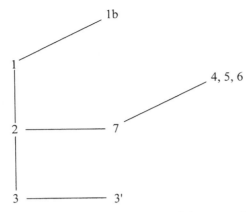

Figure 44.1. The multidimensional structure of the entry *fresh* in the *OED*

an existing definitional practice. However, Cognitive Linguistics may also suggest ways of dealing with the links between the senses of lexical items that go beyond common practice. Swanepoel (1992, 1998) and Van der Meer (2000), for instance, argue for devoting more explicit attention to the motivational link between core senses and figurative subsenses. Such motivational links could specifically involve conceptual metaphors in the Lakoffian sense (Van der Meer, Swanepoel), or even image schema (Swanepoel). Interestingly, Van der Meer's suggestion is part of a critical appraisal of the *New Oxford Dictionary of English*, which is probably the first dictionary to refer explicitly to prototype theory as the basis of its organizing principles (see Hanks 1994). Up to a point, then, Van der Meer's comments can be read as the suggestion that an even greater influence of the Cognitive approach could be lexicographically useful.

In the same line of thought, we should also mention the possible influence of Cognitive Linguistics on a very specific subdiscipline of lexicography, namely, on terminography, the study and description of professional and scientific terminology. Temmerman (2000) convincingly shows that the tenets of Wüster's highly influential Vienna school of terminography (which is firmly based on structuralist principles) do not hold out when confronted with the way in which concepts are developed and terms applied in actual professional and scientific discourse. Temmerman's analysis of biotechnological terminology demonstrates that all the lexical and semantic phenomena that Cognitive Linguistics focuses on (like structured polysemy, metonymy, and metaphor) occur in specialized terminologies just as much as in the general vocabulary. Even more importantly from the present point of view, she suggests ways how these insights into the structure and function of specialized terminologies may lie at the basis of new descriptive practices in terminography.

However, while all of these extensions of current lexicographical and terminographical practice basically take the form of suggestions for further developments, there is one form of cognitively inspired semantics that has led to a full-fledged lexicographical project. Fillmorean frame theory (see Cienki, this volume, chapter 7) has proved a highly stimulating framework for the description of lexical meaning, both theoretically and lexicographically. The FrameNet project that is currently being carried out in Berkeley is a large-scale attempt to build a digital lexicon according to the principles of frame theory. The theoretical background of the approach, as derived from frame theory as described in chapter 7 of this *Handbook*, was developed in publications such as Fillmore and Atkins (1992, 2000). Detailed information about the principles, purposes, and procedures within the FrameNet project are provided in a thematic issue of the *International Journal of Lexicography* (Fontenelle 2003). A full description of the project, together with the current release of the actual database, may also be found at the site of the Berkeley FrameNet project (http://www.icsi.berkeley.edu/~framenet).

Basically, the information provided in the FrameNet database consists of three types of information. First, there is a description of the frames. This description in itself consists of different kinds of information. As an example, let us have a look at the Grant-permission frame. (The examples quoted here were derived from the FrameNet Web site in November 2003. It should be borne in mind that the FrameNet project is far from being completed: no definitive value should be attributed to the examples.) The description begins with a global definition of the frame:

> In this frame a Grantor (either a person or an institution) grants permission for a Grantee to perform an Action or for an Action to occur. This frame does not include situations where there is a state of permission granted by authority or rule of law. The permission for the Action may be limited to certain Conditions.

> The core FEs (frame elements) are then described separately:

> *Action*: The Action is the activity of the Grantee that the Grantor permits.
> *Grantor*: The Grantor is the individual or group of individuals vested with the authority to grant permission with respect to a specific domain and who grant permission to the Grantee.
> *Grantee*: The Grantee is the individual who is given permission to engage in a certain Action.

Further, it is indicated how the frame in question relates to other frames. In the present case, for instance, Grant-permission is said to use the Communication frame, that is, it may take over elements from that frame. Finally, the LUs (lexical units) that exemplify the frame are listed:

> *allow.v, greenlight.v, leave.n, let.v, okay.v, permission.n, permit.v, sanction.v, suffer.v, the go-ahead.n, the green light.n, the okay.n.*

The second basic type of information provided by FrameNet consists of the individual description of the lexical units. The description of the frames does not, in fact, exhaust the description of the lexical items that exemplify the frame. For instance, it is one of the basic insights of frame theory that words may vary individually in the patterns of frame element realization they allow. For example, given a description of the Commercial-transaction frame as "These are words that describe basic commercial transactions involving a Buyer and a Seller who exchange Money and Goods," the typical patterns for the verbs *buy* and *sell* differ in their configuration of frame patterns:

> *buy*: Buyer buys Goods from Seller for Money
> *sell*: Seller sells Goods to Buyer for Money.

This implies that the description of the frames need to be complemented with a description of the individual valence patterns exhibited by the lexical items. This is all the more so because lexical units may feature in different frames. Take the example of *suffer* in the Grant-permission frame. It also occurs in the Catastrophe frame, defined as:

> The words in this frame involve an Undesirable_Event which affects the Undergoer negatively. No agent need be involved.

Within the Catastrophe frame, *suffer* occurs in a number of valence patterns. In the following corpus-based examples, we successively find a passive construction with a *by*-phrase, a passive construction without a *by*-phrase, an intransitive use, a transitive use, and a construction with a *from*-phrase expressing the frame element Undesirable_Event. The FrameNet project comprises an exhaustive description of these valence patterns.

> When I returned to the drawing room, a clergyman was talking about [the hardships] Undesirable_Event being *suffered* [by children] Undergoer in Berlin.
>
> The problems in applying the rule arise when [the damage] Undesirable_Event which has been *suffered* is not financial. [DNI] Undergoer
>
> And [social services] Undergoer *suffered* too, as they always will when wealth creation is despised. [DNI] Undesirable_Event
>
> [Both countries] Undergoer have *suffered* [prison violence, disorder and breakouts] Undesirable_Event.
>
> A year-long survey of Edinburgh has shown [much of the city] Undergoer to be *suffering* [from severe air pollution] Undesirable_Event.

The set of examples just given illustrates the third main feature of the FrameNet database: for each of the LUs (lexical units) in the frames, the database provides a set of corpus-based examples illustrating the valence patterns and the configurations of frame elements that the LUs occur in. The examples are annotated, in the sense that the relevant frame elements are tagged. (In the examples, DNI stands for "definite null instantiation"—a frame element that is missing but whose identity is understood from the context.)

The FrameNet database mainly tries to serve two audiences (apart from theoretical linguists): researchers in natural language processing, who may profit from the FrameNet information for any application that has to deal with word sense disambiguation, information extraction, and machine translation; and lexicographers, who may profit from the semantic definitions, the combinatorial descriptions, and the corpus-based examples provided by FrameNet.

4. FURTHER PROSPECTS

When dealing with the relationship between theoretical lexicology and practical lexicography, one should definitely not assume that theoreticians in principle have the answers and that lexicographers simply have to follow: the relationship is not a one-sided one, and as I have stressed on an earlier occasion (Geeraerts 1997: 5), there should be a relationship of mutual inspiration between both disciplines. The present chapter has basically looked from lexicological theory as developed within Cognitive Linguistics to lexicographical practice rather than the other way round, but to round off, we may now reverse the perspective: to what extent is existing lexicography a source of inspiration for Cognitive Linguistics—or to what extent could it be?

Although much of the work done in historical lexicology by cognitive linguists (see Grondelaers, Speelman, and Geeraerts, chapter 37, this volume) took inspiration from the great historical dictionaries like the *Oxford English Dictionary*, there are important aspects of current lexicographical practice that Cognitive Linguistics has only marginally touched upon, in spite of the fact that the lexicographical approach has proved extremely rewarding for lexical analysis at large and for the study of polysemy in particular. Specifically, a collocational approach to lexical description, systematically singling out the constructional patterns that lexical items occur in and identifying different meanings through differences in collocational patterns, is a methodological focus for many current lexicographical projects (see, e.g., Moon 1998). However, collocational methods to get a grip on polysemy are not (yet) among the standard equipment of cognitive linguists. There are, in fact, two aspects to such a collocational approach: it is a corpus-based approach, and it generally uses a quantitative method for the analysis of the corpora. So to what extent does Cognitive Linguistics incorporate these two methodological approaches?

First, the use of corpus materials was already part of early studies like Rudzka-Ostyn (1988), Schulze (1988), Geeraerts (1988), Dirven and Taylor (1988), or Goossens (1990). Typically, however, these were studies carried out by European cognitive linguists, while the early American studies were predominantly based on an introspective methodology. For the broader community of Cognitive Linguistics, the importance of corpus materials became a topic only since Barlow and Kemmer (2000), and as we saw in the description of the FrameNet project, using a corpus-based methodology is becoming more and more natural.

Second, the use of quantitative data within Cognitive Linguistics is more recent than the use of corpus materials, but there are now various lines of research within Cognitive Linguistics using quantitative models and/or methods: Tomasello's work on language acquisition (see chapter 41, this volume), Bybee's work on linguistic change (see chapter 36), and the work by Grondelaers, Speelman, and Geeraerts on sociolinguistic variation (see chapter 37). The use of corpus materials, in short, is slightly more widespread in Cognitive Linguistics than the use of quantitative methods, but neither is as yet a dominant approach.

What Cognitive Linguistics could learn from current lexicography, then, is a combination of a corpus-based approach and a quantitative approach to tackle the collocational and combinatorial properties of lexical items. An interesting step in that direction may be found in the research program recently defined by Gries and Stefanowitsch (Gries 2003; Gries and Stefanowitsch 2003), connecting Construction Grammar (see Croft, chapter 18, this volume) and quantitative corpus linguistics. To conclude, although Cognitive Linguistics appears to offer an exciting perspective for the further development of lexicography and lexicographical theory, the interaction could be carried much further than is currently the case.

REFERENCES

Ayto, John. 1983. On specifying meaning. In Reinhard R. K. Hartmann, ed., *Lexicography: Principles and practice* 89–98. London: Academic Press.

Barlow, Michael, and Suzanne Kemmer, eds. 2000. *Usage-based models of language.* Stanford, CA: CSLI Publications.

Dirven, René, and John R. Taylor. 1988. The conceptualisation of vertical space in English: The case of *tall.* In Brygida Rudzka-Ostyn, ed., *Topics in cognitive linguistics* 379–402. Amsterdam: John Benjamins.

Fillmore, Charles J., and Beryl T. Atkins. 1992. Towards a frame-based lexicon: The semantics of RISK and its neighbours. In Adrienne Lehrer and Eva Feder Kittay, eds., *Frames, fields, and contrasts: New essays in semantic and lexical organization* 75–102. Hillsdale, NJ: Lawrence Erlbaum.

Fillmore, Charles J., and Beryl T. Atkins. 2000. Describing polysemy: The case of 'crawl.' In Yael Ravin and Claudia Leacock, eds., *Polysemy* 91–110. Oxford: Oxford University Press.

Fontenelle, Thierry, ed. 2003. FrameNet and frame semantics. Special issue of *International Journal of Lexicography* 16.

Frawley, William. 1981. In defense of the dictionary: A response to Haiman. *Lingua* 55: 53–61.

Geeraerts, Dirk. 1985. Les données stéréotypiques, prototypiques et encyclopédiques dans le dictionnnaire. *Cahiers de Lexicologie* 46: 27–43.

Geeraerts, Dirk. 1987. Types of semantic information in dictionaries. In Robert Ilson, ed., *A spectrum of lexicography* 1–10. Amsterdam: John Benjamins.

Geeraerts, Dirk. 1988. Where does prototypicality come from? In Brygida Rudzka-Ostyn, ed., *Topics in cognitive linguistics* 207–30. Amsterdam: John Benjamins.

Geeraerts, Dirk. 1990. The lexicographical treatment of prototypical polysemy. In Savas L. Tsohatzidis, ed., *Meanings and prototypes: Studies in linguistic categorization* 195–210. London: Routledge.

Geeraerts, Dirk. 1997. *Diachronic prototype semantics: A contribution to historical lexicology.* Oxford: Clarendon Press.

Goossens, Louis. 1990. Metaphtonymy: The interaction of metaphor and metonymy in expressions for linguistic actions. *Cognitive Linguistics* 1: 323–40.

Gries, Stefan Th. 2003. Towards a corpus-based identification of prototypical instances of constructions. *Annual Review of Cognitive Linguistics* 1: 1–27.

Gries, Stefan Th., and Anatol Stefanowitsch 2003. Collostructions: On the interaction between words and constructions. *International Journal of Corpus Linguistics* 8: 209–43.

Haiman, John. 1980. Dictionaries and encyclopedias. *Lingua* 50: 329–57.

Haiman, John. 1982. Dictionaries and encyclopedias again: Discussion. *Lingua* 56: 353–55.

Hanks, Patrick. 1994. Linguistic norms and pragmatic exploitations, or why lexicographers need prototype theory, and vice versa. In Ferenc Kiefer, Gabor Kiss, and Julia Pajzs, eds., *Papers in computational lexicography* 89–113. Budapest: Linguistics Institute.

Kilgarriff, Adam. 1997. I don't believe in word senses. *Computers and the Humanities* 31: 91–113.

Lara, Luis Fernando. 1989. Dictionnaire de langue, encyclopédie et dictionnaire encyclopédique: Le sens de leur distinction. In Franz Josef Hausmann, Oskar Reichmann, Herbert Ernst Wiegand, and Ladislav Zgusta, eds., *Wörterbücher/ Dictionaries/ Dictionnaires* 1: 280–87. Berlin: Walter de Gruyter.

Moon, Rosamund. 1998. *Fixed expressions and idioms in English: A corpus-based approach.* Oxford: Oxford University Press.

Peeters, Bert, ed. 2000. *The lexicon-encyclopedia interface.* Oxford: Elsevier.

Putnam, Hilary. 1975. The meaning of meaning. In Hilary Putnam, ed., *Mind, language, and reality: Philosophical papers* 2: 215–71. Cambridge: Cambridge University Press.

Rey-Debove, Josette. 1971. *Étude linguistique et sémiotique des dictionnaires français contemporains.* The Hague: Mouton.

Rudzka-Ostyn, Brygida. 1988. Semantic extensions into the domain of verbal communication. In Brygida Rudzka-Ostyn, ed., *Topics in cognitive linguistics* 507–54. Amsterdam: John Benjamins.

Schulze, Rainer. 1988. A short story of *down.* In Werner Hüllen and Rainer Schulze, eds., *Understanding the lexicon: Meaning, sense and world knowledge in lexical semantics* 394–410. Tübingen, Germany: Max Niemeyer Verlag.

Stock, Penelope F. 1983. Polysemy. In Reinhard R. K. Hartmann, ed., *LEXeter '83: Proceedings of the Exeter lexicography conference* 131–40. Tübingen, Germany: Max Niemeyer Verlag.

Swanepoel, Piet. 1992. Linguistic motivation and its lexicographical application. *South African Journal of Linguistics* 10: 49–60.

Swanepoel, Piet. 1998. Back to basics: Prepositions, schema theory, and the explanatory function of the dictionary. In Thierry Fontenelle, Philippe Hiligsmann, Archibald Michiels, André Moulin, and Siegfried Theissen, eds., *Euralex '98 Proceedings* 655–66. Liège, Belgium: Université de Liège, Département d'anglais et de néerlandais.

Temmerman, Rita. 2000. *Towards new ways of terminology description: The sociocognitive approach.* Amsterdam: John Benjamins.

Van der Meer, Geart. 2000. Core, subsense, and the New Oxford Dictionary of English. In Ulrich Heid, Stefan Evert, Egbert Lehmann, and Christian Rohrer, eds., *Euralex 2000 Proceedings* 419–31. Stuttgart: Institut für Maschinelle Sprachverarbeitung.

CHAPTER 45

COGNITIVE LINGUISTIC APPROACHES TO LITERARY STUDIES: STATE OF THE ART IN COGNITIVE POETICS

MARGARET H. FREEMAN

1. INTRODUCTION

In his statement, "Language is the child of the literary mind," Turner (1991, 1996) reverses the traditional view that literature is a special, exotic subcategory of language by arguing that human language capabilities arose from the cognitive mapping projections of parable and story. Although Turner's argument has not as yet received wide acceptance in either field of linguistics or literature (but see Modell 2003), the emergence of Cognitive Linguistics has encouraged the development of new relations between the two disciplines (see Geeraerts 1999 for a comprehensive survey of the historical development of linguistic semantics and literary theories). Just as literary texts may serve as legitimate data for understanding the principles of language structure and use, linguistic analysis offers new perspectives on literary production, interpretation, reception, and evaluation

(Bizup and Kintgen 1993; Hart 1995; Jahn 1997; Crane and Richardson 1999; Jackson 2000).

Historically, a certain amount of tension has existed between the disciplines of linguistics and literature. For those of us engaged in bridging the two, the particular form this tension takes—namely, that literary criticism contributes nothing to linguistic enquiry, and vice versa—has always seemed anomalous. However, this anomaly may have roots deeper than being simply a matter of turf wars. Recently, Burrows (2003) has characterized the split between scientific method and literary criticism as a comparison between Descartes's retiring to his 'stove' to contemplate the foundations of knowledge and Montaigne's retiring to his tower to write his *Essays*:

> Descartes's stove and Montaigne's library tower have given us two ways of living and thinking that are at root divergent. Stove people think that you can strip everything away and rebuild reality from precepts; tower people reckon that writing about and exploring or refining beliefs is the best you can do. For tower people, the process of writing and arguing is what thinking is; it is not concluding. (Burrows 2003: 21)

Though the ways of the stove and the tower may appear fundamentally incompatible, this chapter surveys recent work in applying cognitive linguistic approaches to literature that carry with them both the air of the tower and the heat of the stove.

Literary critics have long been familiar with such topics as perspective, point of view, flashbacks, foreshadowing, and so on that cognitive linguists are just now exploring. One question that inevitably arises is what new insights Cognitive Linguistics provides in literary studies that literary criticism has not already discovered. The corollary, what literary criticism can contribute to Cognitive Linguistics, is almost always never asked (but see Brandt and Brandt 2005a). In its focus on the processes of literary creation, interpretation, and evaluation, Cognitive Linguistics contributes scientific explanations for the findings of literary critics and thus provides a means whereby their knowledge and insights might be seen in the context of a unified theory of human cognition and language. To this extent, the stove is not incompatible with the tower; to the contrary, neither functions completely or well without the other.

Although "literature" in its broadest sense refers to all written texts, this chapter restricts its scope to the more narrowly focused term used to cover the literary genres of fiction, poetry, and drama, written instances of humor, multimedia forms such as film, and religious writings that display literary qualities, such as the Bible and mystic poetry. All these writings are oriented toward the expressive, the emotive, and the aesthetic; it is here that the more inclusive approach of Cognitive Poetics, particularly as practiced by Tsur (1992, 1998, 2003), may serve as a guide for further developments in the interdisciplinary area of linguistics and literature. As Hamilton (2000: 3) notes, "Cognitive poetics can provide a sensible epistemology for the event of interpretation."

The past few years have seen an explosion in interest in cognitive approaches to literature.[1] These approaches include the development of methodologies for describing both the production and reception of literary texts. Since the work presented in this chapter describes a symbiotic relationship between literary and linguistic objectives, I have organized it according to challenges common to both. Each section highlights aspects important to literary and linguistic study and describes work that suggests possible directions for future study.

2. PROTOTYPICALITY AND THE NOTION OF LITERATURE

Several researchers have turned their attention to illuminating the nature of literature and its various genres through prototypicality theory as opposed to a classical, feature-based theory of categorization (Meyer 1997; De Geest and van Gorp 1999; G. Steen 1999b). From the perspective of literary criticism, the category "literature" has been so enlarged in the postmodern period as to include whatever a particular reader chooses to consider "text," whether oral or written or even the nonlinguistic "signifiers" of culture. Under these circumstances, G. Steen wisely calls for an empirical research program to develop a taxonomy of discourse, in which literature may be positioned within the domain of discourse in general. He argues for a taxonomy in which "a prototypical approach emphasizes the hierarchical order of fuzzy concepts in a domain, using the same attributes for every level of conceptualization" (1999b: 116). The seven attributes he identifies are content, form, type, function, medium, domain, and language. The more abstract the level, the more certain attributes are unspecified. Thus, the basic level "novel" may be characterized by values of all seven attributes, whereas the superordinate term, "literature," is characterized by domain ('artistic'), content ('fictional'), and function ('positively affective'), but not by the other four. The advantage of G. Steen's taxonomy is that it quickly identifies when theories of literature mix values belonging to different attributes, as Meyer (1997) does. In his analysis, the addition of the attributes of medium, language, and form to the term "literature" makes it less superordinate as a category and closer to the level of genre. In Meyer's prototypical definition of literature, works that contain more features would be considered more literary or better examples of the category than those that contain less.

In their focus on the basic level of literary genre, De Geest and van Gorp (1999) reveal the complexities of applying a prototype approach. They point out that identifying the "best" or more typical example of a literary category is not at all the same as an aesthetic evaluation: "the 'best' texts are almost by definition exceptional cases which clearly are, at least in some aspects, atypical" (1999: 43). As the discussion of G. Steen's taxonomy has noted, the greater the superordination of the category, the harder it is to establish prototypical instances; consider, for example, the difference between "poem" and "sonnet." However, even the lower-level category is more problematic than it seems. Although the sonnet exists at a more subordinate level than the poem and thus might be more readily defined in prototypical terms, De Geest and van Gorp show that it is just as problematic; it would be strange, if not absurd, to consider a Petrarchan sonnet more prototypical than a Spenserian one, or a Spenserian than a Shakespearian. And then, what does one do with so-called sonnets whose rhyme, meter, structure, or number of lines vary from these established forms?

Like G. Steen and Meyer, De Geest and van Gorp indicate that literary texts and genres must be considered along their evaluative and axiological components, considering norms, values, and models, as well as the author's intentions and the reader's expectations. They suggest that the concept of norm has to include not just what is proscribed but what is permitted. One possibility for achieving a prototypical theory of literature would be to adopt De Geest and van Gorp's (1999: 41) recognition that "the so-called 'prototype' need not exist in reality, since it is generally assumed to be a kind of hypothetical cognitive construction, a theoretical 'fiction,'" much like Lakoff's Idealized Cognitive Model that structures a conceptual domain. The "prototype" of a literary work would then include in its description an atypical example of its genre.

This rather radical proposal—that the category of literary works needs to accommodate atypicality as prototypical—appears to undermine the very notion of prototypicality theory, so that literary critics might well question the relevance of applying it to literature in the first place. This is one example of the conflict between the stove and the tower. Understanding the nature of literature involves explaining its role in the workings of the embodied human mind. It might be argued that this begs the question: why should the methodology applied to understanding literature (and the other arts) be necessarily a scientific one? Talmy's (2000: 479–80) discussion of the parameter of protoypicality in the context of evaluation provides one answer: it is only by judging with respect to cultural norms that one can determine the relative status of a literary work as conforming to or challenging them. As Talmy notes, "Thus, it appears that certain long periods in Chinese art and literature maintained themselves with great conservatism, while this century in the West has rewarded authorial experimentation" (480). In this light, the expectation that a literary work be atypical may be seen as the prototypical attitude to literature held by contemporary Western critics. Only by looking at literature using the same methodology that is applied to looking at other activities of the human mind can we fully comprehend the nature of the distinctions between creative and conventional expressions and trace the changes in their prototypical status through time.

All the research surveyed in this chapter may be understood as examples of this principle. A case in point is Ravid and Hanauer's (1998) study of how adult speakers of Hebrew show evidence of having a prototypical theory of rhyme. Their scientific analysis and empirical research confirm literary intuitions about the way readers respond to the kind of rhyme schemes that occur in a variety of poetic texts. One finding that ran counter to Ravid and Hanauer's predictions—that Hebrew speakers tolerated contrasting coda consonants but not contrasting vowels in the post-stress syllable of modernistic rhymes—may possibly signify a dynamic shift of category boundary in process as Hebrew speakers grow more familiar with the rhyming practices of modernist poets. Whether Hebrew speakers in the future tolerate both post-stress consonants and vowels as members of the same rhyme category would be a hypothesis for such dynamic change and subject to further empirical research.

A dynamic theory of prototypicality over time could explain how literary decisions as to what constitutes a literary text are made. For example, though Wordsworth, in his second preface to the *Lyrical Ballads,* remarked that readers might question whether the poems included could be considered poetry at all, literary critics today perceive them to be classic examples of the genre of Romantic Poetry, a possible indication of category change over time. Evidence for a dynamic as opposed to static construal of prototypes is provided by two studies of prototypicality that involve literary texts. Głaz's (2002) lexicological study of the concept domain of Earth looks at the use of the term in six novels by Kingsley Amis, alongside data collected from the 1995 editions of *The Times* and *The Sunday Times.* Głaz combines Fuchs's (1994) dynamic model of semantic space with Langacker's (1987, 1991) network model to show how the use of a term opens a window onto its entire lexical network, with meaning construed by shifts in both intracategorial and extracategorial tensions set up by the context. Gibbs (2003: 38) recognizes that "prototypes are not abstract, pre-existing conceptual structures, but are better understood as products of meaning construal." These include interpreting context-sensitive meaning in literary texts, the judgment of novelty by skilled readers, and the fact that an "embodied view of meaning construal nicely captures at least some of what people see as poetic during their reading experiences" (39). Applying a dynamic view of prototype theory might well serve as a research agenda for understanding how prototypical judgments of literature change over time.

3. CONCEPTUAL STRUCTURE IN HUMAN COGNITION AND NARRATIVE

The aims of the tower are different from those of the stove. Literary critics focus on the emotional and aesthetic effects of literary works, cognitive linguists on accounting for the way language characterizes meaning. From a cognitive perspective, literary critics are engaged in mapping the meanings of texts from various contextual domains. They are interested in the results of these mappings, not the means by which they accomplish them. Analyses of these means, however, can reveal the principles on which the mappings are made. Exploring general cognitive constraints on mapping provides a framework for evaluating the effect of individual writers who violate these constraints. Research into the cognitive systems and constraints on human language processing provides a mechanism for precise description of the motivations for both literary production and reception. Talmy's (2000: 479–80) work reveals the extent to which the approaches of the stove and the tower may be made compatible.

Talmy's discussion in the final chapter of his two-volume work on Cognitive Semantics is the most comprehensive account to date of the cognitive system that gives rise to literature. Although he uses the term "narrative structure" to describe this system, he does not mean narrative in its narrow sense but in the sense of its function "to connect and integrate certain components of conscious content over time into a coherent ideational structure" (2000: 419). In this respect, his approach correlates closely with Turner's cognitive reversal in exploring the structures of "the literary mind" that distinguish us as human beings.

Talmy's description of the framework of the narrative cognitive system includes three parts: domains, strata, and parameters. Domains include "the spatiotemporal physical world with all its (so-conceived) characteristics and properties; the culture or society with its presuppositions, conceptual and affective structuring, values, norms, and so on; the producer or producers of a narrative; the experiencer or experiencers of a narrative; and the narrative itself" (Talmy 2000: 422). Strata refer to the basic structuring systems (temporal, spatial, causal, and psychological) that operate within and across domains. Parameters are the general organizing principles that apply across all the strata, such as relating structures to each other, relative quantity (scope, granularity, density), degree of differentiation, combinatory structure, and evaluation. Explorations of literary works tend to focus on one or more aspects within or across these three areas. With its many examples drawn from literary works, Talmy's system serves both as an exemplary model for the taxonomy of discourse G. Steen calls for and as a way of integrating and uniting into a coherent theory the various theoretical stances of literary criticism.

Although its theoretical framework ties together work on other literary approaches such as text and possible world theories, reader response, psychoanalytic approaches, and so on, the fairly recent appearance of Talmy's work means that it has not yet had a direct effect on cognitive approaches to literature. One problem is the pervasive practice of using different terminology to address similar phenomena. For example, it is unclear how Talmy's theory of domains, strata, and parameters complements or differs from Brandt's (2004) model for literary text construction. Sternberg's (2003a, 2003b) work provides an extensive analysis and rigorous criticism of various cognitive approaches to narrative theories. However, several studies discussed in this section fall under the framework of Talmy's theory as it applies to perspective and construal by author or reader and mental space projection and deixis.

3.1. Perspective and Construal

There is already copious research on narratology that focuses on the processes of scene construal and perspective from the point of view of author and reader (for a useful overview, see Van Peer and Chatman 2001). For instance, the concept of "implied" author comes from literary criticism's awareness of the dangers of assigning "intentionality" to real writers of texts. New Criticism attacked intentionality, in its early phase, because it suggested that the author of a text had a specific intention in mind, which could be accessed by a "true" reading of the text. Poststructuralist critics, in challenging the stability of the text itself, also sought to undermine the idea of intentionality in the writer. However, following new discoveries in psychology and neuroscience, literary critics are beginning to reappraise the roles of writer, reader, and text. With the rise of Cognitive Linguistics came the idea that conceptual metaphorical structure could provide insights into the human mind, so that a natural move is to explore what these structures might reveal about the author's conceptual attitudes and motivations (Holland 1988; Crane 2000).

Kardela and Kardela (2002) discuss the conflicting metaphorical realities of the "implied author" and those of the "unreliable" narrator by exploring the extended metaphor that structures the narrative of Ishiguro's novel *The Remains of the Day*. In objecting to one literary critic's reading of the novel as having only one narrative perspective, the authors show the need to invoke an implied author to establish the extended conflict metaphor, thereby accounting in a principled way for the degree of unreliability evidenced by the narrator. In a similar manner, Kedra-Kardela and Kardela (2000) extend the literary meaning of "subjectivity" as representing a character's thoughts and feelings to embrace the notion of the focalizer/narrator's viewpoint, which includes world knowledge, beliefs, and values. By adopting Langacker's methodology of subjective and objective grounding of perspective in scene construal, they are able to show in three stories by Elizabeth Bowen how shifts in scene construal reveal the extent of alienation and reconciliation the protagonists experience with respect to their homes, family, and society.

Reader response theories have focused on the way readers construct meaning from text. Cognitive psychologists have begun to explore constraints on reader responses to literary texts, as indicated by Gibbs and Bogdonovich's (1999) empirical studies on the role of mental imagery in interpreting image metaphors in literature. Their findings indicate that readers of Andre Breton's poem "Free Union" more frequently respond to image metaphors like *My wife whose hair is brush fire* by mapping concrete images than by mapping their more complex knowledge about the source domain. They conclude: "People indeed *must* create concrete imagistic mappings to understand novel image metaphors" (1999: 43). These findings are particularly suggestive when considering exactly what interpretive strategies literary critics use. Interpretations often depend on the critic's choice of image mappings across metaphorical domains (M. Freeman 2000, 2002a). Gibbs and Bogdonovich's study is important in showing that "theories of metaphor must distinguish between different kinds of conceptual mappings in explaining the aesthetic qualities of metaphorical statements" (1999: 43).

Compatible with this approach is extensive work by Miall (1989) and Miall and Kuiken (2001) on the way readers comprehend and evaluate literary narratives through their subjective experience of emotions and feelings. This "affect," they argue, is: (i) *self-referential*, in enabling readers to identify with a story; (ii) *cross-domain*, in being able to transfer schemata from one domain (such as setting) to another (such as relation between characters); and (iii) *anticipatory*, in providing readers with the capability of comprehending the narrative's progress. Miall (2000) shows how the empirical testing of literary notions of canon renewal, style, and empathy in narrative reveals the innate qualities of literary texts.

3.2. Mental Space Projection and Deixis

Some literary studies have used mental space theory to explore creative aspects of literary technique. Harding (2001) discusses Hemingway's use in one short story of counterfactual spaces in the discourse of two protagonists to reinforce the negative affect governing their situation. Irandoust (1999) cites passages from French literary works to show that tense markers like the past-perfect construction can create narrative perspective through concealed parallel spaces or "reference frames" that enrich linear narrative sequencing with subjective information. Mental space theory and deictic projection can account for a poet's idiosyncratic grammar (M. Freeman 1997). Epistolary letters provide clear examples of deictic projection since the letter writer will often project into the imagined reality space of the letter recipient. Readers of the epistolary sections of A. S. Byatt's novel *Persuasion* are drawn into these projections as their own cognitive abilities trace the deictic triggers that move them from one mental space to another (Herman 1999).

Parallel to these literary approaches is the work of the Discourse and Narrative Research Group at the State University of New York at Buffalo on the ways in which narrative deictic techniques illuminate general cognitive processes of human understanding (Duchan, Bruder, and Hewitt 1995).

4. METAPHOR AND BLENDING IN LITERARY TEXTS

Metaphor, metonymy, and the figurative tropes of classical rhetoric have always been identified as an integral part of literary texts. The explosion of metaphor studies at the end of the last century has led to fresh ways of conceiving the tropes and to the emergence of coherent views of metaphor and metonymy that are still very much under development. This development is reflected in Kittay's (1987) seminal work on metaphor, which is situated in the context of the traditionally understood divide between semantics and pragmatics, while at the same time it develops a theory of metaphor closely allied to modern cognitive science. Her theory of "semantic field" spells out the way a "content domain" (analogous to "conceptual domain" or "Idealized Cognitive Model") is linguistically articulated and forms the basis of her understanding of metaphor structure, especially as it is represented in literary texts. She shows that John Donne's poem "The Bait" has a more complex metaphorical structure than Wordsworth's poem "On the Extinction of the Venetian Republic" and that metaphor in Shelley's poem "Song to the Men of England" is less successful. Kittay's application of semantic field theory to metaphor anticipates Fauconnier and Turner's (2002) theory of the structure of multiple domain mappings and also provides suggestive criteria both for determining the distinctions between standard and novel metaphors and for evaluating the relative success of a particular literary metaphor.

Kittay's suggestion that metaphors may be evaluated according to the extent to which the vehicle field restructures the topic field may provide a useful heuristic for the evaluation of literary texts. Recognizing the existence of literary metaphor is a case in point. Cognitive metaphor analyses have revealed the absurdity of the position of some critics that the works of Tolstoy and Jane Austen are nonmetaphorical by revealing just how successful Tolstoy (Danaher 2003a, 2003b) and Austen (Peña Cervel 1997–98; Wye 1998) are in tapping the underlying metaphorical systems of all cognitive thought. Fernandes's (2002) PhD dissertation focuses on metaphors and cultural models which are central to the work of four contemporary Francophone women novelists (Condé, Djebar, Beyala, and Belghoul). Such work extends the concept of metaphor from its use in individual examples to entire conceptual domains.

4.1. The Structure of Extended Metaphor and Its Literary Effects

Lakoff and Johnson (1980, 1998) identified the structural schemas and extended metaphors that underlie some of the most basic ways we conceptualize our experiences of life. These extended metaphors, as Werth (1994: 80) has noted, can consist of "an entire metaphorical 'undercurrent' running through a whole text, which may manifest itself in a large number and variety of 'single' metaphors." This metaphorical undercurrent brings structural unity to a literary text and contributes to the emergence of a text's theme, as Popova (2002) shows in her study of the metaphorical mappings of smell in Süskind's novel *Perfume*. In his studies on conceptual metaphors in Shakespeare's plays, D. Freeman (1993, 1998,

1999) explores the extended metaphors that build the theme of each play on the principle that a theory of metaphor depends upon a theory of mind. His cognitive analyses show how figurative patterns generalize to other patterns, such as plot and scene, and provide interpretations detailed and coherent enough to be compared against competing interpretations.

Studying such structuring metaphors provides a principled way to explain how writers are influenced by the metaphors of their culture while at the same time they are selecting and refining those metaphors to shape their own thinking and attitudes about the world around them. While literary metaphors often subvert conventional and stereotypical cultural attitudes (see M. Freeman 1995), Kövecses (1994: 132) concludes that what Tocqueville saw in his travels through America "must have been thoroughly influenced by the unoriginal, ready-made, and subconscious ideas" that constitute the basis of the PERSON metaphors he uses to describe American democracy. That writers adopt certain metaphors from a range of metaphor systems deeply embedded in their culture is explored further in Csábi's (2000, 2001) articles on Thomas Paine's arguments for the separation of America from Britain and the immigration experiences of American Puritans.

Like Kövecses and Csábi, Bertuol (2001: 21) is interested in the "influence that common knowledge and beliefs shared by the members of a linguistic community exert on the poet's choice of metaphors." However, Bertuol is not claiming that this influence determines a poet's choices; if this were true, then it would be difficult if not impossible to explain individual, creative, and revolutionary thinking. His study of the works of Margaret Cavendish, a seventeenth-century poet writing on scientific matters, shows how mathematical knowledge at that time influenced people's views of reality. The cultural choice the poet makes of the seventeenth-century conceptual metaphor UNIVERSE IS MATHEMATICS enables her to argue that "*irrationalia*, such as female nature and fancy, cannot be penetrated and controlled" (Bertuol 2001: 37).

Exploring the relations of a writer's metaphorical perspective to his or her culture also provides a means for explaining the extent of a writer's popularity. Kimmel (2001) analyzes the metaphor of CENTER AND ALTERITY in Conrad's *Heart of Darkness* to see whether it sheds light on "the scope of variation" and "prevailing cultural dispositions" of Victorian England. He concludes that Conrad's use of the metaphor reflects the Victorian psychopolitical mindset of a self-model that Europeans have been subconsciously sharing for a long time and explains why Conrad's novel resonated so strongly with its Victorian audience.

4.2. Creative and Conventional Metaphors

Turner's reversal in claiming the literary mind generated language removes the problem of attempting to discover how conventional language could give rise to creative language. In the case of metaphor, deeply entrenched or conventionalized metaphors presumably began as novel or creative metaphor. However, old habits die hard, and the language, if not the spirit, of much metaphorical work in Cognitive Linguistics tends to reflect a conventional to creative direction, as reflected in two of Lakoff and Turner's (1989) frequently quoted passages: "Poetic thought uses the mechanisms of everyday thought, but it extends them, elaborates them, and combines them in ways that go beyond the ordinary" (67); "Poetic language uses the same conceptual and linguistic apparatus as ordinary language" (158). Though these statements might appear reductionist, all Lakoff and Turner are saying is that the underlying *apparatus* or *mechanisms* of poetic and conventional language and thought are the same, not that the two are conflated. Several studies have explored the extent to which creative metaphors arise from extension, elaboration, and combination in such writers as Henry James (Čulić 2001), Eavan Boland and Adrienne Rich (McGrath n.d.), and Hemingway (Strack 2000). In a detailed and thorough explanation of conceptual orientation metaphors that combine to create such conventional expressions as *down and out* to mean 'destitute and unfortunate', Sweetser (2004) shows how the same co-orientations of metaphorical mappings occur in a pivotal speech in Shakespeare's tragedy *Julius Caesar*. Although she does not specifically claim that such mappings become literary when they form a single complex model, her notion that this in fact is what occurs in Shakespeare's passage suggests one possible way of distinguishing creative from conventional metaphor.

The prevailing assumption in these studies is that a continuum exists between creative and conventional use of metaphor and that devices such as elaboration, extension, and compression account for the distinction between them. G. Steen (1994, 2001b) challenges this assumption as presumed rather than proven and calls for cognitive psychologists, linguists, and literary critics to work toward a better understanding of how we identify and process metaphor. To this end, G. Steen (1999a, 2001a) has developed and tested for reliability a five-step procedure for metaphor identification that is based on conceptual metaphor theory and blending. Several issues for cognitive research emerge from G. Steen's studies, including how to account for the distinction between conceptual and linguistic metaphor and how to identify metaphorical projections when the target domain is not identified. G. Steen's reliability studies indicate that the technical ability to identify metaphor, especially in literary text, is something that has to be learned, a finding that has implications for both pedagogy and metaphor theory.

4.3. Blending as a Metaphorical Structure

So far as I know, no researcher to date has considered exploring metaphor as a category, though many different types of metaphor are discussed, such as "conventional," "creative," "banal," "extended," and so on. Many of the arguments over the structure of metaphor may in fact rest in the failure to recognize that there may be many different metaphorical types and structures. As noted in section 4, Kittay's work explores some of the possible structures metaphor might have. Although Fauconnier and Turner's work on conceptual integration networks or "blending" does not specifically refer to metaphor, all metaphors at some stage in their creation involve blending, so that the analysis of single-, double-, or multiple-scope blending might very well be productively applied to metaphor structure. As in all cognitive linguistic applications to literature, work in this area has only just begun, but increasingly, more researchers are applying blending analysis to literary texts.

Blending provides an elegant explanation for creativity in its theory of an "emergent structure" created by the blend. It explains, for example, the rhetorical effects in haiku texts of juxtaposing phrases by *kireji* (cutting letters) and *kake-kotoba* (multiple puns); and it provides a better reading of the frequent use in haiku of personification and allegory through indirect mapping across spaces and recruitment from common cultural knowledge (Hiraga 1999a, 1999b). Blending reveals the structure of prototypical and borderline allegories, from Dante to Pynchon (Sinding 2002) as well as the mixing of genres that can define literary history (Sinding 2005). Blending enables F. Steen (2002) to show how an Aphra Behn novel, by mapping the rhetoric of power onto the rhetoric for love, may have functioned as both literature and political propaganda. Oakley's (1998) article on conceptual blending, narrative discourse, and rhetoric provides an exemplary account of blending and how it operates in Art Spiegelman's *Maus* to link the more immediate story of Richelieu's relationship to his "ghost brother" to the larger story of the Holocaust. Matthew's (2003) dissertation explores temporal compression blends in literature. Coulson (2003) explores conceptual blending in political and religious rhetoric.

Conceptual schemas and blending also address questions of literary structure and style, such as reconfiguring literary allusion, constructing a lyric subject, establishing the roots of African American poetry, and comparing literary styles (L. Ramey 1996, 2002). In her exploration of the way Edmond Rostand creates "artistically right Form-Meaning blending" in his verse drama, *Cyrano de Bergérac*, Sweetser (2006) provides many intriguing suggestions as to how stylistic iconicity creates art. Poetic styles can be identified, described, and compared according to which image schemas are chosen as a structuring principle for a writer's poetics (M. Freeman 2002b). Tobin (2006) shows how the emergent structure of a blend can become culturally entrenched and institutionalized over time within a given discourse community.

Recent work by Brandt (2004) refines and elaborates Fauconnier and Turner's original blending model to articulate the roles of culture, context, emotion, evaluation, and ethics in the creation of meaning. In his discussion of Baudelaire's poem, *Les Chats*, Brandt shows how his model characterizes literary texts. The model suggests that the dynamic schemas of form and feeling are integral to meaning production and processing and thus supports Langer's (1953, 1967) argument that both are crucial in establishing a theory of all art.

5. Embodiment, Iconicity, and Neurology in Literary Form and Affect

Literary critics in stylistics, especially those influenced by New Criticism, structuralism, and the work of the Russian formalists, have long recognized the importance of formal, emotional, and aesthetic effects in literary works. As a natural extension from the principle of the embodied mind and in line with literary critical work in this area (McGann 1991), some cognitive linguists are beginning to explore literary "meaning" that arises from formal textural qualities or "pastiosity" (to borrow a term from graphology), where physical, sensory modalities fuse with linguistic and metalinguistic forms (M. Freeman 2000). As a corollary to reader response theory in literary criticism, several cognitive studies have begun to use empirical research to determine such literary affects. These include sensory modalities beyond sight and sound, the way language in poetic texts iconically reflects its meaning, and how these might be governed by cognitive constraints in the brain.

5.1. Sensory Modalities of Embodiment: Empirical Research

Certain general cognitive constraints have been shown to govern figurative use. In a series of psychological experiments, Todd and Clarke (2001) were able to show in a principled way the cognitive similarities and differences between simile and metaphor, with simile being harder to process. In simile, synaesthesia, and zeugma, Shen (1997) found that Hebrew poets across different schools and periods prefer mapping from the more accessible term. They provide psychological evidence from empirical experiments to support this constraint. Whenever the two terms in simile differ in their relative concrete and abstract levels or degree of salience, the preferred direction of mapping is from more to less. In zeugma (Shen 1997) and synaesthesia (Shen and Cohen 1998), poets were found to prefer naming the more prototypical term first and to prefer mappings that went from senses more closely related to the body, such as touch and taste, to those less closely related, such as sound and sight; readers found these easier to understand. Gibbs and Kearney's (1994) work on poetic oxymoron produced similar results. Shen (1997: 67) concludes that studies such as these show "not only that poetic uses of figuration constrain our cognitive system, but that poetic figures are themselves constrained by general cognitive constraints."

5.2. Iconicity of Form and Meaning

Embodiment takes on a special form with respect to structural and visual iconicity. Recent research on signed languages has given cognitive linguists crucial new insights into the relationship between form and meaning: it is almost impossible to ignore the pervasive iconicity present in signed language structure. Taub (2001) makes the first major advance since Charles Sanders Peirce in building a modern cognitive theory of the nature of iconicity, applicable equally to linguistic and semiotic systems in any language. Applying her theory to American Sign Language (ASL) poetry as well as to the structure of ASL grammar, Taub's chapter on Ella Mae Lenz's work provides new insights for both literary and linguistic theorists. Wilcox (2001) centers on the issues of productivity and creativity in the use of metaphor in ASL and analyzes the unique role of visual iconicity in the poetics of a visual-gestural language.

Hiraga's (1998, 2002, 2005) discussion of the metaphor-icon link in poetic texts provides a cognitive account of how iconicity and metaphor can be fused in grammar and language. Hiraga shows how two poems by George Herbert and Percy Bysshe Shelley differ in degree and types of iconicity. Herbert's poem exhibits imagic iconicity overtly, while Shelley's poem exhibits diagrammatic iconicity covertly. Hiraga's thesis is important because it suggests one definition of poetic language: foregrounding metaphor-icon links makes language poetic because form and meaning are closer together in literary than in nonliterary language in the sense of sharing and sometimes fusing sensory features. In this sense, Berntsen's (1999) discussion of the "embodied" nature of modernist poetry may be extended to all forms of poetic language, regardless of school or period.

Recent research on iconicity in literature (Nänny and Fischer 2003) suggests that the iconic relation between form and meaning may very well be a defining characteristic of literary texts. Ljungberg (2001) explores the way iconic patterning in Margaret Atwood's poetry and prose draws the reader into participatory relationship with the text. The icon's potential for abstraction (Ljungberg 2004) is beautifully captured in Moretti's (2005) study of maps, graphs, and trees in developing abstract models for literary theory.

5.3. Neurological Constraints and Affordances

A more general view of human cognition is taken in Danaher's (1998) study of metonymy in Gogol, where Danaher draws attention to the need for cognitive linguists to step beyond their conventional boundaries of showing how cognitive systems motivate and constrain linguistic structure to explore the fundamental principles which underlie human cognition itself. Benzon (2000) explains the ability of the neural self to animate imaginary characters in literary fictions. Zunshine (2003) provides insight into Virginia Woolf's style by exploring findings on autism and cognitive experiments on our ability to imagine representations of mental states. Richardson (2001) reexamines from a cognitive neuroscience perspective the extent to which literary Romanticism was historically deeply implicated with research and speculation on the brain.

Some cognitive psychologists have begun to explore aspects of literary form and affect from a conceptual-emotional perspective. In addition to Miall's and Kuiken's work mentioned in section 3.1, Getz and Lubart (2000) explain creative metaphor in terms of emotional information processing. Their Emotional Resonance Model of creative associative thought reveals how "feeling tones" or "emotional traces, acquired through self-involving experiences, play a key role in the production and interpretation of creative metaphors" (285). Getz and Lubart show that whereas the conventional metaphor *X is a burdock* meaning 'X is a prickly person' has little creative potential, Tolstoy's feelings about seeing a burdock one day created an emotional trace in his mind that became linked with his memories of the Chechen leader and thus provided the potential for creative metaphor in his story *Hadji Murat*. The role of emotion in memory (Modell 2003) is reflected in literary stylistics work, such as that of Brearton and Simpson (2001) on language, form, and memory in Michael Longley's poetry and McAlister's (2006) essay on trauma and identity in Helen Weinzweig's novel, *Basic Black with Pearls*. The importance of feelings in situational context in developing the dynamic schemas that serve to construct meaning can be seen in Brandt and Brandt's (2005b) elaboration of the original blending model.

6. FURTHER APPLICATIONS

This chapter has focused primarily on studies of literary texts inspired by the work of cognitive linguists as defined in this *Handbook*. Following is a brief survey of related research.

6.1. Multimedia Art Forms

Several researchers have begun to explore these cognitive processes in other art forms. Zbikowski (1999, 2002) applies blending to the analysis of early nineteenth-century art songs. A text-music blend creates a much richer structure than is provided by text or music alone. His blending analysis of different musical settings of Wilhelm Müller's "Trockne Blumen" shows how the music constrains our interpretation of the text to produce somewhat different descriptions of the miller's character and motivations. Forceville (1999) considers conceptual structural metaphor across verbal and pictorial domains in the novel, screenplay, and film versions of Ian McEwan's *The Comfort of Strangers*. He shows how both Pinter in his screenplay and Schrader in his film employ pictorial metaphors to support the underlying metaphor COLIN IS A CHILD, which describes the novel's adult protagonist. An even more integrative approach to multimedia dimensions is Narayan's (2001) research on comic books, which describes multiple embeddings in blended spaces where such narrative elements as focus and viewpoint are sometimes created jointly by images and "voice-overs."

Rohrer (2005) defines mimetic blending as a blend that self-referentially embeds itself into subsequent blends and shows how this iterative chaining serves as a literary device in Mario Vargas Llosa's novel *Aunt Julia and the Scriptwriter*, and its film version *Tune in Tomorrow*, to provide metafictional commentary on issues such as the ability of art to create fictive emotion. The use of grammatical voice in a dynamic discourse situation in a Tagalog video melodrama reveals the underlying scenarios that affect whether or not the agency of the participants will be profiled (Palmer 1998). Palmer's study suggests that cognitive analysis may reveal how emotional discourse in literature is governed by the social and power relationships that give rise to dramatic conflict and resolution.

6.2. Religious Texts

Tsur's (2003) latest contribution to his theory of Cognitive Poetics studies "how religious ideas are turned into verbal imitations of religious experience by poetic structure" (7). Ranging widely over metaphysical, baroque, and romantic poetry, Tsur explores all the many different aspects of human cognitive processes in a comprehensive and detailed manner to show how poets attempt to represent the ineffable.

One of these ways is of course through metaphor, and the articles in Boeve and Feyaerts's (1999) edition of *Metaphor and God-talk* provide a cognitive linguistic perspective on religious discourse. Other book-length studies include discussion of an extended metaphor describing the deity in the context of Hebrew cultural beliefs and practices (Sienstra 1993) and a study of the Bible through metaphor and translation (Feyaerts 2003). From another perspective, M. Ramey (1997) reviews the religious preconceptions of biblical exegesists that govern their interpretations of St. Paul's views on the body and the resurrection and suggests that a blending analysis of particular Pauline passages in the New Testament comes closer to Paul's eschatological and ethical stances. Van Hecke (2001) explores polysemy or homonymy from a cognitive perspective in a Biblical Hebrew verb and root to provide new insights into the way Hebrew functions. In 2002, a Royal Netherlands Academy of Arts and Sciences colloquium brought together scholars in Hebrew semantics, biblical studies, and Cognitive Linguistics to discuss "The Book of Job: Suffering and Cognition in Context," which resulted in the publication of several cognitive articles (van Wolde 2003). Noteworthy in that volume is Geeraerts's (2003) analysis because it not only argues for an ironic reading of the controversial speeches of God in the Book of Job, but suggests ways humor in a text can be characterized and described.

6.3. Humor

Humor in general has caught the attention of cognitive linguists as evidenced by the large number of proposals submitted to the Eighth International Cognitive Linguistics Conference (Brône, Feyaerts, and Veale 2006). The cognitive structure of jokes and their reception are explored in several cognitive studies (Coulson 2001;

Coulson and Kutas 2001; Goel and Dolan 2001). Feyaerts (1997) shows how metonymic extension patterns provide a constant renewal of the humorous expressive meanings in the conceptual domain of the German terms for stupidity.

Conceptual metaphor approaches reveal how writers create literary humor through manipulation of conventional metaphorical schemas (Sun 1994) or by juxtaposing literal and metaphorical meaning (Jurado 1994). Jurado, for example, shows how the Roman poet Horace exploits the orientation metaphors GOOD IS UP and BAD IS DOWN to argue that 'up' is 'good' as long as it does not literally go too far. Donald Barthelme's short stories are a good example of how the interplay between the literal and the metaphorical structures humor. In "Some of Us Had Been Threatening Our Friend Colby," Barthelme plays with what would happen if we actually responded literally to the notions of common metaphorical expressions like *going too far* and *I'll kill you for that*. This interplay between the metaphorical and the literal to create humor is further explored by Jurado and Gregoris (1995) in several examples from the Roman dramatist Plautus.

6.4. Dreams

Another aspect of written texts is the prolific and extensive work on dream research. With the development of new methodologies in neuroscientific studies of the brain, several researchers have begun to explore cognitive linguistic approaches to dream content analysis. Notable in this area is Domhoff's (2003) study that presents a new neurocognitive model of dreams using empirical research and including an extensive bibliography of related research.

6.5. Literary Translation

The task of translating one language into another poses a great challenge for translators of literary texts. Here, Cognitive Linguistics provides a special contribution. Tabakowska's (1993) study applies Cognitive Grammar principles to literary translation. Defining translation equivalence in terms of units larger than a single sentence, Tabakowska notes that these units overlap with Langacker's notions of image and scene construal. In a series of case studies, Tabakowska shows how Cognitive Linguistics contributes to the art and practice of translation by (i) providing systematic explanations for the ease or difficulty of translation; (ii) describing the techniques of style through "pairing individual dimensions of imagery with particular linguistic means" (1993: 130); and (iii) identifying the reasons in some cases for the impossibility of translation. She concedes that "it takes a poet to translate poetry" (133) but argues that Cognitive Linguistics can help provide better understanding of the images and techniques in poetic text.

Wójcik-Leese (2000) also employs Langacker's theory of scene construal to analyze the strategies of free verse composition and to provide principled reasons for preferring one translation over another. Focusing on free verse as a visual, rather than phonic, form, she applies Figure/Ground orientation to the structure of a Polish poem by Adam Zagajewski to show the importance of the formal elements of ordering and placement of words and phrases, along with delimiting punctuation. Translators, she suggests, ignore the significance of such formal patterning at their peril.

Understanding conceptual metaphoric networks might also help translators achieve greater equivalence in their translations, as Holm (2001) shows in analyzing two translations into Danish of the Spanish poet Garcia Lorca. Holm claims that Cognitive Linguistics provides a better possibility for assessing not just whether a given translation of a metaphor can be said to provide the "equivalent effect" in the target language or not, but what the "effect" consists in and by which criteria "equivalence" can be achieved.

Typological differences in languages affect narrative style with implications for literary translation. Slobin (1996) compared the verb-framed language of Spanish with the satellite-framed language of English in verbs of motion in ten novels. He discovered significant differences between the two languages with respect to rhetorical style, descriptions of movement, and relative allocation of attention to movement and setting. He notes that "Spanish speakers and writers have apparently developed a 'rhetorical set' that favors separate clauses for each segment of a complex motion event" (1996: 217). When he compared translations of the novels, he found that Spanish translators faced greater problems than their English counterparts did. In a subsequent paper, Slobin (1997) enlarged his study to include other satellite-framed (Germanic and Slavic) languages as opposed to verb-framed (Romance, Semitic, Turkic, and Japanese) languages, with similar results. He is careful to note, however, that cultural factors can modify the sharp distinctions of linguistic typology that he found in his studies. These studies serve as a model for Cognitive Linguistics approaches to literary translations.

7. THE POETIC CHALLENGE

Like cognitive linguistic approaches, Cognitive Poetics attempts to describe how poetic language and form is constrained and shaped by human cognitive processes. Tsur's theory of Cognitive Poetics is more inclusive of the cognitive sciences in general than studies in Cognitive Poetics that draw from linguistics and stylistics (Stockwell 2002; Gavins and Steen 2003) and therefore provides one way of evaluating the directions such studies should take.

Cureton, (1992, 1997, 2000, 2001) and Tsur (1992, 1998) both challenge Cognitive Linguistics' failure to attend to the formal aspects of literary works, such as the temporal dimension of meter and rhythm. Although differing in their theories of rhythm, both believe that rhythm is a general cognitive process and make significant claims about the formal and prosodic features of poetry that need to be explored in order to fully account for the role of rhythm in human cognition and language.

Conspicuous by its absence in this chapter is the role of phonology and phonetics in poetic discourse. In its infancy, Cognitive Phonology has not yet reached the stage of providing theoretical and methodological applications to literature. However, since literary iconicity often depends on sound patterning, as Alexander Pope showed more than two hundred years ago in his *Essay on Criticism*, cognitive studies of phonetic iconicity in poetic texts could contribute much to a cognitive theory of phonology.

Brain studies of connections between the emotive qualities of the senses and their aesthetic effects indicate additional potential areas for exploration of the affective dimension of poetic language. In his appraisal of what it would take to have a "cognitive science of poetics," Hogan (2003b) takes us back to a Sanskrit theory of poetry based on aesthetic response being the result of experiencing *rasa* (usually translated, according to Hogan, as 'sentiment' but akin to emotion, with no precise English language equivalent): "These rasas are evoked in a reader by words, sentences, topics, and so on, presented in a literary work. This is, of course, in part the result of literal meanings. But it is also, and crucially, a function of the clouds of nondenumerable, nonsubstitutable, nonpropositional suggestions that surround these texts" (2003b: 51).

The poetic challenge we face is to incorporate these formal and affective aspects—Langer's (1953, 1967) "form" and "feeling"—into an adequate, productive, and plausible theory of aesthetic creation and response. Until we do, we will not be able to claim we have fully accounted for human cognition in language.

8. CONCLUSION

Can stove and tower people communicate productively with each other, or are their approaches, as Burrows (2003) suggests, "at root divergent"? A symposium held at the Getty Museum in spring 2002 brought together cognitive scientists and art historians to discuss "Frames of Viewing: The Brain, Cognition, and Art." Stimulating and insightful as these discussions were, proceedings were marred by the contempt shown by some art historians for what they saw as the crude naïveté of the cognitive scientists in their approach to the arts. Certainly, the expertise in sophisticated analyses evidenced by art historians, musicologists, and literary critics should not be ignored. As the research discussed in this chapter reveals, researchers have been quick to see the advantages of applying cognitive linguistic research to the literary arts; unfortunately, there is no indication that the reverse is true. So far as I have been able to determine, with the exception of discussions of cognitive poetics and stylistics (Semino and Culpeper 2002), there have been no critical exchanges with existing literary theory, nor any indication that the Cognitive Linguistics approach is recognized within the field of literary studies or that literary studies can contribute to cognitive linguistics. This may change with the publication of results from the conference at the University of Helsinki in 2004 on "Cognition and Literary Interpretation in Practice" (Veivo and Polvinen 2005) and the results from the 2005 Cognitive Poetics Workshop at the University of Tel Aviv (http://www.tau.ac.il/~tsurxx/Workshop_folder/WorkShopSite.html), although I am not optimistic. It is sobering to note that the recent special issue on New Directions in Poetics of the *Publications of the Modern Language Association* includes no mention of Cognitive Poetics.

Despite this disheartening comment, the work reviewed in this chapter strikes a more positive note and is just a sample of research being accomplished. Researchers are already showing that Cognitive Linguistics can contribute to literary theory by providing insight into such matters as the changing status of literary appreciation through time, the evaluation of quality in both literary texts and criticism, the empirical testing of literary choices and judgments, and the development of a theory of literature. More broadly, the emerging field of Cognitive Poetics, which includes these approaches, has already shown that the literary mind is indeed fundamental to the processes of human cognition.

NOTES

I am grateful to all those who sent me information about their cognitive work in literary studies, without which I would not have been able to write this chapter. I also thank Eve Sweetser for her contributions, especially regarding ASL work, the editors of this volume, and Beth and Don Freeman for helpful suggestions on earlier drafts. Needless to say, all errors of commission and omission are mine.

1. A growing body of literature reflects the current interest of cognitive linguists and literary scholars in the ways Cognitive Linguistics can illumine literary texts and the challenges and opportunities literary texts raise for Cognitive Linguistics. Special issues of the *Journal of Pragmatics* (1995), *Poetics Today* (1999), *Language and Literature* (2002), and the *European Journal of English Studies* (2004) have focused on cognitive approaches to metaphor in literary texts; other special issues on cognitive approaches include *Journal of English Linguistics* (2002), *Style* (2002), *Poetics Today* (2002, 2003), and *Language and Literature* (2005, 2006); articles now regularly appear in such journals as *Language and Literature, Literary Semantics, Metaphor and Symbol, Mosaic, Poetics Today, Style*, and the *Journal of English Linguistics*. In addition to the citations mentioned in this chapter, there are books by Turner (1987), Spolsky (1993), Bex (2000), Semino and Culpeper (2002), Hogan (2003a), Popova, Freeman, and Freeman (forthcoming), Brône and Vandaele (2009); and three textbooks: Stockwell (2002), Gavins and Steen (2003), and Kövecses (2002). Associations that have sponsored special sessions and disciplinary areas featuring cognitive approaches to literary texts include the Poetics and Linguistic

Association (PALA), the Modern Language Association (MLA), the International Cognitive Linguistics Association (ICLA), the European Society for the Study of English (ESSE), the International Association of Literary Semantics (IALS), the International Association of Empirical Aesthetics (IAEA), the Western Humanities Alliance (WHA), and the University of North Texas annual Languaging conference. Several Web sites include information on cognitive approaches to literary texts, such as the home page of the coglit discussion group http://www.ucs.louisiana.edu/~cxr1086/coglit/, blending at http://www.wam.umd.edu/~mturn/WWW/blending.html, metaphor at http://www.let.vu.nl/pragglejaz, literature, cognition, and the brain at http://cogweb.english.ucsb.edu/Culture/WoF/eventsrtc.html, iconicity at http://home.hum.uva.nl/iconicity/, and the Cognitive Poetics Project at http://www.tau.ac.il/~tsurxx/index.html. Further links are available at these Web sites for additional related research.

REFERENCES

Benzon, William L. 2000. First person: Neuro-cognitive notes on the self in life and in fiction. *PsyArt: A Hyperlink Journal for the Psychological Study of the Arts*, article 000619. http://www.clas.ufl.edu/ipsa/journal/2000_benzon01.shtml (accessed November 29, 2005).

Berntsen, Dorthe. 1999. How is modernist poetry "embodied"? *Metaphor and Symbol* 14: 101–22.

Bertuol, Roberto. 2001. The *Square Circle* of Margaret Cavendish: The 17th-century conceptualization of mind by means of mathematics. *Language and Literature* 10: 21–39.

Bex, Tony, ed. 2000. *Contextualized stylistics: In honour of Peter Verdonk*. Amsterdam: Rodopi.

Bizup, Joseph, and Eugene R. Kintgen. 1993. The cognitive paradigm in literary studies. *College English* 55: 841–57.

Boeve, Lieven, and Kurt Feyaerts, eds. 1999. *Metaphor and God-talk*. Frankfurt am Main: Peter Lang Verlag.

Brandt, Per Aage. 2004. *Spaces, domains and meaning: Essays in cognitive semiotics*. Frankfurt am Main: Peter Lang Verlag.

Brandt, Line, and Per Aage Brandt. 2005a. Cognitive poetics and imagery. *European Journal of English Studies* 9: 117–30.

Brandt, Line, and Per Aage Brandt. 2005b. Making sense of a blend: A cognitive-semiotic approach to metaphor. *Annual Review of Cognitive Linguistics* 3: 216–49.

Brearton, Fran, and Paul Simpson. 2001. "Deciphering otter prints": Language, form and memory in Michael Longley's poetry. *The honest Ulsterman: Special feature on Michael Longley* 110: 17–31.

Brône, Geert, Kurt Feyaerts, and Tony Veale, eds. 2006. Cognitive linguistic approaches to humor. Special issue of *Humor, International Journal of Humor Research* 19.3.

Brône, Geert, and Jeroen Vandaele, eds. 2009. *Cognitive poetics: Goals, gains and gaps*. Berlin: Mouton de Gruyter.

Burrows, Colin. 2003. Friskes, skips and jumps. Review of *Michel de Montaigne: Accidental philosopher*, by Anne Hartle. *London Review of Books* 25: 21–22.

Coulson, Seana. 2001. *Semantic leaps: Frame-shifting and conceptual blending in meaning construction*. Cambridge: Cambridge University Press.

Coulson, Seana. 2003. Reasoning and rhetoric: Conceptual blending in political and religious rhetoric. In Elzbieta H. Oleksy and Barbara Lewandowska-Tomaszczyk, eds., *Research and scholarship in integration processes* 59–88. Lódz, Poland: Lodz University Press.

Coulson, Seana, and M. Kutas. 2001. Getting it: Human event-related brain response to jokes in good and poor comprehenders. *Neuroscience Letters* 316: 71–74.

Crane, Mary Thomas. 2000. *Shakespeare's brain: Reading with cognitive theory.* Princeton, NJ: Princeton University Press.

Crane, Mary Thomas, and Alan Richardson. 1999. Literary studies and cognitive science: Toward a new interdisciplinarity. *Mosaic* 32: 123–40.

Csábi, Szilvia. 2000. The war of independence: A cognitive linguistic analysis of Thomas Paine's *Common Sense.* MA thesis, Eötvös Loránd University, Budapest.

Csábi, Szilvia. 2001. The concept of America in the Puritan mind. *Language and Literature* 19: 195–209.

Čulić, Zjena. 2001. A cognitive approach to innovative metaphors derived from root analogies. *Studia Romanica et Anglica Zagrabiensia* 45/46: 25–63.

Cureton, Richard D. 1992. *Rhythmic phrasing in English verse.* London: Longman.

Cureton, Richard D. 1997. Linguistics, stylistics, and poetics. *Language and Literature* 22: 1–43.

Cureton, Richard D. 2000. Jakobson revisited: Poetics, subjectivity, and temporality. *Journal of English Linguistics* 28: 354–92.

Cureton, Richard D. 2001. Telling time: Toward a temporal poetics. Odense American Studies International Series, no. 48. Odense: Center for American Studies, University of Southern Denmark.

Danaher, David S. 1998. Metonymy in cognition, literature, and phenomenology: A case study. Paper presented at the Fourth Conference on Conceptual Structure, Discourse, and Language (CSDL-4), Atlanta, GA, October 10–12.

Danaher, David S. 2003a. A cognitive approach to metaphor in prose: Truth and falsehood in Leo Tolstoy's 'The Death of Ivan Il'ich.' *Poetics Today* 24: 439–69.

Danaher, David S. 2003b. Conceptual metaphors for the domains TRUTH and FALSEHOOD in Russian and the image of the black sack in Tolstoi's "The Death of Ivan Il'ich." In Robert A. Maguire and Alan Timberlake, eds., *American contributions to the thirteenth international congress of Slavists*, vol.2, Literature 61–75. Bloomington, IN: Slavica.

De Geest, Dirk, and Hendrik van Gorp. 1999. Literary genres from a systemic-functionalist perspective. *European Journal of English Studies* 3: 33–50.

Domhoff, G. William. 2003. *The scientific study of dreams: Neural networks, cognitive development, and content analysis.* Washington, DC: American Psychological Association.

Duchan, J. F., Gail A. Bruder, and Lynne E. Hewitt, eds. 1995. *Deixis in narrative: A cognitive science perspective.* Hillsdale, NJ: Lawrence Erlbaum.

Fauconnier, Gilles, and Mark Turner. 2002. *The way we think: Conceptual blending and the mind's hidden complexities.* New York: Basic Books.

Fernandes, Martine M. 2002. Les écrivaines françaises en liberté: Une analyse cognitive de l'hybridité dans le roman postcolonial féminin. PhD dissertation, University of California at Berkeley and Paris IV University.

Feyaerts, Kurt. 1997. Die Bedeutung der Metonymie als als konzeptuelles Strukturprinzip: Eine kognitiv-semantische Analyse deutscher Dummheitsausdrücke, PhD dissertation, Catholic University of Leuven, Belgium.

Feyaerts, Kurt, ed. 2003. *The Bible through metaphor and translation*. Frankfurt am Main: Peter Lang Verlag.

Forceville, Charles. 1999. The metaphor "COLIN IS A CHILD" in Ian McEwan's, Harold Pinter's, and Paul Schrader's *The Comfort of Strangers*. *Metaphor and Symbol* 14: 179–98.

Freeman, Donald C. 1993. 'According to my bond': *King Lear* and re-cognition. *Language and Literature* 2: 1–18.

Freeman, Donald C. 1998. 'Catch[ing] the nearest way': *Macbeth* and cognitive metaphor. In Jonathan Culpeper, Mick Short, and Peter Verdonk, eds. *Exploring the language of drama: From text to context* 96–111. London: Longman.

Freeman, Donald C. 1999. 'The rack dislimns': Schema and rhetorical pattern in *Antony and Cleopatra*. *Poetics Today* 20: 443–60.

Freeman, Margaret H. 1995. Metaphor making meaning: Dickinson's conceptual universe. *Journal of Pragmatics* 24: 643–66.

Freeman, Margaret H. 1997. Grounded spaces: Deictic-self anaphors in the poetry of Emily Dickinson. *Language and Literature* 6: 7–28.

Freeman, Margaret H. 2000. Poetry and the scope of metaphor: Toward a theory of cognitive poetics. In Antonio Barcelona, ed., *Metaphor and metonymy at the crossroads: A cognitive perspective* 253–81. Berlin: Mouton de Gruyter.

Freeman, Margaret H. 2002a. Cognitive mapping in literary analysis. *Style* 36: 466–83.

Freeman, Margaret H. 2002b. Momentary stays, exploding forces: A cognitive linguistic approach to the poetics of Emily Dickinson and Robert Frost. *Journal of English Linguistics* 30: 73–90.

Fuchs, Catherine. 1994. The challenges of continuity for a linguistic approach to semantics. In Catherine Fuchs and Bernard Victorri, eds., *Continuity in linguistic semantics* 93–107. Amsterdam: John Benjamins.

Gavins, Joanna, and Gerard J. Steen, eds. 2003. *Cognitive poetics in practice*. London: Routledge.

Geeraerts, Dirk. 1999. Hundred years of lexical semantics. In Mario Vilela and Fatima Silva Porto, eds., *Actas do 1° encontro internacional de linguística cognitiva* 123–54. Porto, Portugal: Faculdade de Letras da Universidade do Porto. (Also published in *Versus: Quaderni di studi semiotici* 88/89 [2001]: 63–87)

Geeraerts, Dirk. 2003. Caught in a web of irony: Job and his embarrassed God. In Ellen van Wolde, ed., *Job 28: Cognition in context* 37–55. Leiden: Brill.

Getz, Isaac, and Todd I. Lubart. 2000. An emotional-experiential perspective on creative symbolic-metaphorical processes. *Consciousness and Emotion* 1: 89–118.

Gibbs, Raymond W., Jr. 2003. Prototypes in dynamic reading construal. In Joanna Gavins and Gerard J. Steen, eds., *Cognitive Poetics in practice* 27–40. London: Routledge.

Gibbs, Raymond W., Jr., and Jody Bogdonovich. 1999. Mental imagery in interpreting poetic metaphor. *Metaphor and Symbol* 14: 37–44.

Gibbs, Raymond W., Jr., and Lydia R. Kearney. 1994. When parting is such sweet sorrow: The comprehension and appreciation of oxymora. *Journal of Psycholinguistic Research* 23: 75–89.

Głaz, Adam. 2002. *The dynamics of meaning: Explorations in the conceptual domain of* EARTH. Lublin, Poland: Maria Curie-Sklodowska University Press.

Goel, Vinod, and Ray Dolan. 2001. The functional anatomy of humor: Segregating cognitive and affective components. *Nature Neuroscience* 4: 237–38.

Hamilton, Craig. 2000. Cognitive poetics and H. D. *The Journal of Imagism* 5: 3–9.

Harding, Jennifer. 2001. "We could have stayed in Paris": A cognitive analysis of counterfactual spaces in narrative discourse. Paper presented at the 7th International
  Cognitive Linguistics Conference, Santa Barbara, CA, July 22–27.

Hart, Elizabeth F. 1995. Cognitive Linguistics: The experiential dynamics of metaphor.
  Mosaic 28: 1–23.

Herman, Vimala. 1999. Deictic projection and conceptual blending in epistolarity. *Poetics
  Today* 20: 523–41.

Hiraga, Masako. 1998. Metaphor-icon link in poetic texts: A cognitive approach to iconicity. *Journal of the University of the Air* 16: 95–123.

Hiraga, Masako. 1999a. "Blending" and an interpretation of haiku: A cognitive approach.
  Poetics Today 20: 461–81.

Hiraga, Masako. 1999b. Rough sea and the milky way: 'Blending' in a haiku text. In
  Chrystopher L. Nehaniv, ed., *Computation for metaphors, analogy and agents* 27–36.
  Berlin: Springer Verlag.

Hiraga, Masako. 2002. The interplay of metaphor and iconicity: A cognitive approach to
  poetic texts. *Theoria et Historia Scientiarum: International Journal for Interdisciplinary
  Studies* 6: 179–244.

Hiraga, Masako. 2005. *Metaphor and iconicity: A cognitive approach to analyzing texts.*
  Houndmills, UK: Macmillan.

Hogan, Patrick Colm. 2003a. *Cognitive science, literature, and the arts.* New York:
  Routledge.

Hogan, Patrick Holm. 2003b. *The mind and its stories: Narrative universals and human
  emotion.* Cambridge: Cambridge University Press.

Holland, Norman. 1988. *The brain of Robert Frost: A cognitive approach to literature.*
  London: Routledge.

Holm, Nanna. 2001. Metaphor and translation: A comparative study of two translations
  into Danish of Federico García Lorca's "Poeta en Nueva York." MA thesis, University
  of Aarhus, Denmark.

Irandoust, Hengameh. 1999. The past participle: Moving across conceptual spaces. *Cognitive Linguistics* 10: 279–302.

Jackson, Tony. 2000. Questioning interdisciplinarity: Cognitive science, evolutionary
  psychology, and literary criticism. *Poetics Today* 21: 319–47.

Jahn, Manfred. 1997. Frames, preferences, and the reading of third-person narratives:
  Towards a cognitive narratology. *Poetics Today* 18: 441–68.

Jurado, Francisco García. 1994. El vestido ascendente y el vestido descendente: Un aspecto
  significato de la mentalidad indumentaria en la obra de Horacio. In Rosario Cortés
  Tovar and José Carlos Fernández Corte, eds., *Bimilenario de Horacio* 295–98. Salamanca, Spain: Universidad do Salamanca.

Jurado, Francisco García, and Rosario López Gregoris. 1995. Las metáforas de la vida
  cotidiana en el lenguaje plautino como procedimiento de caracterización de los pe-
  sonajes. *Studi Italiani di filología clásica*, Terza Serie 13: 233–45.

Kardela, Anna, and Henryk Kardela. 2002. The "unreliable narrator": A cognitive linguistic
  analysis of truth in Kazuo Ishiguro's *The Remains of the Day.* In Joanna Burzynska and
  D. Stanulewicz, eds., *Beyond philology* 2: 121–45. Gdańsk, Poland: Gdańsk University
  Press.

Kedra-Kardela, Anna, and Henryk Kardela. 2000. Subjectivity in Elizabeth Bowen's short
  stories: A cognitive linguistics approach. In Sven-Johan Spånberg, Henryk Kardela,
  and Gerald Porter, eds., *The evidence of literature: Interrogating texts in English studies,*
  331–48. Lublin, Poland: Marie Curie-Sklodowska University.

Kimmel, Michael. 2001. Penetrating into the *Heart of Darkness*: An image-schematic plot-gene and its relation to the Victorian self-schema. *View[z]: Vienna English Working Papers* 10: 7–33.

Kittay, Eva Feder. 1987. *Metaphor: Its cognitive force and linguistic structure*. Oxford: Clarendon Press.

Kövecses, Zoltán. 1994. Tocqueville's passionate "beast": A linguistic analysis of the concept of American democracy. *Metaphor and Symbolic Activity* 9: 113–33.

Kövecses, Zoltán. 2002. *Metaphor: A practical introduction*. Oxford: Oxford University Press.

Lakoff, George, and Mark Johnson. 1980. *Metaphors we live by*. Chicago: University of Chicago Press.

Lakoff, George, and Mark Johnson. 1998. *Philosophy in the flesh: The embodied mind and its challenge to Western thought*. Chicago: University of Chicago Press.

Lakoff, George, and Mark Turner. 1989. *More than cool reason: A field guide to poetic metaphor*. Chicago: University of Chicago Press.

Langacker, Ronald W. 1987. *Foundations of cognitive grammar*. Vol. 1, *Theoretical prerequisites*. Stanford, CA: Stanford University Press.

Langacker, Ronald W. 1991. *Foundations of cognitive grammar*. Vol. 2, *Descriptive application*. Stanford, CA: Stanford University Press.

Langer, Susanne K. 1953. *Feeling and form: A theory of art*. New York: Charles Scribner's.

Langer, Susanne K. 1967. *Mind: An essay on human feeling*. Baltimore: Johns Hopkins Press.

Ljungberg, Christina. 2001. Iconic dimensions in Margaret Atwood's poetry and prose. In Max Nänny and Olga Fischer, eds., *The motivated sign* 351–66. Amsterdam: John Benjamins.

Ljungberg, Christina. 2004. Between 'reality' and representation: On the diagrammatic use of photographs and maps in fiction. *Visio* 9: 67–78. (Special issue on 'Peirce and the Question of Representation,' ed. Jean Fisette)

Matthew, David A. 2003. Bodies of blended times: Time compression figures and the imagination of the future. PhD dissertation, University of Florida.

McAlister, Sean. 2006. The explosive devices of memory: Trauma and the construction of identity in narrative. *Language and Literature* 15: 91–106. (Special issue on 'Blending,' ed. Barbara Dancygier)

McGann, Jerome. 1991. *The textual condition*. Princeton, NJ: Princeton University Press.

McGrath, Barbara J. N.d. Reconceptualizing poetic and cultural landscapes: Evan Boland's and Adrienne Rich's revisionist uses of metaphor. Manuscript.

Meyer, Jim. 1997. What is literature?: A definition based on prototypes. *Work papers of the Summer Institute of Linguistics, University of North Dakota Session* 41. http://www.und.edu/dept/linguistics/wp/1997.htm (accessed December 15, 2003).

Miall, David S. 1989. Beyond the schema given: Affective comprehension of literary narratives. *Cognition and Emotion* 3: 55–78.

Miall, David S. 2000. On the necessity of empirical studies of literary reading. *Frame. Utrecht Journal of Literary Theory* 14: 43–59.

Miall, David S., and Don Kuiken. 2001. Reader response: Empirical research on literary reading. http://www.ualberta.ca/~dmiall/reading/index.htm (accessed December 15, 2003).

Modell, Arnold H. 2003. *Imagination and the meaningful brain*. Cambridge, MA: MIT Press.

Moretti, Franco. 2005. *Graphs, maps, trees: Abstract models for a literary theory*. London: Verso.

Nänny, Max, and Olga Fischer. 2003. *Iconicity in language and literature.* 4 vols. Amsterdam: John Benjamins.

Narayan, Shweta. 2001. Conceptual integration in multimodal narratives. Paper presented at the 7th International Cognitive Linguistics Conference, Santa Barbara, CA, July 22–27.

Oakley, Todd V. 1998. Conceptual blending, narrative discourse, and rhetoric. *Cognitive Linguistics* 9: 320–60.

Palmer, Gary B. 1998. *Sana'y Maulit Muli:* Emotion, denial of agency, and grammatical voice in a Tagalog video melodrama. Paper presented to the Annual Meeting of the American Anthropological Association, Philadelphia, December 2–8, 1998, and to the Linguistics Colloquium, University of the Philippines, Diliman Campus, February 11, 1999.

Peña Cervel, M. Sandra. 1997–98. Pride and Prejudice: A cognitive analysis. *Cuadernos de Investigation Filologica* 23–24: 233–55.

Popova, Yanna. 2002. "The fool sees with his nose": Metaphoric mappings in the sense of smell in Patrick Suskind's *Perfume. Language and Literature* 12: 135–51.

Popova, Yanna, Donald C. Freeman, and Margaret H. Freeman, eds. Forthcoming. *Literature and the embodied mind.* Berlin: Mouton de Gruyter.

Ramey, Lauri. 1996. The poetics of resistance: A critical study of Michael Palmer. PhD dissertation, University of Chicago.

Ramey, Lauri. 2002. The theology of the lyric tradition in African American spirituals. *Journal of the American Academy of Religion* 70: 347–63.

Ramey, Martin. 1997. The problem of the body: The conflict between soteriology and ethics in Paul. PhD dissertation, Chicago Theological Seminary.

Ravid, Dorit, and David Hanauer. 1998. A prototype theory of rhyme: Evidence from Hebrew. *Cognitive Linguistics* 9: 79–106.

Richardson, Alan. 2001. *British romanticism and the science of the mind.* Cambridge: Cambridge University Press.

Rohrer, Tim. 2005. Mimesis, artistic inspiration and the blends we live by. *Journal of Pragmatics* 37: 1686–1716.

Semino, Elena, and Jonathan Culpeper, eds. 2002. *Cognitive stylistics: Language and cognition in text analysis.* Amsterdam: John Benjamins.

Shen, Yeshavahu. 1997. Cognitive constraints on poetic figures. *Cognitive Linguistics* 8: 33–71.

Shen, Yeshayahu, and Michael Cohen. 1998. How come silence is sweet but sweetness is not silent: A cognitive account of directionality in poetic synaesthesia. *Language and Literature* 7: 123–40.

Sienstra, Nelly. 1993. *YHWH is the husband of his people.* Kampen, Netherlands: Kok Pharos.

Sinding, Michael. 2002. Assembling spaces: The conceptual structure of allegory. *Style* 36: 503–23. (Special issue on 'Cognitive Approaches to Figurative Language')

Sinding, Michael. 2005. *Genera mixta:* Conceptual blending and mixed genres in *Ulysses. New Literary History* 36: 589–619.

Slobin, Dan I. 1996. Two ways to travel: Verbs of motion in English and Spanish. In Masayoshi Shibatani and Sandra A. Thompson, eds., *Grammatical constructions: Their form and meaning* 195–219. Oxford: Clarendon Press.

Slobin, Dan I. 1997. Mind, code, and text. In Joan L. Bybee, John Haiman, and Sandra A. Thompson, eds., *Essays on language function and language type* 437–67. Amsterdam: John Benjamins.

Spolsky, Eleanor. 1993. *Gaps in nature: Literary interpretation and the modular mind.* Albany: State University of New York Press.

Steen, Francis. 2002. The politics of love: Propaganda and structural learning in Aphra Behn's love-letters between a nobleman and his sister. *Poetics Today* 23: 91–122.

Steen, Gerard J. 1994. *Understanding metaphor in literature.* London: Longman.

Steen, Gerard J. 1999a. From linguistic to conceptual metaphor in five steps. In Raymond W. Gibbs, Jr., and Gerard J. Steen, eds., *Metaphor in cognitive linguistics* 55–77. Amsterdam: John Benjamins.

Steen, Gerard J. 1999b. Genres of discourse and the definition of literature. *Discourse Processes* 28: 109–20.

Steen, Gerard J. 2001a. A reliable procedure for metaphor identification. In John Barnden, Mark Lee, and Katja Markert, eds., *Proceedings of the workshop on corpus-based and processing approaches to figurative language—held in conjunction with Corpus Linguistics 2001* 67–75. Lancaster, UK: University Centre for Computer Corpus Research on Language.

Steen, Gerard J. 2001b. A rhetoric of metaphor: Conceptual and linguistic metaphor and the psychology of literature. In Dick Schram and Gerard J. Steen, eds., *The psychology and sociology of literature: In honor of Elrud Ibsch* 145–63. Amsterdam: John Benjamins.

Sternberg, Meir. 2003a. Universals of narrative and their cognitivist fortunes (I). *Poetics Today* 24: 297–395.

Sternberg, Meir. 2003b. Universals of narrative and their cognitivist fortunes (II) *Poetics Today* 24: 517–638. (Special issue on 'The Cognitive Turn? A Debate on Interdisciplinarity')

Stockwell, Peter. 2002. *Cognitive poetics: An introduction.* London: Routledge.

Strack, Daniel C. 2000. Deliver us from *nada*: Hemingway's hidden agenda in *For Whom the Bell Tolls. Kitakyushu University Faculty of Humanities Journal* 59: 97–127.

Sun, Douglas. 1994. Thurber's fables for our time: A case study in satirical use of the great chain metaphor. *Studies in American Humor* 3: 51–61.

Sweetser, Eve. 2004. "The suburbs of your good pleasure": Cognition, culture, and the bases of metaphoric structure. In Graham Bradshaw, Tom Bishop, and Mark Turner, eds., *Shakespeare International Yearbook.* Aldershot, UK: Ashgate.

Sweetser, Eve. 2006. Whose rhyme is whose reason? Sound and sense in *Cyrano de Bergérac. Language and Literature* 15: 29–54. (Special issue on 'Blending,' ed. Barbara Dancygier)

Tabakowska, Elzbieta. 1993. *Cognitive linguistics and poetics of translation.* Tübingen, Germany: Gunter Narr Verlag.

Talmy, Leonard. 2000. *Toward a cognitive semantics.* Vol. 2, *Typology and process in concept structuring.* Cambridge, MA: MIT Press.

Taub, Sarah. 2001. *Language from the body: Iconicity and metaphor in American Sign Language.* Cambridge: Cambridge University Press.

Tobin, Vera. 2006. Ways of reading Sherlock Holmes: The entrenchment of discourse blends. *Language and Literature* 15: 73–90. (Special issue on 'Blending,' ed. Barbara Dancygier)

Todd, Zazie, and David D. Clarke. 2001. Interpretations of metaphor and simile in poetry. Paper presented at the Society for Text and Discourse Conference, Santa Barbara, July 13–14.

Tsur, Reuven. 1992. *Toward a theory of cognitive poetics.* Amsterdam: North Holland.

Tsur, Reuven. 1998. *Poetic rhythm—structure and performance: An empirical study in cognitive poetics.* Frankfurt am Main: Peter Lang Verlag.

Tsur, Reuven. 2003. *On the shore of nothingness: A study in cognitive poetics*. Exeter, UK: Imprint Academic.

Turner, Mark. 1987. *Death is the mother of beauty: Mind, metaphor, criticism*. Chicago: University of Chicago Press.

Turner, Mark. 1991. *Reading minds: The study of English in the age of cognitive science*. Princeton, NJ: Princeton University Press.

Turner, Mark. 1996. *The literary mind*. New York: Oxford University Press.

Van Hecke, Pierre. 2001. Polysemy or homonymy in the root(s) r'h in Biblical Hebrew: A cognitive-linguistic approach. *Zeitschrift für Althebraistik* 14: 50–67.

Van Peer, Willie, and Seymour Chatman, eds. 2001. *New perspectives on narrative perspective*. Albany: State University of New York Press.

van Wolde, Ellen, ed. 2003. *Job 28: Cognition in context*. Leiden, Netherlands: Brill.

Veivo, Harri, and Merja Plovinen, eds. 2005. *Cognition and literary interpretation in practice*. Helsinki: University of Helsinki Press.

Werth, Paul. 1994. Extended metaphor: A text-world account. *Language and Literature* 3: 79–103.

Wilcox, Phyllis P. 2001. *Metaphor in American Sign Language*. Washington, DC: Gallaudet University Press.

Wójcik-Leese, Elzbieta. 2000. Salient ordering of free verse and its translation. *Language and Literature* 9: 170–81.

Wye, Margaret E. 1998. *Jane Austen's Emma: Embodied metaphor as a cognitive construct*. Lewiston, NY: Edwin Mellen Press.

Zbikowski, Lawrence. 1999. The blossoms of "Trockne Blumen": Music and text in the early nineteenth century. *Music Analysis* 18: 307–45.

Zbikowski, Lawrence. 2002. *Conceptualizing music: Cognitive structure, theory, and analysis*. Oxford: Oxford University Press.

Zunshine, Lisa. 2003. Theory of mind and experimental representations of fictional consciousness. *Narrative* 11: 270–91.

CHAPTER 46

COGNITIVE LINGUISTICS AND CULTURAL STUDIES

RENÉ DIRVEN,
HANS-GEORG WOLF, AND
FRANK POLZENHAGEN

1. INTRODUCTION: THE RELATION BETWEEN THOUGHT, LANGUAGE, AND CULTURE

Language and cultural theory, as developed in pre–cognitive linguistics and anthropology, has a long tradition, beginning with Humboldt and drastically reshaped by Saussure. In the nineteenth-century Humboldtian tradition, language, thought/ *Geist*, and culture form an inseparable unity. Humboldt assumes the relationship between thought and language to be bidirectional rather than unidirectional. In language, thought/*Geist* is articulated; yet language at the same time gives shape to thought. Likewise, the Humboldtian view assumes mutual correspondences between culture and language: to Humboldt, language is characteristic of the cultural will of a people and reincorporates the "real world" into the property of thought/ *Geist*. In strong contrast to this unified view of cognition, language, and culture, Saussure, the father of modern linguistics, sees language not as a mere form of thought, but as a self-contained system with its own organization and classification of "content." In other words, for Saussure, semantics is an autonomous realm at the interface between phonological/grammatical/cultural form, on the one hand, and cognition, on the other. In fact, this view meant the beginning of a split between semantics as part of the language faculty and other cognitive faculties. Saussure's view became known as structural semantics, with its complete separation of language and thought. The opposition between the Humboldtian and the Saussurean views of semantics can be summarized as in figure 46.1—which is based, in strongly adapted form, on Bickel (2000: 162)—emphasizing the holistic nature of Humboldt's approach.

In the 1940s and later, Humboldt's ideas received a new impetus in Whorf's relativity hypothesis (see, e.g., Joseph 1996; Lee 1996; Koerner 2000), which sets up links between "habitual thought" in a given society, the cultural form of aspects of behavior, and semantics. This cognitive reorientation in linguistic anthropology led to a shift from the then dominant Saussurean paradigm toward a more sophisticated reinterpretation of the Humboldtian model, as represented in figure 46.1a. Although Cognitive Linguistics generally does not subscribe to linguistic relativity, it clearly sticks with the Humboldtian conception of the relation between thought, language, and culture, which is laid down in a number of cognitive models, or rather cultural models, as we will see.

This chapter is organized as follows: section 2 discusses various cultural models and their mental locus; section 3 opposes universal and culture-specific aspects in cultural models; section 4 opposes two models of deixis: corporeal deixis and environmental deixis; and finally, section 5 focuses on cultural variation and exemplifies how radically different cultural models can be created in one language, that is, English as a world language.

2. Various Cultural Models

2.1. Cultural Models and Their Mental Locus

A culture's collective wisdom and experience is laid down in knowledge structures, variously called cognitive models, cultural models, folk models, or folk theories. The study of cultural models as "cognitive schemas that are intersubjectively shared by a social group" (D'Andrade 1987: 112) is the predestined meeting ground of cognitive anthropologists and (cognitive) linguists. For the former, language data are among the best available clues for the reconstruction of patterns of cultural knowledge; for the latter, these models promise to provide an explanatory basis of linguistic usage (see Quinn and Holland 1987: 24). This common interest has guided a rich interdisciplinary exchange. An early manifestation thereof is Holland

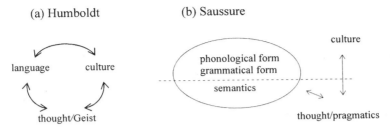

(a) Humboldt   (b) Saussure

language   culture

thought/Geist

culture

phonological form
grammatical form

semantics

thought/pragmatics

Figure 46.1. Humboldtian compared to Saussurean semantics

and Quinn's (1987) influential volume *Cultural Models in Language and Thought*. The articles collected in this book readily reflect the various approaches to the field and some of the major theoretical controversies. One such controversy concerns the locus of culture. Significantly, the book's original title was to be "Folk Models," a term which expresses the assumption that a community's cultural wisdom resides in the community's collective mind rather than in the minds of the individual members (see Keesing 1987: 370 for criticism of this label and Gibbs 1999 for further discussion). The cognitivist position, by contrast, holds that "individual minds are the primary locus of linguistic and cultural knowledge" (Langacker 1994: 26), and from this perspective cultural patterns are largely subsumed under the general notion of "cognitive models." The term "cultural model" intends to transcend this problem in that it embraces the notion of "distributed representation," which allows for the explanation of uneven and partially shared distribution of cultural schemas in individuals and across members of a given group (see Sharifian 2003). A second controversy concerns the composition of cultural models and the connection to closely related terms developed in Cognitive Linguistics, such as schema, frame, scenario, and script (see Palmer 1996: chapter 5 for a review of these notions; see also Palmer, this volume, chapter 39). Here, a particularly debatable issue is the role of conceptual metaphors within a cultural model. For some authors (e.g., Quinn 1987, 1991, 1997), they are merely culture-based means to explain aspects of experience; for others (e.g., Lakoff and Kövecses 1987), they constitute these models. Both controversies are instantiated in the following sections.

2.2. Americans' Cultural Model of Marriage

For the reconstruction of a cultural model, cognitive anthropologists set up a procedure of interviewing and language data analysis, strongly based on metaphor. For her cultural model of marriage, Quinn (1987) interviewed husbands and wives in eleven marriages (fifteen hours of tape recording) and applied the techniques of key words, metaphor grouping, and reasoning analysis. The most frequent key words were *commitment, love,* and *fulfillment*. She identified the following eight templates, in her terminology "proposition-schemas," around which the metaphors used to explicate these schemas are grouped:

1. MARRIAGE IS ENDURING
2. MARRIAGE IS MUTUALLY BENEFICIAL
3. MARRIAGE IS UNKNOWN AT THE OUTSET
4. MARRIAGE IS DIFFICULT
5. MARRIAGE IS EFFORTFUL
6. MARRIAGE IS JOINT
7. MARRIAGE MAY SUCCEED OR FAIL
8. MARRIAGE IS RISKY

Some of these metaphor clusters, or their entailments, are reflected in the following interview fragment (numbers refer to one of the corresponding items in the above list):

> That we have changed so much (3) and that we have been able to work (5) through so many basic struggles (4) in our marriage and be at a place now where we trust each other (6), we love each other (6), we like each other (6), we appreciate each other (2), and feel pretty confident (2) about being able to continue that way (1) and to continue (1) working (5) any other stuff that comes up (3). Just seems pretty amazing to me. It could have gone in so many different directions . . . and that it didn't is incredible (8). But I think both of us take a whole lot of credit (5) for the direction it went (2), that we worked at it (5) really hard (4). (Quinn 1987: 176)

The model of marriage emerging is that marriage is on the positive side a joint enterprise, enduring, and mutually beneficial, but on the negative side, an unknown affair at the outset, difficult to cope with, requiring lots of efforts to make it go, hence risky, and bound either to succeed or to fail.

Importantly, Quinn (1987, 1991, 1997) regards the above proposition-schemas as primary and the various conceptual metaphors (like MARRIAGE IS A JOURNEY, MARRIAGE IS A JOINT ENTERPRISE) grouped around them as derived. She thus assumes that cultural models are constituted by nonmetaphorical "cultural postulates," a view which is at odds with Lakoff and Kövecses's (1987) claim that conceptual metaphors hold the constitutive role. This issue has received much attention in subsequent discussions of cultural models. In a critical review of Quinn's findings, Gibbs (1994: 197–207), for instance, holds that the marriage model may well be structured by a set of frequently occurring metaphorical models alone, based on salient source domains like JOURNEY and PRODUCT. Kövecses (1999) proposes a further reanalysis of the marriage model in terms of the constitutive metaphor view. He argues that the model of marriage cannot be detached from the concept of love, a point also observed by Quinn but not pursued in her analysis. Crucially, according to Kövecses, the concept of love is centered around the metaphorically conceptualized notion 'unity of two persons', and this structure is mapped to the model of marriage. Many of Quinn's data are indeed expressions of the metaphor MARRIAGE IS THE PHYSICAL UNITY OF TWO COMPLEMENTARY PARTS, which is but a special instance of the NONPHYSICAL UNITY IS PHYSICAL UNITY metaphor underlying the conceptualization of various social, legal, psychological, political, and other unities, and the concept of love in particular. It is against the background of the UNITY metaphor that marriage is expected to be shared, beneficial, lasting, and so on. Kövecses thus concludes that the proposition-schemas identified by Quinn are, in fact, themselves derived from basic conceptual metaphors (but see Kövecses 2005). He provides this treatment of the marriage model in a general discussion of the relation between conceptual metaphors and cultural models.

Many descriptions of other cultural models have become available now. For example, Kövecses (1995a) developed the cultural model of American friendship. The Holland and Quinn (1987) volume itself contains a range of cultural models, for instance, Sweetser (1987) on *lie*, Kay (1987) on language, Holland and Skinner (1987) on gender types, D'Andrade (1987) on the mind, Lakoff and Kövecses (1987) on the emotion of anger, and, working from different assumptions and a different theoretical background, Lutz (1987) on Ifaluk emotion theory. The latter will be discussed now in more detail.

2.3. Ifaluk Emotion Theory: Action Schema for Fago 'Love'

Seemingly in line with D'Andrade or Quinn, Lutz (1987) understands the term *emotion theory* as a folk theory reflecting the cultural knowledge or wisdom that underlies the behavior in the domain of emotional experiences of a given cultural group, here the people on the Ifaluk atoll in the Micronesian islands. But instead of following a one-way route from language to underlying cognitive models, as D'Andrade or Quinn do, Lutz engages upon fieldwork to study these people's emotional behavior as well as their use of emotional terms. Their linguistic use is thus seen as part of an action schema triggering other emotion events in order to reach certain goals—this "action" aspect is not totally absent from Quinn's analysis (see section 2.2).

It is worth mentioning that Lutz represents the tradition of "social constructionism," which claims that all emotions are cultural constructs built up by a given social group (for further discussion, see Kövecses and Palmer 1999: 247–49). This entails that emotions, like many other cognitive categories, are not universal, and certainly not innate, but that they are learned by the members of a social group in their interaction with their caregivers. Thus, for example, the Ifaluk people share with other cultures the category LOVE (small capitals here designate a concept which is the abstract summary of the meanings of partly overlapping terms in various cultures). Their concept *fago* covers the emotional range of 'compassion/love/ sadness', but is not comparable to any of these three English concepts, neither separately nor in combination. The English terms are not a paraphrase of *fago* but only vague glosses for it. Living on a coral island measuring half a square mile, at most fifteen feet above sea level, often threatened by typhoons, the 400-odd Ifaluk people have developed a cooperative and nonaggressive life pattern, partly in response to these natural conditions (Lutz 1988: 83). Situations that trigger the feeling of *fago* are, first of all, minor catastrophes such as illness, departure from an island, or lack of food. The hidden goal or action schema is then "Change the situation by filling the need of the unfortunate party" (Lutz 1987: 301). Possible actions inspired by *fago* are as diverse as giving food, crying, talking politely, or, in the negative case, not speaking (Lutz 1987: 295). The latter reaction seems to be associated with major disasters like death. In such events, a report says, "We really felt bad inside. It was like our insides were being torn. We beat our chest and scratched our faces because a *fago* was so strong" (Lutz 1988: 125). But *fago* is also felt by a woman who "hears her younger brother singing from his canoe in the lagoon" (Lutz 1988: 121). Alongside this feeling for a close person who is potentially in danger, *fago* may also be appealed to by parents in order to promote gentle and generous behavior in their children (Lutz 1988: 136). In Wierzbicka's (1992: 143) interpretation of such findings, *fago* is claimed to be a polysemous term, but this interpretation may well be an instance of ethnocentrism, which means that we project or even impose our Western categories on those of other cultures.

Lutz (1987: 296) sees another important difference with Western patterns: "In talking about the emotions, the Ifaluk treat them as fundamentally social phenomena rather than, as in the case of American ethno-theory, as predominantly internal psycho-physiological events that are simply correlated with social events." As the subtitle of Lutz's (1988) study indicates, she therefore sees Ifaluk emotion theory as a basic challenge to established Western thought, which centers on the individual and is individualistic in its orientation.

3. UNIVERSAL AND CULTURE-SPECIFIC ASPECTS IN CULTURAL MODELS

3.1. The Universal Bodily Basis of Language and Thought

Apart from the social versus the individualistic, psychophysiological conceptions in the cultural models of emotions, there is another fundamental contrast, that between culture-specific and universal dimensions of experience. Obviously, Lutz's "social construct" view of emotions entails a culture-specific emphasis, whereas Lakoff and Kövecses's "individual and psychophysiological" view creates room for an outspoken universalist conception. Indeed, since all humans have the same bodies and hence the same fundamental bodily experiences, we may expect there to be a strong universal basis for our conceptualization of emotions.

In his 1992 paper "Anthropology and Linguistics," Keesing welcomes Cognitive Linguistics as a new evolution in linguistics in an experientialist direction:

A crucial element in the new linguistics is the importance of experience, particularly *bodily* experience—the subjectivities of being embodied as a human in our
kind of world—in shaping language. Consistently, across languages, we find
a kind of embodied subjectivity in which experience-rich (especially visual) domains are used in characterising more abstract domains. (603)

It is to be expected, then, that universal bodily experience is fertile soil for universal
conceptualizations of emotions and abstract thought in general.

In order to avoid any circularity in our argument, we will first, in section 3.2,
apply the notions of bodily experience and universalism to an entirely different
domain than emotions, that of language acquisition; in particular, we will apply it
to the acquisition of sound systems in languages—the first domain for which the
reality of "bodily experience" holds. While generative theories of language acquisition saw an unexplained link between the biological body and the functioning of
a mental "Language Acquisition Device" (LAD), recent language acquisition research has emphasized that it is especially the perceptual apparatus and the factor of
attention that have a strong impact on the evolution of language acquisition and
learning. As will be shown in section 3.2, we are born as universal beings, but
gradually narrow down our perceptual apparatus to the linguistic and cultural environment we live in. Things may be fundamentally different in the area of emotions and thought: since our bodily experience is very much the same all over the
world, we possess the same pre–conceptual image schemas, such as CONTAINMENT,
VERTICALITY, BALANCE, and so on. According to Lakoff and Johnson (1999: 508–9),
these image schemas form the experiential basis from which we develop spatial
conceptualizations and, on the basis of these, by metonymic and metaphorical extensions, abstract conceptualizations. The rise of conceptual metaphors based on
pre–conceptual image schemas may well be a universal phenomenon, as will be
discussed in section 3.3.

3.2. Born as Universal Hearers, Socialized as Culture-Specific Sound Perceivers

One of the areas of our world that are most easily accessible to nonspeculative
research is language itself, especially the perceptual or auditive aspects of the sound
system of language. The predominating Western cultural model or—given its naive
character—folk theory of people's language capacities is reflected in the "expert"
model of Lenneberg's (1967) hypothesis of the biological foundation of language.
This theory holds that the LAD stops playing a role around the period of puberty and enters a postcritical phase in which it loses its flexibility so that all later
language learning is believed to be highly cumbersome and ineffective. But recent
language perception research, as summarized in Bohn (2000), suggests that already
at the age of twelve months babies have narrowed down their attention for all
possible nonnative language sounds and only discriminate the sounds of their

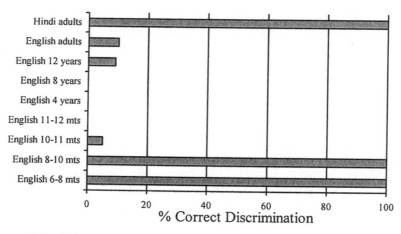

Figure 46.2. Discrimination performance of various age and language groups for the Hindi dental-retroflex contrast in Werker and Tees (1984).

mother tongue. The sensitive period for discriminating consonant sounds in foreign languages ends even before the end of the first year of life.

As can be seen from figure 46.2, English babies of ten months old can discriminate Hindi sounds, but at eleven months this ability begins to disappear. Later in adult life, discrimination performance remains very weak. Evidence has also become available now that the decline in perceptual abilities is not sensory in nature, but rather due to reorganization of attention. This means that the child's mind, which is initially open to all possible human speech sounds and language phenomena, narrows down its attention to the one or two, perhaps three, languages in his or her social and ecological environment. This also means, as is now clear from a fairly large number of studies, that the initial abilities are not lost due to some kind of attrition, but can be reaccessed in adults. Furthermore, Johnson and Newport (1989) have shown that the critical period for the kinds of abilities tested by them, especially the ability to give correct judgments about the grammaticality of sentences, ends at the age of seven, long before puberty. Thus, apart from refuting Lenneberg's theory of a biological foundation of language and supporting the experientialist basis of language acquisition, the above facts simultaneously confirm Zlatev's (1997) critique of Lakoff and Johnson's understanding of "embodiment." In his view, Lakoff and Johnson see the human body and bodily experiences as divorced from the social context and the environment in which they operate. Zlatev's correction is the notion of "situated embodiment": the human body and our bodily as well as other experiences are by necessity situated in an environment, including a physical and a social or cultural environment. Up to the tenth month, the sound-discriminating baby may live in a universalist limbo, but from then onwards his or her cultural environment makes the baby rapidly focus exclusive attention on the facts of this cultural environment.

3.3. Universal and Culture-Specific Aspects in Models of anger in English and Chinese

Lakoff and Johnson (1980) developed the theory of (partially) universal conceptual metaphors in human thought which underlie many different linguistic metaphors. Kövecses (1986, 1995b, 2002: chapters 12–13) and Lakoff and Kövecses (1987) applied this theory to the area of emotions. One of the conceptual metaphors for the expression of the notion 'anger' in English is ANGER IS HEAT or ANGER IS A HOT FLUID IN A CONTAINER. Yu (1998) adopted this model and tested it out in a comparison between English and Chinese metaphors and metonymies of emotion. His conclusion is that Chinese and English see ANGER in a similar way; however, instead of associating 'anger' with heat, Chinese stresses the cause of heat, namely fire, which is most of all linked to one of the many internal organs, as seen in the English glosses for Chinese emotion terms such as *fire head, liver fire, heart fire, belly fire* (Yu 1998: 53–54). Instead of the LIQUID metaphor, Chinese utilizes the HOT GAS metaphor, which is again linked to the container holding it: *spleen gas, heart gas, liver gas, belly gas* (55). Central, then, to the Chinese conceptualization of ANGER are the internal organs, which are the location for both the fire and the gases—almost of necessity, one might say, since in the logic of the metaphor gases need a closed container and the immediate presence of the fire for the heating of the contents in the container to expand and eventually to explode. This particular view of the human body is in line with traditional Chinese medical thought and practice, more particularly with the highly specialized art of mastering internal pressures and blockages in the body structure, known as acupuncture. Now, the interesting and remarkable phenomenon is that even though Chinese medical tradition may have strongly shaped the concrete linguistic metaphors for ANGER, these nevertheless go back to the same conceptual metaphors as English metaphorical expressions. Instead of relativizing or weakening the Lakoff and Johnson approach, Yu's findings strengthen it, as they show that the different medical "ideology" and philosophy in Chinese culture have not had any fundamental influence on the basic conceptual metaphors for emotions. Thus, Yu's survey of the many concrete instances in the Chinese linguistic expression of general conceptual metaphors shows both the universal character of the Chinese conceptualization of abstract domains such as emotion, or of other domains such as time and event structure, while simultaneously showing the uniquely concrete way of expressing or "framing" the respective conceptual metaphors. While the Chinese language views the world in a more concrete way, since it exploits bodily experience and its contact with the world more systematically and more profoundly, this bodily self-experience does not relativize the reality of very general, universal conceptualizations. As such, Yu offers evidence both for the correctness of Lakoff and Johnson's universal claims (at least to the extent that that they are confirmed in other languages) and for the great, colorful variety of culture-specific realizations of universal conceptual metaphors. But as we saw for language acquisition, the cultural factor may equally well be dominant. This is also the case in environmental deixis, as we will see now.

4. Environment or Speaker as Deictic Center? Two Models of Deixis

As embodied beings, we are, using Zlatev's (1997) terms again, not just bodily beings, but situated bodily beings, implanted in our environment and the world at large. This two-sided reality is the basis for two models of deixis.

4.1. Corporeal and Environmental Deixis Models

As the Ifaluk's handling of emotions (see section 2.3) has shown, a central factor in culture is interactive discourse. In discourse, the participants position themselves, and all the entities in their perceived or conceived world, with respect to a deictic *origo*, which is the speaker's position in space, time, the discourse progression, and his or her whole cultural world. Languages may have a multitude of expressions for spatial deixis, time deixis, person deixis, and so on. With regard to spatial deixis in particular, the speaker must locate things according to a certain reference point or reference framework. Languages can organize the link between the deictic *origo* and the other entities in the world in essentially two different ways: in terms of corporeal and environmental deixis.

In line with the strong bodily orientation of human experience, the form of spatial deixis which is probably most frequent is bodily or *corporeal deixis*. Given the central position of the human body in the metaphor systems of languages (see section 2.3), it is only natural that also in the structuring of deixis the human body is taken as the organizing principle. The two axes of horizontality (*in front of, behind*) and verticality (*above/up, under/down*) and the left-right axis all cut through the speaker's body as the deictic center. The principle of corporeal deixis is even so self-evident that it has been considered by most linguists, including cognitive linguists, as the default case, if not the universal one (Talmy 1983). But it is far from universal. A number of languages take a different model of spatial deixis, in which speakers' highly salient geographical environment constitutes the organizing principle. This is known as *environmental deixis*. Since this model may well be the nondefault instance, it will be discussed in more detail.

The discovery of noncorporeal principles of deixis organization is to a large extent the merit of the Cognitive Anthropology research group at the Max Planck Institute in Nijmegen, The Netherlands (Hill 1996; Levinson 1997; Senft 1998; Bickel 2000; etc.). For reasons of economy and coherence, we will only concentrate on Bickel's (2000) analysis of a Nepalese community, the Belhare, who live in the Himalayas foothills. This physical/geographical environment is so strongly pronounced that it is hardly surprising that it has overridden the centrality of the human body as the organizing principle for spatial deixis. Giving this sloping environment, the horizontal and vertical dimensions are conflated so that the main orientations are the equivalents of *down(hill)* and *up(hill)*. The third dimension is 'across (the hill)'. Belhare also makes a distinction between locating things and persons either directly from the deictic center (expressed by -*u* forms) or indirectly from a second reference point (expressed by -*o* forms). The forms used in Belhare can be diagrammed as follows whereby ϕ represents the direct link to the deictic center, and ϕ' the indirect link (based on Bickel 2000: 169).

Direct link	Indirect link	
ϕ	ϕ'	
tu	*to*	'above', i.e., behind
mu	*mo*	'below', i.e., in front of
yu	*yo*	'across', i.e., on the same level, i.e., left or right

It is remarkable that this system of environmental space is not only an organizing principle for spatial deixis, but also for temporal deixis. Furthermore, this deixis model needs to be used to locate entities both indoors and outdoors, even inside a room in the dark. As such, one has to decide which side of a table is 'uphill' and which one is 'downhill'. When having a drink in a pub with one's friends, one can only draw the waiter's attention to a friend's empty glass by explicitly locating this friend's position and shouting "Hey! Up there, his/her (glass) is finished" (Bickel 2000: 177). Here, the speaker locates the friend with the empty glass in the direction of a path leading to the top of the hill. Various social practices in the Belhare community reflect these 'up' and 'down' trajectories. In mat-weaving, one begins by orientating uphill. Metaphorically, when weaving downwards, one weaves for a corpse. When making sacrifices on an altar, the building-up phase uses leaves pointing to the top of the Himalayas; after the sacrifice, ritual food is thrown away downhill, to the south. Inside the house, the hearth, which has a strong sacred value, is placed uphill, to the north, farthest away from the entrance, thus marking where 'up' is in the house. Moreover, these deictic structurings apply not only to a familiar background of clearly structured space, but also to unknown territory. For instance, when visiting the Nepalese capital, Kathmandu, soccer players from Belhare on a playground used a sudden inclination in the landscape to locate the 'downhill' side and 'uphill' side of the field (Bickel 2000: 181). What Bickel's analysis has shown is the strong connection between Whorfian patterns of behavior in the Belhare country and their patterns of linguistic structure. In other words, "in eastern Nepal . . . the cultural formality of social practices does indeed show 'affinities' to linguistic patterns" (Bickel 2000: 161).

5. Cultural Variation: Different Cultural Models in One Language

Given that English has developed into various first- and second-language varieties around the world—labeled World Englishes by sociolinguists—one can expect that cultural specifics and different cultural models in the cognitive systems of their speakers should be reflected in the respective varieties of English (see Eggington 1997: 30). Evidence of this environmentalization of English in the particular cultural settings all over the world is provided, for example, by Wolf (2001), Wolf and Simo Bobda (2001), and Wolf and Polzenhagen (2009) with respect to the cultural model of "community" in African English, which is critically at odds with the Western model of self (see Wolf 1994). One linguistic manifestation of conceptualizations of the African community model consists of the particular African English use of kinship terms, which differs markedly from that in Western varieties.

Metaphorical and metonymic use of kinship terms can be found in both Western and African varieties of English. The following examples taken from computer corpora of British English (FLOB) and American English (FROWN) are representative of the Western cultural model:[1]

(1)   a. The father of sociology, Adam Ferguson. (FLOB)
      b. Lynden Pindling, the founding father of Bahamian independence. (FROWN)
      c. The most influential figure in this process was Tony Pastor, often called the father of American vaudeville. (FROWN)
      d. Hawthorne was a true son of clerical New England in his formal and even stately style. (FROWN)

It is the conceptual metaphor of PROCREATION that underlies these expressions; here, academic disciplines (1a), historic-political events (1b), or cultural genres (1c) are metaphorically structured as being the CHILD of a person important to their formation. In turn, in (1d), a person is metaphorically conceived as the CHILD of a particular region at a particular point in history on the basis of characteristics associated with both that person and that region, making use of the metonymy that certain characteristics stand for the whole person. These metaphors are based on and reflect a biological kinship model centering in the notion of 'descent' (see Turner 1987 for a detailed account of Western kinship metaphors). Importantly—reminding us of Lutz's characterization of Western thought as "individualistic"—they occur as individual entities in isolation rather than being tied to an interrelated network of community metaphors. In sharp contrast with this, in African English, kinship-based conceptualizations are part of a broad and full-fledged community model; that is, they have a different range and different elaborations, to use the terms proposed by Kövecses (2002: 183–84) with respect to cultural variation of metaphor and metonymy. Due to the interchangeable conceptual metonymy COMMUNITY FOR KINSHIP/KINSHIP FOR COMMUNITY, African thought concentrates on social group awareness, as is evidenced below (see Wolf 2001: 279–80, for references):

(2)   a. I greet my fathers.
      b. The family head of the Bakweri community.
      c. Three policemen molesting their grandson (i.e., a member of the wider Cameroonian community).
      d. My child, daughter of our people.

The members of all kinds of communities are readily conceptualized as CHILDREN, BROTHERS, SISTERS, FATHERS, and so on, depending on the specific relationship between them. Examples include political parties as well as ethnic and regional groups, and the nation as a whole, as illustrated in the examples in (3) from Cameroon and Nigerian English:

(3)   a.   The Santa CPDM [a political party in Cameroon] is planning a mass decamping because none of their sons was appointed into the new government. (Ntoi, cited in Wolf 2001: 280)

    b.   In as much as the Igbo nation is trying to unite with itself and with its South-South brothers because the Igbo people know that they cannot do without neighbouring brothers, non-Igbo brothers and non-brothers believe they cannot do without us. There must be a kind of marriage or rethinking between these two brothers. (Chijioke Nwosu 2000)

These examples raise the problem of cultural perspective and cultural presupposition as a crucial element in the notion of cultural model. This problem is interwoven with the problem of assigning the descriptive label "metaphor" or "metonymy" to these examples and the interpretation of the cognitive domains involved. Whereas the conceptualizations underlying the kinship references above in British, respectively American English, go across domain boundaries and are thus clearly metaphorical, the matter is less straightforward in the case of the African English examples. One could argue that in a traditional village setting, community and kinship are indeed one domain and that this "traditional" understanding is used to structure and explain more complex forms of "modern" social organization. Yet this still does not mean that in African thought, the domains of 'community' and 'kinship' are as clearly demarcated as in the West.

The range of different kinship-based cultural models is, however, but one aspect of cultural variation in this context. Another aspect is the phenomenon of highly complex cultural modes, consisting of the blending of various single cultural models. This becomes manifest, for instance, in the expression *son of the soil*, which is pervasive in African English. This and similar expressions are based on a complex model of spiritual and social existence (see Wolf 2001) and evoke the image of a plant nurtured by the soil (Medubi 2003). Indeed, the understanding of a community as a family is closely tied to the concept of nurture; roughly speaking the family is expected to provide nurture and care. Thus, one crucial part of the African kinship model is that it is built on a reciprocal eating and feeding pattern. In a nonmetaphorical sense, the father of a family is expected to provide the food for the family members, while he is the first in line to draw on the available food, an understanding that exists in various cultures. Yet this pattern is extended to any kind of community and is elaborated in various ways (see Schatzberg 2001). Linguistically, this illustrates the second type of cultural variation distinguished by Kövecses: different elaborations of conceptual metaphors and metonymies. It is the notion of nurture that is central to the African kinship-based model, rather than the notion of descent, which was found to be primary in the Western model (see above).

Consequently, eating-related metaphors, which highlight the aspect of nurture, are pervasive in the community domain and in political discourse (see, e.g., Bayart 1993; Geschiere 1997; Schatzberg 2001). One such elaboration is the metaphor LEADERSHIP IS EATING AND FEEDING, coupled with the metonymy FOOD FOR RE-SOURCES, as in the examples in (4):

(4)   a. Leadership positions are for some synonymous with "license to eat". (Kaigarula, cited in Schatzberg 2001: 41)

  b. AD [Alliance for Democracy, a political party] would openly campaign for Obasanjo's PDP [Peoples Democratic Party] to triumph....What kind of democracy is that? Back stabbing democracy for a meal of porridge. Democracy of protecting and promoting self interest which we called YCIC [You Chop I Chop, chop being the Pidgin English word for 'eat'] arrangement. (Ayetigbo 2002)

  c. They have given him plenty to eat. [said in Cameroon when a new government official is appointed]

  d. They have taken food off his plate. [said in Cameroon when a government official is dropped]

The salience of these and various related cultural models in African English becomes evident in an elicitation of keywords (see above, and Wierzbicka 1999) in computer corpora of African varieties of English (in comparison to corpora of native Western varieties of English). Not only do numerous lexical items from the domains of 'community', 'wealth', 'money', and 'food' appear as key words there, but they form collocative clusters as well, significantly signaling the culturally deeply entrenched structural mapping within or across the domains involved (see Wolf and Polzenhagen 2009).

Such findings support a moderate version of linguistic relativity. They speak, however, against strong deterministic claims about the impact of language on thought and culture, as the various varieties of English reflect the respective socio-cultural patterns rather than rigidly transferring Western models of thought. From a critical perspective, this kind of contextualization—or environmentalization—of English can be understood as a "counter-penetration of the new varieties found in Africa and Asia" (Brutt-Griffler 2002: 178) into conceptualizations dominant in Western native varieties of English (see Eggington 1997).

6. CONCLUSION

Culture, language, and thought are not abstract entities, but basic patterns of behavior, discourse, and reasoning in a given community. They co-occur in each concrete instance of interaction between members of that community. The cultural and linguistic forms express, and are in turn interpreted on the basis of, cultural models. These are knowledge structures representing the collective wisdom and experience of the community, acquired and stored in the individual minds of the community's members. Given the situatedness of humans as "bodies in the mind" within a specific environment, it is predictable that cultural studies will meet with and be subject to a set of tensions and contradictions.

    a. *The existence of cultural models either in the form of a conceptual unit, that is, a proposition, or else in the form of a conceptual metaphor.* The propositional view is Quinn's postulate and as such is as respectable as any other postulate. The metaphorical view is Kövecses's and is almost a necessary consequence of Lakoff and Johnson's cognitive metaphor theory: human abstract thought feeds on conceptual metaphors, which themselves are rooted in bodily based image schemas. Future research will always be torn between the propositional or nonmetaphorical view and the metaphorical view of cultural models.

    b. *The tension between the social and the individualistic nature of cultural models.* The "social" view seems to dominate in the research of non-Western models; it is found, for instance, with Ifaluk emotion theory or can be observed in African interpretations of kinship metaphors reflecting the social bonds and the union of the group. The "individualist" view is characteristic of Western models of emotional experience and can be observed in the use of kinship metaphors focusing on the individual 'procreation' aspects, which are ideally geared to conceptualizing inventions (as individual achievements of a singular mind), the creation of new trends, or currents.

    c. *The tension between the universal and the cultural-specific.* The universalist view of cultural models finds support in (potentially) universal conceptual metaphors, as found for the domains of emotion, time, event structure, and many more. The cultural-specific view is substantiated in the concrete linguistic realizations of underlying conceptual metaphors. Here the two poles seem to be in harmony. But the culture-specific may also tend to dominate as in the process of language acquisition by closing down the perceptual apparatus for universal sound patterns and focusing on the sound patterns (and life patterns more generally) of one's own cultural environment.

    d. *The tension between two possible types of bodily experience.* In the individualist Western conception, each single body is experienced as the center of the universe and serves as the basis of spatial orientation, which is reflected in corporeal deixis. Given the universality of human bodily experience, it is not astonishing that corporeal deixis should constitute the default case. But as a more refined conception of embodiment, the notion of situated embodiment incorporates and integrates man's physical and social environment in his or her holistic bodily experience. This type of bodily experience makes room for a different type of deixis: environmental deixis. This latter type of deixis requires a continued effort on the part of language users to find "environmental" reference points so that their behavioral thought and linguistic practice strongly determine one another in a mildly linguistic-relativity sense, thus supporting the Humboldtian and Whorfian view of the inseparable unity between culture, language, and thought.

NOTES

1. The Freiburg-LOB Corpus of British English (FLOB) and the Freiburg-Brown Corpus of American English were compiled at the English Department of the University of Freiburg, under the supervision of Christian Mair. Both corpora are on the New ICAME Corpus Collection CD-Rom, version 2, 1999 (http://helmer.aksis.uib.no/icame/newcd.htm).

REFERENCES

Ayetigbo, Ayodele. 2002. Back stabbed, frontally bruised Nigeria/Africa will survive: The U.S. African Voice. http://www.usafricanvoice.com/back_stabbed.htm (accessed July 8, 2003)

Bayart, Jean François. 1993. *The state in Africa: The politics of the belly.* London: Longman.

Bickel, Balthasar. 2000. Grammar and social practice: On the role of 'culture' in linguistic relativity. In Susanne Niemeier and René Dirven, eds., *Evidence for linguistic relativity* 161–91. Amsterdam: John Benjamins.

Bohn, Ocke-Schwen. 2000. Linguistic relativity in speech perception: An overview of the influence of language experience on the perception of speech sounds from infancy to adulthood. In Susanne Niemeier and René Dirven, eds., *Evidence for linguistic relativity* 1–28. Amsterdam: John Benjamins.

Brutt-Griffler, Janina. 2002. *World English: A study of its development.* Clevedon, UK: Multilingual Matters.

Chijioke Nwosu, Brady. 2000. Let's leave everything to posterity. *This Day Online.* http://www.thisdayonline.com/archive/2001/10/25/20011025polo8.html (accessed February 22, 2002).

D'Andrade, Roy. 1987. A folk model of the mind. In Dorothy Holland and Naomi Quinn, eds., *Cultural models in language and thought* 112–47. Cambridge: Cambridge University Press.

Eggington, William. 1997. The English language metaphors we plan by. In William Eggington and Helen Wren, eds., *Language policy: Dominant English, pluralistic challenges* 29–46. Amsterdam: John Benjamins.

Geschiere, Peter. 1997. *The modernity of witchcraft: Politics and the occult in postcolonial Africa*. Charlottesville: University of Virginia Press.

Gibbs, Raymond W., Jr. 1994. *The poetics of mind: Figurative thought, language, and understanding*. Cambridge: Cambridge University Press.

Gibbs, Raymond W., Jr. 1999. Taking metaphor out of our heads and putting it into the cultural world. In Raymond W. Gibbs, Jr., and Gerard J. Steen, eds., *Metaphor in cognitive linguistics* 145–66. Amsterdam: John Benjamins.

Hill, Deborah. 1996. Distinguishing the notion 'place' in an Oceanic language. In Martin Pütz and René Dirven, eds., *The construal of space in language and thought* 307–28. Berlin: Mouton de Gruyter.

Holland, Dorothy, and Naomi Quinn, eds. 1987. *Cultural models in language and thought*. Cambridge: Cambridge University Press.

Holland, Dorothy, and Debra Skinner. 1987. Prestige and intimacy: The cultural model behind Americans' talk about gender types. In Dorothy Holland and Naomi Quinn, eds., *Cultural models in language and thought* 78–111. Cambridge: Cambridge University Press.

Johnson, Jacqueline S., and Elissa L. Newport. 1989. Critical period effects in second language learning: The influence of maturational state on the acquisition of English as a second language. *Cognitive Psychology* 21: 60–99.

Joseph, John. 1996. The immediate sources of the Sapir-Whorf hypothesis. *Historiographia Linguistica* 21: 212–21.

Kay, Paul. 1987. Linguistic competence and folk theories of language: Two English hedges. In Dorothy Holland and Naomi Quinn, eds., *Cultural models in language and thought* 66–77. Cambridge: Cambridge University Press.

Keesing, Roger M. 1987. Models, "folk" and "cultural": Paradigms regained? In Dorothy Holland and Naomi Quinn, eds., *Cultural models in language and thought* 369–93. Cambridge: Cambridge University Press.

Keesing, Roger M. 1992. Anthropology and linguistics. In Martin Pütz, ed., *Thirty years of linguistic evolution* 593–609. Amsterdam: John Benjamins.

Koerner, Konrad E. F. 2000. Towards a 'full pedigree' of the 'Sapir-Whorf hypothesis': From Locke to Lucy. In Martin Pütz and Marjolijn Verspoor, eds., *Explorations in linguistic relativity* 1–24. Amsterdam: John Benjamins.

Kövecses, Zoltán. 1986. *Metaphors of anger, pride, and love: A lexical approach to the study of concepts*. Amsterdam: John Benjamins.

Kövecses, Zoltán. 1995a. American friendship and the scope of metaphor. *Cognitive Linguistics* 6: 315–46.

Kövecses, Zoltán. 1995b. Anger: Its language, conceptualizations, and physiology in the light of cross-cultural evidence. In John R. Taylor and R. A. MacLaury, eds., *Language and the cognitive construal of the world* 181–96. Berlin: Mouton de Gruyter.

Kövecses, Zoltán. 1999. Metaphor: Does it constitute or reflect cultural models? In Raymond W. Gibbs, Jr., and Gerard J. Steen, eds., *Metaphor in cognitive linguistics* 167–88. Amsterdam: John Benjamins.

Kövecses, Zoltán. 2002. *Metaphor: A practical introduction*. Oxford: Oxford University Press.

Kövecses, Zoltán. 2005. *Metaphor in culture: Universality and variation*. Cambridge: Cambridge University Press.

Kövecses, Zoltán, and Gary R. Palmer. 1999. Language and emotion concepts: What experientialists and social constructionists have in common. In Gary B. Palmer and Debora J. Occhi, eds., *Languages of sentiment: Cultural constructions of emotional substrates* 237–62. Amsterdam: John Benjamins.

Lakoff, George, and Mark Johnson. 1980. *Metaphors we live by*. Chicago: University of Chicago Press.

Lakoff, George, and Mark Johnson. 1999. *Philosophy in the flesh: The embodied mind and its challenge to Western thought*. New York: Basic Books.

Lakoff, George, and Zoltán Kövecses. 1987. The cognitive model of anger inherent in American English. In Dorothy Holland and Naomi Quinn, eds., *Cultural models in language and thought* 195–221. Cambridge: Cambridge University Press.

Langacker, Ronald W. 1994. Culture, cognition, and grammar. In Martin Pütz, ed., *Language contact and language conflict* 25–53. Amsterdam: John Benjamins.

Lee, Penny. 1996. *The Whorf theory complex: A critical reconstruction*. Amsterdam: John Benjamins.

Lenneberg, Eric. 1967. *Biological foundations of language*. New York: John Wiley.

Levinson, Stephen C. 1997. From outer to inner space: Linguistic categories and non-linguistic thinking. In Jan Nuyts and Eric Pederson, eds., *Language and conceptualization* 13–45. Cambridge: Cambridge University Press.

Lutz, Catherine A. 1987. Goals, events, and understanding in Ifaluk emotion theory. In Dorothy Holland and Naomi Quinn, eds., *Cultural models in language and thought* 290–312. Cambridge: Cambridge University Press.

Lutz, Catherine A. 1988. *Unnatural emotions: Everyday sentiments on a Micronesion atoll and their challenge to Western theory*. Chicago: University of Chicago Press.

Medubi, Oyinkan. 2003. Language and ideology in Nigerian cartoons. In René Dirven, Roslyn Frank, and Martin Pütz, eds., *Cognitive models in language and thought: Ideology, metaphors and meanings* 159–97. Berlin: Mouton de Gruyter.

Palmer, Gary B. 1996. *Toward a theory of cultural linguistics*. Austin: University of Texas Press.

Quinn, Naomi. 1987. Convergent evidence for a cultural model of American marriage. In Dorothy Holland and Naomi Quinn, eds., *Cultural models in language and thought* 173–92. Cambridge: Cambridge University Press.

Quinn, Naomi. 1991. The cultural basis of metaphor. In James W. Fernandez, ed., *Beyond metaphor: The theory of tropes in anthropology* 56–93. Stanford, CA: Stanford University Press.

Quinn, Naomi. 1997. Research on shared task solutions. In Claudia Strauss and Naomi Quinn, eds., *A cognitive theory of cultural meaning* 137–88. Cambridge: Cambridge University Press.

Quinn, Naomi, and Dorothy Holland. 1987. Culture and cognition. In Dorothy Holland and Naomi Quinn, eds., *Cultural models in language and thought* 3–40. Cambridge: Cambridge University Press.

Schatzberg, Michael G. 2001. *Political legitimacy in Middle Africa*. Bloomington: Indiana University Press.

Senft, Gunter. 1998. *Frames of spatial reference in Kilivila: Studies in language, cognition and the conceptualization of space*. LAUD Paper no. 424. Essen, Germany: Linguistic Agency of the University of Duisburg-Essen.

Sharifian, Farzad. 2003. On cultural conceptualisations. *Journal of Cognition and Culture* 3: 187–207.

Sweetser, Eve. 1987. The definition of 'lie': An examination of the folk models underlying a semantic prototype. In Dorothy Holland and Naomi Quinn, eds., *Cultural models in language and thought* 43–66. Cambridge: Cambridge University Press.

Talmy, Leonard. 1983. How language structures space. In Herbert L. Pick, Jr., and Linda P. Acredolo, eds., *Spatial orientation: Theory, research and application* 225–82. New York: Plenum Books.

Turner, Mark. 1987. *Death is the mother of beauty: Mind, metaphor, criticism.* Chicago: University of Chicago Press.

Werker, Janet F., and Richard C. Tees. 1984. Phonemic and phonetic factors in adult cross-language speech perception. *Journal of the Acoustical Society of America* 75: 1866–78.

Wierzbicka, Anna. 1992. *Semantics, culture, and cognition: Universal human concepts in culture-specific configurations.* Oxford: Oxford University Press.

Wierzbicka, Anna. 1999. *Emotions across languages and cultures: Diversity and universals.* Cambridge: Cambridge University Press.

Wolf, Hans-Georg. 1994. *A folk model of the "Internal Self" in light of the contemporary view of metaphor: The self as subject and object.* Frankfurt am Main: Peter Lang Verlag.

Wolf, Hans-Georg. 2001. *English in Cameroon.* Berlin: Mouton de Gruyter.

Wolf, Hans-Georg, and Frank Polzenhagen. 2009. *World Englishes: A cognitive sociolinguistic approach.* Berlin: Mouton de Gruyter.

Wolf, Hans-Georg, and Augustin Simo Bobda. 2001. The African cultural model of community in English language instruction in Cameroon: The need for more systematicity. In Martin Pütz, Susanne Niemeier, and René Dirven, eds., *Applied cognitive linguistics,* vol. 2, *Language pedagogy* 225–59. Berlin: Mouton de Gruyter.

Yu, Ning. 1998. *The contemporary theory of metaphor: A perspective from Chinese.* Amsterdam: John Benjamins.

Zlatev, Jordan. 1997. *Situated embodiment: Studies in the emergence of spatial meaning.* Stockholm: Gotab Press.

....

CHAPTER 47

COGNITIVE LINGUISTICS, IDEOLOGY, AND CRITICAL DISCOURSE ANALYSIS

....

RENÉ DIRVEN, FRANK POLZENHAGEN, AND HANS-GEORG WOLF

1. INTRODUCTION: IDEOLOGY, A VAST RESEARCH FIELD OUTSIDE COGNITIVE LINGUISTICS

....

Since the late 1970s, the linguistic study of ideology and discourse has been the home territory of Critical Discourse Analysis (CDA). The development of this research framework is thoroughly documented in Caldas-Coulthard and Coulthard (1996) and in Toolan's (2002) four-volume reader, which covers the movement's intellectual roots in the social sciences and its precursors (e.g., Bakhtin 1982, 1986; Bourdieu 1991), the various theoretical approaches of its major proponents (e.g., Fowler and Kress 1979; Fairclough 1989, 1992, 1995; Wodak 1989; Hodge and Kress 1993; van Dijk 1993, 1997, 1998), and a number of central case studies. A more concise overview of the field can be found in Blommaert and Bulcaen (2000) and in Blommaert (2005). CDA is a highly heterogeneous research program. Its dominant linguistic approach has its footing in Functional Grammar, in particular Systemic-Functional Grammar as developed by Halliday (1985), who himself has made major contributions to the field (e.g., Halliday 1978). Yet there is also a cognitive strand, notably through the work of van Dijk (e.g., 1997, 1998), and there is a strong discussion on further interdisciplinarity (e.g., Wodak and Chilton 2005) and on further methodological and theoretical pluralism, including an opening toward Cognitive Linguistics (e.g., Chilton 2005; O'Halloran 2003). Given the diversity and vastness of the field, the label "critical linguistics" has been introduced, which also comprises approaches such as feminist linguistics and ecolinguistics.

From the past decade on, the issue of ideology and discourse has received increasing attention from scholars working within the Cognitive Linguistics framework, and the aim of this chapter is to survey the particular contributions and insights this theoretical perspective may yield beyond the analytic methods applied so far by CDA scholars, keeping in mind the David and Goliath relationship between the two (see also Stockwell 1999). Given the convergence with CDA work, this survey of cognitive linguistic ideology research intends to implicitly and explicitly strengthen the common interests of the two frameworks.

First, some terminological clarifications may be in order. The terms "discourse" and "ideology" have been applied in several different ways and against various theoretical backgrounds. For the scope of the present chapter, a methodological distinction is made between a broad and a narrow understanding of the two notions, largely abstracting from competing theoretical positions. Discourse, then, can refer (i) to long-term discursive practices in social interactions, constituting social practices in a broad, Foucaultian understanding (e.g., the discourse on AIDS), or, (ii) more narrowly, to actual written or spoken textual material like this chapter or book. Both CDA and the cognitive linguistic approach address these two levels of discourse, although detailed text-linguistic analyses are still the hallmark of CDA.

Likewise, two understandings of ideology, a broad one (ideology i) and a narrow one (ideology ii), can be distinguished. The broad view holds ideology to be "a system of thought" which is not taken in any philosophical or political sense, "but rather as an implicit or explicit set of norms and values which provide patterns for acting and/or patterns for living within a given social network" (Dirven 1990: 565). CDA scholars may conceive of these largely unconscious norms as "preideological" or as "common ground" (see van Dijk 2002; Wolf and Polzenhagen 2003: 250) and generally tend toward a more restricted understanding of ideology. In CDA, ideology is seen, first of all, as a "modality of power," that is, as attitudes with respect to social relations of dominance. Leaning on Bourdieu, Fairclough (2003: 9), for instance, states that "ideologies are representations of aspects of the world which can be shown to contribute to establishing, maintaining and changing social relations of power, domination and exploitation." As implied above, however, from a cognitive linguistic perspective, such overt ideologies are not separated from conventional conceptualizations shared by a particular social group; in other words, the broad and narrow understanding of ideology are highly intertwined. As one of the first cognitive linguistic ideology researchers, Lakoff states the link in an interview with Pires de Oliveira as follows:

> Ideologies have both conscious and unconscious aspects. If you ask someone with a political ideology what she believes, she will give a list of beliefs and perhaps some generalisations. A cognitive linguist, looking at what she says, will most likely pick out unconscious frames and metaphors [and other conceptual units; our addition] lying behind her conscious beliefs. . . . It is there that cognitive linguists have a contribution to make. (Pires de Oliveira 2001: 37)

It is the particular strength of Cognitive Linguistics that it allows for and aims at an analysis of ideology on both levels. What both levels share is the notion of perspective. Cognitive Linguistics thus relates "ideology in language" to conceptual and linguistic phenomena that establish specific, though often unconscious, perspectives on the world, be it in the broad or in the narrow sense of ideology, or predispose speakers to such perspectives.

This double layer of unconscious and conscious ideologization will determine the structure of this chapter, in addition to the distinctions to be made in the tools of analysis. The first cognitive linguistic analyses all remain within the narrower framework of metaphor research à la Lakoff and Johnson (1980), but gradually further and more powerful conceptual tools are developed. Phenomena that establish potentially ideological perspectives are traced on different levels of linguistic description. Section 2 outlines the ideological dimension of metaphor, with the emphasis on covert ideology in the discourse domain of economics. Section 3 develops the notions of "ideological deixis" and "iconographic frames of reference," with the focus on overt ideology in political discourse. Section 4 explores grammatical means that reflect deep-rooted unconscious norms within a sociocultural group. Section 5, finally, discusses the pervasiveness of metaphor and the role of cultural models in the highly abstract domain of science and addresses their more often than not ideological orientation, more specifically in the metalanguage of biological and linguistic discourse.

2. TRADITIONAL COGNITIVE LINGUISTIC METAPHOR RESEARCH ON IDEOLOGY: THE CASE OF ECONOMIC DISCOURSE

Traditionally, cognitive linguistic research on ideology has mainly focused on one tool of conceptualization: metaphor. This approach has been applied to numerous domains, and we will survey, in an exemplary way, cognitive linguistic studies along these lines in the domain of economy, more specifically of economy in Western popular discourse. Generally, as can be expected in a free-market economy context, this domain is shaped by metaphors of competition, conflict, and even hostility. For example, Boers (1997), from his corpus analysis of editorials in *The Economist*, notes that metaphors of economic HEALTH and FITNESS are coupled with metaphors of an economic RACE and that accounts of economic activity as WAR and FIGHTING occur just as frequently. These observations are further confirmed by Eubanks (2000) and by Koller's (2002) study on metaphors in the discourse on business mergers. Likewise, White and Herrera (2003) have worked out the metaphorical models in the press coverage of telecom corporate consolidations. They describe a complex blend of metaphors, including BUSINESS IS A JUNGLE, where COMPANIES are PREDATORS and PREY, BUSINESS IS WAR, and BUSINESS IS COLONIZATION. In the former two, competition between companies is conceptualized as a struggle for survival. In the logic of this scenario, companies are ORGANISMS in an inhospitable habitat, an environment that requires reckless struggle—kill or be killed—to avoid extinction. White and Herrera (2003) focus on a particular instantiation of this scenario, in which companies are DINOSAURS in a prehistoric Jurassic Park. The underlying metaphorical network is expressed, for instance, in the following example (1):

(1)   Rapacious feeders, for a century or more the telephone companies have grown even fatter and more complacent, grazing on hunting grounds where none could challenge them. (taken from White and Herrera 2003: 291)

Unlike the DINOSAUR metaphor, which is dominated by blind instincts and inevitable cause-effect chains, the second set of metaphors, BUSINESS IS WAR and BUSINESS IS COLONIZATION, prioritizes the strategic aspect and the underlying hegemonic intentions. In a similar vein, Wolf and Polzenhagen (2003) have analyzed the conventional nature of such metaphors as TRADE IS WAR, TRADE NEGOTIATIONS ARE BATTLES, and, less combatively, TRADE NEGOTIATIONS ARE CONTESTS in the press coverage of a U.S.-Japanese trade dispute. The conventional use of the above metaphors can be described as "common ground," as "pre-ideological," to use van Dijk's (2002) terms, thus reflecting an ideological position not drawn upon deliberately by a group of speakers (also see Wolf and Polzenhagen 2003: 250). Rather, these metaphors are part of the stock of deeply entrenched and commonly shared conceptualizations among Western speakers of English and other European languages.

Crucial to an understanding of the ideological function of these metaphors is the notion of "perspective." Throughout the various theories of metaphor, a recurrent characteristic determining the nature of metaphor has been that it presents its target from a particular point of view. This is, for instance, directly expressed in Black's (1993) notion of "perspective," in Davidson's (1981) "seeing-as," and, within Cognitive Linguistics, in Lakoff and Johnson's (1980) notion of "highlighting and hiding" and, more generally, in Langacker's (e.g., 1987) notion of "profiling." The "highlighting-and-hiding" function, for instance, can be seen at work in the above-mentioned metaphors from the economic domain: they highlight aspects of (social) Darwinism, aggression, and domination, and hide, among other things, the mutually beneficial nature of trade and the social responsibilities of economic "players." Importantly, as an experiment by Boers (1997) has shown, exposure to different metaphors in an economic scenario may give rise to a perception of the economy as a cooperative enterprise, for example, as a team sport (Cubo de Severino, Israel, and Zonana 2001), or it may even affect the decision-making processes of the participants involved, in accordance with the metaphors used. Thus, rather than merely reflecting a particular "rhetorical style" in the field, metaphors are often indicative of a particular "style of economics" itself (see section 5 for a related analysis). This is manifest in the following abstract from course material published by a school of management, proposing alternatives to the dominant competitive metaphors in the economic domain (see Wolf and Polzenhagen 2003: 265):

> *Metaphors we market by*: • Market as jungle • Customers as targets • Marketers as hunters . . . • Products as mousetraps • Promotions as baits and lures • Sales-people as baiters and switchers . . .
> *Toward a new marketing metaphor*: • Marketers as gardeners • Customers as plants • Loyalty as roots • Profits as harvest • Marketing as seed, feed, greed, and weed.

This highlighting-and-hiding function of metaphor links up to the broad understanding of "discourse" in CDA, in that a discourse defines, describes, and delimits what it is possible to say and what it is not possible to say ("and by extension— what is possible to do or not to do") and that it "provides a set of possible statements about a given area" (Kress 1989: 7; see also Wolf and Polzenhagen 2003: 254).

In addition to ideology in economic discourse, metaphor and blending theory has been applied in the analysis of ideology in various other social domains such as conservative and liberal politics in the United States (Lakoff 1996), nation building in South Africa (Dirven 1994), the American constitutional battle around impeachment (Morgan 2001), British (un)parliamentary discourse (Ilie 2001), the school domain (Urban 1999), the domain of law (Winter 2001), the hidden ideology of the Internet (Rohrer 2001), and so on.

3. NEW PATHS IN COGNITIVE LINGUISTIC RESEARCH ON OVERT IDEOLOGY: POLITICAL RHETORIC

This section outlines two recently developed Cognitive Linguistic analytic tools: "ideological deixis" and "iconographic frames of reference." Each of these new approaches is illustrated here with case studies from the domain of political rhetoric.

As Langacker (1991: 499) has pointed out, a speaker grounds what he or she says in the speech situation, that is, minimally in relation to the place and time coordinates of the speaker at speech act time, and in the participants' commitment to cooperating. Recently in Cognitive Linguistics the concept of deixis has been widened to include a societal function: the speaker's vantage point relates not only to the physical coordinates of location in space, to time, and to discourse participants, but also to the attitudinal or ideological anchoring of the speaker's beliefs and values in his or her cultural world. As Hawkins (1999) observes, ideology is akin to time and space in that it constitutes a cognitive domain that plays a role in the meaning-making process of deixis. In view of the fact that in any process of reference the speaker tries to direct the interlocutor's attention to a given referent, ideological deixis involves assessing the effect that a referential act is to have, assessing the current attitude of the audience toward the referent, and determining how best to manipulate various conceptual tools to achieve the intended rhetorical effect with this particular audience. In any process of reference, the speaker tries to direct the interlocutor's attention to a given referent.

A study by Botha (2001) shows how ideological deixis is used for nation-building purposes by new South African leaders, especially President Mbeki. He analyzes how they make use of the positive connotations of the images of a "new birth" and a splendid, colorful "rainbow" in the coinage of new compounds such as *African Renaissance* and *rainbow nation* in order to transmit the idea and the ideology of a new and integrated, multiethnic South African nation. In order to emphasize the strong unity of this rainbow nation, Mbeki exploits the flexibility of the deictic center in the person of a nation's leader and relates the first-person singular pronoun in *I am an African* not only to the whole of Africa as a continent, but also to his own country South Africa, and to each of its eleven officially recognized linguistic and ethnic groups. In order to achieve this identification of the leader with each of these groups, Mbeki makes different vantage point shifts and speaks as the African who reappears in each and every national group:

(2)   I owe my being to the Khoe and the San whose desolate souls haunt the great
       expanses of the beautiful Cape; In my veins courses the blood of the
       Malay slaves who came from the East; I am the grandchild of the warrior men
       and women that Hintsa and Sekhukhune led.

Each of the ethnic groups have their own ideologies, grown through and from their own history, and by means of his vantage shifts in ideological deixis, Mbeki identifies with each of these groups which are integrating through him in the rainbow nation and the African continent.

The second recent notion is that of "iconographic reference," which was developed in Hawkins (2001) and applied, *inter alia*, to the Nazi propaganda machinery in its representation of Jews as lower parasites during the Third Reich. As the "parasite" image may suggest, an iconographic reference exploits the discursant's experience or view of the referent by means of a powerful iconographic image, that is, a conventionalized semantic unit as in Hawkins's examples of a *parasite*, a *monster*, a *villain*, or in Mbeki's use of a *rainbow nation*. Iconographic reference is a dynamic process which selects one such attribute or element from a wider iconographic frame of reference. In the case of Nazi anti-Jew propaganda, the frame of reference is an old and deeply entrenched cultural model known as the

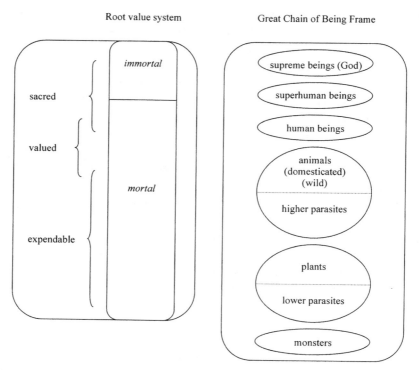

Figure 47.1. The Great Chain of Being iconography (based on Hawkins 2001: 44)

Great Chain of Being (see, e.g., Lovejoy [1936] 1960 for the history of this model in Western thought). This is a vertical scale on which beings are hierarchically ordered in aesthetic, moral, and rational terms (see Lakoff and Turner 1989: chapter 4). Those that are in the top are valued higher than those that rank low, as illustrated in figure 47.1, and the schematic iconographic images selected from this scale thus bear a direct conceptual link to a basic value system grounded in fundamental human experience, a "root value system" in Hawkins's (2001) terminology.

The GREAT CHAIN OF BEING frame serves as the source domain in numerous metaphorical processes, for instance, and most importantly for the present chapter, in the language of oppression. As a chain of dominance, it can be readily used as a chain of subjugation. This frame and its related value system are referred to, for example, when members of particular ethnic, social, or religious groups are conceptualized and labeled as lower life-forms (e.g., *animals, beasts, parasites*) or even as below life-forms (e.g., *chattels* or *goods*). Thus, in the Nazi exploitation of the Great Chain model, the Aryan race is at the superhuman level (*Übermensch*), whereas the Jewish race is located at the lowest level possible, even below plants. Simultaneously, this iconographic reference implies the notion of lack of productivity and living on the resources of other species. In the line of Hawkins's analysis, Santa Ana (2003: 208) traces the same mechanism in the anti-Latino discourse in the United States.

Lakoff's (1992) analysis of metaphors in the American rhetoric during the first Gulf War can also be reinterpreted in terms of iconographic frames of reference. Hawkins's concept of iconographic reference readily allows the setup of antithetical elements, such as the *Übermensch-parasite* antithesis. Similarly, Lakoff (1992: 466) invokes the FAIRY TALE frame with a hero and a villain, and a victim. Lakoff (1992) identifies two scenarios instantiating this frame, which were employed in the justification of the war: (i) *The Self-Defense Scenario*, where Iraq is villain, the United States is hero, the United States and other "civilized" nations are victims, and the crime is a death threat, and (ii) *the Rescue Scenario*, where Iraq is villain, the United States is hero, Kuwait is victim, the crime is kidnap and rape. The former scenario proved to be less agreeable to the American public; the latter, however, was readily embraced and subsequently maintained. Tellingly, George Bush declared victory before the congress as follows: "The recent challenge could not have been clearer. Saddam Hussein was the villain; Kuwait the victim." Numerous other metaphors employed in the American Gulf War rhetoric are based on the FAIRY TALE frame. Although trend-setting, Lakoff's approach was also criticized by various authors, especially for its data-collecting methods, which were not corpus-based, but rather impressionistic. Pancake (1993) was the first to use real corpus evidence and presents further analyses of metaphor use in this context. Equally elaborating on Lakoff (1992), Rohrer (1995) starts from a written-to-be-spoken corpus and provides an analysis of Bush's speeches during the Gulf War. Sandikcioglu (2000, 2001) analyzes the American news reports in the magazines *Time* and *Newsweek* and situates the Gulf War news coverage in the wider "Us versus Them" antithesis (Western model versus Orient), in which the West constructs itself as civilized, powerful, mature, rational, and stable, as opposed to a barbaric, weak, immature, irrational, and unstable Orient. These orientalist conceptualizations have far-reaching inferences. They present "Us" and "Them" as incompatible, with a marked moral asymmetry built in. An immature and irrational Other cannot be trusted or negotiated with, it can only *have some sense talked into it* and be *taught a lesson* in a *didactic war*, to use illustrations from Sandikcioglu's (2001: 176) Gulf War corpus data.

4. THE COVERT IDEOLOGY OF ALIENATION AND SEXISM IN GRAMMAR

As a highly abstract and unconsciously operating system, grammar, by definition, can only incorporate covert ideology. This holds at least for those areas of grammar where no variation, and consequently no choice, is possible. But when variation is possible, the choice offered by the alternatives may pave the way to overt ideology.

This is in fact the proper field of stylistics. It comes as no surprise, then, that CDA and its underlying framework of functionalism have mainly researched this variation-bound ideology. Prominent objects of analysis are grammatical means that lend themselves to hiding agency, in particular passivization and nominalization (see, e.g., Simpson 1993: chapter 4), and that may thus encode specific ideological perspectives. From a cognitive linguistic point of view, we can go much further and claim that ideology may enter at any level of grammatical conceptualization, even the most abstract ones. We already saw an example in Botha's discussion of ideological deixis at the beginning of section 3. The present section focuses on two additional instances, one from the area of tense (Grundy and Jiang 2001) and one from the area of declension (Nesset 2001). Grundy and Jiang's (2001) analysis exemplifies the link between grammatical constructions and underlying ideological models against a sociocultural background, thus establishing the bond with the notion of Cultural Models (see Dirven, Wolf, and Polzenhagen, this volume, chapter 46), and Nesset's (2001) study makes a cognitive linguistic contribution to a feminist critique of sexism in language.

Grundy and Jiang (2001) analyze some specific features in Hong Kong English, in particular the nonconventional use of the bare past. Against the background of mental space theory (Fauconnier 1997), Grundy and Jiang discuss the representation of "anomalous" sentences which are found especially in public address messages in Hong Kong, such as (3), with a past perfect instead of the expected present perfect form:

(3)   Last bus had departed.

In the present perfect form *(The) last bus has departed*, the present of the reader would be set as the reference time from which the event (the departure of the bus) is viewed. The past perfect form in (3), by contrast, prompts the reader to locate the event relative to a past viewpoint space. Yet this past viewpoint space remains completely unspecified; no material is provided or inferable for its interpretation, and it is impossible for the reader to recover the reference time. Note that "non-anomalous" uses of the past perfect, such as (4)

(4)   When we arrived, the last bus had (already) departed.

contain linguistic material (here, *when we arrived*) which makes the past reference time recoverable for the reader and provides the contents of the viewpoint space, thus establishing the Ground in relation to which the Figure (here, the departure of the bus) is in focus. Grundy and Jiang (2001: 122) observe that (3) presents the departure of the bus and the posting of the message as distinct events. It "hides" the person from whom the message originates, and it enables this person to reject an involvement in the inconvenient event which he or she reports and to decline responsibility for it. Grundy and Jiang argue that this "hiding oneself" strategy is an expression of a "how-can-I-act-in-order-to-ensure-that-no-blame-attaches-to-me" mentality, which is an inherent part of Hong Kong ideology.

In a wider context, virtually all the debates in the Hong Kong government center around deciding who is to take the blame and who is not for the situations that arise. A recent example is the debate on their handling of the SARS outbreak. The outcome of the work by a commission set up to investigate the government's crisis management was captured by a headline-like advertisement at a newspaper stand saying "Faults found, but no one to blame" (personal observation). As Grundy and Jiang (2001) argue, the deeper cause of this "no-blame-attaches-to-me" ideology is in all likelihood the typical historical and political situation of the British Crown Colony and its present relation to the People's Republic of China. Although Hong Kong citizens enjoy economic opportunities and domestic freedoms, they are constantly reminded that they are not responsible for the political structure they are part of and the decisions it makes for them. In such a climate of alienation, individuals protect themselves from the consequences of decision making in a context where it is not for them to be decision makers.

An even more abstract grammatical area is the system of declensions. Nesset (2001), working on Russian, investigated the class II or *a*-declension class for nouns, which includes short forms of given proper names, nonfeminine common nouns, and nouns denoting female persons. Short forms of given names instantiate a FAMILIARITY schema, for "persons who stand out from the multitude by virtue of their intimate relationship to the speaker" (Nesset 2001: 214). An example would be *Dima* (< *Dimitrij*). Nonfeminine common nouns in the *a*-declension class have an underlying MARGINALITY schema, which involves an evaluation scale (while evaluation is absent in the masculine Ø-declension class); that is, this declension class includes persons "who stand out from the multitude by being placed at an end point of a scale" (Nesset 2001: 214). Examples from the extreme ends of the scale would be *voevoda* 'commander of army in medieval Russia' and *sluga* 'servant'. The two subcategories share the semantic component 'persons who stand out from the multitude', which constitutes a general NONPROTOTYPICALITY schema, instantiated by the two more specific schemas. The third subcategory, nouns denoting female persons, is related to the other two in conclusive ways. Nesset argues that in the grammatical system of Russian, men are conceptualized as the multitude or the unmarked case, while reference to women needs additional specification of the sex (also see Howard 2001). He points out that multitude should not be understood numerically, but rather in a representational sense of what is normal or unmarked in a society. Thus, it becomes evident that the three subcategories constitute a well-defined category, as all three instantiate the general NONPROTO-TYPICALITY schema (Nesset 2001: 217–18). Furthermore, Nesset suggests that the subcategories in the *a*-declension class interrelate in even closer ways. First, he connects the subcategory of female persons to that of nonfeminine common nouns with its evaluational and polar scale. To that purpose, Nesset draws on Simone de Beauvoir's idea of the category WOMAN being associated with "extreme" qualities, which he condenses in terms of metaphors—or, perhaps better, metonymies, since these qualities are associated in the underlying cultural model as attributes to the

category—that relate SIN AND VICE and VIRTUE to WOMAN. Second, Nesset holds
that there exists a relationship between the subcategory for female persons and that
for short forms of given names (which, as will be recalled, instantiates a FAMIL-
IARITY schema), thus making the internal coherence of the *a*-declension class come
full-circle. Applying Lakoff's (1987: 93) "domain-of-experience-principle," which
states that "if there is a basic domain of experience associated with *A*, then it is
natural for entities in that domain to be in the same category as *A*," Nesset finds that
both subcategories pertain to the "private sphere." The private domain of experience is that of home and of relationships to family and friends, whereas the public
domain is that of broader social structures. Therefore, Nesset argues, the belief that
"woman's place is in the home" is implied in and perpetuated through grammatical
categorization, which always applies to any occurrence of the given category. Thus,
there is no stopping the sexist bias laid down in the Russian declension system.

Nesset (2001: 224) concludes "that sexist ideologies may be so deeply entrenched
in the grammar of a particular language as to pervade inflectional classes—an area
which is traditionally viewed as devoid of semantic structure." Nesset's analysis
demonstrates the descriptive and explanatory power of Cognitive Linguistics in
explorations into ideologies hidden in grammatical categories.

5. IDEOLOGY AT THE LEVEL OF SCIENTIFIC DISCOURSE

Ideology abounds not only in the most abstract area of language, which is grammar,
but also in the most abstract type of discourse, which is scientific discourse, here
especially by means of conceptual metaphor. The role of metaphor in scientific
writing and thinking has, of course, long been noticed, and it has been assessed in
different ways. One position has it that metaphor is redundant in scientific writing:
at best it is seen as illustrative, at worst as deceptive, and therefore to be avoided.
Evidently, this position correlates with the view that what may be conveyed metaphorically can also be expressed literally. Conversely, there is the position that
metaphors have a constitutive role in scientific theories. Evidently, this position
correlates with the view that human conceptualization is largely metaphorical. Jäkel
(1997: chapter 8), for instance, provides a cognitive linguistic analysis of what he
calls the "science scenarios," that is, different models of scientific theory, of leading
Western philosophers and identifies their respective dominant conceptual metaphors. Most importantly, he observes that the critique of a competing scientific
theory is often directed against the criticized theory's metaphorical model. Paradigmatic changes in science generally go along with a rejection of old metaphors
and the introduction of new ones. Finally, midway between the positions of met-

aphor as either redundant or constitutive is the view that it is a useful and valuable heuristic tool, with a limited scope.

Significantly, various sciences use each other's fields as source domains in the metaphorical conceptualization of their own domains as target domains. One example is provided by the collective volume by Naumann, Plank, and Hofbauer (1992) on the osmosis between linguistics and geology in the nineteenth and twentieth centuries. Another example is Maasen, Mendelsohn, and Weingart's (1995) collective volume—with the telling title *Biology as Society, Society as Biology*—which discusses the case of biology and the social sciences using each other's scientific field as a metaphor for their own field of research. The most prominent example of a mapping from biology to the social sciences is certainly Darwinism, in all its various elaborations (see, e.g., Weingart 1995 for a discussion). In turn, biologists were inspired by models in the social sciences (see Bowler 1995 on social Darwinism).

In the following, we outline a particular instance of biology and linguistics making recourse to each other's domains: the LIFE IS LANGUAGE metaphor in biology and its converse LANGUAGE IS AN ORGANISM in linguistics. The former is paradigmatic in the recent biosemiotic approach in biology, which develops a full-fledged semiotic view of biology (see Sebeok, Hoffmeyer, and Emmeche 1999, for a comprehensive overview). Two advocates of this approach, Emmeche and Hoffmeyer (1991), discuss salient linguistic metaphors in biology and outline more specifically the history and application of the LIFE IS LANGUAGE conceptualization in its different forms. An early manifestation thereof is the theologically motivated NATURE AS THE GREAT BOOK metaphor, which has a history as old as theology itself and had its climax in the late Middle Ages: in nature, one can read the eternal power and divinity of the Almighty. Modern manifestations range from LIFE AS A MEMORY SYSTEM and LIFE AS LEARNING to ORGANISMS AS INFORMATION PROCESSING SYSTEMS, which are traced by Emmeche and Hoffmeyer in different theories of evolutionary and molecular biology. Specifically, they provide a detailed critical discussion of proposed analogies between living beings and the Saussurian model of language. Here, similarities are assumed between, among other things, *langue* and *genotype*, *parole* and *phenotype*, *new words* and *new mutations*, *linguistic communication* and *genetic communication*, *signifiant* and *DNA triplets*, and *morpheme* and *gene*. Emmeche and Hoffmeyer (1991) show the advantages and limits of this particular mapping. If, for instance, the gene is seen in analogy to a morpheme as the smallest meaning-bearing unit, this fails to account for the substantial and not abstract nature of a gene and misses the fact that a gene is only truly meaningful through and in the process of its biochemical interpretation. Without the appropriate interpretation device, it is no more than a DNA sequence. In their own biosemiotic approach, Emmeche and Hoffmeyer thus advocate a Peircean rather than a Saussurean perspective on language, which includes the indispensable interpretant. The gene is seen, correspondingly, as a triadic sign (see figure 47.2).

Emmeche and Hoffmeyer's arguments show that, when applied uncritically, the transfer of entire models developed elsewhere faces the inherent risk of yielding one-sided or even inappropriate perspectives on the envisaged target field. This

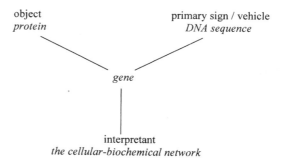

Figure 47.2. The sign relation of the gene

may become even more crucial when scientific discourse is used and referred to in the presence of a nonspecialist public. A relevant study is that by Nerlich and Dingwall (2003), who examine the rhetoric during the announcement of the deciphering of the human genome in June 2000. They provide a critical analysis of the metaphors employed by leading politicians (Clinton and Blair), by scientists, and by the media. The most pervasive metaphor drawn upon was DNA IS A CODE, which is highly conventional in genetics. Like Emmeche and Hoffmeyer (1991), Nerlich and Dingwall point to the limits of this conceptualization. It suggests, among other things, a genetic determinism which is clearly untenable, as a living being cannot be reduced to its genome—indeed, genetic processes involve a multitude of other components in that they are highly context-sensitive. Nerlich and Dingwall (2003: 403) note that the CODE metaphor itself reflects a reductionist and outdated model of human communication and that the genetic discourse has retained linguistic analogies which stem from the 1960s. The CODE metaphor, specifically, evokes the ideology of control: that "faulty" genes may simply be eliminated and that the genetic code can be easily "reprogrammed." In addition to the related ethical problems, this image conveys a false picture of genetic processes and is thus potentially misleading for nonspecialists. Nerlich and Dingwall argue that modern cognitive and contextual models of language may yield far more appropriate analogies.

The LIFE IS LANGUAGE metaphor in biology has a well-known counterpart in linguistics, LANGUAGE IS AN ORGANISM, with a long tradition in linguistic discourse. Its impact is, first of all, evident in the present established linguistic terminology: tone groups have *heads*, *bodies*, and *tails*, morphology speaks of *stems* and *roots*, phrase structures are *trees*, creole languages have a *life cycle*, sociolinguists conventionally speak of *language death* and *language revival*, to give just a few examples. As a full-fledged model of language, however, LANGUAGE IS AN ORGANISM evolved in the nineteenth-century romantic tradition, alongside the newly developed evolution theory (see e.g., Kucharczik 1998). As Haugen (1972: 326) rightly observes, the biological model was rejected in mainstream twentieth-century linguistic theory and replaced by different metaphors, in particular LANGUAGE IS AN INSTRUMENT (with the rise of Prague School functionalism) and LANGUAGE IS A STRUCTURE (with Bloomfieldian structuralism). The biological model and its metaphors were, however, maintained, to various degrees, in linguistic theories which have affinities to the romantic Humboldtian tradition. Whorf (1956: 84), for example, draws on it in the following passage:

> The relatively few languages of the cultures which have attained to modern civilization promise to overspread the globe and cause the extinction of the hundreds of diverse exotic linguistic species, but it is idle to pretend that they represent any superiority of type.

And within a very recent trend in linguistics—ecolinguistics—the ORGANISM metaphor is again paradigmatic and merges with a full readaptation of the biological model (e.g., Mühlhäusler 1996).

Again, it is important to notice that the perspective inherent in scientific models may have significant ideological implications, beyond the immediate scientific discourse. Geeraerts (2003) analyzes this dimension with respect to views of linguistic standardization, a highly controversial political issue. He distinguishes two "cultural models" under which the different views on standardization may be subsumed: the Rationalist Model, grounded on Enlightenment thinking, and the Romantic Model, rooted in the eighteenth- and nineteenth- century romantic tradition. The linguistic-philosophical basis of the Rationalist Model favors a view of LANGUAGE AS AN INSTRUMENT and sees standard and global languages, against this background, as neutral media of social participation and emancipation. This model clearly dominates past and contemporary language policy. The Romantic Model, by contrast, sees language primarily as a medium of expressing one's identity (see Kristiansen 2003 for a cognitive linguistic approach to this issue). Geeraerts (2003: 38–39) rightly places contemporary critical approaches such as the "linguistic human rights" movement (e.g., Skutnabb-Kangas 2000; Maffi 2001) in the broader Romantic Model. In this specific instantiation of the model, standard and global languages are regarded as media of social exclusion and a threat to local identities (see Geeraerts 2003: 40, 55), on the basis of the language-as-identity view, and often against the background of the biological model of language. From a critical perspective, both the scientific basis and the political impact of a model need to be scrutinized, or as Geeraerts (2003: 27) concludes: cultural models in the social sphere, including science, "may be ideologies in two different respects: either when their idealized character is forgotten (when the difference between the abstract model and the actual circumstances is neglected), or when they are used in a prescriptive and normative rather than a descriptive way (when they are used as models of how things should be rather than of how things are)." And evidently, such criticism, in turn, depends on one's own scientific and ideological position (see Silverstein 1979: 193).

6. CONCLUSION

The overall aim of this chapter has been to illustrate that the theoretical apparatus developed in Cognitive Linguistics may elegantly account for the expression of ideology in language, by relating the ideological dimension of linguistic phenomena to general conceptual principles. It is a particular strength of the cognitive linguistic approach that it makes it possible to describe these phenomena, diverse as they may appear, against a common theoretical background. As the above sections have shown, this approach explicitly analyzes linguistic expressions against the background of their underlying sociocultural, group-specific models. Here, linguistic patterns are taken as a strong but not sufficient indicator of ideological patterns; that is, they need to be related to a wider social context. When pursued systematically, this commitment to an integrative analysis should make the critical approach relatively robust against possible overinterpretations or even misinterpretations of linguistic data (see, however, the criticism in Hutton 2001).

The critical perspective, however, goes beyond the merely descriptive level. This becomes particularly apparent in the various applications of conceptual metaphor theory instantiated in several sections of this chapter. True to the thought expressed by Lakoff in the quote in the introductory section regarding the unconscious use of metaphors, the cognitive linguistic analysis may contribute to raising a critical awareness of how discourse domains are conceptualized. Being conscious of the metaphors we use, and hence their ideological nature, may enable and encourage us to continually search out models that capture and develop alternative views of the target domain in question. Here, Cognitive Linguistics offers analytic tools for a critical assessment of ideologies, yet it is not about providing "ideal ways" of conceptualizing.

REFERENCES

Bakhtin, Mikhail. 1982. *The dialogic imagination*. Ed. Michael Holquist. Trans. Caryl Emerson and Michael Holquist. Austin: University of Texas Press.

Bakhtin, Mikhail. 1986. Speech genres and other late essays. Ed. Caryl Emerson and Michael Holquist. Trans. Vern W. McGee. Austin: University of Texas Press.

Black, Max. 1993. More about metaphor. In Andrew Ortony, ed., *Metaphor and thought* 19–42. 2nd ed. Cambridge: Cambridge University Press.

Blommaert, Jan. 2005. *Discourse: A critical introduction*. Cambridge: Cambridge University Press.

Blommaert, Jan, and Chris Bulcaen. 2000. Critical discourse analysis. *Annual Review of Anthropology* 29: 447–66.

Boers, Frank. 1997. 'No pain, no gain' in a free market rhetoric: A test for cognitive semantics? *Metaphor and Symbol* 12: 231–41.

Botha, Willem. 2001. The deictic foundation of ideology with reference to African Renaissance. In René Dirven, Roslyn Frank, and Cornelia Ilie, eds., *Language and ideology*, vol. 2, *Descriptive cognitive approaches* 51–76. Amsterdam: John Benjamins.

Bourdieu, Pierre. 1991. *Language and symbolic power*. Cambridge: Polity Press.

Bowler, Peter J. 1995. Social metaphors in evolutionary biology, 1870–1930: The wider dimension of social Darwinism. In Sabine Maasen, Everett Mendelsohn, and Peter Weingart, eds., *Biology as society, society as biology: Metaphors* 107–26. Dordrecht, Netherlands: Kluwer Academic Publishers.

Caldas-Coulthard, Rosas Carmen, and Malcolm Coulthard, eds. 1996. *Readings in critical discourse analysis*. London: Routledge.

Chilton, Paul. 2005. Missing links in mainstream CDA: Modules, blends and the critical instinct. In Ruth Wodak and Paul Chilton, eds. *A new agenda in (critical) discourse analysis: Theory, methodology and interdisciplinarity* 19–51. Amsterdam: John Benjamins.

Cubo de Severino, Liliana, Daniel A. Israel, and Victor G. Zonana. 2001. Globalisation for beginners in Argentina: A cognitive approach. In René Dirven, Roslyn Frank, and Cornelia Ilie, eds., *Language and ideology*, vol. 2, *Descriptive cognitive approaches* 215–34. Amsterdam: John Benjamins.

Davidson, Donald. 1981. What metaphors mean. In Mark Johnson, ed., *Philosophical perspectives on metaphor* 200–219. Minneapolis: University of Minnesota Press.

Dirven, René. 1990. Metaphor and ideology. *Revue Belge de Philologie et d'Histoire* 68: 565–75. (Special issue on 'La pratique de la métaphore: How to do things with metaphors,' ed. Jean-Pierre Van Noppen)

Dirven, René. 1994. *Metaphor and nation: Metaphors Afrikaners live by*. Frankfurt am Main: Peter Lang Verlag.

Emmeche, Claus, and Jesper Hoffmeyer. 1991. From language to nature: The semiotic metaphor in biology. *Semiotica* 84: 1–42.

Eubanks, Philip. 2000. *A war of words in the discourse of trade: The rhetorical constitution of metaphor*. Carbondale: Southern Illinois University Press.

Fairclough, Norman. 1989. *Language and power*. London: Longman.

Fairclough, Norman. 1992. *Discourse and social change*. Cambridge: Polity Press.

Fairclough, Norman. 1995. *Critical discourse analysis*. London: Longman.

Fairclough, Norman. 2003. *Analysing discourse: Textual analysis for social research*. London: Routledge.

Fauconnier, Gilles. 1997. *Mappings in thought and language*. Cambridge: Cambridge University Press.

Fowler, Roger, and Gunther R. Kress. 1979. Critical linguistics. In Roger Fowler, Bob Hodge, Gunther Kress, and Tony Trew, eds., *Language and control* 185–213. London: Routledge.

Geeraerts, Dirk. 2003. Cultural models of linguistic standardization. In René Dirven, Roslyn Frank, and Martin Pütz, eds., *Cognitive models in language and thought: Ideologies, metaphors, and meanings* 25–68. Berlin: Mouton de Gruyter.

Grundy, Peter, and Yan Jiang. 2001. The bare past as an ideological construction in Hong Kong discourse. In René Dirven, Roslyn Frank, and Cornelia Ilie, eds., *Language and ideology*, vol. 2, *Descriptive cognitive approaches* 117–34. Amsterdam: John Benjamins.

Halliday, Michael A. K. 1978. *Language as social semiotic: The social interpretation of language and meaning*. London: Edward Arnold.

Halliday, Michael A. K. 1985. *An introduction to functional grammar*. London: Arnold. (2nd ed., 1994; 3rd ed., 2004)

Haugen, Einar. 1972. The ecology of language. In Anwar S. Oil, ed., *The ecology of language: Essays by Einar Haugen* 325–39. Stanford, CA: Stanford University Press.

Hawkins, Bruce. 1999. Matters of life and death: The role of iconographic reference in the language of oppression. In Jef Verschueren, ed., *Language and ideology: Selected papers from the 6th International Pragmatics Conference* 206–17. Antwerp, Belgium: International Pragmatics Association.

Hawkins, Bruce. 2001. Ideology, metaphor and iconographic reference. In René Dirven, Roslyn Frank, and Cornelia Ilie, eds., *Language and ideology*, vol. 2, *Descriptive cognitive approaches* 27–50. Amsterdam: John Benjamins.

Hodge, Robert, and Gunther Kress. 1993. *Language as ideology*. London: Routledge.

Howard, Harry. 2001. Age/gender morphemes inherit the biases of their underlying dimensions. In René Dirven, Bruce Hawkins, and Esra Sandikcioglu, eds., *Language and ideology*, vol. 1, *Theoretical cognitive approaches* 165–95. Amsterdam: John Benjamins.

Hutton, Christopher. 2001. Cultural and conceptual relativism, universalism and the politics of linguistics: Dilemmas of a would-be progressive linguistics. In René Dirven, Bruce Hawkins, and Esra Sandikcioglu, eds., *Language and ideology*, vol. 1, *Theoretical cognitive approaches* 277–96. Amsterdam: John Benjamins.

Ilie, Cornelia. 2001. Unparliamentary language: Insults as cognitive forms of ideological confrontation. In René Dirven, Roslyn Frank, and Cornelia Ilie, eds., *Language and ideology*, vol. 2, *Descriptive cognitive approaches* 235–63. Amsterdam: John Benjamins.

Jäkel, Olaf. 1997. *Metaphern in abstrakten Diskursdomänen*. Frankfurt am Main: Peter Lang Verlag.

Koller, Veronika. 2002. "A shotgun wedding": Co-occurrence of war and marriage metaphors in mergers and acquisitions discourse. *Metaphor and Symbol* 17: 179–203.

Kress, Gunther R. 1989. *Linguistic processes in sociocultural practice*. 2nd ed. Oxford: Oxford University Press.

Kristiansen, Gitte. 2003. How to do things with allophones: Linguistic stereotypes as cognitive reference points in social cognition. In René Dirven, Roslyn Frank, and Martin Pütz, eds., *Cognitive models in language and thought: Ideologies, metaphors, and meanings* 25–68. Berlin: Mouton de Gruyter.

Kucharczik, Kerstin. 1998. 'Organisch'—"Um den beliebten aber vieldeutigen Ausdruck zu gebrauchen": Zur Organismusmetaphorik in der Sprachwissenschaft des 19. Jahrhunderts. *Sprachwissenschaft* 23: 85–111.

Lakoff, George. 1987. *Women, fire, and dangerous things: What categories reveal about the mind*. Chicago: University of Chicago Press.

Lakoff, George. 1992. Metaphor and war: The metaphor system used to justify war in the Gulf. In Martin Pütz, ed., *Thirty years of linguistic evolution: Studies in honor of René Dirven on the occasion of his sixtieth birthday* 463–81. Amsterdam: John Benjamins.

Lakoff, George. 1996. *Moral politics: What conservatives know that liberals don't*. Chicago: University of Chicago Press.

Lakoff, George, and Mark Johnson. 1980. *Metaphors we live by*. Chicago: University of Chicago Press.

Lakoff, George, and Mark Turner. 1989. *More than cool reason: A field guide to poetic metaphor*. Chicago: University of Chicago Press.

Langacker, Ronald W. 1987. *Foundations of cognitive grammar.* Vol. 1, *Theoretical prereq-uisites.* Stanford, CA: Stanford University Press.

Langacker, Ronald W. 1991. *Foundations of cognitive grammar.* Vol. 2, *Descriptive appli-cation.* Stanford, CA: Stanford University Press.

Lovejoy, Arthur O. [1936] 1960. *The great chain of being: A study of the history of an idea.* New York: Harper and Row.

Maasen, Sabine, Everett Mendelsohn, and Peter Weingart, eds. 1995. *Biology as soci-ety, society as biology: Metaphors.* Dordrecht, Netherlands: Kluwer Academic Pub-lishers.

Maffi, Luisa, ed. 2001. *On biocultural diversity: Linking language, knowledge, and the en-vironment.* Washington, DC: Smithsonian Institution Press.

Morgan, Pamela S. 2001. The semantics of an impeachment. In René Dirven, Roslyn Frank, and Cornelia Ilie, eds., *Language and ideology,* vol. 2, *Descriptive cognitive approaches* 77–106. Amsterdam: John Benjamins.

Mühlhäusler, Peter. 1996. *Linguistic ecology: Language change and linguistic imperialism in the Pacific region.* London: Routledge.

Naumann, Bernd, Frans Plank, and Gottfried Hofbauer, eds. 1992. *Language and earth: Elective affinities between the emerging sciences of linguistics and geology.* Amsterdam: John Benjamins.

Nerlich, Brigitte, and Robert Dingwall. 2003. Deciphering the human genome: The se-mantic and ideological foundations of genetic and genomic discourse. In René Dirven, Roslyn Frank, and Martin Pütz, eds., *Cognitive models in language and thought: Ideologies, metaphors, and meanings* 395–428. Berlin: Mouton de Gruyter.

Nesset, Tore. 2001. How pervasive are sexist ideologies in grammar? In René Dirven, Bruce Hawkins, and Esra Sandikcioglu, eds., *Language and ideology,* vol. 1, *Theoretical cog-nitive approaches* 197–226. Amsterdam: John Benjamins.

O'Halloran, Kieran. 2003. *Critical discourse analysis and language cognition.* Edinburgh: Edinburgh University Press.

Pancake, Ann S. 1993. Taken by storm: The exploitation of metaphor in the Persian Gulf War. *Metaphor and Symbolic Activity* 8: 281–95.

Pires de Oliveira, Roberta. 2001. Language and ideology: An interview with George Lakoff. In René Dirven, Bruce Hawkins, and Esra Sandikcioglu, eds., *Language and ide-ology,* vol. 1, *Theoretical cognitive approaches* 23–48. Amsterdam: John Benjamins.

Pope, Alexander. [1732] 1891. *An essay on man.* London: Cassell.

Rohrer, Tim. 1995. The metaphorical logic of (political) rape revisited: The new wor(l)d order. *Metaphor and Symbolic Activity* 10: 113–31.

Rohrer, Tim. 2001. Even the interface is for sale: Metaphors, visual blends and the hid-den ideology of the internet. In René Dirven, Roslyn Frank, and Cornelia Ilie, eds., *Language and ideology,* vol. 2, *Descriptive cognitive approaches* 189–214. Am-sterdam: John Benjamins.

Sandikcioglu, Esra. 2000. More metaphorical warfare in the Gulf: Orientalist frames in news coverage. In Antonio Barcelona, ed., *Metaphor and metonymy at the crossroads: A cognitive perspective* 299–320. Berlin: Mouton de Gruyter.

Sandikcioglu, Esra. 2001. The otherness of the Orient: Politico-cultural implications of ideological categorisations. In René Dirven, Roslyn Frank, and Cornelia Ilie, eds., *Language and ideology,* vol. 2, *Descriptive cognitive approaches* 161–88. Amsterdam: John Benjamins.

Santa Ana, Otto. 2003. Three mandates for anti-minority policy expressed in U.S. pub-lic discourse metaphors. In René Dirven, Roslyn Frank, and Martin Pütz, eds.,

Cognitive models in language and thought: Ideologies, metaphors, and meanings 199–227. Berlin: Mouton de Gruyter.

Sebeok, Thomas A., Jesper Hoffmeyer, and Claus Emmeche, eds. 1999. Biosemiotica. Special issue of *Semiotica* 127, 1/4.

Silverstein, Michael. 1979. Language structure and linguistic ideology. *Chicago Linguistic Society* 15, vol. 2 (parasession): 193–247.

Simpson, Paul. 1993. *Language, ideology and point of view.* London: Routledge.

Skutnabb-Kangas, Tove. 2000. *Linguistic genocide in education: Or worldwide diversity and human rights?* Mahwah, NJ: Lawrence Erlbaum.

Stockwell, Peter. 1999. Towards a critical cognitive linguistics? In Annette Combrink and Ina Biermann, eds. *Poetics, linguistics and history: Discourses of war and conflict* 510–28. Proceedings of PALA XIX, Potchefstroom University, South Africa, March 29–April 1. CD edited and produced by Peter Stockwell and Martin Wynne (available at http://www.pala.ac.uk/confs/potch/CD/home.htm). Published for PALA by the Humanities Computing Unit, Oxford University. (Available at http://www.nottingham.ac.uk/~aezps/research/papers/CRITCOG.PDF)

Toolan, Michael, ed. 2002. *Critical discourse analysis: Critical concepts in linguistics.* 4 vols. London: Routledge.

Urban, Nancy Y. 1999. The school business: Rethinking educational reform. PhD dissertation, University of California, Berkeley.

van Dijk, Teun. 1993. Principles of critical discourse analysis. *Discourse and Society* 4: 249–83.

van Dijk, Teun. 1997. *Discourse as structure and process.* London: Sage.

van Dijk, Teun. 1998. *Ideology: A multidisciplinary approach.* London: Sage.

van Dijk, Teun. 2002. *Discourse, knowledge and ideology: Reformulating old questions.* LAUD Paper no. 546. Essen, Germany: Linguistic Agency of the University of Duisburg-Essen.

Weingart, Peter. 1995. 'Struggle for existence': Selection and retention of a metaphor. In Sabine Maasen, Everett Mendelsohn, and Peter Weingart, eds., *Biology as society, society as biology: Metaphors* 127–51. Dordrecht, Netherlands: Kluwer Academic Publishers.

White, Michael, and Honesto Herrera. 2003. Metaphor and ideology in the press coverage of business consolidations. In René Dirven, Roslyn Frank, and Martin Pütz, eds., *Cognitive models in language and thought: Ideologies, metaphors, and meanings* 277–323. Berlin: Mouton de Gruyter.

Whorf, Benjamin L. 1956. *Language, thought, and reality: Selected writings of Benjamin Lee Whorf.* Ed. John B. Caroll. Cambridge, MA: MIT Press.

Winter, Steven L. 2001. *A clearing in the forest.* Chicago: University of Chicago Press.

Wodak, Ruth, ed. 1989. *Language, power and ideology.* Amsterdam: John Benjamins.

Wodak, Ruth, and Paul Chilton, eds. 2005. *A new agenda in (critical) discourse analysis: Theory, methodology and interdisciplinarity.* Amsterdam: John Benjamins.

Wolf, Hans-Georg, and Frank Polzenhagen. 2003. Conceptual metaphor as ideological stylistic means: An exemplary analysis. In René Dirven, Roslyn Frank, and Martin Pütz, eds., *Cognitive models in language and thought: Ideologies, metaphors, and meanings* 247–77. Berlin: Mouton de Gruyter.

CHAPTER 48

....

COGNITIVE LINGUISTICS AND PHILOSOPHY

....

PETER HARDER

1. INTRODUCTION

....

How one sees the relationship between Cognitive Linguistics and philosophy depends on what one takes to be the role and nature of philosophy. The approach followed below is the one presented by J. L. Austin (see Austin 1970: 232): it views philosophy as constituting the overarching arena for discussions about the nature of the world and our knowledge about it, within which independent disciplines have gradually crystallized into domains of their own. The decisive factor in the process that creates such independent areas is the rise of a descriptive practice that is generally recognized as adequate for a particular area of inquiry. When such a method becomes established, work within the field "graduates" from the stage of philosophical argument to systematic investigation in well-defined terms. To some extent, such areas then point the way for the rest of philosophy to follow; already in antiquity, the systematicity of mathematics endowed it with the status of a paradigmatic form of knowledge that was a source of inspiration for the rest of philosophy. In more modern times, the most epochal instance of this is the process that gave rise to natural science with physics as the paradigm discipline.

This process of "cultural modularization of knowledge" means that the territory of philosophy is gradually diminishing. There is, for instance, no longer anything corresponding to "philosophy of nature," in which the constitution of matter is discussed. In contrast, there is still an area of "philosophy of mind" because discussions about the nature of the mind have not in the general opinion reached a stage of solidity in which they can be discussed in isolation from the overall framework. Austin envisaged a period in which also the area of language might come to constitute an independent domain—and this is a natural perspective for viewing the relationship between Cognitive Linguistics and philosophy.

Even for areas that have reached the stage of independence, however, philosophy retains the function of keeping order in the universe from an overall perspective. The question of how different areas with different approaches relate to each other cannot be answered by any single discipline. In this view, philosophy is an arena of inquiry, not a body of definitive results. To say that something is a philosophical question may occasionally suggest that you can say whatever you like about it. The reason for that impression is that philosophical questions only arise in cases where there are no straightforward answers to a question, but where we must go back to more basic and general principles. A fair number of such questions can still be found in Cognitive Linguistics.

Taking Austin's approach means that the chief aim below is to address some foundational issues that I view as important for the theory and practice (goals and methodology) of Cognitive Linguistics. I will make no attempt to express *the* philosophical position of Cognitive Linguistics (there is none) or to follow up all references to philosophical issues in the cognitive linguistic literature (e.g., to Aristotle's views on the nature of concepts or Merleau-Ponty's on embodiment). The points I will take up are those that call for a continuing clarification process that would also be useful to Cognitive Linguistics.

The main issue to be addressed is the nature of the object(s) of investigation. No consensus has been achieved, either inside or outside Cognitive Linguistics, on the precise status and properties of mental entities, including their relation both to the human body that generates them and to the outside cultural and physical environment. That issue and its implications will be a leitmotif below.

For obvious reasons, the status of mental entities is crucial also to philosophy—and since Cognitive Linguistics makes claims about the mind that bear upon what philosophers have said, this aspect of the problem constitutes an issue in its own right.

In order to discuss that problem, it will be necessary to touch on some of the basic concerns of philosophy. These include the relationship between ontology (i.e., the nature of reality, including the objects under description) and epistemology (the question of how we can acquire true knowledge of reality). The latter is concretely manifested in the form of methodology (what are the appropriate scientific, descriptive procedures that reflect our epistemological stance?). Thinking about the mind is historically bound up with dilemmas that span all these levels, with a rough polarity between, on the one hand, idealism and rationalism, which share a commitment to mental foundations of understanding, and on the other hand, empiricism, which takes actual experience, entering the mind via the senses, as the foundation of knowledge.

The aim of both positions, however, is to arrive at true knowledge of the world—that is, whatever may be the nature of mental representations, there are criteria which these representations have to live up to in order to work "properly" from a philosophical point of view. These criteria involve epistemology as well as ontology: our thoughts must work reliably and tend toward valid conclusions about reality. Below, the word *validity* will be used with reference to both dimensions. The criteria of validity, which are central to philosophy, constitute a major difference of perspective between philosophy in its metaposition, viewing all areas from above, and Cognitive Linguistics as a discipline in the process of carving out its own domain. The implications of that difference constitute another main theme below.

Thinking about mental entities has had a turbulent history in the twentieth century. An account of the developments that led up to the emergence of Cognitive Linguistics may therefore be illuminating in order to pave the way for a discussion of the principles involved. Especially in relation to the "first cognitive revolution" (see Sinha, this volume, chapter 49), including Generative Grammar, which constitutes the immediate predecessor to Cognitive Linguistics, the process of development is an important part of the present picture. The account below will therefore begin with a historical account.

2. LINGUISTICS AND THE PHILOSOPHY OF SCIENCE IN THE TWENTIETH CENTURY

The history of linguistics in the twentieth century is profoundly influenced by developments in the overall philosophical perspective. Other disciplines, for example, biology, have to a greater extent developed as a result of increasing domain-specific knowledge leading to the rise of, for example, a molecular dimension of the subject. Developments in linguistics, in contrast, have been marked by revolutions from above.

Already in Classical Antiquity, linguistics (or "grammar" as it was then called) experienced a partial liberation from its philosophical beginnings with the morphological school of the Alexandrian grammarians. The tradition they founded was extremely durable, continuing uninterruptedly until the twentieth century—even today, most people who have had any experience with school grammar probably think of grammar in their terms, as classes of words with different sets of inflections. But the liberation from philosophy was only partial; the semantic foundations of this pattern of description remained bound up with classical ontological assumptions going back to Plato and Aristotle. These included an assumption that linguistic categories directly mirror mental categories, which again mirror the categories of the world. The "speculative" approach (from Latin *speculum* 'mirror') was applied through intuitive "hermeneutic" (interpretive) description (with unclear empirical control, which is why the word *speculative* gradually acquired a new sense and a doubtful reputation) and, throughout that entire period, did not undergo much change. Therefore, it was vulnerable to radical twentieth-century changes in philosophical assumptions about the world and about principles of scientific description.

The underlying cause of these changes had to do with the paradigmatic status of natural science understood as carrying the beacon of progress—not only intellectually but also technically and socially. From the Renaissance onwards, the emergence of a world picture based on blind, objective laws, supported by demonstrations of the technical possibilities created by insight in these laws, gradually changed the picture of human knowledge. A central trend was the erosion of faith in systems of intuition-based "ideas" in favor of faith in scientific method, both inside philosophy itself and in the general intellectual climate. From the beginnings of philosophy, epistemology and ontology had been intimately connected, while the relations between them had varied. The triumphs of scientific method tipped the balance decisively in favor of a greater weight attached to epistemology—that is, in favor of the question of "how" rather than "what." The result was that world knowledge became increasingly subservient to the dictates of methodology, whatever the consequences might be for the familiar picture of the world. Being intuitively obvious was no longer the same as being taken for granted.

Although this development had been at work since the sixteenth and seventeenth centuries, some of the potential consequences only became apparent in the twentieth. Behaviorism, which defined psychology in terms of overt behavior only, was a radical consequence of this way of thinking, eliminating the mind entirely as part of the scientific world picture. Since scientifically reliable insight could only be achieved by observations of overt behavior (methodology), it followed in practice, if not in theory, that responsible psychologists could not accommodate such a thing as the mind in their world picture (ontology). From a philosophical perspective, this conclusion was not by any means obvious (see Russell 1956: 293); and jokes like that of the two behaviorists who met and said, "How am I?—You're fine!" showed a continuing awareness of the apparent absurdity of the position. Within psychology, it had all the destructive influence that only a denial of the chief object of description can have on a scientific discipline (see Sinha, this volume, chapter 49). The fact that psychologists were willing to pay this price shows how powerful the epistemological and methodological considerations were. In linguistics, Bloomfield revised his linguistic system to make it fit with the assumptions of behaviorist psychology, excising all reference to mental objects.

Psychologists and their linguistic followers in America, however, were the only scholars who went so far as to deny the existence of the mind. Within philosophy, the development away from the familiar world picture toward principles of scientific method took another form, called "the linguistic turn." The idea was, roughly speaking, that scientific status is bound up with the *formulation* of scientific problems and solutions, rather than with the actual substance that they dealt with (see Carnap 1934). By fixing the properties of the scientific metalanguage, in practice a version of formal logic, the philosophy of science could be a guardian of the reliability of knowledge without getting involved with the actual world. The inspiration came from the use of mathematics as a tool for the precise formulation of physical laws (the model of true scientific knowledge noted above). One of the aims of tightening up criteria for what counted as tenable forms of thought was precisely to get rid of the whole inherited but prescientific ontology, as expressed in volumes of what was seen as mere verbiage (since it was not expressed in the language of formal logic).

Within linguistics, there were domain-internal tendencies that could derive inspiration from this view of what counted as reliable knowledge. The structural revolution occurring in the wake of Saussure was also motivated by a desire to get rid of the ontological ballast from antiquity. Saussure insisted that words as linguistic entities were severed from meanings understood as preexistent entities in the mind or in the world. The classical, in the etymological sense, speculative grammar, in which language mirrored immutable ideal reality (such that substantives denoted substances, etc.), was thus rejected in favor of a picture that focused on structural relations between linguistic forms.

This transfer was further promoted by a movement toward structure within philosophy itself. Carnap (1928) set up the concept of "logical syntax" to capture the logical analysis of the structure of the world and suggested that science can essentially only describe structures. It is not surprising that in European structuralism this parallel was a major source of inspiration. The abstract and formal nature of structural relations, as opposed to intuitive content in the form of ideas or concepts, had the same aura of rising above inherited muddles in linguistics as it had in philosophy. It is perhaps not inappropriate to point to modernist developments in art (see Ortega y Gasset [1925] 1976) to give an idea of the pervasive drift in the early twentieth century away from a baggage of assumed, presupposed substance, toward imposing a new abstract order on experience. In this movement, the alien flavor is a virtue, precisely because it demonstrates a successful break with accepted (hence suspect) criteria of naturalness.

Although this movement was by no means restricted to philosophy, its most powerful manifestation remained the alliance between physics as a model science, on the one hand, and formal modeling as the paradigm for scientific description, on the other. The reason Generative Grammar achieved its dominant position in modern linguistics is that it presented an application of this model of description to language and launched it at the point when the behaviorist barriers against theorizing about the mind were ready to be dismantled. The rise of cognitive science, the "first cognitive revolution" around 1960, came about not because mental entities as we intuitively know them suddenly became scientifically respectable, but because the restrictions imposed by behaviorism were becoming obsolete.

Chomsky (1959) achieved his most spectacular breakthrough with his review of *Verbal Behavior* by B. F. Skinner, the main exponent of behaviorism as applied to the psychology of language. The force of his argument had two sources: it introduced more advanced descriptive techniques, and it was directed against a position that was intuitively unattractive because of its reduction of human powers to reflexes. The complexities that Chomsky introduced thus combined the thrust of increased scientific sophistication with a defense of human dignity. Moreover, in being a founding member of the newborn discipline of cognitive science, Generative Grammar was part of a movement that appeared to mark a wholly new epoch in all sciences dealing with human nature, combining exciting new vistas with rigorous scientific precision. Only much later did the limitations of the formal apparatus that was at the core of the first cognitive revolution become an issue.

The sudden scientific acceptability of complex theories of cognition can primarily be attributed to the invention of the computer. If a machine could handle complex information processing in ways that could not be handled by simple stimulus-control relations between events, the credibility of trying to understand human information processing in those simplistic terms was gone. The first step in Generative Grammar was the demonstration that the formal model that could be distilled out of behaviorist principles of description was simply too impoverished to account for the known structure of linguistic facts. The scientific legitimacy that was already accorded to formal modeling in physics was thus simply transferred to formal modeling in linguistics. It is therefore natural that Generative Grammar should understand itself as carrying the beacon of true scientific principles of description.

In the generative context, the frequently invoked term *empirical* refers to the conception in terms of building a formal model, deriving empirical predictions from it, and testing them against the data, which had now been finally extended to linguistics. Previous forms of linguistics were assigned the status of alchemy in relation to chemistry, with Bloomfieldian linguistics as the primitive precursor to the true science of language. The identification with hard science was confirmed when Generative Grammar allied itself with a semantics based on logical, truth-conditional foundations (i.e., the level of "logical form").

Philosophically, however, the situation became rather more complex when Chomsky reinterpreted his own philosophical position in rationalist terms, claiming that the nucleus of the formal system must be innate in the human mind. As pointed out by Itkonen (1992: 73), this is a wholly external maneuver in relation to the anatomy of Generative Grammar per se, which (in good accordance with the model science of physics) was originally predicated on the "physical properties of utterances" (Chomsky 1975: 127), just as in the thinking of his Bloomfieldian predecessors.

It is sort of odd for a science to invent a new and more attractive object of description while retaining the descriptive apparatus, and this is an important clue to Chomsky's way of thinking. Apart from the rejection of behaviorist oversimplification, Chomsky's early writings were not initially motivated by new insights in language, but by the idea of putting linguistics on a new scientific footing. From that point of view, it is natural that the exact nature of language, or rather "grammar," as an object would have to depend on what fitted best into the new scientific footing. A grammar that is inherent in the basic wiring of the human mind is much more congenial to his formal system than one viewed as a property of actual, messy empirical talk. Chomsky's repeated insistence on internal language as the only proper object of linguistic description (for a recent reaffirmation, see Chomsky 2000) reflects a basic commitment to formal, metalinguistic precision as the criterion of scientific status. This claim is maintained in spite of the fact that the hard-nosed attitude of precision coexisted with a rather soft intuitive underbelly when it came to relations with the data. His postulated underlying structures are prevented from having empirical status in terms of the criteria of hard sciences because of the problem of experimental access to mental as opposed to physical entities. When it became apparent that there were no compelling reasons to prefer Chomskyan intuitions over intuitions less regimented by rather idiosyncratic principles of formalization, the time was ripe for a new Second Generation Cognitive Science in which Cognitive Linguistics had a central role (see also Sinha, this volume, chapter 49).

3. COGNITIVE LINGUISTICS AND THE REBELLION AGAINST METHODOLOGICAL IMPERIALISM

Cognitive Linguistics represents a radical break with the earlier twentieth-century trend of shaping linguistics in ways that reflect philosophical views of what counts as scientific description. Cognitive Linguistics focuses squarely on mental, conceptual entities as legitimate objects of description in their own right. Historically, this can be understood as reflecting increasing permissiveness in the philosophical climate. The first generation of cognitive scientists remained careful in their outline of a science of the mind because the fear of the science police was still present: their way of mapping out the science of the mind was designed to prove that such a science would not revert to prescientific forms of description. When discussions about the nature of mental entities had become generally accepted, the need to stay within established "formalist" bounds of scientific respectability was no longer acutely present and diminished in favor of a desire to bring new kinds of phenomena to light.

From that perspective, an important mission of Cognitive Linguistics, as part of the new generation of cognitive science, was to show that established barriers prevented a full investigation of the field. The most uncontroversial achievement of Cognitive Linguistics is probably that it opened language description to a rich new landscape of conceptual phenomena and mechanisms interrelated in multiple ways with the whole of human experience and shaped in accordance with patterns of human imagination. In addition to these positive qualities, Cognitive Linguistics was also very much aware of being everything that Generative Grammar was not: nonformal, nonmodular, non-truth-conditional, and so on. Cognitive Linguistics saw itself as a liberation from misguided earlier philosophical positions.

This is true especially when it comes to methodology. Langacker (1987: 31) has gone on record as being wary of devoting too much importance to methodology as opposed to the actual object of description. Both Langacker (1999: 26) and Lakoff and Johnson (1999: 79) espouse the open-minded doctrine of "converging evidence," that is, of letting all methodologies be used and see what they collectively point to.

When it comes to ontology as opposed to methodology, the position of Cognitive Linguistics is more well-defined and follows from the core area of the approach. The central domain of Cognitive Linguistics is cognitive, conceptual structures defined by their content rather than their formal structure alone. In accordance with this, Langacker (1987: 97) has made explicit his commitment to the conceptualist approach to meaning. This commitment is made in direct contrast to the views expressed by Lyons (1977: 113) as a representative of first generation cognitive science. Generative Grammar and Truth-conditional Semantics saw no independent role for a purely conceptual-semantic level, because it would be an expendable "middleman" between the two central levels of formal-syntactic structure and logical form.

However, the conceptualism adopted by Langacker and other cognitive linguists should not be understood as aggressively oriented against other ontological commitments—rather, its function is specifically to defend the legitimacy of the central elements in the theory, regardless of what other elements they may share the universe with. This ontology goes naturally with attributing a central methodological role to intuition: since mental content is only accessible to human subjects, there is no way of getting at the central data without them.

The basically optimistic feeling about the sturdiness of its object of description and of the intuitive descriptive practice that goes with it has served Cognitive Linguistics well in its investigation of the central phenomena of its field. These include construal, imagery of different kinds, mental spaces (this volume, chapters 3, 14, and 17), and the way these are associated with different linguistic categories. But the problems that worried most of modern psychology and philosophy about the nature of mental entities have not evaporated entirely. Cognitive Linguistics would not have been possible without a certain consensus about the value of intuitions.

Still, as had been noted at earlier points in the history of psychology, intuitions do not always provide clear-cut answers. One of the points where conceptual disagreement is frequent in scholarly circles is when it comes to the question of how much to lump together under one concept. Where this is usually a problem at the metalevel (involving the scientific terminology), in Cognitive Semantics it involves the object of description, linguistic meanings. The problem was brought to the forefront by Sandra and Rice (1995) in relation to the issue of polysemous networks of meaning, as they have become familiar from the analysis of the preposition *over* in Brugman (1981) and Lakoff (1987). Sandra and Rice found that it was very difficult to confirm the existence of cohesive semantic links in polysemous networks of meaning by experimental means. The question this raises, as expressed in the title of their article, is whether the mental constructs posited in network analyses reflect any other mental object than the linguist's mind (see also Rice, Sandra, and Vanrespaille 1999). The article thus directly challenges the scientific status of intuitions.

The discussion continued in a series of articles in *Cognitive Linguistics* (Croft 1998; Sandra 1998; Tuggy 1999; see also Sanders 1997). Whereas Croft and Sandra stress the limitations of what can be postulated on the basis of intuition-based linguistic evidence, Tuggy defends the possibility of using linguists' intuitions as a source of information about mental entities. This is not the place to enter into the discussion, but it shows that there is a methodological, hence philosophical, dilemma for Cognitive Linguistics here: while convergent evidence makes it possible to relax constraints on methodology, divergent evidence brings back the issue. In particular, the latter calls for a clarification of criteria of what exactly is meant by "psychologically real." The question of what the relation is between mental content as it manifests itself intuitively and mental content as manifested in experimental findings is a philosophical question, which cannot be answered simply by looking at the data. At this point, the foundational question of the nature of the object of description raises itself as part of the road to further progress, bringing us back to the central issues raised in the introduction.

4. Conceptual Structures and the Philosophy of Mind: Internalist and Externalist Perspectives

The question of the nature of mental entities is also becoming more salient in relation to the issue of how the domain of cognitive phenomena is to be defined in relation to phenomena inside as well as outside the individual subject. The general tendency is to use the word *cognition* to cover as broad a range of phenomena as possible, rejecting narrow compartmentalization and stressing the essential *continuity* of all cognitively imbued domains. This is motivated both by opposition to the modular and formal approach of the previous generation of linguists and cognitive scientists and by the development toward applying the central insights of Cognitive Linguistics to more and more areas.

From an internalist perspective, concerned with everything that goes on inside the cognizing subject, this broad use of the term makes it natural to understand most forms of response and processing as coming under the label "cognition." Lakoff and Johnson (1999: 17) even see the amoeba as a "categorizing" entity, because it distinguishes between two sets of objects by either moving toward them or away from them. However, a continuity that generalizes mental phenomena "downwards" to include mechanisms that other authors see as clearly nonmental (e.g., Johnson-Laird 1988: 24) raises a philosophical issue with those natural scientists who would like to generalize "upwards" from purely physical, neurological reactions in order to eliminate all reference to mental phenomena from scientific description. If we generalize from the physical level, the ontological dilemma of "reductionism" arises (several kinds of apparently different objects are "reduced" to one kind in the theory). Conversely, if we attribute mental life to objects that do not obviously manifest it, the possibility of using Occam's razor arises, pruning away unnecessary additions to the world picture. Either way, there is a need to clarify the ontology of the object domain.

From an externalist perspective, the strategy of emphasizing continuity means that all sorts of human experience—from bodily movement via everyday interaction to religion, ideology, and politics (see Dirven, Hawkins, and Sandikcioglu 2000; Dirven, Frank, and Ilie 2001)—are part of the domain of cognition and conceptualization. The continuity between conceptualizations as they operate inside and outside the individual head is stressed, for example, by Gibbs (1999). Notwithstanding the virtues offered by this all-encompassing approach, it means that the realm of cognitive objects comes to be somewhat heterogeneous. I will try to show where this may become problematic, beginning with the descriptive practice that takes its point of departure in the individual.

The emphasis within Cognitive Linguistics on bodily grounding (see below) means that the internalist perspective is generally given priority as a source of explanation. In this, there is a continuity with first-generation cognitive science. Lakoff and Johnson (1999: chapter 2) outline a picture of cognitive architecture which accords with a rule of thumb among cognitive scientists stating that 95% of all thought is inaccessible to consciousness: "Our unconscious conceptual knowledge functions like a 'hidden hand' that shapes how we conceptualize all aspects of our experience" (1999: 13). Chomsky is generously said to "deserve enormous credit" (Lakoff and Johnson 1999: 472) for bringing into linguistics the notion of unconscious cognitive structures. In this picture, the explanatory status of "tacit knowledge" thus survived from Chomsky to Cognitive Linguistics, while the specification of what it consists of radically changed.

The emphasis on an object that belongs in the mind of the individual without being directly accessible raises a philosophical dilemma, which is taken up by Geeraerts (1999). Geeraerts's own background for raising the issue is his work on diachronic semantics (see, e.g., Geeraerts 1997), which shows how empirical processes of lexical change can be accounted for with the tools of Cognitive Linguistics. He presents the dilemma in the form of a classical dialogue that brings out in counterpoint the contrasting difficulties of the idealist as opposed to the empirical orientation. Although the idealist position is illustrated with quotations from Wierzbicka rather than "mainstream" Cognitive Linguistics, the reliance on intuitive analyses is similar enough to make the dilemma relevant. The clear-cut idealist position is criticized because too firm a reliance on intuitively accessible concepts is liable to seal off the results of the investigation from criticism—in effect not living up to the empirical commitments of scientific activity. Wierzbicka's project derives from Leibniz's idea of "the alphabet of human thought" and could naturally be described as rationalist in orientation (although in terms of a rationalism quite different from Chomsky's).

The orientation toward conceptualization as taking place in processes of language use has not been equally emphasized, although in principle the commitment to language as part of human interactive experience has never been in doubt. Barlow and Kemmer (2000) explicitly set out to place Cognitive Linguistics in a broader picture of linguistic models that share the goal of basing linguistic description on usage.

This brings us back to the externalist perspective and the problem of the heterogeneous domain of cognitive phenomena. Unlike an item in one's personal mental dictionary, the process whereby naming practices are shaped in a speech community over time does not belong in the internal arena of the cognitive unconscious of an individual. In a philosophical context, the question is what follows from the fact that the object of description is not exactly the same when one is investigating diachronic prototype semantics as when investigating the hidden hand of "backstage cognition." The difference in ontological commitments between the two approaches, as pointed out in Geeraerts (1999), cannot be straightforwardly cashed out in terms of decidable empirical issues. Conceptualization is clearly involved in both phenomena—but if it is too easily assumed that the same kind of thing is going on in both cases, the external, historical, and social factors contributing to the shaping of concepts are at risk of becoming invisible, overshadowed by the emphasis on the role of the individual human body/brain/mind viewed as an integrated system. This issue has also been addressed in a number of contexts by Chris Sinha, whose psychological perspective has reflected an orientation toward the dependence of cognitive structures on cultural and discursive processes (see Sinha 1988, 1999).

The polysemy issue raised in the previous section involved two perspectives on the same object, namely, semantic networks in the mind. The present issue is more complex, because it involves two sets of related but different objects. The need for clarification of the interaction between the internal and the external domain of cognitively constituted phenomena should not lead to a classical form of dualism. A reversal to Descartes's division into separate realms of body and mind would both be against the scientific world picture and against the idea of the embodied mind.

Exactly how best to avoid this, however, is not a settled issue. Both cognitive science and the philosophy of mind are still faced with the question of how to address the basic problem of accommodating mental phenomena in a nondualist world picture.

There are positions available that suggest directions one might take. With the scope of phenomena it wants to accommodate, Cognitive Linguistics finds itself somewhere in the same landscape as the biologically based philosophy of mind and cognition developed by Maturana and his associates (see Maturana and Varela 1980). In it, organism and environment are understood to be mutually determined: the organism can only be understood as an aspect of the larger system it interacts with, and the environment is created by the way the organism itself responds to the "medium" in which it finds itself. This approach stresses the closure that comes about around the fused spheres of inner and outer processes, the so-called *autopoiesis*, in which the events that happen and the state of the organism itself are in a form of equilibrium that can only be understood from within (see also Varela, Thompson, and Rosch 1991). This approach has influenced cognitive science independently of Cognitive Linguistics (see Maturana 1975; Winograd and Flores 1986) but is congenial in its broad view of cognition and in emphasizing the embodied nature also of environmentally shaped processes.

In continuation of this perspective, Clark (1997) discusses the implications of the human ability to extend cognitive processes into the external domain, including as a paradigm case the dependence on language as a public medium. As a consequence of Clark's perspective, an element of distance is interposed between body and mind, that is, between bodily processes including those of the brain and the mind as a property of the human subject. While this perspective emphasizes the embodied status of action and cognition, it thus renders problematic the extent to which the body "in the flesh" (see Lakoff and Johnson 1999) remains the seat of all forms of mental content. In his final chapter, Clark emphasizes the difference between a person's *mind* (which includes his links with external objects) and the brain as a bodily organ. Minds are to some extent socially constituted.

One clear implication of the argument above is methodological. To the extent that the processes giving shape to meaning and conceptualization occur in the social sphere rather than in the individual mind, the methods of the social sciences need to be taken into account. One challenge is how to include methods addressing social variability in accounting for conceptual distinctions as part of language use (see Geeraerts 2003). The new theoretical platform proposed by Croft, including the diachronic (2000) as well as the synchronic (2001) dimensions, draws on foundational elements that have been extended from natural science (biology) to the social side of language. It will be interesting to see how the understanding of cognition, and of the appropriate way of handling it, will develop in the expanding universe of Cognitive Linguistics.

5. THE CHALLENGE FROM COGNITIVE LINGUISTICS TO PHILOSOPHY

The nature of mental entities, however, is not only a philosophical problem—it is also a problem for philosophy. The new light thrown upon conceptualization by results from Cognitive Linguistics also puts the ball in the other court: how should philosophy respond? This point was raised by Johnson (1992) and followed up in Lakoff and Johnson (1999). Johnson claims that if Cognitive Linguistics is to be worthy of its name, then its results with respect to how the mind works must have implications for philosophical positions on how the mind relates to reality. By claiming that mental function is grounded in the body and imaginatively structured in a way that reflects specifically human experience, Cognitive Linguistics has defined a new position in the philosophical landscape. This position contrasts, on the one hand, with a belief in absolute objective foundations of knowledge and, on the other hand, with a deconstructionist rejection of any kind of foundation whatsoever.

Of special philosophical interest is the way in which the bodily basis, with force dynamics as a key example (see Talmy 1988), affects mental domains such as knowledge and reason. In the case of reasoning, we understand the force of physical compulsion as a source domain recruited to conceptualize the force of a logical argument. A similar example is the relationship between knowing and seeing, where the perceptual term "seeing" is recruited to serve as an indicator of the cognitive relationship that is the result of seeing (as when you explain something and then ask, *You see?*) (see Sweetser 1990). Among other philosophical key areas are the concepts of subjective versus objective, of selfhood, of social relations, and of ethics, all of which are illuminated by being seen in the context of their anchoring in embodied experience.

This manifesto was followed by a discussion in *Cognitive Linguistics* (Gorayska 1993; Johnson 1993; McLure 1993; Sinha 1993), offering different views on exactly what kind of force the findings of Cognitive Linguistics can rightly be claimed to have with respect to philosophy. One possible interpretation of the article is that Cognitive Linguistics has proven Philosophy (with a capital P) wrong, an interpretation Johnson (1993: 69) denies, while admitting that his title is perhaps misleading in that perspective. Sinha (1993: 53) offers a weaker alternative, namely that Cognitive Linguistics, like any new theory, raises the issue of how its results should be interpreted philosophically, but Johnson's reply suggests that this may not go far enough; results of Cognitive Linguistics are repeatedly referred to as *challenging* established philosophical positions, although the exact implications are still to "emerge dialectically" from reflections on the philosophical dimensions of Cognitive Linguistics. From a slightly different perspective, the issue is whether Cognitive Linguistics is going to provide positive answers to some of the philosophical questions for which Johnson sees these answers as relevant. At this point, Sinha and Johnson seem to find each other in their belief that it is simply too early to tell.

In *Philosophy in the Flesh* (Lakoff and Johnson 1999), the themes of Johnson's article are fully developed in the form of a comprehensive set of claims concerning the consequences that results obtained within Cognitive Linguistics should have for philosophy. The chief targets are, as before, abstract disembodied reason coupled with objective facts, on the one hand, and total relativism, on the other. According to the most radical claim expressed in the book (Lakoff and Johnson 1999: 14–15), traditional philosophical thought, as we know it, can and should be set aside on the basis of empirical results based on embodied cognition and achieved within Cognitive Linguistics. If we look at this strain in the book, it inscribes itself in the twentieth-century tradition of science-based denunciations of speculative preempirical thinking (see section 2 above). As I will argue below, this is problematic for methodological reasons (see section 6).

This somewhat hard-hitting level of argumentation, however, is interwoven with a rather more cautious strain. In that respect, the point of the book is to show how the nonconventional forms of conceptual organization that cognitive linguists have been pursuing may be used to enrich philosophical thinking about basic issues in human life and thought. This "weaker" stance can be seen as a continuation of the more constructive view on the issue, on whose relevance Johnson (1993) and Sinha (1993) agreed, but which they found it too early to explore thoroughly. Among the specific problems that belong here is the question of exactly how much of the philosophical understanding of concepts like time and causation can be ascribed to literal content and how much is dependent on metaphorical enrichment recruited from other domains.

After *Philosophy in the Flesh*, a renewed philosophical discussion of Lakoff and Johnson's position arose in *Cognitive Linguistics*; and again, it proved difficult to achieve consensus on the basic issues. Rakova (2002) argues that an uncompromising belief in the "experiential" or "embodied" status of concepts can only result in extreme empiricism, or loss of powers of abstraction (including the kind that is involved in logical thinking). In their reply, Lakoff and Johnson (2002) point out that the undesirable consequences only follow if traditional assumptions of analytic philosophy are taken for granted. In their view, Rakova's criticism is invalid if the alternative premises are adopted, according to which (i) the embodied mind transcends a rigid dichotomy between empiricism and rationalism, (ii) embodied conceptualizations can be more or less adequate in relation to a body of empirical data, and (iii) abstraction arises naturally from more concretely embodied conceptualizations.

The disagreement reflects that there exist two readings of the book. On the strong reading, where Cognitive Linguistic positions are put where philosophy used to be, the issues Rakova raises are valid criticisms. On the weaker reading, where Cognitive Linguistics does not replace but rather grounds disembodied philosophical reasoning, Lakoff and Johnson are justified in saying that this poses no threat to the concerns Rakova raises. Either way, these are issues in need of clarification, as stressed by Krzeszowski (2002) and Sinha (2002).

6. The Hermeneutic Perspective: The Cognitive Unconscious versus the Content of Understanding

There is one important reason why it is problematic to determine the precise implications of embodiment for the philosophy of mind. The reason lies in the distinction, more significant for philosophical than for linguistic purposes, between conceptualizations as part of the equipment that we carry around in our heads and conceptualizations that we form in the process of understanding something, such as the nature of the world (or the content of a text, see below). Cognitive Linguistics naturally takes its point of departure in the mental equipment, whereas philosophy begins with the task of understanding the world. Beginning at the cognitive linguistic end, I will try to show where the path toward the philosophical end raises philosophical issues with implications for linguistics as well.

When it comes to mental equipment, a central issue concerns the ontological commitment to the cognitive unconscious, which was carried over from Chomsky but was provided with a different content (see section 2). In spite of the new content, it raises the same methodological problem of access that affected Chomskyan competence. A similar problem bears upon the simulation paradigm in cognitive science in general: however great an achievement it is to create a simulation that works, the simulation in itself does not prove that this is the way things actually work in the simulated object. The discussion in Lakoff and Johnson (1999: 38–42) with regard to successful simulations within the "Neural Theory of Language" project also illustrate the relevance of this issue in a cognitive linguistic context. On general methodological principles, such models must be regarded as attractive scenarios rather than definitive truths. Only data from the neural system itself (see Lakoff 2003) bear directly on the issue of what constitutes the neural reality underlying language.

Searle (1992: 152; 1995: 128) has presented a general epistemological argument against totally tacit knowledge. His central point is that we do not know what mental states such as knowledge are, if we set them apart from consciousness—simply because there is no access to mental states (as opposed to physical states) except via subjective consciousness. Searle thus does not want to rule out mental states that, for a variety of possible reasons, happen to be unconscious; the problem arises if we simultaneously claim that these are mental states and that we can never be conscious of them.

Chomskyan tacit structures are suspect because they transplant properties that essentially belong to the scientific metalanguage into the brain. Conversely, one might object that attributing conceptualizations from Cognitive Linguistics to a tacit level is problematic for the opposite reason: in doing so, we locate at an inaccessible level of knowledge the kind of phenomena we might intuitively very well have conscious awareness of. Among the things we do that are said to be "inaccessible to conscious awareness and control" are "anticipating where the conversation is going" and "planning what to say in response" (Lakoff and Johnson 1999: 10–11). It would be natural to suggest that such processes are sometimes conscious and that sometimes they are not. Also, such processes are clearly part of the process of coping with cognitive tasks with very direct ties with conscious mental content. Anticipation and planning lend themselves to direct comparison with actual outcomes: if things work out differently from what we had planned and anticipated, that is something we tend to be aware of. This being so, however, it is not clear exactly how much hidden determination is to be attributed to the structures that Lakoff and Johnson attribute to the unconscious mind, as compared with the less covert kind of influence that is associated with (more or less) conscious processes of construal and interpretation.

I think it would be fair to say that the conceptualizations uncovered by Cognitive Linguistics are generally assumed to be unproblematically applicable across the domain affected by the distinction suggested above: they are both part of the equipment we draw on in trying to understand and the result of processes of understanding. Such flexibility, however, means that there are certain claims with respect to those structures that become problematic. Above (section 5), we saw how Lakoff and Johnson (1999: 14–15) invoked the science-based pattern of thinking that seeks to prove traditional thinking wrong by pointing to empirical findings. If conceptualizations are bound up with ongoing processes of understanding, however, it is not clear whether the scientific foundations of the account are strong enough to make that claim compelling.

If we look at the way in which Cognitive Linguistics has distanced itself from Generative Grammar, it has moved toward a position that is in many respects closer to that of the humanistic tradition than of modern science. The fact that Cognitive Linguistics is moving into territory associated with the humanities is also reflected in the growing commonality of interest between Cognitive Linguistics and the theory of literature (see, e.g., Stjernfelt 1995; Turner 1995; Freeman, this volume, chapter 45), which is perhaps the domain in the humanities that is most remote from scientific methodology and where hermeneutic practices still reign supreme. This has implications for the philosophical perspective within which Cognitive Linguistics must situate itself and which includes the hermeneutic perspective, as pointed out repeatedly by Geeraerts (1992, 1993, 1999). Cognitive Linguistics has in effect opened up the territory that was consigned to oblivion by the science police and their allies, including Chomsky. That is essentially the territory that was allocated to the humanities by Dilthey in the nineteenth century when the split between science and humanities was becoming unbridgeable, with the area of *Verstehen* being opposed to that of *Erklärung* (see Geeraerts 1999: 184). One implication of this is the need to reserve a place in Cognitive Linguistics for the process of interpretation, that is, of assigning (additional) meaning to input in order to understand it (more fully).

In this context, it is relevant that Cognitive Linguistics does not place great emphasis on the distinction between coded meaning and utterance meaning. While this may—in contrast to a "wastebasket" approach to the role of context—be beneficial, it bypasses the question of what the actual processes are whereby complex linguistic utterances are assigned meaning in actual interaction. The tradition of Dilthey and Gadamer, with its emphasis on the historical life of conceptualizations and on how actual empirical processes of understanding work, is a necessary dimension in the landscape in which Cognitive Linguistics belongs. That is not to suggest that the continuity between conceptual structures viewed as resources and conceptual structures viewed as constituting the content of understanding should be rejected, but we need to recognize the two different jobs they are doing. For example, to succeed in understanding something one has never understood before is not the same thing as calling up a preexisting understanding from one's subconscious mind. Moving into the area of processes of understanding therefore raises issues that are different from asking about the grounding of existing concepts.

Ending up in the neighborhood of the humanities is not a regrettable consequence of rejecting Chomskyan formal linguistics (as some might think). As pointed out by Itkonen (1978), in the absence of the experimental verification that underpins physical models, Chomskyan concepts, too, must be understood as humanistic interpretations of linguistic data and must be judged on that basis. While this is inconvenient for the generative ambition of rising above the vagaries of the humanities, there is less reason for Cognitive Linguistics to shy away from being in the company of the humanities; it just needs to be considered what that implies for the conception of cognitive *science*. The social sciences, in comparison, have lived explicitly with the issue of how to incorporate the dimension of *Verstehen* since Max Weber (see Weber [1925] 1972).

Seeing conceptual analysis in the context of the humanities also opens up the issue of what the implications are of language being a sign system in addition to being a cognitive accomplishment. Linguistic meanings are meanings only because they are tied to an expression, which functions as the vehicle. Again, this is congenial with Cognitive Linguistics; the symbolic nature of grammar is one of the foundational assumptions of Cognitive Grammar (see Langacker 1987). In terms of the cognitive perspective, however, both *signans* and *signatum* are cognitive entities, and the Saussurean insistence on the independence of entities within a sign system from the entities denoted by signs is clearly alien to Cognitive Linguistics (cf. the "encyclopedic" view of meaning). The type of sign that is most obviously congenial with Cognitive Linguistics is perhaps Peirce's "icon," since the grounding of signs in experienced reality provides them with an iconic basis. However, in general, the results of Cognitive Linguistics are clearly central also from a semiotic perspective, since the formation and organization of complex signs draw on the whole area of mechanisms of meaning creation that is explored in Cognitive Linguistics from construal to blending. (This relationship has been explored, e.g., in work at the Aarhus Centre for Semiotic Studies, see Brandt 2004). Saussure envisaged a discipline of semiology of which linguistics would only be one part, where all other sign systems would be accommodated as well. The two enterprises are similar in terms of breadth of scope; but exactly what the relation would be between such a broad-ranging semiology and the rival umbrella discipline of cognitive science will only become clear once the interface between social processes of understanding and cognitive systems has been satisfactorily mapped.

7. VALIDITY: GROUNDING, ABSTRACTION, AND DECONSTRUCTION

Above we started with conceptualization seen as mental equipment, from the point of view of Cognitive Linguistics and cognitive science. I will now turn around and view the issue from the philosophical end, that is, that of conceptualization as a way of arriving at true knowledge of the world. This reversal of perspective is necessary in order to understand how matters stand when Cognitive Linguistics is viewed not from its own home ground, but as a potential contribution to a philosophical agenda. That is where the question of validity becomes central.

The interesting situation here is that of the human mind at work, trying to understand something. Understanding involves recruiting a conceptual model to apply it to the case at hand. But after a conceptual model has been found, two additional questions arise: (i) What follows if I choose one conceptualization rather than another? and (ii) How do I know which way of understanding the case at hand is the best one?

Cognitive Linguistics has its main strength in exploring the models in themselves, including the mappings that link up different models. It has less to say about what follows from using them in particular cases—aside from those consequences that can be read directly off the models in themselves. In the case of metaphorical mappings, the difference between seeing marriage as a journey and seeing it as a desert island is transparent as far as the conceptualization in itself goes. However, it is not clear exactly what actually happens when the model is applied to the object one is trying to understand. To tackle a very basic aspect of conceptualization as viewed in Cognitive Linguistics, the problem can be illustrated by the procedure of tracing metaphors back into the source domain of bodily experience. In the most radical interpretation, pointing out what model lies behind a given conceptualization of the target domain would mean that the source domain was the ultimate content of understanding of the thing conceptualized (and I assume nobody believes that). Force as applying to arguments is not the same as force used in physical compulsion—otherwise there would be no difference between reasoning about a matter and fighting it out. Lakoff (1993: 216) expresses this by the "target domain override" principle that rules out metaphors destroying the inherent structure of the target. But if a target overrides whatever does not fit, it remains open exactly what follows from applying a given conceptualization to that target.

Davidson (1978) argues that metaphorical meaning is in fact too indeterminate to qualify as part of the description of language. The idea is that while one can be precise about nonmetaphorical meaning, one cannot be precise about a metaphorical meaning until the metaphorical mapping is complete and the source domain meaning has become part of the target domain and hence "flattened" into a determinate, truth-conditional meaning. To take a familiar example: Going from London to New York is a journey in a determinate sense, but we do not know exactly what LOVE IS A JOURNEY means until we have completed the work of mapping the metaphor onto the target domain. A primitive result of such a mapping would be something like 'love is an experience where, after the relationship has come into being, you move through a succession of new situations, rather than remaining in the same initial position'—which is again determinate. Until the metaphorically transferred meaning has become literalized in its new domain, Davidson claims, it can mean so many different things that its readings are non-determinate.

Against this, Collin and Engstrøm (2001) point out that metaphorical meaning as something both nonliteral and determinate can be defended when taking an explicitly process-oriented view of meaning. The whole process of recruiting metaphorical meaning has a determinable content, even though not all of the potential of using the metaphor is determinable at a given stage. This theory is like Davidson's in that it explicitly goes beyond understanding metaphor purely as a mapping—it insists that metaphor needs to be "brought to bear" and thus to make a difference in understanding in order to make sense. But it retains the emphasis on the mapping as a process rather than to look simply for the products of the mapping as if they might just as well have been literal all the way through.

Once the implications of a conceptualization (metaphorical or not) have been determined, we face the question of whether it is a good way of understanding what we are dealing with. This problem reflects one of the really basic issues that radically divide the philosophical tradition from the position outlined by Lakoff and Johnson, namely the fear of "psychologism," that is, of mistaking the nature of reality for what we take to be reality. Lakoff and Johnson (1999) take up this issue in relation to Frege, to whose "rabid antipsychologistic bent" (468) they trace the failure of analytic philosophy to consider the role of embodied meaning. What Frege and later analytic philosophers failed to realize, they say, was the capacity of embodied reasoning to give rise to shared meanings (440). However, the whole point of philosophy from Plato onwards (with the position of Hume as an exception) has been to establish a way of talking that keeps clear of the traps that ordinary mental impressions and opinions are liable to fall into. Frege's views were not the more or less accidental cause of this aberration in modern philosophy—it is the whole philosophical enterprise that is at stake.

From the point of view of the philosophical tradition, shared and grounded meaning is therefore not enough. Truth is the traditional philosophical criterion, which in a usage-based perspective can be seen as one way of being adequate for the job a conceptualization is recruited to do—in this case, to provide an account of the true nature of reality. Whether a conceptualization is adequate is not determined by its grounding; in fact, if we know what job the conceptualization is doing, it is simply irrelevant exactly how that conceptualization is grounded or neurally wired (from the philosophical perspective). Something else is at stake here. This, in fact, might be seen as a challenge from philosophy to Cognitive Linguistics.

In order to understand more and more complex issues, philosophy pursues strategies of abstraction that move their concepts further and further away from bodily grounding, neutralizing differences between alternative ways of experiencing and conceptualizing. The question of validity, in the case of abstraction, translates into the issue of whether we manage to "carve nature at the joints," that is, whether the abstract concepts we set up are genuinely applicable to the domain we are trying to understand. Even in the case of mathematics, which is not inherently about anything, the same issue exists. To see how mathematical abstractions emerge from the human perspective (see Lakoff and Núñez 2000) means to understand mathematics in an important way that has been overlooked before and makes the concepts accessible from a new angle. But what makes these mathematical concepts what they are is still the way they fit into the whole web of mathematics. Even if you can see where they come from, you also need to see what follows from them in order to be able to claim that you understand them.

This difference is not a matter of disagreement between Cognitive Linguistics and philosophy but is due to the basic difference of perspective that I outlined at the beginning of this chapter. Philosophy understands itself as the metadiscipline entrusted with the job of keeping order, which includes standing as guardians of the basic tools of science, such as rational inquiry. Cognitive linguists could simply decide that they do not want to compete with philosophy in this domain, since it is external to its primary domain. But rationality in the sense of accountability to nonarbitrary principles of description is part of the picture of Cognitive Linguistics that defines it as being in opposition not only to objectivism, but also to deconstructionism. It is therefore worth pursuing the issue one final step further.

The ontology that goes with this "mid-position" understands the world picture as reducible neither to subjective choice nor to features of the objective world alone. Although in this description Cognitive Linguistics is situated far from the extremes, it finds itself in a territory that is not entirely its own. Among its neighbors are, at the most skeptical end, Derrida, then Rorty (1996) and Putnam (1992), and at the somewhat more confident side, Searle (who accepts the "enlightenment vision" that the world exists independently of us but we can come to know it "within the limits set by our evolutionary endowments," 1998: 4). One reason why the mid-position is not so well-defined as it might appear is that "objectivism" is a problematic label to stick on mainstream philosophy, where the pragmatic dimension has come to play an increasing role in the last generation. The term "objectivism" suggests a complacent belief in the unchallengeablity of objective fact; but, as discussed above, the driving force in the modern philosophical tradition is actually a radical skepticism about traditional would-be facts and extreme diligence in finding ways of falsifying even the most innocuous-looking claims. If the traditional premises of the search for knowledge are abandoned, something else must take their place if we are to avoid ending up at the other end of the spectrum, in the company of Derrida.

Derrida has said a number of things that suggest total skepticism about what kind of reality, if any, is to be found behind interpretations, and in that respect the difference with Cognitive Linguistics is clear-cut, in the way suggested by Johnson (1992). However, when it comes to actual descriptive practice, it may be hard to tell the difference between conceptualizations of the world being shaped by the hidden hand of our cognitive unconscious or by historical deceptions masquerading as facts (see Derrida 1972). As an illustration, one might in fact look for Derrida-type hidden hands that are also behind the conceptual models serving as hidden hands in Lakoff and Johnson (1999). The folk models that end up in the cognitive unconscious, such as the "strict father model" that Lakoff and Johnson (1999) use to deconstruct Kantian moral philosophy, have a history of oppression behind them. The cognitive unconscious includes a vast repository of historical processes of conceptualization, including those driven by power and manipulation. An appeal to models inscribed in the body itself thus does not safeguard us from Derrida-type skepticism.

The kind of work that is needed here can be exemplified with Lakoff (1996), which looks at the role played by competing models of the family in actual human practice. This type of analysis, however, needs to be explicitly placed in relation to the foundational issues: how do we discover these models, and how can we place them in relation to those aspects of reality with which they are causally involved? The fact that postmodernism as a real-life movement is driven (among other things) by a desire to increase the number of (self-)interpretations that a human body makes available, transcending for instance stereotypes of gender and sexuality, means that the precise status of models grounded in the body is not purely an esoteric issue of epistemology, but also a question of where Cognitive Linguistics wants to stand between a fundamentalism of the body and an indeterminacy of interpretations that questions the very existence of definable implications of bodily grounding.

Perhaps the closest one can get to placing Cognitive Linguistics "as such" in the philosophical landscape is Hilary Putnam's "internal realism" (see Lakoff 1987; Geeraerts 1999). In his discussion of irrealism and deconstruction, Putnam (1992) emphasizes the distinction between what is in the description itself and what the description points to. We may be justified in deconstructing descriptions that lay claim to any form of absolute truth—but unless we accept the commitment to "reconstruction," that is, to putting better descriptions in their place, we are ontologically irresponsible (see Putnam 1992: 133). Failure to do that would be to let bloody-minded irrationalism take over the site demolished by deconstruction (Hitler's world view would be just as good as anybody else's). Because it distances itself from objective truths while rejecting total relativism, realism based on embodiment belongs naturally in the terrain defined by Putnam's position.

8. Conclusion

We began with the picture in which philosophy gradually gives birth to independent fields, while remaining as the arena of inquiry about overall fundamental issues. Above I have tried to point out some ways in which types of inquiry pursued within the domain of Cognitive Linguistics have implications involving these overall issues. Two main perspectives have recurred, the ontological and the epistemological/methodological, with natural affinities between them.

Cognitive Linguistics arose as a new approach by rejecting ontological and methodological assumptions that constrained language description to abstract formalisms based on a narrow view of permissible objects and of methods of description. Its achievements are based on pointing to new phenomena (an enriched ontology) as well as on a less restrictive methodology. I have tried to show that with an expanding domain of objects brought under the purview of Cognitive Linguistics, issues arise which can only be clarified by maintaining communication lines with the philosophical arena of inquiry. The overall reason for this is that we cannot go from neural wiring to historical tradition and social variation while assuming that the same concepts and methods will apply in the same way. Taking up the philosophical issues does not suggest that the generous ontological assumptions of Cognitive Linguistics should be abandoned in favor of earlier narrowness—only that we need to be precise about the different properties of conceptual structures as we move from one end of the scale to the other.

Another dimension of the relationship between philosophy and Cognitive Linguistics concerns the implications of cognitive linguistic findings for philosophy. Just as the findings of modern physics changed the way philosophers thought about knowledge, so the findings of Cognitive Linguistics can be expected to change the way philosophers think about the mind. Caution suggests that we do not specify the necessary changes in philosophy too categorically; there is room for different ways of understanding the world (as also stressed by Lakoff and Johnson 2002). We need to know how to choose between them in actual cases, and problems of that kind are outside the core domain of Cognitive Linguistics. Therefore, the agenda of validity remains, reserving a niche for philosophical scrutiny of the adequacy of alternative conceptualizations.

The most remarkable achievement of Cognitive Linguistics in relation to philosophy reflects its central ambition within its own domain. Cognitive Linguistics has documented the power and systematicity of imaginative forms of thinking that were previously regarded as beyond the pale of serious consideration and thereby demonstrated how much richer the activities of conceptualization and thinking are, compared with the orthodox views of less than a generation ago: human reason is more than we used to think.

REFERENCES

Austin, John L. 1970. *Philosophical papers*. Oxford: Oxford University Press.

Barlow, Michael, and Suzanne Kemmer, eds. 2000. *Usage-based models of language*. Stanford, CA: CSLI Publications.

Brandt, Per Aage. 2004. *Spaces, domains, and meaning: Essays in cognitive semantics*. Frankfurt am Main: Peter Lang Verlag.

Brugman, Claudia. 1981. Story of *Over*. MA thesis, University of California at Berkeley. (Published as *The story of Over: Polysemy, semantics, and the structure of the lexicon*. New York: Garland, 1988)

Carnap, Rudolph. 1928. *Der logische Aufbau der Welt*. Berlin-Schlachtensee: Weltkreis-Verlag. (English translation published as *The logical structure of the world: Pseudoproblems in philosophy*. London: Routledge and Kegan Paul, 1967)

Carnap, Rudolph. 1934. *The philosophy of science*. Baltimore, MD: Williams and Wilkins.

Chomsky, Noam. 1959. Review of *Verbal Behavior*, by B. F. Skinner. *Language* 35: 26–58. (Also in Jerry A. Fodor and Jerrold J. Katz, eds., *The structure of language: Readings in the philosophy of language* 547–78. Englewood Cliffs, NJ: Prentice-Hall, 1964)

Chomsky, Noam. 1975. *The logical structure of linguistic theory*. New York: Plenum Press. (First available in 1955 as mimeograph, MIT Library, Cambridge, MA)

Chomsky, Noam. 2000. *New horizons in the study of language and mind*. Cambridge: Cambridge University Press.

Clark, Andy. 1997. *Being there: Putting brain, body, and world together again*. Cambridge, MA: MIT Press.

Collin, Finn, and Anders Engstrøm. 2001. Metaphor and truth-conditional semantics: Meaning as process and product. *Theoria* 67: 75–92.

Croft, William. 1998. Linguistic evidence and mental representations. *Cognitive Linguistics* 9: 151–73.

Croft, William. 2000. *Explaining language change: An evolutionary approach*. London: Longman.

Croft, William. 2001. *Radical construction grammar: Syntactic theory in typological perspective*. Oxford: Oxford University Press.

Davidson, Donald. 1978. What metaphors mean. *Critical Inquiry* 5: 31–47. (Also in Donald Davidson, *Inquiries into truth and interpretation* 245–64. Oxford: Clarendon Press, 1984)

Derrida, Jacques. 1972. *Positions*. Paris: Editions Minuit.

Dirven, René, Roslyn Frank, and Cornelia Ilie, eds. 2001. *Language and ideology*. Vol. 2, *Descriptive cognitive linguistic approaches*. Amsterdam: John Benjamins.

Dirven, René, Bruce Hawkins, and Esra Sandikcioglu, eds. 2000. *Language and ideology*. Vol. 1, *Theoretical cognitive approaches*. Amsterdam: John Benjamins.

Geeraerts, Dirk. 1992. The return of hermeneutics to lexical semantics. In Martin Pütz, ed., *Thirty years of linguistic evolution* 257–82. Amsterdam: John Benjamins.

Geeraerts, Dirk. 1993. Cognitive linguistics and the history of philosophical epistemology. In Richard Geiger and Brygida Rudzka-Ostyn, eds., *Conceptualizations and mental processing in language* 53–79. Berlin: Mouton de Gruyter.

Geeraerts, Dirk. 1997. *Diachronic prototype semantics: A contribution to historical lexicology*. Oxford: Clarendon Press.

Geeraerts, Dirk 1999. Idealist and empiricist tendencies in cognitive semantics. In Theo Janssen and Gisela Redeker, eds., *Cognitive linguistics: Foundations, scope, and methodology* 163–94. Berlin: Mouton de Gruyter.

Geeraerts, Dirk. 2003. The inevitability of a variationist cognitive linguistics. Plenary lecture given at the 8th International Cognitive Linguistics Conference, Logroño, Spain, July 20–25.

Gibbs, Raymond W., Jr. 1999. Taking metaphor out of our heads and putting it into the cultural world. In Raymond W. Gibbs, Jr., and Gerard J. Steen, eds., *Metaphor in cognitive linguistics* 145–66. Amsterdam: John Benjamins.

Gorayska, Barbara. 1993. Reflections: A commentary on "Philosophical implications of cognitive semantics." *Cognitive Linguistics* 4: 47–53.

Itkonen, Esa. 1978. *Grammatical theory and metascience.* Amsterdam: John Benjamins.

Itkonen, Esa. 1992. Remarks on the language universals research II. *SKY: The Yearbook of the Linguistic Association of Finland* 53–82.

Johnson, Mark. 1992. Philosophical implications of cognitive semantics. *Cognitive Linguistics* 3: 345–66.

Johnson, Mark. 1993. Why cognitive semantics matters to philosophy. *Cognitive Linguistics* 4: 62–74.

Johnson-Laird., Philip N. 1988. *The computer and the mind.* London: Fontana.

Krzeszovski, Tomasz P. 2002. Problems that are not supposed to arise? *Cognitive Linguistics* 13: 265–69.

Lakoff, George. 1987. *Women, fire, and dangerous things: What categories reveal about the mind.* Chicago: University of Chicago Press.

Lakoff, George. 1993. The contemporary theory of metaphor. In Andrew Ortony, ed., *Metaphor and thought* 202–51. 2nd ed. Cambridge: Cambridge University Press.

Lakoff, George. 1996. *Moral politics: What conservatives know that liberals don't.* Chicago: University of Chicago Press.

Lakoff, George. 2003. The brain's concepts. Plenary lecture given at the 8th International Cognitive Linguistics Conference, Logroño, Spain, July 20–25.

Lakoff, George, and Mark Johnson. 1999. *Philosophy in the flesh: The embodied mind and its challenge to Western thought.* New York: Basic Books.

Lakoff, George, and Mark Johnson. 2002. Why cognitive linguistics requires embodied realism. *Cognitive Linguistics* 13: 245–63.

Lakoff, George, and Rafael E. Núñez. 2000. *Where mathematics comes from: How the embodied mind brings mathematics into being.* New York: Basic Books.

Langacker, Ronald W. 1987. *Foundations of cognitive grammar.* Vol. 1, *Theoretical prerequisites.* Stanford, CA: Stanford University Press.

Langacker, Ronald W. 1999. Assessing the cognitive linguistic enterprise. In Theo Janssen and Gisela Redeker, eds., *Cognitive linguistics: Foundations, scope, and methodology* 13–59. Berlin: Mouton de Gruyter.

Lyons, John. 1977. *Semantics.* 2 vols. Cambridge: Cambridge University Press.

Maturana, Humberto. 1975. The organization of the living: A theory of the living organization. *International Journal Man-Machine Studies* 7: 313–32.

Maturana, Humberto, and Francisco Varela. 1980. *Autopoiesis and cognition: The realization of the living.* Dordrecht, Netherlands: Reidel.

McLure, Roger. 1993. On "Philosophical implications of cognitive semantics." *Cognitive Linguistics* 4: 39–47.

Ortega y Gasset, José. [1925] 1976. *La deshumanización del arte e ideas sobre la novela.* Madrid : Revista de Occidente. (English translation published as *The dehumanization of art, and notes on the novel.* Princeton, NJ: Princeton University Press, 1948)

Putnam, Hilary. 1992. *Renewing philosophy.* Cambridge, MA: Harvard University Press.

Rakova, Marina. 2002. The philosophy of embodied realism: A high price to pay? *Cognitive Linguistics* 13: 215–44.

Rice, Sally, Dominiek Sandra, and Mia Vanrespaille. 1999. Prepositional semantics and the fragile link between space and time. In Masako Hiraga, Chris Sinha, and Sherman Wilcox, eds., *Cultural, typological and psycholinguistic issues in cognitive linguistics* 107–27. Amsterdam: John Benjamins.

Rorty, Richard. 1996. *Truth and progress: Philosophical papers.* Vol. 3. Cambridge: Cambridge University Press.

Russell, Bertrand. 1956. On propositions: What they are and how they mean. In Ronald C. Marsh, ed., *Logic and Knowledge* 285–320. London: Macmillan. (First appeared in *Proceedings of the Aristotelian society* 2 [1919]: 1–43.)

Sanders, Ted. 1997. Psycholinguistics and the discourse level: Challenges for cognitive linguistics. On Morton Ann Gernsbacher (ed.) *Handbook of Psycholinguistics* and Morton Ann Gernsbacher and Talmy Givón (eds.) *Coherence in spontaneous text.* *Cognitive Linguistics* 8: 243–65.

Sandra, Dominiek. 1998. What linguists can and can't tell you about the human mind: A reply to Croft. *Cognitive Linguistics* 9: 361–78.

Sandra, Dominiek, and Sally Rice. 1995. Network analyses of prepositional meaning: Mirroring whose mind—the linguist's or the language user's? *Cognitive Linguistics* 6: 89–130.

Searle, John R. 1992. *The rediscovery of the mind.* Cambridge, MA: MIT Press.

Searle, John R. 1995. *The construction of social reality.* Harmondsworth, UK: Penguin.

Searle, John R. 1998. *Mind, language and society: Philosophy in the real world.* New York: Basic Books.

Sinha, Chris. 1988. *Language and representation: A socio-naturalistic approach to human development.* Hemel Hempstead, UK: Harvester-Wheatsheaf.

Sinha, Chris. 1993. Cognitive semantics and philosophy. *Cognitive Linguistics* 4: 53–62.

Sinha, Chris. 1999. Grounding, mapping, and acts of meaning. In Theo Janssen and Gisela Redeker, eds., *Cognitive linguistics: Foundations, scope, and methodology* 223–55. Berlin: Mouton de Gruyter.

Sinha, Chris. 2002. The cost of renovating the property: A reply to Marina Rakova. *Cognitive Linguistics* 13: 271–76.

Stjernfelt, Frederik. 1995. We can't go on meeting like this: A cognitive theory of literature? The fall of the wall between linguistics and theory of literature. *Nordic Journal of Linguistics* 18: 121–36.

Sweetser, Eve. 1990. *From etymology to pragmatics: Metaphorical and cultural aspects of semantic structure.* Cambridge: Cambridge University Press.

Talmy, Leonard. 1988. Force dynamics in language and cognition. *Cognitive Science* 12: 49–100.

Tuggy, David. 1999. Linguistic evidence for polysemy in the mind: A response to William Croft and Dominiek Sandra. *Cognitive Linguistics* 10: 343–68.

Turner, Mark. 1995. *The literary mind.* New York: Oxford University Press.

Varela, Francisco J., Evan Thompson, and Eleanor Rosch. 1991. *The embodied mind: Cognitive science and human experience.* Cambridge, MA: MIT Press.

Weber, Max. [1925] 1972. *Wirtschaft und Gesellschaft: Grundriss der verstehenden Soziologie.* Tübingen, Germany: J. C. B. Mohr Paul Siebeck Verlag.

Winograd, Terry, and Fernando Flores. 1986. *Understanding computers and cognition: A new foundation for design.* Norwood, NJ: Ablex.

CHAPTER 49

COGNITIVE LINGUISTICS, PSYCHOLOGY, AND COGNITIVE SCIENCE

CHRIS SINHA

1. INTRODUCTION

1.1. Cognitive Science and Its Forebears

Cognitive Linguistics is one of the principal branches of Second Generation Cognitive Science—the alliance of new approaches emerging from what has been called the second cognitive revolution of the last decades of the twentieth century (Harré and Gillett 1994). The phrase "second cognitive revolution" may be overstated, emphasizing discontinuity over continuity in the historical development of cognitive science and suggesting that a unitary new paradigm has replaced that of Classical Cognitive Science. There can, however, be little doubt that contemporary cognitive science is much less consensual in its fundamental assumptions than was the case a quarter of a century ago.

Classical Cognitive Science emerged as a result of both technological and intellectual developments after World War II.[1] The development of computer science, the renewed focus by psychologists on human, as opposed to animal, behavior, and the formal rigor of early Generative Linguistics combined to convince many scientists that the behaviorist injunction to ignore the inner workings of the "black box" of the mind was no longer either necessary or desirable. This "first" cognitive revolution led eventually to a coherent set of shared theoretical propositions (e.g., the rejection of general-purpose learning mechanisms in favor of innate, domain-specific knowledge; the key role of mental representations in the organization of behavior) and methodological preferences (the primacy of formalization and algorithmic representations), deriving from the confluence of Generative Linguistics with Information Processing theory. The classical consensus has been challenged in Cognitive Linguistics and allied approaches, and although it would be premature to claim either that the classical paradigm is dead or that a new paradigm now commands universal assent, a cluster of common themes have emerged in recent cognitive research which suggest something of what the future holds for the interdisciplinary science of the mind.

I return to these contemporary themes below, but the first aim of this chapter is to shed light on the history of the sciences of mind within which the development of Cognitive Linguistics can be situated. Cognitive Linguistics is a relatively new discipline, but it is one which draws on a long history. I will try to show that it is the modern inheritor of an older tradition, antedating the behaviorist ascendancy in mid-twentieth century psychology which preceded Classical Cognitive Science. This tradition, centered in psychology but drawing heavily on biology, linguistics, philosophy, anthropology, and sociology, was a kind of cognitive science *avant la lettre*. It is represented in the German *Sprachpsychologie* (psychology of language) tradition from Wundt, through Gestalt psychology, to Bühler; in Baldwin's and Piaget's Genetic Epistemology; in Bartlett's sociocognitive theory of memory; in Vygotsky's and Mead's sociogenetic theories of the development of language and cognition; and, of course, by social-psychologically oriented linguists in the United States (Boas, Sapir, Whorf) and Europe (Meillet, Bakhtin, Volosinov), as well as Prague School functionalism (Jakobson, Mukařovský, Trubetzkoy) (see also Nerlich and Clarke, this volume, chapter 22).

This tradition remained the main alternative to Behaviorism up until World War II, but it was largely neglected in the cognitive science of the 1950s and succeeding decades, which viewed human (natural) cognitive processes as an arbitrarily limited subset of theoretically resource-unlimited, universal computational procedures. Despite the intense research effort generated by the classical program over a period of more than thirty years and despite massive technical advances, its ultimate contribution to *psychological* science is debatable. This is in no way to deny the real advances registered by cognitive psychology during the period of hegemony of the classical paradigm. However, these advances involved an implicit or explicit break with the premises of the Classical Cognitive Science program and a reworking of key ideas in prebehaviorist cognitive psychology.[2]

It is a measure of the poverty of Behaviorism that psychology was compelled to concede disciplinary leadership in Classical Cognitive Science to formalist linguistics and computer science. In the Classical Cognitive Science scheme of things, the role of psychology (and psycholinguistics) was first to explore human "performance" limitations and second to quarry data for formal modeling. In both roles, psychology was cast as an under-laborer to formal theory, with its research superprogram of Artificial Intelligence. Cognitive psychologists were not in much of a position to protest at this treatment, since Behaviorism had inflicted on psychology a kind of amnesia, in which the mind was purged from theory, and theory scourged from the mind. Psychology, emerging from its mindless dogmatic slumber, could only gratefully, but disastrously, borrow dualistic mentalism from Generative Linguistics. Behaviorism (for which the mind is supernumerary) and Formalism (for which the body is merely contingent) thus framed, in fearful symmetry, the disembodied Cartesian mind of Classical Cognitive Science.

1.2. The Psychology of Higher Mental Processes

The main focus of this chapter will be on cognitive psychology, which has been the source of many of the theoretical concepts employed by Cognitive Linguistics. Acknowledging this inheritance both restores to psychology its "bridge discipline" status between the biological, social, and language sciences and highlights the new insights that Cognitive Linguistics affords for what have traditionally been known as the "higher mental processes": memory, reasoning, and language.[3]

The higher mental processes are considered, in the tradition to which Cognitive Linguistics reaches back, to be the locus of a specifically *human* psychology (not necessarily species-unique in every respect, but uniquely developed as an ensemble of capacities in the human species); to constitute the domain proper to *cognitive* psychology (as opposed to, say, psychology of perception); and to occupy the problematic and indeterminate zone at which biologically based psychological processes, shared by human organisms with other mammals, interface with, and are perhaps transformed by, the processes of social life, symbolization, and cultural tradition. The higher mental processes are thus both the focus of a cognitive subdiscipline of psychology and an interdisciplinary meeting point between psychology, neuroscience, linguistics, philosophy, semiotics, and the social sciences. Because of the crucial role played by symbolization (sign-function) in *mediating* (i) all higher mental processes and (ii) individual and social aspects of psychological functioning, psychology of language can be considered to be paradigmatic of the psychology of higher mental processes.

Both Behaviorism, for which higher mental processes effectively do not exist, and Classical Cognitive Science, for which *all* mental processes are "symbolic," in a restricted and nonsemantic sense, are radically opposed to the tradition in cognitive psychology and psychology of language to which Cognitive Linguistics historically refers. This is not a question only of theoretical orientation, but also of the *scope* and *methodology* of psychology of language. In the psycholinguistics born of the "first cognitive revolution," the principal questions concern the processing of formally defined language structure, and the methodology is almost exclusively experimental. In the older tradition of psychology of language, research topics in linguistic and nonlinguistic cognition were closely connected, and language was viewed as a window to the general properties of higher cognition, in the study of which experimental methods should be complemented by methods proper to the nature of language.

Consider, for example, the range of linguistic work carried out by Wilhelm Wundt, founder, in Leipzig in 1879, of the first university laboratory of experimental psychology (see Wundt 1880, 1900, 1901).[4] Wundt contributed to the late-nineteenth-century debate in linguistic theory regarding the structural and semantic primacy of word versus sentence; he was the inventor of the tree-diagram notation for analyzing syntactic structure; he was the originator of the term "holophrase" to denote children's early one-word utterances; and he discussed the complex relationship between grammatical subjecthood, agency, and foregrounding, employing these terms in essentially the same sense as modern cognitive-functional linguists (Blumenthal 1985; Verfaillie and Daems 1997; Seuren 1998; Talmy, this volume, chapter 11). Wundt also investigated what we would now term the cognitive basis of language change and the role in this of metaphor (see Bybee, this volume, chapter 36). In short, Wundt saw linguistics not merely as an adjunct to, but as a complementary discipline to, psychology. As well as interdisciplinarity, Wundt advocated a multimethodological approach to the science of the mind, upholding the complementary roles of experimental psychology and *Völkerpsy-lkerpsychologie* (cultural, or anthropological, psychology), based upon field-linguistic methodology. Wundt's towering status in the language sciences, as much as in psychology, probably lies behind the assertion by Boas that "the purely linguistic inquiry is part and parcel of a thorough investigation of the psychology of the peoples of the world" (Boas [1911] 1966; cited in Palmer 1996: 11).

Current research in Cognitive Linguistics is motivated by a similar research program, in which linguistic theory is unified and synthesized with findings regarding other aspects of higher mental processes. This chapter therefore emphasizes the historical connectedness of Cognitive Linguistics with nonbehaviorist and pre-formalist cognitive psychology, as well as the affinities between Cognitive Linguistics and other currents in contemporary cognitive science. Where possible, the development of the application of key psychologically derived notions in Cognitive Linguistics is traced from their historical roots up until the present day; however, their specific current applications in Cognitive Linguistics are not detailed, since this would duplicate material to be found elsewhere in this *Handbook*.

2. Conceptual Foundations in Psychology

2.1. "Rule" versus "Schema"

The single most important theoretical concept in traditional and formal linguistics is the *rule*, adopted by Classical Cognitive Science in the specific form of the *algorithm*. Cognitive Linguistics is a usage-based, not a rule-based, theory. The Cognitive Linguistics unit of analysis that most readily corresponds to "rule" is "schema," which is employed in a variety of different contexts (e.g., image schema, event schema, construction schema) and recurs throughout this *Handbook* (see chapters 4, 9, 18, and 41). The functional equivalence between "rule" and "schema" was already pointed out by Kant, who was the first to employ the term in the context of cognitive representation: "Indeed, it is schemas, not images of objects, which underlie our pure sensible concepts.... The concept 'dog' signifies a rule according to which my imagination can delineate the figure of a four-footed animal in a general manner, without limitation to any single determinate figure such as experience, or any possible image that I can represent *in concreto*, actually presents" (Kant [1781] 1929: 182–83).

Kant here presents us with two hypotheses that have been fruitfully explored in cognitive psychology and Cognitive Linguistics. The first is that some kind of regularity, or organizing principle, mediates between perception (what he called "intuitions"), on the one hand, and linguistic (or discursive) concepts, on the other. The second hypothesis is that this regularity is "rule-like" in guiding the application of linguistic concepts and in "abstracting" from the particularity that attends any particular mental image. Kant himself was well aware that the "schema" notion raises as many questions as it purports to solve, but he also realized that these were essentially *psychological* questions which philosophy was unequipped to answer.[5]

Foremost among these are: (i) If schemas are *stored representations* (in memory), how do they get to "abstract" from specific objects or episodes and yet be flexible enough to accommodate new instances of the category to which they apply? (ii) What degree of internal structure and differentiation (or "partitioning"; see Nelson 1985) do schemas possess, and how do they fit into larger structures of knowledge and memory? Question (i) was reformulated as follows by Rumelhart, McClelland, and the PDP Research Group[6] (1986: 20): "On the one hand, schemata are the structure of the mind. On the other hand, schemata must be sufficiently malleable to fit around most anything." A plausible computational and neuropsychological answer to question (i) only emerged in the PDP research of Rumelhart and his colleagues in the 1980s. Question (ii) reemerged in cognitive science research as the issue of how lower-level elements and subschemas could be slotted into structural positions in "frames" or "scripts" (Minsky 1975; Schank and

Abelson 1977), work which in turn influenced both Fillmore's (1982) "frame semantics" and Lakoff's (1987) analysis of lexical meaning in relation to Idealized Cognitive Models.

The concept of "schema" is therefore of extremely wide application. It has been applied both to perceptual categorization and to higher cognition; and in relation to the latter, it has been used in theories of memory, language, action and motor planning, and reasoning. The "schema" notion has been criticized on exactly these grounds—that its breadth of application renders the concept vacuous. This criticism was in fact voiced by one of the pioneer cognitive psychologists most frequently cited as promoting the schema notion in the psychology of memory, Sir Frederic Bartlett, who wrote:

> I strongly dislike the term 'schema'... to refer generally to any rather vaguely outlined theory.... It does not indicate what is very essential to the whole notion, that the organised mass results of past changes of position and posture are actively *doing* something all the time; are, so to speak, carried along with us, complete, though developing, from moment to moment. Yet it is certainly very difficult to think of any better single descriptive word to cover all the facts involved. (Bartlett 1932: 201)

Bartlett acknowledges that he is appropriating the term "schema" from the neurologist Sir Henry Head, who proposed its usage in relation to movement, posture, and the body in space:

> The sensory cortex is the storehouse of past impressions. They may rise into consciousness as images, but more often, as in the case of spacial [*sic*] impressions, remain outside central consciousness. Here they form organised models of ourselves which may be called schemata. Such schemata modify the impressions produced by incoming sensory impulses in such a way that the final sensations of position or of locality rise into consciousness charged with a relation to something that has gone before. (Head 1920: 607; cited in Bartlett 1932: 200)[7]

Head's formulation was important to Bartlett primarily because it offered an alternative account to the theory of the memory "trace," which was essentially the idea that each specific "sense impression" leaves an individual "copy" of itself in the brain. Bartlett (1932: 201), in fact, criticized Head's formulation, cited above, for using the expression "storehouse of sensory impressions," which "gives away far too much to earlier investigators.... Schemas, are, we are told, living, constantly developing, affected by every bit of incoming sensational experience of a given kind. The storehouse notion is as far removed from this as it well could be." This counterposing of two deeply opposed views of memory anticipates the point made by Rumelhart, McClelland, and the PDP Research Group (1986: 20) that, in contrast with locally addressed memory, distributed memories are both content addressable and *reconstructive*:

> There is no representational object which is a schema. Rather, schemata emerge at the moment that they are needed from the interaction of large numbers of much simpler elements working in concert with one another. Schemata are

not explicit entities, but rather are implicit in our knowledge and are created by the very environment that they are trying to interpret—as it is interpreting them.

The best known evidence offered by Bartlett for the reconstructive nature of memory involved the repeated reproduction of an unfamiliar story, at various intervals after its reading. To heighten the unfamiliarity of the narrative material, and thus (Bartlett supposed) to increase the extent to which the schematic conventionalization of the remembered material would result in distortions, Bartlett used the now-famous *War of the Ghosts* story—"adapted from a translation by Dr. Franz Boas of a North American folk-tale" (Bartlett 1932: 65).[8] His discussion of this and other experiments anticipated not only subsequent work on narrative schemas, but also a number of other themes in contemporary cognitive psychology and cognitive science.

2.2. The Role of Imagery in Language Comprehension and in Cognition

The role of imagery in thinking, reasoning, and problem solving has always been an important (and disputed) topic in cognitive psychology (Johnson-Laird 1983; John-Steiner 1987), and one of obvious relevance to Cognitive Linguistics. Bartlett suggested that studying memory of narrations of dramatically vivid events would lead to a better understanding of the "conditions and functions of imaging." A similar line of reasoning was followed in a well-known experiment by Bransford and Johnson (1973) investigating the relationship between visual setting and text comprehension (see figure 49.1).

Subjects' ratings of the comprehensibility of the text were higher when the picture was presented as prior context. Later, Shepard and Metzler (1978) showed that the time taken to mentally rotate objects is proportional to the angle of rotation, a finding which suggests that visual reasoning makes direct use of imagery, rather than calling upon symbolic algorithms. Shepard and Metzler's work on imagery is widely regarded as having seriously undermined the theoretical presuppositions of Classical Cognitive Science. More recently, research by McNeill and his colleagues on the relationship between speech and gesture leads them to the unequivocal conclusion that "language is inseparable from imagery" (McNeill 2000: 57).

2.3. Affect, Consciousness, and Metacognition

Bartlett (1932: 207) regarded the schema as constituting an "organized setting" whose constituents are mobilized for recall through what he called *attitude*: "a complex psychological state or process [which is] very largely a matter of feeling, or

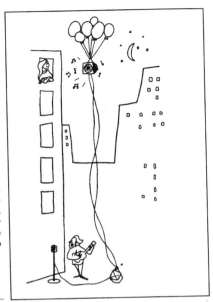

Reprinted from Bransford and Johnson (1973: 392, 396).

If the balloons popped, the sound wouldn't be able to carry far, since everything would be too far away from the correct floor. A closed window would also prevent the sound from carrying, since most buildings tend to be well insulated. Since the whole operation depends upon a steady flow of electricity, a break in the middle of the wire would also cause problems. Of course, the fellow could shout, but the human voice is not loud enough to carry that far. An additional problem is that a string could break on the instrument. Then there could be no accompaniment to the message. It is clear that the best situation would involve less distance. Then there would be fewer potential problems. With face-to-face contact, the least number of things could go wrong.

Figure 49.1. Text and pictorial context

affect." Attitude is a product of the capacity of the organism to treat schemas as *objects* of cognition:

> To break away from [domination by immediate experience] the 'schema' must become, not merely something that works the organism, but something with which the organism can work. . . . So the organism discovers how to turn round upon its own 'schemata', or, in other words, it becomes conscious. (Bartlett 1932: 208)

In modern terminology, Bartlett is drawing attention to the mutual relationships between consciousness, metacognition, and emotion. The cognitive process which is involved in "turning round upon" existing cognitive systems is designated by Karmiloff-Smith (1992) "Representational Redescription" and is implicated across many domains of cognitive development, including language development. Representational redescription underlies the capacity to analyze, or partition, and to reconstruct or transform schemas. It makes sense, too, to relate it to the ability to construct interschematic mappings and blends, as proposed by conceptual integration theory (see Turner, this volume, chapter 15). A hint of this may even be found in Bartlett's discussion of constructive imagination: "Material from any one 'scheme' may be set next to material from any other 'scheme'. . . . It is not in constructiveness that constructive imagination is peculiar, but in the range and play of its activity, and in the determination of its points of emphasis" (1932: 313).

2.4. Schema, Self, and Autobiographic Memory

A closely related topic is that of the neurocognitive foundations of the self, self-consciousness, and identity. Autobiographic memory has been a major topic of recent research, pioneered by the cognitive psychologist Neisser (Neisser and Winograd 1988; D. Rubin 1996). Neisser's career is of particular interest in that he was one of the original promoters of the Information Processing paradigm, which was cognitive psychology's disciplinary signature in the heyday of Classical Cognitive Science (Neisser 1967). Later, he developed a critique of the Information Processing paradigm (Neisser 1976), based upon insights from Gibson's (1979) ecological psychology. However, Neisser supplemented and extended Gibsonian ecological theory with a schema-based theory of memory and perception, which attempts to remedy the main and glaring deficiency of ecological perceptual realism—namely, that it offers no theoretical purchase upon higher cognitive processes.

Research by Neisser and others on autobiographic memory has confirmed Bartlett's contention that memory is *reconstructive*, and such research has been decisive in recent years in undermining claims—themselves based upon Freud's adherence to a version of the "memory trace" theory—of the infallibility of "repressed" childhood memories. Even more radically, perhaps, current research in cognitive neuroscience points to a conclusion already drawn by Bartlett: that the apparently incontestable originary and unitary self of Cartesian theory of mind is itself a sociocognitive construction. Bartlett (1932) wrote: "Memory is personal, not because of some intangible and hypothetical persisting 'self'... but because the mechanism of adult human memory demands an organization of 'schemas' depending upon an interplay of appetites, instincts, interests, and ideals peculiar to any given subject" (218), and "we have so far no ground for denying the existence of a substantial, unitary Self, lurking behind all experience, and expressing itself in all reactions. We know only that the evidence... does not necessitate such a hypothesis" (309).

Bartlett anticipates in his triad of hypotheses—(i) the reconstructive nature of memory, (ii) the key role of consciousness in "turning round upon" schemas and treating them as cognitive objects, and (iii) the emergent, "attitudinal" nature of the self—the most recent findings of cognitive neuroscience. Antonio Damasio (1999: 221–25) proposes:

> We store records of our personal experiences in [a] distributed manner, in as varied higher-order cortices as needed to match the variety of our live interactions. Those records are closely coordinated by neural connections so that the contents of the records can be recalled and made explicit, as ensembles, rapidly and efficiently.... The key elements of our autobiography that need to be reliably activated in a nearly permanent fashion are those that correspond to our identity, to our recent experiences, *and to the experiences that we anticipate, especially in the near future....* The images which represent those memories explicitly are exhibited in multiple early cortices. Finally, they are held over time by working

memory. They are treated as any other objects are and become known to the simple core self by generating their own pulses of consciousness. . . . A key aspect of self evolution concerns the balance of two influences: the lived past and the anticipated future. . . . The memories of the scenarios that we conceive as desires, wishes, goals, goals and obligations exert a pull on the self of each moment. No doubt they also play a part in the remodeling of the lived past, consciously and unconsciously, and in the creation of the person we conceive ourselves to be, moment by moment. (emphasis added)

Before leaving this topic, it is worth pointing out that even if the "originary Cartesian self" is a construction, even in some sense an illusion, the existence of a sense of persistent identity, a nonfractured autobiographical self, is a fundamental necessity for psychological well-being and even survival. As is dramatically demonstrated by research by Chandler and Lalonde (2000) on adolescent suicide in indigenous (First Nation) and European descent Canadian communities, the emergent autobiographical self is also deeply interwoven with, and in some sense dependent upon, the *situatedness* of self in collectively shared sociocultural schemas, narratives, attitudes, and ethical-political *topoi*. Self, like schema, both rests upon, and lends order to, meaning.

2.5. Meaning, Embodiment, and Society

The psychology (and linguistics, at least in the United States) of the middle of the last century, from Behaviorism through Classical Cognitive Science, was predicated upon a flight from meaning. Behaviorism reduced meaning to stimulus-response connections, and Classical Cognitive Science marginalized and subordinated it to syntactic form. Cognitive Linguistics places meaning once again at center stage in language and cognition and views meaning as being a broader category than linguistic semantics *senso strictu*. This is again consonant with Bartlett's (1932: 227) view:

We can take any constituent part of a setting and find that it 'leads on to' some other, related part. We can then say that its significance goes beyond its own descriptive character. . . . All the cognitive processes . . . from perceiving to thinking, are ways in which some fundamental 'effort after meaning' seeks expression.

A crucial part of Bartlett's way of thinking was that schemas were *conventionalized* and *shared by social and cultural groups*. The concept of schema thus interfaces human neurobiology with the social context of cognitive process, a perspective shared by contemporary theorists in psychological anthropology (Shore 1996). A topic which is currently emerging as central to much cognitive semantic research is the dynamic tension between sources of semantic motivation in the human body and nervous system, in the properties of the physical world, and in cultural schemas (see Palmer 1996; this volume, chapters 2, 39, 46, and 47). Perhaps the major challenge facing Second Generation Cognitive Science is how to move, not just beyond Cartesian mind-body dualism, but also beyond the dualism of individual and society that has bedeviled cognitive psychology and cognitive science. In this, too, Bartlett was a visionary forerunner of modern cognitive science: he maintained *both* that psychology was an essentially biological science *and* that understanding cognition demanded attention to its social situatedness.

2.6. Dynamism and Development

We have already noted that the dynamic character of Bartlett's notion of schema lends it an affinity with Parallel Distributed Processing (PDP) and with cognitive neuroscience. Bartlett's schema is not a fixed entity but a developing, organized, and organizing relational structure. The psychologist most associated with the development of schematization in ontogenesis, however, is Jean Piaget.[9] Piaget must be counted as a major, if somewhat ambiguous, forerunner of Cognitive Linguistics and of current Cognitive Linguistics inspired work in developmental psychology (Mandler 1996). Piaget's (1953) account of sensorimotor development in infancy is one in which successive reorganizations and coordinations of action schemas, arising from bodily movement and interactions with the physical world, lead to increasingly abstract cognitive representations (or internalized operational structures). The dynamic processes that underpin cognitive development are designated as *assimilation, accommodation,* and *equilibration.* These biologically inspired mechanisms were criticized, until recently, as being vague and imprecise; however, PDP computational modeling has shown how they can be specified as emergent properties of learning in connectionist networks (Plunkett and Sinha 1992; Elman et al. 1996). Assimilation is the process by which the schema incorporates (and conventionalizes) new instances; accommodation is the process by which the schema is modified by successive exposures to different instances; and equilibration is both the manner in which these two complementary processes achieve successive states of stable interaction and the process by which schemas are assimilated and accommodated *to each other.* For Piaget, all schemas originate in basic bodily *actions*; for example, to grasp a cup (assimilate the cup to the grasping schema), the hand must shape itself to the cup in anticipation of the act of grasping (accommodation).

Piaget believed that perception was subordinate to action, and he downplayed the role of imagery: an assumption which is, of course, not shared by Cognitive Linguistics and is contradicted by the work of, for example, Mandler (1996) and McNeill (2000). He regarded what he called "figurative thought" as developmentally nonprogressive, and in some sense primitive. This was because he sought to formalize his stage theory of cognitive development in terms of the mathematical theory of groups, an aspect of his research program which most developmental psychologists now consider unsupported. Piaget's neglect of the imagistic and iconic aspect of cognition was shared by other psychologists, such as Bühler and Vygotsky (discussed below); it can be counted as a major contribution of Cognitive Linguistics to cognitive science that it has directed attention to the centrality of visuo-spatial imagery and iconicity in language and cognition.

A more productive feature of Piaget's developmental theory is his employment of the developmental biological notion of *epigenesis* (Waddington 1977). Piaget rejected both environmentalism and nativism in favor of a constructivist and organismic theory of development. Again, this notion has sometimes been criticized as a banal "interactionism," but this criticism fails in the light of modern findings in developmental neurobiology (Changeux 1985) and in the light of recent findings of the Human Genome Project. Furthermore, at a formal level, there are striking parallels between Waddington's concept of an "epigenetic developmental land- scape" and the mechanism of gradient descent learning in an *n*-dimensional space that is the essence of PDP modeling. The era of formalism in linguistics was also the era of nativism in psychology; Second Generation Cognitive Science inaugurates an era of Cognitive Linguistics and of epigenetic and emergentist theories of devel- opment (Sinha 1988; Zlatev 1997; MacWhinney 1999).

2.7. Linguistic Schemas and Metaphor

A crucial notion in Cognitive Linguistics is the linguistic schema (*construction schema, utterance schema*), with its semantic basis in event schematization (see Croft, this volume, chapter 18). Although it has not been possible to determine with certainty the first usage of the term "schema" for linguistic construction, it can be traced at least as far back as Bühler's employment of the term "syntactic sche- mata" in a 1908 report of experiments on language comprehension, which he described as "something that...*mediates* between thoughts and words; a knowl- edge of the sentence's form and the relations of the sentence's parts to each other" (Innis 1982: 34).

Bühler also employed the schema notion in his analysis of metaphor, which clearly anticipated some key results of cognitive linguistic research. First, he held that "every linguistic composite is metaphorical in some degree, and the meta- phorical is no special linguistic manifestation" (Innis 1982: 43). Second, he viewed metaphor as a *cognitive*, not merely linguistic, phenomenon, with nonlinguistic parallels: "There exists outside of language in the most various representational techniques more remote and closer parallels to the linguistic procedure of fusion accomplished by metaphor" (Innis 1982: 43). Third, he proposed (in a way that anticipates conceptual blending theory—Fauconnier, this volume, chapter 14) that every metaphorical utterance involves a *Sphärenmischung* or 'mixing of spheres', where "sphere" is a conceptual meaning (*Sphären-schema*): "A word's range of meaning can be denoted as a sphere and the word itself as a schema opening onto it," just as a syntactic schema "opens onto a particular sphere in the language, allowing only certain items to be included" (Innis 1982: 49).

Bühler, who was one of the first proponents of Gestalt psychology, also used Gestaltist concepts in his theory of metaphor (to explain the combination of semantic surplus and semantic reduction that is involved in metaphor). This is then an appropriate point to conclude our discussion of the schema notion and move on to Gestalt psychology.

2.8. Gestalt, Figure/Ground, Prototype

Bartlett employed the schema notion as an alternative to the associationist theory of memory advanced by Ebbinghaus (1897), who invented the experimental method of having subjects memorize lists of nonsense syllables, which was later widely used by behaviorist psychology of "verbal learning." Gestalt psychology was based upon a similar rejection of associationism, in the field of psychology of perception. The term was employed first by von Ehrenfels (1890), who argued from the fact two melodies can be recognized as identical, even when no two notes in them are the same, that what is recognized as identical is the melody's *Gestalt quality*. The problem of how to account for Gestalt properties in perception was extended by Max Wertheimer to include higher cognitive processes (such as number concepts from a cross-cultural perspective). In 1913, he proposed that "the contents of our consciousness are mostly not summative, but constitute a particular characteristic 'togetherness'.... Such structures are to be called *Gestalten*" (Ash 1985: 308). Koffka took this argument a stage further in 1915, arguing for a revision of the concept of "stimulus," which should no longer be seen as a pattern of excitation, but as referring to whole, real objects, in relation to an actively behaving organism. He concluded that "the unambiguous sensation exists only for the psychologist; it is a product of the laboratory" (Ash 1985: 312). This is one of the earliest statements in psychology of the case for "ecological validity"; it should be noted that such considerations did not, in the view of Koffka and the other Gestaltists, *invalidate* laboratory experimentation, but rather called for both new data interpretations and more naturalistic approaches to experimentation. Gibson (1979) advanced similar arguments half a century later in his ecological theory of perception.

Koffka argued that Gestalt qualities of "wholeness" characterize motor action, as well as perception. The next step, to apply Gestalt theory to learning and problem solving, was taken by Köhler. He observed that chimpanzees appeared to exhibit a spontaneous grasp of means-ends relationships and claimed this to be evidence of learning through "insight" (Köhler [1917] 1973). Köhler pioneered modern naturalistic studies of animal behavior, filming the chimpanzees solving the experimental tasks he set them and arguing that this ethological record was more valid and revealing than repeated trial laboratory experimentation.

We have seen (in section 1.2) that Wundt had already employed the notion of *foregrounding* in his analysis of the psychology of the sentence. Foreground and background are the psychological basis, for Wundt, of the linguistic categories of subject and predicate. In fact, Wundt considered the operations of selective attention to be fundamental to higher mental processes, which are dynamically structured by a distinction between the foreground (focus of attention) and the background. The experimental demonstration of the existence of central attentional control in perceptual processing formed, indeed, a major part of his attempt to refute associationism. Edgar Rubin (1914) reported experiments on Figure/Ground perception and reversal, and Köhler attempted to construct a physically based neurophysiological explanation for the segregation in perception of the Figure and for the laws of "Good Gestalt" (e.g., figural closure: the tendency to perceive, for example, an arc beyond a certain circumference as an incomplete circle). Köhler (1924: 256) drew upon both electrical field theory and fluid dynamics to argue that physical systems tend toward "the simplest and most regular groupings," calling this "tendency to simplest shape" the *Prägnanz* of the Gestalt (cited in Ash 1985: 319; see also Rosenthal and Visetti 2003).

It has often been maintained that the attempt by Köhler to ground neuropsychology in physics was a theoretical dead end. This may be so for his detailed formulations, but Gestalt notions have proved more resilient, in the long term, than the Behaviorism that appeared to have won out in the late 1930s. Recent years have witnessed a new interest in physical and mathematical models of self-organizing systems, including biological, cognitive, and linguistic forms (Thom 1976; Prigogine and Stengers 1984; Petitot-Concorda 1985). In terms of specific psychological concepts, Gestalt psychology has probably contributed to Cognitive Linguistics, directly and indirectly, more than any other single cognitive psychological approach. Prototype theory, which treats categorization in terms of goodness of exemplification and organization around central tendencies and which is based upon interactive stochastic processing of microfeatures rather than a "checklist" of atomic macrofeatures, has obvious affinities with the Gestalt notion. Figure/Ground is a fundamental concept in Cognitive Semantics and Cognitive Grammar (see this volume, chapters 11, 13, and 17), as well as in the recently developed vantage theory of categorization (MacLaury 1997).[10] As the song says about Joe Hill, Gestalt psychology never died. It is alive, well, and living at a new address under the name of Cognitive Linguistics.[11]

This is ironic, for Bühler came to criticize Gestalt psychology mainly because he considered that it paid insufficient attention to the psychology of language (Bühler 1927) and to the specifically human dimension of symbolization. In proposing that the same mechanisms were operative in both perception and higher mental processes, Bühler argued, Gestalt psychology neglected to ask what might be *specific* to the higher mental processes.[12] This is a live issue for Cognitive Linguistics, inasmuch as we still have a great deal to learn about the relationship between the preconceptual and the conceptual basis of language (between perception, action, and symbolization). Barsalou, Solomon, and Wu (1999) and Mandler (1996) discuss how perceptual information may be transformed cognitively and developmentally into symbol-like internal representations; some such representational redescription of imagistic perceptual (and motor; see Jeannerod 1994) neuropsychological formats must play a crucial part in linguistic conceptualization. The recent turn to an *embodied* cognitive science (Lakoff and Johnson 1999) requires us, in the spirit of Köhler, to "abandon the idea of neat dividing lines between perception, cognition and action" (Clark 1997: xiii). Bühler would still, however, have maintained that embodied action and perception is not the whole story of symbolization and that in order to understand this, we need to move beyond the individual organism.

2.9. Representation and Symbolization

Representation is perhaps *the* most important, and most contested, foundational concept in modern cognitive science. Cognitive Linguistics takes the view that linguistic structure is motivated by conceptual representation and communicative function, thereby placing the representational function of language at the center of its concerns. As a *usage-based* theory of language, Cognitive Linguistics rejects the strict dichotomy in traditional, Saussurean linguistics between *langue* and *parole*, as well as the generative linguistic postulate of the autonomy of syntax. Cognitive Linguistics, though distinctive, new, and unparalleled in earlier linguistic theories in terms of its detailed working-out of the cognitive-functional perspective, has many precursors in linguistic theory (Nerlich and Clarke, this volume, chapter 22), one of which in particular—the *Sprachtheorie* (language theory) of Bühler ([1934] 1990)—deserves special attention as a full-fledged, linguistically sophisticated psychology of language.

Bühler rejected *langue* as the basis for psychology of language, though not as a basis for linguistic description, which he considered to be a necessary precondition for a psychology of language. He viewed speaking as *representational action* and language as the *mediating vehicle* of such action, elaborating this general perspective in the "Organon" (Tool/Vehicle) model of linguistic communication.[13] His best-known contribution to linguistic theory was the formulation of a theory of deixis of person and place, which remains to this day a standard model from which most current theories of deixis take off. I will focus here, however, on the general features of Bühler's language theory, beginning with the foundations in phonology of his attempt to integrate sign-theory into the psychology of language and speech.

Bühler was an active participant in the discussions of the Prague Linguistic Circle, and, as Innis (1982) points out, he was probably the first psychologist to recognize the profound implications of Trubetzkoy's and Jakobson's analyses of the phoneme and phonological representation, for a theory of perception. Bühler's Gestalt psychological background undoubtedly played an important role in his realization that in perceiving speech sounds, we perceive *linguistic* material, not untransformed "sensations." In modern terminology, he understood that speech sound perception is *categorical*. Categorical perception has been extensively studied in visual as well as in auditory modalities (Harnad 1987), and we now know it to be characteristic of human perception at all ages. Perceptual categories also have internal structure: they are organized around typicality (Rosch 1977). Infants' early speech sound perception is categorical in nature (Eimas et al. 1971); infants learn to apply words to typical category members before atypical ones (Meints, Plunkett, and Harris 1999); and they display preferences for typical over atypical members of lexical categories (Southgate and Meints 2000).

Bühler, however, was primarily interested in working out the consequences of the lesson that the "sign character" of language has a psychological reality which goes, as Bruner (1974) would later put it, "beyond the information given": what is "there to be perceived" is, at a physical level of description, just sound, but what we *actually* perceive is meaningful speech. His question was then: how does language operate, as a symbol system? Bühler focused his answer on two properties which he considered to be unique to human natural languages and which distinguished *symbol systems* from *signals.*

First, symbol systems have a "two class" character: every language has both a lexicon and morphosyntactic rules, and this two class character underlies the *productivity* of natural language.[14] Bühler was aware that historical language change involved the recruitment of lexical items to grammatical constructions (Heine 1997), but he insisted that these "two classes of posits" needed to be distinguished in linguistic theory. The distinction between lexicon and syntax is fundamental to both Generative Grammar and Classical Cognitive Science, in which the lexicon consists of a set of symbols, and the grammar of a set of *non-meaningful* rules for generating legal symbol strings. Cognitive Linguistics rejects the absolute distinction between lexicon and grammar, but I would argue nevertheless that Bühler was closer to a Cognitive Linguistics position than a Generative one, since he considered grammatical constructions, as well as lexical items, to be symbolically meaningful (see the discussion above of "syntactic schemas"). Both the lexical and the combinatorial aspects of "two class" symbol organization were thus, for Bühler, contributory to sentence or utterance meaning.

Bühler argued, furthermore, that "one class" systems of *signals* can be considered as "codes," but that language, as a symbolic system, is *not a code.* There is not the space here to explore this issue in depth, but it is plausible to argue that this aspect of Bühler's language theory points toward a deep theoretical inadequacy of generative linguistic theories: they are "code" theories, not theories of genuinely symbolic systems. Bühler was also aware of the role played by imagistic or iconic "relational faithfulness" (structural likeness) in motivating constructions.

> [Language employs] not a materially faithful . . . but a relationally faithful rendering (through intermediate constructions) . . . what physicists nowadays naturally count as 'mapping'. . . . The set of case forms [function linguistically] only because [the represented states of affairs] are understood and perceived according to the schema of human or animal action. . . . The schema is projected image-like. . . . It is traced out by the [construction]. ([1934] 1990: 213, 219)[15]

Second, Bühler argued that conventional symbol systems are grounded in an *intersubjective* meaning-field in which speakers *represent*, through symbolic action, some segment or aspect of reality for hearers. This representational function is

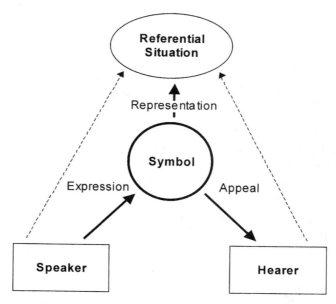

Figure 49.2. A modified variant of Bühler's Organon Model (broken lines represent joint attention)

unique to symbolization and is precisely what distinguishes a *symbol* from a *signal*. A signal can be regarded as a (coded) *instruction to behave* in a certain way. A symbol, on the other hand (and using a deliberately updated terminology), directs and guides, not the *behavior* of the organism receiving the signal, but their *intentional stance* or (minimally) their *attention*. This, in a nutshell, is Bühler's Organon theory of language, diagrammed in figure 49.2.

Figure 49.2 modifies Bühler's own diagram in two main ways. First, it makes explicit that the relationship of Representation is one obtaining between the Symbol (or linguistic expression) and a Referential Situation (which is linguistically conceptualized by the linguistic expression).[16] This representational relationship exists within a sign-field which is coconstituted with the other two sign-functions: Expression (obtaining between the Speaker and the symbolic sign) and Appeal (obtaining between the symbolic sign and the Hearer). The symbol *expresses* the speaker's communicative intention and *appeals* to the hearer to direct their own intentional processes toward the referential situation *represented* by the symbolic sign.[17] Functionally, these three metafunctions of the symbolic sign find structural realization in the person-deixis system of natural languages: I (expression), You (appeal), and He/She/It (representation).

The second modification introduced into Bühler's original diagram is the depiction by means of dotted lines of the way in which the symbol coordinates the "joint attention" of the speaker and hearer, directed toward the symbolically represented referential situation. In linguistic symbolization proper, this joint attention is expanded and developed into the symbolized communicative *intention* of the speaker and the *intentional reading* of speaker's meaning by hearer. However, in the prelinguistic coordination of joint attention by gesture or gaze, occurring productively from about 9-to-10 months of age, we can substitute for the symbolic sign an indexical communicative sign (e.g., pointing), while preserving the same general sign-field structure. This modification helps us to see how Bühler's Organon model can illuminate the process of early language acquisition, as well as mature language use (see Tomasello, this volume, chapter 41).

To conclude this brief discussion of Bühler's psychology of language, two significant advantages it possesses over other well-known sign theories can be highlighted. First, unlike other versions of the "semiotic triangle" (e.g., Ogden and Richards 1923), Bühler's model places symbolic representation in the context of communication: the Organon model is both cognitive and functional. Second, although Bühler's binary distinction between "signal" and "symbol" does not invalidate Peirce's better-known triadic classification of index, icon, and symbol, it is in many ways more psychologically and functionally illuminating. The essential difference between Bühler's signal and symbol is that the symbol combines intentionality, conventionalization, and structural elaboration, and these aspects of human symbolic communication emerge ontogenetically (and probably evolved phylogenetically) in just this order of development. By contrast, communication by signals involves *none* of these properties. Nonhuman communication systems have either only a signal character or employ symbols unsystematically (Sinha 2004; Tomasello, this volume, chapter 41).

Bühler was far from being the only psychologist of language to underline the significance of symbolization as fundamental to higher mental processes. The Russian psychologist Vygotsky (e.g., Vygotsky [1930] 1978, [1934] 1986), for example, developed an account of the developmental transformation of individual cognitive processes via the internalization of culturally established forms of "semiotically mediated" social interaction, a view with clear affinities to Bühler's view of language as a mediating instrument of representation.[18] The sociogenetic theories of Vygotsky, and of his American pragmatist contemporary Mead (1934), lend a developmental counterpoint to Bühler's functional-cognitive analysis of linguistic representation and are key resources for researching and understanding the social interactional grounding of language and cognition.

Bühler's language theory, less well known than Vygotsky's cultural-historical psychology, deserves the central place accorded to it in this brief historical survey because of the remarkably prescient manner in which he anticipated numerous themes in Cognitive Linguistics. In acquainting ourselves with this work, we are not engaging in a mere antiquarian exercise, but in a dialogic exploration of the intellectual foundations of what Tomasello (1998) justly calls *The New Psychology of Language*. This dialogue is productive, not merely reproductive, because Bühler's writings invite us, across the gulf of a world war and more than a half century of cognitive science, to rethink the concept of representation.

3. REPRESENTATION AND THE DEVELOPING, SITUATED, EMBODIED MIND

What is representation? The standard answer, in Classical Cognitive Science, was that representations are internal states of a cognitive mechanism. Given the assumption that the cognitive mechanism is computational, it follows that representations are computational states (or, if we define computation in terms of procedures, then perhaps representations are the inputs and outputs of procedures). The totality of such internal representations at any time constitutes the current knowledge of the cognitive mechanism. Knowledge is therefore a kind of internal code, which stands in a "representational" relation to the world outside the cognitive mechanism. Such internal representations can be communicated from one cognitive mechanism to another, by "recoding" them in natural language. On such an account, the semantic relationship between language and the world is derivative from the relationship between internal (mental) representations and the external world. The particular instantiation or implementation of the cognitive mechanism (in a biological organism, or in a computer, or in any other device capable of functionally realizing the computational states and transitions called for by the theory) is irrelevant to the goal of formalizing the theory. This classical, "representationalist" theory of mind has been challenged by a number of currents of thinking, most of which emerged in the mid-1980s and whose confluence makes up Second Generation Cognitive Science.

3.1. Back to the Body and Brain

Classical Cognitive Science was relatively unconcerned with the biological foundations of human cognition. Insofar as it did concern itself with the biological interface between the cognitive system and the real world, it conceived these in terms of the manipulation of symbolically rendered "inputs." The body was subordinated to the computational mind. The turn to an *embodied* cognitive science has involved, first, a growing understanding of the constitutive role played in human cognition and language by the human body itself (Johnson 1987); second, a (connectionist) computational research program which consciously seeks to constrain its hypotheses in ways which are compatible with what is known about the microstructure and functioning of the human brain; and third, the rise of cognitive neuroscience in the last decade of the twentieth century, which promises to become as foundational for Second Generation Cognitive Science as Artificial Intelligence was for Classical Cognitive Science.

Connectionist computational models do not directly "map" the structure of external reality. Rather, they map the input-output regularities that constitute the cognitive model's adaptive (internal and/or external) environment. Representation ceases to be itself a model; it becomes a property of the functional coupling of the model (or system) with its environment. Furthermore, in "dynamic systems" approaches, this coupling itself becomes to a large extent nonrepresentational. Apparently intelligent behavioral strategies can emerge from morphology in dynamic functional interaction with environment (Clark 1997). It is clear that the reformulation of the notion of representation is squarely on the cognitive science agenda (Sinha 1988; Gibbs and Matlock 1999).

3.2. Return to Reality

Classical Cognitive Science was formalist in method and mentalist in theory, having as its goal the formal description of internal cognitive states and processes. Second Generation Cognitive Science does not deny the existence of internal states, nor rule them (as behaviorism did) out of bounds for scientific inquiry. However, the boundary between "external" and "internal" is more permeable in Second Generation Cognitive Science than it was in Classical Cognitive Science—the mind is now viewed as being no more separable from the world than it is from the body. The philosophical basis of Classical Cognitive Science was *objectivist* (Lakoff 1987), based upon the idea of a correspondence mapping between external world and internal mental representation. Classical Cognitive Science, even though it claimed to be realist, was in fact hopelessly enmeshed in the insoluble antinomies of Cartesian dualism. Second Generation Cognitive Science is realist, but not objectivist. It seeks its grounding of the mind not in "mental representation," but in the activity, movement, and engagement of the organism with its environment: a point of view which clearly resonates with the pragmatist tradition (Putnam 1999; Rohrer 2001; this volume, chapter 2).

3.3. The Developmental Perspective

Classical Cognitive Science was not much concerned with development, some of its most famous proponents even arguing that it does not really exist (Piatelli-Palmarini 1980). Chomsky's "argument from the poverty of the stimulus" was generalized from language to cover all aspects of cognition, resulting in the modular nativism which dominated theories of cognition in the recent past.[19] In contrast, there is a natural affinity between Cognitive Linguistics and developmental, constructivist approaches to language acquisition (see Fauconnier, this volume, chapter 14). A main aim of future research will be to clarify the developmental relationship between conceptual and preconceptual aspects of cognition, by exploring the developmental relationship in human cognition between the emergence of intentional, representational communication, the capacity to employ schematic cognitive representations, and the development of full-fledged linguistic conceptualization. More generally, development and emergence are set to become central themes of Second Generation Cognitive Science, at all levels from neural plasticity to the sociocultural context of human cognition and communication. The new cognitive science is biologically based in the new epigeneticism.

3.4. Socially Situating the Self

The formalism and mentalism of Classical Cognitive Science were congenial to the epistemological individualism that it inherited from the Cartesian philosophical tradition. Questions of knowledge (and representation) are posed in this tradition exclusively in relation to the individual knower (or speaker/hearer). For most of its history, psychology too has had a predominant focus on the individual organism and the individual mind. We have also seen, however, that there have been repeated efforts, by psychologists such as Bartlett, Bühler, Mead, and Vygotsky, to locate cognition and language in their social context of situation.

In reaction against the individualism and mentalism of Classical Cognitive Science, some contemporary social constructionists have argued that the aim of explaining human action with reference to inner mental states is wholly misguided (sometimes appealing in support of this stance to Wittgenstein's philosophy of language, e.g., Coulter 1989). Anticognitivism is also often antinaturalist, implicitly or explicitly arguing that there is a fundamental and unbridgeable gulf between neuroscience and the explanation of socially intelligible action and interaction.[20] The cognitive anthropologist Edward Hutchins (1999: 1) argues that such anticognitivism merely mirrors the inadequacies of traditional cognitivism:

> For much of cognitive science, cognition is exclusively something that happens inside people's heads. . . . The social and physical environments of thinking are what thought operates on, but have no part in thought itself. On the other hand, for some proponents of situated action and situated cognition . . . mental models are figments of analysts' imagination. In a reaction against the excesses of early artificial intelligence, these authors deny the relevance of mental models to human action. Both of these views seem wrong to me.

Hutchins here articulates a conviction, shared by an increasing number of researchers in Cognitive Linguistics and cognitive science, that human cognition is best viewed as dually grounded in organismic properties adapted to the ecology of human life and in the socio-communicative processes which construct that ecology (see also Sinha 1988, 1999a; Hutchins 1995; Shore 1996; Itkonen 1997; Harder 1999; Tomasello 1999). Such a cognitive science, grounded in "situated embodiment"

(Zlatev 1997), requires the methodological "recognition of the complementarity, not opposition, of the objectivizing stance of naturalism, and the reflexive stance of the sciences of meaning. This bi-perspectivism, or perspectival complementarity, [can be] called a 'socionaturalistic' approach" (Sinha 1999b: 34). Representation, because embodiment of culture extends beyond the individual human body (Sinha and Jensen de López 2000), is not something existing in a different, "mental" sphere from the physical world. Rather, it is both consequence of and part of the shaping of the world by human agency and the signifying of the world in acts of human, intersubjective communication.

4. IMPLICATIONS FOR COGNITIVE LINGUISTICS

In tracing the historical debts owed by Cognitive Linguistics to psychology and its affinities with the *ensemble* of other currents making up Second Generation Cognitive Science, I hope to have reinforced the basic proposition which unites all subscribers to the scientific program of Cognitive Linguistics: that language can best be made sense of by recognizing that it is structurally and functionally continuous with, motivated by, and emergent from nonlinguistic cognitive processes. It would be mistaken, however, to conclude from this that the future of Cognitive Linguistics in the emerging landscape of the "new" cognitive science is likely to be uncontested.

I wish to highlight, in conclusion, two especially problematic issues. The first concerns the status of linguistics in the interdisciplinary context of cognitive science. Generative Linguistics was constitutively influential in Classical Cognitive Science, and I have argued that this was, in part, a consequence of the marginalization and "forgetting" of important currents in prebehaviorist psychology which, in turn, have been deeply influential upon Cognitive Linguistics. It follows from this that Cognitive Linguistics does not *in and of itself* constitute the sought-for new paradigm in cognitive science. Rather, it is a major contributory current to an emergent new *interdisciplinary* science of mind. The second issue concerns the relations between the biological and the historical, sociocultural grounding of language and mind. Language, from a psychological perspective, is not simply an expression of human organismic capacity; rather, it is the most important symbolic mediator between developing organism, psychological subjectivity, and culturally evolving surround. It is, in my view, the adequacy with which Cognitive Linguistics addresses this dynamic, processual, relational complex that will be decisive for its lasting disciplinary contribution to the science of the embodied mind in society.

NOTES

....

I am grateful to the following for their help with references: Dorthe Berntsen (autobiographical memory; e.g., Berntsen 1998); Ocke-Schwen Bohn (infant speech perception; e.g., Bohn 2000); Brigitte Nerlich (history of psychology and linguistics; e.g., Nerlich and Clarke 1998). I also wish to thank the editors for their extensive and helpful comments. This chapter is dedicated to the memory of George Butterworth and Steen Folke Larsen, with whose shades I continue to converse about psychology.

1. Gardner (1985), in his now-classic history of cognitive science, dates the emergence of the interdiscipline to the Hoxon Symposium of 1955, which is close to another widely cited landmark date, that of Chomsky's famously devastating review of Skinner's *Verbal Behavior* (Chomsky 1959).

2. It is important to note that not all cognitive psychologists endorsed the Classical Cognitive Science program, or indeed viewed themselves as working in cognitive science. Nevertheless, the grounding assumptions of this program deeply permeated the discipline, and to an extent still do so. One problem in establishing interdisciplinary dialogue is the way in which this has led to different appropriations of the terms "cognitive," and especially "cognitivist," by linguists and psychologists. For the former, this designates an adherence to the Cognitive Linguistics paradigm; for the latter, an adherence to Information Processing and related "classical" paradigms. I will be using the latter. There were always, of course, psychological dissenters from cognitivism, but these tended to counterpose an ecological or social constructionist vision, leaving the heartland of cognition to the classical cognitivists.

3. In a way, we can say that Cognitive Linguistics has restored to psychology the status of "propaedeutic science" accorded it by Wundt (Blumenthal 1985), which it forfeited in a Classical Cognitive Science dominated by linguistics and computer science.

4. A bust of Wundt, along, among others, with one of Karl Bühler, can be viewed at the Max Planck Institute for Psycholinguistics in Nijmegen. Wundt was skeptical about the application of experimental methods to language, because he considered naturalistic observation and linguistic analysis more appropriate methodologies. Bühler (who debated with Wundt over the appropriateness of experimental methods for studying higher mental processes in general) can be credited with founding modern experimental psycholinguistics: "He moved psycholinguistics into the laboratory, something George Miller had to accomplish again half a century later" (Levelt 1981: 190).

5. Brigitte Nehrlich (p.c.) points out that "Kant ([1781] 1929) saw the schema as a *procedure* (*Verfahren*) of the productive imagination" and that "Kant's distinction between an image and a procedure of imagination, i.e., a schema, is similar to Wittgenstein's (1953) conception of static and dynamic meaning in *Philosophical Investigations*."

6. PDP stands for 'Parallel Distributed Processing', a strongly connectionist approach to cognition and learning.

7. Head was by no means the first to employ the term "schema" after Kant. Herbart employed it in his early-nineteenth-century associationistic psychology and also coined the terms "assimilation" and "accommodation," but this can safely be considered prehistory.

8. Bartlett's reference to the Boas source is to the *Annual Report of the Bureau of American Ethnology Bulletin* (26: 184–85). There is a text of at least one story, narrated by the Chinook Charles Cultee, and translated by Franz Boas, in the *Bureau of American Ethnology Bulletin* 26 (Washington, DC: Government Printing Office, 1901). This reference

is from Elliott (2003), who discusses a story about the familiar Native American trickster character Coyote on a salmon fishing expedition, which bears little resemblance to "The War of the Ghosts."

9. Piaget was a biologist by training and did not designate himself as a psychologist; for his interdisciplinary science of cognitive development he used the term (coined by James Mark Baldwin) *genetic epistemology.*

10. We have already noted Bartlett's use of the term "organized setting" as synonymous with "schema," and it is interesting in this light that he clearly identifies, with reference to Rubin's Figure/Ground experiments, schema with Ground, entitling one of his subsections "The Scheme, or Setting, which makes Perceiving possible" (Bartlett 1932: 32).

11. Gestalt psychology was much weakened by the fact that many of its founders were victims of the Nazification of the German (and later, Austrian) universities and compelled to emigrate to the United States. Wertheimer was a Jew, closely associated with Marxist and socialist philosophers, and a friend of Einstein. He was among the first professors dismissed by the Hitler regime. Köhler was one the few German professors to publicly protest at the Nazi purges of the universities and to try to defend his assistants accused of "communist activities." Karl Bühler was associated with progressive educational circles, and his wife, Charlotte, was Jewish. Charlotte Bühler was a developmental psychologist and psycholinguist who founded Gestalt therapy. Karl Bühler "spent the last 23 years of his life in total oblivion in America" (Levelt 1981), his psychology of language neglected; the work of the other Gestalt psychologists mentioned here was received with interest and respect in the United States, but lacked the institutional strength of behaviorist psychology.

12. This criticism was also to be leveled, decades later, against Gibson's ecological psychology.

13. The name of the model is taken from Plato's *Cratylus.*

14. This discussion of productivity was not original to Bühler and can also be found in Wundt, but Bühler developed it particularly clearly.

15. The symbolic field of language, according to Bühler, is both an *intermediary* and an *organizer* ("an ordering and coordinating implement," Bühler [1934] 1990: 217); in the quotation in the main text the term "construction," employed by Bühler in designating one kind of such "implement" is accordingly substituted for the now unfamiliar expression "field implement."

16. Bühler employed the designation "objects and states of affairs" for what I name referential situation, and "sender" and "receiver" for what I designate as, respectively, Speaker and Hearer.

17. The symbolic sign-field thus also functionally incorporates the pre- or subsymbolic aspects of meaning or signification: "[The complex linguistic sign] ... is a *symbol* by virtue of its coordination to objects and states of affairs, a *symptom* (index) by virtue of its dependence on the sender, whose inner states it expresses, and a *signal* by virtue of its appeal to the hearer, whose inner or outer behavior it directs as do other communicative signs" (Bühler [1934] 1990: 35). Note that in Bühler's theory *representation* is a relationship between symbol and world, not synonymous with or reducible to speakers' "inner states."

18. There is a tragic parallel between Bühler's expulsion by the National Socialists and the condemnation in the Soviet Union of Vygotsky's psychology as a "bourgeois deviation" during the Stalin era.

19. The argument from the poverty of the stimulus, as developed by Chomsky with respect to language, whether its premises were really correct or not, at least had the virtues of originality, relevance, and intellectual substance. The same cannot be said for arguments

such as that, since witches and ghosts are never actually perceived, concepts of religion and magic are innate.

20.   See note 2 for usage of the terms "cognitivism" and "anticognitivism." It should also be noted that while it is undoubtedly the case that Wittgenstein's later philosophy is antagonistic to cognitivism, it is not in my view inconsistent with the kind of (socio) naturalism delineated in the following paragraph.

REFERENCES

Ash, Mitchell. 1985. Gestalt psychology: Origins in Germany and reception in the United States. In Claude E. Buxton, ed., *Points of view in the modern history of psychology* 295–344. London: Academic Press.

Barsalou, Lawrence W., Karen Olseth Solomon, and Ling-Ling Wu. 1999. Perceptual simulation in conceptual tasks. In Masako Hiraga, Chris Sinha, and Sherman Wilcox, eds., *Cultural, psychological and typological issues in Cognitive Linguistics* 209–28. Amsterdam: John Benjamins.

Bartlett, Frederic C. 1932. *Remembering: A study in experimental and social psychology.* Cambridge: Cambridge University Press.

Berntsen, Dorthe. 1998. Voluntary and involuntary access to autobiographical memory. *Memory* 6: 113–41.

Blumenthal, Arthur 1985. Wilhelm Wundt: Psychology as the propaedeutic science. In Claude E. Buxton, ed., *Points of view in the modern history of psychology* 19–50. London: Academic Press.

Boas, Franz. [1911] 1966. *Introduction to Handbook of American Indian languages.* Lincoln: University of Nebraska Press.

Bohn, Ocke-Schwen. 2000. Linguistic relativity in speech perception: An overview of the influence of language experience on the perception of speech sounds from infancy to adulthood. In Susanne Niemeyer and René Dirven, eds., *Evidence for linguistic relativity* 1–28. Amsterdam: John Benjamins.

Bransford, John D., and Marcia K. Johnson. 1973. Consideration of some problems of comprehension. In W. G. Chase, ed., *Visual information processing* 383–438. New York: Academic Press.

Bruner, Jerome. 1974. *Beyond the information given: Studies in the psychology of knowing.* London: Allen & Unwin.

Bühler, Karl. 1927. *Die Krise der Psychologie.* Jena: Fischer.

Bühler, Karl. [1934] 1990. *Theory of language: The representational function of language.* Trans. Donald F. Goodwin. Amsterdam: John Benjamins.

Chandler, Michael, and Christopher Lalonde. 2000. Cultural continuity as a hedge against suicide in Canada's First Nations. *Transcultural Psychiatry* 35: 191–219.

Changeux, Jean-Pierre. 1985. *Neuronal Man: The biology of mind.* Oxford: Oxford University Press.

Chomsky, Noam. 1959. Review of *Verbal Behavior,* by B. F. Skinner. *Language* 35: 26–58. (Also in Jerry A. Fodor and Jerrold J. Katz, eds., *The structure of language: Readings in the philosophy of language* 547–78. Englewood Cliffs, NJ: Prentice-Hall, 1964)

Clark, Andy. 1997. *Being there: Putting brain, body, and world together again.* Cambridge, MA: MIT Press.

Coulter, Jeff. 1989. *Mind in action.* Oxford: Basil Blackwell.

Damasio, Antonio. 1999. *The feeling of what happens: Body, emotion and the making of consciousness.* London: Heinemann.

Ebbinghaus, Hermann 1897. *Grundzüge der Psychologie.* Leipzig, Germany: Veit.

Eimas, Peter D., Einar R. Siqueland, Peter Juszyk, and James Vigorito. 1971. Speech perception in infants. *Science* 171: 303–6.

Elliott, Michael A. 2003. Coyote comes to the Norton: Indigenous oral narrative and American literary history. *American Literature* 75: 723–49.

Elman, Jeff, Elizabeth Bates, Mark Johnson, Annette Karmiloff-Smith, Dominico Parisi, and Kim Plunkett. 1996. *Rethinking innateness: A connectionist perspective on development.* Cambridge, MA: MIT Press.

Fillmore, Charles J. 1982. Frame semantics. In Linguistic Society of Korea, ed., *Linguistics in the morning calm* 111–37. Seoul: Hanshin.

Gardner, Howard. 1985. *The mind's new science: A history of the cognitive revolution.* New York: Basic Books.

Gibbs, Raymond W., Jr., and Teenie Matlock. 1999. Psycholinguistics and mental representations. *Cognitive Linguistics* 10: 263–69.

Gibson, James. 1979. *The ecological approach to visual perception.* Boston: Houghton Mifflin.

Harder, Peter. 1999. Partial autonomy: Ontology and methodology in cognitive linguistics. In Theo Janssen and Gisela Redeker, eds., *Cognitive linguistics: Foundations, scope, and methodology* 195–222. Berlin: Mouton de Gruyter.

Harnad, Stevan. 1987. *Categorical perception.* Cambridge: Cambridge University Press.

Harré, Rom, and Grant Gillett. 1994. *The discursive mind.* London: Sage Publications.

Head, Henry. 1920. *Studies in neurology.* Oxford: Oxford University Press.

Heine, Bernd. 1997. *Cognitive foundations of grammar.* New York: Oxford University Press.

Hutchins, Edwin. 1995. *Cognition in the wild.* Cambridge, MA: MIT Press.

Hutchins, Edwin. 1999. Mental models as an instrument for bounded rationality. Manuscript (paper submitted for the 'Dahlem Workshop on Bounded Rationality: The Adaptive Toolbox'), Department of Cognitive Science, University of California at San Diego.

Innis, Robert. 1982. *Karl Bühler: Semiotic foundations of language theory.* New York: Plenum Press.

Itkonen, Esa 1997. The social ontology of linguistic meaning. *SKY: Yearbook of the Linguistic Association of Finland*: 49–81.

Jeannerod, Marc. 1994. The representing brain: Neural correlates of motor intention and imagery. *Behavioral and Brain Sciences* 17: 187–245.

Johnson, Mark. 1987. *The body in the mind: The bodily basis of meaning, imagination, and reason.* Chicago: University of Chicago Press.

Johnson-Laird, Philip. 1983. *Mental models.* Cambridge: Cambridge University Press.

John-Steiner, Vera. 1987. *Notebooks of the mind: Explorations of thinking.* New York: Harper and Row.

Kant, Immanuel. [1781] 1929. *Critique of pure reason.* London: MacMillan.

Karmiloff-Smith, Annette. 1992. *Beyond modularity: A developmental perspective on cognitive science.* Cambridge, MA: MIT Press.

Köhler, Wolfgang. [1917] 1973. *Intelligenzprüfungen an Anthropoiden.* Berlin: Springer Verlag.

Köhler, Wolfgang. 1924. *Die physischen Gestalten in Ruhe und im stationären Zustand: Eine naturphilosophische Untersuchung.* 2nd ed. Erlangen, Germany: Verlag der Philosophischen Akademie.

Lakoff, George. 1987. *Women, fire, and dangerous things: What categories tell us about the mind.* Chicago: University of Chicago Press.

Lakoff, George, and Mark Johnson. 1999. *Philosophy in the flesh: The embodied mind and its challenge to Western thought.* New York: Basic Books.

Levelt, Willem. 1981. Déja vu? *Cognition* 10: 187–92.

MacLaury, Robert E. 1997. *Color and cognition in Meso-America: Constructing categories as vantages.* Austin: University of Texas Press.

MacWhinney, Brian. 1999. *The emergence of language.* Mahwah, NJ: Lawrence Erlbaum.

Mandler, Jean. 1996. Preverbal representation and language. In Paul Bloom, Mary A. Peterson, Lyn Nadel, and Merrill F. Garret, eds., *Language and Space* 365–84. Cambridge, MA: MIT Press.

McNeill, David. 2000. Analogic/analytic representations and cross-linguistic differences in thinking for speaking. *Cognitive Linguistics* 11: 43–60.

Mead, George Herbert. 1934. *Mind, self and society.* Chicago: University of Chicago Press.

Meints, Kerstin, Kim Plunkett, and Paul Harris. 1999. When does an ostrich become a bird? The role of typicality in early word comprehension. *Developmental Psychology* 35: 1072–78.

Minsky, Marvin. 1975. A framework for representing knowledge. In Patrick Winston, ed., *The psychology of computer vision* 211–77. New York: McGraw-Hill.

Neisser, Ulrich. 1967. *Cognitive psychology.* New York: Appleton-Century-Crofts.

Neisser, Ulrich. 1976. *Cognition and reality.* San Francisco, CA: Freeman.

Neisser, Ulrich, and Eugene Winograd, eds. 1988. *Remembering reconsidered: Ecological and traditional approaches to the study of memory.* New York: Cambridge University Press.

Nelson, Katherine. 1985. *Making sense: The acquisition of shared meaning.* Orlando, FL: Academic Press.

Nerlich, Brigitte, and David Clarke. 1998. The linguistic repudiation of Wundt. *History of Psychology* 1: 179–204.

Ogden, Charles, and Ivor A. Richards. 1923. *The meaning of meaning: A study of the influence of language upon thought and of the science of symbolism.* London: Routledge & Kegan Paul.

Palmer, Gary, 1996. *Toward a theory of cultural linguistics.* Austin: University of Texas Press.

Petitot-Concorda, Jean. 1985. *Morphogenèse du sens.* Paris: Presses Universitaires de France.

Piaget, Jean. 1953. *The origin of intelligence in the child.* London: Routledge and Kegan Paul.

Piatelli-Palmarini, Massimo, ed. 1980. *Language and learning.* London: Routledge and Kegan Paul.

Plunkett, Kim, and Chris Sinha. 1992. Connectionism and developmental theory. *British Journal of Developmental Psychology* 10: 209–54.

Prigogine, Ilya, and Isabelle Stengers. 1984. *Order out of chaos: Man's new dialogue with nature.* London: Heinemann.

Putnam, Hilary. 1999. *The threefold cord: Mind, body and world.* New York: Columbia University Press.

Rohrer, Tim. 2001. Pragmatism, ideology and embodiment: William James and the philosophical foundations of cognitive linguistics. In René Dirven, Bruce Hawkins, and Esra Sandikcioglu, eds., *Language and ideology*, vol. 1, *Theoretical cognitive approaches* 49–81. Amsterdam: John Benjamins.

Rosch, Eleanor. 1977. Classification of real-world objects: Origins and representations in cognition. In Philip Johnson-Laird and Peter C. Watson, eds., *Thinking: Readings in cognitive science.* Cambridge: Cambridge University Press.

Rosenthal, Victor, and Yves-Marie Visetti. 2003. *Köhler.* Paris: Les Belles Lettres.

Rubin, David, ed. 1996. *Remembering our past: Studies in autobiographical memory.* Cambridge: Cambridge University Press.

Rubin, Edgar. 1914. Die visuelle Wahrnehmung von Figuren. In F. Schumman, ed., *Bericht über den 6. Kongress für experimentelle Psychologie.* Leipzig, Germany: Barth.

Rumelhart, David, James L. McClelland, and the PDP Research Group. 1986. Schemata and sequential thought processes in PDP models. In James L. McClelland, David Rumelhart and the PDP Research Group, eds., *Parallel distributed processing: Explorations in the microstructure of cognition,* vol. 2, *Psychological and biological models* 7–57. Cambridge, MA: MIT Press.

Schank, Roger C., and Robert P. Abelson. 1977. *Scripts, plans, goals and understanding.* Hillsdale, NJ: Lawrence Erlbaum.

Seuren, Pieter 1998. *Western linguistics: An historical introduction.* Oxford: Blackwell.

Shepard, Roger N., and Jacqueline Metzler. 1978. Mental rotation of three-dimensional objects. *Science* 171: 701–3.

Shore, Bradd. 1996. *Culture in mind: Cognition, culture and the problem of meaning.* New York: Oxford University Press.

Sinha, Chris. 1988. *Language and representation: A socio-naturalistic approach to human development.* Hemel Hempstead, UK: Harvester-Wheatsheaf.

Sinha, Chris. 1999a. Grounding, mapping and acts of meaning. In Theo Janssen and Gisela Redeker, eds., *Cognitive linguistics: Foundations, scope, and methodology* 223–55. Berlin: Mouton de Gruyter.

Sinha, Chris. 1999b. Situated selves. In Joan Bliss, Roger Säljö, and Paul Light, eds., *Learning sites: Social and technological resources for learning* 32–46. Oxford: Pergamon.

Sinha, Chris. 2004. The evolution of language: From signals to symbols to system. In D. Kimbrough Oller and Ulrike Griebel, eds., *Evolution of communication systems: A comparative approach* 217–35. Cambridge, MA: MIT Press.

Sinha, Chris, and Kristine Jensen de López. 2000. Language, culture and the embodiment of spatial cognition. *Cognitive Linguistics* 11: 17–41.

Southgate, Victoria, and Kerstin Meints. 2000. Typicality, naming and category membership in young children. *Cognitive Linguistics* 11: 5–16.

Thom, René. 1976. *Structural stability and morphogenesis: An outline of a general theory of models.* Reading, MA: Benjamin.

Tomasello, Michael, ed. 1998. *The new psychology of language: Cognitive and functional approaches to language structure.* Vol. 1. Mahwah, NJ: Lawrence Erlbaum.

Tomasello, Michael. 1999. *The cultural origins of human cognition.* Cambridge, MA: Harvard University Press.

Verfaillie, Karl, and Anja Daems. 1997. The priority of the agent in visual event perception: On the cognitive basis of grammatical agent-patient asymmetries. *Cognitive Linguistics* 7: 131–48.

von Ehrenfels, Christian. 1890. Über Gestaltqualitäten. *Vierteljahrschrift für wissenschaftlichen Philosophie* 14: 249–92. (Also in Ferdinand Weinhandel, ed., *Gestalthaftes Sehen.* Darmstadt: Wissenschaftliche Buchgesellschaft, 1960)

Vygotsky, Lev. [1930] 1978. *Mind in society: The development of higher psychological processes.* Cambridge: Harvard University Press.

Vygotsky, Lev. [1934] 1986. *Thought and language.* Cambridge, MA: Harvard University Press.

Waddington, Conrad H. 1977. *Tools for thought.* St. Albans, UK: Paladin.

Wittgenstein, Ludwig. 1953. *Philosophical investigations.* Trans. G. E. M. Anscombe. Oxford: Basil Blackwell.

Wundt, Wilhelm. 1880. *Logik: Eine Untersuchung der Prinzipien der Erkenntnis und der Methoden Wissenschaflicher Forschung.* Stuttgart: Enke.

Wundt, Wilhelm. 1900. *Völkerpsychologie: Eine Untersuchung der Entwicklungsgestze von Sprache, Mythus und Sitte.* Vol. 2, *Die Sprache.* Leipzig, Germany: Engelmann.

Wundt, Wilhelm. 1901. *Sprachgeschichte und Sprachpsychologie: Mit Rücksicht auf B. Delbrücks "Grundfragen der Sprachforschung."* Leipzig, Germany: Engelmann.

Zlatev, Jordan. 1997. *Situated embodiment: Studies in the emergence of spatial meaning.* Stockholm: Gotab Press.

INDEX

....